The Papers of Dwight David Eisenhower

THE PAPERS OF DWIGHT DAVID EISENHOWER

COLUMBIA UNIVERSITY: XI

LOUIS GALAMBOS, *EDITOR*

EXECUTIVE EDITOR
DAUN VAN EE

SENIOR ASSOCIATE EDITOR
ELIZABETH S. HUGHES

ASSOCIATE EDITOR
JOSEPH P. HOBBS

ASSISTANT EDITORS
WILLIAM J. CALDERHEAD   CECELIA T. MARCINKO
ESTHER GILLER   CHRISTINE MOSELEY MILLOFF
ROGER T. JOHNSON

EDITORIAL ASSISTANT
GERALD J. CONTI

THE JOHNS HOPKINS UNIVERSITY PRESS

BALTIMORE AND LONDON

308.1
Ei 83c
V.11

*This book has been brought to publication with the generous assistance of the William S. Paley Foundation, Inc.,
and the National Endowment for the Humanities.*

The Johns Hopkins University Press, Baltimore, Maryland 21218
The Johns Hopkins Press Ltd., London

All illustrations in this volume are from the
Dwight D. Eisenhower Library, Abilene,
Kansas, unless indicated otherwise.

Frontispiece: Columbia University, Columbiana Collection.

Library of Congress Cataloging in Publication Data
(Revised for volumes 10 and 11)

Eisenhower, Dwight D. (Dwight David), 1890–1969.
The papers of Dwight David Eisenhower.

Vol. 6 edited by A. D. Chandler and L. Galambos;
v. 7–   by L. Galambos.
Includes bibliographies.
CONTENTS: v. 1–5. The war years.—v. 6. Occupation,
1945.—v. 7–9. The Chief of Staff. —v. 10–11. Columbia University.
1. World War, 1939–1945—United States.   2. World
War, 1939–1945—Campaigns.   3. Eisenhower, Dwight D.
(Dwight David), 1890–1960.   4. Presidents—United States—
Correspondence.   I. Chandler, Alfred Dupont, ed.
II. Galambos, Louis, ed.   III. United States. President.
(1953–1961: Eisenhower)   IV. Title.
E742.5.E37   1970   973.921′092′4 [B]   65–27672
ISBN 0–8018–1078–7 (v. 1–5)
ISBN 0–8018–2061–8 (v. 6–9)
ISBN 0–8018–2720–5 (v. 10–11)

o

Contents

Volume X

Columbia University

Volume XI

Columbia University

The Papers of Dwight David Eisenhower

Columbia University

IV

The University and the American Way

DECEMBER 1949 TO JUNE 1950

8

Marshaling Columbia's Resources

TO MILTON STOVER EISENHOWER   *December 19, 1949*

Dear Milton: It seems that everybody can enjoy "freedom of speech" except me. Because some .22 caliber reporter decides that I am a candidate for President, I am not allowed to open my mouth except for something so innocuous as sulphur and molasses for spring fever. I grow very, very weary of the whole business. I am about to blow up.[1]

Of course, I recognize that your advice is sound, in view of the interpretations that other people insist upon making of a man's words, in terms of his intentions. I shall undoubtedly follow your advice.[2] In fact, I have already made up my mind to stop speaking entirely. I may even go to the extent of breaking tradition here and getting someone else to make the annual Commencement Address. Unless I do, someone will be certain to see nefarious purposes in my talk. Incidentally, I have not yet seen a single one of my talks reported accurately.

Any way, thank you for writing. *As ever*

[1] Before leaving for Texas on December 1, Eisenhower had addressed the St. Andrew's Society's 193d anniversary banquet (Nov. 30). The General had cautioned the eleven hundred members and guests of the society that individual freedom should not be exchanged for personal security. "Somewhere along the line," he had told his audience, "we have lost some respect for mere thrift and independence"; luxuries had become too important. "Maybe we like caviar and champagne when we ought to be out working on beer and hot dogs" (transcript in EM, Subject File, Speeches; see also *New York Times*, Dec. 1, 1949).

Eisenhower's speech had triggered renewed speculation about his political aspirations and harsh criticism from the Columbia University student newspaper. The *Columbia Daily Spectator* had attacked Eisenhower's speech in a December 5 editorial. The *Spectator* had said that "being content with beer and hot dogs has never been part of the American tradition we know. The one we know assures any citizen that he may some day eat champagne and caviar and in the White House at that" (*New York Times*, Dec. 6, 1949). During Eisenhower's stay in Texas (see no. 607) his office fielded numerous letters commenting on the speech and the *Spectator* editorial. One alumnus of the class of 1909 wrote Eisenhower (Dec. 9) that "the editorial in 'Spectator' . . . indicates how far you are straying from the American way of life. There must be someone over in the history department who could give you a refresher course on what American democracy really means." Eisenhower's assistant, Kevin McCann, replied in Eisenhower's absence, describing the General's busy schedule on behalf of the university. Columbia, McCann wrote, "the finest school of its kind in the country, although a few of its alumni may exhibit a lamentable lack of good taste and good judgment, is very close to General Eisenhower's heart," and he advised the alumnus that Eisenhower would see the correspondence upon his return (Dec. 12, 1949, EM, Coleman Corr. See also McCann to Frederiksen, Dec. 7, 1949; Andersen to Eisenhower, Dec. 1, 1949, and McCann to Andersen, Dec. 17, 1949; McCann to Krieg, Dec. 15, 1949, and Krieg to McCann, Dec. 26, 1949, with enclosures; Roberts to Eisenhower, n.d., with enclosed transcript of broadcast; papers in EM, Columbia Corr.; *Time*, Dec. 16, 1949; *U.S. News & World Report*, Dec. 16, 1949; *Newsweek*, Dec. 19, 1949; and the *Columbia Daily Spectator*, Dec. 9 and

15, 1949. For Eisenhower's recollection of this incident see *Mandate for Change*, p. 8).

When Eisenhower made similar speeches before the local chambers of commerce in Houston (Dec. 7), Galveston (Dec. 8), and Fort Worth (Dec. 15), public speculation about his political intentions became even more intense, and newspapers reported that President Truman believed Eisenhower to be a political candidate (*New York Times*, Dec. 10, 1949; transcripts of the Houston and Galveston speeches, in EM, Subject File, Speeches; *New York Times*, Dec. 7, 1949; *Fort Worth Star Telegram*, Dec. 8, 15, 16, and 17, 1949; and Jones to Benton, Jan. 16, 1950, in EM, Benton Corr.). For background on the pressure Eisenhower was receiving from various friends and politicians to run for the presidency see no. 602; on his reaction to the press see no. 562. See also the next document.

[2] On December 14 Milton Eisenhower had sent his brother a copy of a *Washington Evening Star* article (Dec. 6) that dealt with the *Spectator* editorial. Milton commented, "No doubt you have read the enclosed, as well as other criticisms. They are becoming numerous." He said that the General's trip to Texas "did appear to the newspaper reader, to be a political trip. As a symbol and hero, you have been free of criticism. As a suspected politician, you will get plenty. I'm sure you haven't intended to give the impression of having become more receptive to a possible political future, but newspaper readers are bound to obtain such an impression. You don't need my advice—but I'd quit making speeches on everything but education" (same file as document).

This experience and his brother's advice apparently convinced the General to alter his course. In January Eisenhower would give Provost Grayson Kirk the responsibility for all public speaking engagements concerning the university (*New York Times*, Jan. 7, 1950), and it would be February 1950 before Eisenhower addressed an audience outside of the university. He would not discuss political questions at that time. A copy of Eisenhower's address, delivered at the Moles' tenth annual award dinner in New York City on February 9, 1950, is in EM, Subject File, Speeches. For further developments see no. 609.

607

Eisenhower Mss.

December 19, 1949

To Frances Hardwick Bloomfield Metcalf

Dear Fran:[1] Your note from New Mexico reached me as I got back to New York where I found, also, your very nice present of pheasants.[2] Within a few days I am to have a luncheon for some of my University friends and I shall serve them my pheasants as a surprise. Naturally, Mamie and I thank you both very sincerely for your thoughtfulness.

While I did not see the editorial in the Denver Post to which your letter refers, I assure you that I am not a candidate for any political office.[3] It seems that a number of columnists and writers are having a great deal of sport these days discussing the possibility of my becoming a politician. I sometimes think they do it on the basis of a sporting event—soon I expect to see the odds quoted along with those on the races at Pimlico.

In any event, nothing has so far happened to change my convictions which I so earnestly tried to present logically and completely in the letter I made public almost two years ago.[4]

This note brings to you both our very best wishes for a fine holiday season and a Happy New Year.

Again, many thanks for your very nice present.

With warmest regards to you both, *Cordially*

[1] Metcalf and her husband, Stanley Warren Metcalf (president of the Columbian Rope Company, in Auburn, New York), had known the Eisenhowers since the 1930s, when the two couples had lived in the Philippines.

[2] Metcalf's letter of December 11 is in EM. Eisenhower had returned to his university office this same day after a two-week visit to Texas. The Eisenhowers had visited friends in San Antonio, and the General had made brief visits to Houston, Galveston, and Fort Worth. Eisenhower had also spent a week at Sid Richardson's San José Island (Dec. 9–14). For background see nos. 582 and 592. See also Eisenhower to Richardson, December 19, 1949, in EM; nos. 606, 622, and 634; and Lyon, *Portrait of the Hero*, p. 408.

[3] Metcalf had written that the December 9 *Denver Post* headline had reported that Truman had said Eisenhower was a candidate for the Republican presidential nomination. Although she said she would do everything she could to help Eisenhower get elected, Metcalf expressed hope that the headline was not true. For background see no. 606.

[4] Galambos, *Chief of Staff*, no. 1998.

608   *Eisenhower Mss.*

TO GEORGE CATLETT MARSHALL   *December 19, 1949*

Dear General:[1] Mamie and I were happy to receive your holiday greetings. Your note was awaiting me when I returned from a two weeks visit to Texas.[2]

On one or two occasions I've been invited to New York affairs that you were attending. To my regret I've never been free to accept. However, I now have February 16th luncheon on my calendar as a fixed date—I understand you are to be here to open the Red Cross Drive.[3]

If, whenever you are compelled to come to this city, you should find yourself with 30 or more minutes of free time, I wish you'd give me the chance to try to come to see you. There are numbers of things I'd like to talk over with you—at least briefly.

I know that Pinehurst must be lovely now—and you are thoroughly enjoying it.[4] So while I hope that you do not have to leave it too frequently—I shall still look forward to your New York visits.

Merry Xmas and Happy New Year to you and yours from all the

Eisenhowers (Now included in the number are 2 grandchildren.)[5] *Cordially*

[1] This letter was handwritten. For background on Marshall, who had been appointed president of the American Red Cross (ARC) in September, see no. 246; and *New York Times*, September 23, 1949.

[2] Marshall's note, which was also handwritten, was dated December 1949 (EM). Marshall had sent the Eisenhowers Christmas greetings and had said that he hoped to see them in New York. For Eisenhower's trip to Texas see nos. 582, 592, and 607.

[3] Eisenhower, who was a member of the ARC board of directors, had opened the organization's 1949 campaign in Chicago (see no. 381). Although he had been unable to attend an October 1949 ARC luncheon at which Marshall had been a guest, Eisenhower had agreed to be a guest of honor and a member of the luncheon committee for the inauguration of the 1950 fund-raising drive on February 16. Marshall would also be a guest of honor and the principal speaker (see papers in EM, Chester Corr., and EM, Subject File, Clubs and Associations; and *New York Times*, Feb. 17, 1949). For developments see nos. 616 and 617.

[4] Marshall had written that he was leaving for his home in Pinehurst, North Carolina, where he would spend the winter. He said, however, that he planned to travel ten thousand miles for the Red Cross in January and February.

[5] John and Barbara Eisenhower's children, Dwight David II and Barbara Anne.

609   *Eisenhower Mss.*

To Edwin Palmer Hoyt   *December 20, 1949*

Dear Palmer:[1] Your two letters together with the copy of the speech you made on November 19th were waiting for me when I returned from Texas yesterday afternoon. The speech was an excellent one and I read every word of it with great pleasure.[2]

So far as your letter of December 2nd is concerned, there is much in it with which I most heartily agree. In fact, except for those parts which touch upon *my* possible and potential responsibilities I go with you every step of the way. As you may know, I try in my own feeble way to awaken interest in our present day problems and to create some alertness against a drift that seems to you and me to be very persistent, not to say alarming.[3]

I should very much like, one of these days, to have a long talk with you. I assure you that these matters absorb a very great deal of my attention, and I most earnestly want to do what I can to sustain the fundamentals of our system even while we adjust the details to the requirements of a mechanized and industrialized civilization. Whenever I get to the point, however, of considering the matter of top leadership, my single and fervent hope is to discover and support some young, vigorous liberal-conservative who can electrify people and lead us into desirable paths. As I have stated publicly and have often told my friends, I still believe that, from every viewpoint, this marks the extent of my responsibility and duty as I see it. I cannot accept the theory that there are no *suitable* individuals who would willingly undertake the task, even if one should eliminate from consideration those who have sought it in the past.

Of this one thing you can be certain: My devotion to what I conceive to be the basis of the American system is unqualified. My efforts in support of that system may be awkward but they will be zealous and untiring. If those who believe in constitutional America are to go down, I am certain of one thing, they will go down fighting and with their flags flying. By the very nature of their task, they cannot give up— they cannot bow to pessimism and discouragement. I number myself among members of this band and I truly hope that the band will always be of such strength and numbers that it will continue to dominate our philosophy and our actions.[4]

Drop in to see me when you come this way. *Cordially*

[1] Hoyt was the publisher and editor of the *Denver Post*.
[2] A copy of Hoyt's address, which he had given at the University of Denver at an inaugural luncheon for the new chancellor, Albert C. Jacobs, is in EM. For background on Jacobs and his new position see no. 440.
[3] The two-party system, Hoyt had written, was "gravely threatened" because the Republicans had only a slim chance to win the presidency. Hoyt was alarmed because the Democrats were "assembling right-wing forces of the South with the left-wingers of the North and adding thereto the battalions of labor, to say nothing of the adherence minorities and the various lunatic fringes. . . ." He said that Eisenhower, however, would offer the party the rallying point it needed. Americans, he said, must look to the middle road Eisenhower had advocated in his Labor Day speech (see no. 532). "In short and fine, I believe that this is the time that you should make up your mind to stand for the nomination for the Presidency of the United States on the Republican ticket." This letter and another of December 14 are in EM. For background on these issues see nos. 371, 491, and 606.
[4] For subsequent developments see no. 638.

610

Eisenhower Mss.,
Service Academy Board Corr.

To John L. Hoen[1]

December 20, 1949

Telegram

You may record my general concurrence with draft of Service Academy Board Report submitted to me for comment under date of 12 December.

While in certain specific features of report my views differ somewhat from those presented in the draft I feel that in no case is the difference a vital one and I do not desire to submit any minority suggestion or recommendation.[2]

The report as drafted represents the majority opinion of the board as I understand it and I congratulate you on a job well done.

[1] Hoen was executive secretary of the Service Academy Board, a group of educators appointed to make recommendations about the education of officers for the services. For background on the board see nos. 299 and 322; on Hoen see no. 403. Eisenhower's longhand draft of this telegram is in EM, Letters and Drafts.

[2] On December 21, 1949, Hoen would transmit to Secretary of Defense Louis A. Johnson a copy of the Service Academy Board's final report and recommendations. The board did not depart from its conclusion of April 1949 that the traditional four-year format of the Military and Naval academies should be maintained (see no. 403). Moreover, the board reiterated its proposal to establish an Air Force academy similar in many respects to the two existing institutions. The final report called upon the Army and the Navy to assist the Air Force with voluntary transfers of cadets and midshipmen to the new academy. One section of the report dealt exclusively with the need for "cross-education" among officers of the three services; the board thought that this form of indoctrination would promote unification within the Department of Defense. The board said: "All instances of Service controversy that have come to the attention of the Board have occurred at, or have been directly derived from, higher levels of command. . . . The Board has found no evidence of a spirit of inter-service friction and jealousy among students or instructors of any academy." The board concluded that the following measures should be taken to facilitate unification: exchange of students and instruction; joint summer training; and provision for a consulting board within the Department of Defense (Department of Defense, *A Report and Recommendation to the Secretary of Defense by the Service Academy Board*, pp. 7–8, copy in EM, Service Academy Board Corr. On the consulting board see no. 516, n. 3).

Johnson would thank Eisenhower on January 27, 1950 (EM), for his work on the board, and he would make the board's conclusions the basis for legislation that he submitted to Congress (see Hoen, "The Service Academy Board Recommends—," p. 43). Congress would eventually act upon some of the recommendations. On June 30, 1950, the age requirements for entrance into the academies would be made uniform (U.S., *Statutes at Large*, vol. 64, pt. 1, p. 304; see also Department of Defense, *A Report and Recommendation to the Secretary of Defense by the Service Academy Board*, p. 11, copy in EM, Service Academy Board Corr.). In 1954 Congress would establish an Air Force academy at a location to be determined later by a special commission (U.S., *Statutes at Large*, vol. 68, pt. 1, pp. 47–49). At the same time, Congress would provide that as many as 12.5 percent of the members of a graduating class at each service academy could be commissioned in a branch of the Armed Forces other than the one for which they had been trained. Several other recommendations made by the board, however, were never put into effect (see Masland and Radway, *Soldiers and Scholars*, pp. 122–27, 477–79).

Eisenhower Mss.

To Herbert Allen Black   *December 20, 1949*

Dear Doctor:[1] It was distressing, not to say shocking, to learn of your illness and that, because of it, the doctors have confined you to the hospital. I do hope that you are improving daily.[2]

I agree with you, of course, that the times are serious and that everyone must be ready to do his duty if we are not to fall prey to false ideas and to political trends that seem to have rather terrifying potentialities. I realize that your changed convictions with respect to myself represent very earnest and serious thought on your part. However, I still feel that, for me, the decisions I made some years ago are correct. I would be very profoundly disappointed and disturbed if ever I should come to believe that circumstances indicated a need for me to enter the political world.[3]

I am, as always, deeply touched by the great compliments paid me by such opinions and convictions as you have expressed. Although I know they represent wild exaggerations, it is nice to know that the source of such exaggerations is in deep and abiding friendship.

Hurry up and get well and I will come down to see you next summer when I come to Denver.[4] *Cordially*

[1] For background on Dr. Black see no. 13.
[2] Black had suffered a stroke and was a patient at the Parkview Hospital in Pueblo, Colorado. There is no letter in EM from Black, who may have telephoned Eisenhower about his illness.
[3] Black had apparently suggested that Eisenhower reconsider his decision not to become a candidate for the presidency.
[4] For later developments see no. 671.

Eisenhower Mss.

To Clifford Roberts   *December 21, 1949*

Dear Cliff: Thank you very much indeed for your letter of December 5th, enclosing the correspondence from Mr. Babcock.[1] I am instantly going to have the project studied by our University counsel and will take it up, when I can, with officials of other colleges.[2]

In the meantime, I think it would be a fine idea if Mr. Babcock would write at length to President Wriston of Brown. He would pass the matter on to the proper committee at once.[3]

I do hope that something can come of it because privately endowed universities are having very tough sledding these days. In any event, it is fine to know that people such as Mr. Babcock and yourself continue to take such a warm interest in the educational problem.[4] *Cordially*

[1] Charles Henry Babcock, a senior partner at Reynolds & Company since 1931, thought that some of the current financial problems of private educational institutions could be solved by revising Section 120 of the Internal Revenue Code (which waived the 15 percent limit on charitable deductions for only those taxpayers who had donated 90 percent of their income for ten consecutive years). Babcock argued that the code limited philanthropic donations, and he suggested that it be liberalized (so that the 15 percent limitation would be waived for each year or for every two consecutive years that a taxpayer donated 90 percent of his income to nonprofit organizations). On November 29 Babcock had sent Roberts copies of his correspondence concerning the code and a draft of the proposed legislation. Babcock had suggested that Eisenhower might be interested in the idea and said that he would await Roberts's advice before writing President Stassen at the University of Pennsylvania (see no. 483) and President Wriston of Brown University (see no. 254. See also Babcock to Harris, Nov. 1, 1949; Babcock to Roberts, Dec. 13, 1949, with enclosures; and above papers in EM, Roberts Corr.; and U.S., *Statutes at Large*, vol. 53, pt. 1, p. 56).

[2] This same day Eisenhower sent Roberts's letter and Babcock's correspondence to Vice-President for Development Paul H. Davis. On December 22 Davis advised Eisenhower that he considered the idea of such importance that he had forwarded the material to university counsel John G. Saxe (see no. 243).

[3] Eisenhower had probably discussed Babcock's idea with Wriston (who was president of the Association of American Universities) at a Council on Foreign Relations meeting on December 20.

[4] For Eisenhower's views on the financing of education see no. 208. For developments regarding this issue see no. 653.

613   *Eisenhower Mss.*

TO JEROME A. FRANKLIN   *December 21, 1949*

Dear Jerry:[1] Thank you very much for your report on the fish pond.[2] I do not know what size bass you are going to put in, in April but I am quite certain that with the preparations you are making, they will grow very rapidly.

A year from now I shall bring down some fishing equipment and leave it there permanently. However, soon there are going to be so many things I like to do at Augusta that I shall either have to stay away or suffer a complete breakdown. With golf, fishing, painting and going to night baseball games, I will have a very crowded schedule. All this does not take into consideration the chance to give old Cliff a good walloping at bridge.[3]

The writing of this note gives me a chance to say, most earnestly and sincerely, Merry Christmas and Happy New Year. Take care of yourself and I hope to see you before too long.[4] *Cordially*

[1] Franklin was a member of the Augusta National Golf Club, in Augusta, Georgia.
[2] In his letter of December 8 Franklin had advised Eisenhower that "Ike's Pond" at Augusta had recently been stocked with two thousand bluegill bream. During the summer the club had cleared land for the pond on the golf course adjacent to the club president's cottage, and Franklin had periodically told Eisenhower about their progress (see Franklin to Eisenhower, July 11 and Oct. 20, 1949; Franklin to Roberts, Sept. 30, 1949; and Eisenhower to Franklin, July 13 and Oct. 24, 1949). In his recent letter Franklin had described the cleaning and fertilizing of the pond and had said that the big-mouth black bass would be added in April. All correspondence is in EM.
[3] For background on club member Clifford Roberts see no. 69.
[4] Eisenhower would go to Augusta in January 1950 (see no. 656). For developments regarding the fish pond see no. 681. In 1953 the pond would be the subject of a *New Yorker* cover (see *New Yorker*, Apr. 18, 1953, 24–25).

614   *Eisenhower Mss., Family File*

To Edgar Newton Eisenhower   *December 21, 1949*

Dear Ed: The prospects of my coming to the Northwest this winter add up to a complete zero. While it is still true that I hope to make one or two visits to the South, they have already been very carefully planned and I don't want to break them. All the rest of my time is completely mortgaged.[1]

Incidentally, from here on out I am going to try to keep my movements just as secret as I know how. I am sick and tired of being accused of seeking a political job every time I open my mouth.[2]

Please express my very deep appreciation to your associates for the compliment of their invitation but explain to them I simply cannot come.[3] *As ever*

[1] In a letter of December 16, 1949, Edgar Eisenhower had said that the General would soon receive an invitation to speak to the board of trade of Vancouver, British Columbia. Edgar said that it would please him very much if he could accept the invitation (EM).
[2] "I see," Edgar had said, "the political prophets are still building a fire in your chimney." For Eisenhower's sensitivity on this point see no. 606, to Milton.
[3] The next day, December 22, Eisenhower would write to Edgar again. This time he would thank Edgar for sending a holiday fruit cake and would tell him that Janis, Edgar's daughter, would soon receive a music box—cigarette case that had been given to Eisenhower in Europe. "I just wanted to send it," Eisenhower said, "as a little Christmas token" (EM).

To Paul Thomas Carroll   *December 21, 1949*

Dear Pete:[1] Thank you very much for your nice Christmas letter. It is pleasing to know that you and your family are so enjoying Leavenworth. I can understand how your work would be most intriguing for you and, so long as your family finds a lot to do there, I can understand, too, why the place seems so satisfactory to you.[2]

Mamie and I have just returned from Texas. In general, the trip was a highly satisfactory one, although I have come to the conclusion that I am one person in the United States who does not enjoy the privilege of "freedom of speech." If I open my mouth on any subject from poverty to flat feet, I am accused of political aspirations. However, I grow used to it and am developing a philosophy somewhat akin to that of the blind mule who insisted on running into the brick wall.[3]

Both of us send you and your family our very best wishes for a fine Christmas and a Happy New Year. Incidentally, our immediate family will be largely together for this Christmas. John and Barbara with their two youngsters will come down from West Point and Mamie's father and mother are already here. We shall have a real family gathering. *Cordially*

[1] Lieutenant Colonel Carroll was now the Assistant Director in the Operations and Training Department at the Command and General Staff College, Fort Leavenworth, Kansas. For further background see no. 25.

[2] In his letter of December 15 (EM) Carroll had described his new job and said that his wife Ruth and their sons "find a world of activities to keep themselves happy and occupied."

[3] Carroll had written that he was following Eisenhower's "comings and goings" closely and that the General's recent speeches had touched on "things that have needed saying for a long time." For background on these speeches see no. 606. On Eisenhower's trip see no. 607.

616   *Eisenhower Mss.,*
Harry Woodburn Chase Corr.

To William Howard Chase   *December 21, 1949*

Dear Mr. Chase: Your note of the 14th has caught me in the press of work that accumulated during a two weeks absence from the city.[1] While I have the feeling that I *should* be able to give you a number of anecdotes or stories in which General Marshall figured, at this moment only one comes to mind. It is inconsequential but, in some revised form, *may* help Mr. Chester.

I'm sorry I can't do better. It accompanies this note.[2] *Sincerely*

[1] Chase, Director of Public Relations for the General Foods Corporation since 1945, had written Eisenhower to explain that Colby Mitchell Chester (the former chairman of the board of General Foods [1935–43] and now chairman of the New York chapter of the American Red Cross) was going to introduce General George C. Marshall at a Red Cross luncheon on February 16 (for background see no. 608) and wanted "to point up his remarks" with a personal anecdote about Marshall. Chase, who had unsuccessfully checked Eisenhower's *Crusade in Europe* for such a story, said that "for self-evident reasons, I am turning to you for help" (same file as document). Eisenhower's handwritten draft of this letter is in EM, Letters and Drafts. For background on his recent trip to Texas see nos. 582, 592, and 607.

[2] See the next document.

617

Eisenhower Mss.,
Harry Woodburn Chase Corr.

To William Howard Chase[1]

December 21, 1949

I once had General Marshall as my house guest and, upon his arrival, personally conducted him to his room. My little Scottie dog accompanied us, a dog of which I was very proud. The dog was obviously delighted with the attention we gave him and grew very excited as we walked to the General's room. Arriving there, the General and I started discussing arrangements for his convenience, and the dog, apparently still trying to attract our attention, hopped up on the bed, barking and jumping until, in a final spasm of excitement, he did what all little puppies do when they can contain themselves, or their bladders, no longer.

General Marshall apparently detected a look of acute embarrassment on my face because he took it all with a grin and said "Apparently the dog doesn't realize who's to sleep here—or" and he paused a second and then added—"or maybe he does!!"[2]

[1] See the preceding document. A handwritten copy of this anecdote is in EM, Letters and Drafts.

[2] This incident took place in Algiers in January 1943 (see Butcher, *My Three Years With Eisenhower*, p. 247; on Eisenhower's dog Telek see Chandler, *War Years*). On January 3 Chase thanked Eisenhower for the anecdote, saying that it would be of great help to Chester (same file as document).

To Henry Clay Williams   *December 21, 1949*

Dear Henry:[1] When I returned from a recent trip to Texas, I found your letter, acknowledging the receipt of my book.[2] It was a small token, indeed, of my indebtedness to you for many months of splendid, loyal service. I hope you understand that I profoundly appreciate all that you did for me during the war.

This note brings to you my very best wishes for a fine Christmas and a Happy New Year. Because I cannot possibly make an intelligent guess as to any item that might appeal to you as a nice little Christmas present, I am enclosing a small check which I hope you will accept in the spirit that it is sent. Please use it merely to buy some little item that you might otherwise deny yourself.[3] *Sincerely*

[1] During the Second World War, T/4 Williams had been a member of Eisenhower's personal staff (see Chandler and Galambos, *Occupation, 1945*; and Galambos, *Chief of Staff*). He was now employed as a clerk by the Chicago Post Office Department.

[2] After the publication of *Crusade in Europe*, Eisenhower had distributed autographed copies of the book to his family, friends, and former associates (see no. 237), but he had been unable to locate Williams. Aide Robert Schulz had tried unsuccessfully to reach Williams in Dallas and San Francisco (see Schulz to Williams, Feb. 11, 1949) and had finally written the National Association of Combat Units in an effort to find a current address for Williams (Oct. 26, 1949). The Associated Press had picked up the story, and Williams had written Schulz (Nov. 11) that on October 30 he had been confronted at work by a flock of newspaper reporters who asked him numerous questions about his association with Eisenhower (see *New York Times*, Oct. 31, 1949). Schulz had talked to Williams on the phone and had sent him a copy of *Crusade in Europe* on October 31. Williams had then written Eisenhower (Nov. 11), "For this priceless gift and for me to have been remembered, I sincerely thank you Sir, a thousand times." All correspondence is in EM.

[3] The previous Christmas Eisenhower had remembered former members of his personal staff with gifts of savings bonds for their children (see for instance Eisenhower to the McKeoghs and to E. R. Lee, both Dec. 18, 1948, and Eisenhower to W. I. Murray, Dec. 20, 1948, in EM; a list of the recipients of the bonds is in EM, Subject File, Christmas, 1948–1949). On January 11 Williams thanked Eisenhower and said that he was "having a sizzling good time with 'Crusade in Europe.' " For developments regarding Williams see no. 821.

TO JOHN FLOWERS CRUTCHER   *December 21, 1949*

Dear Dixie:[1] I fairly shuddered to read in your recent note that someone in my office ever addressed you as "madam." Your house may be big, but I doubt that it held you for the next half hour or so after that one.[2]

I did not know that you were such a good friend of the Floyd Parks family. While I knew that you were acquainted with him in the Tanks long years ago, I was not aware that you had many later opportunities to see him. I have always regarded him as one of my finest friends and as a very fine officer.[3]

Quite naturally I am delighted that you are again sending me the Readers Digest. It is the one periodical that I seem to get time to read— and I always seem to enjoy it. My very profound thanks.

This note, of course, brings to you earnest wishes for a fine holiday season and a Happy New Year. *Cordially*

[1] Crutcher, now a cattle breeder in Henning, Tennessee, had served in the Tank Corps with Eisenhower (for background see Chandler and Galambos, *Occupation, 1945*, no. 101).

[2] Crutcher had been sending Eisenhower a gift subscription to *Reader's Digest* magazine since the Second World War. On December 18 he had written that he had again renewed the subscription. He asked Eisenhower not to acknowledge the gift because he knew how busy the General was, and he said that he did not want a letter from an aide. "Last year," Crutcher wrote, "he called me 'Madam' or 'Madame.'"

[3] Crutcher wrote that the Floyd L. Parks family had visited him en route to Washington. For background on Parks see no. 584.

TO EDWARD EVERETT HAZLETT   *December 22, 1949*

Dear Swede: Apparently my most recent letter to you tended to excite you a bit.[1] I hope it did not raise your blood pressure beyond the blow-off point.

I think that now I have a clear picture of your estimate of Sherman.[2] While it is true that this estimate is somewhat different from what I thought it was, some months ago, yet my own acquaintanceship with the man, added to what I thought, originally, was your opinion, gave me a composite reading that was not greatly different from the one you now present. No harm has been done.

Churning around in the back of my mind is the impression that I may have already answered your letter on this point. If I have, just take this repetition as another indication of approaching senility, and throw the thing in the wastebasket. At least, nothing will be hurt if I send you, even for the second time, very best wishes from Mamie and me for a fine Christmas and a 1950 crowded with good things for all the Hazlett family. *Cordially*

[1] Eisenhower's letter is no. 598. In his reply, dated December 8, 1949 (EM), Hazlett had said that he was "amazed at the thought and work" that Eisenhower put into his letters and that he was also surprised at Eisenhower's "gentle tolerance" of his "sometimes crackpot ideas."

[2] Hazlett, who in his letter of November 2 had criticized Chief of Naval Operations Sherman for his snobbishness (see no. 598), had clarified his views in his later letter. He told Eisenhower of his great respect for Sherman's "brilliance" and "cooperativeness." Hazlett said that his only reservation was that Sherman was not generally popular within the Navy and therefore would not be able to "make a recalcitrant and conservative Navy *like* what he forced down its throat." He was, Hazlett added, "sarcastic, a bit of a snob, and hard to know." For developments see no. 716.

621   *Eisenhower Mss.*

To J. MEYRICK COLLEY   *December 22, 1949*
Personal

Dear Mr. Colley:[1] It is true that I was a supply officer in Leon Springs, Texas in 1917.[2] However, I was on duty with the 57th Infantry and if you were in the first Officers Training Camp at that place, someone else would have been responsible for the issue of your uniform. However, if you were in the 57th Infantry, then you are right in holding me responsible.[3]

I was especially intrigued with the latter part of your letter.[4] Frankly, I believe that the great problem of today is that of advancing the culture, living standards, opportunities and a personal security of all of our citizens, but *without* sacrificing fundamental parts of our individual rights and privileges (which are the essence of our American system) and without material loss in those qualities of initiative, enterprise and sturdiness that have been so largely responsible for our unique material development. If we go completely to the socialized state, I firmly believe that all of these will be lost—at least they will be lost to such an extent that we will become nothing less than a regimented state.

You remark that you are an engineer and, therefore, accustomed to accepting facts. It is also true that human beings have in the past, in human affairs, produced new sets of facts. It would have been easy to say, in the winter of 1777, that the Revolutionary War was lost. During that bitter winter, Washington lost more than 3500 men from his little army just by reason of starvation, cold and disease. His spirit and the determination of a small band of patriots in each of the colonies brought about, finally, a set of facts that, in the midst of that winter, would have been called just the dreams of a visionary.

I must confess that sometimes I fully—and very often partially—share the somberness of your general outlook. Yet I do insist that for people who were raised as were those of our generation, who have enjoyed and profited from the priceless opportunities that America has offered us, who realize that without freedom there can be no dignity for the individual and who know that if we are to become fully socialized, we will become also fully regimented—on these people lies a burden of responsibility to work as hard as they may to preserve the essentials of our great system, even while we struggle to insure that its fruits reach every last one of all our citizens.

Quite naturally, there is no place in a short letter to discuss these matters in detail. Moreover, I have no intention of indulging in any particular public discussion of them, either in a written or verbal form. When I cannot escape appearances, I rarely fail to reaffirm my loyalty to what I conceive to be the American system, but beyond that I think the job is largely one for businessmen, economists and public and professional leaders. After all, I am just an old soldier and not supposed to know too much.

I do thank you for the nice things you had to say about my book. I did work hard on it.[5] *Sincerely*

[1] Colley was an engineer from Gastonburg, Alabama. His letter of November 30 is in EM.

[2] Colley had just finished reading *Crusade in Europe*, and he wrote, "Since time has softened to some extent my intense indignation over the uniform you issued me at Leon Springs in 1917 (I understand you were Supply Officer there in May of that year), I wish to add one more expression of pleasure to the many you must have already received."

[3] Captain Eisenhower had been regimental supply officer of the 57th Infantry at Leon Springs, Texas, from June until September 1917 (see Eisenhower, *At Ease*, pp. 126–32). In a reply of January 3 Colley said that he was in the first officer training camp and Eisenhower was thus exonerated "of all blame in the affair of the uniform."

[4] Colley was interested in Eisenhower's discussion in the last chapter of *Crusade in Europe* of the conflict between communism and democracy. No one, he said, would disagree with Eisenhower's "unequivocal rejection of statism and . . . the desire to improve the position of the more unfortunate," but these two tenets seemed directly opposed and impossible to reconcile. There was "no practical means of substantial and rapid improvement in the position of the general run of people other than by governmental effort; either direct assistance or governmental influence in economic spheres." He hoped that if Eisenhower ever published anything on this subject, he would analyze the problem.

[5] On January 3 Colley thanked Eisenhower for his letter and wrote, "The concept that men can, by concerted and consistent effort, 'produce' new facts, as differ-

entiated from new ideas, appeals to me. I think perhaps I have been aground on that shoal for a long time and have become so anesthetized by the great plethora of 'new ideas' that I have failed to remember the difference between fact and fancy—no matter how often the latter may be reiterated." He admitted that if the nation "could be presented with the 'fact' that social betterment for the whole is no more than merely good business practice and, conceivably, may be had without the eternal interference of bureaucratic mediocrity (and that's going to be a hard fact to bring about) I think the battle will be nearly won." Colley added, "For 'an old soldier' you are commonly regarded as doing very well." All correspondence is in EM.

622   *Eisenhower Mss.*

To AMON GILES CARTER, SR.   *December 22, 1949*

Dear Amon:[1] This is merely to tell you once more how grateful Mamie and I are to you and Minnie for the many wonderful courtesies you extended us during our recent trip. It was fun to be with you down at Sid's island and we thoroughly enjoyed our stay at the Club. On top of all this, the luncheon that Minnie gave at your house was truly an enjoyable and attractive affair. We are grateful.[2]

There was one thing I heard at the Chamber of Commerce meeting that puzzled me a little and concerning which I had no chance to ask you. I heard the so-called "Trinity River Project" spoken of in glowing terms; it was implied that the Federal Government should prosecute that Project energetically.[3] Quite obviously, I do not know much about the Trinity River Project, but I have heard from some of our railroad friends that it comprises a deliberate attempt to induce the Federal Government to provide, at great public expense, an unnecessary competition for the railways of that region.[4]

I realize that my ignorance of the facts may be responsible for such questions as are now in my mind, but I know that people like you and Sid and the others that I like and respect in Texas are definitely opposed to unnecessary Federal intervention in state and local matters, and cannot be led to violate this principle by anything, merely because it promises *temporary* local advantage.[5]

I do hope you will continue to give some thought to Columbia and the suggestions that I made to you concerning it. I honestly believe that this institution deserves support from such individuals as you and other prominent Texans, even though I recognize that your first obligation is to your local colleges.[6] The national viewpoint and national thinking are so important that we must have a good solid minority of all our young people, from every state, trained in institutions that are truly national in character and purpose, and where each student can meet representatives from all over the country, indeed, from all over the world.

Mamie and I send to you and Minnie and to the members of your family our very best wishes for a Merry Christmas and a Happy New Year.

With warm personal regard, *Cordially*

[1] For background on Carter see no. 482.

[2] After their visit to Sid Richardson's San José Island, the Eisenhowers had spent a day in Fort Worth, Texas, and had lunched at the Carters' home (Dec. 15). That evening they had attended the city's annual chamber of commerce meeting (see Maddox to Eisenhower, Dec. 21, 1949, and Eisenhower to Maddox, Dec. 23, 1949, in EM). For background on the trip see no. 607. On Carter's wife, the former Minnie Meacham Smith, see Galambos, *Chief of Staff*, no. 1950.

[3] For many years landlocked Fort Worth and Dallas residents had dreamed of opening up their cities to the Gulf of Mexico by making the Trinity River navigable. Improvements to the 511-mile stretch of river had been started in 1902 but had been abandoned in 1922, and attempts to renew these efforts had been short-lived (see Lynn M. Alperin, *Custodians of the Coast: History of the United States Army Engineers at Galveston* [Galveston, 1977], pp. 72–74; Walter Prescott Webb, ed., *The Handbook of Texas*, 2 vols. [Austin, 1952], vol. II, p. 802; and Harry Hansen, ed., *Texas: A Guide to the Lone Star State*, American Guide Series, rev. ed. [New York, 1969], pp. 255–57).

[4] Eisenhower had probably discussed the project with Ernest Othmer Thompson (LL.D. Texas Technical College 1934) and Jonathan Catlett Gibson (LL.B. George Washington University 1923). Eisenhower had met Thompson, a member of the Texas Railroad Commission, at Sid Richardson's home on December 12, and Gibson, the vice-president and general counsel for the Atchison, Topeka, and Santa Fe Railway System, at Carter's December 15 luncheon. Gibson and his wife (the former Maude Lucile Allen) had also traveled with the Eisenhowers as far as Chicago on the return trip to New York (see papers in EM, Gurley Corr. and Thompson Corr.).

[5] There is no response from Carter in EM, but he had always been a proponent of the river's canalization (see Jerry Flemmons, *Amon: The Life of Amon Carter, Sr. of Texas* [Austin, 1978], p. 275).

[6] See no. 634. See also Eisenhower's June letter to Carter about this subject, no. 482. In November 1950 Carter and Sid Richardson would contribute substantially to Columbia's American Assembly program (see no. 1097).

623   *Eisenhower Mss.*

TO THEODORE S. WATSON   *December 22, 1949*

Dear Mr. Watson:[1] Of course, I should be delighted to meet you and Mr. Kleburg as citizens interested in the public good and the country's future. However, I cannot make an engagement with an understanding that there is to be discussed organization for partisan political activity or my own specific participation in politics.[2] Public statements that I have made in the past reflect—as clearly as I could make them—my personal attitude toward political office.

Nevertheless, I hope that the next time Mr. Kleburg is in town that the three of us can get together here in my office for a chat. As you may know, I did have lunch with him in San Antonio early this month and at that time came to appreciate his tremendous energy and the intensity of his convictions about public affairs.[3] I was personally attracted to him and any chance to talk to him will always be most welcome.[4] *Sincerely*

[1] In a letter of December 8 Watson had explained that he had been a senior partner of a New York Stock Exchange firm until his retirement in 1938; in 1944 he had served under Eisenhower as a regional transportation officer for Scotland. He was now the chairman of the Fairfield County, Connecticut, Republican finance committee. Kevin McCann helped the General prepare this reply.

[2] Watson had recently returned from a month-long trip through the South, and he said that he had visited Robert Justus Kleberg, Jr., who was "intensely interested in endeavoring to change our Country's trend, under the present Administration, to a Welfare State." (Kleberg, a Texas rancher since 1916, was the president of the vast King Ranch, Inc. [see Tom Lea, *The King Ranch*, vol. II (Boston, 1957); and Charles J. V. Murphy, "Treasure in Oil and Cattle," *Fortune* 80 (August 1, 1969), 110–14].) Watson, who said Kleberg was anxious to use his influence "to organize the South for you, if you should be the Republican candidate," asked if Eisenhower would see Kleberg when the rancher next came to New York. Watson offered the General the use of his apartment for their meeting (EM).

[3] Eisenhower had met Kleberg at Hal Mangum's dinner in San Antonio on December 3 (see list of guests in EM, Mangum Corr.); on Eisenhower's visit to San Antonio see no. 592.

[4] On December 27 Watson wrote Kleberg. He described his letter to Eisenhower and quoted the General's reply. He asked Kleberg to advise him when he planned to be in New York and said, "I consider the tenor of his letter very encouraging, considering that no candidate is willing to get out on a limb at this early date." In January Kleberg would write Eisenhower about Watson's letter; see no. 697 for developments.

624   *Eisenhower Mss.*

To WALTER BEDELL SMITH   *December 22, 1949*

Dear Beetle: Your book, a copy of which just reached my desk, is one of the nicest appearing volumes I have ever seen.[1] In addition, the few short excerpts from it that I read in the New York Times convinced me that I will find it an intensely interesting volume—even if my knowledge of its author had not convinced me of this before I saw any part of it.[2] Thanks also for the inscription. Regardless of responsibility for the idea, I shall obey your behest and take your book as my "homework."[3]

Mamie and I send our very best wishes to you and Nory[4] for a splendid Christmas and a Happy New Year. *Cordially*

[1] Smith's book, *My Three Years in Moscow*, would be published in January 1950.
[2] *My Three Years in Moscow* had been serialized in the daily and Sunday *New York Times*.
[3] Shortly after Smith had assumed his post in Moscow, Eisenhower had advised him to keep a diary or write frequently so that a personal record of his service as Ambassador could be preserved (see Galambos, *Chief of Staff*, no. 838).
[4] Smith's wife.

625   *Eisenhower Mss.*

To Louis Marx   *December 22, 1949*

Dear Louis:[1] That boy Spencer Bedell is certainly a precocious youngster.[2] The composition of his Christmas shopping list, as I can testify, demonstrated imagination and experience, while his taste in ties is superb. If he has not yet been promoted to Executive Vice-President of the Marx interests, I'm certain it's only because he has decided against taking the job.

While I am told that he speaks a language that is somewhat beyond the limits of my understanding, I'm sure I can impose upon you to inform him that the ties, the 8-ball and the golf-ball soap, the lotion and the cologne made up one of the nicest presents I ever saw; for which I am most grateful to him.

My warmest regards to him and to his parents, together with best wishes from Mamie and me for a fine Christmas and a 1950 crowded with good things for the whole family. I hope, of course, to see you *before* Christmas; I'm waiting for you to come pick out your particular item from among the Eisenhower Atrocities, so that I can dispose of others.[3]

My profound thanks for your thoughtfulness![4] *As ever*

[1] Eisenhower's handwritten draft of this letter to toy manufacturer Louis Marx is in EM, Letters and Drafts.
[2] Marx's wife, the former Idella Ruth Blackadder, had given birth to Spencer Bedell Marx on August 28, 1949 (see memo from Schulz to Eisenhower, with Eisenhower's handwritten draft of a cable, Sept. 1, 1949). For background on Idella Marx see Galambos, *Chief of Staff*.
[3] The "Eisenhower Atrocities" were paintings by the General (for background on Eisenhower's hobby see no. 51). Although Eisenhower would not see Marx before Christmas, they would talk on the phone on December 23, 1949 (see Eisenhower's desk calendar).
[4] On January 7, 1950, Eisenhower would go to Scarsdale, New York, for Spencer

B. Marx's christening; the General and Walter B. Smith would be the child's godfathers. All papers are in EM.

626

To Arthur Elsworth Stoddard   *December 23, 1949*

Dear Mr. Stoddard:[1] The member of your group, who stressed the ineffectiveness of talk and speeches that are restricted to a small and exclusive audience, hit the nail on the head. Your planned Freedom Dinner seems to me to be a sound implementation of his idea—particularly if you do not stop at the foremen level but can include representatives of the machine hands, clerks, typists, truckmen and others who seldom, if ever, hear more than one side of the story.[2]

It will be the kind of gathering I should truly like to attend if it were possible. Unfortunately, I cannot make a trip to Omaha for a long time to come.[3]

The schedule that confronts me for the remainder of the academic year is so extremely crowded in the first quarter and so badly chopped up in the second quarter that I cannot even consider a trip more than a few miles west of the Hudson at any time between now and the middle of June. Nevertheless, I hope that you will go ahead with the idea of the Freedom Dinner. I should like to learn, also, of the reaction in Omaha to such an affair.[4]

With warm personal regard and with best wishes for the Holiday Season and the New Year. *Cordially*

[1] In 1916 Stoddard had joined the Union Pacific Railroad Company as a student helper; on March 1, 1949, he had been named the firm's president. During World War II Stoddard, who had attained the rank of colonel, had served as Deputy Director General of Military Railways in SHAEF's G−4 division (1943−45) and as Europe's general manager of the first military railway service (1945−46). He was now a brigadier general in the U.S. Army Officers' Reserve Corps. Eisenhower extensively revised assistant Kevin McCann's draft of this letter (see copy in EM, Letters and Drafts).

[2] Stoddard had written that at a recent luncheon of Omaha businessmen someone had suggested that instead of talking among themselves about political and economic problems, they should be talking to "people who don't hear it at lunch every day and who ought to be thinking about the future of America." Various civic organizations had agreed, and a dinner for a thousand people was planned for not only "executives and junior executives, but . . . other employees, including foremen, who seldom have an opportunity to attend dinners or public affairs functions." The theme would be freedom, he wrote, and he asked Eisenhower to be the principal speaker. If it was a success, such meetings might spread to other cities and "introduce some straight American thinking to people who have been too

much inclined to accept tbe policies of 'give away' politicians" (Dec. 19, 1949, EM).

[3] Eisenhower added this paragraph to McCann's draft of the letter.

[4] There is no further correspondence in EM regarding this dinner. On Eisenhower's reluctance at this time to accept speaking engagements see no. 606.

627   *Eisenhower Mss.*

To Walter D. Fletcher   *December 23, 1949*

Dear Mr. Fletcher:[1] Thank you for your letter of December 21st. I shall take steps at once to see that news of Mr. Harriman's gift is not published in any way. I shall expect you, as we agreed, to make the announcement to the Trustees at our next meeting.[2]

I agree also that any future plans that involve either this money or any other gift from Mr. Harriman should be discussed with him before implementation.[3]

This note brings to you also my best wishes for a fine Christmas. *Sincerely*

[1] Fletcher was the attorney who represented W. Averell Harriman and his brother E. Roland. For background on Fletcher and the Harrimans see no. 605.

[2] The Harrimans were in the process of making two gifts to Columbia: one, securities valued at fifty thousand dollars; the other, Arden House, the Harriman home, which was to be given to the university for as yet undetermined purposes (see no. 605). According to Fletcher, the conditions of the gift were (1) that if a satisfactory proposal were developed for Arden House, Columbia would use the fifty thousand dollars to further that plan; and (2) that if no such proposal were accepted and Arden House were not given to the university, Eisenhower would decide how to use the funds (in cooperation with Fletcher, who was a university trustee). Fletcher requested that no publicity be given to the Harriman gifts and that no announcement be made to anyone except to Columbia's board of trustees (CUF).

Eisenhower and Fletcher had discussed these matters at a dinner honoring the Shah of Iran at the Men's Faculty Club on December 19. It was there that the two agreed that Fletcher would announce the Harriman gift to the trustees at their next meeting. On the day following the dinner (Dec. 20), Eisenhower wired Averell Harriman to express his gratitude: "I fully appreciate and shall carefully respect the purposes that lead to your action and extend my thanks for the personal compliment implicit in it" (EM).

[3] Fletcher had also requested that in the event that Arden House was given to Columbia, all public statements on this subject should first be submitted to W. Averell Harriman for his approval. For developments see no. 689.

To EDWARD VERNON RICKENBACKER   *December 23, 1949*

Dear Eddie:[1] Thank you very much for your thoughtful Christmas letter. It presents, most eloquently, a message that I try to carry to people every time I am called upon to utter a word in public or where I have a chance for serious conversation in private. Not only do I agree with what you say, but I urge you to use every possible means at your command to keep on spreading that type of information and exhortation to every single soul that you can reach.[2]

With the season's greetings to you and yours and the devout hope that the coming year will bring all America the promise of happiness by closer bringing back to us renewed understanding of the scale of values that lie at the foundation of America's greatness. *Cordially*

[1] Rickenbacker, who had been an aviator hero of World War I, was currently president of Eastern Air Lines. For further background see Galambos, *Chief of Staff*, no. 1940.

[2] In his letter, dated Christmas 1949 (EM), Rickenbacker had said that selfishness, greed, and indifference could lead America down "the road to ruin." Rather than wanting something for nothing, Rickenbacker said, Americans should rededicate themselves to the spiritual welfare of the country; they should concern themselves less with the material things of life.

To CLARENCE M. MALONE   *December 27, 1949*

Dear Mr. Malone:[1] Thank you very much for sending on to me a copy of your letter and of the article from the Wall Street Journal. I most heartily agree with the things you had to say in your letter, and I hope that the Journal will go to work on the matter.[2]

With very best wishes for a fine New Year to you and yours and the hope that your extraordinary and selfless efforts in conservation will bring, in 1950, solid and satisfying results throughout the nation. *Cordially*

[1] For background on Malone, a conservationist, see no. 58.

[2] On December 23, 1949, Malone had sent Eisenhower a letter that he had written to the editors of the *Wall Street Journal*; he had also enclosed a typewritten copy of the article that had inspired his letter (EM). Malone asked Eisenhower to comment on both documents. The article, "Crop Confusion" by Kenneth M. Scheibel, had appeared on the front page of the December 20, 1949, *Wall Street Journal*. Scheibel expressed concern about several programs sponsored by the Department of Agriculture and the Department of the Interior, programs that he described as expensive

and of contradictory purposes. He said that on the one hand the programs encouraged high production but on the other hand they also tried to discourage it.

In his letter, dated December 22, Malone agreed basically with Scheibel's analysis of the government's agricultural and conservation programs. Malone thought that the reason the agencies overlapped and worked at cross-purposes was that until recently the business world had taken no part in dealing with the farmers' problems. He asked permission to circularize the Scheibel article and suggested that the *Journal* publish another piece that would explain how private enterprise could work with government to develop an agricultural program that would save taxpayers money without penalizing the farmers.

630   *Eisenhower Mss.*

To Aksel Nielsen   *December 27, 1949*

Dear Aksel: Thank you very much for your nice Christmas letter. It was extraordinarily kind of you to go to the train to start Mr. and Mrs. Doud on their journey.[1] I think you are right in believing they are in somewhat better frame of mind than they have been for a long time. The next time I see you, we should have a long talk about some of the troubles that have beset them.

Of course, your idea about politics, so far as I may be involved, was most appealing to me.[2] In fact I frequently have adopted as a defense measure, when attacked by people who say I am refusing to do my duty when I refuse to enter the political field, a reply that attempts to throw the burden on my questioner. For example, I have said several times to visitors "Well, if you think this is my duty—what is yours?" Then I run through an entire catechism asking whether each belongs to his own precinct organization, whether he goes to his precinct or district caucuses, whether or not he has rigidly voted, contributed, and done everything else in support of his party that an active and interested citizen should do.[3] It is astonishing how frequently, when these questions are asked, the subject turns to hunting, fishing and the like.

In any event, your basic assumption is correct—that no one individual by himself can do anything about the current situation. It is group effort and there has got to be a lot of shoulders put to the wheel. This can only be done along the same, sensible lines you suggest. If they will do that, I believe they will be astonished to find they have a hundred good individuals, each of whom would be suitable to carry the flag for them in the top spot.[4]

Anyway, 1950 is almost upon us so Mamie and I send to you and Helen[5] our very best wishes for the happiest of New Years.

In this we, of course, include Virginia[6] and her nice husband. We sincerely hope that 1950 will be the best year that any of you has ever had. *Cordially*

P.S. If you run into Al Jacobs, my best to him.[7]

[1] Mamie Eisenhower's parents, the John S. Douds, had left Denver on December 17 for a visit with the Eisenhowers in New York. They had arrived on December 19 and would stay until March 5 (see papers in EM, Family File). For developments see nos. 671 and 680. For background on Nielsen see no. 77.

[2] In his letter of December 22 (EM) Nielsen had said that all of the energy being directed towards getting Eisenhower to run in the 1952 election should be harnessed in a grass-roots movement to stop political maneuvering. He had discussed this idea with many politicians. They wanted to see Eisenhower run for the presidency, but they didn't want to give up "their own political strings to see that happen." Nielsen had argued that if Eisenhower were elected he could not do much without a cooperative Congress. But the politicians replied that Eisenhower "could sweep them off their feet like Roosevelt did." This, Nielsen said, would be only a temporary solution.

[3] Eisenhower had asked his brother Edgar these same questions in October, when the latter had criticized the country's labor-management relations. The government, Eisenhower had argued on different occasions, could not solve the nation's problems without the active support of its citizenry (see no. 566).

[4] See also no. 609. For developments see no. 638.

[5] Nielsen's wife.

[6] Nielsen's daughter.

[7] Albert C. Jacobs, the former provost at Columbia University, had recently become Denver University's chancellor (see no. 440). Nielsen hoped to get better acquainted with Jacobs. "I have never seen a man take Denver by storm as he has," Nielsen wrote. "It is the greatest thing that has ever happened to the University."

631   *Eisenhower Mss.*

To Charles Vincent McAdam   *December 28, 1949*

Dear Charlie:[1] Cliff Roberts has just forwarded to me a copy of an article written by Mr. McLemore who, I understand, works for your syndicate.[2] The story was apparently published in the newspapers while I was in seclusion on an island off the Texas coast so this is the first time I have seen it.[3]

I think I have never met Henry McLemore, but quite naturally am flattered by his far more than generous comments with respect to me.

Because of your friendship, I have no doubt that you suggested the article—so I am grateful to you both. In any event and in spite of the embarrassment of reading nice things about myself, I like the article because of its last four or five lines in which it preaches the same thing in which I believe, namely, reward for work and opposition to the attempt of government to make mediocrity attractive.[4]

It just occurs to me that it has been a long time since I have seen you. This is something that should be remedied very soon.[5] In the meantime Mamie and I send to you and yours our best wishes for a splendid New Year. I truly hope that all goes well with you. *Cordially*

[1] For background on McAdam, president of the McNaught Syndicate, see no. 260.

[2] Henry McLemore, a syndicated columnist since the 1920s, had been with the McNaught Syndicate since 1940. Roberts had sent Eisenhower McLemore's article and several newspaper clippings, along with an undated covering note. He said that McAdam had asked him to bring the McLemore story to Eisenhower's attention, and he also advised the General that it was actually McAdam, not McLemore, who deserved credit for the article.

[3] The article, which was not to be released before December 13, 1949, commented on the recent attack by the *Columbia Daily Spectator*, Columbia's student newspaper, on Eisenhower's November 30 speech before the St. Andrew's Society (for background see no. 606). The article suggested that the newspaper change its name from Spectator to Spectacle and wondered if anyone on the editorial board had asked, What are our chances of ever serving our nation as well as the man we are getting ready to criticize? For background on Eisenhower's trip to Texas see no. 607.

[4] The article said that the Columbia editors should recognize that "there can be no happiness that's handed out. It keeps you warm, that free stuff, but if you deserve the designation of a man it will never give you real happiness, because *that* you must make for yourself." The current government trend "to take care of the inefficient, instead of rewarding workers," was making mediocrity attractive, and this was not right.

[5] On January 5 McAdam thanked Eisenhower for his letter and wrote, "I am at your command. You name the time and place . . . and I'll be Johnny-on-the-spot." All papers are in EM.

632   *Eisenhower Mss.*

To Bob Hope   *December 28, 1949*

Dear Bob:[1] Thank you very much for a most attractive and unusual Christmas card—but more than this for your thoughtfulness in remembering us.[2] You got exactly the kind of smoking jacket that I am sure I needed, sometimes I think I still do.

This note brings to you and yours my very best wishes for happiness and contentment throughout 1950 and, in fact, for all the years to come.[3] *Cordially*

[1] Hope was a popular radio and motion picture comedian greatly admired by the General for his entertainment tours of military bases overseas during World War II (Summersby, *Eisenhower Was My Boss*, p. 84). Hope had spent Christmas 1948 with American troops in Europe.

[2] Hope's holiday greeting to the General and Mrs. Eisenhower was written atop a silhouette of the comedian's famous profile. It read in part, "Sorry I can't get

over to your place this Xmas—staying in with the family. Gee! they got me the keenest smoking jacket." Accompanying this message was a humorous caricature of the Hope family at Christmas. Bob, the central figure, was bound to his chair in a strait jacket. Dolores, his wife, was pictured lighting up Hope's cigar as their children, Linda, Anthony, Honora, and William, looked on (n.d., EM).

[3] For developments involving Hope see no. 673, n. 5.

633   *Eisenhower Mss.*

To John Davison Rockefeller III   *December 29, 1949*

Dear John:[1] To say that I am grateful for your generous gift to Columbia University is a woefully feeble expression by which to describe the lift that your note gave us.[2] Fundamentally, my reason for being here is because I believe that Columbia has an ideal background and is ideally situated to be uniquely effective in re-awakening respect and support for those things that have been responsible for the spiritual, intellectual and material greatness of America. Receipt of such a gift as yours not only increases Columbia's opportunities to serve our people effectively— from the personal angle it gives me the definite feeling that the donor shares my hopes and convictions.

I understand the reasons that lead you to desire anonymity, and shall respect them.[3] Nevertheless, I hope that you will come to look upon this university as next after your own in your affections and esteem which is the kind of personal relationship we dare to covet with you and your brothers.

This note brings to you and yours my sincere wishes for a fine New Year. May all 1950 be crowded, for you, with happy and satisfying experiences. Again—personal and official thanks and warm personal regard. *Sincerely*

[1] For background on Rockefeller see no. 113. This handwritten letter was sent by special delivery on December 30.

[2] In a letter of December 28 Rockefeller had advised Eisenhower that he was making a gift to the university because of Columbia's contribution to American education and "more particularly in appreciation of your own leadership and what you stand for personally. . . ." He said that he hoped Eisenhower would feel free to use his contribution "in any way that would be most helpful. . . ."

[3] Rockefeller had written, "Since my brothers and I have, generally speaking, found it best to limit our gifts to educational institutions to those with which we have had some personal relationship, I would ask that my contribution be considered as from an anonymous donor" (EM).

TO HUGH ROY CULLEN   *December 29, 1949*

Dear Roy:[1] You may have heard that on my way out of Houston to take the road to Galveston I had the opportunity to visit the University of Houston campus, in company with Dr. Oberholtzer.[2] While Major Schulz and some of the others protested bitterly against my stealing the time for the expedition, I was so interested in what you were doing there that I merely disregarded well-meant advice and as a result had a most enjoyable half-hour visiting the several parts of the University grounds. I truly congratulate you on the progress made, and I am sure you are feeling a tremendous sense of satisfaction in the work that is being done there.[3]

Of course, as I have told you, I hope to interest you also in Columbia University. While I firmly believe that your first concern in the education of our youth should involve local Houston and Texas problems, yet I am quite sure that you recognize also the value of assuring support for such institutions as this one, where purposes and objectives are completely national in scope and where faculties and student body are representative of every state and territory. One of the basic reasons for the existence of such a national institution is to prepare our young people for effective citizenship in a free country. Columbia stands for free competitive enterprise.

The next time that I may be fortunate enough to have an opportunity for a long talk with you and Mrs. Cullen,[4] I hope to lay before you in some detail my hopes and aspirations for the future of this great institution, and my firm belief that it deserves some measure of support from all those citizens who believe in the fundamentals of our economic, governmental, and social system. I realize, of course, that political parties properly concern themselves with various and sometimes devious methods of applying these principles to the problems of the moment, but I am convinced that, regardless of particular political affiliation, one of our tasks today is to revive in all of us an acute respect for values that must be preserved if America is to retain its position of leadership in the world and to continue as the land of individual liberty and opportunity.[5]

Again, Mamie and I send to you both our very sincere wishes for a Happy New Year.[6] *Cordially*

---

[1] For background on Cullen see no. 602.

[2] On December 7 the Eisenhowers had had lunch with the Cullens at their Houston home, and the following morning Eisenhower had met Edison Ellsworth Oberholtzer at a Columbia alumni breakfast (Oberholtzer [Ph.D. Columbia 1934] had been part-time president of the University of Houston from 1927 until 1945, when he had become full-time president). After his visit to the University of

Houston that morning, Eisenhower had gone to Galveston. For background on the Eisenhowers' trip see no. 607. See also Eisenhower to Cullen, November 26, 1949; McCann to Oberholtzer, December 1, 1949; and Kilman and Wright, *Hugh Roy Cullen*, pp. 277–79.

[3] The University of Houston, which had become a four-year institution in 1934, had occupied temporary quarters on the grounds of a high school until Cullen had agreed to chair a fund-raising drive to build the school a campus. His initial donation had been one of time and effort. Subsequently he had contributed considerable amounts of money. In 1939 he had provided $260,000 for the construction of a building in memory of his son. This gift grew to $345,000, and by 1949 his contributions to the school totaled well over $5 million (see Kilman and Wright, *Hugh Roy Cullen*, pp. 190–95, 232, 253; David G. McComb, *Houston: The Bayou City* [Austin, 1969], pp. 149–50, 237–39; "A Man Who Likes to Give Away Millions," *U.S. News & World Report*, Feb. 11, 1955; and Cullen to Eisenhower, July 13, 1949. All correspondence is in the same file as the document).

[4] The former Lillie Cranz.

[5] For background on Cullen's interest in Eisenhower as a political candidate see no. 602.

[6] For further developments see no. 989.

635   *Eisenhower Mss.*

To Frank Smithwick Hogan   *December 29, 1949*

Dear Frank: It was neither through intent nor forgetfulness that I missed your swearing-in cermony yesterday.[1] Just as I was preparing to leave the house, we were called upon by two friends of more than thirty years standing and who were in the city for a matter of two or three hours only. They had come by taxi to 60 Morningside merely in the hope that we might be in. I simply did not have the heart to go away and leave them, particularly when they are already in their high seventies and my opportunities to see them in the future will be few indeed.

My desire to attend the ceremony was based upon more than personal friendship, although this alone would have been reason enough, but I felt that by attending I also could have symbolized something of Columbia's pride in your unique career and accomplishments. All of us here on the hill are very proud of you, and I am sorry that I could not gather with your other friends and admirers to be with you on such a significant occasion.[2] *Cordially*

[1] Hogan had been sworn in for his third four-year term as the District Attorney for New York County on December 28; on December 22 he had written to Eisenhower explaining that the General's attendance at the ceremony would make him very happy. Eisenhower had replied on the twenty-seventh that he would try to change an existing commitment so that he could come. For further background on Hogan see no. 10.

² Hogan replied, "Your absence . . . has its compensation since it resulted in your sending me a letter which I prize very much" (Jan. 4, 1950). All correspondence is in EM.

636   *Eisenhower Mss.*

TO GORDON GRAY   *December 30, 1949*
Confidential

Dear Mr. Secretary:[1] In reply to your letter of the 16th, I trust you will understand that I have had no opportunity to discuss exhaustively the Hoover Commission recommendations with any individuals who have had a specific knowledge of the Army Engineer Corps.[2] Consequently, my comments are based upon personal experiences and convictions rather than upon the broader considerations that must have been decisive in the formulation of the Hoover Commission recommendations.

Fundamentally, I, of course, agree that similar governmental functions should be grouped into a specific administrative network. Only thus, as a general proposition, can wasteful duplication be avoided. However, because I am not familiar with the specific engineering projects that now come within the purview of Department of Interior responsibility, I am unable to comment upon the wisdom of adding also to that Department's responsibilities all those civil functions now performed by the U.S. Army Engineers.

From a strictly military viewpoint, it would be a serious error, in my opinion, to confine the peace-time activities of our Army Engineers to the inconsequential engineering work incident to the peace-time training of the Army. Lack of troops and of money, and, therefore, of extensive training opportunity, would prevent our engineers from gaining the basic skills and, more important, the broad and practical experience that is absolutely essential to successful engineering work during a war.[3] To illustrate the point that I am trying to make here: In 1943 on the little island of Gozo near Malta, the U.S. Army Engineers prepared a satisfactory fighter strip in about twelve days, in a location where engineer officers of our Allies had estimated that the work could not possibly be accomplished in less than three months. This could have been vital to success, and it is my conviction that differences of this particular kind originate in the type of training and experience that men undergo in time of peace.[4]

It is possible, of course, that in lieu of the river and harbor work now performed under the authority and responsibility of the U.S. Army Engineers, there might be assigned to the Engineer Corps other governmental work deemed more akin to the specific problems of war engineering. Likewise, it may be contemplated that the officers of the Army Engineers should be employed on vast governmental projects in time of peace, but under the direction of the Interior Department of the Government.

On the first of such possible alternatives, I would offer no comment because I think the manner would be largely technical and professional. To the second of these possible alternatives, I would offer the objection that while individuals might, under such a plan, secure technical and professional training, there would be little opportunity for gaining experience in positions of great responsibility and therefore the Army's senior Engineers in time of war would very likely not be so competent as they are now. Here, I have particular reference to those vast wartime construction, repair and maintenance projects that demand the utmost in imagination, energy, professional ability as well as a discipline that is created out of a lifetime experience in unswerving devotion to duty.

Manifestly, these comments are presented, as I noted earlier, strictly from the Army viewpoint. I admit that other considerations may be of overriding importance, but I strongly urge that these special factors be not lost sight of in the making of the final decisions.[5] *Very sincerely*

---

[1] Eisenhower revised the initial draft of this letter (see copy in EM). For background on Secretary of the Army Gray see no. 471.

[2] The Hoover Commission (see no. 57 for background) had recommended that the civil functions of the Army Corps of Engineers be taken over by the Department of the Interior, and Gray had been asked to present President Truman with his views regarding this proposal. Throughout the Roosevelt and Truman administrations the Army had successfully lobbied against this idea, but the popular support aroused by the Hoover Commission's report in 1949 had renewed the congressional debate. With his letter to Eisenhower, Gray enclosed two documents: the commission's *Nineteenth and Concluding Report* (Washington, D.C., 1949), which stated that the Army Corps of Engineers, whose authority in river development lay outside the purview of the Secretary of the Army and the President, conflicted with and duplicated the Bureau of Reclamation's jurisdiction (pp. 5–6, 27–33); and House Document No. 122 (81st Cong., 1st sess.), which consolidated the commission's *Report of the Department of the Interior* [no. 14] *and . . . Appendixes L. M. and Q . . .* (Washington, D.C., 1949). Gray asked Eisenhower to comment on the proposal's probable effect "on our overall military capabilities in peace and in war" (EM). For background see Pemberton, *Bureaucratic Politics*, pp. 1, 31, 44–46, 99–107. Copies of Gray's enclosures are also in OS/D, 47–50, Clas. Numeric File, CD 12-2-29.

[3] Two members of the commission, former Alabama congressman Carter Manasco and Arkansas senator John Little McClellan, had disagreed with the commission's recommendation. In their dissenting argument they had quoted excerpts of statements Eisenhower had made praising the Corps of Engineers and the value of its civil-works training. The point General Eisenhower is making here parallels their argument (see Hoover Commission, *Report of the Department of the Interior* [no. 14], pp. 81–89).

[4] See Eisenhower, *Crusade in Europe*, p. 171, for his recollection of this incident. On the Corps's wartime service see Blanche D. Coll, Jean E. Keith, and Herbert H. Rosenthal, *The Corps of Engineers: Troops and Equipment*, U.S. Army in World War II, ed. Kent Roberts Greenfield (Washington, D.C., 1958); and Lenore Fine and Jesse A. Remington, *The Corps of Engineers: Construction in the United States*, U.S. Army in World War II, ed. Maurice Matloff (Washington, D.C., 1972).
[5] On January 4 Gray thanked Eisenhower for this letter (EM). On March 13 President Truman would present Congress with twenty-one reorganization plans that would implement many of the Hoover Commission's recommendations, but the President would not include the proposal discussed in this document (see *New York Times*, Mar. 14, 1950; and Pemberton, *Bureaucratic Politics*, pp. 124–25).

637   *Eisenhower Mss.*

To William Stuart Symington   *December 30, 1949*

Dear Stu: Our hopes of going with you to Puerto Rico this winter have collapsed about our heads.[1] There are many reasons for this, but a principal and decisive one is that Mamie's parents intend to stay with her at least until early February.[2] They are aging so rapidly that she would, under no circumstances, leave them here while she went off on a vacation trip. I would be particularly anxious to have her with me when I come to Puerto Rico so I feel we simply must drop out this time.

However, I still intend to get to Augusta National during late January if that is humanly possible. Under the circumstances I have just described this means that I would have to go without Mamie, but I should still like you for my guest. Unless Mamie were there I doubt that Eve[3] would like to come, but I am certainly anxious for you to see the golf course and to play it once. Maybe we could also get Dave Calhoun to come for a couple of days.[4]

Can't you mark your calendar for a few days, say from the 19th to the 26th of January, and then spend as much of that week with me at Augusta as possible—always providing that no calamity overtakes me and stops me from going. It happens to be a club where I cannot just send you a card. Guests are most welcome but must be accompanied by their particular host. I know that you and Dave would enjoy it tremendously. It is a grand golf course and the food is delicious. A fine gang of men belongs to the Club.[5]

In any event, let me hear from you when you have time to write. Mamie and I are most bitterly disappointed that we cannot join your expedition. The place and crowd sound delightful, but above all we would have liked to have spent a few days with you and Eve.

Happy New Years to you and yours. *Cordially*

[1] In November the Eisenhowers and Secretary of the Air Force Symington had discussed plans for a January vacation in Puerto Rico (Symington to Eisenhower, Nov. 29, 1949); in Symington's letter of December 22 he had said that he was counting on the General to set a date for the trip.
[2] On the Douds' visit to New York see no. 630.
[3] On Symington's wife, the former Evelyn Wadsworth, see Galambos, *Chief of Staff*.
[4] Symington had written that the David R. Calhouns, Jr., and the Lauris Norstads would join the Symingtons and Eisenhowers in Puerto Rico. For background on Calhoun see no. 581; on Norstad see no. 73. See also Calhoun to Eisenhower, December 20, 1949, and Eisenhower to Calhoun, December 23, 1949. All correspondence is in EM.
[5] Symington and Calhoun would visit Augusta as Eisenhower's guests in January. For the trip see no. 656. See also nos. 673 and 687.

638   *Eisenhower Mss., Diaries*

DIARY   *January 1, 1950*

This was not dated originally. It was *approximately* Jan 1, 1950[1]

This begins my attempt to keep some notes of my own in a form that I can later read. I do not like to dictate them, while my penmanship, in spite of my earnest efforts, quickly degenerates into a hopeless scrawl that, within a matter of days, is entirely meaningless to me. So I take advantage of this extraordinary present[2] from the I.B.M. (Tom Watson) to begin my own training on the typewriter and to kill two birds by practicing on notes that I should like to remember.[3]

All through the notes I have made since the war's end runs the strain of annoyance, or irritation, of my seeming inability to draw completely clear of public suspicion that I seek some political office, without baldly and arbitrarily making certain statements that I believe no American has the right to make! Those notes are scattered over periods of months and are characterized chiefly by their irregularity and haphazard composition. They have ordinarily been dashed off in crowded minutes, with little time to insure exactness of expression or even to check on the thought expressed. Nevertheless, I know, without referring to the little black book in which they are to be found, that my statements as to their reflection of a worrisome ~~political problem for my~~ personal ~~solution~~ problem is absolutely correct.[4]

To describe accurately the position in which I now find myself will take far more time than I can devote to this laborious business today! However I can make a start and perhaps I can find the opportunity during the coming week to put down the essentials of the situation. Admittedly the doing so promises no return to anybody—least of all me! No, here I think I'm wrong! I believe my effort, if successful will tend to clarify my mind to some degree and thus give me greater confidence that I am not straying from what I believe to be principle in any of my statements, conversations or decisions affecting any part of this confusing problem.

First the personal angle.

I do not want a political career; I do not want to be publicly associated with any political party, although I fervently believe in the two party system and further believe that, normally, a citizen is by no means performing his civic duty unless he participates in all applicable activities of his party, to include participation in precinct caucuses.

Consequently, it seems necessary to give reasons for regarding ~~myself~~ own as an exceptional rather than a normal case.

My basic purpose is to try, however feebly, to return to the country some portion of the debt I owe to her. My family, my brothers and I, are examples of what this country with its system of individual rights and freedoms, its boundless resources and its opportunities for all who *WANT to work*, can do so for its citizens, regardless of lack of wealth, political influence or special educational advantage. Nowhere else on earth has this type of material, intellectual and spiritual opportunity been so persistently and so successfully extended to all. Regardless of all faults that can be searched out in the operation of the American system, I believe without reservation that in its fundamental purposes and in its basic structure it is so far superior to any government elsewhere established by men, that my greatest possible opportunity for service is to be found in supporting, in renewing public respect for, and in encouraging greater thinking about these fundamentals. Since I believe that All Americans, even though they do so unconsciously or sub-consciously, actually support these basic tenets of Americanism, it follows that in the field in which I should work, (that is, the bringing of these basic tenets to our CONSCIOUS attention,) there is no difference between the two great parties. Therefore I belong to neither. *Their* function is to bring before the people the chance to choose between two different methods in the application of the principles to specific problems and to allow the people to choose between two specific slates of candidates. It seems to me that there are cogent reasons why I should eschew this partisan field of citizenship effort.

In the first place I shall never lose my direct and intimate interest in the legitimate aspirations and the welfare of our veterans of World War II.[5] They, I hope, have confidence that I shall try to discharge toward them every obvious obligation— and they comprise BOTH Democrats and Republicans. Whatever name or reputation I have, they made for *me*—I cannot

conceive of their believing that I was showing proper appreciation of this fact if I should join a political party. (At least I
am sure that those of the opposite party would look at me with
a jaundiced eye.)

In the second place I have been a soldier—necessarily without
political affiliation all my life. I should like to be of some help
from time to time in that type of governmental problem for
which I have been educated. That classification is military.[6] If
my counsel is ever desired in that kind of question, I should
like to be available no matter what political party might happen
to be in power at the moment. In other words, I should like
to remain just what I've always been, a military officer instantly
responsive to civil government, regardless of its political com-
plexion. In the third place I accepted, after long urging, the
Presidency of Columbia in the belief that in this post and with
the help of these great faculties I could do more than anywhere
else to further the cause to which I am devoted, the reawakening
of intense interest in the basis of the American system. Having
assumed the responsibilities of this post I do not believe it
appropriate for me to ~~publicly~~ proclaim a loyalty to a particular
political party. We have here men and women of all parties,—
our alumni and supporters, upon whom we are dependent for
our existence, likewise come from all parties. My joining a
specific party would certainly antagonize some. In my conviction, even partial adherence to a specific party or any partial
entry into the political field would demand from me an instant
resignation from Columbia. But here (in Columbia) is the place
I THINK I can do the most good for all—even if that most
is a rather pitiful amount.

I believe that the Army of the United States is this country's most
devoted, most efficient and best informed body of its size now existing.
The Army upholds the Constitution, our basic governmental document
and the foundation of the system that places the civil power of the
government in the master's position over the military. The good Army
officer has always been particularly careful to remain loyal to this
concept—both in deed and thought and, beyond this, in appearance!!!
Many people regard a soldier's entry into politics as an effort to overturn
this concept. Such a thought springs from prejudice and woeful ignorance—but it is idle to claim it does not exist. Consequently many
individuals in the army would fear that my entry into the political field
was showing a disregard of the possible consequences to the army's
reputation—they might even feel that I was "letting the Army down."
This, by itself, might be of only minor consequence. But the possibility
of false interpretation on the part of the public—inspired by political
partisans to whom no dirty trick is unknown—could be very serious

to the welfare of the Army, which, I repeat is the finest organization in government—any government.

There is an angle to this same subject that is important, though little noticed. It is the danger—once we become accustomed to thinking of our military leaders as potential political leaders—that their selection (which is done by the party in power at the time of selection) will certainly be based as much upon political considerations as upon their demonstrated military capacity. Such a grave occurrence in time of war could defeat the nation. That this line of reasoning is not baseless is demonstrated by the history of France throughout the 19th and early 20th centuries.[7]

As between the so-called concept of the welfare state and the operation of a system of competitive enterprise there is no doubt where I stand. I am not on any fence. In the same way I am not on any fence with respect to my attitude toward a possible nomination to political office. I want none of it and believe that to change my attitude would be bad both for me and for what I HOPE I can do in the line of public service. ~~But~~ People will believe me when I say that I'm against the handout state but nevertheless a militant liberal. They will not believe me when I say I am not interested in a political office—even the presidency. We are just NOT capable, in this country, of conceiving of a man who does not want to be president. Too many men running for political office have said just that, so the response is, "OH YEAH!" Well, the obvious course is to say nothing and to continue to preach what I believe, regardless of criticism by the columnists.[8]

Many men have appeared at my office or at my home to volunteer their services if and when I decide I have responsibilities in the political field.

Governor D.[9]
Russell Sprague[10]
    Brownell[11]
Sam Pryor—Connecticut—Panam.[12]
Arthur Gardner—2211 30th St., N.W. Washington
                (Decatur 8455)
[an associate of mine in World War I][13]
Dave Calhoun—St. Louis
Bill Robinson
Pete Jones—in special way.
Ed Clark—
Jimmy Byrnes—
Mrs. Luce
Dozens whose names appear in confidential file.
Lucius Clay
Russ Forgen
Wes Mac Afee (Pres., Union Elec.)

Eberstadt)
) in house of former
Hoover)[14]

The last thing that an office-seeker seems to think of is just plain honesty. If he can be devious he thinks he's smart; he'd rather be evasive than direct. He wants to give pat answers—he will never, for a second, admit that the true course, usually, is a middle one—between extremes. He hasn't the guts to be "middle of the road." He's afraid of attacks & "me too" from both sides. My speech in St. Louis on Sept. 3 to lawyers was on this point.[15]

In the back of this book are two memos, written by my two best friends in New York. Neither is a politician—one is a banker, the other a newspaperman.[16] They take opposite sides in arguing the question "Should Gen. E. now associate himself definitely with the Republican party and participate in the ensuing struggles between the two parties—specifically in the Congressional elections of the coming fall?" Why they happened to decide to write and give me their thoughts on this question, I do not know. But I am keeping them because each summarizes, fairly accurately, the arguments brought to me by many others—some on one side, some on another. Eberstadt, Byrnes, Dewey, Hoover, Sprague, Brownell among the more widely known politicians, and dozens of people on the business and industrial side, have talked to me on the same subject—but the answer remains the same.

Today the New York Sun ceases to exist as a separate paper. It has been bought up by the Scripps-Howard Chain. The one point that makes the incident of some significance is the explanation given by the ex-publisher of the Sun for its demise. His printed statement is pasted on this page—particularly because of his contention that labor leaders have become so unreasonable in their demands that they are defeating their own ends, i.e., by forcing small industry into bankruptcy they are creating conditions in which the workingman cannot fail to suffer.[17]

Another important reason for noting here the passing of The Sun is found in that paragraph of the final editorial of explanation that states what the paper stood for during its existence. These are the things in which I believe.[18] If a paper that has preached these things cannot secure enough support to operate successfully, the question is, "Are these principles, as guides to American action, now to go into the discard. If they are I am wasting a lot of energy—but I'll go down fighting. The cartoon below appeared in the final issue of the SUN.[19]

[1] This sentence appears in longhand at the top of a partially typewritten diary entry. Since Eisenhower refers in the last paragraph to a cartoon that appeared in the *New York Sun* on January 4, 1950, he wrote at least part of this entry on or after that date.

[2] Eisenhower inserted an asterisk between *extraordinary* and *present* and wrote "this typewriter" in longhand in the margin.

[3] Thomas John Watson, Jr. (B.A. Brown 1937), executive vice-president of IBM,

had informed Eisenhower on November 15, 1949 (EM), that he was sending him a new IBM executive typewriter "as a reminder of our admiration." The machine had arrived on November 18, and Eisenhower had thanked Watson on the following day (EM), remarking that he would keep the machine by his desk in order to find out "whether or not it is possible for a fellow of my age—as clumsy as I am—to learn to run one of these things satisfactorily."

[4] Earlier diary entries concerning Eisenhower's thoughts about a political career include nos. 491, 542, 543, 581, and 602.

[5] Eisenhower had a longstanding interest in the problems of veterans (see nos. 205, 228, and 233).

[6] Eisenhower had continued to perform this task since he had been at Columbia. He had, for instance, presided at meetings of the JCS and had served as adviser to the President and Secretary of Defense from January to August 1949. For background see nos. 294 and 521.

[7] Eisenhower's reference may have been to the frequent changes in government in France during the years of the Second Empire and the Third Republic. There had been nineteen governments and sixteen war ministers between 1870 and 1888, and the advancement of an army officer's career had become dependent upon his political views and his religious affiliation (Paul-Marie de La Gorce, *The French Army: A Military-Political History*, trans. Kenneth Douglas [New York, 1963], pp. 9, 50–54).

[8] In the coming weeks Eisenhower's name would appear in newspaper headlines as a result of speculation about his political prospects. He would rank high as a favored candidate for the governorship of New York when the results of a poll of Republican party county chairman in New York were announced (*New York Times*, Jan. 7, 1950). Eisenhower was not eligible, however, to run for the governorship because he had not been a resident of New York for five years. The *New York Times* would report on January 8, 1950, that Carlos Pena Romulo (A.M. Columbia 1921), president of the U.N. General Assembly, had nominated Eisenhower to be named "Man of the Half-Century." Romulo had been Resident Commissioner of the Philippines (in Washington, D.C.) until the establishment of the Republic of the Philippines on July 4, 1946 (for background see Chandler, *War Years*; and Chandler and Galambos, *Occupation, 1945*). On January 9 Roy A. Roberts, president and general manager of the *Kansas City* (Missouri) *Star*, would assert that Eisenhower could be drafted to run for the presidency in 1952 (*New York Times*, Jan. 10, 1950). On January 20 Senator Robert A. Taft, Republican of Ohio, would remark that he thought Eisenhower would become "a strong candidate . . . for high public office" (*ibid.*, Jan. 21, 1950). On January 21 the Alabama State Democratic Executive Committee would consider a Dixiecrat party proposal to pledge southern presidential electoral college votes to Eisenhower in order to ensure that one of the major parties selected him as its candidate. The plan was essentially an invitation to the Republicans to join forces with the Dixiecrats behind Eisenhower (*ibid.*, Jan. 22, 1950).

[9] Governor Thomas E. Dewey, of New York (for background see no. 33). In June 1950 Dewey would tell newsmen that Eisenhower "would make a fine President" (see *New York Times*, June 19, 1950).

[10] John Russel Sprague (LL.B. Cornell 1910) had been county executive of Nassau County, New York, since 1938. He was also a member of the Republican National Committee of New York State.

[11] Herbert Brownell, Jr. (LL.B. Yale 1927), had been chairman of the Republican National Committee from 1944 to 1946. He had been manager for Thomas E. Dewey's presidential campaigns in 1944 and 1948.

[12] Samuel F. Pryor, Jr., was vice-president, assistant to the president, and director of Pan American Airways. For background see no. 581.

[13] Arthur Gardner (Ph.B. Yale 1910) had enlisted in the Army in 1917 and in

a short time had attained the rank of captain in the Tank Corps. In 1926 he had embarked on a twenty-year career as a businessman in Detroit, Michigan. In 1946 he had become Assistant to the Secretary of the Treasury in the Truman administration.

[14] For background on David R. Calhoun, Jr., see no. 581; on William E. Robinson see no. 28; on W. Alton "Pete" Jones, no. 388; on Edwin N. Clark, Galambos, *Chief of Staff*, no. 1456; on James F. Byrnes, no. 602; on Clare Boothe Luce, no. 542; on Lucius D. Clay, no. 490; on J. Russell Forgan and J. Wesley McAfee, no. 581; and on Ferdinand Eberstadt and Herbert C. Hoover, no. 57. Eisenhower's reference is probably to a meeting with Hoover and Eberstadt that had taken place in Eberstadt's home.

[15] Eisenhower had spoken before the American Bar Association convention in St. Louis, Missouri, on September 5, 1949 (see no. 532).

[16] The banker was Clifford Roberts, a partner in the firm of Reynolds & Company, investment bankers; the newspaperman was William E. Robinson, executive vice-president of the *New York Herald Tribune*. Roberts had argued that Eisenhower's concern for the welfare of the nation ought to make him put aside his distaste for partisan politics and help stop "the current trend of socialism and the serious threats to our liberty." He wanted Eisenhower to support members of the Republican party during the 1950 congressional elections, if only to save the two-party system from extinction. He predicted that the only significant Republican victory in 1950 would be the reelection of Senator Robert A. Taft of Ohio. This might in turn lead to Taft's nomination as the party's candidate for the presidency in 1952, but Taft would probably lose the presidential election and doom the country to four more years of Democratic ascendancy. Roberts thought that Eisenhower might "be compelled to publicly oppose the Taft nomination because of the probability of his defeat and because of his isolationist convictions." To oppose Taft successfully, Roberts advised, would be to make certain that "you would be drafted for the nomination, even against your wishes."

Robinson maintained that Eisenhower should not join the Republican party. Political affiliation might diminish his "potential influence among the youth of the nation," make suspect the impartiality of his decisions as president of a major university, and confirm the opinions of those political writers who had doubted the sincerity of his denials of political ambition. Robinson cited Eisenhower's influence as a spokesman for independent voters as another reason for staying out of partisan politics during 1950. Robinson, who agreed with Roberts's evaluation of the Truman administration's "Socialistic doctrines," hoped that Eisenhower would husband his political resources until the Republicans called upon him to lead the independent voters to their side. Both Roberts's and Robinson's memoranda are undated and are in EM, Roberts Corr. Copies are also in the William E. Robinson Papers, Dwight D. Eisenhower Library, Abilene, Kansas. For an analysis of the memoranda see Lyon, *Portrait of the Hero*, pp. 405–6.

[17] Thomas Wheeler Dewart, president and publisher of the *Sun*, had issued a statement on January 4, 1950, explaining why he had sold the *Sun* to the *New York World-Telegram*, one of the many newspapers belonging to the Scripps-Howard group of companies. Dewart had declared that union demands for higher wages had left him no other choice and he had warned that similar demands were causing "an unprecedented and increasing number of casualties among newspapers which once were great and strong" (*New York Times*, January 5, 1950. A copy of Dewart's printed statement of January 4, 1950, is attached to Eisenhower's entry in EM, Diaries).

[18] Among the ideas that Dewart had listed as having received the support of the *Sun* were "constitutional government, sound money, reasonable protection for American industry, economy in public expenditures, preservation of the rights and

responsibilities of the several states, free enterprise, good citizenship, equality before the law, and . . . all the finer American traditions." The newspaper had opposed "Populism, Socialism, Communism, governmental extravagance, the encroachments of bureaucracy and that form of governmental paternalism which eats into the marrow of private initiative and industry" (*New York Times*, Jan. 5, 1950). For Eisenhower's ideas on similar subjects see for example nos. 445, 474, and 482.

[19] The cartoon, which Eisenhower attached to his diary entry, was "State of the Union" by Reuben Lucius "Rube" Goldberg. It depicted the continental United States about to plunge into a sea of debt. Pictured as inhabitants of the country were a number of square dancers as well as a piano player labeled "Harry" who was calling out the following cadence: "Do-si-do and crash the gate, dance around the welfare state! Swing your partners take the lead, everything is guaranteed! Promenade and feel no pain, get aboard the gravy train! Do-si-do it's all for free, circle left and vote for me!" Goldberg (B.S. University of California 1904) had drawn cartoons for the *Sun* since 1938. He would join the staff of the *New York Journal-American* after the *World-Telegram* acquired the *Sun*.

639   *Eisenhower Mss.*

To Carl Vinson   *January 3, 1950*
Confidential

Dear Mr. Chairman: I find it quite difficult to comply effectively with your request that I furnish a rough outline and specific ideas for the report that your Committee will have to make covering your recent investigation of the Armed Services.[1] My difficulty arises out of several reasons but the principal one is that I have not followed the testimony in detail—I do not even have a list of witnesses.[2]

In spite of these considerations, I assume that you are still clear in your own mind that you want to minimize the space that the report will give to the futile business of attempting to reach a judicial decision in past quarrels affecting particular weapons, techniques, procedures and other technical matters, which decisions even if they could be perfectly formulated, do not now comprise the basic concern of the average citizen who is contemplating the future security of our country. Instead, I understand that you want to turn your mind constructively to the future—that you want to indicate methods that, as a result of this investigation, you believe must apply in the future if we are to achieve the broad unity of purpose and coordination in execution that any sensible man sees as mandatory to maximum security, with minimum expenditure.

Nevertheless, and here I clearly have nothing but assumption to go on—it would appear that you cannot wholly ignore the questions and some of the statements that first gave rise to and, later, characterized the investigation by the Committee. If what I have so far said conforms to your thinking, then the answer should be, it seems to me, to prepare a report in which the major points of difference are identified, the conflicting testimony of several individuals is briefed under each such question, and then the whole used to show the need for a different approach to security development, rather than for mere identification of right and wrong in all these past incidents. The above represents the impression I carried away from our personal meeting immediately after the adjournment of the Committee at noon on Thursday, October twentieth.[3] It is in line with this understanding that I have prepared and send to you the following confidential memorandum.

One or two observations apply. I send you this as a personal effort to assist you in your difficult task and the paper has no official standing of any kind. It is personal between you and me. Naturally there will be vast gaps even in those paragraphs or parts of the report which I shall suggest as desirable. Obviously, I shall have to omit all of the opening and introductory paragraphs because I do not even know the authority for the investigation or whether or not any resolutions were passed in Congress directing it.

I think that these explanations are sufficient to describe my attitude in attempting such a difficult thing and why my effort must be incomplete. It will comprise, in fact, little more than suggestions for expansions.

With best wishes, *Sincerely*

CONFIDENTIAL SUGGESTIONS SUBMITTED TO CHAIRMAN VINSON IN ACCORDANCE WITH HIS PERSONAL REQUEST

- - - - - - - - - - - - - - - - - - -
Report by the Committee
- - - - - - - - - - - - - - - - - - -

I

In this section should go all of the preliminary and introductory matter that is customary in the preparation of these reports or that seems to be indicated in the circumstances.

II

BRIEF REVIEW OF THE UNIFICATION EFFORT

At various times during the past years, particularly after the airplane first became recognized as a significant weapon in warfare, a three-part organization of our Defense forces was suggested—the whole to be coordinated or directed by a single civilian executive head. However, the movement which led to the current, three-part organization of our Defense forces was really initiated during World War II.

As the end of that conflict became foreseen by some of our uniformed leaders, the question of future military organization came up for discussion. Without recounting the details of divergent views, it is pertinent to note that, by inter-Service agreement, there was appointed a joint Board to study the subject of post-war defense organization. There was implied, at the very least, a conclusion that pre-war organization of our armed forces was no longer appropriate. This Board was headed by Admiral Richardson of the Navy.

The Board made a long and exhaustive study of the matter, securing testimony from every prominent Army, Navy and Air Force officer in our World War II forces. Incident to its labors the Board traveled around the world to secure field, as well as Washington, opinion. Originally, there appeared to be almost unanimity of field opinion, in all Services, as to the necessity of a three-part organization of our Defense forces, headed by a single civilian Secretary. This unanimity never prevailed in Washington.[4]

Shortly after the cessation of hostilities, the President of the United States, in his capacity as Commander-in-Chief of the Armed Forces, decided that a unified organization was necessary to the security of our country. He announced the basic decision, and invited frank discussion and opinion from all the Services on the proposal in the hope of producing a plan acceptable to all before its submission to Congress. It then developed that the Navy Department had, apparently unanimously, become extremely doubtful of the wisdom of this move and all Navy opinion, both at home and in the field, was eventually thrown on the side of retention of the old organization.

It would appear fruitless to describe here the long and tedious procedure that finally resulted in the adoption of the so-called Unification Act of 1947. Likewise, this report includes no account of the operations of the Defense Department during the early months of its existence.[5]

However, the first executive head of the new Department, James Forrestal, decided, during the course of some year and a half of service as such, that the law should be amended so as to concentrate greater authority in the civilian Secretary. He finally came to believe that unification would have to come about more as the product of civilian authority than as the result of complete agreement among the Armed Services.

Again the Navy, as a body, was opposed to the proposition. The other Services were almost as unanimously in support. After additional months of hearings and discussions, certain amendments of the character recommended by Secretary Forrestal and the President of the United States were enacted in the law.[6]

During this entire time, indeed from early 1946 until the present date, the principle of unification and its application to our nation's security organization have been complicated by certain very serious differences in professional opinion and conviction involving strategy, tactics, weapons and organization.

All advocates of every theory of American security turn back to the experiences of World War II for historical example—for illustration—to prove the soundness of their own arguments. The difficulty is that these experiences were frequently as different, one from the other, as is the center of a continent from an ocean expanse. They were as varied as the climates and territorial characteristics of the different quarters of the globe—almost as diverse as the personalities of the participants in the fighting of World War II.[7]

The obvious lessons of the war are not the same to the men who conducted an island-hopping campaign through the far reaches of the Pacific in the general direction of Japan as they are to men who, day after day, carried the destructiveness of American bombing into the heart of Hitler's homeland. Officers who prepared and led amphibious operations against island fortresses of definitely known and limited strength are left with a far different picture of war than those who conducted even greater amphibious operations which were, nevertheless, nothing more than preludes to vast continental campaigns, in which the full disposable strength of the enemy's homeland became involved.

It was only human that each man would gain a tremendous respect for the particular weapon, machine or type of unit with which he personally was identified in the war and that he should tend later to magnify or at least support the importance of that particular weapon, machine or unit in considering the future of our country's security.

Thus is explained one of the basic reasons for the great differences that have characterized the professional convictions of our highest commanders during the several years just past.

On the part of the Navy there was also a lively suspicion that the Navy would be at a disadvantage in any tripartite councils, due to the fact that the other two Services were originally one. The validity of such a suspicion cannot be wholly discounted, although, most certainly, it would be counterbalanced in some degree by the history of smouldering and bitter opposition that existed in the twenties and thirties between the ground officers and the air officers of the Army. The most explosive incident of this contest was the Mitchell trial; but that trial was merely a dramatic illustration of a mutual distrust and antagonism that lasted even up to the outbreak of World War II.

In any event, rigidly held professional opinions, in all Services, and Navy fear of a minority position in council stood in the way of achieving that degree of unification and resultant economy that the President and the Congress so fervently anticipated when the law of 1947 was enacted.

An added, and possibly a principal, cause for discontent and inter-Service quarrel was a feature which would appear to be an inescapable part of unified policy and dictated by considerations of efficiency. It is the practice of allocating, by the Bureau of the Budget in the name of the President, of an over-all maximum financial ceiling to the Armed Services, out of which total sum the support for all Services for any given year must come. Thus was created a contest among the leaders of each Service for the lion's share of the defense dollar—especially since the total sum that could be safely allocated, with due consideration for the financial stability of the country, could not possibly equal the aggregate of the Service recommendations, when these were based strictly upon professional considerations. With the certainty staring them in the face that all Services would have to live and operate on an austerity basis, the ingenuity and the fervor developed by each Service in advancing its own claims, ran head-on into an equal ingenuity and fervor in each of the other Services.

During organizational and operational activities in the Defense Department, members of this Committee have been frequently invited into consultation with executive officials. It has been evident that a great amount of patience, tolerance and persuasion has been employed in the effort to assure basic agreements that would permit and lead to efficiency and effectiveness in our Security arrangements.

Eventually, however, civilian authority, in the person of the Secretary, began to be applied more and more specifically and with greater and greater impact on the operations and functions of the Services. This led to several results. In one instance, at least, Congressional intervention provided about eight hundred million dollars more for one of the Services than had been budgeted for it by civilian Executive authority.[8] In other instances, rumblings of discontent and unhappiness began to reach the ears of Congress and the public. Finally, certain of these rumblings broke out so dramatically and in such apparent disregard for the traditional civilian control over Armed Services that investigation by this Committee was indicated as desirable, even mandatory.

III

BASIC QUESTIONS OF THE INQUIRY
NAVAL PRESENTATION

The general charge of the Navy, whose witnesses first appeared before the Committee, was that in the tripartite system of control the Navy was always at a disadvantage.[9]

More specifically, the Navy charged that too much of the National Defense dollar had been placed in the manufacture, procurement and maintenance of the giant Air Force airplane, designated the B-36. This charge was expanded to include the statement that, within the Air

Forces, far too much money and attention was given the big bomber at the expense of "tactical" aviation.

Navy witnesses said that the B–36 would be completely helpless to carry out a successful bombing mission against modern defenses—and held also that at the heights from which it would attempt to bomb, its destructive effect could be described only as "area" bombing. This type of operation was bitterly assailed by Navy men as ineffective, expensive and inhuman. Moreover, the Navy held that our strategic plans placed too great a reliance on the effect of an early bombing offensive featuring the A-bomb, in deterring and damaging a potential enemy. It was claimed also that the Army and Air Force failed completely to understand Naval problems and principles and that, because of this, the Navy had been hampered and impeded in its efforts to produce the type of weapons essential to future security of the country.

Numerous Naval witnesses, some of whom qualified as experts in specialized technical and professional lines, appeared before the Committee either to support these general charges or to amplify and expand each into technical channels and problems.

In the addenda to this report appear the records of all testimony submitted. Here, it is deemed sufficient to state that unanimously the Navy witnesses urged upon the Committee the validity of the charges out-lined above, together with the need for some kind of intervention— possibly Congressional—that would assure to the Navy freedom of action and the necessary appropriations to produce and maintain the kinds of weapons and the number of units that the Navy should decide was necessary for the country's security. Implicit in the Navy's argument was the contention that no other Service can have any valid opinion whatsoever as to the need for the particular kind and type of Navy weapon.

AIR PRESENTATION

The representatives of the Air Forces challenged almost every statement made by the Navy. As might be expected, this was particularly true with respect to the Naval allegations respecting the B–36. Professional Airmen defended the fitness of the B–36 to carry out the job for which it was designed, namely, long distance bombing with heavy bomb loads even, when necessary, on a transoceanic and intercontinental basis. The Air Force also challenged the right of the Navy to criticize this weapon in view of the Navy's assertion that each Service should be free to design, procure and maintain those weapons which it believed best in its own field.[10]

Moreover, the Air Force representatives, in turn, deprecated the need for aircraft carriers in the Navy, except for those carriers specifically designed for the elimination of hostile submarines. The Air Force admitted that the existence of a certain number of aircraft carriers of the Essex and similar classes would be most convenient upon the outbreak of any war, but insisted that, in view of the necessity for cutting security expenditures, this particular item was of such relatively low value as to deserve no allocation of peace-time Defense funds.

To the Navy charge that the Air Forces were devoting too much money to long-range bombers at the expense of tactical and pursuit aircraft, the Air Forces argued that our possession of long-range bombers and the A-bomb was one of the greatest deterrents to Russian aggression that now exists. They argued further that, if Russia were freed from this deterring influence, that country would logically turn from the manufacture of Air defensive equipment to the production of offensive equipment. In other words, the Communists would be free, without danger of retaliation, to begin preparing for bombing attacks on the United States.

The Air representatives urged that strategic bombing was not only the function of the Air Forces, they believed also that strategic bombing had been a significant factor in the attainment of victory in World War II and would become more and more significant to victory in any future war, as the years go by. Because they claimed this field as their own, both, they said, by logic and by Service agreement, they unequivocally denied the need of the so-called "super carrier" in the Navy. They insisted that that carrier is intended for no other reason than for participation in strategic bombing. They insisted that through it the Navy intends to disregard its traditional and legal mission of controlling the seas and intends to intervene directly in the role and mission of another Service. This, in the Air contention, is not only duplication but is defiance of law and of logic.

As in the case of the Navy, the Air Forces produced a variety of witnesses. Generally speaking, their purpose was to establish in the minds of the Committee a high degree of confidence in the main contentions just enumerated.

ARMY PRESENTATION

In general, the tone of the Army presentation was set by the Chief of Staff General J. Lawton Collins, who took a most conciliatory attitude toward the whole unfortunate affair. This attitude he maintained even in discussing the one subject that has reportedly been of such acute contention between the Army and Navy, namely the size and the missions of the Marine Corps. General Collins maintained that, while the Army believed that the Marine Corps should be confined to its own specific functions and, consequently, accurately tailored amounts of money should be devoted to its maintenance, no one in the Army had ever advocated the abolition of the Marine Corps. Its function as an arm of the fleet and as a mechanism for developing amphibious doctrine was admitted. In answer to questions, it appeared that the Army would consider unwise the allocation of funds to the Marine Corps for the purpose of preparing to organize forces of the size used in World War II, when the Marines were such an important part of the island-hopping campaign across the Pacific. General Collins specifically denied the accuracy and validity of the charges made by the Marine General Cates before the committee to the effect that the Army was seeking the annihilation of the Marine Corps.[11]

Through his entire presentation General Collins pledged again and again the intention of the Army to do its part in making unification work.

Succeeding witnesses from the Army were not brought forward merely to substantiate the statements of the head of the delegation. General Clark, until lately in command of the Sixth Army Area in San Francisco, presented the results of an experimental unification project in the field. He asserted that, in field operations, true unification could save millions of dollars for the Government, but said also that much of his effort in the field had been defeated by the Navy, apparently in the belief that if success were permitted in the nine Western states, which formed the experimental area, the anti-unification arguments of the Navy in Washington would be weakened. His testimony dealt with concrete administrative affairs and was, therefore, interesting. His complete text is found in the appendices.[12]

General Clark believed that the prospects for success in future unification were dependent upon the ruthless elimination from positions of high command of all officers who did not subscribe to it, in principle.

IV

PRESENTATION BY THE OFFICE OF THE SECRETARY OF NATIONAL DEFENSE

Secretary Johnson requested a number of individuals to appear before the Committee. Some of these were officials of his own office. Some were individuals who, by reason of past experience, were familiar with the general problem of unification. The first to appear was General Omar Bradley, Chairman of the Joint Chiefs of Staff and Commander, during the war, of the Twelfth Army Group in Europe.

General Bradley addressed himself largely to the charges and complaints lodged with the Committee by the Naval representatives. In effect, he denied their validity, individually and collectively. He charged a complete lack of cooperation on the part of the Navy in attempting to solve the problems of the Security Establishment and gave as a reason for this lack of cooperation the determination of the Navy to prove that a unified control will not work. He seriously questioned the loyalty of anyone in the Services who, in the face of contrary orders from his civilian superiors, would bring these questions into the open. So far as he dwelt upon professional argument and specific value, he generally supported the Air position as opposed to the Navy.[13]

General Bradley, who has been a member of the Joint Chiefs of Staff since February 1948, attempted to refute the charges that within that body the Navy was invariably subjected to 2–1 coercion: that the Navy was not treated as a full partner in the business of devising the proper defense structure for the country.

While, running through General Bradley's testimony was a thread of conciliation or at least some implied hope that these grave differences could be finally adjudicated, he was obviously vastly disturbed and indignant as a result of the charges and complaints presented at the hearing by the Naval representatives.

The Secretary of Defense arranged for a number of other witnesses to appear before the Committee. They included General of the Army Dwight D. Eisenhower, General of the Army George C. Marshall, ex-president Herbert Hoover and finally the Secretary himself. Mr. Johnson took the stand to give the Committee a general summing up of all the whole argument.

Except for Secretary Johnson, none of the witnesses mentioned referred specifically to the questions under dispute. They addressed themselves to the larger question of unification, urging its necessity now and in the future and, in certain instances, gave at least some suggestion of how unification could be made to operate more effectively.

By implication, General Eisenhower expressed great concern over the fact that Navy complaints and arguments had been dragged out in the open and thus had become a matter of acute interest in our daily newspapers.[14] Both Generals Marshall and Eisenhower made the obvious point that much of the inter-Service contest centered around the Budget. Secretary Johnson denied specifically the major charges launched by the Navy against the functioning of the Department of Defense. He explained the reasons for forced savings within the Departments and defended vigorously his decision of last spring to cease work on the so-called "super-carrier." He joined with the three preceding witnesses in arguing that unification must be made to work and promised the Committee that he was ready and anxious in every possible way to secure this result.[15]

V

COMMITTEE ACTION

After thorough consideration of the circumstances which had first indicated the necessity for this investigation and of the detailed and conflicting testimony submitted to it by witnesses, the Committee arrived at certain basic conclusions. The first of these deals with the adequacy of laws now existing for effective unification.

While it is obvious that individual members of the Committee feel that certain provisions of existing laws could be changed with advantage to the proper functioning of the unification idea, yet the general conclusion was that there should be no attempt at this time to make radical changes in these laws. Some of these ideas for partial revision would tend to make even yet tighter the control exercised by the civilian Secretary, in the name of the President, over the whole structure; others would advocate revisions looking toward more decentralization and, therefore, the diminishing of the authority of the Secretary of Defense. At this time when differences between the Services—some of which differences revolve around the question of the adequacy of the laws— have been so acutely brought to the attention of the public and have become a matter of serious concern to all, it would seem to be most unwise to undertake the process of revision with renewed arguments that could not fail to prolong and possibly even intensify the heat and rancor of the quarrel. In addition, the Committee clearly felt that such errors as have occurred within the Security Establishment are probably far more the fault of administration than of the existing legal structure. This is particularly true since the revision of the original law, a process that was completed in the Congressional Session just past.[16]

Having disposed, for the moment, of the question of required revision of the law, the Committee addressed itself next to one point that had come up from time to time during the course of the investigation, either directly or by implication. This point involved the propriety of the methods used by the Navy in attracting public notice to information, facts, statistics and charges which, it was contended by some, should have been kept confidential within the limits of executive discussion. It was definitely charged that, when men in uniform feel capable and qualified to defy orders of civilian superiors, we are coming dangerously close to violating that basic concept of American political life, which makes the military organization completely subordinate to civilian orders.

The Committee notes the obvious fact that the original unification law instituted a very great change in the Security organization of this country. Among other things, it probably confused a number of individuals as to the particular source of civilian authority. The law left in each Service a Secretary, traditionally the mouthpiece of civilian authority for that particular Service. It then set up over the three Service Secretaries another civilian Secretary. Among these Secretaries it is clear that differences have arisen, a circumstance that could not fail to become public and to have a very definite effect in confusing the minds of men, minds already disturbed by rejection of their professional advice. In addition, as already indicated in this report, it was only some months ago that general public discussion of all these issues was not only permitted but seemingly encouraged. Spokesmen for both sides of the unification argument in 1945–47 eagerly took advantage of opportunities to appear in public and to express themselves in the columns of the public press. It seems clear to the Committee that Service custom and precedent in this regard suffered a great, but tacitly approved change, coincident with the beginnings of the intensive discussion of unification when it was still only a proposal. Consequently, the Committee believes that to attempt at this moment to apply, against the officers now accused of implied insubordination, the strictest codes of military discipline would be grossly unfair. Moreover, it would probably compel the Committee to go back for some years to the record and history of each Service to discover whether other violations, probably less dramatic but equally serious in character, should warrant censure and whether, also, they helped to inspire the present upheaval that has attracted so much public attention. In these circumstances and, realizing that officials already set up in the several Service Departments hold specific and legal responsibility for the discipline of their commands, the Committee advises no further Congressional action of any kind on this point.

In analyzing conflicting testimony bearing upon the technical and professional issues at stake, the Committee reaches a somewhat similar conclusion to that explained in the paragraphs just preceding. It should be obvious that if professional men cannot clearly decide, for example, between the value of a "fleet" carrier as opposed to the value of a group or larger unit of long range bombers, then the question is one of those that probably can never be completely resolved unless, unfortunately, placed to the ultimate test of war. However, it is pertinent to state here that it was clear, in all this testimony, that each officer was presenting the case from the particular situation he himself pictured, probably based on his own specialized war experience.[17] Thus, it appeared to the Committee that each man before it was probably earnestly of the belief that his own testimony represented the full truth. Manifestly, someone was wrong—it is more probable that each party to the argument was, in varying degree, wrong. The professional question that should be sifted to the bottom is the worth of these several weapons based against their cost, and the probability of their future emergency need. This process, let it be noted, is part of the actual making of a war plan, obviously the business for professionals.

The Committee had, of course, from records and from testimony, the opinions of such bodies as the Research and Development Board and individuals who have been testifying on these matters before Committees of Congress for these past several years. Integration of all these views does not change the Committee's decision, implied above, that no civilian body can of itself reach, through deliberative processes, final answers that can be adequately weighed against the facts of the past and the probability of future wars. Although scientific people have pointed out that if the United States believes it may need heavy bombers before

1952 the B–36 is the best available, this does not answer the general charge that all heavy bombers of current design are so vulnerable as to make their building nothing else but a costly blunder—or the contrary argument that the heavy bomber provides the cheapest, surest and most effective way of delivering significant bombing attacks.[18]

The Committee believes, therefore, that, as always before, we must depend upon and encourage a continuation of the process of exploration, study, and coordination among our officers of the several Services to preserve for America a satisfactory doctrine of defense, to have ready applicable plans and to devise units, suitably equipped to meet the most probable circumstances of any emergency.

It is a truism that the situation at the beginning of any war is, for the defender at least, always radically different from any that was anticipated. It is this truth that makes impossible the complete and detailed reconciliation of divergent and professional views in the problem of utilizing available appropriations so as to produce the maximum in security.

If every detail of the opening phases of any war of the future could be foreseen with certainty, then it is entirely probable that the professional issues so bitterly contested in the current investigation could not only be decided easily, but would never have arisen.

This kind of observation does not, of course, take into account Service prejudices and jealousy and personal thirst for power and recognition. The Committee does not attempt to minimize the importance of these undesirable qualities but makes observations with respect to them. In the first place, they are natural human qualities and though men who aspire to positions of leadership must learn a large measure of self-control in self-seeking, the qualities themselves are never eliminated. It is the considered judgment of the Committee that, in this particular incident, this type of motive had only a bare minimum of influence.

Reasoning along the line just indicated, the Committee was compelled to decide that whatever good was to come from the public airing of both sides of this controversy would be found, so far as the past arguments were concerned, in bringing to bear upon them the full glare of public opinion and the clear realization on the part of the Services that the American people expect them to resolve their differences and to perform their professional duties not only with efficiency and effectiveness but also with dignity and decorum.[19]

With respect to the future, however, the Committee's conclusions are far more specific. The question presented to the Committee, as a result of this long and exhaustive inquiry, is:

> —How can unification be made to work
> and how can this Committee, as the
> agent of the House of Representatives
> best cooperate to that end?

The first half of this question, of course, presupposes that in the lower echelons of command, and in many administrative areas, unification is now a working fact; the objective must be the extension of unification in letter and spirit throughout the entire Defense structure. This objective cannot be achieved by persuasion, although indoctrination—at the unit level in all Services, in the classrooms of the Academies, in all Service schools, by instruction, association and joint exercises—is essential. The chief instrument for the development of unification in letter and spirit, however, is the discipline and fidelity to duty that are uniquely characteristic of all the Armed Services.

Given clear-cut doctrine and clear directives in every matter that concerns unification, and assured the support of their civilian superiors, all officers of the Services can exact of those below them unquestioning obedience to the letter of unification—a relatively short space of time will convert this obedience into a firm acknowledgment of unification and loyalty to its spirit.[20] In sum, unification—already at work—can be made to work throughout the Defense Establishment if the discipline of the Armed Forces is recognized as the chief instrument toward its development.

The answer to the second part of the question is actually a corollary to the preceding.[21] The Committee's relationships with the National Defense Establishment and the Services must be premised on the fact that unification is no longer a controversial subject—it has been enacted, to a large extent implemented and must be sustained, unless the past acts of Congress are revoked and the Services be returned to competitive bidding for Congressional favor.

Above all, immediately it is determined, or is evident from the start, that complaint or attack on unification is intended to resurrect dead controversy or inflame opinion, the committee should in no wise lend its dignity and prestige to those inciting dispute. Particularly, it must be recognized that the press and other media of communications and their guaranteed freedom of speech, can be misused and abused by those[22] more interested in sensational impact on the public than in constructive strengthening of the Services. One man, recognized by the Committee and given a hearing that his charges do not merit, can undo the work of many thousand men and many months.

Association of the Committee with the Services, at all levels and in all areas, should be far closer than was thought necessary in the past. Only by such association can the members of the Committee gain the factual knowledge that will re-enforce their personal convictions about unification and that will guard them against acceptance of irresponsible charges.[23]

One of the obvious obstacles to smooth and effective cooperation in the higher echelons in the Service Command is to be found in the processes by which annual appropriations are distributed to each. It is obviously impossible to provide an impregnable and indestructible defense for the United States with any array of forces, machinery, equipment and organization that could conceivably be maintained at any cost below that of National Bankruptcy. We are not, however, concerned with considerations of absolute defense—rather we deal always in relative terms. A concept of perfect defense would envision such an overwhelming preponderance of force in all the categories that the practical result would be single power domination of all the world.[24]

Because of these inescapable circumstances professional opinion will always find grave deficiencies in the amounts provided for defense. This applies to the total sum that can be made available as well as to that part of the sum that each Service receives.

Manifestly, each service will attempt to secure the greatest possible portion of the aggregate sum in any year in order that it may find itself in a position to meet, with some degree of effectiveness, its own assigned and traditional responsibilities. Much of the heat in recent inter-Service controversy has sprung directly *from this process of attempting to distribute deficits* among the three, with the consequent jealousy with which each has viewed every allocation made to other Services. When civilian authority is forced to intervene and make decisions in this delicate matter, it is easy to see where one of the Services can quickly convince itself that it is the victim of special considerations or special lobbying ability on the part of others. It then seeks relief from any possible source, including the Congress.

The Committee believes that much can be done to lessen the intensity of this struggle and thus to remove one great obstacle from the path of successful coordination and cooperation.

Manifestly, the Congress cannot escape its constitutional duty of raising and maintaining defense forces. This particular Committee cannot escape its duty of examining, analyzing, and reporting upon every recommendation made by the professional Services.[25] Moreover, the Committee is convinced that by coordinating the performance of this legislative duty with the functions of the Executive Department, there will result improved confidence among all the agencies responsible for defense.

Normally, the Services begin the development of the annual defense budget something like a year in advance of the opening of the Congressional session which is to consider that appropriation. There is a long series of adjustments, conferences, reviews and revisions that takes place within various echelons of the Executive Department in order to produce a reasonably balanced budget for the Services and within the aggregate limiting figure tentatively fixed by the President, through his Bureau of Budget.

All of this work is done in rough conformity to an outlined strategic plan that the Services have agreed upon among themselves as applicable to the world situation then current. This budget-development work is tedious and arduous, and requires a very great deal of mutual concession and compromise in order to produce a document that is reasonably acceptable to the several Services, to the civilian heads of the three departments, and to the Secretary of Defense.

When a Congressional session opens, therefore, there is normally presented to this Committee certain plans and recommendations from the Services which conform to the concepts and ideas upon which all of this budget work has been proceeding for many months. Since it is the clear duty of this Committee to use its judgment in passing upon recommendations involving policies, plans, methods and procedures, it is almost inevitable that certain changes will have to be made, and these changes necessarily re-open the whole budgetary process and require adjustments all the way back to the very beginning. The entirety of each Service's deficiencies, fears, warnings—and resentments are thus thrust into the open forum of debate at one time.—There has been neither step by step coordination between Committee and the Secretary of Defense, nor has the Committee had opportunity to inform itself progressively of the many important factors applying to this critical problem. Circumstances tend to encourage expensiveness in presentation.

This whole process is disjointed and uncoordinated in spite of the best will in the world on the path of both the Secretary of Defense and the Committee. It is bound to create a considerable amount of irritation and may even incite charges of bad faith. When this occurs, mutual antagonism of course increases and reaches a peak.

The Committee proposes to make impossible this particular kind of difficulty by keeping itself progressively and constantly informed of development of plans and policies at the same time that there is being constructed the budget intended to implement both plans and policies. It is hoped that at every stage of discussion and of concession and conciliation, the Committee or its representatives, thus informed of the considerations leading to each decision, will be a virtual participant in these months of work, and can give constant assurance to each Service that its particular point of view has been considered and digested by the representatives of the law-making body of the Government. All this can be done, the Committee knows, because of the specific invitation of the Secretary of Defense. Thus will result coordination without surrender of responsibility by any part of Government.

Of course, a very considerable degree of cooperation has existed in the past, but it has been spasmodically and accidentally accomplished rather than deliberately planned. It is the conclusion of the Committee that by undertaking to perform this duty in this timely fashion, there will not only be complete confidence on the part of each military Service that it cannot possibly become the victim of injustice or prejudice, but a smooth-working procedure should develop that will do much to achieve the whole unification.[26]

[1] Eisenhower had been involved in the House Armed Services Committee's investigation of unification and strategy; Congressman Carl Vinson (see no. 294) was chairman of that committee. For background on the investigation, which initially had focused upon the B–36 bomber, see no. 574. A number of earlier versions of both this letter and Eisenhower's draft report are in EM; most of these versions have extensive revisions in Eisenhower's handwriting.

[2] In November General Gruenther had sent Eisenhower an "Analysis of Testimony Presented to the Armed Services Committee of the House of Representatives Investigating the B–36 and Related Matters." The Army's Plans and Operations Division, which had prepared the document, was very critical of the Navy's role in the entire affair and had concluded that the *"one basic issue"* had been *"unification itself."* A copy of the analysis, dated November 3, 1949, is in P&O, 49–50, 452.1, Case 6/6. See also Andrus to Gruenther, December 12, 1949, *ibid.*, Case 6/7; and Gruenther to Eisenhower, November 12, 1949, and Schulz to Gruenther, January 5, 1950, both in EM.

[3] Eisenhower had testified before Vinson's committee on October 20 (see no. 570).

[4] For background on the board headed by Admiral James O. Richardson see Chandler and Galambos, *Occupation, 1945,* no. 206, n. 1. This paragraph, the following paragraph, and the two preceding paragraphs would become the opening section of the House Armed Services Committee's report (see House Committee on Armed Services, *Unification and Strategy,* 1950, p. 1). In the last sentence of the following paragraph the committee would change Eisenhower's "retention of the old organization" to "a type of reorganization more closely related to the prewar system."

[5] In regard to the events leading up to the passage of the National Security Act of 1947 and the establishment and initial operation of the National Military Establishment see Galambos, *Chief of Staff.*

[6] See no. 327 for information on the National Security Act amendments of 1949.

[7] This and the following seven paragraphs were incorporated, with only a few minor editorial changes, into the final report of Vinson's committee (see House Committee on Armed Services, *Unification and Strategy,* 1950, pp. 4–5).

[8] Eisenhower was referring to President Truman's decision to hold in reserve the funds voted by Congress that were in excess of the amount Truman had asked for (see no. 296, n. 7).

[9] The Navy's presentation is discussed in the notes to nos. 556 and 560.

[10] For the Air Force testimony see no. 570.

[11] Collins, whose October 20 statement had been described by the *New York Times* as "generally conciliatory," had been speaking in rebuttal of the statement of General Clifton Bledsoe Cates (LL.B. University of Tennessee 1916), the Commandant of the Marine Corps since January 1, 1948. Cates had entered the Marine Corps during World War I; during the Second World War he had led combat troops at Guadalcanal, Tinian, and Iwo Jima. During the House Armed Services Committee hearings Cates had claimed that "the Army General Staff group," in violation of the 1947 National Security Act, was close to success in its "unremitting effort to deprive the Marine Corps of the status which the Congress had given it." The Marine Corps had been hampered in its efforts to defend itself, claimed Cates, because it had been excluded from the JCS (see no. 402). During Cates's testimony one congressman had reminded the committee of Eisenhower's 1946 proposals to limit the size and functions of the Marine Corps (see Galambos, *Chief of Staff,* no. 816), and Cates had testified that it was his belief that the Army General Staff

was still trying to accomplish these goals (House Committee on Armed Services, *National Defense Program—Unification and Strategy: Hearings*, 1949, pp. 365–94, 543–64; *New York Times*, Oct. 21, 1949).

[12] General Mark W. Clark, former commanding general of the Sixth Army, had assumed command of the Army Field Forces on October 1, 1949. On October 20 he had described his efforts to unify the Army, Navy, Air Force, and Marine installations and activities in nine western states during 1948 and 1949. This project, which had been initiated by former Secretary of Defense Forrestal, had been successful in reducing costs by eliminating duplication of facilities and services. His testimony is in House Committee on Armed Services, *National Defense Program—Unification and Strategy: Hearings*, 1949, pp. 567–82.

[13] For General Bradley's testimony see no. 574.

[14] In an earlier version of this draft report (in EM, Vinson Corr.) Eisenhower had been far more specific in his description of his own testimony. He omitted from the final version these sentences: "He [Eisenhower] stated that he refused to be a party to anything that could possibly be considered an aid and comfort to a potential enemy of the United States. Obviously, he felt that the evidence of this disunity and seething antagonism within our Defense Establishment was seriously disturbing and that the publicity attending the quarrel could not fail to encourage Soviet hopes for the weakening of America. The General felt that the effect was probably not dissimilar to that of the prolonged strikes now current in two of our major industries, so far as the effect upon the Soviet General Staff is concerned." See nos. 570 and 573.

[15] Both Secretary of Defense Louis Johnson and former Secretary of State George C. Marshall had testified before the House Armed Services Committee on October 21, 1949. Marshall had described his personal experiences with problems associated with unification from the 1920s until the end of his service as Chief of Staff of the Army in 1945. Johnson had emphasized the accomplishments of the Defense Department in securing a greater measure of efficiency and economy. He had also described Eisenhower's connection with the events leading up to the cancellation of the super aircraft carrier *United States* (see nos. 412 and 413). Their testimony may be found in House Committee on Armed Services, *National Defense Program— Unification and Strategy: Hearings*, 1949, pp. 597–635.

[16] In spite of this advice, the House Armed Services Committee would recommend significant changes in the national security acts of 1947 and 1949. The committee would call for rotation among the services of the chairmanship of the JCS; a limitation on the length of the term of service of the JCS chairman to two years in peacetime; the addition of the Commandant of the Marine Corps to the JCS; and mandatory consultation by the Secretary of Defense with the House and Senate appropriations committees before appropriated funds could be withheld by executive action (House Committee on Armed Services, *Unification and Strategy*, 1950, pp. 46, 49–50).

[17] Vinson's committee would include this sentence in its report, adding the words "and his professional education and training" at the end (*ibid.*, p. 33).

[18] The committee would adopt this paragraph, slightly modified, as one of its conclusions (*ibid.*, p. 34).

[19] This and the preceding three paragraphs would also appear in the House Armed Services Committee's report (*ibid.*, pp. 33–34). The committee would add the words "and with full receptivity to one another's professional judgments" to the last sentence of this paragraph.

[20] In this final version of his draft committee report Eisenhower here omitted three sentences that had appeared in an earlier draft: "Any officer who cannot win this obedience, by every tradition of all Services, is unworthy of command. Any officer, given the law of the land and a straightforward directive, who will not enforce

such obedience, is derelict in duty. In either case, he should be removed from command."

[21] At this point in an earlier draft had appeared these words: "While the Committee should at all times be ready to hear the presentation of sound civilian or military protest against the application of unification or any other matter concerning the National Defense—. . . ." Eisenhower had deleted this preliminary clause and had begun the next sentence with the words "The Committee's relationships. . . ."

[22] In an earlier draft Eisenhower had used the words "irresponsible self seeking critics"; later he substituted the word *those* as it appears here.

[23] Eisenhower had deleted the following sentences from the end of an earlier version of this paragraph: "In such association, the members of the Committee must henceforth recognize that their most important objective is the development of unification, since in the development of arms, training methods and morale, the Armed Forces are already assured the necessary means and support. For unification—which welds the three Services into a single defense team—they must have the interest, support and vigilance of the Committee—above all, its insistence that unification is a matter of military discipline and its help in the maintenance of discipline."

[24] This and the following ten paragraphs would appear in the House Armed Services Committee report. The committee would, however, modify this discussion of budgetary procedures by taking into account the fact that the Appropriations Committee, not the Armed Services Committee, dealt with budget matters (House Committee on Armed Services, *Unification and Strategy*, 1950, pp. 50–52).

[25] At this point in an earlier draft had appeared this sentence: "In discharging this function there has heretofore been little synchronization, as to time, between Committee examination of applicable policy and methods on the one hand, and the division and allocation of forces to implement such policies, on the other." Eisenhower had deleted this sentence and had substituted the next sentence in its place.

[26] Representative Vinson would thank Eisenhower in a letter of January 7, 1950. In his letter (in EM) Vinson would suggest that he and Eisenhower "have a personal visit of some length to see whether or not our minds can meet fully on these fundamental problems." This meeting would not take place, however, and on March 1, 1950, Vinson would send Eisenhower a copy of his committee's report. The House Armed Services Committee would add these words to the end of Eisenhower's draft: ". . . and a fully rounded national defense." The Committee's report would also differ from Eisenhower's draft in other, more fundamental ways. It would be less critical of the Navy for bringing interservice conflicts to the attention of Congress and the public. It would also present the Navy's situation in a more favorable light by focusing on the testimony of the aggrieved Navy witnesses and by condemning the removal of Admiral Denfeld as an act of reprisal for his testimony (see no. 598). The report would in general agree with the Navy's claim that its views had not been taken into account by the JCS and the Defense Department and that the Navy itself was the most competent judge of whether a weapon such as the super aircraft carrier was best suited to carry out the missions of the Navy. The committee would support unification, but it would also qualify its support by saying, "Blind support should not be given to 'unification' as a word; its meaning should always be examined to determine whether the particular concept being applied or proposed is the proper one" (see House Committee on Armed Services, *Unification and Strategy*, 1950, esp. pp. 52–56; and Vinson to Eisenhower, Jan. 7 and Mar. 1, 1950, and Eisenhower to Vinson, Mar. 4, 1950, both in EM).

TO RICHARD C. BYRD

January 3, 1950

Personal and confidential

Dear Mr. Byrd:[1] I have just read your letter of December 14th, which was awaiting in my office when I returned from a recent trip to Texas.[2]

Quite naturally I am deeply complimented, not to say flattered, by the sentiments you express with respect to me. I appreciate also the disinterestedness and unselfishness of your attitude.

However, I must tell you that my convictions with respect to my possible public duties have not changed from those expressed in the letter I made public in January 1948.[3] I cannot believe that it is either appropriate or wise for me to enter the political field and, therefore, I must disapprove of any attempt to organize any club or to begin any movement that might lead people to believe that I acquiesce in the suggestion that I should stand for political office.[4]

I know you will respect my position as I respect the public spirited purposes that inspired you to write to me. I trust that you will come to see the logic and wisdom of my conclusions.

Again, my thanks. *Sincerely*

[1] Byrd (LL.B. Washburn University of Topeka 1947) was a member of the Ottawa, Kansas, law firm of Gleason, Anderson and Byrd. He was secretary of his county's Republican central committee and a precinct committeeman in the city of Ottawa. An earlier version of this letter, with Eisenhower's extensive revisions, is in EM, Letters and Drafts.

[2] Concerning Eisenhower's trip to Texas see no. 607. Byrd had written to Eisenhower (EM) explaining that "would be king makers" in the Republican party did not realize that the party could not elect a President in 1952 unless Eisenhower agreed to be its candidate. Byrd proposed that the Republicans organize "Eisenhower for President Clubs" throughout the country. He pledged his support for such an effort "first in Kansas, then in other states." Byrd had not discussed his plan with the highest party leaders in his state, but he assured Eisenhower that "your unanimous popularity in Kansas makes their approval a certainty."

[3] See Galambos, *Chief of Staff,* no. 1998.

[4] Numerous individuals had recently offered Eisenhower their support in the event that he decided to seek elective office. See nos. 491, 542, 543, 581, 602, and 638.

TO FRANK COPELAND PAGE

January 4, 1950

Dear Frank:[1] The reason I have not earlier replied to your Christmas note is that it was quite the nicest one I got—I wanted to think it over awhile. Possibly I wanted only to revel in the glow inevitably resulting from the flattering and overgenerous commendation that I found in your letter.

In any event, I had the distinct feeling that you, for one, sense what I am trying to do no matter how awkward or futile I may be in the effort.[2]

It has been far too long since I have seen you, but life in New York seems to inflict upon me a series of defeats. These consist in yielding always to the demands of things that I "must" do rather than to personal desire.[3] Do you suppose it is a sign of advancing age when apparent duty and obvious pleasure are no longer synonymous? While that seems an odd question to put in a note, I really think it would make a fine subject to argue out over a highball.

To you and yours Mamie and I send our very best wishes for a successful and happy 1950. For ourselves, we record as one of our fondest wishes that we get to see more of you this year than we have in the past. *Cordially*

[1] Page was a vice-president of the International Telephone and Telegraph Corporation. For background see Galambos, *Chief of Staff*.
[2] Page had recalled in his letter of December 20, 1949 (EM), that Eisenhower had outlined a program of action when the two had talked in Frankfort, Germany, in June 1945. Since then Page had followed reports of Eisenhower's activities, and he congratulated him on his success in carrying out his program. With regard to the proposals that Eisenhower enter politics, Page counseled, "If lightning is going to strike, and I would like to see it strike, you can't stop it. However, the most important thing is to say what you think, when you think it, and not try to figure the public reaction." This was a modification of Page's advice of the previous year, when he had told the General to stay out of politics (see Galambos, *Chief of Staff*, no. 2032).
[3] Eisenhower probably had in mind the fact that early that morning he had attended a "Dawn Patrol" breakfast of the Greater New York Councils of the Boy Scouts of America at the Waldorf Astoria. Carlos P. Romulo, president of the U.N. General Assembly, had spoken at the gathering and had announced that he had nominated Eisenhower to be "Man of the Half-Century." For background on Romulo see no. 638.

On this same day Eisenhower accepted a nomination to serve on the national board of directors of the United Service Organizations (USO). The letter of acceptance as drafted by Kevin C. McCann, assistant to the president of Columbia University, explained Eisenhower's general policy of declining all such invitations but cited the USO as an exception to the rule. Eisenhower added the following postscript to the letter: "Struggling with a complicated and crowded calendar I am moved to express the pious hope that the Board of Directors holds meetings most infrequently!!"

Harvey Samuel Firestone, Jr. (A.B. Princeton 1920), president of the USO and chief executive and chairman of Firestone Tire and Rubber Company, sent Eisenhower a telegram on January 25, 1950, announcing that the USO would be deactivated on January 31, 1950, and placed in a "stand-by position available for service if called upon in the event of a national emergency." As a consequence, Eisenhower would not have to attend the meeting of the board of directors previously scheduled for February 4, 1950. All of the correspondence is in EM, USO Corr. Concerning one of Eisenhower's earlier encounters with the USO see Galambos, *Chief of Staff*, no. 978. During 1949 Eisenhower had served as honorary chairman of the New York USO campaign.

642

TO GEORGE ANTHONY HORKAN, JR.   *January 4, 1950*

Dear Bo:[1] Of course, I am delighted to fill out the form that came with your letter and to comply with the additional requirement that the seconder of a nomination must write a letter to the Chevy Chase Board. However, I am sending both these documents to you instead of sending them directly to the Chevy Chase Board, for the reason that I notice instruction No. 1 says, "No name shall be posted on the list of candidates until duly proposed and seconded by two resident members."[2]

While my membership in Chevy Chase was, for some years, a resident one, I changed to a non-resident status about a year ago. Consequently, this would seem to make it impossible for me to be your actual seconder.

There is still the possibility that a letter from a non-resident member might be acceptable. In this case, you could send on to the Board the attached letter and withhold the other document.[3]

Naturally, if you want both papers to go forward, it is quite all right with me. I merely didn't want you to be making an error if such it is.

We had quite a New Year's celebration. John and Barbara, with the two children, came down both Christmas and New Year's Day and we had lots of fun. The youngsters are getting along now to the point where even their granddad admits they are personalities and not merely animated putty.[4] In fact, if you would like to really get the low-down on young David, just plan on spending half a day or so with me. In that time I should be able to do him partial justice at least (provided, of course, you give me the floor without interruption, except for questions).

This note brings to you both my very best wishes for a fine New Year. My love to that charming wife of yours[5] and, of course, warmest regards to yourself. *Cordially*

[1] Horkan (J.D. George Washington University 1948) had been associated with the law firm of McClure & Updike in Washington, D.C., since October 1, 1949. He had previously worked for the firm of Miller & Chevalier, and he was a lifelong friend of the Eisenhower family's. For background see Galambos, *Chief of Staff*, no. 984.

[2] In a letter of December 28, 1949 (EM), Horkan had asked Eisenhower to support his nomination for membership in the Chevy Chase Club. Eisenhower

had been elected a resident member of the club in August 1946 (see Galambos, *Chief of Staff*, no. 1016), but effective October 1, 1948, he had become an "absent member" (Eisenhower to Board of Governors, Chevy Chase Club, Apr. 9, 1948, EM, Subject File, Clubs and Associations). Eisenhower had previously recommended Kenneth C. Royall and John Edwin Hull for membership in the club (those supporting letters and letters that Eisenhower would write for other friends are in *ibid*. For background on Royall see no. 46; on Hull see *Eisenhower Papers*, vols. I–IX).

[3] In his letter of recommendation of January 5, 1950 (EM), Eisenhower stated that he had known Horkan for twenty-five years and was "proud to claim his friendship." An earlier draft of the letter dated January 4 is in EM, Letters and Drafts. Horkan would be elected a resident member on May 8, 1950, and he would thank Eisenhower for his help on May 23, 1950 (EM).

[4] John S. D. Eisenhower and Barbara Jean Thompson Eisenhower were the General's son and daughter-in-law (for background see no. 1). Dwight David Eisenhower II would be two years old on March 31, 1950 (for background see no. 27). Barbara Anne Eisenhower would be one year old on May 30, 1950.

[5] The former Evelyn Maddox.

643   *Eisenhower Mss., Subject File,*
                                                       Clubs and Associations

To Hamilton Fish Armstrong   *January 5, 1950*

Dear Mr. Armstrong: Thank you very much for your thoughtful memorandum and your personal note.[1]

Quite naturally, I should be glad to see and talk to you at any time that we can arrange an hour convenient to us both. However, my feeling at the moment is one of gravest doubt with respect to the preparation of an article such as you suggest. The first reason is not so much the pressure on personal time as what I might call preoccupations of the mind. Seemingly I simply do not get the opportunity for contemplation that is necessary to me before I can decide that an idea of mine is ready either for utterance or for discard. Another circumstance is that I have been importuned by certain publishers to do a series of articles, in which would be one somewhat of the type you suggest. I have consistently refused to undertake such a chore and I feel that if I did attempt to do anything at all in this line I would have to make some rather laborious explanations to the others involved.[2]

Of course, it is very flattering to me to feel that you consider that I might contribute something of value to the study of this important problem, and I most profoundly appreciate your opinion. Consequently, I have tried to be perfectly frank in my reply and I repeat that I am quite ready to talk the matter over further if you should so desire.[3]
Cordially

[1] Armstrong was editor of *Foreign Affairs* (for background see no. 269). In his letter and memorandum of December 30, 1949 (same file as document), Armstrong had outlined his reasons for asking Eisenhower to elaborate on some remarks that he had heard the General make to the effect that military action should be an instrument of political policy. An article in a journal such as *Foreign Affairs* might be a good opportunity, Armstrong had suggested, to explain how this idea was related to the current difficulties of the National Military Establishment in defining its responsibilities. Armstrong had also asked Eisenhower to address the problem of the lack in a democracy of a strong awareness of military realities. Specifically, Armstrong had asked the General to evaluate the extent to which political and military considerations had influenced certain wartime decisions. "I have in mind," he had written, "things like the decision to use the atomic bomb at the time and place when it was used, and for the purposes which it was meant to achieve; the decision to halt Patton's armies short of Prague; and the decision to withdraw the forces of the Western Powers from forward areas in Germany and to occupy three previously-arranged zones."

[2] In March 1949 William E. Robinson, of the *New York Herald Tribune*, had asked Eisenhower to write a series of articles (see no. 395).

[3] Eisenhower's appointment calendar indicates that he would meet with Armstrong on the morning of February 14, 1950.

644   *Eisenhower Mss.*

TO HARVEY SEELEY MUDD   *January 5, 1950*

Dear Mr. Mudd:[1] Although I am quite sure that Professor Kerr has already acknowledged receipt of your generous and welcome gift to the Lamont Observatory, the Treasurer's official slip, just now on my desk, inspires me to add my personal thanks.[2] You have been a great friend of Columbia—more than this, it is of course my earnest conviction that gifts such as yours imply a realization on the part of the donor that giving to a worthy educational cause is a direct investment in the future of America.

At this moment, also, I have just seen a circular invitation to a dinner given by the Columbia University Alumni Association of California on the night of January 13. You are to preside and you are going to have Professor Rabi as a guest speaker. I do not know whether you are personally acquainted with Professor Rabi, but I assure you that he is one of the men upon whom I lean most heavily—from whom I might almost say, I derive inspiration. His brilliant mind is matched by his sound common sense and his unswerving devotion to America.

With you presiding and Professor Rabi speaking at the dinner, it is certain to be a great success. I know this, in spite of the fact that I have never heard him speak in public.[3]

This note brings to you my sincere wishes for happiness and success throughout 1950. *Sincerely*

[1] Mudd was president and managing director of Cyprus Mines Corporation. For background see no. 216.

[2] Paul F. Kerr was professor of mineralogy and executive officer of the geology department at Columbia University (for background see no. 235). He had played an important part in the negotiations (in the fall of 1948) that had led to the establishment of the Lamont Geological Observatory at Palisades, New York. Concerning the contributions that had made the observatory possible see no. 302. Mudd's gift during FY50 was a thousand dollars (see Columbia University, *Report of the Treasurer, 1950*, p. 268).

[3] Isidor I. Rabi was professor of physics at Columbia University (for background see no. 325). Mudd wrote Eisenhower on January 16 (EM) praising Rabi's speech at the Alumni Association dinner. In the same note he acknowledged receipt of this letter from Eisenhower.

645   *Eisenhower Mss.*

To Bryant Edward Moore   *January 5, 1950*

Dear Bryant:[1] While my answer to your letter of the 3rd will reflect instantaneous reaction more than considered judgment based upon discussion with others, I must say that I most heartily approve the project for hanging General Lee's portrait in the Library.[2] To me, he has always typified the virtues in the American character, while the devotion that he inspired among his followers—in spite of circumstances that would cause disruption in most armies—is one of the most brilliant features in American military history.

I realize that some argument could be advanced to support an accusation that every regular army officer who entered the Southern forces was guilty of violation of an oath, in spite of the fact that formal resignation of the commission always intervened. Any such contention, I think, is invalid. The first ninety years of our history prove that people were uncertain as to whether the first loyalty was to the State or to the Federal Union and we know, at the very least, that Lee followed the dictates of his own conscience.[3] I feel certain that the entire body of graduates would approve of the project. For what it is worth, that is my opinion. If I should have any further thoughts on the matter, I shall write to you instantly.

This note brings to you and Mrs. Moore very best wishes from Mamie and me for success and happiness in 1950.[4]

With warm personal regard, *Cordially*

[1] Major General Moore was superintendent of the U.S. Military Academy. For background see no. 322.

[2] Moore had written on January 3, 1950 (EM), asking for Eisenhower's opinion of a proposal to hang a portrait of Lieutenant General Robert E. Lee (USMA 1829) in the main room of West Point's library. The project had been planned for 1952, the year during which the academy's sesquicentennial, as well as the hundredth anniversary of the year Lee had become superintendent of West Point, would be celebrated.

[3] The considerations that had led Lee to resign his commission in the U.S. Army on April 20, 1861, are recounted in Douglas Southall Freeman, *R. E. Lee: A Biography*, 4 vols. (New York, 1934–35), vol. I, pp. 431–43.

[4] A committee headed by Gordon Gray would plan the unveiling of a portrait of Lee in the post library at the U.S. Military Academy on January 19, 1952. It would be the first picture of a West Point graduate in a Confederate uniform to be hung at the academy. The portrait would be the work of Sidney Edward Dickinson, and its unveiling would mark the 145th anniversary of Lee's birth, on January 19, 1807 (*New York Times*, Jan. 20, 1952. For background on Gray see no. 471).

646   *Eisenhower Mss.*

To Roy Wilson Howard[1]   *January 5, 1950*
Telegram

My regret in saying goodbye to an old, old friend is tempered by the assurance that it is to live on in the united World-Telegram and The Sun. In this venture are now combined more than a century of great newspaper traditions and achievement with a nationwide organization of which you are the head.[2] New York and all America will be the richer through your purpose that the joined strength of the World-Telegram and The Sun will produce one of the country's most comprehensive and colorful newspapers. My congratulations to you and to your staff.[3]

[1] Howard was editor and president of the *New York World-Telegram and The Sun* and president of Scripps-Howard Newspapers (for background see Galambos, *Chief of Staff*; concerning the recent sale of the *Sun* to Howard see no. 638, n. 17). Kevin C. McCann, assistant to the president of Columbia University, drafted this telegram, and Eisenhower rewrote it (see the version in EM, Letters and Drafts). The telegram was published in the *New York World-Telegram and The Sun* on January 6, 1950.

[2] In 1931 Howard had brought about the merger of the *New York World* and the *Telegram*, two newspapers that had been in existence since the 1860s. The *New York Sun* had been founded in 1833 (see *New York World-Telegram and The Sun*, Jan. 5, 1950).

[3] On January 12 (EM) Eisenhower would thank Howard for sending him a copy of Hansen, *The World Almanac for 1950*. The book had been an annual publication

of the *New York World-Telegram*. Concerning Eisenhower's objection to an error of fact in the book see no. 660.

647   *Eisenhower Mss.*

To Percy Poe Bishop   *January 6, 1950*

Dear Percy:[1] While this is in no sense an answer to your very interesting and thoughtful letter of November 22nd, I cannot help seizing a moment to say "Happy New Year to you and yours." We often think of you two and of the children and always with affectionate interest and fond memory.[2]

Referring again to your letter, I find that, except for those portions that have a personal application to myself, I am in complete agreement with your observations and conclusions.[3] Here in the University and in this city I am a member of several organizations that are getting down to earth in the effort to bring home to the public the need for the kind of education that you speak of—and ways and means of bringing that education to all our citizens. It is no easy problem and must be approached cautiously, not to say wisely, in order that a good purpose will not be defeated by false charges of Fascism, Communism, politics or any other expressions by which some of our demagogues are accustomed to influence our citizenry.[4]

Mamie joins me in most sincere wishes to you and yours for the best of everything in 1950.

With warm personal regard, *Cordially*

[1] Major General Bishop, a friend of the Eisenhowers' since their years in the Philippines, had retired from the Army on May 31, 1941. For background see Chandler and Galambos, *Occupation, 1945*.

[2] Bishop was married to the former Grace Waldron Calvert.

[3] In his letter of November 22, 1949 (EM), Bishop had observed that the American people had been converted to "the something-for-nothing philosophy" and that it was time for men such as Eisenhower to make their voices heard. The formation of a "non-partisan" political party under Eisenhower's leadership might, he argued, reverse the current trend of affairs. On the other hand, Bishop thought that Eisenhower was the only presidential candidate whom the Republicans might choose who could carry the next election. In order to win, however, the Republicans would need to emphasize "solvency in government, honesty and integrity in government and preservation of the American Way in opposition to the Welfare State." Bishop had praised Eisenhower for his recent statements on these problems, but, he had concluded, "someone must wake up the Republican party. . . ."

[4] For Eisenhower's views on citizenship education at Columbia University see no. 346. He had recently emphasized the importance of the subject in a speech at a fund-raising dinner on behalf of the Eisenhower Foundation (see no. 532). Moreover, Eisenhower was a trustee of the American Heritage Foundation, whose work

he had commended in no. 168. During the spring of 1950 the public school systems in New York, New Jersey, Connecticut, and Pennsylvania would institute a program of citizenship training under the auspices of Teachers College. Eisenhower would pledge the support of the appropriate schools and departments of the university (see *New York Times*, Jan. 20, 1950; and no. 727).

648   *Eisenhower Mss., Family File*

To Milton Stover Eisenhower   *January 7, 1950*

Dear Milton: Instantly, upon the receipt of your letter, I referred it to Ralph Furey who is our Director of Athletics. The sad news is that our schedule through 1952 has been rigidly fixed.[1]

The only suggestion of a positive character that came out of our conference was that it might be possible for us to arrange a basketball game in Manhattan, if that would be desirable from your viewpoint. This suggestion, to my mind, represents a failure to appreciate the fine public reaction that almost inevitably would have derived from a football game between the two schools. However, I pass it along to you for any consideration your people might want to give it. If your Director of Athletics and your basketball coach are interested in any way, I would suggest a direct communication with Ralph Furey, Director of Athletics, Columbia University.[2]

There is little in the way of news to put into this letter. I am having my usual troubles in thinking up new alibis with which to respond to insistent invitations; when I have a series of quick failures, as I am having this coming week, I get the devil at home for going to so many "stag" dinners. But I am getting to the point that whenever I can sell out for a confidential, off-the-record meeting, lunch, or dinner, I am glad to do so.[3]

In New York State there is an argument going on as to the wisdom of organizing eleven colleges of a junior type—that is, of a two years' duration—to be sustained at public expense. I know that the presidents of most of our privately endowed colleges oppose this bill. I am strongly in favor of it. But, of course, I have very little in the way of experience or actual knowledge to back me up.[4]

What do you think of the matter, as a general proposition?[5] Please note attached copy of letter I sent to Dr. Case, whom I admire very much.[6] *As ever*

[1] In a letter of December 29, 1949 (same file as document), Milton S. Eisenhower had asked whether Columbia University might consider scheduling a football game with Kansas State College during the fall of 1950. As president of the latter institution, he had been hesitant to make this proposal before this time because

Kansas State had had a series of bad seasons. It appeared that the team was improving, however, and the General's brother had decided to broach the subject of a football game. "I don't know what there would be in it for Columbia, your coach, or your team," he admitted, "unless it might be a 'breather' and also a lot of interesting publicity." General Eisenhower wrote on the bottom of the letter: "Provost—Confer with Furey—Dean—etc—etc from viewpoint of Columbia's good only." Ralph J. Furey was Director of the Department of Physical Education and Intercollegiate Athletics (for background see no. 168).

[2] Grayson L. Kirk, provost of Columbia University, had sent a memorandum to Eisenhower on January 6 (same file as document) reporting that Furey had informed him that Columbia's football schedule had already been arranged through the 1952 season (for background on Kirk see no. 515). Furey had suggested that the two schools make plans for their basketball teams to compete. Milton would reply (Jan. 9, same file as document) that the director of athletics at Kansas State would discuss the situation with Furey at a meeting of the National Collegiate Athletic Association (NCAA) in New York City on January 10 (a draft of a talk that Eisenhower planned to deliver at the meeting is in EM, NCAA Corr.). After Milton S. Eisenhower was elected president of Pennsylvania State College (on Jan. 21, 1950 [see no. 679]), however, these plans were apparently abandoned.

[3] In the afternoon of this same day the Eisenhowers would travel to Scarsdale, New York, to attend the christening of Spencer Bedell Marx, the son of Louis and Idella Ruth Blackadder Marx (for background see no. 625). On January 8 the General attended a stag dinner as the guest of Charles Erwin Wilson (E.E. Carnegie Institute of Technology 1909), president and chief executive officer of General Motors Corporation. On January 9 Eisenhower had lunch with the trustees of Columbia University, and in the evening he was the guest of William H. Burnham at the Metropolitan Club. Burnham was an investment banker in New York City (for Eisenhower's reaction to the dinner see no. 663). Eisenhower would initiate a fund-raising campaign for Columbia's proposed Riverside Engineering Center at a luncheon at the Men's Faculty Club on January 10, and in the evening he attended a meeting of the Council on Foreign Relations. On the eleventh Eisenhower had lunch with John Charles Walter (E.E. Columbia 1904), president of the Alvey-Ferguson Company, and Charles Edward Wilson, president of General Electric Company, at the Waldorf Astoria, and in the evening he had cocktails and dinner with the Society of Older Graduates of Columbia University. On the following day Gilbert Holland Montague (LL.B. Harvard 1904), a leading authority on antitrust law, was the host for a dinner in honor of the Eisenhowers. The General's appointment calendar for January 13 has the note "Sick—at home."

[4] A master plan for the establishment of eleven two-year colleges had been under study by the trustees of the State University of New York since the summer of 1949. The trustees had held public hearings on the need for higher-education facilities, and representatives of various localities had urged that the state carry the burden of the community colleges. State law required that the communities pay for one-half of the cost of building the junior colleges and two-thirds of the cost of operating them (*New York Times*, Aug. 31, 1949; Sept. 21, 1949; and Jan. 16, 1950).

[5] In his reply Milton S. Eisenhower would express agreement with his brother's views. He would argue that the establishment of junior colleges would increase enrollments at four-year institutions, observing that "the number of transferees from junior to senior institutions is high—and constantly increasing." He would dismiss the argument that junior colleges did not provide an education of the same quality as that at senior institutions.

[6] For background on Everett N. Case, president of Colgate University, see no. 322. We were unable to find a copy of the letter to Case in EM.

To James Bryant Conant *January 7, 1950*

Dear Jim:[1] I remember that in one of the books you wrote I found the advocacy of the two-year college. I am a convert to that idea, but I am frank to say that I have not carefully studied the conflicting considerations that would determine whether the mass of these two-year colleges should be publicly or privately supported.[2]

I have just written a note to Dr. Case (whom I like tremendously), asking him for a further explanation of his views on this subject. Enclosed is a copy of that letter, which I send to you in the hope that you can tell me in a paragraph or two where I may be going a little haywire in my thinking and where I may possibly be on the right track. I have such a woeful ignorance in many of the important considerations applying to these questions that I simply must depend on my friends to help me out. I hope you will not think it too much of a chore.[3]

With warm personal regard, *Cordially*

[1] President Conant of Harvard University. For background see no. 285.

[2] In his reply of January 10 (EM) Conant would refer to his *Education in a Divided World: The Function of the Public Schools in Our Unique Society* (Cambridge, Mass., 1948), pp. 200–204. This part of the book argued for cooperation among local, state, and federal governments in the building of community colleges. The arrangement should be similar, Conant believed, to the program worked out for financing public elementary and secondary schools. Federal funds should be distributed according to need, but special consideration should be given to states that were already making exceptional progress in the field of post–high school education. "If this pattern is established," Conant had written, "one need not fear Federal control at this stage of education any more than at the lower levels." Conant pointed out that his book had been concerned solely with public education and that by omitting any mention of privately financed junior colleges or of a two-year terminal curriculum at private universities he did not mean to eliminate them as possibilities. Conant thought that New York's plans to build four-year colleges to be supported by taxes were not feasible. "To my mind we have enough four-year colleges and universities," he had informed Eisenhower. He thought that state funds might be more effectively spent on scholarships for students who needed to be educated away from home.

[3] In his letter Conant merely mentioned that he had "read with interest" the General's letter to Everett N. Case, president of Colgate University. Eisenhower's letter to Case is not in EM. For background on Case see no. 322.

To John Gillespie Jackson *January 7, 1950*

Dear John: Your memorandum, of course, reflects what I originally thought was the general desire of the Trustees for the establishment of a retirement plan for the Trustees.[1] However, as we agreed some weeks ago, the matter is of such extreme delicacy that the development of even minority opposition within the Trustees, was sufficient in my mind to drop it for the moment. How or when it can be brought up again, I am most uncertain.[2]

I am particularly grateful to you for taking the trouble to summarize your thinking, which roughly coincides with mine, along this line into a single memorandum. I shall file the memorandum with the official records of the University, making certain that one copy goes into the records of the Trustees.[3] *Cordially*

[1] For background on the issue of establishing a mandatory retirement plan for future members of the board of trustees see no. 585. The plan had been considered at the December meeting of the board, which Eisenhower had been unable to attend. On January 5, 1950, Jackson had informed Eisenhower that the resolutions on retirement had been tabled by the trustees. Jackson nevertheless enclosed a memorandum (in both CUF and EM, Columbia Corr.) again advocating the adoption of such a plan. He argued that when a man retired from business his associations and contacts were reduced and "his value and usefulness as a Trustee are correspondingly lessened." He stated that the board must act, not just advise, and that the physical disabilities that came with age could prevent members from carrying their share of the committee work and other responsibilities of the board (see also Trustees, *Minutes*, Dec. 5, 1949, CUF).

[2] Eisenhower dictated a draft of this letter on January 6, and he subsequently made numerous handwritten changes in the draft. The letter was originally marked "*Personal*," and the General deleted the following sentences at the end of this paragraph: "But I am quite sure that one thing can be done. This is to talk the matter over, very informally and without commitment of any kind, with every individual who is hereafter asked to become a Trustee. This, it is possible, may eventually bring about the result that we believe desirable" (copy in EM, Letters and Drafts).

[3] When one of the trustees had been unable due to illness to attend any meetings for two years, the board approved (Mar. 6, 1950) a resolution naming him an honorary trustee for life and vacating his position. The board would also approve Eisenhower's proposed change in the bylaws to make this sort of "retirement" possible in future cases of this sort (Trustees, *Minutes*, Mar. 6, 1950, CUF).

651   *Columbia University Files*

To Grayson Louis Kirk   *January 7, 1950*

Attached hereto are self-explanatory documents. Three items of action with respect to the Higgins Fund are now on the program for the remainder of this academic year.

A. Submission of comments on the attached draft of "Rules of Procedure." I have personally gone over the draft and see no important point except, possibly, on page 4 under Section V, Paragraph No. 1. The certification required in the last sentence should include also the word "research," in my opinion.[1]

B. Our annual estimate for the expenditure of $185,000. This, I think, should be submitted to the Trustees no later than March 15.[2]

C. The preparation of the detailed statistical report covering expenditures for the current academic year. This should go to the Trustees as soon after the close of the fiscal year, as possible.[3]

In Items A and B above, the Vice President in Charge of Education[4] should be consulted and his advice will govern. As to Item C, I wish that you would make certain that our Comptroller is fully aware of his responsibilities ~~here~~ in this matter and keeps his records so well up to date that the report can be submitted promptly after the close of the fiscal year.[5]

[1] This change in the "Rules of Procedure" would become the subject of Eisenhower's February 20, 1950, letter to the secretary of the board of control of the Eugene Higgins Trust (see no. 711).
[2] Columbia University's estimate for FY 1951 allocated income from the Higgins Trust to education and research in the fields of biochemistry, botany, chemistry, chemical engineering, civil engineering, electrical engineering, mechanical engineering, metallurgical engineering, geology, physics, and zoology (see Eisenhower to Board of Control of the Eugene Higgins Trust, Mar. 31, 1950, CUF).
[3] See Board of Control of the Eugene Higgins Trust, *Reports 1950–1951*, CUF.
[4] George B. Pegram. For background on Pegram's appointment to this post see no. 361.
[5] William H. Lane, Jr., was controller of the university. For background on Lane see no. 290.

652   *Eisenhower Mss.*

To Robert Daniel Murphy   *January 9, 1950*

Dear Bob:[1] How nice of you to send me a New Year's note.[2] It had slipped my mind for a moment that you are now in Brussels; you are becoming almost a permanent exile from these United States.

Just five years ago now we were punishing the Germans very badly as they attempted to retreat out of the Bulge.[3] It is hard to believe that it will soon be five years since you and Lucius and I were struggling with the Russians and the involved problems that we met in Berlin.[4]

May 1950 bring everything to you for which you hope. Please give my very best to those charming daughters of yours[5] and, of course, with warmest regards to yourself, *Cordially*

[1] Murphy had been U.S. Ambassador to Belgium since September 1949. For background see no. 218.

[2] In his note of December 31, 1949 (EM), Murphy had expressed concern about the effects upon Eisenhower of "the nice, quiet tempo of New York."

[3] By January 9, 1945, the Allied armies had almost succeeded in pushing back the thrust that the Germans had made in December through the Belgian Ardennes. For Eisenhower's wartime view of the situation see Chandler, *War Years*, nos. 2226–48. For his later account of the Battle of the Bulge see Eisenhower, *Crusade in Europe*, pp. 358–65. See also Cole, *The Ardennes*, pp. 606–76; and John S. D. Eisenhower, *The Bitter Woods*, pp. 405–30.

[4] Murphy had been Eisenhower's political adviser on German affairs, and he and Eisenhower and Lieutenant General Lucius D. Clay (in April 1945 Deputy Military Governor and Deputy Chief of Staff, United States Forces, European Theater of Operations [USFET]) had helped to set up the Military Government of Germany. For background on Clay see no. 490. Murphy would describe their work in *Diplomat Among Warriors* (Garden City, N.Y., 1964), pp. 245–46, 248–64, 280–97. On Clay and Eisenhower's handling of problems with the Russians see Clay, *Papers*, vol. I, pp. 3–126; and Clay, *Decision in Germany*, pp. 7–59. See also Chandler, *War Years*, no. 2395; and Chandler and Galambos, *Occupation, 1945*.

[5] Catherine Taylor Murphy, Rosemary Murphy, and Mildred Margaret Murphy.

653   *Eisenhower Mss.*

To Henry Merritt Wriston   *January 9, 1950*

Dear Wriston:[1] My legal staff here at Columbia did not look with too much favor on Mr. Babcock's suggestion for changing the ten to two in Section 120 of the Internal Revenue Code.[2] In fact, it appears that our people believe that the educational world must gird up its loins for a fight to keep what we already have in tax concessions. Apparently it is felt that some members of Congress are getting ready to blast us— their excuse being instances of universities engaging in competitive industry.[3]

In spite of all the above, I hope that the Legal Committee gives thorough study to the recommendation for revising Section 120.[4]

If you learn of any significant development in the matter, won't you let me know. I'm anxious to discuss the matter again with my friend, Mr. Babcock.[5] *Cordially*

[1] Wriston was president of both Brown University and the Association of American Universities (AAU) (for background see no. 254). Eisenhower's handwritten draft of this letter is in EM, Letters and Drafts.

[2] Charles H. Babcock wanted to see Section 120 of the tax code revised to encourage philanthropic donations to educational and charitable organizations, and in December Eisenhower had referred Babcock's idea to his vice-president in charge of development, Paul H. Davis (for background and for explanation of the change from "ten to two" years see no. 612). After studying Babcock's suggestion, John G. Saxe, university counsel, had written Davis (Dec. 29) that his tax expert had confirmed a rumor that Congress wanted to restrict, rather than enlarge, university

exemptions. The most important issue universities faced now, he said, was legislation that might "repeal or restrict the exemption on its *income*," and he advised Davis that only after the threat to existing exemptions was resolved should the universities initiate revisions of the tax code. Davis had sent Eisenhower Saxe's memorandum and a brief on January 3, 1950 (papers in EM, Roberts Corr.).

[3] Saxe was right. On January 23, 1950, President Truman asked Congress to revise the tax laws, eliminating the loopholes that allowed educational institutions to misuse exemptions and "in a few instances to gain competitive advantage over private enterprise through the conduct of business and industrial operations entirely unrelated to educational activities" (U.S., Congress, House, *Revision of the Tax Laws*, 81st Cong., 2d sess., 1950, H. Doc. 451). For developments see no. 903; see also Millett, *Financing Higher Education*, p. 375.

[4] On January 11 Wriston wrote that he had forwarded Eisenhower's comments to M.I.T.'s president, James Rhyne Killian, Jr., chairman of the AAU's Committee on Financial Support and Taxation (EM).

[5] Eisenhower had met with Clifford Roberts and Babcock on January 5, and on the sixteenth Eisenhower wrote Babcock that he would continue to discuss the idea "with everyone who seems to have any interest in the subject" (EM). In February 1950 Killian would testify before the House Ways and Means Committee regarding university exemptions and would recommend that Section 120 be revised. Instead of advocating Babcock's plan, however, Killian proposed that the 15 percent limitation on gifts be changed to 20 percent (U.S., Congress, House, Committee on Ways and Means, *Revenue Revision of 1950*, vol. I, *Excise Taxes*, 81st Cong., 2d sess., 1950, p. 502). Killian's suggestion would finally be incorporated in the tax law in 1952 (see U.S., *Statutes at Large*, vol. 66, p. 443).

654   *Eisenhower Mss.*

TO RAYMOND CHARLES MOLEY   *January 9, 1950*
Personal

Dear Mr. Moley:[1] Thank you very much for sending on to me the article by Kyle Palmer.[2] While you remarked that no reply was expected, yet because you seemed impressed by Mr. Palmer's presentation, I am moved, on a very confidential and off-the-record basis, which I know you will permit, to make a point or two that may have a bit of bearing on the subject.

In some of his argument I can see the workings of an astute mind, but I cannot possibly agree with all he says. For example, his final paragraph: "Nevertheless, whether the general gets in or stays out, he will never get very far playing footsy with his political conscience." I do not understand him here—it looks a bit like wise-cracking. But—"get very far"!! I don't want to go anywhere. I have got a hard job this moment. I just hold to certain fundamental convictions, and I try to work for them, nothing else.

Next, "playing footsy with my . . . conscience." Frankly, I think I have a right to resent that. I may blunder—I may be habitually wrong—but at least I try to follow what I think is conscience. Possibly Mr. Palmer meant some special conscience when he chose the adjective in his sentence—but, again, I am too simple to recognize the existence of several kinds of conscience.

Finally, "whether he gets in or stays out." Now, what in the name of all that's good does a man have to do, and how many times must he do it, to show that he has deliberately—not just accidentally—stayed out.[3]

I believe in good morals, but do I have to become a preacher in the pulpit? Because I believe in social progress, in honest government, in diffused authority, in community and individual responsibility, in paying-as-you-go, do I have to become a politician? Such reasoning, it seems to me, divorces from a *cause*, which is the important thing, all except those who want to run for office. If this is good sense, I must be very stupid indeed.[4] *Sincerely*

---

[1] Moley (Ph.D. Columbia 1918), a contributing editor of *Newsweek* magazine since 1937, had been a professor of public law at Columbia University before becoming Assistant Secretary of State in 1933. He had been an adviser—a member of the so-called Brain Trust—to Franklin D. Roosevelt, but he had become disillusioned with the New Deal and had resigned in 1937.

[2] Kyle Dulaney Palmer was political editor of the *Los Angeles Times* and, as Moley had described him in a letter to Eisenhower dated January 7 (EM), "a writer, practical observer and participant of a very extraordinary character." Palmer had argued in a column published on New Year's Day that Eisenhower and the Republican party had much in common. The General, he had said, ought to help the party gain control of the Eighty-second Congress during the election of 1950. Truman and his advisers, in Palmer's opinion, had "embarked upon a long-range program calculated to keep them in power indefinitely." Eisenhower could foil these plans and at the same time displace certain self-interested Republican leaders if he were to join the GOP and stop "playing footsy with his political conscience."

[3] For Eisenhower's recent thoughts on political office see nos. 638 and 640.

[4] Moley would reply (Jan. 12, EM) that he thoroughly agreed with Eisenhower's views. He had visited Texas at the same time as Eisenhower, and he had been impressed by the reactions of the people who had heard Eisenhower's speeches (for background on the speeches see no. 606). He concluded that the times required Eisenhower's "moral leadership." The General wrote back on January 16 (EM) suggesting that he and Moley arrange a meeting at which they could discuss their views at length.

---

655 *Eisenhower Mss.*

To James Ernest Beery *January 11, 1950*
Personal

Dear Colonel Beery:[1] After thinking over, for some time, the contents of your letter I send you the following:

You will understand, of course, that I speak very hesitantly and without any confidence at all that I am on the right track, but I believe that this letter represents, more or less, the way I would tackle your problem today if I were in the same circumstances.

I rather believe that you would get more satisfaction out of the years to come and that you would be taking best advantage of your past education and experience if you should now pursue some additional courses under the GI Bill of Rights and then enter the teaching profession.

There is a very great dearth of qualified teachers throughout the country, and I am quite certain that if you should enter a local university, for example, Richmond University, and keep your nose to the grindstone, you could get both your master's and your doctor's degree within a reasonable period. Thereafter, I am certain you will have no trouble finding employment.

Of course, I believe you should choose your subject with some regard for your own personal likes and inclinations. If I should attempt such a thing, I would take history as my subject. You might choose anything because my impression is that our shortage of teachers applies in every field.

In any event, I am quite sure that I would not return to our active military service. You have now dropped sufficiently behind your own classmates that you would probably feel a bit handicapped and I rather suspect also that you would never be entirely free of worry that the effects of your injury might again make themselves manifest. In such an event you could not escape the feeling that all the intervening time had been completely wasted.

By no means would I exclude a business career if some decent opportunity were opened up to me, but in the absence of such an opportunity I am quite certain I should personally attempt to follow the first course that I outlined.

I realize that this may be of slight, if any, use to you, but in any event it is what I believe. *Sincerely*

[1] Lieutenant Colonel Beery (USMA 1932) had retired from the Army in August 1947; he was currently living in Richmond, Virginia. He had commanded the 257th Field Artillery Battalion from January 1943 to July 1945, and he had been decorated by General Charles de Gaulle after the liberation of Bordeaux, France. Beery had written to Eisenhower on December 30, 1949 (EM), asking for advice as to how he should spend the rest of his life. He was considering taking a position in industry, returning to active duty, or entering a program of graduate study leading to a doctoral degree.

To Robert Winship Woodruff   *January 11, 1950*

Dear Bob:[1] I expect to come to Augusta National, arriving there sometime on January 19th. I hope to be there for a week and I think Cliff,
Bill Robinson, Pete Jones, and possibly a couple of my St. Louis
friends—Stu Symington and Dave Calhoun—will all be there at the
same time.[2]

I am getting off this note today so that you will understand you are
expected, demanded, ordered, and advised to be there for the entire
week. Aside from your personal company, I am determined that there
must be one man on the spot whom I have an outside chance of beating
at golf. You are the only one who qualified so I hope you will make
it.[3]

At the end of the week I must run over to Alabama for a day or
two. I have a friend named Ed Bermingham who is one of Columbia's
great supporters and who contributes constantly to our income. I have
a number of things I must talk over with him and so expect to spend
2−3 days on his plantation.[4] I am hopeful that Mamie will come down
to be with me for a day or so. But she now has her parents in New
York, and I doubt that she will come.[5]

I do most earnestly hope that you will not fail to be over at the Club
when all of us are there. *Cordially*

[1] Woodruff was chairman of the executive committee and director of the Coca-
Cola Company. For background see no. 258.
[2] Clifford Roberts was a partner in the firm of Reynolds & Company, investment
bankers (see no. 69). William E. Robinson was executive vice-president of the
New York Herald Tribune (see no. 28). W. Alton "Pete" Jones was president,
director, and a member of the executive committee of Cities Service Company
(see no. 388). Eisenhower would arrive in Augusta, Georgia, on January 20 and
remain there until January 26.
[3] Woodruff replied (Jan. 16, EM) that he would try to join Eisenhower at Augusta,
and he invited the General to spend January 30−31 at Ichauway Plantation in
Newton, Georgia. Eisenhower would stay at the plantation from January 30 to
February 2, 1950 (see no. 690). Concerning Eisenhower's return trip to New
York City on February 2 see no. 673.
[4] Edward J. Bermingham was a retired investment counselor who owned Enon
Farm in Midway, Alabama (for background see no. 381). Eisenhower would stay
at the farm January 26−30, 1950.
[5] John S. Doud, Mamie Eisenhower's father, would contract pneumonia in late
January 1950, and Mrs. Eisenhower would stay in New York to care for him
(see no. 671).

Eisenhower Mss.

To Thomas John Watson, Sr. *January 11, 1950*

Dear Tom:[1] First, my grateful thanks for the very nice luncheon you gave to the Provost the other day at the Union Club. It was a nice tribute to him and, as usual, you did the thing in your own inimitable way.[2]

I am sorry that you missed the Trustees Meeting, but I hope that it was not because of any indisposition—merely some business pressure. The same slate of officials was elected and off-hand I can think of no unusual feature that came up.[3] A couple of unusual Christmas gifts were reported, in each instance the donor commending Columbia's firm stand in favor of basic American principles.

The invitation from the men of the Presbyterian Church finally reached me, and I have simply had to decline. One point influencing me is that for the past six days I have had neither luncheon nor dinner with Mamie, and this even includes Sunday evening. I am again getting into the rut and round of engagements; and, as you know, the evening of March 6th will be the Trustees Meeting. I simply have to limit my appearance, particularly when I am supposed to make a speech.[4] *Sincerely*

[1] Watson was chairman of the board of the International Business Machines Corporation and a trustee of Columbia University.
[2] Watson had been host at a luncheon in honor of Grayson L. Kirk, provost of Columbia University, at the Union Club on January 6. For an account of the luncheon see *New York Times*, January 7, 1950; the guest list is in the same file as this document. For background on Kirk see no. 515.
[3] See Trustees, *Minutes*, January 9, 1950, CUF.
[4] This was no doubt a reference to Eisenhower's January 10 declination of an invitation from the Men's Club of the Fifth Avenue Presbyterian Church in New York City. On both the invitation and letter of declination see EM, Subject File, Invitations. In regard to Eisenhower's busy schedule from January 7 to January 13, 1950, see no. 648.

Eisenhower Mss.

To Anna Eleanor Roosevelt *January 12, 1950*

Dear Mrs. Roosevelt: Of course, I concur in your feeling that there will be educational usefulness in the program you are initiating in February.[1] I know of no problem that more needs open and full discussion than the dividing line between the responsibility of central government and local or individual enterprise.[2]

Nevertheless, so far as my own personal participation in a radio panel on the subject is concerned, I find myself unable to accept. Many months ago I had to develop what amounts to a policy in this regard when several radio organizations asked me to take part in single broadcasts or series of broadcasts—all of them largely of a forum or panel discussion type. I gave the suggestions considerable thought and turned them over to members of the University staff for extended study. The net result was a final decision that none of them should be accepted; the reasons— lack of time, establishment of precedents, etc.—seemed adequate and valid to me.

Since then, every request has been refused on the strength of that somewhat prolonged study. The number of refusals based on it has built a habit into a well-defined policy that cannot be ignored. You will appreciate my position, I am sure. Should I now make an exception, I would certainly be guilty of a breach of good faith and would embarrass a number of friends.[3]

My best wishes to you for success in giving the radio and television audience broad and full information on issues of public moment. *Sincerely*

[1] Mrs. Roosevelt, widow of Franklin D. Roosevelt, had been a U.S. delegate to the U.N. General Assembly since December 1945 and chairman of the U.N. Commission on Human Rights since April 1946 (for background see Chandler, *War Years*; and Galambos, *Chief of Staff*). Mrs. Roosevelt had invited Eisenhower (letter of Jan. 6, EM) to join her on a radio and television program she was initiating to discuss such issues as "government versus individual and local responsibility in such areas as health, education and social security." Mrs. Roosevelt hoped that Eisenhower could appear on the first broadcast of this public-service program, on the evening of February 5, 1950; she asked the General and Mrs. Eisenhower to have supper with her afterwards.

[2] For Eisenhower's views on this subject see nos. 445, 447, and 482.

[3] Calendars of the correspondence with various individuals who had asked Eisenhower to speak on their radio programs are in EM, Principal File, Cross Reference Cards and Cross Reference Sheets, s.v. "Radio."

659   *Eisenhower Mss.*

To Francis S. Murphy   *January 13, 1950*

Dear Mr. Murphy:[1] Thank you very much for your letter. It came just as I had finished a "thank-you" note to Bill Burnham to tell him that his party was quite the most enjoyable stag affair I have attended in New York City.[2] It was an unusual gathering with distinguished people, some of them my friends, and I formed an instant liking for all those that I was then meeting for the first time.

The story on Wesleyan College is already in the hands of some of my assistants. I did not waste a second in handing it to them because we need to widen markedly our circle of friends so as to carry Columbia's message on an intimate basis to more and more people in this country. The Wesleyan idea may have in it something we can use promptly and effectively.[3]

While I do not possess what might be called "leisure reading time," I am nevertheless going to glance through your pamphlet within the next hour. That should at least give me a chance to mark the paragraph or pages that I am determined to read in detail. It looks like it would be truly interesting.[4]

With the hope of resuming, one of these days, the conversations of the other evening.[5] *Cordially*

[1] Murphy, publisher of the *Hartford* (Conn.) *Times*, was a trustee of the University of Connecticut and a member of the U.S. Civil Service Loyalty Board for New England. He was also a member of the Army Advisory Committee.

[2] Murphy had been present with Eisenhower at William H. Burnham's dinner on January 9. Eisenhower's letter to Burnham is no. 663.

[3] The alumni of Wesleyan University of Connecticut had conducted a fund-raising campaign during which twenty-five hundred self-educated businessmen had been asked to become "associates" of the university. Murphy had asked Eisenhower in a letter of January 11 (EM) whether he knew about the campaign. Murphy reported that university officials thought this strategy might be applicable to financially troubled colleges in other sections of the country. For background on Wesleyan's associates plan see *New York Times*, November 29 and December 4, 1949.

[4] Although Murphy had expressed doubt that Eisenhower would have any leisure time, he had sent along an enclosure that he thought the General "might like to glance through." It was a booklet Murphy had written about a trip he had taken to South Africa.

[5] Murphy and Burnham would meet with Eisenhower at Columbia University at 11:00 A.M. on February 20, 1950. See no. 710 for developments.

660   *Eisenhower Mss.*

To Orlando Ward   *January 13, 1950*

Dear Pink:[1] I am still trying to get through the text of your OVERLORD draft and have made sufficient progress so that I can promise to send the whole thing back in a matter of two or three weeks. My comments constitute nothing but scribbled notes or marks on the draft itself—but in some instances these may be helpful to your authority.[2]

Incidentally, I wonder whether your Division takes upon itself such chores as bringing historical errors to the authors of contemporary reference works such as "The World Almanac."[3] On Page 744 of the 1950 issue I find in the "Highlights of World War II" a number of errors. For example, the text says that Lt. Gen. George S. Patton with 3rd U.S. Army attacked south and west of St. Lo July 26. At that moment the 3rd Army was not in the battle and neither was George Patton. It occurs to me that someday such contemporary documents as these may be looked upon almost as source material so I would think it wise to call attention to glaring errors when they come to official notice.[4]

If all of this is outside your responsibility, just throw this note in the wastebasket.[5] *Cordially*

[1] Major General Ward was Chief of the Historical Division, Special Staff, USA. For background see no. 373.
[2] Eisenhower had promised to read proofs of the Historical Division's *Cross-Channel Attack*, by Gordon A. Harrison. For background see no. 583.
[3] On the circumstances in which Eisenhower received this copy of the *Almanac* see no. 646.
[4] Lieutenant General George S. Patton, Jr., had been scheduled to enter the battle on July 24, 1944, but there had been a change in plans. Patton's army did not "begin functioning" until August 1, 1944 (see Chandler, *War Years*, no. 1869). For Patton's account of his activities during this time see Patton, *War As I Knew It*, pp. 95–98; see also Ladislas Farago, *Patton: Ordeal and Triumph* (New York, 1964), pp. 445–64.
[5] Ward replied (Jan. 17, EM) that he would write to the individuals responsible for the "Highlights of World War II" section of Hansen, *The World Almanac for 1950*, informing them of the error that Eisenhower had found. Ward admitted that the Historical Division ought to spend more time looking for errors in contemporary reference works but said that such activity delayed the writing of the division's own histories.

Major Robert L. Schulz, Eisenhower's aide, wrote the following note at the bottom of Ward's letter: "Returned by hand 19 Jan 1950." Schulz was probably referring to the *Cross-Channel Attack* manuscript.

661

Eisenhower Mss.

To James Stack

January 13, 1950

Dear Jim:[1] It was quite astonishing to me to find that you would consent to enter politics; it was even more astonishing to learn that your doctors agreed.[2] I understand, of course, that your local situation could easily be such as to induce you to attempt a task that you would otherwise avoid like the plague. In any event, I wish you all kinds of luck and do sincerely hope that the strain will not be so much as to damage you physically.

Recently I went out to Louis Marx's house to participate in the christening of his son. During conversation he took time off to praise your work in his company and he did so in glowing terms.[3] He said there was no "guff" about it—that on your own efforts and with your own shrewdness and imagination you had developed a volume of business far over and above any they had anticipated. He was very enthusiastic.

It was he that told Mamie and me about the loss of your baby. Mamie and I want you to know how distressed we are and how deeply we sympathize with you both, particularly with Elsa.[4] Such occurrences are always tragic and when they happen to one's best friends they seem particularly useless and cruel.

With our love to you both, *As ever*

[1] Colonel Stack (USA, ret.) had served as aide to Eisenhower from July 1945 to June 1947 (for background see no. 427). In a letter of January 9 (EM) Stack had mentioned that he might run for Mayor of Tacoma, Washington. Stack was dissatisfied with the political situation in Tacoma. He said that his supporters within the business community were distressed that the incumbent municipal leaders "prefer to maintain the town on a 'status quo' basis. . . ." Regarding Stack's earlier refusals to run for office in the state of Washington see Galambos, *Chief of Staff*, nos. 1733 and 1839.
[2] According to Stack's letter of the ninth, his doctors had said that participation in political activities might improve his health. "I just am not constituted," he had concluded, "so I can sit passively while things move around me."
[3] On the christening see no. 625. Stack was a toy distributor in Tacoma, and he had business ties with Louis Marx & Company, toy manufacturers. For background on Marx see no. 493.
[4] Eisenhower had sent a night letter to James and Elsa Stack on January 7 (EM) expressing sympathy, and Stack had acknowledged this in his letter of the ninth.

662   *Eisenhower Mss.*

To James Strom Thurmond   *January 16, 1950*

Dear Governor Thurmond:[1] Someone recently told me that South Carolina officials were beginning to look around for a potential replacement for General Summerall when he may be retired as head of the Citadel.[2] At the same time I learned that Major General Henry B. Sayler is just now retiring from the Army and very much desires to be considered for the position as head of the Citadel.[3]

If you are beginning the search for a possible successor to the distinguished man and soldier who has held the position so long, I would urge that you consider General Sayler's application.

He was a classmate of mine at West Point and graduated #38 in a class of 164. He has had long and distinguished service in the Army, chiefly as an Ordnance officer. The highlight of his service came during World War II when he was the Chief Ordnance Officer for the entire

American force in Europe. In that position he was extraordinarily successful. In such a matter as social and personal acceptability he and his family qualify in every respect. Mrs. Sayler is a native of Savannah, Georgia.

I am enclosing a few excerpts from General Sayler's record. Should you want any further information from me I shall certainly be glad to attempt to furnish it. In any event, my very deep appreciation for such consideration as you can give this recommendation.

Won't you please pay my respects to Mrs. Thurmond[4] and with warm personal regard to yourself,[5] *Sincerely*

[1] For background on Thurmond, the Governor of South Carolina, see no. 106.
[2] Since 1931 General of the Army Charles Pelot Summerall (USMA 1892) had been president of The Citadel, a military college in Charleston, South Carolina. Summerall, now eight-two years old, had retired from the Army in 1931 (see also Chandler, *War Years*, no. 825, n. 1; and Galambos, *Chief of Staff*, no. 733).
[3] See no. 531. Sayler, who had retired on November 30, 1949, had recently sent Eisenhower the names of those on The Citadel's board; he had written, "I am sure your judgment as to what to use is better than mine." In the margin of Sayler's letter Eisenhower marked Thurmond's name (n.d.).
[4] The former Jean Crouch.
[5] Eisenhower sent Sayler a copy of this letter, and on January 29 Sayler thanked him and said, "Due to the age of C.P.S. [Charles P. Summerall] there is always a possibility of this post becoming vacant at any time." For additional developments see no. 672.

663   *Eisenhower Mss.*

To WILLIAM H. BURNHAM   *January 16, 1950*

Dear Bill: Your party was a huge success.[1] Please don't worry about staying too late at my house. While it is true that I have been much on the go lately that particular hour was one that I enjoyed thoroughly because it was so well spent in fine company.

The pleasing circumstance of your dinner, from my viewpoint, was the obvious desire of those present to learn about the university situation of today. There was no insistence upon limiting the conversation to personal political comment and speculation, and I truly appreciated the opportunity to tell such a distinguished group about some of our educational problems with special reference to Columbia.

You can understand that I take very seriously the fact that I agreed to come to a place like this and to attempt giving some assistance in the solution of its problems. Consequently, when people argue loosely, casually, but with great force that I should leave Columbia and enter into some mad whirlpool of political activity, one of the reasons that

I get a bit furious is that they seemingly forget that both my heart and mind are involved in making progress on my present job.

Possibly all this is not making too clear why your particular dinner was sort of a unique experience. In any event, I had a whale of a good time, and I am grateful to you, particularly for your skill in assembling such an unusual group of individuals.

I have not written a separate note to Mr. Lawrence because I understood that I was exclusively your guest. However, I am also obligated to him for his part in making the evening such an enjoyable one.[2]
As ever

[1] Eisenhower had been the guest of Burnham, a Wall Street investment banker, at a dinner at the Metropolitan Club on January 9. Burnham had written to Eisenhower on January 10 (EM) thanking him for attending and for inviting Burnham and three of the guests to 60 Morningside Drive for after-dinner drinks.
[2] Arthur B. Lawrence was a senior partner in F. S. Smithers & Co., the firm with which Burnham was associated. In a letter of January 16, 1950 (EM), Burnham informed Eisenhower that he was still receiving compliments about Eisenhower's remarks at the January 9 dinner. "It is pleasant to have as a guest one who generates such enthusiasm and affection," he said.

664   *Eisenhower Mss.*

To John Davison Rockefeller, Jr.   *January 18, 1950*

Dear Mr. Rockefeller:[1] This morning I had a meeting with my committee at which Professor Krout was also present.[2] Everybody was pleased, indeed, with the opportunity to explore ways and means by which Columbia's connection with Riverside Church can be developed. All of the individuals involved expressed, also, the greatest satisfaction in the opportunity to work with Dr. McCracken.[3]

I think that for the moment we may leave the whole program in the hands of the capable and enthusiastic people who will be representing the two institutions.

Thank you very much for initiating this whole plan. I am hopeful that much good will come out of it and I do assure you of my deep and personal appreciation. I am grateful, also, for your offer to pick me up any Sunday when I might have a chance to go to Riverside. After I return from my impending short vacation, I shall hope to find some early chance to go over there with you.[4] I most thoroughly enjoyed the two occasions when I have gone with you and my only difficulty is a habit of using my Sundays for a period of complete rest and relaxation.[5] Then, of course, I hope to attend, occasionally, the services at the Chapel on the campus.

With warm personal regard, *Sincerely*

[1] Rockefeller, son of the founder of Standard Oil Corporation, had been chairman of the building committee of the Riverside Church, near Columbia University. The church, which had opened on October 5, 1930, was affiliated with the Northern Baptist Convention, but its congregation included people of many denominations (see Raymond B. Fosdick, *John D. Rockefeller, Jr.: A Portrait* [New York, 1956], pp. 220–24). Rockefeller had written to Eisenhower on January 11 (EM) inviting Columbia's faculty and students to participate in the activities of the Riverside Church. He offered to meet with Eisenhower to discuss ways to bring the church and the university into a closer partnership.

[2] John A. Krout was dean of the Faculty of Political Science, Philosophy and Pure Science at Columbia University. The committee to which Eisenhower refers was one that he had recently appointed to confer with representatives of the Riverside Church. Its chairman was Chaplain James A. Pike, and its other members were Provost Grayson L. Kirk and Vice-President in Charge of Development Paul H. Davis (for background on Pike, Kirk, and Davis see nos. 577, 515, and 156, respectively). Eisenhower's desk calendar indicates that he had met with this committee on the morning of January 17, not the eighteenth.

[3] Robert James McCracken (D.D. McMaster University 1946) had been pastor of the Riverside Church since October 1946 and a lecturer in practical theology at Union Theological Seminary since May 1948. He would meet with Chaplain Pike on March 2, 1950. They would discuss the possibility of appointing one of the ministers on the staff of the Riverside Church to act as counselor to Protestant students at Teachers College. Pike would report that Eisenhower had "indicated that he would find a way of providing funds for a program resulting from the Riverside minister's campus efforts." Pike and McCracken would consider proposals for organizing discussion groups, planning joint programs of music, and increasing collaboration between the church and the university in other areas. See "Summary of the Sense of the Meeting of the Joint Committee on Relationships between Columbia University and Riverside Church Held at the Men's Faculty Club on Thursday, March 2, 1950, at 1 P.M.," EM, Pike Corr.

[4] Concerning the vacation see no. 656.

[5] The first occasion had been October 16, 1949, when Eisenhower had taken part in the Laymen's Sunday services at the Riverside Church (see the correspondence in EM, McCracken Corr.). The other occasion had probably been January 15, 1950 (see Rockefeller's January 17 letter to the General, in EM).

665   *Eisenhower Mss.*

To Edwin Norman Clark   *January 18, 1950*

Dear Ed:[1] With further reference to the historical project, I had a long conference with the History Department this morning. I find that while the idea of research into military history struck them as somewhat novel, it is likewise true that by the time the conference was over there was a tremendous enthusiasm developed. The individuals to whom I talked are going to start a little quiet research to see what would be needed in the way of libraries, equipment, research, space, etc. I am hopeful that some of the personal libraries that have been accumulated in the past by such soldiers as General Pershing and others might be donated to us.[2]

I could not provide much information on the Military Institute. Moreover, I could not remember whether your concept of teaching or researching military history in Columbia was necessarily tied up with the project of bringing here the Military Institute.

I am going to Washington tomorrow for Hap Arnold's funeral; thereafter, I shall spend a few days in Georgia but shall be back here in early February.[3] Could you find the time to drop me a note outlining your views very roughly? I am sure that in the main I have not mistaken either your basic idea or your future plans, but it will save me much time here in dealing with others if I had a short memorandum.[4]

With warm regard, *Cordially*

[1] Clark was a business consultant and executive in New York City (for background see Galambos, *Chief of Staff*, no. 1456). He was currently head of a fund-raising campaign for the benefit of the American Military Institute (for background on the institute see no. 500; and "Headquarters Gazette (continued)," *Military Affairs* 14, no. 3 [1950], 133–59). Negotiations were under way to alleviate the institute's financial difficulties by bringing it under the auspices of Columbia University. The institute especially needed new sources of support to continue the publication of *Military Affairs*, its quarterly journal. Eisenhower hoped to make the organization part of a program for military studies at Columbia. On the plans for the latter see no. 730; see also Donald Armstrong to Eisenhower, December 7, 1949, and Eisenhower to Armstrong, December 22, 1949, both in CUF.
[2] General of the Armies John J. Pershing had died on July 15, 1948 (see no. 119, n. 3).
[3] Eisenhower would leave New York on the following day and would attend the services for General of the Air Force Henry H. "Hap" Arnold at Arlington National Cemetery. That evening Eisenhower would board a train in Alexandria, Virginia, and would travel to Warrenville, South Carolina, and from there to Augusta, Georgia. On his vacation plans see no. 656.
[4] We could not locate such a memorandum from Clark in EM, but there is an undated memorandum regarding the reorganization of the institute in EM, Winnacker Corr. For more developments see no. 765.

666   *Eisenhower Mss.*

To JOHN A. WELLS   *January 18, 1950*
Personal and confidential

Dear Mr. Wells:[1] It is unusal to get such an extremely thoughtful letter as yours.[2] Unfortunately, it came without the extract from Joe Keenan's *League* Reporter which was mentioned in the text. Consequently, I do not have the advantage of information as to your basic beliefs, which, you indicated, are roughly outlined in that document.[3]

Certain parts of your letter do not seem to be applicable because you address them to "any candidate for public office," which I am *not*.

In spite of this observation, I should like to make it clear that if there is one individual in whom I am concerned, it is the so-called average citizen of the United States. I am not particularly impressed by propaganda terms, but I do not believe that the average citizen can contemplate "statism" with any degree of complacency unless he places a far different definition on the word than I do. Real statism exists in Russia and if there is any liberalism in it, then I most certainly have attached a wrong meaning to that word all my life.

My industrial work week, during the last years I spent in civil life in 1909, '10 and '11 was 84 hours. On the farm it was longer.[4] Remembering the meager wage I received for such hours, and the fact that instantaneous discharge was usually the penalty for even mild complaint, it is hardly to be expected that my sympathies today would lie exclusively with industrialists. I have far more respect for the man who works with his hands, or the soldier who carries the gun, than I do for many who, by reason of some stroke of fortune or opportunity, have achieved sufficient wordly success so that they may complacently class themselves as "nice people." Yet, to bring up the specter, now, of conditions that existed in New York in 1873 is, to my mind, as far wide of the mark as to confuse every decent program for the social and economic betterment of our people with socialism or communism.[5] I am quite certain that no one can justifiably accuse me of ever opposing anything which I believed would work for the long-run good of the mass of Americans. But, in my opinion, anyone who hopes, through unwarranted concentration of power in Washington, to serve the long-run good of our country is blind both to the facts of human nature and of history. The only thing that I have continually "opposed" is unwarranted concentration of power in the Federal government.[6] That, I shall continue to do.

I repeat that I am appreciative of the thoughtful character of your letter and should you, by any chance, be up in this neighborhood some day, I suggest that you inquire from my office as to the possibility that I might be free at the moment. I think a conversation might prove very interesting; the more so, as I have a lively suspicion that what appear to be differences in idea are largely differing definitions of the same terms.[7] *Sincerely*

[1] Wells (LL.M. Harvard 1936) was a member of the law firm of Dwight, Royall, Harris, Koegel, and Caskey. He had served as counsel for the Office of Price Administration in 1942, for the New York State Moreland Commission Investigating Workmen's Compensation Law in 1943, and for the Navy Price Adjustment Board from 1944 to 1945.

[2] In his letter to Eisenhower (Jan. 13, EM) Wells had mentioned that he had been an active member of the Republican party in New York City for twelve years. He and other members of the progressive element in the party hoped that Eisenhower would accept the Republican presidential nomination in 1952, but they disliked his recent public criticisms of the "welfare state" and "statism." Wells argued that Americans were concerned that another depression might occur, and they refused therefore to relinquish "certain minimum guarantees" of economic security. "The average man and woman has no great faith in his or her individual ability, no matter how great that may be, to take care of himself or herself, let alone their families, in any and all events."

[3] The excerpt from the *League Reporter*, a publication of Labor's League for Political Education of the AF of L, would arrive after Eisenhower had left New York City (regarding his trip to the South see no. 656). Joseph Daniel Keenan was Director of the League, and he had included in the *Reporter* for December 26, 1949, an editorial attacking certain statements that Eisenhower had made during a speech on November 30, 1949, the same that Eisenhower had defended in no. 606. The editorial focused on the General's allegation that Americans were excessively concerned with obtaining "security." Eisenhower's Army retirement pension had assuaged his financial worries, according to the editorial, and he was no longer able to sympathize with less fortunate people. "No, Ike, we're not looking for caviar and champagne," the editorial had concluded. "We're looking for candidates who are champions of the people. For awhile, we thought you were the man, Ike!"

[4] Eisenhower had held several jobs after graduating from high school (see Eisenhower, *At Ease*, pp. 103–4).

[5] In his letter of the thirteenth Wells had quoted an account of the numbers of New York City residents who had died of starvation and exposure after the panic of 1873.

[6] See, for example, nos. 326 and 442.

[7] Eisenhower made extensive changes in a draft of this reply to Wells. The version in EM, Letters and Drafts, does not include this final paragraph.

667 *Eisenhower Mss.*

To John Singleton Switzer

January 18, 1950

Dear Jack: Thank you very much for your nice letter. It was most interesting, particularly that part about the possibility of a scholarship.[1]

I am not quite clear whether your organization is to supply this scholarship or only the travel. If the first is correct, we will be very glad to make arrangements through our Admissions Office for a suitable student to come to us. If, however, we are to supply also the tuition and living expenses, the case becomes more complicated. We have a policy here never to assign a scholarship to any one student. Scholarships must be competed for by all comers, and the awards are made on the basis of the records submitted. Competition is very keen, as the number of applicants far exceeds the number of scholarships available. Your candidate would therefore have first to be admitted to study at the

University and then have his qualifications passed upon by the scholarships committee. We will be very glad to have any of your candidates compete but we cannot guarantee the result. Applications for scholarships must be on hand by March first to be considered for the academic year 1950—51.

I do hope that you will understand how appreciative we are here in Columbia that you thought of this University in connection with the project you have in mind. Even if the project does not come off, I am still grateful.[2]

I am quite astonished that you should have to show cause for retention on the active list. But I suppose it has to do with age and grade or service and grade features of the law.[3]

Mamie joins me in warm greetings to you and Edith.[4] We do hope that you both are well and happy. *As ever*

[1] Colonel Switzer (A.B. University of Michigan 1916) was commanding officer of the Hokkaido Civil Affairs Region in Japan. On behalf of the American Scholarship Committee for Hakkaido, he had asked Eisenhower in a letter of December 17, 1949 (EM), whether Columbia University would be interested in a scholarship for a Japanese student. Switzer promised to give further details of the plan in a later letter, and he explained that his committee "contemplated paying costs to and from—maybe more, if fund raising here is successful." Eisenhower had referred Switzer's letter to Provost Grayson L. Kirk.

[2] In a letter of May 5, 1950 (EM), Switzer would describe the progress his committee had made in the screening of applicants for the scholarships. The committee expected to have sufficient funds to send three or four students to the United States, but he did not mention plans for any to matriculate at Columbia University.

[3] In a postscript to his letter of December 17, 1949, Switzer had mentioned that he had recently been asked "to show cause why I should be retained on the active list." Switzer would report, however (letter of Apr. 18, EM), that a board of inquiry had determined that he should remain on active duty.

[4] Switzer's wife.

668   *Columbia University Files*

To Paul Herbert Davis   [*February 3, 1950*]

For V.P. Davis:[1] This creates in me a fear directed entirely to money angle. (Otherwise I like the letter very much.)[2] But if we can raise this amount of money—the question arises as to how much we are cutting into support for *other* Columbia projects. Please see me![3]

[1] Eisenhower's undated note to Vice-President in Charge of Development Davis is at the bottom of a February 2, 1950, letter that Frederick Cecil Mills had written to George B. Pegram (vice-president of the university). Eisenhower had originally

addressed the note to Pegram but had changed the name to Davis. For background on Pegram and Davis see no. 361. Mills (Ph.D. Columbia 1917) had been a professor of economics and statistics at Columbia since 1931.

[2] In the fall of 1949 Eisenhower had asked Mills and a committee of four professors to investigate the feasibility of a study to examine the cause and effect of the growth of government activities in America and to seek to define the line that should separate government and personal responsibilities. With his letter to Pegram, Mills had enclosed a draft letter for Eisenhower's signature explaining the proposed inquiry (Feb. 2). Two studies were suggested. The first project would consist of a series of conferences that would assemble well-informed leaders from many fields to investigate resources and organize existing knowledge relevant to this broad issue. These inquiries could be completed in two years at a cost of $250,000. The second project would consist of semi-independent examinations of specific areas of concern—such as taxation, fiscal policies, and social security—each lasting two to four years. It was estimated that a comprehensive group of these latter studies would cost $2 million, but $350,000 would support "selected strategic investigations. . . ." (same file as document. See also Mills to Pegram, Dec. 16, 1949, with enclosed "Summary Statement of the Problem and of Anticipated Results of Proposed Study of Governmental Activities" and Pegram to Eisenhower, Dec. [?], 1949, both in EM, Mills Corr. For background on Eisenhower's interest in this issue see nos. 555 and 588).

[3] Eisenhower saw Davis on February 4, 1950. There is no indication in EM that Eisenhower ever sent the committee's letter; the first fund-raising letter concerning the study would not be issued until the fall of 1950 (see no. 979). For further developments see no. 1039.

669   *Eisenhower Mss.*

To EDWARD JOHN BERMINGHAM   *February 3, 1950*

Dear Ed: Here's a memo that explains, rather well, the current situation in private institutions of learning.[1] I've heard much advice, since coming here, of the "go easy" variety—people saying that the financial situation would easily take care of itself. That's bosh![2]

The Trustees best acquainted with the situation are Adrian Massey, Bert Putnam, Geo. Warren, Marcy Dodge.[3] Of these, the first named has taken the trouble to inform himself in detail. If you know him you might be interested, some day—in talking to him about it. Incidentally, he agrees with Paul Davis—as I do.

I've sent a note to John Cahill, asking to arrange a visit.[4] *As ever*

[1] Eisenhower and Bermingham had apparently discussed university matters during the General's recent visit to Bermingham's Enon Farm (see no. 656 for background). With this handwritten letter, Eisenhower enclosed several items, including a memorandum Paul H. Davis had prepared concerning the university's development program. For background on Bermingham's interest in the development issue see no. 381.

² On Eisenhower's fund-raising efforts see no. 622; for background on the university's finances see nos. 242, 417, and 986.

³ Adrian Mitford Mass*ie*, executive vice-president of the New York Trust Company, had been a trustee at Columbia since 1947. For background on trustees Albert W. Putnam, George E. Warren, and Marcellus H. Dodge see nos. 209, 243, and 41, respectively.

⁴ See no. 674.

Bermingham replied (Feb. 7) that whatever fault there was in the development program could be attributed to "aggressiveness." The university could not emulate highly trained industrial sales forces, Bermingham said; there was "inherent danger in turning loose a thousand men, more or less, without grooming." In another letter of the same date Bermingham noted that he knew all of the trustees Eisenhower had mentioned except Massie, and he offered to see them if Eisenhower wanted him to do so. All correspondence is in EM.

670   *Eisenhower Mss.*

To Lewis Herold Brown   *February 3, 1950*

Dear Mr. Brown:[1] Thank you for sending me the article written by Bruce Barton.[2] When Bruce expresses himself on international problems, I sometimes find my views to be in opposition to his.[3] But when he talks about basic guides to a prosperous American future, the situation is quite otherwise. I like his forthrightness and his common sense approach.

Incidentally, I particularly liked the statement in your note that at this time the identity of leaders and flag-bearers is of far less importance than is the need for the development of and the adherence to basic ideas.[4] *Cordially*

¹ For background on Brown, chairman of the board of the Johns-Manville Corporation, see no. 331.

² Barton's article, "Fateful Year," warned that deficit spending and the politicians' appeal to selfish interests had to be stopped. Full employment and prosperity were wonderful concepts, he wrote, "but what happens when the waiter comes around with the check?" Barton feared that in 1952 a leader would not emerge who would be willing to end the current trends (King Features Syndicate, 1949). For background on Barton see no. 178.

³ Barton was an isolationist (see Barton to Eisenhower, Dec. 18, 1950).

⁴ Brown had written that although Eisenhower was not a presidential candidate, the General could offer his leadership to the nation's youth in the war against socialism. He added, "No matter who the candidate is, we need leadership in the field of basic ideas" (Jan. 25, 1950. All papers cited are in EM).

Eisenhower Mss.

TO HERBERT ALLEN BLACK   *February 3, 1950*

Dear Dr. Black:[1] You will be interested to know that something over
two weeks ago Mr. Doud contracted a case of pneumonia but was able,
with the aid of all these fancy new drugs, to shake it off successfully.
He is up and around the house again and is very cheerful.[2] However,
we are keeping the night nurse on for a while longer because he likes
her and she seems to know how to handle him so well. Mrs. Doud
was in bed for a while also with what was apparently nervous exhaustion.
She was up and around again when I returned from the South last
evening where I have been for about ten days.[3]

I have had some encouraging reports on your continuous improvement. One of these came from Mr. Davis of Chicago.[4] I know that it
must be a great trial for a person of your temperament to remain in
bed, but I am hopeful that you will not be too impatient but will
faithfully follow the instructions of your "doctor"—far better, for example, than Mr. Doud ever followed yours.

Your friends are all looking forward to the day when you can be up
and around once more. I especially hope that you are in fine fettle by
the time Mamie and I get out to Colorado this summer. You must
come up to Denver to have a visit with us.[5] *Cordially*

[1] For background on Black see no. 13.
[2] Mamie Eisenhower's parents, the John S. Douds, had been visiting the Eisenhowers in New York since December (see nos. 630 and 680).
[3] For the trip see no. 656.
[4] Joseph Davis, a Chicago attorney and an old friend of Black's, had written
Eisenhower about the doctor's condition. Davis's letter is not in EM, but see
Eisenhower to Davis, February 3, 1950, EM. For background on Black's illness
see no. 611.
[5] In March Black would reply from Hot Springs, Arkansas, thanking Eisenhower
for his encouraging letters (see no. 752. See also Davis to Eisenhower, Mar. 28,
1950, EM). On the Eisenhowers' summer vacation see no. 884.

672   *Eisenhower Mss.*

TO HENRY BENTON SAYLER   *February 3, 1950*

Dear Henry: When I was in Georgia I had a letter from Governor
Thurmond saying that the Board of Regents at The Citadel has had
someone under consideration to whom he refers as "a distinguished
army officer."[1] He said that, in the event the Board did not select that
individual, he would present your name for consideration.

While I have no reason for any such conclusion, I have had a faint hunch that the man to whom he referred was Witsell.[2] This morning's paper says that Witsell has been reappointed Adjutant General of the Army and, consequently, if my hunch is correct, your own chances might be markedly improved.

The reason for sending this kind of guesswork on to you is that it is just possible that additional letters written, particularly to *other* members of the Board, by friends of yours might have a very good and decisive effect.[3]

My love to all the family. *Cordially*

---

[1] Eisenhower had written South Carolina Governor J. Strom Thurmond in January about Sayler's desire to become president of The Citadel (for background see no. 662). Thurmond's reply of January 20, 1950 is in EM. For Eisenhower's trip to Georgia see no. 656.

[2] For background on Major General Edward F. Witsell see no. 220.

[3] As it turned out, General Charles P. Summerall, president of The Citadel, would not retire from his post until 1953, and General Mark W. Clark would succeed him (see *New York Times*, June 13 and Oct. 24, 1953). For background on Clark, who had become Chief of the Army Field Forces in August 1949, see no. 464, n. 8.

673   *Eisenhower Mss.*

To William Stuart Symington   *February 3, 1950*

Dear Stu: With regard to the Augusta proposition of which I spoke to you, I think that Cliff will be back from South America sometime shortly after the middle of the month. At that time, I will ask him to get the ball rolling and you should hear about the matter promptly.[1]

Of course, I was delighted to get the chance to talk to you yesterday.[2] I was particularly glad to see the evidence of a spirit of conciliation that was implicit in the agreement on research and development.[3]

Because of my deep conviction that all of this furor about the H-Bomb makes unification a hundred times more important than it was in the past, I am always delighted with every accomplishment along this road.[4]

I am, of course, deeply grateful to you for the ride and I congratulate you on the new constellation; she is a beauty. It was also fortunate that Colonel Lowe was coming on up to New York to pick up Bob Hope.[5] We had a quick trip up to LaGuardia, even though the authorities on the field took up about an hour deciding that we could land. As quick as they gave permission, we slid in with no trouble whatsoever. Captain Thomas is obviously a grand pilot.[6]

I can't say for certain when I can come to Washington. But if you are up here in the meantime, give me a ring and possibly we can get together.[7] *Cordially*

[1] In January 1950 Secretary of the Air Force Symington and St. Louis banker David Calhoun had been Eisenhower's guests at Augusta National Golf Club (see no. 637 for background); before Eisenhower had left Augusta, he and Clifford Roberts, chairman of the club's executive committee, had discussed inviting the two men to join the club. Eisenhower wrote Helen N. Harris, office manager at Augusta National, this same day and advised her that he had since talked to Symington, who "would deeply appreciate receiving such an invitation" (EM, Subject File, Clubs and Associations). Symington would receive an invitation from club president Robert T. Jones, Jr., on March 3 and would accept on March 6 (same file as document). For developments regarding Calhoun see no. 687.

[2] On February 2 Eisenhower had met Symington at Turner Air Force Base in Albany, Georgia. Eisenhower was returning to New York after a fourteen-day vacation, and Symington was returning to Washington after a trip to Texas. The two men had lunch at the base officer's dining room and flew to Washington, D.C., in a new Super Constellation, a plane introduced by Lockheed in 1950 (see Eisenhower's desk calendar; and *Encyclopedia of Aviation* [New York, 1977] p. 49).

[3] Eisenhower was probably referring to a recent JCS agreement regarding the assignment of responsibility for guided missiles, a pact that Secretary of Defense Johnson would approve in March (see Historical Section, Joint Chiefs of Staff, "Chronology of Changes in Key West Agreements, April 1948–January 1958," [Feb. 7, 1958], in CCS 337 [4-2-49], B.P., pp. 11–12).

[4] The September 1949 detection of an atomic explosion in the Soviet Union had prompted months of debate concerning the need for the United States to develop the hydrogen, or "super," bomb. On January 31, 1950, President Truman settled the question when he announced that the Atomic Energy Commission (AEC) had been directed to continue its work "on all forms of atomic weapons," including the H-bomb. The President's decision, which (according to David Alan Rosenberg) "publicly confirmed the United States' commitment to a strategic arms race with the Soviet Union," and the events leading up to it are discussed in Rosenberg, "American Atomic Strategy," 62–87; Warner R. Schilling, "The H-Bomb Decision: How to Decide Without Actually Choosing," *Political Science Quarterly*, 76, no. 1 (March 1961), 24–30; Richard G. Hewlett and Francis Duncan, *A History of the United States Atomic Energy Commission*, vol. II, *Atomic Shield, 1947–1952* (University Park, Pa., 1969), pp. 362–409; Truman, *Memoirs*, vol. II, *Years of Trial and Hope*, pp. 294–309; Lilienthal, *Journals*, vol. II, *Atomic Energy Years*, pp. 580–634; and Acheson, *Present at the Creation*, pp. 344–49. For Truman's statement see *Public Papers of the Presidents of the United States, Harry S. Truman, January 1 to December 31, 1950* (Washington, D.C., 1965), p. 138; and *New York Times*, February 1, 1950.

[5] On February 3 Secretary Symington would award comedian Bob Hope a medal for entertaining overseas troops during and after the war. Eisenhower flew to New York with Lieutenant Colonel Andrew Stevenson Low, Jr. (USMA 1942), who would return to Washington with Hope for the ceremony (see desk calendar, and *New York Times*, Feb. 4, 1950).

[6] According to Eisenhower's desk calendar, the tower control "forgot" Captain W. W. Thomas and his passengers for forty minutes.

[7] Symington's reply of February 14 is in EM. Eisenhower would see the Secretary in Washington on Febrary 23, 1950 (see no. 716, n.14).

To John Thomas Cahill   *February 4, 1950*

Dear John:[1] While on a trip to Alabama I happened to have quite a talk with Ed Bermingham.[2] He feels that you and I might have a chat with some profit to Columbia interests, particularly in the field of athletics. While I hesitate to impose upon a busy man, I should be quite pleased to have such an opportunity.

I find myself in an embarrassing situation—having no free luncheon hours during the coming week; so I am writing this note to find whether there would be any other hour of the day when we might arrange a meeting convenient to both of us. If agreeable to you, would you have someone in your office call mine to determine when we might get together? Almost any place would suit me since I am quite ready to come downtown if this would be helpful from your viewpoint.[3]

Involved in Mr. Bermingham's suggestion were certain alumni interests and activities and realizing that you had passed the Presidency of the Federation on to Frank Hogan, I had at first thought that it might be well for me to see him directly.[4] Mr. Bermingham was quite certain, however, that I should talk to you alone because he felt that you would be in a better position to do whatever might seem desirable than would anyone occupying an official position in the University.[5]

All this sounds quite mysterious. Actually, it is quite simple.[6]

With personal regard, *Sincerely*

[1] For background on Cahill see no. 495.

[2] Eisenhower had just returned from a visit with friends in Alabama and Georgia (see no. 656). Bermingham, who had been Eisenhower's host in Alabama, was actively involved in Columbia affairs—at this time he was particularly involved with problems between the Alumni Football Committee and Coach Lou Little. On Bermingham see no. 381; for Bermingham's concern with Little's difficulties see no. 593.

[3] See the chronology for Eisenhower's busy luncheon schedule. Cahill and the General would meet on Friday, February 10, at 3:00 P.M.

[4] On June 1, 1949, Hogan had been elected president of the Alumni Federation of Columbia University, succeeding Frank W. Chambers. For background on Hogan see no. 10; on Chambers, no. 304.

[5] When Eisenhower saw Cahill (see n. 3, above), Hogan was also at the meeting.

[6] Cahill immediately launched a study of the problems in Columbia's athletic department. Among the steps taken to ease strained relationships would be plans to provide Little with an additional assistant, one who would serve as his chief of staff. On February 24, 1950, Cahill wrote Bermingham that he had looked into the "Little situation" and felt "reasonably sure that all is well now." In a letter to Cahill (Feb. 28), Bermingham replied, "Your fine hand has smoothed a situation which could have developed into a messy affair. I know it concerned the General and you have relieved him of considerable worry in that direction." Both letters are in EM, Bermingham Corr.

To Gordon Gray   *February 4, 1950*

Dear Gordon: While in Alabama the other day, someone told me that you had accepted the position of President of the University of North Carolina.[1] Instantly, for several reasons, I determined to write you a note.

In the first place, it gives me a slight feeling of advancement in the Society of College Presidents when I learn of another that I can class as a younger recruit. Secondly, I think you will thoroughly enjoy the work, particularly at an institution with such a distinguished record as North Carolina. Finally, there is in Chapel Hill one of my oldest and best friends, a retired captain of the Navy. His name is Everett Hazlett and he was at one time connected with the University as head of its Naval ROTC.[2] He was retired for heart trouble and my impression is that his physical condition permits him almost no social life. However, I am certain that if ever you run into him you will be struck by his wisdom and sound common sense.

So—congratulations on your new job.[3] *Cordially*

[1] Secretary of the Army Gray would be elected to head the Chapel Hill university on February 6, 1950 (see *New York Times*, Feb. 7, 1950). He would resign his Defense Department post in April and serve as a special assistant to President Truman until November. In October 1950 he would be installed as the president of the University of North Carolina (see no. 471). For background on Eisenhower's January visit to Alabama see no. 656.
[2] For background on Edward Everett Hazlett see no. 36.
[3] Gray replied that he was honored to join the distinguished Society of College Presidents and happy to be able to give Eisenhower "a slight feeling of advancement." He also said he looked forward to meeting Hazlett (Feb. 9, 1950, EM).

To Paul Herbert Davis   *February 4, 1950*

Re: Associates

Why could not an Associate[1]
  (*a*) Contribute to general purposes,[2] or
  (*b*) Select from among a series of approved projects the one he wants to support?[3]
Meetings of Associates will be difficult and may *kill* interest. I'll talk to you about this at your convenience.[4]

[1] Eisenhower and Davis, who was vice-president in charge of development, had probably discussed the Columbia Associates during a meeting on this same day (appointment calendar; Eisenhower's handwritten draft of this note is in EM, Letters and Drafts). The Associates had been organized in 1948 to draw business and professional men into the financial development and educational planning of the university (see no. 214). The annual membership fee of one thousand dollars per associate was expected to be a "major item of development . . ." (Davis to Eisenhower, June 6, 1949, EM, Columbia University Corr.), but enrollment had fallen far short of the 550 associates originally projected ("Columbia Associates," May 28, 1949, EM, Columbia University Corr.). By the fall of 1949 only twenty-seven men were members of the organization, and others had withdrawn, one dubbing it a "millionare's club." For background see nos. 485 and 509.

[2] On February 20 James D. Wise, president of the Columbia Associates, would write to Eisenhower on the subject of member contributions (CUF). Wise said that he had considered the many proposals made for the use of Associate funds and suggested the following: "Dues paid by members of Columbia Associates will go to the general funds of the University, except that a member desiring to do so may stipulate that a portion, but not more than one half, of his dues shall go to a particular University purpose." Eisenhower would concur with Wise's proposal (letter of Feb. 23, 1950, CUF), and the Associates would approve this policy at their May 11, 1950, meeting (see n. 4 below).

On the same day that Eisenhower sent this message to Davis, he also wrote to Wise concerning copies of George Sylvester Counts's *The Country of the Blind: The Soviet System of Mind Control*, which had been sent by Wise to each Associate (EM). Counts (Ph.D. University of Chicago 1916) had been a professor of education at Columbia Teachers College since 1927 and was the author of several books on education and communism. *The Country of the Blind*, which Counts had written with Nucia Lodge, explained "the all-embracing system of mind control in the Soviet Union" (Counts to Eisenhower, Aug. 9, 1949, EM). Eisenhower told Wise that the book should give each member "additional reasons for earnest support of Columbia in talking to all their friends" (EM).

[3] Among the projects supported by the Associates were the Columbia nutrition center (see no. 826); the Graduate School of Business (see no. 599); and the American Assembly (see no. 1039).

[4] At the Associates' May 11 meeting their Policy Committee would vote the transfer of $41,546.73 from the Associates account to the general-purposes fund of the university. The remaining sum of $1,591.27 had been previously designated to specific university purposes by the individual donors (see Wise to Eisenhower, May 17, 1950; and Columbia Associates Policy Committee Meeting, May 11, 1950, both in EM, Columbia University Corr.).

677   *Eisenhower Mss.*

To Kenneth Dewey Johnson   *February 4, 1950*

Dear Dean Johnson:[1] Attached is a letter which will, I am sure, interest you very much.[2] While I am certain that much of the writer's concern— especially that part that involves the New York School of Social Work—

is not well founded, yet the letter itself does demonstrate the good intent and purposes of its author.[3]

Because the writer is quite a friend of my wife's I should not like the letter to be widely distributed, but if you can conveniently find the time to give me your reactions, comments and suggestions with respect to the allegation she makes, I will be very grateful to you.[4] *Sincerely*

[1] Johnson was dean of Columbia University's New York School of Social Work (for background see no. 605).

[2] Mrs. C. Walter Allen, of Denver, Colorado, a friend of Mrs. Eisenhower's, had written to the General to criticize the operations of the New York School of Social Work. She charged the school with weakening the rights of individuals by training welfare workers who spread the destructive forces of "ismatic philosophies." She suggested that the curriculum emphasize the principles of democracy and rebuild in the welfare field a belief in individual and community responsibility (Jan. 26, 1950, EM).

[3] The New York School of Social Work was a graduate division of Columbia University (see Columbia University, *Bulletin of the New York School of Social Work* 45, no. 1 [1951], *Dean's Report 1950–51*).

[4] Johnson would reply to Mrs. Allen's allegations on February 8, 1950 (EM). In an attached memorandum, he would describe the school's historical and current positions on "the rights and responsibilities of the individual citizen." The curriculum, he said, stressed the interaction between scientific method and democratic social values, and the admissions policy emphasized the selection of students with potentialities for functioning inside our democratic system. On February 9, 1950 (CUF), Eisenhower would send Johnson's memorandum to Mrs. Allen, along with an invitation to visit the New York School of Social Work. For further developments see no. 857.

678   *Eisenhower Mss.*

TO CHARLOTTE GIBBS BLESSE PRICHARD   *February 4, 1950*

Dear Charlotte:[1] I cannot tell you how happy I am to know that you have found a niche in which you can feel some contentment and where you know that you are helping to develop youngsters into fine American citizens.

Of course, I should like to accept your invitation if it were at all possible.[2] But my schedule has such a bad habit of becoming completely rigid and so crowded for months in advance that I have to avoid adding anything to it outside of the "must" category. While it is true that I get away for an occasional short holiday, these are placed on my calendar by the doctor and I have finally come to admit that they are essential parts of my schedule. I no longer seem able to keep up the pace that I could 20 years ago.

So, when the formal invitation, of which you speak, comes to me,

I shall be forced to decline. But I do want you to know that I do so with real regret, because of your interest in the school.

I spoke to Mamie on the phone after your note came to my desk a few minutes ago and she asked to be included in sending to you and your lovely daughter[3] our warm greetings and affectionate regards. *Cordially*

P.S. Although your note was dated the 24th, I got it only today because I have just returned from a trip to the South.[4]

[1] Mrs. Prichard was the widow of Eisenhower's West Point classmate Major General Vernon E. Prichard, who had died in a boating accident in July 1949 (for background on Prichard see nos. 505 and 532). Mrs. Prichard had once served as a hostess at The Principia, a school for the children of Christian Scientists, in St. Louis, Missouri. After General Prichard's death she had returned to The Principia as a dormitory housemother in the upper school.
[2] In her letter of January 24 Mrs. Prichard had asked Eisenhower to address The Principia students in April 1950 (EM).
[3] Carlotta Prichard.
[4] See no. 656.

679   *Eisenhower Mss., Family File*

To Milton Stover Eisenhower   *February 4, 1950*

Dear Milton: Just this morning I returned to my desk after a two-weeks' trip to Georgia and Alabama.[1] While absent, I read a little notice in the paper that you had accepted the Penn State job. Quite naturally, all of us are highly pleased that you are coming back to the East. While I know that sentiment bound you rather tightly to KSAC, I believe that in the long run the move will bring you greater satisfaction and contentment.[2] I truly hope that Helen[3] and the youngsters[4] feel the same way about it.

Incidentally, with your departure from Kansas, the only real connection the family will have with the State is through Roy's widow and one of the children.[5] It seems odd, doesn't it?

There is no doubt in my mind that Tommy Stephens would be by far the best artist that you could get for the portrait.[6] Chandor is the only other artist in the country who, to my mind, produces a truly great portrait. . . .[7] On the other hand, Tommy Stephens, being a very human and understanding fellow, is quite likely, because of friendship, to forget his own interest entirely. I sometimes fear that he is going to die in a garret.

In one or two instances, I have asked him, as a favor to me, to paint some particular person where financial considerations did not permit the imposition of his established fee. This established fee is roughly, I believe, something like $3500 to $5000, depending upon the size of the portrait. However, the two, to which I referred, were both painted for $2500 each and, I am sure, that he would be more than glad to do the same again. I think he would be particularly interested in having one of his portraits in the Middle West. I know that he has gone to San Francisco to paint, to Atlanta, and to other places. But, so far as I know, he has never been in that particular region. With this rough guess upon the amount that I think would be involved, would you let me know as soon as possible whether I should consult him about the matter?

Incidentally, I would suggest that, if you have Tommy do it, you invite him out to your home and put him up for the few days that he would be there. The reasons for this suggestion are several, but the most important one is that it would operate greatly in your favor. It would shorten the time needed for the sittings and would make it most convenient for you. Also, he would get a better portrait because of your relaxation and surroundings. Another reason is that he is a very personable and interesting sort of human. All of you would enjoy having him around and he would help you immeasurably in your painting.

When you receive this note, I would suggest that you telephone me because, if you are to get Tommy, we ought to let him know in plenty of time.[8]

My very best love to the family, *As ever*

[1] For Eisenhower's trip see no. 656.

[2] Milton Eisenhower had been president of Kansas State College of Agriculture and Applied Science since 1943 (see Chandler, *War Years*, no. 950). On January 21, 1950, he had been elected president of Pennsylvania State College (*New York Times*, Jan. 22, 1950). Dr. Eisenhower's decision to accept the offer was based on several factors. The position enabled him to move closer to his family and to return to his ancestral state of Pennsylvania. His interests in national and world affairs also attracted the educator to the East (Milton S. Eisenhower to Dwight D. Eisenhower, Jan. 30, 1950, EM, Family File; Neal, *Reluctant Dynasty*, pp. 216–19). The announcement ended speculation that he would become a candidate for the governorship of Kansas in 1950 (*ibid.*, pp. 217–18; see nos. 705 and 716, n. 6).

[3] Milton's wife, the former Helen Elsie Eakin.

[4] Dr. Eisenhower had two children: Milton Jr. ("Buddy") and Ruth Eakin.

[5] Roy J. Eisenhower, brother to Dwight and Milton, had died in 1942. Edna Eisenhower, Roy's widow, lived in Junction City, Kansas (for background on Mr. and Mrs. Roy Eisenhower see *Eisenhower Papers*, vol. I–IX; and Bela Kornitzer, *The Great American Heritage: The Story of the Five Eisenhower Brothers* [New York, 1955], pp. 99–103). A daughter, Patricia Eisenhower, lived in Kansas with her husband, Thomas B. Fegan.

[6] The student council of Kansas State College planned to have a portrait painted of Dr. Eisenhower before he resigned as college president as "a lasting tribute to a man who has a brilliant future ahead of him" (Harman to Dwight Eisenhower, Mar. 23, 1950, EM). In a letter of Janaury 30 Milton had written the General

for information about Thomas Stephens, whom he hoped would be selected to paint the portrait (EM, Family File). For background on Stephens see no. 51.
[7] Douglas Chandor, born in Woldingham, England, had come to the United States in 1926. Among the prominent subjects of his paintings were Winston Churchill, Bernard M. Baruch, and presidents Herbert Hoover and Franklin D. Roosevelt. For further background on Chandor see Galambos, *Chief of Staff*, no. 1024.
[8] Thomas Stephens would not paint this particular portrait. The student council would select Elmer Westley Greene, Jr., of New York City. Greene, a native of Boston, had studied at the Massachusetts School of Art and the art school of the Boston Museum. He had painted portraits of Pope Pius XII; Erwin N. Griswold, dean of the Harvard Law School; and President Herbert Hoover. In a letter of April 17, 1950 (EM, Family File), Milton would tell the General that his own portrait (now in the foyer of Eisenhower Hall at Kansas State University) was "excellent." On March 23 the president of the student council at Kansas State would solicit a donation from Eisenhower to help in the purchase of his brother's portrait. Eisenhower jotted on the letter, "What next?" On April 3, however, he sent a check for fifty dollars (see papers in EM, Harman Corr.).

680   *Eisenhower Mss.*

To Aksel Nielsen   *February 4, 1950*

Dear Aksel:[1] Last evening I returned from a trip to the South where I had some very good bird shooting but no luck at all with the fish.[2] Mr. Doud was sick when I left New York, having had a light attack of pneumonia. Dr. Snyder and nurses pulled him through but, of course, at his age, recovery is quite slow. Just when he will be able to come back to Denver, I am not quite certain. Fortunately, this time, he did not seem to have any serious heart complications as he did two years ago. While he was down, Mrs. Doud also had to take to her bed for about a week due, I think, almost entirely to exhaustion.[3]

While in the South, I spent several days with Mr. Edward Bermingham.[4] One evening I began discussing with him some of the work that he carries on at his cattle ranch in Wyoming. I made the remark that when an individual raised purebred cattle that the proceeds were classed as capital gains rather than as normal income. Since he had never heard of this before, I promised him to ask you to send along the particular notation or reference that would give him full information on the matter. Consequently, would you mind writing to him at Enon Farm, Midway, Alabama, to give him this information? He is a very fine man and I have the impression you may have met him either last summer or summer before last in Denver. He visited me briefly both years, in connection with a Columbia luncheon.

It seems to me that there was something else that I wanted to write to you about this morning but, since I cannot recall to my mind what it is, I shall have to wait until another time.

With all the best, *Cordially*

[1] For background on Nielsen see no. 77.

[2] On the trip see no. 656.

[3] Mrs. Eisenhower's parents, the John S. Douds, had become ill during their stay at 60 Morningside Drive (see no. 671). Dr. Howard M. Snyder, Sr., was Eisenhower's friend and physician (see no. 1).

[4] See no. 381 for background on Bermingham, who owned the Double Diamond Ranch in Duncan, Wyoming. On February 9, Nielsen sent Bermingham information regarding reportable gains upon the sale of draft, breeding, and dairy animals (EM, Nielsen Corr.). In a letter of February 13 Bermingham thanked Eisenhower for his help and said that he did not think his own accountants had taken advantage of the long-term capital-gains provision as outlined by Nielsen's accountants (EM).

681   *Eisenhower Mss.*

To JEROME A. FRANKLIN   *February 6, 1950*

Dear Jerry:[1] Herewith two pamphlets on fish pond development which I picked up in Alabama. The one pamphlet emphasizes certain important details in dam construction; the other tells more about the actual stocking of the pond. Incidentally, I find a notation in the one pamphlet that the best document on stocking and managing is the "Alabama Agricultural Experiment Station Bulletin 254." I have no doubt that the document could be procured for a few cents.

With respect to our dam construction, I was particularly concerned about whether we had allowed a sufficient additional height for settling. The pamphlet says, "For dams extremely well packed, a minimum of 6 inches should be added to every 10 feet in height to take care of settling." If our dam was extremely well packed, then apparently we should have added 1½ feet to the finally desired height to provide for settling.[2]

There are also paragraphs on the spillway that seem important, although I should doubt that in our own we would need concrete paving. I believe though that we should be certain that the *width* of the spillway will never allow the water to run over the dam—otherwise we'd lose a lot of money.[3]

I realize that you may have had far better documents than these to guide you when you were building the dam. But there may be something in these of sufficient value to warrant your reading them. If you think they are worth it, you might file them at the office.[4] *Cordially*

[1] Since July 1949 Franklin, a member of the Augusta National Golf Club, had kept Eisenhower informed about the progress in constructing a fish pond at the club. For background see no. 613.

[2] Franklin replied (Feb. 15, EM) that during construction a heavy tractor had been run back and forth over the clay dam; he did not think it would settle more than six inches.

[3] Franklin enclosed sketches of the overflow pipe and the spillway. He agreed that a concrete base would not be necessary for the clay-based spillway, which was twelve feet wide.

[4] On February 17 Eisenhower wrote to Franklin, "The complete explanation that you sent to me embarrasses me just a bit—after all, I keenly realize that you not only have been the moving spirit in the development of our Club's fishing facilities, but, also, that you know far more about it than I ever will." This reply, as well as further correspondence, is in EM.

682   *Eisenhower Mss.*

To Clarence Dillon   *February 6, 1950*

Dear Mr. Dillon: A recent visit to Ed Bermingham's home in Alabama reminded me that I should like, if possible, to see you again at luncheon, to continue the conversations that we began some weeks ago at your house.[1] A quick examination of my calendar shows free luncheon hours on March 9th and 10th. And I wonder whether you could conveniently come up to 60 Morningside Drive on either of those dates. Should you be able to accept, I intend to write a note to Ed to find out whether, by some happy chance, he might be in town the same day. Except for him, I have not thought of inviting anyone else.[2]

You will be glad to know that during my three-day visit at Enon Farm, which was a most enjoyable affair, I found both Ed and Mrs. Bermingham to be in the very best of health and spirits.[3]

With warm personal regard, *Cordially*

[1] Eisenhower, Dillon, and Bermingham had met at Dillon's home on November 7, 1949 (see no. 593).

[2] On February 8 Dillon would accept Eisenhower's invitation for Thursday, March 9 (EM. Eisenhower's note to Bermingham is no. 693). The three men would discuss preliminary plans for the establishment at Columbia of an institute for the study of war and peace. For Dillon's important role see nos. 730 and 810. For background on the Institute of War and Peace Studies see no. 1056.

[3] See no. 656.

To Robert Lawrence Stearns

Dear Dr. Stearns:[1] Upon my return from a recent southern trip, I received your nice letter of January 19.[2]

I hope that you realize how privileged I felt to associate with you and other distinguished educators in the work of the Board of which you were Chairman. My personal gratitude goes especially to you, not only because of extraordinary consideration you constantly showed to all of us, but for acting as our agent in procuring and presenting the little memento to Mr. Hoen.[3]

I hope this coming summer to make my customary visit to Colorado and, if I do, shall certainly attempt to come to Boulder for a personal visit, if this should prove convenient to you.[4]

Please convey my greetings to your nice family and with warm personal regard, *Cordially*

[1] Stearns was president of the University of Colorado and chairman of the Service Academy Board (for background see no. 322).

[2] On Eisenhower's trip see no. 656. Stearns's letter (EM) included the information that Secretary of Defense Louis A. Johnson had approved the final report of the Service Academy Board. Johnson had arranged for Stearns to present a copy of the report to President Truman on January 13, 1950.

[3] John L. Hoen had been executive secretary of the Service Academy Board (for background see no. 403). In his letter of January 19 Stearns had acknowledged that he had received from Eisenhower a check to cover part of the cost of an "appreciation presentation" for Hoen. According to Stearns, the suggestion for the gift had come from Eisenhower and Rear Admiral James L. Holloway, Jr., superintendent of the Naval Academy (for background on Holloway see no. 322). Hoen had presented the Service Academy Board's final report to the Armed Forces Policy Council on January 24, 1950, and the council had commended the board for its work (Johnson to Eisenhower, Jan. 27, 1950, EM). For background on the Service Academy Board's final report see no. 610.

[4] The Eisenhowers would spend about seven weeks in Denver during the summer of 1950 (see no. 873).

To Charles Edward Wilson

Dear Mr. Wilson:[1] I have just finished reading, in a document entitled BIG PROGRESS AND BIG BUSINESS GO TOGETHER, the statement you made before a Congressional Committee.[2] Your whole case seemed to me to be admirably stated and I was particularly struck by your ability to answer detailed questions, apparently without calling on any staff assistance.[3]

Certainly, I believe you may have done something to convince thinking people that the words "big" and "evil" are not necessarily synonymous.[4]

With warm personal regard, *Cordially*

[1] Charles Edward Wilson had been president of the General Electric Company since 1940. Educated in the New York City public schools, Wilson had been with General Electric since 1899, working in the departments of accounting, production, engineering, manufacturing, and marketing. During World War II he had served as executive vice-chairman of the War Production Board (WPB), and in December 1950 he would be appointed Director of the Office of Defense Mobilization.

[2] On November 30, 1949, Wilson had testified before the House Judiciary Committee, which was conducting a study of monopoly power; the document to which Eisenhower refers, however, is not in EM.

[3] Wilson had emphasized the benefits of large-scale economic enterprises at the investigative hearings on monopolies and conspiratorial action by large corporations. He had contended that very few true monopolies existed in any field and had said that limitations to corporate size would prove detrimental to the American economy. Wilson, who was without staff assistance, had nevertheless countered detailed charges involving the assets, affiliations, employees, products, and policies of the General Electric Company.

[4] Wilson had defended corporate bigness: "To say that any company is too large, on the basis of any absolute standard, is the height of defeatism. For no company and no industry in the American economy is yet big enough to bring enough goods to enough people" (U.S., Congress, House, Committee on the Judiciary, *Study of Monopoly Power*, 81st Cong., 1st sess., 1949, p. 1237).

685 *Eisenhower Mss.*

To Errett P. Scrivner

February 6, 1950

Dear Congressman Scrivner:[1] Thank you for your thoughtful letter and for the personal compliment implicit in it. I should, of course, always be ready to talk with individuals who are earnestly concerned with the future of this country.[2] I never fail to gain something from informal discussions on such subjects with people I respect. Of course, I assume that what you have in mind is a very small, informal gathering where discussion would be on the conversational basis and would not involve a "speech."

However, I am at a loss to suggest any time and place for such a meeting. In recent weeks I have been coming to Washington only on special occasions and have no idea when I shall again be there. Because my schedule has a habit of becoming quite rigid and inflexible for many weeks in advance, I could scarcely plan a special trip. In spite of all this, if I should find myself in Washington with a luncheon or dinner hour to spare, I shall certainly give you a ring with the idea of gathering with you and any of your friends that might be immediately available. While I do not flatter myself that I can add much in the way of wisdom to the type of discussion you have in mind, it is always a pleasant experience for me to renew contacts with old Kansas friends, to say nothing of what I gain otherwise.[3] *Sincerely*

[1] Scrivner (LL.B. University of Kansas 1925), a Republican, had represented Kansas's Second District in Congress since 1944.

[2] In an undated, handwritten letter (EM) Scrivner had told Eisenhower of his concern about socialist trends and public lethargy in the nation. He praised Eisenhower's leadership in World War II and said he hoped that the General would not "bar the door" to any possible opportunities that might come his way. Should such opportunity arise, Scrivner wrote, "it is your patriotic duty to accept the responsibility it would place upon you." He asked Eisenhower if he would be willing to meet with a group of congressional leaders to discuss the problems facing the country at this time.

[3] Eisenhower's appointment calendar does not show that such a meeting with Scrivner took place.

686   *Eisenhower Mss., Diaries*

DIARY   *February 7, 1950*

General Snyder[1] and I have decided that it is not possible for me to remain in New York and at the same time resist sufficiently the demands upon my time so that I can maintain a schedule indefinitely. Moreover we have found that whenever I return from a vacation it is only a matter of a very few weeks until I am showing again the effects of strain, long hours and tension.[2] Reservation of a day or half day each week (aside from Sundays) fails because of my giving way to some insistent demand for a conference, meeting, luncheon or similar chore. So now we are to try something different: we are reserving one full week out of each two months, to be completely blacked out of my calendar. Preferably I am to leave the city during the "no work" week, but if not then I am to lock the front door of my house. This ought to work . . . but only today I have broken into the March week to accommodate the meeting of the Boy Scouts National Executive Council.[3] That's the way it goes. (And it is only Feb. 7, 1950).

[1] Major General Howard M. Snyder, Sr., was Eisenhower's physician.

[2] Eisenhower had recently returned from a vacation in the South (see no. 656).

[3] Eisenhower was a member of the National Executive Board of the Boy Scouts

of America (see no. 40). He had agreed to attend a board meeting scheduled for March 16 at the Biltmore Hotel in New York City, but on the day of the meeting Major Robert L. Schulz, Eisenhower's aide, informed Thomas J. Murphy, secretary to the chief scout executive, that the General was out of town and would not attend (R. L. Schulz to Eisenhower, Feb. 6, 1950; and T. J. Murphy to R. L. Schulz, Mar. 13, 1950, both in EM, Subject File, Clubs and Associations). General and Mrs. Eisenhower did, in fact, leave town. On Sunday, March 12, they arrived at the Seaview Country Club in Absecon, New Jersey, where they spent several days with friends (the George E. Allens and the Ellis D. Slaters). The Eisenhowers would return to New York on Saturday, March 18. See the chronology in these volumes for the General's full schedule during February and March 1950.

To David Randolph Calhoun, Jr.   *February 7, 1950*

Dear Dave: By this time you may have received a formal invitation from Augusta National to join the Club as a member.[1] You seemed to like the place so tremendously that I decided to go to the "Invitations Committee" and ask them whether they would extend such an invitation. This is a bit of a shortcut to the procedure at that particular Club; but there happened to be so many members of the Committee present when you were there, and all were so enthusiastically pleased with the opportunity of meeting you, that I thought it best not to defer the matter. Since that time, I have also put up Stuart's name.[2] I rather think that you are sufficiently acquainted with the Club, its membership, its facilities and possibly even its customs that I need to discuss none of these. The only point probably worth mentioning is that, normally, a very complicated procedure precedes the extending of any invitation to a prospective member. This procedure is designed to protect members against pressures that are sometimes applied by others who want to join the Club. Because of this, I would merely ask you to keep the whole matter confidential until after you receive the invitation and make your final decision.

As I remember, the initiation fee is $1000 and the dues are $240 a year, including tax.[3]

After you left, my back became so painful that I had to stop playing golf. It continued to bother me while I went on short hunting trips in Alabama with Ed Bermingham and in Georgia with Bob Woodruff. However, it didn't bother me enough to keep me from trying every day and I must say that I got a very good bag of quail and turkey.[4]

Give me a ring when you come up this way, for I am always happy to see you.[5] *Cordially*

P.S. The reason for not writing to you about this earlier is because

I got back from the South at the end of last week. I've just heard about our failure to get together on a date at the Links. Sorry!

[1] On February 6 Helen N. Harris, office manager at Augusta National, had written Eisenhower that a "preparatory letter" should be sent to Calhoun before a formal invitation was sent by club president Robert T. Jones, Jr.; since Eisenhower had proposed Calhoun for membership, she said, he should write the letter (EM, Subject File, Clubs and Associations). For background see no. 673.

[2] See *ibid*.

[3] Calhoun would accept Jones's February 15 invitation on March 6 (see papers in EM, Subject File, Clubs and Associations; and in EM).

[4] See nos. 656 and 690.

[5] Eisenhower would next see Calhoun at an April 3 dinner Calhoun and J. Wesley McAfee arranged in Eisenhower's honor (see Schulz to Calhoun, Feb. 15, 1949, and Calhoun to Eisenhower, Feb. 29, 1950, both in EM. For background on McAfee see no. 581).

688   *Eisenhower Mss.*

To Marcellus Hartley Dodge   *February 8, 1950*

Dear Marcy: Thank you very much indeed for your two notes, both dated yesterday.[1]

In connection with the one concerning Dean Pegram, your memorandum states exactly what I think should be done.[2] Yesterday, another suggestion was made to me on which I do not feel capable of giving an opinion because of my lack of experience in universities. It was that the University should, by all means, have a permanent portrait of such a distinguished scholar and long-time member of the Columbia family as is Dean Pegram. If this is true (and I am taking no stand either for or against at this moment), would you consider it proper to include in your memorandum a recommendation that we secure the same artist here in the University that the Trustees commissioned to paint a portrait of me?[3]

With respect to the creation of a new position of Director for Scientific Research and John Dunning's assignment to it, I answer your specific question concerning salary with the opinion that, at first, it should be about $15,000 per year. In the particular instance of which we are now speaking, we cannot be completely certain as to how this task will develop in importance and responsibility. Therefore, I think we should leave ourselves some leeway, even though I agree that Dunning should be substantially advanced in salary if he is to take this position.[4]

There is a point with respect to our Monthly Meetings about which I should like to talk to you sometime at your convenience. So the next time you happen to be going past my office, won't you drop in to see whether or not I am free? It merely concerns opportunity for "informal" talk![5]

With warm personal regard, *Cordially*

[1] Eisenhower had received two notes from Dodge (dated Feb. 7, EM) concerning university business.

[2] The note contained two recommendations by the Committee on Education regarding the retirement of Vice-President George B. Pegram. The first, to be submitted to the Committee on Honors, would make Pegram vice-president emeritus of the university. The second, to be submitted to the trustees under provision of the revised statutes, would confirm Pegram's appointment as special adviser to Eisenhower for one year, dating from July 1, 1950. For background on Pegram see nos. 337 and 361; for developments see no. 722.

[3] Eisenhower's portrait, painted by artist Elie Christo-Loveanu, hangs in the Butler Library at Columbia; the university would not, however, commission a portrait of Dean Pegram (letter from Marion E. Jemmott, Secretary, Columbia University, July 31, 1980, EP).

[4] In his second note Dodge informed Eisenhower of a memorandum (prepared for the Committee on Education and to be submitted to the trustees) authorizing John R. Dunning's appointment to the newly created position of director for scientific research (for background on Dunning see no. 191). "If you will allow me to make the suggestion," Dodge wrote, "I doubt if the purpose of the creation of this office will be accomplished unless you pay him more than you have had in mind. Personally I believe he will earn a Dean's salary in this important office." On June 1, 1950, the statutes of the trustees would be amended to provide for a director for scientific research, who would "assist the Vice President of the University in matters relating to research and instruction in the Physical and Biological Sciences and in Engineering, including undertakings to secure funds for the support of research" (CUF). Dunning would become dean of the School of Engineering on July 1, 1950; for developments see no. 739.

[5] Dodge replied (Feb. 16, EM) that he had put the proposed portrait of Dean Pegram on the agenda for the next meeting of the Committee on Education. He considered the Dunning appointment so important that he planned to obtain informal approval from members of the Committee on Education rather than wait until the regularly scheduled meeting on February 27. With Eisenhower's approval, he wrote, the initial salary of fifteen thousand dollars would be attached to the position.

689   *Eisenhower Mss.*

To William Averell Harriman   *February 8, 1950*
Telegram

Fletcher informs me you plan early trip home.[1] Investigations and plans involving possible public service use of Arden House by Columbia are progressing with faculty and administrative officers showing increasing optimism and enthusiasm.[2] All these plans are in fluid state and I am anxious to have long talk with you and hope you can have luncheon and afternoon with me while you are in New York City. If this is possible can you let me know most convenient time for you?[3] Am personally badly tied up to and including February 20 but thereafter till end of month am committed only on 23rd.[4] *With warm regard*

[1] Walter D. Fletcher, a Columbia trustee and Averell Harriman's attorney, had met with Eisenhower the morning of February 8. Harriman, Truman's Special Representative in Europe for the Economic Cooperation Administration, would arrive in New York City from Paris on February 16, en route to Washington, D.C., where he would testify before House and Senate committees concerning the extension of U.S. aid to Europe (*New York Times*, Feb. 17, 1950).

[2] For background on the proposed uses of Arden House, a gift to Columbia University from the Harriman family, see no. 605.

[3] In a wire of February 10 Harriman suggested Sunday, February 26, for their meeting, and on the same day Eisenhower confirmed the date in a night letter to Harriman at the Hotel Talleyrand in Paris (both wires in EM). The two met at 60 Morningside Drive as planned; and they agreed to meet again on April 23 (Eisenhower to Harriman, Feb. 28, 1950, EM). For developments on the Arden House project, which would ultimately become the American Assembly, see no. 771.

[4] Eisenhower would leave Columbia on this same day for New Haven, Connecticut, to attend the *Yale Daily News* annual banquet, honoring retiring Yale president Charles Seymour. On February 9 Seymour thanked Eisenhower for coming to the banquet and for the "kindly things" he had said in tribute. "It was great fun seeing you," wrote Seymour, "but I realize the effort involved in your visit" (EM). See the chronology in these volumes for Eisenhower's heavy schedule during February.

690   *Eisenhower Mss.*

To Edward John Bermingham   *February 8, 1950*

Dear Ed: Of course, long ago I should have written you a bread and butter note but I think that both apology and explanation can be combined in the simple statement that my schedule, since returning to New York, has been very greatly similar to the one that I left behind me when I started South in the middle of the month. Moreover, I have had little doubt that you thoroughly understood how much I enjoyed the hospitality that I experienced at Enon Farm and how much I appreciated the many personal courtesies extended to me by you and Mrs. Bermingham and by your admirable staff.[1]

As I suppose Bob Woodruff told you, he has a very large holding in his Ichauway Estate.[2] He frequently has two hunting parties out at the same time. Consequently, he has a large number of dogs. I meant to ask him what he does with his surplus puppies—that is, whether he sells them off or gives them away—but I don't recall posing the question. In any event, he keeps approximately 75 grown dogs, out of which number they attempt to keep 25 or 30 constantly in condition for hunting. Since the weather is much warmer—or so it seemed to me—than it is in Alabama, they use more dogs on a 2½ hour hunt than you do. We frequently carried 12 dogs with us in the wagon and worked them, by pairs, for half an hour. Thus, we usually worked five pairs and had one reserve when we came in.

As you would expect in such a large tract, the hunting varies considerably, although the whole area is quite flat. The final day of my visit, one pair of hunters got 20 birds, the other 2. However the latter pair flushed 6 coveys.

Bob has many birds but I should estimate that, acre for acre, not more than you have. One afternoon we were in an area that is shot over only once in a great while. In that area we flushed, I think, about 10 to 12 coveys in two hours. This did not differ greatly, as I remember, from our afternoons on your plantation.

Bob uses all types of traps and snares against vermin. He believes in controlled burning but does not consider that this has much effect on the elimination of rats. These, he catches in a kind of trap that can take 10 or 12 rats in a single catch.[3] He completely shares your belief that Southern agriculture will be prosperous only on the basis of making the pine tree its principal crop. He says he has no trouble in conducting his burning in such a way as to protect seedlings and young trees.[4]

One day we had a turkey shoot. The shoot is conducted as a drive, with all of the guns stationed along one side of a large timbered area through which the beaters come, making all the noise possible. I was astonished to find how fast the turkey flies when on full wing but I was very lucky and missed none. However, my entire shoot was accomplished within a period of two minutes.

The whole process of organizing the drive, stationing and starting the beaters, deploying and instructing the shooters and, finally, gathering and taking them back home for a barbecue is all a highly organized and very colorful business. We got 22 birds altogether and I think there were 22 shooters.

One afternoon I went fishing in Ichauway Creek and we confidently expected to nail a number of big bass. My companion, the estate manager, accompanied me, in a separate boat on the opposite side of the creek. He caught two little bass by the use of a fishing method called "jigger fishing." I didn't have a strike.

Tell Dobson[5] that jigger fishing consists in the rigging up of a long bamboo pole (15 or 20 feet) with a very short line, not over about 18 inches in length. On the end of the line is a single hook with a pork rind bait (or something similar). The boat is then steered very silently along the shore line just far enough out so that the bamboo pole will reach to the water's edge. The fisherman achieves a sort of quiver or vibration in the end of the bamboo pole as he trails the bait just along or just under the water's surface at the very edge of the shore line. (Incidentally, a good length of line is wound around the rod all the way back to the handle. This method of tying on, I assumed, was merely to avoid cutting a line into short pieces.)

Frankly, the method seemed to be fairly effective if you just want to catch fish—I couldn't say too much of it as a thrill in sport.

Possibly all the above represents nothing but sheer boredom for you, but I send it along on the outside chance that you may find in this rambling account something of slight interest.

I have just sent a note to Mr. Dillon, asking him to come to lunch on March 9 or 10 if he can do so. I told him that, in the event of a favorable reply, I would write to you to find out whether, by some happy chance, you would be in town on that day. If that miracle should occur, I would hope that you would also consent to come to lunch.[6]

In the meantime, my renewed and grateful thanks to you both—I shall never forget my days at Enon. *Cordially*

[1] Eisenhower had recently returned from a visit with the Berminghams at their home in Midway, Alabama. This letter to Bermingham was preceded on February 3 by a handwritten note of appreciation from Eisenhower to Bermingham's wife, Katherine (EM). For background on the trip see no. 656.

[2] Eisenhower had also visited Robert W. Woodruff at his plantation home in Newton, Georgia (see *ibid.*).

[3] See no. 693 for more on the subject of controlled burning.

[4] Bermingham replied (Feb. 19, EM) that he was involved in educating the people of Bullock County, Alabama, about timbering. He had persuaded the editor of a local newspaper to run a series of editorials on the subject; he had also arranged to meet with timber experts who had agreed to instruct him in the latest scientific methods.

[5] *H*obson Creswell was Bermingham's estate superintendent. In an undated handwritten note to Eisenhower, Bermingham said that when he read to Hobson the part of this letter describing fishing at Ichauway Plantation, Hobson "chuckled & seemed not at all unhappy that you had no luck. His great ambition is to give you a lively time on the lake" (EM).

[6] For background see no. 682; for developments regarding their meeting see no. 693.

691   *Eisenhower Mss.*

To Michael F. Hogan and Ann M. Hogan   *February 9, 1950*

Dear Mr. and Mrs. Hogan:[1] Your son Frank has just told me that you have passed your fiftieth wedding anniversary and are planning, next Saturday, to celebrate the occasion with a family gathering.[2] Although I've not had the honor of meeting you, I hope you will permit me to invoke my admiration and friendship for your son as my excuse for sending you felicitations and warm greetings on your arrival at this memorable milestone.[3]

May all that's good be ever yours—and may you have many more years to enjoy gatherings together. Especially I wish you the happiest of family reunions on Saturday, next.[4] *Most sincerely*

[1] The Hogans, of Waterbury, Connecticut, were the parents of Frank S. Hogan, District Attorney of New York County. For background on Hogan see no. 635. Eisenhower's handwritten draft of this letter is in EM, Letters and Drafts.
[2] Hogan had telephoned Eisenhower's office this same day to inform the General that his parents would celebrate their golden wedding anniversary on February 11 (Schulz to Eisenhower, EM, Hogan Corr.).
[3] Since June 1949 Hogan had been president of Columbia's Alumni Federation.
[4] On February 14 Hogan would thank Eisenhower for the message. In his reply of February 17 Eisenhower told Hogan that it had been "nothing but genuine pleasure" to greet his parents and that he would file carefully a "delightful note" received from Hogan's mother. All correspondence is in EM.

692

To William H. Adams   *February 10, 1950*

Dear Mr. Adams:[01] I have been informed that Norwich University may possibly consider, for the post of President, certain army officers of distinguished records. I am sure you will understand that I have more than a perfunctory interest in Norwich, not only because of its fine record in the field of military education but because, as you may know, I have the distinction of holding an honorary degree from the University.[2]

This explains, I hope, my temerity in suggesting that you consider the qualifications of Major General George A. Horkan of the United States Army. I have been informed by a friend that he would be definitely interested in being considered for the position.[3]

I have known General Horkan since he was a Captain in the Army, somewhere around the year 1925.[4] His family roots are in Georgia as are his wife's, and both are of the highest character and most pleasing and congenial personality.

After combat service in World War I, General Horkan, who is 55 years old, joined the Quartermaster Corps and has spent most of his career in the business and logistic side of the Army's activities. He took his A.B. degree at Georgetown University and some years later graduated from Babson Institute. He had command of Camp Lee, Virginia, during World War II and established there a very enviable record in military administration and in human relations. He was presented the Distinguished Service Medal by the Government.

I realize that it is impossible in a letter to do more than urge the worthiness of any individual for consideration. Consequently, I can only say that if you should become interested in General Horkan as a possible prospect for your presidency, I will be glad to answer, specifically and in detail, anything that I possibly can about him and his charming family.[5]

With my apologies for imposing upon your time for the reading of this letter, *Sincerely*

[1] William H. Adams was chairman of a nominating committee for the presidency of Norwich University, in Northfield, Vermont.

[2] On June 9, 1946, General Eisenhower had received the honorary degree of Doctor of Military Science at the 127th commencement of Norwich University (EM; *New York Times*, June 10, 1949). The school was the nation's oldest private military institution. Established as the American Literary, Scientific, and Military Academy in 1819, it had adopted a new charter and the name Norwich University in 1835. In January 1972 Norwich would merge with Vermont College, a private women's school in Montpelier, Vermont.

[3] Since 1948 Major General George A. Horkan had been Chief Quartermaster to the European Command in Heidelberg, Germany. Horkan had asked a former staff member, Colonel Frank Maxim, to inquire about the Norwich University presidency. Maxim, aware of Eisenhower's friendship with Horkan, wrote to William Adams, suggesting that he contact Eisenhower concerning Horkan's qualifications (memorandum, Schulz to Eisenhower, Feb. 6, 1950, and Schulz to Horkan, Mar. 6, 1950, both in EM, Horkan Corr.). For background on Horkan see *Eisenhower Papers*, vols. I–IX.

[4] In 1928 Eisenhower and Horkan had worked together on the Battle Monuments Commission in Paris, France (see Chandler, *War Years*, no. 2035). The relationship between these old Army friends would last throughout their careers.

[5] Horkan, who would not be selected as president of Norwich University, would succeed General Herman Feldman as Quartermaster General in October 1951. (Additional correspondence on Horkan's career is in EM.) The university would appoint instead another friend of Eisenhower's, Major General Ernest N. Harmon (ret.). In a letter to Eisenhower of March 15, 1950, Adams explained his committee's reasons for the choice. Harmon had attended Norwich University for one year before going on to West Point and later had served Norwich for four years as commandant of cadets. In addition, he had been professor of military science and tactics at the school (EM). For further background on Harmon see *Eisenhower Papers*, vols. I–IX.

693 *Eisenhower Mss.*

TO EDWARD JOHN BERMINGHAM *February 10, 1950*

Dear Ed:[0] Mr. Dillon is coming to lunch with me on March 9. Would you by some miraculous chance, be in town on that date? If so, I will expect you to have a bite with us.[1] I had thought some of asking one or two of my University associates to lunch with Mr. Dillon but have decided not to do so this time. I do hope that he can meet Grayson Kirk who is a very fine individual and a wonderful personality.[2]

I like to have comments and criticisms on our plans, particularly from the viewpoint of appropriateness, effectiveness and good taste. There are many, many ways to go wrong in the business of mobilizing support for a great institution such as this. By reason of my lack of experience, I am very apt, I should think, to overlook many, if not all, of these risks and dangers. But I do know if we attempt nothing, we face certain ruin—so I must try to push ahead and depend upon good friends to shout a warning when we steer too close to "verboten" territory.[3] *Cordially*

P.S. I note from your most recent letter that your dropping of the subject of "burnings" from conversations with Bob Woodruff was deliberate on your part. I think I have already explained in a recent letter to you that Bob agrees with you about the futility of burning in the task of pest extermination. I believe his theory is merely that the "sedge" grass is completely useless and is even poor cover for quail. Therefore, he should burn it off once in a while. At least, he never gave me any better explanation than this.[4]

P.P.S. Had a talk with John Cahill & Frank Hogan re: football.[5]

---

[1] Clarence Dillon had accepted Eisenhower's invitation to lunch (see no. 682). On February 13 Bermingham would accept this invitation from the General (EM).

[2] Grayson Kirk was the provost of Columbia University.

[3] Dillon would make an important financial contribution toward the establishment of Columbia's Institute of War and Peace Studies in the future (see no. 1142).

[4] In his letter of February 7 Bermingham had told Eisenhower that he preferred not to discuss with Woodruff the subject of controlled burning of acreage inhabited by bobwhite quail populations (see no. 690 for background). According to Bermingham, burning did not destroy the vermin that attack quail but it did destroy the balance of nature. On February 19 Bermingham wrote again on this subject (this letter and other related correspondence on this question are in EM. See also Dan W. Speake, "Effects of Controlled Burning on Bobwhite Quail Populations and Habitat of an Experimental Area in the Alabama Piedmont," *Proceedings of the Twentieth Annual Conference, Southeastern Association of Game and Fish Commissioners, October 24–26, 1966, Asheville, North Carolina* [Columbia, S.C., 1967], pp. 19–32).

[5] For background on the recent difficulties involving football at Columbia see no. 674. Eisenhower added this second postscript by hand.

To Arthur Hays Sulzberger   *February 10, 1950*

Dear Arthur:[1] I am in complete agreement with the ideas expressed in your note to me under date of February 7.[2] I have never yet understood some of the methods that we use for the performance of some of our most important work and I think that this matter of selecting candidates for honorary degrees is a very important function. Specifically, I most heartily agree with your idea that we should have several meetings during the course of the year, certainly a minimum of three, and do this job deliberately and carefully.[3] *Cordially*

[1] Eisenhower had appointed Sulzberger, who had been a life trustee of Columbia University since 1944, chairman of the Honors Committee. The members of the committee were Eisenhower, Frank D. Fackenthal, Harris K. Masters, Walter H. Sammis, Frederick Coykendall, and George L. Harrison.

[2] On February 7, 1950, Sulzberger had written to Eisenhower criticizing the "wholesale-rush-manner" in which honorary degree candidates had been selected by the Honors Committee at the trustees meeting on February 6 (EM). In its report to the trustees at that meeting, the Honors Committee had nominated the following candidates for honorary degrees to be awarded at commencement 1950: For the Doctor of Science degree, Charles Proctor Cooper, vice-president and director of the American Telephone and Telegraph Company; and John Fairfield Thompson, president and director of the International Nickel Company of Canada, Ltd. For the Doctor of Letters degree, Eleanor Robson Belmont, social and philanthropic worker; and Edward Morgan Forster, novelist. For the Doctor of Sacred Theology degree, Charles Kendall Gilbert, bishop of the New York diocese; and Robert James McCracken, pastor of Riverside Church. For the Doctor of Laws degree, Camille Gutt, chairman of the board and managing director of the International Monetary Fund; Paul Gray Hoffman, Administrator of the Economic Cooperation Administration; Robert Abercrombie Lovett, former Under Secretary of State; Harold Raymond Medina, judge of the U.S. District Court of the Southern District of New York; and Laurence Adolph Steinhardt, U.S. Ambassador to Canada (Report of Committee on Honors, Feb. 6, 1950, EM, Columbia University Corr.). Sulzberger told Eisenhower that he wanted to "take steps now to correct the situation for next year." He was particularly concerned about the candidates whose names had not been acted upon; about whether or not these should be carried forward; and about the order of preference in which they should be considered.

[3] Sulzberger's suggestion that several meetings be held during the year to consider candidates would be approved by the committee at its meeting on May 1, 1950. The committee further agreed that Sulzberger should inform his committee of recommendations as received and should indicate in each case what action was necessary (Minutes, Committee on Honors, May 1, 1950, EM, Columbia University Corr.).

    At the Columbia commencement on June 8, honorary degrees would be bestowed upon all those nominated, with the exception of novelist Edward Morgan Forster and Laurence A. Steinhardt. Steinhardt, scheduled to receive a Doctor of Laws degree, had been killed in an airplane accident (*New York Times,* June 9, 1950). Two whose names were not on the original list also were honored: Albert C. Jacobs, chancellor of the University of Denver and former provost of Columbia

University; and Trygve Halvdan Lie, Secretary General of the United Nations since 1946. Both received the Doctor of Laws degree. For plans to award honorary degrees to Chilean president Gabriel Gonzales Videla and Charles Edward Wilson, president of the General Electric Company, see nos. 735 and 823, respectively.

695 $\qquad$ *Eisenhower Mss.*

To Aksel Nielsen $\qquad$ *February 13, 1950*

Dear Aksel: Here is my thought about the successor to D. D. Domino.[1]

Why not, out of the proceeds of his sale as beef, pay to Carl a fair cost of his maintenance?[2] Put the remainder, if there is any, in a temporary reserve fund.

Next, out of the calves you expect to be dropped this spring, pick a certain number of cows in order of priority that you select. The first one of these that drops a *bull* calf is the one selected as the dam of the calf in which you and I will now be interested as partners.

We give this particular calf every care and loving attention and give him every chance for developing into a really fine bull. On the average, he should at least develop to the point where, as a yearling, he would bring around $900 to $1000 level as a prospective range bull. Of course, if he shows better than this, we hang on to him. But, if he turns out to be just a good high average we let him go.

Then, if we let him go, we take the proceeds and add it to the little reserve we accumulated in paragraph 2, above, and you go to a sale of good Hereford stock, preferably, where the animals for sale are not over one or two months old and where you might get one of the exact blood lines you want for somewhere around $1000. In any event, you buy the very best prospect you can for whatever money has been accumulated through the steps so far taken. We then begin to devote our loving care to this new prospect, but with this added advantage. Assuming that he does not turn out to be the perfect animal we should like to acquire, we will still have introduced into your range and for such use as you may want, a very fine blood line that is new so far as your own herd is concerned.

Now that I have put all this down, you can possibly find a fatal flaw in its somewhere along the line and show that it is completely cockeyed. In any case, you invited me to try to produce a new idea. If you don't like this one, you think of a better. Anyhow, it is a plan that, in its entirety, would carry us forward at least two years. And think of the fun we would have during that time watching our little pets develop.[3]

Thanks a lot for sending the information to my friend, Ed Bermingham.[4] *Cordially*

[1] Eisenhower's bull, a gift from his old friend Nielsen, had become ill in January and had not responded to the several types of treatment administered by a veterinarian. "Therefore," wrote Nielsen on February 9, "we decided that the thing to do was to send him to the market as beef and of course bull beef doesn't sell for too much." Nielsen estimated that D. D. Domino brought a disappointing $250, compared with $950 for other cattle at the sale. Nielsen wanted to know what Eisenhower wanted to do regarding the $250 and also whether or not he wanted to try his luck at raising another bull calf. Nielsen said that he would like to see Eisenhower continue in the "bull business," even though such losses were to be expected (EM).
[2] Carl A. Norgren, a friend of Eisenhower's and Nielsen's, who had boarded D. D. Domino. For background see no. 489.
[3] In a letter of April 5 Nielsen told Eisenhower that he had picked out five cows that were "good individuals," bred to very good bulls, and would be calving before long (EM). For developments see no. 881.
[4] See no. 680.

696   *Eisenhower Mss.*

To Hal L. Mangum   *February 13, 1950*

Dear Hal:[1] Every time you get out of my sight something happens to you. I cannot conceive of a worse combination than a broken back and virus pneumonia, all complicated by a fever of 105. Are you engaged in the business of just showing the doctors how tough you can be? At least, I see that you have instinctively done the right thing, which is to go off to your ranch and get away from all annoyances until you are completely recovered.[2]

It is, of course, too bad that you had to accept such a markdown on your cattle, particularly when they are as healthy as any others in the world. I agree with you that, so long as you have an outlet that will keep things going on a reasonable basis for the present, they should work out well in the long run.[3] I was a bit astonished to note that your ranch was overstocked, because I recall at one time you were running more than 20,000 head and now I believe you told me that you are running 14,000 or 15,000.

Mamie and I and her folks are all disappointed that you cannot get here during their visit with us.[4] However, the main thing is your health and the whole family joins me in sending love and best wishes to you. *Cordially*

[1] For background on Mangum, a rancher from San Antonio, Texas, and an old friend of Eisenhower's, see no. 592; and Galambos, *Chief of Staff.*
[2] On February 9, 1950, Mangum had written to Eisenhower describing his recent series of illnesses. The Texan told Eisenhower that he was returning to his ranch, La Babia, in San Geronimo, Mexico, to recover from his weakened state (EM).

[3] Mangum had said that he had recently sold twenty-eight hundred head of cattle to the Joint Mexican–United States Foot and Mouth Disease Commission. For background on Mangum's role in the campaign to eradicate this disease see Galambos, *Chief of Staff*, nos. 1246 and 1637.

[4] Mangum had been invited but was unable to visit the Eisenhowers in New York on Christmas Day, 1949 (Eisenhower to Mangum, Dec. 19 and 25, 1949, EM). Mrs. Eisenhower's parents, the Douds, had been staying at 60 Morningside Drive since December (see no. 630). For developments involving Mangum see no. 756.

697   *Eisenhower Mss.*

To ROBERT JUSTUS KLEBERG, JR.   *February 13, 1950*

Dear Bob:[1] There was no need at all for you to explain that Mr. Watson had misinterpreted your meaning and intention with respect to me. I have complete faith that my friends would never deliberately embarrass me; so when someone else attaches erroneous meaning to a casual remark, I don't even note it sufficiently well to remember it.[2]

Actually, the only disappointment in my entire Texas trip was the need for making a couple of speeches and my failure to get down to visit you and your family.[3] This failure I hope some day to correct so long as you have been so kind as to ask us to come see you at a future opportunity.

Just a day or so ago I had a note from Hal Mangum in Eagle Pass, written just as he was recovering from a severe attack of virus pneumonia.[4] I do hope that he takes care of himself; he is a most wonderful and lovable character.

After seeing you, I spent a few days on Sid Richardson's ranch on San Jose Island.[5] I had a perfectly marvelous time but Sid assured me that at your place so many things were done so much better that I had not seen that part of Texas until I came some day to King Ranch.[6]

With warm personal regard, *Cordially*

[1] For background on Kleberg see no. 623.

[2] On January 30 Kleberg had sent Eisenhower a copy of a letter he had received from Theodore S. Watson. Watson's letter (Dec. 27) described his correspondence with Eisenhower concerning the General's political candidacy and Kleberg's willingness to help consolidate support in the South (for background see no. 623). Kleberg wrote that he knew Watson only slightly. "I am just a little afraid that he may have, in his letter to you, given you an impression that in some way I was interested in forming a group to commit you to some course of action. Of course, nothing could be further from the truth, or more absurd from a cowboy's way of thinking!" He reiterated, however, a conversation he had had with Eisenhower in San Antonio in December 1949 (see *ibid.*), when they had discussed the need for a change in Washington. "While I think there may be other men

that could do the job, as matters now stand I do not think there is any chance to elect anyone else but yourself."

[3] On Eisenhower's speeches see no. 606; on his trip see no. 607.

[4] See the preceding document.

[5] For background on Richardson see no. 113.

[6] For developments regarding Kleberg see no. 926.

698   *Eisenhower Mss.*

To Robert Hiester Montgomery   *February 13, 1950*

Dear Bob:[1] The invitation from the American Institute of Accountants is not an easy one to turn down, solely and simply because it is presented by you.[2] But I have no escape from a negative answer. While my schedule is free, at the moment, from any commitments for the first week of October, I know positively that the official University calendar—now in preparation—will inundate me with campus engagements which cannot be cancelled or postponed. The busiest weeks of the year are the final week of September and the first two weeks of October.

I have a tentative speaking engagement here in New York City for September 25—subject to cancellation any time up to September 1—but I cannot add another speaking engagement to the schedule, particularly one that would require an out-of-town trip.[3]

Any invitation from you has a top priority on my time, both as an old friend and as an outstanding member of the Columbia family, so it is particularly difficult to decline.[4] Moreover, I have deeply appreciated the way you have resisted outside pressures to make demands upon me.[5] But the sort of situation that confronts me both in the physical scheduling of my time and in an undesirable frequency of public appearances, with consequent wear and tear upon my health and disposition, compels a negative answer.[6] I hope you will explain the situation to the executives of the Institute.

The next time you are in New York City, I hope we can get together for a long visit, during which, very briefly, I will spread before you the facts of academic life that seldom permit me to do those things which I should most like to do.

Mamie joins me in best wishes to Nell[7] and you. *Sincerely*

[1] Montgomery, who was a lawyer and an accountant, had known Eisenhower since the 1930s, when the two had worked together on the War Policies Commission's plan for wartime industrial mobilization (for background on Montgomery see Chandler and Galambos, *Occupation, 1945*, no. 171). An undated draft of this letter, with the General's numerous handwritten changes, is in EM, Letters and Drafts.

[2] Montgomery had asked Eisenhower to address the American Institute of Ac-

countants at its annual meeting in Boston on October 2. A past president of that organization (1935–37), Montgomery described the membership as being of an informed, widely connected class highly representative of free enterprise (Feb. 9, 1950, EM).

[3] Eisenhower apparently canceled the speaking engagement for September 25, because his appointment calendar indicates that he played bridge that evening.

[4] From 1912 until 1914 Montgomery had been an instructor at Columbia's School of Business. He had become an assistant professor of accounting in 1914, and from 1919 until 1931 he was a professor and member of the school's administrative board.

[5] Montgomery had written, "This is the first thing I have asked you to do since I met you in 1932—and God knows I have been importuned often enough!!"

[6] For Eisenhower's efforts to gain more time for relaxation see no. 686. In a reply dated February 20 Montgomery said that he fully understood Eisenhower's reasons for declining the invitation. He cautioned the General to care for his health and invited him to visit the Montgomery home in Coconut Grove, Florida. Montgomery's letter and Eisenhower's reply of February 25 are in EM.

[7] Montgomery's wife, the former Eleanor Foster.

---

699   *Eisenhower Mss.*

To Robert Lowry Biggers   *February 13, 1950*

Dear Bob:[1] The last thing that could have occurred to me was the need for your apologizing for spending the afternoon with us. We thoroughly enjoyed the day and I had specifically and deliberately avoided all entanglements and engagements for the afternoon so that I could keep you as long as you could stay.[2]

With regard to the painting: I cannot write a book concerning my hobby because I don't know anything about it. But I do most emphatically know that anyone else can do better things than I. I not only have no talent, no instruction and no experience—I am totally incapable of drawing anything accurately.[3] So when you get the set of materials I hope to send you in a day or so, just sit down with a grin and start playing with them. No matter what happens, I assure you that you will have a lot of fun.[4]

For the past several days we have been very busy socially and Mamie and I have had several opportunities to use the new car.[5] Both of us bubble with satisfaction each time we get into it; I am going to make a report to Mr. Keller immediately.[6]

When you come this way, give me a ring and please bring with you an example of your painting.

With warm personal regard,[7] *Cordially*

[1] Biggers had been president of the Fargo Motor Corporation, a division of the Chrysler Corporation, in Detroit, Michigan, since 1937. He would become vice-

president of the Chrysler Corporation in 1956. Biggers periodically assisted Eisenhower in selecting Chrysler automobiles and frequently offered to arrange transportation for the General. Their friendship would continue for many years.
[2] On February 9, 1950, Biggers had spent the afternoon with General and Mrs. Eisenhower in New York. In a letter of February 10 he had apologized to Eisenhower for overstaying his welcome but attributed his lengthy visit to the graciousness of his hosts (EM).
[3] Biggers had apparently suggested that Eisenhower write a book on painting. "Your achievements in the field of Art astound me," Biggers wrote. "Never did I expect to meet Michelangelo face to face." For background on Eisenhower's hobby see no. 51.
[4] Eisenhower had inspired Biggers to try his hand at painting and would send him a supply of art materials. In a letter of February 24 Biggers thanked Eisenhower for the equipment and said he looked forward to the challenge of painting.
[5] Eisenhower's new 1950 seven-passenger Crown Imperial limousine had been delivered the same afternoon that Biggers visited the Eisenhowers (Feb. 9). Eisenhower had planned to purchase a new car in July 1949, but he had changed his mind and continued to drive his 1940 Chrysler Windsor. Several months later, however, Eisenhower had asked Biggers to help him make arrangements to obtain a new car (Biggers to Eisenhower, Dec. 27, 1949, EM).
[6] Eisenhower would write to K. T. Keller, president of the Chrysler Corporation, that he and Mrs. Eisenhower were delighted with the beauty, comfort, and usefulness of the new car. He said, "For many years we, and those close to us have used Chrysler products and . . . there is no need whatsoever of 'selling' us on the idea of Chrysler" (Feb. 13, 1950, EM). Keller would acknowledge Eisenhower's "nice letter" and send his own note of thanks to the General on February 16, 1950 (EM). See Galambos, *Chief of Staff*, for background on Keller.
[7] Biggers would have Newton B. Drury, Director of the National Park Service, send Eisenhower a color print of the Grand Teton National Park—Jackson Hole National Monument (Feb. 17, 1950, EM). In a note to Biggers of February 28, Eisenhower said that he was looking forward to painting the scene (EM).

700   *Eisenhower Mss.*

To William Edward Robinson   *February 13, 1950*

Dear Bill:[1] In connection with the matter of which you spoke to me, my attention was recently called to the great abilities, in P.R. field, of Earl Newsome.[2] He is head of one of our principal P.R. concerns— his accounts include, Ford—Standard of New Jersey—etc., etc. He is young—enthusiastic—keen; might be just the man you want.[3] *As ever*

[1] Robinson was executive vice-president of the *New York Herald Tribune*. A typed copy of Eisenhower's handwritten letter to Robinson is in EM.
[2] Eisenhower, chairman of the Aid to Europe Group, Council on Foreign Relations, had apparently recommended Edwin Earl Newsom as a candidate for membership on his committee. The General enthusiastically endorsed Newsom, who was a public relations counsel and senior partner in his own firm, Earl Newsom

and Company, of New York City. Newsom had received an A.B. from Oberlin College in 1921 and had done some graduate work at Columbia University. He was public relations adviser for Columbia's medical school and had offered assistance to the university's development program (Memo, P. H. Davis to Eisenhower, June 27, 1949, EM, Newsom Corr.). For background on the Council on Foreign Relations see no. 269.

[3] Robinson agreed with Eisenhower that Newsom was able and resourceful. He replied (Feb. 17, 1950, EM) that he would submit the public relations executive's name and recommend him as a candidate. Robinson added, however, that because Newsom lacked political experience, he might not qualify. For developments see no. 721.

701   *Eisenhower Mss.*

To George Herman Mahon   *February 13, 1950*

Dear Mr. Chairman:[1] The essence of my reply to your letter of the 11th is that, as always, I am at the complete disposal of any governmental body that may feel that I can be of the slightest help in the solution of our security problems.[2] In this particular case, the performance of a suggested duty could be nothing but pleasure, in view of my long time friendship for the members of the Subcommittee.[3]

With respect to the specific item of the time of the appointment, I interpret your letter to mean that the schedule of the Subcommittee can permit a considerable amount of leeway. Consequently, while assuring you that I am always ready, when necessary, to break any engagement in order to respond to such a request as yours, I am listing here the periods that would be most convenient for me, in the thought that you may find one of them suitable from the standpoint of your committee. If this should not prove to be the case, will you please so advise me?

I could spend the *morning* of Tuesday, February 21, with you or, I could meet with you any time on the day of Friday, February 24. These are the first two periods that are free on my calendar. In late March I am planning three or four days in Washington, but I assume that you will want to finish up the work of the Subcommittee before that time.[4]

I think that an off-the-record, informal meeting would be best for the reasons that I no longer have official responsibility with respect to our security forces, and an informal atmosphere would promote candor and frankness among the whole group. However, here again, I am always ready to conform to the desires of responsible governmental bodies, such as yours.[5]

With warm personal regard to you and to your associates, *Cordially*

[1] Congressman Mahon (LL.B. University of Texas 1925) represented Texas's Nineteenth District. A Democrat, he was chairman of the House Subcommittee on Department of Defense Appropriations.

[2] On February 11 Mahon had asked Eisenhower to meet with his committee for informal discussions of the national armaments budget for fiscal 1951. "As you know," Mahon had written, "all of us on the Subcommittee have the highest regard for you and feel that your advice would be extremely helpful" (EM). Eisenhower had participated in the preparation of the proposed 1951 budget for the Department of Defense. See no. 348, n. 11, for the General's work with the JCS on the allocation of defense funds to the armed services.

[3] The members of Mahon's committee included Harry R. Sheppard (Democrat, representing California's Twenty-first District); Robert L. F. Sikes (Democrat, representing Florida's Third District); Albert J. Engel (Republican, representing Michigan's Ninth District); and Charles A. Plumley (Republican congressman at large, Vermont).

[4] Eisenhower would meet with Mahon's committee on Friday, February 24 (see telegrams, Eisenhower to Mahon, Feb. 17, and Mahon to Eisenhower, Feb. 17 and 20, 1950, EM).

[5] In his testimony before Mahon's committee Eisenhower would defend the $13.5 billion budget. Allocations under the total figure included $4.018 billion for the Army; $3.881 billion for the Navy; and $4.434 billion for the Air Force. The remainder had been earmarked for the Office of the Secretary of Defense and contingent items. Among the points that Eisenhower made during the closed-door session were (1) that democracies, unlike dictatorships, cannot sustain total preparedness until a state of war actually exists; (2) that total defense in modern war is not possible because of the great expense; and (3) that the United States must allocate enough money and use it wisely enough that its powers of retaliation would be effective following a surprise attack (*New York Times*, Feb. 25, 26, 1950). For further developments see no. 753.

702

Eisenhower Mss.

[*February 13, 1950*]

To Richard Gill, Jr.,
Michael Doud Gill, Ellen Doud Moore,
and Mamie Eisenhower Moore

Dear Richy, Michael, Ellen, Mamie:[1] Thank you very much indeed for the nice Valentine tie. It's exactly the kind I like—I shall wear it the next time I want especially to impress some friend.

Soon you all will be packing to start homeward. Mamie says you are to go to Washington.[2] One advantage is that there are fine schools there—including colleges. But you have to make good grades now—or, later, the colleges won't take you.

Give my love to your mother and dad and take good care of yourselves.

All of us send love to the entire family—and—thanks again for the lovely tie. *Devotedly*

[1] Eisenhower's nephews and nieces, the children of Mrs. Eisenhower's sister, Mabel Frances Doud Moore. For background on the Gill and Moore children see no. 430.

[2] Major George Gordon Moore, Jr., had been stationed in the Panama Canal Zone since January 1948. He had been promoted to lieutenant colonel in January 1949, and the family would soon move to Washington, D.C., where Moore would be assigned to the Office of the Quartermaster General (EM).

703

TO JOSEPH CAMPBELL[1]

February 15, 1950

At a recent meeting of the Bicentennial Committee, it was suggested that we should attempt to have Morningside Heights, Inc. request the cooperation of Mr. Robert Moses and other appropriate city officials in pushing the beautification of Morningside Heights in anticipation of our Bicentennial year.[2] The thought was expressed that, since there will be—during the course of 1954—a number of conventions here at Columbia University which attract representatives from all over the nation and the world, the city would be especially interested, now, in a beautification program.[3]

I shall leave it to you to develop this idea: if at any time you feel that you need my assistance, please let me know. In the meantime, you should keep the Chairman of the Bicentennial Committee advised of any significant agreement or progress.[4]

[1] Campbell, a member of the Bicentennial Committee on Organization, was university treasurer and vice-president in charge of business affairs. He was also treasurer of Morningside Heights, Inc., a non-profit organization started in 1947 by area institutions to upgrade the Morningside neighborhood on New York's upper West Side.

[2] Campbell had been unable to attend the Bicentennial Committee's February 8 meeting. (For background on the bicentennial see no. 495.) Arthur H. Sulzberger, the committee's chairman, had called Robert Moses after the meeting and advised Eisenhower that Moses was already working with the president of Morningside Heights, Inc., David Rockefeller. Sulzberger said, however, that he had alerted Moses to the 1954 bicentennial year date (Feb. 8, 1950; see also Sulzberger to Eisenhower, Mar. 10, 1950, both in EM). Moses (Ph.D. Columbia 1914), the public-works official, had begun his career in 1913 as a municipal investigator for New York City, and since 1924 he had been president of the Long Island State Park Commission and chairman of the State Council of Parks. He was also the New York City park commissioner, the administrator of city parkways, co-ordinator of suburban and state systems, and a member of the New York City Planning Commission. For further background see Robert A. Caro, *The Power Broker: Robert Moses and the Fall of New York* (New York, 1974); and Cleveland Rodgers, *Robert Moses: Builder for Democracy* (New York, 1952). See also Moses's autobiography, *Public Works: A Dangerous Trade* (New York, 1970).

[3] See the following document.

[4] For later developments see *New York Times*, October 1, 1951.

To Joseph Patterson Binns   *February 15, 1950*

Dear Colonel Binns:[1] Recently I had a most thoughtful note from your Mr. Philippe who had read in the papers that Columbia University will be celebrating its Bicentennial in 1954. Because he realized that a number of significant ceremonies would probably be staged by the University during that year, he suggested that we now make tentative reservations of desired rooms in the Waldorf to assure availability when needed.[2]

I am quite sure that Mr. Philippe's estimate is an accurate one; there is no doubt in my mind that at some time or times during 1954 we will have need of Waldorf facilities. However, it appears impossible, at this moment, for our Bicentennial Committee to determine the exact nature and time of the celebrations that may then prove to be appropriate. At this moment, we can do no better than make what might be called intelligent guesses. This, I am sure that the Committee—which is headed by Mr. Arthur Sulzberger of the New York Times—will do as soon as possible, and will send to Mr. Philippe appropriate notification.

The purpose of this note is merely to ask you to be as understanding as is practicable, consistent with your own requirement for producing at the earliest opportunity a firm schedule for the utilization of these facilities. In other words, I am asking you to be as flexible as you can with us. Possibly, you could arrange to send us specific notices before closing us out completely from any period that our Committee may designate as one in which we are especially interested.

From time to time I assume that Mr. Sulzberger or his representative will be in touch with you or one of the others in the Waldorf organization. I assure you that we shall do our best to substitute concrete engagements for these indecisive suggestions just as quickly as it can be done.

With deep appreciation of your consideration and with warm personal regard.[3] *Cordially*

---

[1] Binns, executive vice-president and general manager of the Waldorf-Astoria Hotel, had begun his career as a room clerk at the Chalfonte-Haddon Hall in Atlantic City in 1928. In 1942 he had entered the Army Air Forces, and in 1946 he had been discharged with the rank of colonel. Since 1946 he had also been vice-president of the Hilton Hotels Corporation.

[2] Eisenhower sent Director of Catering Claudius C. Philippe's letter to Arthur Sulzberger, chairman of the Bicentennial Committee, and at the committee's February 8 meeting the letter was given to Provost Grayson Kirk. The committee had decided that there would be three formal gatherings during the 1954 celebration—concerning Columbia and New York City, Columbia and the nation, and Columbia and the world—and Kirk agreed to write the hotel, giving approximate

dates for the events (Feb. 8, 1950, minutes, in CUF; see also Sulzberger to Philippe, Feb. 3, 1950, CUF). For background on the bicentennial see no. 495.
[3] The following day Eisenhower attended a luncheon at the Waldorf and discussed this matter with Binns. Binns advised Eisenhower in a letter of February 16 that the hotel would avoid making any permanent bookings that might conflict with the university's needs during the bicentennial. It would be helpful, he wrote, if the hotel could be given "the roughest kind of an idea of the general time and type of ceremony which might require Waldorf facilities" (EM). Eisenhower sent Binns's letter and this document to Sulzberger, and the three men met for lunch on March 6, 1950 (see also Sulzberger to Binns, Mar. 22, 1950, in EM). For developments regarding the bicentennial see no. 800.

705   *Eisenhower Mss.*

To Harry Cecil Butcher   *February 15, 1950*

Dear Butch:[1] Thank you very much for your note about young ————.
While I am uncertain as to what may be done in such cases, I shall have the thing investigated at once.[2]

Your comment about Milton's transfer to Pennsylvania made me chuckle. Specifically, I refer to the suggestions: "But if he wants a political future, it seems to me he is losing his investment in Kansas." Why, in the name of all that's holy, does everyone always have to think of the word politics in connection with the name Eisenhower? Milton has never hinted to me that he wanted any political career—to the contrary, I know of one instance at least where he turned down one very bright opportunity to enter that field.[3]

It is fine to know that your station is doing so well. I hope that you grow bigger and better every day, so much so that soon you will be seeking opportunities to contribute to Columbia University.[4] *Cordially*

[1] For background on Butcher see no. 33.
[2] Butcher had written Eisenhower on February 10, 1950, on behalf of a young man who had applied for admission to Columbia University. According to Butcher, the applicant was a "precocious but diabetic young man"; Butcher also enclosed a letter from his friend Lester Cohen, a Washington, D.C., lawyer, who represented the boy's father (there is no copy of Cohen's letter in EM; in addition, a part of Butcher's letter is missing). This particular applicant had been placed in group 3, the category for those persons with a remote chance of acceptance. Subsequent correspondence would confirm, however, that he was accepted at Columbia University following Eisenhower's inquiry into the matter.
[3] On Milton Eisenhower's move to Pennsylvania State College see no. 679. There had been much speculation about Dr. Eisenhower's political ambitions. Republicans and Democrats courted him as a prospective candidate for a senatorial seat in 1948, the governorship of Kansas in 1950, and the presidency in 1952 (Neal, *Reluctant Dynasty*, pp. 204–5, 217–18). Milton Eisenhower chose, nevertheless, to remain aloof from direct political participation in order to pursue his interests

in education and government as an administrator and an adviser to eight presidents (Milton Eisenhower, *The President Is Calling*; see also no. 716).
[4] Butcher had described his radio station, KIST, in Santa Barbara, California, as having "beaten the tar" out of the other stations in the ratings (EM).

706   *Eisenhower Mss.*

To Grayson Louis Kirk[1]   *February 15, 1950*

Memorandum for the Provost: This morning Lord Boyd Orr, Chancellor of Glasgow University, visited me to extend a verbal invitation for me to attend the Quincentenary of that institution in the summer of 1951. I believe the particular convocation which they would like me to attend is to be held on June 21 of that year.[2]

I have just had an invitation from Chancellor Hutchins of the University of Chicago to visit the "School of Humanistic Studies" at Aspen, Colorado during the coming summer. This school is apparently run by Chicago University, and the invitation covers the period of a week during which time I would be expected to deliver two 30-minute talks. There is a nice little honorarium involved except, of course, that it would be valuable to Columbia, since I never accept such things personally.[3]

Will you please consider the above two suggestions and determine, in agreement with any other members of the staff that you may desire to consult, whether from Columbia's viewpoint there seems to be any important reason why either of these should be accepted.[4] So far as my personal convenience is concerned, I should think that I might be able to attend the affair at Aspen quite easily; to go to Scotland would be much more of a chore because I would probably go by ship instead of airplane.[5]

[1] For background on Kirk see no. 515.
[2] Eisenhower had met with Lord John Boyd Orr and Lady Boyd Orr in New York the morning of February 15, 1950. Boyd Orr, a Scottish scientist and a former director of the United Nations Food and Agricultural Organization, had arrived from London with his wife on February 2 for a two-week visit in the United States. At a Columbia Associates luncheon on February 17, Eisenhower, together with Boyd Orr, would propose the establishment of a new research center on nutrition and agricultural techniques at Columbia University (*New York Times*, Feb. 3 and 18, 1950). For background on the nutrition center see no. 431.

On July 3 Eisenhower would receive the official invitation from Professor C. J. Fordyce, clerk of Senate College at Glasgow, to celebrate the five-hundredth anniversary of the founding of the university. The General would also be invited to receive the honorary degree of Doctor of Laws (letter of June 28, EM, Glasgow Corr.).

[3] Eisenhower had received a telephoned invitation from Robert Maynard Hutchins

the morning of February 14, 1950, to visit the Institute of Humanistic Studies in the summer of 1950. The Aspen institute, which had developed out of the highly successful Goethe Bicentennial celebration held in 1949, was organized to hold annual educational and musical programs. For background on Hutchins see no. 282.

[4] There is no copy of a reply from Kirk in EM.

[5] Eisenhower would decline Hutchins's invitation (letter of Feb. 20, EM) because of his previously scheduled summer commitments. He originally accepted the Glasgow invitation in letters to Boyd Orr on July 3 and 5, and to Fordyce on July 3. On April 5, 1951, however, Eisenhower wrote to Boyd Orr as follows: "In accepting your gracious invitation in July of last year, I did so in the capacity of President of Columbia University. . . . Since then, however, I have received my new appointment. . . . In an organisation of twelve nations, the demands [on my time have] become geometric in character." For Eisenhower's appointment as commander of the NATO forces see no. 1136. Boyd Orr would reply that he regretted not having "the honour of conferring the degree" on Eisenhower, but he wished the General "all success in the great task which has been laid upon you" (Apr. 20, 1951). All correspondence concerning the invitation to Scotland is in EM, Glasgow Corr.

707   *Eisenhower Mss.*

TO KENNETH WILLIAM DOBSON STRONG   *February 15, 1950*

Dear Kenneth:[1] My records show that I am guilty of failure to answer your most recent letter to me—written on October 27, last. I have no completely valid excuse, but I must say that these days I am busy enough so that, frequently, I find myself neglecting correspondence with friends—and this has always been most important to me.[2]

During the winter I have heard nothing more of Sir Frederick Sheddon and his efforts to restore free interchange of military information among some of the wartime Allies.[3] It is, however, also true that I have been going down to Washington infrequently in the last few months so I am not aware of what steps, if any, have been taken in our Defense Establishment in this regard.[4]

Recently, I have seen little of my old SHAEF staff.[5] Occasionally, I run into Beedle Smith and Lucius Clay, both of whom have written books. Because of a full schedule I have had no opportunity to finish reading either one of them. But, for me at least, Clay's book deals with the far more interesting episodes of post-war history so that it is the one I shall try to get through first.[6]

Tell Jock that I recently had a letter from Simonds up at Kingston who renewed the invitation to me, first extended by Jock when he was commandant at that school. As usual, I found myself unable to go. But I still hope that some day I will find it possible to run up to that locality and spend a day or two at the school.[7]

As time goes on, I realize that one encounters, with constantly decreasing frequency, friends and associates of the war days. Nevertheless, I am quite certain that from time to time you bump into some of my old and valued friends. When you can identify them as such, please convey to each my warmest greetings and regards. I think instantly of such people as Gale, Morgan, Jumbo Wilson, Tedder, both Cunninghams, Foord, Jimmy Gault, Louis Gregg, and all the dozens and dozens of others. Tell Jock I hope he will do the same.[8]

With warm person regard,[9] *As ever*

[1] Major General Strong was Director of the Joint Intelligence Bureau at the Ministry of Defence in London. For background see no. 480.

[2] Strong had written Eisenhower on October 27, 1949, concerning Sir Frederick Geoffrey Shedden, Secretary of the Australian Defence Department, and various wartime friends (EM).

[3] For background on Shedden see no. 480.

[4] Strong had explained to Eisenhower that Shedden understood the position of the U.S. government and that the problem under discussion was of such gravity that the authorities in Australia would need to show "positive evidence of an attempt to rectify the matters about which there was complaint." Strong had described the problem as one of "confidence . . . between the two parties," and he hoped that the Americans would not discount Australia's potential importance as an ally in time of war.

[5] For background on the staff see Eisenhower, *Crusade in Europe*, pp. 220, 433–35.

[6] Generals Walter Bedell Smith and Lucius Clay had both written books concerning their military experiences. For Eisenhower's reaction to Smith's *My Three Years in Moscow* see no. 624; for developments on Smith see no. 950. For background on Clay and his volume, *Decision in Germany*, see no. 652; for developments involving Clay see no. 783.

[7] On Major General John F. M. "Jock" Whiteley see no. 480. Lieutenant General Guy Granville Simonds, commandant of the National Defence College and Canadian Army Staff College in Kingston, Ontario, had written on January 3, 1950, inviting Eisenhower to visit and address the National Defence College in the spring. Simonds's letter and Eisenhower's letter of declination are in EM.

[8] For background on Lieutenant-General Sir Humfrey M. Gale and Field Marshal Lord Henry M. "Jumbo" Wilson see *Eisenhower Papers*, vols. I–IX. On Lieutenant-General Sir Frederick E. "Freddie" Morgan see no. 357. Marshal of the Royal Air Force Arthur W. Tedder would leave the Air Ministry to go to Washington, D.C., as chairman of the British Joint Services Mission and United Kingdom representative on the standing group of the Military Committee of NATO in March 1950. For background on Tedder see no. 84. For background on admirals of the fleet Lord Andrew B. Cunningham and Sir John H. D. Cunningham see no. 259; on Brigadier Edward J. Foord see no. 568; and on James F. "Jimmy" Gault see no. 601. In regard to Group Captain Sir Louis Greig see *Eisenhower Papers*, vols. I–IX.

[9] Strong would reply to Eisenhower in a letter of June 17, 1950 (EM). For developments see no. 865.

TO JULIUS CECIL HOLMES   *February 20, 1950*

Dear Julius:[1] As I remember the conversations respecting possible return of King Leopold to Belgium in 1945, they conformed quite accurately to the account Grassett gives in his letter to you.[2] Incidentally, this is the first word I have had of Grassett for a long, long time. When you get a chance, won't you please convey to him my warm regard?

You may recall that, upon the liberation of Belgium, I made an early trip to its capital. The Belgian government was in complete control and Prince Charles was acting as Regent. I believe that the first time I went to Brussels we had no American ambassador but, on a later trip, I recall that Ambassador Sawyer was present.[3]

In any event, I was always somewhat influenced in my actions toward King Leopold by the fact that a Belgian government, recognized by both Britain and America, was functioning in Brussels. I had close contact with that Government and, consequently, anything that it desired respecting any of its citizens, including the King, could have been easily communicated to me. There was no need for me to be a party to any kind of cabal, either for or against any individual.[4]

So far as the King and his family are concerned, I recall that I directed that he have proper protection and should not want for food. He was informed that Allied Headquarters always stood ready to help in any legitimate and proper way with transport, housing and so on. To say that I "impeded" his return could not possibly be regarded as an accurate statement of the case unless it would be interpreted to mean that I did not actively plan with King Leopold to secure his return to Belgium. Frankly, it was a matter that was obviously none of my business so long as the established government of Belgium made no official request upon me.[5]

I believe that, if any concrete, official evidence would ever have to be brought forward regarding SHAEF's negotiations with King Leopold, G−5 and other General Staff files would probably provide some written record of the pertinent incidents.[6]

It was good to hear from you again—I wish you would write to me with a bit more frequency. I never lose my interest in British friends and the British Services, and you always have some comment to make about them. Equally, I never lose my interest in any of that legion of loyal friends that served with me in SHAEF.[7] So, from numerous standpoints, I value every message I have from you.

My very best to any of our old associates that you may encounter.[8] Also, won't you extend my greetings to your charming wife?[9] With warm regard, *Cordially*

[1] Julius C. Holmes was Minister Counselor in London. For background see no. 30.

[2] Holmes had written Eisenhower that Lieutenant General Sir Arthur Edward Grasett, former Chief of the SHAEF Civil Affairs Section (G−5), had noticed press dispatches regarding Eisenhower's involvement in the liberation of Belgium in 1945. Grasett had sent Holmes his own account of the events, apparently refuting allegations that Eisenhower had impeded the return of King Leopold III (Feb. 8, 1950, EM; Grasett's letter to Holmes is not in EM). For background on Grasett, who had been Lieutenant Governor and Commander in Chief of Jersey, in the Channel Islands, since 1945, see Chandler, *War Years*, no. 1601, n. 2. On King Leopold III and the Belgian royal question see Chandler and Galambos, *Occupation, 1945*, no. 141; and E. Ramón Arango, *Leopold III and the Belgian Royal Question* (Baltimore, 1961).

[3] On November 9, 1944, when Eisenhower had spoken before the Belgian parliament in Brussels, Charles, Leopold's brother, was Prince Regent (Chandler, *War Years*, no. 2111). On September 6, 1945, Eisenhower had returned to Brussels at the invitation of the Prince and U.S. Ambassador to Belgium Charles Sawyer to receive various decorations and awards (Chandler and Galambos, *Occupation, 1945*, no. 265). For background on Sawyer see *ibid.*, no. 244. Peter Lyon discusses Eisenhower's method of handling the sensitive Belgian problem in *Portrait of the Hero* (pp. 314−15).

[4] In July 1945 the U.S. State Department, with Truman's approval, had directed U.S. military authorities to give no air transportation to Leopold and his family unless it was specifically requested by the Belgian government. In August, however, the U.S. II Corps was instructed to provide Leopold with facilities to the Swiss border; on October 1 the King, his second wife, Marie Liliane Baels (a commoner given the title Princess de Rethy), and the royal children (princes Baudouin and Albert) departed for Switzerland (Chandler and Galambos, *Occupation, 1945*, no. 141, n. 4; State, *Foreign Relations, 1945*, vol. IV, *Europe* [1968], pp. 132−34; James Page, *Leopold III* [London, 1960], pp. 53−54. For background on Princess de Rethy see Page, *Leopold III*, pp. 31−33).

[5] Leopold and his family had spent the years 1945−50 in exile in Switzerland. Discussions between Leopold and the Belgian government had resumed, however, and as a result of the elections of June 1949 a referendum on the subject of the return of the King would be favorably passed in March 1950 (by 57.68 percent of the voters). In July the regency of Prince Charles ended as the reign of King Leopold began.

Half the population of Belgium, nevertheless, was unwilling to accept the monarch. Massive anti-Leopold strikes and demonstrations paralyzed the nation. To avert revolution, Leopold finally abdicated and delegated power to his son Prince Baudouin, who became King on September 7, 1951, his twenty-first birthday. This struggle left a heritage of bitterness, but Baudouin, as King in his own right, would eventually gain the good will of the people (Page, *Leopold III*, pp. 53−61; and Arango, *Leopold III and the Belgian Royal Question*, pp. 196−208).

[6] The official policy of SHAEF, Civil Affairs Division (G−5), was one of non-interference in Belgian internal affairs (F.S.V. Donnison, *Civil Affairs and Military Government: North-West Europe, 1944−1946*, History of the Second World War, ed. J.R.M. Butler [London, 1961], pp. 111−23). For developments see no. 1015; see also no. 781.

[7] For background on Eisenhower's SHAEF staff see the preceding document.

[8] Holmes's reply would include a report on Great Britain's electoral campaign. He also wrote that he had sent a copy of Eisenhower's February 20 letter to General Grasett, who was enjoying an immense success as the current governor of Jersey.

Another friend Holmes mentioned was Lewis W. Douglas, U.S. Ambassador to Great Britain, who would be in New York in March (Feb. 27, 1950, EM).

[9] Holmes told Eisenhower that his wife, "Hennie" (Henrietta), had just spent two months in the United States because of her father's death.

Eisenhower Mss.

To Matthew Bunker Ridgway   *February 20, 1950*

Dear Matt:[1] I think that your letter to the Dutch Investigating Committee is completely appropriate in view of the paucity of information in the facts.[2] Frankly, I have been trying to figure out the exact purpose of the investigation—it has the appearance of an attempt to fix some blame upon a particular group or a particular individual; consequently, it would be very dangerous to submit any testimony except where this is backed up by official records or by clear memory. In my own case, I must admit that while I think my memory is clear enough as regards general plans and intentions, it is most uncertain with respect to important details.

If you think it at all appropriate, you might add, as an enclosure to your note, two paragraphs from the book I wrote, CRUSADE IN EUROPE. The ones to which I refer begin on page 416 with the words "We knew" and end on page 417 with the word "capitulate."

This would be of no great moment except that it does show that it was my personal decision that we should not take a general campaign into Holland in the spring of 1945.[3]

This suggestion may be valueless and, if so, please disregard it. In any event, I apologize for all of the trouble to which you have been put because of this communication.[4] *Cordially*

[1] Lieutenant General Ridgway was Deputy Chief of Staff for Administration, U.S. Army. For background see no. 599.

[2] Eisenhower had asked Ridgway to prepare a reply to L. A. Donker, chairman of the Commission of Inquiry on Government Policy 1940—45, of the Second Chamber of the States-General (The Hague), which was investigating "events connected with the German attack on The Netherlands and the Policy of the Cabinets in power in subsequent years." In a letter of December 15, 1949 (COS, 1949, 091 Netherlands), Donker had asked Eisenhower for information on the formulation of Allied policy concerning the Netherlands in 1944 and 1945. The investigation involved a number of very specific activities associated with the return of the Netherlands government to the southern part of Dutch territory after its liberation; these included, for instance, the Allied command's views regarding the Dutch government's presence there (including distinctions made by SHAEF between the government, the Queen, and the cabinet). In connection with the termination of hostilities in April 1945, the commission asked for information concerning Netherlanders who operated as informants from within occupied ter-

ritories of Northwestern Holland and for Eisenhower's opinion of the views held by the Allied High Command regarding the liberation of that area (see letter from D. van Galan Last, Netherlands State Institute for War Documentation, Sept. 23, 1980, EP; and papers in COS, 1949, 091 Netherlands).

In his draft reply, Ridgway said: "For the most part the records [of the Department of the Army] show only events and decisions as they transpired. Factors and persons influencing these decisions are not usually recorded." Ridgway provided some information on SHAEF policies but said there was "no record of difference of opinion between the Allied Commanders on the desirability of returning liberated parts of Holland to the control of the Netherlands Government." SHAEF had not made any distinction "between the Government, the Cabinet, and the Queen" (Feb. 16, 1950, EM). Ridgway's reply to the Commission of Inquiry on Government Policy 1940–45 would be dispatched on February 23, 1950 (P&O, 49–50, 091 Netherlands, Case 20; another copy is in EM).

[3] An extract from Eisenhower's own record, *Crusade in Europe*, would be enclosed with Ridgway's letter to the Dutch commission, and a copy is in EM. On pages 416–17 he wrote, "I still refused to consider a major offensive into [Holland]. Not only would great additional destruction and suffering have resulted but the enemy's opening of dikes would further have flooded the country and destroyed much of its fertility for years to come."

Perhaps a more significant factor in the postponement of further attempts to invade Holland before and during 1945 was the failure of operation MARKET-GARDEN. MARKET-GARDEN, the combined air-ground offensive in the battle of Arnhem, which took place in September 1944, ended in tragedy. In the nine days of the operation Allied losses were higher than in the twenty-four-hour period of D-day (Charles B. MacDonald, *The Siegfried Line Campaign*, U.S. Army in World War II, ed. Stetson Conn [Washington, D.C., 1963], pp. 200–201. See also Chandler, *War Years*, nos. 1945, 1968, n. 3, 1978, n. 2, and 2233; Cornelius Ryan, *A Bridge Too Far* [New York, 1974]; and Pogue, *Supreme Command*, pp. 281–88, 307–18. For a summary of the events in the Netherlands in the years 1944–46 see Donnison, *North-West Europe, 1944–1946*, chap. 7). In 1945 serious famine afflicted the population in the western Netherlands. At least ten thousand people died from starvation because of the Germans' failure to sustain the civilians under their authority. Hundreds of thousands more would doubtless have lost their lives had the liberation been delayed for two or three more weeks (*Malnutrition and Starvation in Western Netherlands, September 1944–July 1945* [The Hague, 1948], pt. 1).

[4] Ridgway thanked Eisenhower for his letter of February 20, 1950. He would send the General a copy of his reply to the commission (Feb. 23, 1950, EM).

To Paul Herbert Davis   *February 20, 1950*

1. Some time ago I invited Charles E. Wilson to be the head of a combined industrial-university committee, the purpose of which would be to study ways and means by which corporations could help universities, particularly Columbia.[1] Mr. Wilson accepted, but I have heard nothing more of this project. As I

recall it, Dr. Dunning was one of the chief instigators of the idea.[2] Will you please look up this matter and let me know what its present status is?[3]

2. Francis Murphy, prominent Hartford publisher, extends an invitation to me to come up to Hartford on any day in May of my own choosing.[4] He wants me to come to a luncheon at the Hartford Club for about 100 people. At this luncheon the talk would be informal and off the record if I should so desire. After luncheon, he wants me to go to the Bradley Air Field to break ground for the start of a new building that the city is planning at this airport. No speech of any sort would be expected at this ceremony.

He then proposes that we return to Hartford for the purpose of having a small cocktail-reception affair for the Columbia alumni at Hartford. This, he says, could be done at the Hartford Club and points out that there are a great many influential Columbia alumni in the city and that they have never been visited by any prominent Columbia official.

Will you please discuss this matter with appropriate individuals, including George Cooper and Mr. McCann, to determine whether it is a worthwhile project, from the standpoint of the University?[5] From one standpoint, it is less objectionable than many similar invitations in that there would be no evening engagement involved. I would start home immediately after the cocktail party.

[1] This memo was hand-delivered on February 20 to Vice-President in Charge of Development Davis. Eisenhower had written to Wilson on January 13 to ask him to chair the Committee on Corporate Participation, which had been organized as part of the university's development program. For background on Wilson, president of General Electric Company, see no. 684.

[2] John R. Dunning was the newly appointed dean of the School of Engineering and the Director of Scientific Research at Columbia (see no. 688).

[3] On April 3 Davis would inform Eisenhower that Dunning and Philip Young, dean of the Graduate School of Business, had met with Wilson and that he had agreed to head the Corporate Participation project (memo, CUF).

[4] Francis S. Murphy, publisher of the *Hartford Times* in Hartford, Connecticut, and chairman of the Connecticut Aeronautics Commission, had visited Eisenhower this same morning. For further background see no. 659.

[5] George V. Cooper (A.B. Columbia 1917) was chairman of the Alumni Club Reorganization Committee; Kevin McCann was Eisenhower's assistant. Davis conferred with Cooper and McCann on this same day (Feb. 20, 1950). Based on Cooper's report that "Columbia alumni activity in Hartford is practically nil," Davis and McCann agreed that there were other areas of the country that merited Eisenhower's prior attention (see memo, Davis to Eisenhower, Feb. 20, 1950, CUF). In spite of this recommendation, Eisenhower would accept Murphy's invitation. On May 23, 1950, the General visited Hartford, where he spoke at the groundbreaking ceremonies for the new terminal building at Bradley Field. In the afternoon he was Murphy's guest at a sheep-bake at Times Tower on Avon

Mountain, and he was honored at a reception given later by the Columbia University Alumni Club of Hartford at the Hartford Golf Club. He would return to Columbia the same evening (see EM, Murphy Corr., for the trip arrangements; and *Hartford Times*, Apr. 26, May 1, 11, 1950).

711   *Columbia University Files*

To Leonard Tyson Scully   *February 20, 1950*

Dear Mr. Scully:[1] Replying to your letter of January 6, 1950, with which was enclosed a third draft of proposed rules of procedure for the Board of Control of the Eugene Higgins Trust, I can say that this draft of the rules appears to me to be quite satisfactory with one exception. The exception is the second sentence under *V. Reports*, paragraph 1, which reads as follows:

"Each such statement shall contain a certification that such income has been expended solely for education in natural and physical science,"

Since, to some future administration, this might seem to limit the certification to "education" rather than research, I suggest that there be inserted a quotation from the Higgins' will, to make this clause read as follows:

Each such statement shall contain a certification that such income has been expended solely "for education in natural and physical science and to that end to promote the general advancement of science by investigation, research and experiment,"[2]

Sincerely

[1] Scully (A.B. Columbia College 1932) was secretary to the board of control of the Eugene Higgins Trust.
[2] Eisenhower had sent this recommendation to Provost Grayson Kirk for action in January (see no. 651). University vice-president George B. Pegram drafted this letter for Eisenhower. In its final form, the clause would read: "for education and research in natural and physical science. . ." (Board of Control of the Eugene Higgins Trust, *Reports 1950–1951*, CUF).

712   *Eisenhower Mss.*

To George Catlett Marshall   *February 21, 1950*

Dear General:[1] It is a physical impossibility for me to accept your flattering invitation to address the opening ceremonies of the anniversary celebration at International House.[2] On the 23rd of April, I shall be out of town, returning that night from a round of visits in the South, and on the 24th I must make the principal address before the Associated Press meeting here in New York City. These commitments are of long standing.[3]

However, if there is any other way in which I can help or if there is any assistance that my associates here at the University can lend, I hope you will call on me again.[4] As you have noted, the ties between International House and Columbia University have been most close and friendly; Columbia would certainly be honored by any kind of participation in the ceremonies that you thought fitting.

I should add that I deeply regret my own inability to be with you on that occasion; but every day now I find that personal inclination means nothing when opposed to the facts of a calendar that is established months in advance. *Cordially*

[1] Marshall, who was president of the American Red Cross, was also serving (since May 1949) as chairman of the board of trustees of New York International House. A home for foreign students attending New York colleges and universities, International House had been established in 1924 through the generosity of John D. Rockefeller, Jr. Over the years some twenty thousand students from sixty foreign countries had lived there.

[2] In a letter of February 15 Marshall had asked Eisenhower to give the main address at ceremonies in observance of the twenty-fifth anniversary of the founding of International House. Marshall had said that it seemed especially appropriate that Eisenhower participate in view of the close ties between International House and Columbia University. McCann drafted this reply for Eisenhower; a copy of his draft, with Eisenhower's handwritten changes, is in EM, Letters and Drafts.

[3] From April 10 until April 23 General and Mrs. Eisenhower would stay at the Augusta National Golf Club in Augusta, Georgia (see no. 774). For the text of Eisenhower's address before fourteen hundred members and guests at the annual Associated Press luncheon see *New York Times*, April 25, 1950.

[4] Marshall would ask Eisenhower to meet with friends of International House at a luncheon to be held on April 4. He said that Eisenhower would learn of the center's future financial needs, "not with a view to any contribution or pledge from you at that time, but rather in the hope that the situation will appeal to you . . . so that you will feel you would like to have an active part in helping us to make these potentialities a reality." In a handwritten note to McCann at the bottom of Marshall's letter, Eisenhower wrote "I shall be glad to go. Please give me sufficient briefing before that date so that I don't appear *too* stupid" (Mar. 21, 1950, EM). On April 4 Eisenhower would meet with Marshall's group at the Hotel Commodore in New York City.

713   *Eisenhower Mss.*

TO ERNEST DALE   *February 21, 1950*

Dear Mr. Dale:[1] I should be glad to talk to you about military organization at any time that we might find an hour convenient for us both.[2]

The "general's staff" or, as it came to be known, the "general staff" is of comparatively recent origin. Its real beginnings are found in the group of able young lieutenants that Frederick the Great personally trained and used as immediate assistants in the conduct of his battles. But "staffs" of men—the term meaning nothing more than non-combatant specialists—have existed for centuries.[3]

These gradually became organized, segregated by profession, and specially trained for war uses. The quartermasters, doctors, ordnance officers and so on, are examples. A few types, because of particular reasons, became both fighters and non-fighters, the engineers, for example.

The common factors in the functions of all staffs include:

a. Essentially non-combatant, and without power of command. (For particular phases of staff support, this latter is not true, but the command exercised is only for a *supporting* effort—it is not a fighting command.)

b. They advise the commander.

c. They assist the commander in executing his plan and orders. (For "special" staffs, this function involves often a sizeable "operation"—but it invariably involves, also, a staff supervision in lower echelons.)

The "general staff" is the group that absorbs and analyzes the facts and statistics applying to all commands, fighting and non-fighting, and presents a consolidated picture to the commander on which he bases his decision. It then translates these decisions into detailed orders and later supervises execution. Therefore, a general staff must include among its members a sufficient number and variety of specialists so that the basic orders are intelligible to specialists—and capable of execution. While I agree that there is a vast difference between the general staff and specialist staffs—I do not go along with the conclusion that they are "diametrically different."[4] *Sincerely*

[1] Dale (Ph.D. Yale 1950) had been an instructor in labor economics at Columbia's School of Business since 1946.

[2] Eisenhower's recent visit to the School of Business had prompted Dale to write on February 15. (Dean Philip Young and Eisenhower had toured the school on February 10.) At that time Dale and the General had talked briefly about the structure of working groups, a subject Dale had been studying for a book he planned to publish in collaboration with Lyndall Fownes Urwick, a British authority on management. A copy of Eisenhower's handwritten draft of this letter is in EM, Letters and Drafts.

[3] Dale had asked Eisenhower's opinion about the "two diametrically contradictory senses" in which the word *staff* was used in the U.S. Army. According to Dale, the word was used to mean the " 'staff' officer who assists the commander in carrying out his functions or command," but it also meant the "specialist who . . . is much more concerned with supplying specialized knowledge to the executives down the line."

[4] On March 21 Dale thanked Eisenhower for this letter. He said that he had been in touch with Urwick in England and that his coauthor thought that the use of the word *staff* in the U.S. Army had caused confusion in American industrial organization. Urwick thought that as a result business writers had mixed up their definitions of *staff* and *line*. Dale wrote, "If there are not two classic relationships, but three—line relationships, specialist or functional relationships, and staff relationships—it would do a great deal to clarify thinking about top organization if we could get some definition and agreement on this very thorny subject." Dale asked Eisenhower about this question and other problems in military organization. Eisenhower directed Schulz to arrange a full-hour appointment for Dale; the meeting would be held on May 3. All correspondence is in EM.

Dale would publish his book, *Staff in Organization*, coauthored with Urwick, in 1960 (New York: McGraw-Hill). Chapter 5, "The Military Use of Staff," and chapter 6, "Comparison of Military and Business Staffs," discuss in depth the confusions and conflicts in business resulting from the influence of military terminology on organizational structure (pp. 56–118; see also their appendix A, pp. 215–20).

714   *Eisenhower Mss.*

To Bernard F. Gimbel   *February 21, 1950*

Dear Bernard:[1] I always like to see you; so, if the prospect of discussing the subject in your letter of the 16th will bring you up here, I assure you that nothing is necessary but a telephone call.[2]

So far as the Baker Field matter is concerned, I have accepted at face value the arguments and reasons presented to me by people who have long been serving at Columbia.[3] But that is no reason why we should not have a good long talk about them. Possibly you have some angles that none of us ever considered.[4] I do not entertain much hope in this regard, however, because I am told that two or three years ago this matter was up over a period of months and very earnestly thrashed out.[5]

But I repeat my warm invitation for you to come up. *Cordially*

[1] Gimbel was president of Gimbel Brothers, operators of large department and speciality stores. In 1948 he had been elected president of the New York Convention and Visitors Bureau, a non-profit agency that promoted travel business for the city of New York. He was reelected to this post in 1949 and again in 1950.

[2] Gimbel's letter concerned a request from the directors of the New York Convention and Visitors Bureau that Columbia University consider moving its home games with the Army and Navy football teams from Baker Field to either Yankee Stadium or the Polo Grounds. Gimbel had explained that at a recent meeting of the bureau's board "it was felt very strongly" that holding these events at the larger baseball stadiums would be "in the best interest of all concerned. . . ." He asked Eisenhower to meet with a committee representing the bureau to discuss the matter (EM).

[3] Gimbel had enclosed with his letter a previous request directed to Ralph J. Furey (Columbia's Director of Intercollegiate Athletics) by Royal W. Ryan, executive

vice-president of the Convention and Visitors Bureau (for background on Furey see no. 168. In reply, Furey had written that despite the limited accommodations at Baker Field, university policy dictated "that whenever possible, intercollegiate sporting events should be conducted in a purely intercollegiate atmosphere . . ." (see Ryan to Furey, Jan. 10, and Furey to Ryan, Jan. 18, 1950, both in EM, Gimbel Corr.).

[4] On the morning of May 9 Eisenhower would meet with Gimbel, Ryan, and two other members of the bureau's committee, Brigadier General John R. Kilpatrick (president of Madison Square Garden) and Frank L. Andrews (president of the Hotel New Yorker), to discuss the football situation (see the General's desk calendar, and Gimbel to Eisenhower, May 3, 1950, EM). As a result of this meeting, Furey, who was also in attendance, agreed to present the bureau's proposal to the university's Committee on Athletics at its regular meeting on October 4 (see note 5 below).

[5] On October 6 Furey would inform the General that the Committee on Athletics had voted unanimously to continue the policy of scheduling home football games at Baker Field. He enclosed a copy of his letter to Gimbel of the previous day, outlining this decision (both documents are in EM, Furey Corr.).

715   *Eisenhower Mss.,*
                                                    Margaret B. Pickel Corr.

To Grayson Louis Kirk[1]   *February 22, 1950*

Yesterday, the Buildings and Grounds Committee voted, as a preliminary step, the provision of a very considerable sum for the renovation of 301 Philosophy Hall.[2] This, of couse, must be approved by the Finance Committee and the Board of Trustees before actual obligations (other than those already undertaken) may go into effect.

I wish you would see Dean Pickel;[3] give her preliminary information on a confidential basis so that she may instantly devise a somewhat different program from that contained in the suggested budget that was made up in 1947. That budget contemplated the total expenditure of somewhere around $20,000 and I do not see how we can honestly ask the Trustees to invest more than $10,000 in this entire venture. But, with this information, she should be able to devise a program that would make the best possible use of some thousands of dollars. And she should have it ready before the Business Vice President wants to start in on the actual work.[4]

[1] Kirk was Columbia's provost.

[2] Eisenhower had attended a meeting of the Buildings and Grounds Committee the afternoon of February 21. The room in question, 301 Philosophy Hall, was a multipurpose room used by women graduate students, student organizations, and the university community at large for meetings and social functions.

[3] Margaret Barnard Pickel (Ph.D. Columbia 1936) was dean of university women at Columbia. She had been appointed to her present position by late Columbia

president Nicholas Murray Butler in 1945; prior to that she had been an adviser to women graduate students and had served as head of Johnson Hall, the university's residence for women.

[4] Kirk requested from Dean Pickel a revised proposal for refurnishing the room, and on March 6 she submitted cost estimates based on the 1947 budget. Kirk in turn, forwarded the plan to Joseph Campbell, vice-president in charge of business affairs. On March 16, W. Emerson Gentzler, Columbia's business manager, notified Dean Pickel that he had been authorized to proceed with the work of renovation (EM. See also Gentzler to Kirk, March 20, 1950, CUF).

716   *Eisenhower Mss.*

To Edward Everett Hazlett   *February 24, 1950*

Dear Swede: Naturally, I cannot challenge your assertion that I had to take the red ink, but I do repudiate your additional postulate that I had to "like" it.[1] To prove my point I am taking advantage of your approaching anniversary (or its approximation, in view of the leap year uniqueness of your birthdate) to send you a new typewriter ribbon. If on arrival, it appears to be packaged in a way that you do not like, I hope that you will find it possible to exchange for one you really want.[2] My additional hope is that, in black print, I shall occasionally get a letter that is as interesting and completely intriguing as your latest one to me.

In its reading, it took me half of the first page to decide that you had not gone a bit balmy. This, because of the fact that I had not previously seen the story about the "best dressed men"; I had not even heard of it.[3] My reaction is that some people must have a hell of a lot to do if they have time to devote themselves to such drivel. My clothes are made by a Jewish friend of mine who has been in the mass tailoring business all his life. He has one or two tailors who make clothing on the "special order" basis. Since my friend keeps my measurements on hand, he comes up here with a new suit every several months, usually of a cloth and cut of his own choosing. So far as my own intervention in such matters is concerned, one of Mamie's chief causes of complaint is that I will not even buy a pair of socks for myself. She keeps in constant touch with my friend Moaney (a negro who has lived with me since the very first days of the war)[4] in order that she can keep me stocked with the necessaries of decent existence. This constitutes my entire knowledge of my own sartorial requirements and equipment.

Gordon Gray strikes me as being a citizen of fine character and sensibilities. He is endowed with good judgment and a likeable personality. I do not suppose that you would class him as an intellectual giant, but such people are usually uncomfortable characters to have around anyway. I understand that he is a wealthy individual—which won't be any handicap in the running of a modern university. I predict that he will eventually achieve a high place in the affections of the University family in Chapel Hill, including the faculty portion.[5]

Like you, I was somewhat astonished that Milton finally made up his mind to leave Kansas State.[6] He was well situated there and his standing with the Regents and the Legislature was well exemplified when his most recent budget was not only approved in detail but, in certain important particulars, was increased over the amounts he requested. Recently the authorities completely remodeled his house, to include full air conditioning—something that is really more than a convenience in Kansas summers, as you well know. His state-wide standing was comparable and he was in constant demand in all the larger centers as a speaker and a distinguished guest. Moreover, he has been offered the Presidency of several other universities, including one or two quite large ones where pay and perquisites far exceeded what he was getting at Kansas State. Some of these he refused to consider for a single moment because of what he deemed to be unsatisfactory academic standards.

In my opinion, the decisive factors in finally taking him to Pennsylvania State were purely personal. First, he has gotten to the point where the doctors urge upon him some regular outdoor recreation and Kansas offers little or none of this in the only thing he really likes— fresh water fishing. Pennsylvania's streams and lakes are numerous, and most of them provide exactly the kind of outdoor sport that he loves. On top of this is the fact that his wife's parents live in Washington, D.C. One of our brothers lives near Pittsburgh and so, by coming East, both sides of the family tend to find greater family companionship than they do in the West. You must realize that, since our father and mother died, there remains in Kansas among our close relatives only Roy's widow and one of her daughters. Of course, the greatly increased pay and emoluments that go with the presidency of Penn State can scarcely be considered as drawbacks.

I have read some of the same comments that you have concerning my alleged dissatisfaction with my present position![7] They are merely examples of distortion and inaccuracy. It is true that in attempting, at times, to explain to my friends the difficulties of my present life, I have dwelt upon the conflicts that arise between the details of university administration, unusually persistent adhesions from a past life, and, finally, the demands that arise out of my earnest effort to be of some help to people who are struggling manfully to support the essentials of the American way of life. Actually, I believe that if a man were able to give his full or nearly full attention to such a job as this, he would find it completely absorbing. On a campus like Columbia's, the greatest opportunity is that of meeting constantly with fine minds, in every kind of discipline. Because I love to partake in or, at least, to listen to discussions on such subjects as economics, history, contemporary civilization, some branches of natural and physical science, public health and engineering, you can see that living with a distinguished faculty gives to me many wonderful hours that I could never have in any other environment. Sometimes, however, my loyalties to several different kinds of purposes lead me into a confusing, not to say almost nerve-wearing, kind of living. At such times, just as anyone else would do, I unquestionably express myself in tones of irritation and resentment, and I have no doubt that a chance listener could interpret some of these expressions as irritation with my "apparently" sole preoccupation — that of administering the affairs of this great University. Actually, such outbursts (which, of course, are nothing but a manifestation of a soldier's right to grouse) are directed at myself for allowing confusion and uncertainty to arise where system and serenity should prevail. I hope you can make out what I am getting at but, in any event, I do assure you that, if I were convinced that I had made a mistake in coming to Columbia, I am not so stupid as to fail to recognize the instant and obvious cure. As long as I am here, you can believe that I am not only interested in the task, but I still believe it to offer a way in which I may render some service to the public at large.

With respect to my political difficulties, it is a curious fact that, while little mention of them is made nowadays in the public press, I am by no means free of the problem.[8] A quite steady stream of visitors, to say nothing of correspondence, reaches me under one excuse or another, and with the frequent consequence of long political discussion that rarely fails to drag me, as an individual, into future speculation. I have heard much of my "clear duty" and have learned to answer this by inquiring as to the comparable duty of my caller. It is astonishing how frequently the conversation can instantly be turned, by this query, into other channels. However, the attempt sometimes backfires, particularly when I learn that an individual has devoted time and effort and a great portion of his substance to the attempt to counteract government by bureaucracy and the discernible drift toward statism. Since I abhor these two things, you can see that occasionally I get myself into a conversational morass.

Fortunately, these incidents are not of great frequency, but on the other side of the picture, they usually involve people of prominence, who, therefore, cannot be disregarded. In some instances, I have the utmost respect for their expressed convictions. Some are businessmen, some are avowed politicians, some seem to be only public-spirited citizens and some can be considered no less than statesmen. In any case, I am merely trying to let you see that the problem is not entirely a thing of the past. It often plagues me at present and some people seem to think it has a future. This last, at least, I do not admit.

I do not recall the exact terms in which I previously expressed to you my opinion of Louis Johnson.[9] I am quite sure, however, that those terms have never included the word "profound." I am convinced he is honest but he is, of course, avowedly a *politician and he is impulsive.* These last two factors lead him to believe that the public likes rapid, even spectacular, decision. Couple this attitude with a conviction that we had better economize or we are going to lose the things that are of the greatest value to us, and I think it is not too difficult to understand his general motivation.

You will recall that, for a number of weeks after Mr. Johnson first took office, he insisted upon my remaining rather regularly in Washington to consult with him and with other responsible officials of the Security Establishment. In recent months, he has not continued this insistence. While I am obviously welcome in his office, he no longer seems to sense the need he once expressed constantly and urgently. This change, I have no doubt, comes about because of increased confidence on his own part as well as a possible feeling that I do not fit into a situation which, after all—from his viewpoint—is political and partisan as well as professional and national. Moreover, he has Bradley as Chairman of the JCS and cannot, by any means, ignore his position and counsel. I know that you do not consider him an ideal public servant in his present post; but will you name any individual—who could be considered reasonably available—that you would think ideal?

I admire and like Spike Fahrion so it is not difficult for me to go along with a great portion of the Service quarrel analysis that he sent to you.[10] I must remark, however, that it is almost impossible for any Service person to achieve a completely objective and disinterested viewpoint toward the development and incidents of that whole unfortunate episode. Actually, I think that you and I could probably come as close to achieving this attitude as could anyone; you, for the reason that you are naturally fair and just by temperament and were removed from the scene both geographically and functionally, while I, because of my wartime post and the way in which I was used, while in Washington, by the Commander in Chief. You, of course, saw nothing but a rather amusing and even slightly ridiculous aspect to the last two sentences of Spike's presentation. Yet to such people as Bradley and Vandenberg, those two sentences, which for many months have been bandied about Washington's cocktail lounges, presented something more than mere cause for a chuckle. They were acutely aware of the fact that the proposition was more than once suggested with some seriousness, at one time, apparently, with deadly earnestness. So far as I am concerned, I have always felt that if we could see anything logical in turning the whole job over to one Service I would be very glad to have the others bow out of the whole picture, no matter which ones might be involved.

But I have earnestly supported the proposition that each Service has an indispensable role in the provision of reasonable national security and that, if it will only perform that role adequately, it will have little time to devote to invasion of the missions of others. I think the sad part of the whole business is that each Service is seemingly incapable of confining itself to its own obvious tasks, but rather feels a compulsion—in order that it may demonstrate its own importance and indispensability—to assert a competency in the performance of other Security tasks which it does not and should not possess.

You may have read my testimony before the Investigating Committee or, if not, you may have seen the recent article, in U.S. News and World Report, in which I expressed my views on these points.[11] Certainly I believe that there is in each Service the brains to do the job right if only each can become *respectful of the importance of its own task* and does not feel it necessary to try to grab off the jobs of others.

So far as Mr. Johnson's economy measures are concerned, there is a very long story involved. I do know that he has asserted a hope of saving money without hurting combat strength—and after many, many years in Washington, both in subordinate and in higher positions of authority and responsibility, I must say that I know of no way of forcing the Services to cut administrative and overhead cost to the bone except by arbitrary action. This does not mean that I would support every move that Mr. Johnson has made, although I understand that he has several times referred to his current proposals as the "Eisenhower Budget." Last spring when I was in Washington, my job was to propose a division of the available money, under varying assumptions as to quantity, so as to carry out as nearly as we possibly could the essentials of the agreed upon strategic plan. This says a very great deal in a relatively short sentence. Particularly, it says a lot in the way of difficult problems. My experiences in the attempt to achieve some success are far too long and involved for me to attempt to describe them in anything less than a full volume. But I would be quite ready to wager that, if I could send to you the full record of all of the efforts that were made, of all the different types of approaches that were used, and could show you the responses received from each of the Services, you would agree that the answers recommended were about as logical and as nearly correct as any individual could make them. Such a wager I would make with some confidence because of the fact that I kept pounding away until the actual percentages of the total budget—that had to be allocated on my judgment (that is, outside the roughly agreed upon conclusions of all three Services)—were extremely small. While I am relying upon a weakening memory, I am quite certain that, even in the smallest of the several budgets on which we worked, the percentage could not have been more than three or, at the very maximum, four. So you will see that from my viewpoint the heat and intensity that characterized the quarrel were unjustified and evidenced to me a flagrant failure to place national convictions and requirements above those of Service.[12]

I realize that I have never before attempted to explain some of these things to you in such detail. I would probably be even more explicit in this particular exposition except for the obvious requirements of secrecy in all of the deliberations and functioning of the Chiefs of Staff and of their relationships with their civilian superiors. But I should like you to believe that there are many sides to this whole argument and it has been a weary battle to get men to forget self and to turn their minds to the critical situation in the world and to think of nothing else. It is because I believe that Sherman possesses a sensitive and logical concern for the national picture, as opposed to any more narrow one, that I spoke so warmly of his appointment.[13] He has, so far as I know, both the ability to do the job and the will to do it properly. Each of these qualifications is extraordinarily important in this day and time.

Along with a letter of such length must come my profound apology, but I just felt today like attempting to give you a fuller explanation of some of the events of the past, and of which I have some knowledge, than I have given you before.

As a sort of postscript to the above, I must tell you that I agree with your opinion that no personal aide should be with any General too long. For this reason, as much as I appreciate his services and as grateful as I am to him, I have constantly urged my present aide to transfer to other duties. Moreover, no one has ever been on my personal staff for one single second except by his own preference. The only thing that I have not done is to insist upon a transfer against the expressed desire of the individual concerned. I must remark also that where you recalled the length of my service with MacArthur at 5 years, you should have used the figure "9."[14] *As ever*

---

[1] Hazlett had sent a letter to Eisenhower (Feb. 19, 1950, EM) that he had typed using a red typewriter ribbon.

[2] Eisenhower would soon send Hazlett a new typewriter ribbon, as well as a new typewriter (see no. 734).

[3] Hazlett had teased Eisenhower for having been named best-dressed man of the year: "You are certainly the first Jayhawker ever to get such an accolade and will probably be the last one. I'm afraid we can't blame it on Abilene—we'll have to give the credit to Mamie."

[4] For background on John A. Moaney see no. 1.

[5] Secretary of the Army Gordon Gray had recently been selected as the next president of the University of North Carolina (see no. 675). Hazlett had told Eisenhower that every person he had spoken to in Chapel Hill was enthusiastic about Gray's selection, "except for a couple of oldsters, who admit he is fine but chew their long grey beards about his lack of 'academic' background."

[6] Hazlett had commented on Milton Eisenhower's decision to leave Kansas State College to become president of Pennsylvania State College (see no. 679). Hazlett

had said that he hated "to see him leave his native prairies" because Milton "seemed such a natural for the job."

[7] Hazlett had said that according to some reports General Eisenhower was "completely bored" with his job as Columbia's president. Hazlett doubted that these reports were accurate, but he also thought Eisenhower might have organized himself "out of a job—a procedure of which I highly approve—except for matters of high policy."

[8] Interest in Eisenhower as a possible presidential candidate had continued, in spite of his public statements that he was not a candidate for office (see, for example, nos. 602 and 697). Hazlett had said that speculation on Eisenhower's political future had ended.

[9] See no. 519. Hazlett had criticized Louis Johnson's economy measures and had characterized the Secretary of Defense as "a blow-hard and a prevaricator who is really weakening national defense."

[10] For background on Hazlett's brother-in-law, Rear Admiral Frank G. Fahrion, see no. 519. Fahrion had told Hazlett that the Navy had mishandled the recent congressional inquiry into the B−36, unification, and military strategy (for background see no. 639). Fahrion regretted that the real issues involved had not been presented properly and that the best naval testimony had been overshadowed by the "yapping of our naval aviators." Hazlett had also quoted Fahrion as saying, "Someone facetiously said last night that the solution to the whole problem was to have the Army join the Marines, and the Air Force the Naval Air, then make Johnson Sec[retary of the] Nav[y] and the whole problem of unification would be solved. Not so farfetched at that, when you consider we [i.e., the Navy] have been running a unified show for many years."

[11] See nos. 570 and 639 for details of Eisenhower's testimony before the House Armed Services Committee. The article to which Eisenhower refers is "Harmony in the Armed Services: An Exclusive Interview With General Eisenhower," *U.S. News & World Report*, February 3, 1950, 13−18. Eisenhower had described the interservice cooperation that had prevailed during World War II, as well as other problems associated with matters of military strategy and the defense budget. He had predicted that harmony among the services would prevail and that a "way will finally be found down the big, broad middle of common sense, logic and conciliation. . ." (see telegram, Eisenhower to Lawrence, Jan. 23, 1950; Lawrence to Eisenhower, Feb. 21, 1950; and other papers in EM, Lawrence Corr.).

[12] For background on the FY51 defense budget see no. 533. At a press conference on January 10 Secretary Johnson had said that the FY51 defense budget had been "largely worked out by General Eisenhower and the Joint Chiefs" and had referred to the completed budget as "Ike III" (see "Minutes of Press Conference Held By Secretary of Defense Louis Johnson," EM, Johnson Corr.; for developments see nos. 701 and 753).

[13] For background on Admiral Forrest P. Sherman, the new Chief of Naval Operations, see no. 598.

[14] Hazlett had urged Eisenhower to release Major Schulz from service as the General's aide. He had admitted, however, that Eisenhower's "being hooked up with [General Douglas] MacArthur as long as you were (5 years?)" had not harmed Eisenhower's career (on Eisenhower's service with MacArthur in Washington and in the Philippines see Eisenhower, *At Ease*, pp. 212−32).

General Eisenhower had left New York City the evening of February 23. He had traveled by train to Washington, where he had met with the Military Appropriations Subcommittee of the House of Representatives (see no. 701) and with officials of the Department of Defense on the following day. He had returned to New York on the twenty-fourth.

To William Samuel Paley   *February 25, 1950*

Dear Bill[1]—I've, by no means, forgotten the project re: Columbia Trustees of which we spoke. The vacancy is in sight—but the former Trustee involved is so old and ill that we are proceeding as delicately as possible.[2]

I saw in the paper that you are now the papa of an 8 pound (plus) girl. My congratulations to you; my best wishes to the mother.[3] *As ever*

---

[1] A typed copy of this note, which was handwritten, is in EM. For background on Paley, chairman of the board of directors of the Columbia Broadcasting System, see Galambos, *Chief of Staff*. See also no. 176; and Eisenhower to William Paley, January 28, 1949, in EM.

[2] Eisenhower was referring to the vacancy on Columbia's board of trustees soon to be created by the failing health of life trustee Joseph Peter Grace. For background see no. 304; for developments see the following document.

[3] Kate Cushing Paley had been born on February 15, 1950. Paley's wife was the former Barbara Cushing Mortimer.

To Grayson Louis Kirk   *February 28, 1950*

Herewith a rough draft which I should like to have put in proper form for submission to the Chairman of the Trustees at the earliest possible moment. He intends to introduce it at the next meeting of the Trustees on Monday next.[1]

*   *   *   *   *   *   *   *   *

Due to failing health Mr. Joseph Grace has been unable to attend any meeting of the Trustees during the past two years. Because of this he verbally informed the Chairman of the Trustees that he felt a resignation was in order and assured the Chairman that his resignation would be forthcoming at any moment the Trustees might deem advisable.[2]

Since that time Mr. Grace's health has further deteriorated and it is considered extremely inadvisable even to mention the matter to him. Nevertheless, it is quite important that we have a full membership on the Board because of the great amount of committee work.

The Charter of the University provides that whenever any Trustee misses five consecutive meetings the Trustees may, at their discretion, declare a vacancy and upon their doing so, the absentee member ceases to be a Trustee.[3]

It is, of course, extremely important that nothing be done that could in any way hurt the feelings of Mr. Grace or his family; on the contrary, the hope is that they will understand the lasting appreciation felt by the entire body of Trustees toward such an old and distinguished member as Mr. Grace.

This situation has been thoroughly studied and explored by the Committee on Education, which recommends as follows:

- *a*) That, to provide a proper position for Mr. Grace during his lifetime, the Trustees create the position of Honorary Trustee and appoint Mr. Grace to it.
- *b*) That the action of the Trustees be held confidential.
- *c*) That the Clerk, Mr. M. Hartley Dodge, be authorized and directed to communicate with Mr. Peter Grace to inform him of the action taken by the Trustees.[4]
- *d*) That, upon the creation of this vacancy that Mr. William Paley, who has already been approved by the Nominating Committee, be appointed to fill it.[5]

To carry these proposals into effect, the following resolution is offered:

Resolved that Section ———— of the bylaws is amended so as to add, after the words ———— and who may thereupon, at the discretion of the Trustees, be appointed Honorary Trustee, a position hereby created.[6]

Whereas Mr. Joseph Grace who has been a Trustee of Columbia University since ————[7] and who has been prevented, by reason of failing health, from attending Trustee Meetings during more than two years and who has, because of this fact, verbally informed the Chairman of the Trustees of his readiness to resign his post in order that an active member could be appointed thereto, and whereas the son of Mr. Joseph Grace has informed the Trustees by letter that his father is now too ill to participate further in the affairs of the University, now be it resolved that the Trustees declare, under the provision of ————[8] of the bylaws, that the position of Trustee held by Mr. Joseph Grace is declared vacant and he is hereby appointed[9] to the position of Honorary Trustee of Columbia University, to be held by him during his lifetime.

Resolved that William D. Paley[10] who has already declared his willingness to serve as a Trustee of Columbia University is hereby elected as a Trustee to fill the vacancy created by the appointment of Joseph Grace as Honorary Trustee.[11]

[1] After Eisenhower had prepared this memorandum for Provost Kirk's attention, he was informed that Kirk was out of town. Eisenhower then asked Associate Provost Joaquin Enrique Zanetti (Ph.D. Harvard 1909) to put the draft in the proper form for Frederick Coykendall, chairman of the trustees. In his memo to Zanetti (Feb. 28, 1950, same file as document), Eisenhower said that he was

anxious to have the completed paper returned this same day because he would be absent from the university for two days and he wanted to dispatch it to Coykendall before his departure (see no. 720 for the trip).

[2] See no. 304 for background.

[3] Columbia University's Charter of 1810, Section VI, states that the trustees shall have the power to "make and declare vacant the seat of any trustee who shall absent himself from five successive meetings of the board. . ." (Elliott and Chambers, *Charters and Basic Laws*, p. 152).

[4] Grace's son, Joseph Peter Grace, Jr.

[5] See the preceding document.

[6] Zanetti changed this paragraph to read: "Resolved, That the By-Laws be amended by inserting in Chapter II a new paragraph, to be numbered 9a, as follows: 9a. Whenever any Trustee shall have absented himself, for reasons beyond his control, from meetings of the Trustees as provided in 9, he may, by vote of the Trustees, be elected an Honorary Trustee, an office which is hereby created."

[7] June 3, 1918.

[8] 9.

[9] Zanetti substituted the word *elected* for *appointed*.

[10] William S. Paley.

[11] Eisenhower's resolution would be approved by the trustees at their meeting on March 6. On March 13 Peter Grace thanked the trustees for making his father an honorary trustee (telegram, P. Grace to M. H. Dodge, EM, Dodge Corr.). Paley's election as life trustee would be announced on March 24 (*New York Times*). For developments see no. 968.

719   *Eisenhower Mss., Van Sant Corr.*

To Grayson Louis Kirk   *February 28, 1950*

Please note next to last paragraph of the attached memorandum brought to me this morning by Mr. Van Sant and Mr. Forsheimer of the Horace Mann School.[1]

I promised that I would have our staff give me a statement of our understanding of our relationship with the Horace Mann School and if this understanding conforms to the one presented in the cited paragraph, I would write a letter to the school confirming this point.[2]

Will you please give me the necessary draft for a suitable reply?[3]

Please also note that point is made that, in recognition of the long term relationship between this University and the Horace Mann School, I should attend a dinner honoring Dr. Tillinghast on May 22. I was promised that I would have to make no major speech, but my two visitors thought it important that I should be there. Will you please give the opinion of the staff to Mr. McCann?[4]

[1] John T. Van Sant, controller of the Horace Mann School, a boys' private school in New York City, and Carl H. Pforzheimer, Sr., chairman of the school's board of trustees, had met with Eisenhower the morning of Monday, February 27. The

paragraph to which Eisenhower referred concerned reciprocal financial arrangements between Teachers College and the Horace Mann School, which had originally been part of Columbia University and Teachers College. Traditionally, sons of faculty at Teachers College were admitted to Horace Mann with liberal scholarships, and Horace Mann faculty received similar privileges at Teachers College and Columbia University. It was a policy that Horace Mann administrators hoped to continue ("Memo for General Dwight D. Eisenhower," Feb. 27, 1950, CUF).

[2] Kirk asked Secretary of the University Richard Herpers to investigate the financial arrangements between the schools (for background on Herpers see no. 552). In a memorandum of March 8 (CUF) Herpers reported to Kirk that there was no written agreement regarding scholarships to Columbia for sons of faculty members at Horace Mann. It was once the custom of the university to provide for such children from budgeted scholarship funds. The arrangement was, according to Herpers, "just an unwritten gentlemen's agreement." In 1946, however, Horace Mann School had become an independent educational corporation, and at that time the university had changed its policy toward scholarship assistance. Aid for sons of Horace Mann faculty members was provided only to those teaching there since before 1946. Faculty members appointed after 1946 received no consideration for their sons. Herpers concluded that perhaps Columbia should reciprocate with some scholarship assistance since Horace Mann had continued to make available scholarships to sons of Columbia faculty.

[3] Eisenhower's reply to Van Sant, drafted by McCann, suggested that Van Sant and Kirk work out "a mutually agreeable chord" between the two institutions regarding scholarship assistance (Mar. 20, 1950, EM). It would not be until 1953, however, that the trustees of both Columbia and Horace Mann would approve an exchange agreement (see "Memorandum in Regard to the Recent Agreement Made between Columbia University and the Horace Mann School, May 6, 1953," attached to the letter from Margaret Hartmann, Administrative Assistant, Office of the President, Horace Mann School, July 29, 1980, EP).

[4] McCann would report that so many invitations had been turned down for the final two weeks of May that "an exception in this case may cause us some trouble" (handwritten note on memorandum, Eisenhower to Kirk, Feb. 28, 1950, CUF). The Van Sant–Pforzheimer memo of February 27 (see n. 1 above) had called it "particularly fitting" that Eisenhower, as president of Columbia University, speak at a dinner honoring Charles Carpenter Tillinghast, retiring principal of the Horace Mann School. Tillinghast (A.M. Columbia 1917), who would soon become professor emeritus of education at Teachers College, had headed the school for thirty years (see *New York Times*, May 22, 23, 1950; and R. A. McCardell, ed., *The Country Day School: History, Curriculum, Philosophy of Horace Mann School* [Dobbs Ferry, N.Y., 1962], pp. 39–44). In his March 20 reply to Van Sant, Eisenhower would decline the invitation to attend the dinner, but he would authorize Van Sant to use his name as a sponsor of the affair (W. F. Russell to J. T. Van Sant, Mar. 27, 1950, same file as document).

720   *Eisenhower Mss., Flexner Corr.*

To Grayson Louis Kirk   *March 1, 1950*

1. Dr. Flexner came to see me, apparently, with your concurrence.[1]
2. He argues—

a) That there is plenty of money to finance a really intelligent and comprehensive future expansion of any great university provided,
   1) That the plan was based upon a real investigation within the university to examine into quality, usefulness and need of educational activities, and
   2) That the plan drawn up as bold, imaginative and forward looking (for next 50 years)
b) That no university has had such an examination (nothing to compare with his work in medical schools of 30 years ago)
c) That an outsider would have to do this—specifically, someone qualified as he is.
d) He would charge total of $7500–$10,000.
e) He would help raise money, specifically and directly hinting that Mr. Rockefeller would be definitely and continuously interested (with money) in such a development.[2]

3. He was most emphatic on the point "No Publicity."
4. He has undoubtedly talked with you along same lines. I finally promised to tell the Trustees about this.

Will you please draw up a memo and bring to me on Friday to accomplish this?[3]

---

[1] Abraham Flexner (M.A. Harvard 1906) had been a lifelong critic of educational institutions. As secretary of the General Education Board of the Rockefeller Foundation in 1917, he had convinced John D. Rockefeller, Sr., to contribute fifty million dollars to promote the reform of medical education in the United States. Flexner had also solicited the funds that formed the endowment for the Institute of Advanced Study at Princeton, New Jersey, and had been director of the institute from 1930 to 1939. He had enrolled in several courses at Columbia University since 1947, including one in American history taught by Allan Nevins (for background on Nevins see Galambos, *Chief of Staff*, no. 1934). Nevins had notified Kevin C. McCann, assistant to the president of Columbia University, that Flexner wanted to have an interview with Eisenhower "to discuss some matters of University policy"; he had described Flexner as an adviser to John D. Rockefeller, Jr. (see Nevins to McCann, Feb. 17, 1950, EM, Flexner Corr.). McCann had replied that an appointment had been set for Flexner for the morning of February 28 (McCann to Nevins, Feb. 24, 1950, *ibid.*). Eisenhower's appointment calendar indicates that his February 28 meeting with Flexner was actually the second time the two had met (see the calendar entry for June 9, 1949).

[2] John D. Rockefeller, Jr., was a member of the Columbia Associates (for background see no. 247).

[3] In a memorandum to Eisenhower of March 6, 1950 (EM, Flexner Corr.), Provost Grayson L. Kirk analyzed Flexner's philosophy of fund-raising. A private university needed to examine the purposes that it was best qualified to fulfill, Flexner believed, and these purposes should be brought to the public's attention. Kirk told Eisenhower that Flexner's type of survey might help administrators at Columbia and that his connections with philanthropists might bolster the university's development program. On the other hand, Kirk pointed out, Flexner's "rigid" views concerning the inappropriateness of schools of business, education, and

journalism in a university setting might lead him to dissuade potential donors from giving aid to Columbia. Kirk mentioned that he had discussed this matter with the president and secretary of the Carnegie Corporation and that they had advised against giving Flexner any official connection with the university. Flexner wanted an appointment as a special assistant to the president or the vice-president at a salary of from four thousand to five thousand dollars per year for two years.

On this same day Eisenhower traveled to Philadelphia to accept an honorary degree from Temple University. The convocation was the highlight of "Moving-Up Day," when student leaders at Temple took office for a new year of service. Milton S. Eisenhower, the General's brother, also received an honorary degree from Temple on this day. On March 2 Eisenhower would speak at Franklin and Marshall College, in Lancaster, Pennsylvania (a transcript of his remarks is in EM, Subject File, Speeches). He would return to New York City that evening.

721   *Eisenhower Mss.*

To WALTER HAMPTON MALLORY   *March 4, 1950*

Dear Mr. Mallory:[1] I most heartily concur with Graeme Howard's recommendation that Phil Reed be added to the Committee, if he will accept.[2] I believe we should have American business a little more heavily represented than it is—especially since Leffingwell had to resign.[3]

I agree also that, on the assumption our finances will permit us to do so, we should attempt to secure George Kennan to help us out in the preparation of our political conclusions. I respect the man's mind as well as his integrity and knowledge.[4]

Won't you consider also the possibility of adding Earl Newsom to our Committee? I know his work and reputation better by indirect report than by personal contact. However, I have had at least one—and most satisfying—conversation with him, and I am particularly attracted because of his very sound understanding of public relations. He is a dynamic and likable individual.[5] *Cordially*

[1] Mallory was Executive Director of the Council on Foreign Relations (for background on Eisenhower's involvement with the council see no. 269).
[2] In a letter of February 28 (EM) Graeme K. Howard, vice-president and a director of the international division of Ford Motor Company, had suggested to Eisenhower that Philip Dunham Reed (LL.B. Fordham University 1924) be added to the Aid to Europe Group of the Council on Foreign Relations. Reed, who was chairman of the board of the General Electric Company, had served with the War Production Board and as Chief of the Mission for Economic Affairs in London during World War II (for background see Chandler, *War Years*). He was currently a director of the Council on Foreign Relations, a trustee and member of the research and policy committee of the Committee for Economic Development, and president of the International Chamber of Commerce. Reed would agree to join the Aid to Europe Group (letter to Eisenhower, Mar. 27, 1950, EM).
[3] Russell C. Leffingwell, chairman of the board of directors of J. P. Morgan &

Company, had resigned from the Aid to Europe Group in September 1949 (see no. 494, n. 6). He had, nevertheless, continued to serve as chairman of the board of directors of the council.

[4] George Frost Kennan, counselor of the Department of State, was a member of the Council on Foreign Relations (for background on Eisenhower's previous work with him see *Eisenhower Papers*, vols. VI–IX). Kennan was currently in Rio de Janeiro, Brazil, attending a conference of U.S ambassadors to South America. Howard had assured Eisenhower in his letter of February 28 that if Kennan were to accept a position with the Aid to Europe Group, funds would be found to "make the chore sufficiently attractive." Eisenhower wrote to Kennan on March 20, 1950, asking him to join the group, and Kennan replied (Mar. 30, EM) that he would try to help the group at least until he began his work at the Institute for Advanced Study in Princeton, New Jersey, in the fall of 1950.

[5] For background on Edwin Earl Newsom, a public relations consultant, see no. 700. Eisenhower had met with Newsom on June 27, 1949. They would have lunch together on March 8, 1950 (see no. 726). Newsom would not, however, become a member of the group (see letter from Janice Murray, Archivist, Council on Foreign Relations, Inc., Sept. 23, 1980, EP).

The evening of March 3, Eisenhower had spoken at a dinner for the members of the Columbia College Forum on Democracy (for a summary of his remarks see *New York Times*, Mar. 4, 1950). He would speak the evening of March 5 at the mid-season gambol of The Lambs, a fraternal organization for people in the entertainment business. On January 31, 1950, the club had elected Eisenhower an honorary member to succeed the late General of the Armies John J. Pershing.

722   *Eisenhower Mss.,*
                                                      Columbia University Corr.

To the Trustees   *March 6, 1950*

Memorandum to the Trustees: Due to the approaching retirement date of Vice President George Pegram,[1] the matter of reassignment of top administrative personnel has been under study.

Incident to this study, there has been examined also the operation of the organizational system devised and approved by the Trustees some months ago, at which time it was agreed that the plan should be constantly studied to the end that, when considered desirable by the President, appropriate recommendation for modification should be submitted to the Trustees.[2]

In general, the soundness of the new organization has been established. But there is one place where difficulty occurs which can be, in my opinion, easily corrected. This particular difficulty involves some overlapping of function, particularly in the minds of the entire University family, between The Vice President and the Provost. A certain amount of overlapping in the prescribed duties of these two officials is inescapable; this circumstance leads to an exaggerated concern in the minds of those who have daily work to transact with these two officials. However, a single official—in this price range—can, with suitable assistants, absorb the duties of both.

A plan to correct the existing difficulty has been submitted in almost identical terms by Dr. Krout, Dr. Kirk and individual Trustees. It involves only slight change in the By-laws.

The plan is as follows:

>(*a*) Appoint and confirm, as of June 30, 1950, the Provost of the University as Vice President, thus permitting one man to carry the responsibilities of both offices.[3]

>(*b*) Provide for this official three principal assistants, one of whom, the Director of Student Affairs, is already provided in the statutes.[4]
>
>A second position, that of the Director for Scientific Research, has already been approved by the Committee on Education and is submitted to the Trustees today. (The individual named to this position is still under consideration as Dean of Engineering.)[5]
>
>The third position, that of Associate Provost, exists in fact but apparently has no statutory authorization. Consequently, the only action required of the Trustees at this time, other than the appointment of Dr. Kirk as Vice President and Provost of the University, is to authorize by statute the office of the Associate Provost.[6]

I submit these two recommendations with the request that they lay over until the April meeting for action by the Trustees.[7]

---

[1] George B. Pegram would retire as vice-president for education on June 30, 1950. At a meeting of the trustees on March 6 Eisenhower would recommend that Pegram be appointed special adviser to the president of the university for a one-year term beginning July 1, 1950. The board would approve this resolution (Trustees, *Minutes*, Mar. 6, 1950, CUF). On the origins of the recommendation see no. 688.

[2] On this organizational system see no. 361.

[3] Grayson L. Kirk, provost of Columbia University, informed Eisenhower in a memorandum of this same day (same file as document) that no revision of the statutes or of the bylaws would be necessary to bring this change into effect. The appropriate action would be to pass a resolution appointing the provost as vice-president, with the explanation that the duties of the two offices were to be combined. The trustees would pass a resolution approving Kirk's appointment as vice-president on April 3, 1950, and he would assume the duties of vice-president effective July 1, 1950 (see Trustees, *Minutes*, Apr. 3, 1950, CUF). For background on Kirk see no. 515. For Eisenhower's views on the duties of the two offices see no. 843.

[4] Eisenhower was probably referring to the post of director of student interests. Kirk assured him that the position was already on a statutory basis (see Kirk to Eisenhower, Mar. 6, 1950, same file as document).

[5] For background on this recommendation see no. 688, n. 4. The board would

approve the appointment of Professor John R. Dunning, a physicist, to this post (see Trustees, *Minutes*, Mar. 6, 1950, CUF).

[6] J. Enrique Zanetti had held this office since July 1948, although it was not yet on a statutory basis. Apparently, no action would be taken on this proposal at the April meeting of the trustees (see Trustees, *Minutes*, Apr. 3, 1950, CUF). In 1951, the board would adopt an amendment to the statutes that would make specific provision for an associate provost (Trustees, *Minutes*, May 7, 1951, CUF).

[7] Eisenhower had made numerous changes in an earlier draft of this memorandum (see the version in EM, Letters and Drafts).

723
Eisenhower Mss.

To George A. Sloan
March 6, 1950

Dear Mr. Sloan:[1] I have been sweating blood over my next January's schedule but I am nevertheless, putting opposite the January 11 date the name United States Steel in very faint lettering and with a big question mark.[2] However, I am hopeful that I may be able to give Irving Olds a final answer before November; possibly by October 1.[3] I am concerned that he does not wait around so long to see whether I can come that he may miss out on getting someone else who would be equally or even more acceptable.[4]

This gives me a chance to tell you again what a nice time we had the other evening. It is difficult to explain the truly enjoyable reaction that I always experience when I find a dinner is very small and is in the home of my host.[5] I think I am achieving an all time high in hatred for big parties held in public places.

Won't you extend my warm greetings to Mrs. Sloan[6] and assure her also that Mrs. Eisenhower and I are most grateful for the very fine evening at dinner and the opera. *Cordially*

[1] Sloan (LL.B. Vanderbilt 1915) was a director and member of the finance committee of the United States Steel Corporation. He had been president of the Cotton-Textile Institute from 1929 to 1935 and had served as its chairman from 1932 to 1935 (see Louis Galambos, *Competition and Cooperation: The Emergence of a National Trade Association* [Baltimore, 1966], pp. 109–11, 134, 152–57, and 270). From 1940 to 1944 Sloan had been commissioner of commerce for the city of New York and chairman of the Mayor's business committee. Since 1946 he had been chairman of the board of the Metropolitan Opera Association, having served as its president from 1941 to 1945.

[2] Eisenhower had been invited to be guest of honor at the United States Steel Corporation's fiftieth annual dinner, to be held at the Waldorf-Astoria Hotel in New York City. The General had apparently inquired about the possibility of rescheduling this event, but Sloan had replied (Mar. 2, EM) that the date was "fixed by U.S. Steel in order to secure certain accommodations at the Waldorf which were necessary for this particular gathering."

[3] Irving S. Olds, chairman of the board of directors of the United States Steel

Corporation (for background see no. 269), had thanked Eisenhower for tentatively accepting this invitation; Olds agreed to wait until the fall for a firm decision (Feb. 6, 1950, EM).

[4] Eisenhower would be on military leave in Europe at the time of this affair. Olds sent Mrs. Eisenhower a handwritten letter the following day (Jan. 12, 1951), expressing his regrets "for personal selfish reasons that the serious international situation prevented General Eisenhower from being our guest of honor" (EM).

[5] The General and Mrs. Eisenhower had dined with the Sloans the night of February 28; afterwards they had attended a performance of *Tosca* at the Metropolitan Opera House. Sloan's "confidential" invitation (Jan. 8) is in EM; see *New York Times*, March 1, 1950, concerning the special pageant featured at the opera.

[6] Formerly Florence Lincoln Rockefeller.

724   *Eisenhower Mss.*

To Lewis Bergman Maytag   *March 7, 1950*

Dear Bud:[1] My acquaintance with Ed Bermingham extends back to the summer of 1948. As you know, he was a partner in Dill & Reed & Co. and is a graduate of Columbia University.[2] Every contact I have had with him leads me to regard him as a gentleman of the highest standards and connections. I like him very much indeed and respect his judgment. I shall be more than happy to second your nomination of him as a member at Augusta.

Recently, I suggested to Cliff the addition of Secretary Symington and of Dave Calhoun to the Club, and I understand that both of them have been accepted.[3] I place Ed Bermingham in the same category of friends as I do those two.

I just called Cliff on the phone and he knows all of the background and business associations of Ed Bermingham, even though he has never met him personally. He enthusiastically agreed with the suggestion and said that if you would write to him, they would get the whole matter disposed of in short order. Because of this, I am enclosing a short note that may be satisfactory as a second—if not, I will do whatever is required of me by the Club authorities.[4]

A recent note from Ed said that you had been a bit under the weather but, since your letter does not mention the difficulty, I assume that you are now better.[5] At any event, I am looking forward to meeting you on the practice team at Augusta, I hope, on the morning of April 11, approximately at ten-thirty.[6] *Cordially*

[1] Maytag, a past president of the Maytag Company, manufacturers of washing machines, had asked Eisenhower in a letter of March 2 (EM) for his opinion regarding the proposed membership at Augusta National Golf Club for Edward J. Bermingham. Maytag was a vice-president and a member of the executive committee at Augusta National.

[2] Bermingham had been a partner in the investment firm of Dillon, Read & Company. For further background see no. 381; and Lyon, *Portrait of the Hero*, p. 388.

[3] Clifford Roberts, a partner in Reynolds & Company, an investment firm, was chairman of the executive committee at Augusta National. Regarding Eisenhower's efforts on behalf of Secretary of the Air Force W. Stuart Symington and David R. Calhoun, Jr., president of the St. Louis (Mo.) Union Trust Company, see nos. 673 and 687.

[4] Eisenhower's note is not in EM. Bermingham would accept an invitation to join Augusta National in May 1950 (Bermingham to Eisenhower, May 14, 1950, EM).

[5] There is no note along these lines in EM.

[6] On Eisenhower's vacation in Augusta, Georgia, from April 10 to April 22, 1950, see no. 774.

725   *Eisenhower Mss.*

To William Stuart Symington   *March 8, 1950*

Dear Stu: I have gone over the secret memorandum you sent to me and which I signed on 3 November 1947.[1] I have no personal objection to its de-classification and such use as the Defense Establishment may want to make of it. However, I note that General Collins obviously collaborated with me in the preparation of the document. Because he is now Chief of Staff, I think it is only proper that the matter should be referred to him. I am sure that he will concur in my attitude; but I should like to be sure that he has no objection to its publication.[2]

Bob Schulz will call someone in your office to read this memorandum to you because it may be delayed in reaching you.[3]

With warm personal regard, *Cordially*

[1] Secretary of the Air Force Symington had requested Eisenhower's permission to remove the classification "secret" from a memorandum that Eisenhower had signed while serving as Chief of Staff of the Army. The memorandum (no. 1840 in Galambos, *Chief of Staff*) argued in favor of retaining tactical air support as a function of the Air Force.

[2] General J. Lawton Collins, Chief of Staff of the Army since August 1949, would notify Symington in a memorandum of March 9 (copy in EM, Symington Corr.) that the paper had been declassified. Collins would also indicate that Eisenhower had informed him that he "remains fully convinced of the soundness of the principle of complementary roles and consequent inter-dependence of the three components of the armed Services. However, he also is firmly convinced that this principle is sound only if the principle of a unified commander is likewise applied whenever elements of two or more services are supporting one another." For Eisenhower's views on unified command see nos. 321 and 639.

[3] Major Robert L. Schulz was Eisenhower's aide. Symington thanked Eisenhower in a letter of March 11 (EM) for "the speed in the handling" of this request. Symington would publish the document in his semiannual report, contained in

Department of Defense, *Semiannual Report of the Secretary of Defense, July 1 to December 31, 1949*, pp. 233–34, as a statement of principles that, he asserted, continued to represent his own views as well as those of Eisenhower, Collins, and General Hoyt S. Vandenberg, Air Force Chief of Staff.

726   *Eisenhower Mss.*

To Edwin Earl Newsom   *March 9, 1950*

Dear Mr. Newsom:[1] Quite naturally I am still turning over in my mind many of the items of information you gave to me yesterday afternoon, to say nothing of the elements of advice regarding my personal situation and problems. Because of your obvious disinterestedness and your sympathetic approach, I value all this more than I can say; I am especially grateful for the time you took out of your busy life to go over all of these matters with me.[2]

I am now busy trying to put together in one short document a resume of the Columbia projects that constitute what I might term the immediate portions of my dream for this institution's enlarging usefulness in this time of trouble and confusion.[3] Taking advantage of your very enthusiastic reaction to my mention of these things, I intend, within a day or so, to send you a very short description with the request for your advice as to the best method of forwarding the story to the Ford Foundation. Realizing that there is no chairman or executive director yet appointed, I feel that I must ask your advice on this procedural matter even though, at this time, these many details of budget and similar features could be presented only in the roughest sort of way.[4]

This morning I asked my assistant, Mr. McCann, to try to arrange a meeting with you. But I assure you that we will try to be considerate in our demands upon your time. I shall always be grateful for your unselfish offer to be helpful both to me and to the work you so clearly understand and which I am trying—though I admit sometimes fumblingly—to perform.[5] *Cordially*

[1] Newsom was a public relations consultant who had been an adviser to Henry Ford II. For background on Newsom see no. 700.
[2] Newsom and Eisenhower had lunched at 60 Morningside Drive on March 8.
[3] In May, June, and July 1950 Eisenhower would send to various friends a summary of his plans for the university. One version of the letter is no. 826.
[4] On the Ford Foundation see no. 419. In December 1949 Henry Ford II, president of the Ford Motor Company, had offered the position of managing director of the Ford Foundation to Paul G. Hoffman, administrator of the ECA (see no. 1007). Hoffman would announce his acceptance of the job in September 1950 (see *New York Times*, Sept. 27, 1950).
[5] Newsom would promise Eisenhower (letter, Mar. 15, 1950, EM) that he would

make certain that the Ford Foundation gave "proper consideration" to the document that Eisenhower had mentioned. Newsom had talked with Kevin C. McCann, and he would meet him for lunch on March 16. Eisenhower would have lunch with Newsom at 60 Morningside Drive on July 11, 1950.

727   *Eisenhower Mss.*

To William Fletcher Russell   *March 9, 1950*

Dear Will:[1] Last evening John D. Rockefeller, III expressed to me a tremendous interest in the program for Citizenship Training. As you know, he is the head of the "Williamsburg" project and one of his basic purposes in the restoration of that colonial town is to create and sustain interest in American history and American institutions. Consequently, he sees some possible relationship between his own efforts and those that we are making with the end of the Carnegie Corporation.[2]

Mr. Rockefeller heard of this project through Mr. Dollard[3] and as a result has arranged for his chief assistant in the Williamsburg project to call upon Professor Vincent.[4] I did not get the name of the assistant but I assured Mr. Rockefeller there would be no difficulty whatsoever in arranging such meetings as may be necessary in order for this individual to familiarize himself completely with our project.

Beyond this, Mr. Rockefeller expressed such a personal interest in our plan that I invited him to sit in on our next "top level" meeting. I explained that at some future time I thought there would be tentative progress reports submitted to a group composed of Mr. Dollard, Mr. Larsen,[5] yourself and me. I told him that he would be welcome at such a meeting, a sentiment which I sincerely trust you share.

Unless you see some objection, therefore, will you make a note in your appointment book to send a special invitation to Mr. Rockefeller to attend the next meeting? I informed him that I thought it would possibly be some months before such a meeting would be held.[6] *Sincerely*

[1] Russell, president of Teachers College and Director of the Citizenship Education Project, had been Director of the National Citizenship Education Program, Department of Justice, from 1941 to 1945 and chairman of the Advisory Committee on Human Relations of the Board of Education of New York City from 1945 to 1947 (for further background see no. 67). Russell's Citizenship Education Project would begin with a focus upon the enhancement of civic pride among high school students. An emphasis on practical experience in the exercise of citizenship in local communities would become an outstanding feature of the program. Regarding the project's goals see William F. Russell, "Preliminary Discussion of a Proposal for a Substantial Program by Columbia University and Teachers College for Education for Americanism," n.d., EM, Columbia University Corr.; and Columbia University, Teachers College, *Improving Citizenship Education: A Two-Year Progress Report of the Citizenship Education Project* (New York, 1952).

[2] Rockefeller was chairman of the board of trustees of Colonial Williamsburg, president of the Rockefeller Brothers' Fund, and a trustee of the Rockefeller Foundation. Eisenhower's appointment calendar indicates that he had seen Rockefeller at a dinner the evening of March 6, 1950 (see also Galambos, *Chief of Staff*, no. 839). The Carnegie Corporation of New York had granted four hundred thousand dollars to Columbia to support the project's two-year experimental program (Carnegie Corporation of New York, *Reports of Officers, 1950*, pp. 39, 50).

[3] Charles V. Dollard was president of the Carnegie Corporation of New York (for background see no. 204; see also Dollard to Eisenhower, Jan. 20, 1950, EM).

[4] William Shafer Vincent (Ph.D. Columbia 1944) was visiting professor of education at Columbia University Teachers College and executive officer of the Citizenship Education Project. He had taught at Pennsylvania State College and had been executive secretary of the Pennsylvania School Study Council from 1946 to 1949.

[5] Roy Edward Larsen (B.A. Harvard 1921), president of Time, Inc., was chairman of the National Citizens Commission for the Public Schools, an organization established in May 1949 to distribute information regarding improvements in public-school education. On Eisenhower's attempt to coordinate the work of the Citizenship Education Project with that of Larsen's group see no. 775. Larsen was also a trustee of the Committee for Economic Development (CED); Eisenhower would agree to become a CED trustee in April 1950 (see no. 732).

[6] We have been unable to determine whether Rockefeller attended the next meeting of the administrators of the Citizenship Education Project. Eisenhower's appointment calendar indicates that he talked with Rockefeller on April 6 and met with him at 60 Morningside Drive on May 12, 1950 (see no. 774).

728   *Eisenhower Mss., Vincent Corr.*

To Grayson Louis Kirk   *March 9, 1950*

Memorandum for Mr. Kirk:[1] Professor Vincent, on duty at Teachers College, is on loan to us from Penn State College. He is in charge of the Citizenship Training project that has attracted such favorable comment from many sources, and which is financially supported by the Carnegie Foundation.[2]

Professor Vincent's wife[3] was once a victim of polio and is still partially disabled. For this reason they are almost compelled to live in Butler Hall, where they now reside. However, they have been able to secure, so far, the tiniest of apartments. Since it now appears that Professor Vincent will be on duty with us for a considerable period, they are most anxious to get more commodious accommodations. Would you ask the appropriate official to place them high on the priority list for a larger apartment when and if one becomes available.

Please inform President Russell of Teachers College of whatever action you take.[4]

[1] Kirk was provost of Columbia University (see no. 515).

[2] William S. Vincent was executive officer of the Citizenship Education Project (see the preceding document).

[3] The former Janet Newton.

[4] Kirk would inform William F. Russell, president of Teachers College, that the Vincents' two-room apartment was "one of the most desirable" in Butler Hall and that there were eight persons ahead of the Vincents on a waiting list for the scarce three-room apartments. Kirk concluded that "we ought to let the situation stand as it is for the time being" (Mar. 11, 1950, CUF).

729   *Eisenhower Mss.*

To William Rea Furlong   *March 9, 1950*

Dear Admiral Furlong:[1] So far as I know, I have never at any time or place given the World Federalists a statement supporting their position toward world government. I have talked, during the past four years, to a number of them—including Cord Meyer, Jr., who, I think, is their principal leader.[2] While I am convinced that eventually there must be some type of federated control if there is to be world-wide confidence in peace, I am also wholly convinced that the world is not *now* ready for such a development, and that it is a mistake to work for it as an alternative to strengthening and supporting the United Nations. This will continue so long as the two-world pattern exists.

I understand that, in many local publications, the World Federalists and similar groups have named me as a supporter of their proposals on the strength of a paragraph or two in CRUSADE IN EUROPE. For your information, I quote the sentences most commonly reproduced.

"Nowhere perfect, in many regions democracy is pitifully weak because the separatism of national sovereignty uselessly prevents the logical pooling of resources, which would produce greater material prosperity within and multiplied strength for defense. Such division may mean ideological conquest. The democracies must learn that the world is now too small for the rigid concepts of national sovereignty that developed in a time when the nations were self-sufficient and self-dependent for their own well-being and safety. None of them today can stand alone. No radical surrender of national sovereignty is required—only a firm agreement that in disputes between nations a central and joint agency, after examination of the facts, shall decide the justice of the case by majority vote and thereafter shall have the power and the means to enforce its decision."[3]

This is a long-term and, I believe, a sound objective; beyond it, I do not go. Certainly, I have never endorsed a plan as specific and detailed as that of the World Federalists.[4] There are far too many complications in the present world situation that require solution before we can even think of a federalized world. *Sincerely*

[1] Rear Admiral Furlong, USN, ret. (USNA 1905; M.A. Columbia 1914), was national commander of the Military Order of the World Wars, a patriotic organization of veteran officers. During World War II Furlong had been commandant of the navy yard at Pearl Harbor.

[2] For background on the United World Federalists and Cord Meyer, Jr., see no. 436. In a letter of March 2, 1950, Furlong had told Eisenhower that in February he had spoken against world government before a joint committee of the Virginia house of representatives and senate. On that occasion a number of world federalists had been present, including Alan Cranston, national president of the organization, and Paul Saunier, an officer of the Virginia state group. According to Furlong, Saunier had named Eisenhower as one who favored world government. The purpose of his letter, said Furlong, was to ascertain from Eisenhower the truth of Saunier's statement (EM).

[3] See Eisenhower's memoir *Crusade in Europe*, pp. 476–77.

[4] The specific plan for world government that the United World Federalists envisioned was based on strengthening the United Nations, giving to that body such legislative, executive, and judicial powers as were necessary to keep peace under law. Among the powers to be incorporated in a new world constitution were provisions (1) prohibiting the possession by any nation of armaments and forces beyond an approved level required for internal policing; (2) requiring control by the world federal government of the dangerous aspects of atomic energy and other scientific developments easily diverted to mass destruction; and (3) requiring such world inspection, police, and armed forces as would be necessary to enforce world law and provide world security. Eisenhower's growing correspondence on this subject primarily involved requests for his support for the movement. See, for instance, Eisenhower's letters to D. S. Bussey, January 3, 1949, to F. R. von Windegger, January 10, 1949 and to F. Thayer, January 28, 1949; and Kevin McCann to A. M. Stevens, November 15, 1949, all in EM. For developments see no. 908.

730   *Eisenhower Mss.*

To EDWARD JOHN BERMINGHAM   *March 10, 1950*

Professorship for Causes, Conduct and Impact of War

prepared by a brilliant Historian.[1]

Dear Ed:[2] As you can see, we'd make the essential start with $15,000 per year ($12,000 if permanency guaranteed). With an additional $10,000 per year the professor would have needed help and go expand his capacity for research and teaching.

Another 10,000 would make the whole thing a splendid enterprise—

with a yearly institute or seminar attended by representatives of government, business, other universities, etc.

This 15,000 per year is necessary as a basic start.

But 35,000 per year would make it a complete—and greatly needed—affair.[3]

[1] Eisenhower added this title in longhand at the top of the first page of a three-page, typed draft of a letter (which he had probably dictated). He also wrote the body of this letter by hand at the bottom of the typed draft. Both letters are in Bermingham Papers, Eisenhower Library, Abilene. Only a typed copy of Eisenhower's longhand note is in EM.

The three-page letter was an outline for a proposal to establish one professorship of military history, one position for a research associate, and one position for a teaching assistant, all of which would comprise an institute of military studies at Columbia University. Such an institute might sponsor conferences and seminars to be attended by "historians, economists, military analysts, and active military leaders." The first priority would involve determining the yearly salary for the holder of the professorship of military history. The letter suggested that if a permanent endowment could be established twelve thousand dollars might be a reasonable salary. If the supporters of the project were able to fund the position for only a term of years, the fifteen thousand dollars per year might be necessary. The additional ten thousand dollars per year would supply the salaries of the research associate and the teaching assistant. Another allowance of ten thousand dollars would pay for "library facilities, conference meetings and other expenses if the full work of an institute is to be undertaken."

[2] Bermingham, a retired investment counselor, was a member of Columbia University's Fund Committee and of the Columbia Associates (for background see no. 381). He had met with Eisenhower and Clarence Dillon (see no. 693) on March 9. At that meeting Eisenhower had remarked that millions of dollars were spent each year "to find ways and means to overcome the two great killers, cancer and tuberculosis, but no money had been provided for study or research of the greatest killer of them all—war." Bermingham had asked Eisenhower to send him a memorandum on this subject, and Eisenhower had provided him with the letter discussed in n. 1 above.

[3] Bermingham would reply on March 20, 1950, that the fund-raising campaign for the proposed institute should begin with modest goals. "I am concerned only with the mechanics of determining ways and means of securing the funds necessary for its inception and sufficient to carry it along successfully," he would say. An endowment was something that the promoters of the project "can ponder." Bermingham's letter is in Bermingham Papers. For developments see no. 764.

731   *Eisenhower Mss.*

To WALTER W. STRONG   *March 10, 1950*

Dear Mr. Strong: I appreciate the kindly spirit and good intent of your letter.[1] I emphatically agree with you that the problems facing our people, and the world, are today of a most serious character. Moreover, satisfactory solutions are going to be reached only through earnest study and thoughtful never-ending effort.

But I cannot agree with you that these answers are going to be more readily found by pessimism and defeatism. In a considerable experience that has been somewhat characterized by very difficult problems, involving—at times—burdensome responsibilities and depressing truths, I have never yet found a long face to be helpful. Unless we approach our work with optimism and cheerfulness, I do not believe that we will persuade many people to work with us. Moreover, I do not see how anyone could be expected to spend his life, constantly watching for the roadside and way-laying photographer; if they insist in printing only those photographs that show a grinning face, particularly of an old soldier, I doubt that the circumstance is of such great moment as to cause justifiable concern.[2]

I repeat my appreciation of your interest.[3] *Sincerely*

[1] Strong, of Long Beach, California, had written (Mar. 4, EM) to suggest that the General only allow the publication of pictures of himself revealing "a serious, determined mood indicating a realization of the weight of the problems facing the nation and with the will to deal firmly with them." Strong also hoped that the Republicans would nominate Eisenhower as their presidential candidate in 1952.
[2] Eisenhower would speak at the closing luncheon of the Columbia Scholastic Press Association convention on March 11, 1950. The *New York Times* (Mar. 12, 1950) quoted him as saying that "everybody has had to face A-bombs and social unrest. Don't let them make pessimists and defeatists out of you!"
[3] The General would vacation at Seaview Country Club, in Absecon, New Jersey, March 12–18, 1950 (on the trip see no. 686).

732

Eisenhower Mss., Subject File, Clubs and Associations

To James Forbis Brownlee   *March 17, 1950*

Dear Mr. Brownlee:[1] I have had an opportunity to read some of the CED papers and can say no less than that I am deeply impressed by them and am heartily in accord with their tenor. I am grateful for your giving them to me.[2]

Because I now more fully appreciate the work of the Committee, I have seriously considered your proposal that I become a Trustee— principally in the hope that I might be able promptly to decide that I could become an active participant. Certainly, I would profit greatly from the association and the discussions, even though I might add little to the advantage of those associated with me.

I find that in explaining to you how little time I might be able to give, I was not exaggerating the facts of my daily routine. Because of the many commitments I seem constantly forced to make to organizations on the campus and elsewhere, my free time for quiet discussions and informal panels simply evaporates. What gaps still exist in my schedule must be reserved for public functions and that sort of thing, which, however much I dislike them, are nevertheless inescapable because of my job here.

The CED is too important an organization to be burdened by a drone—and, as a Trustee, I could scarcely be more than that. My own conviction, therefore, is that I should send you my regretful declination. But my interest in your work is such that, if you still believe that some good might come out of the association—regardless of the obvious difficulties—won't you give me a ring?[3]

I should add that I greatly appreciate the compliment implicit in your proposal and—if it were not for the circumstances I have outlined—I should be quick to accept without further discussion. *Sincerely*

[1] Brownlee (B.A. Harvard 1913) had been president of Frankfort Distilleries from 1935 to 1943. He had been a member of the Business Advisory Council for 1937 to 1939, a member of the War Production Board in 1942, Director of the Transportation War Food Administration in 1943, Deputy Administrator of the Office of Price Administration (OPA) from 1943 to 1945, and Deputy Director of the Office of Economic Stabilization in 1946. He was currently a consultant to several corporations and chairman of the business-education committee of the Committee for Economic Development (CED). A group of businessmen and academicians had founded the CED in 1942 as a planning agency with the purpose of finding the means of maintaining a high level of employment and economic activity after World War II. After the much-feared postwar depression had not developed, the CED had devoted itself to research on fiscal policy as an instrument for controlling the business cycle (see Robert M. Collins, *The Business Response to Keynes, 1929–1964* [New York, 1981]; and Karl Schriftgiesser, *Business and Public Policy: The Role of the Committee for Economic Development, 1942–1967* [Englewood Cliffs, N.J., 1967], pp. 1–48). Eisenhower made numerous handwritten changes on a draft of this letter by his assistant, Kevin McCann; a copy is in EM, Letters and Drafts.

[2] Brownlee had expressed his hope that Eisenhower would accept an invitation to become a trustee of the CED, and he had enclosed with his letter of February 24 (same file as document) an undated memorandum titled "The Committee for Economic Development: Who It Is, What It Is, And Why." Brownlee had also given Eisenhower several CED studies when they had conferred at Columbia University on February 6, 1950 (see also William Benton to Eisenhower, Oct. 4, 1949, EM).

[3] Brownlee would reply (letter of Mar. 29, same file as document) that he and the other CED trustees understood the demands upon Eisenhower's time; they still wanted him to join the organization and "give to the work only such time as your interests of special subjects may dictate." Eisenhower would accept in a short note of April 3, 1950 (*ibid.*), on the condition that he would not be considered a "deadbeat." After his election, Eisenhower would send a formal letter of acceptance, explaining that his calendar "already looks like a crowded infantry battalion" and that he would not be able to attend a CED conference on May 18 and 19, 1950 (see Eisenhower to Williams, May 2, 1950, *ibid.*; and a longhand copy of the letter in EM, Letters and Drafts).

To Philip Caryl Jessup *March 18, 1950*

My dear Jessup:[1] I am writing to tell you how much your University deplores the association of your name with the current loyalty investigation in the United States Senate.[2]

Your long and distinguished record as a scholar and a public servant has won for you the respect of your colleagues and of the American people as well. No one who has known you can for a moment question the depth or sincerity of your devotion to the principles of Americanism. Your University associates and I are confident that any impression to the contrary will be quickly dispelled as the facts become known.[3] *Sincerely*

[1] Jessup was Ambassador at Large of the United States and Hamilton Fish Professor of International Law and Diplomacy at Columbia University (for background see no. 515). On March 8, 1950, Senator Joseph Raymond McCarthy (LL.B. Marquette 1935), Republican of Wisconsin, had accused Jessup of "unusual affinity" for Communist causes (see U.S., Congress, Senate, Committee on Foreign Relations, *State Department Employee Loyalty Investigation: Hearings*, 81st Cong., 2d sess., 1950, S. Res. 231, pt. 1, p. 28). The initials on the carbon copy of this letter indicate that Grayson Kirk, provost of Columbia University, assisted Eisenhower in drafting it.

[2] Jessup would testify before a Senate subcommittee on March 20, 1950. Senator Millard Evelyn Tydings, Democrat of Maryland and chairman of the subcommittee, would read into the record this letter (*ibid.*, p. 271), as well as a letter from General of the Army George C. Marshall, currently president of the American Red Cross (see no. 712).

[3] In a letter of March 20 (EM) Jessup thanked Eisenhower for his support and asked for an opportunity to discuss his situation. Eisenhower replied (Mar. 22, EM) that he would be glad to see Jessup at any time. The two men met at Columbia University on March 25. Jessup would ask in a letter of March 30 (CUF) for an indefinite extension of his leave of absence from the university, and Eisenhower would grant the request (Apr. 3, CUF). Meanwhile, President Truman had announced on March 27, 1950, that Jessup would continue indefinitely as Ambassador at Large (*New York Times*, Mar. 28, 1950).

734 *Eisenhower Mss.*

To Edward Everett Hazlett *March 20, 1950*

Dear Swede:[1] Had I known that I could possibly have impressed you so much with one miniature typewriter, I would have sent you one a long time ago.[2]

I am sorry to hear that you and Ibby have had this virus pneumonia. Mamie's father had a siege of it when he was visiting us this winter and I think it was only this new drug, aureomycin (possibly that is nearly correct), which pulled him through. This note brings my fervent hope that you both are well again.[3]

I cannot recall the man from Abilene named Alexander. Your story of the love life of his father left me a bit amazed; I did not realize that we had an Abilenite who was so light-footed and light-hearted as to jump out of one matrimonial venture in order to get tangled up with a senorita. It must have been the Naval influence![4]

I was interested to read your observations about Crommelin.[5] By the way, you may have seen an account of one incident that occurred just after he reached San Francisco. (If I told you about this in a former letter, just please skip it here.) He asked for a press conference and talked rather wildly about a "Prussian General Staff in the Pentagon." Apparently failing to stir up comment as he had hoped, he finally fired a gun which he hoped would be of really big caliber. It was something about as follows: "I am particularly disturbed that a man in uniform who is definitely a candidate for the Presidency, but who will not announce his allegiance to either political party, is free both to influence decisions within the Pentagon and to present his views to the Congress." There was a bit more to the story, as reported to me by Forrest Sherman, but that will give you some idea of the fantastic lengths to which the man goes in order to attract attention. I think that you understand, as clearly as anyone else, that I have gone to the Pentagon or to the Congress only when ordered or insistently requested to do so. Moreover, I have constantly pled that we should forget the quarrels of the past and, particularly, the attempt to fix blame for unfortunate outbursts. I have constantly urged that we turn our attention to the future on the basis of *mutual cooperation and understanding.* Crommelin, I think, cannot fail to know this as well as anybody else. But I think, also, that he has gotten so avid for acclaim and headlines that he will say anything in order to achieve that purpose.[6]

With respect to the handling of the case, I must say that I feel sorry for the Navy, particularly for Sherman. While it has been my practice always to ignore this type of thing and so deny to the offender the opportunity to appear as a martyr, yet there finally comes a point where the very good name of the Navy (or any other Service in which such an incident occurs) is involved. The country expects its Armed Services to be models of discipline and deportment and the spectacle of successful insubordination is one to create fear in the minds of the public that their traditions of service and subordination to civilian authority are deteriorating. It seems to me to be another case of "whether you do or whether you don't, you are bound to regret it."

No one respects courage and gallantry in battle more than I do. Goodness knows that I have had more reason than most people to be eternally grateful that in a pinch a young American exhibits an extraordinary disregard for the dangers of the battlefield. Nevertheless, I feel that we cannot, in succeeding years of peace, constantly excuse, condone and ignore serious offenses committed by individuals, whether civilian or military, merely because their physical courage has been established beyond a doubt.[7]

These are merely observations—I have no exact knowledge of any kind applying to this case, and my information is based entirely on what the newspapers have said and what Forrest Sherman has told me. Incidentally, Forrest called me to apologize for what he called "an unwarranted attack on one of the Navy's friends." Personally, the whole thing bothers me not a whit; I don't believe I have mentioned it to anyone but you. But I repeat that my sympathy is with those who have to handle such disagreeable cases.

With respect to young Wingfield, I will, on your suggestion, always be glad to see him. However, he should be careful to telephone or otherwise communicate with my office (Mr. McCann, UNiversity 4-3200, Ext. 2773) well in advance of the proposed visit so that we can find a free period and set up the engagement.[8]

Love to Ibby and, as always, warmest regards to you. *As ever*

---

[1] For background on Captain Hazlett (USN, ret.) see no. 36.

[2] Eisenhower had sent Hazlett a typewriter ribbon packaged in a new Royal Quiet Deluxe portable typewriter. Hazlett had thanked Eisenhower in a telegram (Feb. 28, 1950, EM) and later had written, "One of those fine, generous impulses of yours! One that was made without thought of repayment, and one that can never be repaid. . . . Aside from our marriage and the birth of our two gals, it was definitely the nicest thing that ever happened to me" (Mar. 14, 1950, EM; see no. 716).

[3] Hazlett had written that he and his wife had virus pneumonia. Eisenhower's father-in-law, John S. Doud, had been stricken in late January 1950 (see no. 671).

[4] Hazlett had included an anecdote about the father of his protégé, Walter Alexander. The senior Alexander was said to have fled his first wife, married again in Mexico, and then sired Walter's Mexican half-brother, who also served in the U.S. Navy.

[5] Captain John Geraerdt Crommelin, Jr. (USNA 1923), was a graduate of the National War College. During World War II he had served aboard the U.S.S. *Enterprise* in the Pacific, and he had been Chief of Staff aboard the U.S.S. *Liscombe Bay* when it was sunk in the Makin Island campaign off the Gilbert Islands (*New York Times*, Dec. 15, 1943; Mar. 16, 1950). In his letter Hazlett had written, "I don't know Crommelin personally but understand he is a very able and gallant aviator whose judgment is warped to the extent that he has now become a zealot in a lost cause . . . every ounce of publicity shoves him further down the path of martyrdom. . . . A dignified and official silence is the best answer." Hazlett's remarks were prompted by the fact that Crommelin had repeatedly made public statements critical of the unification policies and leadership of the U.S. Department of Defense. His disclosures and the release of confidential Navy correspondence (including statements by then Chief of Naval Operations Admiral Louis E. Denfeld, Vice-Admiral Gerald F. Bogan, and Admiral Arthur W. Radford concerning the "despondency" of Navy morale) had helped initiate the congressional hearings

on the roles and relationship of the services and the capabilities of the B—36 bomber. For background see Hammond, "Super Carriers and B—36 Bombers," p. 467 and esp. pp. 507—13; and nos. 639 and 716. For a comprehensive study of the subject see Philip A. Crowl, "What Price Unity: The Defense Unification Battle, 1947—50," *Prologue: The Journal of the National Archives* 7, no. 1 (Spring 1975), 5; Coletta, "Defense Unification Battle," pp. 6—17; Wolk, "Defense Unification Battle," pp. 18—26; and Richard F. Haynes, "The Defense Unification Battle, 1947—50: The Army," *Prologue: The Journal of the National Archives* 7, no. 1 (Spring 1975), 27—31.

[6] On Admiral Forrest Percival Sherman, Chief of Naval Operations since November 1949, see no. 598. One of Crommelin's favorite themes had been "the Prussian-mindedess" of the military high command of the United States (*New York Times*, Mar. 16, 1950). Without naming General Eisenhower, Crommelin had told the Pacific Traffic Association of San Francisco: "I abhor the influence which a powerful potential Presidential candidate in Army uniform, who did not and has not declared his political party affiliations, could have on decisions of Congress" (*New York Times*, Jan. 11, 1950).

[7] Following a series of unheeded warnings, Sherman had advised disciplinary action against Crommelin. The reprimands included a transfer to Western Sea Frontier Headquarters in San Francisco and a furlough at half pay (which involved the officer's virtual retirement). Sherman wrote to Secretary of the Navy Francis P. Matthews, "The good of the service and the welfare of the entire national defense structure require that there be an end to intemperate public criticism of responsible officials and agencies of the national defense establishment by officers on active duty in the Navy. I conclude, therefore, that for the present, Captain Crommelin's further employment in an active capacity will be detrimental to the best interests of the Navy and of the country" (*New York Times*, Mar. 16, 17, 1950). For developments see no. 766.

[8] Hazlett had described Alvin Wingfield, Jr., the "smart and ambitious" young man who had delivered the typewriter. Wingfield was the district manager of the Royal Typewriter Company, Inc., in Raleigh, North Carolina, and a former officer under the General's European command. Hazlett had agreed to write a letter of introduction and recommend Wingfield to Eisenhower. Wingfield would finally meet the General on May 19, 1950 (Schulz to Wingfield, Dec. 16, 1950, EM).

735   *Eisenhower Mss.*

To Arthur Hays Sulzberger   *March 20, 1950*

Dear Arthur:[1] This morning I sent to you a letter from Marcy Dodge, who feels that we should tender an honorary degree to Al Jacobs this year. While I realize that this matter has been previously considered by the Committee, yet the whole selective process was, this year, on a most hurried and unsatisfactory basis. Consequently, because of Marcy's strong feeling in the matter, I decided to send his letter on to you.[2]

For myself, I favored the inclusion of Jacobs' name on the list but abandoned the idea because of representations made to me that it was traditional in Columbia to keep the honorary degree list down to something like a total of eight. While I do not share Marcy's feeling of urgency in the matter, I do believe that inclusion of Jacobs' name would be a very fine gesture, with a good effect on the whole University family.[3]

Just a few minutes ago I had a letter from Tom Watson, supporting the idea that we should give an honorary degree to President Gonzales Videla of Chile. This suggestion, received from the State Department, is already in your hands. But I send you the following extract from Tom's letter.

"I think it would be very appropriate for Columbia to invite him to receive an Honorary Degree during his visit.

"President Gonzales Videla is on the young side and is a most enthusiastic and agreeable person. He will be accompanied by his wife, their daughter and her husband, and the Minister of Interior and his wife, all of whom are very fine people."[4]

Cordially

[1] Sulzberger was publisher of the *New York Times* and chairman of the Columbia University trustees' Committee on Honors (for background on the committee see no. 694).

[2] M. Hartley Dodge, chairman of the board of the Remington Arms Company and clerk of the board of trustees of Columbia University, had informed Eisenhower on March 14 (EM) that Syracuse University planned to give Albert C. Jacobs, chancellor of the University of Denver, an honorary degree in June 1950. Jacobs had been provost of Columbia University from July 1947 to October 1949, and Dodge thought that Columbia should confer a degree upon him in June 1950 (for background on Dodge see Galambos, *Chief of Staff*).

[3] Jacobs would be one of twelve recipients of honorary degrees from Columbia University in June 1950. For background on the other eleven see no. 694.

[4] Thomas J. Watson, Sr., chairman of the board of directors of IBM, was a trustee of Columbia University. His praise for Gabriel Gonzales Videla was expressed in a letter of March 14 (EM). Eisenhower replied on this same day (Mar. 20, *ibid.*), explaining to Watson that the Committee on Honors was already considering the Chilean president for an honorary degree. Sulzberger also favored this proposal. He had sent the members of the Committee on Honors a memorandum (Mar. 9, EM, Columbia University Corr.) that, among other things, denied that Gonzales Videla had censored the Chilean press. Sulzberger quoted Arthur Krock, of the *New York Times* Washington bureau, who had assured him that the allegations against the Chilean president were false and that "'the State Department gives Chile a clean bill of health on the question of freedom of the press.'" Sulzberger also noted that in a letter of February 15, 1950 (*ibid.*), Frederick Edward Hasler, a New York City banker and past president of the Pan American Society of the United States, had praised the Chilean president's accomplishments, noting that he had outlawed the Communist party and "strengthened the faith not only of his own people but that of all believers in constitutional government."

In a letter of March 22 (EM) Sulzberger would inform Eisenhower that the Committee on Honors had approved the awarding of a degree to Gonzales Videla during the president's visit to New York. Eisenhower would instruct Provost Grayson L. Kirk (memorandum, Mar. 23, EM, Columbia University Corr.) to arrange a special convocation for April 18, 1950. Columbia University Vice-

President George B. Pegram would preside at the ceremony because Eisenhower would be on vacation (see no. 774). A formal invitation would go to Gonzales Videla on April 3, 1950, over Eisenhower's signature. Eisenhower's changes in his staff's March 28, 1950, draft of the invitation appear in EM, Letters and Drafts.

736 *Eisenhower Mss.*

To Regis J. Colasanti *March 21, 1950*
Personal and confidential

Dear Mr. Colasanti: Thank you very much for your recent letter and for the very great personal compliment you pay me.[1]

I have not seen the editorial to which you refer but I assure you that it never bothers me in the slightest to find that my opinions and convictions are not fully shared by others. The complete right to argue with anyone is one of the priceless privileges we have in America.

Nevertheless, I would not want my recent remarks to some young high school students to be misinterpreted to mean that I accuse newspapers of deliberately misleading the public. I merely said that the news in my daily paper was so constantly discouraging (reports of strikes, of difficulties abroad, of Communistic domination in China, etc., etc., etc.) that I was beginning to avoid reading them in order to preserve my optimism. As you can see, I was speaking in a semi-jocular vein because I was suggesting to this great band of students that they do not lose faith in the power of America to solve her problems.

With specific reference to the H-bomb, I did not criticize newspapers particularly. I simply pointed out that I thought no one was doing a real service to the public if he went around threatening us all with complete extinction without warning and, as a result, producing among us a tension that would be an obstacle to clear thinking and reasonable action. As a practical matter, if we are all to be destroyed in the twinkling of an eye, what is there to do about it?[2]

Again my thanks for your interesting letter. *Sincerely*

[1] Colasanti, of Aurora, Colorado, had assured Eisenhower (letter, n.d., EM) that he agreed with the General that American newspapers had exaggerated the threats posed by the A-bomb and the H-bomb. Colasanti referred to editorials in the March 14 issue of the *Denver Post* concerning Eisenhower's remarks at the closing luncheon of the Columbia Scholastic Press Association convention on March 11, 1950. He maintained that many journalists had belittled the ideas of "one of our greatest and most respected Army Generals, Gen. Dwight D. Eisenhower."
[2] The *New York Times* (Mar. 12, 1950) had quoted Eisenhower's remark of March 11 as follows: "'No matter how strong may be that hydrogen bomb—which after all, remember, is still just an idea—it can be produced for good or evil. It is up

to us.'" On President Truman's recent authorization of hydrogen bomb production see no. 673, n. 4.

737   *Eisenhower Mss.*

TO PAUL HERBERT DAVIS[1]   *March 21, 1950*

Attached is a copy of a letter which is self-explanatory.[2]

This donation came from a man that I met only once, the occasion being a short, off-the-record speech at the University Club to some 200 outstanding businessmen. The significance of this gift is that it evidences the readiness of many people to give to worthy causes, once that cause is presented in clear and unmistakable language and promises attainment of objectives that they themselves believe important. On the particular occasion to which I refer, the speech and the subject are sufficiently outlined in the attached letter.

All this indicates to me that if we would follow up closely and urgently the opportunities created by this type of speech delivered by prominent University officials, we would vastly multiply the amount of money presently coming into the University coffers.[3]

[1] This letter was addressed to "Paul H. Davis (or his assistant)." Davis was vice-president in charge of development at Columbia University (for background see no. 361).

[2] In a letter of March 14 (CUF) George Malvin Holley, Jr., executive vice-president of Holley Carburetor Company, had praised Eisenhower's talk at the A. & H. Kroeger Organization dinner forum (held at the University Club in New York City, Mar. 7, 1950). Holley recalled Eisenhower's remark that one hundred shares of stock from each firm represented at the dinner would "fortify" the General in his work at Columbia University (a list of the people who attended the dinner is in EM, Subject File, Entertainments). Holley sent instead a check for two thousand dollars from the Holley Foundation, and he said that Eisenhower could use this to buy one hundred shares of stock or "to spend to the advantage of the University." On this same day Kevin C. McCann, Eisenhower's assistant, drafted a thank-you letter to Holley for Eisenhower's signature (CUF).

[3] For developments see no. 742.

738   *Eisenhower Mss.*

TO BEATRICE PATTON WATERS   *March 21, 1950*

Dear Bee:[1] A note from you is never an imposition upon my time— quite the contrary. I must admit, however, that because I cannot help thinking of you in terms of Camp Meade and 1919, it is something of a shock to realize that such a little girl can write and spell just like a grown-up person.[2]

Quite naturally, I will be glad to see Mrs. Tidball if she should like to come in to see me. All she would have to do would be to call my office to find out when I would have a free moment. There will be no difficulty about it at all.[3]

However, please be sure, before she comes, of her realization that the chances of my coming to Mt. Vernon to speak at a dinner are just about as close to zero as they can possibly be. The constant chore of appearing in public places and of making public talks has become more than burdensome. For some months I have been rigid in my refusal to take on any more obligations of that kind for this calendar year.

Of course, I heartily support her project and, consequently, would find a talk with her interesting and intriguing.[4] You are one of the few people who knows just how close my friendship with your Daddy was. I am delighted that this move to honor his memory is being made, in the country where he fought during two wars. I know that you will understand and be sympathetic to the reasons for my failure to come to the dinner, and I know, also, that you will not interpret this to mean any lessening of my devotion to George's memory.

With warm regard to you both, *Cordially*

[1] Mrs. Waters was the eldest daughter of the late General George S. Patton, Jr. (for background on her see Galambos, *Chief of Staff*, no. 545; on Patton see *Eisenhower Papers*, vols. I–IX).
[2] Eisenhower and Patton had begun assignments at Fort George G. Meade, Maryland, during the spring of 1919. Eisenhower had served as executive officer and later as commander of various tank battalions until January 1922; Patton had commanded the 304th Tank Brigade until September 1920 (see Eisenhower, *At Ease*, pp. 169–79).
[3] In a letter of March 9 (EM), Mrs. Waters had asked Eisenhower to grant an interview to Mrs. Charles Tidball, of Mount Vernon, New York. Mrs. Tidball wanted Eisenhower to speak at a dinner to be held in Mount Vernon to raise funds for the commissioning of a bust of Patton to be sent to Thionville, France. Eisenhower wrote at the top of Mrs. Waters's letter: "Dear Bee—Glad to see your friend—please tell her that chances of my 'speaking' are practically nil."
[4] Eisenhower's appointment calendar does not indicate a meeting with Mrs. Waters or Mrs. Tidball during 1950.

739

Eisenhower Mss.

To Lucius Du Bignon Clay

March 21, 1950

Dear Lucius:[1] I sent the telegram you requested in order to induce Mr. McCormick to help out on the European Aid job. I assume that you have already received his negative reply. It would appear that our combined influence is not as great as we might like![2]

You will recall that I talked to you, even if somewhat theoretically, about the possibility of a Columbia post for you. I thought you would be interested in knowing that the affected faculties have recommended the nomination of Professor John Dunning for the post. I assume that his appointment will be approved in due course. But in the meantime this information is very secret.[3]

I have been expecting, almost daily, news of your return to New York. There were so many possibilities open to you at the time of our last visit that I could imagine no very long delay in your accepting one of them. Do let me know, when you can, as to your final decision. The outcome here has, very definitely, disappointing features for me because of the flickering hope I had that we might again be real partners in some enterprise. However, I am largely consoled by the fact that you are quite likely to find the job of your choice to be far more interesting than you would have anything that we could have arranged.[4]

Love to Marjorie[5] and the very warmest regard to yourself, *Cordially*

[1] General Clay had retired from the Army on May 31, 1949, and had served briefly as president of Ecusta Paper Corporation in Pisgah Forest, North Carolina (for background see no. 490).

[2] Clay was national chairman of the Crusade for Freedom, a project sponsored by the National Committee for a Free Europe. He had asked Eisenhower to send a telegram to Fowler McCormick, chairman of the board of International Harvester Company, encouraging him to become vice-chairman of the committee that would organize the crusade. McCormick (B.A. Princeton 1921) had been a member of an ordnance advisory committee during World War II and had also served on the War Department Manpower Board. On March 15, 1950 (EM) Eisenhower had sent McCormick a telegram supporting Clay's request, but in a cable of the following day (EM) McCormick had declined the post.
The Crusade for Freedom would begin on September 4, 1950, and would continue for six weeks. If would include a fund-raising drive to benefit the radio broadcasting program of the National Committee for a Free Europe (for background on the committee's work see no. 428). Eisenhower would launch the crusade with a nationwide radio speech that would be broadcast from Denver, Colorado, on September 4, 1950 (see no. 962).

[3] Eisenhower had suggested to Clay (letter, Nov. 9, 1949, EM) that they discuss "the possibility of your becoming a college professor or dean or president," and Clay had then attended the Hamilton Day dinner at Columbia University on February 16, 1950. In his reply (Mar. 23, EM) to this letter from Eisenhower, however, Clay would say: "I thought that on my recent visit with you we had definitely written off the Columbia prospect and I have not given it further thought since then." Clay would claim that he was not "suited to academic life." The position involved in this correspondence was the deanship of the School of Engineering (on the appointment see "Second Revised List, Suggestions for the Deanship—School of Engineering," n.d., EM, Columbia University Corr.; nos. 688 and 783; and *New York Times*, June 14, 1950).

[4] For developments see no. 783.

[5] Clay's wife.

To Frederick Coykendall

Dear Mr. Chairman:[1] I suggest that Mr. Paley would be a fine addition to the Development Committee.[2] I suppose there are certain routine regulations to be observed in assigning him, but I just pass along to you the thought. *Sincerely*

[1] Coykendall was president of the Cornell Steamboat Company and chairman of the board of trustees of Columbia University. A longhand draft of this note is in EM, Letters and Drafts.
[2] William S. Paley was chairman of the board of directors of the Columbia Broadcasting System (for background see *Eisenhower Papers*, vols. VII–IX). Columbia University would announce Paley's election to life membership on the board of trustees on March 23, 1950 (*New York Times*, Mar. 24, 1950. For background see nos. 717 and 718). There is no indication in EM that Paley would become a member of this particular committee (on the committee see no. 488).

Diary

I give up on the typewriter. I've turned over my new electric machine to one of the secretaries. Am too awkward—and too old to learn.[1]

Last week Mamie and I spent five days, with George & Mary Allen, at the Sea view Club at Atlantic City. I'm convinced that the only way I can maintain a reasonable average of activity is to go away from this city at least as often as once every 2 months.[2]

Monday I had Harvey Mudd, Mr. Krumb, Mr. Lovejoy & John Dunning for lunch to see the idea of an Engineering Center.[3]

That evening I spent (5–10) at the Council on Foreign Relations, following an hour's meeting of the Board of the Metropolitan Museum.

Tuesday I went out to Newark, to address an alumni meeting.[4] Today I spent the morning in the College—lunch at Faculty Club— at 4:30 I go to a meeting of the Committee to support Medical Education,[5] tonight to some d—— dinner. I believe the name is Sibleys.[6] A few nights ago I went to a dinner for the Garretts (Ambassador to Ireland) given by Mrs. Garrett's sister.

Duke & Duchess of Windsor also guests. We were out very late.[7]

Tomorrow night I lecture (1 hr) on Peace. The donor of the money to support a yearly lecture on the subject insists that I deliver the first one!![8]

[1] Eisenhower had begun typing some of his diary entries in January 1950 (see no. 638).

[2] On the vacation see no. 686.

[3] Harvey S. Mudd was president and managing director of the Cyprus Mines Corporation (for background see no. 216). Henry Krumb (E.M. Columbia 1898) was a consulting mining engineer; he had been a trustee of Columbia University from 1941 to 1947. John Meston Lovejoy (E.M. Columbia 1911) was president of Seaboard Oil Company. John R. Dunning, a professor of physics at Columbia, would become Director of Scientific Research and dean of the School of Engineering during the summer of 1950 (for background see no. 688). Walter Hull Aldridge (E.M. Columbia 1887), president of Texas Gulf Sulphur Company, had also been present at the luncheon on March 20. Plans for building an engineering center at an off-campus site had been under study for several years prior to the start of Eisenhower's tenure at Columbia (for background see no. 242; and Finch, *A History of the School of Engineering*, pp. 121—22. For developments see no. 1122).

[4] See the next document.

[5] This was a meeting of the National Fund for Medical Education. For Eisenhower's recollection of the discussions there see no. 793.

[6] George H. Sibley (LL.B. Harvard 1923) was vice-president, general attorney, and director of E. R. Squibb & Sons Inter-American Corporation. He was also a trustee of American University and a former vice-chairman of the executive committee of the National Republican Committee.

[7] The host at the dinner on March 11 had been Robert Livingston Clarkson, chairman of the board and a member of the executive committee of the American Express Company. His wife, the former Cora G. Shields, was the sister of Mrs. George A. Garrett (the former Ethel Shields Darlington). The Senate had confirmed the appointment of George Angus Garrett to be Ambassador to Ireland on March 16, 1950. He had been Minister to Ireland since April 10, 1947, while the U.S. Mission there had held legation status. Previously he had been a resident partner in the firm of Merrill, Lynch, Pierce, Fenner & Beane, investment bankers. The Duke of Windsor was the former King Edward VIII of Great Britain, and the Duchess of Windsor was the former Wallis Warfield Simpson.

[8] Eisenhower would deliver the first of an annual series of lectures called the Gabriel Silver Lecture on Peace. Leo Silver, a retired industrialist, had established an endowment and named the lecture series in memory of his father (transcripts of the speech are in EM, Letters and Drafts; EM, Subject File, Speeches; *New York Times*, Mar. 24, 1950; and *Vital Speeches of the Day* 17, no. 13 [1950], 386—91).

742   *Columbia University Files*

To Paul Herbert Davis   *March 22, 1950*

With further reference to the check sent to you yesterday from Mr. Holley in the amount of $2,000, you will note that Mr. Holley's letter specifies that the money is to be spent as I direct.[1] At a meeting yesterday of the Buildings and Grounds Committee, I was so struck by the desperate need for money that I told Mr. Campbell I would be quite ready to put the $2,000 where he might direct.[2] However, since thinking this over, it occurs to me that this is sort of a futile gesture since whatever money is spent on B. & G. must come out of our total assets.

Therefore, since I want to report to Mr. Holley exactly what his money was spent for, I should like to think of something that would enlist his continuing interest in our University. So, as I have already passed my word to Mr. Campbell and would have to go through with the arrangement if he insisted, I am quite sure that he will see the wisdom of the proposal I am now making; I shall send him a copy of this memorandum. Consequently, will you undertake to give me specific suggestions concerning the use of the check, in line with the above ideas?[3]

Herewith a check for $100 which was handed to me last evening at a meeting of Columbia alumni in the Essex Hotel in Newark. Mr. Cox, whose name appears upon the check, and Mr. Koch informed me that this is merely the first installment on a sum that the alumni club (Essex County Club, I think) intends to provide in order to establish a scholarship. Consequently, the money should be set aside for that purpose.[4] Will you please communicate with Mr. Cox to assure him that the conditions indicated in the above paragraph will be carried out?

[1] For background see no. 737.

[2] Joseph Campbell was vice-president in charge of business affairs and treasurer of Columbia University (for background see nos. 392 and 514).

[3] There is no reply from Davis in EM. It is possible that someone else handled this matter, since Davis was at home convalescing at this time; he planned to return to work on March 27 (Davis to Eisenhower, Mar. 22, 1950, EM). Eisenhower would inform Holley in a letter of April 3, 1950 (CUF), that Columbia would use the gift for a fellowship in the Graduate School of Business. Eisenhower said that Philip Young, dean of the Graduate School of Business, would write to Holley and explain his plans for the school. The General also invited Holley to visit him and Young at his first opportunity (for background on Young see no. 54). Young would inform the staff of the Graduate School of Business (memorandum, Aug. 31, 1950, EM) that a two-thousand-dollar fellowship from the Holley Foundation would be available to a deserving student from the vicinity of Detroit, Michigan.

[4] Eisenhower had met with the directors of the Alumni Club of Essex County, New Jersey, on November 17, 1948. Davis had described the group as "one of the few truly active and effective alumni clubs of Columbia" (see Davis to Eisenhower, Nov. 17, 1948, EM, Essex County Alumni Corr.). William Henry Dickerson Cox (LL.B. Columbia 1922), a partner in the law firm of Cox & Walburg of Newark, was president of the club, and Arnold T. Koch (LL.B. Columbia 1923), a member of the law firm of Haggerty, Myles & Wormser of New York City, was a member of the club and chairman of Columbia's University Fund Committee. On this same day Eisenhower wrote to Cox (CUF) thanking him for the check and asking him to contact Davis concerning his plans for the scholarship. Cox replied (letter to Davis, Mar. 24, CUF) that his club was not yet able to provide additional funds for a scholarship. Cox hoped that the money that he had given Eisenhower on the twenty-first would constitute a portion of a scholarship for a boy from New Jersey.

Dear Mr. Osborne:[0] In recent years I have received from parents of West Point cadets a number of letters that have reflected the same possibilities of student maladjustment that I find in yours.[1] As a first observation I should tell you that in almost every case the youngster has finally found some reason for changing his conclusions and has gone on to successful graduation and a satisfying career.

I congratulate you on the letter that you wrote to your son. It wisely refrains from argument and merely makes suggestions that may possibly lead the young man to alter his views, on his own account.[2]

With respect to the curriculum, the procedures and the faculty at West Point and Annapolis, I will give you the briefest kind of summation of the conclusions reached by a Board, of which I was a member, and which was appointed by the late Secretary Forrestal and continued under Secretary Johnson, to study these subjects. The President of the Board was Dr. Stearns, head of Colorado University. Other members included Dr. Moreland of M.I.T., Dr. Baxter, head of Williams College, Dr. Middlebush, head of the University of Missouri, Dr. Stoddard, head of the University of Illinois and other distinguished educators. I was on the Board solely to represent the viewpoint of the Defense Department.[3]

Some surprising facts were developed by this inquiry. Among other things, it was found that where colleges gave to their graduating students examinations covering the entire four-year course, the West Point and Annapolis graduates led all others in the grades obtained. This in itself is not necessarily very meaningful, but alongside of this finding were others to the general effect that in the social sciences and humanities the young men at these institutions received a well-rounded course of instruction, which they seemed to absorb very well indeed.

The Committee found that in the field of character building the two schools were almost unique in their specific devotion to this particular objective, and in the success they achieved.

With respect to the quality and composition of faculties, it is true that the Committee had certain criticisms to make. It was recommended that both West Point and Annapolis seek greater opportunity for exchanging professors with civilian institutions and that the systems of both schools be somewhat modified so as to include within the faculty both civilian and military members. The Committee, by no means, completely condemns the system in vogue at either Academy; nor would it claim perfection for the practices at any of our civilian institutions. It did make a number of specific recommendations for improvement at the Academy, and in all of these, I personally agreed.[4] What I am trying to get at is that, while no reasonable person would make exaggerated claims for West Point and Annapolis, I am equally sure that any disinterested examination will show that they not only present unique advantages in training officers for the professional security forces, but their scope of teaching and instruction is remarkably comprehensive. Some of the professors at West Point and Annapolis are very favorably and widely known in their own specialties; their reputation is not purely local.

I can well understand that young men in the two Academies, particularly in their first year, find the courses rather irksome. Classes are so designed that every man must get his lesson every day and recite every day. Moreover, it is considered a duty to have the lesson well prepared. I personally believe that in the long run this kind of program is a good one for future officers but I, of course, admit that such a plan requires that care be exercised by the faculty in order to stimulate creative and independent thinking.

I do not presume, of course, to suggest anything that you should write to your son in order to help him get a little bit better understanding of the experiences through which he is now going; you know him and I don't. So, in spite of my interest in your problem, the only thing I can do is to give you one or two hints of schemes that have worked in the past.

Frankly, I go on the assumption that your youngster really would like the place once he should get through his plebe year—at least this is the experience of 99 and 9/10 per cent of the lads who go there. Consequently, during the first—and, admittedly, very tough—year, it might be well, now and then, to express a little admiration for people who have seen tough jobs through to the finish. In addition (and here I almost blush at the over-generous complimentary things you have already said to your son about me), you might occasionally include in your letters an undertone of admiration about servicemen of the past—the Farraguts, the Shermans, the Lees, the Jacksons, and so on.[5] Because West Point puts so much emphasis on physical fitness, erect carriage and general alertness, it might be wise occasionally to express some great respect for the showing of the corps of cadets in ceremonial parades, etc. In one case I know that a father helped his son a lot by the simple expedient of sending to his son pictures of the U.S.C.C.[6] clipped from newspapers. The boy suddenly got the idea that he was proud to be a member of the corps.

These few little things will possibly suggest to you one way in which I believe you can be helpful to your son. I know the depth of your concern because, quite naturally, you want him to begin his career in some profession or activity in which he will find great satisfaction—especially in the sense that he renders a real service to his country and to society. I do assure you that the young man will receive a very fine under-graduate education in West Point, if he sticks it out. Moreover, I rather feel that any boy who decides to quit during the first year of the course never fails thereafter to have a certain lingering disappointment that he did not fight the matter out. A resignation *after* the first year is over and the going is easy is a vastly different thing.[7]

I am sorry to be of so little help to you but I can think of nothing else to offer. *Sincerely*

[1] Osbor*n*, of Detroit, Michigan, had a son at West Point who disliked "the circumscribed viewpoint and education of the faculty." According to the father's letter (Mar. 17, EM), the son, who had completed a year of college training before receiving an appointment to the Military Academy, was now thinking of leaving West Point.

[2] Osborn had enclosed a copy of a letter he had written (Mar. 15, EM) to his son. He had counseled the youth to read "some very sober and thought-provoking news" in the issue of *Time* magazine that he was sending. "This country of ours is in a fix, a bad one too," he had advised. "You guys at West Point are very much the men of the hour." Osborn had conceded that the faculty might be "inbred," but he had asked his son to temper his opinions of the institution with the realization that men such as Eisenhower had graduated from West Point.

[3] Eisenhower had been vice-chairman of the Service Academy Board (for background on the members of the board see no. 322).

[4] On the board's recommendations see no. 610.

[5] David Glasgow Farragut, son of Revolutionary War hero George Farragut, had won decisive victories with flotillas of Union warships in battles at New Orleans and Mobile Bay. Union General William T. Sherman (USMA 1840) had become famous for his brilliant campaigns against the South's armies and the region's productive capacity in Georgia, South Carolina, and North Carolina (for Eisenhower's views on Sherman's postwar political statements see no. 96). Confederate General Robert E. Lee was also the son of a noted Revolutionary War soldier— Henry "Light-Horse Harry" Lee. The younger Lee had led the Army of Northern Virginia during the Civil War (concerning the plans to honor Lee during the Military Academy's sesquicentennial celebration see no. 645). Thomas Jonathan "Stonewall" Jackson (USMA 1846) had acquired his nickname as a result of holding his troops "like a stone wall" against the advance of the Federal army during the first battle of Bull Run. He subsequently had become Lee's most trusted lieutenant.

[6] United States Corps of Cadets.

[7] Osborn would thank Eisenhower in a letter of April 12 (EM), noting that his son had recently decided to remain at West Point.

744   *Eisenhower Mss.*

To John Stephens Wood   *March 23, 1950*

Dear Congressman Wood:[1] Even if it had been possible for me to accept your original invitation to appear before your Committee, my testimony would, of necessity, have been couched in general terms. For this there are sound reasons. In the first place, I am not a lawyer and, consequently, am not in a position to discuss the adequacy of existing agencies of government to execute the provisions of such a law as is contemplated in H.R. 7595. In the second place I have had very little time in which to read the Bill and, consequently, cannot comment upon its specific provisions with the assurance that I might possibly gain from an exhaustive study.[2]

In these circumstances, I think that the following summarizes what I would have said if I could have found it possible to appear before the Committee:

We should make certain that there is adequate protection against Communist infiltration into American life and institutions. In devising laws for this purpose, it seems apparent that we might incur other dangers, against which we should also be on guard. Among these risks would be, certainly:

a) The danger of placing restrictions upon the Constitutional rights and freedoms of the individual that would weaken the very system of free government we are attempting to protect;

b) Giving to some bureau or agency of government an unwarranted combination of executive, judicial and quasi-legislative powers, thus again violating a basic concept of our federal government, even though the purpose is to preserve our system;

c) Building up another and possibly useless bureau or agency of government, where existing agencies, with some slight addition in strength, might logically and properly carry out missions laid upon them by the Congress. I think we should carefully avoid the practice of creating new bureaus or boards and of incurring all the disadvantages and evils that result therefrom.

There will, of course, always be argument as to the best method of combatting the various "isms" that from time to time threaten our institutions. Those who believe that restrictive legislation serves only to drive such forces underground also believe that these false ideas gather greater strength when they are spread clandestinely and in the dark than when preached in the open, subject to public scrutiny and exposure.

On the other hand, the spectacle of democratic government, helpless to defend itself against the false propaganda and lies of an ideology that openly proclaim its readiness to destroy by force every kind of government based upon the dignity of man, *is, of course, intolerable.*

To sum up, I should say that it is my impression, in spite of my ignorance of the existing law, that we probably need certain additional legislation to enable us effectively to combat misguided and vicious persons within our own borders. But we must be exceedingly careful, even to the extent of leaning over backward, to avoid the enactment of legislation which, by its character, would in itself tend to place unwarranted restrictions upon our guaranteed freedoms or which would be adding unnecessarily to the bureaucratic power of government—in effect pushing us away from real democratic government.

I have grave doubts that you will find this statement worthy of presentation to your colleagues, because of its very general character. However, it represents about all that, under the circumstances, I feel justified in saying at this time. If it has no value to you, please discard it.[3] *Sincerely*

[1] Wood, Democrat from Georgia and chairman of the House Committee on Un-American Activities (HUAC), had invited Eisenhower (letter, Mar. 2, 1950, EM) to testify on March 23, 1950 at 10:30 A.M. about proposed legislation to combat subversive activities. Kevin C. McCann, the General's assistant, had drafted a reply of March 6 (EM) for Eisenhower's signature. The General could not leave New York on the twenty-third, the letter said, but he would provide a written statement on the legislation that was being considered. Wood responded (Mar. 13, EM) with an invitation to testify on March 21, 22, or 24. "If you find this also to be impossible," he wrote, "the Committee will feel honored to receive from you a statement of your views. . . ." Eisenhower made numerous changes in two early drafts of the letter above (see the versions in EM, Letters and Drafts).
[2] Supporters of H.R. 7595 hoped to force Communist organizations to register with the Attorney General. Provisions of the bill explained that "a clear and present danger to the security of the United States" required registration of every Communist political organization and every Communist-front organization. Members of such groups were to be excluded from employment in the federal government and denied passports for travel to foreign countries. The drafters of the bill also envisioned a "Subversive Activities Control Board," which was to conduct public hearings to determine whether or not the members of certain organizations could be classified as Communists. After numerous amendments, H.R. 7595 would become law as the first part of Title I of the Subversive Activities Control Act of 1950, a bill which Congress would pass over President Truman's veto on September 23, 1950 (cf. U.S., Congress, House, Committee on Un-American Activities, *Hearings on Legislation to Outlaw Certain Un-American and Subversive Activities*, 81st Cong., 2d sess., 1950, pp. 2111−22; and U.S., *Statutes at Large*, vol. 64, pt. 1, pp. 987−1003. On the origins of the law see William R. Tanner and Robert Griffith,"Legislative Politics and 'McCarthyism': The Internal Security Act of 1950," in *The Specter: Original Essays on the Cold War and the Origins of McCarthyism*, ed. Robert Griffith and Athan Theoharis [New York, 1974], pp. 174−89).
[3] There is no reply from Wood in EM. HUAC would not publish Eisenhower's letter in House Committee on Un-American Activities, *Hearings on Legislation to Outlaw Certain Un-American and Subversive Activities*, 1950.

745   *Eisenhower Mss.*

To Francis Wilfred De Guingand   *March 23, 1950*

Dear Freddie: It was nice to have your note and, of course, I am highly flattered by the high regard in which you seem to hold the talk I made last September 3 at St. Louis.[1] Incidentally, I am trapped into making another long speech this evening, this time on "peace." The circumstances are that a very wealthy man has left a certain amount of money to our University with which to sponsor a yearly lecture on this subject. But one condition was that I should deliver the first lecture. Peace happens to be one of those subjects that is easy enough to talk about— for hours—but it is certainly difficult *to do* anything about. Consequently, a talk becomes more of a sermon and exhortation to spiritual greatness than a blueprint for practical action. This characteristic in the speech is, for the soldier, nothing less than a tragedy—however, I think I shall get through the ordeal.[2]

Just now I am toying with the idea of going back to the United Kingdom for a visit in the first part of 1951. I have two invitations, the first of which is to come to London in January for the ceremony of depositing the Roll of Honor in its proper place in St. Paul's Cathedral; the second one involves a visit to Glasgow University in June. I am quite sure that, if my prospective hosts of the January affair can possibly shift it to June so that I could fulfill both engagements in one trip, I shall most certainly go.[3]

As you know, I am especially anxious to make a trip down into your part of Africa but I seem to be completely balked in my efforts to come there. I do not want to make such a trip without Mamie and, since she will not consider making such a long trip by air, there seems to be no solution because I simply cannot spare the time to come by ship.

Our wartime Boss really put on a terrific campaign in February. Strangely enough, I like him so well that I am rather glad that he did not go in as a result of a nip and tuck election. Could he have gone in with a solid 50 votes majority, then I should have been highly delighted.[4]

Occasionally, I hear from our good friends in the United Kingdom. My latest letter was from Jimmy Gault who had just been spending a week with Pug Ismay. Jimmy, who has been very sick, is definitely improving but is not yet well. Pug seemed to be in fine shape.[5]

Mamie and I send to you and yours our very fondest regards. *As ever*

P.S. I heard a rumor last evening to the effect that Bedell Smith is very sick. This, I have not had a chance to verify, although my informant said that Beetle had an operation for an active stomach ulcer. If I find out anything definite about the matter, I shall send you a message.

Bedell just called me on phone, Had an operation is improving rapidly[6]

---

[1] De Guingand, who had been Field Marshal Montgomery's Chief of Staff during World War II, was chairman of the board of Tube Investments South Africa, Ltd., in Johannesburg (for background see *Eisenhower Papers*, vols. I–IX). In

his letter of March 17, 1950 (EM), De Guingand had mentioned that he had read a transcript of Eisenhower's address delivered before the convention of the American Bar Association in St. Louis, Missouri, on September 5, 1949. "I was terribly impressed," he said, "with what you had to say and I do not think I have ever seen the democratic issues of the present day more clearly or vividly expressed" (on the speech see no. 532). De Guingand also expressed his hope that Eisenhower would accept a nomination to become a candidate for the presidency of the United States in the next election.

[2] See nos. 741 and 908.

[3] Eisenhower would dedicate the American Roll of Honour at St. Paul's Cathedral in London on July 4, 1951. The roll of honor listed the names of the U.S. citizens who had died during World War II while based in the United Kingdom (for background see Chandler and Galambos, *Occupation, 1945*, no. 404; and Galambos, *Chief of Staff*, nos. 1069 and 1127). Eisenhower would not be able to visit the University of Glasgow in 1951 (see no. 706).

[4] The Conservative party and its supporters, led by Winston S. Churchill, prime minister of Great Britain during World War II, had secured 297 seats in the House of Commons in the general election in February 1950. The Conservatives had held the Labour party to 315 seats, and it appeared that Labour's thin majority would necessitate another general election before the end of the year (*London Times*, Feb. 25 and Mar. 2, 1950). Churchill had returned as Leader of the Opposition in the House of Commons when the new Parliament had assembled on March 1, 1950. On his longstanding friendship with Eisenhower see *Eisenhower Papers*, vols. I–IX.

[5] James F. Gault had served as Eisenhower's military assistant from 1943 to 1945 (see *ibid.*). On Gault's illness see no. 266; in a letter of March 6 (EM) Gault had informed Eisenhower that although he was "getting fitter every month," he was still not strong enough to travel to the United States. Lord Hastings L. "Pug" Ismay was currently honorary and advisory chairman of the Council for the Festival of Britain, to be held in 1951 (for background see no. 259).

[6] General Walter Bedell "Beetle" Smith, commanding general of the First Army, had undergone surgery at Fort Jay Hospital, Governors Island, New York (*New York Times*, Mar. 28, 1950). Eisenhower would visit Smith during the afternoon of March 24. Later that month Smith would enter Walter Reed Army Medical Center in Washington, D.C., to continue his convalescence (*New York Times*, Apr. 1, 1950).

746   *Eisenhower Mss.*

TO WILLIAM AVERELL HARRIMAN   *March 25, 1950*

Dear Averell:[1] I am delighted to hear that you can attend the group meeting on Monday, April 24, at the Council on Foreign Relations, the evening after your visit at my home here on the campus.[2]

For the Monday discussion I doubt that you will need any "material" since we are primarily concerned with public reaction in each of the European countries to our European aid program. Of course, it would be nice if there is available any particular documentation for the views you will express, but I am quite sure you are the real expert on this matter. On the other hand, if you should be accompanied by an assistant or staff member who is a specialist on the subject, and you can bring him with you, I know the group would be delighted to have him too.

I should add that I am looking forward with keen anticipation to a long chat with you at the house, Sunday afternoon, April 23. *Cordially*

[1] Harriman was President Truman's special representative in Europe for the Economic Cooperation Administration (for background see *Eisenhower Papers*, vols. I–IX). Eisenhower had invited Harriman to meet with the Aid to Europe Group of the Council on Foreign Relations on April 24, 1950 (on this group see no. 269). Eisenhower, who was head of the group, wanted Harriman to lead a discussion on "psychological reactions in European countries to American Aid." Kevin C. McCann drafted this letter for General Eisenhower.

[2] On the planned visit to 60 Morningside Drive on April 23, 1950, see no. 771. In a telegram of March 24 (EM) Harriman had indicated that he would be present at the meeting on Monday, April 24. He had asked what "material" he should bring.

747   *Eisenhower Mss.*

TO FRANCIS JOSEPH TOOHEY   *March 27, 1950*

Dear Toohey:[1] I am just as concerned as you are with the nefarious plottings of the Communists. Certainly, I would not for one moment tolerate about me or defend a man who might be in any way tainted by active support or sympathy for Communists' designs.

In the case of Philip Jessup, I have known him personally quite a while now.[2] Moreover here at the University are men in whose judgment I have complete faith; they—who have known him a great many years—are unanimous in their praise of him as outstanding in his loyalty to American principles and in his readiness to sacrifice personal interest in the country's service. Under the circumstances, I had absolutely no alternative—when he was publicly attacked—but to voice my personal views. As his superior officer here at Columbia, silence on my part very probably would have been considered against Phil Jessup by those attacking him. I am enclosing with this letter a copy of a public letter written by my great friend Henry L. Stimson, who is, to my mind, one of the greatest Americans alive. He expresses my views on this general subject very accurately.[3]

Nevertheless, I am glad that you decided to write me about the matter boldly and bluntly. And, any time you think I have made a mistake, I hope you will point it out to me. *Sincerely*

[1] Toohey (USMA 1913) currently lived in Grand Rapids, Michigan. He had retired from the Army in 1933 and had owned a business in California until 1946.

In his letter of March 21 (EM) he had expressed chagrin at reading about Eisenhower's recent letter to Ambassador at Large Philip C. Jessup (no. 733). Toohey asked Eisenhower not to defend Jessup and not to interfere with the Senate's investigation of charges of disloyalty among personnel in the State Department. Toohey wrote, "I have been talking you up politically as THE ONE who would clean out such RATS—as the next President. . . ." Kevin C. McCann drafted this reply for Eisenhower.

[2] On Jessup see no. 515.

[3] Henry Lewis Stimson (A.M. Harvard 1889) was retired and living in Huntington, New York; he had served as Secretary of State from 1929 to 1933 and Secretary of War from 1940 to 1945. On his friendship with Eisenhower see *Eisenhower Papers*, vols. I–IX. The *New York Times* had published (Mar. 27, 1950) an open letter from Stimson inveighing against the Senate's conduct of its investigation of State Department employees. In the executive branch of the government, Stimson maintained, there were established procedures by which such sensitive problems could be resolved "by men of both parties and unimpeachable integrity." The Senate's public inquiry could only harm the reputations of innocent people and disrupt the foreign affairs of the nation. Stimson concluded, "This is no time to let the noisy antics of a few upset the steady purpose of our country or distract our leaders from their proper tasks."

748   *Eisenhower Mss.*

To Orlando Ward   *March 28, 1950*
Personal

Dear Pink:[1] I have read over the particular section of the document you sent me entitled "Origins and Background of the Stilwell Mission to China."[2] I am replying without the benefit of any notes; while I did keep a few memoranda of those days, these are stored away somewhere and are not now easily accessible.[3]

My first impression is that, either too much is being made of the fact that General Drum and General Marshall did not see eye to eye about the purposes of the project of sending the former to China, or too little effort has been made to develop the background—the situations and conditions that were the soil in which General Marshall's ideas sprouted and grew.

The account talks blithely of sending American troops, arms and equipment, etc., etc., and of proper strategic objectives. The truth is that, at the moment, there was not a uniformed man in sight who was available for assignment; arms and equipment were so short that General Marshall was practically desperate. About all, except deficits, that he had to distribute was morale—possibly it would be better to say, hope.

By various ways and means, he attempted to inspire officers, troops and civilians to unusual effort and to hang on pending the time that America's strength could gradually begin to make itself felt. For example, you will find that in the very early stages of the war, he, on his own initiative, took a number of specific actions with respect to the Philippine affair that were calculated to keep up the spirits of the American garrison and of the Filipinos themselves. Part of his idea—at least as he expressed it to me—in sending *a very high ranking officer to China was to provide a symbol of American intent.* He felt that high rank in this individual was important, and so far as I know, he favored General Drum solely because of the esteem in which he held the latter.

I do not mean to say that there is untruth in the account as written. But I believe that it shows lack of real feeling and understanding of the situation then existing, and ignores the staggering problems that faced General Marshall.

As for myself, I was a newly arrived Staff Officer, engaged in trying to take as much of the burden off General Marshall as I possibly could. I do not question in any way the motives that led General Drum to the conclusions that he reached; I do not say that those conclusions were wrong; I merely contend that attempts—involving incidents of eight years ago—to place argument against argument and then to interpret those arguments into terms of motives and reasons of affected individuals are to my mind largely abortive.

In this particular instance, I am reinforced in my view when I read on a few pages and find General Stilwell praised in glowing terms, apparently with the purpose of comparing either Marshall or Drum unfavorably to him. I do not see that it is a function of an *official* military history to pass judgments upon the qualifications of people. It seems to me that the concern should be with incident, with fact, with plans and with results. Of course, the record of argument is fact and it should be included. But I see no point in trying to translate these into indices of qualifications and character.

It happens that, in this particular instance, all three of the individuals under discussion are old friends of mine. I have liked and admired them for years. I thought that General Drum was one of the ablest men I had known and I still regret that he did not go to China because *I believe that he would have accomplished more than any other man then in the Army could.* Nevertheless, I repeat that I do not, in any slightest way, quarrel with his own reasoning and his own decision.

But, as well as I think I knew those men, I would certainly not attempt to translate my knowledge of them then or later into a complete evaluation of capability and personality. I have, in the past, publicly recorded my admiration for certain methods that General Marshall used in the war and for certain qualities he displayed, but I would not consider it appropriate to go farther than that.[4] I cannot possibly see how we are going to write objective and dispassionate history if we constantly mix it up with personal opinions of character, to say nothing of personal friendships and prejudices.

I know that you will have the reaction that there is nothing very helpful in this letter. I can only say that so far as alleged facts are set down in the document, I do not recognize any as a misstatement. But, for your eyes, I thought I would present my feeling about this personality business entering too strongly into the attempt to write objective history. That, I think, belongs to the field of personal biography—which so often degenerates into nothing more than a historical novel.[5] *Sincerely*

[1] For background on Major General Ward, Chief of the Historical Division, Department of the Army, see no. 373.

[2] Ward had enclosed with a letter of March 23 (EM, Historical Division Corr.) a draft of the first chapter of a history of the China-Burma-India theater of World War II. Ward wanted Eisenhower's comments on the manuscript and especially on the section concerning the appointment of a general to visit China in early 1942. Lieutenant General Hugh A. Drum had been the first choice for this assignment, but Secretary of War Henry Stimson and General George C. Marshall, Chief of Staff of the Army, had decided after several meetings with Drum that the general's dissatisfaction with the limited scope of the mission would make him unfit for the job. Stimson and Marshall had then selected Major General Joseph W. Stilwell to go to China. For a complete account see Pogue, *Marshall*, vol. II, *Ordeal and Hope*, pp. 355–61. For background on Drum see no. 787; on Stimson see the preceding document; on Marshall see no. 75; and on Stilwell's appointment see Chandler, *War Years*, no. 102, and Herbert Feis, *The China Tangle: The American Effort in China from Pearl Harbor to the Marshall Mission* (Princeton, 1953), pp. 14–17. An earlier version of Eisenhower's letter, in EM, Letters and Drafts, includes the General's numerous changes.

[3] These memoranda include nos. 34, 39, 43, 44, and 60 in Chandler, *War Years*.

[4] See, for example, Eisenhower, *Crusade in Europe*, pp. 16, 34, 40, and 209.

[5] Ward would admit in his reply (Apr. 3, EM) that he had not read the manuscript before sending it to Eisenhower. He now agreed, however, that the authors of the piece had devoted too much space to allocating blame, and he said that he thought Eisenhower's letter would remedy the problem. "I am particularly glad to get your letter at this time," he said, "as there have been other instances of like writing and I can use your advice to great advantage as the writers have great respect for your views."

749 *Eisenhower Mss.*

To Carl H. Nelson *March 28, 1950*
Personal

Dear Mr. Nelson:[1] Quite naturally, I found your letter intensely interesting.

I would be the first to concede that you would know General Lee more intimately than did I. Except for the war years, my contacts with him have been of a sketchy nature, involving nothing more than a few personal conversations. I have known him for years by reputation—

and he was always known as one who "got things done." In any event, I note that much of what you have to say confirms the estimate I expressed in my book about him. Possibly, however, I did not sufficiently detail some of the Cromwellian traits, that I thought I saw in him, to present a truly clear picture.

Certain of his qualities were valuable, especially his driving force and almost arbitrary methods in executing his duty. In any event, you will note that, except for one or two individuals, I did not pretend in the book to describe people at any great length. Usually, I merely hinted at their general character and qualifications for the very simple reason that limited space would not permit me to do more.[2]

I assure you that I appreciate not only the over-generous sentiments that you expressed with respect to my book but, likewise, I am grateful for the trouble you took to write me. *Sincerely*

[1] Nelson, of Whittier, California, had been chief stenographer in the office of Lieutenant General John C. H. Lee during World War II. In an undated letter (EM), Nelson had expressed partial agreement with Eisenhower's favorable description of Lee in *Crusade in Europe*, pp. 235–36. Nelson had argued, however, that Lee's concern with the niceties of military form had occasionally left his subordinates no choice but to cater to his whims even though more pressing problems of the war required attention.

[2] In February 1945 Eisenhower had evaluated Lee's performance and had placed his name nineteenth on a list of general officers most important to ETOUSA (see Chandler, *War Years*, no. 2271). Lee had retired from the Army in 1947 and was currently vice-president of the Brotherhood of St. Andrew in the United States.

750   *Eisenhower Mss.*

To Frank Copeland Page   *March 28, 1950*

Dear Frank:[1] I am grateful for your letter, even though it had such flattering references to myself that I felt like blushing.

Someone told me that my speech of the other evening is to be printed; I believe that the Carnegie Foundation intends a great many thousands for distribution.[2] In any event, when it has been printed, I shall see that you are sent a couple dozen copies.

I was quite interested in your thought about concentrating on a religious approach to the job of increasing or restoring our respect for integrity, morality and high principle in public life.[3] I have frequently mentioned this need in speeches but your letter leads me to believe that I have not emphasized it as much as I should have. I shall look for a good opportunity to try it.

Not long ago, I had a chance to say hello to Arthur,[4] but your note reminded me that it had been far, far too long since I had seen you. I hope that all goes well with you, and this note brings you my very best wishes and regards. *Cordially*

[1] Page was a vice-president of the International Telephone and Telegraph Corporation. In a letter of March 24 (EM) he had congratulated Eisenhower on his Gabriel Silver Lecture on Peace (March 23; on the speech see nos. 745 and 908). Page believed that the speech should be printed and widely circulated, especially at Columbia University Teachers College. He wanted one or two dozen copies himself when they became available.

[2] Eisenhower was probably referring to the Carnegie Foundation for the Advancement of Teaching.

[3] Page had recalled that he had asked President Truman three years earlier to call together the most prominent religious leaders in America to initiate "a definite move toward a religious renaissance." Nothing had been accomplished in this regard, however, and Page asked Eisenhower to stress "public integrity, principles, and high public morality" at the first appropriate opportunity.

[4] Arthur W. Page, brother of Frank C. Page, was a business consultant in New York City (for background see no. 452).

751   *Eisenhower Mss.*

To William Fletcher Russell   *March 28, 1950*

Dear Will:[1] Herewith an extract from a letter from Frank Page.[2] I do not send this to you to impress you with my oratorical ability—rather to see that you have the benefit of a recommendation from a man whom I consider outstanding.

"I have just finished reading the best speech that I have read in a long time and I want to congratulate you on it.

"I have two suggestions: One, that it should be called to the attention of the British Ambassador or the British Information Service and have them give it wide distribution in England. The other, that it should be put in a pamphlet and made an obligatory part of the course at Teachers College. Unfortunately, our teachers don't study and read such material. I hope it is published in a pamphlet and if it is, I would like to get a dozen or two copies."[3] *Sincerely*

[1] For background on Russell, president of Teachers College, see no. 67.

[2] Eisenhower's reply to Page is the previous document.

[3] In his reply (Mar. 30, EM) Russell thanked Eisenhower for the extract. Russell said he had tried unsuccessfully to obtain copies of the speech and that when they were available he would distribute three hundred at Teachers College.

To Herbert Allen Black

Dear Dr. Black:[1] It was fine to have such a long and interesting letter from you. I think Mrs. Doud must have given you a somewhat false impression concerning my health. The fact is that I feel very well indeed. But experience here has shown that the only possibility of keeping up a normal pace is to take my recreation in small bunches. Every day that I am in New York City is a crowded one. For example, just a few minutes ago I was desperately trying to find on my calendar tomorrow, enough time to run out and see a friend of mine who is extremely sick.[2] The only way I could do it is to cancel one engagement which has already been on my books for several weeks. As a result of this kind of thing, Mamie and I now run off for a few days at a time. The last one of these occurred only recently, and Mrs. Doud must have thought I was sick. To the contrary, I never felt better—but no man could take the day-by-day punishment here without making some arrangements for relieving the monotony and the pressure.

I am, of course, highly complimented that Mr. Karston should want me to address District 200 of Rotary International.[3] But I already have had to decline numerous invitations for the months of May and June, some of them involving meetings before national organizations. I find myself constantly involved in a need to make speeches, and there is nothing that constitutes such a drain upon my energy, my nervous system and my disposition as a stream of public appearances, especially when newspapers seem always to be searching for some isolated phrase or sentence that can be made to sound startling or terrifying.[4] The result is that I try to keep public appearances to the very minimum. But, even so, I feel that I make too many.[5] Of course, I should like to come to that region and, of course, I should like to meet exactly the kind of people that make up the Rotary International, but I am certainly not going to be able to indulge such desires until the time comes when other pressures on me are somewhat relieved.

So far as "fee" for speaking is concerned, I have never accepted any honorarium for any appearance in spite of the fact that, in certain instances, very handsome ones have been offered.[6] Such considerations, however, have nothing to do with my decision.

It is nice to know that you are counting on being back in Colorado this summer, and with time that you can devote to fishing. My own suggestion is that we go up to Aksel's ranch where we batch and do our own cooking—although this year I may take with me a colored man who has been with me for ten years.[7] In any event, the fishing is very easy—on a creek within 200 yards of the house. It is high and cold and isolated. We love it and I think you would. While the place belongs to Aksel, I am quite certain that he would approve of my tendering you an invitation in his name, when we go up there.[8] Such an expedition would not involve the need for meeting a whole group of other guests that might be present. Anyway, we can talk over these things when I get out there this summer. Just what date that will be, I do not yet know.

Warm personal regards and best wishes for your complete recovery, *Cordially*

[1] Black, the Douds' personal physician for many years, was recuperating from a stroke (for background see no. 671). He had written (Mar. 23, EM) from Hot Springs National Park, Arkansas, a health resort which he recommended highly to General and Mrs. Eisenhower. Elivera C. "Min" Doud had recently telephoned Black from Denver, and she had mentioned that the Eisenhowers were "away for a rest and that it was to be a regular routine each month" (for background see no. 686).

[2] The reference is probably to General Walter Bedell Smith, who had recently undergone surgery at Fort Jay Hospital, Governors Island, New York (for background see no. 745, n. 6). Eisenhower's appointment calendar does not indicate that he visited Smith on March 29, 1950.

[3] Black had asked Eisenhower to speak at a conference of District 200 of Rotary International on May 15, 1950. C. Emmett Karston, a member of the board of directors of Rotary International in Hot Springs, was chairman of the arrangements committee for the district conference.

[4] This was probably a reference to criticisms of Eisenhower's Gabriel Silver Lecture on Peace (Mar. 23, 1950). The General had contended that the United States had disarmed to the point that its safety could be threatened. Strong negative reactions to this remark were mentioned in the *New York Times*, March 24, 25, and 26, 1950. Eisenhower would appear before a subcommittee of the Senate Committee on Appropriations on March 29 to defend his statement (see the next document).

[5] Eisenhower would speak at a dinner arranged by the Columbia Alumni Clubs of Westchester County, New York, on this same day (see *New York Times*, Mar. 29, 1950).

[6] Black had said that the club would pay for Eisenhower's expenses and for "whatever fee you may charge for the address."

[7] Eisenhower's reference was to Master Sergeant John A. Moaney, a member of Eisenhower's household staff since 1942 (for background see *Eisenhower Papers*, vols. I–IX).

[8] Aksel Nielsen, president of the Title Guaranty Company in Denver, Colorado, owned a ranch near Cheesman Lake, in central Colorado. Eisenhower's appointment calendar indicates that he and Nielsen would go fishing in Colorado in August 1950 and that Eisenhower would visit Black in Pueblo, Colorado, on September 17, 1950.

To the Military Sub-Committee of the   [*March 28, 1950*]
Appropriations Committee of the Senate[1]
Memorandum for the record

Because I have been invited before this body to amplify an allusion regarding our national security position that I made in an address on the evening of March 23rd at Columbia University, I present first a brief background of pertinent circumstances.

The entire speech, of an hour's duration, dwelt on the general subject of "international peace." In the development of this subject I argued that the nations of the world would necessarily include universal disarmament as an inescapable step in reaching effective peace agreements. Because of the insistence of my argument on this point I thought it wise to caution against precipitous or unilateral action on the part of the United States, and argued that our country had already disarmed to the limit of safety, until all other countries, in coordination, are prepared to go along with us in implementation of this purpose.

Giving this caution I indicated that, because of my constant and deep concern for the safety of this country, I could not advise anything more in current reduction, and observed that in certain details we had probably gone below the line of reasonable safety.[2]

In this connection it must be understood that I have always, in repeated public statements concerning our nation's security, argued against hysteria, war mongering, jingoism, or any tendency to exaggerate the strength of others or to belittle our own. Moreover I have urgently recommended against padding of Military Budgets and only recently advised Mr. Mahon's sub-committee in the House, that I believe that a general level of something toward 14 billions of dollars for military purposes represented a fair compromise between considerations of security and economy.[3] I believe that this nation, when truly *united*, possesses an overbalance of actual and potential power vis-à-vis any other country.

Moreover, we must not forget that because war has become all-inclusive in its nature, any adequate preparation against it should properly involve many facets of our national complex. Clearly, there is an economic and industrial side to this great problem as well as moral and intellectual ones. There are problems of research, both in the physical and social sciences. There is the tremendously important problem of intelligence, because it is on our calculations of risk that we make our estimates for security.

If we should deem war imminent, then there would be no expense too great and no preparation too elaborate to meet what we would see as an impending crisis. I am not talking in the terms of crisis; rather, I think that we should strive to answer this question on the basis of a period of indeterminate length. Since the purpose is to defend a way of life at the heart of which is the guaranteed freedom of the individual, we must not so over-burden or tax the resources of the country that we practically enslave or regiment people in the very effort to keep them free from foreign aggression. To wreck our economy would be as great a victory for the Soviets as they could remotely hope for in a war. Only a highly competent and comprehensive intelligence service—in itself something that involves no small item of cost—can keep us, on the one hand, from any unnecessary waste of our resources and, on the other, from incurring risks that are intolerable to a free nation. In our intelligence activities, we not only need the finest brains available, we also need adequate financial support.

It is necessary also to mention another point connected with official activities carried on last year with civilian and military parts of our Federal Government. I should make clear that I am not consciously quarrelling with the views of anyone else.[4] So far as I know my views are not greatly different, except on a few details, to those still entertained by responsible officials, including my old associates on the Joint Chiefs of Staff and the Secretary and Deputy-Secretary of Defense.[5]

In the fall of 1948 I was called to Washington by the late Secretary of Defense, Mr. Forrestal, and asked to assist the Joint Chiefs of Staff in the development of plans and, on such plans, to help determine the size of forces that should be maintained in time of peace. As a further requirement we were asked to make estimates of the cost of such forces. This request from the Secretary of Defense was reinforced by a similar one from the President, and I instantly agreed to attempt the performance of this duty.[6]

This arrangement was prior to the recent revision of the defense law and I agreed to serve until some way could be found to regularize an appointment for some officer still professionally engaged in security activities. As soon as General Bradley could be appointed to that post I ceased functioning, and so everything I say today is based upon a memory of events of some time past.[7]

The first Joint Meeting on this subject that I attended was in the office of the President, where the Chiefs of Staff presented their estimate of what they believed to be required for the *1950 defense budget*.[8] I did not comment in any way upon the presentation but after studying the problem for some time in New York, returned to Washington for a conference with the President. My purpose was to determine his estimate of the amount of money that *could* and *should* be devoted to the purposes of national defense for the *fiscal year '51*. I considered very wise his rough and tentative decision that the amount would be of the order that had been appropriated the previous year. The target was to be not over

15 billion dollars, which would *include* the amounts set up for stock piling and for meeting any increased pay and allowances of the Services. I presented this information to the Joint Chiefs of Staff in January 1949 at my first formal meeting with them on the 1951 budget.[9] The budget for 1950 had not yet been passed by Congress. For the next six months, with time out for a sickness of mine, we worked incessantly on the problem.

Working to this rough level, which I believed should not, under conditions then existing be exceeded because of the need for economy, the Chiefs of Staff attempted to reach agreement on how the amount— about 14 billion, plus dollars, for military purposes exclusive of stock piling—would be divided. Naturally the agreements were not 100 percent perfect, for the very simple reason that the aggregate amount was not equal to the amounts sought by the Services. However, we pushed ahead and by the middle of June I was prepared to recommend the general division of money along lines that, while not completely and exactly conforming either to my personal views or to the consolidated views of the Chiefs of Staff, did conform to their ideas as well as I could devise.

About this time the new Secretary of Defense stated that he had orders to prepare another budget from which a substantial sum would be lopped off—roughly, as I remember, about one billion dollars.[10]

The Chiefs again went through the same process of allocation, although, of course, it now became more difficult to achieve any unanimity of opinion. In the final version of their reduced budget— because there was no way of telling where the greatest difficulty would arise in the required elimination of force—I recommended to the Secretary that he hold in reserve some 200–300 million out of the entire sum, to apply to those shortages in any service that would later appear to him as the most critical.

I informed the Secretary that I *believed* that this entire reserve would probably have to be devoted to Air Force procurement of airplanes— since I felt that we had probably cut that item too deeply, but that I did not have complete data on which to provide a truly factual estimate.[11]

These cuts in the original estimates were intended by the Secretary of Defense, he stated, to eliminate any water from the estimates—to reduce administrative costs through streamlining, but with the hope that combat strength would not be affected.

I earnestly supported him in all his efforts and plans for reducing administrative costs in the Services and of securing whatever economy was possible through efficiency in operations. Particularly I consider wise his efforts to trim personnel to the bone.

So you will see that while I have been in agreement with the purposes of the Secretary of Defense—and have often expressed the opinion that somewhere in the region of 14–15 billion dollars was probably the most reasonable level at which to stabilize, for the present, our security expenditures, and have, in addition, generally supported the rough allocation of funds made in the final and reduced estimates—I have never been asked to support unequivocally and in detail every deletion made, or the exact distribution of the last dollar affected. I do not even know the details of the budget as finally presented to the Congress, since I assume that changes must have been made since I last saw its bare outlines some months ago. I am not the author of this particular budget but I was instrumental in helping to make the allocations of the sums that the Chiefs of Staff and I understood to represent the available maximum.

I should add that every recommendation I ever made was, before presentation, discussed in detail with Admiral Denfeld and Generals Bradley, Vandenberg and Gruenther—the last named in his capacity as head of the Joint Staff.

Now with respect to specific items in which I think we have probably carried economy to the point where it seems to cross the line that represents a "respectable posture of defense." All of these I have, in the past, called to the attention of civilian officials responsible for our defenses.

a. The defenses of Alaska. I consider that our failure to make provision for the stationing of reasonable garrisons at the principal airfields in that area is a clear mistake.[12]

b. Some deficiencies in the projected procurement of aircraft.

In the final, reduced version of the budget on which I worked for so many weeks, it was contemplated, with my agreement, that for the present we should content ourselves with the maintenance of 48 *modern* groups in the regular service and with something like a dozen or so in the National Guard. These latter would be supported by other units flying older airplanes. (The first post-war plan of defense had contemplated 70 groups of Regular Air Force, with 27 in the National Guard. These figures, expressed in groups, are not too meaningful, because of the constant changes in the models in types of aircraft and in numbers assigned to groups.) Partially because of the inclusion of the enormous bomber plane in our Air Force, I decided to agree to the indicated reduction in numbers of groups. I am now informed that projected procurement of airplanes will not maintain the *48 Regular* and dozen National Guard units. This I regard as a dipping close to or below the line of reasonable safety.[13]

c. From informal statements made to me I understand that antisubmarine activities in the Navy are maintained at a lesser level than I became convinced, by Navy officials some months ago, was vital to our safety. While I have not discussed this point with Admiral Sherman, whose judgment I would unhesitatingly accept, I feel that it is a field in which we are at the lowest acceptable level—possibly below. A wide variety of equipment is involved, and the problem is one of great difficulty.[14]

d. In *modernization* of Army equipment we have lagged. [While I learn that a start has now been made in rectifying this, for five years almost nothing was done. I would personally feel easier if our tank, antiaircraft and vehicular programs could be somewhat more broadly supported.][15]

e. Plans for national industrial mobilization are among the most important—and *least expensive* of all preparatory measures—we can make. Here is needed a vigorous purpose and effort that I have never, in many years of service, seen applied in the full measure that I think necessary. I do not believe that a great deal of money is required—this you would have to learn from the head of the National Resources Board and the heads of the Munitions Boards and the several Supply Chiefs, but the vast and important category of things that could be accomplished by vigorous, incessant and adequately supported effort might be a decisive factor to us in any future emergency. An expert in this field is Mr. Baruch.[16]

f. A number of items in the administrative field must be carefully watched. In time of peace "logistics" is a forgotten word, but in war it looms up insistently. Sufficiency of transport (including land, air and sea transport) must be ours, as, likewise, hospital, evacuation and rehabilitation organizations. While I applaud, without reservation, every wise cut in these peacetime activities, I grow concerned that we may sometimes apply the pruning knife too enthusiastically because of their seeming unimportance in peace. But I assure you that the unimportance is only seeming.

Without even mentioning details of lesser importance, I trust that Committee Members appreciate that we have, in this eternal contest between necessary economy on the one hand and the need for security forces on the other, pushed as far in favor of the former as it seems wise to go. My qualms as to excessive cuts in specific instances, are, I think, understandable. Although I earnestly subscribe to the conviction that there is no absolute security to be obtained through maintenance of armaments, I still believe that, as of today, our greatest chance of avoiding war is reasonable readiness for it. Moreover, I believe that without military force to back up moral integrity, intellectual honesty and economic strength, our determined efforts to establish a peaceful world cannot succeed.

At least it should be clear that because of the tremendous importance of the conflicting considerations of security and economy, eternal care and study, by all concerned, are necessary if we are not to go too far in either direction.

Finally—let me say that I would not advise a radical increase in our expenditures for national security. Our purpose is, in conjunction with other free countries, to establish a sound safe position for ourselves in a world where force is still a central factor. The cautions I have voiced I deem important—but not really so important as unified purposes and intent among us at home—and the existence of firm mutual understandings with our international associates. The greatest weapon in our entire arsenal is a readiness among us to work earnestly and selflessly for a common cause—ironing out details as they arise, and without allowing them to interfere with attainment of our major objective—security.[17]

[1] Apparently this memorandum was prepared to aid Eisenhower during his appearance before the subcommittee of the Senate Committee on Appropriations in Washington, D.C., the afternoon of March 29, 1950 (an earlier draft, which includes Eisenhower's numerous changes, is in the same file as this document). The invitation to testify had come in a telegram of March 24 (EM) from Senator Elmer Thomas (A.B. DePauw University 1900), Democrat from Oklahoma and chairman of the subcommittee concerned with armed services appropriations.

Eisenhower would travel by plane from New York to Washington, D.C., the morning of the twenty-ninth and would attend conferences at the Pentagon with Deputy Secretary of Defense Stephen T. Early, Secretary of the Air Force W. Stuart Symington, and Lieutenant General Alfred M. Gruenther, Deputy Chief of Staff for Plans and Combat Operations. These meetings would be followed by lunch with Vice-President Alben W. Barkley. After Eisenhower's testimony before the appropriations subcommittee, he would meet again with Early, Symington, and Gruenther, as well as General Wade H. Haislip, Vice Chief of Staff, U.S. Army. Eisenhower would spend most of the following day with the Educational Policies Commission (on this group see no. 387). He would have lunch with Sid W. Richardson, a philanthropist and oil executive from Texas, and in the afternoon he would meet with Major General Wilton B. Persons, formerly Director of the Office of Legislative Liaison, Office of the Secretary of Defense (for background see no. 534). The evening of March 30, General and Mrs. Eisenhower would attend a Columbia University alumni dinner in Washington. On the thirty-first Eisenhower would confer with the Educational Policies Commission during its morning and afternoon sessions, and he would again have lunch with Richardson. On Saturday, April 1, the General would meet with the Educational Policies Commission in the morning and play golf at Burning Tree Country Club in the afternoon. By Sunday, April 2, Eisenhower would be back at Columbia University. Copies of the agenda and schedule of meetings of the Educational Policies Commission are in EM, Subject File, Clubs and Associations.

[2] The speech, titled "World Peace—A Balance Sheet," had included the following passage: "And here it seems appropriate, in view of my insistent belief that the world must finally disarm or suffer catastrophic consequences, to assert my conviction that America has already disarmed to the extent—in some directions even beyond the extent—that I, with deep concern for her *present* safety, could possibly advise, until we have certain knowledge that all nations, in concerted action, are doing likewise" (see no. 741; EM, Subject File, Speeches; and *New York Times*, Mar. 24, 1950).

[3] On Eisenhower's informal discussions with members of the House Subcommittee on Department of Defense Appropriations on February 24, 1950, see no. 701. Representative George H. Mahon, Democrat of Texas, was chairman of the subcommittee.

[4] Eisenhower might have been referring to President Truman's comment to news-

men on March 2, 1950, that "the national defense situation is in better shape than it has ever been in times when we were not at war" (*Public Papers of the Presidents: Truman, 1950*, p. 183; and *New York Times*, Mar. 3, 1950).

[5] Secretary of Defense Louis A. Johnson had announced during a press conference on March 27 that he did not agree with Eisenhower's statement that the nation had disarmed too much. He had pointed out that the General had been aware of cutbacks in the proposed budget for defense spending during FY51 and that he had not sent any protests to government officials (see *New York Times*, Mar. 28, 1950).

[6] Eisenhower had advised Forrestal on the preparation of the FY50 budget during the fall of 1948. For background see nos. 183, 223, and 303.

[7] Concerning the amendments to the National Security Act of 1947 see no. 327. On the appointment of General Omar N. Bradley as chairman of the JCS see no. 517.

[8] The date of this meeting was probably December 9, 1948. Regarding the discussions see no. 294.

[9] The second conference with Truman had probably occurred on January 24, 1949 (see President's Appointment Books, Harry S. Truman Library, Independence, Missouri). On the negotiations with the JCS see no. 348.

[10] Truman had decided on July 1, 1949, that spending for the armed services during FY51 should not exceed $13 billion. Gruenther had mentioned this in a confidential memorandum of March 28, 1950, prepared for Eisenhower's use during his appearance before the subcommittee of the Senate Appropriations Committee the following day (copy in EM, Subject File, Hearings).

[11] According to Gruenther's memorandum of the twenty-eighth, the setting aside of a sum to be used at the discretion of the Secretary of Defense had been considered prior to Truman's budget cut of July 1, 1949. It had been "automatically eliminated," however, by Truman's order to remain below the $13 billion ceiling. Eisenhower nevertheless had continued to press for the restoration of $200 million to the allocation for the Air Force (see no. 506).

[12] See the following document.

[13] For background see nos. 506 and 533. The defense budget as submitted by President Truman in January 1950 had called for $1.35 billion for Air Force aircraft procurement; Eisenhower had recommended that $1.4 billion be allocated for this purpose. During the congressional hearings on the FY51 budget, however, Air Force spokesmen had said that $1.55 billion was needed to provide and maintain a forty-eight-group force with modern airplanes (House Committee on Appropriations, *Department of Defense Appropriations for 1951: Hearings*, 1950, pt. 3, pp. 1315–17). The Air Force also planned to equip with modern aircraft eleven of the twenty-seven National Guard groups then in existence (see Senate Committee on Appropriations, *Department of Defense Appropriations for 1951: Hearings*, 1950, p. 823). For background on the B–36 bomber program see no. 378.

[14] Secretary of Defense Louis A. Johnson would recommend to Congress in April 1950 that the allotment for anti-submarine equipment be increased substantially (see no. 782).

[15] Eisenhower would pursue this subject at greater length in a letter of March 30 to the chairman of the Subcommittee on Department of Defense Appropriations of the House Committee on Appropriations (see no. 755).

[16] Financier Bernard M. Baruch had been chairman of the War Industries Board in World War I and an adviser to the Director of War Mobilization in World War II (for background see Chandler, *War Years*, no. 2456; and Robert D. Cuff, *The War Industries Board: Business-Government Relations during World War I* [Baltimore, 1973]). Baruch had agreed to participate in a seminar on industrial mobilization at Columbia University during the spring of 1950 (see no. 555).

[17] During a press conference on March 30, 1950, President Truman would declare that Eisenhower's testimony before the subcommittee of the Senate Appropriations Committee had been "fundamentally in complete agreement with the policies which we have pursued right along" (see *Public Papers of the Presidents: Truman, 1950*, p. 233; and *New York Times*, Mar. 31, 1950). Secretary Johnson would telephone Eisenhower on April 3 to assure him that action would be taken on his recommendations. A summary of the conversation is at the bottom of Eisenhower's appointment calendar for this day. Johnson would tell reporters the following day that there was no disagreement between the General and him (see *New York Times*, Apr. 5, 1950). For developments see no. 782. A transcript of Eisenhower's testimony of March 29, 1950, is in EM, Subject File, Hearings; and in Senate Committee on Appropriations, *Department of Defense Appropriations for 1951: Hearings*, 1950, pp. 679—704. See also *New York Times*, March 30, 1950.

754   *Eisenhower Mss., Vinson Corr.*

To Elmer Thomas   *March 30, 1950*

Dear Mr. Chairman:[01] In accordance with our agreement at the hearings before your Subcommittee on the afternoon of March 29, I submit herewith a memorandum to supplement the testimony I then presented.

As a first and important point, I must inform you that I inadvertently omitted from my testimony one item that appeared prominently upon my notes and which I failed, except for one short reference, to mention. This involves the modernization of certain types of Army equipment. While this item has been urged by professional leaders of the Army in each of the years following the close of World War II, it has always been eliminated, or practically eliminated, from annual budgets because of overriding priorities in other directions. The time has come when we cannot afford longer to delay the modernization of such types as tanks, antiaircraft artillery, recoilless weapons and various classes of vehicular equipment. While I understand that a start is being made in this year's budget in this direction, I feel I should call the attention of your Committee to the very bad situation resulting from the negligence of past years.[2]

A specific item that I promised a member of the Committee—Senator Ferguson, I think—I would mention in this memorandum is the identity of the stations that I believe should be garrisoned in Alaska.[3] I believe that as a minimum we should place garrisons on the major airfields in the Fairbanks-Anchorage area. The Service Staffs might recommend small garrisons at a few other stations, particularly in the establishing of a radar screen in Alaska, but the Fairbanks-Anchorage area is of clear importance. I reaffirm my belief that not less than a reinforced infantry battalion and antiaircraft artillery should be stationed and properly quartered at each one of our major fields.[4]

In an effort to establish priorities, among the items I mentioned as suffering the risk of malnutrition I find myself in somewhat of a dilemma, because such priorities must be calculated for so many types of potential situations. However, while clearly recognizing nothing sacrosanct in the order in which I place these, I give you the following:

   a. Garrisons in Alaska.

   b. Modernization of aircraft and Army equipment, and reinforcement of our anti-submarine facilities.[5]

   (Note: I believe that the level of airplane procurement that I have recommended for the Air Force, under existing conditions, can be accomplished for about $1,500,000,000 annually. Any additional funds provided for this purpose must not be at the expense of the other two services whose needs are not now satisfied.)[6]

   c. Intelligence.

   d. Industrial mobilization.[7]

I repeat the caution that none of these items can be treated or acted upon by itself. One peculiarity of a military establishment is that it is, in a crisis, only as strong as its weakest link. Therefore, there must be coordinated progress, and it would be erroneous to devote available resources exclusively to those items toward the top of the list, with no attention to those at the bottom. In spite of this observation, I still believe that some defense of Alaska is so important that it should be considered before the others, both in time and in importance.

If your Subcommittee should desire anything further of me, I shall, as always, be available to do it.[8] *Sincerely*

---

[1] Senator Thomas, Democrat from Oklahoma, was chairman of the subcommittee of the Senate Appropriations Committee, before which Eisenhower had testified on March 29, 1950 (for background see the preceding document).

[2] These views coincided with those expressed by Major General E. L. Ford, the Army's Chief of Ordnance, who had appeared before Thomas's subcommittee on March 28, 1950. Ford had explained that 73 percent of the money budgeted for the procurement program for FY51 would be spent on new light tanks, on the T-33 antiaircraft fire-control system, on 75-millimeter antiaircraft guns, and on new transport and tactical vehicles (Senate Committee on Appropriations, *Department of Defense Appropriations for 1951: Hearings*, 1950, p. 409. See also House Committee on Appropriations, *Department of Defense Appropriations for 1951: Hearings*, 1950, pt. 2, pp. 753–54; and J. Lawton Collins, "Modern Weapons for Today's Army," *Army Information Digest* 5, no. 6 [1950], 3–9).

[3] Senator Homer Ferguson (LL.B. University of Michigan 1913), Republican from Michigan, and other committee members had questioned Eisenhower about the adequacy of the Alaskan defenses. It had been Senator Thomas, however, who had asked for the names of the sites most in need of protection (see Senate Committee on Appropriations, *Department of Defense Appropriations for 1951: Hearings*, 1950, pp. 686–87).

[4] Eisenhower had mentioned this problem in a December 1948 letter to the former Secretary of Defense, the late James V. Forrestal (see no. 303). In August 1949 the Joint Intelligence Committee of the JCS had reported that the Soviet Union had 350 aircraft in areas adjacent to Alaska. With these planes the Russians could strike at American sea lines of communication; they could also undertake some airborne operations "against weakly-held United States bases in Alaska and the Aleutians" (JCS 1952/8, Aug. 25, 1949, CCS 373 [8-23-48]; see also JCS 1295/2, Dec. 20, 1945, CCS 660.2 Alaska [3-23-45], Sec. 3, and Lucas to Stone, Apr. 9, 1948, *ibid.*, Sec. 4). For developments see no. 782.

[5] In April 1950 Secretary of Defense Louis A. Johnson would propose to Congress an increase of $79 million in the FY51 allocation for anti-submarine equipment (see no. 782).

[6] In September 1949 Eisenhower had proposed an allocation of $1.4 billion for aircraft procurement for the Air Force during FY51 (for background see no. 533). By the time President Truman submitted his budget to Congress in January 1950, the amount set aside for aircraft procurement for the Air Force had become approximately $1.35 billion (see House Committee on Appropriations, *Department of Defense Appropriations for 1951: Hearings*, 1950, pt. 3, p. 1327; and Senate Committee on Appropriations, *Department of Defense Appropriations for 1951: Hearings*, 1950, pp. 31, 61). Secretary Johnson would recommend in April 1950 that $1.55 billion be spent on aircraft for the Air Force during FY50 (see no. 782).

[7] See Senate Committee on Appropriations, *Department of Defense Appropriations for 1951: Hearings*, 1950, pp. 684, 690–91.

[8] Eisenhower sent copies of this letter to Secretary of the Army Gordon Gray, to General Wade H. Haislip, Vice Chief of Staff, U.S. Army, and to Congressman George H. Mahon, chairman of the House Subcommittee on Department of Defense Appropriations (for background on Gray and Haislip see nos. 675 and 599, respectively; Eisenhower's covering letter to Mahon is the following document). Senator Thomas would print this letter in Senate Committee on Appropriations, *Department of Defense Appropriations for 1951: Hearings*, 1950, pp. 703–4.

755   *Eisenhower Mss.,*
Vinson Corr.

To George Herman Mahon   *March 30, 1950*

Dear George:[01] In the confusion of the questioning during my appearance before the Senate Appropriations Subcommittee on Armed Services Appropriations, I apparently neglected to mention one of the most critical subjects in our national defense which I feel merits greater attention.[2] That is the subject of modernization of Army equipment, a field in which we have lagged. Although I have learned that a start has now been made in rectifying this, the fact remains that for five years almost nothing was done. I would personally feel easier if our tank, antitank, antiaircraft and vehicular programs could be more broadly supported.

Because my failure to discuss this critical subject may have caused misunderstanding among committee members and the press as to my views, I feel that this information should be brought to your attention.

I am attaching a copy of a letter I am sending to Senator Thomas to clarify this misunderstanding.[3] *Sincerely*

[1] Mahon, Democrat from Texas, was chairman of the Subcommittee on Department of Defense Appropriations of the House Committee on Appropriations. Eisenhower had discussed the FY51 defense budget at an off-the-record meeting with members of Mahon's subcommittee on February 24, 1950 (for background see no. 701).

[2] For information on this appearance by General Eisenhower see no. 753. Major General William H. Arnold, Chief, Budget Division, Office of the Comptroller, Department of the Army (see no. 380), delivered this letter to Mahon on March 31, 1950.

[3] See the preceding document.

9

New Programs,
Old Problems

To Hal L. Mangum   *April 3, 1950*

Dear Hal:[1] Thank you for your very nice note and its appealing invitation.[2] While it is impossible to change plans now to come down to the ranch, we both certainly wish that we could accept. We have already made definite plans to go down to Georgia a week from today and will be there for about eight days. That will be my final absence from the University during this academic year. Unfortunately, Mamie does not like to fly—as you well know—and this circumstance always leads me to look for places for short vacation periods within a night's run of New York. By leaving here next Sunday afternoon, we will be at Augusta, Georgia early the following morning, whereas it takes two days to reach San Antonio. Possibly we should get to work on schemes for making Mamie air-minded.[3]

Day before yesterday, I saw Arthur Seeligson in Washington. He and Ramona are coming up here this week, and Mamie is to have a dinner for them on Friday night.[4] You should most certainly be here, because there is no question but that in your absence you will be talked about! Arthur told me that you had had quite a struggle with your health during the latter part of the winter. I do hope that you are feeling fit again and are quite your old self. Your letter did not mention the cow situation—so I assume that it is neither particularly the better nor particularly the worse than when you last wrote.[5]

Again our most sincere thanks for a lovely invitation and our real regret that we cannot come.[6] *As ever*

[1] For background on Mangum see no. 696.

[2] Mangum had invited General and Mrs. Eisenhower and "anyone else" they cared to bring to relax at La Babia, his cattle ranch in Mexico. "You look tired," he had written in his letter of March 31 (EM), enclosing as proof some newspaper clippings picturing Eisenhower on March 29 testifying before the Senate Appropriations Committee in Washington (see no. 753).

[3] The Eisenhowers would stay at the Augusta National Golf Club, in Augusta, Georgia, from April 10 until April 22 (see no. 774).

[4] Eisenhower had seen Seeligson on April 1 at the Burning Tree Country Club in Bethesda, Maryland, near Washington, D.C. On Friday, April 7, the Eisenhowers would entertain Seeligson and his wife, Ramona, at 60 Morningside Drive. For background on the Seeligsons see no. 582.

[5] On Mangum's poor health and his problems with his herds see no. 696.

[6] On March 31, the same day that Mangum had written to Eisenhower, he had also written to Major Robert L. Schulz, the General's aide (EM). Mangum had said that if the Eisenhowers could not visit him in Mexico, he would come to New York to see them. As it turned out, Mangum would visit the General on May 9. All correspondence is in EM. For developments see no. 849.

To Milton Stover Eisenhower   *April 3, 1950*

Dear Milton: I shall instantly reserve the period October 3-6 for your inauguration.[1] It requires me to break a date with the Educational Policies Commission, but it is possible that the Commission will change its dates.[2] In any event, your inauguration will take priority.

You are informed correctly as to my promise to go to Pittsburgh on October 19.[3] I am a bit sorry that your own inauguration is not close enough to that date so that I could have gone to both places on the same trip and still have two or three days to spend with you. However, it won't be too much of a chore to make two trips to western Pennsylvania.

In the same mail that brought your note, I had one from Gardner Cowles, suggesting that I have a dinner with him and his brother. I am to fix a date for some time in May when I am to see them. He originally proposed April 12, but I shall be out of the city then.[4] *As ever*

[1] Milton Eisenhower was the newly elected president of Pennsylvania State College (see no. 679). On March 30 Milton had written that his inauguration had been tentatively set for October 4 and 5. He hoped that Dwight, as well as their brothers Earl, Edgar, and Arthur, would attend the ceremonies and stay an extra day for a reunion (EM). For developments see no. 790.

[2] On April 5 Eisenhower would write to William G. Carr, secretary of the Educational Policies Commission, to inform him that he could not attend the meetings scheduled for October 5, 6, and 7. In a letter of April 14 Carr asked Eisenhower whether he could be present if the commission extended the meeting dates through October 8. "So many old friends, relatives and others are involved in the Pennsylvania get-together," replied Eisenhower (May 5), "that I dare not disrupt something that happens only once in a lifetime. . . ." Correspondence is in EM, Subject File, Clubs and Associations. On the commission see nos. 387, n. 4, and 492.

[3] On March 24, at a meeting with James M. Bovard, president of the board of trustees of the Carnegie Institute, Eisenhower had agreed to be the principal speaker at exercises commemorating Founder's Day and celebrating the opening of the Pittsburgh Exhibition of Paintings at Carnegie Institute. Correspondence regarding the address and trip arrangements are in EM, Bovard Corr. The speech is in EM, Subject File, Speeches. See also the *New York Times*, October 20, 1950; and no. 1042.

[4] In a second note, also dated March 30, Milton Eisenhower urged the General to meet his good friends the Cowles brothers, whom he described as "wonderful gentlemen" (EM). They were Gardner "Mike" Cowles (A.B. Harvard 1925), president of Cowles Magazines of New York; and John Cowles (A.B. Harvard 1920), president of the Minneapolis Star and Tribune Company, Minneapolis, Minnesota. "I'm sure they want to talk to you about politics," Milton said, "and this will be most annoying to you. . . . I hope you can stand this one bit of unpleasantness because you will like the Cowles brothers immensely otherwise." A private luncheon would be arranged for May 12 at the Waldorf Towers in New

York, but Eisenhower was ill on that day, and the luncheon had to be postponed indefinitely. Eisenhower would, however, meet the Cowles brothers on two separate occasions in July 1950. He would have dinner with John on July 7 in Minneapolis, and Gardner Cowles would visit the General at Columbia on July 13. All correspondence regarding these meetings is in EM. For developments see no. 910.

758   *Eisenhower Mss.*

To Hoyt Sanford Vandenberg   *April 3, 1950*

Dear Van:[1] I am sorry that we had such a brief moment together at Burning Tree Club on Saturday. However, I was being pulled and hauled around by good friends that I had not seen for many months; so I suppose I should not have expected a real opportunity to talk to you.[2] Recently, I have received two letters, both of them dealing with specific problems of our Air Forces and our Air defenses.[3] I think it would be useless to send them on to you to become matters for "staff study" in your headquarters, but they do raise in my mind certain questions that I should like to talk to you about some day. While I do not expect to come to Washington for a number of weeks, if you should happen to be coming this way, won't you try to include an extra hour when we could have a chat?

Since neither letter involves something that demands instant and emergency action, even if you should agree with its argument, I think that a leisurely talk would be far better than to try to handle them on a formal basis.[4] *Cordially*

[1] General Vandenberg was Chief of Staff of the United States Air Force.
[2] Eisenhower had played golf with James C. Black and Arthur A. Seeligson on Saturday, April 1, at the Burning Tree Country Club in Bethesda, Maryland, near Washington, D.C. The General had been in the capital since March 29 (see no. 753). For background on Black see no. 62; on Seeligson see no. 582.
[3] See the next two documents.
[4] In a note of April 11 Vandenberg would thank Eisenhower for this letter and would promise to arrange a meeting at the first opportunity (EM). On Thursday, April 20, Vandenberg traveled to the Augusta National Golf Club, in Augusta, Georgia, to see Eisenhower, who was vacationing there (see no. 774).

759   *Eisenhower Mss.*

To Julius Earl Schaefer   *April 3, 1950*

Dear Earl:[1] Thank you very much indeed for your very interesting— and most informative—letter. Manifestly, I cannot answer it promptly and in detail because you raise a number of technical questions on which I would not be remotely qualified to have an opinion. Parenthetically, I should like to say, however, that for a long time I have had a growing feeling that the increasing complexities of aircraft were demanding, on the ground, such a high degree of maintenance skill that some reorganization of the Air Forces might become necessary.[2]

With regard to your fear that we will not have any modern aircraft on M-Day, you may have seen that I recommended an expenditure of $1,500,000,000 a year for Air Force procurement of aircraft. This figure, although failing to represent the complete ambitions of the Air Force partisans, does mean to me not only a reasonably sized and healthy Air Force in being, but it should assure us a capacity for expansion in emergency.[3]

I am saving your letter in order to discuss with Van the several questions you raise. I have just returned from Washington and, so, may not see him for some weeks but I have already written him a note asking him to drop in to see me when he is up this way. I hope such a chance will come before too long.[4]

In the meantime, my very best to you and to Mrs. Schaefer.[5] I truly hope that both of you are having a wonderful vacation. At least you are in one of God's garden spots. I love that section of Texas.[6] *Cordially*

---

[1] Schaefer, an old friend of Eisenhower's, was vice-president and general manager of the Wichita, Kansas, division of the Boeing Airplane Company (for background on Schaefer see *Eisenhower Papers*, vols. I–IX).

[2] On March 29, 1950, Schaefer had written Eisenhower a long letter about U.S. air-defense structure (EM). He did not intend to be critical, Schaefer had said, but he did wish to present what he hoped were "worthwhile and pertinent" views on the subject. Schaefer was concerned about delays in production of the B–47 Stratojet, which was being manufactured at the Wichita Division plants of the Boeing Airplane Company. The six-jet bomber, he said, was designed to have the speed and range necessary to carry the atomic bomb beyond the Ural Mountains. He called it "a highly technical airplane and very promising," but he said there were many problems that their technicians had not yet solved. "Don't let anyone tell you we are ready with the B47," he said, ". . . it isn't ready yet and won't be for months." It would take time to overcome technical maintenance problems which he said could not be licked by the average " 'tech sgt,' however good he may be." Technical skills and ingenuity beyond those of the best of the noncommissioned officers were necessary to maintain the B–47. Such experts, Schaefer pointed out, were in great demand in industry, but serving the Army or the Air Force was not appealing to them. For a discussion of the need for trained specialists and technicians able to keep pace with the rapid technical progress in aviation since the end of World War II see House Committee on Appropriations, *Department of Defense Appropriations for 1951: Hearings*, 1950, pt. 3, pp. 1260–67.

Schaefer compared the technical operational problems in the B–47 Stratojet with those that had occurred in the B–36 bomber. He said that "some of these same problems and more will prevail when the B47 gets into service." The B–36, he thought, was not altogether the answer to U.S. defense needs. In Schaefer's opinion, it was "too slow and too vulnerable against Interceptors" (for background on the

B–36 see nos. 336, n. 5, and 378). Schaefer asked Eisenhower to keep all these thoughts in mind whenever he heard or read of General Vandenberg's problems in building an effective air force. For more information on the development of the B–47 and the continuing problems in its production see Alexander McSurely, "AF Pushes Buildup of B–47 Jet Bomber," *Aviation Week*, April 16, 1951, 13–14; and "Stratojet Delays Worry Air Force," *ibid.*, January 14, 1952, 34. See also Charles D. Bright, *The Jet Makers: Aerospace Industry from 1945 to 1972* (Lawrence, Kans., 1978), pp. 32–39.

[3] Schaefer thought that it was "very dangerous" to include B–29 bombers and other World War II aircraft as part of the U.S. striking force: "Many of our accidents today, I feel, are caused by the boys trying to fly World War III missions with World War II airplanes." Some of the B–29's and the B–50's were being modified and equipped for refueling at Wichita plants, he said, but for the most part these airplanes are not "ready NOW." Schaefer was concerned over plans predicated on M-day in an atomic age. (M-day is Mobilization Day, the day total military and industrial mobilization is ordered. It may precede or follow the commencement of hostilities.) "M day," he said "could well have been when Russia accomplished atomic fission."

On March 29 Eisenhower had testified before a subcommittee of the Senate Committee on Appropriations concerning the national defense budget for FY51. In a memorandum dated March 30, 1950 (no. 754), supplementing his testimony of the day before, Eisenhower had said that the level of airplane procurement that he had recommended for the Air Force could be accomplished under existing conditions for about $1.5 billion annually. For more information on Eisenhower's testimony see no. 753.

[4] Eisenhower's note to General Vandenberg is the preceding document.

[5] Catherine Rockwell Schaefer.

[6] Schaefer had written to Eisenhower from McAllen, Texas, located in the southern part of the state.

760

Eisenhower Mss.,
Hoyt S. Vandenberg Corr.

To George M. Jasper

April 3, 1950

Dear Mr. Jasper:[1] Your letter carries the first intonation [intimation?] I have seen that the "Flying Wing" was rejected without thorough test. I thought the opposite was true.[2]

While obviously I am not qualified even to discuss such matters as the comparative technical excellence of airplanes, I do have great faith in the brains and purposes of the leaders of our Air Force.[3] Consequently, I am going to discuss with them the questions you raise.[4] More than this, I cannot do.

I am naturally encouraged to know that citizens, like yourself, are giving earnest concern to these matters and trying to inform themselves on important facts concerning our defenses. I hope that you will always continue to do so. *Sincerely*

[1] Jasper was vice-president of Barrett Herrick & Company, a New York investment firm.

[2] On March 30 Jasper had written to Eisenhower (EM, Vandenberg Corr.) to ask why contracts had been canceled for the "Flying Wing," a boomerang-shaped bomber manufactured by Northrop Aircraft, Inc., of Hawthorne, California. Jasper said that he had read about Eisenhower's recent testimony before a congressional committee, and in view of the General's opinion that the United States Air Force was "insufficient," Jasper questioned the decision to cancel the "Flying Wing." He had corresponded extensively with both Northrop Aircraft and the Air Force; the replies from the Air Force had been, he said, "very inadequate and greatly lacking in interest. . . ." Eisenhower directed that General Hoyt Vandenberg, Air Force Chief of Staff, receive a carbon copy of this reply to Jasper, as well as a copy of Jasper's letter to Eisenhower. For background on Eisenhower's appearance at the Senate committee hearings on Department of Defense appropriations for 1951 see no. 753; and *New York Times*, March 30, 1950.

[3] The "Flying Wing" had been designed by John Knudsen Northrop, president of Northrop Aircraft, on the theory that since only the wings contribute to the buoyancy of an airplane, the fuselage and the tail were unnecessary. The unconventional, wedge-shaped craft made its first flight in 1940. Since then, Northrop had produced a series of "Flying Wing" designs for the U.S. air forces, but in January 1949 the Air Force had announced sweeping revisions in allocations of its procurement funds and canceled the contracts for thirty Northrop YB-49 "Flying Wing" bombers (*New York Times*, Feb. 10, 1949). According to Air Force spokesmen, the change had been part of a move to acquire more long-range strategic bombers, such as the B–36 and the B–50, in order to raise the effectiveness of the Air Force in as short a time as possible. For more information see *New York Times*, January 12 and 15 and August 18, 1949. See also the preceding document; and Bright, *The Jet Makers*, p. 191.

[4] Eisenhower would discuss this matter with General Vandenberg (see no. 758).

761   *Eisenhower Mss., Subject File,*
Clubs and Associations

To John Arthur Brown   *April 4, 1950*

Dear Mr. Brown:[1] By a coincidence, your cordial letter reached my desk just after I had spoken to a friend of mine named John Brooks, who asked my permission to nominate me for membership in the United States Seniors' Golf Association. I had some reluctance to join, but solely because of the miserable brand of golf that I play; from every other angle his suggestion seemed so appealing that I told him I would be delighted to be a member of such a distinguished group. Moreover, because our common friend John Jackson had been the first ever to mention this matter to me, I asked Mr. Brooks, as a personal favor, to request Mr. Jackson to second the nomination.[2]

With this explanation out of the way, I assure you that I should be greatly pleased to join your Association either as a Regular member as indicated above, or as an Honorary member as suggested in your letter to Mr. Jackson. I would feel a great sense of distinction in either arrangement.

With respect to the specific date of June 27, I cannot give quite so definite an answer. I have tentatively planned to go to Canada sometime toward the end of June, and it is possible that I may be absent from the country when your tournament is held. Would it be possible for me to defer making final answer to this specific invitation until my plans can crystallize? I assure you that I would like very much to be with you that evening and regret that I cannot give you an affirmative answer at this moment.[3]

May I voice the profound hope that the United States Seniors' Golf Association never permit an invited dinner guest to make a "speech"? I am sure that it is one group that is of sufficient wisdom and experience to assert its independence of an incomprehensible custom of turning a nice dinner into a dreary oratorical contest.[4] *Sincerely*

[1] Brown had been president of the United States Seniors' Golf Association since June 25, 1947.

[2] Eisenhower had received a letter of invitation from Brown to be the honorary guest at the annual tournament and dinner of the United States Seniors' Golf Association on June 27, 1950, at the Apawamis Golf Club in New York. Two friends, John St. Clair Brookes, Jr., of the Washington, D.C., law firm of Hogan & Hartson, and John G. Jackson, a Columbia trustee and New York City lawyer, had apparently encouraged Eisenhower to join their group and had hoped to nominate him (Mar. 30, 1950, EM).

[3] Brown would reply (Apr. 6, EM) that "the Association would be complimented in having you as an honorary member . . ." and that he would suggest such action to Jackson and Brookes at the annual meeting. Brown also added that in reference to June 27, the matter would stay open until Eisenhower's plans matured (EM).

[4] The General would be unable to attend the tournament, but on July 27, while he was on an extended vacation in the West, Kevin McCann (assistant to the president) would be notified of Eisenhower's election as an honorary member in the United States Seniors' Golf Association. McCann acknowledged this "great compliment" in a letter on July 28 to the secretary of the association, Sherrill Sherman. All correspondence is in the same file as this document.

762   *Eisenhower Mss.*

To Curtis H. Gager   *April 4, 1950*

Dear Mr. Gager:[1] Thank you very much for your note and its attached clipping. Every sane man understands that rigid economy in governmental expenditure has become a must. It is tragic that the world situation is such as to demand huge expenditures for the maintenance of sizeable military forces and for helping potential allies abroad. But these, as well as all other expenditures, should be measured in terms of sheer necessity.² *Sincerely*

¹ Gager was a vice-president and a director of the General Foods Corporation. He had joined General Foods in 1929 and had been associate advertising and merchandising manager from 1932 to 1937. In that year he had become general manager of the corporation's Walter Baker Division, and he had subsequently served as its president from 1938 until 1944.

² In a handwritten note Gager had asked the General to "hammer the point that—adequate military safeguards require—absolute economy in other areas of government" (n.d., EM). The editorial that accompanied his note was titled "Incompatibles" (*Wall Street Journal*, Mar. 28, 1959, p. 8); it contended that an "increasingly dangerous propped-up economy" had resulted from a mixture of mutually incompatible economic systems advocated by statesmen and publicists in the United States. The editorial called for immediate reductions in government expenditures (for previous correspondence from Gager advocating "economy-mindness" in government, see Gager to Eisenhower, Dec. 7, 1949, EM; for more on Eisenhower's views concerning the budget and national defense see no. 753).

763   *Eisenhower Mss.*

To CARL A. SPAATZ   *April 4, 1950*

*Dear Tooey:*¹ While you told me that you were sending me a letter from Lowell Weicker, there was no such document accompanying your note. If you will send it on, I shall get busy on whatever it requests or suggests.²

Your fishing trip must have been lots of fun. I have heard much of Acapulco but have never been there. In fact, my most vivid impression of the place was obtained from a photograph about three years ago when you and Stu Symington were standing behind a great catch of marlin and other fish—I think sailfish.³

Respecting your fearing that we may be slowly losing the battle with the Communists, it is certainly accurate to remark that we have no apparent cause for self-congratulation at the moment. I note that you did not cite evidence of an external character to justify your fear but rather you said, "too great a percentage of our people ready to accept anything at all from the Government for nothing in return" etc.⁴ To counteract the thinking or lack of thinking that you believe responsible, you even suggest that universal military training might have some virtue.⁵

I should like to talk to you about these things. For the moment, I would content myself with saying that I most emphatically agree that we need a true reawakening in this country to the facts of the world situation and to our own opportunities and responsibilities. I believe that such a reawakening can be accomplished if there would be a concerted drive toward that end by, say, a hundred inspired and respected leaders in our country. I think the movement would gradually gather momentum and would soon sweep the country. I have been astonished to see how much has been accomplished here at Columbia by a few determined leaders; I am certain that 99 per cent are beginning to identify "paternalism" as one of the greatest dangers to the sturdiness and individual independence of our people.[6]

As you know, I have always believed in universal military training. However, I have always argued for it solely on the basis of military usefulness—never as a means of indoctrination. While this latter would be a tremendous by-product of a proper training course, yet I could not admit that we have to put our youth in military formations in order to instruct them properly. Some day when I see you, we will talk about these vital subjects.[7]

This note brings my love to Ruth[8] and your nice family and my warmest regards to yourself. *Cordially*

[1] General Spaatz (USAF, ret.) was now living in Washington, D.C. (see no. 154).
[2] Spaatz, who had written to Eisenhower on March 31, 1950 (EM), had enclosed he said, a letter from Lowell Palmer Weicker, a former member of Spaatz's staff during World War II. There is no indication in EM that Eisenhower ever received the enclosure.
[3] Spaatz had said that he had just returned from a fishing trip in Acapulco, Mexico. W. Stuart Symington, newly appointed chairman of the National Security Resources Board, had been Secretary of the Air Force since September 1947.
[4] Spaatz had said, "There is too great a percentage of our people ready to accept anything at all from the Government for nothing in return, too much of our valuable petroleum wasted on the highways, and most of all too great a percentage of the population ready to do almost anything but work."
[5] "I believe a strenuous campaign should be put on for universal training," Spaatz had written, "more with the idea of indoctrinating the youth with Americanism than anything else."
[6] Eisenhower felt strongly about this issue (see, for instance, no. 638).
[7] For Eisenhower's views on universal military training see Chandler and Galambos, *Occupation, 1945*, nos. 114–16 and 206.
[8] Spaatz's wife, the former Ruth Harrison.

764   *Eisenhower Mss.*

To Gretchen H. Waldo   *April 4, 1950*

Dear Mrs. Waldo: I have been quite intrigued by the ideas set forth in your letter of the 31st.[1]

With respect to my suggestion for establishing a Chair for Peace, it was my thought that we should devote the efforts of some of our great scholars to the studying of the matters that seemed to be forever disturbing the peace of the world. Consequently, I should think that such scholars ought to study the causes of war, its conduct and its effect upon our social and political mechanisms. Such studies have been too long neglected and I believe that dispassionate analysis might bring to light some pertinent and practical suggestions for increasing the health and strength of world peace.

As to your idea that we might establish a Department of Peace, with its head in the President's Cabinet, I think that most people would assume that that is what our Department of State is for. While I suppose that a definite series of responsibilities could be placed upon the head of such a Department, I have the feeling that such duties would inevitably conflict with those assigned to the Secretary of State.[2] I really believe that Mr. Baruch's scheme was something over and above the establishment of a new Department. I think that he wanted to establish a commission made up of representatives of business, of the professions, of governmental activities, etc.[3] His idea was that what we now call peace—specifically the cold war—could be best waged by the Government, with the aid, advice and counsel of such a body. This, I assume, is somewhat different from your own suggestion.

I repeat that I was greatly intrigued by your letter. Thank you for writing to me and I do assure you that I share your very great concern in the maintenance of peace.[4] *Sincerely*

[1] Mrs. Waldo, of Boston, Massachusetts, was a Red Cross nurse's aide working with the national blood program. She had expressed interest in Eisenhower's plan to establish a chair for peace at Columbia University (for background on this project see no. 730). During a speech on March 23, 1950, Eisenhower had made public his plans to establish this chair and possibly an institute for the study of the causes and consequences of war. For background on the speech see no. 741; for developments concerning the institute see no. 765.

[2] Mrs. Waldo had written to George C. Marshall shortly after he had become Secretary of State in January 1947 suggesting that a department of peace be established within the federal government (on Marshall see no. 75). Marshall had apparently taken no action on her proposal, but she had heard reports of a recent speech by financier Bernard M. Baruch in which he had made a similar suggestion, and she now urged Eisenhower to organize "a permanent group of non-partisan men-of-good-will . . . to work for Peace" (Mrs. Waldo's letter is in EM). Baruch, speaking at the Naval War College, in Newport, Rhode Island, on March 31, 1950, had suggested that "a central 'think body,' should be created, to survey the whole of the cold war, re-examining our policy and advising the President." The speech was printed as " 'Pacing Ourselves': Cold War Strategy," *Vital Speeches of the Day* 16, no. 13 (1950), 391–94.

[3] Baruch had outlined these plans during the summer of 1949 (see no. 449).

[4] In a letter of April 22 (EM) Mrs. Waldo thanked Eisenhower for his comments and tried to answer his criticisms of her proposal.

To EDWIN NORMAN CLARK   *April 5, 1950*

Dear Ed:[1] We have had various talks about reorganizing the American
Military Institute and affiliating it with a Chair for Peace at Columbia
University.[2] As you know, I think that this could result in real benefit
to the country. It is almost incomprehensible that no American university has undertaken the continuous study of the causes, conduct and
consequences of war—the greatest ill to which our civilization is heir.

I have had extended discussions regarding this with the heads of the
various departments concerned here at Columbia and find that all are
most enthusiastic.

Unfortunately, Columbia like most other American universities is
currently operating at a deficit and cannot embark on such an undertaking without outside help.[3] I understand that you feel such outside
help may be forthcoming from American individuals and foundations
who appreciate the importance of the work.

You have told me that if Columbia's decision was in favor of the
affiliation you wanted to discuss the matter of the necessary finances
with certain individuals. Should it develop that any of these interested
individuals might want to discuss the subject with me personally, I
should be delighted to have them for lunch. I regret that I shall be
absent from the city until about April 20th, but I would appreciate it
if you would invite those interested to lunch with us and some of our
senior faculty members here at the University Club at 12:30 o'clock
on April 25th.[4] *Sincerely*

[1] Clark was a business executive and consultant in New York City (for background
see Galambos, *Chief of Staff*, no. 1456). Eisenhower rewrote an earlier draft of
this letter (EM, Letters and Drafts).
[2] On the American Military Institute see no. 665; on plans for the chair for peace
see no. 730. Eisenhower's appointment calendar indicates that he had conferred
with Clark on January 6; February 6, 21, 27; March 3; and April 5, 1950.
[3] On Columbia University's financial situation see no. 417.
[4] According to General Eisenhower's appointment calendar John A. Krout, dean
of the graduate faculties, attended the luncheon (for background on Krout see no.
361; concerning Eisenhower's vacation from April 10 to April 22 see no. 774).

766   *Eisenhower Mss.*

To HARRY CECIL BUTCHER   *April 5, 1950*

Dear Butch:[1] It is completely out of the question for me to come to
Santa Barbara during the month of May. While I have not yet received
the "petition," there is no other answer that I shall be able to make.[2]

I cannot quite follow the reasoning of people who will give up an evening or a luncheon period to hear someone like Crommelin. While I understand that, upon occasion, he has dragged me into his diatribes, insisting that I am a nefarious influence in Washington, this in itself has nothing to do with my feeling toward him. I simply believe that he is completely warped, practically an egomaniac and, consequently, is not deserving of too much attention.[3]

It was nice to have news of Thor Smith. I [He?] was one of our best and one that I hope to see again one of these days.[4]

With my best to you both,[5] *Cordially*

[1] For background on Butcher see no. 33.

[2] Butcher had written to Eisenhower about a petition to "draft" the General to speak in Santa Barbara, California, during National Defense Week May 13–20. The General's former naval aide had enclosed with his letter an article from the April 2 edition of the *Santa Barbara News Press*, which stated that a roster of some two hundred signatures was in the mail, along with personal letters of invitation; Eisenhower, however, would not be able to attend the celebration (Apr. 3, 1950, with enclosure, in EM).

[3] Butcher told Eisenhower that he had declined to introduce Captain John Geraerdt Crommelin, Jr., a guest of the Channel City Club of Santa Barbara, a civic group that invited speakers to address its members at their luncheon meetings. Butcher said that he had wanted to avoid any implied endorsement of the controversial naval officer, an action which might involve Eisenhower. For background on Crommelin, who would retire from the U.S. Navy on June 1, 1950, to pursue a political career, see no. 734. Because of his combat record he would be promoted by Secretary of the Navy Francis P. Matthews to rear admiral on the retired list. Crommelin would mount an unsuccessful campaign for the U.S. Senate in the November 1950 election, running as an independent Democrat from Alabama; he would lose to the incumbent Democrat, Lister Hill (*New York Times*, June 1, and 4, Nov. 8, 1950).

[4] Thor M. Smith was assistant to the publisher of the *San Francisco Call-Bulletin* and a former public relations officer with Eisenhower. He had told Butcher that Crommelin had made himself "a worn out story to the San Francisco Press because he feverishly accepted all invitations to speak, including even small groups of Boy Scouts and Girl Scouts."

[5] The reference is to Butcher's wife, Mary Margaret ("Mollie").

767

DIARY

Another kind of typewriter!

I am quite sure that some of the nervous tension that the doctor (and others) seem frequently to detect in me[1] (as far as I got)

Barnard Trustee Meeting tonight.[2]

There is probably no more complicated business in the world than that of picking a new dean within a university. Faculties, including the retiring dean, feel an almost religious fervor in insisting upon acceptance of their particular views. These are as varied as there are individuals involved, and every man's opinion is voiced in terms of urgency.——The result is complete confusion & I cannot see why Universities have followed such a custom! But I'll be d—— glad when we have a new dean of engineering and the fuss, fury & hysteria die down!![3]

Some of my Republican connections in Kansas have broadly hinted or openly stated that I should declare my association with them. They know of course that I believe we must have a Republican victory in '52; from this they do a lot of arguing that, in my opinion, fails to look very far into the future.[4]

[1] Eisenhower used a typewriter to this point. The rest of the entry is handwritten.
[2] Eisenhower would attend a dinner meeting of the trustees of Barnard College this evening.
[3] For Eisenhower's correspondence regarding the retirement of James K. Finch, dean of the School of Engineering, and the appointment of his successor, John R. Dunning, see nos. 434, 688, 739, and 783.
[4] Eisenhower was probably referring to U.S. Senator Harry Darby (M.E. University of Illinois 1929), who had been Republican National Committeeman from Kansas since 1940. Darby, an industrialist and a farmer-stockman of Kansas City, Kansas, would ultimately become the dominant leader from Kansas in the growing movement to draft the General for the Republican presidential nomination. Other Republicans from Kansas who worked for Eisenhower's candidacy were Governor Frank Carlson (see no. 113); U.S. congressmen Albert M. Cole (First District) and Clifford R. Hope (Fifth District); and Roy A. Roberts, president and general manager of the *Kansas City Star* (see no. 638).

768   *Eisenhower Mss.*

To ———   *April 6, 1950*

Dear Mrs. ———:[1] I have always observed the custom of agreeing to see anyone in an organization that I head, where this becomes necessary to examine into any question that such individual believes to involve injustice.[2] However, it is manifestly necessary in such cases that my appropriate assistant has first had opportunity to adjust any differences of opinion that may have caused the misunderstanding and is therefore prepared to provide me his side of the case.[3]

So far as opportunity to see me, personally, is concerned, this will be possible after the 24th of April. I am about to leave the city and will not be available in my office until that date.[4] However, if you still want to see me when I come back, I should like to make certain—in the meantime—that you have called upon Vice President Joseph Campbell who has general supervision of all residence hall personnel. He is out of town this week but I believe will be back at his desk on Monday morning, next.[5] *Sincerely*

[1] This letter was written to a member of the staff of Columbia University.

[2] In a letter of April 4, 1950, Mrs. ———— had appealed to Eisenhower as a " 'Country girl' from Dixie" writing to a " 'Country boy' in New York"; she had asked for a personal hearing to discuss "a great injustice" concerning her application for a particular position in the school.

[3] Kevin McCann, assistant to the president, had reported to Eisenhower about this situation, explaining that the decision to turn down her application had been agreed upon by everyone concerned because "a young woman is not the best fitted to manage a residence hall for medical students." According to McCann, the applicant had nevertheless persisted in discussing this matter with many at the university who were not concerned with the administration of residence halls. McCann pointed out that Dr. Rappleye, dean of the Medical School, was emphatic that the decision should not be "short-circuited by Mrs. ———— appealing directly to the President" (memorandum, McCann to Eisenhower, Apr. 5, 1950, EM).

[4] Eisenhower would vacation in Augusta, Georgia, from April 10 to April 22 (see no. 756).

[5] Judging by Eisenhower's appointment calendar, the applicant would not meet with the General.

769   *Eisenhower Mss.*

TO KENYON ASHE JOYCE   *April 7, 1950*

Dear Kenyon:[1] As of now, I can see no possible chance to come to Bohemian Grove this summer. Early last fall I received a letter from President Sproul of the University of California, informing me that the Board of Trustees or Directors of the Grove would send me an invitation if I thought I could accept. For a while I thought that I could do so, but finally felt that the complications of my life would force me to decline. Since then, I have talked the same prospect over with Mr. Collier of the Standard of California, with my friend Pete Jones here in New York, with Mr. Hoover and with others.[2] It goes without saying that I should very much like to attend—your own personal invitation makes the whole prospect more appealing than ever.

But my plans are so confused and involve so many tentative activities that I feel it mandatory to avoid making any more commitments, no matter how attractive the invitation.[3]

To give you some inkling of how difficult it is to carry out even the simplest of purposes in this direction, I have been carrying on negotiations for some weeks involving possible engagements in Britain and France for June *1951*. When a man begins putting on his calendar fixed engagements for that distance ahead, you can see that he gets quickly into difficulties for which there seems to be no way of getting out.[4]

I hope you will assure your associates, as I do you, of my very deep and lasting appreciation of their courtesy. *Cordially*

[1] For background on Major General Joyce (USA, ret.) see *Eisenhower Papers*, vols. I–IX. In his letter of April 4 (EM) Joyce had requested that Eisenhower attend the upcoming Bohemian Grove encampment. Joyce currently resided in San Francisco, California, where he was a service member of the Bohemian Club (on the club see no. 388).

[2] A longhand draft of Eisenhower's declination of Robert G. Sproul's invitation is in EM, Letters and Drafts (for background on Sproul see no. 113). On June 13 (EM) Eisenhower would write to Sproul again, explaining that he would in fact be present at Bohemian Grove during July 1950 as the guest of Harry DeWard Collier, chairman of the finance committee of Standard Oil Company of California. For developments see no. 804. On W. Alton "Pete" Jones see no. 388; and on former President Herbert Hoover see no. 57.

[3] Eisenhower would arrive at the Bohemian Grove encampment on July 20, in time to engage in only a few of the planned activities (see the agenda enclosed in Collier to Eisenhower, May 9, 1950, EM; on the Eisenhowers' trip to California see nos. 884 and 887).

[4] On Eisenhower's travel plans for June 1951 see no. 841.

770   *Eisenhower Mss.*

TO DAVID ANDREW SIMMONS   *April 7, 1950*

Dear Mr. Simmons:[1] It was only when I received the brochure you have prepared, entitled "Americans for Eisenhower," that I realized you were actually contemplating the formation of any kind of organization to which my name would be attached.[2] I immediately looked up my past correspondence and find that, under date of February 24, you sent me a clipping and a short memorandum describing the organization that had just been chartered in the State of Texas.[3] I regret that I was not more alert at that moment in examining your memorandum and in letting you know that I could not fail to suffer some embarrassment if you should carry out your purpose as outlined.

Quite naturally, any American is certain to be highly complimented by the knowledge that any other individual should consider him qualified for political leadership. Nevertheless, I am so earnestly attempting to devote my efforts to matters that I deem to be non-partisan—to sound education and the basic values in American life—that any movement designed to attract attention to my name in a partisan sense is certain to embarrass me in what I am trying to do.[4]

So, while I acknowledge and uphold your right to follow your own convictions as an American citizen, I, nevertheless, cannot help saying that I hope you do not push any program which bears my name in its descriptive title.[5] *Sincerely*

[1] Simmons (LL.B. University of Texas 1920) was an attorney from Houston, Texas. In 1944–45 he had been president of the American Bar Association; before that he had been president of the Houston-Galveston District Bar Association, the Texas Bar Association, and the American Judicature Society.

[2] Simmons had sent Eisenhower a three-page brochure about a nonprofit educational and literary corporation called Americans for Eisenhower. The purpose of the group, according to Simmons (its organizer and president), was to analyze (1) the American form of government, (2) the great Americans of the past and present, and (3) the principles, practices, and platforms of all political parties in the United States. The results of such studies, he said, would be disseminated through publications, educational talks, or radio broadcasts (EM).

[3] In a letter dated February 4, 1950 (not Feb. 24), Simmons had told Eisenhower that Americans for Eisenhower had been issued a charter by the state of Texas under Title 32, Article 1302, Section 105 of the Revised Civil Statutes of Texas. It was, he said, "a small beginning" (EM). According to the enclosed clipping from the February 4 issue of the *Houston Post*, Simmons had said that Americans for Eisenhower had "nothing to do with politics." Nevertheless, Simmons had for some time corresponded with Edgar Eisenhower, the General's brother, concerning the 1952 presidential election. "The formula is quite simple," he had written to Edgar on January 5, 1950. "Those who believe in the American form of government, no matter with which of the great parties they are affiliated, must see to it that General Eisenhower is nominated by both parties in every state in the Union." Simmons sent copies of the letter to both General Eisenhower and his brother Milton (EM, Simmons Corr.).

[4] See no. 767, n.4.

[5] On April 10 Simmons agreed to defer an organization drive but reserved the right to express his views as to the needs of the country (EM). For Eisenhower's continuing problems with such groups see no. 788.

771   *Eisenhower Mss.*

To Kenneth Dewey Johnson   *April 7, 1950*

Dear Kenneth:[1] The next time you see Congressman Reece, tell him not only did I, for the first and last time, use my absentee voting privilege in 1948 but I shall never get over a feeling of regret that I was finally compelled to shift my voting residence to another State. Only someone from Kansas can realize what a hold that State gets on a man.[2]

I realize that you have had to go to Washington for a few days, but I am still hopeful that you can be here Sunday afternoon the 23rd to meet with Averell Harriman and some others for discussion of the Arden House project.[3] *Cordially*

[1] Johnson was dean of the New York School of Social Work at Columbia University (see no. 605).

[2] In a letter of April 5 Johnson said that he had recently seen Republican Congressman Edward H. *Rees* (from Kansas's Fourth District). According to Johnson, Rees's "proudest boast" was that Eisenhower had been one of his constituents. "He told me to tell you," Johnson wrote, "that he forced me to testify under oath in response to his questions as to whether or not you made use of your absentee ballot when he was up for reelection in '48" (EM). In October 1949 the General had registered to vote as a nonpartisan in the state of New York (*New York Times*, Nov. 15, 1949, and Oct. 24, 1950). See Eisenhower's memoir *At Ease*, pp. 64–108, for an affectionate account of his boyhood in Kansas.

[3] Johnson, who had been a special assistant to the Secretary of War after World War II (1946–47), had written Eisenhower that for the next several days he would be in Washington, D.C., for consultations with Gordon Gray, retiring Secretary of the Army (Apr. 3, 1950, EM). For background on Gray see no. 675.

The Arden House project concerned proposed uses of the Harriman family estate, which W. Averell Harriman and his brother, E. Roland Harriman, had given to Columbia University (for background see no. 605). Eisenhower and Harriman had met in February 1950 to discuss Arden House (see no. 689), and they had agreed at that time to talk again on April 23 at Morningside Drive. In a letter of April 3 Johnson, whom Eisenhower had asked to chair a special committee to study possible uses of Arden House, had acknowledged that his committee was behind schedule but that good progress, nevertheless, was being made (EM). Others who would attend the April 23 meeting, in addition to Johnson and the Harriman brothers, were Kevin C. McCann, John R. Dunning, John A. Krout, Grayson L. Kirk, Walter D. Fletcher, and Philip Young.

On April 26 Eisenhower wrote Johnson: "I thought you would like to know that Averell Harriman seemed to be very favorably impressed by our discussion last Sunday afternoon, in spite of the fact that we had so little in the way of definite plan or crystallized conviction to offer him. I have heard also that he, in turn, has inspired his brother Roland to take a terrific interest in the matter and so it would appear that things are coming along in pretty splendid fashion" (EM). For developments on Arden House, which would ultimately become the home of the American Assembly, see no. 844.

772   *Eisenhower Mss.*

To William Fletcher Russell[1]   *April 7, 1950*

Herewith a file of correspondence and information dealing with a program in Texas for promoting interest in conservation of natural resources and in *American Citizenship*. The real sparkplug of this program is Mr. C. M. Malone of Houston who tells me that some years ago he had some correspondence with you when you were engaged in a publicity campaign against Communistic growth.[2]

It occurred to me that our own program in Citizenship Training might be somewhat enriched by the experiences of the "Friends of the Land." It would seem axiomatic that the more we can get our youngsters interesting themselves in the practical problems of their own locality (and conservation is always one of these), the more effective our training will be.

In any event, if you see any possible benefits out of cooperation with Mr. Malone's group, I suggest that you write to him directly. I am certain that, on his side, he would welcome any such communication.[3]

[1] Russell was president of Teachers College and director of the Citizenship Education Project (see no. 727).

[2] The file that Eisenhower sent Russell was probably information that Clarence M. Malone, vice-chairman of the board of directors of the Second National Bank of Houston, had enclosed with his letter to Eisenhower of February 28, 1950 (EM). Eisenhower and Malone were directors of Friends of the Land, a conservation organization sponsoring an essay contest for high school students in Texas (see no. 113).

[3] According to his appointment calendar, the General met with Malone on this same day.

773   *Eisenhower Mss.*

To Thomas James Hanley, Jr.   *April 7, 1950*

Dear Tom:[1] Possibly I am low in imagination today but I don't seem to think of words that strike me as particularly descriptive of Beukema's long service to our Class and, at the same time, few enough in number to go on a cigarette box.[2]

In submitting the following, I do it apologetically and with the hope that someone of you can do a lot better—and without half as much thought as I have tried to give to this.

To HERMAN BEUKEMA
For never failing service to his
classmates.
U.S.M.A., '15

Or alternatively,

To HERMAN BEUKEMA
In lasting appreciation
U.S.M.A., '15

Again, I say this is terrible but it is the best I can do.[3] *Cordially*
P.S. You didn't ask me for a check. Doesn't the Treasurer need money?[4]

[1] Major General Hanley, USAF, who had graduated from the United States Military Academy with Eisenhower in 1915, had been Chief of the Military Personnel Procurement Division since 1948.

[2] Hanley had written to Eisenhower (Apr. 5, 1950, EM) concerning the 1915 class reunion June 3–5 at West Point. He had asked Eisenhower to write an inscription for a cigarette box for Colonel Herman Beukema, who had headed West Point's Department of Economics, Government and History. Beukema would be presented with the gift in appreciation for "his efforts in behalf of the class during his tour of duty at the Academy." For background on Beukema see Galambos, *Chief of Staff*, no. 874.

[3] In a letter of April 19 Hanley thanked Eisenhower, saying, "I am sure that we will take your first effort, but I am waiting . . . [to] . . . have a unanimous vote" (EM).

[4] In his letter of April 19 Hanley informed the General that the treasury was in good shape and money might be needed only if a majority at the reunion favored a class book. The General and Mrs. Eisenhower would arrive at West Point on Saturday, June 3, and would stay for the three-day celebration. Events on the itinerary included a steak fry at Round Pond Lodge on Saturday; a barbecue on Sunday; the presentation of the class gift to sons of graduates on Monday, and a family party that day at Bear Mountain Inn. For more details see Hanley to classmates, April 7, 1950, in EM.

774 *Eisenhower Mss.*

To John Davison Rockefeller, Jr. *April 7, 1950*

Dear Mr. Rockefeller: Mrs. Eisenhower and I are running off on Sunday afternoon for a few days in Georgia.[1] I could not leave without thanking you again for your courtesy to me on yesterday afternoon.[2]

I enjoyed the luncheon very much and was proud to be included on the guest list at a function where you were to be honored; but far more than this, I appreciated the opportunity to discuss with you problems that have had very great weight upon me. I am instantly investigating the possibilities of the kind of analysis you suggested. While I regret that Mr. Flexner is not a very much younger man, I am sure we can find the kind of individuals needed. It will be most interesting—and, I hope, helpful—to see what they develop.[3]

With renewed expression of my appreciation, *Sincerely*

[1] The Eisenhowers would leave New York City on Easter Sunday, April 9, via the "Commodore," a special car of the Pennsylvania Railroad. They would arrive in Warrenville, South Carolina, on Monday, the tenth, and drive to the Augusta National Golf Club, in Augusta, Georgia, for their vacation. On April 22 they would return to New York via the "Commodore."

[2] On April 6 Eisenhower had attended a luncheon for Rockefeller given by the Chamber of Commerce of the State of New York. Rockefeller, who had been a member of the chamber for fifty years, had become a life member and had been elected an honorary member as well. Of the forty-eight honorary members who had been elected over the years, Rockefeller joined Eisenhower and former president Herbert Hoover, who was also present on the occasion, as the only three who were living (*New York Times*, Apr. 7, 1950).

[3] Eisenhower had probably discussed with Rockefeller the question of eighty-three-year-old Abraham Flexner's proposal that he be retained by Columbia to conduct a critical analysis of the university as an aid in fund-raising (see no. 720).

775   *Eisenhower Mss.*

TO ROY EDWARD LARSEN   *April 8, 1950*

Dear Roy: Thank you for the trouble you took in writing the letter that you addressed to me under date of April 4.[1] I assure you that there has never been any doubt in my mind as to your attitude toward our own effort here at Columbia in the Citizenship Program and I have never suggested any amalgamation of the efforts.

It is true that whenever I find individuals interesting themselves in a program that has purposes related to those of your Group or of the one carried out at Columbia, I always suggest a meeting with the idea that we exchange viewpoints and information and so increase the effectiveness of all. Obviously, you felt the same way about the matter when you asked Mr. Schacter to see me.[2]

Only this morning I suggested to Mr. Malone of Houston, who is a prime mover in the conservation efforts of the "Friends of the Land," that he investigate Columbia's program to determine whether we could not, with advantage, exchange some views and information.[3] I think all of us should continue to do this, but I emphatically agree with you that to attempt amalgamation of these various efforts with the reselling job to our several supporters that would necessarily ensue, would very largely slow up and possibly damage the whole thing.

Please do not worry as to whether or not I shall understand your position, and be certain also that I shall always look forward to any opportunity to talk about these things to you. The basic objectives of all these programs are very close to my heart and I merely want to do what I can.[4]

With warm personal regards, *Cordially*

[1] Larsen, president of Time, Inc., was chairman of the National Citizens Commission for the Public Schools. In his letter of April 4 (EM) he had said that the Citizenship Education Project undertaken by Columbia University Teachers College interested him, but he had also said that his commission could not get involved at that time in the school curriculum matters that the project was considering (for background see no. 727).

[2] Harry William Schacter (A.B. Columbia 1921) was president of Kaufman Straus Company, a department store in Louisville, Kentucky. He had discussed with Eisenhower (Mar. 21) his plans for a citizens community council program, which would centralize the organization of self-improvement groups in small American communities. Schacter's experiences with the Committee for Kentucky had con-

vinced him that reform could be accomplished most rapidly through a consortium. The Committee for Kentucky, which had been organized in 1943, promoted the idea that local communities should mobilize their own resources to solve local problems (for background see Karl Detzer, "Kentucky on the March," *Reader's Digest* 55 [October 1949], 67–70; and Harry W. Schacter, *Kentucky on the March* [New York, 1949]). Larsen had enclosed with his letter a copy of a letter he had written on the same day to Schacter. Larsen expected that Schacter's work would assist his own, since "any awakening of local interest in local problems will inevitably strengthen local institutions, including the public schools."

[3] Eisenhower's appointment calendar indicates that he had met with Clarence M. Malone, vice-chairman of the board of directors of the Second National Bank of Houston, on April 7. Regarding Malone's interest in the Friends of the Land see no. 113.

[4] Larsen replied (Apr. 14, EM) that he was glad that Eisenhower agreed with him "about the difference between exchanging views and merging of projects." Larsen had heard from Schacter, who also shared their opinion. Eisenhower would see Larsen at a citizenship conference at Teachers College on May 5, 1950. The General would issue a statement to the National Citizens Commission for the Public Schools on October 10, 1950, emphasizing the importance of schools in preparing an informed citizenry. A copy is in EM, Subject File, Messages.

776   *Eisenhower Mss.*

To John Allen Stephens   *April 8, 1950*

Dear Mr. Stephens:[1] This letter should be read in the light of my known and publicly expressed admiration for General W. B. Smith, who was my loyal and efficient Chief of Staff throughout the war in Europe.[2] Nevertheless, while I may be a prejudiced witness, I believe the following to be strictly impartial.[3]

There is no doubt in my mind that General Smith could interpret and apply intellectually to any specific argument the terms of the labor agreement, in so far as there was not demanded special qualifications of a legal or other professional character. He is alert, quick, positive and fearless. He has never concerned himself with such questions as personal popularity and so, while I know that some individuals have not particularly liked him, I have known none who, having worked with him, failed to respect him.[4]

He has not been in good health for some years—his difficulty being digestive. He is now undergoing hospitalization. Because of this, he is frequently abrupt in manner and impatient of any ineptitude that he encounters. But so far as integrity, force, keenness and executive ability would qualify him for this job, I doubt that you could find a better, subject to the reservation respecting his health.[5]

Should you like to consult further about this matter, I shall always be glad to see you.[6] *Cordially*

[1] Stephens had been vice-president and director of the United States Steel Corporation of Delaware since 1943.

[2] Lieutenant General Walter Bedell Smith had been commander of the First Army, Governors Island, New York, since 1949 (for background see no. 410).

[3] Stephens had written to Eisenhower in a "confidential and personal way" for an evaluation of Smith, who was under consideration as chairman of a three-man board of arbitration for the United Steelworkers of America and the steel-producing subsidiaries of United States Steel. Stephens said that before talking with Smith, his organization was "desirous of learning from those who know him whether, in their judgment, he possesses the qualifications which experience has led us to conclude are essential in this position" (Apr. 6, 1950, EM).

[4] In the same letter, Stephens had pointed out that the most important functions of an arbitrator were to interpret and apply provisions of agreements without fear or influence. "In other words, he should continuously interpret the labor agreement in a judicial manner and . . . not be concerned with advancing any causes or philosophies beyond that of justice to both parties under the agreements."

[5] Smith, who was recuperating from a minor operation, had been transferred in March from Fort Jay Hospital, Governors Island, New York, to Walter Reed General Hospital in Washington, D.C. He would undergo more surgery in May for a chronic peptic ulcer (*New York Times*, Apr. 1, May 3, 1950).

[6] Stephens would thank Eisenhower for his "frank letter" (Apr. 12, 1950, EM). In October President Truman would appoint Smith to succeed Rear Admiral Roscoe N. Hillenkoetter as Director of the CIA (for developments see no. 950). Sidney L. Cahn would become chairman of the arbitration board (*New York Times*, May 13, 1950).

777   *Eisenhower Mss.*

To RICHARD W. COURCHAINE   *April 8, 1950*

Dear Mr. Courchaine:[1] A letter such as yours, from a World War II veteran, always gets a prompt answer from me. I have not read the article in the Saturday Evening Post to which you refer, but I assure you that I have never in any way advocated the abolition of the Marine Corps.[2]

It seems fundamental to me that the Navy is for the control of the seas and I have always believed that, in order to carry out this mission, it needs certain, specially equipped land troops. This is the Marine Corps, and they are normally used in the seizing of small forward bases that the fleet needs to *control the seas*. Consequently, I believe that we need Marine forces in the numbers and kinds of units, primarily, for these particular purposes.

Large-scale land fighting is the business of the Army. The Army, therefore, produces forces required for the conduct of campaigns, covering continents in area and months in time. We should not give this mission to both forces, because, if we are merely carrying out a contest of seeing who can have the most of every kind of unit, for every kind of fighting, then we are going to break our Treasury.[3]

I trust that this clears up the question you have in your letter. I repeat that I tremendously admire the Marine Corps and believe it absolutely necessary for its own functions. But my further belief is that, unless it is designed, organized, led and trained for *these special functions*, then it is getting into a field for which a heavily taxed country is already maintaining another type of force.[4]

Quite naturally, I am more than flattered by your expression of confidence in me and your overgenerous comments as to my personal qualifications. I appreciate your writing to me.[5] *Sincerely*

[1] Courchaine, of Haverhill, Massachusetts, had enlisted at age seventeen and served three years in the U.S. Marine Corps.

[2] In his handwritten letter (Apr. 4, 1950, EM) Courchaine had said he was concerned about Eisenhower's attitude toward the Marine Corps after reading a magazine article that charged the Army and the Air Force with attempts to reduce the size and effectiveness of the Marine Corps. The ex-Marine told Eisenhower that he was "very surprised" to read that the General was a "foe" of the Marines. Courchaine's letter had been prompted by an article entitled "The Marine Corps Fights for Its Life," published by Richard Tregaskis in the February 5, 1949, issue of the *Saturday Evening Post*. According to Tregaskis, Eisenhower had proposed that the Marine Corps be maintained solely as an "adjunct of the Fleet" and participate only in minor shore combat operations. For Eisenhower's April 2, 1946, memorandum to the Joint Chiefs of Staff, the document on which Tregaskis based his allegations, see Galambos, *Chief of Staff*, no. 816.

[3] For Eisenhower's views on defense spending and the roles and missions of the services see nos. 368, 519, and 598.

[4] Eisenhower commented on the Marine Corps as the subject of contention between the Army and Navy in no. 639.

[5] Courchaine said that he and his fellow marines thought that Eisenhower was "a pretty good Gen. . . . [and] . . . would make a good President of the United States."

778   *Eisenhower Mss.*

To Joseph Biddle Priestley   *April 8, 1950*

Dear Dr. Priestley: I was glad to get your letter with its explanation of one reason why we had so many men discharged or rejected because of mental difficulty.[1]

The figures I gave were quoted to me by an officer from the Surgeon General's office of the Army and, as I understood them, were meant to cover the aggregate loss in *all the armed services*.

Nevertheless, whatever the cause and whatever the extenuating circumstances, I still think that at the very least we must guard against repeating that experience in another great emergency. We cannot afford either that kind of wastage or mistakes that deny us the use of that many competent men.[2]

I am grateful for the trouble you took in writing to me. *Sincerely*

[1] Priestley, of Des Moines, Iowa, had said in a letter of April 4 (EM) that he had recently read Eisenhower's statement that over two million men had been rejected or discharged from Army service during World War II because of mental disease. Priestley, who had served as Chief of Surgery in the Army, said that while he had been stationed at Camp Crowder, the post commander had informed the CO of the hospital there that he "had to get rid of one thousand men, the names of which he sent over to the hospital." The men had been hospitalized, and most of them were subsequently discharged as psychoneurotics. This had happened "repeatedly," he said, and the numbers of the mentally disabled were thus inflated and inaccurate.

[2] In 1948 Eisenhower had started a project at Columbia University to study this problem (see no. 155).

779
Eisenhower Mss.,
Miscellaneous Corr., Pakistan

To George Crews McGhee
April 24, 1950

Dear Mr. McGhee:[01] I am happy to inform you that the Trustees of Columbia University will award the Prime Minister of Pakistan, Lia-quat Ali Khan, the honorary degree of Doctor of Laws.[2] In order to save the time of the Prime Minister, the award will be made *in camera* in the Trustees' Room on Monday, May 8th, at 5 p.m. This is a standard procedure with the University and has distinguished precedents, as for example in the case of the President of Venezuela, who received a similar degree *in camera* in the summer of 1948.[3]

The University is very glad to accept your suggestion and to contribute to the strengthening of this country's relations with the Government of Pakistan.[4] *Sincerely*

[1] McGhee had been U.S. Assistant Secretary of State for Near Eastern, South Asian, and African Affairs since 1949.

[2] McGhee had written to Eisenhower on April 21 in the "hope [that] the University will find it possible to make this award" (CUF). On this same day (Apr. 24) Eisenhower notified Khan of the decision to honor him with a degree and added, "We welcome this opportunity to manifest to you and to the world the high regard we have for your great accomplishments and our desire to strengthen the intellectual bonds that unite your country with this University" (EM). Associate Provost Joaquin Enrique Zanetti drafted both this note and the document printed above.

[3] Eisenhower would confer the award upon the Prime Minister, who was on a state visit and tour of the United States, in a brief ceremony on May 8 at Columbia University's Low Memorial Library. The citation accompanying the degree read

in part: " 'Liaquat Ali Khan, administrator and statesman . . . whose long political career has not only revealed warm sympathy for the underprivileged, but has included a host of practical measures to improve their lot; and . . . whose ability as a statesman had been tested in his country's struggle for independence among the freedom-loving nations of the world' " (*New York Times*, May 9, 1950). In 1948 Eisenhower had presented the honorary degree of Doctor of Laws to President Rómulo Gallegos (see no. 111, n. 5).

[4] McGhee had advised Eisenhower that "the Department of State considers that the according of such an honor to Liaquat Ali Khan will go far to strengthen relations between the United States and Pakistan . . ." and that it would be "eminently fitting if an American university with the prestige enjoyed by Columbia could give him a degree, and I know the Prime Minister and his Government would cherish this honor" (CUF).

Some officials at Columbia University, however, disagreed. In a handwritten memorandum to Eisenhower, University Provost Grayson L. Kirk, a specialist in international affairs, opposed the move and advised that "although the Pakistani representatives would like it—because of Nehru's degree—our position can be that the Nehru degree was earned by his general career of leadership, and not by the mere fact that he is head of a state" (Kirk to Eisenhower, n.d.; for background on the degree conferred upon Prime Minister of India Pandit Jawaharlal Nehru, see no. 512). In reply, Kevin McCann, assistant to the president, pointed out that Eisenhower had been given a free hand by the trustees regarding Khan's degree and therefore, "because of the political impact on Pakistan and the addition of a new 'common bond' between Moslem Liaquat Ali Khan and Hindu J. Nehru, we should give the former an honorary degree—that is if the State Department asks us to give one" (memorandum, McCann to Kirk, Apr. 11, 1950, EM).

In late May 1950 the government of Pakistan would pledge twenty-five thousand dollars annually for ten years to Columbia University for the development of a center of Pakistani studies as part of a projected Near and Middle Eastern institute (for background see no. 544; papers concerning Pakistan's contribution are in CUF and in same file as document). The centers of Pakistani and Iranian studies both would open with the winter session of 1951. The Turkish government also decided to allocate funds in its 1951 budget for the establishment of a center of Turkish studies at Columbia, and this center would open in 1952. For further background see Cowan, *A History of the School of International Affairs*, pp. 40–89; and Columbia University, *Educational Future*, pp. 147–49.

780 *Eisenhower Mss.*

To Robert Wood Johnson

April 25, 1950

Dear Mr. Johnson:[1] Thank you very much for your letter of the 19th which I had my first opportunity to read only this morning.[2]

The idea expressed in the second paragraph of that letter is one in which I am in rough, but most earnest accord.[3] I believe that a great university, such as Columbia, is not discharging its full duty to the public when it concentrates its sole attention on the "training of future leaders" even though that training may have in view the discharge of the great responsibilities of citizenship in a free country. I believe, specifically, that the university should seek constant and enduring contacts with America of today—with business, with the professions, with governmental officials on a personal basis, and with all who are part of the complex organism that we call our nation. I believe that, through these contacts and continuing relationships, the wisdom of practical business and professional men will be brought into the university while the great scholars will be enabled, constantly, to turn over to living, day-by-day America the products of their reflections, studies, observations and research.

I am instantly turning over your letter to President Russell of Teachers College with the suggestion that he contact your organization promptly. I am quite certain you will be pleased with the attitude you will find that he represents and with the constructive suggestions he will be able to make for implementing the idea you propose in the final paragraph of your letter.[4]

It just occurs to me that I shall also send a copy of your letter to Dean Philip Young of our School of Business, you will unquestionably have a similar interest and may, likewise, contact your organization.[5]

I am grateful for your letter and for the ideas you express. *Sincerely*

[1] Johnson was chairman of the board of Johnson & Johnson, surgical dressing manufacturers. During World War II Johnson had risen from colonel to brigadier general in the Army Ordnance Department while also serving as chairman of the Smaller War Plants Corporation and vice-chairman of the War Production Board. Johnson had written to Eisenhower on April 19 (EM) expressing agreement with the General's recent statements on the need for individualism and decentralized government in America.
[2] Eisenhower had been on vacation in Augusta, Georgia, until April 22 (on the trip see no. 774).
[3] Johnson had described what he thought to be an ideal educational program. He envisioned thirty or forty million adults receiving "education at work," that is, attending classes taught by academicians "at the place of work, mostly on company time."
[4] Johnson had praised President William F. Russell of Teachers College for the sentiments the latter had expressed on the subject of citizenship education in the April 17, 1950, issue of *Life*. Russell was Director of the Citizenship Education Project, a program organized to increase civic pride among high school students (for background see no. 727). Johnson had offered the facilities of his company to the project while it was in its experimental stage.
[5] On Young see no. 54.

781   *Eisenhower Mss.*

To Robert Daniel Murphy   *April 25, 1950*

Dear Bob:[1] I think you have already been sent a copy of the letter I wrote to Julius Holmes, giving an account of SHAEF's relationships, in 1945, with King Leopold. The fact is that the whole affair did not make too deep an impression upon my mind; consequently, it does not live too vividly in my memory. Nevertheless, any intimation that I actually impeded his return to Belgium is completely erroneous. I not only had no reason to take a stand in the matter but, since there was a Belgian government functioning—one that was recognized by both America and Britain—there was no need for me to attempt any independent analysis of the Belgian political situation. I contented myself with issuing orders to see that King Leopold should have whatever he might require in the way of subsistence and protection and I had someone (probably Grasett) inform him that transportation would always be available to return him to Brussels when this should be requested, both by the Belgian government and by him.[2]

You will understand that this represents my impressions—the only thing to which I should take oath is that I did not take any stand in the matter and have no opinion or feeling one way or the other concerning the wisdom of his returning to Brussels.

I hear that Lucius Clay is in the city this morning and I have been trying to get in contact with him on the telephone. So far, I have had no success. There is a group here at the University which is very anxious to have him accept a position with us.[3]

Please convey my greetings to your charming daughters, and with warm regards to yourself,[4] *Cordially*

[1] Murphy had been U.S. Ambassador to Belgium since September 1949 (for background see no. 218).

[2] For information on the Belgian royal question see no. 708. Murphy had written to Eisenhower requesting information on the General's involvement in the liberation of King Leopold of Belgium by American troops in 1945 (Apr. 11, 1950, EM). Murphy reported that since the referendum over the Belgian royal question had resulted in assertions about the Allied attitude at that time, he wanted a copy of the letter Eisenhower had written to Holmes on February 20, 1950, along with General A. Edward Grasett's letter; these, he said, would give him a "clearer understanding of exactly what transpired." Eisenhower provided Murphy with the former but could not send the latter because it had been addressed to Holmes (Schulz to Murphy, Apr. 20, 1950, EM). For Murphy's account of the issue see Murphy, *Diplomats Among Warriors*, pp. 327–28. For developments see no. 1015.

[3] For developments concerning Lucius D. Clay and the possibility of a Columbia post see no. 739.

[4] Catherine, Rosemary, and Mildred Murphy.

To Louis Arthur Johnson   *April 25, 1950*

Dear Louis:[1] I have just read a copy of the statement that General Gruenther tells me you propose to deliver before the Senate Appropriations Committee, tomorrow, the 26th.[2] As I understand its terms you recommend

    (*a*) A construction program for Alaska that represents the maximum possible in the short Alaskan building season.[3]

    (*b*) An increase in anti-submarine activity in accordance with Admiral Sherman's views, and authorization for modernization of naval aircraft.[4]

    (*c*) An amount of about $1,550,000,000 for airplane procurement for the Air Force.[5]

    (*d*) Increased provision for modernization of Army equipment.[6]

    (*e*) Adequate provision for intelligence and industrial mobilization.[7]

So far as I can determine your recommendations accord exactly with what I personally believe should now be done. I hope the Committee agrees with you in detail.[8]

With warm regard.[9] *Cordially*

[1] This letter to the Secretary of Defense was probably drafted by General Alfred M. Gruenther in Washington, D.C. A copy of the letter, initialed by Eisenhower, is in EM. In an accompanying note Gruenther wrote, "Here is the letter in type. I got McDuff to sign it, and I must say he does a better 'Ike' than you do" (Apr. 26, 1950, EM, Johnson Corr.). Lieutenant Colonel Robert Joseph McDuff had been assigned to the Office of the Joint Chiefs of Staff, Washington, D.C., in September 1949 (for background on McDuff see Galambos, *Chief of Staff*, no. 533, n. 7). Other members of the defense establishment who had seen the letter were Secretary of Defense Johnson; Deputy Secretary of Defense Stephen T. Early; and Marx Leva, who since August 1949 had been an assistant secretary of defense (for background on Early see no. 551; on Leva, no. 288). According to Gruenther's note, they were all pleased.

[2] On April 26 Johnson would submit successive statements before closed sessions of the armed services subcommittees of both the House and the Senate appropriations committees. His appearance had come as a result of testimony by Eisenhower before these same committees, after which Johnson had ordered a reappraisal of the 1951 defense budget by the Joint Chiefs of Staff (for Eisenhower's testimony at that time see nos. 701 and 753).

His purpose, Johnson would tell the congressional committees, was to "discuss the adequacy of the military budget in the light of world conditions." A reevaluation of U.S. military requirements, he said, was appropriate following recent developments in the "constantly changing world situation." He cited the September 1949 atomic explosion in Russia, which had occurred somewhat in advance of its anticipated date; and the subsequent decision by the President to proceed with the construction of the H-bomb. Among other world events that had increased the need for U.S. military strength were the "fall of China, the serious situations in southeast Asia, the break in diplomatic relations with Bulgaria and deteriorating relations with other satellite countries, the Soviet assumption of control over the armed forces of Poland, Soviet naval expansion, the increased Soviet pressures in Germany, the recent attack on a naval aircraft in the Baltic, and the recent Soviet demands relative to Trieste." Accordingly, Johnson would recommend an increase of $350,000,000 in the military budget for the 1951 fiscal year, raising proposed armament expenditures from $14,114,460,000 to $14,464,460,000. The Secretary's new proposal was a revision both of his own and of President Truman's earlier budget requests (see *New York Times*, Apr. 5, 27, 1950).

[3] In his testimony before the Senate military subcommittee Eisenhower had said that he believed the defense of Alaska was so important that it should be given highest priority. He specifically recommended that garrisons be built for Alaskan air bases (for the General's views on Alaska see no. 754; see also nos. 753 and 808). In his own testimony, Johnson would not request additional funds for military construction in Alaska; rather, he would explain that the $130 million already available and the $100 million appropriation request for 1951 would bring funds for construction to $230 million—an adequate amount to provide housing for the military forces in Alaska. "This is in no sense a criticism of General Eisenhower," said Johnson, who thought that the General had not known that funds were available for Alaskan construction when he appeared before the congressional committees: "I leaned over backward not to contact him. . . . I leaned over backward so that no one would accuse me of influencing him in his testimony. So, it is a criticism of myself and not a criticism of General Eisenhower."

[4] Johnson would explain that the President's budget included a readjustment to increase by $79 million the original allocation of $40 million for anti-submarine equipment. He said that when Admiral Denfeld was Chief of Naval Operations he had refused an allocation of up to $100 million for anti-submarine equipment but that when Admiral Sherman had become Chief of Naval Operations he had requested and had received $79 million. Johnson would also ask for $50 million in cash for conversion and operation of additional destroyers and small ships required for anti-submarine defense. For contract authorization for aircraft procurement for the Navy he would ask $100 million.

[5] Johnson's recommendation of an additional $200 million for procurement of aircraft for the Air Force was $50 million above Eisenhower's suggested figure of $1.5 billion (for background see no. 754).

[6] Of the total $41 million increase requested by Johnson for Army materiel procurement, $10 million would be used for new signal equipment for mobile striking forces; $17 million for heavy ordnance; and $7 million for modernized portable bridges and other new engineering equipment. Additional requested increases included $5 million to rebuild and modernize equipment for the National Guard, as well as $16 million for armories for the National Guard and the Organized Reserve. For Eisenhower's recommendations on modernization of Army equipment see no. 755.

[7] Johnson would say that intelligence was a field in which large sums of money were not involved and one which did not lend itself to discussion in open session. The Secretary would offer to discuss the matter in detail in executive session if the committees desired. Plans for industrial mobilization were well advanced, according to Johnson. He would point out that industrial mobilization, "in its broader aspects," was by law the responsibility of the National Security Resources Board. The funds, totaling $100 million already included in the President's budget were adequate, he believed, to cover that portion of industrial mobilization planning which was the responsibility of the Department of Defense.

[8] Both House committees—the full Committee on Appropriations and its subcommittee—would accept immediately Johnson's recommendations. The Senate subcommittee had placed in its record of proceedings a special communication

from the President in which he concurred with the $350 million supplemental estimates of appropriation for the Defense Department budget for 1951 (for Johnson's statements and testimony before both committees see U.S., Congress, House, Committee on Appropriations, *Department of Defense Appropriations for 1951: Additional Supplemental Hearings*, 81st Cong., 2d sess., 1950, pp. 1–11; and Senate Committee on Appropriations, *Department of Defense Appropriations for 1951: Hearings*, 1950, pp. 837–58). A note at the bottom of one of Eisenhower's appointment calendars for April 27 indicates that Johnson telephoned the General that day to thank him for this letter. According to the note, Johnson "did not have [a] chance" to use the letter during his appearance before the Senate subcommittee.

[9] A dramatic escalation in appropriations for defense would come during the summer and fall of 1950, when North Korea invaded South Korea and Chinese Communists attacked the U.N. forces in South Korea. By year's end supplemental appropriations to the original $13.5 billion defense budget for fiscal 1951 had brought the total to more than $42 billion (see *New York Times*, Dec. 16, 21, 22, 23, 1950; and January 2, 3, 7, 1951).

783   *Eisenhower Mss.*

To Felix Edgar Wormser   *April 25, 1950*

Dear Felix: Thank you very much for your note of the 19th.[1] This whole process of securing a new Dean has developed unexpected and, sometimes, astonishing frictions. I am quite certain that, had we all been a unit in the beginning, we could have gotten Lucius for the job. Now I think the chances are 100 to 1 against it. However, I am expecting a telephone call from him today and maybe I shall learn something new.[2]

Of course, I am grateful for your continued and lively interest. *Cordially*

[1] Wormser (E.M. Columbia 1916) was vice-president of St. Joseph Lead Company and president of the Lead Industries Association of New York City. In a letter to Eisenhower of April 19 (EM) he had praised General Lucius D. Clay and proposed that Clay be selected as the dean of the School of Engineering. For background on Clay see no. 55; on the consideration of Clay for the deanship see no. 739.

[2] The results of a survey of opinion among the faculty of the School of Engineering had shown in early April that five departments out of seven were "solidly behind" the selection of Clay. James K. Finch, soon to retire as dean of the School of Engineering, had ranked Clay first among the candidates under consideration and had reported that this was also the consensus among the alumni he had consulted (See Finch to Eisenhower, Apr. 17, 1950, EM). Clay would talk with Eisenhower at Columbia the afternoon of April 26, and on the same day the directors of Continental Can Company would elect Clay to be chief executive officer and chairman of the firm's board. He would accept the position (see *New York Times*, Apr. 27, 1950).

To Robert Paul Leary   *April 26, 1950*

Dear Cadet Leary:[01] Memory can be a treacherous thing, so I hope that you will not attempt to elevate the following to the status of "source material." With this apology, I give you the following as my recollection of my meeting with Secretary Morgenthau in the summer of 1944.[2]

At the time of my meeting with Secretary Morgenthau, Allied Forces were engaged in breaking out of the beachhead and were still a long way from the German border. Consequently, at Allied Headquarters, exhaustive and objective thinking about the problem of occupying Germany had been done *only* by that portion of the staff whose duty it was to prepare the studies, plans and orders that were to apply once we should gain entrance into Germany territory. That part of the staff was then under the direction of Brig. Gen. Wickersham.[3]

When Secretary Morgenthau visited me, the specific subject of his conversation was the rate of exchange to be established between the German mark and the American dollar. I agreed with him that this rate of exchange should not be at a level to favor the German economy. This discussion quite naturally broadened the scope of our conversation to include a general concept of our future purposes in German occupation. Secretary Morgenthau expressed himself very emphatically on this general subject and in rough accord with the general provisions that finally came to be known as the "Morgenthau Plan."

Specifically I agreed with the need for impressing upon the German people a sense of war guilt—at least to the extent of preventing them from absolving themselves from blame in bringing a man of Hitler's type to power in 1933. Moreover, I felt that if the German people, at any time before German rearmament had progressed to the point that the Treaty of Versailles was obviously violated, had clearly and definitely disapproved of the Hitlerian philosophy they could have eliminated him.

I stated to Secretary Morgenthau that the German General Staff should be broken up, that its archives and records should be confiscated or destroyed, that its schools and training centers should be eliminated and that supervision should be exercised to see that it could not be reborn and function under some subterfuge. I thought that certain individuals of Germany should be punished for bringing on the global disaster of World War II. I stated that membership in the Gestapo and in certain other organizations was prima facie evidence of war guilt and the burden of proof should be on any such member to show that he was not guilty of any war crime.

The same applied to high position in the Nazi party. Consequently, I believed that all members of these groups should be brought before properly constituted tribunals for trial.

Economically, I argued that Germany should not be permitted to maintain what could be called "war industries." But I was emphatically against the destruction or choking off of natural resources. I recall that I had previously heard some extreme suggestions to the effect that the Ruhr mines should be flooded and destroyed. To any such proposal I was definitely opposed because I do not believe that peace can be promoted in the world through destruction of natural resources.

I was in favor of reparation as decided upon by Allied Tribunals, but was against a "scorched earth" policy.

From the above you can see what my general impressions were of that particular time. When I came, later, to specific study of these various questions, my recommendations were always for the elimination of war industry but for the application of reason and caution in the destruction or dismantling of other industries because of my fear that we might make the German people, particularly those of Western Germany, permanently dependent upon the United States for subsistence and the barest necessaries of life. I wanted to make sure that through a combination of manufacture and agriculture, Western Germany (or Germany, as a whole) could be self-supporting. I did not believe in 1944 and I do not believe now that Western Germany can exist as a "pastoral" state unless some other nation should undertake responsibility for meeting part of the basic needs of the population.

With respect to your second question, it did not occur to me at the time to question or examine into Secretary Morgenthau's purposes or his motivations.[4] I have always assumed him to be a serious and upright public servant. While I later concluded that he wanted to apply a much stricter and harsher plan to the German people than I did, I never felt that he did so merely through any thought of hate or revenge. He possibly believed that only through the methods he advocated could Germany be rendered impotent in waging aggressive war. That nation, from 1866 to 1939, certainly had a bad record in this regard.

I realized that this can be of very little help to you in the preparation of a real study, but it is the best my memory can give you.[5] *Sincerely*

P.S. I must repeat that, at the time of my talk with Sec. Morgenthau it was just that—nothing more. I have not yet given the whole subject of occupation sufficient study to venture the formulation of specific recommendations!

---

[1] Leary was a member of the class of 1950 at the United States Military Academy. In a letter of April 12 he had asked Eisenhower about his role in the origins of a postwar plan for Germany, the so-called Morgenthau Plan. He would use the

information, he said, for a term paper in a course he was taking on international relations (EM).

[2] On August 7, 1944, Secretary of the U.S. Treasury Henry Morgenthau, Jr., and two aides had visited Eisenhower at his advance command post at Portsmouth, England. Their conversation that day had concerned plans for the future occupation of a vanquished Germany. According to the several accounts of the meeting, there is agreement that an exceedingly hard peace for Germany—a peace that would have rendered Germany economically and militarily powerless—was discussed. The question, however, of who inspired the plan—Eisenhower or Morgenthau— has been the subject of a good deal of controversy. For background see Chandler, *War Years*, no. 2087; Chandler and Galambos, *Occupation, 1945*, nos. 386 and 471; and Galambos, *Chief of Staff*, no. 1684.

[3] For background on Brigadier General Cornelius W. Wickersham, whose per- formance in the establishment of American military government in Germany Eisenhower described as "brilliant" (*Crusade in Europe*, p. 435), see no. 170.

[4] Leary had asked whether Eisenhower thought the Morgenthau Plan "a policy of hate or merely a near-sighted program of a sincere man."

[5] On May 8 Leary would thank Eisenhower for his letter (EM). The cadet said, however, that the information concerning the Morgenthau Plan was of secondary importance compared with the lesson in leadership he learned. "The lesson," he said, "is that a truly great man does as fine a job on trivial matters as upon the most important task. You have given me an excellent principle to shoot at in my service career."

785   *Eisenhower Mss.*

To H. R. RAMSDELL   *April 26, 1950*

Dear Mr. Ramsdell:[1] I did not receive your letter of April 10 until my return, yesterday, from a trip to Georgia.[2] You understand, of course, that I no longer hold any official position in our security forces— consequently, I cannot act directly on your suggestions.[3]

Needless to say, your proposal was most interesting to me. I agree that it is highly desirable—even essential—to succeed in getting the truth about the United States understood better in all the populations back of the Iron Curtain.[4] The method you suggest is one way of doing it. There is one disadvantage in employing this particular method. It is that totalitarian governments sometimes establish the death penalty for anyone caught reading a foreign leaflet, pamphlet or any kind of paper that comes from anywhere except the propaganda system of that particular country. Since secret police are everywhere, the risks are apparent. During World War II we had to be very careful in supporting subversive elements in occupied territories, so as to avoid exposing them to this kind of punishment.[5]

I, however, assure you that friends of mine, in Washington, who have to study and work with these things will have your idea brought to their attention. Certainly, as parents of fine American boys and veterans of World War II, you and your wife have a right to have your suggestions carefully considered by those in authority.[6]

Thank you for writing me.[7] *Sincerely*

[1] Ramsdell headed H. R. Ramsdell Real Estate and Insurance Company, of Live Oak, California.

[2] For the trip see no. 756.

[3] In his letter Ramsdell had suggested the use of message-carrying balloons as a method of disseminating information to the peoples of the Soviet Union. "They could be released by the millions at points in Europe selected by Meteorological Experts, so that a certain number of them would be sure to land in Russia." They would, he said, "carry the real truth direct to the Russian people . . . without endangering a single American life" (see Senate Select Committee to Study Governmental Operations with respect to Intelligence Activities, *Final Report*, bk. IV, 1976, p. 29).

Ramsdell's suggestion was not new. The use of balloons to disseminate propaganda had been proposed as early as 1854 in a letter written by a Russian exile to a French war minister. Radio broadcasts, however, eventually proved a quicker and more effective propaganda weapon. The Free Europe Committee (FEC) would combine the two methods during the spring and summer of 1954 in a propaganda campaign known as "Operation Veto," directed at the population behind the Iron Curtain. Balloons containing millions of anti-Soviet leaflets, stickers, posters, etc., were dropped in coordination with explanatory radio broadcasts to the peoples of Czechoslovakia (see William E. Daugherty, with Morris Janowitz, *A Psychological Warfare Casebook* [Baltimore, 1958], pp. 332–37). For Eisenhower's involvement with organizations to assist peoples behind the Iron Curtain see nos. 303 and 428.

[4] The State Department's postwar program to provide information about the United States to peoples of other countries was summarized in an article by Assistant Secretary of State William Benton entitled, "Self-Portrait—By Uncle Sam" (*New York Times Magazine*, Dec. 2, 1945; for additional background see Galambos, *Chief of Staff*, no. 1863).

[5] Concerning the effectiveness of leaflet propaganda during World War II see Martin F. Herz, "Some Lessons from Leaflet Propaganda," in *Propaganda in War and Crisis*, ed. Daniel Lerner (New York, 1951), pp. 416–33. See also Paul M. A. Linebarger, *Psychological Warfare* (Washington, D.C., 1954), esp. pp. 244–308.

[6] Ramsdell had mentioned that he and his wife, Ena, were parents of sons who had served in the Pacific and in Europe during the war.

[7] In a letter of May 9 Ramsdell would agree with Eisenhower that reprisals by totalitarian governments were a major disadvantage of his proposal. He insisted, however, that "many people have died for Freedom's sake and many more will die before Freedom is won everywhere" (EM).

Lately a couple of "Gallup Polls" have put me back into the political gossip columns—although, there never has been a complete cessation of loose talk about me as a presidential possibility![1]

A few evenings ago Gallup reported running me against Pres. Truman. Bad business! but nothing to do about it. I hope that Pres. is too philosophical to take real note of the 60−30 report against him.[2]

Public speaking gets to be more & more of a burden. I can limit, very well, the appearances before big audiences—prepared speeches, etc. But *every* luncheon & dinner, some, even, that appear to be social only—seems certain to bring around the moment where a host declares—"I'm sure Gen. E. will be kind enough, etc." How I hate it! Sometimes I think I'm trapped by my liking for people![3]

Am going to try my first *New York* golf this p.m.[4]

[1] In recent months much speculation had arisen concerning Eisenhower as a possible candidate in the presidential election of 1952. A poll by public opinion statistician Dr. George Horace Gallup (Apr. 24, 1950) had posed the question, "Of course, it's still a long time away, but if the 1952 presidential election were being held today, and Dwight Eisenhower were running for President on the Republican ticket against Harry Truman on the Democratic ticket, how do you think you would vote—for Eisenhower or Truman?" Sixty percent of those interviewed had chosen Eisenhower; 31 percent had chosen Truman; and the remaining 9 percent were undecided (see George H. Gallup, *The Gallup Poll: Public Opinion, 1935−1971*, 3 vols. [New York, 1972], vol. II, *1949−1958*, p. 905). In a poll of April 5, Eisenhower had headed the list of possible nominees for the Republican party with 37 percent, over Taft with 17 percent; Warren with 5 percent; Vandenberg with 5 percent; Bricker with 3 percent; and an assortment of others. As a second choice for the Republican ticket, the bulk of the followers of Dewey, Warren, Vandenberg, and Stassen picked Eisenhower as an alternative candidate (*ibid.*, pp. 901−2).

[2] In the December 19, 1949, issue of *Newsweek* President Truman was reported as having declared his own conviction that Eisenhower would run as the Republican candidate for the presidency in 1952. Truman, rumored to be thinking about running again, was said to regard the General as a formidable candidate because of his personal popularity and his middle-of-the-road political orientation. According to the article, however, the President considered Eisenhower's tactics amateurish, and he thought that the General allowed associates and enthusiastic audience response to lead him to overstate his own opinions (see no. 491).

On October 30, 1950, DeWitt Wallace, founder and editor of *Reader's Digest*, would send Eisenhower the results of yet another Gallup poll undertaken for his magazine (for background on Wallace see no. 448). Wallace reported that in a cross section of one thousand Protestant clergymen of different denominations, ages, and sections of the country 71 percent had chosen Eisenhower for the presidency in 1952; 13 percent had chosen Truman; and 10 percent were undecided. "You are the *only* person in sight," Wallace said, "who can give *real leadership* to this country" (EM). For background on Eisenhower as a possible candidate in 1952 see nos. 581 and 638.

[3] Eisenhower's extemporaneous speeches critical of Truman's policies had triggered more speculation concerning his political aspirations. In a letter to his brother Milton he had resolved to "stop speaking entirely" (see no. 606). For developments involving political pressures see no. 788.

[4] General Eisenhower left his office at 11:30 A.M. to play golf with George Allen, former boxing champion James "Gene" Tunney, and Ellis "Slats" Slater at the Blind Brook Country Club.

787   *Eisenhower Mss.*

To Louis Marx   *April 29, 1950*

Dear Louis:[1] I shall be on the lookout for the plastic animals. I have never attempted that kind of painting, but so long as you have stuck your neck out by announcing your desire for a completed set, I shall try to dress them up, brand them with my own mark and send them to you. It will be fun to try something different.[2]

So far as Bernhardi is concerned, I find that our calendar from now on through the month of May is nothing less than a "mess."[3] However, Mamie and I fight to keep free the hours from about 4:30 until about dinner time for friends who can drop in to see us. Normally the only time we break this habit is when I play golf, but even so I am always back by 5:15 or 5:30 and can, of course, always break a golf date. So I suggest that instead of your trying to make some formal date which would fit our very inflexible schedule you simply wait until Bernhardi arrives, and then give us a ring from 12 to 24 hours in advance merely saying when you are going to bring him by.[4] If Idella should be in town she would probably not mind coming along and listening to men chinning over the war days and events.[5]

Of course, there is always the possibility that at the last minute Mamie and I might be able to go out on some other kind of a date, but it would be scarcely less than a miracle if this should happen. In any event, I am most anxious to see Bernhardi again and I am, of course, grateful that you are trying to make this possible. *Cordially*

[1] Louis Marx, president of Louis Marx & Company, toy manufacturers.

[2] In a letter of April 24, 1950, Marx had told Eisenhower about his company's line of plastic animals (dogs, farm and wild animals, etc.). He had suggested that Eisenhower paint and initial the figures and give them as Christmas presents. On April 28 Marx had informed the General that a shipment of animals was on its way (EM). "Paint some of them up," he said. "Put your initials on the under belly. . . . I would like a set—I can tell you that, if you ever get around to it." Marx would send more animals on June 1 and would continue to supply Eisenhower with assorted cowboys, animals, and paints (see Marx to Eisenhower, June 1 and 22, 1950, EM). For developments see no. 856.

[3] Marx had invited the General and Mrs. Eisenhower to his home on May 4 for

cocktails and dinner in honor of Prince Bernhard of the Netherlands. The Prince would arrive in New York on May 2 for a two-week visit to the United States to stimulate trade and to open a Holland fair in the Gimbel Department Store in Philadelphia on May 6 (*New York Times*, May 3, 6, 15, 1950). Prince Bernhard, an old friend of Marx's and Eisenhower's, had been Commander in Chief of the Netherlands forces in World War II (for background see Chandler, *War Years*, nos. 910 and 1510).

[4] Mrs. Eisenhower had also suggested that a visit be arranged on a mutually convenient day (memorandum, Schulz to Eisenhower, Apr. 28, 1950, EM). According to his appointment calendar, however, Eisenhower would meet with Marx, Prince Bernhard, and John J. Raskob at a scheduled luncheon party given by Lieutenant General Hugh A. Drum (ret.) on May 3 at the Empire State Building (Drum to Eisenhower, Mar. 18, 1950, EM, Miscellaneous Corr.). Drum and Raskob were, respectively, president and vice-president of Empire State, Inc., the corporation that managed and operated the Empire State Building. Drum had headed the Eastern Defense Command and the First Army during World War II (see Chandler, *War Years*, no. 34). Raskob was a prominent industrialist who had held executive positions with both the du Pont Company and the General Motors Corporation. In 1928 he had served as chairman of the Democratic National Committee, managing Alfred E. Smith's presidential campaign. In a letter of May 24 Eisenhower would thank General Drum for the luncheon and "the opportunity of renewing old memories . . ." (EM).

[5] Marx's wife, the former Idella Ruth Blackadder, would attend the luncheon (for background on Mrs. Marx see Galambos, *Chief of Staff*).

DIARY   *April 29, 1950*

Some time ago I listed in these notes the names of men who have been urging me to go into politics. I've tried to put down the names only of those who seem to be in position to cause some ripple of interest—who seem to have convictions on the matter and therefore deserve the courtesy of a hearing.[1] None has changed my mind an iota—probably Mr. Hoover has shaken me more than anyone else— and strangely enough he did not urge me to do anything. He simply talked from the *assumption* that *duty might* compel me to do something I would not choose to do.[2]

A man named Simmons from Houston and one named Wenke from Ft. Collins, Colo. have recently started embarrassing movements— but I *think* we've got them stopped.[3] The most studied document I've received on the subject is from Graeme Howard—a most conscientious (sometimes I think humorless) individual, who has an important job with Ford Motor Co. He concludes that I must (a) announce Republican affiliations now; (b) speak this summer, in favor of outstanding Senatorial and Congressional candidates (Republican, of course) and (c) thereafter merely await the *inevitable* nomination. All this or else I'm failing to do my duty to this nation and, finally, I will come to realize I have so failed—and will die an *embittered* & disappointed man!!!⁴

All very pretty; but I still don't believe it.

The international situation deteriorates even though we see, occasionally, favorable editorials. I wonder how long the few remaining areas in S.W. Pacific can hold out!!⁵

Our leadership is too intermittent; Communism is on the job every minute of every day of the 365. Our V.I.P.'s are concerned only when there is a crisis—Iran—Greece—Trieste—Berlin—etc.⁶

As to China, we wrote a white paper to show how right we were!!⁷ God, such stupidity. When we liberated those areas of Europe in W.W. II where *resistance* movements were strong, we learned to be careful to prevent later lawless action by the former guerrillas. (MacA. and the P.I. did not learn this.)⁸ What do our bosses think that the Chinese commies are now going to do? I believe Asia is lost with *Japan, P.I., N.E.I.*⁹ *and even Australia under threat.* India Itself is *not* safe!¹⁰

---

¹ For the names of those who were pressuring the General to declare himself a political candidate see nos. 581, 602, and 638.

² See no. 638.

³ Eisenhower had recently written to attorney David A. Simmons, of Houston, Texas, to ask him not to proceed with plans for forming a group called Americans for Eisenhower (see no. 770). On April 28, the day before Eisenhower made this entry in his diary, his friend and adviser William Burnham had telephoned from Houston to say that he had talked to Simmons and that Simmons had agreed to call off Americans for Eisenhower—temporarily. Burnham would also work to dissuade a Dallas, Texas, group calling itself Americans for National Coalition from organizing to draft the General as a presidential candidate (Burnham to Eisenhower, May 4, 1950, EM). Paul E. Wenke, an attorney, and Robert L. White, a commercial printer, both of Fort Collins, Colorado, had formed the "Dear Ike" Club, which required its members to write Eisenhower at Columbia and ask him to accept the Republican nomination for the presidency in 1952. Members were also asked to write ten or more friends telling them about the plan (correspondence concerning the club and its sponsors is in EM, P.E. Wenke Corr. and R. L. White Corr.).

⁴ Howard headed the international division of the Ford Motor Company (for background on him see no. 269). The "studied document" to which Eisenhower refers is not in EM.

⁵ Eisenhower was probably referring to the Philippines, Formosa, South Korea, and Japan (see American Assembly, *The United States and the Far East* [New York, 1956]).

⁶ For the General's concern with crises in these areas see *Eisenhower Papers*, vols. VI–IX. For studies of increasing tensions worldwide see Kolko and Kolko, *Limits of Power*; Feis, *From Trust to Terror*; and Yergin, *Shattered Peace*. For personal accounts by "our V.I.P.'s," as Eisenhower calls them, of involvement with postwar problems and the spread of communism see Truman, *Memoirs*, vol. II, *Years of Trial and Hope*; and Acheson, *Present at the Creation*.

⁷ This was the *China White Paper*, originally published by the U.S. Department of State as *United States Relations with China with Special Reference to the Period 1944–1949* in 1949. Authorized in March 1949 by President Truman, its most

ardent enthusiast was Secretary of State Dean Acheson, who had urged on Truman the preparation of an account of U.S. relations with China, to be published "when the collapse came" (Acheson, *Present at the Creation*, p. 302). When the *China White Paper* appeared in August 1949, a storm of controversy broke over its contents and over Acheson's depressing conclusion, which read in part: "The unfortunate but inescapable fact is that the ominous result of the civil war in China was beyond the control of the government of the United States. Nothing that this country did or could have done within the reasonable limits of its capabilities could have changed that result; nothing that was left undone by this country has contributed to it. It was the product of internal Chinese forces, forces which this country tried to influence but could not. A decision was arrived at within China, if only a decision by default" (State, *China White Paper*, p. xvi). Some saw the *China White Paper* as pro-Communist; others saw it as anti-Communist. To some it was a deliberately slanted document favoring the Truman-Acheson administration; still others called it an ill-timed violation of the codes of official privacy. Almost no one accepted it at face value. For more information about the *China White Paper* and the controversy over its publication see Acheson, *Present at the Creation*, pp. 302–3, 306–7; and Gaddis Smith, *Dean Acheson*, The American Secretaries of State and Their Diplomacy, vol. XVI, ed. Robert H. Ferrell (New York, 1972), pp. 115–21.

[8] Eisenhower is referring to General Douglas MacArthur's policy of returning to civil administration all areas in the Philippines liberated from the Japanese in 1944 and 1945. American and Filipino forces serving in the Philippines during the liberation were subject to civil authority and were not considered armies of occupation (Douglas MacArthur, *Reminiscences* [New York, 1964], pp. 235–37, 250–51). At the same time, the vigorous and powerful Philippine resistance army, the Hukbalahap, refused to surrender its arms and became a source of civil unrest in the islands. Known as the Huk Rebellion, the uprisings were heavily influenced by the PKP, the Communist party of the Philippines. For more information see Douglas MacArthur, *Reports of General MacArthur*, prepared by his General Staff, vol. I, *The Campaigns of MacArthur in the Pacific* (Washington, D.C., 1966), pp. 295–325; Benedict J. Kerkvliet, *The Huk Rebellion: A Study of Peasant Revolt in the Philippines* (Berkeley, 1977); Smith, *Philippine Freedom*; and Robert Ross Smith, *The Hukbalahap Insurgency: Economic, Political, and Military Factors* (Washington, D.C., 1963).

[9] The Philippine Islands and the Netherlands East Indies.

[10] The spread of communism in the Far East was of growing concern to Eisenhower. In Japan there were continuing disputes over the repatriation of Japanese war prisoners from the Soviet Union and over the conclusion of terms for a peace treaty that would be acceptable to both the Western powers and to the Soviet Union. In the Philippines the Communist-led Huks (discussed in n. 8 above) had recently mounted new attacks on the island of Luzon. The Netherlands East Indies (NEI), which in 1949 had become the fully sovereign United States of Indonesia, were in the throes of a civil war and seemed ripe for infiltration by Chinese Communists. In Australia Communist activity had created such tension that legislation had been introduced to outlaw the party on grounds that it sought the overthrow of the government. India, while admitting that it had more in common with the West than with the Soviet Union, was nevertheless attempting to remain neutral (see Harold M. Vinacke, *Far Eastern Politics in the Postwar Period* [New York, 1956]; and Charles B. McLane, *Soviet Strategies in Southeast Asia: An Exploration of Eastern Policy under Lenin and Stalin* [Princeton, 1966], esp. pp. 351–483).

On behalf of the Trustees of the University, I have accepted with regret the resignation of Paul H. Davis as Vice President in Charge of Development.[1] Mr. Davis has been of important assistance to Columbia in devising development programs and in the high quality of his professional work in the development field.[2] I feel that Columbia's position with respect to gift procurement has been vastly improved through the services of Mr. Davis.[3] Both personally and officially I regret his resignation and am happy to know that he will stay with us long enough to assist in such reorganization as is made necessary thereby.[4]

I therefore offer the following resolution:

Resolved That the action of the President in accepting the resignation of Paul H. Davis is approved to be effective at such date in 1950 as may be mutually agreed upon between the President and Mr. Davis.

The Trustees express their gratitude to Mr. Davis for the high quality of the professional service and for the great personal zeal and loyalty with which he has served Columbia. They hereby authorize the payment to him of his full salary to include December 31, 1950.

[1] Davis had held this position since March 1949 (for background see no. 361).

[2] For background on the program see nos. 438, 488, and 669.

[3] Eisenhower would write Davis on May 11 to acknowledge his decision to leave Columbia University to establish a development and public relations firm in California. "I am pleased with the progress and results that the Development team has attained," the General told Davis. "There is every indication that the accomplishments of the Columbia Development Program will be increasingly apparent to all as the ultimate record unrolls" (EM). The *New York Times* would report that "Columbia received $10,000,000 in gifts, grants and bequests in the three completed fiscal years that Mr. Davis directed the fund-raising campaigns" (May 2, 1950).

[4] On May 9 Eisenhower would write to all of those cooperating in the development program to assure them that Davis's departure would not mean a setback in these activities. He would ask that they continue to support the various phases of the program (CUF). In June Eisenhower would have an informal committee review the university's policies and procedures, and in a memorandum of June 28 Provost Grayson L. Kirk would announce that development activities would be "decentralized" (while being coordinated through the Office of Development). "Separate budgets will be set up for these decentralized activities as of July 1, 1950" for Columbia College and for the graduate schools of business, medicine, science, and engineering. Dean Philip Young would serve as Acting Coordinator of Development (Kirk to all deans and directors and to the Office of Development staff, EM). For background on the decentralization of Columbia's administration see no. 479; for developments see nos. 834 and 930.

To Milton Stover Eisenhower   *May 1, 1950*

Dear Milton:[1] Ed's note to you indicates that the Bar Association and the Golf Tournament have such high September priority on his schedule that he will probably be absent from your inauguration.[2] I do hope that Earl and Art can make the grade.[3] Certainly I'll be there if above ground and still able to walk![4]

Love to all. *As ever*

[1] A handwritten copy of this document is in EM, Letters and Drafts.
[2] Milton Eisenhower's inauguration as president of Pennsylvania State College had been planned for October 4 and 5 (for background see no. 757). Milton had sent the General a copy of a letter from their brother Edgar, who was a lawyer in Tacoma, Washington (Apr. 25, 1950, EM, Family File, Milton S. Eisenhower Corr.). Edgar had written that unless the inauguration immediately followed his September trip to the East Coast, he could not attend the ceremonies. Edgar planned to play in the Fred Waring Golf Tournament in Pennsylvania; he would also attend the American Bar Association convention in Washington, D.C. Both events would keep him in the East for most of the month of September, and he felt that he could not justify a longer absence from his office. As it turned out, Edgar would attend Milton's inauguration (see Edgar Eisenhower to Dwight Eisenhower, Sept. 14, 1950, EM, Family File; and *New York Times*, Oct. 6, 1950).
[3] Earl Eisenhower would attend Milton's inauguration, but Arthur, another brother, would not be able to attend because of the death of a member of his banking firm. For background on the Eisenhower brothers see no. 37; for developments see no. 915; and for Milton Eisenhower's inauguration see no. 997.
[4] General Eisenhower would be there.

791   *Eisenhower Mss.*

To Winston Spencer Churchill   *May 1, 1950*

Dear Winston:[1] There is in Great Britain today one of America's outstanding authorities in history. His name is Edward Mead Earle and he is now delivering a series of lectures at Oxford, in All Souls College.[2]

He and I have discussed a project for establishing in an American university a Chair of Military History. I have found that at no place in our civilian educational institutions do we study war as a social phenomenon—as a cancerous growth on the body of world society. Disinterested studies on the causes, conduct and consequences of war should do something, I think, to give us factual bases for many of the so-called "peace" discussions that otherwise remain mere exercises in dialectics or academic logic. What I really believe should be started by some university is what might be called an Institute of Peace, with a professor of military history as its directing head.[3]

I wondered whether you might find it convenient to have a secretary ask Dr. Earle to come to see you while he is in Britain, just to chat informally with him about these matters. I should very much like to get your ideas as to whether or not there might be definite value in such an effort. Most certainly, I do not want to attempt something that would not promise a more practical result than publication of a new and abstract condemnation of war.

In any event, if you talk to Dr. Earle about these things, I think that the sending to him of a mere word would insure his coming promptly to call upon you.[4]

Naturally, this note brings to you my continued and sincere wishes for your health, happiness and success. *Cordially*

[1] Churchill was currently serving as a Member of Parliament and Leader of His Majesty's Opposition.
[2] Earle was Chichele Lecturer at Oxford from April to June 1950. He was on leave from the Institute for Advanced Study at Princeton, New Jersey (for background see no. 252). He had reminded Eisenhower in a note of April 27 (EM) that the General had promised to write him a letter of introduction to Churchill. Earle planned to discuss informally with Churchill the proposal for a professorship in military affairs at Columbia University. He also hoped to ask Churchill if he would like to give a short series of lectures at Columbia "on the role of war in statecraft."
[3] For background on this proposal see no. 730.
[4] There is no indication in the Churchill correspondence or in the Earle correspondence in EM that the two men met during 1950. Earle and Eisenhower would discuss the chair of military history at Columbia on July 14, 1950. Eisenhower would eventually invite Earle to rejoin the Columbia University faculty, but Earle would decline (see Earle to Eisenhower, Oct. 14, 1950, EM). Earle would, however, serve as one of four special consultants when Columbia organized the Institute of War and Peace Studies in 1952 (*New York Times*, Dec. 10, 1951).

792 Eisenhower Mss., Diaries

DIARY   *May 2, 1950*

Yesterday my mother would have been 88 years old, had she lived.[1]

In a recent issue of "Life" Magazine was a most flattering story by Quentin Reynolds. It was written about me and my activities at Columbia.[2] This week another article came out—this time in "Harpers"—which castigated me, on the ground that here the students & faculties hate me—and I return the sentiment with interest.[3]

If I could solve the money problems of the University* I would not only regard this as almost an ideal place, but I'd have great opportunity

& time for personal study. But its the nagging money problem that keeps me going always—including nights. And so I get tired out.

* I hear we may avoid an operating deficit this *year*—but at the cost of deferring truly *needed* maintenance.[4]

[1] Ida Elizabeth Stover Eisenhower had died on September 11, 1946, at the age of eighty-four. For background on her see *Eisenhower Papers*, vols. I–IX. For the General's affectionate recollection of his mother see pp. 305–7 of Eisenhower's memoir *At Ease*.

[2] Reynolds's article, entitled "Mr. President Eisenhower," had appeared in the April 17 issue of *Life*, pp. 144–60 (for background on Reynolds, an author and editor, see Galambos, *Chief of Staff*, no. 1906). Reynolds praised Eisenhower for his skill at putting ideas to work and for his insistence that graduates of Columbia University be "exceptional Americans," as well as exceptional students. The General was credited with inspiring the establishment of Columbia's nutrition center, its Citizenship Education Project, and its studies on the conservation of human resources (see nos. 300, 431, and 727). According to Reynolds, the students liked Eisenhower for his interest in their athletic programs and his practice of dropping into classrooms. Eisenhower's mind, he wrote, was dedicated to "logical analysis" and "enlightened judgment," two propositions which suggested that the General might be a "tough steer to try to ride in the American political rodeo."

[3] Richard H. Rovere's article, "The Second Eisenhower Boom," appeared in the May 1950 issue of *Harper's* magazine, pp. 31–39. Rovere (A.B. Columbia 1937) had been a staff writer for the *New Yorker* since 1944 and a contributing editor to *Harper's* since 1949. His was a study of the "Eisenhower phenomenon," which, he said, revealed "the democratic electorate as an essentially frivolous body which worships success for its own sake. . . ." The General's memoir *Crusade in Europe*, "sometimes comes close to splendor," said Rovere, but it was nevertheless a "rather austere, chilly book. . . ." Rovere credited Eisenhower with great personal popularity among his troops, but he was dismayed at the General's lack of political skill during World War II. As a university president, Eisenhower was "anything but a success." There was, Rovere wrote, "intense hostility toward him on the part of the majority of both faculty and student body." The problems stemmed, not from any administrative ineptitude on Eisenhower's part, but from the fact that this interest in education was not very serious and that consequently, claimed Rovere, he did not function as president. It was Rovere's conviction that "none of the people who have supported [Eisenhower] as a Presidential candidate has ever given acceptable evidence that the man is suited for the job or that he could develop the gifts the job requires."

[4] Columbia University's deficit for FY50, after providing for the amortization of the mortgage loan of 1948, would be $417,132.92 (for background see no. 210). Depreciation and deferred maintenance during FY50 would be estimated to be $1,391,165.14 (see Columbia University, *Report of the Treasurer, 1950*, pp. 5, 53).

Dear Bob:[01] I have been highly intrigued by developments in the effort
to secure lay support for medical education.[2] I frequently gather the
impression that businessmen are more ready to attempt the adjustment
of traditional views and attitudes and more ready to make concessions
in the interchange of ideas than are some of our professional medical
friends.

At the meeting, some time ago, at the Cloud Club, I was struck by
the fact that, in reply to your suggestion that medical schools might
do something to help themselves, the curt answer was made, "We tried
that and it did not work."[3] Now there may be some very definite reasons
why your idea of the attached clinic would hurt a medical teaching
center. But that reason was not an obvious one and I, personally, thought
that a more convincing answer was indicated.

But beyond this, there seems to me to be a series of factors that need
some study. For example, here are some considerations.

  a) Admittedly, medical education is the most expensive item in
      the whole problem of higher education. If universities were
      relieved of this burden, their other problems would be much
      easier to solve.

  b) The real reason that universities do not try to duck this burden
      is because they believe that resulting federal responsibility for
      medical education would eventually compel the socialization
      of medicine.

  c) The entire financial burden for higher education may, never-
      theless, be too much for private donation to carry. This would,
      in turn, require a decision on the specific part of the educational
      job that should be assigned to government.

This cost possibility inspires some speculation along the following
lines. If we must abandon some portion of higher education to government, is it not logical (or, let us say, less harmful) to choose medicine
as the proper item? This would, first of all, take up the most expensive
and costly item. Next, it would involve an item that has little to do
with the social, political and cultural development of the country. In
fact, I have heard at least one of our doctors claim that they are immune
from and very little interested in political systems and orders. This
thesis was upheld on the ground that doctors are important to any kind
of society and, therefore, they are less concerned than other professions
in world trends and in the conflict of ideology. If this is only faintly
true, then we would certainly be justified in applying it in reverse.
Another thought is that if we assume complete socialization of medicine,
would not the socialistic trend still be easier to stop on the basis of *one*

subject than to let the process continue to creep into all educational and social ventures. By abandoning one costly subject completely to the government, we might be able to establish a defensive line more easily than by contemplating a lesser deterioration in *all* activities.

Now, I do not believe any such line of reasoning to be sound—but I do believe that doctors, themselves, should be confronted with *possibilities* that could finally become fact unless they work as hard and intelligently for the salvation of medical education as they want the rest of us to work.

Doctors, particularly the American Medical Association, have raised funds to fight against proposed legislation that they class as "socialization." I believe that last year each member of the Association was taxed a given amount to fight certain Bills then before Congress. A proper question here is, what have these doctors done, *either individually or collectively, to help educational institutions that have, almost without exception, presented to each of these practicing doctors, during his school years, the equivalent of some ten to twelve thousand dollars*. In other words, is not a group of laymen entitled to know that the medical profession itself is so deeply concerned with these various preliminary steps in the socialization process of their own profession that each member in it will make *reasonable* sacrifices and will render a modicum of support in order to combat this trend? For the life of me, I cannot see why we should be so concerned about the doctors unless each of them, presumably and keenly aware of all the potential dangers of the situation, is ready to donate some one or two hundred dollars a year to a cause in which he not only believes but in which his own personal fortunes are involved. An average of 100 dollars a year from 150,000 doctors would go a long way toward solving the entire problem.

You can see from the above that this subject troubles me mightily. I do not, for one second, suggest any defeatist approach. But if doctors and university officials are going to look to a layman's group for real support, then all the cards should be placed on the table and there should be such clear evidence of the effective cooperation on the part of educators and of medical men that we are not compelled to suspect anybody of seeking a free ride.

This letter I mean to be personal and confidential. It merely sets forth some of the ideas that plague me as I seek an effective solution here at Columbia where, we have, probably the best and certainly one of the most expensive systems of medical education in the world.[4]
Sincerely

[1] Woodruff was chairman of the executive committee and a director of the Coca-Cola Company (for background see no. 258).
[2] Concerning Eisenhower's involvement in this plan see no. 285.
[3] On March 22 Eisenhower and Woodruff had attended a meeting of the National Fund for Medical Education in the Cloud Club in the Chrysler Building, New

York City (see Schulz to Eisenhower, Mar. 20, 1950, EM, Woodruff Corr.; and S. Sloan Colt to Eisenhower, Mar. 10, 1950, EM. See also no. 567).

[4] Eisenhower would soon express concern over his personal commitment to the work of the National Fund for Medical Education (see no. 806). In correspondence at this time with Russell W. Davenport, an editor associated with *Life* magazine who was currently moderator of Life Round Tables, a series of panel debates on important questions of the day, Eisenhower discussed a related subject: health insurance legislation. For background on Davenport see Galambos, *Chief of Staff*, no. 753; and no. 871 in this volume. All correspondence is in EM; see esp. Eisenhower to Davenport, April 3, 1950.

794   *Eisenhower Mss.*

To Douglas Elton Fairbanks, Jr.   *May 3, 1950*

Dear Mr. Fairbanks:[1] For some days, I have intended to drop you a note of congratulation on the excellence of the talk you delivered in the middle of March at the Waldorf.[2] Everyone who studies seriously today's international situation and problems arrives finally at the conclusion that the battle is going to be won by forces of freedom only if each of us gets out his spiritual armor, shines it up, and goes out to fight until victory is attained. This, of course, is inherently necessary for the solution of any real problem of democracy—the very meaning of the word compels each, voluntarily, to do his part. Your talk is properly directed toward inspiring each of us to believe that this *method* of functioning is still effective. All that is needed is the faith that this is so.[3]

I hope you keep repeating the same idea over and over again.[4] *Sincerely*

[1] Fairbanks, a popular motion picture actor and producer, served as a volunteer in many international organizations of the postwar era. From 1946 to 1950 he was fund-raising chairman for the Cooperative for American Remittances to Europe (CARE) and national vice-chairman of the American Association for the United Nations (for which he wrote supportive articles and speeches); and he undertook several missions to Europe for the ECA (Marshall Plan). Fairbanks had received numerous awards in recognition of his public-spirited activities and his contribution to international understanding.

[2] Fairbanks had been one of four speakers at a dinner given at the Waldorf-Astoria Hotel in New York City (Mar. 14, 1950) in honor of Federal Judge Harold R. Medina by the anti-communist organization Common Cause, Inc. Medina, who had recently presided at a trial in which eleven Communists were convicted of conspiracy to overthrow the government, had decided not to attend the dinner because he feared that "the dignity and reputation of the court would suffer. . . ." But Republican policy adviser John Foster Dulles, Democratic former Postmaster General James A. Farley, and military analyst Major George Fielding Eliot had all joined Fairbanks in speaking on the meeting's theme, "What's Ahead for America?" (*New York Times*, Feb. 25, Mar. 10 and 15, 1950). Eisenhower had

apparently asked to see a copy of Fairbanks's speech, which the actor sent to Mrs. Eisenhower (Apr. 10, 1950, EM).

[3] Fairbanks, who had recently been on a European tour, had expressed his conviction that America must provide a clearer exposition of its motives and objectives to the peoples of the world. He said that in order for America to determine what *must* happen in the future, the meaning of its goal, "peace in a world . . . of free men," must be restated clearly and vigorously to counter the strident voices from behind the Iron Curtain. The Communists, he insisted, offered to deliver the suffering, the confused, and the anxious from chaos in exchange for "rigid, perfect, unquestioned Order" (full text in EM). On this theme see Eisenhower's address at the 196th commencement of Columbia University (*New York Times*, June 9, 1950); see also no. 606, n. 1.

[4] Fairbanks would continue to send Eisenhower his political essays (see copies in EM).

795   *Eisenhower Mss.*

To WILLIAM O'DWYER   *May 9, 1950*

My dear Mr. Mayor:[01] Under date of October 25, 1949 I wrote to Mr. Spencer Young, Treasurer of the City of New York, in regard to a tax lien on property owned by Barnard College and used for educational purposes.[2] Mr. Young has subsequently replied to my letter and I believe has discussed this matter with you.[3]

Mr. Spencer C. Young knows all the details, and I certainly hope that you and he will agree that the lien can be bought in by Barnard at the price suggested, in view of all the circumstances.[4]

Barnard, which is part of Columbia University but is financially separate, has been severely affected by the rise on costs and expenses since the war. The Treasurer of the College advises me that the accumulated deficit will amount to over $500,000 by June 1950, which is almost equal to the unrestricted endowment funds of the College, and that the operating deficit for the current year will be about $100,000.[5]

Barnard does an important service in providing a higher education to the girls of the City. Of the 1100 students of the College, 450 reside in the City and of these over 100 receive scholarship aid.[6]

I urge that every consideration which is fair and proper be given by the City in the settlement of this tax lien, since the benefit from any such settlement will accrue soley to an educational institution which is doing a very real service to the citizens of New York.[7] *Sincerely*

[1] William O'Dwyer had been Mayor of New York City since 1946 (for background see no. 175). Amidst a controversial investigation of police corruption in New York City O'Dwyer would resign his post on September 1, 1950, to assume duties as U.S. Ambassador to Mexico (*New York Times*, Sept. 1, 19; Oct. 12, 1950).

[2] A more extensive draft of this letter, dated May 1, 1950, and written in part by

Columbia's Vice-President for Business Affairs and Treasurer Joseph Campbell, is in EM, Letters and Drafts. Copies of the May 9 version were sent to Young and to New York City Deputy Mayor, William Reid.

[3] Eisenhower's letter to Young of October 25, 1949, concerning Barnard College, and Young's replies of November 3, 1949, and January 17, 1950, are not in EM.

[4] Eisenhower had written in the draft that the tax lien amounted to $12,157.68, of which $6,547.50 represented principal and $5,610.18 interest on property purchased by Barnard in 1936 (see *New York Times*, Feb. 12 and Dec. 6, 1936, concerning Barnard's acquisition of real estate on Riverside Drive). The General explained that the lien had arisen because of "doubt as to whether taxes were due in respect of the half-year after Barnard bought the property . . ." and that interest had accrued "on account of the long delay on the part of the City in ruling on the point." Eisenhower consequently suggested that the city not charge Barnard the interest, and accept their offer of $3,500 for the lien as a "very fair disposition of the matter in view of the dubious fairness of charging the College, a clearly exempt, educational institution, for real estate taxes while it held the land and used it for educational purposes" (EM, Letters and Drafts).

[5] In a letter of February 16, 1949, Dean Millicent C. McIntosh had alerted the alumnae of Barnard College to the school's financial difficulties. "If the College is to continue, and to go forward," she said, "we must raise a very large sum of money within the near future" (EM, McIntosh Corr.; for background on Dean McIntosh's initial efforts to help the school see no. 359). In April 1950 Barnard had announced a hundred-dollar-per-year increase in tuition, which Dean McIntosh felt was necessary to help offset the school's hundred-thousand-dollar budget deficit (*New York Times*, Apr. 6, 1950). Barnard's development fund had also undertaken an ambitious campaign drive to raise $10 million by June 1, 1951. Of this sum, $4.5 million was needed as an endowment for faculty salaries, scholarships, and curriculum enrichment; the remaining $5.5 million would be set aside for construction of a new building and improvement of existing facilities (*New York Times*, May 24, 1950). Income generated by these activities, including a million-dollar contribution from John D. Rockefeller, Jr., would help Barnard decrease its operating deficit and approach a balanced budget for the first time since 1944 (*New York Times*, Apr. 19, 1950; see also *ibid.*, Feb. 11, 1951).

[6] Barnard College, the women's undergraduate liberal arts affiliate of Columbia University, had a separate board of trustees, a separate faculty, separate finances, and a separate development fund (Palmer to Eisenhower, Mar. 3, 1950, EM, Barnard Corr.). In 1950 approximately 30 percent of the students were on partial scholarship and 60 percent were registered at the placement bureau for employment while attending college. For more information see *ibid.*; and Columbia University, *Educational Future*, pp. 85–86.

[7] O'Dwyer's reply of July 15, 1950, is not in EM. Eisenhower later wrote (Aug. 2, 1950) the Mayor, "It is most unfortunate that a solution to the problem within the means of Barnard College cannot be worked out; I'm certain that this is as much regretted by you as it is by me." Joseph Campbell apparently drafted the General's reply.

To WILLIAM HARRISON STANDLEY   *May 9, 1950*

Dear Admiral Standley:[1] Thank you very much for your thoughtful
letter. I am more than glad to see that, in our basic conclusions concerning military people in politics, we see eye to eye.[2]

Although I am highly flattered by your personal references, I have—
certainly up to now—found no reason for revising the public statements
I have already made concerning my desire to abstain from any political
activity. In fact, I am so busy trying to do my job at the University
that I have little time even to think of such things.

I do appreciate your writing. *Sincerely*

[1] For background on Admiral Standley, who had retired in 1946, see no. 206.
[2] In a letter of May 1, 1950, Standley had urged Eisenhower to declare himself
a candidate in the presidential election of 1952. The Admiral said that he did not
believe that military men generally possessed the "appeasing qualities" required in
political office, but "these are no ordinary times and heroic measures are necessary."
He likened the course of the present government administration to a "socialistic
toboggan . . . daily gaining increased momentum," and he called on Eisenhower
to save the country from dictatorship (EM).

To EVERETT STRAIT HUGHES   *May 10, 1950*

Dear Everett:[1] I know that you have not yet returned to the United
States but I am sending this note on to Washington so that when you
do get back to the Westchester you will learn that I received your letter
(and enclosure) from Algiers.[2]

Until I received your message, it had never occurred to me to want
to go back to Algiers—that was one place for which I never expected
to experience any homesickness.[3] But the mental picture of you sitting
under a palm tree, and with nothing more serious on your mind than
the extraordinary picture you sent me, was responsible for a sudden
desire to go down and buy a plane ticket and start back to the Mediterranean.[4] Instead, I will go, incessantly, to luncheons and dinners,
at the latter usually making a few banal remarks which are supposed
to pay for the meal, and lose a bit more of my disposition because of
a realization that I never seem to be boss of my own time.[5] The hours
that I get to spend actually on the campus are the best ones I have.
(This does not mean that I no longer look forward to a day's fishing
in the country.) Anyway, I know that you both had a wonderful time—
I hope that your health is as good as your memory is.[6]

Love to Kate and warmest regards to yourself. *Cordially*

[1] During World War II Major General Hughes (USA, ret.) had served as deputy commander of the North African Theater of Operations, U.S. Army (NATOUSA) (for background see no. 66; see also Chandler, *War Years*, no. 896).

[2] Hughes, who lived at the Westchester Apartments in Washington, D.C., had been on vacation with his wife Kate. The return address on his handwritten letter read: "Under a date palm in the garden of the St. George Hotel, Algiers, 7 April, 1950." The letter and a typed copy are in EM.

[3] Eisenhower and the Allied Force Headquarters (AFHQ) had transferred from Gibraltar to Algiers on November 23, 1942 (see Chandler, *War Years*, nos. 613, 631, 641, and 651, and the entries from November 13, 1942, to December 31, 1943, of the chronology, vol. V. See also Eisenhower, *Crusade in Europe*, pp. 115–34; and Butcher, *My Three Years with Eisenhower*, pp. 173–350, esp. pp. 198–99 and 207–8).

[4] In his letter, Hughes had described his activities and the changes that he had noticed in Algiers. "The St. George has been completely renovated and in some respects and in a minor fashion the interior has been remodeled. The carpets worn threadbare by British and American feet have been replaced. The only reminder of the war days is a plate on your old office door stating in effect that General Eisenhower labored here."

[5] For Eisenhower's annoyance with public speaking and luncheons see no. 786; on his lack of leisure time see no. 38.

[6] The Hugheses had arrived in Algiers on April 4, had flown to Marseilles on April 8, and would travel to Venice, Heidelberg, Paris, and Oberammergau before returning to the United States on June 3.

798   *Eisenhower Mss.*

TO GEORGE VAN HORN MOSELEY   *May 10, 1950*

Dear George:[1] I shall send Mr. Gunby an autographed photograph at once. He was a Columbia student for a while but, apparently, was unable to stand our rigid winters and actually completed his education at Emory University.[2]

I hope you will not worry about the things that you see newspaper columnists saying about a possible political career for me.[3] It seems to me that my actions in 1947 and '48 should have demonstrated that I was quite serious when I said that I wanted no part of a political career.[4] Consequently, I do not make political statements and do not discuss political subjects publicly.[5] I believe that our country needs a reawakening in fundamental values, in those things to which all of us (excepting always the lunatic fringe) should adhere. There are plenty of politicians to struggle and fight for office. There ought to be more people preaching such simple things as the love of and preservation of freedom, both political and economic freedom. We should realize that individual liberty is the greatest gift a man can have and we should watch every move of government and of the politicians to satisfy our own minds that that liberty is not being endangered by any new proposal or project.

It is because of my almost fanatical belief in the American system—that is in a capitalistic economy and a political republic—that I am occupying the job I now do and so frequently undertake tasks that would be otherwise distasteful. It is my ambition to see every American become consciously aware of these basic truths and to attempt to apply them in making his own day-by-day decisions. Such an ambition involves no entry into the political field.

With warm personal regards, *Cordially*

[1] For background on General Moseley see no. 368.

[2] In a letter of May 2 Moseley had asked Eisenhower to send a photograph of himself to Eugene Gunby, judge of the court of ordinary of Fulton County, Atlanta, Georgia. Moseley said that he had recently seen Judge Gunby, whom he described as an "outstanding citizen of Georgia," and that Gunby's "greatest wish" was to have Eisenhower's photograph (EM). In February 1950, however, Gunby himself had already written to Eisenhower and asked for an autographed picture. His letter of February 3 is in EM, as is a note from Eisenhower's assistant, Kevin McCann, to Gunby, dated February 6, which accompanied an enclosed autographed photograph of Eisenhower. Nevertheless, on May 17 Eisenhower directed Major Robert L. Schulz to forward another inscribed photograph (Schulz to Gunby, EM).

[3] Moseley's concern had come as a result of recent press and radio speculation on Eisenhower's candidacy in the 1952 presidential election. Moseley feared that people such as those who backed Wendell Willkie and Thomas E. Dewey as presidential candidates would choose to support Eisenhower. For example, he said, Walter Winchell, the radio commentator, was such a person. "You just can't afford to be in such company," Moseley admonished, "or to permit the public at large to feel that you are accepting any such support." He cautioned Eisenhower not to "let anything happen now to set you back in the George Marshall class—our dear friend—who made a great record as a soldier and killed himself completely as Secretary of State. Today he is, in fact, a 'pathetic figure.' "

[4] There are many examples in the Eisenhower papers of the General's efforts in 1947 and 1948 to end speculation about his political ambitions. See, for example, Galambos, *Chief of Staff*, nos. 1614, 1625, 1966, 1969, and esp. 1998.

[5] Eisenhower was sensitive about this (see his letter to his brother Milton in December 1949, no. 606). In an undated note he had apparently enclosed with his original letter of May 2, Moseley included a statement that the General could make to help "clear up the situation." The statement reaffirmed Eisenhower's refusal to participate in any political activity and reminded the public that Eisenhower had given no individual or organization the right to include him in their plans (EM). We have no evidence that Eisenhower ever used Moseley's statement.

799   *Eisenhower Mss.*

To Allen Alderson Zoll II   *May 15, 1950*

Dear Mr. Zoll:[1] I sincerely appreciate the personal courtesy implicit in your suggestion that I examine, prior to publication, the results of your

Columbia investigation.[2] This I cannot do, since such examination might possibly be interpreted in some quarters as my acquiescence in criticisms based upon methods, assumptions and conclusions concerning which I could know little, if anything.

My own conclusions as to the loyalty, ability and high purposes of individuals must be based either upon my own experience or upon the published findings of some duly constituted tribunal.[3] *Sincerely*

[1] Zoll was founder and executive vice-president of the National Council for American Education, an organization dedicated to attacking communism in American schools. Through the council, Zoll had published a number of reports, the "red-ucator" series, which printed the names of allegedly pro-communist faculty and administrators and described their activities and the organizations to which they belonged.

[2] On May 2 Zoll had written Eisenhower to suggest that the General examine his report on Columbia faculty before its publication. According to Zoll, the report would list "93 of the Columbia faculty with their more than 500 Communist-front affiliations." He said that his organization had never before offered to discuss data with any of the universities it had analyzed, but "because of the great admiration that a number of the officers and governors of this Council bear toward you personally . . . we are willing to show it to you before publication." Zoll enclosed with his letter two reports on the "Communist-front affiliations" of professors at Harvard and at the University of Chicago. The Columbia report, "Red-ucators at Columbia University," would be published by the National Council for American Education on May 15, 1950.

[3] On May 4 Kevin McCann had telephoned Walter Gellhorn (LL.B. Columbia 1931) to inquire about Zoll. The next day Gellhorn, who had been a member of Columbia's faculties of law and political science since the 1930s, had written McCann that he had "a dim remembrance of [Zoll] as a professional specialist in anti-semitism." Gellhorn referred McCann to a recently published book by Arnold Forster, titled *A Measure of Freedom* (New York, 1950), and enclosed copies of pp. 74–79, in which Zoll was described as a former "fascist propagandist" turned professional patriot (EM, Zoll Corr.). Eisenhower's original draft of the reply to Zoll is in EM, Letters and Drafts. McCann helped draft the final reply, and a copy was sent to William Russell, president of Columbia's Teachers College. For more on Zoll and his activities see MacIver, *Academic Freedom in Our Time*, pp. 59–61; Iversen, *The Communists and the Schools*, pp. 245–56; and Frederick Woltman, "Zoll, Hate-Monger, Promotes New Racket," *New York World-Telegram*, August 25, 1948. For background on Eisenhower's earlier encounter with allegations about Communist infiltration at Columbia see nos. 115 and 131.

On May 31 Eisenhower would reply to Robert Donner, of Colorado Springs, Colorado, who had seen Zoll's "Red-ucators at Columbia University" and had written the General (May 26) to express his concern about the "manner in which radical educators have been at work subverting education, indoctrinating American youth and organizing student opinion to the left." In his letter to Donner, drafted by McCann, Eisenhower said he disagreed with Donner's implication that Columbia is "shot through with Communist propagandists." All correspondence is in EM.

To Universities and Colleges[1]   *May 15, 1950*

It is an honorable custom for universities to mark their centennial years by suitable observances. During the year 1954, Columbia University in the City of New York will take note of the two-hundredth anniversary of its establishment as an institution of higher learning.

In considering what would be the most appropriate theme for Columbia to emphasize in its celebration, the Trustees, aided by a committee representing the Faculties, students and alumni, have agreed that there is one principle which all free universities unfailingly must defend. This is the ideal of full freedom of scholarly inquiry and expression, the right of mankind to knowledge and to the free use thereof.

For many centuries the civilized world has held that this principle is essential to human liberty, welfare and progress. Unhappily, it is now being subjected to serious and systematic attack in many lands. Our Trustees, accordingly, have concluded that it would be appropriate to ask institutions of higher learning throughout the world to join in reaffirmations of their faith in the freedom of inquiry and expression. Our plans for a convocation in New York are in preparation.[2] Meanwhile, we are suggesting that each participant find its own manner of marking this privilege, which is man's natural right, but not always his legal one. The nature and methods of such observances would vary greatly from institution to institution, possibly taking the form of convocations, special lectures, courses of instruction, publications, and the like. But no matter what forms such observances may take, if they center on the year 1954, their concentrated effect will focus world-wide attention on the belief that, through the free and just use of all the knowledge he can acquire, man may triumphantly insure the peace and progress for which he strives.

Columbia will make this ideal the central theme of its Bicentennial celebration in 1954. Should you find it possible to participate at that time in this demonstration of faith and belief, we would be happy to exchange with you and other institutions such information and plans as may be mutually of interest.

The cause which we seek to serve far transcends any of our individual institutions. We invite your collaboration in it, and shall welcome such comments on this letter as you, at your convenience, may care to send me.[3] *Sincerely*

---

[1] After months of discussion and preparation the Bicentennial Committee sent this letter to more than three hundred U.S. and foreign universities and colleges. The same letter, with a few minor changes, also went to some three hundred fifty libraries and museums. Eisenhower, who was a member of the Bicentennial Committee, had prepared a preliminary draft of the letter early in the year (Kirk

to Herpers, Dec. 13, 1949; Feb. 8, 1950, minutes of the committee, with attached drafts; Herpers to Dallas, May 5, 1950, with enclosures; and May 16 press release of the Public Information Office, Columbia University, all in CUF). In March the task of reconciling the different ideas had been turned over to Provost Kirk, and Kirk had produced this version. After minor changes, the committee, including Eisenhower, had accepted this draft (see Sulzberger to Kirk, Mar. 7, 1950; Sulzberger to the members of the Bicentennial Committee on Organization, Mar. 15 and Mar. 21, 1950; Sulzberger to Kirk, Mar. 21, 1950; and Columbia University Bi-Centennial, Minutes of Joint Meeting of Committee on Organization and Program Committee, Apr. 13, 1950, all in CUF). Several additional minor changes were introduced before Eisenhower sent out this final version (see also Sulzberger to Committee Members, Jan. 6, 1950, with enclosures, EM; *Columbia Daily Spectator*, May 16, 1950; and *New York Times*, May 16, 1950). For background on the bicentennial see no. 495.

[2] See nos. 496 and 704.

[3] By May 27 Kirk would report to Arthur Sulzberger that he had already received over forty replies and that most of them had been "extremely co-operative and enthusiastic." Kirk's letter and other materials involving the bicentennial are in CUF.

801   *Eisenhower Mss.*

To Robert Winship Woodruff   *May 17, 1950*

Dear Bob:[1] I have just heard that someone is trying to put the squeeze on the General Electric Board to get it to subsidize an Owen D. Young professorship in the Harvard University Business School.[2] While I have also heard that Mr. Young himself has never been queried on this subject, I have been told that his real educational interest lies with St. Lawrence University. I learned that Mr. Young and many members of his family are supporters of that school and that, if any memorial professorship were to be established for him, the logical location would be that particular school.[3]

From my own viewpoint, it is frankly a lot more personal. His son is head of our own Business School and, if there is to be a professorship established in his name, I think Philip Young and the Columbia School of Business should be among the first to receive consideration.[4]

I don't want to appear in the position of knifing any worth-while effort in the educational field, but I am also determined to give Philip Young, who I consider to be one of the most effective men in the university world today, all the help that I possibly can.[5] So, you will see that I hope you, as a member of the General Electric Board, will remember these things if this particular question should ever come before you.[6]

With warm regard, *Cordially*

[1] Woodruff was chairman of the executive committee of the Coca Cola Company and a director of the General Electric Company (for background see no. 258).

[2] Young, an attorney and industrialist, was honorary chairman of the board of the General Electric Company. Soon after he had joined GE as general counsel in 1913, he had become the firm's vice president; he had been chairman of the board from 1922 to 1939 and from 1942 to 1944. For further background see no. 486.

[3] Young had entered St. Lawrence University, in Canton, New York, in 1890. He had received an A.B. degree in 1894 and had served as a trustee of the university from 1912 to 1934. He was awarded more than twenty-five honorary degrees from colleges and universities both in the United States and abroad. Both Harvard and Columbia had honored him with honorary LL.D. degrees in 1924 and 1925, respectively.

[4] For background on Dean Philip Young and the Graduate School of Business see no. 54. Young, a graduate and trustee of St. Lawrence University, had received an M.B.A. from Harvard University in 1933.

[5] For the General's evaluation of Young see also no. 599.

[6] Woodruff would reply that he intended to "take any affirmative action I consistently can in support of your position." Woodruff said the proposed professorship had not been officially discussed but the idea probably arose because "twenty-five years ago Mr. Owen Young made some profound observations and predictions concerning the Harvard Business School which apparently have more or less materialized. . . ." He added that a choice between the institutions involved would be "an extraordinarily difficult decision to make" (May 23, EM). For developments see no. 814.

802   *Eisenhower Mss.*

To Renée du Pont Donaldson   *May 18, 1950*

Dear Mrs. Donaldson:[1] Thank you very much for your thoughtfulness in writing to me after our meeting at Nevis.[2] I cannot tell you how gratified I am to know of your continuing interest both in that property and in the aspirations of Columbia. I assure you that Mr. Kirk will fulfill his promise to you at the very earliest opportunity.[3]

This note gives me a chance to say again that it was an honor to meet you and your brother[4] on the day of the dedication of the Cyclotron—not only do I look forward to seeing you both again, but I shall hope also for the pleasure of meeting your husband.[5] *Sincerely*

[1] Mrs. Donaldson, of Millbrook, New York, had written to Eisenhower on May 12. Her letter is in EM.

[2] Eisenhower and Mrs. Donaldson had met on May 2 on the occasion of the dedication of the Columbia synchro-cyclotron. The powerful atom smasher had been built at Nevis, the sixty-eight-acre estate located at Irvington-on-Hudson, New York; this property had been given to Columbia University in 1935 by Mrs. Donaldson's mother, the late Alice du Pont, whose husband, the late senator Thomas Coleman du Pont, had bought it in 1920. The cyclotron—under construction since February 1947—had been built for Columbia's nuclear physics

research center, in cooperation with the Office of Naval Research (see *New York Times*, Dec. 15, 1946; Dec. 7, 1947; Nov. 5, 1948; Mar. 19 and May 3, 1950).
[3] Mrs. Donaldson had said that she was concerned over the fate of the remaining property on the Nevis estate. It seems, she wrote, "to have 'fallen between two chairs.'" Provost Grayson Kirk had apparently promised Mrs. Donaldson that he would study additional uses for Nevis. In a handwritten note at the bottom of Mrs. Donaldson's letter, Eisenhower said, "Mr. Kirk—Here is one contact it would seem that you should personally maintain. Could you see me about it?"
[4] Francis V. du Pont, the son of T. Coleman du Pont (see n. 2 above).
[5] John Wilcox Donaldson.

803   *Eisenhower Mss.*

TO HERBERT BAYARD SWOPE   *May 19, 1950*

Dear Herbert:[1] A virus got between me and a quick reply to your last letter.[2] However, I did take advantage of the respite from routine to initiate inquiries on the possibility that some of our people might study comprehensively the agricultural situation. I have found that several times the matter has been discussed informally by various faculty members, but each time the decision was to stay out of the field.[3]

Other schools are far better fitted by location and environment to study agricultural problems, and our people feel that the job should be left to them. This is not an expression of the "Let George Do It" attitude, but a realist appraisal of the situation.[4] Nevertheless, for my personal enlightenment I am fortunate in having a brother—newly appointed head of Penn State—who makes the subject his particular field of study and interest.[5] *Cordially*

[1] Swope was a journalist and policy consultant for governmental, industrial, and commercial concerns (for background see no. 212).
[2] Eisenhower had been ill from May 9 through May 18 (see his appointment calendar). There is a draft of this letter by assistant Kevin McCann with Eisenhower's handwritten changes in EM, Letters and Drafts.
[3] In his letter to Eisenhower (May 9, EM), Swope had suggested that the General have his "alleged experts" study the nation's agricultural policies. Swope had pointed out that only a small proportion of the billions of dollars for federal farm subsidies ever reached the dirt farmers.
[4] Eisenhower deleted a statement in McCann's draft to the effect that Columbia University was inappropriately situated for this study because of its geographical location and environment.
[5] This sentence, in Eisenhower's handwriting, was added at the end of the draft. Milton Eisenhower, the General's brother, had been elected president of Pennsylvania State College on January 21, 1950 (see no. 679). He had served as an assistant to the Secretary of Agriculture from 1926 to 1928; Director of Information for the U.S. Department of Agriculture from 1928 to 1940; and Land-Use Coordinator from 1937 to 1942. From 1944 to 1947 and from 1950 to 1953 Dr. Eisenhower was on the executive committee of the Association of Land-Grant

Colleges and Universities. He would be president of that organization from 1951 to 1952. For further background see Kornitzer, *The Great American Heritage*, pp. 222–32 and 237–38; and Milton Eisenhower, *The President Is Calling*, pp. 70—92. See also *idem, The Wine is Bitter* (New York, 1963), pp. 111–26, for his interest in agricultural reform in Latin America.

804 *Eisenhower Mss., Subject File,*
Clubs and Associations

To HOLLOWAY JONES *May 19, 1950*

Dear Mr. Jones:[1] I have just received through Mr. H. D. Collier the gracious invitation of the Board of Directors to attend the 1950 Midsummer Encampment at Bohemian Grove.[2] I am indeed flattered that your Club should want me to join in this year's encampment. Unfortunately, I cannot follow my personal inclination to send a quick and affirmative answer. My hesitancy to accept is due only to extremely unsettled plans for the summer, which are guided principally by my family's desire that I remain in Colorado as long as possible, at the home of my wife's parents.[3] But if I should find it possible to come I shall, with great delight, take advantage of your invitation. Won't you assure your Directors of my deep appreciation? I shall send a definite reply, through Mr. Collier, no later than July 1.[4] *Sincerely*

[1] Jones was secretary of the Bohemian Club and a member of the club's board of directors (for background see no. 388). Lieutenant Colonel Robert L. Schulz, Eisenhower's aide, drafted the first four sentences of this letter, and Eisenhower added the remaining three (draft in Schulz Coll., EP).
[2] Harry D. Collier, chairman of the finance committee of Standard Oil Company of California, had invited Eisenhower to Bohemian Grove in a letter of May 9 (EM).
[3] On the Eisenhowers's vacation plans see the next document.
[4] Eisenhower had made a similar explanation to Collier in a letter of the previous day (EM). There is no copy of a "definite reply" in EM, Collier Corr., or in the same file as this document. In any case, Eisenhower would be Collier's guest at Stowaway Camp in the Bohemian Grove from July 20 to July 24, 1950. For developments see no. 873.

805 *Eisenhower Mss.*

To ROY ALLISON ROBERTS *May 20, 1950*

Dear Roy:[1] Of course, I should like to join the wonderful fishing party that will be on Mr. Davis's houseboat from August 25th to August

30th.[2] While I have not communicated with Milton since receiving your letter, he has previously told me that he expects to be very busy this summer getting settled at Pennsylvania State. So, I doubt that he would be in a position to accept.[3] For myself, I will be going to Colorado no later than August 1, and ordinarily we do not start back this way until about the fifteenth of September. All of this would seem to add up to hopeless complications for the two of us this summer.[4] I think that the only safe thing is to tell your friend, Mr. Davis, that, while I am extraordinarily appreciative of his kindness and thoughtfulness, I cannot possibly plan to be with the party. I have had to say the same thing in the case of invitations involving visits this summer to Aspen, Colorado—Bohemian Grove in Colorado[5]—participation in the American Senior golf tournament—attendance at the General Electric outings in the Great Lakes—two trips to Canada—and so on.[6] Every one of them proposes something that I would most earnestly like to do. But Mamie and I are always so anxious to spend a goodly part of the summer with her parents in Colorado that I must forgo such pleasurable expeditions.

With respect to your friends of the National Aeronautical Association, please tell them that it is completely out of the question for me to come to St. Louis on June 13.[7] I appreciate the distinction implicit in their invitation, but I cannot possibly break away from the many New York City engagements that are already on my calendar for that particular period. I believe that my Aide gave you this information a week ago.

Drop in to see me the next time you are in the City. *Cordially*

[1] Roberts was president and general manager of the *Kansas City* (Mo.) *Star* (for background see no. 160).

[2] Roberts had invited Eisenhower to join him on a fishing trip hosted by Don Davis, president of the Minnesota and Ontario Paper Company, aboard his houseboat on Rainy Lake, near International Falls, Minnesota. Davis had also invited Eisenhower's brother Milton, General Lucius Clay, and John Cowles. Roberts, who had previously vacationed with Davis, had said that the fishing on the lake was "the greatest . . . I have ever tackled" (May 9, 1950, EM).

[3] For Milton Eisenhower's inauguration as president of Pennsylvania State College see no. 915.

[4] The General's vacation plans for the summer of 1950 were extensive (see no. 865, n. 2). He would depart from New York City on July 14; visit the Grand Canyon on July 17 and Yosemite National Park on July 18; and then spend two weeks on the West Coast in Oakland, Bohemian Grove, and San Francisco, California. He would stay in Denver, Colorado, from July 28 to September 17 (see nos. 873, 884, and 900).

[5] The General's staff should have changed this to *California*.

[6] For Eisenhower's invitations to the School of Humanistic Studies in Aspen, Colorado, see no. 706, nn. 3 and 5; to Bohemian Grove in California, no. 887, esp. n. 4; to the annual tournament and dinner of the United States Seniors' Golf Association, no. 761; to the National Defense College and Canadian Army Staff College in Kingston, Ontario, no. 707, n. 7; and to the Canadian National Exhibition in Ottawa, Viscount Alexander of Tunis to Eisenhower, June 25,

1950, EM. Finally, for Eisenhower's invitation to the General Electric Company's Association Island in Lake Ontario see Charles E. Wilson to Eisenhower, March 23, 1950, EM.

[7] In the same letter, Roberts had asked Eisenhower to reconsider an invitation to speak before the National Aeronautical Association. Aide Robert L. Schulz had already informed Roberts that it was impossible for the General to attend the June 13 dinner in St. Louis (May 15, 1950, EM).

806 *Eisenhower Mss.*

To Samuel Sloan Colt *May 20, 1950*

Dear Mr. Colt:[1] A virus attack that removed me from action last week provided a measure of leisure to study my official University schedule, particularly as it is affected by my commitments to various organizations such as the National Fund for Medical Education.[2] I learned that I had too far overextended myself from the Columbia base even though in every instance the organizations were engaged in work or operations closely allied with or of great interest to the University. While most of them demand no more than a few hours a season, the sum of all becomes a major inroad on my time. I decided that, as my term of membership or office neared an end in each of them, I would submit my resignation.

On my return to my office, your letter awaited me in the stack of correspondence on my desk.[3] Certainly, the success of the National Fund is essential to the maintenance of our independent medical schools— unless we give up some part of their independence and seek govern- mental subsidy.[4] Because of that circumstance, I was—and still am— reluctant to decline re-election to the Council. Nevertheless, since a drastic cut in my outside commitments is absolutely essential to the effective performance of inescapable tasks, the only possible alternative would be to agree that my name might continue on the Advisory Council roll, but with the clear understanding that I would not be able to live up actively to even the minimum demands of that position. I do not feel that a merely nominal association should be tolerated in an enterprise so important as the National Fund, and I feel that you should not accept anyone on such a basis.

As a consequence of these things I hope you will withdraw my name from nomination for re-election, explaining to the Trustees my decision and the reasons for it. On the other hand, if you should still see an advantage in retaining my name on the list I shall accept your decision.[5] In either event I shall continue to try to help further the purpose of the National Fund for Medical Education.[6] *Sincerely*

[1] Colt (B.A. Yale 1914) had been president of Bankers Trust Company since 1931. He had recently been elected a member of the executive committee of the Committee for Economic Development (CED). For background on the CED see no. 732. Eisenhower made extensive changes in Kevin C. McCann's draft of this letter (EM, Letters and Drafts).

[2] For background on Eisenhower's activities on behalf of this organization see no. 387.

[3] In his letter (May 15, 1950, EM) Colt had included an announcement that the trustees of the National Fund for Medical Education would elect the advisory council at the fund's annual meeting on June 7. Eisenhower had been a member of the council during 1949/50, and Colt asked if he wanted to have his name presented for reelection.

[4] Eisenhower had set forth his views on government subsidies for medical schools in no. 793.

[5] In his reply (May 31, EM) Colt would urge Eisenhower to renew his membership on the advisory council "at least until the time that the Fund has advanced beyond the exploratory stage."

[6] Eisenhower would continue as a member of the advisory council during 1950 and 1951. He would not attend the annual meeting on May 16, 1951, but he would send a telegram describing his interest in the work of the fund. Colt would read the telegram to the 175 men and women at the meeting, and they would elect Eisenhower to membership on the newly formed Medical, Educational and Scientific Advisory Council for the 1951/52 term (see address by Colt and minutes of the annual meeting, May 16, 1951, EM, National Fund for Medical Education Corr.). The fund would continue to acknowledge Eisenhower's role in its founding, and the author of its pamphlet, "A Solution for the Financial Crisis Confronting the Medical Schools," would recall in October 1951 that Eisenhower had "emphasized that the nation's strength primarily depended upon the sound mental and physical health of its citizens and that the medical schools were the foundation stones for the building of sound national health" (see enclosure, Cotter to the Board of Trustees and Members of Advisory Council, Oct. 29, 1951, *ibid.*).

807   *Eisenhower Mss.*

TO JAMES THOMSON SHOTWELL   *May 20, 1950*

Dear Dr. Shotwell:[1] I am tentatively scheduled to meet Louis Johnson today.[2] I shall seek an opportunity to ask him about the printing of the record of the Nuremberg Trials.[3] As I understood the last part of your letter, the Endowment can do little about this matter until *after* the documents are printed. However, the printing once accomplished, the Endowment intends to interest itself in giving the documents an effective distribution.[4] *Sincerely*

[1] Shotwell had been president of the Carnegie Endowment for International Peace since 1949. He would become president emeritus when Dr. Joseph E. Johnson, a former State Department officer and U.N. adviser, succeeded him as president on July 1, 1950 (*New York Times*, May 5, 1950). For background on Shotwell

see no. 167. On the Carnegie Endowment and Eisenhower's election to its board of trustees see no. 63.

[2] According to his appointment calendar, Eisenhower met with Secretary of Defense Louis A. Johnson in Washington, D.C., on May 20, 1950. For background on Johnson see no. 401.

[3] Shotwell had written Eisenhower on May 17, 1950 (EM), concerning the publication of the Nuremberg trial records (see no. 553). Shotwell feared that Johnson wanted to cut off funds for the printing of the fifteen-volume series, even though nearly a third of the set had already been completed. "If we are to have a study of war including the conspiratorial planning for it and the nature of its impact," Shotwell said, "it would seem to me that this series of volumes would be absolutely indispensable to scholars and lawyers and might help to clarify our thinking so as to be of very great service to the cause of peace."

[4] "If anything can be done about this," Shotwell had written, "the Endowment itself would have a very real interest in ensuring the distribution of this material to the proper repositories where it could be most effectively used." He would later inform the General (letter of May 24, EM) that Secretary Johnson had in fact given instructions for the continuation of the project.

808

Eisenhower Mss.

TO THOMAS DONALD CAMPBELL

May 20, 1950

Dear Tom:[1] Of course, I share your concern about Alaskan defenses, but I do not share your optimism about the ease of operating land forces in Arctic regions. Certainly, it can be done, but the terrain and climate of Alaska favor, in my judgment, the defense, and favor it so strongly that garrisons of only reasonable size should be able to protect our major air bases there.[2] Moreover, we should not belittle the usefulness of Alaskan air bases to anyone intending to bomb the United States. The farther forward we can push an air base, the more effective the operation.[3]

With respect to the oil affair, I am in your corner.[4] Possibly we two can get together one of these days and thrash the whole thing out in a long conversation.

Best of luck. *Cordially*

[1] Campbell's firm, the Campbell Farming Corporation, was one of the world's largest wheat growers, operating a sixty-five-thousand-acre wheat farm near Hardin, Montana, and a seven hundred-square-mile cattle ranch near Albuquerque, New Mexico. For more information about Campbell, who had attained the rank of brigadier general in the Air Force, see *Eisenhower Papers*, vols. VI–IX. This letter was taken to Washington, D.C.—where Eisenhower was on May 20—for dispatch; on the trip see no. 819, n. 5.

[2] Campbell had twice written to Eisenhower on the same subject—once on May 10 and again on May 15 (both letters are in EM). On May 10 he had just returned to the United States from Alaska, where he had studied living conditions, the training program, and the ground transportation for U.S. forces there. He had

made the trip at the request of General Hoyt S. Vandenberg, U.S. Air Force Chief of Staff. Campbell had called Alaska a "natural training ground for arctic warfare," but he was concerned that the United States had been delinquent in training operations with the result that "our officers are hopelessly uninformed and inexperienced. . . ." Ground transportation in the Arctic, Campbell said, was not a serious problem. He pointed out that Alaska was not much colder than Montana, Minnesota, or Maine and that heavy tonnage had been transported for years in those areas (May 10, EM). For developments see no. 929.

[3] Campbell had said that he would not be surprised if, on any night, Russia launched a sneak attack on the United States. According to him, "It will be by airplanes over the North Pole and submarines equipped with atomic bombs on our West Coast" (May 10, EM). For Eisenhower's concern about the defense of Alaska see nos. 753, 754, and 782.

[4] Campbell had discussed the Navy's search for oil at Point Barrow, at the most northerly point of Alaska on the Arctic Ocean. Known as Naval Petroleum Reserve Number Four, the exploration had continued since 1944. Campbell said that even though the work was being "well done under severe arctic conditions," the plan to pump crude oil, if discovered, through a pipe line to Fairbanks and Anchorage was "perfect nonsense." Campbell proposed that work be stopped on the Point Barrow project and the money be used for defense against submarines. For more information about the Navy's petroleum reserve at Point Barrow see *New York Times*, June 12, 1949; October 7, 1950; and November 10, 1951.

809   *Eisenhower Mss.*

To Albert Coady Wedemeyer   *May 20, 1950*

Dear Al:[1] Thank you very much for your interesting letter. While I do not recall the exact circumstances under which I met Mrs. Axtell, I do remember telling some person that you were a student and a scholar.[2] The occasion for the statement was a conversation in which she informed me that she expected soon to meet you. In any event, if I have overbuilt you, I hope that I did not hurt you in the lady's estimation—my distinct impression was that she would like the scholarly type!!!

I read Mr. Chapin's article with real interest.[3] Needless to say, I am always flattered when any American expresses such overgenerous and complimentary sentiments with respect to me as are contained in his article. However, I continue an effort, which I admit quite frequently appears to be hopeless, of attempting to make people see that at this point in our history we should be working for the promotion and veneration of ideas and ideals and not making ourselves dependent on any particular personality.[4] Nevertheless, Mr. Chapin's idea, in some form or other, is presented to me incessantly. People, high and low in all estates, frequently oversimplify a problem and, therefore, get a far too simple answer.

Of course, I am delighted that Cargill continues to give you such wonderful service.[5] Except that I considered it unfair to him, I would most certainly have asked him to leave the Service in 1945 and to stay with me the rest of my life as a personal member of my household staff. I agree with all the nice things you have to say about him.

While I have been quite cordially and frequently invited to come to the Bohemian Grove, we have so far been unable to find a way of saying "yes." If we can possibly get there, I shall most certainly look you up.[6] *Cordially*

[1] Wedemeyer had been commanding general of the Sixth Army, Presidio of San Francisco, California, since August 1949 (for background see no. 8).

[2] Wedemeyer had told Eisenhower that he had recently met "a Mrs. Axtell" at a cocktail party. He complimented the General on being a "good 'picker' for Mrs. Axtell is a very lovely looking and charming woman" (May 8, 1950, EM).

[3] Wedemeyer had apparently sent publisher William Wallace Chapin's editorial from the May 5, 1950, issue of the *Argonaut*, an historic California weekly (for background see no. 164). In the editorial, "General Eisenhower and the Presidency," Chapin supported Eisenhower as the Republican party candidate for the presidency in 1952.

[4] Chapin had described Eisenhower as "a man with ideas" who had the ability to learn and "who knows what o'clock it is in our time world. . . . The sequence of events has shown us again and again that this military man has all the qualifications for the most exalted position in the choice of the American people. . . . We believe that the Republication Party is all but certain to win, if it is sufficiently clear-sighted to nominate General Eisenhower as its standard-bearer in the next presidential campaign" (p. 3).

[5] Sergeant Cargill was a former member of Eisenhower's personal household staff. When the General had assumed presidential duties at Columbia, he had advised Wedemeyer to "take Cargill on" and had given him a very strong recommendation. Wedemeyer now said that even though Eisenhower had been very positive, he had been "guilty of understatements. . . ."

[6] Concerning Eisenhower's visit to Bohemian Grove see no. 887.

Eisenhower Mss.

To Edward John Bermingham   *May 22, 1950*

Dear Ed:[1] Since you, Mr. Dillon[2] and I first talked about the "Peace Institute," I have been encouraged by numbers of people (including our friend, Hap Flanigan)[3] to enlarge and embellish the program so far as to make it a great center of study of war's causes, conduct and consequences, as well as an effective means of drawing together frequent convocations of business and professional men so that they, with our academic staff, can increase their understanding of these things and carry this understanding back with them for instant application in their daily lives and in the daily conduct of our Government. Many of our friends are afraid that we 'may develop just another—even though a particularly valuable—academic study of these things, with the results to be buried in dusty tomes residing in a few obscure libraries. As a result, I have enlarged my concept of the "institute" and "forum" features of the program, both to insure the practicality of the answers developed and their availability to all interested parties.

One of our friends, Edwin Clark, who has been very interested in the proposition, has approached a number of foundations, particularly the private foundations like the Whitney, and a few others. Each of these has expressed an interest in the proposition and a desire to help.[4] If Mr. Dillon and his friends could produce for a limited number of years—say five—support at the rate of something like $35,000, I am quite sure that we can secure from other sources enough to do a real job, including the continuation of the quarterly magazine known as "Military Affairs." (Maybe I am wrong in that name, but, anyway, it has a subscription list of 1200 that we do not want to lose.)[5]

I outline these things briefly for you so that, when you see your Chicago friends, you will be armed with this additional information.[6]

As to the physical layout of my offices, that is the least of my personal worries, except that I always get upset when I see anyone working in an office which has no outside exposure. I do have one or two people forced to work that way, and I resent it. But we have to make the best of a building which was never designed for office use in the first place.[7]

I sincerely and earnestly hope that by this time Mrs. Bermingham is fully recovered from the difficulty she had in Europe.[8] *Cordially*

---

[1] Bermingham was a retired investment counselor and one of the businessmen whom Eisenhower had asked to help raise money to establish an institute of military studies at Columbia (see no. 730). Bermingham had written on May 10 (EM) that he agreed to make an annual contribution to the institute. Subject to the consent of the trustees of Columbia University, Bermingham was also willing to provide funds for this undertaking from the Bermingham trust agreement.

[2] Clarence Dillon was the head of Dillon, Read and Company (see no. 593 on his early meeting with Bermingham). According to Bermingham's letter, Dillon had now agreed to find ways of financing the work of the institute. A longhand draft of Eisenhower's note of thanks to Dillon is in EM, Letters and Drafts.

[3] Horace C. "Hap" Flanigan (C.E. Cornell 1912) was vice-chairman of the board of Manufacturers Trust Company.

[4] On Edwin N. Clark's fund-raising efforts see no. 665. Clark had probably contacted the William C. Whitney Foundation, an organization making grants to projects during their formative period. On May 17, 1950, Eisenhower had met with Clark and Major General Julius Ochs Adler (A.B. Princeton 1914), who was vice-president, treasurer, general manager, and a director of the New York Times Company, as well as commander of the 77th Infantry Division, ORC (Organized Reserve Corps). On November 22, 1950, Adler would send Eisenhower a check for fifty thousand dollars from the New York Times Company to be used primarily for the institute. Adler's letter of transmittal is in EM.

[5] See "Report of Status of Funds, American Military Institute," *Military Affairs*

14, no. 3 (1950), 164. Regarding the proposal that Columbia University take over the publication of *Military Affairs* see no. 665.

[6] In his recent letter Bermingham had promised that he would ask Sewell Lee Avery, Robert Douglas Stuart, and Robert E. Wood for assistance in funding the institute. Avery (LL.B. University of Michigan 1894) was chairman of the board of Montgomery Ward and Company, chairman of the board of U.S. Gypsum Company, and a trustee of the University of Chicago. Stuart was vice-chairman of the board of directors of the Quaker Oats Company. Wood was chairman of the board of Sears, Roebuck & Company.

[7] Bermingham had added the following postscript to his letter: "Every time I call I am increasingly depressed with the physical layout of your offices. You could be greatly helped with some changes." Eisenhower's offices were located in Low Library. Concerning his changes in the office arrangements see Eisenhower, *At Ease*, p. 342.

[8] Bermingham would reply (May 24, EM) that his wife, the former Katherine Carpenter, had recovered. She was "looking back with some enjoyment on a very strenuous European jaunt" which the Berminghams had taken during the spring of 1950. In the same letter, Bermingham would assure Eisenhower that forty thousand dollars could be raised for the institute.

811   *Eisenhower Mss.*

To William Fletcher Russell[1]   *May 22, 1950*

The two attached pamphlets were brought to me by Mr. Crider, Editor of The Boston Herald. He apparently has been instrumental in helping organize the groups that are carrying forward the outlined citizenship programs.[2]

I send them to you for three reasons:

   a. It is possible that from them we may gain some worthwhile ideas;

   b. Mr. Crider asked me to allow my name to be used in the furthering of the work these particular groups are doing, and I told him that I would be guided by the advice of my own staff and particularly, in this case, by advice from you;

   c. As we uncover more and more of the various groups that are working on specific parts of the citizenship training program (i.e., Roy Larsen's group — the Kentucky program[3] — different institutional programs such as that at Syracuse[4] — the one listed in the attached documents), I become more and more impressed with an eventual need for some kind of articulation or coordination but *without* amalgamation or integration. It may well be that you and your assistants may eventually find a great field of service in attempting to act as the connecting link between these various programs. Obviously, we want to avoid the confusion and waste that would be inevitable in uncoordinated duplication and possible working at cross-purposes.

I suspect that either Mr. Crider or one of the people actively working on the program that he has been sponsoring will attempt to get in touch with you or with Mr. Vincent.[5]

No reply is necessary, but when next I see you I will be glad to talk with you concerning this and related subjects.

[1] Russell, president of Teachers College, was director of the Citizenship Education Project, a program designed to increase civic pride among high school students (for background see no. 727).

[2] John Henshaw Crider (B.Litt. Columbia 1928), editor in chief of the *Boston Herald* and a recent recipient of a Pulitzer Prize for distinguished editorial writing, had met with Eisenhower on May 19. The pamphlets had probably been prepared by the Civic Education Project of the Educational Research Corporation in Cambridge, Massachusetts. One of the project's pamphlets for secondary-school students was called "Know Your Isms," and the *Herald* had published it in twenty-two installments between April 16 and May 10. Each excerpt had included warnings of the dangers that fascism and communism posed to the American way of life.

[3] Roy E. Larsen was president of Time, Inc., and chairman of the National Citizens Commission for the Public Schools; the Citizens Community Council Program had originated in Kentucky. For background see no. 775.

[4] The cornerstone of the citizenship program at the Maxwell Graduate School of Citizenship and Public Affairs at Syracuse University had been a freshman course called "Responsible Citizenship," first offered in 1924. During 1947 and 1948 a special staff of citizenship teachers had changed the format of the freshman course to include "practical projects" such as visits to the offices of government administrators and attendance at meetings of civic groups (see Syracuse University, Maxwell Graduate School of Citizenship and Public Affairs, *The Maxwell Graduate School of Citizenship and Public Affairs: Twenty-fifth Anniversary, 1924–1949* [Syracuse, 1949], pp. 17, 40–42).

[5] Professor William S. Vincent was executive officer of the Citizenship Education Project (for background see no. 727, n. 4).

812   *Eisenhower Mss.*

TO WILLIAM SAMUEL PALEY   *May 23, 1950*

Dear Bill:[1] William G. Carr of the Educational Policies Commission informs me that he has invited you to attend the special EPC session on home television and its influence on young people. I hope you can accept.[2] The Commission is one of the most important groups in the educational field. In a way, it comprises, a General Staff to the entire educational system of the country. Your advice and counsel to it members will be reflected, in time, in practically every American classroom.[3]

While I cannot attend the session myself, I have gone to every meeting since I became a member of the Commission and I would be there in October, if it were not for my brother Milton's inaugural in Pennsylvania State.[4] Only something that happens (of that sort) once in a lifetime could prevent me from joining you for the October meeting.[5]

Sincerely

[1] Paley was chairman of the board of the Columbia Broadcasting System (for background see no. 740).

[2] In a letter of May 17 Carr, secretary of the Educational Policies Commission (EPC), had asked Eisenhower to encourage Paley to attend a special conference on the "Effects of Home Television on Children and Young People" on October 5, 6, and 7 at the Westchester Country Club in Rye, New York. The commission had decided at its thirty-fifth meeting in March to invite spokesmen from the television industry to review with them "evidence concerning educational and social effects of television in the home, and to seek suggestions as to what can be done to make these effects useful and constructive, and to minimize harmful effects" (EM, Paley Corr.).

[3] For background on the EPC see no. 387, n. 4.

[4] Eisenhower had been a member of the EPC since January 1, 1949 (see n. 3 above). For the General's additional correspondence with Carr and for background on Milton Eisenhower's inauguration see no. 757.

[5] On May 16 Carr had acknowledged Eisenhower's declination to the October conference (EM, EPC Corr.). Eisenhower had previously prepared a letter of resignation to the chairman of the commission because of his inability to give a reasonable portion of "time, effort, and thought in order to further your important work." Typewritten instructions at the top of the page indicated that the letter was not to be sent but should be retained in the files (Mar. 31, EM, EPC Corr.).

813   *Eisenhower Mss.*

To Thomas John Watson, Sr.   *May 23, 1950*

Dear Tom:[1] Long before this, I should have answered the nice note you sent me the day after your party. I was delighted with the opportunity to be among those present when you received such a nice tribute from the American Arbitration Association.[2]

I only wish that I could have been more eloquent in my particular part of the program—but I do assure you that I could not have been more sincere.[3]

As you know, from the very beginning, you were a most influential factor in my coming to Columbia. This was not merely because of your skill as a salesman; it comprised also the implication that you would always be my partner in seeking the good of this great University.[4] I realize, of course, that your beloved Lafayette has, likewise, some claim upon your affection and support. In fact, I share your feelings toward that institution. But, by and large, I count you one of the loyal, even partisan members of the Columbia family.[5]

So I had this additional reason for gratification when you were the guest of honor before such a distinguished company as attended the dinner the other evening.[6] *Cordially*

[1] Watson was chairman of the board of the IBM Corporation. He was active in domestic and international arbitration as a director of the American Arbitration Association (for background see Galambos, *Chief of Staff*). A copy of Eisenhower's letter to Watson was sent to George B. Pegram, special adviser to the president of Columbia University.

[2] Eisenhower had been the principal speaker at a dinner for Watson sponsored by the American Arbitration Association on May 16, 1950, at the Waldorf-Astoria Hotel in New York City. Watson was honored for his twenty-five years as a "supporter of the wider use of arbitration as a method of settling commercial disputes between business men engaged in international commerce" (*New York Times*, May 1, 1950). In a letter of May 17 the business executive had thanked the General for "the personal tribute you paid to me last night, not only by your mere words, but also by the fact that you were there" (EM). According to his appointment calendar, Eisenhower had become ill the afternoon of May 9 and had canceled most of his engagements through May 18. On May 15 Watson had telephoned to assure the General that he did not have to attend the dinner.

[3] In his address Eisenhower had said that "war is the most despicable, the most dreadful thing to which men can resort, made possible only by the spiritual values it evokes in courage and team play." These spiritual values, he continued, could be better utilized in the cause of peace. Peace must bring to "all men living together the confidence that bodily harm will not be used to make them agree— that violence cannot bring about right." On the subject of international trade, the General asked that American exports not only bring a profit but help to develop positive qualities in mankind throughout the world (*New York Times*, May 17, 1950; see also "World Peace through World Trade," *Arbitration Journal* 5, no. 2 [1950], 96–97).

[4] For Watson's role in Eisenhower's decision to assume the presidency of Columbia University see Galambos, *Chief of Staff*, nos. 1528, 1551, and 1552; and Rodgers, *Think*, pp. 201–11. Concerning the application of IBM equipment at Columbia see Rodgers, *Think*, pp. 135–48; on the establishment of the Watson research center see *ibid.*, pp. 179–80; and for IBM's financial contributions to the university see *ibid.*, p. 281.

[5] Watson had been vice-president of the board of trustees of Lafayette College, in Easton, Pennsylvania, and had received the honorary degree of Doctor of Laws from that institution in 1934. Eisenhower had received a Doctor of Laws degree from Lafayette in 1946 (see Galambos, *Chief of Staff*, no. 722).

[6] Among those who attended Watson's tribute were: Spruille Braden, president of the American Arbitration Association, who presented a gold medal to Watson; Cardinal Francis Spellman, who delivered the invocation; Dr. Ralph C. Hutchinson, president of Lafayette College; James A. Farley, former Postmaster General of the United States; Richard C. Patterson, Jr., Ambassador to Guatemala; and James W. Gerard, former Ambassador to Germany. Watson would reply to Eisenhower (May 29, EM), "No one could possibly have more interest in the success of the University under your direction than I, and I want you to always count on me as a loyal supporter of you and the other members of the Columbia family."

To Robert Winship Woodruff   *May 23, 1950*

Dear Bob:[1] With further reference to my note of May 17 I have just
learned from Philip Young that his father disapproves of the use of
his name in subsidizing a professorship at Harvard Business School.[2] *As
ever*

¹ Eisenhower's handwritten letter to Woodruff concerned the proposed Owen D.
Young professorship at Harvard University (for background see no. 801).
² In his reply of May 30 Woodruff said, "The next time I see you . . . I will
tell you an interesting story about the action taken by the [General Electric] Board
relative to the matter we recently discussed" (EM). The board of directors of
General Electric would establish a professorship in honor of its president, Charles
Edward Wilson, at the Graduate School of Business Administration of Harvard
University. The Wilson professor would be concerned with "the over-all approach
to business problems required by top management" and "the relationship of business
to government and to the community as well as with internal matters" (*New York
Times*, Aug. 15, 1950).

To George Ephraim Sokolsky   *May 23, 1950*

Dear Mr. Sokolsky:[1] When you told me of your talk before the Chaplains,
I failed to absorb from your casual statements the fact that you had
actually delivered a powerful and moving appeal for the adjustment of
our codes and standards to eternal values. I should think that every
minister, rabbi and priest in the U.S. would be glad to have a copy.[2]
    I thank you for letting me see it—I hope I shall profit from it as
much as I should.[3] *Sincerely*

¹ Sokolsky was an author, lecturer, and industrial consultant whose syndicated
columns and editorials for the *New York Sun* and other newspapers frequently
maintained that the future of America depended on the adherence to the inseparable
principles of democracy and capitalism (for further background see no. 333).
² A draft of this letter with Eisenhower's handwritten changes is in EM, Letters
and Drafts. Sokolsky had sent Eisenhower a copy of the address, entitled, "Watch-
men, What of the Climate?" which he had delivered to the Military Chaplains
Association. The General apparently had discussed the speech with Sokolsky when
they had met on May 17 (May 18, 1950, EM).
³ In his speech, Sokolsky had challenged ministers (whose profession he called
one of "watchfulness over the character and morals of men and women, and
particularly over the young") to act as "warriors of our day . . . in an everlasting
war against a retreat from moral law." He attributed the dire conditions of society
to man's "unwillingness to live with his neighbors on a moral basis." Sokolsky
concluded with the thought that "America's mission to all the world . . . is the

brotherhood of man in the law of God" ("Convention Addresses," *The Military Chaplain* 21, no. 1 [July 1950], 8–9).

816   *Eisenhower Mss.*

To Thomas Jeffries Betts   *May 24, 1950*

Dear Tom:[1] Thank you for your note of May 17th.[2] The only suggestion I have seen about the possibility of service for me in connection with the Atlantic Union has been in the newspapers.[3] However, I assure you that, if ever I have any duty of the kind you mention, I shall instantly take advantage of your very acceptable offer. I should like very much to have you with me again under the kind of circumstances that you describe.[4] *Cordially*

[1] Betts had been a colonel in the U.S. Army since April 1, 1946, and would retire as brigadier general on July 31, 1953. He had been Chief Intelligence Officer assigned to the Bikini atomic bomb tests in 1946; U.S. military attaché in Warsaw, Poland, in 1947–48; and subsequently a geopolitical planner in the Central Intelligence Agency. For further background see Chandler and Galambos, *Occupation, 1945*, no. 109.

[2] In his letter (EM) Betts had offered his services in the event that Eisenhower assumed official duties in connection with the North Atlantic Alliance. Betts described his own chief asset as a "broad and objective knowledge of the world and of the comparative values of the great forces which dominate it today." He said he was willing to serve in a military capacity or as a retired Army officer (EM).

[3] For Eisenhower's views on the Atlantic Union see no. 1009. Eisenhower was probably referring to speculation in the *New York Times* that he was the "logical choice" to head the North Atlantic Treaty powers (for background on the North Atlantic Treaty see nos. 375 and 539). Journalist Raymond Daniell, reporting on the May 1950 conferences of the North Atlantic Pact organization in London, had written: "The name that pops into everyone's head seems to be that of Gen. Dwight D. Eisenhower, who, having liberated Western Europe, is regarded as its potential savior now." Daniell pointed out that there was "some question whether General Eisenhower should be regarded as a soldier or a citizen" and that some European nations felt that the Russians might misinterpret his appointment to the post as a "war-like move." "On the other hand," Daniell added, "there is a feeling that the mere creation of the post would have that effect and that if the step must be taken at all it would be better to put at its head a man who at least would have a good chance of producing results" (May 17, 1950; for subsequent articles by Daniell concerning this issue see *New York Times*, May 18 and 19).

[4] For Eisenhower's appointment as Supreme Commander of the NATO forces see no. 1134. Betts would not accompany Eisenhower to Europe, but the General would invite many of his wartime comrades to serve with him "under the brave new banners of NATO." They would include former aides Kevin McCann and Lieutenant Colonel Robert L. Schulz, who were then serving as assistants to Eisenhower at Columbia University (see Galambos, *Chief of Staff*, no. 1551), Colonel Charles Craig Cannon, another aide-de-camp (see *ibid.*, nos. 618 and 1976), and Colonel Paul T. "Pete" Carroll, a former staff member in the Pentagon

(see *ibid.*, no. 2052). "All these officers gave Eisenhower their devotion and unquestioning loyalty. They could provide advice, a smartly administered headquarters, a balanced checkbook, a smooth flow of appointed visitors, some laughter, occasional good companionship, and constant sympathetic support . . ." (Lyon, *Portrait of the Hero*, p. 422; see also no. 1137).

817   *Eisenhower Mss.*

TO WILLIAM ROBERT ROSS   *May 24, 1950*

Dear President Ross:[1] Quite naturally I am flattered by the cordiality of your invitation to be with you in Greeley next August 17.[2] While it is true that, under present plans I shall be in Colorado at that time, it is still a bit early to pin myself down—without providing for some escape clause—to a fixed date. To do so might operate to spoil important family vacational plans.[3]

However, since I understand from your letter that I would not be expected to make any lengthy or formal address, but would be coming to Colorado State College of Education on the specified date for an *informal* and friendly visit, I would be happy, in view of your belief that such a visit would be gratifying to your assembled teachers, to put it on my tentative calendar.[4] If this is satisfactory, I could give you a final and firm answer about August 5th or 6th—after my arrival in Denver.[5]

Since my purpose in coming, if I find myself able to do so, would be to use this method of showing my high regard and respect for the teaching profession and for your College as a teaching institution, I would be inclined to feel that the award of an Honorary Degree should not be contemplated. This would be in keeping with the informality of the day and the uncertainty of my ability to attend.[6]

If you do not feel it possible for you to wait for a firm answer, of course I have no alternative but to tell you of my regret that I cannot come. On the other hand, if you accept the conditions outlined above, I shall do my best to fit the date into my schedule. In any event, I trust that you need no assurance of the distinction I feel in the receipt of your invitation.[7] *Sincerely*

[1] Ross (Ph.D. Colorado State College of Education 1940) had been president of Colorado State College of Education, at Greeley, Colorado, since 1948. The institution had originally been established as the State Normal School in 1889 and had been renamed Colorado State College of Education in 1935. It would be Colorado State College after 1957, and the University of Northern Colorado in 1970. A draft of this letter, with Eisenhower's handwritten changes is in EM, Letters and Drafts.

[2] Ross had invited Eisenhower to the convocation and sixtieth anniversary cele-

bration of the founding of Colorado State College of Education (Apr. 26, 1950, EM).

[3] Eisenhower would be on vacation from July 14 to September 17 (see no. 805, n. 4).

[4] In the same letter, Ross had said that should the General interrupt his vacation in Colorado to attend "our home-grown and friendly meeting . . . many teachers would be more wisely inspired to carry on their work as the most hopeful long-term alternative to war" (May 24, 1950, EM).

[5] Eisenhower would ask Ross to write him in Denver (July 6, EM). Ross would reiterate his request on August 1, saying, "We will leave no stone unturned to make your visit as pleasant and free from tensions as possible. . . ." He added that he hoped to have a small dinner party in the General's honor to be attended only by the school's Columbia-affiliated professors, the members of the board of trustees, and some visiting guests (EM).

[6] Ross had written the General, "We shall consider it a happy privilege to confer on you an honorary degree of Doctor of Education" (Apr. 26, EM).

[7] In a letter of August 11 Eisenhower would inform Ross that he would be unable to come to Greeley after all, because of family, university, and quasi-public committments (EM). Concerning other invitations that Eisenhower declined in the summer of 1950 see no. 805, n. 6.

818   *Eisenhower Mss.*

To Stafford LeRoy Irwin   *May 24, 1950*

Dear Red:[1] Enclosed are two documents which are self-explanatory. They are, as you will see, prepared by representatives from the "enslaved countries." This group seems to be currently residing in Munich.[2]

Occasionally, Europeans passing through New York drop in to see me and tell me something of the existing situation in that region. However, this particular case appears to be somewhat different and I am not certain of what they want when they ask for my *moral* support.[3]

In any event, I pass these on to you to ask whether you or the Chief of Staff or the State Department sees any virtue in my attempting to encourage these people. If you could give me your comments and advice, I will be governed thereby.[4]

I trust that I am to see you at West Point for our Reunion.[5] *Cordially*

[1] Major General Irwin had been Assistant Chief of Staff, G–2, U.S. Army, since November 1948. He had been commander of the Replacement and School Command, Army Ground Forces, from June to August 1946, and commander of V Corps from September 1946 to October 1948.

[2] The documents pertained to the Military Commission of the Anti-Bolshevik Bloc of Nations (ABN), which had been organized in Munich, Germany, on March 19, 1950. One was a letter from Munich of May 6, 1950, announcing the formation of the Military Commission; the other was a list of "Basic Principles of Cooperation between the Members of the ABN Military Commission," dated March 19, 1950. The ABN included representatives of twenty nations governed

by Communist regimes. The signers of the documents asked for moral support and offered to cooperate with Western leaders in any future attempt to "break up the USSR of today, free the world from Russian imperialism and the nations from Communist slavery." Copies are in the same file as this document.
[3] Regarding Eisenhower's association with groups involved in political warfare against the Soviet Union see no. 303, n. 19.
[4] Irwin would reply on May 26 (EM) that he had sent the ABN papers to the CIA. For developments see no. 828.
[5] General and Mrs. Eisenhower would join the members of the class of 1915 and their wives at West Point from June 3 to June 5. On the planned festivities see no. 773.

819   *Eisenhower Mss.*

To Joseph Lawton Collins   *May 24, 1950*

Dear Joe:[1] There are three men now on the retired list who commanded American armies in active operations and did so with brilliant success. They are Bill Simpson, Eichelberger and Lucian Truscott.[2]

Since it is my understanding that all retired officers above the grade of Major General receive identical pay, I have often felt that it would be a most deserving and graceful thing if these three men could be promoted to four-star rank on the retired list. It is one of those things which I intended to get at when I was still Chief of Staff; but, for some reason or other, the job of demobilizing the Army and getting it started on the upward path of development always seemed to cut out opportunities to do with things of this kind.[3]

If you should think this suggestion unwise, I suggest that you merely throw this letter in the wastebasket and do nothing about it—not even acknowledge it. On the other hand, if you think well of the idea and you and the Secretary should like to present it to Chairman Vinson and Senator Tydings, you are at liberty to quote me as being in urgent support.[4]

I accepted an invitation to come to Washington the other day with a very lively hope of seeing you for a chat. I might have known that you would have to be away some place, speaking. But I did get a chance to chat a few minutes with Matt Ridgway.[5]

All the best. *Cordially*

[1] General Collins had been Army Chief of Staff since August 1949 (for background see no. 8).
[2] Lieutenant General William Hood Simpson, former CG of the Ninth Army, had retired in November 1946. Lieutenant General Robert Lawrence Eichelberger, former Eighth Army CG and consultant on Far Eastern affairs to the Secretary of the Army since 1949, had retired in December 1948 (see no. 6). Lieutenant General Lucian King Truscott, Jr., former CG of the Fifth Army, had retired in

September 1947 (see no. 924). For background on these U.S. Army officers and their roles in World War II see *Eisenhower Papers*, vols. I–IX.

³ For Eisenhower's problems with Army promotion and reduction policies after World War II see no. 16; and Galambos, *Chief of Staff*, nos. 589, 668, and 2003.

⁴ Eisenhower was referring to Secretary of the Army Gordon Gray (for background see no. 675). Carl Vinson was chairman of the House Armed Services Committee, and Millard E. Tydings was chairman of the Senate Armed Services Committee (for background see nos. 294, n. 2, and 733, respectively. There is in EM no further correspondence from Collins concerning this subject). Simpson, Eichelberger, and Truscott would finally attain the rank of full general in 1954, along with eight other lieutenant generals of World War II. On July 19, 1954, the House would unanimously approve legislation authorizing Eisenhower, as President of the United States, to promote officers who according to a House committee report would have attained the four-star rank "except for administrative delays and the press of World War II." The committee concluded that these promotions were "in keeping with the rank accorded other Army officers who held similar wartime commands during the same limiting periods" (*New York Times*, July 20, 1954; U.S., *Statutes at Large*, vol. 68, pt. 1, p. 492).

⁵ On May 20, 1950, Eisenhower had a full schedule in Washington, D.C. According to his appointment calendar, he met with Secretary of Defense Louis A. Johnson; President Harry S. Truman; and Lieutenant General Matthew B. Ridgway (for background on Ridgway, Deputy Chief of Staff for Administration, U.S. Army, see no. 599). Eisenhower later reviewed the Armed Forces Day Parade, met with Ridgway again at the Pentagon, and then departed at 3:00 P.M. for New York City.

820   *Eisenhower Mss.*

TO FREDERIC RENÉ COUDERT   *May 26, 1950*

*Dear Mr. Coudert:*¹ I am looking forward to our luncheon with Tom Finletter on Monday, the 29th; I shall be at the Century Association at one o'clock.²

So long as my friends of the Union Club want a portrait of me by Mr. Alfred D. Smith, I shall of course agree to sit for him.³ While, ordinarily, the sitting for a portrait—except where there is involved an artist who has already painted a number of pictures of the sitter—is a time-consuming chore, I could not possibly be so discourteous as to refuse to cooperate in the case of the Union Club.⁴ So, while some years ago I resolved never again to sit for any artist except Mr. Thomas Stephens, I have made an exception in the instance of the artist commissioned by the Trustees of Columbia and will do so in the case at hand.⁵

I think that the best time for me would probably be between July 7 and July 15. If Mr. Smith could communicate with my office to make necessary engagements during that period, I am sure that something satisfactory can be worked out. Unfortunately,⁶ I could probably arrange for a preliminary sitting—if the artist should want it—about June 12, 13 or 14.[7]

With warm personal regards, *Cordially*

[1] For background on Coudert, an attorney and trustee of Columbia University, see no. 72. Coudert and Eisenhower were fellow members of the Century Association, which included authors, artists, and "amateurs of letters and the fine arts," and the Union Club, the oldest social club in the United States.

[2] Coudert had written several times to confirm his luncheon date with Eisenhower and Secretary of the Air Force Thomas K. Finletter (May 11, 23, 1950, EM). The General would thank Coudert for "a most enjoyable luncheon [which] . . . served to increase my already very high opinion of Tom Finletter" (May 31, EM).

[3] Coudert had asked Eisenhower, on behalf of the Union Club, to consent to have his portrait painted by Al*bert* Delmont Smith. Smith, also a member, had recently completed a painting of Admiral Thomas C. Kincaid which was to be included with portraits of Generals Grant, Sherman, Sheridan, and Pershing in the Union Club gallery. Coudert wrote, "The President [Beverley Robinson] of the Union Club is very anxious to have your portrait to add to the collection of very fine portraits already in the Club of our great military leaders since General Washington. . . . As Beverley Robinson has written; 'I would give three cheers if we could actually accomplish this'" (May 23, 1950, EM).

[4] Eisenhower had declined an invitation from the Union Club president to sit for a portrait in April 1949. He had written to Robinson, "I find sitting for a portrait, even if only for a very few hours, as wearing and tiring as several days hard work" (Apr. 25, 1949; along with other correspondence in EM, Subject File, Clubs and Associations).

[5] For Eisenhower's experiences with portrait artists and for background on Thomas Edgar Stephens see no. 493. For information on the General's portrait for the trustees of Columbia University see no. 688, n. 3.

[6] Eisenhower may have used the word *unfortunately* because of his distaste for this chore (see n. 4, above).

[7] Eisenhower would be informed in a memorandum of June 6 that Smith had suggested a one-hour sitting at 2:00 P.M. on June 13 and a half-hour sitting at 9:00 A.M. on June 15 (Schulz to Eisenhower, EM). According to the General's appointment calendar, an additional session was necessary at 3:00 P.M. on July 10. Smith would invite Eisenhower to view the finished painting several months later. He wrote, "Though the portrait is not entirely satisfactory to me; it does convey, in a way, the message I wished to transmit: courage, force and determination. Which is written all over your face. Humor, is also there but, I am afraid and sorry, it is concealed in this portrait. . . . As an alibi for its absence I will blame it on our present political and social unrest" (Feb. 5, 1951, EM). In a handwritten message of February 10, 1951, Smith told Eisenhower that the portrait had been approved and was on display at the Union Club. He sent a photograph to show changes in the portrait that the General had suggested. Smith wrote that he hoped the changes had "removed some of the toughness you mentioned" (EM).

To Henry Clay Williams   *May 26, 1950*

Dear Williams:[1] Today I heard of an opportunity that I think might interest you and might possibly bring to you a most successful and enjoyable career.

One of my friends is Mr. Freeman Gosden who is one member of the radio team of "Amos 'n' Andy." This show, which has enjoyed a tremendous success for many years, is soon to be put on television and for this they need certain individuals to take the parts of the fictitious characters they have created over the years in their radio show.[2] Mr. Gosden explained to me that they still need one man who possesses both intelligence and understanding and who can be trained to take a part which is important in their show. They want a fairly good-sized man with a good voice, and who can read well![3]

I explained to him that I was sure that you had never had any training or education in the theatrical profession but he seemed to feel that, if you should be found to possess the particular qualifications—other than technical—that they are looking for, they might be able to give you the technical instruction required.[4]

Of course, there is a great deal more involved in such a job than mere application, but the rewards seem to me to be sufficiently attractive that it would be well worth your while to apply and, if given a reasonable chance, *to work hard to make good.* I have the impression that, if they take you on for the job, you would be offered a very fine salary.

Of course, you may already be embarked on some career that attracts you more than the one I suggest herein. If not, won't you write instantly to

> Mr. Freeman Gosden
> Savoy-Plaza Hotel
> Fifth Avenue and 59th Street
> New York City

He seemed so interested when I told him about you and your general capabilities and qualifications that I believe he would give you every possible chance to make good. He would arrange for someone in Chicago to come see you, make a recording of your voice and to submit to him a professional opinion on your qualifications for the job.

The only thing further I can say in the matter is that I like Mr. Gosden very much indeed and I am certain that, if you make it, you would find him one of the best men you ever worked for or with.[5]

Best of luck and good wishes.[6] *Sincerely*

P.S. Let me hear from you!

[1] Williams, who worked for the Chicago Post Office Department, had been a member of Eisenhower's personal household staff in Europe (for background see no. 618). A draft of this letter, with the General's handwritten changes, is in EM, Letters and Drafts.

[2] Freeman F. Gosden was a writer, producer, and performer who had created "Amos 'n' Andy," a radio program that aired in 1929 with the National Broadcasting Company (NBC) and in 1939 with the Columbia Broadcasting System (CBS). Gosden, who played Amos, and co-creator Charles J. Correll, who played Andy, had engaged in a year-long search to find black actors to take over their characters in the show when it transferred to television in the fall of 1950 (*New York Times*, June 18, 1950).

[3] Eisenhower had recommended Williams for the role of Kingfish, a dominant character who posed the greatest casting problem for Gosden. Most actors, Gosden said, failed to grasp the real nature of Kingfish, a good-hearted man with a devilish streak (*ibid.*).

[4] The *New York Times* would report that Eisenhower had recommended "a former soldier" for the part (June 18) and that President Harry S. Truman had suggested that a Kingfish might be found in the great schools of the South (June 21).

[5] On May 30 Williams would thank the General and assure him that "I shall not fail to exercise every single bit of physical, mental and spiritual property that I might accidentally possess to justify your faith in me" (EM). Eisenhower would send Gosden a copy of Williams's letter, and on June 7 Gosden would inform the General that the auditions were under way; Williams would be flown to New York for additional coaching. Eisenhower replied on June 9 that his former staff member appeared heavier in civilian clothes than he remembered (Gosden had enclosed a recent picture of Williams with his letter). "I truly hope," added the General, "he is not too much of a dud" (EM). On June 17 Williams gave Eisenhower an account of his acting difficulties. "One must forget for the time being, everything that has ever happened in one's life and actually live and be this character," he wrote, but "I shall use every available moment and method to make myself the fabulous 'Kingfish'" (EM).

[6] As it turned out, Tim Moore, of Rock Island, Illinois, would be selected as Kingfish; Alvin Childress would take the role of Amos; and Spencer Williams, Jr., that of Andy (*New York Times*, Nov. 12, 1950). In a letter of October 19 Williams apologized to Eisenhower for failing to make the show. He sent a leather briefcase in honor of the General's birthday in "sincere and humble appreciation for having had a great boss" (EM). Eisenhower thanked Williams and added, "You can chalk up your efforts to a worthwhile experience" (Nov. 3, EM). The General would later receive films of three "Amos 'n' Andy" television shows from Gosden (July 24, 1951, EM).

822 *Eisenhower Mss.*

To Pierre Joseph Koenig *May 27, 1950*

Dear General Koenig:[1] Today Irving Geist delivered to me the plaque designed by your friend Albert de Jaeger.[2] In commissioning such a fine artist to execute a plaque bearing my likeness, you have paid me a compliment which I shall always treasure. Because it comes from a valued friend and comrade of World War II and my former associate on the Berlin Control Council, its significance is multiplied for me.[3]

Mr. Geist has told me of the wonderful work you are doing to promote the welfare of disabled Veterans in France. It is gratifying to know that you have undertaken this task.[4] I share your concern about the readiness of the free world to meet the demands of any emergency.[5] But it seems to me that recent diplomatic developments, particularly the conferences between the foreign ministers of the democratic countries, give some hope that all of us are awakening to the value of "time."[6]

I assure you again of my grateful thanks for the compliment of your thoughtful gift. Please accept my warmest wishes for your continued health and happiness. *Cordially*

P.S. When Mr. Geist returns to your country, I shall ask him to bring a message of greetings to those attending your celebration on July 14. I think you will not consider this presumptuous on my part.[7]

[1] General Koenig was Inspector General of the French forces in North Africa. He had been Commander in Chief of the French occupation zone in Germany from July 1945 to August 1949 (for background on Koenig's relationship with Eisenhower see *Eisenhower Papers*, vols. I–IX). A draft of this letter, with Eisenhower's handwritten changes, is in EM, Letters and Drafts.

[2] According to his appointment calendar, Eisenhower had met with Irving Geist, a New York philanthropist and board chairman of the Knickerbocker Ford Motor Company, at 9:30 A.M. on May 26, 1950.

[3] In a letter of April 22 (EM) Koenig had asked Eisenhower to accept as a memento of the General's work with the Allied Control Council in Berlin a medal engraved by French artist Albert de Jaeger. Eisenhower had represented the United States and Koenig had represented France on this central Allied governing council (see no. 93).

[4] Koenig was honorary president of the Home du Blessé, a charitable organization devoted to serving France's seriously disabled veterans of the first and second world wars. Geist had also promoted the interests of U.S. veterans of World War II (June 9, 1950, EM, Germain Corr.; see *New York Times*, June 25, July 22, and Dec. 31, 1950).

[5] In his letter Koenig had said that he had followed "with the greatest attention" Eisenhower's recent declarations and felt that "too many people forget the lessons of the past and believe that they will always have at their disposal sufficient time to mobilize the resources without which wars are lost." "I fear," he continued, "that the Democratic world will repeat over again its errors of the period before 1939" (Apr. 22, 1950, EM). Koenig was probably referring to remarks in Eisenhower's March 23 address at the Columbia University Gabriel Silver Lecture series (see no. 741) and his supplemental testimony before the Senate Appropriations subcommittee (see no. 753) concerning deficiencies in the military preparedness of the United States. Eisenhower had said on the former occasion that, "until war is eliminated from international relations, unpreparedness for it is well nigh as criminal as war itself" (*New York Times*, Mar. 24, 1950). In regard to the General's appearance before the Senate subcommittee see nos. 754, 755, and 914; and *New York Times*, May 19, 1950.

[6] Eisenhower was apparently referring to the May conference in London of the twelve foreign ministers of the North Atlantic Treaty nations. The pact members had taken specific steps to strengthen the alliance of the free nations of the West.

These measures included the creation of a permanent deputies' committee to provide continuity and direction for the organization's program (see no. 816, n. 3); an understanding by the foreign ministers of the guiding principles of the committees of the North Atlantic Pact; directives for the unified treatment of military and economic aspects of defense; agreement upon the creation of balanced collective forces as the most effective use of resources; and the establishment of a planning board for ocean shipping (*New York Times*, May 19, 1950; see also *ibid.*, May 16, 17, and 18). For background on the North Atlantic Treaty see nos. 375 and 539.

[7] Geist had invited Eisenhower to a celebration in Paris on behalf of the permanently disabled French veterans of World War II (Geist to Eisenhower, June 12, 1950, EM). The General declined but asked that Geist hand-deliver a check enclosed with another letter to Koenig. Eisenhower wrote, "Because of my respect and affection for my French associates in the Mediterranean and European campaigns in that war, I should like to be accounted, at least modestly, among your supporters in this effort" (Eisenhower to Koenig, June 1, 1950, EM).

---

823   *Eisenhower Mss.*

To Arthur Hays Sulzberger   *May 27, 1950*

Dear Arthur:[1] I submit to you for consideration by the Honors Committee the name of Charles E. Wilson (of General Electric) for Honorary Degree of Doctor of Laws in 1951.[2]

Mr. Wilson is so well known that I think there is no need to attempt to outline his qualifications. One significant item of information that may not be common knowledge among our Trustees is that some months ago Mr. Wilson undertook the task, at my request, of heading a committee to develop ways and means by which universities and corporations—with specific reference to Columbia University—could work more effectively together.[3]

I would have recommended Mr. Wilson for Honorary Degree this year but was under the mistaken impression that he had already been awarded one.[4] This error rose because of the fact that we previously gave a Degree to Charles E. Wilson of General Motors.[5] *Cordially*

---

[1] Sulzberger was chairman of the Columbia University trustees' Committee on Honors. For background on the committee's revised methods of selecting honorary degree candidates see no. 694.

[2] For background on Wilson, president of the General Electric Company, see no. 684. John Charles Walter, president of the industrial supply company of Alvey-Ferguson, had written to Eisenhower concerning Wilson, whom he considered "the greatest industrialist of our time" (for background on Walter see no. 648, n. 3). He asked that Eisenhower "very seriously consider awarding him [Wilson] an honorary degree" because of his excellent executive and administrative record and "his various other activities for the good of industry, education and the country."

Walter added that the president of GE was very "sympathetic toward Columbia" and interested in the future of the university (May 24, 1950, EM).

[3] For Wilson's role as head of Columbia's corporate participation project see no. 710, n. 1.

[4] For the recipients of honorary degrees at Columbia's 1950 commencement see no. 694.

[5] On May 27 Eisenhower thanked Walter for his letter, which corrected the "erroneous impression" that Columbia had already awarded an honorary degree to Wilson (EM). In an undated memorandum to clarify the situation, it was pointed out to Provost Grayson L. Kirk that Charles E. Wilson of General Electric had never received an honorary degree, while Charles E. Wilson of General Motors had received one in 1949 (EM, Walter Corr.; see *New York Times*, June 1, 1949). Eisenhower wrote Walter that he would nominate Wilson at the earliest possible moment but that all arrangements for the current year had been completed and a degree could not be awarded until 1951 (May 27, 1950). The president of General Electric would be honored with a Doctor of Laws degree on June 7, 1951, at Columbia's 197th commencement (*New York Times*, June 8, 1950).

824   *Eisenhower Mss.*

To Charles L. Matter   *May 27, 1950*

Dear Charles:[1] There seems to me no doubt, after reading your letter, that you and I are second cousins.[2] My grandfather married a girl named Matter, and I know also that the house he built in Elizabethville was later sold to a man named Romberger. Since your great-grandfather was the father of my grandmother, it is clear that the relationship is that of second cousins.[3]

Of course, I was glad that you took the trouble to write to me. It is always nice to learn something about the various branches of the family which has, since about 1870, scattered all over the United States and, in some instances, members have gone back to Europe. Before that year my family on my father's side had apparently never left Pennsylvania after coming there first in 1741. On my mother's side the entire family had lived in the Shenandoah Valley of Virginia through roughly the same periods.[4]

I am sorry that you had such a catastrophe on your farm as described in your letter. I hope, however, that things are working out well for you.[5]

Please give my warm regards to your family, and I assure you again of my thanks for the family information you provided me.[6]

I enclose a short note for your little daughter.[7] *Sincerely*

[1] Matter was a farmer in Millersburg, Pennsylvania.

[2] Matter's letter to Eisenhower (May 21, 1950, EM) was addressed to "My dear Cousin and Former General." It contained information from a history of the

Matter family which had led him to conclude that he was related to the General. Matter wrote that since Rebecca Matter, daughter of his great-grandfather, Henry Matter, had married Jacob Eisenhower, the General's grandfather, "You and I would be second cousins [*sic*]. If that is O.K." (EM).

[3] Matter said that he had consulted with a man named Ira Romberger, of Elizabethville, Pennsylvania, who had confirmed that his farmhouse had been formerly owned by Jacob Eisenhower (EM). For more information on Eisenhower's ancestors see Kornitzer, *Great American Heritage*, pp. 1–8, esp. pp. 5–6 for Milton Eisenhower's description of the Eisenhowers in Elizabethville, Pennsylvania.

[4] In Eisenhower's own genealogical chart of the eight generations of his family in North America, he set down 1741 as the date for the arrival of the first Eisenhower in America and "about 1729" for the arrival of the first member of his mother's family, the Stovers. The General wrote, "Progenitors of both David J. and Ida Elizabeth Eisenhower landed in America just before the middle of the eighteenth century. The Eisenhower name was originally spelled 'Eisenhauer,' and the Stover name 'Stoever.' The Eisenhowers settled in Pennsylvania and the Stovers in Virginia" (*ibid.*, pp. 2–3). In 1878 Jacob Eisenhower and his family migrated from Pennsylvania to Dickinson County, Kansas. For further background see Neal, *Reluctant Dynasty*, pp. 1–9. A genealogy entitled "Eisenhower Family in America," by Ross K. Cook (Chandler and Galambos, *Occupation, 1945*, no. 341), published in the *New York Genealogical and Biographical Record* of April 1945, is in EM, Subject File, Genealogy.

[5] Matter told Eisenhower of a fire in 1947 which had destroyed his "barn, milk house, hog stable, water house . . . three horses, 4 milk cows, 2 bulls, 2 heifers and all our grain." He said, "Now this I have only mentioned so you may know we are only common folks who appreciate one like you to know you must be one of our kind" (EM).

[6] Matter would later send Eisenhower a much more detailed genealogy of the Matter family ([May 30, 1950], EM).

[7] Eisenhower wrote in his letter to Mary Joanne Matter, "I just wanted to drop you a note to say that I'm delighted to discover I have a little girl cousin of whose existence I did not know before . . ." (May 26, 1950, EM).

825

Eisenhower Mss.,
President's Committee on the
State of the University Corr.

To Harry James Carman

May 29, 1950

Dear Dean Carman:[1] For some time I have felt that the University should undertake a systematic assessment of its aims, organization and functions.[2] Much of our development planning has been carried on without adequate consideration of the relationship between an individual project and the over-all requirements of the University.[3] What has been lacking is a comprehensive statement of what we believe to be the proper and essential activities, given our history, our financial status, and our metropolitan setting, in which we should engage, and the aims and purposes which we should seek particularly to serve.

If agreements can be reached on these general and fundamental considerations, our existing functions, organizations and physical facilities can then be evaluated in terms of their adequacy to help us achieve these goals. In this way, we can best determine those activities and facilities which require special priority in our development program.

To carry on such a study, I have decided to appoint a "President's Committee on the State of the University," to be composed primarily of the deans and directors of the respective academic divisions. Dean Krout will act as chairman and there will be a small steering committee to assist him.[4] At the present time, the inquiry will not extend to our affiliated organizations.[5]

Such a procedure of self-examination could be lengthy. I hope, however, that we can conclude our task before the end of the fall semester and thereupon submit our findings to expert outside criticism. In order, therefore, to expedite this matter before the end of the present academic year, I am asking the committee to hold an organizational meeting in the Trustees' Room on Thursday, June 1, at 11:30 A.M. I hope very much that you can be present at that time.[6] *Sincerely*

[1] Later this year Carman, dean of Columbia College since 1943, would return to the faculty as Moore Collegiate Professor of History. He would be succeeded as dean by Professor Lawrence H. Chamberlain (Ph.D. Columbia 1945), of the Department of Public Law and Government, on July 1, 1950 (for background on Carman see no. 353). Copies of this letter, drafted in part by Provost Grayson L. Kirk, were sent to deans and directors of Columbia's academic divisions.

[2] For background on this general situation and the principles and the plans for Columbia University see Eisenhower's series of letters to alumni (nos. 332, 346, and 374). On the function of the private university see no. 326. On May 31, 1950, Eisenhower would write of his own "hopes and purposes so far as Columbia University is concerned" (see the next document).

[3] Among the projects that were developing during Eisenhower's administration at Columbia were the nutrition center, the Arden House project, the chair for peace, the Gabriel Silver Lectures, the Higgins Trust, the Conservation of Human Resources Project, Friends of the Land, the Nevis Cyclotron, and the Citizens Training Program. For background on development see nos. 124 and 438; on the decentralization of development see no. 479; and for further events see no. 930.

[4] John A. Krout had been dean of the Faculty of Political Science, Philosophy and Pure Science since April 1949. He would assume additional responsibilities as associate provost on July 1, 1950 (for background on Krout see no. 361).

[5] The affiliated organizations of Columbia University included the Columbia Ambassadors, the Columbia Associates, and the Columbia University Affiliated Clubs within the Alumni Federation (for background see no. 124).

[6] According to his appointment calendar, Eisenhower would meet with the "Presidents Examination Committee" on June 1 (see no. 883). This committee would not report its findings, however, until after Eisenhower had left to assume command of the NATO forces (see papers in CUF).

Eisenhower the hunter at Ichauway, Robert W. Woodruff's plantation at Newton, Georgia, January 1950.

General Eisenhower addresses members of the Harvard Business School Club at a dinner in honor of Columbia's Graduate School of Business, May 26, 1949.

General Eisenhower dedicates Columbia University's new cyclotron,
April 2, 1950. Also present, *L to R*, are John R. Dunning, dean of the
School of Engineering; Rear Admiral Thorvald A. Solberg, USN;
and Isidor Isaac Rabi, professor of physics.

Photo courtesy Captain John Mott, MVO, RN, Culzean

Culzean Castle, Maybole, Ayrshire, Scotland

Governor Thomas E. Dewey (*second from left*) receives from Eisenhower
a report on the New York State hospital system prepared under the direction of
Professor Eli Ginzberg (*second from right*), November 1949. Robert T. Lonsdale,
New York State Commissioner of Social Welfare, looks on.

Low Memorial Library, Columbia University

General Eisenhower holds a press conference at Columbia, May 3, 1948.

L to R: John Sheldon Doud, Mamie Doud Eisenhower, John S. D. Eisenhower,
Barbara Eisenhower, Elivera Doud, and Anne Eisenhower held by
her proud grandfather; in the foreground is David Eisenhower.
Denver, Colorado, August 1950.

Secretary of the Army Frank Pace, Jr., confers with General Eisenhower at the
Pentagon, Washington, D.C., October 28, 1950.

General Eisenhower and Field Marshal Bernard Law Montgomery at Columbia University, November 29, 1950.

The General rides at Ichauway, Robert W. Woodruff's plantation at Newton, Georgia, January 1950.

To Leonard Franklin McCollum   *May 31, 1950*

Dear Mr. McCollum:[1] At Bill Burnham's luncheon, as I remember it,
I told you that I would write you, when I could, of my hopes and
purposes so far as Columbia University is concerned.[2] Of course, on
such a subject I can write at such length that not even a series of letters
would exhaust the possibilities.[3] Consequently, I must restrict myself
to the most general terms. [As I see it, the chief responsibility of our
educational institutions is to establish a sharper understanding of the
American system, a sharper appreciation of its values and a more intense
devotion to its fundamental purposes.] I say this because for many years
I have been greatly concerned with what seems to be a progressive
change in basic thinking—possibly I mean aspirations—in our country.

Traditionally, we Americans have been chiefly concerned with opportunity for social, economic and political betterment under a system
that insured individual freedom and complete equality before the law,
free from governmental control other than that necessary to make certain
that liberty did not degenerate into license. Now, many of us seem to
want only a powerful central government which will insure us against
the need for initiative, sacrifice or foresight by the individual. For
instance, it seems to me we no longer believe that a livelihood can be
earned only by a day's toil; we no longer in prosperous times feel a
compulsion thriftily to set aside savings for a rainy day. Sometimes it
seems to me that pride in work and thrift—the dignity of work and
thrift—has been lost in a new belief that the government owes us a
living because we were born.

Obviously, economic and industrial changes have compelled government to intervene more frequently and intimately in our daily lives
than was the case even a generation ago. No citizen is any longer a
fully self-dependent being. Modern conditions make us interdependent
and this circumstance has encouraged all of those who naturally lean
toward paternalism in government to insist that only through centralized
control of our government can justice, efficiency and economy be maintained. You and I agree that this type of thinking is completely false
but we must also agree that it does have a tremendous appeal to a great
many people and that it can be made to appear logically necessary
particularly in those times when our economic system undergoes a
recession. Moreover, the need for constant revision and adaptation in
methods and procedures encourages neglect and even contempt for the
fundamental principles.

There are all shades and varieties of encroachment upon the foundations of our system. Some are entirely insidious and evil; some are

essentially humanitarian and sometimes necessary and others the product of fuzzy-minded thinking. The problem of our day and time is how to distinguish between those things that government *must* do to perpetuate and maintain freedom for all—freedom from economic as well as political slavery—while, on the other hand, we combat those paternalistic and collectivistic ideas which, if adopted, will accomplish the lessening of individual rights and opportunities and finally the collapse of self-government.

In such matters, there is magnificent opportunity, challenge and work for the country's universities—our great centers of research, of investigation, of independent thinking. While they are conventions of learned men, to my mind, *they are of little worth unless they have underlying purposes for training and imparting of knowledge.* Nor can they fulfill their mission, if they concentrate their efforts only on the material betterment of their graduates. They must attempt satisfaction of the human soul's social, political and economic cravings.

In this country, we know that individual freedom of the basic rights of free speech, worship, self-government are at the core of our deepest desires and aspirations. Our universities must, therefore, aid in the perpetuation of these and be alert against all the insidious ways in which freedom can be lost. If the things that we fear as threats to the American system are the product of faulty leadership, shallow thinking and sheer neglect, it seems to me that only through education, led by our great and understanding universities, are we going to get back on the right track.

My own belief is that Columbia University has an outstanding faculty capable of taking the initiative in the study and analysis, from a national viewpoint, of the great social, political and economic problems. Other institutions, of course, can perform equally valid and useful service. But Columbia is singularly free from real or fancied ties to any group, class, section or dogma. It has a high reputation for academic excellence. By using its prestige, we can do something effective to pass on our basic ideals and our freedom intact to our grandchildren.

It is in this light that I should like my friends to think of Columbia and of the work to which I am personally dedicated. In order to make progress, much is needed—money, in very considerable amounts. *Most independent universities exist today on deficit financing.* I suppose that every one of them can instantly tick off a number of great projects that await implementation because there simply is not available the necessary money. Here at Columbia we most certainly find ourselves in that position; on many fronts we are ready to advance and we know that action will redound to the public good and the strengthening of all American institutions. Yet, we must stand idle; or, rather we must spend much of our time cultivating possible sources of money so that we may get to work on the problems that cry for solution.

It is of these ideas and of these hopes for Columbia and our country that I wish you would sometimes talk to our friends in Texas.[4] This, I suggest with no intention of distracting them from their interest in Texas educational institutions. My philosophy of democracy insists upon local and community responsibility as the basis for free government. I would be the last to urge the neglect of local problems or local ways toward their solution. However, the moral and intellectual strength of Columbia is a tremendous power for good in this country. Every year, many thousands of its graduates go back to their homes across the nation. Somewhere around four thousand enter the teaching profession each year. Their impact is felt in every State and in every American community worthy of the name. The faculty members here—more than three thousand of them—are equally representative of the nation. Beyond that, they are outstanding authorities in all of the specialized fields that comprise the national economy and are enthusiastic believers in the American system. Because of all this, I firmly believe that those who help Columbia help America.

Special studies and projects that we plan to initiate when possible include:

(a) Establishment of a great center outside New York City where business and professional men, members of city, state and national government, and university scholars can meet in forums and round table discussions of the important political, social and economic problems of the day. There should be an attempt to determine a logical dividing line, under modern conditions between governmental control, authority and supervision on the one hand—and the freedom and responsibility of the citizen on the other.[5]

(b) Establishment of a Nutrition Center, a project looking toward the bettering of the physical welfare of all through scientific knowledge of foods: their comparative values, their production, preservation, etc.[6]

(c) Peace Institute—At no place in America is there presently studies of the causes, conduct and consequences of war. We spend millions on physical cancer of the individual body but none on the greatest and most destructive cancer that society as a whole has endured.[7]

(d) Human resources—Our experiences in World War II were alarming in their indication of the tremendous burden we incur by producing such a large percentage of mental defectives. Causes, prevention and cure are mandatory.[8]

(e) There are many others—both old and new in the sciences, the social sciences and humanities.

Forgive this very lengthy exposition. Your first reaction may be that

I will have little left to say about the University when we meet next week. I assure you the contrary is true; I have not even scratched the surface of what I believe can be done toward the accomplishment of those things in which we both so earnestly believe and which can be best furthered and supported in our great universities.[9] *Sincerely*

[1] McCollum (A.B. University of Texas 1925) had been president of the Continental Oil Company of Ponca City, Oklahoma, and Houston, Texas, since 1947. Before that he had worked for the Humble Oil Company and the Carter Oil Company, both subsidiaries of the Standard Oil Company of New Jersey. At this time he lived and worked in Houston, Texas, and he was a close friend of William H. Burnham, Eisenhower's friend and adviser.

[2] Burnham had written the General on April 4 (EM) to say that he would be in Texas for about three weeks and that he would like to use his free time there to help in raising funds for Columbia. Burnham had asked to see Eisenhower to discuss the matter, and on Thursday, April 6, the two men had met in Eisenhower's office. On May 4 Burnham had sent Eisenhower a long report memorandum summarizing his activities in Texas on behalf of the university. "In thinking over the problem of obtaining funds for Columbia from these Texas people," he wrote, "I have reached the conclusion that it would be better if you had a sort of Texan emissary of good will, who would talk to them about what you are trying to do at Columbia. L. F. McCollum, who is joining us for luncheon on Monday, is . . . one of the most popular people in the industry, as well as one of the most brilliant, and is a very patriotic and generous American. . . . I have not said anything to him about this, but I thought on Monday you might mention you would like to have him help you out in Texas. I imagine that he might do it" (EM). The Monday luncheon took place on May 8 in New York City. It was then that Eisenhower, McCollum, and Burnham discussed the university, with the result that the letter to McCollum which is printed above (and several other versions of it) would become the key document in a major drive to raise funds for a number of specific projects at Columbia.

On May 9 Eisenhower told Burnham in a brief note that he was "greatly intrigued by Mr. McCollum." In a reply of May 15 Burnham wrote that McCollum had been "deeply impressed" at the May 8 luncheon and that he had told Burnham that "he knew ten men who would give a million dollars" to Columbia. Burnham said that McCollum now had an entirely different conception of Eisenhower's college presidency (both letters are in EM).

Meanwhile, a copy of the final version of this letter to McCollum would be given to Burnham on June 6 (an early draft of the letter, showing Eisenhower's handwritten changes and additions, is in EM, Letters and Drafts). On June 8 Burnham returned what came to be known as the "McCollum letter," with his own slight revisions. He asked Eisenhower's approval of the changes, after which he planned to make copies of the letter to send to his friends and to take along with him (see typewritten notation on copy 1, Eisenhower to McCollum, EM). The several versions of the McCollum letter and the names of persons who would be given copies of it are in EM, McCollum Corr.). Among those to whom Eisenhower himself would send the letter (with revised and appropriate opening and closing paragraphs) were Samuel Goldwyn, motion picture producer (June 14, 1950, EM, Letters and Drafts); Harry A. Bullis, chairman of the board, General Mills, Inc. (July 10, 1950, EM); Donald S. Kennedy, president, Oklahoma Gas & Electric Company (July 10, 1950, CUF); and Robert B. Whitney, banker (July 10, 1950, EM).

³ Eisenhower had recently written to Dean Harry Carman concerning an assessment of the "aims, organization, and functions" of Columbia (see the preceding document).

⁴ McCollum and Burnham would give a luncheon for a group of Texans on July 13, 1950, at Burnham's apartment in New York City. The guest list included John H. Blaffer, Lamar Fleming, Jr., Walter Golston, and H. J. Porter of Houston; Joseph H. Frost and Edgar G. Tobin of San Antonio; Robert J. Kleberg, Jr., of Kingsville; and H. L. Hunt of Dallas. In addition to Eisenhower, McCollum, and Burnham, Dean Philip Young would also attend the luncheon (see telegram, Burnham to Schulz, June 28, 1950; Burnham to Eisenhower, July 6 and 10, 1950; and guest list, July 13 luncheon, Burnham Corr., all in EM). Burnham would later write to Eisenhower about a half-million-dollar endowment which had been proposed to the luncheon guests on that occasion. "This the Texans are sure we will accomplish speedily. I am not nor either are you I believe, as sanguine as they are of the results, but I do know they are working—and I must admit that from experience I have found that the Texans usually come through" (July 28, 1950, EM).

⁵ This project would ultimately become the American Assembly, established at Arden, the Harriman estate, which had been given to Columbia University by the Harriman brothers (for background on the plan see no. 605; and for developments see no. 1039).

⁶ For Eisenhower's interest in establishing a nutrition center at Columbia University see nos. 431 and 706.

⁷ For background on Eisenhower's involvement in the efforts to raise funds for a proposed institute of war and peace studies see nos. 810; for developments see no. 1056.

⁸ For Eisenhower's concern about this problem see nos. 155 and 1121.

⁹ On June 6 Eisenhower would entertain McCollum, Burnham, and Dean Philip Young at lunch at 60 Morningside Drive. The purpose of the meeting was a briefing for a luncheon on June 15, which McCollum would host at the University Club, 4 West Fifty-fourth Street, in New York City. In addition to Eisenhower, Young, and Burnham, those in attendance would include Frank W. Abrams, chairman of the board, Standard Oil Company of New Jersey; Charles R. Cox, president, Kennecott Copper Company; Howard C. Sheperd, president, National City Bank of New York; LeRoy A. Wilson, president, American Telephone & Telegraph Company; Clarence Francis, chairman of the board, General Foods Corporation; and Robert W. Woodruff, president, Coca-Cola Company (see guest list, luncheon at the University Club, EM, Burnham Corr.). Both Burnham and McCollum would continue to play important roles in helping to raise funds for specific projects at Columbia, especially for the American Assembly. For additional developments see nos. 877 and 979.

827

Eisenhower Mss.

To Louis Arthur Johnson

June 1, 1950

*Dear Louis:*¹ This letter is based upon information brought to me by colleagues in Columbia University who are deeply interested in National Defense. I have been told by them that The Management Committee of the Department of Defense has apparently decided to move the Special Devices Center from Sands Point, Long Island, New York, as a means of reducing operating costs.[2] I recall that, after extensive investigation, many on our Service Academy Board were very enthusiastic about this Center, not only because of its past achievements and future promise, but because it is a notable example of inter-service cooperation. It seemed to them to provide an ideal foundation for genuine unification.[3]

I am also told that moving from the present location, which appears to be nearly ideal, will involve such losses of personnel as may disrupt an operating team of scientists that has taken a long time to build.

You know how earnestly I have supported your efforts to achieve economy, but I think it would be desirable to review the losses, both tangible and intangible that might be involved in the projected move, before making a final decision that might possibly turn out to be penny-wise and pound-foolish. In any event, I'd deeply appreciate your taking a close look at the matter.[4]

With personal regard, *Cordially*

[1] Johnson was Secretary of Defense.

[2] On August 10, 1949, Johnson had issued a directive establishing a Management Committee to recommend to the Department of Defense ways of reducing expenditures. He had reported to Congress the initial findings of the committee on October 21, 1949 (see House Committee on Armed Services, *National Defense Program—Unification and Strategy: Hearings*, 1949, pp. 582–83, 624–30). The Department's plans to move the Special Devices Center from Sands Point, New York, to another location had come to the attention of Ben D. Wood, director of the Columbia College Bureau of Collegiate Educational Research (for background on Wood see no. 338). After World War II the Navy had moved the Special Devices Center to Sands Point so that pilots could undergo flight training on the ground by using equipment that simulated the operations of aircraft. In recent months the Army had taken an interest in this work and had decided to open an Army section at the center (see De Florez to Wood, May 25, 1950, and De Florez to McNarney, May 22, 1950, both in EM, Wood Corr. A short history of the center is in "Report of the Teaching and Testing Methods Panel to the Service Academy Board," Nov. 8, 1949, pp. 51–67, in EM, Service Academy Board Corr.).

[3] In a letter of May 26, 1950 (EM), Wood had informed Eisenhower that the members of the Teaching and Testing Methods Panel of the Service Academy Board had been especially enthusiastic about the Special Devices Center when they had inspected it during July 1949. Economies in defense expenditures were probably necessary, Wood had conceded, but he doubted that the money that might be saved by moving the center could offset the "very real psychological losses in terms of breaking up an enthusiastic team that has taken many years to develop."

[4] Eisenhower made numerous changes in two staff-drafted versions of this letter (see EM, Letters and Drafts). The Special Devices Center would continue to operate at Sands Point, New York, and as the Naval Training Service Center, it would celebrate its tenth anniversary in 1956 (see *New York Times*, Aug. 12, 1956; see also Henry Lefer, "Navy's Special Devices Center; Better Training, Less Expense," *Aviation Week*, Sept. 26, 1955, 35, and "Naval Center Develops Training Devices for Use by Services," *ibid.*, Sept. 17, 1956, 99).

To Stafford LeRoy Irwin   *June 2, 1950*
Confidential

Dear Red:[1] Thank you very much for your letter. In my office we shall instantly make a record of Colonel . . .'s address and functions so that we may in the future call upon him for such help as he can give us in dealing with foreign business.[2]

There is a very definite difficulty involved in attempting to make advance arrangements for such contacts. Sometimes foreigners come to see me through University channels—such individuals as visiting professors or occasional visitors to the institution—and sometimes they come with notes of introduction from prominent people I have met abroad.[3] Usually there is no advance warning that the person involved intends to bring up any political, military or other subject of interest to our security establishment. We will be able to make some application of the procedure you suggested, and it will be most helpful to know the identity of the person we should contact.

In the case of the documents I have already sent to you, I trust that as soon as the CIA has evaluated the documents they will send to me, through you, a suggestion for the reply I should make. Even if this is only to be a noncommittal sort of acknowledgment of receipt—I still think that it is unwise to ignore such things completely unless they are known to have a hostile source.

I absolutely agree with your conviction that great caution must be observed in giving any kind of encouragement whatsoever. In fact, that is the reason I sent the recent documents on to you.[4]

It will be fun to see you at the Reunion. I expect to reach there early Saturday afternoon and I shall have to leave Monday afternoon.[5]

With warm regard, *Sincerely*

[1] Major General Irwin was Assistant Chief of Staff, G–2, U.S. Army (for background see no. 818).
[2] In a letter of May 26 (EM) Irwin had offered to make available a person in the New York field office of the CIA to assist General Eisenhower in dealing with foreign organizations and individuals who contacted him in regard to military or intelligence matters.
[3] See, for example, no. 463.
[4] Recently Eisenhower had sent Irwin two items that he had received from the Anti-Bolshevik Bloc of Nations (ABN) (for background see no. 818). Irwin would inform Eisenhower on June 9 (EM) that the CIA was currently evaluating the ABN documents and that the agency would make suggestions as to the appropriate type of reply. Irwin would quote the agency's conclusions in a letter to Eisenhower of July 11 (EM): " 'The Stetzko group [ABN] is one of several such groups attempting to obtain predominance. Even a brief reply of acknowledgment is capable of being misinterpreted to others. . . . It is our recommendation that no reply should be made to the ABN.' "

General and Mrs. Eisenhower would join the members of the class of 1915 and their wives at West Point, New York, from June 3 to June 5. On the planned festivities see no. 773.

829   *Eisenhower Mss.*

To Edward Bishop Dudley, Jr.   *June 3, 1950*

Dear Ed:[1] Thank you very much for your note and for the clippings you sent with the account of your daughter's wedding.[2] I must say that she was a beautiful bride—I can imagine that you were very proud.

The new set of woods has arrived, and there is no question about their effect on my long shots. Unfortunately, I cannot keep in my mind all the details of the swing as I was finally executing it at Augusta. This is probably because I get to play so rarely. I believe I have been out a total of five times since returning from the South.[3]

I truly hope you will get to come through New York on your way to Colorado Springs. I shall be quite busy through the eleventh, but for the following five days I will be relatively free.[4] After that, I go to Canada for a few days. I hope to reach Colorado about the first of August and, if I have not seen you before then, you can expect a call from me very quickly thereafter.[5]

I assume that Spaulding will soon send me a bill for the clubs.[6] My only possible regret with respect to them is that they don't carry the name "Bobby Jones" instead of just "Spaulding."[7] In any event I am most grateful to you for rushing the order through. *Cordially*

[1] Dudley, a golf professional at the Augusta National Golf Club, had written to thank Eisenhower (May 30, EM) for the letter the General had sent Dudley's daughter prior to her wedding (Eisenhower's longhand note of May 9 is in EM, Ruth E. Dudley Corr.).

[2] Dudley had enclosed with his letter several clippings of the *Augusta* (Ga.) *Chronicle* account of the wedding, including a picture of his daughter in her bridal gown.

[3] The Eisenhowers had vacationed at Augusta National April 10–22, 1950.

[4] Dudley would remark in a letter to Eisenhower of December 21, 1950 (EM): "Sorry, we missed our game in New York. Had hopes of getting back before the cold weather set in."

[5] Regarding the trip to Canada see no. 839; on the summer vacation in Colorado see no. 805.

[6] In his letter Dudley had mentioned that he hoped Eisenhower had received the set of new woods and that they were "just what you wanted." A. G. *Spalding* & Bros., a sporting goods firm, had manufactured the golf clubs, and there is no indication in EM that the company would send Eisenhower a bill.

[7] Robert T. "Bobby" Jones, Jr., was a golf champion and president of the Augusta National Golf Club.

To Henry F. Rennhack   *June 3, 1950*

Dear Mr. Rennhack: Thank you very much for your letter. I was most interested to hear from one whose work will be permanently represented on a medal of mine.[1]

With respect to your son: I normally do not attempt to influence any Senator or Congressman in his selection of young men for West Point and Annapolis, for the reason that many of my friends send in such requests to me, and it would be difficult, indeed, for me to distinguish among the merits of the several applicants. Nevertheless, I am interested in the fact that your son has tried so persistently and earnestly to realize his ambition, and I would not hesitate to send an appropriate message to Senator Ives or to Senator Lehman if I should have any opportunity to meet and talk to your son so that I could base my recommendation on personal knowledge. Consequently, if your boy could come up to my office at a convenient time, and I could establish with him a personal acquaintanceship, I would not hesitate to express my opinion in the matter. Because my days are so crowded, it would be necessary, if he should want to come to see me, to communicate with my office as soon as possible. The date would probably have to be made some days in advance.[2]

The telephone number of my office is University 4-3200, or he may address a letter to me. *Sincerely*

[1] Rennhack, of Valley Stream, New York, had mentioned in a letter of May 31 (EM) that Gorham Manufacturing Company had selected him to engrave a medal to be awarded to Eisenhower. Rennhack's main purpose in writing, however, was to ask for help in securing an appointment to the Naval Academy for his son, Elliott Rennhack. The youth had been offered a second alternate appointment to the academy, and Rennhack asked Eisenhower to write letters to congressmen from New York recommending his son for a principal appointment.
[2] Mrs. Henry F. Rennhack would thank Eisenhower in a note of June 9 (EM), explaining that her son would arrange for an interview after the middle of June. On July 10 Eisenhower would meet with him, and the same day the General would write letters of recommendation to U.S. senators Irving M. Ives and Herbert H. Lehman. For developments see no. 889.

To Wallace C. Speers   *June 3, 1950*

Dear Mr. Speers: Thank you very much for sending me a copy of the letter giving the impressions you formed during your latest trip to

Europe.[1] Quite frankly, I agree with the concern you express over the frequency with which we hear the word "war" spoken in this country, sometimes with such a casual attitude as to give the impression that the speaker is not overly disturbed by the prospect he seems to see. I realize that this is not so—but it does indicate a failure to think seriously and accurately, because otherwise our whole attention would be absorbed in ways and means for preventing or postponing such a tragedy.

It might interest you to know that our apparent failure to comprehend all of the certain consequences and implications of war as a social cancer has inspired us here at Columbia to launch a project for establishing an "institute for the study of war and peace." So far as we know, there has been no university that has given concentrated and objective thought to the causes, conduct and tragic consequences of war. We intend to establish professorships, research staffs and, far more than this, to conduct institutes and forums in which we hope that businessmen, professional men and governmental leaders will join with us from time to time so that, as facts and truths are unearthed and emphasized, they will become immediately useful to people who are conducting the affairs of our country. The effort will be to prevent their withering away in dusty tomes on library shelves. I am happy to report, also, that this idea has evoked the enthusiasm of numbers of our friends—the prospects are that we shall secure adequate support to begin the project by the end of the next school year.[2] *Very sincerely*

[1] Speers, who was first vice-president and a director of James McCutcheon & Company, was also founder and chairman of the Laymen's Movement for a Christian World. He had sent Eisenhower a copy of a letter he had written to president Truman on May 31, 1950 (EM), expressing his alarm at finding so much talk in the United States about war with the Soviet Union. In Europe, which he had recently visited, Speers had heard no mention of the possibility of a war. Upon returning, he had written to the president to express the hope that Truman could resolve the current crisis "without any signs of appeasement, but also without getting the world into a war." Speers argued that "a new type of dynamic statesmanship" would be as essential to the preservation of peace as the strength of the U.S. Armed Forces (copies of Speers's letter and Eisenhower's reply are also in CUF).

[2] For developments see no. 1056.

832   *Eisenhower Mss.*

TO BRYANT EDWARD MOORE   *June 3, 1950*

Dear Bryant:[1] Between July twentieth and thirtieth, there will be in New York City an officer of the Scots Guards who served under me in the European campaign. He was a very gallant man, but like so many of that group is extremely diffident.[2]

He wants to visit West Point, and were I to be in this region at the time of his visit, I would be truly honored to bring him up for a day. Because I shall be in California and Colorado at that time,[3] I will be denied the opportunity to do this personally, but, with no objection on your part, shall ask my Aide, Lt. Col. Robert L. Schulz, to bring my old comrade up there. I particularly want him to call on you if you should then be at the Point, and I am writing this note to ask your permission for my Aide to bring him in for a call.

If I could impose upon you a bit further, would it be possible for you to detail some junior officer to conduct him on a visit around the institution? In this way, his own natural diffidence will not prevent him from seeing the main points of interest.[4]

I do hope that you will not consider this request an imposition, but I am most anxious to show every possible courtesy to my friend. His name is Major Sir Charles MacLean. *Cordially*

[1] Major General Moore was superintendent of the U.S. Military Academy (for background see no. 322).
[2] Eisenhower was referring to Sir Charles Hector MacLean, eleventh baronet of Dowart and Morvaren and twenty-seventh chief of clan MacLean. MacLean, a major in the Scots Guard during World War II, had retired in 1949. On May 30, James F. Gault, Eisenhower's British military assistant during World War II, had written to Lieutenant Colonel Robert L. Schulz (Eisenhower's aide), asking him to make arrangements for MacLean's visit to West Point (see also no. 841).
[3] On the Eisenhowers' summer travels through several western states see nos. 884, 887, and 900.
[4] In his reply (June 9, EM) Moore would assure Eisenhower that he would be very glad to show West Point to Sir Charles. Schulz (who had been promoted from major to lieutenant colonel on May 15, 1950) would receive instructions to contact Lieutenant Richard Harriman Maeder (B.A. Boston University 1943) at West Point regarding the visit. For developments see no. 842.

833   *Eisenhower Mss.*

To Julius Earl Schaefer   *June 7, 1950*

Dear Earl:[1] Of course, I should be glad to see Colonel Howse at any time that our two schedules will permit us to arrange a meeting.[2]

I have always been somewhat embarrassed about the so-called "Eisenhower Foundation."[3] I rather cringe when I think of anyone starting on a money-raising campaign when my family name is connected with the project. My brothers and I gave our consent when the matter was presented to us as a project for memorializing the Kansas veterans of

World War II and when it was explained to us that, by using the name of "Eisenhower Foundation," greater support would be secured, particularly if I would provide a collection of wartime mementos. In the past, I have sent on a number of souvenirs of various kinds, including scrap books, pictures, material objects, decorations and so on. Moreover, I have frequently told the directors of the Foundation that, if a suitable place was provided, I would be delighted to add to this type of material from among the things that I have.[4]

You can understand that the very name of the Foundation prevents me or any one of my brothers from taking an active supporting part. Such agreements as we have given in the past to the project, therefore, springs exclusively out of our affection and admiration for Kansas.

When Colonel Howse comes to New York, tell him to call my office, UNiversity 4-3200, Ext. 2773 and speak to Col. Schulz, and I am sure we can arrange some meeting.[5] *Sincerely*

[1] Schaefer, vice-president and general manager of the Wichita, Kansas, division of Boeing Airplane Company, had mentioned in a letter of June 2 (EM) that he was helping to raise funds for the construction of a building in Abilene, Kansas, to house Eisenhower's World War II trophies. He said he would be host at a meeting of the steering committee in Wichita, Kansas, on June 14, and he offered to pass on to the group any suggestions that Eisenhower might wish to make (for background on Schaefer see *Eisenhower Papers*, vols. I–IX).

[2] Schaefer had described Colonel Alfred E. Howse as "a very dear friend, and a great admirer of yours." Howse had served in several procurement and supply positions with the U.S. Army Air Forces during World War II, and from April to August 1945 he had been Administrator of the Surplus Property Board. He was currently chairman of the Howse Company, in Wichita, Kansas, and campaign chairman of the Eisenhower Foundation.

[3] For background on the foundation see no. 278. Milton S. Eisenhower would advise his brother (letter June 9, EM, Subject File, Eisenhower Foundation) that the building to be constructed in Abilene would cost between $350,000 and $400,000. The architect's preliminary specifications of June 10, 1950, are in *ibid.*

[4] Schaefer would allow the Associated Press to quote the last two sentences of this paragraph in an article that would appear in the *New York Times* on June 16, 1950. According to the dispatch, the executive committee of the Eisenhower Foundation hoped to raise five hundred thousand dollars for the construction of the building.

[5] In a memorandum of June 23 (EM, Subject File, Eisenhower Foundation) Lieutenant Colonel Schulz would inform the General that Howse would be in New York City during the following week; Eisenhower and Howse would meet on June 26. For developments see no. 854.

To Edwin Earl Newsom   *June 7, 1950*

Dear Mr. Newsom:[1] Just today I learned that you are going to absorb
Colonel Chet Hanson into your organization. This point came to my
attention when I was discussing with Bill Burnham and Phil Young
the possibility of getting hold of a fine young organizer to help out Phil
Young in the job of developing our great program for tying the University family and the business family much closer together.[2] This note
is to say that one of us may be on your doorstep before long, insisting
on the loan of Chet Hanson. He is one of the young fellows I admired
all through the war.

With warm personal regard, *Cordially*

P.S. And don't give way to irritation and throw this note into the
wastebasket before you have read it at least twice.[3]

[1] Newsom was public relations counsel and senior partner in his own firm, Earl
Newsom and Company, of New York City (for background see no. 700). On this
same day Eisenhower would inform Roscoe C. Ingalls, a member of the Blind
Brook Club, in Port Chester, New York, that he had sent a letter to the club's
admissions committee supporting the nomination of Newsom for membership.
Ingalls (B.S. Columbia 1912), a partner in the investment securities firm of
Ingalls and Snyder, had requested this in a letter of June 2 (EM). The secretary
of the Blind Brook Club would tell Newsom he had been elected to active membership
in December 1950 (see W. G. Chandler to Newsom, Dec. 29, 1950, EP).
[2] Lieutenant Colonel Chester Bayard Hansen (B.S. Syracuse University 1939) had
been aide to General Omar N. Bradley since 1942 (for background on his experiences during World War II see Omar N. Bradley, *A Soldier's Story* [New York,
1951]; on his postwar work see Galambos, *Chief of Staff*, no. 1843). Hansen was
currently connected with the JCS at the Pentagon in Washington, D.C., and he
would not become involved in Columbia's development program. When he resigned
from the Army after the Korean War, however, he would join Newsom's firm
(1956) (see letter from Hansen, Nov. 26, 1980, EP). William H. Burnham was
an investment banker in New York City. Philip Young was dean of Columbia's
Graduate School of Business (for background see no. 54). He was serving temporarily as Acting Coordinator of the activities of the Office of Development. For
subsequent events see no. 930.
[3] When Newsom replied (June 12, EM), he said that he knew Hansen might
want to work for Eisenhower and that he would be free to do so.

835   *Eisenhower Mss.,*
                                                     Columbia University Files

To Louis Morton Hacker   *June 9, 1950*

Dear Professor Hacker:[1] Thank you for the memorandum giving an
account of your last year's operations in the School of General Studies.[2]

I am in complete agreement with your hopes and ambitions and I share your concern because of the meager facilities available to you. Before you start overseas for your summer vacation, I want you to know that, come what may, you shall have at least one room for your counseling service next year.[3] I hope you will have a good time, and please drop in to see me as soon as possible after we both return from our summer vacations.[4]

I shall circulate your memorandum to the Provost and a number of other interested individuals in the University. In fact, I think I shall send a copy to each Trustee.[5] *Sincerely*

P.S. I meant also to say—"Congratulations to you and your able staff for a great record!"[6]

---

[1] In 1949 Hacker had succeeded Harry M. Ayres as Director of the School of General Studies (for further background see no. 448). A copy of this document is also in EM.

[2] Hacker had reported (June 7, copies in CUF and EM) that the school now offered majors in 30 fields of study and approximately 1,000 different courses. In the 1949/50 school year, over 9,500 students had registered for over 45,000 classes; 404 had graduated with B.S. degrees; and the school had contributed over $1.8 million to the university's income. Hacker said the school planned to expand but needed new basic facilities. He observed, "We cannot maintain sound human relations and continue to have the confidence of our students unless we can furnish working space to our staff and privacy to staff Advisers and students. . . ." These were immediate needs, he wrote, but on a long-term basis, the school needed a building of its own (copies in CUF and EM). For background on the school and its problems see no. 156.

[3] See no. 875.

[4] Hacker would see Eisenhower on November 1.

[5] See the next document.

[6] On October 6 Hacker would send Eisenhower an excerpt from a recent *Boston Post* editorial praising the school's decision to accept students who had not graduated from high school. The article stated, "Whether Columbia's president, General Eisenhower, initiated this educational reform or simply gave it final approval is not known but it certainly marks real progress under his leadership." Eisenhower wrote at the bottom of this letter, "Dear Louis—I'm shining in reflected glory" (EM).

836

Eisenhower Mss.,
Columbia University Files

To Grayson Louis Kirk

June 9, 1950

Memo for Provost Kirk: Herewith copy of report from Professor Hacker and copy of my reply.[1] Please have copies made and provide it to each member of our informal "headquarters staff" and send a copy to each Trustee.[2]

It occurs to me that it might be wise in the fall to add Hacker to our little headquarters team.

[1] See the previous document.

[2] Provost Kirk would reply (June 13, 1950, CUF) that copies of Dean Louis M. Hacker's report on the School of General Studies had been sent to all trustees, to Joseph Campbell (vice-president in charge of business affairs and treasurer), to Lawrence H. Chamberlain (soon to become dean of Columbia College), to John R. Dunning (Director of Scientific Research), to John A. Krout (Dean of the Graduate Faculties), and to Kevin C. McCann, assistant to the president. For Eisenhower's response to one of the trustees who commented on the situation at the School of General Studies see no. 875.

837   *Eisenhower Mss.*

To Edward H. Rees   *June 9, 1950*

Dear Congressman Rees:[1] At the moment I have no extra copy of the Commencement talk I made yesterday but, as you requested, shall send you one soon. While I do not believe that it has sufficient significance to warrant its inclusion in the Congressional Record, I have no objection to your carrying out your suggestion of inserting it, should you so desire. Of course, I am complimented that you should think it worthy of such treatment.[2]

With personal regard and best wishes, *Cordially*

[1] Congressman Rees, a Republican from Kansas's Fourth District, had written Eisenhower (June 8, EM) to ask for a transcript of the speech the General had delivered at Columbia's commencement exercises that day. Rees also had requested permission to enter the speech in the *Congressional Record*.

[2] Lieutenant Colonel Robert L. Schulz, Eisenhower's aide, would send Rees a "final corrected copy" of the speech on June 12. Rees would place that version in the *Record* the following day, and he would thank Eisenhower in a letter of the fourteenth (EM). (The version in U.S., Congress, House, *Congressional Record*, 81st Cong., 2d sess., 1950, 96, pt. 16:A4473–74, differs slightly from the transcripts in EM, Subject File, Speeches, and in *New York Times*, June 9, 1950.) Congressman Robert F. Rich, Republican from Pennsylvania's Fifteenth District, had quoted part of the speech in Congress on June 12 (see U.S., Congress, House, *Congressional Record*, 81st Cong., 2d sess., 1950, 96, pt. 6:8476).

To Clifford Roberts   *June 9, 1950*

Dear Cliff:[1] I shall look forward to seeing Gene Sarazen's book.[2] Thanks for thinking of me. *Cordially*

P.S. In spite of the high price of American Cyanimide and of Dow Chemical, I wonder if those two do not warrant a reasonable investment at this time, even if we should contemplate holding them only for a few months. Let's talk about it when we can.[3]

[1] Roberts, a partner in the investment firm Reynolds & Company, was frequently one of Eisenhower's golfing companions.

[2] Sarazen, an American professional golfer, had been U.S. Open champion in 1922 and 1932; U.S. Professional Golfers Association champion in 1922, 1923, and 1933; British Open champion in 1932; and Masters champion in 1935. In collaboration with Herbert Warren Wind, he had written *Thirty Years of Championship Golf: The Life and Times of Gene Sarazen* (New York, 1950). Roberts had asked Sarazen to inscribe a copy of the book for Eisenhower (memorandum, June 7, 1950, EM).

[3] During 1949 the American Cyanamid Company had tallied the largest volume of sales and net total of earnings in its history (see *New York Times*, Mar. 2, 1950); and during the fiscal year ending May 31, 1950, the Dow Chemical Company had experienced a 23 percent rise in sales (see *ibid.*, May 30, 1950). Eisenhower's appointment calendar indicates that he discussed stocks and bonds with Roberts during a telephone conversation on June 16, 1950.

839   *Eisenhower Mss.*

                                                 June 10, 1950

To Harold Rupert Leofric George Alexander

Dear Alex:[1] It appears that, at long last, I am going to get a chance to spend a day or two fishing in Canada, on the Moisie. It, therefore, seems proper that I should send you a note of apology because I shall venture within the limits of your "area" but without being able to call at your command post to make my number and to pay my respects.[2]

Of course, you know how much I should like to come to see you. But my schedule will be very tight and we are to take off directly from here to the Northeast and, so, will miss Ottawa by many miles.

I should like to be remembered to your charming family and, as always, with warmest regards to yourself. *Cordially*

P.S. I am told by some of the Club members that you fished on the Moisie last year, so you will know where I am. I have never even been on a salmon stream, so I suppose that my awkwardness will provide great sport for the veterans.[3]

[1] Viscount Alexander of Tunis, Governor General of Canada since 1946, had been Supreme Allied Commander of the Mediterranean Theater during the last year of World War II (for background see *Eisenhower Papers*, vols. I–IX).

[2] Eisenhower, accompanied by Kevin C. McCann, his administrative assistant, would fly from New York to the Moisie Salmon Club, at Seven Islands, Quebec, on June 16. Their host for the following nine days would be William L. McLean, Jr. (A.B. Princeton 1917), vice-president and treasurer of the Bulletin Company, publisher of the *Evening Bulletin* and the *Sunday Bulletin* of Philadelphia. Eisenhower and McCann would return to New York on June 25 (on the arrangements for the trip see EM, McLean Corr.).

[3] Alexander would reply (June 16, EM) that he had been on the Moisie River during 1949. Eisenhower would answer in a longhand letter of July 1 (EM) that although the water had been high on the Moisie, he had caught a few salmon, ranging in size from nineteen to thirty pounds.

840   *Eisenhower Mss.*

To Bernard Edwin Hutchinson   *June 10, 1950*

Dear Mr. Hutchinson:[1] There is obviously no difference whatsoever in the basic views we both hold with respect to today's outlook. I think that, unless I misunderstood you, we would find our differences confined to problems of method, practices and procedures, not to principles.[2]

With respect to a possible golf date or week end, you could get rich by going on the short side of any prospects I have. My summer schedule is getting as crowded as that of the academic months, but, so far, it does continue to contain a couple of recreational trips.[3] I do hope, however, that, if you get back this way, you will give me a ring. Possibly, we could fix up an afternoon together, and though my golf may be lousy, I think that the Scotch at my Club is at least average of any in the neighborhood. Certainly, I shall be looking forward to seeing you again.[4] *Sincerely*

[1] Hutchinson was a vice-president and director of Chrysler Corporation (for background see no. 127). On June 7 he had written Eisenhower (EM) to ask if they could continue the exchange of ideas that had begun at a dinner on May 31, 1950, given by William Lambert Kleitz (B.A. Cornell 1915), president of Guaranty Trust Company of New York. Hutchinson hoped that they might get together some weekend in order to "mix a little golf and Scotch whisky with our philosophizing."

[2] We could not determine what the areas of disagreement were, but Hutchinson had listed two points of agreement in a letter of March 10, 1950 (EM). These were "the indivisibility of freedom" and the importance of linking "our whole

concept of human life in both its political and economic aspects to an over-all spiritual basis."

³ On these plans see the preceding document and nos. 884, 887, and 900.

⁴ In a note of June 20 (EM) Hutchinson would suggest that they have dinner in New York City on June 27, but Eisenhower would reply (telegram, June 26, EM) that his schedule was "unfortunately crowded with prior engagements." For further developments see no. 892.

On this same day Eisenhower would deliver a speech before the Nassau County Bar Association, in Mineola, New York (a transcript of his remarks is in EM, Subject File, Speeches). On the following day he would travel to Hempstead, New York, to receive an honorary degree from Hofstra College (see *New York Times*, June 12, 1950).

841   *Eisenhower Mss.*

TO JAMES FREDERICK GAULT   *June 12, 1950*

Dear Jimmy:[1] I enclose a copy of a letter I have written to Bryant Moore.[2] From it, you will see that I am, unfortunately, going to be a long way from New York City when your friend, Major MacLean, reaches here.[3] Nevertheless, I hope he will call immediately upon Colonel Schulz for any assistance we here may be able to give him. I clearly remember the day we inspected his battalion. In fact, unless my memory plays me false, you stayed over with your old battalion to celebrate some heathenish Scottish tradition. As I recall, it degenerated into a dance, and that with no ladies present.[4]

Enclosed also is a copy of a note I have just sent to Sir Charles.[5]

My prospective visit to Britain is more than a rumor, although the details have not been settled. For your information, Lord Boyd Orr has asked me to be in Glasgow for the 500th Anniversary of the University. This is to be on June 21. Current plans call for me to be in London on July 4 to accept, on behalf of the American Forces, the scroll to be deposited in St. Paul's Cathedral. It is even possible that I may come over the first of June to participate in an annual French celebration of the D-Day landing. None of these engagements is firmly fixed, except on a most informal basis, but they are the prospects now in the offing.[6]

If I do come, Mamie will be with me and we shall, of course, spend some time at Culzean Castle.[7] We will hope that you and Peggy[8] could come up; we wouldn't know what to do there without you. *As ever*

¹ Gault had been an officer in the Scots Guards before becoming Eisenhower's British military assistant in July 1943. He had served with Eisenhower until August 1945 (for background see *Eisenhower Papers*, vols. I–IX).

² See no. 832.

³ Eisenhower was referring to Major Sir Charles Hector Fitzroy MacLean (for background on him see *ibid.*).

[4] In a letter of May 30 (EM) to Lieutenant Colonel Schulz, Eisenhower's aide, Gault had mentioned that MacLean had commanded a squadron of the 3rd Battalion of Scots Guards when Eisenhower had visited the battalion after a severe battle.
[5] See the next document.
[6] On the carbon copy of this letter in EM the word *confidential* appears in the margin beside this paragraph. Gault had noted in his letter of May 30 that he had heard rumors that Eisenhower would visit Scotland during 1951 (for background on the invitation from Lord John Boyd Orr, a Scottish scientist, see no. 706). Although Eisenhower would decline the latter invitation, he would dedicate the American Roll of Honour at St. Paul's Cathedral in London on July 4, 1951. The roll of honor was a list of the names of the U.S. citizens who had died during World War II while based in the United Kingdom (for background see Galambos, *Chief of Staff*, no. 1127). Eisenhower would also attend the seventh anniversary celebration of D-day in France (see no. 876).
[7] For background on Culzean Castle, Ayrshire, Scotland, see Chandler and Galambos, *Occupation, 1945*, no. 444; and no. 587. For developments see no. 863.
[8] Gault's wife, the former Margaret Ella Campbell.

842   *Eisenhower Mss.*

To Charles Hector Fitzroy MacLean   *June 12, 1950*

Dear Sir Charles:[1] From Jimmy Gault I have just learned that you are contemplating a stay in New York City between the twentieth and thirtieth of July, during which period you should like to visit West Point.[2]

I most sincerely regret that I personally shall be out of the city at that time, since my plans call for me to be in the western part of the United States in the latter half of July.[3] Nevertheless, my Aide, Lt. Colonel Robert L. Schulz, will be here in the city at our office and will be more than delighted to take you to West Point for the visit. I have already communicated with the Superintendent of West Point, who commanded the 88th Division in Italy, and he extends also a cordial invitation for you to spend a day at the place.[4]

I remember well our meeting in a little Belgian town just as your battalion came out of battle.[5] Because of that memory, my regret at missing a friend of Jimmy Gault's is all the greater.[6] *Sincerely*

[1] MacLean had been a major in the Scots Guards during World War II (for background see no. 832).
[2] James F. Gault, who had served with MacLean in the Scots Guards and later with Eisenhower during World War II, had brought MacLean's visit to Eisenhower's attention (see the preceding document).
[3] On the trip see nos. 884, 887, and 900.
[4] Major General Bryant E. Moore, currently superintendent of the U.S. Military Academy, had commanded the 88th Infantry Division in Italy from November 1945 to October 1947 (for background see no. 322).

⁵ On this incident see the preceding document, n. 4.
⁶ MacLean would thank Eisenhower and Schulz in letters of June 20 (EM). See also Schulz's note of July 11 (EM) scheduling the visit to West Point for July 21, 1950.

843   *Eisenhower Mss.*

TO GRAYSON LOUIS KIRK[1]   *June 13, 1950*

SUBJECT: Administration

To make effective previously issued instructions to you that in the combined office of Vice President—Provost you are to take over the major portion of the University administrative load, I give below some of the points that I deem to be of particular importance. This list is not meant to be exclusive; it mentions only a few of those activities to which you should give personal attention and supervision.

1) In general, to include within the purview of your responsibility, under the bylaws of the Trustees and the delegated authority of the President, those duties which pertain both to the Vice President of the University and to the Provost.[2]

2) To take cognizance of all interior administrative matters and to handle them roughly as follows:

   a) Immediate action in all those things in which there is previously established policy or precedent.

   b) In any case of unusual character or where there exists no established policy, to have made appropriate studies and analyses before bringing the matter to the attention of the President for decision.

   c) To take over, so far as appears appropriate and in keeping with present circumstances, the functions of the President in prescribed ceremonials, meetings, and conferences.

   d) To maintain liaison with appropriate Committees of the Trustees. Important Committees with which the Provost will be concerned are Education and Development.[3] (Normally, Mr. Campbell will do the same with Finance and Buildings and Grounds.)[4]

   e) In maintaining this liaison, to direct such follow-up as to make certain that appropriate action is taken to implement agreed upon programs and plans, and to inform the Trustee Committees of the nature of this action.

   f) To accomplish that coordination between the several branches and officials of the University as is necessary to make certain that our administrative organisms do not work at cross purposes.

g) To serve as Deputy Chairman for the informal University committee that meets bi-monthly in the President's office.

h) Any other duties that normally devolve upon the President but which can be efficiently and appropriately performed by his chief assistant.

It is realized that, to carry out this type of assignment, you must have proper assistance in your own office to relieve you of detailed administrative duty. It is important that the University officers should have one individual, who is rather constantly available on the campus and to whom they can look as the mainspring of the administrative machine, that you must not permit your attention to be diverted by routine administrative detail from this all-important and vital duty.

In planning personal absence from the campus, please check with me so that, normally, one of us is always present.

[1] Provost Kirk would assume the additional duties of vice-president in charge of education on July 1, 1950 (for background see no. 722). Eisenhower made numerous changes in a draft of this memorandum (see the copy in the same file as this document).

[2] On these duties see no. 361, n. 8.

[3] On matters of concern to the trustees' Committee on education see no. 688. On the Development Committee see no. 488.

[4] Joseph Campbell was treasurer and vice-president in charge of business affairs of Columbia University. Regarding Eisenhower's encounters with the Committee on Finance see no. 209. On a recent meeting with the Buildings and Grounds Committee see no. 715.

844 *Eisenhower Mss.*

To William Averell Harriman *June 13, 1950*

Dear Averell:[1] I think you probably know Philip Young who is head of Columbia's Business School and who is the son of Owen D.[2] I have placed him in direct charge of Columbia planning with respect to Arden House and since doing so we have made real progress. We have been particularly successful in interesting a number of firms who are willing—in some cases even anxious—to sponsor short conferences and institutes at Arden House.[3] Generally speaking, each of these conferences would deal with some specific part of the basic political and social questions of which you and I have so often talked. A few would unquestionably deal with more scientific subjects, while two courses each year would deal with advanced business management. In any event, we have gone so far that both Dean Young and I feel certain that, shortly after the beginning of the new school year, we will place before you definite and concrete plans through which Arden House can be used effectively for educational and public service.[4] While these plans will undoubtedly contemplate some continuing help from you and Roland—which you have generously implied to be your purpose—I assure you that we are beginning to enlist support on a fairly wide basis. The specific plans we submit to you will have the approval of our own Trustees.[5]

One of our biggest problems will be to get the house refurnished and ready to operate. This is one of the important details on which we are now working.[6]

Of course, had either Philip Young or I been willing to attempt the project on a hit-and-miss, shoestring basis, we would have started some time back. But I am quite certain that something like this must be done well or not at all.[7]

I shall send a copy of this letter to Roland so that he will understand, also, that by next October this whole thing will be so crystallized and so carefully planned that nothing further will be needed to reach a final and definite decision.

On Friday I am going up to Canada for about five days in the hope of "killing" a salmon, something I have never done.[8] If you should be in New York during the next two days, possibly I will get to see you. But, in any event, I hope you won't have to stay abroad too long.[9]

In the meantime, I know that you realize that I deeply appreciate your generous and public spirited attitude, to say nothing of your patience, in the Arden House project. I am more certain than ever that we are going to make something really fine out of the whole idea.[10]

With warm personal regard, *Cordially*

[1] For background on Harriman see no. 605.

[2] On Young see no. 54; for background on his father see no. 486.

[3] Arden was the Harriman family estate, which had been given to Columbia by brothers W. Averell and E. Roland Harriman (for background see no. 605). Eisenhower frequently referred to plans for Arden as "the forum," "the conference plan," or "the conference center." The project would soon become the American Assembly (see nos. 588 and 826; for subsequent development see no. 945).

[4] See no. 1039.

[5] The trustees would give full approval of the conference plan at their meeting on October 2, 1950 (*ibid.*).

[6] See no. 605, n. 6. By August 1949 Eisenhower had received an estimate of the capital outlay necessary to refurnish and prepare Arden House for public use. The total sum would be $105,850 (Harriman Property Estimate, Aug. 31, 1949, EM, American Assembly). As work progressed, it became clear that a great deal more money would be needed to ready the house for the American Assembly. Following a conference with Averell Harriman on September 7, 1950, Philip Young reported to Eisenhower that Harriman had agreed to give the project another $100,000 for "kitchen repairs, etc." (Schulz to Eisenhower, and Eisenhower to Harriman, both Sept. 8, 1950, EM, Young Corr.; see also *New York Times*, May 21 and 23, 1951).

[7] Eisenhower expressed similar sentiments in his accompanying note to Roland

Harriman. The General's note of June 13, 1950, and Roland Harriman's reply, dated June 15, 1950, are both in EM.

[8] "Killing" salmon means to catch and to keep the salmon for eating; it is a traditional expression common to the sport of salmon fishing (letter from Lefty Kreh, Outdoor Editor, *Baltimore Sun*, Mar. 15, 1981, EP). For the trip to Canada see no. 839.

[9] Harriman would soon have a new job. For developments see no. 852.

[10] For Eisenhower's continuing interest in the conference plan see no. 877.

845   *Eisenhower Mss.*

To Edward Peck Curtis   *June 13, 1950*

Dear General Curtis:[1] I am grateful for the opportunity that you, as Honorary Chairman of the dinner honoring James Wadsworth, have given me to submit this brief notation of my appreciation of his public service.[2]

Perhaps the best way to express my feeling is to say that he has, through a long and active career, provided, to me, a shining example of enlightened patriotism and unselfish service. Wisdom, integrity and courage are invariably recognized as his distinguishing characteristics, and these, capped by a personality of warmth and understanding, mark him as a statesman and leader of men.

It is sad to know that he now feels it necessary to leave public life. But I sincerely hope that he carries with him a realization that millions of his countrymen will always feel indebted to him for reminding us, through his deeds and actions, that the Republic still breeds men of character and stature.

Won't you please extend to him assurance of my very warm and lasting regard? *Cordially*

[1] Curtis had been General Carl Spaatz's Chief of Staff in the European and Mediterranean campaigns of World War II. He was currently vice-president in charge of motion pictures and supervisor of general European business for Eastman Kodak Company (for background see *Eisenhower Papers*, vols. I–IX). Eisenhower made extensive changes in two earlier versions of this letter (in EM, Letters and Drafts).

[2] Curtis had written Eisenhower (June 12, EM) asking for a letter of appreciation for the services rendered the Military Establishment by Congressman James Wolcott Wadsworth, a Republican from the Forty-first District of New York (for background see Galambos, *Chief of Staff*, no. 892). Wadsworth planned to retire from Congress at the end of his current term, and Curtis was seeking letters of commendation from Wadsworth's former associates. The letters would be bound into a volume and presented to Wadsworth at a dinner in his honor on June 24. Apparently the dinner would be held in Rochester, New York, and Curtis had assumed that Eisenhower would not want to attend. "You will be delighted to know, I am sure," he had written, "that as a result of my influence you are not being asked to attend the dinner."

To Georges Frederick Doriot   *June 14, 1950*

Dear General Doriot:[1] Ed Clark[2] has sent me the 1949 Annual Report of your company, American Research & Development Corporation, from which report I learn that you are the President of the Company.

Permit me to congratulate you both on your position and on the announced purposes of the company. Obviously, one of the prime factors in our progress is venture capital and venture capital operations. This is particularly so at a time when, because of disturbing factors and uncertainty, people dislike to take risks and have a tendency to forget about new ideas and new developments.

With best wishes for your continued success and with kindest personal regards,[3] *Sincerely*

[1] Doriot (B.S. University of Paris 1920) had been a brigadier general in the U.S. Army during World War II. He was currently professor of industrial management at the Graduate School of Business Administration, Harvard University, and the president of American Research and Development Corporation, an investment firm (for background see Galambos, *Chief of Staff*, no. 876).

[2] Edwin N. Clark was a business consultant and executive in New York City (for background see Galambos, *Chief of Staff*, no. 1456). The initials at the top of the carbon copy of this letter in EM indicate that Clark drafted this letter. Eisenhower made numerous changes on the copy in EM, Letters and Drafts.

[3] Joseph W. Powell, Jr., vice-president of American Research and Development Corporation, would reply (June 19, EM, Doriot Corr.) that Doriot had left for Paris and that Eisenhower's letter had been forwarded to him. When Doriot returned to the United States, Powell said, he would want to talk to Eisenhower about the company's activities.

847   *Columbia University Files*

To Grayson Louis Kirk   *June 14, 1950*

SUBJECT: Mr. Phelps Barnum[1]

The above-named graduate of Columbia's School of Architecture came to see me this morning. He presented certain mild criticisms and suggestions which I think will be interesting to you, particularly in your post of Vice President of the University.[2] I gathered the following from his conversation:

(*a*) That he is a very successful architect.

(*b*) He is quite anxious to help Columbia and believes that our School of Architecture should be the finest in the country. He believes that we already have the best architectural *library* in the country.

(*c*) He thinks that we have erred in our, alleged, failure to bring in different types and kinds of successful architects from this city to take a far greater part in our instructional and lecture periods in our School of Architecture.

(*d*) Because of the allegations made in "*c*" above, Mr. Barnum thinks that Columbia is getting a reputation for being a mere *academic* School of Architecture, rather than the vital kind it could be if it would use on its instructional staff, the practical knowledge of experts.

(*e*) He believes that we are too ritualistic in our adherence to dogmatic requirements for graduation. Pointing out that a man is a college graduate when he enters the School of Architecture, Mr. Barnum feels that if he demonstrates a capacity to graduate in three years, or even two years, after entering that we should be flexible enough to accommodate this kind of student. In fact, he says that Columbia lost his own son as a student of architecture because of our refusal to give him any credit for taking architecture as a major in Yale University. Apparently, the lad was a brilliant student in his undergraduate courses.

(*f*) I have the distinct impression that Mr. Barnum would be delighted if you would voluntarily call upon him for advice and counsel—in other words, to seek an opportunity at luncheon or anywhere else to talk the matter over with him. Possibly, he would be even more flattered if we would ask him to do a little lecturing. In any event, I shall say nothing to Dean Arnaud personally.[3] The matter is in *your* hands.

[1] Phelps Barnum (B. Arch. Columbia 1917) was a New York architect whose designs included the rebuilt Stoa of Attalos of ancient Athens and the Sterling-Winthrop Research Institute, near Rensselaer, New York. During World War II he had directed the construction of numerous airports in Central and South America.
[2] For background on Kirk's new post see no. 843.
[3] Leopold Arnaud (M.S. Columbia 1933) was dean of the School of Architecture.

848   *Eisenhower Mss.*

To Mark Wayne Clark   *June 15, 1950*

Dear Wayne:[1] I suggest Friday morning, July 14, as our meeting date. I will keep the entire morning free and will hope that you can stay to lunch. I would suggest something about nine o'clock as a time to be here.[2] *Cordially*

[1] General Clark had been Chief of the Army Field Forces, Fort Monroe, Virginia, since October 1949.

[2] Clark had visited Eisenhower in his office at Columbia the morning of June 9. The two generals had discussed Clark's forthcoming book about the Second World War, *Calculated Risk* (New York, 1950), and they had agreed to meet again soon to go over the galley proofs. In his letter of June 13, 1950 (EM), Clark had written: "I believe I have your views on the American setup in the Tunisian campaign and on ANVIL. However, our next visit will give me an opportunity to make sure that they are lined up correctly." Clark would confirm the appointment for July 14, remarking that he would be "more than delighted" to have Eisenhower's suggestions (June 18, 1950, EM). For developments see no. 910.

849   *Eisenhower Mss.*

To Hal L. Mangum   *June 15, 1950*

Dear Hal:[1] Thanks for your very fine letter.[2] I had a hunch as to the reasons that inspired your recent letter and telegram and I most deeply appreciate your concern and thoughtfulness.[3] I must say that, while I don't know very much about Sid Richardson's politics, my belief is that, judging from what he has said to me, he is about as far from being a New Dealer as anything I can imagine.[4] In any event, I agree with you that it is well for me to avoid as much as I can being caught in positions where people believe there is some kind of political aspect or purpose involved.[5]

Thank you very much for sending me the note from John Garner.[6] I am returning it herewith and wonder whether, at some convenient time, you would not pass on to him an expression of my very warm and respectful greetings. He is a man I have always admired, as you know.[7] *Cordially*

[1] For background on Mangum see no. 696.

[2] Mangum had written Eisenhower that he had visited with Robert Kleberg, Jr., and Tom Armstrong (June 13, 1950, EM; see no. 697). Eisenhower had met both of these men at a luncheon given by Mangum in San Antonio on December 3, 1949. According to Mangum, Kleberg was concerned now that Eisenhower would come under the influence of "New Dealers" (for background on Kleberg see no. 623).

[3] In a telegram and a letter both dated June 6, Mangum had advised Eisenhower against having "too close [an] association" with Kleberg and Armstrong. Mangum felt they might later embarrass Eisenhower (telegram, Mangum to Eisenhower, June 6, 1950, EM).

[4] In his letter of June 13 Mangum had recalled a reference by Kleberg to Eisenhower's "New Dealer friend," Sid Richardson (for background on Richardson see no. 113).

[5] On this general problem see no. 638.

[6] John Nance Garner, who had served as Vice-President under Franklin D.

Roosevelt from 1933 to 1944, had guided much of the important New Deal legislation through Congress. A copy of his note is not in EM.

[7] Mangum's health would deteriorate. Unable to recover from virus pneumonia and the flu, he died on August 3, 1950, in San Antonio, Texas (telegram, R. Dickson to Eisenhower, Aug. 3, 1950, EM).

850   *Eisenhower Mss., Diaries*

DIARY   *June* [ ], *1950*[1]

Recently I wrote a letter to Mrs. Cecil Killien, a member of the University staff who is retiring after long service.[2] In her reply she used a sentence, "Columbia has been a more interesting and colorful place since you became its head." The remark is interesting only by way of showing that not *all* the old-timers resent the effort to bring Columbia and the world into closer, *cooperative*, effort.[3]

[1] Eisenhower apparently made this entry in his diary in late June.

[2] Mrs. Cecil P. Killien had been a secretary at Columbia University for thirty-six years. From October 1914 until her retirement in June 1950 she had worked in the departments of chemistry, Greek and Latin, history, public law and government, and zoology. On June 2 Eisenhower had written to express appreciation for her long service to the university and had wished her well in the "more leisurely years ahead" (EM).

[3] Mrs. Killien's letter of June 14 is in EM. Eisenhower was sensitive about recent reports that he and the Columbia faculty did not get on well (see no. 792, for instance, for his reaction to two magazine articles about his Columbia presidency). In his two years at the university, Eisenhower had directed a reorganization of the school's administration, as well as its far-reaching Development Plan. He had been an enthusiastic participant in the establishment of such projects as the nutrition center, citizenship education, and studies of the conservation of human resources. He had worked hard to improve alumni relations, had pushed the plans for the American Assembly, and had been involved directly in the proposals for the forthcoming observance of Columbia's bicentennial. This was the "closer, *cooperative*, effort" to which he referred.

851   *Eisenhower Mss.,*
                                               Michael J. Quill Corr.

TO GRAYSON LOUIS KIRK   *June 26,1950*

SUBJECT: Negotiations with Maintenance Workers[0]

When Vice President Campbell reported to me this morning that our Maintenance Union was calling a meeting tomorrow night in order to secure authority for a strike, I learned the matter at issue seems to be exclusively wages, since the contract, which has another year to run, specifically provides that negotiations may be reopened during the life of the contract only on the matter of wages. I understand that the Union is demanding something like 15¢ an hour "across the board" increase.[1]

The Vice President in Charge of Business has, through his representatives, informed the Union that the University simply does not have the money to meet this demand and has called attention to the fact that the cost of living, which has previously been the basis of arguments for increase, has now dropped. Since the University actually granted increases on the cost of living argument, it would now appear that the Union is no longer concerned with the validity of this particular argument.

A year or so ago, Michael J. Quill, who is head of the International Union to which our own local board belongs, visited me in my office.[2] We discussed the University situation in a complete and extremely friendly manner and that conference was terminated on the definite understanding that, if, after that date, either Mr. Quill or the University should have reason to feel dissatisfied with the actions of the other party to the agreement, an immediate conference between the two of us would be sought by the party that felt aggrieved. Mr. Quill has made no attempt to see me. Consequently, there is an implication that he is not wholly confident of the justice of the demand now made upon us. This conclusion, however, is somewhat nullified by the fact that a Mr. Faber,[3] presumably an important subordinate of Mr. Quill's, has attended one or two conferences between the University and the local group.

I had a somewhat similar experience with the Executive Committee of our local Union. I was promised that, at any time the Committee should feel itself unable to attain justice from our Business Sections, the members would immediately come to my office to tell me about the matter. While such affairs fall almost wholly within the province of the Treasurer and the Vice President in Charge of Business, the University's deep concern for each of its employees is such that final action in any dispute must always have approval of the Trustees, even where this has to be obtained by informal methods.

I am particularly anxious that the whole series of wage classifications be examined in the light of comparative pay for similar institutions in this region. While I realize that under certain circumstances this University need not always be the highest in every category of pay, yet, in general, Columbia should not fall behind, in its broad averages of pay, those scales established for similar positions in similar institutions elsewhere in this region.[4]

While manifestly we cannot effect any large and general upswing in wage scales, this fact makes it even more important that in no category are we guilty of any slightest injustice or lack of consideration.

Since we are wholly dependent upon student fees and gift and endowed income for operating this University, we obviously cannot continue to operate if our total expenditures markedly exceed the aggregate of this income and any reasonable expectancy for increase.[5]

I shall expect you to keep in close touch with these negotiations through Vice President Campbell and keep me informed from time to time.[6]

[1] The meeting with Joseph Campbell, vice-president in charge of business affairs and treasurer of Columbia University, was the first item on Eisenhower's appointment calendar following his return from a ten-day vacation in Canada (on the trip see no. 839). The maintenance employees were members of Local 241 of the Transport Workers Union of America, CIO.

[2] For background on Michael J. Quill, international president of the Transport Workers Union, CIO, and his meeting with the General see no. 457.

[3] Gustav A. Faber, secretary-treasurer of the Transport Workers Union.

[4] The *New York Times* (June 28, 1950) would report the opinion of W. Emerson Gentzler, business manager of the university, that the wages paid to maintenance workers at Columbia were "fair" compared with the wages paid by similar institutions.

[5] Columbia University's deficit for FY50 would be $417,132.92 (see Columbia University, *Report of the Treasurer, 1950*, p. 5).

[6] There is no further correspondence on this subject in EM. Negotiations would continue between university officials and representatives of Local 241 until July 11, 1950, when the maintenance employees would vote to accept a settlement providing for wage increases of four to eight cents per hour (see *New York Times*, July 12, 1950).

852   *Eisenhower Mss.*

To WILLIAM AVERELL HARRIMAN   *June 26, 1950*

Dear Averell:[1] Your picture has been ready for some weeks, but I have not known exactly what to do with it. I had it framed in a plain natural wood so that it would probably be suitable for a den, especially if you have a very dark corner in yours.[2]

The salmon did not suffer too much during my week on the Moisie. We had high water most of the time, but I did catch a few and, for the first time in my life, I learned something of the technique of "killing" a salmon.[3] Incidentally, the black flies are plentiful but are no problem at all if one uses the insect repellent developed by the Army during the war. It is called 6−12.[4]

I am quite anxious to talk to you about your new job; in fact, there are developments going on in this country that seem to me to indicate a very poor approach to most of our problems and, because of this, I should like to have a real chin with you. While I do not flatter myself that I could be helpful in the post I understand you are to take, I have no doubt that, with the shoe on the other foot, you could do much to allay some of my doubts and misgivings. This country is such a big, splendid, wonderful and always potentially powerful nation that I am convinced the solutions of our internal problems will go a very long way toward achieving our international aims, particularly that of preserving the peace.

While I am expecting to be in the West for a period this summer, I shall always be at your command when I am in the East.[5] You have only to give me a ring and I can find, within a day or so, an opportunity to run down to Washington to see you.

With warm regard, *Cordially*

[1] President Truman had appointed Harriman his Special Assistant on Foreign Affairs on June 16, 1950. The former Ambassador to the Soviet Union was currently serving as Special Representative to the Economic Cooperation Administration in Paris, France (for background on Harriman and his role in developing Columbia University's plans for the American Assembly see no. 605; and *New York Times*, June 17 and July 2, 1950).

[2] This was probably a painting of Sun Valley, Idaho. It would be delivered to Harriman on September 15, 1950 (see no. 972).

[3] On "killing" salmon see no. 844, n. 8; on Eisenhower's fishing trip in Canada see no. 839.

[4] Workers at the Rutgers Experiment Station in New Jersey had developed the chemical compound called Rutgers 612 prior to World War II (see Ebbe Curtis Hoff, ed., *Preventive Medicine in World War II*, vol. II, *Environmental Hygiene*, The Medical Department of the United States Army, ed. John Boyd Coates, Jr. [Washington, D.C., 1955], pp. 255–56).

[5] For Eisenhower's travel plans see nos. 884, 887, and 900.

853   *Eisenhower Mss., Family File*

TO EDGAR NEWTON EISENHOWER   *June 26, 1950*

Dear Ed:[1] The story told you was one which, as is usual in such cases, had a slight element of truth in it, although it is incorrect.[2] When that particular Howard Johnson Restaurant was started, the originators were two friends of mine. They offered me an opportunity to go in on a "silent basis" and with a very minor percentage—as I remember about 5 per cent. When someone discovered that I had this minor interest in the restaurant and made a news item of it, I immediately withdrew from the venture, because I will not have my name connected with any commercial activity of any kind. In fact, the only stocks I own are held in the name of a bank—so far as I know, my own name does not appear anywhere as a stockholder in any business of any kind.[3]

As to the "operation" part of the story, that is completely in error. I was never even inside the restaurant nor inside the building where it was established. My interest in it was exactly like yours in any business in which you own a few shares of stock—nothing more. *As ever*

[1] General Eisenhower's brother (for background see no. 36).

[2] In a note of June 12 (same file as document), Edgar Eisenhower had recounted a story he had heard to the effect that the General was "one of the owners and operators" of a Howard Johnson restaurant in Washington, D.C.

[3] For background on Eisenhower's personal investments see no. 19.

854   *Eisenhower Mss.*

To Julius Earl Schaefer   *June 27, 1950*

Dear Earl:[1] Col. Howse came in to see me yesterday morning and we had quite a long talk. Nevertheless, he may report to you that I rather wandered off the reservation in attempting to describe to him my attitude toward the "Eisenhower Shrine." We got into such broad subjects, and I so thoroughly enjoyed meeting him, I am afraid I was more garrulous than instructive. I am certain, however, that he and I share the one basic thought that a mere "Eisenhower" shrine would be meaningless and not worth the effort, but that the use of a name to personalize a really worthwhile objective is something else again.[2]

It has been some years since I have read the basic provisions of the charter of the Foundation, but as I recall the document, it contains an outline of purposes that is worthy of any effort. Largely, those purposes touched upon, directly or indirectly, are the matter of citizenship training and citizenship performance.[3] It is this kind of thing that I am certain all my brothers would approve of. And I think that we should all remember that, while my name has been somewhat more publicized than that of some of my brothers, all of us are in this thing together. This merely suggests another reason why we should be particularly careful not to allow the project to descend to any kind of personal glorification. With you and Col. Howse on the job, I am quite certain it will never do so.[4]

With warm personal regard, *Cordially*

P.S. Thank you for giving me the opportunity to meet such an interesting and personable individual as Col. Howse.

[1] In a letter of June 25 (EM) Schaefer, vice-president and general manager of Boeing Airplane Company and vice-president of the Eisenhower Foundation, had summarized his reasons for sending a telegram to Colonel Alfred E. Howse, a businessman in Wichita, Kansas, and campaign chairman of the Eisenhower

Foundation, on June 24. Both men were raising money to finance the construction of a building in Abilene, Kansas, to house Eisenhower's World War II trophies (see no. 833). In his telegram Schaefer had advised Howse of several problems involved in the latter's suggestion that "a peace tone" be emphasized during the campaign to raise funds for the building. Schaefer had argued that a peace theme might be interpreted as a statement of opinion regarding the situation in Korea or as evidence that "our Midwest isolationist reputation" had some basis in fact.

[2] In a letter of July 5 (EM) Schaefer would inform Eisenhower that Howse had called a special meeting of the trustees of the Eisenhower Foundation on July 1, 1950. Howse had reported on Eisenhower's reluctance to concern himself with a project that would be focused on one individual. Schaefer summarized the events of the meeting as follows: "Colonel Howse made your position with respect to the memorial and mementoes as well as, your citizenship goals very clear to everyone. The Executive Committee and the Board of Trustees gave him full authority to carry out the program as you passed it on to him." Howse would confer again with Eisenhower in New York City on July 13, and on the following day the *New York Times* would carry an article outlining the Eisenhower Foundation's plans for promoting citizenship training in the public schools of Kansas. Educators planned to orient the program toward youths unable to attend college. The *Times* would also quote Howse's prediction that the foundation would construct a "modest" building to house Eisenhower's World War II trophies during the spring of 1951. As it turned out, the building would be dedicated on November 11, 1954.

[3] Regarding this part of the charter see Galambos, *Chief of Staff*, no. 1023.

[4] In a letter of July 6 (EM) Howse would place in perspective the General's role in the foundation: "The emphasis has been changed from a memorial to General Eisenhower to a project sponsored by the people of Kansas for the purposes of developing citizenship education and of illustrating the possibilities of a democratic way of life. You are cooperating in this project because of your boyhood residence in Kansas and your affection for the people of Kansas." At the top of the letter Eisenhower would write the following message to Kevin C. McCann, his assistant: "*McCann* Nice note! Will you please make it one of your chores to keep in constant touch with this whole project? I don't want to be in position of dealing with it, too much, personally."

855   *Eisenhower Mss.*

To Charles Henry Caldwell   *June 27, 1950*

Dear Caldwell: I am more than grateful for your letter of June 13 and for the suggestions you made in it.[1]

First of all, please do not set aside any elaborate space for my use during the summer. Except for the meeting of the Air Force Board, last year, I found it necessary to go out to Lowry only two or three times during the entire month.[2] The maximum that I could conceivably need in the matter of space would be a small office for a secretary in which I could have a desk on the very few occasions that I would expect to come out to the Post. I would truly appreciate the monitoring of telephone calls by such secretary, since, at times, the useless answering of the telephone becomes a terrific burden.

Beyond this, if the corporal you mention would be agreeable to going on furlough during the period I expect to be in Denver—from something like the first of August until the middle of September—I would be more than glad to employ him at whatever rates are normal in the region during that period. Should you consider this too long a period for him to be absent from post duties, I would still be glad to make the same arrangement, pending the time I could secure a good and satisfactory civilian chauffeur.[3] If any official duties should arise involving a need for any other kind of assistance, I shall be quick to discuss the matter with you because of the cordial suggestions you have made.

With very deep appreciation and warm personal regard, *Cordially*

[1] Brigadier General Caldwell (USMA 1925), CG of Lowry Air Force Base, near Denver, Colorado, had written (EM) to tell Eisenhower that a two-room suite at the base would be available for the General's use during his visit to Denver later in the summer. Caldwell had also offered to prepare a telephone-monitoring system linking the General's living quarters with his office at the base.

[2] Eisenhower had attended meetings of the Service Academy Board at Lowry on August 8 and 9, 1949 (for background see no. 517).

[3] Caldwell had mentioned that a corporal could be available "in a non-official capacity and in civilian clothing" to drive for the General, Mrs. Eisenhower, or her parents, the Douds. Eisenhower did in fact employ a corporal during the first few days of his visit to Denver (see Eisenhower to Caldwell, Aug. 4, 1950, and Eisenhower to Sample, Aug. 5, 1950, EM). A civilian chauffeur would replace the corporal on August 1 (see Johnson to Eisenhower, July 31, 1950, and Eisenhower to Johnson, Aug. 3, 1950, EM).

856   *Eisenhower Mss.*

To Louis Marx   *June 27, 1950*

Dear Louis:[1] Sunday evening I got home from a week's absence and got out the Plastic Figures to start painting.[2] Frankly, I am having one dickens of a time. I cannot make more than one out of three or four figures stand up and, even then, they fall over in the slightest breeze. Secondly, the paints apparently need some kind of mixing medium that I cannot discover. I am thinking of using gasoline. What I do is smear myself from head to foot, which I did the other evening.

In any event, when you come back, give me a ring and we will take a whirl at this business together. This evening I am going back to my paints and see whether I can do a little bit better job.[3]

Both Mamie and I send you and your nice family best wishes for a fine European tour.[4] *Cordially*

[1] Louis Marx was an old friend of the Eisenhowers'; his firm, Louis Marx & Company, manufactured toys.

[2] Eisenhower had returned to New York City on June 25 from his fishing trip in Canada (see no. 839). Marx had periodically supplied Eisenhower with his company's line of assorted plastic figures and paints (see no. 787). The latest shipment of cowboys, cowgirls, steers, horses, and dogs had been delivered on June 21 (EM).

[3] The toymaker would apologize for this inconvenience and ask the General to postpone his painting venture until Marx returned from England (telegram, Marx to Eisenhower, July 10, 1950, EM).

[4] Marx, his wife Idella, and their children Jacqueline ("Jackie"), Patricia ("Patsy"), and Louis, Jr., would sail to France to visit their eldest daughter, Barbara, a student at the Sorbonne, and then travel to Marx's factory in England before returning to the United States in August (Marx to Eisenhower, June 22, 1950, EM).

857   *Eisenhower Mss.*

To Mrs. C. Walter Allen   *June 27, 1950*

Dear Mrs. Allen:[1] This morning I had a letter from ex-Governor Vivian saying that he had discussed with you our previous correspondence about social services.[2] Receipt of this letter reminded me that your friend, Edward Carroll, never came to see me in my office. Possibly, he never got to New York.[3]

You could not hate "bureaucracy" more than I, but when you get into the specific field of welfare, I have no recourse except to turn to people who studied the subject far more than I have. My own information is limited to operation of one or two institutions in which I am specifically interested and the work of our academic department in this regard. I think that some time it might be a nice thing for you to come back here and visit our School of Social Work for several days. Possibly you could needle them into doing some of the things that you think should be done, whereas they might be able to explain to you something of what they are actually doing.[4] *Sincerely*

[1] Mrs. Allen, of Denver, Colorado, had written to Eisenhower early in 1950 regarding some criticisms of the New York School of Social Work (for background see no. 677).

[2] John Charles Vivian (LL.B. University of Denver 1913), Governor of Colorado from 1943 to 1947, had been the Republicans' unsuccessful candidate for a seat in the U.S. Senate in 1948. In his letter (June 20, EM) Vivian had expressed his conviction that the administration of public welfare should be the concern "largely, if not entirely" of local rather than federal government. He believed, moreover, that "practical laymen trained in the work" should sponsor welfare

programs, instead of "highly technical, professional social service workers" who tended to advocate "a strictly federal viewpoint." Mrs. Allen shared these opinions, Vivian had assured Eisenhower.

[3] Edward J. Carroll was director of economic research for Sharp & Dohme, Inc., manufacturers of pharmaceuticals and biologicals in Philadelphia, Pennsylvania. Mrs. Allen had informed Eisenhower (Mar. 5, 1950, EM) that Carroll was "particularly well informed on the inside picture" of welfare work in the United States. She had hoped that Eisenhower and Carroll might meet when the latter visited New York during the middle of March 1950.

[4] On August 21, 1950, Eisenhower would address a gathering of alumnae of the Wolcott School in Denver, Colorado, a finishing school that Mrs. Eisenhower had attended for one year. Mrs. Allen would be present for the occasion (see Allen to Eisenhower, Aug. 24, 1950, EM).

858   *Eisenhower Mss.*

To Howard Stix Cullman   *June 27, 1950*

Dear Mr. Cullman: Thank you for your very cordial letter. If all goes well, I shall most certainly be with you at the dinner honoring Richard Rodgers and Oscar Hammerstein. They are among Columbia's most brilliant alumni.[1]

If you were contemplating any particular part in the program for me, I should like, at this early date, to suggest a very minor role. I note that your letter says "could be with us at the dinner to present the award" which might mean that you would expect me to make a rather extensive talk. On the other hand, it may merely mean that after suitable preliminaries carried on by others, you would like for me to perform the actual presentation with only one or two words, in each case, directed particularly to the recipients. If this latter is your intention, I would be quite pleased to take part.[2]

I have two reasons for making a point of this. One is that I try to avoid too many public speeches and I am committed to one on October 19.[3] The other is that I am so often forced because of unexpected duties, to cancel engagements at the last moment that I try very earnestly to limit the number in which my appearance or non-appearance makes any great difference to the scheduled program.

I trust that all this is clear to you. In any event, I am delighted at the prospect of meeting with you to honor two such outstanding citizens.[4]

With best wishes, *Cordially*

[1] Cullman (A.B. Yale 1913) was Commissioner of the New York Port Authority, chairman and vice-president of Cullman Brothers, Inc., cigar leaf tobacco merchants, and president of the Hundred Year Association of New York, Inc. The latter organization would hold its annual dinner, at which Richard Rodgers and Oscar Hammerstein II would be honored, on October 22, 1950. In his letter of

June 19 (EM) Cullman had asked Eisenhower if he could come to the dinner to award gold medals to Rodgers and Hammerstein. Rodgers, a composer and producer, had been a student at Columbia from 1919 to 1921. He was currently head of a committee to plan a new arts center at Columbia (see *New York Times*, Feb. 9, 1950. Eisenhower's appointment calendar indicates that he met with Rodgers the morning of June 27 and that they had lunch at 60 Morningside Drive on July 10, 1950). Hammerstein (A.B. Columbia 1916) was an author and librettist. The General had presented university medals for excellence to both men at commencement ceremonies on June 1, 1949.

[2] Cullman would reply (June 30, EM) that Eisenhower could limit his remarks to "a few words" while presenting the medals. On October 13 Cullman would send copies of a memorandum (EM) to Eisenhower and to each of the major speakers at the dinner notifying them that the program would be changed to allow the General to leave early in order to catch a train to Chicago (on the trip see no. 1043).

[3] Eisenhower would speak at the Carnegie Institute, in Pittsburgh, Pennsylvania, on October 19, 1950 (for background see no. 757).

[4] A picture of Eisenhower presenting the medals to Rodgers and Hammerstein would appear in the *New York Times* on October 23, 1950.

859

Eisenhower Mss.,
Amos F. Eno Corr.

To Grayson Louis Kirk

June 28, 1950

SUBJECT: Amos F. Eno Fund[1]

I return this matter to you for some further consideration. I feel that it is greatly to our advantage to establish the finest kind of relations with the surviving members of families of which the head may have donated generously to Columbia. Consequently, while I approve of telling Mr. and Mrs. Steffanson that we do perpetuate the name of Amos F. Eno through the Treasurer's Report each year, I would want also to know that this action would seem to be fully satisfactory to them.[2]

I—and I assume that they—have seen plaques on the University grounds expressing deep appreciation for the beneficence of some former donor. I am sure, therefore, that it is this kind of thing they have in mind. I am quite certain that for a very minimum expenditure, such a thing could be done. But if it is considered out of taste or is too expensive if we do it properly, then of course we have a problem.

I should like your definite recommendation on the matter.[3]

[1] Amos F. Eno had been a wealthy merchant and owner of real estate in New York City. He had fought in the Civil War with the 7th New York Infantry Regiment, rising to the rank of colonel by the war's end. Prior to his death in 1915, Eno had named Columbia University as a residuary legatee in his will, and

after the settlement of the estate in 1923, the university had received a bequest of more than $2 million (see *New York Times*, Apr. 18, 1923).

[2] In 1917 Hokan Bjornstrom Steffanson had married Mary Pinchot Eno (niece of Amos F. Eno). Steffanson, a chemical-engineering graduate of the Stockholm Institute of Technology in Sweden, had entered the wood-pulp business in New York in 1909. Mrs. Steffanson, a devotee of music, had been a member of the board of governors of the Philharmonic-Symphony Society for thirty years. Eisenhower had assured the Steffansons in a letter of May 26, 1950 (EM), that he had asked Provost Kirk to investigate ways "to recognize the generosity and public spiritedness of Mrs. Steffanson's uncle." Kirk had turned the matter over to Joseph Campbell, vice-president in charge of business affairs and treasurer of the university, and Campbell had informed the provost in a memorandum of June 13 (CUF) that there was no building or plaque at Columbia University commemorating Eno's bequest. Campbell had argued, however, that the treasurer's report annually included Eno's name and that this was a far better way of familiarizing people with Eno's generosity than was placing a plaque somewhere on the campus. Columbia University, *Report of the Treasurer, 1950*, pp. 148–49, indicates that the net value of the properties that formed the Amos F. Eno Endowment was currently estimated to be $7,112,802.24.

[3] There is no further correspondence on this subject in EM.

860   *Eisenhower Mss.*

TO ARTHUR HAYS SULZBERGER   *June 28, 1950*

Dear Arthur: Thank you for your letter about Admiral Strauss.[1] While I have met him briefly, I can by no means claim him as a friend. But your opinion, so emphatically expressed, is good enough for me.

So far as I know, we have no immediate prospect of a vacancy on our Board.[2] Nevertheless, we have agreed in the past that, as occasion arises for any Trustee to make a recommendation concerning a membership, he should instantly submit the name to the Nominating Committee. I would suggest that you do so in this case; I think Bert Putnam is the Chairman.[3]

So far as I am personally concerned, I shall have no hesitancy whatsoever in supporting an individual of whom you have such a high opinion. However, for the next Trustee in point of time, to be elected, I have tentatively promised Mr. Masters to support a candidate of his— immediately after Bill Paley was elected.[4] I shall hope to talk to you about this soon.[5]

It will be nice to see you, no matter what the excuse. *Cordially*

[1] Sulzberger was publisher of the *New York Times* and a trustee of Columbia University. He had written Eisenhower (June 22, EM) to ask if he knew Lewis Lichtenstein Strauss, who had recently resigned from the U.S. Atomic Energy Commission to become financial adviser to Rockefeller Brothers, Inc. (see *New York Times*, June 23, 1950). Sulzberger planned to nominate Strauss to be a life

trustee of Columbia University. Strauss had been associated with Kuhn, Loeb & Company, a Wall Street banking house, from 1919 to 1947, and he had served in the Navy during World War II, rising to the rank of rear admiral. He was currently president of the Institute for Advanced Study in Princeton, New Jersey, and a trustee of Hampton Institute.

[2] Frank S. Hogan, president of the Alumni Federation of Columbia University, had announced on June 8, 1950, the nomination of Robert Wilson Watt (B.S. Columbia 1916), president and a director of the Seaboard Surety Company, to serve a six-year term as an alumni trustee (see *New York Times*, June 9, 1950). The board of trustees would elect Watt to membership on October 2, 1950 (see *ibid.*, Oct. 3, 1950). For further developments concerning the board of trustees see no. 968.

[3] Albert W. Putnam, a member of the law firm of Winthrop, Stimson, Putnam & Roberts, was chairman of the trustees' Committee on Nominations (see Trustees, *Minutes*, Jan. 8, 1951, CUF).

[4] Harris K. Masters was a consulting engineer with the Molybdenum Corporation of America and a trustee of Columbia University (see Galambos, *Chief of Staff*, no. 1674). William S. Paley, chairman of the board of CBS, had become a trustee during March 1950 (see nos. 717 and 718).

[5] A note at the bottom of one of Eisenhower's appointment calendars for July 11, 1950, indicates that on that day he discussed over the telephone with M. Hartley Dodge, chairman of the board of the Remington Arms Company and clerk of the trustees, Sulzberger's proposal to fill a vacancy on the board. We have been unable to find more information regarding this proposal. Sulzberger would suggest in a letter of November 14 (EM) that the university confer upon Strauss an honorary degree, and Eisenhower would reply in a note of November 16 (EM) that he would be glad to support this recommendaton. Strauss would receive the degree at commencement ceremonies on June 1, 1954 (see *New York Times*, June 2, 1954).

861   *Eisenhower Mss.*

To Arthur William Sidney Herrington   *June 28, 1950*

Dear Arthur: Your letter intrigued me mightily and I shall take it home and talk it over with the family czarina.[1] Frankly, I think my biggest problem would occur in trying to persuade her to make the trip by air. Her opinion about airplanes is just about what yours would be about a skunk in the living room. Nevertheless, I am counting a little bit on her curiosity being so great that she would consent to go anyway. And, if that is the case, I shall write to you again with the idea of doing some *tentative* (very tentative) planning.[2]

In the meantime, when you are in New York, give me a ring and let us try to have lunch together at least.[3]

Thanks again for your very cordial suggestion.

[1] Herrington, chairman of the board of Marmon-Herrington Company, had described in his letter of June 21 (EM) his visit to Pakistan during December 1949

and January 1950. He wanted Eisenhower to accompany him on a hunting trip to Pakistan during the coming winter (for background on Herrington see Galambos, *Chief of Staff*, no. 1758).

[2] There is no indication in EM that the General wrote to Herrington again on this subject.

[3] Eisenhower would renew this invitation in a note of September 21 (EM), and in a letter of the following day (EM) Herrington would suggest that General and Mrs. Eisenhower have dinner with him and his wife in New York City on September 25. A note at the bottom of the letter indicates that the Eisenhowers would decline the invitation.

862

Eisenhower Mss.,
William R. Stewart Corr.

To Harry James Carman

June 28, 1950

Dear Harry:[1] Here is a letter I have just received from an alumnus in Chicago. I send also a copy of my tentative reply.[2] Would you have someone (possibly Dean McKnight) study the letter carefully and reply to Mr. Stewart in any way that may seem to be appropriate?[3]

[1] Carman would relinquish his position as dean of Columbia College on July 1, 1950, and return to the faculty as Moore Collegiate Professor of History (for background see no. 353).

[2] William Robert Stewart, a publishers' representative in Chicago, Illinois, had attended Columbia University. He had complained to Eisenhower (June 9, EM) that the committee that awarded scholarships to incoming freshmen had passed over the recommendations of the Chicago Alumni Club, of which Stewart had been scholarship chairman. "I doubt," Stewart had written, "if we will ever again be able to present to Columbia as many fine names of well-rounded boys as we were able to give this year." Stewart had noted that Princeton University had recruited one of his top prospects by awarding him a scholarship larger than the one Columbia had offered. Stewart wanted to discuss the problem with Eisenhower during a visit to Morningside Heights that he planned for the autumn of 1950. In his tentative reply dated June 29 (EM) Eisenhower described "a feeling of bewilderment and even frustration" over the loss of students to other members of the Ivy League. He agreed to discuss the matter when Stewart visited New York in the fall.

[3] Nicholas M. McKnight, dean of students, would reply (June 14, same file as document) that Columbia University had reduced its scholarship appropriations during the preceding year in an attempt to balance the FY50 budget. Funds for the entering freshman class had been especially scarce, because, as McKnight explained, "the outstanding commitments to students already here must be met first" (for background on McKnight see no. 586).

On September 14 Stewart would write Eisenhower again (EM), complaining about two instances in which Columbia University had awarded scholarships to students in the Chicago area who had not met the requirements that were apparently essential for admission. Kevin C. McCann, assistant to the president, would draft a reply (Sept. 25, EM) for Eisenhower's signature and also Eisenhower's letter of October 2 (EM) describing the scheduling problems that would prevent the General from meeting with Stewart during October and early November. According to the appointment calendar, the General would not be able to meet with Stewart during 1950.

863   *Eisenhower Mss.*

To James Frederick Gault   *June 28, 1950*

Dear Jimmy:[1] So far as the notices you want to publish about the Winant Volunteers going to Culzean Castle, I have no particular choice between the two drafts except that No. 1 Draft is shorter.[2] If the Reverend Tubby Clayton should be disposed to use the first one, will you ask him to consider the slight revisions that I have suggested in pencil?[3] You will note that these suggestions were made merely to put the thought in a bit more informal phraseology.

In the same mail with your letter came a note from Sir Charles MacLean.[4] I am sure that we will be able to do everything possible to make his New York stay an enjoyable one. But I hope you will warn him, however, that this city is likely to be so hot and sweltering at that time of the year that he should be prepared to have the lightest kind of clothes. I should say "pajama" thickness would be about right.

I shall keep you in touch with next year's plans as they develop. I rather doubt that anything definite will be known until late next winter.[5]

Love to Peggy[6] and, as always, my very best to yourself, *As ever*

[1] For background on Gault see no. 14.
[2] In a letter of June 19 (EM) Gault had mentioned that he had made the arrangements for the Winant and Osler Volunteers to stay at Culzean Castle, Ayrshire, Scotland, during August and September 1950. The Winant Volunteers were from schools and colleges in the United States, the Osler Volunteers were from Canada, and both groups would do settlement work in the East End of London during 1950. Eisenhower was honorary chairman of the American sponsoring committee of the Winant Volunteers.
[3] Gault had enclosed with his letter two drafts of notices regarding the Winant Volunteers drawn up by Reverend Philip B. "Tubby" Clayton, vicar of All Hallows Church in London and chaplain to King George VI. Neither draft is in EM.
[4] For background on MacLean and his plans see no. 832 and MacLean's thank-you note to the General (June 20, EM).
[5] Eisenhower was probably referring to his travel plans for June and July 1951 (see no. 841).
[6] Gault's wife, the former Margaret Ella Campbell.

To Philip Sporn

Dear Mr. Sporn:[1] Thank you very much for your cordial note about John Dunning's appointment. I trust that you will not be displeased to learn that I am showing it to John in person. Since there was voiced some criticism in the selection of a scientist as Dean of Engineering, I want him to know that there are many other people of brains and distinction who thoroughly approve the selection.[2]

Thank you again for writing. *Very sincerely*

[1] Sporn, president and a director of American Gas and Electric Company, American Gas and Electric Service Corporation, and numerous other companies, had congratulated Eisenhower in a letter of June 16 (EM) on the appointment of John R. Dunning as dean of the School of Engineering.

[2] Dunning would assume his new duties on July 1, 1950 (see no. 739). Concerning the problems of selecting a new dean see nos. 767 and 783.

To Kenneth William Dobson Strong

Dear Kenneth:[1] Your letter came just as I was in the midst of planning the last details of my summer vacation. It is a rather complicated affair this year, involving California, Oklahoma and Colorado.[2] When you add the uncertainties caused by railroad strikes, you can see that the thing becomes difficult enough that one is tempted to stay right here and swelter in the heat.[3] That is exactly what I would do except that I am getting so old that such things irritate me and everybody is glad to get me out of their way.

While you reported yourself, in your letter, as being on the optimistic side with respect to the international situation, I wonder what you think, this minute, about the Korean situation. In the general picture, I have consistently, ever since the cessation of hostilities, argued that there would be no deliberately planned war within five years and that, in my opinion, the only real danger of war, within the matter of a decade, was one of the "powder keg" variety or one arising out of complete miscalculations on the part of our potential enemies as to the determination of the free world to protect itself.[4]

It is because of such beliefs—which, of course, could be expanded and amplified for hours—that I believe the United Nations, in taking the stand it has now taken in Korea, must be absolutely firm and must, if necessary devote its full strength to hold and maintain the position that it has announced for itself. Failure to do this would be interpreted as nothing less than another kind of Munich, and it is clear what the result of that would be. So, as of this morning, I still concur in your note of optimism, but that optimism is based upon an assumption that the United Nations will stand absolutely firm in the present crisis and not allow its fears, as to what may happen elsewhere, to deter it from taking whatever action may be necessary.[5]

If you come to the States, of course I want to see you and will always arrange some date, even if I have to break a few appointments. On my part, I intend to come to Europe in late May and shall probably stay there until after July 4. I trust, however, that you will not wait for such plans as that to develop before writing to me again.[6]

With warm personal regard, *Cordially*

---

[1] Major General Strong, Director of the Joint Intelligence Bureau at the Ministry of Defence in London, had included in a letter of June 17 (EM) news about Eisenhower's friends in Britain (for background on Strong see no. 480).

[2] On the Eisenhowers' travel plans see nos. 884, 887, and 900.

[3] On June 25 railroad-yard employees of five companies operating through the midwestern and western sections of the country had walked off their jobs seeking shorter hours and higher wages. The striking workers were members of the Switchmen's Union of North America, AFL. Negotiations between the union and the companies were still under way at the time Eisenhower wrote this letter (see *New York Times*, June 26, 27, and 30, 1950). The strikers of all the companies except the Chicago, Rock Island and Pacific Railway Company, would return to their jobs on July 6, 1950, after President Truman threatened "drastic action." On the same day he would take steps to postpone for sixty days a strike by the Pullman Conductors' Division of the Order of Railway Conductors (see *Public Papers of the Presidents: Truman, 1950*, pp. 516–18; and *New York Times*, July 7, 1950). The walkout on the Rock Island Railroad would end on July 8 when Truman ordered the Army to seize and operate the system (see U.S., *Federal Register* 15, no. 132 [July 11, 1950], 4363–65; and *New York Times*, July 9, 1950).

[4] North Korean forces had attacked South Korea on June 25, 1950 (June 24 in Washington, D.C.). The U.N. Security Council had convened in New York and had passed a resolution expressing "grave concern" regarding the situation and calling for an immediate cease-fire. The Soviet Union's representative had been absent, and Yugoslavia's delegate had attended the session but had abstained from voting. On June 26 President Truman had ordered U.S. air and naval contingents in the Far East to support the South Koreans, and on the following day the U.N. Security Council had adopted a resolution asking member countries to aid that country. The Russian delegate had again been absent, and Yugoslavia's had voted against the measure (see *New York Times*, June 25, 26, 27, and 28, 1950; Truman, *Memoirs*, vol. II, *Years of Trial and Hope*, pp. 331–41; Acheson, *Present at the Creation*, pp. 402–11; Trygve Lie, *In the Cause of Peace: Seven Years with the United Nations* [New York, 1954], pp. 327–34; Glenn D. Paige, *The Korean Decision, June 24–30, 1950* [New York, 1968], pp. 79–233; Kolko and Kolko, *Limits of Power*, pp. 567–87; and P. Wesley Kriebel, "Unfinished Business— Intervention under the U.N. Umbrella: America's Participation in the Korean War, 1950–1953," in *Intervention or Abstention: The Dilemma of American Foreign Policy*, ed. Robin Higham [Lexington, Ky., 1975], pp. 114–19).

A note at the bottom of one of Eisenhower's appointment calendars indicates that he had telephoned President Truman on June 27 at approximately 6:30 P.M. to congratulate him on his stand. The General had called again from New York on June 28 at 8:20 P.M. to inform the President that General Omar N. Bradley, chairman of the JCS, had been advised of Eisenhower's views on the situation. On Eisenhower's visit to the Pentagon, in Washington, D.C., the afternoon of the twenty-eighth see no. 870. For Eisenhower's views on Korea in the postwar period see Galambos, *Chief of Staff*, nos. 728, 1439, 1492, 1900, and 2039.

[5] The morning's *New York Times* carried reports that the Russian government had sent a note to U.N. Secretary General Trygve H. Lie declaring that the Nationalist Chinese member of the Security Council had had "no lawful right" to participate in the deliberations concerning Korea. The Soviets had argued, moreover, that the Security Council could not approve military action without the concurrence of all five permanent members—the United States, Great Britain, France, Russia, and China. The same issue of the *Times* quoted Eisenhower as follows: "The best check for sustaining world peace was to take a firm stand, and when our Government guaranteed the Government of South Korea, there was no recourse but to do what President Truman did."

[6] On the carbon copy of this letter in EM, *1951* appears in the margin beside this paragraph, and *Confidential* appears beside the paragraph above it. Eisenhower probably wanted the confidentiality to apply to his travel plans rather than to his views regarding the war in Korea (see no. 841, n. 6).

866   *Eisenhower Mss.*

TO CLARE BOOTHE LUCE   *June 29, 1950*

Dear Mrs. Luce:[1] On a plane trip yesterday I read Bob Hutchins' essay on the *Summa Dialectica*. My interest in his idea was amply sufficient to surmount my instinctive dislike (possibly born of my ignorance) of pretentious words and terms. I thank you for sending me a copy.[2]

I intend to make use of it by circulating it among some of our scholars.[3] If I get significant reaction, I'll drop you a note.

The intensity of the current international "mess" shows no sign of diminishing this morning. Incidental to a trip to Walter Reed yesterday, I stopped at the Pentagon to see some of my old friends.[4]

One gets the feeling that Washington considers it is swimming in strange and swift currents—and there are rocks, rapids and terrors on every hand.[5] *Sincerely*

[1] Mrs. Luce, a Republican, had represented Connecticut's Fourth District in the U.S. House of Representatives from 1943 to 1947 (a longhand draft of this letter is in EM, Letters and Drafts).

[2] Robert M. Hutchins was chancellor of the University of Chicago (for background see Galambos, *Chief of Staff*, no. 1784). Mrs. Luce had enclosed with her letter of June 15 (EM) a memorandum by Hutchins proposing a multivolume *Summa Dialectica* embracing "the whole range of human learning and discourse, as it is represented in the materials of the western tradition and in the life of contemporary thought." Such a work was not feasible due to the completion of *The Great Ideas:*

A *Syntopicon of the Great Books*, a two-volume work soon to be published by Encyclopaedia Britannica, Inc., in cooperation with the University of Chicago. Hutchins had likened the latter set to "a philosophical dictionary, an encyclopedic survey of ideas, an index to the whole tradition of western thought. . . ." The word *syntopicon* referred to the fact that the set synthesized 3,000 topics under 102 headings. The research staff at the University of Chicago that had compiled the syntopicon would now be available to amass the larger work, and Hutchins had concluded with a projected annual budget for the enterprise of $75,000 to $100,000 (see Hutchins, "A Program of Syntopical Research," June 1, 1950, CUF).

Mrs. Luce had discussed the syntopicon with Eisenhower on June 14. In her letter of the following day she had assured him that should Columbia University come into collaboration on the *Summa Dialectica*, "there's little doubt that you would go down in the annals of Education as one of *its* greatest Generals!" For further background see *New York Times*, April 20, 1950.

[3] Eisenhower would give Hutchins's memorandum to Provost Grayson L. Kirk (see the following document).

[4] The "mess" was the beginning of the Korean War (see the preceding document and no. 870).

[5] Eisenhower would reiterate these sentiments upon his return from a second trip to Washington, D.C. (see no. 886).

867   *Eisenhower Mss.*

To Grayson Louis Kirk   *June 29, 1950*

I do not know whether you have heard of the Syntopicon prepared under the auspices of the University of Chicago.[1] There is now proposed a considerable expansion of that type of research. The project is explained in an essay by Robert Hutchins, copy attached.[2] Apparently, the University of Chicago hopes to secure the cooperation of other universities or at least parts of the staff of other universities in pursuit of this work.

I send you this document, which was given to me by a citizen having no connection with the University, so that you may determine whether there is any local desire to participate in this type of project. I think that the idea itself is intriguing—but I have no suggestion to make and shall wait whatever formal or informal report you may believe to be appropriate.[3]

[1] See the preceding document.
[2] Robert M. Hutchins was chancellor of the University of Chicago.
[3] There is no further correspondence on this subject in EM.

To Theodore Scarborough Petersen   *June 29, 1950*

Dear Mr. Petersen: Thank you very much for your letter and the nice invitation it conveyed.[1]

At the moment, my California schedule is in a rather topsy-turvy state due to uncertainties arising out of current difficulties on railways. If we are able to use railway transportation, Mrs. Eisenhower will accompany me to the Coast and, consequently, my dates of arrival and departure will not coincide with those that would obtain if I were to come out by commercial plane. Since she positively refuses to use airplanes, you can see that the switchmen's strike and rumblings of other railway troubles leave my plans a bit uncertain.[2]

This minute I am trying to get Fred Gurley on the phone and possibly some of these doubts will be resolved.[3] In any event, I have promised to be in San Francisco on Thursday noon, July 20, for a luncheon that Mr. Collier is to give. I think that, immediately thereafter, we are to take off for the Bohemian Grove, returning to San Francisco on Monday or Tuesday of the following week.[4] I am a little uncertain as to the travel time involved between the Grove and San Francisco, but it would seem to me that I should be rather safe in planning for a luncheon with you on the day of our return, provided we could, by an early start, reach San Francisco by luncheon time.

The unfortunate thing about the whole business seems to be that the railroad situation will not be completely clarified for some days. But, tentatively, I think that we should be safe in planning for luncheon on Monday, July 24.[5] Fred Gurley of the Santa Fe and a friend of his and mine, James Black of Washington, will be with me, under tentative plans, on the Santa Fe car provided by Fred.[6] I am not only appreciative of your nice invitation; I would most certainly be delighted to meet the small group of San Franciscans that you contemplate assembling. Consequently, I shall try to provide you definite information at the earliest possible date.

I realize that an answer as indefinite as this is not wholly satisfactory, but I do hope you will bear with me until I can get all the snarls untangled.

With personal regards and, again, my thanks. *Cordially*

[1] Petersen, president of Standard Oil Company of California since 1948, had written to invite Eisenhower (June 26, EM) to a luncheon or dinner in San Francisco, "where a group of fifteen or twenty of our people might join you in an informal discussion."

[2] On the labor problems of the nation's railway companies see no. 865.

[3] For the coordination of trip plans with Fred G. Gurley, president and chairman of the executive committee of the Atchison, Topeka and Santa Fe Railway Company, see no. 873.

[4] For background on Harry D. Collier, chairman of the finance committee of Standard Oil Company of California, see no. 769. Regarding the Bohemian Grove encampment see no. 887.

[5] Petersen would reply on July 3 that he had tentatively arranged a luncheon for July 24. Eisenhower would respond (July 6) that July 25 was a more convenient date. Both letters are in EM. Scheduling of the luncheon would also be the subject of no. 887.

[6] James C. Black was manager of the Republic Steel Corporation, in Washington, D.C. (for background see no. 62).

869   *Eisenhower Mss.*

To MICHAEL JAMES McKEOGH   *June 29, 1950*

Dear Mickey:[0] My records provide no evidence that I ever sent you a book.[1] I am not only chagrined, I am positively astounded. Had I been called before a court of law to testify on the point, I would have gladly sworn that your name was one of the very first I put down on my list. In sending out copies of my own book, I must confess that I felt somewhat guilty of unwarranted egotism in the assumption that my friends would want to have it. However, in the case of all those individuals who went through the war with me on my personal staff, I felt that at least the book might serve as a little memento of our long and exciting months together.

In any event, I am correcting the error of omission this morning and one is on the way to you. I regret that I do not have one of the "special" edition left in my possession, but the copy I send you is one of the original printing.

Affectionate regards to you and your nice family, *Sincerely*

P.S. I am sending also a book to Pearlie.[2] Both of them are signed as of December 1948, the month I sent out the original group.[3]

[1] McKeogh, Eisenhower's orderly during World War II, was currently a salesman for radio station KIST in Santa Barbara, California. Eisenhower's appointment calendar indicates that McKeogh had visited him at Columbia University on June 28 (for background on McKeogh see no. 33). Concerning the distribution of inscribed copies of Eisenhower's memoir *Crusade in Europe* see nos. 237 and 246.

[2] McKeogh's wife, the former Pearl Hargrave (for background see *Eisenhower Papers*, vols. VI–IX).

[3] McKeogh thanked Eisenhower for the books in a letter of July 18 (EM). For developments see no. 919.

Calendar says Friday but it feels like I've lost a day.

On Wednesday I went to Washington. First W. R. Hospital, then a number of friends in Pentagon. Haislip—Collins—Matt Ridgway—Al Gruenther. (Couldn't see Brad—he was sick).[1]

I went in expecting to find them all in a dither of effort—engaged in the positive business of getting the troops, supplies, etc. that will be needed to settle the Korean mess. They seemed indecisive—which was natural in view of indecisiveness of political statements.[2] I have no business talking about the basic political decision—(to support or not to support S. Korea) [It happens that I believe we'll have a dozen Koreas even if we don't take a firm stand[3]—but it was not on that basis that I talked to my friends.] My whole contention was that an appeal to force cannot, by its nature, be a partial one. This appeal having been made, for [God's] sake, get ready! Do everything *possible* under the law to get [us?] going.[4]

Remember, in a fight we (our side) can never be *too strong*! I urged action in a dozen directions—and left a memo for Brad. We must study every angle to be prepared for *whatever* may happen—even if it finally comes to use of A-bomb (which God forbid.)[5]

---

[1] Eisenhower had traveled to Walter Reed Army Medical Center, in Washington, D.C., accompanied by his physician, Major General Howard M. Snyder, Sr. (USA, ret.), the afternoon of June 28 (on the results of his physical examination see no. 874). Afterward he had visited General Wade H. Haislip, Vice Chief of Staff, U.S. Army; General J. Lawton Collins, Chief of Staff, U.S. Army; Lieutenant General Matthew B. Ridgway, Deputy Chief of Staff for Administration, U.S. Army; and Lieutenant General Alfred M. Gruenther, Deputy Chief of Staff for Plans and Combat Operations. On Omar N. Bradley, chairman of the JCS, see Schulz, memo for record, June 29, 1950, EM, Bradley Corr.

[2] See *Public Papers of the Presidents: Truman, 1950*, pp. 491–92, 496, 498–99, and 502–8; *Department of State Bulletin*, July 3, 1950, pp. 3–8; and *ibid.*, July 10, 1950, pp. 43–50.

[3] Eisenhower had treated this theme more fully in no. 865.

[4] Early this same morning, President Truman had approved the request of General of the Army Douglas MacArthur, CINCFE, that one U.S. Army regimental combat team be committed to the fighting (for background on MacArthur see no. 33). Truman had met with his advisers and the JCS later in the morning and had then decided to give MacArthur authority to use all Army forces available to him (see Truman, *Memoirs*, vol. II, *Years of Trial and Hope*, pp. 342–43; MacArthur, *Reminiscences*, pp. 332–36; J. Lawton Collins, *War in Peacetime: The History and Lessons of Korea* [Boston, 1969], pp. 19–24; and James F. Schnabel, *Policy and Direction: The First Year*, U.S. Army in the Korean War, ed. Maurice Matloff [Washington, D.C., 1972], pp. 74–79). American infantrymen would engage the North Koreans in direct combat on July 5. For developments see *ibid.*, pp. 82–86; and no. 920.

[5] For Eisenhower's views on the use of the atomic bomb see Chandler and Galambos, *Occupation, 1945*, no. 195; and Galambos, *Chief of Staff*, no. 1957.

871   *Eisenhower Mss.*

To Russell Wheeler Davenport   *June 30, 1950*

Dear Mr. Davenport:[1] On a plane trip yesterday I got to read the memorandum you sent to me on the Social Security project.[2] I did not read the long memorandum on "Federal Old Age and Survivors Insurance."[3]

I think you have put your finger accurately upon a point that is significant today in almost everything that our Government does. If we lose our faith in private initiative—if we do not check the tendency to surrender all initiative to the Government in solving social problems—I can foresee the outcome—and I dislike it intensely.

I particularly liked your idea about Community Councils. That same idea is the basis of a system now being developed in Teachers College for practical citizenship training in communities.[4] One effect of your Councils would be to put the pressure on the governmental bodies that could most easily be reached, namely, the *local* mayors and governors. Where we do have to have governmental intervention, let us keep it local!

Emphatically I agree with your idea that legislation should concern itself more with *encouraging private* industry and communities to do necessary things than in organizing the activity and compelling its performance under Federal Government. In fact, I have talked often on this one particular point and I believe that an effective spur would be the granting of some relief in taxes to individuals and corporations that establish social security systems within the limits recognized by the government as satisfactory.[5]

I sincerely hope that you may be able to resume your work next fall.[6] *Sincerely*

[1] Davenport had been moderator of the Life Round Tables since March 1948. He had been a consultant publishing officer for Columbia Broadcasting System until 1947 and head of the experimental department of Time, Inc., from July 1947 to March 1948 (for further background see no. 793).

[2] Eisenhower had drafted this letter on June 29. Two earlier versions are in EM, Letters and Drafts. On the trip to Washington, D.C., on June 28 see the preceding document.

[3] There are no copies of the memoranda in EM, but Davenport's recently published articles on these subjects included "The Greatest Opportunity on Earth," *Fortune*, October 1949; and "Pensions: Not IF But HOW," *ibid.*, November 1949.

[4] On the Citizenship Education Project at Teachers College see no. 727.

[5] On this theme see also no. 538.

[6] Davenport, who had been a policy adviser to Republican presidential candidate Wendell L. Willkie in 1940, would soon be listed among the New Yorkers under consideration as the Republican party's candidate for U.S. senator; Eisenhower's name would also appear on the list (see *New York Times*, Aug. 5, 13, 15, and 18, 1950). Davenport would become chairman of the campaign policy committee of the Republican candidate for the mayoralty of New York City in the fall (see *ibid.*, Sept. 22, 1950). For developments see no. 1105.

V

"Now that we are at war"

JULY 1950 TO DECEMBER 1950

10

Conflict in the Far East

To Carl Milton White   *July 1, 1950*

Dear Dean White:[1] Thank you for sending me the excerpt from Prof. Burgess' talk.[2] "He must have been a great man; he agrees with me!"[3] This goes for the first two paragraphs.[4] In this modern day, with government growing more and more influential, I wonder whether or not he'd revise his 3rd paragraph?[5] *Sincerely*

[1] White (Ph.D. Cornell 1933) had been Director of Libraries and dean of the School of Library Service at Columbia since 1943. This note to him was hand-written by Eisenhower. A typed copy is in EM.

[2] In his letter (June 27, EM) White had said that he had found a speech that John William Burgess had given in 1911 at the decennial celebration of Nicholas Murray Butler's appointment as president of Columbia. So pleased was White with Burgess's "estimate of the importance of the Presidency of Columbia" that he enclosed an excerpt from the speech for Eisenhower. According to White, the speech had been published in the *Columbia University Quarterly* 14 (1911–12), 12–13.

Burgess (Ph.D. Princeton 1883; LL.D. Amherst 1884) had become dean of Columbia's graduate faculties of Political Science, Philosophy, Pure Science, and Fine Arts in 1890. He had come to Columbia from Amherst in 1876, where he had been professor of history and political science. Burgess, who had played an important role in transforming Columbia from a college into a university, had retired in 1912 as emeritus professor of political science and constitutional law.

[3] Eisenhower was probably paraphrasing the following: "My idea of an agreeable person is a person who agrees with me," from *Lothair* (1870), a romantic novel by British statesman and novelist, the Earl of Beaconsfield, Benjamin Disraeli (1804–81).

[4] In the first two paragraphs of the speech Burgess had said that he hoped Butler would "never abandon academic life for governmental position," not because he was less fit for such a role but because Butler could "do more for the people of New York and of these United States and of the world, as the president of this University and as an eminent American citizen, free to form and express his own opinions in his own way, and to labor for their realization untrammelled by party or administrative considerations."

[5] Here Burgess said that he had heard from his childhood "the fact bemoaned" that the best men were not to be found in government work, and it was his conclusion that the best men should not, in fact, be in government positions. "In the genuine and lasting Republic," he said, "the finest work for culture and civilization must be done outside of governmental positions, by great personalities and by private combinations of great personalities, exercising their power through rational and moral suasion and influence, rather than through force and compulsion." Burgess believed that individual liberty and individual initiative could be crushed by men in government stations who "address themselves immediately and assiduously to the expansion of their jurisdiction and the intensification of their power." See also John W. Burgess, *Reminiscences of an American Scholar: The Beginnings of Columbia University* (New York, 1934).

To Fred G. Gurley   *July 1, 1950*

Dear Fred:[1] After yesterday's telephone conversation, I have little to give you in the way of additional information, except the item that Rosie[2] will *not* accompany Mamie to California. Rosie will use that period for her vacation and will later join us in Denver. I think we will all have a great time—if your car is running at that time! We are planning on leaving here the evening of the 14th which, I trust, will be in plenty of time. You did not give the hour that we should have to be in Chicago, but I do not want to leave before evening if I can help it because I have an important engagement that day.[3] Please let me know at once if I am assuming something here that I shouldn't.

A Mr. Blyth has asked me to luncheon on July 23, and I gather from his letter that he thinks someone has approved that idea. But you and I agreed that we would not return from the Bohemian Grove until possibly the 24th; at any rate, we were not counting on being back in San Francisco on Sunday noon. So I am writing to Mr. Blyth to give him this information.[4] The wife of a partner of Mr. Blyth, a lady named Mrs. Ford, has written Mamie, inviting the ladies to lunch at a "Redwood" place on the 21st or 22nd. This, I think, is all to the good, as it will allow them to see the Redwoods under admirable conditions, while we are visting at the Grove.[5]

I cannot think of anything else important at this moment, but I have no doubt we will be communicating with each other from time to time.[6] Love to Ruth.[7] *As ever*

[1] In January 1950 Gurley, who was president of the Atchison, Topeka and Santa Fe Railway System, had asked Eisenhower to be his guest at the Bohemian Grove encampment in July 1950 (for background on the Bohemian Club see no. 388). Eisenhower had declined the invitation, as he had the similar invitations from others who had urged him to visit the California camp (see, for instance, no. 769). See also Gurley to Eisenhower, Jan. 25, 1950; Eisenhower to Gurley, Feb. 3, 1950; Eisenhower to H. D. Collier, May 18, 1950; and Eisenhower to Robert G. Sproul, June 13, 1950, all in EM). By the end of May, however, Eisenhower had changed his mind and was making plans with Gurley for a trip by train and automobile to Bohemian Grove, near San Francisco, California. He would be the guest of H. D. Collier (for background on Collier's invitation see no. 804).
[2] Rose Wood was Mrs. Eisenhower's personal maid.
[3] Among those whom Eisenhower would see on Friday, July 14, were General Mark Clark, Dean Philip Young and Luther Lee, William E. Robinson, and, according to an entry in Eisenhower's appointment calendar, a "Mr. 'D' of Penna." This was Republican Governor James H. Duff of Pennsylvania. Eisenhower also saw Professor Edward M. Earle, Dean John A. Krout, and former congresswoman Clare Booth Luce.
[4] Charles R. Blyth (B.S. Amherst 1905), a banker from San Francisco and a member of the Bohemian Club, was president of the investment banking house of Blyth and Company. In a letter of June 27 Blyth had invited the Eisenhowers

to his home in Burlingame, California, for an informal buffet luncheon and swimming party. Blyth's invitation and Eisenhower's declination of July 1 are both in EM.

[5] Mrs. Bernard W. Ford had apparently invited Mrs. Eisenhower and her traveling companions, Mrs. James C. Black and Mrs. Fred G. Gurley, to lunch at a camp located in the area of the California redwoods. Her invitation to Mrs. Eisenhower is not in EM, but the General told Blyth that Mrs. Eisenhower was "accepting in today's mail" (July 1, 1950, EM).

[6] For the continuing arrangements with Gurley regarding the trip to the West see no. 884.

[7] Mrs. Gurley.

874   *Eisenhower Mss.*

TO WILLIAM STUART SYMINGTON   *July 3, 1950*

Dear Stuart:[1] The day after I saw you I ran down to Walter Reed for a complete examination and found that I had probably been doing some useless worrying about my knee. While the pains were very real and very upsetting when they occurred at the top of a backswing, the experts pointed out that they were in no sense a prophecy that I was going to suffer a new dislocation. Consequently, they gave me some exercises and a new type of bandage.[2] Since seeing you I have played golf twice, with no bad results. In fact, in my most recent game I made two astonishing birdies which, considering the odds at which they put me in the birdie game, netted me $108.00. I practically wrecked the club, because no one had ever heard of such an astonishing performance. It was like beating the Irish Sweepstakes.[3]

The Korean mess does not seem to clear up very rapidly.[4] I have to come to Washington soon to testify before a Senate Committee. I think I shall run into the Pentagon to get a briefing. I am constantly questioned by friends as to the "situation." While it is true that I can always answer that I know only what I read in the papers, the questions do serve to keep my curiosity at fever pitch and I should like to satisfy it.[5]

With best regards, *Cordially*

[1] Symington was chairman of the National Security Resources Board. He and Eisenhower had played golf at Deepdale Club in Great Neck, New York, on June 27.

[2] On Eisenhower's Washington, D.C., trip (June 28, 1950), which had included a visit to Walter Reed Army Medical Center, see no. 870. In a note of June 29 (EM) the General had confided his worries about his knee to another golfing companion, Clinton R. "Cupe" Black, chairman of the board of the C. R. Black Corporation, insurance brokers in New York City: "If I faithfully exercise my leg with a machine they gave me," the General had remarked, "the doctors say that I may continue to try to play. I suppose I should underline that word 'try.' " For developments see no. 891.

[3] Eisenhower's appointment calendar indicates that he had played golf only once between June 28 and July 3.

[4] On July 4, Eisenhower would describe the situation in an address before forty-seven thousand Boy Scouts at their second national jamboree at Valley Forge, Pennsylvania. The *New York Times* would summarize the speech in its issue of July 5, 1950. The following is from the transcript in EM, Subject File, Speeches:

> At the moment, a friendly Republic suffers outrageous invasion. The South Koreans' only crime has been the desire to live their own lives as they choose, at peace with the rest of the world. The American decision to assist them was inescapable. The alternative would be another kind of Munich, with all the disastrous consequences that followed in the wake of that fatal error 12 years ago. Now, our decision must be carried to its conclusion by whatever means are necessary. In firmness for decency and readiness for any eventuality lies the only possible route to the peace and friendliness with all the world we so earnestly seek. The end is difficult to see. But, for us in Valley Forge, where every field and hill and stream reminds us of George Washington, how can we doubt eventual success, if we meet these issues firmly?

[5] Eisenhower would travel to Washington, D.C., on July 5 (see no. 886).

875   *Eisenhower Mss.*

To WILLARD VINTON KING   *July 3, 1950*

Dear Mr. King:[1] Thank you very much for your note of June twenty-seventh. The address on it brings me the welcome news that you are now enjoying the wonderful climate of Colorado.[2]

I have already arranged for Louis Hacker to have some additional office and consulting space this coming year, which is his great need.[3] In fact, I told a few assistants around here that if they did not secure better accommodations for Louis Hacker I was going to turn over my own office to him, because I knew I could personally run someone else out of his accommodations. This more or less bombastic threat seemed to produce the necessary action and it is reported to me that Louis is very happy indeed with the arrangements that have been made for his next year's program.[4]

It is always nice to hear from you. With best regards, *Cordially*

[1] King (A.B. Columbia 1889), a retired banker, was a member of the Columbia board of trustees.

[2] King, who lived in Convent, New Jersey, had written from Colorado Springs. Copies of his letter are in EM and CUF.

[3] Louis M. Hacker, Director of the School of General Studies, had submitted a report in June delineating the school's needs; Eisenhower had had copies of the report and his reply sent to the university trustees (for background see no. 835). King had commented that the income from the school was amazing. He cautioned,

however, that "we Americans do have our waves of fashion, and this wave of fashion for getting education may wane, so it might not be wise to rush too fast into construction." He said he was writing "with due hesitation."

[4] For further developments see papers in EM, Hacker Corr.; see also Curtis to Eisenhower, October 19, 1950, and Eisenhower to Curtis, October 30, 1950, in EM.

876   *Eisenhower Mss.*

TO HASTINGS LIONEL ISMAY   *July 5, 1950*

Dear Pug:[1] Tentatively I am planning to come over in the early part of June to participate in a French ceremony on D-Day, June sixth. This particular part of my program has not been fixed and it may possibly be omitted.[2] In any event, I am counting on being in Scotland by June 21st, when I have a tentative engagement in Glasgow.[3] I will spend the next ten days or so in Culzean and, of course, Mamie and I would be delighted if you and your good Lady could come up during that time.[4] Since it isn't shooting time, I suppose that there is some salmon fishing on the river. In any event I think that you and I could spend a couple days reminiscing. If we couldn't we are the most extraordinary old soldiers I ever heard of. If, of course, I go to France in early June, I shall probably stay at Culzean longer than the ten days. I have no intention of travelling about Europe, and while Mamie and I might want to go to Norway and Sweden for a matter of two or three days, we certainly are not going to make any tour.[5]

On a wild guess I would say we would come down to London on the night of July 1st and remain there until July 5th at least, but after that date will come home on the first suitable liner. I have to make all my schedule on the basis of sea transport since Mamie refuses to fly in the absence of dire emergency.[6]

This gives you all that I can even guess at in the matter of my next summer's schedule. I shall be looking forward with great delight to seeing you again, and in the meantime will send you any detailed information that I may obtain.[7]

With warmest regards, *As ever*

[1] For background on General Ismay see no. 259. Eisenhower had sent birthday greetings to his old wartime colleague and in the postscript had said, "In 1951, I hope to greet you personally on your birthday" (June 19, 1950, EM). On June 27 Ismay had thanked Eisenhower for the birthday wishes and asked for specific dates of the visit so that he would not "get too full up with public engagements." Ismay was honorary and advisory chairman for the Council for the Festival of Britain, which was scheduled to begin in May 1951. He said that he would keep

all his news until they met next year. "You wouldn't believe," he said, "how much I look forward to it." All correspondence is in EM.

[2] On June 6, 1951, Eisenhower, who had become commander of the North Atlantic Treaty forces, would participate in a D-day commemoration ceremony in Sainte-Mère-Église, in northwest France. The small village had been the first to be liberated by Allied forces after the Normandy invasion. On the same day Eisenhower would visit the Allied landing site at Omaha Beach; the U.S. cemetery at Saint-Laurent; and the British cemetery at Bayreux (see *New York Times*, June 7 and 10, 1951).

[3] This engagement would be canceled (see no. 706).

[4] Culzean is the castle in Ayrshire, Scotland, in which there was an apartment reserved exclusively for Eisenhower during his lifetime—a gift to the General from the Scottish people after World War II (see no. 14; and Chandler and Galambos, *Occupation, 1945*, no. 444).

[5] None of these plans would materialize. In April 1951 Ismay would travel to Paris to visit Eisenhower, who would then be commanding the NATO forces (see Bowers to Ismay, Apr. 17, 1951, and Ismay to Eisenhower, Apr. 18, 1951 both in EM).

[6] As it turned out, Eisenhower and Ismay would meet in London on July 4, 1951 (Eisenhower to Ismay, July 7, 1951, EM).

[7] For developments see no. 959.

877   *Columbia University Files*

TO FRED FARREL FLORENCE   *July 6, 1950*

Dear Mr. Florence:[1] Your encouraging letter started my day off exactly right. I am deeply indebted to Mr. Burnham for presenting to your attention our developing plans here at Columbia.[2] I truly believe that we shall succeed in subjecting the great and crucial questions of today to objective and enlightened study and analysis. We should arrive at conclusions based upon fact and logic rather than prejudice and vote seeking. Moreover, by using the conference or round-table method of study, results will reflect not only the intellectual contemplation of the scholar but the practical experience and knowledge of the business man. Finally, the ideas developed at such conferences will not be buried away on the dusty shelves of some library, but will live in the hearts and minds of the people who attended the conferences and who will make immediate and effective use of them.

I am deeply grateful for your readiness to assist in the development of these ideas.[3]

With best wishes, *Sincerely*

[1] Florence, of Dallas, Texas, had been president of the Republic National Bank of Texas since 1929. He was a director of a number of other Texas banks, a member of the executive committees of several industrial companies, and active in civic organizations in Dallas.

[2] Florence had recently talked with William H. Burnham, who had been in Dallas on June 29 and 30 to inform a select group of Texans about the proposed conference plan to be sponsored by Columbia University (for background see no. 826; and the itinerary for Burnham's California-Texas trip, June 19–July 5, 1950, and other correspondence with Eisenhower in EM. See also no. 844).

In his letter of July 1, 1950, Florence had told Eisenhower that he was enthusiastic about arranging a "National Conference" among leaders in business, economic and social life (CUF). He had told Burnham, he said, that he wished to assist the project. "It is apparent," he said, "there would be no difficulty in arousing very great interest in such a plan throughout the Southwest, and it would be supported both in time and whatever money is essential."

[3] Burnham, in a memorandum to Eisenhower dated July 6, 1950, said that Florence and William H. Wildes (a resident of Dallas who was president of the Republic Natural Gas Company) had agreed to "arrange for sponsorship of one conference" (EM). In November 1950 Florence would contribute one thousand dollars to the American Assembly (see "The American Assembly Contributions, 1950," p. 7, EM, American Assembly Corr.).

878   *Eisenhower Mss.*

To George Shellenberger   *July 6, 1950*

Dear Mr. Shellenberger:[1] I am delighted that you had a chance to hear Mr. Burnham explain something of the plan we are developing here at Columbia University for bringing scholars, businessmen, professional men, labor officials and Government officials all together in order to discuss and analyze selected topics in the intricate, difficult, problems of today.[2] It would be too much to hope that in such discussions prejudiced presentation could be entirely eliminated.[3] However, since these presentations would be thrown into a common hopper of analysis and digestion, and since part of the conference would be made up of scholars and professors who would be presumably disinterested in their approach—seeking only the truth—there should be definite hope that logic would characterize any conclusions reached. In any event each individual present at any gathering would be exposed to the viewpoints of his contemporaries and under conditions where no immediate battle objective (such as the winning of a strike) would be involved.

The function of the university in all this process would be to provide an atmosphere of disinterested and objective research by men who have spent their lives in this kind of theoretical study and investigation. Published conclusions would be looked upon, by the public, as honest. My thought is, further, that great good would come out of this both for the people who come in from outside the university and for the academic groups here. Contact with the experience and hard-headed logic that would be brought in by successful men of affairs would be good for teachers.

I am convinced that we, today, are too much dependent upon the statements of persons of whom we have a right to suspect of self-seeking, for much of our advice and counsel in problems of the greatest moment. I want to see logic, fact, and statistics take the place of prejudice, emotion and vote seeking. Consequently, I should like to see a great university such as this take the lead in helping develop such a system of analytical study.

With many thanks for your interesting letter, *Sincerely*

[1] Shellenberger, of Los Angeles, California, was executive vice-president of the Merchants and Manufacturers Association.

[2] This is another example of William H. Burnham's efforts on behalf of Eisenhower and the proposed conference plan to be sponsored by Columbia. For background on what would soon become the American Assembly see the preceding document; and no. 826. Burnham had met Shellenberger at the California Club in Los Angeles on June 26. The occasion was a luncheon given for Burnham by Guy Witter, a senior partner of Dean Witter and Company, a large investment banking firm in the West. The purpose of the luncheon, which was attended by fifteen Californians, primarily businessmen from the Los Angeles area, was to discuss Eisenhower's ideas on the Columbia conference plan. Burnham would later write Eisenhower, "Again long discussion about why you went to Columbia, what you were trying to accomplish. Then conference plan was thrashed out. Unanimous approval of idea and execution. Think at least two conferences could be obtained from this luncheon. . . . Politics were persistently brought up" (memorandum, July 6, 1950, EM). Later, in an undated note, Burnham would recall that the luncheon was a "pleasant affair and I was greatly impressed by the sincerity of most of them in hoping you would be a candidate [for the presidency] more for the country's sake than for their own. . . ." In a letter to Robert L. Schulz, Eisenhower's aide, Burnham would explain that Shellenberger was "extremely interested" in the conference plan and that although Shellenberger's name was not "used in public," he was, nevertheless, in a position to throw a "good deal of weight around in So[uthern] California and would be a fine assist." Burnham asked Schulz to remind Eisenhower that a letter from Shellenberger would be forthcoming and to see that is was "noted properly" (n.d., EM, Burnham Corr.).

[3] In his June 27 letter (EM) Shellenberger had expressed his fear that the members of the study group would not be objective. Shellenberger cited specifically the heads of the big unions, very few of whom, he said, are "statesmanlike or objective in their analysis of and attitude toward important public problems." He hoped that the men assigned to the tasks of exploring problems could put aside their personal or group attachments. "Perhaps under your able leadership union officials selected could be induced to do this," he said, "but ordinarily—and I do not mean to be critical or unfair—" the union leader's job is one of "demanding, attacking, tearing down or creating division rather than one of cooperation, upbuilding and general assistance to our economic improvement." In spite of Shellenberger's concerns, Eisenhower would soon seek participation in the conference plan from organized labor (see no. 904).

To ———   *July 6, 1950*

Dear Colonel ———:[1] I was both shocked and distressed to receive the information contained in your letter to me, dated July 2nd. It is a great pity that, after all these years of service, you should approach the end of your active service with the necessity of defending yourself before a court martial.[2]

Obviously, I occupy no position of responsibility in the Services and it would be highly inappropriate for me to question the judgment, common sense or qualifications of those who are responsible for the discipline of the Army. The most, therefore, that I can possibly do in your behalf is to write one of your superiors to give him my impressions of you as an officer, through the years that I have known you. While you have not served in a direct and intimate capacity under my command, we have been sufficiently close at different periods that I have direct knowledge of your general reputation for ability and integrity. All this I shall communicate to appropriate officials; more I cannot do. Of course, I am very greatly sympathetic with a friend in trouble, but any attempt at direct intervention on my part would not only be futile, it would be completely out of order.

With my very best wishes for your vindication,[3] *Sincerely*

[1] This officer was currently serving at Letterman General Hospital, Presidio of San Francisco, California.

[2] The colonel had writen to explain to Eisenhower the "unjust way the current Army is treating one of your old friends, after his thirty two years of service without any official blemish." He said that prior to his retirement, a court-martial charge was drawn against him for which he insisted "there is no guilt on my part." The charge apparently concerned misappropriation of government property and failure to discharge financial obligations. The colonel asked Eisenhower to intervene "to prevent an unnecessary Courtsmartial [*sic*] and its consequent humiliating publicity" (July 2, 1950, EM).

[3] See the following document.

880   *Eisenhower Mss.*

To ALBERT COADY WEDEMEYER   *July 6, 1950*
Personal and confidential

Dear Al:[1] The attached letter from a Colonel . . . in your area and a copy of my reply tells a story with which you may already be familiar. They also tell everything I know about the particular incidents for which Colonel . . . now faces court martial and, also, all that I know about him.[2]

On two or three different occasions, he and I have served in the same post or station and he has always enjoyed a reputation for being an efficient officer, devoted to his family and of fine character. I have not served with him on such an intimate basis that I could give you personal judgments on these matters but, quite naturally, my sympathies are aroused, especially when he is at the end of his career and his offenses seem to be fairly well on the "petty" side. Obviously, he dreads the publicity, particularly as he has a boy in the Service.

Of course, if the evidence would indicate that a scorching reprimand would not serve the ends of justice, I would be the last to attempt to intervene, from the outside, in a matter where your own sense of duty must prevail.[3] I would be rather interested in your final action in the matter and if—when it is all over—you let me know what you decided, I will be grateful.[4]

I hope that this letter adds nothing to your daily burdens.

With warm personal regard, *Cordially*

[1] Wedemeyer had been commanding general of the Sixth Army since August 1949. For background on him see no. 8.
[2] See the preceding document.
[3] Wedemeyer replied (July 11, EM) "that careful consideration was given to every facet of his case before charges were drawn. . . . I would have preferred to give him a sharp admonition in the premises, but objective analysis of the allegations and evidence indicate clearly that the man has been lacking in integrity as well as negligence in the performance of his duties." Wedemeyer added that the latter could be handled appropriately by an admonition, but the former, involving "moral turpitude," must be adjudicated by a court-martial.
[4] For developments see no. 920.

881   *Eisenhower Mss.*

To Aksel Nielsen   *July 6, 1950*

Dear Aksel: Your letter had good news about the calf. I am trying to figure out a name for him and I think we should call him "Dandy Domino." In that way we have my initials and we keep also the name of his strain. (I assume he is a Domino calf.)[1] In any event, I am most certainly looking forward to meeting him, come August 1.[2]

I am delighted you told me about the information you received on the Wyoming fishing, starting August 11. My feeling is "To Heck With It." While I have an idea who they are talking about, I am not interested in going on any fishing party where there are VIPs more important than the rainbows. So far as I am concerned, there ain't no such animal when I am on a Rocky Mountain stream.[3]

Love to all the family and, as always, my very best to yourself.
Cordially

P.S. Please tell your secretary to keep track of all the hooks I order so that I can make proper refund to your petty cash fund when I come. Will you have her call Wright and McGill to see whether they make a No. 18 hook? While I asked you to get me a hundred of the 18's when I wrote you before, two boxes of 16's came. I assume this is because they make no 18's—but it may have been accidental. Thanks for all your trouble.[4]

[1] On July 3 Nielsen had written that Miss Byers White Aster, Horn Brand 80, had produced a bull calf that would now belong to Eisenhower (EM). Twice before, Nielsen had tried to give a bull to the General, but the young animals had developed problems and had been sent to the stockyards (see no. 77; and Galambos, *Chief of Staff*, no. 1158). Nielsen would reply on July 10 (EM) that the name Dandy Domino was already in use; they would finally settle on the name Denison Domino (Nielsen to Eisenhower, Sept. 21, 1950, EM; see also no. 1047).
[2] For Eisenhower's annual vacation trip to Denver see no. 917.
[3] The VIP in this case was the General himself. Nielsen had learned of the elaborate plans to guard a "very important individual" during the week of August 11, when he would be on a fishing trip in Wyoming. According to Nielsen's information, the entire stream and the approach to the property would be guarded by Army personnel and the FBI. Nielsen had then discovered that the party to be protected was Eisenhower, whom Nielsen thought "wouldn't want that kind of fanfare."
[4] Wright & McGill Company, in Denver, Colorado, manufactured and wholesaled fishing tackle. On July 10 (EM) Nielsen informed Robert L. Schulz, Eisenhower's aide, that no. 18 fish hooks were out of manufacture (see also Schulz to Nielsen, July 14, 1950, EM).

882   *Eisenhower Mss.*

To Fred D. Fletcher   *July 6, 1950*

Dear Mr. Fletcher:[1] Thank you very much for telling me about your experience at Bremerton Navy Yard. I have sent that information to General Bradley who is Chairman of our Joint Chiefs of Staff. Consequently, your warning should come to the attention of all the Services and not solely to the Naval Department.[2]

Needless to say, I am greatly appreciative of your interest and I thank you for taking the trouble to write me about your findings and your conclusions.[3] Naturally, I am complimented by the overgenerous personal references that your letter contains, but I do agree with your proposition that all of us had better be thinking very seriously about the great problems of today and the directions we are going in seeking solutions.[4] Moreover, I enthusiastically agree with the observations you made concerning my very fine friend, Bernard Baruch.[5]

With best wishes, *Sincerely*

[1] Fletcher was an attorney from Klamath Falls, Oregon.

[2] Fletcher had written Eisenhower on June 27, 1950, to explain that the security regulations regarding visitors to the Puget Sound Naval Shipyard at Bremerton, Washington, were inadequate. An excerpt from his letter was forwarded to General Omar N. Bradley on July 6, 1950 (EM). For background on Bradley, who would be promoted to General of the Army in September 1950, see no. 517.

[3] On July 13, 1950, Admiral Forrest P. Sherman, Chief of Naval Operations, would reassure Fletcher that "as a result of rather extensive experience, it has been found advisable in peacetime to permit visitors to enter naval shipyards under competent escort. Under such conditions visitors do not obtain information which could not otherwise be obtained quickly by unfriendly agents without such a visit." Sherman pointed out, however, that since the date of Fletcher's letter "the general situation [i.e., the Korean War] has caused a considerable increase in security measures and the termination of casual visiting on board ships and naval stations" (EM). For more information concerning efforts to safeguard U.S. military installations see *New York Times*, June 30 and August 6, 1950.

[4] Fletcher had expressed his belief that the United States needed as its president a man "who has given his life to the science of making war." Eisenhower, he said, would be elected if war threatened.

[5] Fletcher had remarked that the United States owed "a real debt of gratitude" to Baruch. For background on Baruch see nos. 555 and 753; for developments see no. 914.

883   *Eisenhower Mss.*

To John Davison Rockefeller, Jr.   *July 6, 1950*

Dear Mr. Rockefeller:[1] Picking up your suggestion for conducting a complete examination of Columbia University's purposes and objectives as well as its existing facilities and requirements, I have taken action that I thought you might have a bit of interest in hearing about.[2]

After long study, we decided to conduct the investigation in two stages. The first one is self-examination carried out under a small group of my ablest, younger assistants.[3] This examination is to be completed early in the coming academic year. The purpose of this particular examination, other than to give us an immediate basis for correction and improvement, is to provide to outside investigators a program on which to start. We have felt the University so large, some of its functions necessarily so overlapping and some of its purposes and plans so hidden or lost in old records that any investigating body called in from the outside would require many months in order to establish a line of departure for themselves. This is what we are now doing—later we shall get in the cold-blooded experts to tell us where we might be wrong.[4]

I trust you have a most enjoyable and restful summer.[5]

With personal regard, *Cordially*

[1] In April Eisenhower had attended a luncheon for Rockefeller given by the Chamber of Commerce of the State of New York. At that time the two men apparently had discussed plans for increasing financial contributions to Columbia University (see no. 774).

[2] Eisenhower had appointed a President's Committee on the State of the University to conduct a systematic evaluation of the institution's aims, organization, and functions (for background on the initiation of this committee see no. 825). Eisenhower and Rockefeller had previously discussed the possibility of retaining eighty-three-year-old Abraham Flexner to conduct such an analysis of the university, but that particular manner of implementing the study had been rejected. For background on Flexner, whose connections with the senior John D. Rockefeller and the Rockefeller Foundation dated back to 1917, see no. 720.

[3] John A. Krout, who would be appointed associate provost of Columbia University later in the month, had been selected to head a small steering group which would assist him in the initial stages of the investigation. For background on him and the other members of Columbia's academic divisions who were invited to participate in the work of this committee see no. 825.

[4] There is no further evidence in EM concerning the work of the examination committee. In 1957, however, the trustees of Columbia University would publish the report of an inquiry into the functions of the university. See *Columbia University, Educational Future*, for a comprehensive survey of the institution's postwar growth and educational objectives.

[5] Rockefeller planned to spend the remaining summer months with his family in Seal Habor, Maine.

884   *Eisenhower Mss.*

To Fred G. Gurley   *July 6, 1950*

Dear Fred:[01] I believe I have not written to you since receipt of your most recent letter to me. In any event, Mamie and I heartily approve of the idea of stopping at the Grand Canyon and of making the trip you suggest through the Yosemite. We shall arrive in Chicago in the morning of the fifteenth, ready to go on the "Grand Canyon" as you suggested. Incidentally, if you consider it smoother and better riding to put the car in front, that is O.K. with us.[2]

As to plans after we come back to San Francisco from the Grove, we have talked very little. I do not even know whether you intend to come on east with us as far as Denver or whether you expect to stay around in California for a while. Naturally we want to remain with you as long as possible, but we are equally anxious that our presence must not create any burden upon you in the nature of inducing you to give up any part of your own vacational plans. My own thought on all this has been that we could well afford to wait until we meet on the fifteenth and, between there and San Francisco, we can certainly arrive at our "post-Bohemian Grove program." As of now, we have no real ideas except that we do want to be back to Denver no later than on or about August 1st.[3]

I just heard that possibly Jerry Brandon might be on the same train. Wouldn't that be something?[4]

I believe that I have told you I have tentatively accepted a luncheon for us with Mr. Petersen. I think there is still some question whether it is to be the 24th or 25th, depending on the time we get back to San Francisco from the Grove.[5]

I don't think of anything else at this minute except to tell you that Mamie and I are getting most terribly excited about the beginning of the expedition, at noon on the fifteenth.

Our very best to you both. *Cordially*

[1] Gurley, president of the Atchison, Topeka and Santa Fe Railway System, would accompany the Eisenhowers on an excursion through several western states in July.

[2] The Eisenhowers would leave New York City on July 14; on the following day they would stop in Chicago, where they would join the Gurleys and several other friends aboard a special train. They would then turn southward to Kansas City, Missouri, for a short visit with Arthur B. and Louise Sondra Grieb Eisenhower. The group would arrive at Grand Canyon National Park in Arizona on the sixteenth, and the couples would take part in a guided tour of the Grand Canyon on the seventeenth. They would visit Yosemite National Park, California, on the eighteenth, before moving on to Oakland, California, the next day. General Eisenhower would enter the Bohemian Grove encampment near San Francisco, California, on the twentieth. For background see no. 873.

[3] The Eisenhowers would arrive in Denver, Colorado, on July 28 and would remain in Colorado until September 17 (see no. 805).

[4] Jerry D. Brandon was president of Brandon Equipment Company, a newly organized railway supply firm in Chicago (for background see Galambos, *Chief of Staff*). Gurley would advise Eisenhower in a letter of July 7 that Brandon had recently been elected to membership in the Bohemian Club and that he would accompany the Eisenhower party on the trip from Chicago to San Francisco. On July 10 Gurley would write to Eisenhower again, this time about plans for luncheons and dinners in the General's honor at Bohemian Grove on July 21 and 22. Both letters from Gurley, together with Eisenhower's telegram of July 12 approving the arrangements, are in EM.

[5] On the luncheon with Theodore S. Petersen, president of Standard Oil Company of California, see no. 868.

To John Merrill Olin

Dear Mr. Olin:[1] This morning Bob Woodruff brought out to me quite the handsomest gun I have ever seen.[2] He tells me that you are largely responsible for its unusual and distinctive features. If there is any detail that you overlooked to make it perfect I have been unable to discover what that particular item could possibly be.[3]

My deep gratitude comes to you for the personal part you took in building such a gun—I shall be proud of it in public and gloat over it in secret.

With best wishes, *Sincerely*

[1] Olin was president of Olin Industries, Inc., manufacturers of ammunition and firearms in East Alton, Illinois. He had been assistant to the president of the Western Cartridge Company from 1914 to 1918 and vice-president and director from 1919 to 1944. He became head of Olin Industries in 1944, when the Western Cartridge Company, the Winchester Repeating Arms Company, the Olin Corporation, and other firms were consolidated.

[2] According to his appointment calendar, Eisenhower had met with Robert Winship Woodruff at 8:30 A.M. on July 6, 1950, for breakfast at 60 Morningside Drive. At that time Woodruff had presented the General with a Model 21 Winchester double-barrel shotgun which apparently was intended to be used for turkey shooting. For background on Woodruff see no. 258.

[3] On July 21 Olin would tell Eisenhower that he had "derived great pleasure" in working out the details of the shotgun. He wrote, "Inasmuch as I killed my first wild turkey at Bob's plantation, I can appreciate your enthusiasm. I am satisfied that once the turkey shooting germ bites, it causes a life long inoculation" (EM). For the General's own description of his introduction to turkey shooting at Woodruff's Ichauway Plantation in Newton, Georgia, see no. 690; see also no. 582 concerning Eisenhower's interest in hunting.

Diary

Yesterday I was in Washington. Went before a Senate Sub-Committee in the morning; lunch with the President; visit with Averill Harriman, and, later with Mr. Finletter, Mr. McCone, Gen. Norstad and *Averill*, Saw Louis Johnson for a moment.[1]

1. The Sub-Committee hearing was on American propaganda. Our people *assume* that the world knows something about us;—our system of govt; our international policies; our economic system, etc. Actually we know very little about others, but they know far less about us, and

it is essential in the world struggle that the world know something about our

> good intentions.
> latent strength.
> respect for rights of others.

Since our opponent has to depend on lies, and we can tell the truth the advantage would seem to be all with us. But the truth must be nailed, banner-like, to a staff—and we must do that by convincing the whole world that our announced intentions of peace *are* the truth.

2. *Lunch:* Both Geo. Marshall and I told the Pres. that his decision of a week ago must be *earnestly* supported. Speed & strength; both are needed. We encountered good intentions but I'm not so sure that we met full comprehension.[2]

Later, in talking to others named above (except Johnson) was encouraged to believe that he, the Pres. would be getting the same advice from his other advisers as he did from G.C.M. and me.

Johnson complacently said, "I've given MacArthur all he asked for;"—and I had the impression that mere saying "approved" meant, to the Sec. that all was well. As [to] inquiries as to the time element— he said "Pretty good." God, how I *hope*!

But there seems no disposition to begin serious mobilizing! I *think* that it is possible that military advisers are too complacent when talking to H.S.T.[3]

---

[1] Eisenhower had traveled by plane from New York to Washington, D.C., on the morning of July 5 to testify on the subject of an expanded international information and education program (his testimony is in U.S., Congress, Senate, Subcommittee of the Committee on Foreign Relations, *Expanded International Information and Education Program: Hearings on S. Res. 243*, 81st Cong., 2d sess., 1950, pp. 26–36). The General had visited the office of W. Averell Harriman, President Truman's Special Assistant on Foreign Affairs, after appearing before the committee and before going to Blair House for lunch with the President. Also present at the luncheon were General of the Army George C. Marshall, president of the American Red Cross; General Omar N. Bradley, chairman of the JCS; and Admiral Forrest P. Sherman, CNO (see President's Appointment Books, Harry S. Truman Library, and *Denver Post*, July 12, 1950). One of Eisenhower's appointment calendars for this day indicates that his next stop was the Pentagon, where he met with General Hoyt S. Vandenberg, Chief of Staff of the Air Force; Lieutenant General Lauris Norstad, Deputy Chief of Staff for Operations and Acting Vice Chief of Staff, U.S. Air Force; Secretary of the Air Force Thomas K. Finletter, and Under Secretary of the Air Force John Alex McCone. Eisenhower then telephoned W. Stuart Symington, chairman of the National Security Resources Board, and visited Secretary of Defense Louis A. Johnson before leaving the Pentagon for his return flight to New York that evening.

[2] On June 26 Truman had decided to order U.S. naval and air forces in the Far East to support South Korea in its efforts to repel the invading North Koreans. Four days later Truman had ordered American troops to intervene directly on the side of the South Koreans (for background see nos. 865 and 870). Eisenhower

would recall his comments at the July 5 luncheon in *Mandate for Change*, pp. 82–83.

[3] For further developments see no. 920.

887   *Eisenhower Mss.*

To Harry DeWard Collier   *July 10, 1950*

Dear Mr. Collier:[1] In reference to your letter of July 5th, I have accepted the invitation of Mr. Petersen for luncheon either on the 24th or 25th. He was to determine the exact date after conference with you.[2] I rather hoped to stay at Bohemian Grove through Sunday, the 23rd, so that he would have three full days to meet as many members and guests as possible. Consequently, I recently wrote to Mr. Blyth saying that I would not be back in San Francisco on the 23rd.[3]

Incidentally, I should be greatly pleased if Major General Kenyon Joyce, now living at 1000 Mason Street in San Francisco, could be invited either to your luncheon or Mr. Petersen's. He is a very old and dear friend of mine.[4]

As to golf, later, at Pebble Beach, I will be ready to do whatever the other members of my party should like. My first and primary purpose is to accept your wonderful invitation to the Bohemian Grove and to have a day or two with you and Mr. Petersen and other friends. I believe that, if we should plan a golf expedition, we can do it after we get there.[5]

With warm personal regard, *Cordially*

P.S. I *think* I'd prefer the 25th over the 24th for the Petersen lunch — but I'll be guided by your, and his, decisions.[6]

[1] For background on Collier, chairman of the finance committee of Standard Oil Company of California, see no. 769.

[2] Theodore S. Petersen, president of Standard Oil Company of California, had invited Eisenhower to a luncheon in San Francisco, California (see no. 868).

[3] Eisenhower would be Collier's guest at Bohemian Grove from July 20 to July 24, 1950. He had recently declined an invitation from Charles R. Blyth, president of Blyth and Company of San Francisco, to visit his home on July 23. For background see no. 873.

[4] Joyce had invited Eisenhower to Bohemian Grove in April 1950, but Eisenhower had declined at that time (see no. 769).

[5] Eisenhower would not be able to play golf at Pebble Beach, south of San Francisco (see Edgar S. Lewis to Eisenhower, July 27, 1950, EM).

[6] According to Eisenhower's appointment calendar, the luncheon would take place on July 25.

To Leonard Townsend Gerow   *July 10, 1950*

Dear Gee:[1] Just a few minutes ago Mamie and I received a very shocking invitation—it was to attend a party incident to your retirement from active service.[2] While—with no more evidence than that of my own date of birth—I realize that the calendar has made this irrevocable decision, I still cannot think of the United States Army without you as one of its active members.[3] One thing is certain, from the day I met you, on or about September 10, 1915, until this day, there has not been a single moment that I have not been proud of our friendship and of my association with you and when I have not considered you an outstanding example of what the regular army officer of the United States should be.[4]

I do not know where you and Mary Louise intend to live after retiring, but I most earnestly hope that the circumstances of our future lives will be such that I may be privileged often to see you.[5]

Additionally, I realize, as I go back over the years in my memories, that I owe to you a great debt for friendly guidance and help—a debt that I have never even thought of repaying because I know that you gave these things to me gladly and with the hope of making me a better member of our Army. Possibly hundreds of other officers will be thinking the same thing, as you leave the active list.[6]

In any event, my very best wishes come with my lasting admiration and my deep affection.

Good luck! *As ever*

[1] Lieutenant General Gerow had been in command of the Second Army, Fort George G. Meade, Maryland, since January 15, 1948. He had been commandant of the Command and General Staff School in Fort Leavenworth, Kansas, from 1945 to 1948. On his service during and before World War II see *Eisenhower Papers*, vols. I–IX.

[2] Eisenhower declined the invitation to Gerow's retirement party in another letter on the same day. He explained to Gerow that since he would be vacationing in the West and could not attend the celebration scheduled for July 31, "I feel impelled to write you a bit of a note. . . . It does not even come close to expressing my feelings but it will give you some faint inkling of my deep sense of obligation and affection" (EM).

[3] Gerow, who was two years older than Eisenhower, would retire after thirty-nine years of service on July 31, 1950. He would be honored in ceremonies on that day at Fort Meade, Maryland (see *New York Times*, Aug. 1, 1950).

[4] Eisenhower had known Gerow since their days together as lieutenants with the 19th Infantry at Fort Sam Houston, Texas. The two men had been classmates at the Command and General Staff School in Fort Leavenworth, Kansas, in 1925 and neighbors when Eisenhower attended the Army War College in Washington, D.C. (Alden Hatch, *Red Carpet for Mamie* [New York, 1954], pp. 69, 142, 145, and 147; for Eisenhower's reminiscences concerning Gerow see Eisenhower, *At Ease*, pp. 202–3, 238–39).

⁵ Gerow would reply on July 13 (EM) that he and his wife planned to move to Virginia or Florida but that "after being told where to live for thirty-nine years it is difficult to make a decision now when we are free to do so." The Gerows would eventually settle in Cocoa, Florida.

⁶ Gerow thanked Eisenhower for "the finest tribute I have ever received. It is all the more appreciated because of the depth and sincerity of your friendship, and I know you meant exactly what you said." In 1951 Gerow would return briefly to active service as head of an investigative panel concerned with the reduction of overseas forces. His name would later be included in legislation authorizing the promotion of eleven Army officers with the grade of lieutenant general in World War II to the rank of full general (see no. 819).

889   *Eisenhower Mss.*

To Herbert Henry Lehman   *July 10, 1950*

Dear Senator Lehman:[1] Sometime ago I learned about a young man who is applying to you for an appointment to Annapolis. He is the son of an engraver at Gorham's. The family asked me to support the boy's application for an appointment, but this I declined to do until I could have a chance of meeting the young man to discuss with him his past record and future ambitions. The young man's name and address are:

> Mr. Elliott Rennhack[2]
> 57 Haig Road
> Valley Stream, N.Y.

This morning he came to my office; he is presently a student at Purdue University, pursuing there a course in metallurgical engineering. From his statements, it appears that he has done fairly well in his academic courses, except in the subject of surveying. He is a well-built, healthy individual and has obviously participated in many extra-curricular activities, especially athletics.

While I cannot, of course, present to you the kind of analysis that would be possible if I had known the young man for a number of years, I am of the opinion that he is a clean-cut, decent young American who has the ambition of becoming a Naval officer. I am writing a similar letter to Senator Ives because I did not ask the young man the political affiliations of his family, and I have no idea whether this factor is of particular importance in this kind of situation.[3]

I apologize for intruding upon your time but I assure you that I am merely trying to be helpful to an American family that strikes me as being earnest and hard-working.

Acknowledgment of this letter is, of course, not necessary. I have no other request than that, in handling the case, you give it such personal attention as you may find feasible.[4]

With best wishes and personal regard, *Sincerely*

[1] Lehman (B.A. Williams College 1899) had been a Democratic senator from New York since January 3, 1950. For background on Eisenhower's association with him in 1945 see Chandler and Galambos, *Occupation, 1945*, no. 478.

[2] For background see no. 830.

[3] Eisenhower's letter of this same date to Senator Irving M. Ives is in EM. Ives, a Republican, would reply (July 19, EM) that he had no vacancies among his appointments to the Naval Academy. He would mention incidentally that Eisenhower had been his instructor while he was in training with a provisional officers battalion at Fort Leavenworth, Kansas, between November 1917 and February 1918. "I have not been surprised at your subsequent outstanding success in the service of your country and of the world," he would remark. "I only hope that you can be persuaded to undertake the one job which yet remains to be done and which only you can do." In a note of July 31 (EM) Eisenhower would thank Ives for "the overgenerous estimate you place upon my capabilities for service."

[4] Lehman would inform Eisenhower in a letter of July 13 (EM) that he had one opening for an appointment to the Naval Academy. The U.S. Civil Service Commission would conduct an examination of the applicants for this vacancy, and Lehman had notified Elliott Rennhack of the time and place of the testing.

890   *Eisenhower Mss.*

To Robert Wood Johnson   *July 10, 1950*

Dear Mr. Johnson:[1] Thank you for your telegram of the 6th. While I am not informed as to the specific plans of the Government in popularizing, throughout the country, the principles of freedom, I firmly believe that a committee of citizens would make a very splendid advisory council in this regard.[2]

I am certain that anybody holding official responsibility for this task would be highly delighted with your offer of service. Because Senator Benton has taken such a leading part in sponsoring the necessary Bills in Congress, it might be best to write to him about the matter.[3] I should think that he would be in a position to give you the exact information as to where your offer should be submitted.

Permit me to express my very deep appreciation of your attitude toward the responsibilities of citizenship. We need this attitude in these days of crisis.[4]

With best wishes and personal regard, *Cordially*

[1] Johnson was chairman of the board of Johnson & Johnson, surgical dressing manufacturers. For further background see no. 782.

[2] In his telegram (EM) Johnson had said that he had been greatly impressed by the General's recent statement "concerning the need of propaganda for freedom." Eisenhower had testified on July 5 before a Senate subcommittee on the subject of an expanded international information program by the United States (on his

testimony see no. 886). Johnson strongly endorsed Eisenhower's suggestion that such a program be under the guidance of a board of "eminent citizens serving without pay. . . ." He offered his help, and concluded, "We must sell ourselves to the world. If there is one thing that our private citizens known how to do, it is to sell" (EM. See also Senate Subcomittee of the Committee on Foreign Relations, *Expanded International Information and Education Program*, 1950, pp. 26–36; and *New York Times*, July 6 and 7, 1950).

[3] In March 1950 Senator William Benton had introduced in the Senate a resolution calling for a "Marshall Plan for Ideas" in the cause of world freedom of information. For background on Benton, who had recently been appointed to the Senate from Connecticut, see no. 283. Copies of Benton's remarks, titled "The Struggle for the Minds and Loyalties of Mankind," and editorial comments on those remarks are in EM, Benton Corr. A copy of Senate Resolution 243, March 22, 1950, is included as well. See also *New York Times*, March 23, 1950.

[4] Eisenhower is referring to the Korean War (see nos. 865, n. 4, and 886).

891   *Eisenhower Mss.*

To Joseph Patterson Binns   *July 10, 1950*

Dear Joe:[1] Thank you for your note. A day after I saw you I went to Washington and had a thorough examination of my knee. The doctor gave me great encouragement and told me to continue at golf. On top of this, he gave me a series of exercises that I have been performing and they seem to be helpful.[2] In any event, when I get back from my summer's vacation, I will get hold of you for another whack at Deep Dale. *Cordially*

[1] Binns was executive vice-president and general manager of the Waldorf-Astoria Hotel in New York City (for further background see no. 704). Eisenhower, Binns, and W. Stuart Symington had played golf at the Deepdale Club, Great Neck, New York, on June 27.

[2] In a note dated July 7 Binns had thanked Eisenhower for the invitation to play golf; he regretted very much, he said, that the General had injured his knee on that day (EM). For background on the injury and treatment for it see no. 874.

892   *Eisenhower Mss.*

To Bernard Edwin Hutchinson   *July 10, 1950*

Dear Mr. Hutchinson:[1] Events, plus the approaching date of my departure from New York City, have combined to push out of my calendar any immediate chance of taking up your offer of June 3.[2] I had been saving this coming Thursday afternoon and was about to wire you when a request came from my old chief, Secretary Stimson, to come to see him that afternoon, to consider with him a problem that is troubling him. Because of my great respect and affection for a man who has grown very, very old in his country's service, I feel that I simply must go.[3]

All this means that, unless I am fortunate enough to run into you around California or Colorado this summer, I must forgo the pleasure of having a long conversation with you until the early fall.[4] I do hope you will keep the possibilities in mind.[5] *Sincerely*

[1] Hutchinson was vice-president, a director, and chairman of the finance committee of Chrysler Corporation. For background see no. 127.

[2] Eisenhower probably meant June *30*. Hutchinson had mentioned in his letter of that date (EM) that he was only two hours away from New York City by airplane and that he would be glad to visit Eisenhower on short notice. On Hutchinson's earlier attempts to meet with Eisenhower see no. 840.

[3] Henry L. Stimson had been Secretary of War from 1940 to 1945 (for background see no. 747). A note at the bottom of Eisenhower's appointment calendar for July 6, 1950, indicates that they had agreed during a telephone conversation that day to discuss on July 13 a letter that Stimson had received from John J. McCloy, High Commissioner for Germany (for background on McCloy see no. 232). Eisenhower would visit Stimson on Thursday, July 13, at Cold Spring Harbor, New York. This was probably the last time Eisenhower saw Stimson before the latter's death on October 20, 1950, at the age of eighty-three.

[4] Concerning the Eisenhowers' vacation in California and Colorado see nos. 884, 887, and 900.

[5] Hutchinson would reply on July 12 (EM) that he usually vacationed in New England and that he would probably not meet with Eisenhower before autumn.

893

Eisenhower Mss.

To Harry Amos Bullis

July 11, 1950

Dear Harry:[1] It was as thoughtful of you to write me a note as it was generous of you to give such a nice dinner last Friday evening.[2] I never enjoyed an evening more. You were a perfect host and had collected together a company of men of whom each had something of interest to add to the conversations. I have tried to write each a personal note— hope I've missed none.[3]

Your nice note encourages me to believe that I did not bore the assembly with my convictions and enthusiasms—I'm so devoted to this country, and want so much to do something about it, that I fear I grow garrulous.[4]

With best wishes and warm regard, *Cordially*

[1] Bullis (A.B. University of Wisconsin 1917), of Minneapolis, Minnesota, was chairman of the board of General Mills. He had met Eisenhower in January 1950

at a New York dinner given in the General's honor by William H. Burnham and Arthur B. Lawrence. For background on the affair see no. 663. A typewritten copy of Eisenhower's longhand letter to Bullis is in EM.

[2] On July 7 Bullis had given an informal dinner at the Minneapolis Club for representatives of leading industries in the area. Eisenhower, the guest of honor, had discussed the role of education in the nation's affairs, giving special emphasis to the proposed Columbia conference plan (see no. 844). In his handwritten note of July 9 Bullis had congratulated Eisenhower on his successful visit in Minneapolis. "You have the common touch . . . and you have a strong spiritual background," Bullis wrote. "Those qualities make you 'unusual' in a world of 'usual' men" (EM).

Bullis had arranged for Eisenhower to travel from New York City to Minneapolis on the General Mills DC−3 executive plane on the day of the dinner. He had returned to New York in the same manner on Saturday morning, July 8, having stayed overnight at the Radisson Hotel. For more information see Bullis to Eisenhower, June 13, 1950; Eisenhower to Bullis, June 15, 1950; Bullis to Schulz, June 16, 1950; letter of invitation, June 19, 1950; and invitation list, July 7, 1950, all in EM, Bullis Corr.

[3] The General's trip to Minneapolis generated a substantial correspondence. Eisenhower sent brief notes, most of which were drafted by Kevin McCann and dated July 11, to a majority of the dinner guests (see Eisenhower to the following: Julian B. Baird, Walter R. Berry, John Cowles, John Crosby, Charles H. Denny, Rudolph Elstad, Daniel C. Gainey, Samuel C. Gale, Frank J. Gavin, Edward J. Grimes, Stanley Hawks, Frank T. Heffelfinger, John L. Hennessy, Clarence E. Hill, R. C. Jacobson, Henry S. Kingman, Frank P. Leslie, Malcolm McDonald, Bradshaw Mintener, Frank J. Morley, Leslie N. Perrin, John S. Pillsbury, C. W. Plattis, Joseph F. Ringland, Harold W. Sweatt, G. Cullen Thomas, J. Cameron Thomson, Harold O. Washburn, Luther W. Youngdahl, and Harry W. Zinsmaster. The notes to Baird and Heffelfinger are in CUF; all others are in EM). Moreover, notes of appreciation, also drafted by McCann, went to Brigadier General Walter W. Hess, Chief of the Minnesota Military District, and to Colonel L. P. Turner, commanding officer, Air Force Reserve Training Corps, both of whom were present for Eisenhower's arrival and departure at the Minneapolis−St. Paul Airport (July 13). Similar notes were sent to Minneapolis Police Chief Thomas R. Jones, who provided two body guards and two officers for police escort for Eisenhower (July 13); and to Jack M. Bates and William A. Stone, pilot and copilot, respectively, of the General Mills plane (July 10). See also no. 904, n. 4; and Eisenhower's letters to Mrs. James F. Bell (July 10) and Thomas Moore (July 11), in EM.

[4] On July 10 Bullis wrote again to the General: "Like Julius Caesar, you came, you saw, you conquered." He thanked Eisenhower for coming to Minneapolis and told him that he had "sold" his audience on the plan for conferences at Columbia among groups of businessmen, labor leaders, and academics. "You not only sold us on your Columbia project, but you made a sale of far greater potentialities— one that only you can 'close' when the proper time comes." In an allusion to Eisenhower as a presidential candidate, Bullis concluded, "When that time arrives, I hope that you will consider, not your own inclinations, but the best interests of our glorious United States of America and then 'close' the sale." On this same day (July 10) Eisenhower sent Bullis a copy of the letter which appears as no. 826 in volume XI. Bullis replied on July 13 that he would send a copy of the letter to each director and major executive of General Mills, as well as to other interested people in the upper Midwest. All correspondence is in EM.

To Eion N. Andrews   *July 11, 1950*

Dear Mr. Andrews:[1] Thank you very much for your thoughtful letter
of July 2.[2] I have read it with a great deal of interest. Such letters are
always helpful to us, especially when they contain concrete suggestions
which may enable us to make our work even more useful to our adult
students.

While our general practice has been to list all final grades either as
passing or failing, I am aware that many institutions do authorize an
instructor to give a final mark (usually called a conditional grade) which
in effect permits a student to repeat his final examination. This is usually
done in instances when a student's mark on the final examination is
far below his previous rating in the course, and thereby creates the
presumption that, for some special reason, the mark is not really representative of what the student is capable of doing.[3]

I am not sure whether the adoption of such a procedure at Columbia
would be desirable, but I will bring this suggestion to the attention of
Director Hacker when he returns to the campus.[4] I assure you that it
will be given careful consideration.

I am also interested in your suggestion that tuition fees for adults be
deductible from income tax returns. I do not know how such an idea
would be regarded in Washington, but I will have it considered by
Director Hacker and it may be that we will undertake to pass the proposal
along to the proper authorities.[5]

May I also add that I am most appreciative of your personal comments. The importance of education to the preservation of a democratic
society is so great that it justifies all our efforts.[6] *Sincerely*

[1] Andrews was an adult student in Columbia's School of General Studies.
[2] Among other issues, Andrews had written about the examination procedure at
Columbia, citing his own difficulties in obtaining permission for reexaminations
as the reason for bringing the matter to Eisenhower's attention. Andrews suggested
that in "borderline" cases grades of D or E be given rather than an F, which
eliminated the possibility of retaking an exam. He pointed out that students can
not put forth their best efforts when examinations are given at the end of "an
arduous day" or when smoking—to relieve tension—is prohibited in classrooms.
His own difficulties, he explained, had resulted from an illness and the obligations
of his full-time job (EM).
[3] Jack N. Arbolino, Assistant Director of the School of General Studies, reviewed
Andrews's letter and on July 8 drafted a reply (Arbolino to McCann, EM, Andrews
Corr.). Instead of using Arbolino's draft, however, Eisenhower finally approved
a draft by Grayson Kirk.
[4] Louis M. Hacker, Director of the School of General Studies, was in Europe at
this time. For background see no. 448.
[5] In his draft reply Arbolino said that this idea had merit but had been found "in

the light of the total economy to be undesirable." There is no correspondence in EM between Eisenhower and Hacker on this subject.

[6] In his conclusion Andrews had said, "Your entry into the field of education has undoubtedly earmarked you as our leader in our fight to preserve the peace and freedom that has been so dearly won, and to help us make sense out of a chaotic world."

---

895   *Eisenhower Mss.*

TO JESSE HOLMAN JONES   *July 11, 1950*

Dear Jesse:[1] As I told you on the phone, I am committed to attending the inauguration of my brother as President of Penn State on October 5th. This precludes my acceptance of the Texas invitation at that particular time.[2]

You are well aware of my very deep and lasting interest in Texas and you know of the great place it holds in my sentiments. Consequently, it is difficult indeed to send such a reply but there is nothing else I can do, as I am sure, you will understand.[3] My brother's inauguration date has been fixed for some months and I could not possibly be absent from that ceremony, particularly since all of my brothers made it a point to attend my own inauguration two years ago.[4]

If, of course, the dates at Texas A. and M. are not finally and completely fixed, I would reconsider this answer.[5] A hasty glance at my calendar indicates that I could possibly get down there in early November, a circumstance that would allow me to fulfill, also, a tentative promise to speak in the Panhandle, but the months of September and October are quite badly jammed on my schedule.[6]

While I would have great doubts that the University could effect this kind of a revision in its plans, yet, if it should like to do so, I suggest that the appropriate official call Mr. Kevin McCann, of my office, on the telephone at once. He will discuss the matter with them to see whether something can be worked out, because I shall personally be in California within a few days. If there is any thought of changing the plan, they should do it very promptly because, every day, my schedule grows more complicated.[7]

I regret to return such an answer to you but, under the circumstances, there is no other alternative. *Cordially*

[1] Jones was a prominent Texas businessman and newspaper publisher (for background on him see no. 113; and Galambos, *Chief of Staff*, no. 1564). According to Eisenhower's "Texas emissary," Leonard F. McCollum (for background see no. 826), Jones had recently expressed an interest in supporting Columbia's Arden House conference programs (Eisenhower to Jones, June 5, 1950, EM).

[2] Jones, who had received an honorary degree from the Agricultural and Mechanical College of Texas in 1936, had urged Eisenhower to accept an invitation to speak at Texas A & M's anniversary observance and inauguration of its twelfth president, Marion Thomas Harrington (B.S. Texas A & M 1922, M.S. 1927; Ph.D. Iowa State College 1941). Jones would remind the General, "There are good reasons why you should be seen and heard occasionally around the country" (July 15, 1950, EM).

[3] The formal invitation had come to Eisenhower from Director of Information and Publications R. Henderson Shuffler. In his letter Shuffler had recalled Eisenhower's participation in the postwar muster service for Texas A & M men who had died in World War II and the "lasting impression" the General had made on "those of us who were fortunate enough to be here at that time" (July 5, EM; see Galambos, *Chief of Staff*, no. 755). The General sent Shuffler a copy of the letter printed above (July 11, EM).

[4] Dwight, Edgar, and Earl Eisenhower would attend their brother Milton's inauguration as president of Pennsylvania State College on October 4 and 5 (see no. 790; for developments see no. 915). For background on the General's inauguration as Columbia's thirteenth president see nos. 149 and 191.

[5] See n. 7 below.

[6] Eisenhower's commitments following his return from Denver, Colorado, on September 18 would include opening exercises for the new academic year at Columbia University and Barnard College; Milton Eisenhower's Pennsylvania State College inauguration; and a succession of Columbia University Alumni Tour visits to Chicago; St. Louis; Indianapolis; Cincinnati; Charleston, West Virginia; and Washington, D.C.

[7] The General would leave for the West Coast on July 14 (see no. 884). In his absence, Shuffler notified Kevin McCann, assistant to the president, that the inaugural ceremonies at Texas A & M could be rearranged in order for Eisenhower to participate in the exercises on November 9 (telegram, Shuffler to McCann, July 18, EM). General Eisenhower would attend. According to his appointment calendar for that day, he reviewed the college's cadet corps at 10:30 A.M.; met with Lieutenant General LeRoy Lutes at 11:30 A.M. (for background see no. 334); and delivered a radio broadcast address at 3:30 P.M. (the full text of Eisenhower's speech is in EM, Subject File, Speeches; see also *Fort Worth Star-Telegram*, Nov. 10, 1950). Later that afternoon the General departed by plane for Houston to attend a cocktail and dinner party hosted by Continental Oil Company executive Leonard F. McCollum (see no. 989). For developments on what Eisenhower described as his "backbreaking" Texas schedule see no. 1000.

896   *Eisenhower Mss.*

To William Stuart Symington   *July 11, 1950*

Dear Stu:[1] I read the enclosures to your note of July 7th.[2]

Mr. Clark's[3] basic principles are (1) the need for legal authority and (2) *single* authority in administering a universal Service Law. With both I agree. The details of laws, reputations, and organization will be very important; individuals who have been experienced in these matters will have to help you. The subject is one for a long talk—I'll see you when you come to Denver, unless a worsening situation abroad brings me back East earlier!!!⁴ *As ever*

¹ Symington was chairman of the National Security Resources Board. A typewritten copy of Eisenhower's longhand letter to him is in EM.
² Symington had sent Eisenhower a letter dated July 7, along with two memoranda dated July 6. According to a notation at the bottom of Eisenhower's reply, printed above, both memoranda were destroyed at Eisenhower's direction; Symington's letter was also destroyed (see R. L. Schulz to A. B. Gaston, July 24, 1950, EM, Symington Corr.).
³ Robert Lincoln Clark (B.A. Dartmouth 1932) was Director of the Manpower Office of the National Security Resources Board. Before accepting his present position in 1949, Clark had served since 1944 as principal budget examiner for the United States Bureau of the Budget. Clark's office was responsible for the development and administration of a skilled manpower program should full mobilization become necessary.
⁴ Clark's memoranda apparently concerned proposed legislation for universal military training and service (for more information about this subject see no. 912; for Eisenhower's meeting with Symington see no. 913). The "worsening situation" was, of course, the fighting in Korea (see no. 874).

897   *Eisenhower Mss.*

To Benjamin Franklin Caffey, Jr.   *July 11, 1950*

*Dear Frank:*¹ I think the idea presented in your letter of July 7th is both valuable and timely; frankly, I am puzzled by your assertion that there is no "guerilla" instruction given in any of our service schools.² Shortly after I became Chief of Staff, I got Brigadier General McLure— who was with the OSS during the war—to prepare a record of World War II operations in the OSS field and, with the help of other people in General Donovan's former program, to devise a program of future training.³ Certainly, guerilla warfare would come within the purview of such a study. And, while I never followed up on the matter, I assumed that something was done.⁴

In any event, I am going to write to Al Gruenther and suggest to him that something along this line be done at once.⁵ I, personally, think that they ought to be studied on a low level at Benning⁶ and on a staff and planning level in more advanced schools.

It was nice to hear from you and I envy you the freedom of your existence. However, I do not envy the locality—not in July and August.⁷ *Cordially*

¹ Since April 1948 Brigadier General Caffey had been the U.S. military attaché in Switzerland. In September 1949 he had returned to the United States because of illness. For background on Caffey see no. 182.

[2] On July 7 Caffey had written Eisenhower to express concern over the lack of instruction in guerrilla warfare techniques in U.S. service schools (EM). He cited the "South Korean debacle" as a case in point: North Korean guerrillas had infiltrated the South Korean Army, he said, and they were also engaging in subversive activities within the South Korean civilian population. He reminded Eisenhower of the value of guerrilla fighters in the European and Mediterranean theaters during World War II (see Chandler, *War Years*). The Russians, he said, were "past masters" of guerrilla warfare, but Americans knew very little about it: "I have never found what I considered an adequate defense against well organized, armed and equipped guerillas, who have good leadership."

Caffey, who had served as Deputy Director of the Organization and Training Division of the War Department General Staff in Washington, D.C., from 1947 until 1948, told Eisenhower that just before ending that assignment, he had directed that a course in guerrilla warfare be included in the curriculum of each of the U.S. service schools. He did not know, however, whether or not such a course had ever been instituted. It was Caffey's suggestion that if Eisenhower thought it worthwhile, he bring the subject to the attention of the Defense Department.

[3] Brigadier General Robert A. McClure had been Chief of the Psychological Warfare Division of SHAEF during World War II. In the spring of 1945 he had become Director of Information Control in the Office of Military Government for Germany (for additional background see no. 89). In September 1950 McClure would be appointed Chief of the Army's Psychological Warfare Department. General William J. Donovan had headed the Office of Strategic Services (OSS) during the war (for background see nos. 60 and 930; for more information on the Office of Strategic Services and the Psychological Warfare Division see Pogue, *Supreme Command*, pp. 84–88).

The specific document to which Eisenhower refers may have been a memo to him, dated June 21, 1947, in which McClure discussed the effectiveness of psychological warfare and recommended more study, research, and training for possible future needs. McClure had prepared the memo at Eisenhower's request. For more information about this paper see Galambos, *Chief of Staff*, no. 1556. See also Chandler and Galambos, *Occupation, 1945*, no. 367; and memo, Lincoln to Eisenhower, March 6, 1946, ABC 385 (1-28-42).

[4] By 1947 courses on the subject of psychological warfare were offered at the National War College, the Command and General Staff College, and the Air College (see memo, Norstad to Eisenhower, July 29, 1947, COS, 1947, 385). In the fall of 1948 the U.S. government was making plans for the establishment of guerrilla warfare organizations to operate in certain areas that were likely to be overrun by an enemy (see memo, Forrestal to JCS, Nov. 20, 1948, OS/D, 47–50, Clas. Numeric File, CD 23-1-22. See also Alfred H. Paddock, Jr., "Psychological and Unconventional Warfare, 1941–1952: Origins of a 'Special Warfare' Capability for the United States Army" [Ph.D. diss., Duke University, 1980]; and two articles by Colonel Donald F. Hall, Chief, Psychological Warfare Division, Office of the Chief, Army Field Forces: "Psychological Warfare Comes of Age," *Army Information Digest* 4, no. 9 [1949], 29–32; and "Psychological Warfare Training," *ibid.*, 6, no. 1 [1951], 40–46).

[5] See the following document.

[6] Fort Benning, Columbus, Georgia. Within the next few months The Infantry School at Fort Benning would introduce a text approved for resident- and extension-course instruction in guerrilla warfare (see The Infantry School, *Operations against Guerilla Forces* [Fort Benning, Ga., 1951]).

[7] Caffey had retired in March 1950 and was living in Orlando, Florida.

To Alfred Maximilian Gruenther   *July 11, 1950*
Personal. Eyes only

Dear Al:[1] I just had a note from a former member of the training division who says that we have no instruction in "gorilla" warfare in any of our schools.[2] I once directed the adoption of a course covering the entire field of OSS, but it is possible that nothing was ever done.

In any event, I think that it is something that would bear looking into—if we have nothing on it anywhere, it is high time that we did so.[3]

Incidentally, has it occurred to you that the G−2 Division in Japan is headed by the same man who headed the G−2 Division in the Philippines in 1941? Is it possible that he is not very alert? This is something that might cause you and your associates a little head scratching.[4]

I wish you would come and see me some time. Tonight is my regular bridge session the final one before I go on leave.[5]

Love to Grace[6] and the best to yourself, *Cordially*

---

[1] Lieutenant General Gruenther was the Army's Deputy Chief of Staff for Plans and Operations.

[2] See the preceding document for background on Brigadier General Benjamin F. Caffey's letter to Eisenhower on the subject of guerrilla warfare. In a note at the bottom of the above document Eisenhower wrote, "My secretary is apparently not acquainted with 'guerilla.'"

[3] On August 7 Gruenther would reply that when next he saw Eisenhower he would tell him about the "gorilla" courses that had been planned (EM). For more information about the Army's concern with unconventional warfare, especially guerrilla warfare, see Weigley, *History of the United States Army*, pp. 517, 542–47.

[4] Caffey had brought this matter to Eisenhower's attention. In his letter of July 7 Caffey had said, "I feel that it was criminal negligence that our Intelligence failed so miserably in the Korean mess. This is the second time that MacArthur had been caught—the first being Pearl Harbor. Yet, he has the same G−2!" Major General Charles Andrew Willoughby (B.A. Gettysburg College 1914) was the Chief of the Far East Command, G−2 (Intelligence Section). He had been Chief of Intelligence on the staff of General Douglas MacArthur during the Philippine campaign of 1941. For background see Louis Morton, *The Fall of the Philippines*, U.S. Army in World War II, ed. Kent Roberts Greenfield (Washington, D.C., 1953), pp. 77–90, 100–114; and Charles A. Willoughby and John Chamberlain, *MacArthur, 1941–1951* (New York, 1954), pp. 23–26, 350–56. On American involvement in the Korean War see nos. 865 and 870.

[5] Eisenhower would leave New York on July 14 for a trip to the western United States (see no. 884). It had been Eisenhower's custom, whenever his schedule permitted, to play bridge with friends on Monday evenings at 60 Morningside Drive. Regular players were George E. Allen, Jerry D. Brandon, William E. Robinson, Clifford Roberts, and Ellis D. Slater. According to Eisenhower's desk

calendar, however, he played bridge on Monday evening, July 10, and not on the eleventh as he states here.
[6] Mrs. Gruenther.

899   *Eisenhower Mss.*

TO THOMAS JOHN WATSON, JR.   *July 11, 1950*

Dear Tom:[1] I understand your situation exactly—in fact, if you would make allowances for the names and different kinds of preoccupations, your letter could well substitute for the many that I have to write.[2] I do hope that you explained your situation to the National Committee— I know that they would appreciate a direct communication from you.[3]

The Boy Scout meeting at Valley Forge was a wonderful experience.[4] I had a thoroughly enjoyable time and the next time they have a convention, I hope to attend but without the responsibility of making a speech.[5]

My grateful thanks for the consideration you gave my request. With warm personal regard, *Cordially*

[1] Watson, son of the chairman of the board of IBM, had been executive vice-president of the corporation since 1949 (for background see no. 638). In May both Eisenhower and Watson had been elected to the board of trustees of the CED (see no. 732).
[2] Watson apparently had declined an invitation from Eisenhower to participate in the Crusade for Freedom campaign sponsored by the National Committee for a Free Europe (for background on this committee see no. 428). Watson had explained that because of his father's lengthy absence from IBM and the subsequent departure of the corporation's president, "I have been forced to divorce myself from all outside activities. . . . Knowing father as you do, I'm sure you can appreciate my desire to make things go as well as possible in IBM . . ." (July 7, EM). Thomas J. Watson, Sr., had left for Europe on May 28 and would not return to New York City until October 5 (for background on him see no. 813. On Eisenhower's previous attempt to secure leadership for the nationwide Crusade for Freedom see no. 739).
[3] Aide Robert L. Schulz would inform the General that Watson had contacted Major General Clarence L. Adcock, executive vice-chairman of the Crusade for Freedom Committee (n.d., EM, Watson Corr.). For developments involving the Crusade for Freedom see nos. 962, 974, and 1001.
[4] Eisenhower had attended the second national jamboree of the Boy Scouts of America on July 4 at Valley Forge Park, Pennsylvania. The invitation had been enclosed in a letter from Boy Scouts president Gerald F. Beal (April 13, EM).
[5] Watson, a member of the executive board of the Boy Scouts, had congratulated Eisenhower on his "courageous and heartening" talk before the scout encampment at Valley Forge. In the address, the General had called for an increased dedication to the ideas set forth in the Declaration of Independence and had emphasized that patriotism was among the greatest of human virtues. Eisenhower had also spoken

of current world conflicts and the U.S. response to the situation in Korea (see no. 874; the full text of the speech is in EM, Subject File, Speeches).

900   *Eisenhower Mss.*

To Michael Doud Gill   *July 11, 1950*

Dear Michael:[1] Your letter came this morning and was more than interesting to your Aunt Mamie and to me.[2] We were intrigued by your stories of the animals in Yellowstone Park and your experiences on the trail and in camp. You are having the kind of vacation that I used to take in my own boyhood, although mine were necessarily confined to the plains of Kansas, while you are in one of the most beautiful spots of the world.[3] I think that the Paint Pots in Yellowstone Park stand out in my memory as the most unusual natural phenomenon I have ever seen.[4]

Recently, I have been down to Washington twice, but neither time was I able to get in touch with your mother. Once she was out when I telephoned and the other time I was so busy throughout the day that I had no chance to call her.[5]

We hope to leave here in two more days to start West to California. We shall stay there two weeks and then go to Denver to spend a month with your Aunt Mamie's parents.[6]

Both of us send our love and best wishes and I am enclosing a tiny present in the thought that you may need some item that this would buy. If not, you can save it until next winter when you can buy your girl a bunch of flowers on Christmas.[7] *Devotedly*

[1] Young Michael Gill was Eisenhower's nephew, a son of Mrs. Eisenhower's sister, Mabel Frances Doud Moore, and her first husband, Richard Gill. For background on the Gill and Moore families see no. 430.
[2] Gill had written to his aunt and uncle from Camp Trails, Yellowstone National Park, Wyoming. There is no copy of his letter in EM.
[3] See Eisenhower's memoir *At Ease* for the General's recollection of his Kansas boyhood; see also Davis, *Soldier of Democracy*.
[4] The Artists Paint Pots are a group of hot springs located in the Gibbon Geyser Basin at Yellowstone National Park. They have been so named because of the brightly colored mineral deposits found in their pools. Eisenhower had seen the Paint Pots in August 1938, on his return to the United States from the Philippines (see Eisenhower, *Diaries*, pp. 31–32).
[5] Mabel Moore and her husband, Lieutenant Colonel George Gordon Moore, Jr., lived in Washington, D.C. Eisenhower had been in Washington on June 28 and again on July 5 (see nos. 870 and 886).
[6] For Eisenhower's trip and visit with his parents-in-law, the John Sheldon Douds, see nos. 884 and 805; see also *Time*, August 28, 1950, p. 32.

The "tiny present" was money; this letter was dispatched by registered mail on July 12.

901   *Eisenhower Mss.*

To WILLIAM HOWARD CHASE   *July 11, 1950*

Dear Mr. Chase:[1] You are somewhat in error when you speculate that there are probably "clever" ways of attracting my interest to an invitation such as yours. Straightforwardness, even to the point of bluntness, in my case, is more effective than anything else. (At least I think it is.)[2]

Frankly, I am so busy at this moment in last-minute preparations for an extended trip—which will include four weeks of vacation as well as a lot of work—that I do not have the time to study my fall and winter schedule to determine whether it is feasible for me to accept the invitation you extend. I am very doubtful, indeed, because I have already been compelled to decline a number of very appealing suggestions. However, I shall have the matter studied by Mr. Kevin McCann, my principal assistant in these matters, and he will probably communicate with you further in a few days. In the meantime, I can only say that I am deeply appreciative of the kind of things you have to say and, certainly, I wish you every success in the purpose you have in mind.[3]

I regret that I cannot give you a prompt acceptance, but I am getting to the point where each new commitment inevitably means a lot of adjustment and sometimes embarrassment.[4]

With personal regard, *Cordially*

[1] Chase was Director of the Department of Public Relations for General Foods Corporation in New York City. He had written Eisenhower on July 6 to invite him to speak at a meeting of the Public Relations Society of America scheduled for December 3–5 in New York (EM).

[2] Chase had said that there were probably other, more clever devices to obtain the General's attention than the straightforward letter he had written; and he had recalled Eisenhower's willingness to furnish an unpublished personal anecdote about General of the Army George C. Marshall for telling at the opening luncheon of the 1950 Red Cross Campaign (see nos. 616 and 617).

[3] Chase had proposed that the public relations profession of America be the "logical task force" to help inspire Americans to further the programs and objectives of Senator William Benton's Senate Resolution 243, "A Marshall Plan for Ideas" (see no. 890). American products had been "extremely effective ambassadors," Chase pointed out. "Why should not the skills that have created mass markets for these objects in this country . . . be devoted to problems on a worldwide scale?"

[4] On July 20 Chase would reply, "Your point on bluntness is well taken. May I, therefore, be blunt?" There followed a strongly worded renewed effort to persuade Eisenhower to address members of the Public Relations Society of America in December. Nevertheless, Kevin McCann, Eisenhower's assistant, would draft a

declination dated August 22, which was dispatched the same day from Denver, Colorado, where Eisenhower was vacationing at the home of Mrs. Eisenhower's parents. Both letters are in EM.

902   *Eisenhower Mss.*

TO JOHN TUPPER COLE   *July 11, 1950*

Dear Tupper:[1] Just tell your daughter to come a-running any time that she wants to delve into the Law Library here.[2] It's located in the Kent Building, on 116th Street, on the same side of the street as Low Library, and to the right of Low as you stand on the sidewalk facing the alma mater statue. All she need do is give her name at the desk; the people there will be expecting her.

I should add that Mamie and I thoroughly enjoyed seeing you the other night and we hope that we will see you often in the future.[3] *Sincerely*

[1] Colonel Cole (USMA 1917) was a member of the Military Staff Committee of the U.S. delegation to the United Nations. During World War II he had served in the European theater with the 5th Armored Division.

[2] In a letter of July 6 Cole had asked Eisenhower to help his daughter, Jean T. Cole, gain permission to use the Columbia Law Library during July and August. According to her father, Miss Cole would be studying the practice of euthanasia, which she had chosen as the subject of her senior thesis (EM). In a penned note in the margin of Cole's letter Eisenhower had requested of McCann, "Please ask whether this [is] possible?"; and across the bottom of the letter the General had drawn an arrow to Cole's signature and had written, "Good friend of mine." McCann, who drafted Eisenhower's reply to Cole, would make arrangements on this same day for Miss Cole to use the law library. Miss Cole would thank Eisenhower for his help on July 13 (EM).

[3] On July 5 the Eisenhowers and the Coles had been among the dinner guests of Lieutenant General and Mrs. Hubert Reilly Harmon, U.S. Air Force, at their quarters at Fort Totten, Long Island, New York. Harmon, like Cole, was a member of the Military Staff Committee of the U.S. delegation to the United Nations (see no. 418, n. 2). Correspondence concerning plans for the Harmons' party is in EM, Harmon Corr.

903   *Eisenhower Mss.*

TO HERBERT HENRY LEHMAN   *July 11, 1950*

Dear Senator Lehman:[1] The Association of American Universities, of which Columbia is a member, has made a comprehensive study of the implications to educational institutions of pending legislation, which, if enacted, would abrogate the long-standing principle of complete tax exemption now accorded to these institutions. I heartily endorse the Association's views in this matter.

A copy of the Report of the Committee on Financial Support and Taxation and a newspaper release relative thereto are enclosed herewith for your information.[2] *Sincerely*

[1] Lehman, a Democrat, represented New York in the U.S. Senate (for background see no. 889). James R. Killian, Jr., president of M.I.T. and chairman of the AAU's committee on financial support and taxation, had written (June 22, EM) to ask the General to write to his state's senators urging them to oppose a bill intended to change the tax-exempt status of certain nonprofit institutions, including universities. The Ways and Means Committee of the House of Representatives had studied such legislation for several months (for background see no. 653).

The initials at the top of the carbon copy of this letter indicate that both Eisenhower and Grayson L. Kirk, provost and vice-president in charge of education at Columbia, contributed to the drafting of this letter. Eisenhower sent a similar note, misdated June 11, 1950, to Senator Irving M. Ives, a Republican from New York. For background on Ives see no. 476.

[2] Both the report and the press release were reprinted in U.S., Congress, Senate, Committee on Finance, *Revenue Revisions of 1950: Hearings on H.R. 8920*, 81st Cong., 2d sess., 1950, pp. 573–77. The report said that changes in tax-exempt status of universities would be "a fatal blow to our educational system." Two of the questions at stake were the tax status of non-educational, business-related activities and "lease-back" transactions, whereby a university would purchase business facilities and lease them back to the seller (thus avoiding property taxes).

Lehman would reply (July 17, EM) that he sympathized with Eisenhower's position and that he would "watch out for the interests of the universities" if and when tax legislation reached the Senate. Senator Ives would express sentiments similar to Lehman's in his answer of July 14 (EM). After the Revenue Act of 1950 became law on September 23, 1950, the government would levy taxes on the "unrelated business net income" of universities (see U.S., *Statutes at Large*, vol. 64, pt. 1, pp. 947–59; see also Millett, *Financing Higher Education*, pp. 376–78).

904   *Eisenhower Mss.*

To Philip Murray   *July 12, 1950*

Dear Mr. Murray:[1] An unusually crowded calendar has prevented me from seeking a conference with you, something that I was particularly anxious to have before I start on an extended trip the day after tomorrow.[2] The subject that I wanted to talk to you about was to secure your approval for labor representation in a series of conferences that Columbia University hopes to hold over the next few years.[3]

The purpose of these conferences is to study on a sort of "town meeting" basis the great problems now confronting our civilization and which will affect the future of the American way of life. The University proposes that these be studied by a convocation of University professors, labor representatives, and individuals from governmental life, from financial, professional and management circles. We want the farmer and the grocer and all the rest.

The aim of the University will be to provide a friendly platform to everybody at these round-table discussions; to maintain an atmosphere of scholarly impartiality and research.

Recently I had an opportunity to discuss this matter at some length with Mr. Jacobson, the Minnesota C.I.O. Secretary-Treasurer. He and I were guests at the same dinner in Minneapolis and he found the project of very great interest.[4]

When I return to this city in September, I shall hope for an early chance to talk the whole matter over with you. In the meantime, I should like to have, if you feel that you can give it to me, an expression of your intention to send representatives to these conferences on the condition that Columbia succeeds in getting them properly financed and supported and that all of the other purposes I have outlined above are achieved.[5] A similar request is being made upon a representative of the A.F. of L.[6]

With best wishes and personal regard, *Sincerely*

[1] For background on Murray, president of the CIO, see no. 330.

[2] For Eisenhower's vacation see no. 884.

[3] The conference plan to which Eisenhower refers was soon to become the American Assembly. For background on the project see nos. 605 and 844; for developments see no. 1039.

[4] R. C. Jacobson, of Minneapolis, was treasurer of the Minnesota State CIO Council. On July 7 he had attended a dinner honoring Eisenhower given by Harry A. Bullis, chairman of the board of General Mills, Inc. (see no. 893). On July 11 Eisenhower had written to Jacobson to thank him for coming to the dinner and to invite him to visit the Columbia campus in the fall (EM).

[5] There is no reply from Murray in EM; Eisenhower would, nevertheless, continue to try to enlist support from organized labor for the American Assembly program (see his telegram to Murray, Dec. 1, 1950, inviting Murray to lunch with other labor leaders on Thursday, Dec. 7 [EM]; see also the next document).

[6] This may have been William Green, president of the American Federation of Labor. There is, however, no record in EM of a request by Eisenhower for Green's support of the American Assembly project. For developments see no. 1083.

To Anna Marie Rosenberg　　　　　　　　　　　*July 12, 1950*

Dear Anna:[1] You have not telephoned me, nor have you been up to
Morningside Heights for many months. I trust that this is only because
you are busy—I would certainly hate to think that I have been listed
in your black book. Now, I am to start off for the West Coast in a
few days to be gone until early September, and before I go, I want to
put before you one point that is of utmost importance to me and to
Columbia.[2]

It concerns a great system of conferences which Columbia is planning
to initiate, possibly as early as next spring. They would extend over a
period of years and would deal with subjects that are of vital importance
to our present-day civilization. Nothing that worries the American
people would be foreign to the curriculum.[3]

Participation in the conferences is to be, we hope, on a "town
meeting" basis. We want capital, labor, management, professions, government and members of the University faculties to attend. Instead of
conducting these conferences on the usual "convention" basis, we will
go to a suburban locality and live together for from three to eight days,
depending upon the subject or subjects under discussion. Sponsorship
by the University would provide three great advantages. The first of
these is an atmosphere of scholarly impartiality in which to study and
discuss the topic of the moment. The next advantage would be that of
securing the intellectual and philosophical approach, as well as the
viewpoint of business people, labor and management alike. Finally, the
conclusions and opinions developed by such a conference would be free
of the taint of self-interest; they would be composites rather than com-
promises and would be cross-sectional rather than narrowly limited.

While the whole financial and programming arrangements have not
been completed, I am, nevertheless, hopeful that we can get all these
matters settled at an early date. But the conferences would be valueless
unless labor is ready and eager to participate, when guaranteed a clear
and unprejudiced platform, just as would be the heads of business and
government.

There are a thousand details connected with the thing concerning
which I would like to talk to you, but times presses and, although I
hope to get you on the phone tomorrow morning, there will still be
little time for a real discussion. I am enclosing a copy of a letter which
I have written to a young friend of mine who is helping me in various
aspects of this matter.[4] If you have time to read it, you will gain some
understanding of what Columbia is trying to do.

What I should like to ask from you is, merely, that when you have
an opportunity, you will support such studies among labor leaders and

recommend their participation with us when these conferences are once inaugurated. You can give them my guarantee of personal and official appreciation and my assurance that, without them, these conferences could neither be successful nor complete.[5]

I am writing a short note to Phil Murray.[6] My associate here, Phil Young, is writing to Matthew Woll with whom we have been in contact on another proposition of which you may have heard, that of establishing a Chair of Labor History in Columbia University.[7]

Until I see you, best wishes and warm regards, *Cordially*

P.S. At a recent dinner, in Minneapolis where I explained this whole program, one of the guests was Mr. Jacobson. He is the C.I.O. representative in that region. He participated intelligently and seriously in the discussion and I am frank to say that I formed, on a short acquaintance, a real liking for him.[8]

---

[1] Mrs. Rosenberg had been a labor and personnel relations consultant since 1924. For background see *Eisenhower Papers*, vols. I–IX, esp. no. 1039 in Galambos, *Chief of Staff*.

[2] For Eisenhower's vacation plans see no. 884.

[3] For background see the preceding document.

[4] This was probably William H. Burnham, Eisenhower's friend and adviser, who had traveled throughout the southern and western United States to explain the goals of the conference plan and other projects at Columbia. The enclosed letter to which Eisenhower refers is probably no. 826, with revised opening and closing paragraphs and other minor changes. For background on the letter and Burnham's efforts on Eisenhower's behalf see no. 826, n. 2.

[5] There is no reply from Mrs. Rosenberg in EM.

[6] See the preceding document.

[7] The idea of establishing a chair of labor history may have originated with William Burnham. On June 8, 1950, he had suggested that Eisenhower discuss the conference plan with leaders of the CIO and the AF of L. "It would prevent their thinking it was all a big business and University combine already prepared for their acceptance," he wrote. Eisenhower's reaction to this was favorable. He penned at the bottom of Burnham's note, "To *Dean Young*: Could we not establish a relationship between a 'Chair on Labor History' and 'Arden House'? Possibly by means of a 'Labor Institute'?" (EM).

Philip Young, dean of Columbia's Graduate School of Business, was very involved in the development of the conference plan. He apparently contacted Matthew Woll, second vice-president of the AF of L. In November 1950 Woll would write Eisenhower that he hoped to report on progress made in connection with the establishment of a Samuel Gompers professorship of labor history. "I am confident," he said, "we will be able shortly to give definite assurance of support that will warrant proceeding in connection with this professorship" (Nov. 8, 1950, EM). There is, however, no further correspondence in EM regarding these plans.

[8] For background on Jacobson see the preceding document, n. 4; on Eisenhower's trip to Minneapolis see no. 893.

To Marvin Jones   *July 12, 1950*

Dear Judge Jones:[1] Not every case is a dry and dusty one; that much is evident from the opinion rendered on Monday. I imagine, however, that you seldom sit in judgment on so romantic a subject as the wartime jeep.[2]

So far as my own war experience was concerned, the jeep was definitely "passenger"—but sometimes I was plagued by the suspicion that the lieutenants thought of the "old man" as nothing but freight, composed mostly of brass.

My thanks to you for letting me know what the courts think of the thing.[3] *Sincerely*

[1] Jones (LL.B. University of Texas 1907) had been appointed judge of the U.S. Court of Claims in April 1940. He had become Chief Justice, U.S. Court of Claims, in July 1947. Eisenhower's letter was originally drafted by Kevin McCann, but the General substituted the word *romantic* for McCann's *colorful* and added the entire second paragraph. The draft, with Eisenhower's handwritten changes, is in EM, Letters and Drafts.

[2] In his letter of July 10 Jones had said that he thought Eisenhower might enjoy the efforts of the U.S. Court of Claims to classify the wartime jeep. The case to which Jones referred was the Union Pacific Railroad Company's suit against the United States to recover additional freight charges on transportation service for shipments of jeeps during World War II. The judge noted that he had seen Eisenhower riding in a jeep and suggested that perhaps the General should have been called as an expert witness to help the court determine whether the jeep was a cargo or a passenger car. "You may get some amusement," wrote Jones, "out of a layman's attempt to rope, tie and brand the thing." Jones's letter and a printed text of the court's opinion and ruling are in EM.

[3] "The jeep," read Jones's opinion, "having been everywhere else, is now in court." He recalled seeing his father haul ploughshares and crosscut saws in a buggy, but that, he said, did not make the buggy a freight vehicle. "Surely the jeep was used for hauling," he wrote. "It was in many respects an all-purpose car. The army called it a truck, but that is not very persuasive, since the army called all wheeled vehicles trucks, including passenger cars. . . ." He found that the jeep was primarily a passenger car and thus ordered that the plaintiff was entitled to recover (see Union Pacific Railroad Company v. United States, No. 47643, United States Court of Claims, July 10, 1950, *Federal Supplement*, vol. 91, pp. 762–65).

To Stafford LeRoy Irwin   *July 13, 1950*

Dear Red:[1] I enclose a paper which is one of three brought to me by a man named Dr. Victor M. Kraus. I have talked to him and found him to be, obviously, a well-educated man. The attached paper is additional data as to his record.[2]

He has a sound background and since he came to this country from Poland, he evidently is well acquainted with the Soviet mind, Soviet organization, and so on.

I suggest that, if you or any other agency of government is interested in following up this lead, you communicate directly with Dr. Kraus.[3]

He provided me with two other short papers but asked that they not be circulated in their present form because they are only tentative in character.[4] *Sincerely*

[1] Major General Irwin was Assistant Chief of Staff, G–2, U.S. Army. For background see no. 818.
[2] Kraus, a former Polish intelligence officer, had met with Eisenhower on July 12 to discuss a proposal to suspend temporarily the release of atomic energy secrets to industry. There is no copy in EM of the paper which Eisenhower sent Irwin.
[3] In a letter of this same day (EM) Eisenhower informed Kraus that he had sent his "original letter" to a friend—that is, Irwin—in Washington, D.C. Irwin would advise Eisenhower (Aug. 8, EM) that he had sent to the Department of State and the Atomic Energy Commission a proposal that Kraus be contacted. Irwin thought that Kraus should not have been alarmed by the announcement in the *New York Times* (June 15, 1950) regarding the release of atomic energy information to the public. According to Irwin, "the scope of the matter originally proposed to be released has been objected to, and will be quite a bit smaller than indicated in the first press release." The United States, Britain, and Canada, according to the account in the *New York Times*, would make available to private industry and to universities enough significant information to allow them to build nuclear reactors (see State, *Foreign Relations, 1950*, vol. I, *National Security Affairs; Foreign Economic Policy* [1977], pp. 499–503, 547, 549–59).
[4] In a letter of July 12 (EM) Kraus had asked Eisenhower not to show anyone two of the short papers that he had left in the General's office. One was an outline of his dissertation, and the other was a four-page essay titled "The Struggle of Our Time: The Problem." The latter document was a prospectus for a new approach to solving the problems confronting the world as a consequence of the development of atomic energy. Both papers are in EM, Kraus Corr.

908   *Eisenhower Mss.*

To Mason D. Wade, Sr.   *July 13, 1950*

Dear Mr. Wade:[1] Thank you for your letter. I must say that I appreciate your directness of approach, and, if it were at all possible, I should give you a full reply. Unfortunately, I am pretty much in the dark as to the nature of the statements in which my name appeared or the quotations ascribed to me. Consequently, I can write you only in general terms.[2]

At no time have I ever endorsed the specific program of the United

World Federalists, and—since I am not acquainted with the proposals presented to the voters of Florida—I do not understand how I can be quoted as supporting the organization's purpose, either in part or in whole. However, because I do not have in my possession full details, either of the content of their presentation or its circumstances, I cannot make a concise statement of my position relative to the proposals of the group. Certainly, however, I have not authorized the use of my name by the United World Federalists or any similar organization—at any time or place, or for any purpose.

Should you be interested in my personal position so far as a world authority is concerned, I enclose a copy of an address which I made in March of this year.[3] In it I have presented as well as I can my attitude toward the United Nations and its mission.

Once again, my thanks for your direct approach.[4] *Sincerely*

---

[1] Wade was national senior vice-commandant of the Marine Corps League in St. Petersburg, Florida. He was also an executive officer of the Florida Committee for American Action, an organization opposing world federalism. This letter was drafted by Eisenhower's assistant, Kevin McCann.

[2] In his letter of July 10 (EM) Wade had asked Eisenhower for a clarification of his position regarding the United World Federalists. Wade said that the organization had used the General's name in support of a "misleading resolution seeking to commit our Government to join with a proposed World Government," a proposition which would be put before Florida voters in November. Wade wrote, "I cannot believe that an American of your attainments and position would knowingly support such a program as that outlined by the United World Federalists." For background on the United World Federalists see nos. 436 and 729.

[3] On March 23 Eisenhower had delivered the first of an annual series of lectures on international peace at Columbia University. On that occasion Eisenhower had taken the following position concerning world authority:

> In a disarmed world—should it be attained—there must be an effective United Nations, with a police power universally recognized and strong enough to earn universal respect. In it the individual nations can pool the power for policing the continents and the seas against *international* lawlessness— those acts which involve two or more nations in their *external* relations.
>
> I do not subscribe to any idea that a world police force or a world organization should be permitted entrance to any nation for the purpose of settling disputes among its citizens, or for exercising any authority not specifically and voluntarily accorded by the affected nation. At this stage of civilization's progress any effort to push to this extreme the purpose of international law enforcement will defeat legitimate objectives. National sovereignty and independence have been won by most at too great cost to surrender to an external agency such powers.
>
> But by the establishment of a United Nations police of properly defined and restricted but effective powers, no nation would surrender one iota of its current national functions or authority, for none, by itself, now possesses a shred of responsibility to police the world. To an international peace organization, a nation would give up nothing beyond its equitable share in men and money. How this organization is to be constituted, or how it is

to be controlled, has yet to be worked out, but with the principles honestly accepted, the procedural problems would be easy of solution.

For background on the speech see no. 741; EM, Subject File, Speeches; and *New York Times*, March 24, 1950.
[4] Eisenhower continued to receive letters about the movement in Florida (see his correspondence with General Sumter L. Lowry, July 15, 1950; William A. Cobb, Sept. 21, 1950; Mrs. C. Raymond Durkee, Sept. 22, 1950; Adelaide Ullian, Sept. 22, 1950; and Richard H. Cooper, Sept. 30, 1950. See also Eisenhower to Arthur E. Elliott, May 29, 1950; to George Kirksey, Aug. 3, 1950; and to Mrs. W. J. Long, Sept. 19, 1950. All correspondence is in EM).

909   *Eisenhower Mss.*

To Louis Arthur Johnson   *July 14, 1950*

Dear Louis:[1] This afternoon I start on a Western tour that will combine University business with a later leave at my wife's home in Denver.[2] I consulted the President on the matter to determine whether he had any desire that I should eliminate this trip from my schedule and he replied in the negative. He understands that I am available on quite instant notice if anything should be desired of me.[3]

My office here at the University will always know how to get in touch with me promptly.[4]

With best wishes and the hope that our present difficulties are soon straightened out.[5] *Cordially*

[1] On July 5 Eisenhower had met with Secretary of Defense Louis A. Johnson, President Truman, and other leading members of the U.S. defense establishment in Washington, D.C., to review the difficult situation in Korea (see no. 886).
[2] The General and Mrs. Eisenhower would leave New York City later this same evening to begin an extensive trip through several western states. For details on their itinerary see nos. 884 and 887; concerning the Eisenhowers' lengthy stay in Denver, Colorado, with Mrs. Eisenhower's family, the John Sheldon Douds, see nos. 805 and 900.
[3] Eisenhower had telephoned President Truman on July 12 to underscore his willingness to cancel personal travel plans should the President advise against his departure for the West Coast. Truman reassured the General that should it be necessary, he would not hesitate to contact him—even for a ten-minute conference (appointment calendar). For Truman's previous remarks on Eisenhower's achievements as a consultant and adviser to the JCS see no. 521.
[4] Arrangements had been made by way of Lowry Air Force Base, near Denver, Colorado, for liaison between Eisenhower and officials in Washington, D.C., (see no. 855).
[5] On this same day Eisenhower sent a similar letter to the Army's Vice Chief of Staff General Wade H. Haislip (EM), with a supplemental request that Haislip inform Secretary of the Army Frank Pace, Jr., of the General's availability for

service despite his travel arrangements. Both Johnson and Pace would later thank Eisenhower for contacting them and would indicate their intention to seek his counsel about the serious problems currently facing the country. Correspondence from Johnson (July 17) and Pace (July 21) is in EM.

Earlier in the year Eisenhower had expressed concern over what he perceived as his diminished role in defense consultation with Secretary Johnson (see no. 716). The General would nevertheless continue to remind defense officials of his availability "for anything that may be required" regarding the crisis (see, for example, nos. 912, 913, and 914).

910   *Eisenhower Mss.*

To Gardner Cowles   *July 14, 1950*

Dear Mr. Cowles:[1] This morning General M. W. Clark came to see me but I had forgotten, at the termination of our conversation the other day, whether or not it was agreed that he was to call your office. Consequently, to avoid embarrassment on either side, I did not mention my earlier suggestion to Look's Managing Editor, Mr. William H. Lowe.[2]

You may be interested in two points. I had an opportunity to read small portions of General Clark's forthcoming book and I found it most intriguing, combining real accuracy with what I thought to be very nice style.[3]

The other item was, when and if the present international crisis seems to lessen in intensity, he will again be interested in some proposition outside the service.[4] *Very sincerely*

P.S. His address is Ft. Monroe, Va.

[1] Cowles was president of Cowles Magazines of New York City. For background see no. 757, n. 4.

[2] On July 13 Cowles and William Hyslop Lowe, Jr., managing editor of *Look* magazine (a Cowles publication), had visited Eisenhower. Among the subjects discussed was General Mark Clark's new book, *Calculated Risk*, which would be published in October 1950 by Harper & Brothers (see *New York Times*, Oct. 22, 1950; and *New York Times Book Review*, Oct. 29, 1950).

[3] On this same day Eisenhower and Clark had gone over the galley proofs of *Calculated Risk* (see no. 848 for Eisenhower's arrangements with Clark to review the manuscript). In September 1950 Cass Canfield, chairman of the board of Harper & Brothers, would send Eisenhower an advance copy of Clark's memoir (for background on Canfield see Chandler and Galambos, *Occupation, 1945*, no. 369). In December 1950 Clark would send Eisenhower a special edition, bound in red leather, hand-tooled, with "IKE" engraved in gold on the cover (see Cass Canfield to Eisenhower, Sept. 5, 1950; and Eisenhower to Mark Clark, Oct. 21 and Dec. 29, 1950, all in EM).

[4] Since August 1949 Clark had been Chief of Army Field Forces at Fort Monroe, Virginia. In his second book (*From the Danube to the Yalu* [New York, 1954])

Clark gives an account of his role as a planner and supervisor of training for the Army and of his subsequent assignments during the Korean War: Commander in Chief, UN Command in Korea; Commander in Chief, Far East; commanding general, U.S. Army Forces in the Far East. For developments on Clark's career after the Korean War see no. 672; see also no. 1038.

911 *Eisenhower Mss.*

To Carl Raymond Gray, Jr. *July 14, 1950*

Dear Carl:[1] I must apologize for the necessary brevity of this letter. I have been very pushed, and I am leaving on a long trip in two hours.[2]

You did not identify for me those points in your letter which are presumably controversial. As I read it through, I could find nothing with which to argue and I am sorry that you did not point out for me any item in which the staff seemed to hold a contrary view. In that way, I could have possibly been of more help.[3]

Of course, I agree with the theory that our railroad units should be taken bodily from the railways and that there should be different age limits than apply in the line and that there should be a centralized control of the railroads within every theater of war. However, if there is some specific point on which you want my opinion, you could send me another letter which will be forwarded to me promptly.[4]

Sorry to be of so little use to you. *Cordially*

[1] Major General Gray was head of the Veterans Administration and Director General of the Military Railway Service. For background see *Eisenhower Papers*, vols. I–IX.

[2] On the trip see nos. 884, 887, and 900.

[3] Gray had written (July 10, EM) to ask Eisenhower to comment on a memorandum of the same date to The Adjutant General (TAG), Department of the Army, on the subject of the Military Railway Service. Gray maintained that since the passage of legislation during the Civil War allowing the President to seize the railroads for military purposes, American railroad men had responded "in a superb fashion" to every call to arms. Their record of cooperation bore witness, Gray argued, to the wisdom of granting the industry a larger voice in the administration of the Military Railway Service. Gray was concerned about the absence of a "workable plan of administration and training," and he wanted TAG to call him into conference immediately.

[4] There is no further correspondence with Gray on this subject in EM.

Dear Louis: Thanks very much for your note of the 20th on the subject of universal military training.[1] As I think I have told you before, I personally supported, while the World War was going on, a system of universal military *service* for our post-war organization. I felt, and so reported to the War Department, that we would probably have to undergo a long period of unsettled international relations pending the time when the United Nations would become fully effective in preserving the peace. Because of this I believed that a democracy such as ours would have to find ways and means of maintaining military forces far larger than any we had tried before to maintain in peace—and that this had to be done without breaking our economy.

A study of military expenditures in a democracy shows that a very large proportion of the cost goes for personnel. The factors above alluded to convince me that for some years following upon World War II we would have to maintain our forces under a system which would provide for a draftee only nominal pay, practically nothing more than cigarette money. I thought that the year and a half (which was the term of service I then thought would be necessary) that he would devote to military service would be simply like taxes that other people would have to pay. Under this system I felt that we would need to maintain only a skeleton cadre who would be remunerated along professional lines.

My correspondence with the War Department toward the end of the War, while I was still in Europe, shows that I finally accepted the convictions of the War Department that our country would not accept such a plan because of the charge that it was "militaristic." My own belief was that it was just the opposite and that it was the only real democratic way in which we could discharge our international obligations in this day and time. However, since the War Department felt so sure on this point, I accepted the theory of universal military *training* and thereafter strongly urged its acceptance.[2]

As I have often told you and other responsible officers in Washington, including the Chief himself,[3] I am always available for any kind of conference or assistance on any subject that you might desire to take up with me. If you should want to send any representative at any time to see me here I will, of course, explain my views in detail. On the other hand, if you should wish me to come to Washington, even for a short conference, the only factor you have to consider is your own judgment as to whether my opinions would be helpful. If you think that they would, I can report to Washington within less than twenty-four hours after receiving your message.[4]

Warm personal regards, *Sincerely*

[1] Secretary of Defense Johnson had informed Eisenhower that President Truman would soon revive the subject of universal military training. According to Johnson, Truman had met on July 20 with representatives of the American Legion and had told them that he planned to support reactivation of UMT legislation in Congress. Johnson said that he wanted the General to be among the first to know of Truman's decision so that Eisenhower could give full and active support to "this important defense measure" (EM).

In October 1945 Truman had presented his original plan for a program of UMT before a joint session of Congress. His proposal required one year of military training for all males when they became eighteen or had completed high school; all young men would receive training before their twentieth birthday. The Congress took no action on the plan, however, and Truman, in an effort to renew enthusiasm for UMT, in December 1946 had appointed a President's Advisory Commission on Universal Training, which presented a revised plan in May 1947. In spite of these measures, interest in military training declined. Among the most compelling reasons for shelving the idea was the power of the atomic bomb. Many reasoned that a new war would undoubtedly be an atomic war and that the need for mass armies was questionable (see Truman, *Memoirs*, vol. I, *Year of Decisions*, pp. 510–12; and Weigley, *History of the United States Army*, pp. 496–501).

[2] For Eisenhower's current views on universal military service and training see nos. 32, 763, and 896. For his immediate postwar correspondence on UMT see Chandler and Galambos, *Occupation, 1945*, nos. 114, 115, 116, 206, 340, 448, and 476.

[3] President Truman (see nos. 909 and 921).

[4] In the coming months, however, Eisenhower would not take part in what would become a formidable campaign to enact legislation for UMT. Both Generals Omar N. Bradley and George C. Marshall would make public appeals for the plan, and Johnson himself would continue to press for enabling legislation, as did Senator Millard E. Tydings, chairman of the Senate Armed Services Committee; Congressman Carl Vinson, chairman of the House Armed Services Committee; and Congressman James W. Wadsworth, a member of Vinson's committee.

In August, however, Truman would announce that he would not propose enactment of UMT legislation at the current session of Congress, declaring that he wanted nothing to impede passage of legislation involving the emergency in Korea. By year's end the President was still firm on that position, and it would be June 1951 before a universal military training and service act would finally be enacted. Even that program would never be implemented (see U.S., *Statutes at Large*, vol. 65, pp. 75–89. See also *New York Times*, Aug. 15, 17, 23, 30, 31, Sept. 22, and Dec. 29, 1950; and June 20, 1951).

913   *Eisenhower Mss.*

To WILLIAM STUART SYMINGTON   *July 31, 1950*

Dear Stu: I hope that you can find some excuse for getting out to Denver for a day or so very soon.[1]

I should like to talk to you about our present situation. (Incidentally, please do not take too lightly what Mr. Baruch is now saying. While you are much closer to this problem than I, I have seen our country, in the past, have real cause for regret that it did not listen a lot more carefully to this man.)[2]

Not long ago I had indirect word that Dave might get out for a little golf. If the two of you could come at the same time it would be wonderful. Please let me know a day or so in advance so I won't be off on a fishing trip.[3]

I have told every individual in our Government, including the Chief himself, that I am always available on an instant's notice for anything that may be required of me in the present crisis. I want you to know that if you should find definite reason for wanting me in Washington, even for a matter of two hours, I would cheerfully make the trip.[4] Alternatively, I shall always be glad to confer, here, with any representative you might want to talk to me. General Caldwell here at Lowry has volunteered the promise that he can always get me to Washington within twelve hours after receipt of necessary notice.[5]

Incidentally, I received only recently, from Ralph Reed, President of the American Express, a copy of a paper submitted to him by a European friend. I inclose it. You may destroy after reading.[6]

With warmest personal regards, *Cordially*

[1] Symington was chairman of the National Security Resources Board. For background on the NSRB see no. 165.

[2] Bernard M. Baruch, who had served as chairman of the War Industries Board in World War I, had testified before the Banking and Currency Committee of the U.S. Senate on July 26. For Eisenhower's views on Baruch's statements see the following document. See also Eisenhower, *At Ease*, pp. 210–11.

[3] Symington had asked in a letter of July 17 (EM) whether Eisenhower planned to visit Colorado Springs, Colorado, with David R. Calhoun, Jr., president of the St. Louis (Mo.) Union Trust Company. He would inquire again in a note of August 4 (EM), and after he telephoned Eisenhower in Denver on August 10, they would agree to meet in Colorado Springs on September 1 (appointment calendar). They would play golf there, and Eisenhower would return to Denver on September 4 (see *Denver Post*, Sept. 1, 1950).

[4] See, for example, no. 909.

[5] Brigadier General Charles H. Caldwell, CG of Lowry Air Force Base, near Denver, had arranged for Eisenhower to maintain contact with officials in Washington, D.C., while the General was on vacation (see no. 855).

[6] Ralph Thomas Reed had been president and a director of the American Express Company since 1944. He had enclosed in his letter of July 19 (EM) an essay dated July 15 from a friend in Europe (a copy is in EM, Symington Corr.). The anonymous author had maintained that the conflict in Korea was only a "further step" in the Soviets' plan for a world war. The Communist party leadership in Moscow would attempt to present an image of impartiality by calling for peace talks, the essayist had continued, but it would be useless to discuss anything with the Russians. Eisenhower would thank Reed for the paper in a note of August 1 (EM), commenting, "A lot of what he [the author] has to say makes sense."

To Bernard Mannes Baruch   *July 31, 1950*

Dear Bernie: It would be most gratifying to me, during this crisis in our affairs, to have a long talk with you.[1]

I most certainly agree with your feeling that this is a time when we should be using every possible method to find out "what is the Soviet industry doing at this time." Moreover, I am delighted with what I have seen in the press concerning the statements that you have made before Senate Committees.[2] While I do not pretend to give specific advice in the matters in which you are the acknowledged master, I am completely sure that we should not treat the present crisis as just a mere inconvenience. It should be our warning to place all of our affairs in order so that we could meet any expansion of the emergency in an effective way. Twice I have gone to Washington and urged that this is no time for dawdling and I felt that everybody there shared my views.[3] Of course, I did not presume to advise in detail along the lines of industrial mobilization and Governmental organization, but I did say to several officials "you had better be talking more to Baruch about these things."[4]

Should anything come up that impels the Government to recall me to Washington, even for an hour or so, I shall make it a point to try to get in touch with you before going. If at any time you should like to get me on the phone, it is easy enough to do so by calling Lowry Air Force Base in Denver.[5]

With my warmest regards, *Cordially*

[1] Baruch, a philanthropist and adviser to several presidents, had tried unsuccessfully to reach Eisenhower by telephone on July 19; he had left a message explaining that he had recently tried to impress W. Stuart Symington with the importance of finding out what was happening in the Soviet's industrial sector at this time (see Schulz to Eisenhower, July 19, 1950, EM, Baruch Corr.). Symington was chairman of the National Security Resources Board (see the previous document).

[2] In his testimony before the Banking and Currency Committee of the U.S. Senate on July 26 Baruch had asked that Congress provide for tighter controls on prices and wages than those that the Senate had proposed in the legislation then under consideration. He had argued that the United States was lagging behind the Soviet Union in mobilizing for war: "Because we permitted the Soviets to gain this headstart in their mobilization, we now face a round of puppet aggressions—where next, who can tell?" The American people would need to make sacrifices if they wished to restore world peace. To believe that the United Nations could achieve its goals in Korea without a greater American commitment was "a futile, illusory hope." Baruch's testimony was reprinted as "All-Out War Effort Now—The Baruch Plan" in *U.S. News & World Report*, August 4, 1950, pp. 60–63. A summary had appeared in *New York Times*, July 27, 1950.

[3] Eisenhower had traveled to Washington, D.C., on June 25 and on July 5 to discuss the war in Korea with high government officials (see nos. 870 and 886. On the current situation of U.S. troops in Korea see no. 920. For President

Truman's views on mobilization see *Public Papers of the Presidents: Truman, 1950*, pp. 527–37, 564; and *New York Times*, July 20 and 28, 1950).
[4] Baruch and Eisenhower had been participants in a seminar on economic mobilization at Columbia's Graduate School of Business on May 18, 1950 (for background see no. 555, n. 3). Their views on the subject had been similar, and Eisenhower had told newsmen after his arrival in Denver, Colorado, on July 29 that Americans ought to pay attention to Baruch's mobilization proposals because the Korean War might require a greater commitment of strength than they had expected. "You can't win anywhere," he had argued, "if you don't win this one." (See *New York Times*, July 30, 1950; and *Denver Post*, July 30, 1950. See also Galambos, *Chief of Staff*, no. 1868).
[5] While Eisenhower was in Denver he would have access to office facilities at nearby Lowry Air Force Base (see no. 855).

915   *Eisenhower Mss., Family File*

TO MILTON STOVER EISENHOWER   *July 31, 1950*

Dear Milton: We are keeping the period around the 4th of October completely free for the ceremony and exercises incident to your inauguration.[1]

I do not expect to be back in New York before September 15th, but in these days anything can happen.[2] In any event I believe that thereafter you and I should definitely plan on spending at least one Sunday a month together. It would certainly be helpful to me. I don't know what the driving time between the two places is but certainly we can work out some schedule that will permit us to get together.[3]

I will ask Bob Schulz to look up the December 9–10 weekend to see whether or not I am already involved in anything. He should be able to drop you a note within a day or so. I am most anxious to see you—for a great number of reasons.[4] *As ever*

[1] Milton Eisenhower's inauguration as president of Pennsylvania State College was scheduled for October 4 and 5. For background see nos. 679 and 757; and for developments see no. 997.
[2] Eisenhower was on vacation in Denver, Colorado, when he wrote this letter. He would not return to New York City until September 18 (see no. 998).
[3] In a letter of July 24 Milton had said that he hoped they might occasionally spend a Saturday or a Sunday together exploring "many aspects of a total educational program" (EM, Family File).
[4] In his letter (see n. 3 above) Milton had said that he had been invited to meet with the Penn State alumni of New York City. He suggested that such a meeting be combined with a weekend visit at Morningside Drive, and he tentatively proposed December 8–10. Lieutenant Colonel Robert L. Schulz, Eisenhower's aide, would reply to Milton on September 2 that the General was indeed expecting the Milton Eisenhowers to visit on December 8, 9, and 10 (EM, Family File).

To Joseph Lawton Collins   *August 1, 1950*
Confidential

Dear Joe:[1] I know how busy you are and almost feel ashamed of myself
for asking for a bit of your time to listen to one of my problems.
However, I know of no one else who could take action in the matter.
I'm telling the full story in this letter—there is no "between the lines"
meaning to it.

Briefly my trouble is this: From the time I left Washington the
Army has been good enough to keep with me my Aide and two Sergeants, who were detailed to me under Presidential regulations several
years ago.[2] Much as I appreciate this I feel that new factors have now
entered the question and we must take certain definite action. The new
factor is the Federal Government's use of the draft to meet the Korean
crisis. Because of this, both the Army and I would, in my opinion,
come under very drastic and justifiable criticism if I were to retain any
enlisted men with me, in the absence of some obvious need such as
would be occasioned by an anticipated recall of some kind of public
service.[3]

Of course, if you are aware of any plan for bringing me back, either
indefinitely or intermittently, into some kind of public service in any
branch of the Government, then you can dismiss this whole business
with a mere notification to me that I had better begin planning for a
tour in Washington. However, I think this possibility to be rather
remote because what the Army needs now is young men who can carry
guns rather than old Generals, of whom we always have a lot.[4]

So, what I propose is: First, that I be allowed to keep an Aide because
of a continuing military correspondence that I can scarcely handle
without some help.

Secondly, both sergeants now with me have been on my personal
staff since the first days of World War II. One of them, Master Sergeant
Leonard Dry, is a top flight mechanic and driver. Much as I would
like to keep him I think that orders should be issued removing him
from detached service with me. Because the Korean crisis might conceivably be solved in the reasonably near future, I should very much
like to see him detailed for duty with the First Army, and with the
understanding that if we are able soon to return to a normal peace time
basis that I might possibly be able to have him once more; moreover,
at First Army Headquarters he would be available to me if I should be
called back to governmental service.[5] Since I have already authorized
Sergeant Dry to take a short furlough in the early part of August, I
believe that while his orders could be issued anytime, the effective date
should be the end of August.[6]

My other Sergeant is John Moaney, a negro. He is 36 years old and his present high rank, that of Master Sergeant, is purely the result of exuberant staff action during World War II. He is not qualified for any kind of service except at some place like Fort Myer or a similar station where General Officers would have need for an orderly of the highest character and all around housekeeping ability but with no special training. In his case I should like to get him discharged for the convenience of the Government. I realize that enlistments have been extended for one year but since he has been continuously in the Army since 1941 and his non-commissioned rank would make his reassignment very awkward, I think that his discharge would be justified. I know that he would have to apply personally for such a discharge and thereafter I would not only take him up in my personal employ but, to play fair with him, I would have to make some provision for him in my will. If I could afford it I'd most certainly like to do the same in the case of Sergeant Dry—but I feel that he is a valuable man to the Army while Moaney is strictly limited in his military qualifications.

This matter must seem, to you, inconsequential in these critical times, but if you should agree *in principle* with what I have suggested, all you would have to do would be to send me brief word to that effect, whereupon I would have my Aide get into communication with the Secretary of the General Staff or The Adjutant General and they could work out all of the details.

No one could possibly be more grateful for all of the consideration shown me than I am and for the many courtesies extended to me by the Army. But the time has come when we must realize that practices which, under normal times are not only thoroughly understood but highly desirable, can become most embarrassing if pursued during this crisis.

You already know my conviction that at this time I could not possibly imagine better hands than yours in which should rest the destinies of the Army. May quick and complete success crown your efforts, and if anytime, anywhere, I could possibly be of any help—just inform me. I would like for you to give Secretary Pace the same message. I recently had a nice note from him.[7]

I apologize for the length of this letter but you can see that I am dealing with the sort of thing that takes a bit of explanation.[8] *Cordially*

---

[1] This letter to the Chief of Staff of the Army was dispatched to Washington, D.C., from Denver, Colorado, where the Eisenhowers were vacationing. For background see no. 805.

[2] Lieutenant Colonel Robert L. Schulz was Eisenhower's aide; Master Sergeant Leonard D. Dry was his chauffeur; and Master Sergeant John A. Moaney was a member of Eisenhower's household staff. For background on these three men see *Eisenhower Papers*, vols. VI–IX.

[3] On June 30, President Truman had signed into law the act extending the Selective

Service Act of 1948 until July 9, 1951 (see U.S., *Statutes at Large*, vol. 64, pt. 1, pp. 318–19). On July 7 Eisenhower had told newsmen in Minneapolis, Minnesota, that the Truman administration's decision to draft men to fight in the Korean War was "a reasonable precaution" (see *New York Times*, July 8, 1950. On Eisenhower's trip to Minnesota see no. 893; on developments in Korea see no. 934).

[4] Eisenhower had made this same remark to reporters in California on July 19 (see *New York Times*, July 20, 1950; and *Denver Post*, July 20, 1950). An Associated Press (AP) story one day later had quoted his description of the Korean War as "a test of the ability of the free world to act." Failure to meet the Communists' challenge might lead to "an outbreak of similar or worse incidents elsewhere" (see *ibid.*, July 21, 1950).

[5] Eisenhower would also write to Walter Bedell Smith, CG, First Army, at Governors Island, New York, asking for approval of this arrangement (see no. 935).

[6] Authorization for Dry's furlough is in EM, Dry Corr.

[7] Secretary of the Army Frank C. Pace, Jr., had informed Eisenhower in a letter of July 21 (EM) that he would call upon him "for advice and counsel on some of the serious problems which are facing us today." Pace had been Director of the Budget before becoming Secretary of the Army on April 12, 1950 (for background see no. 380).

[8] For developments see no. 934.

917   *Eisenhower Mss.*

TO AMON GILES CARTER, JR.   *August 1, 1950*

Dear Amon: Your kind letter of the 13th and your wire to Bob Schulz dated 24 July were handed to me when I reached Denver.[1]

At the moment I am so snowed under with accumulated work that I cannot plan, even tentatively, for my vacational period. However, within two or three days I should be able to give you a fairly definite answer. I hope that this will be satisfactory because I am most grateful for your kindness in thinking of me.[2]

Incidentally, if I should find it possible to come, might I bring one friend with me—if not Bob Schulz, then one of my local friends. The reason I ask this is that I have not personally driven a car in ten or twelve years and I might possibly pile myself into the ditch if I should attempt it.[3]

Please give my kindest regards to your Dad and Sid Richardson.[4]
Cordially

[1] Carter (B.B.A. University of Texas 1941), manager of general advertising for the *Fort Worth Star-Telegram*, was the son of one of Eisenhower's old friends (for background on Amon Carter, Sr., see Galambos, *Chief of Staff*). Amon Carter, Jr., had served in the U.S. Army from 1941 to 1945 and had been a prisoner of war in Germany from 1943 to 1945. In his letter of July 13 (EM) he had invited

Eisenhower to visit a ranch owned by his father near Gunnison, Colorado. Lieutenant Colonel Robert L. Schulz, Eisenhower's aide, had acknowledged the letter in a note of July 18 (EM), and Carter had sent a telegram on the 24th inviting Schulz to come to the ranch also.
[2] In a letter of August 21 (EM) Carter would ask whether Eisenhower had decided to come to Gunnison, and Schulz would reply (Aug. 26, EM) that the General's commitments in Denver would preclude a trip to the ranch.
[3] On Eisenhower's arrangements for transportation while in Denver see no. 855.
[4] Sid W. Richardson was a multimillionaire who lived in Fort Worth. For background see no. 113.

918   *Eisenhower Mss.*

To Frederick Edgworth Morgan   *August 1, 1950*

Dear Freddie: I have read both pamphlets you sent me and found them highly intriguing and interesting. They should be particularly effective in informing readers as to the facts on the Eastern Europe situation.[1]

Because Soviet Russia does not want people to know the facts, it naturally follows that the publication of this magazine is the kind of thing that free nations should undertake. The Soviets can be fairly sure today that the free nations are not going to use force and weapons except on a completely defensive basis and then as a definite war measure. Consequently, they fear truth more than they do threats, and facts more than weapons.[2]

We should flood the world with truth and in such a campaign possibly the magazine "East Europe" could be classed as a "T-bomb."[3] *Cordially*

[1] Lieutenant General Morgan had been one of Eisenhower's British staff officers during World War II (see no. 357). Morgan had enclosed with his letter (June 27, EM) the June 22 issue of *East Europe*, and he had directed Eisenhower's attention to the opening article, entitled "Soviet Military Estimates." The piece was an analysis of the Russians' defense expenditures; the author, using the pseudonym "Pachydermus," concluded "that the Soviet Budget is a war Budget and that the Soviet Union is preparing intensively for war." The issue also included comments on several other aspects of the Soviet's East European policies, as did the July 13 issue, which Morgan had sent Eisenhower along with his letter of July 18 (EM).
[2] Morgan would reply (Aug. 9, EM) that he was gratified by Eisenhower's response and that he hoped the General would take out a group subscription to *East Europe* in the name of Columbia University. Eisenhower would write at the top of Morgan's letter: "Send items to McCann—to find out whether or not Dean White would be interested?" Kevin C. McCann was in New York City handling the General's correspondence while the Eisenhowers were on vacation (for background on the trip see no. 900). Carl M. White was Director of Libraries and dean of the School of Library Service at Columbia University. In his letter of the ninth Morgan would also thank Eisenhower for his "typically common-sense reaction to current

events in world affairs," and he would remind him that he still had an "I'm for Ike" lapel button, which he hoped he would soon have an opportunity to wear.
[3] The American counterpart to the British magazine *East Europe* was a semimonthly, mimeographed digest, *News from Behind the Iron Curtain*, which the National Committee for a Free Europe, Inc., had first issued in July 1950. It was a compilation of information to be broadcast by the committee's Radio Free Europe program, and by January 1952 it had evolved into a monthly magazine. Eisenhower, who had been a member of the committee since May 1949 (see no. 428), would receive copies. For background on Eisenhower's interest in the dissemination of propaganda see no. 785.

919   *Eisenhower Mss.*

To Michael James McKeogh   *August 1, 1950*

Dear Mickey: Thanks very much for your letter.[1] It is indeed difficult for me to give you any sound advice, but I believe that in your situation I should simply wait for instructions from the Army. While I realize that at times you may have some feeling that you are not doing your full duty, by merely waiting for a call, I have the very definite conviction that in the long run this is the best thing you can do both from your own standpoint and that of the Government.

As I remember the regulations of World War II, it would not be easy for you to obtain a commission. As I remember it you never went to college and you are now some thirty-two or thirty-three years of age. These two factors would combine to make it very difficult for you to get a commission unless, of course, because of some special knowledge that you may now possess concerning communications. This might be sufficient to overcome the obvious objections. If you feel that this might be the case I think you could write to the Chief Signal Officer outlining what you believe to be your special qualifications. Even this I would not do unless I received some tentative notice of an impending call to duty. Otherwise I would say that your job is to stay where you are, take care of your family and be as good a citizen as you know how.[2]

I am inclosing Henry Clay Williams' address on a slip of paper with this letter.[3]

Please give my warm regards to Pearlie and best wishes to Captain Butcher.[4] *Cordially*

[1] McKeogh, Eisenhower's orderly during World War II, was currently a salesman for radio station KIST, in Santa Barbara, California (for background see *Eisenhower Papers*, vols. I–IX). In a letter of July 18 (EM) McKeogh had asked Eisenhower for advice on returning to active service in the Army. He wanted to know whether it would be wiser to join immediately or to wait until his reserve unit was activated. He also wondered if he should seek a commission, and if so, in which branch of the Army it should be.

² McKeogh would reply (Dec. 11, 1950, EM) that he was still a master sergeant in the reserve and that he would probably be called back into the Army. He had heard that Eisenhower would soon become Supreme Commander of the NATO forces, and he hoped that the General might find him a place at his headquarters. He was even willing to reenlist if it meant that he could work with the General again. Eisenhower's staff-drafted reply of December 16 (EM) would indicate that McKeogh's offer of service would be kept on file.
³ McKeogh had asked Eisenhower for Williams's address in a postscript to his letter of July 18. Williams, currently living in Chicago, had been a member of Eisenhower's personal household staff during World War II. On his current interests see no. 821.
⁴ Pearlie was McKeogh's wife, the former Pearl Hargrave. Harry C. Butcher, naval aide to Eisenhower during World War II, was owner of radio station KIST. For background on both see *Eisenhower Papers*, vols. I–IX.

920   *Eisenhower Mss.*

TO ALBERT COADY WEDEMEYER   *August 1, 1950*

*Dear Al:*¹ I feel positively ashamed of myself for having placed before you a question that obliged you to take time enough to write such a letter as you did on the 17th.² My only purpose in making the original request was to assure myself that you would study the case personally. You need never to defend to me your own sense of fairness and your own judgment.³ You have too often saved me from bad errors to leave any doubt in my mind of your outstanding qualifications in this regard.

Anyway, I thoroughly appreciate the trouble you took to write me such a letter.⁴

Needless to say I found our conversation the other evening not only stimulating but informative. I have, since then, considered your ideas and convictions and I agree that we must, anticipating future incidents of this kind, develop ways and means of meeting issues without dribbling away our ground troops. This means Air and Navy.

On the other hand I believe that you agree with me that having gotten into this mess we must use every necessary means, including ground forces, to get out of it quickly and successfully.⁵

With warmest personal regards. *Cordially*

¹ Wedemeyer had been commanding general of the Sixth Army, Presidio of San Francisco, California, since August 1949. For background see no. 8.
² Wedemeyer had sent Eisenhower a detailed account of a court-martial investigation about which Eisenhower had written him (for background see nos. 879 and 880).
³ Wedemeyer had explained that records in the Sixth Army Headquarters revealed extensive irregularities on the part of the colonel in question. A subsequent investigation into the matter culminated in a lengthy report that strongly recommended that court-martial charges be drawn against the officer on sixteen counts.

"Some of the specifications," Wedemeyer admitted, "were relatively insignificant. . . . However, the two specifications relating to misappropriation of government property I simply could not in clear conscience fail to have adjudicated by a court martial." Wedemeyer asked Eisenhower to contact him if he felt that "common sense and comity" had not been exercised in the decision (July 17, 1950, EM).
[4] On August 14 Eisenhower would receive a handwritten letter from the colonel in question informing him that the case had been resolved with a "'disciplinary Action' letter" from Wedemeyer; his retirement was proceeding without delay. For later developments in this situation see *New York Times*, Dec. 11, 1954.
[5] Eisenhower and Wedemeyer might have discussed the Korean situation at a dinner on July 20 in San Francisco (see the guest list in EM, Collier Corr.). U.S. ground forces in Korea were retreating, and the U.S. Army divisions, greatly outnumbered and lacking tanks and artillery, had suffered 7,859 casualties by August 5. (See Schnabel, *Policy and Direction*, pp. 80–86, 111–14, 125–28; and Robert Frank Futrell, *The United States Air Force in Korea, 1950–1953* [New York, 1961], pp. 84–92, 100–103).

921   *Eisenhower Mss.*

To WILLARD R. COX   *August 1, 1950*

Dear Willard: Thank you for your nice letter of the 14th, which reached me only Saturday.[1]

I am sorry that I must forgo my annual trip to Wisconsin this year, but I do hope to get back for a few days next year.

As you would suspect, I have reported to the Government my readiness to come to Washington any instant that there might be any desire for my services. More than this I cannot do.[2] Actually they need young fellows who can carry guns far more than they need old Generals.[3]

Warmest personal regards. *Cordially*

[1] Cox, president of the Coca-Cola Bottling Company of St. Louis, Missouri, had expressed regret that Eisenhower would not be able to visit his ranch at Boulder Junction, Wisconsin, but he extended to the General a "perennial" invitation for the future (EM). On Eisenhower's visits to the ranch in 1946 and 1948 see no.122; on his stay during July and August 1949 see no. 426.
[2] Cox had mentioned that millions of Americans would feel that the country's safety was better assured if Washington officials were to summon Eisenhower to duty at the Department of Defense. Eisenhower had offered to cancel his vacation plans in order to consult with military leaders about the war in Korea, but President Truman had told him that this would not be necessary (see no. 909).
[3] See also no. 916, n. 4.

To Paul Burgess Fay, Jr.　　　　　　　　　*August 1, 1950*

Dear "Red":[1] Thanks for your most heartwarming and complimentary letter. I read with special interest the description of your public service activities which you carry on in addition to the necessary business of making a living. I do not see how you can do more—in fact I am especially proud of those citizens who incorporate into their day by day lives the responsibilities of citizenship. Just keep it up.

I am, of course, delighted that you liked the party the other evening. For myself it was one of the most stimulating experiences of my life. I hope that sometime I may see again each person who was there.[2] One of my purposes will be to show that their "selection" of an individual must and should involve someone else.[3] *Cordially*

[1] Fay (B.A. Stanford 1941) had been executive vice-president of Fay Improvement Company, a construction firm in San Francisco, California, since 1946. He had served in the Navy in the South Pacific during World War II, and he had campaigned for John Fitzgerald Kennedy (B.S. Harvard 1940) when the latter had been the Democratic candidate for election to the U.S. House of Representatives from the Eleventh District of Massachusetts (1946). Eisenhower had met Fay at a cocktail party in San Francisco on July 25. The host had been Adolphus Andrews, Jr. (A.B. Princeton 1943), assistant secretary of Pope & Talbot, Inc. The political discussions at the party had prompted Fay to recall in his letter to Eisenhower (July 27, EM) that during the war he and Kennedy had "spent many hours talking of the part we would like to play in the governing of our country when we got home." Fay's business commitments currently limited his political activities to "doorbell pushing, postcard writing and short speeches in front of small groups at election time," but he hoped eventually to obtain both the expertise and the resources that would allow him to devote more time to politics.

[2] As an enclosure to a letter of August 7 (EM) Andrews would send Eisenhower the names and addresses of the guests who had attended his party, and Eisenhower would thank him in a note of August 10 (EM).

[3] Fay had remarked, "If I don't get an opportunity to see you again between now and '52, I'll see you in the White House." Other guests at the party had written letters to Eisenhower expressing similar sentiments (see Larsen to Eisenhower, July 30, 1950, and Miller to Eisenhower, July 26, 1950, EM). Eisenhower would reply to these with notes (of August 4 and 5, respectively) that followed closely the pattern of this letter and of no. 932.

To Donald Sipe Kennedy　　　　　　　　　*August 1, 1950*

Dear Don:[1] In this day and time I doubt that we can permit such affairs as the "Korean Crisis" to affect, materially, a long range plan for improving understanding and exercise of citizenship in the United States. I rather have the feeling that these crises are going to become a nagging part of our lives.[2] Be sure to drop me a note whenever an idea might occur to you that you should like me to hear about. I need the imaginations and advice of my friends very much—sometimes I wonder whether my own are not a bit threadbare.[3] *Cordially*

[1] Kennedy (A.B. University of Arizona 1932) had been president of Oklahoma Gas and Electric Company since 1949. During July Eisenhower had sent him a letter outlining his goals for Columbia University (a draft dated July 10, 1950, is in EM, Letters and Drafts; that version differed only slightly from no. 826). In an undated reply, Kennedy had promised to help raise money for Columbia when his friends returned from their vacations. He worried, however, that he would not have much success until the war in Korea became "more stabilized." On the war see no. 920, n. 5.
[2] See also no. 865.
[3] For developments see no. 1022.

924   *Eisenhower Mss.*

To Lucian King Truscott, Jr.   *August 1, 1950*

Dear Lucian:[1] Numbers of letters, somewhat similar to yours, have reached me in recent days but none of them has made me feel quite so good as yours.[2] It would really be like old times to be in harness, with you by my side. Of course, I hope that this present crisis is quickly eliminated but I am sure that plans should go forward just exactly as if it were going to be a long drawn out affair—with the possibility always with us of an even greater explosion somewhere else.[3]
With warm personal regards. *Cordially*

[1] Lieutenant General Truscott had retired from the Army in September 1947. For background see no. 819.
[2] Truscott had observed (July 24, EM) that the war in Korea was becoming "a sort of creeping emergency, a long haul in which the services of some of the old war horses might be of some use." Truscott said he had written letters to General Omar N. Bradley, chairman of the JCS, and General J. Lawton Collins, Chief of Staff of the Army, offering to serve the nation during the current crisis. It would be better, he had concluded, to "die in harness doing what ever I can than to live to a ripe old age sitting on the side lines."
[3] In May 1951 Truscott would become Coordinator and Adviser for Military Security, Defense Organization, and Public Safety on the staff of the United States High Commissioner for Germany (see *New York Times*, May 25, 1951).

To Haroldson Lafayette Hunt

Dear Mr. Hunt:[0] Your letter of July 17th reached me Saturday, when I finally arrived in Denver.[1]

I respect your judgment and you may be sure that I shall study your letter carefully. Incidentally, it may interest you to know that in two recent public speeches in California I have stated flatly and without qualification "Any citizens of this country who embrace Communism can be considered nothing less than traitors."[2]

Of course, I think that you will agree with me that even in this campaign against subversion we must be very careful to preserve the essentials of Americanism, including, among other things, the complete equality of each of us before the law.[3]

I thoroughly enjoyed our opportunity to talk while in New York, and hope that other opportunities of this kind will come to me because your views are so direct and positive.[4]

Warm personal regards. *Cordially*

---

[1] Hunt, founder of the Hunt Oil Company in east Texas, had visited Eisenhower at Columbia University on July 13 (for background see no. 826). In his letter of the seventeenth (EM) Hunt had argued that Americans needed to inform the Russians that the U.S. government would not permit the spread of communism "over new territory and other nations." He had asked Eisenhower to criticize publicly the Communist sympathizers in the U.S. government who had "surrendered the freedom of hundreds of millions" of Eastern Europeans and Chinese to the Soviets.

[2] We have been unable to locate transcripts of the speeches, one of which was probably delivered at Bohemian Grove on July 22. For background see no. 887.

[3] Hunt had criticized the decision of the board of trustees of the Carnegie Endowment for International Peace not to accept the resignation of Alger Hiss, the organization's president and trustee, until the courts had handed down a judgment. Hunt maintained that so many government officials had testified as character witnesses for Hiss that it had been unlikely that he would be convicted of anything (for background see no. 167). Actually Hunt had the story confused. The board of trustees had "tabled" consideration of Hiss's letter of resignation on December 13, 1948, and had granted him a three-month leave of absence. The executive committee of the trustees had later voted to extend the leave until the annual meeting of the board in May 1949. Hiss had submitted a request to the board that it not consider his name for reelection at the May 5 meeting, and the board had elected James T. Shotwell, Bryce Professor Emeritus of History and International Relations at Columbia University, to succeed Hiss. The trustees deferred action, however, on the portion of Hiss's letter in which he had tendered his resignation as a trustee (the minutes of the May 5 meeting are in EM, Carnegie Endowment Corr.; see also *New York Times*, Mar. 12 and May 6, 1949). Hiss would not be listed as a trustee in Carnegie Endowment for International Peace, *Annual Report, 1950–1951* (New York, 1951), pp. 18, 51.

Hunt had also expressed reservations about the loyalty and integrity of others (for his continuing interest in this subject see no. 961). He had commented,

moreover, that it would be senseless to try to implement Eisenhower's goals for Columbia University as long as free institutions were vulnerable to destruction from within.
[4] Hunt would thank Eisenhower for this praise in a letter of August 16 (EM). He would enclose a draft of a proposal for a peace league to prevent wars. Hunt hoped that Eisenhower would give the paper to someone in a position to suggest changes in the organization of the United Nations. "I am sure," he had written, "that anything constructive which could be offered to bolster up the United Nations would do a great deal of good." The outline set forth an arrangement for "percentage participation" by various nations. The United States, the Soviet Union, and the United Kingdom would control as much as 66 percent of the activities of the league, and no other country was to have more than a 5 percent share in the operations.

926   *Eisenhower Mss.*

To Robert Justus Kleberg, Jr.   *August 2, 1950*

Dear Bob: I have written, and am sending to you along with this note, a rather formidable treatise, similar to one I wrote recently to Bill Burnham, about Columbia's projects.[1] I felt that it might be useful to you occasionally when you are talking to some of your friends about these particular things.[2]

It now looks as if I might get down to Texas for a few days in November. However, the demands for "speaking engagements" have become so great that I have been forced to eliminate any possibility of including recreational time in the program. Just how I can get to Texas and actually spend some time with friends, free of all work, worry and planning, is getting to be a real problem. Already, the mere assumption that I am coming down next fall, has brought me a whole series of invitations to appear publicly.[3] *Cordially*

[1] Kleberg, president of the King Ranch, Inc., was one of the Texans who had attended the luncheon given by William H. Burnham, an investment banker, and Leonard F. McCollum, president of the Continental Oil Company, in New York City on July 13, 1950 (for background on Kleberg see no. 623; on the luncheon see no. 826). The "treatise," dated August 1 (EM), was a modified version of no. 826. Eisenhower would revise his "treatise" and dispatch it to another Texan on August 30 (see no. 953).
[2] For developments see no. 942.
[3] For examples see nos. 989 and 1017. On Eisenhower's itinerary see no. 1000.

To ALFRED MAXIMILIAN GRUENTHER

Dear Al:[1] I enclose a letter I have received from a Chinese citizen who has had long experience fighting the Reds in the Far East. You may or may not find some interest in it. It is possible that you may even find some reason for wanting to see Dr. Liu.[2] In any event, you will see from the copy of my answer, also enclosed, that I wash my hands of the whole matter and leave it in yours.[3]

I am beginning to feel the need for a long talk with my old associates in Washington. I wish that one of you were flying out this way sometime soon, but I know that all of you are busy as you can be. It is faintly possible, especially if I should run into an opportunity to make a very speedy round trip to Washington, that I will drop in someday for an hour or so.[4]

Anyway, good luck to all of you. *Cordially*

[1] Lieutenant General Gruenther was Deputy Chief of Staff for Plans and Combat Operations (see no. 569).

[2] There is no copy of Fred Hian-tsie Liu's letter to Eisenhower in EM. Eisenhower had replied to Liu on this same day (EM), remarking, "I personally believe that the kind of tactics you advocate should be used to the limit of practicability."

[3] Gruenther would respond (Aug. 7, EM) that Liu's ideas were good but that U.S. forces in Korea had not yet had a chance to "get set," let alone undertake new strategies. Gruenther would send Liu's recommendations to Major General Edward Mallory Almond, Chief of Staff to General of the Army Douglas MacArthur (for background see *Eisenhower Papers*, vols. VI–IX). Almond had been Deputy Chief of Staff, GHQ, U.S. Army Forces, Pacific, from November 4, 1946, to February 19, 1949, when he had become Chief of Staff, Far East Command.

[4] Judging by Eisenhower's appointment calendars, he would not be able to visit Washington, D.C., before October 27, 1950. He would meet with Gruenther at Columbia University, however, on October 13 and 20.

To EDGAR NEWTON EISENHOWER

Dear Edgar: I have your note of July 25th and regret that my need for having some little regard for my health has forced me to decline an invitation in which you are interested. When I did so I was not aware of your personal involvement but in any event my decision would have had to be the same.[1]

I arrived in Denver to find my desk flooded with invitations to "speak" and the same thing has been happening to me for a long time. I thought that things would be better this last spring but they were really worse.[2]

I have now included on my fall schedule at least five public appearances within a space of six weeks. To do more is simply out of the question if I am to pay any attention at all to the requirements of my administrative work.

Ever since I have returned from War, I have been intimately associated with one or more scientists who were engaged in the development of nuclear fission—in fact some of the basic patents are owned by several of the professors in Columbia University.[3] In the same way I am intimately associated with men who are giving all of their time and energy to public service—always with little, and occasionally, with no remuneration.[4] So, I am completely sympathetic with the purpose of the group in which you are interested.

With respect to the recording, I would have no objection to making a short one provided I would be given some idea of the kind of thing that is wanted and if it could be done after I return to Columbia in mid-September.[5]

I am puzzled as to what you mean about making a broadcast from State College but such a chore would be subject to the same observations made in the early part of this letter—it would require too much time and effort to do the job right.[6]

I have made this rather lengthy explanation so that if you want to send, to my office at Columbia, a full description of what would be wanted from me in making the recording, I will have some basis for a decision.[7]

I still hope that you can make Milton's inauguration. I plan to be there and hope all the rest do.[8] *As ever*

---

[1] Eisenhower's brother Edgar had expressed disappointment in a letter of July 25 (same file as document) saying that the General had decided not to speak on "Atom for Peace Day" at the University of Michigan on October 2, 1950. In a letter of July 13, 1950, Alexander Grant Ruthven (Ph.D. University of Michigan 1906), president of the university since 1929, had invited Eisenhower to be the main speaker at a dinner in Ann Arbor, Michigan, on the opening day of a drive to raise $6.5 million for an atomic energy research center. Eisenhower had sent a declination on the following day. Both letters are in EM, Correspondence Relating to Declinations, 1950.

[2] See, for example, no. 741.

[3] John R. Dunning, dean of the School of Engineering at Columbia University, had been the first U.S. scientist to demonstrate that splitting uranium atoms released vast amounts of energy. He had also been scientific director for the construction of the synchro-cyclotron at Irvington-on-Hudson, New York (see no. 802; on Dunning's current situation at Columbia see no. 688). George B. Pegram, vice-president emeritus of Columbia University and special adviser to Eisenhower, had helped to organize the studies that had led to the development of the atomic bomb (for background see no. 254). Isidor I. Rabi, Eugene Higgins Professor of Physics at Columbia, had received the Nobel prize for physics in 1944 as a result of his discovery of a method for studying the radio frequency spectra of atoms. Hideki Yukawa (D.Sc. Osaka University 1938), who had received the Nobel prize for

physics in 1949, was currently visiting professor of physics. He had been the first physicist to formulate equations alleging the existence of the meson, a fourth basic particle of subatomic matter. Eisenhower would meet with Rabi and Yukawa on September 26, 1950 (see also Galambos, *Chief of Staff*, nos. 612, 1244, 1468, and 1808).

[4] On Eisenhower's public service activities see nos. 473, n. 4, and 825, n. 3.

[5] Edgar had asked the General to make—in lieu of a personal appearance—a ten-minute recording which would be broadcast on October 2.

[6] As an alternative to the recording, Edgar had suggested that the General deliver "a ten minute broadcast from State College." Edgar had apparently assumed that his brother would be at State College, Pennsylvania, on that date, although their brother Milton's inauguration as president of the Pennsylvania State College would not take place until October 4. As it turned out, the General would arrive in State College on October 3 (see no. 997).

[7] Edgar would quote the fourth paragraph of this letter in a note to Ruthven (Aug. 24, EM, Family File), adding, however, that the General might not satisfy in a speech of ten minutes a nationwide audience that deserved a fifteen-minute treatment of the subject. He would conclude with the observation that "a word from Dwight would be helpful but by golly, I still believe the Michigan alumni can do this without any outside help" (see Ruthven's reply on August 13, and Edgar's note of September 14 [both in *ibid.*], with General Eisenhower's comment typed on the letter). Eisenhower would record a short speech, and it would be broadcast on October 2. The General would describe atomic energy as a resource that Americans ought to put to use in peaceful ways in order to win "the battle for freedom" (see EM, Subject File, Messages; and *New York Times*, Oct. 3, 1950). Ruthven would thank Eisenhower in a note of October 9 (EM).

[8] In April 1950 Edgar had informed his brother Milton that he might not be able to attend the inauguration (for background see no. 790). By September 1950, however, Edgar's plans had changed, and he would notify Dwight in his letter of September 14 (EM, Family File) that he might see him at State College in October.

929   *Eisenhower Mss.*

To Louis Arthur Johnson   *August 2, 1950*

Dear Louis: I have just had a long conversation with Tom Campbell.[1] As you know, he has a great background of experience in land transport and is a member of the American Institute of Constructional Engineers.

He brings to me a story of deep personal concern because of a belief that the government—specifically the security departments—is not fully abreast of modern practices in the purchase and procurement of certain types of motor equipment. As a consequence of this failure, or what he believes to be a failure, he is convinced that the government is not only spending a great deal of money inefficiently but is not obtaining the best, surest and most effective transport in critical areas. This he feels ranges all the way from the Arctic to tropic areas.

For a number of years I have had the privilege of listening to Tom Campbell on an informal basis; he has been kind enough to consider himself as a sort of an unofficial member of my official family. Possibly, I have not always agreed with him, but I have never listened to him without benefit.[2] Because of this personal experience and my confidence in his selflessness and his devotion to our country, I suggest that you send for him at some time when you have at least two hours to devote to the subject and listen to his complete story. You may find—or your technical advisors may find for you—that you cannot agree with all that he says, or there may be factors in the situation of which he is currently unaware.

Nevertheless, I do feel that you will be highly gratified that you have had a full explanation of his views.

This note, of course, requires no answer.[3] It's nothing in the world but a personal suggestion to you that you may follow or disregard as you wish. But I know you will understand that I merely want to be helpful.[4]

With warm regard, and my very best wishes to you in these difficult days.[5] *Sincerely*

[1] Thomas D. Campbell, head of the Campbell Farming Corporation, had met with Eisenhower at 11:00 A.M.; they had gone to lunch at 12:15 P.M. at Lowry Air Force Base, near Denver, Colorado, and discussed subjects ranging from wheat farming to transportation in Alaska during the winter (for background on Campbell see no. 808). Commenting on their conversations, Campbell had noted that Eisenhower, "having grown up in the Kansas farm country, has been a farmer at heart all his life and would go back to the farm tomorrow if he could. I'm also sure that's where he first learned to 'work eight hours twice a day'—which he has been doing ever since" (see *Denver Post*, Aug. 3, 1950).

[2] See, for example, Eisenhower's account of a conversation with Campbell three years earlier in Galambos, *Chief of Staff*, no. 1734.

[3] Secretary Johnson would reply in a letter of August 9 (EM) that he had recently received a letter from Campbell analyzing the problems of heavy overland transport, and he had sent the letter to the chairman of the Munitions Board and to the Secretary of the Army. In addition, he promised to present Eisenhower's recommendation to Hubert Elmer Howard (LL.B. Harvard 1912), chairman of the U.S. Munitions Board and of the NATO Military Production and Supply Board.

[4] Notes at the bottom of this letter indicate that Eisenhower handed a carbon copy to Campbell and dispatched the ribbon copy by air mail.

[5] Eisenhower would deliver an address at the graduation and commissioning ceremonies for the Air Force ROTC summer camp at Lowry Air Force Base on August 4. Referring to the conflict in Korea, he would observe that many of his listeners might wonder, "What the Hell is this fighting about?" As a partial explanation, he would remark, "When they say it is American imperialism that is causing trouble in Korea, that is all bologna and they are liars—nothing else." Greater solidarity would solve the problem, he would argue, and he foresaw a united America "standing before the world as a moral force—a moral force for decency, for good, for fairness, and for justice." A transcript of the speech is in EM, Lowry Air Force Base Corr.

Dear Phillip:[01] Today I received a letter from Marcy Dodge which I inclose. After you have read it will you send it on to Kevin McCann to be kept with my Columbia files?[2]

I am enthusiastic about the idea of organizing a little "Cabinet" such as Marcy suggests.[3] One difficulty which immediately suggests itself is that in a way, work of such a group would be duplicating that of the Development Committee of the Trustees.[4] This could be worked out I think, particularly if Douglas Black would give his attention to it.[5] The great advantage would be that we could enlist enthusiastic Columbians who are not necessarily Trustees—on the other hand, Trustees could also be included. The great difference between the functions of the proposed group and the duties of the Development Committee would be that the new group would be "operational" whereas the Development Committee concerns itself chiefly with policy.[6]

Personally, I think that Bill Donovan would be a natural to head such a group but I will talk to you about that when I return.[7]

In the meantime won't you study the whole idea thoroughly and if you like it, draw up some plan that could be considered by the staff when I return.[8]

It would seem to me that with such a general arrangement the head of our "professional staff " would not need to be of extraordinary calibre.[9]

With cordial regard, *Sincerely*

[1] Phi*l*ip Young, dean of the Graduate School of Business, was Acting Coordinator of Development at Columbia University (see no. 789). For background on Young see no. 54; for developments see nos. 971 and 972.

[2] For background on Marcellus H. Dodge, clerk of the trustees of Columbia University, see no. 41. Copies of this letter and of Dodge's letter to Eisenhower of July 27, 1950, were forwarded to Young, who was on vacation. The originals were sent to Kevin McCann, assistant to the president (MacKenzie to Eisenhower, Aug. 7, EM, Young Corr.).

[3] Dodge had asked Eisenhower to consider Major General Willian J. Donovan to head a "little cabinet of die-hards," which would be formed in connection with development operations at Columbia University. Dodge said he had discussed this idea at a luncheon meeting with Young and Columbia trustees George E. Warren and John G. Jackson. Dodge wrote that "Bill Donovan, former Columbia Trustee, Columbia football man, known to practically every Columbia man I know and respected by all, would be a very good leader" (EM. For background on Donovan, a member of Columbia's College Fund Committee and of the Columbia Associates, see *Eisenhower Papers*, vols. I–IX. For background on Warren and Jackson see nos. 243 and 225, respectively). Eisenhower had thanked Dodge for "an idea that we can apply perfectly" (Aug. 1, 1950, EM).

[4] For background on the trustees' Development Committee see no. 488, n. 4.

[5] On Douglas M. Black, a life trustee of Columbia University, see no. 304, n. 3.

[6] See nn. 8 and 9 below.

[7] Eisenhower would be in Denver until September 17 (see no. 805, n. 4).
[8] Young's recommendations for an effective development organization would include the following: a special adviser to assist the president of the university in his role as chief development officer; a central office, or "home," for development activities of the various schools and departments of the university; a provision for the Development Plan Committee to serve as an independent planning group, divorced from operating responsibility, to review and prepare proposals for the president; and the necessary arrangements to ensure a close working liaison between the president's office and the development units (Oct. 16, 1950, EM, Columbia Corr.).
[9] On December 1, 1950, a Council on Development and Resources would be formed to supersede the existing development groups. This council, with "vast powers" to coordinate all development activities, was "responsible directly to the trustees in determining the relative needs of Columbia's schools and projects and in supervising efforts to meet those needs." Charles A. Anger, a professional fundraiser and newly appointed Executive Director of Development, said the council would determine the relative merits of fund requests, advise campaigners, and correlate appeals "so as to avoid duplication and an 'over-working' of contributors and solicitors." General Donovan was named chairman of the council, which included Black, Dodge, and Warren, representing the trustees; chairman Edward Green of the Development Plan Committee; and Associate Provost John A. Krout, representing the administration (*New York Times*, Jan. 8, 1951).

931   *Eisenhower Mss.*

TO HAROLDSON LAFAYETTE HUNT   *August 4, 1950*

Dear Mr. Hunt:[0] Thank you very much for your note and its attached memorandum.[1] If I should come up to Wyoming I will most certainly stop to see you.[2] In the meantime, I give my quick reaction to your suggestions by saying that the word "constructive" seems to offer more possibilities for putting over what we really mean than does any other word I have heard. We have certainly suffered from the fact that extremists have pre-empted and used, as their own personal property, the more popular descriptive words.[3] *Cordially*

[1] Hunt had suggested (July 28, EM) that the word *constructive* be substituted for *liberal* in everyday usage. He had also enclosed a memorandum entitled "What's In A Name?" which included analyses of various meanings of *liberal, conservative, right, progressive,* and *constructive.* The anonymous author of the paper had argued that *liberal* connoted "change, innovation, improvement, progress and in an indefinite way, consecration to the welfare of the many," but the word had been appropriated by the "radical, left-wing spend-thrift element." *Constructive* was the word to use if good government were the goal one sought. For background see no. 925.
[2] Hunt had mentioned that he had a ranch southwest of Cody, Wyoming, and that Eisenhower ought to visit it if he happened to be in the area.
[3] For developments see no. 969.

To EDWIN C. CALLAN   *August 5, 1950*

Dear Mr. Callan:[0] Thank you very much for the generosity of the sentiments you express toward me in your letter of the 31st. No American can read such things and fail to experience a warm glow of gratitude—but I must still tell you that it is the final paragraph of your letter that pleases me most! Keep right on the ball! The country needs that kind of service.[1]

Ever since Dolph Andrews's party I've considered myself lucky that I was included on his guest list—that was a wonderful crowd of young men.[2]

With warm personal regard, *Sincerely*

[1] Callan, who worked for Brush, Slocumb & Company, an investment securities firm, had met Eisenhower at a cocktail party in San Francisco, California, on July 25. The host had been Adolphus Andrews, Jr., and much of the discussion had concerned politics (for background see no. 922). In his letter (EM) Callan had expressed the hope that the General would accept a nomination to run for the presidency in 1952. He had mentioned in closing that he planned to campaign for local Republicans seeking election during the fall of 1950, and he expected to be ready to canvass for Eisenhower in 1952.
[2] See also the following document.

To EDGAR S. LEWIS   *August 5, 1950*

Dear Mr. Lewis: First I take up the second of your two postscripts. In spite of your injunction, I cannot possibly refrain from answering such an interesting letter![1]

With respect to the other postscript, I occasionally like to indulge, on a very modest scale, my sentiments when I find them opposed to my better judgment. So I enclose a $5.00 bill, which is my bet on Columbia against Princeton this fall. While I hope it returns to me with its mate, I, secretly, have no real optimism on this point.[2]

If, with respect to the serious part of your letter, you will allow me to ignore the personal allusions, I want to tell you right off that it represents, in my opinion, a penetrating analysis of our current situation and of necessary measures. You understand that my conviction as to the wisdom of your conclusions is probably influenced by the realization that they coincide so closely with my own.[3]

Others who attended Dolf Andrews's party have written to me in a somewhat similar vein, but without presenting the clear analysis that you have taken the trouble to set down.[4] I truly hope that you have kept a copy of the letter, because of its clarity and because of the help it could be to you in presenting your views to others. In fact, I am bold enough to ask your permission to use the letter myself, after deleting, of course, your name and address (assuming that you would prefer this) and deleting also those parts that make any personal reference to me. Manifestly, I could not use the letter unless I had the privilege of eliminating this particular part.[5]

You are particularly persuasive in urging the need for honest, straightforward leadership, based upon truth, no matter how unpleasant that truth may be and based also upon a willingness to point out the eventual consequences of proposals, no matter how currently appealing the proposal may seem. Indeed, I think it certain that softness, indulgence, wishful thinking and refusal to face unpleasant facts must be equalled by sterner virtues if we are to preserve the essentials of the American way of life.

Possibly, I could have said all this very promptly and more emphatically by simply noting that the parts of your letter I have discussed gave me a tremendous lift.

Warm greetings to any of Dolf Andrews's guests that you may happen to encounter and with personal regards and best wishes to yourself. *Cordially*

[1] Lewis (A.B. Princeton 1943), of San Francisco, California, had met Eisenhower at a cocktail party in that city on July 25 (for background on the gathering and on Adolphus Andrews, Jr., the host, see no. 922). Lewis's first postscript to his letter of July 27 (EM) had been an assurance that Eisenhower need not answer it, "for you are a busy man."
[2] Lewis's second postscript had been a wager that Princeton would win its football game against Columbia in the fall. Princeton would in fact win all of its games in the 1950 season.
[3] Lewis perceived that American participation in the U.N. intervention in the Korean conflict had been the outcome of the nation's obligation to provide moral leadership on a global scale. The manner in which the U.S. government was waging war, however, would "either cause us eventually to throw in the sponge or force us into bankruptcy." The solution would be to "forego our present luxuries and buckle to the task." Unfortunately, the Truman administration was unprepared to divert its attention from legislation providing citizens "the hand-out, guaranteed security, parities, etc." Lewis argued that Eisenhower was the only man who could "tell the people blunt, unpleasant truths and re-teach our basic principles." He had interpreted Eisenhower's remarks at the party as indications that the General would "govern flexibly in such a manner as to encourage our tradition of free enterprise and individual incentive," and he promised that he and other guests at the party would be enthusiastic supporters of a campaign to elect Eisenhower.
[4] See the preceding document.
[5] In a letter of August 11 (EM) Lewis would grant Eisenhower permission to reproduce his earlier letter "in any way you see fit."

To Joseph Lawton Collins August 10, 1950

Dear Joe: Your reply to my recent personal request was typical—you have always shown me the maximum in personal consideration.[1]

I assure you that I am permanently obligated to you for your prompt and generous action.

I am very anxious to talk to you and for a while thought that I would be coming to Washington for a day or so about this time. Unfortunately I have found that the general crisis in our affairs has enormously increased my correspondence and the demands made upon me in the form of personal visits, telegrams, and telephone conversations. I seem to be pretty well nailed down and except for the fact that the Commanding General at Lowry Field has generously provided me with an office and secretarial help, I frankly don't know what I would do.[2]

If, by any chance, you should be coming this way in the next two or three weeks, please do try to stop for a little while in Denver. In the meantime, the best of luck to you. The news right now looks quite encouraging, which means to me that this is the very time there should be every possible reinforcement flowing into the theater.[3] There is no one that knows better than you do the value of pouring on the heat when you have the enemy shaken up and partially defeated.[4]

Again my thanks, and my love to Gladys.[5] I told Mamie that I was writing to you and she joins me in these sentiments. She is quite heartbroken at the thought that we must lose our beloved Sgt. Dry but she quite realizes the wisdom and necessity for the move. Cordially

[1] General Collins, Chief of Staff of the Army, had notified Eisenhower in a letter of August 4 (EM) that Lieutenant Colonel Robert L. Schulz, Eisenhower's aide, and Master Sergeant John A. Moaney, a member of Eisenhower's household staff, should remain with Eisenhower in spite of the Army's manpower shortage during the Korean War (for background see no. 916). Collins had consented, however, to Eisenhower's request that Master Sergeant Leonard D. Dry, his chauffeur, be transferred to Headquarters, First Army, at Governors Island, New York, effective September 1, 1950. Eisenhower informed Dry of this development in a letter of this same day (no. 936).

[2] The Eisenhowers were currently on vacation in Denver, Colorado. On the trip see no. 805; on the arrangements at Lowry Air Force Base see no. 855.

[3] On August 8 (Korean time) U.S. ground forces had launched their largest attack since their entry into the war. This had been an attempt to break out of the defensive line known as the Pusan Perimeter, behind which the U.N. troops had withdrawn between August 1 and 4. On the eighth the U.N. forces had regained some of the ground that they had lost during more than a month of retreat, but a North Korean counteroffensive on the same day penetrated the Naktong River line of the Pusan Perimeter. For a detailed account of actions by various units see Roy E. Appleman, South to the Naktong, North to the Yalu (June–November 1950),

U.S. Army in the Korean War, ed. Stetson Conn (Washington, D.C., 1960), pp. 266–302, 334–42. See also *New York Times*, August 8, 9, and 10, 1950.

Eisenhower would discuss the Korean War in a recorded message to be broadcast at the groundbreaking ceremonies for the new Leydon-Chiles-Wickersham American Legion post in Denver on August 19. He would refer to American unpreparedness as a factor contributing to the current difficulties, and he would point out an underlying contradiction in the manner in which the U.S. government was waging war: "We have *not* mobilized our industry and our manhood on the scale that we did in recent wars, but young Americans are, nevertheless, serving and sometimes dying on the battle front." A transcript of the recording is in EM, Subject File, Messages. For a summary see *Denver Post*, August 20, 1950.

[4] On Collins's success as a corps commander in World War II see no. 8.

[5] Collins's wife, the former Gladys Easterbrook.

935   *Eisenhower Mss.*

TO WALTER BEDELL SMITH   *August 10, 1950*

Dear Bedell:[01] Inclosed is a copy of a letter I have written to General Collins and a copy, also, of his reply to me.[2]

You know how dependent I have become on Sgt. Dry, but I do not honestly feel that in good conscience I can keep him in my service while the draft is in effect.[3]

Nevertheless, I am anxious that he stay in New York for three reasons:

    a.   If I should be called to any kind of active service, he would be immediately available to me.

    b.   If conditions ever return to the so-called "normal," possibly you and the Department will consider returning Sgt. Dry to me.

    c.   He would be, with your permission, available to me for any kind of emergency service if I should get into a hole.

The first minor emergency that will face me will be the hiring of some individual to replace him (as far as such an extraordinary individual can be replaced). I intend to return to New York shortly after the middle of September and I should like to have your permission to use Sgt. Dry from the date of my return until I can hire a replacement.[4] This should not take too long.

Sgt. Dry now lives at Fort Totten. I assume that he would want to continue living there unless you had satisfactory available quarters on Governors Island, which I would seriously doubt. In view of the uncertainties of the moment and of the future, I wonder whether you could find it possible to allow Dry to keep his quarters until things clarify a lot more.[5]

I realize that I am imposing on you with my personal problems, but you have for so many years been my mainstay that I find it quite natural to be asking you to help me out. *Sincerely*

¹ Lieutenant General Smith, Eisenhower's Chief of Staff during World War II, was commanding general of the First Army. For background see *Eisenhower Papers*, vols. I–IX.
² See the preceding document.
³ Master Sergeant Leonard D. Dry was Eisenhower's chauffeur. Eisenhower had argued in a letter to the Chief of Staff of the Army (no. 916) that Dry should be assigned to duties with Headquarters, First Army, at Governors Island, New York. The Army's manpower shortage had led the Truman administration to draft men to fight in Korea, and Eisenhower preferred under those circumstances to hire a civilian driver.
⁴ The Eisenhowers would remain on vacation in Denver, Colorado, until September 17. On their stay there see no. 900.
⁵ Dry would be transferred to Headquarters, First Army, but he would retain his quarters at Fort Totten. For developments see no. 950.

936
*Eisenhower Mss.,
J. Lawton Collins Corr.*

To Leonard D. Dry
August 10, 1950

*Dear Sergeant Dry:*¹ Because the government has found it necessary to use the draft in obtaining soldiers, I have had to conclude that, unless I should be called to military service, I would have to release the soldiers now serving with me. I wrote the Chief of Staff to this effect, and asked that you be detailed for duty at Headquarters, First Army, so that if conditions should soon quiet down, I could secure your services once more.²

I also told the Chief of Staff that I had granted you a short furlough during the month of August and requested therefore that you not be transferred to regular duty until September 1.³

To all of this he agreed, and so, on September 1, you will be detached from me and sent to Headquarters, First Army, for duty. However, I am going to ask General Smith if he could lend you temporarily to me when I return to New York, pending the time I can secure a reliable and satisfactory driver for the big Chrysler.⁴

Of course, could I have provided for you from personal funds the same remuneration and expectations that you have in the Army, I would have proposed to you that you take your discharge for the convenience of the government and go to work for me privately. However, the certainty and security of your position in the Army, to say nothing of your pay and retired privileges, are something that you cannot possibly give up even for an unusually good civilian salary.

On the other hand you will see from the above that I am hopeful of securing you again, in the future. In any event you will be close by and I trust that we will see each other often. I feel certain that General Smith will do everything possible for the convenience of yourself and your family.

In this letter I shall not even attempt to express the extent of my obligation and appreciation to you. This I will leave for a personal meeting, but I should tell you that since this news has come, Mrs. Eisenhower has been very despondent. She feels that she does not want to live in New York if she does not have you to help her.[5]

Please give our love to Geraldine and to the baby.[6]

With warmest regards to yourself. *Sincerely*

[1] Master Sergeant Dry was Eisenhower's chauffeur.
[2] The letter to the Chief of Staff of the Army is no. 916.
[3] Authorization for Dry's furlough is in EM, Dry Corr.
[4] The letter to Lieutenant General Walter B. Smith, CG of the First Army, is the preceding document.
[5] Dry would reply in a letter of August 17 (same file as document) that he was amenable to Eisenhower's wishes. For developments see no. 950.
[6] Dry's wife and daughter, Mary Alice.

937   *Eisenhower Mss.*

To Kenneth Claiborne Royall   *August 10, 1950*

Dear Kenneth: This is in answer to your note of August 4—I shall attempt no reply to your message of August 1 until I see you.[1]

I think that you have a good idea and certainly I will try to follow your suggestion at my first opportunity. I can probably do this best on Labor Day because on that day I have promised Lucius Clay to go on a nationwide hook-up.[2] In the meantime, of course, I shall do what I can locally.

I can well understand the embarrassment that might come to the Administration if I should be "requested" to make such a statement. I think it far better that I look for a chance on my own.[3] *Cordially*

[1] Royall, a partner in the law firm of Dwight, Royall, Harris, Koegel and Caskey, had been Secretary of the Army when Eisenhower was Chief of Staff (for background see no. 324). Royall, who had marked his letter of August 1 (EM) "*VERY PERSONAL*," had written three pages on the prospects of Republicans who might seek the presidential nomination in 1952. He had recently discussed this subject with Guy George Gabrielson, chairman of the Republican National Committee since August 4, 1949. Gabrielson (LL.B. Harvard 1917), who was also president and a director of Carthage Hydrocol, Inc., and of Nicolet Asbestos Mines, Ltd., had argued that Governor Thomas E. Dewey of New York, was "out of the

question"; that U.S. Senator Robert A. Taft of Ohio either might not want to run or might lose; that Harold E. Stassen, president of the University of Pennsylvania, was a possible candidate; that Governor James Henderson Duff of Pennsylvania was not well known on the national level; that former Congressman Joseph W. Martin, Jr., of Massachusetts was out of the running; and that Governor Earl Warren of California lacked "sufficient stature" (for background on Dewey and Stassen see nos. 491 and 116, respectively; on Taft, Martin, and Warren see no. 104). Duff (LL.B. University of Pittsburgh 1907) had been Attorney General of Pennsylvania from 1943 until 1946, when he had become Governor. Eisenhower had recently met with him (see no. 873).

Gabrielson had told Royall that the consensus of Republican leaders was that Eisenhower ought to declare his allegiance to one party or the other and make it clear whether or not he would accept a nomination if it were offered to him. Royall had replied that to do the latter would be tantamount to becoming "the target of all prospective candidates of all parties" and that Eisenhower would not be able to defend himself without losing prestige. Royall had concluded that as a Democrat he (Royall) probably should not get involved in Republican politics, but he thought that "from the standpoint of the country at large" he needed to tell Eisenhower of the discussion. Royall had promised that except for the letter he was writing, his conversation with Gabrielson would remain confidential.

In his letter of August 4 (EM) Royall had mentioned that during his visit with Secretary of the Army Frank Pace, Jr., on the third, they had agreed that the deteriorating situation in Korea required that someone publicly discuss "the difficulties of the campaign, the odds against our soldiers and the heroism of their conduct to date." Eisenhower had been the first choice of both men for this task, but they thought that a speech by the General would be appropriate only if President Truman were to request it. Truman would probably not take such a step, however, and Eisenhower would have to decide as to "the necessity and propriety of the statement." For background on Pace see no. 380; on the situation in Korea see no. 934.

[2] Eisenhower would launch the Crusade for Freedom, sponsored by the National Committee for a Free Europe, with a radio broadcast from Denver, Colorado, on September 4, 1950 (see no. 962). Eisenhower had assisted General Lucius D. Clay, national chairman of the crusade (and chairman of the board and chief executive officer of Continental Can Company), in the organization of the campaign as early as March 1950. For background see no. 739.

[3] Eisenhower might have had other reasons for making a statement establishing a position apart from the administration's. In a speech at Columbia University three months before the outbreak of the Korean War he had announced his belief that the nation had disarmed too much, and a subcommittee of the Senate Appropriations Committee had asked him to come to Washington to explain what he meant. It seems likely that the Truman administration thought Eisenhower had been disloyal when he told the subcommittee that the President's proposed defense appropriations for FY51 were too low (see no. 753). The setbacks faced by U.S. forces in Korea seemed, however, to bear out the accuracy of Eisenhower's forecast, and this had exacerbated the bad feeling within the administration. Eisenhower would lose patience with this ill will later in the month (see nos. 957 and 958).

To John Allen Krout   *August 10, 1950*

Dear John: Thanks for sending me, on July 28, the message from your friend Frederick Mayer.[1] You will be interested to know that both in California & Colorado the reaction to my "Conference" plan has been extraordinarily favorable.[2] In fact, one man in California was so impressed that he, in his capacity as regent of the University, sent a copy of my letter on the subject to President Sproul. The latter replied at once — much impressed, and with the hint that he might start a similar move *now*.[3] The only reason for telling this is that it reinforces my belief that we should get a move on.

Tomorrow a new group of Texans is coming to see me. I trust that some of them [will] soon begin signing on the dotted line. It would be a just relief.[4]

The pressures on me seem to be as great (or even greater) when away from New York as when there. I begin to doubt the efficiency of the so-called "Holiday."[5] *As ever*

[1] Krout, associate provost and dean of the Faculty of Political Science, Philosophy and Pure Science at Columbia University, was also currently head of a small steering group investigating Columbia's aims, organization, and functions (for background see no. 883). Krout had informed Eisenhower (July 29, EM) that Frederick Miller Mayer (LL.B. Harvard 1924), president and a director of the Continental Supply Company, Ltd., in Dallas, Texas, had seen a fund-raising letter that Eisenhower had written (probably similar to no. 826). It had impressed Mayer as "a remarkable letter, well thought out and persuasively expressed," and he hoped that Eisenhower's plans for Columbia would come to fruition.

[2] Eisenhower had described his conference plan, soon to become the American Assembly, at a luncheon in San Francisco, California, on July 25, 1950 (for background see no. 887). The plan called for the establishment of a conference center for the discussion of subjects of public interest by leaders in business, labor, government, and education (see nos. 605 and 844). Theodore S. Petersen, president of Standard Oil Company of California and host of the luncheon, would notify Columbia University late in 1950 that Standard Oil would contribute twenty-five thousand dollars to the American Assembly (see Petersen to Young, Dec. 29, 1950, EM, Petersen Corr.).

[3] William H. Burnham (see no. 130) had given a copy of Eisenhower's fund-raising letter to Preston Hotchkis (A.B. University of California, Berkeley 1916), president of Founders' Fire and Marine Insurance Company and a regent of the University of California from 1935 to 1936 (regarding Burnham's work on behalf of the American Assembly see no. 877). Hotchkis had sent a copy to Robert G. Sproul, president of the University of California (for background on Sproul see no. 113). When Sproul had thanked Hotchkis for the letter, he had praised it as "a statesmanlike expression of views . . . in addition to being an appealing presentation of the opportunities and needs of a great university" (see Sproul to Hotchkis, July 18, 1950; Hotchkis to Eisenhower, Aug. 4, 1950; and Eisenhower to Hotchkis, Aug. 10, 1950, EM).

[4] Leonard F. McCollum, president of the Continental Oil Company, would host

a luncheon in Eisenhower's honor at the Cherry Hills Club in Denver, Colorado, on August 11 (on McCollum see no. 826). He and seven of the Texans who would attend the luncheon would make contributions to the American Assembly program totaling $11,525 (guest lists are in EM, American Assembly Corr. and McCollum Corr. Lists of contributors are in Columbia University, *Report of the Treasurer, June 30, 1951* [New York, 1951], pp. 258–62; and in EM, American Assembly Corr. For Eisenhower's recollection of the discussion at the luncheon see no. 979). The evening of August 11 Eisenhower would hear the Denver Symphony perform its final Red Rocks concert of the season (see *Denver Post*, Aug. 12, 1950).

[5] On the Eisenhowers' travels since leaving New York see no. 805. Eisenhower spent the morning of this same day at his office at Lowry Air Force Base. He left at midday to attend a luncheon at the Cherry Hills Club accompanied by Burnham, Jerry D. Brandon (president of Brandon Equipment Company, a railway supply firm in Chicago), Fred M. Manning, Sr. (a Texan who had made a fortune in the oil business), and ten top executives of Phillips Petroleum Company (the guest list is in EM, American Assembly Corr. For background on Brandon see Galambos, *Chief of Staff*; on Manning see no. 545). Eisenhower's appointment calendar suggests that he stayed at the club during the late afternoon and that he was there at 5:30 P.M. for the dinner celebrating the wedding anniversary of John S. Doud and Elivera C. Doud, the parents of Mamie D. Eisenhower.

939 *Eisenhower Mss.,*
Clubs and Associations

To Dudley T. Easby *August 11, 1950*
Personal and confidential

Dear Mr. Easby:[01] While naturally I have certain, even if somewhat incomplete, views on the question of beginning evacuation of art treasures from the Metropolitan area, these are so complicated that it would be futile to try to describe them in a letter. The only thought that I should like to present at this moment is this: Recognizing the great desirability of foresight and of prudence in preserving priceless art treasures, and realizing also that in the case of an all out war, the risk of destruction in New York City would be far greater than in central United States, I still would decry any move that could possibly be interpreted as evidence of hysterical fear or even as indicating a lack of confidence. Great as is the value of a masterpiece, human judgment will not make that value greater than that of a human life. Consequently, any suggestion that art treasures should be evacuated for safety's sake would imply an immediate need for a population exodus from the city.

While it would be my opinion that present world tensions might induce the Board to look very favorably upon requests for art exhibits in the central United States, I would urge that favorable action be based solely upon the esthetic values involved — not upon world conditions and risks.[2] It would of course, therefore, be important that the public understand that the move was a "normal" one and not made in anticipation of any kind of emergency.

I request that these views be discussed with no one except proper officials of the Museum because, as I explained above, they are only fragmentary views and the necessary supporting explanations cannot possibly be included here.[3] *Sincerely*

[1] Easby (LL.B. University of Pennsylvania 1931), secretary of the Metropolitan Museum of Art in New York City, had informed Eisenhower in a letter of July 31 (same file as document) that the museum's board of trustees, of which Eisenhower was a member, would meet on August 8 to discuss plans for the evacuation of certain works of art in the event of a national emergency. Easby had known that Eisenhower would not attend the meeting, and he had offered to read to the board any message Eisenhower might give him.

[2] This was probably a reference to a proposal to send "a very important loan exhibition of works of art" from the Metropolitan to the Colorado Springs Fine Arts Center in Colorado (see Taylor to Redmond, July 12, 1950, same file as document). The proposal, a copy of which Easby had sent to the General, included an evaluation of the feasibility of storing art objects in several abandoned silver mines near Colorado Springs if war appeared imminent. The administrators of the Metropolitan planned to let the public know only that the program of renovation that would begin in the fall would result in a temporary shortage of space and would necessitate the loan exhibition to Colorado Springs (on the building program see *New York Times*, May 9 and Nov. 17, 1950).

[3] Easby would thank Eisenhower in a note of August 24, explaining that the only officials to whom he had given copies were the president, the director, and the treasurer. He would also report that the board of trustees had decided at its meeting on August 8 that no immediate steps should be taken but that the search for storage sites should continue. The administrators of the museum would keep Eisenhower informed of their plans, but there is no indication in EM that he would take an active role in the decision making. All of the correspondence is in the same file as this document.

940   *Eisenhower Mss.*

TO EARL MARVIN PRICE   *August 14, 1950*

Dear Earl:[0] Thank you very much for your interesting letter. There is one thing about your ideas—they are stated with a directness and a refreshing bluntness that removes all suspicion of hidden motives.[1]

I think I need hardly take up space to insist that I share your concern about the words "country" and "duty." Frequently however, it would be an easier world in which to live if a man could always be sure of just where "duty" exists.[2]

In any event, thanks for your letter and particularly for the fine picture of classmates and wives that you sent to me.[3] Recently I spent a few days in San Francisco but I was so much on the jump and my time so completely committed that I got to see very few of my old friends.[4] When my visit became further complicated by the sudden illness of my wife, I was forced to abandon all tentative plans for looking up classmates (even though I got all of their addresses from Commanding General, Sixth Army) and finally ended up with visiting with no one except P.A.[5] *Cordially*

[1] Price, Eisenhower's classmate at West Point, had enclosed in his letter of August 3 (EM) an editorial he had written recently for a newspaper. He had asked his readers to "put a Republican like Eisenhower in the White House two years from now." Price had charged that President Truman, Secretary of State Acheson, and Secretary of Defense Johnson had shown themselves to be incompetent; he had urged Eisenhower to enter politics to prevent Americans from becoming "pawns of government planners and . . . of labor unions." Price was head of a blueprinting and photostat company in Bakersfield, California. For background see Chandler, *War Years*, no. 2059.

[2] Price had admonished Eisenhower that he had "a duty and a Country to think of" and that history would not "forgive" him if he did not enter politics. Speculation on Eisenhower's ability to win the presidential election in 1952 continued to appear sporadically in the press (see, for example, no. 638, n. 8). On August 2 the *Denver Post* had announced that a recent poll indicated that residents of Colorado would favor Eisenhower two to one over Truman if the two men were to run for the presidency in 1952. Twelve days later the *Post* included an account of an interview with former U.S. congresswoman Clare Boothe Luce, who had represented the Fourth District of Connecticut as a Republican from 1943 to 1947. She had declared Eisenhower to be the best candidate the Republicans could select to run for the presidency. Party leaders from seven southern states would make a similar announcement on August 16. They would base their opinion on the results of a poll that placed Eisenhower first in a field that included Senator Robert A. Taft of Ohio; Governor James H. Duff of Pennsylvania; Harold E. Stassen, president of the University of Pennsylvania; and Governor Earl Warren of California (see *New York Times*, Aug. 17, 1950). For the opinion of the chairman of the Republican National Committee regarding Eisenhower's standing among these men see no. 937.

[3] Price had sent Eisenhower a picture taken at a thirty-fifth reunion dinner (May 31, 1950) for the members of the class of 1915 living in the San Francisco Bay area. The photograph and a diagram indicating who the people were is in the same file as this document.

[4] See no. 887.

[5] In a letter of July 11 (EM) Lieutenant General Albert C. Wedemeyer, CG of the Sixth Army since August 1949, had offered to make available a car, a chauffeur, and an aide during Eisenhower's visit to San Francisco (for background on Wedemeyer see no. 8). "P.A." was Colonel Paul Alfred Hodgson (USA, ret.), who had roomed with Eisenhower at West Point (for background see *Eisenhower Papers*, vol. I–IX). The Hodgsons currently lived in Mill Valley, California.

To Joseph Campbell   *August 14, 1950*

Dear Joe:[0] I am enclosing twenty-eight (28) checks totaling $16,385. In addition to your formal acknowledgment you may wish to indicate that you have received instructions from me to earmark these contributions for the Conference Center project and that you will return the donation should there be a decision not to establish the program as originally intended.[1]

A question was raised as to a tax exemption clause — I assume that your formal acknowledgment shows such authority for exemption. Please keep a most careful record of all checks and acknowledgments involving the Center.[2]

Where necessary I have indorsed the checks.

With warm personal regard, *Sincerely*

[1] Campbell was vice-president in charge of business affairs and treasurer of Columbia University (for background see nos. 392 and 514; on Eisenhower's conference plan, soon to become the American Assembly, see nos. 605 and 844). Checks totaling $6,025 from five Texans who had attended a luncheon in Denver, Colorado, on August 11 were included in the $16,385 (on the luncheon see no. 938). The names and addresses of the twenty-eight benefactors are in EM, American Assembly Corr.

[2] Eisenhower, currently on vacation in Denver, had sent short acknowledgments to the twenty-eight contributors (see Schulz, memo to New York Office, Aug. 19, 1950, EM, American Assembly Corr. On the vacation see no. 805).

·

942   *Eisenhower Mss.*

To Robert Justus Kleberg, Jr.   *August 14, 1950*

Dear Bob: It would be difficult to try to tell you what a lift I received the other day when your check was handed to me by Jack Porter.[1] It is heartwarming to know that thoughtful friends agree with my idea that there is something we can do about undesirable trends in this country, especially where these are wholly or partially occasioned by lack of knowledge and understanding and by our own failure to get together and work out reasonable solutions. When approval is buttressed by the kind of material support that you have contributed to the program, the prospects of success begin to proceed from the probable to the certain. I am tremendously grateful to you.

With warm personal regards. *Cordially*

¹ Kleberg, president of the King Ranch, Inc., had mentioned in a letter of August 9 (EM) that he was sending a check for ten thousand dollars "to be used for the purposes we discussed" (for background on Kleberg see no. 623). Kleberg had liked the emphasis on good citizenship in Eisenhower's description of his goals for Columbia University (enclosed in no. 926), and he had praised the plan for the conference center to be established at Arden House, the Harriman estate (see no. 605). "I think," Kleberg had written, "that if you can get together some of the best minds in the country, with your personal interest and guidance in their endeavor, we may get some worthwhile answers to the vast and complicated problems with which our country is faced."

Kleberg had hoped that Leonard F. McCollum, president of the Continental Oil Company, could bring the check to Eisenhower, since it might give McCollum an opportunity to show it to other wealthy businessmen, who might then contribute. In any event, H. J. "Jack" Porter, a prominent figure in the Texas oil industry and a leader in the Republican party in that state, had given the check to Eisenhower; this had probably occurred at a luncheon given by McCollum in Denver, Colorado, on August 11 (for background see no. 938).

943   *Eisenhower Mss.*

To H. E. SCHLICHTER   *August 14, 1950*
Personal and confidential

Dear Mr. Schlichter: While I have no hesitancy at all in commenting myself on subjects where I feel I have an opinion worth uttering, yet the kind of subjects raised in your letter of August 1st not only require profound thought and analysis, but frequently there is no short way to present an opinion or conclusion because of conflicting factors.¹

Consequently, I can do scarcely more than to acknowledge receipt of your communication and to express my satisfaction that you are devoting your time and attention to the study of such important matters.

For my part, it has been so many years since I read Homer Lea's books that I scarcely recall the essentials of his arguments and prophecies. However, I do remember that as a youth I was very greatly impressed by his writings and I suspect that a re-reading of them at this time would convince me that he was even wiser than I then thought.²

I think that you overstate the case when you say that war with Russia is "inevitable."³ Certainly I am not going to be a Pollyanna in an attempt to minimize the grimness of the present situation and outlook but it is worthwhile, now and then, to look back upon history. In the same area where the great Russian dictatorship now rules with an iron hand lived once a man who was probably the greatest dictator of all time, Genghis Khan and his immediate successors in power. That dictatorship finally fell apart, not through defeat in war or as a result of war, but because of internal difficulties. Certainly I do not give you this thought with any contention that the same result will be repeated— I merely give it to you to show why I cannot agree with your word "inevitable."[4]

There is no possible question concerning your argument that our Nation should be taught more and more about the facts of international life. We have lived too long with our heads in the sands. Unless we do so, it is certain that we are going to come squarely up to the crossroads of choosing either the path of war or of being bled white economically. No single fact is so necessary in solving the problem that arises out of this situation as a clear knowledge of the strength, tenacity and ultimate goal of the Communists. This also suggests the one thing we must learn, how to produce military force that is characterized at one and the same time by both efficiency and economy. I personally believe that we must begin to realize that we cannot *buy* security—we must provide it for ourselves as an obligation to the state to which we belong.[5] *Sincerely*

[1] In a letter of August 1 (EM) Schlichter, sales promotion manager for Newman Dry Goods Company, in Emporia, Kansas, had asked Eisenhower for his "frank opinion, as far as you can commit yourself, on several subjects."
[2] Schlichter wanted Eisenhower's opinion of the writings of Homer Lea, an American who had attended the Occidental College of the University of the Pacific, as well as Stanford University, between 1894 and 1900; Lea later became a general in the Chinese Army and a military adviser to Dr. Sun Yat-sen, leader of the Kuomintang party of China. Schlichter had praised Lea's *The Day of the Saxon* (New York, 1912) and *The Valor of Ignorance* (1909; reprint ed., New York, 1942), which stressed the need for U.S. preparedness in the face of Japanese, German, and Russian expansionism.
[3] Schlichter had argued that Lea's expectations regarding Russia's "ultimate aims and ambitions" implied that war with Russia was inevitable.
[4] Genghis Khan (ca. 1162–1227), a Mongol chief, had conquered large parts of China, Turkestan, Persia, and southern Russia, but his empire had fallen apart several generations after his death (see Michael Prawdin, *The Mongol Empire: Its Rise and Legacy*, trans. Eden Paul and Cedar Paul, 2d ed., rev. [London, 1967], pp. 23, 222–23, 225, 236–38, 520–23).
[5] Schlichter had maintained that America's military commitment to certain regions of the world was not commensurate with the nation's political and economic involvement there. With regard to Russia, he felt that U.S. citizens needed to "appreciate the strength, tenacity of purpose and ultimate goal of the foe we face. . . ."

944   *Eisenhower Mss.*

To James Cunard Black   *August 14, 1950*

Dear Jim:[0] Thank you very much for your nice letter. I was especially interested in what you had to say about titanium.[1]

I share your anxiety when you contemplate the intervention of persons into the business of organizing our country for economic mobilization where those persons have had no previous experience and particularly when there is reasonable ground to suspect that each is somewhat animated by the bureaucrat's search for additional power and prestige. I do hope that Stuart Symington will be able to keep this whole matter on the rails and above all else keep it out of the hands of politicians who might try to use national crises for furthering selfish ambitions.[2] Our affairs are in such shape that we cannot afford anything but efficiency and selfless devotion on the part of all those who are in positions of authority.[3]

Gladys left on Saturday afternoon[4]—all of us miss her. With warm regards to yourself. *Cordially*

---

[1] Black, manager of the Republic Steel Corporation, in Washington, D.C., had described (Aug. 10, EM) a conversation he had had the previous day with Charles McElroy White, president of Republic Steel, and General J. Lawton Collins, Chief of Staff of the Army. They had discussed titanium, a metallic element used to remove oxygen and nitrogen from steel, and its possible importance in the production of airborne equipment. Black had mentioned that the government might finance the building of a plant to manufacture steel made with titanium. When alloyed with steel, the metal was noncorrosive, resistant to acids, and greater in tensile strength than steel. The National Lead Company and Allegheny Ludlum Steel Corporation had recently formed a jointly owned corporation for the marketing and distribution of titanium (see *New York Times*, Jan. 17, 1950). Remington Arms Company and Crucible Steel Company of America had also pooled their technological expertise and patents for the production of titanium metal and titanium metal alloy products (see *ibid.*, July 27, 1950).

Black had expressed alarm at the Truman administration's plans for the allocation of materials during the war in Korea. He thought that bureaucrats seeking power would deprive industrial leaders of the role that they had played in government during World War II. Charles Franklin Brannan (LL.B. University of Denver 1929), Secretary of Agriculture, and Oscar Littleton Chapman (LL.B. Westminster Law School 1929), Secretary of the Interior, would make allocations on the basis of each company's "political rather than historical position in the industry," Black feared, and he planned to discuss with Senator Edwin Carl Johnson, Democrat of Colorado, the possibility of amending the pending legislation to allow for the administration of allocations by the Department of Commerce. For background on Eisenhower's relations with Johnson see Galambos, *Chief of Staff.*

[2] Eisenhower had written recently to W. Stuart Symington, chairman of the National Security Resources Board, about the problem of mobilizing American industry for war (see no. 913). At hearings on July 24 Symington had testified before the Senate and House committees on Banking and Currency on the importance of granting powers to the President to control and allocate steel, aluminum, lead, and other products to essential industries (see *New York Times*, July 25, 1950). Congress would pass such a bill, the Defense Production Act of 1950, which President Truman would sign into law on September 8, 1950 (see U.S., *Statutes at Large*, vol. 64, pt. 1, pp. 798–822).

[3] Black would reply (Aug. 18, EM) that it was not likely that Symington would "keep this whole situation on the conservative side." Black would conclude with the hope that the country might eventually have a President who was above partisan

politics. Black would play golf with Eisenhower in Denver, on September 9, and he would thank the General for his hospitality in a short note (EM) written on September 11.

[4] Mrs. James C. Black had been Mrs. Eisenhower's traveling companion during a recent trip through several western states (for background see no. 884; on the trip see no. 805).

945   *Eisenhower Mss.*

To Philip Young   *August 14, 1950*

Dear Phillip: Thank you very much for your letter and its accompanying report. I am delighted with the showing that Eli and his associates have so far made.[1]

Recently I have talked to numerous gatherings about our "American Assembly" idea. I have been gratified by the reception. In no case have I found any real objection. The other day I had the pleasure of forwarding some $16,000 in checks to the Treasurer, with instructions to keep the amounts definitely earmarked for the Arden House fund.[2] I have been told that Roy Cullen is also sending us a check for $25,000.[3] This, added to Averill Harriman's gift of a year ago, the bulk of which is still intact,[4] leads me to suggest that if you are well pleased with your man Lee, that we might consider asking him to stay with us permanently. I am thinking of his possible suitability for the job of "Chief Staff Officer" in the whole development project. Certainly we will have to be getting someone into that position at a very early date.[5]

There is no lack of confidence on the part of any of our associates (McCollum, Burnham, and others) as to the procurement of the necessary sponsors of specific conference periods.[6] The biggest trouble seems to be getting the immediate donations of cash for renovating and refurnishing Arden House and for providing the necessary working capital that will justify us in going ahead full speed. However, even in this direction, I am receiving great encouragement and promises of support.[7] With all the best. *Cordially*

[1] Philip Young, who was chairman of the advisory committee of the Conservation of Human Resources Project at Columbia, had sent Eisenhower the study's first progress report and a covering letter on August 4 (EM; for background on the project see no. 481). Young commented that Director Eli Ginzberg and Howard M. Snyder "have the Surgeon General's Office really at work on certain phases of the military manpower problem," and he advised Eisenhower of a recent letter from the Selective Service System expressing its support (for background on Snyder see no. 1). In his six-page report Ginzberg said that since October 1949 "a threefold plan of attack" had been developed. Researchers were exploring (1) the changing patterns of work between 1890 and 1950; (2) the problems of workers who were inadequate and maladjusted in the civilian or military environment; and (3) the

misuse of society's superior or talented performers. Ginzberg also reported that financial arrangements for the five-year study were nearing completion. For further developments see no. 1121.

[2] For background on the American Assembly project see nos. 605 and 844. On the checks see no. 941.

[3] Hugh Roy Cullen, president of Quintana Petroleum Corporation, in Houston, Texas, would inform Eisenhower in a letter of September 11 (CUF) that as soon as the American Assembly fund had reached five hundred thousand dollars he would send a check for twenty-five thousand. Cullen's note was probably a response to Eisenhower's letter of July 12 (EM) explaining that William H. Burnham (an investment banker in New York City) would soon visit Houston to raise money on behalf of the American Assembly. For developments see no. 989. For background on Cullen see no. 602, n. 7. On Burnham's trip to Texas see no. 877.

[4] W. Averell Harriman, President Truman's Special Assistant on Foreign Affairs, had given Columbia University securities valued at fifty thousand dollars to further the plan for the use of Arden House. On Harriman see no. 852; on the gift see no. 627.

[5] Luther J. Lee, Jr. (Ph.D. University of California 1945), was on leave from Pomona College, where he had served as associate professor of government and assistant to the president since 1948. He had been Assistant Field Director for the Business-Education Division of the Committee for Economic Development (CED) during 1949, and he was also on leave from that position in order to help plan the American Assembly program. On the CED see no. 732. For background on Eisenhower's plans for the organization of development activities at Columbia see no. 930, n. 8.

[6] Eisenhower had sent staff-drafted letters of July 11 (EM) to Burnham and to Leonard F. McCollum, president of Continental Oil Company, asking them to act as ambassadors in soliciting funds for the American Assembly. McCollum had accepted the position in a note of July 17 (EM), and Burnham, who for several months had been planning an American Assembly fund-raising campaign, had reaffirmed his readiness to help when he had been host of a special luncheon on July 13. On that event and on McCollum's involvement in the project see no. 826. For background on the Columbia Amabassadors see no. 124, n. 7.

[7] For developments see no. 979.

946   *Eisenhower Mss.*

To William Carl Hoffmann   *August 14, 1950*

Dear Colonel Hoffman: Because I have been moving about rather rapidly for the past several weeks, your letter has had difficulty reaching me.[1]

The kind of thing you have written requires a much longer answer, involving analysis and estimates, than I can possibly give to it in this brief reply but I do want to say that I thoroughly share your apprehension about the failure of the free world to recognize the Communist purpose for what it is and I applaud every intelligent effort to defend [against?] and define Communism whether it attempts to reach us from without or within.

It seems to me that G–2 of the Department of the Army would be interested in your views and the results of your long studies.[2]

With best wishes. *Sincerely*

[1] Lieutenant Colonel Hoffman*n*, G–1 (Personnel Section) at Fort Riley, Kansas, had asserted in his letter of July 28 (with enclosure, EM) that atomic weapons should be used in Korea. Neither this drastic step nor the war itself would have been necessary, he maintained, had Americans not for the previous twenty years taken a "dilatory attitude" toward the Russians' policy of territorial aggrandizement. Hoffmann also worried that the Russians had planted atomic bombs within the United States and that the danger of Communist subversion required that the nation be ready to use atomic weapons against the Soviet Union.

[2] G–2 was the Intelligence Section.

947   *Eisenhower Mss.*

To Grayson Louis Kirk   *August 14, 1950*

Dear Kirk: Thank you very much for your letter.[1] While I realize that it does not require an answer, I want you to know that I approve thoroughly of your action in declining to give any kind of University approval to a group attempting to circulate a document that has been denounced by our State Department as inspired by the Communists. For the moment the exact terminology of the "Stockholm Peace Petition" has slipped from my memory. It is still safe to assume that the State Department has investigated the matter thoroughly before taking the stand that it has.

It would be interesting to learn just who inspired the action of the student group and whether or not it is merely another case of mistaken zeal.[2]

I hope to see you when you come to Denver.[3] *Cordially*

[1] Kirk, vice-president (education) and provost of Columbia, had mentioned in a letter of August 10 (EM) that he had declined the request of a group of students for recognition as the University Peace Committee. They had planned to ask for signatures for the Stockholm Peace Petition, but Kirk had refused to let them circulate the appeal on university property. The petition was the work of the Permanent Committee of the World Congress of the Defenders of Peace, which had met in Stockholm, Sweden, March 15–19, 1950. Secretary of State Dean G. Acheson had denounced the petition as "a propaganda trick in the spurious 'peace offensive' of the Soviet Union" during a press conference on July 12 (see *New York Times*, July 13, 1950). The portion of the Stockholm resolution that Acheson had found to be most objectionable had been a passage declaring that the first nation to use atomic weapons would be "committing a crime against humanity and should be dealt with as a war criminal." The authors of the petition had also called for the outlawing of atomic weapons (see *New York Times*, July 22, 1950).

[2] For background on allegations of Communist influence at Columbia University see nos. 70 and 132.

[3] Kirk had concluded his letter with the observation that he would arrive in Denver, Colorado, after August 22 and that he would remain there until September 7. He hoped to talk with Eisenhower about university matters at that time, but the General's appointment calendar does not indicate that they met.

948   *Eisenhower Mss.*

To William H. Burnham   *August 21, 1950*

Dear Bill: Circumstances simply will not allow me to come to Wyoming, but I do assure you that you paint a good picture of its appealing advantages. When you come down here I can explain better why I cannot consider coming, at least this year.[1]

Would you send me in the form of the briefest kind of a memorandum, your ideas as to one or two important points that I should cover in the Labor Day speech?[2]

I have a draft that has been prepared in New York but my fear is that it merely repeats and repeats "we must answer Communist lies" and does not fully express my personal views about the whole sorry mess.[3]

A word or two from you might get me started on necessary revisions.[4]
Cordially

[1] Burnham had written an undated letter (EM) regarding the accommodations that awaited Eisenhower at the ranch owned by Charlie and Marian Moore in Dubois, Wyoming. Burnham, an investment banker in New York City, was currently visiting the ranch, and he planned to remain there until September 3, when he was to fly to Denver to hear the General's speech launching the Crusade for Freedom on the following day. On Eisenhower's work in organizing the Crusade for Freedom see nos. 739 and 899.

[2] Burnham would reply in a telegram of August 24 (EM) that Eisenhower should ask Lieutenant Colonel Paul T. Carroll to meet with him and Burnham in Denver immediately. Carroll and Burnham could then prepare a rough draft of the speech. Carroll, a member of the Office of the Secretariat when Eisenhower was Chief of Staff, was currently on assignment at the Army War College, at Forth Leavenworth, Kansas. For background on Carroll see Galambos, *Chief of Staff*, no. 2052.

[3] Abbott McConnell Washburn (B.A. Harvard 1937), public services manager of General Mills (who would become executive vice-chairman of the Crusade for Freedom in 1951), had sent Eisenhower background information for the speech under a covering letter of July 25 (EM, Subject File, Clubs and Associations). In his telegram Burnham would mention that this material was "very inane and too milk toast [*sic*]." Kevin C. McCann, Eisenhower's administrative assistant at Columbia, had also received a copy of the information and had used it in drafting the speech. He had sent copies to Eisenhower and to Carroll. The latter had listed his objections to the New York draft in a letter to Washburn of August 17 (EM, Carroll Corr.), and Carroll's revised version of the speech, as well as a draft by

Eisenhower, would go to McCann for further editing (see Schulz to McCann, Aug. 29, 1950, EM, Subject File, Clubs and Associations). Among those who contributed suggestions regarding the speech were William E. Robinson, executive vice-president of the *New York Herald Tribune*, and Victor George Reuther, Michigan state chairman of the Crusade and Educational Director of the United Automobile, Aircraft and Agricultural Implement Workers Union, CIO. Deputy Secretary of Defense Stephen T. Early would also pass judgment on Eisenhower's speech when the latter telephoned him on August 31. A note at the bottom of one of Eisenhower's appointment calendars for that date summarizes the conversation: "DDE called Sec. Early and read excerpts of his labor day address (Crusade For Freedom) especially those that had bearing on Nat'l or internat'l scene & which might be classed as controversial. Mr. Early said 'they were all good.' DDE requested an early opportunity for a friend to friend talk or conference." For background on Early see no. 551. Two drafts of the speech, with Eisenhower's extensive changes, are in EM, Subject File, Clubs and Associations. Transcripts of the final versions are in EM, Subject File, Speeches; and *New York Times*, Sept. 5, 1950.
[4] For developments see no. 962.

949   *Eisenhower Mss.*

TO MAURICE HAROLD MACMILLAN   *August 21, 1950*

Dear Harold: Thank you for your note.[1] If they ever draft me for another of these Allied wars, you will get your call in a hurry.

My warm greetings to any of the old "team" that you may encounter. *As ever*

[1] Macmillan, a member of the Conservative party in the House of Commons, had mentioned in a short note of August 4 (EM) that he had read that Eisenhower might soon be back in uniform. "If it should come," he had written, "I hope we shall serve together." On Macmillan's encounters with Eisenhower during World War II and their contact afterward see *Eisenhower Papers*, vols. I–IX.

950   *Eisenhower Mss.*

TO WALTER BEDELL SMITH   *August 21, 1950*

Dear Bedell:[1] I note by the papers that you are going to undertake the job of the CIA.[2] God knows it needs a firm hand coupled with some imagination and leadership. I scarcely need to say I wish you well, but I cannot help adding expressions of regret because you are leaving Governors Island.

This note brings to you also my very deep appreciation for your consideration in the matter of Sgt. Dry.[3] If, for the moment, you and your successor will merely make him available to me when I need him, it will be quite sufficient. Of course I do hope that someday I may have him back for day by day service, even though he remains, as always, attached to the New York headquarters. He means a very great deal to me, as you know.[4]

Good luck, and as always, warm regard. *Cordially*

[1] Lieutenant General Smith, who had been Eisenhower's Chief of Staff during World War II, was currently serving as CG of the First Army, at Governors Island, New York. For background see *Eisenhower Papers*, vols. I–IX.
[2] President Truman had named Smith to succeed Rear Admiral Roscoe H. Hillenkoetter as Director of the CIA. The Senate would confirm Smith's appointment on August 28 (see *New York Times*, Aug. 19 and 29, 1950).
[3] Dry was Eisenhower's chauffeur. Eisenhower had asked Smith to assign Dry to duties with Headquarters, First Army, at Governors Island (see no. 935).
[4] Smith would reply (Sept. 7, EM) that Dry "is all taken care of and is yours, as I told you." In a telegram of September 17 (EM) Smith would also promise to "make any arrangements for Dry that you wish but strongly urge you not deprive yourself of his services."

951   *Eisenhower Mss.*

TO FERDINAND EBERSTADT   *August 21, 1950*

Dear Ferd: Thank you very much for your note of the 16th.[1]

The greatest obstacle to reasonable arrangement of men's affairs— domestic as well as international—is fear. Moreover, we have great difficulty in assigning priorities and so the question of who fears whom and how much has not only started lots of wars, but it keeps the world upset a great portion of the time.

Your suggestion is designed to develop a greater strength against the free world's principal enemy and it at least recognizes the sorry state in which we now find ourselves.

Incidentally, I inclose a different kind of suggestion that I received the other day. Because I do not know the man, I have not attempted to answer his message, so won't you please merely destroy it when you have looked at it?[2]

[1] Eberstadt was an investment banker who had headed a task force of the Hoover Commission on Organization of the Executive Branch of the Government. Under a covering note of August 16, he had sent Eisenhower a copy of a letter of the previous day (EM) to U.S. Senator H. Alexander Smith, Republican of New Jersey (for background on Eberstadt see no. 57). Smith (LL.B. Columbia 1904), a senator since 1945, was a member of the Committee on Foreign Relations. Eberstadt had congratulated Smith on the stand he and three other Republican members of the committee had taken in a recent statement on foreign policy (see

New York Times, Aug. 14, 1950), but he was concerned that the legislators were not sufficiently aware of the dangers posed by the Russians' penchant for territorial conquest. The Soviet rulers cherished the imperialistic ambitions of their czarist predecessors, he feared, and unrestrained Russian expansionism might lead to World War III. Eberstadt suggested that as Germany and Japan reentered the ranks of the Great Powers they might act as bulwarks against the Soviets, and he hoped that the Republicans in Congress would support legislation that would serve these ends.

[2] A note at the bottom of the carbon copy of this letter indicates that the enclosure was a copy of a telegram from Edwin T. Kame, secretary of the Paul Revere Civil Defense Committee of Texas. We have been unable to locate the message in EM. Eberstadt would thank Eisenhower for the enclosure in a letter of August 24 (EM), describing it as "very interesting and plausible, though I do not, myself, know enough about the Chinese situation to express a definite view on it." Eberstadt said there was "a certain similarity" between Kame's proposition and his own ideas concerning the importance of bolstering the economic and military power of Germany and Japan.

Eisenhower would receive an honorary degree at commencement exercises at the University of Denver on August 23. Chancellor Albert C. Jacobs, former provost of Columbia University, would confer the honor (see *New York Times*, Aug. 24, 1950. For background on Jacobs see no. 440).

952   *Eisenhower Mss.*

To ———   *August 30, 1950*

Dear Doctor:[0] You pose a question that I am unable to answer promptly.[1] I do not have the exact information you need and it would take me some little time to get it. Consequently, I am sending your letter instantly to Headquarters of the Air Force in Washington, with the request that you get as prompt a reply from them as may be possible.[2]

I am quite certain that a personal appeal to General Hershey would be out of order—this because of the fact that he could not possibly make an exception from the standpoint of the draft.[3] On the other hand, the Air Forces may be sufficiently interested that they could accept your son as a volunteer instantly.

I trust that you will get a prompt answer and, of course, hope that your boy will be able to realize his ambition.[4] *Cordially*

[1] This correspondent had asked Eisenhower (Aug. 24, EM) to use his influence with the military authorities in Washington, D.C., to prevent his son from being drafted. The doctor had emphasized that his son wanted to enlist in the Air Force after finishing college.

[2] Eisenhower wrote to Lieutenant General Lauris Norstad, Deputy Chief of Staff for Operations and Acting Vice Chief of Staff of the Air Force, on this same day (EM) enclosing a copy of the doctor's letter and this reply. Eisenhower described him as "an old and dear friend." Norstad would report to Eisenhower (Sept. 6, EM) that his executive officer had telephoned the correspondent and had presented

a choice between two courses of action: (1) the father could ask the local draft board to allow his son to apply for aviation cadet training, which would begin at the end of the current college semester, or (2) the son could enlist in the Air Force immediately and finish his college work by corresponding with his teachers. Norstad thought that the latter was the "only sure way" to avoid the draft, and he indicated that the correspondent had expressed appreciation for this information. Eisenhower would thank Norstad in a note of September 11 (EM).

[3] The doctor had suggested that Eisenhower ask Major General Lewis B. Hershey, Director of the Selective Service System, to prevail upon the local draft board to allow his son to finish college and enlist in the Air Force.

[4] The correspondent would reply in a letter of January 25, 1951 (EM), that his son had recently finished college and had been accepted as an aviation cadet.

953   *Columbia University Files*

TO WILLIAM REYNOLDS ARCHER   *August 30, 1950*

Dear Mr. Archer: Needless to say, I have been more than gratified by the interest you have taken in our project for an "American Assembly" to be sponsored by Columbia University.[1] Moreover, I am particularly distressed that I cannot attend the meeting at Hot Springs to talk over with you some of the great problems now plaguing us.[2]

Because of my inability to meet with you and to have a long personal talk, I am writing a fairly formal letter, and attaching it to this one, in which I attempt to give a short explanation of our projects. I trust that through it you will be able to spread the word of what we are trying to do.[3] *Cordially*

[1] Archer, president of Uncle Johnny Mills, in Houston, Texas, had tried to reach Eisenhower by telephone on August 24. He wanted the General to present his ideas regarding the conference plan to a meeting of the board of directors of the National Association of Manufacturers (N.A.M.) in Hot Springs, Virginia, on September 19 and 20, 1950 (see memorandum, Schulz to Eisenhower, Aug. 24, 1950, CUF; on the N.A.M. see no. 581. For background on Eisenhower's plan for the establishment of a conference center see nos. 605 and 844). Archer had attended a luncheon in Denver, Colorado, on August 11, 1950, at which Eisenhower had described his proposal (see no. 938).

[2] Lieutenant Colonel Robert L. Schulz, Eisenhower's aide, had given Archer a similar message in a telephone conversation on August 28. At that time Archer had asked for a letter describing the conference plan, something that he could read at the N.A.M. meeting. Archer hoped in this way to "put over the deal myself" (see memorandum, Schulz to Eisenhower, Aug. 28, 1950, CUF).

[3] This letter, of this same date, differed in a few details from no. 826, and it included more information regarding the conference plan. Eisenhower added the following in longhand to a copy of the letter of August 1 (EM) which he had sent to Robert J. Kleberg, president of the King Ranch (see no. 926): "It is this particular project of which I have spoken to you previously. It has been so well received and supported by industrial leaders that I feel it is well on its way to an

auspicious beginning. Each conference is to be sponsored by some industrial concern, and labor organizations as well as business have agreed to participate. If we once get the 4–5 hundred thousand needed to establish the place properly, we will be on our way to accomplishment of the greatest thing, in my humble opinion, yet attempted for the health of our free system. Conferences will last, under the pleasantest of surroundings from 3–5 days. We will have discussions on everything from Tito to taxes. The only criterion will be—'Is it important to the U.S.?'—and results will go out at once—they will not rot on book shelves!" A copy of the letter in its final form (CUF) indicates that Eisenhower appended these six sentences to the end of what had been subparagraph *a* in both the letter to Kleberg and no. 826. For developments regarding the conference plan see no. 1039.

954

Eisenhower Mss.

To Ernest A. Bromberger

August 30, 1950

Dear Mr. Bromberger: I am always delighted when I find the interest in our security affairs that is evidenced by your letter to me of August 18.[1] There can be no possible quarrel with the contention that we should not publish anything that could be of any help either to our active or our passive enemies.

With respect to the article you sent along with your letter, I am not too much impressed by it. First, I do not believe that it gives Americans any needed or certainly any very accurate information—but by the same token, I doubt that it was very helpful to anybody else.[2]

In any event, it would appear that Washington has been moving lately to control this matter of official information.[3]

Thank you for writing. *Sincerely*

[1] Bromberger, of Los Angeles, California, had enclosed with his letter a copy of an interview with Joseph Fromm entitled "Plight of Ground Soldier in Korea," *U.S. News & World Report*, August 18, 1950, 14–17. Bromberger thought that the piece had revealed to America's Communist adversaries the weaknesses of the U.S. Army.

[2] Fromm, a *U.S. News & World Report* regional editor currently in Korea, had reported that U.S. Army troops had entered the war without proper physical training and that there was dissatisfaction with the division of command responsibilities among Army, Air Force, and Marine Corps officers.

[3] On July 13 Secretary of Defense Louis A. Johnson had directed that the three services henceforth limit the release of information to newsmen (see *New York Times*, July 14, 1950. On previous attempts to restrict press coverage of defense affairs see nos. 313 and 365).

To John Allen Krout *August 30, 1950*

Dear John:[0] It would seem to me that it would be best to have the memorandum that is to accompany your prospectus on the University's short courses signed by some individual other than myself.[1]

The reason I say this is because I think that this year we should probably send one or two more letters to all Columbia's alumni and these I think I should sign.[2] It would be bad practice to have me sign so many communications to alumni that the recipients' reaction would be to heave the communication into the nearest wastebasket.

However, I am ready to talk to you about the matter if you disagree.[3] With best regard. *Cordially*

[1] Krout, associate provost and dean of the Faculty of Political Science, Philosophy and Pure Science at Columbia University, had sent Lieutenant Colonel Robert L. Schulz, Eisenhower's aide, a draft of a memorandum to be sent to Columbia alumni announcing the initiation of a series of short courses. The enclosed prospectus described the courses and fees for the program (EM, Krout Corr.). For background on Krout see no. 825.
[2] For examples of earlier letters to alumni see nos. 332, 346, and 374.
[3] There is no further correspondence with Krout on this subject in EM.

To William Edward Robinson *August 30, 1950*

Dear Bill: I am delighted that you and all the rest of the group had a nice time in Denver and I hope you realize that none of you could possibly have valued the vacation more than I did. It was wonderful to have you with me.[1]

I am, at this moment, too pressed to write to everybody individually, but I hope that you will take an opportunity to tell each of them how much their visit here meant to me, to Mamie, and the Douds. This includes Cliff and Slats, as well as Schooie and Freeman.[2]

I am sending to you a copy of a letter I just received from a friend of mine in Wichita, Kansas. He is the Vice-President of the Boeing Company, in charge of their Wichita operations. I send also a copy of my reply to him.[3] The reason I send these things is just so you may have some exact information in case you hear the same kind of propaganda that my friend picked up in Wichita. Needless to say, I know that you will consider this information as personal. *Sincerely*

P.S. I don't object to your showing the attached communications to members of our own crowd—on a purely personal basis.

[1] Robinson, executive vice-president of the *New York Herald Tribune*, had written (n.d., EM) that the week he had spent in Denver, Colorado, had been "the most pleasant vacation I ever had."

[2] The Douds were Eisenhower's in-laws. Clifford Roberts, Ellis D. Slater, and Clarence J. Schoo had accompanied Robinson to Denver on August 11. Roberts was a partner in the firm of Reynolds & Company, investment bankers; Slater was president of Frankfort Distilleries; and Schoo was founder and president of General Fibre Box Company. Freeman F. Gosden was was a writer, producer, and performer (for background see no. 821).

[3] See the following document.

957   *Eisenhower Mss.*

To Julius Earl Schaefer   *August 31, 1950*

Dear Earl: Thank you very much for sending on to me the information contained in your letter of August 26.[1]

The actual facts of the budget development are these:

I was called back to Washington by the late Secretary Forrestal sometime in late 1948 to help him in various aspects of the unification problem. Inevitably this led to some connection with the budget work, since the greatest problem of unification is to allot among the services the total amount of money made available by the government.[2]

At no time have I ever been asked what the total amount of money given to the entire security problem should be—my entire responsibility was to help in the distribution of the money made available. However, it was tentatively agreed with both the Secretarty of Defense and with the President that the sum of 15 billion dollars, including stockpiling, would be set aside for security purposes. This was the sum that the Chiefs of Staff thought they were going to have for 1951, but long before our detailed work was finished, we were twice informed that some reductions would have to be accomplished.[3] Insofar as I know, there was no professional man asked for an opinion as to the adequacy of this sum.

The Chiefs of Staff naturally attempted to make the best possible distribution of the remaining sums. (I have forgotten the exact amount of the final limiting figure, but I think it was somewhere around 13.2, including stockpiling. However, I would not vouch for the accuracy of this figure.) The only justification for referring to the successive budgets as "Eisenhower Budgets" was that I was the temporary presiding officer of the group that tried to make the necessary adjustments among the services.

Some several months later I gave a lecture at Columbia University in which I mentioned that our disarmament had gone, in some directions, further than I thought wise. On the basis of this remark, the Senate Committee called me to Washington to explain my meaning.[4] I gave them all the above information and in addition pointed out that I was very deeply concerned about our weakness in the following points: a) Defense of Alaska. b) Inadequacy of airplane procurement. c) Uncertainty as to the Navy's anti-submarine sufficiency, and, d) The almost total failure to modernize Army equipment and procure new items, such as tanks, anti-tank and anti-aircraft weapons.[5]

All the above is of record. I told the Senate Committee that I thought at least 500 million more should be added to the budget that they were then studying, and there was actually added some 350 million dollars.[6]

Shortly after I appeared before the Senate Committee, Secretary Johnson went to New York and made a speech before a rather large assembly in which he brought up the matter of my recommendations to the Senate Committee. At that time, he said that because of my fairly long absence from Washington, I was no longer acquainted with the details of the budget making and certainly, by implication, took full responsibility for recommending the lower rather than the higher figure as adequate for our defense.[7]

In addition to all the above, it is easy enough to find in the recommendations I made when I was Chief of Staff a series of appeals for more and better Army equipment, for universal military training, and for adequate protection of Alaska and other exposed areas.[8]

While I am not concerned about the "threats" that are being made with respect to the circumstances under which the record will be brought out, yet it happens that in this case I think the record would be anything but a comfort to such persons as the one who brought the story to you. In fact, if these people are thinking of the good of our country and not of personal political ambitions, why should such a story ever be brought to you and to a group of Americans at dinner.

In any event, I most sincerely appreciate your concern and the trouble you took to write to me. What some of these so-and-so's cannot possibly realize is that there just might be one American who believes he has enough work to do without trying to be President of the United States.[9]
Cordially

---

[1] Schaefer, vice-president and general manager of Boeing Airplane Company in Wichita, Kansas, had recounted (EM) his recent conversation with Irving Roth, Chief, Aviation Unit, Office of Assistant Comptroller for Budget, Department of Defense. Roth had maintained that the nation had been unprepared for a conflict in Korea as an indirect result of Eisenhower's recommendations to Secretary of Defense Louis A. Johnson regarding the FY51 budget. Eisenhower's miscalculations, according to Roth, had "ended any political ambitions the General might have had for the administration could show & would show if necessary that our Korean embarassment [*sic*] was [at] his door step." Several of Schaefer's friends had also repeated to him recently a statement that Roth had made to the effect that "whenever we get ready to

pull the file on the General he will be a dead duck from that time on." For background
on Schaefer see *Eisenhower Papers*, vols. I–IX.

[2] Eisenhower had advised Secretary of Defense James Forrestal on the preparation
of the FY50 budget during the fall of 1948. For background see nos. 183, 223,
and 303.

[3] On the revisions of the $15 billion figure see no. 435.

[4] On the lecture see no. 741; on the testimony before a subcommittee of the Senate
Committee on Appropriations see no. 753.

[5] Eisenhower had also emphasized these points in a letter supplementing his testimony before the subcommittee (see no. 754).

[6] On the addition of $350 million see no. 782.

[7] The speech to which Eisenhower referred was probably Secretary Johnson's ad-
dress on Armed Forces Day in New York City on May 20, 1950 (see *New York
Times*, May 21, 1950). Johnson would make a similar statement in his testimony
before two Senate committees on June 14, 1951 (see Senate Committee on Armed
Services and Committee on Foreign Relations, *Military Situation in the Far East:
Hearings*, [1951], pp. 2599–2601).

[8] For Eisenhower's recommendations for the improvement of equipment see Galambos, *Chief of Staff*, nos. 883, 1250, 1869, and 2055; on universal military
training see *ibid.*, nos. 630, 656, 688, 761, 1244, 1473, 1538, 1702, 1837,
and 1980; and on the defense of Alaska see *ibid.*, nos. 1086, 1108, 1214, 1678,
and 1797.

[9] Schaefer would thank Eisenhower for this letter in a note of September 5 (EM).
"Let 'em come—I have the answer now," he would write. "Some of these 'so
and so's' are apparently getting desperate."

958   *Eisenhower Mss.*

TO ALFRED MAXIMILIAN GRUENTHER   August 31, 1950

Dear Al: Thanks for your note of the 26th.[1] I can imagine Averell's
chagrin when he found you so well equipped with his trump suit. On
that particular occasion, you occupied the position that I constantly
seek in a bridge game—that of ax-holder over an injudicious bidder.
The only time I get a real feeling of frustration in bridge is when my
partner, with such an opportunity, fails to take advantage of it. (By no
means would I remind you of the time we settled for a three diamond
bid, with six a certainty, and then found you with a potential 1400 set
against our opponents. In fact I have forgotten that incident).[2]

For your very secret and personal information, I am sending you
copies of two letters, one that I have just received from a friend of mine
in Wichita, Kansas; the other a copy of my reply.[3] If I have given, in
my reply, any slightest misstatement of fact, won't you let me know
at once?[4] I am sending this with the injunction that you keep the thing
completely personal and confidential because by no means am I going
to get involved in any argument—particularly if the purpose is to
establish a favorable political atmosphere for myself.

Love to Grace.[5] As ever. *Sincerely*

[1] Lieutenant General Gruenther, Deputy Chief of Staff for Plans and Combat Operations, had outlined (EM) a strategy he had implemented in a recent bridge game. One of his opponents had been W. Averell Harriman, who, on the last rubber "misplaced every card (and played the hand badly in addition) and had apoplexy every time I showed up with another trump." For background on Harriman see no. 852.

[2] For an evaluation of Gruenther's abilities as a bridge player see Galambos, *Chief of Staff*, no. 1820.

[3] See the preceding document.

[4] Gruenther would reply (Sept. 9, EM) that the letter to J. Earl Schaefer contained no misstatements. For developments see no. 986.

[5] Mrs. Gruenther.

959   *Eisenhower Mss.*

To Hastings Lionel Ismay   *August 31, 1950*

Dear Pug: It was fine to have your letter of August 15.[1] Under current plans, I hope to reach the Eastern shore of the Atlantic no later than about June 1, 1951. I plan to participate in the Normandy D-Day celebration next year, after which I currently plan to go to Culzean in Scotland, for ten days or so. On the 21st of June, I am to participate in the celebration of the 500th anniversary of Glasgow University. On July 3 or 4, I take part in the St. Paul's Cathedral ceremony involving the Roll of Honor.[2] I have tentatively agreed also to attend one dinner in London — I believe it is to be given by the English Speaking Union; at least it is a society for the promotion of British-American friendship.[3]

Except for these specific dates, I hope to make full utilization of my time in seeing and being with old friends. Among these, my specific ambitions involve you, Jimmy Gault, Louis Greig, Harold McMillen, Freddie Morgan, Humphrey Gale, Peter Portal, and others that I learned to like and admire so much in the War.[4] I shall hope, of course, that Winston will have an hour or two to give me — I do want to see him and talk to him.[5]

As the details of my plans get really firmed up, I will give you a complete itinerary. *Cordially*

[1] General Ismay, Churchill's military adviser during World War II, had asked for the complete schedule of the Eisenhowers' visit to Great Britain and France during June and July 1951 (EM; for background on Ismay see no. 259). He had mentioned hearing rumors that Eisenhower might soon be recalled to military service. He did not believe that there would be a general war, however, "provided that America continues to be robust and vigilant, and the British Commonwealth are staunch and unswerving in supporting you."

[2] For background on these plans see nos. 706, 841, and 876.
[3] Eisenhower would be the guest of honor at a dinner given by the English-Speaking Union in London on July 3, 1951 (see *New York Times*, July 4, 1951).
[4] On Colonel James F. Gault and Sir Louis Greig see no. 14; on Harold Macmillan see no. 949; on Lieutenant-General Sir Frederick E. Morgan see no. 357; and on Lieutenant-General Sir Humfrey M. Gale and Marshal of the Royal Air Force (RAF) Viscount Portal of Hungerford see *Eisenhower Papers*, vols. I–IX.
[5] Winston S. Churchill would be present with Eisenhower at the dinner on July 3, 1951. Churchill was currently a Member of Parliament and Leader of His Majesty's Opposition.

960   *Eisenhower Mss.*

To Ellis Dwinnell Slater   *August 31, 1950*

Dear Slats: Thank you very much for your nice letter.[1]

Today, I made a few changes in your suggested draft for the American Field Services Foreword. I had to do this because I was not in France during the hostilities of World War I.[2] In any event, it should reach you within a day or so.[3]

I am delighted that you had such a nice time while out here but you did not enjoy the week more than I did. I hope that we can repeat the performance annually.[4] *Cordially*

[1] Slater, president of Frankfort Distilleries, had thanked Eisenhower in an undated letter (EM) for his hospitality during the week Slater and several friends had stayed with the Eisenhowers in Denver, Colorado (for the reaction of one of the other guests see no. 956). Slater had also asked Eisenhower to send him some comments on the American Field Service (AFS) that could be used as a foreword to a booklet describing the group's scholarship program. The AFS sponsored teenage students from foreign countries during one-year visits to the United States.

[2] One of the drafts that Slater had sent Eisenhower included a description of the work of the AFS in carrying the dead and wounded of the Allied forces from the battlefields during both world wars. Eisenhower had changed one sentence from "I witnessed their unselfish courage as they manned their own ambulances and stretchers under fire . . ." to "They became known for their unselfish courage. . . ." The draft with this and other changes, together with a typescript of a version that would be sent to Slater under the date of September 5, are in EM.

[3] Slater would acknowledge receipt of the foreword in a letter of September 15 (EM), and he would promise to send a copy of the booklet before it appeared in published form.

[4] This evening the Eisenhowers would be hosts at a dinner at the Cherry Hills Club in Denver (correspondence concerning the arrangements and a list of the guests are in EM, Subject File, Entertainments). Eisenhower would fly to Colorado Springs, Colorado, on September 1 (for background on the trip see no. 913).

To Haroldson Lafayette Hunt   *September 2, 1950*

Dear Mr. Hunt:[0] The copy of Senator Bridges' statement that you sent
to me was my first intimation that Dr. Jessup had ever delayed a trip
to testify for Alger Hiss.[1] By no means have I ever said that I *knew*
anything about any of these specific cases. Moreover, you have convinced
me that even the kind of public statement that I issued in one case had
best be left unsaid until such matters are settled by courts.[2]

What infuriated me was the manner in which the accusation was
made. But if any individual is ever properly accused in court and judged
guilty of such an offense, I do not need to tell you where I will stand.
Moreover, I agree with your statement that the more highly placed
such an individual is, the greater his crime.

So, while I cannot believe that the only one of these men that I have
known—Jessup—can possibly be guilty either of disloyalty or even of
remotely sympathizing with the Communistic doctrine, I agree that it
is unwise for any individual to make public statements about such cases
until a final and proper adjudication has been made.

It is difficult indeed to talk about these things in letters because of
the various directions in which each thought can move. Possibly, sometime in the future, we can have a couple of hours to talk them over
leisurely. Most certainly I share your concern in these serious days and
times for everything that can affect the good of our country, particularly
the presence of any disloyal man in a governmental position.

With best wishes. *Sincerely*

P.S. I'm reading "Seeds of Treason."[3] Thank you.

[1] Hunt, founder of the Hunt Oil Company in east Texas, had enclosed in his
letter of August 25 (EM) an excerpt from a speech by Senator Styles Bridges,
Republican from New Hampshire. The selection from Bridges's remarks of July 18,
1950, in the Senate (copy in EM, Bridges Corr.) reads: "It was less than 1 year ago
that the State Department issued the infamous 'China White Paper,' a product of the
thinking of Philip C. Jessup—our Ambassaor-at-Large—whose personal prejudices,
and those of his associates in the State Department against the Republic of China, are
too well known to require further comment. Incidentally, my colleagues will recall
that Jessup's last trip to south Asia was delayed while he testified for Alger Hiss. This
White Paper, a monstrous excuse for losing the key to the Orient, was issued on
August 5, 1949" (see U.S., Congress, Senate, *Congressional Record*, 81st Cong., 2d
sess., 1950, 96, pt. 8:10488). Jessup was Ambassador at Large of the United States
and Hamilton Fish Professor of International Law and Diplomacy at Columbia
University. Hiss was the former president of the Carnegie Endowment for International
Peace. For background on Hunt's interest in these men see no. 925. On the *China
White Paper* see no. 788, n. 7.
[2] For Eisenhower's statement see no. 733.
[3] Hunt had sent Eisenhower a copy of Ralph de Toledano and Victor Lasky, *Seeds
of Treason: The True Story of the Hiss-Chambers Tragedy* (New York, 1950). He
had asked Eisenhower to begin reading on page 166 "to determine if the close

associates of Alger Hiss would or would not know if he was innocent." This part of the book concerned developments between Hiss's testimony before the House Committee on Un-American Activities on August 16, 1948, and his conviction for perjury on January 24, 1950, after his second trial.

962   *Eisenhower Mss.*

TO BRUCE BARTON   *September 2, 1950*

Dear Bruce:[0] I'm still doing a pretty fair job dodging speeches[1]—but I'm hooked for a four-network twelve and half minute affair on Monday night—Labor Day. I'm speaking in favor of the "Crusade for Freedom," which is something on the order of being against sin![2]

It will be nice to see you when I get back to New York—along about the middle of September.

With warm regard. *Cordially*

[1] In a letter of August 28 (EM) Barton had complained to Eisenhower about the Truman administration's "policy of universal meddle and muddle." He hoped that Eisenhower would not need to make speeches "to pull the chestnuts of these bungling bastards out of the fire." For background on Barton see no. 178.

[2] Eisenhower would launch the Crusade for Freedom with a nationwide radio speech to be broadcast from Denver, Colorado, on September 4. Sponsored by the National Committee for a Free Europe, the crusade's purpose was to publicize the plight of the peoples of Eastern Europe whose governments were subject to Soviet domination. On Eisenhower's work in organizing the crusade see nos. 739 and 899. On the preparations for the broadcast see no. 948; and *Denver Post*, August 27, 31, September 3, 4, 1950.

963   *Eisenhower Mss.*

TO W. WALTER WILLIAMS   *September 5, 1950*

Dear Mr. Williams: This note is just to bring you my very best wishes for success on September 12th.[1] I am heartened when I find men of your caliber are taking direct and personal interest in our governmental affairs and are willing to shoulder the burdens involved in active participation.

Good luck to you.[2] *Cordially*

[1] Williams (B.S. University of Washington 1916), president of Continental, Inc., a mortgage banking, realty, and insurance firm in Seattle, Washington, was running for U.S. senator, and on September 12 he would compete in his state's Republican primary. He had been chairman of the Committee for Economic

Development (CED) in 1948, and he was currently a member of the executive committee of that organization. Eisenhower had been a trustee of the CED since May 1950 (for background see no. 732). Williams had visited Eisenhower in Denver, Colorado, in early August, and he had noted in a letter of August 15 (EM) that if he won a seat in the Senate, he would "be in a better position than ever to do a job for you in connection with 1952."
[2] Williams would win the Republican primary, but he would lose the general election on November 7 (see *New York Times*, Sept. 14 and Nov. 9, 1950).

964   *Eisenhower Mss., Family File*

TO EDGAR NEWTON EISENHOWER   *September 5, 1950*

Dear Ed:[1] A man named W. Walter Williams is competing in your September 12th primaries for senatorial nomination.[2] This note is just to tell you that upon several occasions I have met Mr. Williams and have been greatly impressed by his integrity and his sincerity, to say nothing of his intelligent comprehension of today's vital problems.

I am not sure that you know him, but if you do not, I should think it would be worthwhile to cultivate his acquaintance. *Sincerely*

[1] General Eisenhower's brother.
[2] See the preceding document.

965   *Eisenhower Mss.*

TO LUCILE SLEINKOFER   *September 5, 1950*

Dear Mrs. Sleinkofer: Your letter to me dated August 28th poses one of the vital problems of our day.[1] It involves the great question of peace in a world that is torn apart by great ideological differences. On our own side, we stand for decency in the conduct of human affairs, for equality of man, the freedom of the individual, and world peace. The other side uses fanaticism to advance a system that means the destruction of all these values that we hold so dear.

So the question is what must we do to preserve a way of life that means so much to us but at the same time do it without becoming nothing but an armed camp.

I shall not, of course, attempt in a short letter to give you too many thoughts and observations on this vast problem. But I do most earnestly believe that in this day and time we must guard our birthright of freedom with the moral, intellectual, economic and military might of this great nation. I use all of these adjectives because, as we are forced to depend upon might and power, it is more than ever necessary that we be certain of our own moral integrity and purpose. Otherwise, we would become no better than the dictators who seek to destroy us.

I realize that such a letter as this offers no practical solution to your boy's problem, but in these times each of us must do what he is called upon to do—each of us must do his own duty to the very limit of his ability. And all of us must retain our faith in good and justice and do our best to preserve the values that we know to be priceless. *Sincerely*

¹ Mrs. Sleinkofer, of Tarrytown, New York, had asked in her letter of the twenty-eighth (EM) for advice as to what young men such as her son might do "to avoid death and destruction" in Korea. Her son, who had recently registered to study at Syracuse University, had been ordered by the U.S. Marine Corps to report for service on September 11. For background on the war in Korea see no. 934.

966   *Eisenhower Mss.*

To H. J. PORTER   *September 6, 1950*

Dear Jack: Your Houston columnist is just like a bunch of others; he assumes that he knows what is in everybody's mind.¹ This seems to be the characteristic of those who practice the profession, so there is nothing to worry about.

I cannot tell you what a tremendous lift I get out of the knowledge that such persons as yourself are supporting me so earnestly in the great idea of establishing an American Assembly. I am not only grateful to you, I am confident that in this particular thing we are working on something that will eventually be of the most vital importance to America and the future of free government.² *Cordially*

¹ Porter, a prominent figure in the Texas oil industry and a leader in the Republican party in that state, had enclosed in his letter of August 30 (EM) a copy of Charlie Evans's gossip column, "Night and Day." Evans had described Eisenhower as a serious contender for the Republican presidential nomination in 1952 and had maintained that Eisenhower had discussed the possibility of support from Texans when Porter and others had met with the General in Denver, Colorado, recently. For background on the meeting see nos. 938 and 942. For Eisenhower's recollection of the discussion on that occasion see no. 979.

Porter had explained that he did not know how Evans had obtained his version of what had transpired. He implied, however, that Evans had concocted his story because of Porter's discussions with the General at the same time that the chairman of the Texas Republican Executive Committee was announcing Eisenhower as his first choice for President in 1952 (see *New York Times*, Aug. 17, 1950). Porter had concluded, "I have decided not to say anything, and let my actions in helping you on the Columbia undertaking do the talking, if any is necessary."

² Porter had also enclosed a copy of one of six hundred letters he had sent on August 30 to people in Texas. The letters described the conference plan (for background see nos. 605 and 844) and appealed for financial support. Eisenhower would receive twenty-six checks as a result of Porter's appeal (see Schulz to Porter, Sept. 16, 1950, same file as document). For developments see no. 1039.

967   *Eisenhower Mss.*

To Harold Edward Stassen   *September 7, 1950*

Dear Governor: After reading your letter of the 3rd, I suggest one change in the "Tentative Draft of Message of Invitation." The final sentence of the first paragraph I would change to read as follows: "We therefore respectfully invite you to join fifty other key citizens, some of each major political party and some of independent views, in a closed session to consider the major aspects of our country's future foreign policy and to discuss our future national security policies and their related economic mobilization policies. Mr. Baruch and General Eisenhower have already agreed to participate in such a discussion, while Admiral Nimitz and General Spaatz will also be invited to take part."[1] This change is suggested as being more appropriate to what you are contemplating in that the affair is not to be a series of formal lectures and "expert" presentation, but rather a round table discussion in which the effort will be to awaken a sense of citizen responsibility in all these matters.

In the final paragraph of the invitation, you suggest a 24-hour convocation. After some reflection on this matter, I rather believe that the initial meeting should last from lunch time through an evening session with the guests themselves then deciding whether they would meet again, and if so, to specify place and date. For those who came from a distance, night accommodations at the Club could still be procured.[2]

As I told you before,[3] I shall be more than glad to join such a group for discussions of the kind proposed, particularly because the purpose is for arousing interest and cannot possibly be misinterpreted as a scheme for undermining the influence and seizing responsibility of properly constituted authority. This I shall be glad to do whether or not you accept the suggestions contained in this letter.[4]

With personal regard. *Sincerely*

¹ Stassen, president of the University of Pennsylvania and former Governor of Minnesota, had enclosed in his letter of the third a draft that contained the following sentence at the end of the first paragraph: "We therefore respectfully invite you to join fifty other key citizens, some of each major political party and some of independent views, in a closed session to consider the major aspects of our country's future foreign policy, to discuss our future national security policies with General Dwight Eisenhower, and our future economic mobilization policies with

Mr. Bernard Baruch" (for background on Stassen see no. 116). Baruch, a philanthropist and adviser to several presidents, had recently made public his views on economic mobilization for the Korean War (see no. 914). For background on Fleet Admiral Chester William Nimitz see *Eisenhower Papers*, vols. I–IX; and no. 519 in this volume. General Carl Spaatz (USAF, ret.), was currently living in Washington, D.C. (for background see no. 154).

[2] Stassen had proposed that the meeting take place at the Westchester Country Club, in Rye, New York, on September 28 and 29. Eisenhower would send him a telegram on the eleventh (EM) explaining that he could stay at the conference only until 11:30 A.M. on the twenty-ninth because he had another engagement later that day. Stassen would reply (telegram, the following day, EM) that he would leave the question of holding sessions on the twenty-ninth to the discretion of the conferees.

[3] Eisenhower had talked with Stassen at Lowry Air Force Base, near Denver, Colorado, on August 21 (appointment calendar), and he had written him a note on September 2 (EM) agreeing to attend the meeting on condition that it take place "on a most informal, give and take, basis."

[4] For developments see no. 984.

968   *Eisenhower Mss.*

To Marcellus Hartley Dodge   *September 7, 1950*
Personal and confidential

Dear Marcy:[1] Just recently young Peter Grace sent to me a very substantial check to help in the establishment of the "American Assembly" which, as you know, I hope to get started soon at Arden House.[2] To my mind this project is not only vitally necessary to the country, but it will develop, for Columbia, the finest possible contacts with worthwhile people all over the United States.

The purpose of this note is merely to say that this example of young Mr. Grace's understanding, confirms favorable opinions I have previously formed of him. Sometime, at your convenience, I should like to talk to you *very confidentially* about the prospect of getting a young man of this kind as one of our Trustees.[3] You remember we once invited young David Rockefeller and I rather think that the same reasons for our interest in him would apply in this case.[4]

Throughout the summer I have held periodic meetings with people to interest them in Columbia's affairs and, while I find that in the average case, a graduate of some other university is not particularly interested in Columbia's *routine* problems, the reaction to the "American Assembly" idea is always favorable—sometimes violently so.[5]

With warm personal regard. *Sincerely*

[1] Dodge was chairman of the board of the Remington Arms Company and clerk of the trustees of Columbia University.

² J. Peter Grace, Jr., president of the W. R. Grace & Company, had contributed five thousand dollars (see Columbia University, *Report of the Treasurer, 1951*, p. 260). For background on the American Assembly see nos. 605 and 844.

³ Dodge would reply (Sept. 8, EM) that Eisenhower's recommendation of Grace confirmed his own good opinion of him. There were currently no vacancies on the board of trustees, but Dodge assured Eisenhower that this suggestion would receive "every and most serious consideration."

⁴ David Rockefeller was vice-president of the Chase National Bank. For background see no. 215.

⁵ Grace had heard Eisenhower describe the American Assembly at a dinner party at the apartment of William H. Burnham, an investment banker in New York City, on July 6, 1950. For Grace's impressions of the evening see Grace to Eisenhower, July 13, 1950, EM. On Eisenhower's other efforts on behalf of the American Assembly see nos. 826 and 938. For later developments see no. 1039.

969   *Eisenhower Mss.*

To Haroldson Lafayette Hunt   *September 7, 1950*

*Dear Mr. Hunt:*⁰ Thank you very much for sending me a copy of Mr. deMille's letter.¹ I agree with what he has to say. I have already tried out your suggestion on a number of my friends and I have yet to find anyone who disagreed with the reasons you give for using the word "Constructive" to describe those people who believe in progress based upon the traditional American concepts of individual freedom and competitive economy, with a minimum of governmental intervention.

Under current plans, it appears that I shall be in Texas in early November. If this works out, I shall hope to see you during that trip.² *Very sincerely*

¹ Hunt had enclosed in his letter of September 1 (EM) a letter from Cecil Blount deMille, a motion-picture producer who was president of Cecil B. DeMille Productions, Inc., in Hollywood, California. DeMille had served briefly as chairman of the Motion Picture Industry Council before relinquishing the position in July 1949 to Ronald Wilson Reagan (B.A. Eureka College 1932). DeMille had praised Hunt's memorandum on the use of the word *constructive*, a copy of which Hunt had already sent to Eisenhower (for Eisenhower's reaction and background on Hunt see no. 931). DeMille had offered to distribute five thousand copies of the brochure, but Hunt had decided that deMille's letter might serve as better advertising, and he had secured deMille's permission to circulate it.

² Hunt would hear Eisenhower speak in Dallas, Texas, on November 11. On the trip see no. 1025.

To MILTON STOVER EISENHOWER	*September 8, 1950*

Dear Milton: This brings you my best for Sept. 15.[1] I know that it must seem strange to you to think of yourself as 51—but all the rest of the boys have to remember that its the baby of the family who has reached the beginning of his 2d half century!

Anyway, the rest of us are proud of what you've done—and so our congratulations are not sent merely because you've lived this long—but because you've lived so effectively.[2]

Love to all the family, *Affectionately*

[1] Eisenhower's brother Milton would celebrate his fifty-first birthday on September 15. The General wrote this letter in longhand.

[2] Milton would begin his longhand reply of the fourteenth (EM, Family File): "Your birthday note has pleased me so much that I'm now resigned to becoming 51—tomorrow." The youngest of the Eisenhower brothers, who was soon to be inaugurated president of Pennsylvania State College, would promise to describe the pressures of his new job when he saw the General in October (see no. 997).

971	*Eisenhower Mss.,*
	Philip Young Corr.

To WILLIAM AVERELL HARRIMAN	*September 8, 1950*
Telegram

Dear Averell: A message from Philip Young tells me about the added help you have given us in order to assure the success of the Conference plan.[1] I have been explaining it incessantly this summer to small gatherings of individuals and have everywhere met with enthusiastic response. Many small contributions are coming in and sizable ones have been promised for support of actual conferences.[2] Because I believe so firmly in the potential value to America of these conferences, I am especially grateful for your generosity and farsightedness which are making them possible.[3] I hope to come to Washington in late October and if I do, I shall hope to see you in person to report still further progress and to express more definitely my deep appreciation and admiration.[4] *Cordially*

[1] For background on Harriman see no. 852. Philip Young, dean of the Graduate School of Business at Columbia University, had telephoned Eisenhower on September 8 to report the results of a four-hour conference during which Harriman had agreed to contribute $275,000 to the conference plan over the next five years (see Schulz to Eisenhower, Sept. 8, 1950, same file as document. For background

on the plan, soon to become the American Assembly, see nos. 605 and 844). Young thought that the program would soon be ready for presentation to the trustees, and he had suggested that Eisenhower bring up the subject at the October meeting of the board. For developments see no. 1039.

[2] For examples of Eisenhower's efforts see nos. 826, 893, and 938. On the contributions see nos. 941, 942, 945, and 968. In the next several days Eisenhower would thank other friends for their support of the conference plan (see the letters to radio and television entertainer Arthur M. Godfrey, Sept. 9, 1950, and to Aksel Nielsen, president of the Title Guaranty Company, Denver, Colorado, Sept. 11, 1950, both in EM). On September 8 Eisenhower would attend a dinner at the Denver home of Claude Kedzie Boettcher, chairman of the boards of directors of American Crystal Sugar Company and Great Western Sugar Company and president of Ideal Cement Company.

[3] Harriman would reply (telegram, Sept. 11, EM): "Greatly appreciate your message. I am enthusiastic about the possibilities under your driving leadership. Look forward keenly to seeing you when you get back."

[4] On the trip to Washington, D.C., October 27–30, 1950, see no. 1045.

972   *Eisenhower Mss.*

To William Averell Harriman   *September 8, 1950*

Dear Averell:[1] When I left New York in late July, I left orders to deliver to you, at your convenience, the picture I painted of Sun Valley. It is possible that my office force has not been able to make delivery because of a lack of information as to appropriate address. In any event, if you still want it—and have not yet received it—I shall get it to you as soon as I return to the city in ten days or so.[2]

Today I dispatched a telegram to you because of a telephone message I just received from Philip Young.[3] I have really encountered a most enthusiastic response to every description I have given of the Conference plan—I am certain it is going to be a great success. For this the main credit, of course, goes to you. *As ever*

[1] For background on Harriman see no. 605.
[2] This was no doubt the same picture Eisenhower had mentioned in no. 852. Sun Valley is located in Idaho. The painting is probably the same as the one titled *Village in the Valley*, plate 49 in Eisenhower, *Eisenhower College Collection: Paintings*. Harriman would reply on September 12 (EM) that he would arrange for someone to come to New York to pick up the picture and deliver it to his residence in Washington, D.C.; his chauffeur would do so on September 15 (see Sharp to Eisenhower, Sept. 15, 1950, same file as document).
[3] See the preceding document.

To ROBERT CUTLER

Dear Mr. Cutler:[01] Thank you very much indeed for your fine letter of September 4th. I am delighted that you see some virtue in the Conference plan — a plan that I truly believe will evolve into something of the greatest significance to America's freedoms.[2]

While my fall calendar is a crowded one, I shall certainly take advantage of your invitation as soon as it is possible to do so. From my knowledge of my schedule, this may be as late as mid-November but I shall try to make it earlier.[3]

Experience at a number of these meetings — particularly when they were on a small and intimate basis — leads me to believe that the most effective session is one conducted during a leisurely afternoon. For example, a lunch followed by a comfortable, round table, session, with say a short period after or during a dinner for such questions as may not have occurred earlier to those present. This is usually not too long to be boring but provides sufficient time for a full explanation.[4]

If I may write to you about the first of October, possibly we can firm up some details.

Thank you again for your very kind suggestion. *Sincerely*

[1] Cutler (LL.B. Harvard 1922) had risen to the rank of brigadier general in the Army during World War II (for background see Chandler, *War Years*, no. 2144). He was currently president and a director of Old Colony Trust Company in Boston, Massachusetts.

[2] Cutler's letter of September 4 is not in EM.

[3] Eisenhower would be the guest of honor at a dinner that Cutler would host in Boston on November 22 (see no. 1094).

[4] Cutler would attend a luncheon at Eisenhower's residence at Columbia on October 10 (the guest list is in EM, American Assembly Corr.). On Eisenhower's recent meetings regarding the conference plan see nos. 826, 893, and 938.

To EDGAR NEWTON EISENHOWER

Dear Ed: If my speech the other evening didn't tell you what you want to know about the "Crusade for Freedom," then I doubt that there is much use of me trying to explain it in a short letter.[1]

My basic opinion about this, as well as about a lot of other things, is fairly simple. It goes something like this:

I, in company with a whole lot of other people, am disturbed about trends, tendencies and developments — or sometime the lack of these —

in both domestic and international affairs. Because of this uneasiness, I am determined to do something constructive about them, so far as it is possible for one individual to do so. In the case of the Crusade for Freedom, I believe there is a clear-cut opportunity to serve our country concretely and immediately. It is because of this conviction that I went to the trouble to work a couple of weeks preparing a talk and then giving it the other night over the radio.[2]

I am sorry to hear that you will be unable to stay over for Milton's inaugural. I realize that to stay around from the 22nd of September to the 5th of October might be difficult for you. However, if you should come through New York City, I hope you can spend a night or two with Mamie and me. We plan to be at 60 Morningside Drive on September 19th.[3] *As ever*

[1] The General's brother Edgar had asked in a letter of September 1 (EM, Family File) for "some idea of what will really be accomplished" by the Crusade for Freedom campaign of the National Committee for a Free Europe, Inc. Eisenhower had opened the crusade with a nationwide radio speech broadcast from Denver, Colorado, on September 4 (for background see no. 962). Edgar, a lawyer in Tacoma, Washington, strongly disliked the man who would serve as state chairman for the crusade, and he wanted to know more about the movement before acceding to requests that he endorse it publicly.

[2] Edgar would reply (Sept. 11, EM, Family File) that his questions were still unanswered and that he had not received a copy of the radio speech. Lieutenant Colonel Robert L. Schulz, Eisenhower's aide, would dispatch a copy of the talk under a covering letter of September 13 (*ibid.*).

[3] Edgar had mentioned in his letter of the first that he planned to visit Washington, D.C., from September 15 to September 22 but that he would not be able to remain in the East until their brother Milton's inauguration as president of Pennsylvania State College on October 4. Edgar's plans would change, however, and he would notify the General (Sept. 14, EM, Family File) that he was no longer going to Washington, D.C., and might attend the inauguration. On Edgar's difficulties in arranging his schedule see no. 790; on the inauguration see no. 997.

975 *Eisenhower Mss.*

To Ernest Nason Harmon *September 11, 1950*

Dear Eddie:[1] It was nice to hear from you. Like yourself, I have told the powers that be that I am available for service if they want me. But I rather think that the need is for young fellows who can tote a gun rather than for old generals to clutter up some headquarters.[2]

With respect to conversations I had with Dr. Cabot, I tried to describe to him a little gadget that we first met in Africa. The enemy used it to prevent, in emergencies, our planes getting quickly into the air. It was a very light weight piece of metal in the shape of a skeleton pyramid.

Because of its construction it always presented a sharp point to any pneumatic tire crossing it and since it was about five inches in height, this meant a wrecked airplane provided the machine had gotten up any speed at all. Our own service experimented with the thing and as I recall finally made them of non-metallic metal in order that they could not be quickly removed by means of a large, magnetized sweep. Like many other things, they were effective the first time they were encountered. But, in the long run they did not amount to much.[3]

It is nice to know that you are devoting your energies to the educational world. One of these days possibly I shall have a chance to talk to you about some of the problems we have in common. *Sincerely*

[1] Harmon, president of Norwich University and a major general recently retired from the Army, had remarked in a letter of September 5 (EM) that as a result of his concern about the trend of events in Korea he had offered to return to active duty; he said, however, that he was probably too old to be of much use. For background on Harmon see no. 692.

[2] See nos. 916 and 921.

[3] Godfrey Lowell Cabot (A.B. Harvard 1882) was president of numerous companies involved in the manufacture of products from oil and natural gas. He was a trustee of Norwich University and of several other institutions. Harmon had recounted in his letter the substance of conversations he had had with Cabot on the subject of devices called chevaux-de-frise, which the Germans had used during World War II. Cabot had heard Eisenhower describe the devices, and he had included research on the items among the projects for which he was giving money to Norwich. On Eisenhower's friendship with Cabot see no. 1054.

976   *Eisenhower Mss.*

To Mark Wayne Clark   *September 11, 1950*

Dear Wayne:[0] It seems almost criminal that you are again back in your old job of training troops for battle. This time, of course, you are the top man instead of the Chief of Staff, but the fact that you face such a necessity less than ten years after you were in the middle of it before, does not speak too well for civilization.[1]

When October rolls around and you still believe that I might do some good by coming to one or more of your camps, I have no doubt that we could arrange the details of such a trip, provided you will give my office a ring at that time. My fall schedule is a rather hectic one, but it would seem likely that a short, over night trip could always be worked into it somewhere.[2]

Soon I shall be going back to New York. I dread the thought because I like this Colorado country so much, but I must get back on the job.[3]

I shall be looking forward to receiving your book.[4] *As ever*

[1] General Clark had been in charge of G−3, the Operations and Training Section of GHQ staff in Washington, D.C., from August 1940 until he became Chief of Staff of the Army Ground Forces in May 1942. He held the latter position for less than two months, and he left for England in June 1942 to take command of II Corps (on those assignments see Clark, *Calculated Risk*, pp. 11−24; on his friendship with Eisenhower see *Eisenhower Papers*, vols. I−IX). Clark, currently Chief of Army Field Forces, had complained in a letter of September 5 (EM) of his difficulties in changing young Americans from "peace lovers to fighters, with sufficient iron in their souls to seek out and kill the ruthless enemy who now opposes us in Korea and who will meet us on future fields of battle." Clark said that speeches by Eisenhower at one or two of the training camps might put the troops on "a sure road to success," and he proposed a visit to Camp Pickett, in Virginia, in late October (see also Clark, *From the Danube to the Yalu*, pp. 23−30).

[2] Clark would thank Eisenhower in a letter of September 23 (EM), taking solace in the reminder that they had succeeded in an immense training task ten years earlier. In a note of October 18 (EM) Clark would ask for a specific date for a visit. There is no reply in EM, but Eisenhower's appointment calendar indicates that he would fly to Camp Pickett the morning of December 7 to address more than twenty thousand soldiers (see also *New York Times*, Dec. 8, 1950). For Eisenhower's continuing interest in the army training program see no. 1038.

[3] On the stay in Denver see no. 805.

[4] On Clark's new book, *Calculated Risk*, see no. 910.

977   *Eisenhower Mss.*

TO FREDERIC RENEÉ COUDERT   *September 11, 1950*

Dear Mr. Coudert:[0] Your memorandum which accompanied your nice note of September 7th is a clear presentation of a very important distinction that we must make if we are not to become confused in our "foreign affairs" activities.[1] I should like very much to talk to you about this and related subjects soon after I get back to New York. There has been some very bungled thinking on such questions.

With warm personal regard. *Cordially*

[1] Coudert, a New York City attorney and a trustee of Columbia University, had congratulated Eisenhower on his radio speech opening the Crusade for Freedom on September 4 (for background see no. 962). In his accompanying memorandum (EM) Coudert had drawn the distinction between revelations to the public of matters concerning foreign policy and revelations of matters concerning military strategy. He had maintained that the formulation of policy, even though it might be in conflict with strategy, was the President's prerogative and that General of the Army Douglas MacArthur was losing sight of this. Coudert had referred specifically to MacArthur's recent unauthorized statements on U.S. policy toward Formosa. The press had widely publicized MacArthur's message to the annual encampment of the Veterans of Foreign Wars (VFW) in Chicago, Illinois, on August 28—a message he had delivered in spite of President Truman's order of the twenty-sixth that MacArthur "withdraw" the statement. MacArthur had described Formosa's safety as vital to that of the United States, saying that its

geographical position made it an irreplaceable link in the chain of air and naval bases in the Far East (see *New York Times*, Aug. 29, 1950). On the day after he had ordered the withdrawal of the message, Truman had sent MacArthur a copy of a letter of August 27 to Warren Robinson Austin, U.S. Ambassador to the United Nations, outlining the seven basic points in U.S. policy toward Formosa (for background on Austin see Galambos, *Chief of Staff*, no. 1198). Truman had suggested that the island's legal status could be determined only by "international action" and that the Chinese Nationalist government currently occupied Formosa at the sufferance of the victorious Allies of World War II (see *Public Papers of the Presidents: Truman, 1950*, pp. 599–600, 602; and *New York Times*, Aug. 30, 1950). For MacArthur's account see his *Reminiscences*, pp. 341–44. Truman would set forth his view of the controversy in *Memoirs*, vol. II, *Years of Trial and Hope*, pp. 354–58.

978   *Eisenhower Mss.*

To Ted Mack   *September 11, 1950*

Dear Mr. Mack:[0] Thank you very much for your note of September 6th—even more so for the prompt and effective action you took in the support of the Crusade for Freedom.[1] It is such positive action as yours that will make the whole campaign a great success. You have done a distinct service for all of us. *Sincerely*

[1] Mack, producer and master of ceremonies of "The Original Amateur Hour," a radio and television show, had expressed (Sept. 6, EM) his agreement with the goals of the Crusade for Freedom, which the General had launched in a speech of September 4 (for background see no. 962). Mack had enclosed the portion of his script for the television show of September 5 that referred to the speech: "General Eisenhower told us in his typical, clear unemotional language how the Communist radio stations are coming right out into the open to 'destroy free government and human liberty.' " Mack had urged all of his listeners to join the crusade and to send contributions to General Lucius D. Clay; Mack and his staff were dispatching a check for one hundred dollars. For background see nos. 739 and 899.

979   *Eisenhower Mss.,*
                                                              American Assembly Corr.

To Leonard Franklin McCollum   *September 12, 1950*

Dear Mc:[01] A short while ago you were kind enough to arrange a luncheon for your friends, to whom I explained certain fundamental ideas I hold about the role of educational institutions in the affairs of our country. In particular I discussed the Conference Program, which I plan to initiate at Columbia University. At that luncheon, several of you suggested that I outline in writing the country's need for this program and the method of operation.[2]

When I came out of World War II, I had a profound conviction that America was in danger for two reasons:

(1) The Communist threat from *without*.[3]

(2) The failure of most of us to remember that the basic values of democracy were won only through sacrifice and to recognize the *dangers of indifference and of ignorance*. Many believe that there is a growing tendency, arising out of this lack of understanding, to sell out the permanent values of our system for gains of the moment.

Deeply concerned by the problems facing our country and believing that educational institutions must assume immediate leadership in studying, explaining, and perpetuating our American system, I ventured to assume the Presidency of Columbia in 1948. My conviction was then and is even greater now that Columbia is ideally situated to pioneer methods by which our educational institutions may be useful to our country in the struggles that lie ahead.

We have always known that democracy could be destroyed by creeping paralysis from within. Bureaucratic controls, deficit spending, subsidies, and just plain hand-outs may, in certain emergencies, be required; but their cumulative effect *could* produce loss of personal initiative and responsibility, lowered production, a stagnated economy, commandeering of property and, finally, dictatorship. To avoid such possibilities every proposed encroachment on individual responsibility and freedom of action must be studied thoroughly, so that its deep-seated, long term consequences will be as well understood as its short term promise. This involves exhaustive study and research.[4]

It seems to me even more important, now that we are at war, that a greater effort be made to study these problems, in conjunction with the serious mess we face abroad. As you know, every war takes away, for its duration, certain privileges, liberties, and rights of citizens. We must be assured that at the end of the conflict we have the same individual benefits which we possessed at the beginning. For if we were to sacrifice lives and our National resources and end up as members of even a semi-dictatorial or regimented state, then the blood of our youth would have been spilled in foreign lands in vain.

To construct a plan that gives assurance of producing reasonable answers to such vital questions has absorbed my attention for the past two years. Within late months this plan has, with the help of such loyal friends and supporters as yourself, been brought to the attention of many influential persons, and the response has been encouraging.[5]

While a full explanation cannot be fitted into the confines of a personal letter, it seems possible to give an outline that may enable you accurately to convey an understanding of it to your friends.

We start with several observations or generally accepted facts:

a. The complexities of modern life make it necessary for most of us to exercise the duties of citizenship without any opportunity to explore, thoroughly, all the facts and factors involved in the problems of democracy. For example:

> Taxes — What rates of taxation are we able to support without mortally wounding our economy? What tax fields should be preempted by, or reserved to, the Federal Government? The State? The Community? What is the effect of unlimited Federal authority to tax upon the independence of the several states and therefore finally, the freedom of the individual?[6]

Dozens of other problems arise in the single field of taxation, but when we cast about a bit further, we grow almost bewildered. Take foreign relations and foreign policy, and look at such specific cases as Berlin, Spain, Tito, Formosa, Korea, Japan, Germany, Atlantic Pact, rearmament of Europe.

Or consider our military forces. With their terrific cost, how do we find the proper dividing line between tragic unpreparedness on the one hand, and unconscionable cost on the other? What about outlawing Communism? Hunting out subversives? How do we correlate peace time economic considerations with security requirements? (Imports, stockpiles, and so on).

Labor-management difficulty and all kinds of industrial strife, socialized medicine and Federal aid (and possible control) of education; and many more.

Today we hear about these things *only* from people who want to be elected or who have some other axe to grind. We vote without the facts!

b. Most business men are so busy meeting payrolls and paying taxes that they have little chance for study and contemplation.

The questions hinted at above bother the business man — he knows that office holders are bungling many of them, but, personally, he has no time to develop specific answers for all the problems of the day. Today we are largely specialists of one sort or another and fields, other than our own, are foreign to our understanding. But in universities, we have great concentrations of men whose only mission in life is to study such problems.

c. The business man and the farmer often distrust the professor as an impractical theorist; as a man who bears little responsibility and knows almost nothing of the actual problems facing any particular group. The professor's opinion of those comprising the "outside" world is not always flattering either — but together these groups represent intellectual comprehension and practical experience. We must bring together all segments of our people to obtain a better understanding of matters that may, if neglected or ignored, bring about our ruin.

d. The planned method of putting the proper individuals together is, first, to identify and describe the subject to be studied. Each study will last from 3—7 days. Each of these periods will be called a conference, but taken altogether, they will constitute "The American Assembly."

The second step is to determine the classifications of professors and scholars who have an interest in the specific questions of the special conference. For example, socialized medicine will certainly involve professors in medicine, law, economics, history, and sociology, possibly more. An expert in each of these disciplines would be picked, from Columbia or some other university, and one of them designated as the *academic leader* of the group. This group, serving as an intellectual task force, will prepare whatever background studies are appropriate—however, they would merely *begin* the conference—because the major proportion of the Assembly would comprise *business leaders, workers and labor leaders, political figures, (always of both parties)* and *professional men* of appropriate classifications. It would not be the intent to hold a conference group in continuous session—the scheduling of time would be such that the Assembly members would be encouraged to break up in small groups where informal discussion would go on in an atmosphere of friendly cooperation. This is the real key to the whole project. At the selected site there are comfortable accommodations, pleasant surroundings, fishing lake, a driving range, soft-ball grounds, and paths for walking through the woods.

e. Answers developed would scarcely be in terms of exact pronouncements, but *there would be an amalgamation of idea with fact, of theory with experience, that should normally produce some clearly agreed upon truths and observations.* These will be carried back by the participants to their own homes and associates, and so will have an immediate effect upon trends and tendencies. Because of the stature of the men attending the assembly, each conference would make news—this would likewise help in dissemination of the proceedings and conclusions. Periodicals and radio and television systems would of course be represented in the Assembly, and these men would certainly develop additional schemes to help in dissemination. The findings of the Conferences would also be published in pamphlet form. The whole effect would be to get the results out so *people could use them*!

f. Such conferences should progressively develop for us a reasonable answer for one of the most vital and almost all-embracing questions of our time which is, "In the modern, complex economy, with its acute interdependencies among great groups of specialists, what is the proper dividing line between the responsibilities and rights of the individual on the one hand, and the necessary controls of the central government on the other?" This must be answered. Soon!

g. An additional advantage of using the University for this type of research is that the conclusions of the Conference would be free of the suspicion of bias and prejudice. Most organizations and institutions are assumed, by the average person to represent a specialized or prejudiced viewpoint. People attending a university assembly would, however, be assured of complete freedom and an impartial platform for the presentation of their own views and the final answers developed would enjoy the same advantage in the public mind.

h. A number of industrial concerns have each expressed a desire to sponsor one or more of these conferences at an average cost of something like $25,000 per conference. (We have a sufficient amount of actual interest to allow us to start operations as soon as we get the necessary capital sums for *initial investment.* This should be $500,000, but I consider the matter so important that, if given $350,000, I would start now!)

Over the past several years, many hundreds of people have consulted with me about problems of the future and have expressed a great fear that unless a radical change occurs we shall destroy our competitive economy and therefore lose individual freedom. *This belief, in varying intensity, is held by millions of our citizens.* The Columbia plan offers no complete answer but it will be an effective start on the intellectual side of the problem. We must have understanding—mere irritation, uneasiness or even winning a single election cannot save us. Other educational institutions will follow the basic example, each in its own way, and the outcome will be a better informed citizenry—informed in those matters that are vital to the preservation of freedom.

In two years of effort to get this great plan started, I have yet to find any person who fails to agree that the vital problems of today require better and more comprehensive studies than they are now getting. The population deserves and must have a better comprehension of the political experiments constantly urged upon us, if American democracy is to survive. This is especially so today because our country is under such tremendous global pressure. We resist Communistic inroads led by Moscow, at the same time that we are called upon to support our weaker friends all over the world in order that the system of free government does not crumble inch by inch and finally leave us an isolated island in a whole sea of enemies.

No one would be so foolish as to assert that success in this plan will assure a fully successful outcome to the larger political, economic and military problems that we face every day. But I repeat that this plan gives us one important avenue by which we may *do something*; something that is vitally necessary. If ever we would lose by default, then we deserve our fate. But failure, I most earnestly believe, is completely unnecessary. We need only to get to work—be tough with ourselves—and be willing to face facts as they exist today. This American Assembly is an important step forward. It is action, not just words.[7] *Sincerely*

[1] McCollum was president of Continental Oil Company (for background see no. 826). There are several other copies of this letter in the same file, as well as in CUF, and some are marked "confidential." Eisenhower signed the ribbon copy "Ike E." on September 14, and his appointment calendar indicates that he had breakfast with McCollum and played golf with him in Denver on the same day.

[2] This luncheon was probably the one in Denver on August 11. For background see no. 938, n. 4.

[3] See Eisenhower, Crusade in Europe, pp. 476–77.

[4] Eisenhower had dealt with these issues in a fund-raising letter of June 1949 (no. 482).

[5] On the conference plan see nos. 605 and 844. On McCollum's role in the fund raising see no. 826.

[6] For Eisenhower's views on federal taxation see no. 871.

[7] McCollum would reply (Sept. 19, EM) that he planned to fly to New York that very day and hoped to assist in getting the American Assembly "moving along at a high speed." He would also suggest that Eisenhower address letters similar to this document and no. 987 (to H. J. "Jack" Porter, a prominent figure in the Texas oil industry and a leader in the Republican party in that state). In the margin of McCollum's letter Eisenhower would write, "McCann—Right away, please"; and a memorandum of September 21 (same file as document) indicates that letters would go out to Porter and to eight other friends of Eisenhower's. Fourteen additional persons would receive this letter or a modified version titled "Memorandum from Dwight D. Eisenhower on the American Assembly" (see nos. 1026, 1032, and 1036; see also Eisenhower to Bermingham, Sept. 29, 1950, and Bermingham to Eisenhower, Oct. 2, 1950, both in Bermingham Mss.). On Porter's fund-raising work on behalf of the American Assembly see no. 966. For developments see no. 1039.

980   *Eisenhower Mss.*

To Douglas Southall Freeman   *September 12, 1950*

Dear Dr. Freeman: You need have no fear that I shall ever forget the time you came to my office in the fall of 1946.[1] What you said to me that day made a deeper and more lasting impression on me than anything else I have yet heard on that subject. Consequently, if ever I, against every inclination, should reach a decision that conforms to your convictions, you will be one of those upon whom I would depend.[2]

This note brings to you my assurance of continued admiration and affection. *Sincerely*

[1] Freeman, a famous Civil War historian, had recalled (letter, Sept. 6, EM) his meeting with Eisenhower in November 1946, when he had told the General to run for President in 1948 (see Galambos, *Chief of Staff*, no. 1152). According to Freeman, Eisenhower's response had been that he "could not and would not" seek that office unless he came to believe that he "alone could do what had to be done." Freeman now asserted that the country faced "the gravest danger" and that the time had arrived for Eisenhower to make a decision.

For other examples of Eisenhower's consideration of this subject see nos. 638 and 786.

981   *Eisenhower Mss.*

To Edward Everett Hazlett, Jr.   *September 12, 1950*

Dear Swede:[1] This will probably be a very short letter but this does not mean that I fail to appreciate every single paragraph and sentence of your fine missive of August 9th. Of course I am delighted that you liked my "Silver" lecture. I worked like a dog on it, during the odd moments of several weeks.[2] Recently I have had to give another talk and again I worked the same way. This latest one, which I delivered on Labor Day, was even more difficult to prepare than the long one that you read. This was because I wanted to say a very great deal in twelve and one-half minutes. To undertake such a chore without allowing the text to become nothing more than a disjointed collection of empty platitudes and aphorisms is rather difficult for an old soldier. During the last days of my ordeal of preparation, I had a couple of friends come to visit me to help out. I am certainly lucky in the friends I have. These two had to come from a considerable distance, interrupting their own vacations, yet they came just as if it were fun to do it.[3]

It is slightly irritating to learn that your typewriter is showing some defectiveness in operation. I remember that when I told Schulz to procure one of them, I told him I wanted one that was noted for its durability and for its general excellence in operation. I hope you will telephone the man who delivered it to you and give him instructions to get on the job with necessary repairs.[4]

The Korean situation seems to be in something of a stalemate over the past several weeks. Most of us are puzzled by some of the developments and certainly all of us are experiencing a definite feeling of frustration.[5] However, we should not fall into the slovenly and easily acquired habit of just blaming others for all our misfortunes. However, it seems quite clear that, in one particular, the civilian authorities of our government must take a very considerable share of blame. They have never been very seriously impressed by professional insistence upon the permanent maintenance of a "task force" or as it is sometimes called, a "striking force."[6] It has always been obvious that a democracy, even one as rich as ours, could not maintain in peace the force in being that could promptly and successfully meet any trouble that might rise in any portion of the globe, particularly if such trouble should occur simultaneously in two or three places. But the existence of a fine, properly balanced, effectively commanded and reasonably strong task force would not only have a deterrent effect upon potential enemies, but would give us a splendid "fire department" basis on which to meet actual aggression.[7]

Beyond all this, however, we must recognize that we, in America, have never liked to face up to the problem arising out of the conflicting considerations of national security on the one hand and economic and financial solvency on the other. We have always felt a long ways removed from any potential and powerful enemy. Our experience has given us the feeling that we have available a cushion of space that would provide, automatically, a similar cushion of time. Consequently, we have not pondered deeply over the individual's obligations to the State, which provides to him protection in his way of life, nor have we been compelled to consider how the discharge of these obligations could most effectively and economically be accomplished.

During World War II, I was so frequently shocked and dismayed by the results of the incomplete training of our youth and by their lack of knowledge of the age-old struggle between individual freedom and dictatorship, that I came, unthinkingly, to assume that after the war our people would at last meet all these issues head on and do something effective about them. As a consequence, all of my thinking during the latter part of the war was based upon the assumption that America would adopt at the war's end some system of universal military *service*, a system whereby every young man would be required to give some 18 months of his time to the government and that the professional element of our security force would, therefore, be held to a minimum. Since such service would, I thought, be performed in discharge of an obligation, there would be no pay other than that for maintenance and a very small monetary allowance.[8] I likewise thought that we would develop means and methods of producing the munitions of war, including stockpiling, without profit to anyone.

In these assumptions I was, of course, proved quite wrong. When I came home, General Marshall told me that we could certainly get no more than a program of universal military training and that it would take a lot of work to put even this compromise across. I took his advice—especially when I found that the President was already sold on this idea—and worked hard for the UMT program. We were defeated even though I am still convinced that the great mass of our people definitely favor the proposition. I am sure that if the law had been passed some of our National Guard divisions would have, before this, been ready to leave for Korea.

With respect to your speculation that Germany may be the next place in which internecine warfare will break out, I should like to observe that if this should be the case, then Russia would, thereby, come very close to declaring open, all out, war. This is because of the fact that *her* troops are in actual occupation of Eastern Germany and in actual *control* of that area. Consequently, if she allows them to move to the attack, she cannot possibly longer hide behind the subterfuge that a "people's government" is attempting to liberate their brothers in another part of the country.[9]

I shall not be able to get down to Gordon Gray's inauguration. The early part of October is already filled with so many engagements on my calendar that I am seriously thinking of going to the hospital for a week or so. I should like to be at his installation—more to have a long talk with you than to attend another ceremony. This is true in spite of the fact that I like Gordon Gray immensely and I am delighted that he is taking over a job that he is going to find a great deal tougher than he suspects.[10]

My love to Ibby[11] and the children. *Cordially*

[1] For background on Hazlett (USN, ret.) see no. 36.

[2] Hazlett had mentioned (letter, Aug. 9, EM) that he had read a transcript of Eisenhower's Gabriel Silver Lecture on Peace (for background see no. 741). Hazlett thought it was excellent, and he wondered how the General could find time to write "such a fine, logical talk" when he was involved in so many activities.

[3] The two friends were William H. Burnham, an investment banker in New York City, and Lieutenant Colonel Paul T. Carroll, currently assigned to the Army War College at Fort Leavenworth, Kansas. On their roles in the drafting of the speech (Sept. 4) that launched the Crusade for Freedom see no. 948.

[4] Hazlett had added a postscript to his letter indicating that he liked the Royal typewriter that Eisenhower had given him (for background see no. 734). He said he had used it so much that certain parts were beginning to wear out. Lieutenant Colonel Robert L. Schulz, Eisenhower's aide, would ask Hazlett in a note of October 3 (same file as document) whether he had had the typewriter repaired, and he would offer to arrange to exchange the machine for another if the repairs were not satisfactory. In a reply of October 31 (EM) Hazlett would discount the complaints of his previous letter, adding that the typewriter was currently working "perfectly."

[5] U.S. troops in Korea continued to hold the defensive line of the Pusan Perimeter against the attacks of the North Koreans (see Collins, *War in Peacetime*, pp. 101–13; and Appleman, *South to the Naktong*, pp. 343–487). For background see no. 934; for developments see no. 1046.

[6] President Truman would have to accept "the major portion of the blame for our lack of preparedness, both militarily and diplomatically," Hazlett had asserted. He thought that Secretary of Defense Louis A. Johnson was also responsible for the setbacks suffered by U.N. forces in Korea because he had concurred in Truman's decision to cut drastically the FY51 budget for defense spending. See also no. 753.

[7] During his second term as President of the United States, Eisenhower would attempt to deal with these problems (see Dwight D. Eisenhower, *Waging Peace, 1956–1961* [Garden City, N.Y., 1965], pp. 290–91; and U.S. Department of Defense, *Annual Report of the Secretary of Defense and the Annual Reports of the Secretary of the Army, Secretary of the Navy, Secretary of the Air Force, July 1, 1958, to June 30, 1959* [Washington, D.C., 1960], pp. 118–20).

[8] On Eisenhower's advocacy of universal military service see no. 912, n. 2; see also no. 1042.

[9] Hazlett had mentioned his concern that the Russians might soon instigate a war to reunite Germany. They would probably use only East German troops, he said, and for that reason the United States should rearm the West Germans.

[10] Hazlett had expressed the hope that the Eisenhowers would stay at his home in Chapel Hill, North Carolina, during the three days of ceremonies marking the inauguration of Gordon Gray as president of the consolidated University of North Carolina in October 1950 (on Gray's resignation as Secretary of the Army the previous winter see no. 675). He was currently President Truman's Special Assistant in Charge of Foreign Economic Policy, as well as publisher of a newspaper and owner of a radio station in Winston-Salem, North Carolina. Eisenhower had informed Gray in a letter of May 27 (EM) that he had already scheduled commitments for October 1950 that would preclude his attendance at the inauguration.

[11] Hazlett's wife, Elizabeth.

982   *Eisenhower Mss.*

To George Catlett Marshall   *September 15, 1950*

I greet your appointment with a deep sense of anticipation and confidence even though I realize that it involves sacrifice for you and again interrupts the personal life you had planned for yourself and family.[1] My very best wishes and my continued admiration and loyalty are yours.[2]

[1] Congress would pass a law permitting General of the Army Marshall to become Secretary of Defense in spite of the clause in the National Security Act of 1947 prohibiting a commissioned officer from holding the position within ten years of his active military service (see U.S., *Statutes at Large*, vol. 64, pt. 1, pp. 853–54; and *New York Times*, Sept. 14 and 19, 1950). On Eisenhower's longstanding friendship with Marshall see *Eisenhower Papers*, vols. I–IX.

[2] Marshall would remark in a note of September 18 (EM), "I accept your good wishes but I think I am entitled to your sympathy too because there are going to be hard days ahead." He would add in longhand an expression of appreciation for Eisenhower's telephone call from Denver, Colorado (see no. 985). The appointment of Marshall followed closely upon Secretary Louis A. Johnson's departure from the office. President Truman had accepted Johnson's resignation on September 12, agreeing with the Secretary's observation that he had made more enemies than friends during his tenure. The resignation of Deputy Secretary of Defense Stephen T. Early was accepted by Truman on the same day (see *New York Times*, Sept. 13, 1950). For background on Johnson see no. 401; on Early see no. 551.

News of the developments affecting the Department of Defense had probably come as no surprise to Eisenhower. His friend William H. Burnham had mentioned in a letter of July 31, 1950 (EM), that Johnson and his aides were "not viewed with too much favor by the White House" (on Eisenhower's personal dissatisfaction with Johnson see no. 957). Moreover, on September 8 the national convention of the Marine Corps League had passed a resolution condemning Johnson's policies as "'short-sighted, inefficient, and dictatorial'" and demanding that Truman fire him (see *Washington Post*, Sept. 9, 1950).

In a few days President Truman would sign into law an act authorizing the promotion of General Omar N. Bradley, chairman of the JCS, to five-star rank (see *New York Times*, Sept. 19, 1950). Eisenhower would send a telegram congratulating Bradley on September 22 (EM. A longhand draft of the message is in the same file). For background on Bradley see no. 517.

983 *Eisenhower Mss., Subject File, Clubs and Associations*

TO THOMAS JAMES HANLEY, JR.   *September 15, 1950*

Dear Gang: To respond to Boye's directive, I picked up my pen in the complacent assumption that from it would immediately start tumbling a stream of memories reaching back over thirty-five years; clear and intriguing recollections of classmates and their families; of their successes and accomplishments.[1] Actually I find, with some dismay, that my memory is as treacherous and uncontrollable as it is ineffective. I easily recall both the routine and the untellable, but the dramatic and the interesting,—to both of which our class has so notably contributed—elude me so completely that I feel empty as a dried up gourd. My only comfort is that at this moment, a lot of other old codgers of 1915 are probably having the same trouble.

But, I doubt that alibis and apologies are, in themselves, going to be considered as satisfactory "Thirty-five years" letters. So here I go, starting with P.A., my oldest friend among all West Pointers and my room mate for four years. I met him in January, 1911; my most recent visit with him was in July, 1950.[2] Just to see him always reawakens memories of booming kicks, slashing thrusts and breath-taking sweeps around the end. Now, the ravages of arthritis have taken their toll, and he was forced to retire at the end of World War II. But the fire and the humor that, for four years, constantly needled my laziness but could endure my stubbornness are still there—and so it's still fun to be with him and his charming Ann.[3]

And Prich—I cannot accustom or reconcile myself to his passing! No need for his classmates to listen to any words about his charm, his debonair courage, his humor and his love of life. But here, may I pay him, once again an appreciative tribute for his great work in the campaign through Italy. He commanded an Armored Division in a region where armor was all but useless; but he never let down and when the big chance finally came he drove out into the northern Italian plains and hastened the rout of the enemy.[4] I wonder whether, on the other bank of the Styx, he and Merillat talk mostly of Jackson and Clausewitz or—with some justifiable condescension— of some of these modern forward pass combinations.[5] Whatever the answer, the two of them still stir wonderful memories, among West Pointers, of the Navy games of our day.

Kahle fought in Italy as an anti-aircraft artilleryman until he shot down all the Heinies, then turned, successfully, to ground fighting![6] Wogan took a bad wound only a few days after he'd brought his division to Europe.[7] Don Davison died while making a brilliant record, in Africa as a constructor of airfields.[8] McNarney became known as the most efficient administrator the Army ever knew and he's still working at it![9]—

Before World War II was too old, Brad became my close official associate and chief ground lieutenant. As far back as our graduation year we were both "F" company zealots and I admiringly wrote his biography for the Howitzer.[10] Early in 1942 I was given the chance to get him for service in the African Theater as a personal assistant, which I promptly, and luckily, did. In the next 3 years he advanced two grades to full general, commanding an Army Group! His stature continues to grow![11]

Maybe my old memory is starting to click a little better because now I'm beginning to remember incidents involving Beukema, Boye, Hanley, Hunt, Jody Haw, Herrick, Harmon, Swing, Warren, Bank, Fox, McNarney, Gillette, Gilkeson, and a lot of others.[12] But after all, they will be writing their own letters, I hope!

Going back behind the days of World War II there was one classmate, Jimmy Ord, whose untimely death, I shall always believe, robbed our country of one of its most brilliant minds and potential leaders. He and I served intimately together for the two or more years just preceding his fatal accident. To his final day, he was the same vivid personality, the same keen thinker, the same witty entertainer that we knew so well in cadet days. The class of '15 lost a lot when he left us, and because he went before his great talents had a chance to flower in positions of responsibility, we'll never know just how profound that loss was and is.[13]

My final paragraph is one of thanks to those who planned the 35 year reunion. If everybody there had as much fun as I did then it was, beyond doubt, the most successful reunion in the history of the U.S.M.A. Beukema, with Pendleton as an assistant seemed to be in charge of the three day jamboree, but for all who were responsible, a cheer and a vote of thanks.[14] And I doubt that even Benny Havens could have attained the perfection as a host that we found in Gene Leone.[15] His party added inches to my waist line, but more to my pleasant memories!

To everyone,

"Here's how!"

---

[1] Brigadier General Frederic William Boye (USMA 1915) would retire from the Army on September 30 to become executive vice-president of the U.S. Equestrian Team in Warrenton, Virginia. In a memorandum of August 11 (same file as this

document) he had proposed that all of the surviving members of the class of 1915 contribute essays of at least three-hundred words to a "thirty-five year book" to be published and ready for distribution by mid-December 1950. All data were to be sent to Major General Thomas J. Hanley, Jr., USAF, Chief of Military Personnel Procurement Service Division.

[2] On the visit with Colonel Paul A. Hodgson (USA, ret.) see no. 940, n. 5.

[3] Anne was Hodgson's wife.

[4] Major General Vernon E. Prichard, USA, had died in July 1949 (see no. 505). Concerning Prichard's performance as the 1st Armored Division's CG from 1944 to 1945 see Galambos, *Chief of Staff*, no. 544.

[5] Eisenhower's references were to West Point classmate Louis Alfred Merillat, Jr. (see *ibid.*, no. 2035); Thomas J. "Stonewall" Jackson, a Confederate general; and to Karl von Clausewitz (1780–1831), a Prussian general and author of *On War*.

[6] Colonel John Frederick Kahle had commanded the 107th Antiaircraft Group in the Mediterranean theater from 1943 to 1945. He was currently a senior instructor for the National Guard of the District of Columbia.

[7] Major General John Beugnot Wogan (USA, ret.) had been the 13th Armored Division's CG until he received a serious wound on April 15, 1945 (see Chandler and Galambos, *Occupation, 1945*, no. 370). He was currently manager of the VA hospital in Oteen, North Carolina.

[8] Major General Donald Angus Davison had died in Bangalore, India, on May 6, 1944, while serving as an observer for headquarters of the Twelfth Air Force.

[9] General Joseph T. McNarney, USAF, had been Chief of the Management Committee of the Department of Defense since August 10, 1949 (see *New York Times*, Aug. 11, 1949; and Joseph T. McNarney, "Economy Makes Sense," *Army Information Digest* 5, no. 5 [1950], 3–6). On McNarney's earlier work as Chief of the Air Force Materiel Command see no. 183.

[10] The *Howitzer* was the class yearbook.

[11] General Omar N. Bradley was chairman of the JCS. He would be promoted to General of the Army on September 20, 1950 (for background see no. 517).

[12] On Colonel Herman Beukema, USA, see no. 773; on Boye and Hanley see n. 1 above. Colonel Jesse Beeson Hunt, USA, had retired in 1946. For background on Colonel Joseph Cumming Haw see Chandler and Galambos, *Occupation, 1945*, no. 29. Haw was currently assigned to the Office of TAG, Department of the Army. On Colonel Charles Curtis Herrick, AUS, see Galambos, *Chief of Staff*, no. 1544. On Lieutenant General Hubert R. Harmon, USAF, see no. 418. Lieutenant General Joseph May Swing was commandant of the Army War College at Fort Leavenworth, Kansas. Colonel Albert Henry Warren, USA, and Brigadier General Carl Conrad Bank, USA, had retired in 1947. Major Tom Fox, USA, had retired due to a disability in 1933 but had returned to active duty from 1940 to 1942. On McNarney see n. 9 above. Colonel Douglas Hamilton Gillette, USA, had been assistant executive director for the renovation of the White House in 1949. Brigadier General Adlai Howard Gilkeson had served in the Office of the Inspector General, Department of the Air Force, from 1948 to 1949.

[13] Lieutenant Colonel James Basevi Ord, USA, had been Assistant Military Adviser to the Philippine Commonwealth from 1935 until his death in 1938 after an airplane crash. On the circumstances surrounding the accident see Eisenhower, *At Ease*, pp. 227–28.

[14] On Beukema's work in organizing the reunion see no. 773. Colonel Henry McElderry Pendleton, USA, had been a senior instructor for the Texas National Guard in Austin since 1948.

[15] Benny Havens was a tavern keeper who had sold liquor and food to cadets during the middle years of the nineteenth century (see Stephen E. Ambrose, *Duty, Honor, Country: A History of West Point* [Baltimore, 1966], pp. 163–64). Eugene Leone,

a famous restaurateur in New York City, had been the host of a barbeque on the second day of the reunion. On June 13, 1950, Eisenhower had signed a staff-drafted letter to Leone (EM) thanking him for his hospitality.

984   *Eisenhower Mss.*

To Harold Edward Stassen   *September 15, 1950*

Dear Governor:[1] After considerable reflection over the recent changes effected in the Defense Department, I have come to the conclusion that the meeting of prominent citizens that you and I discussed, should be deferred—or rather, that I could not at this moment appear before such a body to discuss our security problems of the moment.[2] In view of the close relationships that have existed between General Marshall and me for some years and of my great admiration of him as a military leader, organizer and thinker, I deem it my duty to confer with him in detail before appearing anywhere either publicly or semi-publicly to discuss these matters.[3]

I have pondered deeply this question and I am convinced that even if I should, by chance, make a presentation to which General Marshall should agree in every detail, there would still be created the impression of lack of complete confidence and trust. If you feel that you should like, in any case, to go ahead with this program, then I most earnestly suggest that you invite General Marshall to appear with you for this discussion. In this event, I would be glad to come just as another guest but I repeat that I now believe it would work against the best interest of our country for me to appear as a speaker or discussion leader on this subject, when we have just placed at the head of our official security organization a man of the stature and experience of George Marshall. In these circumstances, it is, of course, best that you do not mention my name at all in conjunction with the proposed study.[4]

[1] Stassen was president of the University of Pennsylvania and a former Governor of Minnesota. A note at the top of the copy of this letter in EM indicates that on this day it was read over the telephone to Edward Larsen, Stassen's administrative assistant. A slightly different version of the letter is in the same file.

[2] The names of six university presidents had appeared at the end of a telegram (Sept. 14) inviting Eisenhower to attend a closed-session conference of "citizens with leadership responsibilities" at the Waldorf-Astoria Hotel, New York City, on September 28. Eisenhower had previously agreed to participate in this discussion on the future of U.S. foreign policy (for background on plans for the meeting see no. 967).

Among the recent changes in the Defense Department to which Eisenhower referred was the appointment of his longtime friend George Marshall as Secretary of Defense. Eisenhower's congratulatory letter to him is no. 982; see it for additional changes in leadership of the defense establishment.

³ Stassen would reply (Sept. 17, EM) that at certain points in the discussion, Eisenhower might want to tell the group to "await General Marshall's analysis and back his recommendations." A note appended to an "Advance Staff Memorandum" would explain that the planning of the conference had not taken into account Marshall's appointment as Secretary of Defense. The conference would nevertheless be "helpful in establishing an understanding public background for solid support for the essential defense steps for the nation. . . ." The memorandum, a proposed agenda, and a "Summary Staff Memorandum as Aid to Discussion," as well as drafts of each are in EM, Subject File, Conferences, Round Table.

⁴ Eisenhower would inform Stassen in a staff-drafted letter of September 21 (EM) that he had decided to attend the meeting. Concerning Eisenhower's consultation with Marshall, who suggested that the program proceed as planned, see the next document. Although Marshall would not be present at the conference, Eisenhower would recount the highlights in a letter to him printed as no. 1042.

985   *Eisenhower Mss.*

TO BERNARD MANNES BARUCH   *September 16, 1950*
Telegram

Have just explained to our mutual friend in Washington the circumstances under which you and I agreed to meet with a group of distinguished men in a closed session for a discussion of security and mobilization problems.¹ I stated that the only purpose was to intensify interest in these matters based upon better understanding of the facts. I did not mention my talk with you but our friend sees no possible embarrassment to him or to me and suggested going ahead with program.² Am grateful that you brought this to my attention. Warm regard.

¹ Baruch was a financier, philanthropist, and an adviser to several presidents. The mutual friend to whom Eisenhower refers was probably General of the Army George C. Marshall, soon to become Secretary of Defense (on Marshall and the changes at the Department of Defense see no. 982). On Eisenhower's concern that he not violate Marshall's confidence and trust by speaking on the subject of national security at a conference at the Waldorf-Astoria Hotel on September 28 see the preceding document.

² On the program see nos. 1016 and 1042.

986   *Eisenhower Mss.*

TO ALFRED MAXIMILIAN GRUENTHER   *September 16, 1950*

Dear Al: Thank you very much for your recent notes.¹
This must be an admission against interest, but I think that in the

bridge situation you describe, I would have done exactly as you did.[2] You had opened on a hand where your action was just barely justified; without the singleton you could easily have passed the hand, waiting to see whether there was anything to be gained by putting in a "spoil" bid. The thing that would have determined my action after partner's double was the former bid of two spades by Pace over Averell's double. This particular sequence of bidding always indicates to me a distribution in favor of the original bid, but no great strength in the hand. (I realize, of course, that a man can use this bid occasionally for a "come on," but the great danger of that kind of bidding is usually the one who is fooled is the partner). I am not going to give the several alternatives that I think Pace could have considered with his hand. But if partners are using, for the original bid, the redouble as a request for rescue, then I think his two spade bid was completely unjustified.

This morning the war news looks very good indeed, since it appears that we have made amphibious landings on both coasts. My local paper reads something as follows: "This is what we have been waiting for— the Marines have landed." Personally, I don't care who does it, I just want the thing over quickly and decisively.[3]

Last evening I had a call from a prominent Washington official who wants to talk to me in company with a Senator. I promised to see them once I have returned to New York. He brought up several points of which I am ignorant and it reminded me that our news coverage here is not very comprehensive. In any event, I am quite anxious to talk to you for a half hour or so and the only reason I don't reach for the phone this minute is that I do not like to discuss such matters over long distance.

I shall reach New York on September 19th, and if it were humanly possible, I would most certainly like for you to come up and spend an hour or so on the 20th, or an early day thereafter. I wonder if that could be done.[4] I would jump on a plane and come down to talk to you but such a visit would cause comment, whereas it is just possible that you and I might be able to get together at my home without anyone noticing. I realize that I am suggesting something that is probably completely impossible, but if you do see any hope for such a thing, please give me a ring or send me a wire.

Love to Grace.[5] *Cordially*

[1] Lieutenant General Gruenther, Deputy Chief of Staff for Plans and Combat Operations, had enclosed in his letter of September 9 (EM) part of the *Washington Post* of the same date. There is no clipping in EM, but the article to which Gruenther referred probably concerned speculation that President Truman would soon appoint either Eisenhower or General Omar N. Bradley to be Chief of Staff of the NATO forces. Gruenther had written, "My own prediction is that one of the two gentlemen will be tagged" (for background on NATO see nos. 375 and 539). Another journalist had made a similar prediction in May 1950 (see no.

816). The most recent rumors had preceded Truman's announcement on September 9 that he would send additional U.S. troops to Western Europe. The President had given no estimate of numbers but had hinted that the extent of the American increase would depend upon the degree to which the Europeans were ready to make matching contributions (see *Public Papers of the Presidents: Truman, 1950*, p. 626; and *New York Times*, Sept. 10, 1950). Truman had based his decision on the recommendations of the JCS and the secretaries of State and Defense. The latter two officials had argued in a memorandum of September 8 to the President that (1) there should be a "Supreme Commander for the European Defense Force" who could organize the separate national forces and "be prepared to exercise the full powers of the Supreme Allied Commander over that force in time of war"; (2) the supreme commander should have "an international staff drawn from the nationals of all of the participating nations"; and (3) the "national contingents" should operate "within overall NATO control and under immediate commanders of their own nationalities." The Secretaries had envisaged two stages for implementing (3): initially, the nations would contribute forces "that would pass immediately to the control of the Supreme Commander, when appointed"; and "in event of war," the nations would make "additional commitments" (see State, *Foreign Relations, 1950*, vol. III, *Western Europe* [1977], pp. 273–75, 290–91).

In a letter of September 12 (EM) Gruenther had recounted a discussion of the previous evening with W. Averell Harriman, President Truman's Special Assistant on Foreign Affairs; Secretary of the Army Frank Pace, Jr.; and someone mentioned only as "Hoffman"—probably Paul G. Hoffman, head of the Economic Cooperation Administration (for background on Harriman see no. 852; on Pace see no. 380; and on Hoffman see no. 726). All four had agreed that Eisenhower would be the best person to fill the position of supreme commander of the NATO forces.

[2] In his September 12 letter (*ibid.*) Gruenther had described the highlight of a bridge game that he, Harriman, Pace, and Hoffman had played on the same evening. See also Gruenther's note of September 13 (EM).

[3] The *Denver Post's* banner headline for this day had been "MARINES BLAST WAY INTO SEOUL SUBURBS." The South Korean capital had been under occupation by troops from the north since July. It had been one of the early objectives of the U.N. offensive that had begun two days previously (Sept. 15, Korean time), when approximately forty thousand U.S. Army and Marine Corps troops had taken part in an amphibious invasion of Inchon, Seoul's seaport (see *New York Times*, Sept. 15 and 16, 1950; and *Denver Post*, Sept. 15 and 16, 1950. See also no. 1046).

[4] Eisenhower, who was currently vacationing in Denver, would return to New York City on September 18. He would confer with Gruenther on October 13 and 20 at Columbia University and again on October 28 in Washington, D.C. On the latter meeting see no. 1045.

[5] Mrs. Gruenther.

987   *Eisenhower Mss.*

TO WILLIAM H. BURNHAM   *September 16, 1950*

Dear Bill:[0] The Columbia Conference Plan has been designed in response to the serious concern with which American Citizens contemplate the possible future of our democracy and individual freedom, based upon a competitive enterprise.[1] The average citizen senses that politicians are, in some instances—and possibly even with the best intentions— leading him down a primrose path whose end could be, in the absence of clear understanding and great vigilance, a socialized form of economy, with resultant regimentation.

Analysis of this broad, general subject indicates that it breaks down into a number of concrete problems. Among these are important ones involving taxation, old age pensions, unemployment insurance, important details of foreign relations, proper medical care for the entire population, support of schools, and so on. The citizen hears these problems discussed only by people seeking elective office, but he, himself, has no time to conduct the vast amount of research necessary to establish the value of the politicians' presentation—he is too busy making a living to devote to these problems the study and time that they deserve.

Here is where the Columbia Plan steps in. It, appreciating all of the above, plans to assign a professorial staff to the historical and intellectual fields of research that can develop a foundation for each of these important problems, and then brings this professorial staff into contact with representatives of business, labor, the professions, and government people, who have to make day by day practical decisions of these affairs. Each of these meetings will be known as a Conference.

Columbia has been fortunate in securing a site where these conferences can take place in the most pleasant surroundings. Each will last from three to six days, depending upon the complexity of the particular problem. Some questions will undoubtedly require several conferences, properly spaced.

Numbers of Corporations have already indicated a desire to sponsor specific conferences at a cost of something like 20 or 25 thousand dollars each. At present we are engaged in securing the financial and material support needed for the professorial and secretarial staffs, for underwriting the program, and for capital investment. This is the work in which you and one or two of your intimate friends have been so effective and productive.

I realize, of course, that this sketchy presentation provides no real understanding of the project to anyone who has not previously heard it discussed. So I have written a longer letter, which I attach hereto, and which you may find useful from time to time when you talk about this matter to others.[2]

With warm personal regard. *Cordially*

---

[1] Burnham had asked Lieutenant Colonel Robert L. Schulz, Eisenhower's aide (telegram, Sept. 13, EM, Burnham Corr.), to send a "conference plan letter" to Robert B. Whitney, assistant vice-president of J. P. Morgan & Co. Schulz probably

sent a document similar to no. 979. Burnham (for background see no. 826) acknowledged receipt of the letter in a telegram to Schulz of September 15 (EM, Burnham Corr.), adding that he wanted to address it to himself and Whitney and to make "suitable changes in first paragraph" (see also a memorandum of September 21 [EM, American Assembly Corr.] and a note of October 3 [*ibid.*] that says that twenty-two other persons received both letters. For developments concerning Whitney see no. 1005. On Burnham's fund-raising campaign see nos. 826 and 877. See also nos. 605 and 844).

[2] The longer letter was probably similar to no. 979. For further developments see no. 1039.

988   *Eisenhower Mss.*

TO WALTER BEDELL SMITH   *September 16, 1950*

Dear Bedell: I hear that Bernard Baruch is giving you a dinner on the night of the 28th. Needless to say, I am delighted to see that our old friend is paying you this compliment and unless the heavens fall, I shall be among those present.[1]

Two men have recently written me asking me to recommend them to you for positions with the CIA. In both instances, they are retired officers, and in answering them, I have sent only non-committal replies. I attach a little slip which you can tuck away among your memoranda and hand someday to your new personnel officer.[2]

You know how much we are going to miss you in New York. I am deeply disappointed that you are leaving but I do agree with the President that there is no one else who can handle the CIA job as effectively as you can.

I shall be seeing you within a few days.[3] *Cordially*

[1] Baruch would host a farewell dinner honoring Lieutenant General Smith in New York City on September 28 (a list of the guests is in EM, Baruch Corr.). Smith was moving to Washington, D.C., to become Director of the CIA. For background see no. 950. On Baruch see no. 753, n. 16.

[2] The enclosed paper gave the names and addresses of the two officers. Eisenhower described one as a man of "splendid character, upright and honest" and said of the other that he had "a good military record." For developments see no. 1070.

[3] In his reply (Oct. 24, EM) Smith would express the opinion that currently CIA personnel were "below the standard I would like to maintain" but that he had "some real good prospects" among the people he had recruited.

To Hugh Roy Cullen   *September 16, 1950*

Dear Mr. Cullen:[0] Thank you very much indeed for your letter of September 11th.[1] I am so convinced that through the Columbia Conferences, which we now refer to as the "American Assembly," there will result such great benefit for America that I am now determined to carry forward the project even if I have to start without the full $500,000 that we deem necessary for underwriting, preparation and capital expenditures. Consequently, I shall write you again as soon as a decision to go ahead has been irrevocably taken, which decision shall, of course, be based upon pledges made.

Mr. McCollum told me yesterday that you intended to cooperate with the head of Rice Institute in some of the details involved in my visit to Houston and Texas A. and M. on November 9th.[2] I have been attempting to arrange the exact details of my schedule and it has not been too easy. However, I hope to be back in Houston on the evening of the 9th and, assuming that your kind suggestion of sometime ago still stands, shall probably count on spending the night with you after whatever affair may be arranged for the early part of the evening.[3]

The next day I am to go out to Houston University, as I have already promised you, and have a very informal and brief visit with the students. Does this conform to your understanding? It has been suggested that on the same day I am to see the students at Rice Institute, but I have not received any formal invitation to that effect. Thereafter, I believe that Mr. McCollum wants me to meet some of the very young members of the Houston community, and right after that I shall have to leave the city.[4]

Again my sincere thanks for your heartwarming message. I have been working very hard to develop a program designed to help solve the great problems involved in perpetuating our form of govenment. I earnestly believe that through the Conference Plan we have made great strides in this direction and it is most encouraging to find that public spirited citizens, such as yourself, endorse the plan and support it in substantial fashion.

Please convey my warm greetings to Mrs. Cullen and with warm regard to yourself. *Sincerely*

[1] In his letter (CUF) Cullen had offered to send a check for twenty-five thousand dollars for the American Assembly as soon as the university had received pledges totaling five hundred thousand dollars. For background on Cullen and his philanthropic activities see no. 634.

[2] Leonard F. McCollum, president of Continental Oil Company, had taken an active part in the fund-raising campaign for the American Assembly (for background see no. 826). On Eisenhower's itinerary for November 9 see no. 895, n. 7.

[3] Cullen would reply (Sept. 19, CUF) that the invitation to stay at his home was

still open. For an account of Eisenhower and Cullen's conversations on the evening of November 9 see Kilman and Wright, *Hugh Roy Cullen*, pp. 285–87.
[4] In a letter of September 25 (CUF) Cullen would notify Lieutenant Colonel Robert L. Schulz that William V. Houston, president of the Rice Institute, planned to invite Eisenhower for a visit on November 10 (see Houston to Eisenhower, Sept. 25, 1950, EM). As it turned out, on November 10 Eisenhower visited the University of Houston in the morning and the Rice Institute in the afternoon. The presidents of the two institutions held a luncheon in Eisenhower's honor, and in the evening the General attended a buffet supper at the Texas Club in Houston (guest lists are in EM, Houston Corr. and Anderson Corr.). For a summary of Eisenhower's remarks at a press conference on the same day see *New York Times*, November 11, 1950; See also *Fort Worth Star-Telegram*, November 11, 1950.

990   *Eisenhower Mss.*

To CLARENCE M. MALONE   *September 16, 1950*

Dear Mr. Malone:[0] Thank you very much for telling me about the developments in your Texas program for conservation.[1]

I think you have taken the right step—and from the success of the Texas club, the National Association should draw a sharp and valuable lesson. If they will immediately get busy and find a dynamic leader in each State and *encourage* rather than *discourage* local development, then we will get somewhere. These things, just as most other things in a democracy, have to get the real impetus from the grass roots; central boards should be for coordination, interchange of information, and representation on a national basis. They should not be for rigid control and direction, with resulting stultification.[2]

Good luck to you and to your entire organization. I see that you have my good friend, Bob Kleberg[3] on your Board of Directors and you are certain, therefore, to have a dynamic supporter. *Sincerely*

[1] In his letter of September 6 (EM) Malone had reported on the activities of Texas Friends of Conservation, a group that had recently broken away from the National Association of Friends of the Land (for background on Malone see no. 58; on Eisenhower's interest in the Friends of the Land see no. 113). Malone believed that Texas Friends of Conservation would be better off after the separation, since the Texans had contributed to the support of the national office but had never received financial help in return.
[2] For Eisenhower's views on decentralization see no. 479.
[3] Robert J. Kleberg, Jr., was president of the King Ranch. For background see no. 623.

To Kaufman Thuma Keller   *September 16, 1950*

Dear K. T.: Yours is the very first letter I have received addressed as "Fellow Bohemian."[1] This really means something to me because I cannot possibly tell you how delighted I am that the Club conferred its honorary membership upon me. I regard it as one of the finest personal distinctions I have ever received.

The subject matter of your letter interests me intensely. While Louis Johnson left the Administration, I have no doubt that your services will still be badly needed and desired along the lines of weapons production.[2]

Within a few days, I shall be back in New York and if ever thereafter you should happen to be passing through that city on your way back and forth to Washington, I do hope that you will give me a ring to see whether we could get together for a brief chat. For me, at least, such an opportunity would be a great treat.

Again my thanks for your cordial welcome to Bohemia.[3] *Sincerely*

---

[1] Keller was president of Chrysler Corporation and a nonresident member of the Bohemian Club (on the club see no. 388). In a letter of September 7 (EM) Keller had mentioned that he had learned that Eisenhower had recently become an honorary member of the Bohemian Club. On Eisenhower's membership see Jones to Eisenhower, August 14, 1950, and Eisenhower to Jones, August 24, 1950, EM, Subject File, Clubs and Associations. On Eisenhower's visit to the annual encampment in July see no. 873.

[2] On the resignation of Secretary of Defense Louis A. Johnson see no. 982. Keller had mentioned that Johnson and President Truman had asked him to assist them in the guided-missiles program. He planned to make "constructive suggestions" on the assumption that the armed services would not listen to "some new wizard's idea which hasn't yet reached the hardware stage. . . ." Secretary of Defense George C. Marshall would appoint Keller to be Director of Guided Missiles for the Armed Forces on October 25 (see *New York Times*, Oct. 26, 1950).

[3] Eisenhower had written to Christian Otto Gerberding Miller, president and chairman of the Pacific Lighting Corporation, on August 31, 1950, describing his pleasure at election to honorary membership. In letters of the same day to Harry D. Collier, Eisenhower's host at Bohemian Grove, and to Joseph J. Geary, president of the Bohemian Club, Eisenhower had expressed similar sentiments. See also H. Rowan Gaither, Jr., to Eisenhower, September 6, 1950, and Eisenhower's September 13 reply; Ford to Eisenhower, September 11, 1950, and Eisenhower to Ford, September 21, 1950. All correspondence is in EM.

To DANIEL I. J. THORNTON   *September 16, 1950*

Dear Dan:[1] Thank you very much for your cordial note of the 13th.[2] While I by no means share your apprehension concerning the need for you and Fred to go to a golf pro, yet I do admit that you possibly should take some lessons in debate and elocution to use on the first tee.

I certainly regret that Fred and I can't run up to your ranch to get some of that good fishing. Time is closing in on me too rapidly and today I am desperately trying to clear up some final items of business in preparation for going back to New York on the week end. How I hate it![3]

I shall look forward to seeing you next summer and possibly then you will renew the invitation to come up to your fishing paradise.

With warm regard, *Cordially*

[1] Thornton, owner of a ranch in Gunnison, Colorado, and a Republican member of the state's senate, would soon replace the GOP's candidate for governor of Colorado and would win the election in November.

[2] Thornton had mentioned in his letter (EM) that he and Fred M. Manning, Sr., owner of an oil-drilling company, planned to hire a golf professional in order to "brush up on our game and protect our financial interests." For background on Manning see no. 545.

[3] Thornton had invited Eisenhower to join him and Manning at the ranch in Gunnison; the Eisenhowers would, however, return to New York City on September 18.

To WILLIAM THOMAS GRANT   *September 16, 1950*

Dear Mr. Grant:[0] Thank you very much for your nice letter of the 11th. I have already sent word to my brother that I cannot come to Kansas City for the Community Chest meeting.[1] I have had to decline several similar invitations from other cities.

Only yesterday I had a little party of my very good friends at the Club and the bar being closed, we polished off the remainder of the "Grant's 12 Year Old." I assure you that all present found it just as delicious as I consider it. I reminded my guests that the donor of the bottle was of the same name as the maker—so we all sent cheers to you.

When I was first planning my trip back to New York, I thought I might possibly be able to stop in Kansas City for a few hours; now it appears that I am to pass through there very early in the morning and so I shall not try to see my brother.[2] However, I am due to have a visit on about the 4th of October when we both attend our baby brother's inauguration as President of Pennsylvania State.[3]

With warm regard. *Cordially*

[1] Grant, of Kansas City, Missouri, was chairman of the board of the Business Men's Assurance Company of America and a friend of the General's brother Arthur (on Arthur see no. 37). In his letter (EM) Grant had repeated Arthur's invitation for the General to launch the Kansas City Community Chest fund-raising drive. Arthur had telephoned on September 8, and Lieutenant Colonel Robert L. Schulz had explained that the General would be in Pittsburgh, Pennsylvania, on the day on which the Community Chest drive was to begin (see Schulz to Eisenhower, Sept. 8, 1950, EM, Family File; on the trip to Pittsburgh see no. 757, n. 3).

[2] The General, currently vacationing, would return to New York City on September 18.

[3] On Milton S. Eisenhower's inauguration see no. 997.

994   *Eisenhower Mss.*

TO HARRY AMOS BULLIS[0]   *September* [*17?*] *1950*[1]

Dear Harry: Thank you for your enthusiastic note about my radio talk and telling me of the schedule that Lucius Clay carried out in Minneapolis. He is a very fine American and I can well imagine that all of you thoroughly enjoyed the day with him.[2]

Frankly, I am delighted that you could find time to participate in the Crusade for Freedom.[3] Entirely aside from the obvious reasons for my support of that movement, I am keen about it because of the opportunity that it offers to every American to do *something* about our country. So often the individual citizen feels helpless and lost in the overwhelming mass of 150 million people. In this instance, he can feel that his signature and his dollar really do something to help our country's cause.

So far as my own limited observations provide any guide, I have concluded that the Crusade is going very well indeed. All of the local officials here in Denver seem to agree with this conclusion.[4]

You will be interested also to know that we have recruited a lot of additional support for the Columbia Conference Plan, which we refer to these days as the "American Assembly." I really believe that very quickly we shall be able to tackle the thing head on, thanks to such fine friends and supporters as yourself,[5] *Cordially*

[1] This document was dated September 5, but the date at the bottom of the carbon indicates that Eisenhower signed it on September 17, and the note from Bullis to which Eisenhower refers was dated September 7.

(telegrams, Sept. 4 and 5, EM) on the success of his nationwide radio speech
opening the Crusade for Freedom on September 4 (for background see no. 962).
Bullis had recounted in his note of the seventh the itinerary of General Lucius
D. Clay, national chairman of the crusade, who had visited Minneapolis, Minnesota, on September 6. On Eisenhower's association with Clay in the planning
for the crusade see nos. 739 and 899.
³ Bullis was chairman for the north central region of the country.
⁴ On local reaction to Eisenhower's speech see *Denver Post*, September 5 and 9,
1950. A list of friends who sent messages of congratulations is in EM, Subject
File, Clubs and Associations. See also Gould to Eisenhower, September 5, 1950,
and Simon to Eisenhower, same date, both in EM.
⁵ Concerning the American Assembly see no. 979.

995   *Eisenhower Mss.*

To FORREST PERCIVAL SHERMAN   *September 21, 1950*

Dear Forrest: Thank you very much for your letter with the memorandum prepared by Admiral Briscoe. I am delighted to have it.¹

I am highly pleased to have you say that you should like to see me
soon. For some weeks now, I have hoped for a chance to talk briefly
to some of my former colleagues and, if it is possible for me to get to
Washington within the next month, I shall certainly call your office
to see whether you are free for a chat.²

Likewise, I was highly delighted with an expression of your conviction that we are making steady progress in unification. That has been
my feeling and impression gathered from contacts with individuals in
the field and it is gratifying to know that the same confidence exists at
headquarters.³ *Sincerely*

¹ Admiral Sherman, CNO, had enclosed in his letter (Sept. 19, EM) a secret
memorandum of the previous day describing three Columbia projects sponsored
by the U.S. Navy. Sherman recalled that Eisenhower had asked for this information
when they had met at the football game between Navy and Columbia in 1949
(for background on Sherman see nos. 345 and 598). The work under way at the
university had "little direct military application at this time," Sherman wrote, but
the research was "important." Rear Admiral Robert Pearce Briscoe (USNA 1918),
Assistant Chief of Naval Operations (Readiness), explained in the memorandum
that the three projects came within the purview of the Navy's intelligence operations, its basic research, and its anti-submarine warfare. Twenty-four other projects at Columbia were in fields of basic research, but Briscoe provided no information about them. For background on Eisenhower's interest in anti-submarine
defenses see nos. 754 and 782.
² Eisenhower would meet with many government officials during his trip to Washington, D.C., October 28−30, 1950, but his appointment calendars do not list
a conference with Sherman.
³ Sherman had expressed "confidence in the future as the result of General Mar-

shall's appointment. . . ." For background on Marshall's new job as Secretary of Defense see no. 982.

996   *Eisenhower Mss.*

To WINSTON SPENCER CHURCHILL   *September 21, 1950*

Dear Winston: I shall leave word for Lord Camrose at appropriate places to the effect that I shall be delighted to see him. I like him for himself but, beyond this, I am eager to hear from a friend of yours an intimate discussion of your current views.[1]

Just recently the New York Times asked me whether I had any objection to your use, in your new book, of my 1942[2] views as expressed in the recorded minutes of a meeting at Algiers. I replied that I had no objection whatsoever to your using the minutes because—while I do not recall the exact details of the presentation I made at those meetings—the minutes certainly expressed what everybody else understood that I meant. Consequently, they were part of history.[3]

I have had a lot of fun since I took up, in my somewhat miserable way, your hobby of painting.[4] I have had no instruction, have no talent and certainly no justification for covering nice white canvas with the kind of daubs that seem constantly to spring from my brushes. Nevertheless, I like it tremendously and, in fact, have produced two or three little things that I like well enough to keep.

This last paragraph was inspired by the fact that, only recently, I saw in one of our magazines some prints of certain of your pictures and I liked them very much indeed, particularly one of a mill by a small lake.[5] *Cordially*

[1] On September 14 Churchill had written Eisenhower to suggest that he meet with Lord Camrose, who would soon be visiting in the United States (EM). First Viscount Camrose, formerly William Ewert Berry, was editor in chief of the *Daily Telegraph* (London) and was Churchill's close friend. On October 12 at 9:00 A.M. Eisenhower and Camrose would meet at Columbia University.

[2] This should read 1943.

[3] Volume IV of Churchill's memoir *The Second World War* was titled *The Hinge of Fate* (Boston, 1950). The *New York Times* would begin publication of excerpts on October 10, 1950, and would continue daily installments (except on Sundays) until November 13. The meetings to which Eisenhower refers were held from May 29 until June 3, 1943, at his headquarters in Algiers. Churchill had called the conference in hopes of persuading American and British military leaders to agree to an invasion of the Italian mainland immediatedly following a successful campaign in Sicily (operation HUSKY, July 1943). While Eisenhower was not opposed to Churchill's wish to invade Italy, he thought it best to evaluate the success of HUSKY before making further commitments in the Mediterranean (*Hinge of Fate*, pp. 812–31). For Eisenhower's views on these matters as expressed at

the Algiers conference see *ibid.*, pp. 816–20, 825, 828; and *New York Times*, November 13, 1950. Eisenhower's own account of the meeting appears in *Crusade in Europe*, pp. 166–69. See also Chandler, *War Years*, nos. 1027 and 1038; and Garland and Smyth, *Sicily*, pp. 12–25.

[4] For background on Eisenhower's painting hobby see no. 51.

[5] Eisenhower had seen an article titled "Greetings by Churchill" (*Collier's*, Sept. 23, 1950, 32–33), in which several of Churchill's paintings were reproduced; an American greeting card company would make them available as Christmas cards. According to *Collier's*, *Mill Pond and Cottage* was painted just before Churchill toured America in the early 1930s. The same painting appears in *Churchill: His Paintings*, comp. David Coombs (Cleveland and New York, 1967), p. 39, where its title is listed as *Le Moulin, St-Georges-Motel* and its date is given as c. 1923.

997   *Eisenhower Mss., Family File*

To Milton Stover Eisenhower   *September 21, 1950*

Dear Milton: As I remember, I am planning on reaching your home on the evening of the third.[1]

Again trusting to memory, I told the Association of American Colleges that I would not officially represent them at the ceremonies because of the personal connections involved.[2] Actually, I would do anything you might prefer, but I rather think that, for the actual ceremony, I should represent this University. I have this impression because I believe that not to do so would create some questions that would need answering. (You may have seen the completely baseless report that I have taken an indefinite leave of absence from Columbia.)

In view of your letter, I shall check up with my officials here and if there is no additional burden involved in acting also as the representative of the Association of American Colleges, I shall probably allow them to designate me in this fashion.[3]

We are certainly looking forward to seeing you. Love to the family. *Cordially*

[1] On October 3 Eisenhower would travel to Pennsylvania to attend his brother Milton's inauguration as president of Pennsylvania State College. On Thursday, October 5, the General joined an audience of fifteen thousand people for the inaugural exercises at Beaver Field. Following the ceremonies, he attended an informal luncheon for delegates and guests at the Nittany Lion Inn (see *New York Times*, Oct. 6, 1950; see also no. 790).

[2] In his handwritten letter of September 14 Milton had said that he had been informed that the General would represent the Association of American Colleges at the inauguration. He would not mind, however, if Eisenhower preferred to be with the family: "Just let me know your wishes" (EM, Family File. See also no. 790).

[3] Eisenhower would represent the Association of American Colleges at the inau-

guration (see letter, Elspeth A. Nunn, Association of American Colleges, Washington, D.C., Aug. 12, 1980; and *Association of American Colleges Bulletin, Report of the Executive Director, 1951*, p. 114, both in EP).

998   *Eisenhower Mss.*

TO AKSEL NIELSEN   *September 21, 1950*

Dear Aksel:[1] Upon arriving home I find that a long-time project of mine for purchase of a farm-home in the Blue Ridge Mountains has suddenly blossomed into a definite possibility. Because my resources are not unlimited, this—if it comes about—will tend to place a ceiling on what I could conveniently invest in Denver.[2] Consequently, for the moment at least, I hope that, in working out a program for you and me to go into things together, you will place an approximate limit of about[3] forty to forty-five thousand in lieu of the figure I originally gave you as the top. If this whole eastern proposition should fall through completely, I will inform you.

We got away from Denver in fine style and all three railroads that we use went to great lengths to make certain of our convenience and comfort.[4]

There was something else that I intended to write to you about this morning—and at the time I thought of it I considered it important—but right now my memory lets me down completely. Possibly I shall think of it later.

In any event, the whole Eisenhower family is deeply obligated to you again for the innumerable courtesies that you extended to us this summer. I have the uneasy feeling that possibly I still owe you some money; if I do, I hope that you will not let any false sense of embarrassment keep you from sending me a bill at once.

Give my love to Helen[5] and to the children and, as always, warmest regards for yourself. *Cordially*

[1] For background on Nielsen see no. 77.
[2] For Eisenhower's comments on his investment in a farm see also *At Ease*, pp. 358–60. Nielsen would report from Denver in a letter of October 13 (EM) that investments in real estate in his area would require patience. "So far as the various local propositions are concerned," he would write, "there is nothing definite up to now." For developments see no. 1003.
[3] On the carbon copy of the document, there is the following longhand note after this word: "as my cash share. If you deem wise I could go to 50–55."
[4] The Eisenhowers had returned to New York City on September 18. On their summer vacation see no. 805.
[5] Mrs. Nielsen.

To HAROLDSON LAFAYETTE HUNT *September 22, 1950*

Dear Mr. Hunt: I deeply appreciate the trouble you took to write me your long letter of the 14th. I am sure that I thoroughly understand your position and I must say that, after the study I have given to this subject since you first mentioned it to me, I have come to accept, for future observance, the principle laid down in your fourth paragraph.[1] I am glad, of course, that you wrote your second paragraph, because the single protest I made was inspired by a conviction that methods were being brought into play which completely abrogated the basic purposes of the Bill of Rights.[2] It is clear that you agree that we should never come to the point where we are ready to tolerate baseless, unsupported and vicious charges made against any individual by someone who enjoys complete immunity for his action. On the other hand I agree that there are instances where only Congressional action can initiate the investigations which will determine and point out the guilty. In such instances I merely would say that there must be some kind of supporting evidence to the charge — otherwise, I think we will be headed on a most dangerous road.[3]

With respect to the Crusade for Freedom in support of which I recently spoke, I do not intend to devote my own efforts to the business of raising money.[4] I am merely anxious to show American citizens that they have different ways in which they can actively participate in the struggle against Communism — in the job of preserving for America the great liberties, rights and blessings that she has given to us all. In this, as indeed I do in all Columbia affairs, I pursue my usual practice of trying to explain and point out principles and opportunities under these principles. I do not personally solicit funds from anyone, even in the Columbia project which I support so warmly.[5] Such individuals as Mr. McCollum, Mr. Burnham, Mr. Manning and Dean Philip Young take over the actual business of securing the necessary financial support.[6] If anyone has given you the idea that I am personally campaigning or seeking donations from anyone for any purpose, they have misinterpreted some word of mine or of my friends'.

Again, my thanks for your letter. *Cordially*

[1] In the fourth paragraph of his letter (EM) Texas oilman H. L. Hunt had criticized Eisenhower for publicly defending Philip C. Jessup from the charge of "unusual affinity" for Communist causes. Jessup was Ambassador at Large of the United States and Hamilton Fish Professor of International Law and Diplomacy at Columbia University (for Eisenhower's opinion of him see no. 733; on Hunt's interest in Jessup see nos. 925 and 961). Hunt had argued that praise from a man of Eisenhower's stature could prejudice a prospective juror in favor of the innocence of a person who might be brought to trial for treason.

[2] In his second paragraph Hunt had noted that Eisenhower had misconstrued Hunt's

attitude as a willingness "to abandon the presumption of innocence in order that convictions be secured." He asserted that he had not advocated depriving people of their rights to due process of law.

³ The latter statement might have been a response to Hunt's remark that one should doubt the loyalty of General Marshall "because of the results of his one year in China, his teamwork with Acheson et al, and the vast amount of liberty which was lost throughout the world during the time General Marshall was Secretary of State" (on Eisenhower's longstanding friendship with Marshall see *Eisenhower Papers*, vols. I–IX. On Marshall's mission to China from 1945 to 1946 see Chandler and Galambos, *Occupation, 1945*, no. 487. On his tenure as Secretary of State from 1947 to 1949 see Alexander DeConde, "George Catlett Marshall [1947–1949]," in *An Uncertain Tradition: American Secretaries of State in the Twentieth Century*, ed. Norman A. Graebner [New York, 1961], pp. 245–66; and Robert H. Ferrell, *George C. Marshall*, The American Secretaries of State and Their Diplomacy, vol. XV, ed. Robert H. Ferrell [New York, 1966], pp. 35–258).

President Truman had announced on September 12, 1950, that he wanted to appoint Marshall to be Secretary of Defense (see no. 982), but certain legislators in both houses of Congress had reacted by questioning Marshall's competence and loyalty (see U.S., Congress, House, *Congressional Record*, 81st Cong., 2d sess., 1950, 96, pt. 11:14750–51, 14835–36, 14950–73, *passim*; and U.S., Congress, Senate, *Congressional Record*, 81st Cong., 2d sess., 1950, 96, pt. 11:14913–31, *passim*. See also *New York Times*, Sept. 13 and 14, 1950).

⁴ Hunt had warned Eisenhower not to dissipate his "wonderful prestige" by asking people for money. Hunt had probably been referring to Eisenhower's nationwide radio address (Sept. 4) launching the Crusade for Freedom (see no. 962). Sponsored by the National Committee for a Free Europe, the crusade was a campaign to publicize the plight of the peoples of Eastern Europe whose governments were subject to Soviet domination.

⁵ This was a reference to a conference plan that had received a significant amount of personal attention from Eisenhower. For background see nos. 605 and 844.

⁶ Leonard F. McCollum was president of the Continental Oil Company, and William H. Burnham was an investment banker in New York City (for background on their fund-raising activities on behalf of Columbia see no. 826). Fred M. Manning, Sr., was a Texan who had made a fortune in the oil business (see no. 545). Philip Young, dean of the Graduate School of Business at Columbia University, was Acting Coordinator of the university's development activities (see no. 789). For further developments see no. 1039.

1000   *Eisenhower Mss.*

To Jesse Holman Jones   *September 22, 1950*

*Dear Jesse:*¹ My Texas schedule is already backbreaking and I had to tell President Harrington that I could not go to the football game. After my appearance at A & M, I come back to Houston for a dinner given jointly by the Presidents of Rice and Houston Universities and the following day—after spending the night with Mr. Cullen—I visit both Rice and Houston. Then I have a luncheon with some young men to whom I will explain the purpose of Columbia's Conference program.[2] That evening I depart for Dallas where I again have luncheon and evening engagements, before leaving for Oklahoma City, the same evening.[3] There, I will repeat!

Of course, if something unforeseen should occur, this formidable schedule might become somewhat less burdensome, but—as it now is—you can see how hopeless it is to plan to be at the football game. Sorry.[4]

With personal regard, *Cordially*

[1] Jones was a prominent financier, builder, and newspaper publisher in Houston, Texas (for background see no. 113). In a letter of July 18, 1950, he had asked Eisenhower to attend the Cotton Bowl game in Dallas, Texas, between Texas A & M and Southern Methodist University on November 11. Marion T. Harrington, president of Texas A & M, had also invited Eisenhower (Aug. 9, EM), but the General had declined the invitation in a note to Harrington of September 5 (EM).

[2] On the visit to Texas A & M on November 9 see no. 895. The presidents of the Rice Institute and the University of Houston would honor Eisenhower at a luncheon on November 10 rather than at a dinner on the ninth. On this and the arrangements with Hugh Roy Cullen see no. 989.

[3] In regard to the trip to Dallas on November 11 see no. 1025; on the stay in Oklahoma City, Oklahoma, on the twelfth see no. 1022.

[4] Jones would hear Eisenhower describe his plans for the American Assembly in Houston on November 10. "It had been explained to me in a way that I had not thought so much of it," Jones would write, "but the approach and reasons you gave today made it clear and practical" (see Jones to Eisenhower, Nov. 10, 1950, EM).

1001   *Eisenhower Mss.*

To WILLIAM MARTIN JEFFERS   *September 25, 1950*

Dear Mr. Jeffers: Thank you very much for your letter of the 15th.[1] I share your reluctance to become associated with any group, until after examination of its record has determined that its aims are in complete conformity with its charter—which is always couched in the most lofty terms.

In the case of "Crusade for Freedom" I felt an unusual confidence. Of course, I cannot vouch for the 100 per cent judgment, loyalty and good sense of every individual who may be supporting it, but I can give you a very short history of my connection with it.

Some eighteen months or more ago, I was approached in Washington to accept membership on the "Committee for Free Europe." The purposes of this Committee of private citizens was to assist the Government in spreading information, particularly in Europe, about the United States, including its purposes, its form of government and related matters. During World War II, I was continually so amazed and sometimes dismayed by the lack of this kind of information in Europe that, when invited to do something definite about it, I suppressed my natural inclination to decline the invitation, and went into its purposes and proposed practices with some care. Finally I agreed that, if Mr. Grew would accept the Chairmanship of the Committee, I would be glad to serve as a member, even though my participation would have to be passive because of the pressure of other business.[2]

The "Crusade for Freedom" is an outgrowth of the activities of the "Committee for Free Europe." When the Crusade was proposed, there was only one man really considered for its head, namely General Lucius Clay. I rate him as one of the most outstandingly brilliant Americans of my acquaintance. His loyalty, courage and his keen intellect are impressive and I think it is sufficient defense of the "Crusade for Freedom" to say that, after full examination, General Clay took over this job in spite of the fact that he had just accepted the position of Chairman of the Board and Chief Executive Officer of a very large corporation and had also accepted the post of Chief of Civil Defense of New York State.[3]

It is my belief that if Communistic propaganda goes unchallenged in the world we are certain to lose, by default, the ideological struggle that is global in scope. If this happens, we have no escape from dictatorship. I am determined to do what I can to help prevent this.

I hope that from this letter you will find some answer to the questions that properly bother you—in fact, I hope that you may even be able to reconsider your answer to Mr. Giannini, for whom I share your admiration.[4]

With personal regard, *Cordially*

P.S. Only a few days ago I was again on the good old Union Pacific, this time on the "Kansas City branch"—it was like going back home.[5]

---

[1] Jeffers, vice-chairman of the board of directors of the Union Pacific Railroad, had listed in his letter (EM) his reasons for refusing to serve on the Pacific Coast Advisory Council of the Crusade for Freedom (on Eisenhower's involvement in the crusade see nos. 739, 899, and 948). Jeffers had argued that the attempt to publicize the dangers that communism posed to traditional freedoms was another instance of "messing around with these communists." He also suspected that the crusade was the work of the "high-pressure publicists," who were less concerned with the menace of communism than with the profits to be earned from the advertising.

[2] For background see no. 428.

[3] On Clay see nos. 739 and 783.

[4] Lawrence Mario Giannini (LL.B. University of California 1920), president and chairman of the executive committee of Bank of America National Trust & Savings Association and West Coast regional chairman of the Crusade for Freedom, had asked Jeffers to join the crusade. The latter had declined, however, in spite of his high opinion of Giannini. Jeffers would admit in a letter of September 28 (EM) that he had probably been "overcautious" in his reaction to the crusade; he was,

he said, glad to read Eisenhower's views, since he hoped that the General would be the Republican candidate for President in 1952.
⁵ The Eisenhowers had left Denver on September 17 and had arrived in New York City on the following day.

1002   *Eisenhower Mss.*

To Clarence Dillon   *September 25, 1950*

Dear Mr. Dillon: Last Thursday evening I read the document you sent me and which I return today.¹ My feeling is that you will want real cooperation in handling this material so that Jim's estate and the public interest will both be served.²

Without going into detail in this letter, I merely repeat what I told you on the phone; namely, that in dealing with Mr. Robinson of the Herald Tribune and Mr. Black of Doubleday, you will be supported loyally and intelligently in seeing that your purposes, objectives and conditions are observed. This was my satisfying experience with them.³

At any later date I shall always be ready, when time is available, to consult with you or others in furtherance of the purposes you expressed to me. *Sincerely*

¹ Dillon, head of Dillon, Read & Company, had sent a copy of the diaries of the late James V. Forrestal with a letter of September 21 (EM) (on Forrestal see no. 425). An earlier draft of the covering letter and a note indicating that the letter was delivered to Dillon's office on September 26 are in the same file.
² Eisenhower's longhand notes with page references to the manuscript of the diaries are in EM, Forrestal Corr. The first of the General's comments contradicts Forrestal's recollection of a disagreement between Eisenhower and Truman over the necessity of bringing the Russians into the war with Japan in 1945 (see Forrestal, *Diaries*, pp. 78–79). "I didn't disagree with *anyone* because I did not know what anyone else had advised," Eisenhower wrote. "I told Pres. T. I felt he didn't need Russians & therefore, by all means, not to *ask* them in."

We have been unable to locate in the published version of the diaries the passages that match the second and third comments. "J.C.S. were *not* under Forrestal in 1946" was Eisenhower's objection to "page 4." "Page 5" evoked the following cryptic observation: " 'Send Nimitz'—at this time Forrestal was Sec. Navy—how could he direct Nimitz to work out unified command."

Eisenhower's fourth comment concerned his negotiations with the JCS regarding the budget requests of the three services for FY50. "Forrestal, when he called me down," Eisenhower recalled, "said the budget he *thought*—ought to be *between* 15 and *16.9*. He felt solvency and economic health demanded that we stick as close as possible to 15. Pointed out that unless prepared to spend 30 or more, could not gain security through arms anyway" (see *ibid.*, pp. 500, 509. For background see nos. 183 and 223). Eisenhower was dismayed that the diaries did not clarify another issue: "The big question that bothered F. so much & is not mentioned here was 'luxury' in the services. One reason he wanted to hold down appropriations was to induce economy in administration, overhead, etc."

Under a general observation on "how poorly an individual may understand the position of individuals," Eisenhower listed four specific objections. The first concerned interpretations of Eisenhower's attitude toward the Marine Corps. The editor of the diaries had used as sources of Eisenhower's views a May 1946 press statement and two JCS papers which appear as nos. 780 and 816 in Galambos, *Chief of Staff* (cf. Forrestal, *Diaries*, pp. 161, 224–25). Eisenhower protested in his notes, "I never opposed Marines except in *large*, ground formations, duplicating Army missions."

The second objection referred to Forrestal's summary of the views expressed by Secretary of War Robert P. Patterson at meetings on May 13 and 14, 1946 (on Patterson see no. 11). Forrestal had recounted that Patterson had not envisaged clear boundaries for the powers of the secretary of a unified department of national defense (see Forrestal, *Diaries*, pp. 161–63). As Eisenhower recalled the situation, "Patterson was positive & definite in his stand for *authority* in hands of Sec. N. D."

The third objection also concerned the status and responsibilities of the secretary of national defense. "I personally told Forrestal, in presence of President & many others," Eisenhower wrote, "that *he*, Forrestal was my idea of a good Sec. Def." The occasion had probably been a meeting at the White House on September 10, 1946, at which, according to Forrestal, Eisenhower had endorsed only the broad concept of a secretary of national defense (see *ibid.*, p. 205).

The fourth objection might also have concerned the unification of the Armed Forces. Referring again to the Secretary of War, Eisenhower contended, "Patterson did not restrain radicals—I handled Army Staff."

Eisenhower's next comment betrayed surprise: "He [Forrestal] told *me* he never demanded resignation of S." This probably referred to then Secretary of the Air Force W. Stuart Symington, who in July 1948 had made a speech to which Forrestal had objected. Forrestal had approached the President about asking Symington to resign but had withdrawn the request when he had learned about "extenuating circumstances" (see *ibid.*, p. 465).

Regarding presidential politics, Eisenhower objected to the manner in which Forrestal had related a conversation alleged to have taken place between Eisenhower and Truman. It concerned Eisenhower's supposed warning that General of the Army Douglas MacArthur would try to run for President in 1948 (see *ibid.*, p. 325). "The only time I ever talked to T. about MacA. was upon his direct question," Eisenhower asserted (on MacArthur's announcement of his availability for the Republican presidential nomination in the spring of 1948 see no. 33). The story about MacArthur had appeared in the same diary entry as the summary of Truman and Forrestal's discussion of the appointment of General Omar N. Bradley to replace Eisenhower as Chief of Staff. The exchange carried the implication of dissatisfaction with Eisenhower's performance. The General said: "I did not want to be C of S and agreed to take task only at urgent request of Pres. Several times I urged release of Brad. from V.A. so I could get out" (on Bradley see no. 1). After publication of the diaries in October 1951, reporters would question Truman about this aspect of Forrestal's diary, and the President would defend Eisenhower as "an excellent Chief of Staff" who had himself recommended Bradley as his successor (see *Public Papers of the Presidents of the United States: Harry S. Truman, January 1 to December 31, 1951* [Washington, D.C., 1965], p. 569; and *New York Times*, Oct. 12, 1951).

[3] The *New York Herald Tribune* had syndicated *Crusade in Europe*, Eisenhower's war memoir; Doubleday & Company had published the manuscript in book form (for background see nos. 71 and 237). On Robinson and Black see no. 28. The *Herald Tribune* would serialize the Forrestal diaries, but the Viking Press would obtain the rights to the book.

To Aksel Nielsen   *September 25, 1950*

Dear Aksel: I spent the week end in Pennsylvania looking for a farm.[1] There was one we made up our minds to buy (189 acres of good farming land) but at the last minute the owner decided to withdraw his offer on the ground that his children didn't want him to sell. There is another layout in the same region that I would personally like to buy, but the houses on it are so hopelessly inadequate that Mamie—who sees in the whole thing a chance to become a lady rebuilder of old houses— was very much against the proposition. So, for the moment at least, I am exactly where I was when I left Denver, although my friend George Allen is continuing to look for some kind of a buy in this area.[2]

The fact is—most confidentially and for your information only— that Mamie simply did not feel too well in the Denver area. She believes it is the altitude and is keen, therefore, on finding a place that we can begin developing in another region. She prefers the Blue Ridge Mountain chain[3] or its eastern slope. Another reason for centering her attention on this particular area is that she feels during the next several years, during which we will presumably be at Columbia, we could go down frequently on week ends to supervise repairs, development and so on.

Nevertheless, I still want to go ahead on the general plan you and I talked about the morning we rode around the outskirts of Denver. This is subject, of course, to a bit of limitation on the amount of obligation—as I suggested to you in the letter the other day.[4] This does not mean that I cannot stretch a point, particularly where there is involved the purchase of land.[5] I feel that it is about as good a hedge against threatening inflation as is available to us.

In any event, I shall be looking forward to the receipt of your plans and suggestions. I am certain we are on the right track.[6] *Cordially*

---

[1] On the weekend in Pennsylvania see Eisenhower, *At Ease*, pp. 358–61; and Lyon, *Portrait of the Hero*, pp. 512–13. For Mrs. Eisenhower's impressions of what would become her long-awaited first home see Dorothy Brandon, *Mamie Doud Eisenhower: A Portrait of a First Lady* (New York, 1954), pp. 262–66.

[2] For background on Allen see *Eisenhower Papers*, vols. I–IX.

[3] After this word on the carbon copy of the document there is the following longhand note: "of course, we shall be coming to Denver every summer as long as any Doud is there—even if we do have to give it up as our future home region."

[4] No. 998.

[5] The last three words of this sentence are underlined on the carbon copy of the document. Regarding investments, Nielsen had written in a letter of September 21 (EM): "As soon as I have something specific to propose to you on the things that we are considering jointly, you will of course hear from me."

[6] For developments see no. 1100.

To Thomas John Watson, Sr.   *September 25, 1950*

Dear Tom: Thank you very much for your nice letter from London.[1] I shall be looking forward to seeing you which will be, as I understand your plans, within a few days.

I saw a good deal of Al Jacobs while in Denver—he is making a very fine name for himself in that region. He works hard and is forming many contacts that will be valuable to Denver University.

I am looking forward to an opportunity to talk to you. Many things have happened since I last saw you, a lot of them of the most extraordinary significance, and it will be interesting to get your views.[2]

Our affectionate regard to you both. *Cordially*

[1] Watson, chairman of the board of International Business Machines and a trustee of Columbia University, had included in his letter of September 15 (EM) congratulations on Eisenhower's honorary degree from the University of Denver. Chancellor Albert C. Jacobs, formerly provost of Columbia University, had conferred the degree upon Eisenhower (for background see no. 951). Watson had also mentioned that he and his wife would sail for the United States on September 22.
[2] Eisenhower would attend a Columbia University alumni luncheon with the Watsons on October 21 (see *New York Times*, Oct. 22, 1950). The General would also meet with Watson on November 1.

To Robert Bacon Whitney   *September 25, 1950*

Dear Bob:[1] So much progress has been made in the past few weeks in the discussion of a Conference Center here at Columbia and the plans for it, we are now far beyond the talking stage and are at the point where material support is immediately necessary to put into effect the decisions we have reached. Within the Columbia family, we call all those friends who assist us in winning financial help, Ambassadors. Consequently, I am taking the liberty of designating you an Ambassador and I hope that you will accept without hesitation.

In this capacity you are in a position, should anyone whom you meet offer financial assistance, to accept instantly. Merely suggest that the check be made out to Columbia University.[2] *Sincerely*

[1] Whitney, assistant vice-president of J. P. Morgan & Company, Inc., had made a contribution during the previous summer to the Columbia conference program, soon to become the American Assembly (see Whitney to Eisenhower, July 21, 1950, EM). At the same time Whitney had confirmed the arrangements for a dinner at the Links Golf Club on Long Island on September 29, 1950 (a list of

the guests and of their contributions to the American Assembly is in the same file as this document).

² For background on the Columbia Ambassadors see no. 124, n. 7; see also no. 945, n. 6. Eisenhower would thank M. Hartley Dodge, chairman of the board of the Remington Arms Company and clerk of the trustees of Columbia University, for a contribution to the program in a note of September 26 (EM).

1006   *Eisenhower Mss.*

To James Bryant Conant   September 26, 1950
Personal

Dear Jim: First, my commiserations upon your illness and assurances of disappointment that you cannot be at the meeting on Thursday, next.[1]

Your memorandum rings the bell with me! Each sentence you have written would, in itself, make a logical subject for a two-hour discussion, but the crux of your memorandum, found near the top of page 4, is your advocacy of universal military *service*.[2] I argued earnestly for this plan before I relinquished command of the American forces in Europe; in fact, before the shooting had stopped in that Theater of War. Later, on the advice and instructions of my official superiors, I supported the plan for universal military *training*, but I did so with the distinct feeling that only optimistic assumptions and estimates could justify a plan that was so obviously a compromise.[3] But, it should be said, if U.M.T. had then been promptly enacted and earnestly executed, there may have been no Korean War.

Incidentally, in my advocacy of a system of universal service, I stressed that young men should perform this service as an obligation to the state; that to pay for it on the basis of competitive wages with industry was unwise.[4]

It is possible that your observation is correct when you say, a little farther down on page 4, "At this point I am sure . . ." While I, personally, agree with every word you say, it is of course true that I cannot be classed as one of your *"academic"* friends.[5]

The particular satisfaction I get out of your memorandum is the fact that someone of your standing in the academic world should have written. It reveals a lot of soul searching.[6]

I do hope that you are soon well. I shall be looking forward to seeing you when you get out and about.[7] *Cordially*

---

¹ Conant, president of Harvard University, had informed Eisenhower in a note of September 22 (EM) that his doctor had advised him that he was not well enough to attend a conference of prominent citizens to be held at the Waldorf-Astoria

Hotel in New York City on September 28. For background on Conant see no. 285; on the conference see no. 1016.

[2] Conant had enclosed in his letter of the twenty-second a memorandum that he hoped the conferees would discuss on the twenty-eighth. He had estimated that to defend Western Europe from Communist aggression would require that the United States keep from three and one-half million to five million men in uniform. Neither the draft nor a program of universal military training (UMT) would be adequate, according to Conant, to meet such a quota. Near the top of page four he had proposed "a universal military *service* of two years for all able-bodied youth *before* they take their place in the industrial life of the country." The physically infirm would serve in other capacities at the same rate of pay, but no one was to receive a deferment. These views were significant departures from his previous statements (cf. Conant, *My Several Lives*, pp. 353–60).

[3] See no. 912, n. 2.

[4] In his memorandum Conant had not mentioned the level of compensation to be paid.

[5] Conant had assumed that his emphasis on every young man's participation would alienate his colleagues. He had written, "At this point I am sure a number of my academic friends in the conference will part company with me. For I should certainly not have college students exempt from this universal conscription of young men."

[6] Universal military service would receive unanimous support from the university presidents at the conference on the twenty-eighth (see no. 1042).

[7] Conant would thank Eisenhower for his positive comments (Oct. 3, EM) and would say that he had heard that the General's remarks at the conference had been "enthusiastically received."

1007   *Eisenhower Mss.*

TO HENRY FORD II   *September 26, 1950*

Dear Mr. Ford: Thank you for sending to me an Advance Copy of the Ford Foundation Report. Its reading gave me a fine feeling! It is good to know that the Foundation's resources are to be used so intelligently and so broadly to assist in solving the vital problems of our time.[1]

I heartily congratulate the author or authors of the document. Excellent as is the whole, I cannot abstain from particular mention of certain passages. For example: The two paragraphs on page 12 beginning "Inevitably linked with the search for peace . . ."[2] The discussion concerning education on page 14 seems equally wise and pertinent; also the final two paragraphs on page 15.[3] Finally, the report would be more than worth while even if it contained only page 17.[4]

The morning paper brings the news that my good friend Paul Hoffman has accepted the Presidency of the Foundation.[5] In my humble opinion you could not have selected a better man. I wish him and you and all those connected with the Foundation a brilliant success in achieving its announced objectives. *Sincerely*

[1] Ford, president of Ford Motor Company, had enclosed in his letter of September 22 (EM) a confidential, advance copy of "Report of the Trustees of the Ford Foundation" (on Eisenhower's interest in the preparation of the report see no. 419). Ford planned to release the paper to the news media on September 26 (see *New York Times*, Sept. 27, 1950).

[2] The passage continued ". . . is the need to strengthen democracy and our own domestic economy." This paragraph and the one that followed concluded that reducing apathy among America's citizens would be the surest path to greater participation in government.

[3] This section and the preceding page dealt with the role of the school system in developing the creative potentialities of the nation's citizens. Education should consist of more than the dissemination of information, the report had continued; it should include an emphasis on the development of character and values. Society required, moreover, that knowledge be linked with its "constructive interests" and that each specialist gather an appreciation of the importance of other fields of study. Emotional maladjustment was often an obstacle to individual development, the authors of the report had maintained, and social tensions were in large measure attributable to the lack of cooperation resulting from inadequate adjustment.

[4] In these general conclusions the authors said that the vitality of democracy required that governments be more efficient and provide greater economic stability and more opportunities for personal initiative and for the development of leadership skills.

[5] Hoffman, Administrator of the ECA, had tried to telephone Eisenhower on the previous day (see Schulz to Eisenhower, Sept. 25, 1950, EM, Hoffman Corr.). Appended to the message regarding the call was the following postscript: "You may have read that Mr. Hoffman had accepted the post as Director of the Ford Foundation." Actually, Hoffman had told reporters on September 25 that he had made no agreement to head the foundation (see *New York Times*, Sept. 26, 1950). He would, nevertheless, be confirmed as president and director of the organization on November 6 (see *New York Times*, Dec. 18, 1949, and Nov. 7, 1950; and no. 726).

1008   *Eisenhower Mss.*

To Horace C. Flanigan   *September 26, 1950*

Dear Hap:[1] As I recall, Howard's place is not too far from Clove Valley. So why not tell him to invite us all to his place for the night, get an early start the next morning, and the three of us have a good shoot.

One reason I suggest his house is that it has been a long time since I've seen him and by you and Mrs. Hap going with Mamie and me to his home we could all have a big visit.[2] Moreover, I want to see whether or not his bass are biting!

It was wonderful of you to think of me. I'll try to suggest a definite date very soon, but so far as I can now foresee, I *think* we could go on Monday evening, October 16, to shoot on October 17.[3] *Cordially*

[1] Flanigan had recently become chairman of the board of the Manufacturers Trust Company (Eisenhower would send a congratulatory telegram on October 2 [EM]).

In his letter of September 20 (EM) Flanigan had invited the Eisenhowers to visit him and his wife, Aimee Magnus Flanigan, at their house in Clove Valley. He had also advised the General that Howard Young, owner of an estate in nearby Ridgefield, Connecticut, might join them for a day of duck and pheasant shooting. For background on Young see Galambos, *Chief of Staff*, no. 1536; on Eisenhower's visit to Young's estate the previous autumn see no. 558.

[2] In the margin of Flanigan's letter of the twentieth Eisenhower wrote "one of these??"; this was followed by his wife's initials. Mrs. Eisenhower replied that she favored Young's house but would leave the decision up to the General (see Schulz to Eisenhower, Sept. 26, 1950, same file as document).

[3] Eisenhower's appointment calendar indicates that he would leave for Ridgefield at 11:30 A.M. on October 16 and would return to New York City the following day.

1009   *Eisenhower Mss.*

To John Orr Young   *September 26, 1950*
Personal

Dear Mr. Young:[1] It is true that I concur in the basic aims and aspirations of organizations seeking to assure world peace through better organization among the free peoples of the world. This I understand to be the purpose of the Atlantic Union. On the other hand, I have never yet fully satisfied myself as to the exact sequence of steps that are best calculated to achieve those ends, but, from the meager study I have been able to give to the arguments advanced in support of various propositions, I think I am in closer agreement with the "Committee for United Europe," than I am with any other group.[2] This does not mean that I may not arrive at a different conclusion; it merely signifies that, up to now, the step-by-step approach appeals to me strongly.

These days there are numerous movements, activities and organized efforts that compel the respect and sympathetic concern of any person who is genuinely interested in the future of freedom, our country, and the peace of the world. But inescapable demands on the time of the individual require—at least in my case—a process of selection in determining those to which he can give active support. For the moment at least, I can do or say nothing further in support of any of the movements looking toward the organizational improvement of the United Nations concept than is indicated in the first sentence of this letter. To attempt more would compel neglect of other duty.

Until I have had the time and opportunity to convince myself of the superiority of some specific proposal over others, I cannot—in good conscience—say more than this.[3] *Sincerely*

[1] Young, a founder of the Young & Rubicam advertising agency and a director of the Atlantic Union Committee, had asked Eisenhower (letter, Sept. 25, EM) to

become an honorary member of the committee, with the title of "Chairman of the Council." The Atlantic Union Committee had invited the nations belonging to NATO to send delegates to a convention to discuss the possibility of a transatlantic federation (for background on NATO see no. 539). The Canadian senate had passed a resolution supporting the idea, and a similar measure was under consideration by the British House of Commons. Young wanted Eisenhower to make a speech supporting the Atlantic Union at a dinner or a mass meeting. He was also conducting a "Draft Eisenhower" for President campaign with advertisements in various newspapers and magazines in preparation for the 1952 election (see Young to Eisenhower, Sept. 12, 1950, EM). There are no indications in EM that Eisenhower had acknowledged Young's efforts in regard to the presidency.

[2] Eisenhower was probably referring to the "United Europe Movement." The group's chairman, Winston S. Churchill, had recently supported the Schuman Plan for the European Coal and Steel Community (see *New York Times*, May 17, 1950). The leaders of the movement favored the reintegration of Western Germany into the economic life of Europe and, to a lesser degree, into Western European defense planning. Churchill and other prominent individuals had spoken on these subjects in London recently (see *Times* [London], July 22, 1950).

[3] On this same day Eisenhower would open the academic year at Columbia with a speech on the subject of democratic concepts. He urged his listeners to "live by the truth" and "to lead America in search of its mission to make all who come under its banner happy, prosperous and free" (see *New York Times*, Sept. 27, 1950).

1010   *Eisenhower Mss.*

TO MIRDZA SILIS-OZOLINS   *September 27, 1950*[1]

Dear Mrs. Silis-Ozolins:[2] While I have never had the privilege of visiting your native country, I have met many Latvians, particularly numbers who were German captives during World War II. I assure you that my affection for them was equaled only by my admiration for the way in which they had withstood the rigors and hardships of captivity and had maintained their pride and morale in spite of the life they led. Consequently, the receipt of a letter such as yours greatly saddens me. I earnestly believe that, like every other people, you have the right to freedom and, when I attempt to put myself in the place of a citizen of your country, I can readily understand the depths of bitterness you feel in the absence of such freedom.

While I no longer occupy any official position in our Government and am not on active military service, I assure you that whenever I hear these matters discussed in this country, the sentiments expressed are similar to those I have put down in this letter. This, however, is a long way from solving the problem. To my mind, another global conflict would, in spite of a possible favorable military outcome, leave the world so prostrated that the liberty we love and the free institutions under which we would hope to live, could possibly not exist.

I am taking the liberty of showing your letter to one or two of my friends in Washington, so as to give them this additional evidence of exactly how a Latvian feels.[3] *Sincerely*

[1] The carbon copy of this letter indicates that the typist had erased *June* and substituted *September*.

[2] Mrs. Silis-Ozolins, a Latvian living in the Federal Republic of Germany, had written Eisenhower on the occasion of the tenth anniversary of the occupation of Latvia by Russian troops on June 17, 1940 (EM). She had asked for help in freeing the Baltic States from Communist control. "It must be done immediately and under your command," she had asserted, "and by the help of the USA military forces." A copy of her letter is in EM.

[3] Eisenhower had sent Mrs. Silis-Ozolins's letter to Major General Stafford L. Irwin, Assistant Chief of Staff, G–2, U.S. Army, requesting advice on how to answer it (see Eisenhower to Irwin, June 27, 1950, EM). On Eisenhower's general agreement with Irwin on matters such as these see no. 828.

On this same day Eisenhower spoke to the students and faculty of Barnard College, reminding them that free access to knowledge would permit them to form their own opinions. The situation was different, he said, in countries in which government propaganda was the only information available (see *New York Times*, Sept. 28, 1950).

1011   *Eisenhower Mss.,*
                                                      Spyros Skouras Corr.

To Willard Cole Rappleye   *September 27, 1950*

Dear Willard:[1] In extension of our telephone conversation, the name of the young Fordham graduate in whom my good friend Spyros Skouras is so deeply interested is . . .[2] I understand that this young man has applied for entry into the Columbia College of Physicians and Surgeons but has been rejected. Mr. Skouras believes that there may be one or two prospective vacancies in the new class and, because of this, urges favorable consideration for the claims of his young friend. . . . He believes that Mr. . . . is a young man of high character and very considerable ability.

I do not know Mr. . . ., but I have not only a real affection for Spyros Skouras, I have found him to be a most public-spirited citizen devoted to our country and fully as ready to work for America's welfare as any native-born citizen of my acquaintance. Consequently, I should like to see every possible consideration given to his request, but I of course realize that students wishing to enter the Medical College must be selected by the faculty and that our standards must be carefully preserved. Because I understand that in your files will be found the

complete scholastic record of Mr. . . ., together with the recommendations of the Fordham faculty, I am not sending forward to you the
transcript that has been furnished me by Mr. Skouras. But should it
develop that you need more information, I assure you that I will be
glad to make further contact with him or, if you so desire, he would
be pleased to furnish, through direct contact, anything you may need.[3]
Cordially

[1] Rappleye was vice-president in charge of medical affairs at Columbia University.
For background see no. 107.
[2] Spyros P. Skouras, president of National Theatres Amusement Company and of
Twentieth Century-Fox Film Corporation, wrote to Eisenhower on this same day
(EM) enclosing this young man's scholastic record.
[3] For further developments see no. 1028.

1012   *Eisenhower Mss.,*
Combined Chiefs of Staff Corr.

TO CEDRIC RHYS PRICE   *September 27, 1950*

Dear Mr. Price:[1] I have had the historians, who are writing of this
period of World War II under the Office of the Chief of Military
History, Special Staff, United States Army, go over your proposed
changes in my Report to the Combined Chiefs of Staff.[2]

They have informed me that you are entirely correct in your proposed
changes in the wording. The changes do make the report more accurately
reflect the events which occurred.

I wish to thank you for the careful scrutiny you have given the page
proof and for your very appropriate changes.[3] *Sincerely*

[1] Price was secretary of the Chiefs of Staff Committee of the Ministry of Defense
in London. This letter was drafted by Lieutenant General Alfred M. Gruenther,
Deputy Chief of Staff for Plans and Combat Operations, and sent to the General
on September 16.
[2] The changes are not in EM. On Eisenhower's report on operations in Europe
from June 6, 1944, to May 8, 1945, see Galambos, *Chief of Staff*, nos. 673 and
900.
[3] Eisenhower had requested in May 1949 that British comments on his final reports
on operations in Europe be referred to the Army. The Historical Division not
only had approved the British changes but had suggested additional amendment
(see Ward to Wedemeyer, July 5, 1949, enclosed in Wedemeyer to Eisenhower,
July 6, 1949, EM, Subject File, Reports).

Eisenhower Mss.

TO ALLAN NEVINS   *September 28, 1950*

Dear Professor Nevins:[1] I am delighted to hear that you are prosecuting vigorously the preparatory work on the new magazine.[2] I have no objection to your quoting me to the effect that "The critical character of these times makes the project of a sound popular magazine of history more important than ever!"[3]

May all success be yours, *Cordially*

[1] Nevins, DeWitt Clinton Professor of American History at Columbia, had asked in a letter of September 21 (EM) for a quotation from Eisenhower to be used to counter objections to a plan to publish "a good popular magazine of history." For background on Nevins see Galambos, *Chief of Staff*, no. 1934. Kevin C. McCann, Eisenhower's assistant, helped prepare this reply.

[2] Nevins had not named the magazine, but he probably meant *American Heritage*. The American Association for State and Local History had founded *American Heritage* in 1947, and Nevins, as president of the Society of American Historians, was currently raising funds to give the magazine a new format. Nevins had been a member of the editorial board of *American Heritage* since September 1949. Eisenhower was listed as one of the subscribers as of June 30, 1950 (see enclosure in Nevins to Eisenhower, July 6, 1950, EM. See also John Higham, with Leonard Krieger and Felix Gilbert, *History* [Englewood Cliffs, N.J., 1965], pp. 83–84; Ray Allen Billington, comp., *Allan Nevins on History* [New York, 1975], pp. 209–11; and William T. Alderson, Jr., "The American Association for State and Local History," *Western Historical Quarterly* 1, no. 2 [1970], 177).

[3] Nevins had suggested this sentence in his letter of the twenty-first.

Eisenhower Mss.

TO ANNA ELEANOR ROOSEVELT   *September 29, 1950*

Dear Mrs. Roosevelt:[1] Of course, immediately on reading through your letter, I found myself in complete agreement with you; confusion or conflict on the community level between the Crusade for Freedom and United Nations Day Committee would be intolerable.[2] While I have no administrative or executive responsibility with the National Committee for Free Europe, I immediately called to suggest that steps be taken to correct any deficiencies in the Committee's presentation of its purpose. To my great relief, I learned that such steps have already been taken and that United Nations Week will be observed jointly by both organizations.[3]

I should add that I am grateful to you for the heart-warming compliment paid the Committee and myself for the work done so far. *Sincerely*

[1] Mrs. Roosevelt, widow of Franklin D. Roosevelt, was chairman of the National Citizens' Committee for United Nations Day (for background see no. 658). Kevin C. McCann drafted this letter for the General.

[2] Mrs. Roosevelt had mentioned (Sept. 22, EM) that the Crusade for Freedom would terminate with the ringing of a bell in Berlin, Germany, on October 24—which would also be United Nations Day. Publicity regarding the ceremony had not indicated that the National Committee for a Free Europe, sponsor of the crusade, shared the U.N. goal of "peace with freedom and justice for all." Confusion had arisen, according to Mrs. Roosevelt, because some citizens wanted to celebrate both United Nations Day and the freedom bell dedication but assumed that they had to choose one or the other. Eisenhower wrote on her letter, "McCann—see me on this—." On the General's work in connection with the crusade see no. 962.

[3] Abbott M. Washburn would send McCann a copy of a letter (same file as this document) that General Lucius D. Clay, national chairman of the crusade, had written Mrs. Roosevelt on September 27. Clay explained that the coordination of the two programs was "in process of being worked out." Washburn, who was a member of Clay's staff (see no. 948), noted at the top of the letter, "Kevin, This should take care of the letter she wrote General Ike, too."

1015

Eisenhower Mss.

To ERNEST O. HAUSER

September 30, 1950

Dear Mr. Hauser:[1] My memory of the detailed happenings in 1945, in which you are so interested, is not sufficiently accurate to provide you with information that could possibly be classed as "history." In general, I had no interest in the Belgian King one way or the other. I had no reason to fear the results of his possible return to Brussels.[2]

Long before we reached the area in which the King was residing in exile, there had been a Belgian government re-established in the country's capitol. I had been in close touch with it and the one clear memory I have of that period is that I was ready at all times to cooperate with this government, which was of course recognized by both the United States and Great Britain.

I realize that this is not the kind of information you are looking for as you prepare an article upon the incidents of those particular days. But, such as they are, the statements made above are reasonably accurate.[3] I have checked them with my friend, who was then my Chief of Staff, General Walter B. Smith. I repeat that none of us had any particular prejudice, feeling or opinion concerning the King of the Belgians as an individual or as to his official place in his own country.

While this reply to your letter is gladly made, it is obviously not of the type that is susceptible to quotes and, therefore, I cannot give you permission to use it in that way.[4] *Sincerely*

¹ Ernest O. Hauser was an associate editor for the *Saturday Evening Post*.

² Hauser, who was preparing an article on the royal crisis in Belgium, had asked Eisenhower for "a fact or two on the events immediately following the liberation of King Leopold III by United States forces in the spring of 1945." Hauser had included in his letter a description of a U.S. Army message issued by SHAEF on June 12, 1945, ordering the detainment of the Belgian King by the commanding officer of the Belgian Fusilier Battalion should Leopold be seen by his unit. Hauser purported that many Belgians believed that SHAEF issued this order to protect the supply lines connecting Antwerp to Central Europe from damage in the event that the return of the King caused disorder. For background on the Belgian royal question see no. 708.

³ Hauser's article in the December 2, 1950, issue of the *Saturday Evening Post* was entitled "How to Get Rid of a King." In it, Hauser concluded that Leopold's "hesitation, his urge to think rather than act, at this hot moment," ruined forever his chances of regaining the Belgian throne.

⁴ Hauser had asked whether he could quote Eisenhower's "informal comment"; in keeping with the General's request, the article would not mention Eisenhower.

11

North Atlantic Command

Dear Governor:[1] I know that you are delighted that your idea developed into an occasion that provoked such universal approval. Clearly, such a result did not come about by accident, and I know that you must have done a lot of very earnest and intelligent work between the time you first spoke to me on this project and its culmination last Thursday at the Waldorf.[2]

Just as I started this note to you, yours of the 30th reached my desk. My part in the whole thing was a minor one, and I was delighted to be included in such a company, discussing such subjects.[3]

Incidentally, the whole day provided new evidence to me that the Conference Program — of which I think I have spoken to you briefly — that Columbia is trying to develop, will produce worthwhile results and will be enthusiastically supported by a very great and influential proportion of our citizenry.[4]

With warm regard, *Cordially*

[1] Stassen was president of the University of Pennsylvania and a former Governor of Minnesota. For background see no. 116.

[2] On September 28 Eisenhower had attended a conference of prominent citizens at the Waldorf-Astoria Hotel in New York City to discuss the nation's foreign affairs and defense policies (lists of the hosts and the guests are in EM, Committee on The Present Danger Corr., and in EM, Subject File, Conferences, Round Table. For background see nos. 967 and 984). Henry M. Wriston, president of Brown University and of the AAU, had presided over the sessions; he would recall in a memorandum of April 22, 1968, that Eisenhower had delivered "an extraordinarily moving and effective argument for strengthening our military posture" (see Henry M. Wriston, "Eisenhower Study Group Letter to President Truman, December 12, 1950," Apr. 22, 1968, pp. 2−3, enclosed in George S. Franklin, Jr., to Eisenhower, Apr. 23, 1968, Council on Foreign Relations Mss., Eisenhower Library, Abilene). Eisenhower had also discussed the problem of universal military service; he would recount his views on that subject in no. 1042.

[3] In his letter of the thirtieth (EM) Stassen had congratulated Eisenhower on "a superb job" and "a very important contribution to the thinking of the outstanding group of citizen leaders. . . ."

[4] On Columbia's conference program see nos. 605 and 844. Eisenhower would use his encounters with those who had attended the Waldorf Conference as a means of introducing his American Assembly plan (see no. 1026. See also nos. 1032 and 1036, n. 7).

Dear Mr. Murchison:[1] Thank you very much for your nice note of the 27th.[2]

As of this morning, Mamie is not planning on coming to Texas with me in early November—I wish she were. I, however, intend to be in the State from somewhere along about the 8th to the 12th of that month and I am trying desperately to save a few hours (possibly on the eighth) on which to visit with Sid and Amon in Fort Worth.[3]

I wonder if, on that day, you might not come to Fort Worth because my whole idea will be merely to renew pleasant, personal contacts and to spend a few hours with my old and good friends. From my viewpoint, you would be far more than welcome—I would appreciate a chance to talk to you again.

Toward the end of my stay in the State, I shall be in Dallas for a part of a day. That day will certainly be very crowded indeed, and it is for this reason that I suggest you might be kind enough to run over to Fort Worth. However, even if a few minutes are afforded us at Dallas, I should certainly prize the opportunity to see you and, of course, to pay my respects to your charming wife and family. As the details of my schedule become crystallized I can figure out whether I am to have such an opportunity and, if so, I shall inform you.

It goes without saying that both Mamie and I are deeply appreciative of your kind offer of hospitality. I have no doubts that Mamie will be writing to Mrs. Murchison very soon. *Cordially*

[1] Murchison, of Dallas, Texas, was a millionaire who had amassed a fortune in oil and now owned or had invested in a variety of businesses throughout the nation.
[2] Murchison said that his wife, Virginia, had invited Mrs. Eisenhower to stay at the Murchison home during Eisenhower's forthcoming trip to Texas. He said the invitation included the General and suggested that he and Mrs. Eisenhower might enjoy seeing a football game in Dallas on October 14 (EM). Apparently, there was some misunderstanding on Murchison's part. Eisenhower's trip to Texas had been scheduled for November, not October. On November 8, 1950, Murchison would reply that he would not be in Dallas during Eisenhower's visit (EM).
[3] Eisenhower would visit Sid W. Richardson and Amon Carter in Fort Worth, Texas, on November 8 (see his letters, nos. 1098 and 1097). The General would be in Dallas on November 11 (see no. 1025). For the General's visit in Fort Worth see the *Fort Worth Star-Telegram*, November 9, 1950.

To Robert Abercrombie Lovett   *October 2, 1950*

Dear Bob:[1] Whenever I pause to take note of the repeated sacrifices you have made in order to render service to our country, I feel ashamed of myself every time I begin to experience discouragement in the feeble efforts that I devote toward support of the American way of life. Every person to whom I have spoken has expressed sentiments of the deepest satisfaction because of your willingness to enter the Defense Department—a satisfaction that I share to the full.[2]

Because I feel as I do, I doubt that you could class this note as one of "congratulations" unless it can serve as an expression of my congratulations to the Government and to our citizens, including myself.[3]

With warm regard and my very best wishes, *Cordially*

[1] Lovett had been Under Secretary of State from July 1947 until January 1949, when he had resumed his banking house partnership with Brown Brothers, Harriman and Company in New York City. For background on Lovett see no. 112.

[2] On September 29, 1949, it was announced that President Truman had appointed Lovett Deputy Secretary of Defense. Lovett would succeed Stephen T. Early and would work directly under his old friend and colleague General George C. Marshall, newly appointed Secretary of Defense (see *New York Times*, Sept. 29, 1949). The appointment would be confirmed by the Senate in November 1949.

[3] In his reply of October 5, Lovett told Eisenhower that he was touched by the kind letter and that because of Eisenhower's heartwarming comments, he would begin his task with greater confidence (EM). For developments see no. 1042.

1019   *Eisenhower Mss.*

To Harry Amos Bullis   *October 2, 1950*

Dear Harry:[1] Thank you very much for your nice note about the conference at the Waldorf[2] and for your personal compliment on my part in it.[3]

I have carefully read every word of the letter you sent out to your Board of Directors. It is a very splendid paper. I am going to save it carefully for my own use in public appearances that I seem to be making all the time.[4] *Cordially*

[1] Bullis was chairman of the board of General Mills in Minneapolis, Minnesota. For background see no. 893.

[2] In a letter of September 29 Bullis had congratulated Eisenhower on his "exceedingly constructive remarks" made the day before (Sept. 28) at a college presidents' conference in New York City (EM). The conference, called by seven university presidents, had been attended by some fifty leaders in business, industry,

and education, who discussed the nation's foreign affairs and defense policies (see nos. 967, 984, and 1016).

[3] Bullis had written and enclosed a six-page typewritten summary of the meeting titled "Confidential Report on Citizens' Conference," which he said he planned to present when the General Mills board of directors met on October 2. Board members would be delighted, he thought, to know that Eisenhower believed that "we do not have to have World War III at this time." According to Bullis's summary of Eisenhower's statement, the General had made the following points: demobilization immediately following World War II had been a mistake; Korea was but one incident in a long campaign by the Communists; a free election in Korea should not be encouraged at this time because the Communists would probably win; the U.S. struggle was not only military but economic, moral, and spiritual as well; Russia did not want global war now—she was not prepared and would not risk it; Russia did not, however, fear an attack from the United States. Eisenhower had also stressed that the United States must maintain a healthy economy; that it was not possible for the United States to defend every danger spot in the world but that mobile, balanced forces should be developed. The United States, Eisenhower had said, might need to spend annually in the twenty billions to build such forces, and the nation had to have universal military service to survive. For Eisenhower's report to General Marshall concerning his statement at the conference see no. 1042.

[4] In a handwritten postscript, Bullis had suggested that Eisenhower might be interested in an attached copy of a letter he had sent to the board of directors of General Mills. For that letter and for Eisenhower's reaction to it see the following document.

1020   *Eisenhower Mss.*

TO WILLIAM AVERELL HARRIMAN   *October 2, 1950*

Dear Averell:[1] I have just seen a letter written by a man in which he includes a summary of the statements you made in an informal discussion or conference around September 14 or 15. The burden of your talk was Russian intentions and capabilities and the policies that the United States must adopt to these.[2]

This note is just to say that if my friend reported you even halfway accurately, you really did a bang-up job—I congratulate you.[3] *Cordially*

[1] Harriman was Special Assistant to the President on Foreign Affairs.
[2] For background on the letter summarizing Harriman's statements see the preceding document, n. 3. Harry A. Bullis had apparently attended the informal discussions on national and international problems in Washington, D.C., in mid-September. Bullis's two-part letter to his board of directors included a section titled "Summary of Remarks of W. Averell Harriman, Assistant to the President" and one titled "Economic State of the Nation: Remarks by Economists." A copy of Bullis's letter is in EM, Bullis Corr.
[3] In a thank-you note of October 5, 1950, Harriman would ask Eisenhower for a copy of Bullis's summary, and on October 13 the General would send the

document to Harriman, remarking "And, again, I say 'Well Done!' " (both letters are in EM).

1021   *Eisenhower Mss.*

To Kenneth Stanley Adams   *October 2, 1950*

Dear "Boots":[1] Thank you very much for your nice letter of the 29th. My friend Bill Robinson had already told me of meeting you and of the enjoyable time he had talking to you. One of two things is certain: either he is easily impressed or you turned on the charm, because he gave me glowing reports about the head of the Phillips Petroleum Company. Since I know him to be a sophisticated, hardheaded Irishman, I am forced to conclude that you were at your scintillating best.[2]

It is possible that I shall pick up your offer of the DC−3. It would be a tremendous help to me if my program can be properly worked out. I doubt that I would want it to come any farther East than St. Louis, even if the weather would permit its use at all. I can leave here late in the evening and make an overnight trip to Chicago, where I have one or two engagements, and an overnight trip to St. Louis. From there on it might be very advantageous indeed to save the time that would be represented in the difference between a train and an airplane trip. However, all this I shall take up with you later, in the event that there is any possibility of using the plane.[3]

It appears for the moment that I shall be able to make only one stop in Oklahoma, which is promised for Oklahoma City. However, I have already told my host there that I should like for him to ask you to any function that he might stage so I imagine you will be getting an invitation from him.[4] While I originally intended to make a stop at Bartlesville, I got tangled up in a Chicago engagement on the return trip that will not permit me to use an extra day in Oklahoma.[5] If I should, then I would get home too late for my wife's anniversary— and that I cannot do.[6] However, I do want to have a talk with you and I am sure that we can get together at Oklahoma City on the day I am there, possibly November 12th.[7] *Cordially*

[1] Adams was chairman of the board of the Phillips Petroleum Company, Bartlesville, Oklahoma.

[2] Adams had told Eisenhower that on a recent trip to New York City he had met William E. Robinson at dinner at the Links Club. For background on Robinson, whom Adams had called a "delightful individual," see no. 28.

[3] Adams had offered to send the Phillips Petroleum Company's DC−3 to New York to take Eisenhower to the West for his forthcoming trip. There is no record in EM that the General accepted this offer. He would begin his journey on November 6 by train (see appointment calendar).

[4] Eisenhower's host would be Donald S. Kennedy (for background see no. 923).
[5] See no. 1061.
[6] Mamie Eisenhower's birthday was November 14.
[7] Eisenhower and Adams would meet at a luncheon in Oklahoma City on November 12 (see the next document).

1022   *Eisenhower Mss.*

To Donald Sipe Kennedy   *October 2, 1950*

Dear Don:[1] I am grateful to you and Streeter Flynn for your readiness to help in a project that I regard as of real importance for the future of our country.[2]

I see that you have planned some golf for the morning of November 12th. I shall start praying for good Oklahoma weather on that day because, by the time I get back to Oklahoma City, I will be so worn out that a round of golf will be a godsend. I am certainly looking forward to seeing you and Streeter—again thanks a lot for your readiness to pick up Bill Burnham's suggestion.[3]

When I originally was planning to come to Oklahoma, I told "Boots" Adams of the Phillips Petroleum Company that I would try to stop at Bartlesville where he was going to have a party. It is now clear that I cannot spare the time and so I wonder whether you would not include him on your list of guests, with possibly one or two of his principal assistants or associates, in the event he would like to bring anybody. He might appreciate inclusion in the golf party on the morning of the twelfth, even if we have to have two or three foursomes.

I do not mean to put the "bee" on you in any sense. I am assuming, of course, that you and "Boots" Adams are friends or at least that you would have no possible objection to asking him to the party.[4] *Cordially*

[1] For background on Kennedy see no. 923 and the preceding document.
[2] Kennedy and Streeter Blanton Flynn, an Oklahoma City attorney, had agreed to head a fund-raising drive in Oklahoma City for the benefit of the American Assembly. Flynn (LL.B. Columbia 1917) was a member of the firm Rainey, Flynn, Green, and Anderson. For more information on the American Assembly see no. 1039.
[3] Burnham, who had helped Eisenhower plan for the initial funding of the American Assembly project, had apparently suggested to Kennedy and Flynn that they sponsor a golf game and luncheon on behalf of the conference plan (telegram, Burnham to Eisenhower, Oct. 1, 1950, EM. See also Kennedy's letter of invitation to Eisenhower, Oct. 4, 1950, and Eisenhower's reply, Oct. 11, 1950, both in EM). For background on Burnham and his role as Eisenhower's adviser see no. 826.
[4] For background on "Boots" Adams see the preceding document. Kennedy would invite Adams for golf and lunch on November 12 at the Oklahoma City Golf and Country Club. Adams would accept the luncheon invitation but would decline

the golf game. Among Kennedy's thirty guests were leading Oklahoma City oil and utilities men, as well as educators, publishers, and lawyers. The guest list is in EM, Kennedy Corr.

1023   *Eisenhower Mss.*

To Fred M. Manning, Sr.   *October 2, 1950*

Dear Fred:[1] Two days ago Indian Summer hit us here and the thermometer has rolled right on up to the mid-eighties. I am convinced that I left Colorado far too early and, this morning, I wish I were calling you up to arrange our daily golf game. In fact, I would be delighted to pay you for birdies every day if I could only have the next week at Cherry Hills.[2]

Exactly when do you expect to be in New York? Whenever you can, I wish you would send the details of whatever plans you may develop for coming East this fall so that, if humanly possible, I can arrange my own plans to be here at the time. I want to take you to two or three of our golf courses. So please keep on playing regularly. I want to see you smack some of these boys down if they are bold enough to give you about an 18 handicap. By the way—last Saturday they entered me in one of our regular days with a 20 and on one nine I turned in a 39, net 29. This would have been catastrophic for the rest of the crowd except that I shot a 47 on the other side.[3]

My plans for my Texas trip are slowly materializing and of course I am counting on seeing you down there during the course of my trip.[4]

My warm greetings to Hazel[5] and to all your nice family, and with best regards to yourself, *Cordially*

P.S. Possibly, if you should "sell" Arthur Ridgstrom on the value of the Conference Program, he might get a *real* contribution from his boss!!!!![6]

---

[1] For background on Manning, of Denver, Colorado, see no. 545.

[2] Eisenhower had recently returned from his annual summer vacation in Denver (see no. 805).

[3] In a reply of October 19, 1950, Manning would say that his plans for coming to New York were indefinite (EM).

[4] Eisenhower would be in Texas November 8–11 (for the trip see nos. 895, 989, and 1017. For developments see no. 1044).

[5] Mrs. Manning.

[6] Arthur G. *Ryd*strom was executive assistant to Claude K. Boettcher, chairman of the Boettcher Foundation, and an officer of a number of Colorado companies. Boettcher and his wife had entertained the Eisenhowers in Denver in September (for background see no. 971). The conference program to which Eisenhower refers was the American Assembly (see no. 1039).

To WILLARD R. COX   *October 2, 1950*

Dear Willard:[1] Thank you very much for your note. As of now, I am expecting to come through St. Louis, possibly as early as October 24th. However, all my plans are very tentative and I shall let you know about them as they develop.[2]

Of course, the information given to you by your two electrical engineer friends was at least partially correct and was, therefore, known to the technical advisors of the Crusade for Freedom.[3] However, what your friends did *not* tell you was that, if radio interference is made so effective in that region that no broadcasts or beamed programs can reach the interior of the country, then the Russians will also be limiting— if not practically eliminating—the use of radio by themselves in their own country.

Moreover, and most important, the Crusade for Freedom is attempting to reach many, many people who are not, at least as yet, behind the Iron Curtain. We need to tell the truth to many nations who, up to now, don't hear a great deal of it.

With warm regard, *Cordially*

[1] For background on Cox see no. 122.

[2] In his letter of September 29, 1950 (EM), Cox had said he hoped to see the General soon. As Eisenhower's plans developed, Cox would host a dinner in Eisenhower's honor on October 24 at the Log Cabin Club in St. Louis, Missouri. The occasion was Eisenhower's five-day tour (Oct. 23–27) to meet with Columbia alumni in Illinois, Missouri, Indiana, Ohio, and West Virginia (for background on the trip see no. 1044). During his visit in St. Louis, Eisenhower would also attend a luncheon given for him by David R. Calhoun at the Statler Hotel (on Calhoun see no. 581. Correspondence concerning plans for the St. Louis trip, including guest lists for both the luncheon and the dinner, is in EM, Cox Corr. and Calhoun Corr.).

[3] Eisenhower had recently helped to launch the Crusade for Freedom in a nationwide radio address which Cox and some friends had heard at a cookout at Cox's home. Among Cox's guests were two electrical engineers, who had suggested that if Russia were to build very strong radio aerials, all radio reception from outside Russia could be blocked (Cox to Eisenhower, Sept. 29, 1950, EM. For Eisenhower's address see no. 962).

To ROBERT V. NEW   *October 2, 1950*

Dear Mr. New:[1] I am more than appreciative of the very appealing suggestion contained in your letter of the 28th.[2] If time permitted, I should certainly seize upon your offer with great delight. However, the fact is that my time in Texas has already been so tightly scheduled that I look at the whole program with something akin to dismay. I shall certainly make a determined effort to see anyone in the city that I am privileged to class as friends, among whom I hope you will permit me to include you.

The basic reason for coming to Texas is because of requests from old and dear friends to be present at a ceremony at Texas A. and M. on November 9. Because I will be there, I shall also make one or two other visits in response to invitations of long standing, some of them of many months, running into years.[3] For example, my invitation to the City Club at Dallas is in this category.[4] There is no other purpose to the trip except that, of course, I always hope to interest people in the work that Columbia University is doing, particularly in the line of helping to solve immediate and vital problems of the day. As you know, it is my conviction that the universities have a great mission in promoting respect for the American way of life and in helping to solve the critical problems that our system must meet if it is to survive.[5]

Again, my thanks for your most hospital suggestion.[6] *Cordially*

[1] New, a Columbia alumnus, was an oil man, formerly in Los Angeles, California, and presently in Dallas, Texas. In 1949 he had given five thousand dollars to Columbia to be used exclusively for cancer research, a project that would be known as the Robert New Study of Cancer Virus. Correspondence regarding the gift is in EM.

[2] New had proposed that he give a cocktail party for Eisenhower on November 11 during the General's visit to Dallas (EM).

[3] For Eisenhower's invitations to Texas A & M, the University of Houston, and Rice Institute see nos. 895 and 989.

[4] In regard to the City Club see the letter to Eisenhower from Thomas E. Jackson, president of the club, September 20, 1950 (EM). Also on November 11 Eisenhower would attend a Columbia alumni breakfast at the Dallas Athletic Club at 8:30 A.M.; a mid-morning coffee-hour meeting with young Dallas businessmen; and, in the evening, a buffet dinner for more than thirty prominent Texans at Dallas's Baker Hotel. Hosts for the affair would be William L. Pickens and H. H. Coffield (see *Forth Worth Star-Telegram*, Nov. 12, 1950).

[5] Eisenhower is referring to the Columbia conference plan (see no. 1039).

[6] On October 19, 1950, New would write that he had been invited by Thomas Jackson to hear Eisenhower speak to the Dallas City Club on November 11. "I consider it an honor and a privilege to attend," he said, "and I know I shall be rewarded with one of your ringing talks on good Americanism. I always enjoy that kind of talk because it is becoming one of the most neglected subjects in our Country" (EM).

1026

To John Hay Whitney

Dear Mr. Whitney:[1] It was fine to see you at The Round Table discussion at the Waldorf, on Thursday last.[2] That conference so definitely exemplified the virtues of a plan that we at Columbia have been developing for the past two years that I am venturing to send you a copy of a memorandum which we, in the past, have used to describe it.[3]

At the end of the Waldorf Conference, the question was posed as to the value of such get-togethers. A number of those present, in later conversation with me, expressed the conviction that such meetings would be extremely valuable and could be more so if the principal topic were somewhat narrowed and concretely stated. Several also thought the sessions should last for a day or longer.

This you will see is our plan. We fortunately have a rural estate where the conferences can be held under the most favorable and pleasant surroundings.

I would be interested to learn of your reactions or suggestions.[4]

With warm regard, *Sincerely*

[1] Whitney, a financier, was senior partner in J. H. Whitney & Company in New York City and a director of various firms.

[2] On this particular conference, which had been held at the Waldorf-Astoria Hotel in New York City on September 28, 1950, see no. 1016 and 1019.

[3] The "Memorandum from Dwight D. Eisenhower on the American Assembly" is printed (with slight variations) as document no. 979. Eisenhower would send copies of his memo, along with the letter printed above, to most of the guests at the Waldorf Conference. The guest list and two drafts of the letter to Whitney are in EM, Subject File, Conferences, Round Table. For subsequent developments involving the American Assembly see no. 1039.

[4] In a reply of October 10 (EM) Whitney said that while he had found the conference at the Waldorf-Astoria "most stimulating," he thought that too much ground had been covered in too short a time, making the conclusions drawn "somewhat superficial." He agreed that a longer program might be more productive, "rather than some effervescent, even if most pleasant, exercise of the brain." He said that he thought the American Assembly plan would be an improvement, and he would be interested to learn more about it. For Eisenhower's further correspondence with Whitney concerning the American Assembly see no. 1079.

1027

To Arthur Michael Godfrey

Dear Arthur:[1] Thank you very much for your note. Of course, I am delighted that you got your promotion and your Navy Wings, but frankly

I am far more delighted to know that you soloed in those jet planes and are now back among us, safe and sound. I am an air enthusiast, but I must say I had my fingers crossed when I learned that you were determined to play around with those things all on your own. They just go too fast to be taken lightly.[2]

Possibly this coming week we can find a date when we can have lunch together, even if a quick one. I must have a few of Bob Woodruff's quail left in my deep freeze and, while mangling one or two of them, you and I could talk over a few of the things in which we are both so interested.[3]

You will be glad to know that I have fully made up my mind to take over the Harriman estate (this is confidential information until public announcement has been made) and to push right ahead with the project. I do not feel that we can afford long to dillydally around. Incidentally, some of the reasons that led me to this particular conclusion may possibly be of some interest to you.[4]

Thanks again for your note. *Cordially*

[1] Godfrey was a well-known radio and television entertainer whose morning program on the CBS network was extremely popular.
[2] In a letter of October 5 (EM) Godfrey had said that he had just returned from a tour of active duty at the Pensacola, Florida, Naval Air Station, where he had earned his Navy wings and had been promoted to full commander in the U.S. Naval Reserve.
[3] For background on hunting quail at Robert W. Woodruff's plantation in Newton, Georgia, see no. 690. Eisenhower and Godfrey would not be able to arrange a lunch date in the coming week; for their continuing efforts to meet see no. 1103.
[4] Eisenhower is referring to the plan to use the Harriman family estate, a gift to Columbia University, as a permanent home for the American Assembly conferences (for background on the Harriman gift see no. 605. For the public announcement concerning the American Assembly conference plan see no. 1039). Godfrey had pledged ten thousand dollars to the project when he and Eisenhower were luncheon guests of Aksel Nielsen at the Denver Country Club in Denver, Colorado, on August 28. In his letter of October 5 Godfrey had reaffirmed his pledge and promised to send a check at Eisenhower's request. Godfrey would soon receive that request (see nos. 1078 and 1103).

1028   *Eisenhower Mss.*

To Spyros P. Skouras   *October 9, 1950*

Dear Spyros:[1] I enclose a very disappointing letter from Dr. Rappleye, Dean of Columbia's College of Physicians and Surgeons.[2] As you know, the president of a great confederated university, such as Columbia, does not interfere in the slightest degree in the selection of students. This applies also to the dean of any particular school or college. So, in reading Dean Rappleye's letter, you should understand that while he could urge sympathetic consideration of the boy's application (as, indeed, both of us did), he could not take issue with the decision reached by his faculty committee.

You know, without my stressing the point, how deeply disappointed I am to send you such an answer. But I really don't see how I could do more for Mr. . . . than I did.[3]

With warm personal regard, *Cordially*

[1] On Skouras see no. 1011.

[2] For background on Eisenhower's efforts to gain reconsideration of the application of Skouras's young friend for admission to Columbia's College of Physicians and Surgeons see *ibid*. A copy of Willard C. Rappleye's letter to Eisenhower of October 4, 1950, is in EM, Skouras Corr. It was with "greatest regret," Rappleye had written, that the young man, a graduate of Fordham University, had been rejected again by the committee on admissions. The Medical School, Rappleye pointed out, had received an unusually large number of applications from students (including several from Fordham) who were better qualified than this candidate. Rappleye would be reluctant, he said, to admit this young man now, as it would jeopardize Columbia's good relationship with Fordham's administration and faculty.

[3] On October 10 Skouras thanked Eisenhower for his help. "It was not my purpose to ask any more than that the boy get sympathetic consideration and that, it is most obvious, you did secure for him" (EM). In a handwritten notation at the bottom of Skouras's letter, Eisenhower directed that it be forwarded to Rappleye. On October 13 Rappleye would write Eisenhower that he was happy that Skouras "understands our problems so thoroughly and that he made such a generous response to your friendly interest in young Mr. . . ." (EM).

1029   *Eisenhower Mss.*

To John Lawrence McCaffrey   *October 9, 1950*

Dear Mr. McCaffrey:[1] I am delighted to have your letter of the fourth with its account of the experience of your company meeting with a group of college professors.[2] Possibly part of my satisfaction with the results you have achieved is explained in the old saw, "His is a great mind, he agrees with me."[3]

For two years, I have been working on a program for bringing together periodically businessmen and college professors, each gathering to have a specific concrete problem to study and each of these problems to be selected on the basis of its degree of interest and concern to the public today. Because I am quite sure you will be interested, I am enclosing with this letter a memorandum that I have used for some time to explain the workings of the plan.[4]

Naturally, I am delighted that you found Professor Otte to be so cooperative and valuable in your conference. I am making sure that a record of your good opinion of him is properly filed here at the University.[5] *Sincerely*

[1] McCaffrey, of Chicago, Illinois, had been president of the International Harvester Company since 1946.

[2] In his letter of October 4, McCaffrey had told Eisenhower about a recent program sponsored by the International Harvester Company. Faculty from several American universities had joined with the company's top management people to study the management philosophy in a large business enterprise and to explore the professional objectives and techniques in higher education (EM).

[3] Eisenhower apparently liked the "old saw" (see no. 872).

[4] The memorandum to which Eisenhower refers is printed, with minor variations, as document no. 979; it is a description of the Columbia conference plan, soon to be announced as the American Assembly (see no. 1039).

[5] McCaffrey had been especially generous in his comments regarding Herman Frederick Otte, who had represented Columbia University at the three-week seminar. Otte (Ph.D. Columbia 1940) was an associate professor of economic geography at Columbia's School of Business. "We came to have a very high regard for Mr. Otte," McCaffrey had written, "and we feel that you are indeed fortunate to have him as a member of the faculty of your great institution. We want you to know how much we enjoyed having him here."

1030   *Eisenhower Mss.*

To ARTHUR HOLLY COMPTON   *October 9, 1950*

Dear Chancellor Compton:[1] I hasten to answer your letter of the 29th both because there is implied in it some misunderstanding of my meaning concerning one point that arose at the meeting at the Waldorf and because, also, I agree so wholeheartedly with what you have to say about the basic objectives of America.

With respect to the first point: all I meant to say was that the only logical reason and the only basic objective of universal military *service* or *training* is to be found in the military field; all other considerations must be secondary and therefore must not be allowed seriously to interfere with the military requirements. I, by no means, meant to disagree with your idea that through various types of activities, a broader and better understanding of America could and should be imparted to all individuals in the armed services.

With respect to your general contention that we must seek and achieve before the world a strong position as champion of the great human values—I subscribe to this thought with whatever strength I possess. I have constantly preached it because I am convinced that, necessary as military and material strength now are to our present and future, unless all people see in our system a workable method by which each may strive for the fulfillment of his own aspirations, then we are doomed as surely as if we today were completely defenseless before the Communistic and Russian purposes.[2]

Not only do I believe these things—I think I can claim that the ideas expounded in your letter also largely explain the reasons for my seeming temerity in joining, two years ago, the society of College Presidents. Since that time I have, with associates here at Columbia, been developing ways and means for improving our usefulness in promoting the understanding necessary to a realization of such objectives. While I am tempted to send, along with this letter, extracts of memoranda, talks and correspondence to amplify this point, I shall save it all until the time when I may have a chance to talk to you.[3]

I am sorry that I did not, at the Waldorf meeting, take sufficient time to explain exactly what I meant when I said it was "visionary" to attempt to attach a formal educational program to any system of military recruitment. In the effort to be concise, I was possibly only confusing.

Thank you again for your letter. *Sincerely*

[1] Compton (Ph.D. Princeton 1916), chancellor of Washington University since 1945 and chairman of the board of trustees of the College of Wooster since 1940, had enclosed in his letter (Sept. 29, EM) a copy of a letter of the same date congratulating Harold E. Stassen, president of the University of Pennsylvania and a former Governor of Minnesota, on the success of a conference held at the Waldorf-Astoria Hotel in New York City the preceding day. Compton recalled that Eisenhower had used the word *visionary* in referring to Compton's suggestions for the education of men in the armed services. In defense of his views, Compton had written, "I should consider it not only the right of each fighting man to know what he is fighting for, but also vital to the morale of the fighting units that the hearts of the men be in their cause." For background on the conference see no. 1016.

[2] Compton had noted in his letter to Stassen that the conferees had not given enough emphasis to the objectives of American foreign policy. This lack of precision in the definition of goals would give the Russians an advantage in the cold war, Compton had argued.

[3] Compton would reply (Oct. 18, EM) that he believed there was no difference in their points of view, and he asked that Eisenhower send him some of the papers he had mentioned.

1031   *Eisenhower Mss.*

TO ROY ALLISON ROBERTS   *October 9, 1950*

Dear Roy:[1] Thank you very much for your letter, and particularly for the copy of the editorial you wrote in your issue of October 1.[2]

I am sure that Mr. Wellington has already told you that the conference group at the Waldorf talked about some of the possibilities that you mention, such as diminishing public interest if our sense of crisis should disappear.³ There was discussed also, at least hastily, the effects of the current inflation, the need for leadership, the need for high taxes, for concentrating our resources on the solution of our most critical problem, and the resentment toward us in other countries of the globe, even, in some instances, where we are trying to help those countries.

Personally, I agree most emphatically with the last sentence of your note. We must be realistic and tough with *ourselves*.⁴ *Cordially*

¹ Roberts was president and general manager of the *Kansas City Star*.
² On October 4, 1950, Roberts had written to Eisenhower about the recent conference called by several university presidents in New York City on September 28 (for background see nos. 1016 and 1019). Roberts had enclosed with his letter a copy of an editorial he had written for the *Kansas City Star*. The editorial, like the conference, concerned current national and international problems. Both Roberts's letter and the editorial are in EM.
³ Roberts had found it necessary to leave the conference early, and he had asked Clarence George Wellington, since 1947 managing editor of the *Kansas City Star*, to attend the meeting in his stead.
⁴ Roberts had said that the United States must guard against complacency. "That is where the punch is needed," he had written, "and where the real danger lies, even more than in what Russia may or may not do."

1032   *Eisenhower Mss.*

To Lewis Herold Brown   *October 9, 1950*

*Dear Lewis:*¹ Thank you very much for your letter of the fifth. I assure you that I do not intend to seek any job other than the one I am now trying to perform. However, I would not go so far as to say that your reasons and mine for my negative attitude could be considered identical.²

Possibly you and I may be running into each other soon—there are some considerations even with respect to your own conclusion upon this matter that you may have overlooked. In any event, it would be fun to talk to you about them.

Everyone who has since spoken to me and who was present at the Waldorf affair of last week has spoken most enthusiastically about the discussion.³

Here at Columbia we have been working on a plan for about two years that is in concept nothing but a very great expansion of the same idea that was exemplified at that meeting. In the thought that you might be somewhat interested I am enclosing a memorandum which gives a brief description of the plan.⁴ *Cordially*

¹ Brown was chairman of the board of the Johns-Manville Corporation (see no. 331).

² Brown had written Eisenhower about the possibility that President Truman might soon name the General to head the NATO forces in Europe (EM). In Brown's opinion, Eisenhower's acceptance of such an appointment would eliminate him from any consideration for the presidency in 1952. He said that he, along with many others, had been doing all he could to make sure of Eisenhower's availability. Brown pointed out that Eisenhower had made his place in history in World War II. It would be a mistake, he thought, to return to Europe in a lesser role. For earlier speculation on Eisenhower's appointment to head the European command see no. 986; for developments see no. 1136. For more information about NATO see nos. 375 and 539.

³ On September 28 Eisenhower had participated in a conference called to consider national and international problems. Brown, who had attended the discussions, had told Eisenhower in the same letter of October 5 that it had been good to hear the General's "very able presentation." For Eisenhower's role in the meeting see nos. 1019 and 1042. See also no. 1016.

⁴ This was Eisenhower's confidential memorandum concering the American Assembly (for background see no. 1026).

1033   *Eisenhower Mss.*

To JOHN COWLES   *October 10, 1950*

*Dear John:*¹ The first two paragraphs of your letter made me both happy and proud; happy that you are so substantially committing yourself to collaborating with us in the development of Columbia's "American Assembly" and proud of the compliment you paid me concerning the off-the-cuff talk I was called upon to make at the Waldorf last week.²

The remainder of your letter leaves me sad and disappointed—every phrase of it builds up a more appealing and attractive picture of the kind of thing that I most enjoy and, therefore, makes doubly bitter the realization that I cannot possibly accept your wonderful invitation.³ On the twenty-second of October I leave here on a tour of addressing Columbia University's alumni clubs. The tour takes me into Pennsylvania, Ohio, Illinois and Missouri and extends over the period, October 22 to October 30. So the entire period of your assembly at Glendalough is blanked out for this schedule of visits.⁴

Because of my disappointment, I am bold enough to ask that you instantly repeat your invitation but with the year 1951 instead of '50 specified as to date. On that basis, I would like immediately to cross that portion of my year's calendar in order to meet with such a wonderful group and for such a delightful purpose.⁵

I have received a number of letters from individuals who attended the meeting at the Waldorf. Most of them are enthusiastic, but they are likewise unanimous in their suggestions that the general problems be broken down into specific suggestions and each be made the topic of a conference by specially selected cross sections of America. Since such suggestions dovetail exactly with our Columbia program, they are gladly received.[6]

With the hope that I shall see you soon to thank you in person for your nice invitation, *Cordially*

[1] Cowles was president of the Minneapolis Star and Tribune Company (see no. 757).

[2] In a letter of October 2 (EM) Cowles had enclosed a check for one thousand dollars as a contribution to the American Assembly, the conference plan to be sponsored by Columbia University (on this proposal see no. 1039). In the same letter Cowles had commended Eisenhower for his part in a recent conference called to discuss problems of national and international import (for background on the meeting see no. 1019).

[3] Cowles had invited Eisenhower to spend a few days in October duck shooting at Glendalough, a game farm in western Minnesota owned by the Minneapolis Star and Tribune Company.

[4] For Eisenhower's trip to meet with Columbia alumni see no. 1044, n. 7. See also the Chronology in this volume for his day-to-day itinerary.

[5] "You are hereby officially invited," Cowles would write in his reply of October 14 (EM).

[6] This, again, is Eisenhower's effort to direct the enthusiastic reactions of those who attend the conference of university presidents toward support for the proposal for Columbia's conference plan (see n. 2 above).

1034   *Eisenhower Mss.*

To L. Clifford Kenworthy   *October 10, 1950*

Dear Mr. Kenworthy:[1] Thank you sincerely for your nice letter of September 29th.[2] I hope that Paul Hoffman passed on to you the word of caution that I have found it necessary to attach to every personal plan that extends any distance into the future.[3] This caution is that I must always make such engagements with the understanding that some unforeseen circumstance could prevent my keeping the engagement. While this is, of course, true in the case of any individual, it seems that with me unexpected things have a way of turning up out of the blue, especially when something is involved that I am particularly anxious to do.

With this established, I go to that portion of your letter that suggests a program of entertainment preceding the parade and football game on January 1st.

As of this moment, I would have some hesitancy about accepting the invitation to the Queen's Coronation on December 28th. Mrs. Eisenhower and I are planning on spending Christmas Day and the

26th with her family in Denver.[4] Since she never travels by air, except in emergency, we would plan on coming to Pasadena by train. While we may arrive by Thursday evening the 28th, it is probable that she would be so tired that I should not permit her to undertake anything further that same evening. Of course, it is always possible that the most suitable train schedule would not bring us to Pasadena before Friday, the 29th. However, I should like to know whether I am right in assuming that we might leave that particular decision until the last moment since I assume that our presence or absence at the ball would not make any great difference in the arrangement for the affair. Your letter does not say whether the football luncheon and the board of directors' guest dinner are stag affairs or whether ladies will attend. In either event, assuming that our train schedule has brought us there on time, we or I—if the affairs are stag—should be able to attend.

With respect to the parade and to the attendance at the game, we would of course do whatever is customarily expected of us.

Paul Hoffman told me that, when he returned to New York somewhere around November 1st or 2nd, he would come to see me to discuss some of these details.[5] I am chiefly concerned in avoiding the kind of appearance where a speech is expected of me. But, of course, I would not like to appear so arbitrary or adamant in these matters that my desires would create an awkward situation. I think, therefore, that some of these details can be much better decided after I have had a chance to talk to Paul Hoffman. But I send you this preliminary letter so that you can get from it whatever information may be essential to you as you proceed with your planning. In any event, I am most sincerely flattered by your kind invitation and am looking forward to the unusual opportunity of visiting Pasadena during the Tournament of Roses.[6]
Sincerely

[1] Kenworthy was president of California's Pasadena Tournament of Roses Association, sponsor of the Tournament of Roses festivities preceeding the annual Rose Bowl football game.

[2] Kenworthy had said how pleased he was that Eisenhower had accepted the association's invitation to be grand marshal of the Tournament of Roses parade on New Year's Day, 1951. His letter, with its several suggestions regarding activities planned for the General and for Mrs. Eisenhower as well, is in EM.

[3] Paul G. Hoffman, who would soon become president of the Ford Foundation, had been influential in persuading Eisenhower to accept the invitation (see R. L. Schulz's memorandum to Eisenhower, Sept. 25, 1950, EM, Hoffman Corr. For background on Hoffman see no. 1007).

[4] For their Christmas visit see no. 1140.

[5] Eisenhower and Hoffman would meet for lunch on November 1 at 60 Morningside Drive.

[6] In a reply of October 17, 1950 (EM), Kenworthy would assure Eisenhower that he fully understood the possibility that unforeseen circumstances might force the

General to change his plans; and indeed, unforeseen circumstances were rapidly developing (see no. 1089).

1035   *Eisenhower Mss.*

TO CRAIG CAMPBELL   *October 10, 1950*

Dear Craig:[1] I have some difficulty in trying to understand your feeling that you are at a crossroad.[2] You apparently have a good and congenial job, a nice family and are embarked upon a life program which promises advancement, economically and intellectually, and the satisfaction that you should attain in providing for the future education for your child or children and a reasonable security for yourself and your wife. Since, now, you must be something like 31 or 32 years of age (obviously guessing), I do not see—unless there has arisen in you some definite and inescapable dissatisfaction with your present job—why this great question mark should arise in your own mind.

Because of the long time that has intervened since your discharge from the army, I can see no possible reason for going back to it unless one of [these] things should be true:

(a) that you would like to make the army your career;

(b) that you are convinced we are very soon to be in a global war which will compel your re-entry into the army and you feel that you should get some refresher training and preparation for active service.

With respect to the first of these possibilities, I would rule it out without hesitation. I shall not waste time discussing the matter because I do not believe that you are seriously entertaining the thought of going back into the army as a career. You would be so junior in rank as compared to your contemporaries in age that you would never be happy unless, of course, there is some special legislative arrangement of which I know nothing.

With respect to the second possibility, I should say that your guess is probably as good as anybody's. My own feeling, however, is that our Communist opponents do not wish to force a global war at this time; if one should come, I think it will be the result of an accident or a miscalculation and not as a result of deliberate intent. This conclusion could change as the months go by but, as of this moment, I believe that most students of war would agree with this estimate. Consequently, I will not belabor the point further.

If, as is implied by your letter, you have just come to the conclusion that you are unhappy in your present work and are rather looking around for something else to do, I believe I would first search for the reason for my own discontent. You have gained a very considerable experience and a wide circle of acquaintances and friends in a particular branch of our economy. Why should you throw these away? It would seem to be the part of wisdom merely to work hard, to increase your usefulness to the company, to broaden your understanding of the whole industry and, even if you do not stay with any particular company, to attempt to develop your talents and qualifications along lines that you have already started.

There would seem to be very little more for me to say because, obviously, there can be some underlying reason that makes all of the above completely useless. I know of nothing that is more important in life than being able to see something a trifle humorous even in disappointments, setbacks and what sometimes seems to be sheer drudgery. If you can do this, I think you can trust your own decisions no matter how important these may be to yourself and to your family.

General Gruenther is in Washington and should be addressed:

Lt. General Alfred M. Gruenther
Deputy Chief of Staff for Plans
3-E-630, The Pentagon
Washington 25, D.C.

General T. J. Davis has retired from the army and is located at:

Route #1
Central, South Carolina[3]

I am sure that both would like to hear from you and possibly both would give you advice that would be in direct opposition to what I have put down here. I have merely tried to figure out what I would do under the circumstances, as I have visualized them in the meager information you gave me.

With greetings to your family and with warmest regards to yourself.[4]
Sincerely

[1] Campbell had been an aide to Eisenhower during World War II. He was presently a petroleum analyst for Humble Oil and Refining Company in Houston, Texas. For background see no. 541; and *Eisenhower Papers*, vols. I–IX.

[2] "I feel that I am again at a cross-road in life and need some sound advice," Campbell had written on October 5 (EM). He had been "toying with the idea of going back into the Army," he said, and he wished to have Eisenhower's views on the matter.

[3] Campbell had inquired about generals Gruenther and Davis.

[4] Campbell would stay with Humble Oil. In a letter of July 3, 1951, he would say, "I am not nearly so disgruntled as when you last heard from me . . ." (EM).

Dear Mr. Robertson:[1] I am disturbed by the things you have to say in your letter of October 6 to Dr. Wriston, a copy of which you sent to me by a note of the same date.[2] It did not occur to me that anyone present at the Waldorf meeting would entertain for an instant the thought that permanent peace could be built on a philosophy of force, on arms alone. I felt that conclusions concerning the need for rearmament was based upon the sad realization of the repeated failures, including the present one, to maintain our own security through weakness. It seemed to me that the action of the meeting in insisting upon adequate and prompt rearmament was to meet an immediate and perhaps a continuing crisis of some years in length—but was not considered to be a permanent solution.[3]

At the meeting it was more than once stated that *permanent* peace would have as its basis a general respect for decency, fairness and justice and a common understanding that these can never be promoted by might alone. I would venture the opinion that almost everyone present has, before this, gone on record as favoring support of the United Nations, of arbitration and the conference table as against the threat and use of force, and is himself convinced that—unless we can achieve this kind of understanding peace in the world—our form of civilization is doomed to destruction.

So, I am compelled to take issue with your implication that we, as a people, have underestimated the need for conciliation or that we have merely *assumed* our neighbor to be hostile. I believe that in the so-called Baruch plan the United States offered unilaterally to make the greatest step toward disarmament in all history in order to promote mutual confidence and understanding in the world; to the end that we might have a decent peace.[4]

Beyond all this, we have the history of the United States. We have always been an unarmed nation, unarmed as compared to the practices and methods of other countries. This has never brought peace. On the contrary, we know that it was the disdain in which both the Kaiser's Germany and Hitler's Germany held us that led them to discount possible American reaction to totally unjust aggresssion.[5]

I am quite sure that 90 per cent or more of the people present at the Waldorf last week will go to any length short of national dishonor or obvious risk of destruction in order to secure and sustain a plan for universal peace and universal disarmament. But most of them probably recall the words of Wilson when he sadly said, after many months of trying to keep out of World War I, "We enter this war only where we are clearly forced into it because there are no other means of protecting our rights."[6] Until we develop the means for assuring to each nation its proper rights and the certainty that it may live in justice and decency, I cannot agree to a repetition of former errors in stripping ourselves of military force. I say all this as one who probably hates war more than any person who is not classed as a fanatic. I consider it not only the greatest cancer that continues to consume the substance of human society, but I think that it is completely stupid and futile. Believing that these views are shared by most of the people who attended the Waldorf meeting, I suggest that they, like myself, proceed at once to the discussion of the practical matters now indicated as necessary, pending the day when world effort may bring forth a universally agreed upon plan for universal disarmament and peace in which we all may have some modicum of confidence.

I would be more than glad, at any convenient time, to pursue a discussion of this subject. I realize that there is little use in attempting to go into it by correspondence. It needs far more exhaustive discussion than letters permit. *Very sincerely*

P.S. Just this minute there arrived your second letter. Thank you for your comments.[7]

[1] Robertson (LL.B. University of Pittsburgh 1910), of Pittsburgh, Pennsylvania, was chairman of the board of Westinghouse Electric Corporation.

[2] Robertson had written to both Eisenhower and Henry M. Wriston, president of Brown University, concerning his reaction to a recent conference called by the presidents of seven universities. The purpose of the meeting had been to discuss the national and international problems facing the United States. Wriston had presided at the session, which had been held at the Waldorf-Astoria Hotel in New York City on September 28, 1950. Robertson's letters to Eisenhower are in EM. For background on the conference see nos. 984 and 1016.

[3] Robertson had attended the conference and was concerned that participants in the meeting believed that world peace was dependent upon total preparation for war. "No one," he said, "seemed to be particularly interested in peace without the doubtful aid of a big stick."

[4] Robertson had said, "We seem so certain of the enemy: first, that he is an enemy (other than a hostile neighbor, prompted by fear); second, that conciliation is hopeless and not worth giving a trial. . . ." For background on Bernard Baruch's plan for international control of atomic weapons see Galambos, *Chief of Staff*, nos. 902, 917, and 946.

[5] According to Robertson, "History has so often shown that getting ready for war doesn't lead to peace but to war. One wonders," he asked, "why America has suddenly decided, as appears to be the case, to adopt a policy so foreign to her."

[6] President of the United States Woodrow Wilson made this statement on the evening of April 2, 1917, when he had addressed a joint session of the Congress to recommend that a state of war be declared between Germany and the United States (*New York Times*, Apr. 3, 1917).

[7] Robertson's second letter (dated Oct. 9, 1950, EM) was in reply to Eisenhower's memorandum about the American Assembly, sent to Robertson on October 3, following the conference discussed above (for background on the Assembly and the memorandum see no. 1026, esp. n. 3). Robertson thought the American

Assembly plan a good one, and he encouraged the General to go ahead with the project (for developments see no. 1039).

1037   *Eisenhower Mss.*

To James Frederick Gault   *October 11, 1950*

Dear Jimmy:[1] Of course I am flattered that your friend Brigadier Jeffries should suggest that I officiate at the unveiling of a portrait of Winston Churchill.[2] If there were the slightest possibility of my creating an opportunity to come to London before Christmas this year, I would, because of my lasting affection and admiration for my old friend, spare no pains to be there. Actually, there is not a single week between now and next spring that does not have its inescapable commitments on my calendar. So, won't you please explain the situation to your friend and tell him that, deeply as I appreciate his thought of me, I cannot possibly participate in the ceremony.

You are right in feeling that I am attempting to keep reasonably confidential my planned trip to the U.K., beginning next June.[3] The only reason for this is that so I will not get my whole itinerary too greatly filled with fixed engagements—I should like to retain the maximum flexibility so that, after I get there, you and I—with Peggy[4] and Mamie—can determine on the spot the things that we would like to do in order to have the most enjoyment out of the whole visit.

As I am tentatively planning at this time, we shall be leaving sometime in May to be certain of being present in Normandy on June 6. I have not yet been informed of the details of that day's celebration: but, since I have been invited regularly on each of the D-Days since 1945 and because I have learned through our military attache that the invitation is to be renewed for next year, I am sure that in good time I will be able to furnish you all the details of the day's activities and ceremonies.[5]

It is possible that, either just before or just after the D-Day ceremony, I may take Mamie over to Luxembourg for a day or two because our lady Minister at that place is quite a friend of Mamie's.[6] Frankly, I should like to avoid any further travel or visits on the Continent. But, again, we must face the possibility that we may feel obligated to stop at some other point which would of course consume a few extra days.

In any event, I should like to be back in Culzean[7] by June 10th or 11th. On the 21st of that month I plan to be in Glasgow to participate in a ceremony at the University.[8] I know nothing at all about the details of the ceremonies in London around July 3rd, 4th or 5th. But, immediately after the 5th, we will certainly be coming home on the first suitable vessel. I will have accumulated work with which to catch up and, of course, we will want to make our annual pilgrimage to Mamie's parents out in Colorado.[9]

Either on the way to or from Normandy, I should like to stop for at least a couple of hours with Grassett on the Island of Jersey, if this should prove convenient. He has been kind enough to ask us to stop there and, since I have never seen the island, I should like to make a very brief visit.[10]

All these are just thoughts. I realize that, long before the event, we may have our plans knocked into a cocked hat, but if I haven't told you all of these tentative plans before now, I thought you might like to have them.[11]

My love to Peggy, *As ever*

[1] For background on Colonel Gault see no. 14.

[2] In a letter of October 4 (EM) Gault had asked Eisenhower to accept an invitation to unveil a portrait of Winston Churchill at the Junior Carlton Club in Pall Mall, London, sometime before Christmas. The invitation had been extended to Eisenhower, through Gault, by Brigadier William Francis Jeffries, secretary of the Carlton Club.

[3] For more information about Eisenhower's plans see no. 841; see also no. 959.

[4] Mrs. Gault.

[5] For background on the celebration of the anniversary of the invasion of Normandy see nos. 841, 876, and 959.

[6] Perle Mesta, United States Minister to Luxembourg since 1949 (see no. 545).

[7] Eisenhower had an apartment in Culzean Castle, near Maybole in Ayrshire, Scotland (see no. 14).

[8] On the invitation to the University of Glasgow see no. 706.

[9] On July 3, 1951, Eisenhower would be guest speaker at a dinner given in his honor in London by the English-Speaking Union. The following day he would participate in memorial ceremonies at London's St. Paul's Cathedral for American servicemen killed during World War II (for background see nos. 959 and 745, respectively).

The annual pilgrimage to Mrs. Eisenhower's parents' home in Denver, Colorado, would be a sorrowful one. On June 24, 1951, Mrs. Eisenhower would fly to Denver from Paris to attend her father's funeral. General Eisenhower, by then Supreme Commander of the NATO forces, would remain in Paris (see *New York Times*, June 25, 1951).

[10] Lieutenant General Sir A. Edward Grasett was Lieutenant Governor of Jersey in the Channel Islands (for background on him see no. 708).

[11] On October 17 Gault would reply expressing his disappointment that the General would not be able to officiate at the unveiling of the Churchill portrait; he said he looked forward, however, to seeing the Eisenhowers in the summer of 1951 (EM). For developments see no. 1045.

Dear Mr. Hilpert:[1] Much as I am chagrinned to do so, I am compelled to acknowledge that there is a definite basis for the biting criticisms you make of military training practices.[2] While I cannot help making the observation, in passing, that I can easily point out to you many glaring and often silly practices in civilian institutions, I cannot see where this would add much to the discussion for the simple reason that I keenly appreciate your desire to be constructively helpful.

Human frailty shows up in many diverse ways and it seems to be axiomatic that when persons attain places of authority or leadership— even where the smallest of organizations or the most routine of functions are involved—they begin to indulge in practices that would seem stupid and silly even to themselves if they could constantly have a mental mirror in front of them.

What I am trying to say is that your criticisms are not universally applicable in the army and that, in your justifiable resentment of the failures in leadership you and your associates obviously encountered far too frequently, you possibly did not take into account human imperfections which, I assure you again, I seem to encounter in civil life as much as I ever did in the military service.[3]

With these observations out of the way—and by no means do I mean them to serve either as an alibi or as lack of appreciation of your effort—I shall send your letter to my old friend General Mark Clark who is now responsible for all training in the ground service.[4] He is a natural born leader and the best trainer of men that I ever knew. He and I have often talked about the kind of failure and weakness that caused you to write your letter and I am certain he can use your letter to good advantage.

Incidentally, one of our difficulties is this: For the Regular Army, we can secure devoted and able men who prepare the manuals, training aids and over-all doctrine that you admire in the military service.[5] But we are normally in times of peace so shorthanded that when the emergency of war hits us, the Army is compelled to expand so rapidly that individuals are made leaders on the basis, almost, of guesswork. It sometimes seems not too astonishing that these men should seek obvious indices of failure or shock (such as shined shoes) rather than dig deeper into the functional progress of a class or unit.

I cannot close this letter without expressing a very lasting and deep appreciation of your thoughtful interest in the problems facing the military. I am grateful to you for the trouble you took in writing to me, and it is because I am forced to agree with many of your observations that I have taken the time to ask you to realize that there are some very definite human reasons for the failures you have encountered. *Sincerely*

[1] Hilpert (M.S. Pennsylvania State College 1948) headed the test facility and proving grounds of the Industrial Power Division of the International Harvester Company at Hodgkins, Illinois. During World War II Hilpert had attained the rank of first lieutenant in the Army Corps of Engineers and had served in both the United States and Europe.

[2] Eisenhower is referring to Hilpert's fifteen-page letter of October 12, 1950 (EM). The letter concerned army training methods, which, according to Hilpert, were so misdirected that the program was held in contempt by most veterans. "It is my opinion," Hilpert had written, "that the situation is not the fault of the men who find themselves in uniform during each war, it is rather the fault of the false set of standards by which the Army judges its efficiency and governs its training and discipline."

[3] Hilpert had given several examples of what he considered misdirected training: carelessness in storing and organizing personal effects was a more serious offense than the miscalculation of a military problem; greater attention was given to keeping things out of shirt pockets than to studying army training manuals; a clean gun at inspection was more the measure of a soldier's skill than was the performance of its mechanism. Hilpert rejected the rationale behind such methods, namely, that a group of men disciplined to follow any order in training, no matter how ridiculous, will probably follow any order in combat. "It is impossible to gain the respect and trust of a man who is continually forced to learn in minute detail things which obviously are not going to increase his military ability." Civilians, Hilpert had pointed out, have to discipline themselves in order to make a living. A civilian, he wrote, knows that his commission depends on how much he sells, not on the wrinkles he left in sheets tucked between the mattress and bed springs.

[4] Clark was Chief of the Army Field Forces (see no. 976). On this same day (Oct. 12) Eisenhower sent Clark a copy of Hilpert's letter and of the reply printed above. In a covering handwritten note, Eisenhower told Clark that if Hilpert's letter did not interest him, "file in the wastebasket." To the contrary, Clark would acknowledge receipt of Hilpert's letter on October 18, and on October 24 he would write Eisenhower at length on the matter. Clark had found Hilpert's description of the "foibles that he encountered in Army training" highly informative, and he summarized for Eisenhower the improved training procedures since World War II. The new mobilization training programs, for instance, included detailed specifications defining post-training expectations. The program, Clark said, was designed to give the officer corps a "reasonable perspective," with continuing stress on leadership. The letters cited here are in EM, Clark Corr.

[5] Hilpert had said that he thought the Army training manuals were accurate and well written and that the training films were "without parallel in their excellence."

To Deans, Directors, and
Departmental Executives⁰
Memorandum. Confidential

At their meeting of October 2, 1950 the Trustees gave their full approval to The American Assembly, a conference program which will function with the cooperation of the schools, colleges, and other divisions of Columbia University. The American Assembly program is one that has been worked on for some time, and it is now possible to start it at an earlier date and under more favorable surroundings than was previously thought possible. At the October 2nd meeting the Trustees accepted from W. Averell Harriman and E. Roland Harriman a gift of property and initial funds for the establishment of The American Assembly, on Harriman Campus of Columbia University, at Harriman, New York.[1]

The Harriman gift constitutes a substantial addition to our educational and financial resources. The full press release will be made on October 18, 1950.[2] Meanwhile I wish to inform you of developments. Your counsel is needed in making the best use of the property and in setting up The American Assembly.

The American Assembly

The Assembly is designed to respond to the concern with which American citizens contemplate the possible future of our democracy and individual freedom based on a philosophy of competitive enterprise. The average citizen senses that pressure groups are in some instances— and possibly with the best of intentions—leading him down a primrose path whose end could be, in the absence of clear understanding and great vigilance, a socialized form of economy with resultant regimentation and stagnation.

Analysis of this generalization shows that it breaks down into a number of concrete problems. Among these are important ones involving taxation, foreign political and economic relations, problems of the aged including old age pensions, unemployment insurance, proper medical care for the entire population, support of schools, and so on. The citizen hears these problems discussed only by people seeking office, or whose positions make suspect their contentions. He, of course, cannot conduct the research necessary to establish the truth or falsity of what he hears. It is clear that in finding the salient facts and solutions to our country's major problems, a team operation is called for, a meeting of many minds. The conference method provides the machinery for such a fruitful meeting.

The conference method involves (a) research before, during, and after the conference or conferences, (b) the actual conference, and (c) the translation of conference findings into non-technical language for wide dissemination through individual members, press, television, radio, magazines, films, booklets, and books. The first step in the process is to identify and describe the subject to be studied. The second step is to select a task force for the conference from the staff of Columbia, and from other organizations and institutions, to prepare necessary background studies. A typical conference would include business leaders, workers, labor leaders, political figures, (always of both parties) and professional men. All groups will contribute their experience and knowledge to the conference—no one will dominate. Answers developed at the conference would not always be in terms of exact pronouncements, but there would be an amalgamation of idea with fact, of theory with experience, that should produce some clearly agreed upon truths and observations. These will be carried back by the participants to their own homes and associates in all parts of the country. Conference findings will be published and broadcast. The whole result will be to get the findings out so citizens can use them.

The Harriman Campus Facilities

The Harrimans have given the University property of some 100 acres, on the west side of the Hudson River, some 48 miles from New York, or an hour's automobile drive. The 96-room house, known as Arden House, is in first-rate condition, with 48 baths, and splendid facilities for housing groups of up to 125 persons, with ample meeting rooms, dining room, and indoor and outdoor recreational facilities. Arden House stands on a 1500 foot mountain. It has sufficient isolation to assure the undivided attention of those attending conferences and other meetings, yet it is convenient to Manhattan.

Benefits to the University as a Whole

The participation in Conferences by faculty members is anticipated as conference leaders, members, or directors of research. This program will attract attention and financial support to Columbia research activities already in existence, and stimulate interest in new research areas. Qualified students will be welcome, within the limit of accommodations, to attend conferences in their fields of interest.

A number of Departments of the University have expressed their interest in using the property for various purposes. Among them might be mentioned the Zoology, Botany, and Geology Departments, which intend to use the estate for field work. The Astronomy Department hopes to use the mountain site for its photographic work on the nearer stars, and for research in radio astronomy. Certain Engineering activities might well be conducted on the property. Teachers College is interested in the estate for possible educational conferences. The foregoing does not preclude the use of the property by other divisions of Columbia.[3]

Finance

The Graduate School of Business has the financial and administrative responsibility for the Harriman Campus. Funds are already in hand to cover rehabilitation and furnishing of Arden House. The Harrimans have pledged an annual sum for three years that will serve as a guarantee to the University that the property can be maintained in a stand-by condition if such a step should become necessary. The University can dispose of the property after five years.

The immediate goal in working capital is $500,000, to be raised from Columbia supporters and Alumni throughout the country. Firm commitment will be secured from companies and other sponsors to underwrite conferences during the five-year period. The financial plans also include the establishment of a permanent endowment fund as the project develops and becomes nationally recognized for its contribution to the public good.[4]

Advice and Counsel

When the Deans and Directors were asked as to potential uses of the property some time ago, the response was helpful in the shaping of The American Assembly. I am gratified that The Graduate School of Business has developed practical methods of financing this program and will administer and operate the Harriman Campus for the benefit of the University. I am asking for the advice and counsel of Deans, Directors, and Department executives on two matters in particular.

(a) A preliminary list of subjects on which conferences may be held has been prepared. Additional subjects are sought.

(b) As stated earlier, it is expected that a number of men and women will be nominated or selected from the Columbia faculty, or that of other institutions, to prepare research or background studies, furnish material while the conferences are in session, and assist in the preparation of findings and conclusions. If you care to make any suggestions as to Columbia personnel who might be available for such tasks, such suggestions will be welcome.[5]

Arrangements for financing The American Assembly will include adequate compensation for staff and research work. Some of this will be done by a permanent group, but most of it by staffs specially selected in the case of each conference. One of the concepts behind The American Assembly program is that a conference represents one stage in the educational process, which starts with research, the facts are then studied and evaluated in the conference, and the conclusions or findings transmitted to the public. With the cooperation of our faculty in this effort, it will be possible to bring the work that Columbia University is doing to a wider audience, gain additional financial support for it, and put authoritative information about current problems into the hands of our citizens who both need it and can use it for the public good. I believe

The American Assembly program can accomplish an enormous amount of good for the University. Your help in enabling it to gain the success it merits will be appreciated. Inquiries or suggestions regarding The American Assembly and projected Harriman Campus activities should be addressed to the Dean of the Graduate School of Business.[6]

[1] There is also a copy of this document in CUF. Eisenhower's reasons for developing the conference plan at Columbia are fully explained in no. 979, as well as in his prospectus, "The American Assembly," dated September 29, 1950, EM, American Assembly Corr. The memorandum printed above was probably written by Eisenhower in cooperation with Dean Philip Young, who, on the day of the trustees' meeting, had urged in a formal letter to Eisenhower that the trustees approve the plan and that they accept Arden Estate from the Harrimans on behalf of Columbia University. Young's letter to Eisenhower, dated October 2, may have been read at the trustees' meeting. Copies of it are in EM, American Assembly Corr., and in EM, Philip Young Corr. On the origins of the conference plan see no. 555; for the Harriman gift see no. 605.

[2] Eisenhower would make the announcement at the Men's Faculty Club following a luncheon sponsored by the Columbia Associates for members and their guests. A list of those attending the luncheon is in EM, Columbia University. For the formal announcement by Eisenhower see *New York Times*, October 19, 1950. See also a copy of the press release issued by Columbia's Public Information Office; and "Note to Reporters" [Oct. 18, 1950], EM, American Assembly Corr.

[3] See no. 605, esp. nn. 3, 4, and 5.

[4] See Dean Philip Young's memorandum to the staff of the Graduate School of Business, August 31, 1950, same file as document; and the financial statement titled "The American Assembly," November 10, 1950, EM, American Assembly Corr.

[5] For developments see no. 1081.

[6] Philip Young, who had worked with Eisenhower as an adviser and consultant on the conference plan since the fall of 1949, would continue his association with the project as its administrator, working through the Graduate School of Business. For subsequent developments see no. 1043.

1040   *Eisenhower Mss., Diaries*

DIARY   *October 13, 1950*

Haven't written in this since going on my summer vacation.[1]

Today Gov. D. called me (I suppose from Albany) saying that if questioned he is going to announce his hope that I would accept a Republican draft in 1952. There seemed to be no double talking about the matter. I merely said I'd say "No comment."[2]

[1] For Eisenhower's 1950 summer vacation see no. 805.

[2] Governor Thomas E. Dewey had apparently telephoned Eisenhower from Albany, New York, the state capital. Dewey knew that the question of presidential candidates for the 1952 election would undoubtedly come up during his forthcoming

guest appearance on "Meet the Press," a nationally televised panel-discussion program (for Eisenhower's reaction to Dewey's public statements see the following document). Dewey had long been interested in Eisenhower as a political candidate (for background on the relationship see no. 491. For Eisenhower's efforts to sort out his feelings about this political situation see nos. 602 and 638).

1041   *Eisenhower Mss.*

To Robert Harron   *October 16, 1950*

Dear Harron:[1] Subsequent to yesterday's broadcast in which Governor Dewey made highly commendatory references toward myself, a number of attempts have been made by individual representatives of the press to question me.[2] On my way to work this morning I promised one of these representatives that, in view of the press interest that has apparently developed concerning my reactions to the Governor's opinions, I would issue sometime during the day a short written statement. I am sending to you the following with the request that you make it available to any representative of the press that may desire it:

"Any American would be complimented by the knowledge that any other American considered him qualified to fill the most important post in our country. In this case the compliment comes from a man who is Governor of a great State and who has devoted many years of his life to public service. So, of course, I am grateful for Governor Dewey's good opinion of me.

As for myself, my convictions as to the place and methods through which I can best contribute something to the cause of freedom have been often expressed. They have not changed. Here at Columbia University I have a task that would excite the pride and challenge the qualifications and strength of any man — I still believe that it offers to such an individual as myself rich opportunities for serving America."
Sincerely

[1] Harron was Director of the Office of Public Information at Columbia. For background see no. 106.
[2] On October 15, 1950, New York State Governor Thomas E. Dewey had endorsed Eisenhower for the Republican presidential nomination in 1952. At the same time he had ruled himself out as a candidate. Dewey's announcement had come during his guest appearance on the television show "Meet the Press." Leo Egan, of the *New York Times*, had asked Dewey if he had thought of anyone who might be a presidential candidate in 1952. The Governor's ready answer had been: "General Eisenhower." To Egan's question, "Have you asked General Eisenhower if he is willing?" Dewey had replied, "I have not." The Governor, however, had actually telephoned on October 13 to put the General on notice that he would soon endorse him for the presidency (see the preceding document). On October 16 the *New York Times* had given Dewey's announcement front-page treatment with triple

headlines. On the following day (Oct. 17) the *New York Times* would print Eisenhower's disclaimer in full on the front page under headlines that read: "Not a Presidential Aspirant, Eisenhower Replies to Dewey" (see also Lyon, *Portrait of the Hero*, p. 413; and Neal, *Reluctant Dynasty*, p. 261).

One week before Dewey's announcement, Eisenhower had said much the same thing in an interview for the *Columbia Spectator*. "So far as I am concerned," the General was quoted, "I put my hand to a job and am doing my best. I don't know why people are always nagging me to run for President. I think I've gotten too old. I have no desire to go anywhere else if I can help do what I want here at Columbia. This is the place for me" (*Columbia Spectator* and *New York Times*, Oct. 17, 1950). This was the third time that Eisenhower had formally and publicly denied having presidential ambitions (see no. 106; and Galambos, *Chief of Staff*, no. 1998). The question of his political candidacy would nevertheless continue to come up (see no. 1061).

1042   *Eisenhower Mss.*

To George Catlett Marshall   *October 18, 1950*

Dear General: Some two weeks ago there was held in the Waldorf-Astoria the meeting of business and professional men, which was still in the planning stage when I spoke to you about it on the telephone, while I was still in Denver.[1] The meeting was, I thought, very constructive and indicated readiness on the part of all those present to think about national problems and to be of assistance in their solution where this seemed possible.

Early in the program I was called upon, personally, to present a general, round-the-world military picture together with a hasty estimate of how the United States was affected by this situation. In the course of this talk I expressed my personal belief that we had come to the point where we should contemplate the use of a system of universal military service for the recruitment of our armed forces, and the building up of trained reserves. This I suggested on the assumption that we should maintain a total of some three million individuals in the armed forces. Of this number, I suggested some 1,200,000 would make up a professional cadre and 1,800,000 men would be serving an obligatory two-year term in the army at nominal pay. Such a system is, of course, not new in the world.[2] Later, during the meeting, a memorandum from President Conant of Harvard was read. With regard to universal service, he took the same stand and urged that there be no deferments for educational reasons. He further specified that the young man should enter the army at eighteen, or upon graduation from high school, so as to allow him to do his two-year term before he entered the industrial stream of the country.[3] If 3,000,000 men should be considered an excessive strength for our armed forces over the next several years, then I would certainly revise my views.[4]

An interesting point is that all seven college presidents present at the meeting voted unanimously for the proposal. Moreover, so far as I could discern, there was no dissenting opinion expressed by any person present. I believe that the entire group numbered some 50. A few years ago, such a result would have been unthinkable.[5]

While these convictions are, I realize, at some variance with your own, I feel that an expression of them cannot damage whatever position you may personally choose to take in a program of so-called "rearmament."[6] Nevertheless, I think you realize, without my saying it, that I certainly want to do nothing to embarrass you in your difficult task; consequently, if you believe that repetition of my personal views would or could embarrass you, then I would like to hear from you as soon as possible, because I am called upon frequently to appear publicly.[7]

Warm personal regards,[8] *Cordially*

[1] Marshall was Secretary of Defense (see no. 982). On the conference in New York City on September 28 see no. 1016. On the Eisenhowers' vacation see no. 805.

[2] General Eisenhower had long been a proponent of universal military service (see nos. 912 and 1006).

[3] On Conant's memorandum see no. 1006.

[4] Marshall would reply (Oct. 23, EM) that he had discussed the subject of universal military service with Robert A. Lovett, soon to become Deputy Secretary of Defense; they had decided that it would be easier to amend the Selective Service Act than to pass a new law likely to arouse great opposition (for background on Lovett see no. 1018; on the recent extension of the Selective Service Act of 1948 see no. 916). Marshall and Lovett would plan a program of universal military training, which would increase in size in proportion to the long-term diminution of the pool of men obtained through selective service. Marshall would emphasize, moreover, the importance of meeting manpower requirements without increasing the cost to the government. The nation could muster "really a great force," Marshall would argue in his letter, with the existing twenty-seven divisions and twenty-two separate regiments of the National Guard "backed by some form of Universal Military Training providing men for the ranks. . . ."

[5] The AAU, at its annual meeting on October 27, would take a stand in favor of two years of military service for all American youth. Twenty-three of the thirty-seven members of the association would support a resolution calling for universal military training (UMT), and the association would release a statement to the press on December 7 (see *New York Times*, Oct. 28 and Dec. 8, 1950). The president of the International Brotherhood of Teamsters (AF of L) would also endorse UMT (see *ibid.*, Dec. 12, 1950).

[6] Marshall had spoken in support of UMT in his first speech as Secretary of Defense (see *ibid.*, Sept. 22, 1950). On subsequent occasions he had blamed the initial defeats of U.N. forces in Korea on the inadequacy of America's military reserves (see *ibid.*, Oct. 7 and 10, 1950). Addressing the seventy-second conference of the National Guard Association on October 24, he would insist that the states strengthen their National Guard units. On the following day President Truman would tell the same assemblage that a law providing for UMT was necessary in order to

rectify the "disgrace" of the government's rejection for physical and mental defects of 34 percent of those drafted (see *ibid.*, Oct. 25 and 26, 1950).

[7] Upon learning that Marshall would become Secretary of Defense, Eisenhower had considered not attending the conference at the Waldorf-Astoria; Marshall had, however, persuaded Eisenhower to go ahead with the meeting (see nos. 984 and 985).

[8] On the next day (Oct. 19) Eisenhower would go to Pittsburgh, Pennsylvania, to speak at the Carnegie Institute (see no. 757). On the same day he would be honored at a reception and luncheon sponsored by Columbia Alumni in Pennsylvania. The guest list is in EM, George V. Copper Corr.

1043   *Eisenhower Mss.*

TO LEONARD FRANKLIN MCCOLLUM   *October 21, 1950*

Dear Mc:[1] Thank you very much for your letter of the 19th. As you suggested, I am sending my reply to your office at 10 Rockefeller Plaza.

Unfortunately, I shall not be here this coming week. I leave Sunday night for Chicago, and I visit, in succession, Chicago, St. Louis, Indianapolis, Cincinnati, Charleston, and Washington before returning home.[2] In addition, I must deliver a lecture at the Defense College on Monday morning, the 30th, so that it will be impossible for me to meet with you and Mr. Sloan, at least during your next visit to this city.[3]

Quite naturally, I am tremendously pleased by the evidence of Mr. Sloan's interest and, most certainly, I shall have a talk with him the first time that an opportunity presents itself. In the meantime, I am inclined to agree with your suggestion that it would be best to have present, when you talk with him, someone who is thoroughly familiar with all recent developments in the project. As usual, I suggest Philip Young.[4] I think that as soon as you get to New York City, it would be a good idea to give him a ring and see whether you could set up some little meeting where you, Mr. Sloan and Philip could go over the project in detail. Philip's enthusiasm and information are impressive — and this will certainly be appreciated by Mr. Sloan.[5]

I was distressed not to get a chance to talk to you personally at the meeting the other day. It seems to me that, more and more, I have fewer and fewer minutes to call my own. But I hope you never forget how deeply obligated I and my associates feel to you.[6]

With warm personal regard, *Cordially*

[1] For background on McCollum see no. 826.

[2] In his letter (EM) McCollum had asked the General to get in touch with him about the American Assembly plan; Eisenhower was referring to his forthcoming trip to meet with Columbia alumni. For more information about these plans see the following document.

[3] Eisenhower had accepted an invitation from Lieutenant General Harold Roe Bull, commandant since July 1949 of the National War College in Washington, D.C., to speak to students on the subject of command in war. (For background on Bull see *Eisenhower Papers*, vols. I–IX. Correspondence regarding Eisenhower's appearance is in EM, Bull Corr.; see esp. Bull to Eisenhower, Sept. 8, 1950. Eisenhower's speech, marked "Restricted," is in EM, Subject File, Speeches.) McCollum had wanted to arrange a meeting between Eisenhower and Alfred Pritchard Sloan, Jr., chairman of the board of General Motors Corporation. According to McCollum, Sloan had expressed a desire to make a significant contribution to the American Assembly fund (EM. For background see no. 1039).
[4] Young, who was dean of Columbia's Graduate School of Business, had worked closely with Eisenhower on the planning and funding for the conference plan.
[5] A gift of five thousand dollars from the Alfred P. Sloan Foundation is listed in Columbia University, *Report of the Treasurer, 1951*.
[6] McCollum had attended the luncheon on October 18, 1950, at which Eisenhower had formally announced Columbia's sponsorship of the American Assembly (see no. 1039, n. 2).

1044   *Eisenhower Mss.*

To Fred M. Manning   *October 21, 1950*

Dear Fred:[1] Thank you very much for your splendid letter. Much as I will be disappointed in failing to see you on November seventh, I could not possibly have approved any other decision than the one you made. I am forced to take along with me an absentee ballot because when my plans were made, way last spring, my office force and I completely overlooked the fact that November 7 would be Election Day.[2]

You can well understand how delighted I am that you have shed a lot of your business worries. You have been carrying a big load for a long time, and I am quite sure that the opportunity to devote yourself a little more intensively to the kind of work you will be doing Election Day, and less of your time to the job of keeping a business running, will bring you a great deal of satisfaction.[3]

The particular meeting that I should like to see you come to on my Texas trip is the one at Oklahoma City on November 12. I understand that we are going to get in a morning of golf and have a small luncheon, at which I will explain the American Assembly plan. It promises to be quite a bit of fun, and I believe that Boots Adams of the Phillips Company will be coming over to Oklahoma City that day. Don Kennedy and Streeter Flynn are my hosts. I am not certain that you know them, although I think it quite likely.[4]

None of the other meetings on the entire trip promises to be so much fun as this one, and, if it sounds good to you, why not let me know at once and I will get busy and ask Don Kennedy to invite you down.[5]

When you get this, I shall probably be out on the road for a week of meetings with different Columbia organizations, but if you would call my office and ask for Mr. McCann,[6] he will take your message and get in touch with me promptly.[7]

When I get to see you, I can tell you in person just how deeply appreciative I am of the effort you are making to keep the Columbia project boiling in the Denver region.[8] *Cordially*

[1] For background on Manning see nos. 545 and 1023.

[2] In a letter of October 19 (EM) Manning had told Eisenhower that he could not accept an invitation to a cocktail party in the General's honor in Chicago on November 7 because the national off-year elections were to be held on the same day (for background on the party see no. 1061).

[3] Manning had said that he had just sold his corporation and now would have more time to work with Eisenhower on any plans he might have for the future. On election day, he said, he would be taking people to the polls.

[4] On Adams, Kennedy, and Flynn and the arrangements for the luncheon in Oklahoma City on November 12 see nos. 1021 and 1022.

[5] In a letter of October 27, 1950, Manning told Eisenhower that he had received an invitation to the luncheon from Kennedy and that he would try to attend (EM).

[6] Kevin McCann, assistant to the president of Columbia University.

[7] The next evening, October 22, 1950, Eisenhower would leave New York for a Columbia alumni tour, with stops in Blue Island and Chicago, Illinois; St. Louis, Missouri; Indianapolis, Indiana; Cincinnati, Ohio; and Charleston, West Virginia. During the five-day trip (Oct. 23–27) the General would meet with and be honored by scores of Columbia alumni at luncheons and dinners. For his day-by-day itinerary see the Chronology in this volume.

[8] Eisenhower is referring to Columbia's American Assembly project. Manning had reported that his representatives in Wyoming, Montana, Utah, Colorado, and New Mexico were a "group of good, solid, worthwhile citizens" who would help make the campaign for funds a success. For more information about the American Assembly see no. 1039.

1045   *Eisenhower Mss., Diaries*

DIARY   *October 28, 1950*

On Monday, October 23, I arrived at the Blackstone Hotel in Chicago to find there a message asking me to call the President. I placed the call immediately and was informed by the President that he should like to have me come to Washington for a conversation, to talk in general terms about an assignment for me involving a command of the Atlantic Pact Defensive Forces. He stated that if I would get in touch with him upon coming to Washington (where I am now) on the weekend of the 28th, he would try to make time with me for a talk and that, so far as he was concerned this would be completely satisfactory.[1]

I was scheduled for a press conference in Chicago and while nothing was suggested by any of the press representatives at that conference which would betray any knowledge on their part of the President's telephone call, I was confronted immediately after the conference by a question from Earl Wilson[2] indicating an accurate knowledge of the incident. I requested that he make no mention of his knowledge because of the embarrassment I would experience during the ensuing week. This he agreed to do, but it appears that some little knowledge did leak out and I was intermittently questioned by other press representatives in the cities I visited—St. Louis, Indianapolis, Cincinnati, Charleston, West Virginia.

I arrived in Washington by a military plane about midnight on Friday, the 27th.[3]

This morning, the 28th, I visited General Collins, Secretary of the Army Pace, and the President; also had a talk with General Gruenther.[4]

The situation seems to be about as follows: The American Chiefs of Staff are convinced that the Commander-in-Chief for the Atlantic Pact Forces should be named immediately. Originally, it was apparently the conception that the Commander should not be named until there were actually large forces to command; that during the formative period a Chief of Staff, heading a large planning, logistic and administrative group, could do the work. The opinion finally prevailed that if a commander's prestige was going to do any good in this problem, it would be best used during the most critical period of all, namely, while we are trying to get each of the nations involved to put forth maximum effort in producing, training and maintaining defensive forces.

It now appears that all of the Chief of Staffs group of the Atlantic union (the group of which General Bradley is Chairman) have concurred in this conclusion and I am informed that they unanimously desire that the Commander should be an American and specifically myself.[5]

From the moment that this possibility was first mentioned, *many months ago*, I have steadfastly stood by one statement. This statement is that I am a soldier and am ready to respond to whatever orders my superiors in the defense forces and the President, as Commander-in-Chief, may care to issue to me. The President is particularly anxious that the matter be not placed upon a cut and dried "order and obey" basis. He apparently wants to be able to announce that if I should take such an assignment, that I am responding to a "request."[6]

There is, however, one major obstacle at this moment to completing the details which would make the assignment effective and public. This is the fact that there are a number of controversial subjects lying in front of the Council of Defense Ministers, and it appears to be the desire of the American and British staffs to handle all of these questions as a bundle—they do not want to agree merely to those points in which other nations offer no objection, and by doing so leave unsolved those parts of the plan to which other nations may object.[7]

Specifically, the most controversial subject of all appears to be that of rearming Western Germany.[8] America and Britain want to proceed with a partial rearmament, and thus throw the Germans into the whole defensive structure. The French have objected to any consideration whatsoever of such a scheme, although later it appears that they have advanced a theory involving a complicated form of partial German rearmament and hodgepodge organization that they feel might be approved by popular French opinion.[9]

In this general argument I appreciate the French position and sympathize with it. However, I am definitely of the opinion that the French leaders should realize that the safety of Western Europe demands German participation on a vigorous scale and should get busy on the job of educating public opinion in France to accept this proposition, subject, of course, to clear evidence that the Germans *cannot* regain a position from which they could threaten the safety and security of France. Because of this belief, I am of the further opinion that the Americans and British are correct in refusing to agree to a plan that would necessarily remain largely a paper one and would give more opportunity for debate than for action. They should hold out for a sensible solution for this vital problem *before agreeing to accept, on behalf of America, responsibility for command.*[10]

I scarcely expect to see this situation clearly and unequivocally resolved. Rather, I suspect that the French may make certain promises and engagements that will at least partially justify a favorable decision on the part of the Americans and British, and that possibly the command will be set up with very great areas of indecision and doubt with respect to the Western German question.[11] If nothing at all is done in the way of resolving these difficulties and I am still asked to command I would have very great doubts as to the wisdom of my consenting to accept the position. It might be better to make an issue of the matter, even though my own attitude might be very seriously misunderstood in this country or abroad. If, however, there is developed any chance whatsoever that this vital point can be settled logically, as before indicated, it seems to me that I have no choice in the matter whatsoever.

As of this moment, I would estimate that the chances are about nine out of ten that I will be back in uniform in a short time.

All this will occasion a very great deal of adjustment in my personal life. Mamie's heart condition deteriorates a bit year by year and I hate to contemplate the extra burden thrown upon her by attempting to set up housekeeping in Europe, particularly when she would also be worried about the condition of her father and mother back in Denver. Actually this phase of the whole business would be the only one that would give me any great private concern.[12] As for myself, I do not think it is particularly important where I am working as long as I feel I am doing the best I can in what I definitely believe to be a world crisis. It will, of course, be a wrench to give up the work I am so earnestly working on at Columbia, but there are some fine young men there that can carry on and I am sure that my friends all over the country who have promised to help will not let them down merely because I have to go away temporarily.[13] As to the period of time in which I might be involved in such an affair, I do not see how a hard and fast estimate can be made. I firmly believe that my own maximum possibilities for service — based upon my alleged prestige in Europe — will begin to diminish very soon after the organizational phases of the proposition begin to show results. We must remember that the whole scheme may be one that will have to remain in effect for ten, fifteen or twenty years.[14] Consequently, it seems to me that it would be important for me to throw in at an early date some acceptable and reasonably young commander to take over and carry on the work for a reasonable length of time. While I realize that I might be able to carry on for five or six years, I think it is bad practice to allow such developments to fall into the hands of older men. Particularly, I would not want to see the habit started of assigning successive commanders who had almost reached the end of their usefulness as soldiers.[15]

At this moment, there is no telling when decision on these matters will be reached.[16]

[1] When President Truman's call came, Eisenhower had just begun a tour of Columbia alumni groups in Illinois, Missouri, Indiana, Ohio, and West Virginia. For background on the trip see the preceding document. On the Atlantic Pact see nos. 375 and 539.

[2] Wilson was a radio commentator and newspaper columnist.

[3] Eisenhower had requested military transport from Charleston, West Virginia, where he had been honored at a luncheon given by Robert S. Spilman, law partner in the firm of Spilman, Thomas and Battle. On the same day Eisenhower had addressed some four hundred guests at a dinner for Columbia alumni at the Daniel Boone Hotel (the luncheon guest list and other correspondence concerning the West Virginia trip is in EM, Spilman Corr.).

[4] General J. Lawton Collins was Army Chief of Staff; Frank Pace, Jr., was Secretary of the Army; General Alfred M. Gruenther was Deputy Chief of Staff for Plans, Army General Staff. Eisenhower had seen President Truman at the White House at 10:30 A.M. For press coverage of his imminent appointment as Supreme Allied Commander of the Atlantic Pact forces see *New York Times*, October 29, 1950.

[5] General Omar N. Bradley, chairman of the Joint Chiefs of Staff, was also chairman of the North Atlantic Treaty Military Committee (see no. 1113).

[6] Eisenhower would continue to stand by his "one statement" (see no. 1050). According to press accounts of the Truman-Eisenhower meeting on October 28, Eisenhower had said that he would accept the assignment if it were offered (see *New York Times*, Oct. 29, 1950; *Time*, Nov. 6, 1950; and *Newsweek*, Nov. 6, 1950. See also Eisenhower's reply to Truman's formal letter of assignment, nos. 1136 and 1139).

[7] Here Eisenhower later added a handwritten footnote/comment: "In late February (1951) Jack Slessor (C/S, Air, Britain) came to my office in Paris. He said this idea belonged to American C/Ss only; that British were confronted with a package—which they did *not* like!" Marshal of the Royal Air Force Sir John Cotesworth Slessor was Chief of the British Air Staff.

[8] By late September 1950 the North Atlantic Council had agreed that while Germany should not be allowed to establish a national army or a German general staff, it should contribute to the defense of Western Europe (see State, *Foreign Relations, 1950*, vol. III, *Western Europe*, pp. 350–53; and *New York Times*, Sept. 27, 1950). Practical implementation of this decision, however, would be delayed and would be a source of contention among the council members.

[9] On October 26 the French National Assembly had endorsed the Paris government's opposition to the creation of a German army. The formation of German divisions, the French believed, would inevitably lead to the resurrection of German militarism. They sought instead acceptance of a plan submitted by French Premier René Pleven: that the German contribution to the defense of Western Europe be accomplished by merging European forces into one army which would include Germans. The army would come under the control of European minister of defense, who in turn would answer to a supranational council of ministers, which itself would be responsible to a European parliamentary assembly. Under the Pleven Plan both the military and the economic structure of Western Europe would develop through preexisting European political bodies (see Robert McGeehan, *The German Rearmament Question: American Diplomacy and European Defense after World War II* [Urbana, Ill., 1971], pp. 62–66; and *New York Times*, Oct. 25, 26, 29, 31, 1950). The new French proposal would, however, fail to win acceptance, and this would stalemate progress at the Atlantic Pact talks (on the defense ministers' deadlock over this issue see no. 1050, n. 8).

[10] On October 26 the North Atlantic Defense Committee had submitted to the North Atlantic Council specific recommendations on a German contribution to Western defense. The paper, which would be known as the American Proposal, spelled out a number of desirable safeguards designed to maintain control of German forces. These measures against the remilitarization of Germany had been designed to reassure France that Germany could never again regain military dominance in Europe (for U.S. reaction to the Pleven Plan see State, *Foreign Relations, 1950*, vol. III, *Western Europe*, p. 406; and McGeehan, *The German Rearmament Question*, pp. 75–80. See also *New York Times*, Oct. 29, 1950).

[11] For developments involving a compromise plan and for Eisenhower's continuing concern over the indefinite political and military arrangements see nos. 1064, 1112, and 1113.

[12] For Eisenhower's account of the changes that would soon come to him and to his family see his memoir *At Ease*, pp. 363–78; and Brandon, *A Portrait of a First Lady*, pp. 266–74. On Mrs. Eisenhower's parents, the John Sheldon Douds, see no. 1037.

[13] Eisenhower is referring to what he would later call his "principal success" as president of Columbia—the American Assembly conference plan (see no. 1039; and Eisenhower, *At Ease*, p. 350).

[14] On February 1, 1951, General Eisenhower added a handwritten footnote here saying, "My own belief is that, in the element of time, *the U.S. should establish clear limits* and should inform Europe of these estimates. This applies to the length of time we should maintain sizeable American forces in Europe."

[15] In May 1952 General Matthew B. Ridgway, five years Eisenhower's junior, would succeed him as Supreme Commander, Allied Powers, Europe (see *New York Times*, Apr. 29, 1952).

[16] For subsequent developments see no. 1134.

Dear General: I have not wanted to bother you with correspondence during the more active phases of your recent campaign, but I cannot longer stay the impulse to express the conviction that you have again given us a brilliant example of professional leadership.[1] I think that your fortitude in patiently gathering up the necessary reserves to make a significant counter-stroke at a time when everyone of those soldiers must have been desperately wanted on the front lines, and your boldness in striking deep into the enemy's vitals with your counter-offensive were particularly shining examples of the kind of thing I mean.[2]

My most sincere congratulations, as well, of course, as my very best wishes to you and your family. With warm personal regard.[3] *Cordially*

[1] Under MacArthur's command, the U.S. X Corps had secured a beachhead at Inchon, South Korea, on Sept. 15, 1950 (Korean time). Army and Marine Corps troops had then severed the communications lines of the North Koreans still fighting the U.S. Eighth Army in the south (for background see no. 934). MacArthur's forces had liberated Seoul, the South Korean capital, by September 28, and a pincer movement by the X Corps and the Eighth Army had trapped large segments of the North Korean Army (see Appleman, *South to the Naktong*, pp. 515–95). By October 1, the North Koreans' retreat had become a rout.

During the second week of September President Truman had approved a National Security Council recommendation to send American forces across the thirty-eighth parallel into North Korea. U.S. Army troops had pursued the enemy across the parallel on October 7 and 8, and by October 19 the Eighth Army was in possession of Pyongyang, the capital of North Korea (see Schnabel, *Policy and Direction*, pp. 177–232; and Martin Lichterman, "To the Yalu and Back," in *American Civil-Military Decisions: A Book of Case Studies*, ed. Harold Stein [Birmingham, Ala., 1963], pp. 584–97). At this point the war broadened, as China became directly involved. Chinese Communist troops had first appeared in action against U.N. forces on October 25, and the Chinese would begin to have a decisive impact on the war as of late November. For developments see no. 1089.

[2] In July 1950 MacArthur had conceived the plan for the landing at Inchon, and he had overruled the objections of Navy and Marine Corps officers to the great risks that the operation entailed (for MacArthur's account see his *Reminiscences*, pp. 346–52. See also Collins, *War in Peacetime*, pp. 123–26; and Schnabel, *Policy and Direction*, pp. 147–50). The Navy's skepticism had made it difficult for MacArthur to gather a large enough amphibious force, but he had ultimately obtained the 1st Provisional Marine Brigade, the 1st Marine Division, and the 7th Marine Division for his assault (see Schnabel, *Policy and Direction*, pp. 159–65, 171–72).

[3] General MacArthur would thank Eisenhower in a letter of November 4 (EM), adding that Eisenhower's note had "brought back so vividly the memories of our intimate relationships over many hard years of effort and travail." MacArthur would publish most of the first paragraph of Eisenhower's letter and the second and third paragraphs of his reply in his *Reminiscences*, pp. 356–57.

TO AKSEL NIELSEN   *October 31, 1950*

Dear Aksel:[1] Thanks for the pictures; they came this morning and I hope to get a chance to look at them this evening.[2]

Lately, I have been on the jump; I feel almost like a drummer. However, I am waking up an awful lot of interest in the American Assembly and if I can just keep at it long enough, we should have the whole project properly on the rails and going full speed ahead.[3]

I am delighted with the news about Denison Domino. Maybe we'll produce a champion yet.[4] *Cordially*

[1] For background on Eisenhower's friend Nielsen see no. 77.
[2] Nielsen had sent Eisenhower (Oct. 13) a series of pictures taken at his Colorado ranch when Eisenhower had visited the Nielsens during the past summer.
[3] See no. 1039.
[4] Nielsen had said that Eisenhower's bull calf, Denison Domino, was doing very well (for background see no. 881).

TO MAXWELL DAVENPORT TAYLOR   *October 31, 1950*

Dear Max:[1] Thank you very much for your birthday greetings.[2] Late newspaper accounts seem to imply that I may have an opportunity to deliver my thanks in person—but I am so busy here that I cannot imagine shaking loose quickly. But if the trumpet blows, I shall try to make assembly.[3] My very best to you both. *Cordially*

[1] Major General Taylor was the U.S. Commander, Berlin, a post he had held since September 1949. Before that he had been Chief of Staff, European Command Headquarters, Heidelberg, Germany. For more background on Taylor see no. 250.
[2] In a letter dated October 14—Eisenhower's birthday—Taylor had commended him for his "inspiration and shining leadership in the past" (EM).
[3] For press reports that Eisenhower would soon be named commander of the North Atlantic defense forces in Europe see, for example, *New York Times*, October 28, 29, 30, and 31, 1950. For Eisenhower's comments and his concern about the problems in Europe see no. 1045.

To Grace Elizabeth Crum Gruenther   *November 1, 1950*

Dear Gracie:[1] In speaking to you about Al's medals, I did not mean to place any burden upon you, but I would like to be your accomplice in getting something that Al might like to keep permanently.[2] I don't have any rigid ideas about the matter but my thought would be to get a small mahogany case with a glass door which could be locked. This would allow changing of the medals when necessary and still keep them securely behind a lock. I think the case should be lined with blue velvet or some other material that would show off the decorations to good advantage.[3]

And have in an inconspicuous place on the back of the case a very tiny brass plate with something on it about like this: To AMG from DDE.

If you will follow through on this, please merely ask whatever firm does the work for you to send the bill directly to me here at the University. I do hope you do not think I am lazy; I just don't see any way of getting the job done except with your help.[4]

The writing of this note gives me a chance, also, to tell you again that your dinner the other night was most enjoyable. The only trouble with spending an evening at your house is that I gain too much weight.

With affectionate regards, and many, many thanks. *Cordially*

[1] Mrs. Gruenther was the wife of Lieutenant General Alfred M. Gruenther, currently the Army's Deputy Chief of Staff for Plans and Operations (for background on them see no. 569).

[2] Eisenhower had dined with the Gruenthers at their home at Fort McNair, Washington, D.C. At the time he had apparently offered to collaborate with Mrs. Gruenther in obtaining this particular gift for her husband. For more on the General's recent stay in the nation's capital see no. 1045.

[3] General Gruenther's military awards included the Distinguished Service Medal with Oak Leaf Cluster, the Legion of Merit, the Bronze Star, the Companion of the Bath (Britain), the Legion of Honor, the Croix de Guerre with Palm (France), the Order of Military Merit (Brazil), and other decorations from Italy, Poland, Belgium, and Czechoslovakia.

[4] As it turned out, the job would be done; a note from General Gruenther in August 1981 pronounced the military medal case in "full service and doing a fine job" (Aug. 8, 1981, EP).

To Edward Everett Hazlett, Jr.   *November 1, 1950*

Dear Swede:[1] I am returning to you the partially written letter that Mr. Graves sent to you some time back. Whenever I read such convincing evidence that I am held high in the esteem of a loyal and obviously thoughtful American, I experience a feeling that I cannot possibly describe. More than likely, it is a combination of a clear realization of my own unworthiness of such an opinion, but this mingled with an equal sentiment of pride.[2]

As to conclusions concerning my future responsibility and duty, I think you know my ideas on this perfectly well. Moreover, the longer I live the more I realize that no individual can predict with confidence anything concerning "tomorrow." At this moment I am confronted with possibilities of profound import; possibilities that had not even crossed my mind as much as a month ago. You yourself mention them in your handwritten note on Mr. Graves' manuscript. You say, "I do hope that this weekend you won't be talked into that Atlantic Pact job."[3]

I am a little astonished at your use of the expression, "talked into." As you know, I am an officer on the active list on which I will always stay, by reason of a special Act of Congress, affecting a few of us, unless I voluntarily remove myself from it. It is clear that my official superiors don't have to do any talking if they actually want me to take any military assignment.[4]

But over and above such considerations and addressing myself to the merits of the case, I would conclude from your statement that you do not attach the same importance to the success of the Atlantic Defense Pact as I do.[5] I rather look upon this effort as about the last remaining chance for the survival of Western civilization. Our efforts in the United Nations have been defeated by the vetoes of hostile groups[6]—but in the Atlantic Pact we are not plagued by the hostile groups and are simply trying to work out a way that free countries may band together to protect themselves. If we allow the whole plan to fizzle out into a miserable failure, it would seem to me that our future would be bleak indeed.

Of course, if the authorities can find anyone else who will tackle the job, and who they believe can perform it, then I hasten to agree with you that that man would probably do it far better than I could.[7] Moreover, I believe, in my present job, I am supporting an effort that will be of unusual significance to the welfare of our people. But I still would not agree that there is any job in the world today that is more important than getting Atlantic Union defensive forces and arrangements off to a good, practical and speedy start.

Of course, all this may be meaningless; I do not want or need any other job. Moreover, I understand from the morning's paper that the Council in Washington seems further than ever from agreement.[8] But the matter still retains its grave importance and so long as it does, any one of us—no matter what his station, his position or what personal sacrifices might be involved—must be ready to do his best. *As ever*

[1] Captain Hazlett (USN, ret.) lived in Chapel Hill, North Carolina. For background see no. 36.

[2] Louis Graves had been editor of the *Chapel Hill Weekly* since 1923. Hazlett described him as a rabid Eisenhower fan and said that he customarily allowed him to read the General's letters. In his letter (which is not in EM) Graves had apparently praised Eisenhower as an ideal choice for the presidency; Hazlett later asked the General not to be "put out" by it, or by Hazlett's own attitude (formerly he had advised Eisenhower not to pursue politics, but now Hazlett had reversed his course [Oct. 31, 1950, EM]).

[3] In recent correspondence (see n. 2 above; and Hazlett to Eisenhower, Aug. 9, 1950, EM) Hazlett had strongly advised Eisenhower to enter politics rather than return to the military via an assignment as head of NATO. For background on NATO see nos. 375 and 539.

[4] On Eisenhower's availability for military service see no. 46. Hazlett hoped Eisenhower would refuse the NATO job even though he respected the General's decision to follow the wishes of his military superiors. "But I still don't like it. I feel that it will be a terrific headache," Hazlett explained, "and will undermine your recently regained health and vigor" (Oct. 31, EM).

[5] "SHAPE doesn't shape up to me as being nearly as important as SHAEF," Hazlett wrote, "militarily it seems like a demotion" (*ibid.*). For similar sentiments comparing Eisenhower's command of the Allied Expeditionary Force during World War II with this "lesser role" at Supreme Headquarters, Allied Powers, Europe, see no. 1032, n. 2.

[6] Eisenhower had presented his views toward the United Nations in a speech initiating Columbia University's lecture series on international peace (see no. 908). At that time, the General had described the United Nations as a visible and working entity but had noted that its progress was being halted by the jeers and vetoes from one sector of the world community. Deteriorating relations between the Soviet bloc and Western nations had adversely affected the United Nations throughout 1950. The Soviet Union had for the most part refused to participate in the workings of the international organization (for background see Leland M. Goodrich, *The United Nations* [1959; reprint ed., New York, 1966], pp. 88–93).

[7] Hazlett had said that his vote for the NATO assignment would go to General Mark W. Clark, currently Chief of Army Field Forces (Oct. 31, EM; for background on Clark see no. 976. For additional speculation concerning the NATO command see nos. 986 and 1045).

[8] The *New York Times* had reported in a front-page article (Nov. 1, 1950) that the defense ministers of the North Atlantic Treaty nations had adjourned their negotiations in Washington, D.C., without creating a supreme command for the defense of Western Europe. Blocked by a French proposal, known as the Pleven Plan, to restrict the participation and unit size of German troops in an integrated force, the Atlantic ministers "never even touched the matter of a supreme command, much less the nationality of its commander or the name of the military leader." Three days prior to this development, the newspaper had announced (Oct. 29) that the designation of Eisenhower's name as Supreme Allied Command in

Europe "appeared to be only a necessary formality today. . . ." For more on these events see nos. 1045 and 1064.

1051   *Eisenhower Mss.*

To Eugene Meyer   *November 1, 1950*

Dear Gene:[1] There has just been called to my attention your fine article on "European Unity Broadened from Goods to Guns," recently published by the Post. This is to tell you how much I was impressed with the article.[2]

I found much value in the subject matter, and in view of what the papers say as to my possible *future* duties, you can understand how badly I feel in need of information.[3]

I hope that your article will be an effective contribution toward strengthening our relations with France and the Western powers, which is so vital at this time.[4] *Sincerely*

[1] Meyer was chairman of the board of directors of the *Washington Post* (for background see the tribute to him on his seventy-fifth birthday in the *Washington Post* [Oct. 31, 1950] and in the *New York Times* [Nov. 1, 1950]; see also Chandler, *War Years*, no. 1081. An earlier draft of this letter, with Eisenhower's handwritten changes, is in EM).

[2] In his article, which had appeared on October 15, 1950, Meyer had presented his own "visitor's" appraisal of the current political and economic situation in Western Europe. Meyer, who had recently returned from a trip to France and England, said he detected a "fresh wind of strength and assurance" blowing in Europe. He described three factors illustrating this "new adventure" in power and solidarity: (1) the Schuman Plan for cooperation in the coal and steel industries of Western Europe; (2) the unity of purpose shown in the efforts to create a consolidated defense to prevent war; and (3) the revitalized spirit in France.

[3] Concerning reports on the General's future responsibilities abroad see the preceding document. Meyer would thank Eisenhower on November 3 (EM) and would enclose a series of five articles on Germany by his wife (for background on Mrs. Meyer, the former Agnes Elizabeth Ernst, see no. 466). These articles were published in the *Washington Post* during the week of October 30, 1950.

[4] For Eisenhower's views on French morale see no. 1072; on relations among the members of the Atlantic Pact see no. 1045.

On this day two Puerto Rican nationalists would attempt to assassinate President Truman while he slept at Blair House in Washington, D.C. As a consequence of the attack, Eisenhower would be assigned police protection (see *New York Times*, Nov. 2, 3, 1950). The General's telegram of concern to Truman (Nov. 1) over what he described as an "unfortunate and disgraceful incident" is in EM.

To ROY WILSON HOWARD   *November 3, 1950*
Private

Dear Roy:[1] Thanks for your letter. In my office we are making a record of your unlisted telephone and of the method by which I can reach you with personal communications, intended for your eye alone.[2]

In my own office, practices somewhat similar to yours are followed. However, if you should want to be assured that only I will see a message, I suggest that you use double envelopes; the outside or mailing envelope to be just an ordinary one, while the interior envelope should carry the word *"Private."*

I am, of course, complimented that you should so generously make yourself available for conversations and personal correspondence with respect to problems that from time to time bother me considerably. Also, I am grateful. Certainly, there are many times when I could profit from the counsel of such an experienced and loyal friend as you.[3]
Cordially

[1] Howard was editor and president of the *New York World-Telegram and The Sun* and president of the Scripps-Howard Newspapers (for background see no. 646).

[2] Howard had sent the General his new phone number and described his office's procedure for forwarding to him unopened all correspondence that was marked "Private" (Oct. 23, 1950, EM).

[3] Howard had told Eisenhower that he was anxious to establish an understanding concerning the confidentiality of their communications. He suggested an agreement whereby what was said between the two men would always be "off the record" unless otherwise specified. "There will not be even a reference to the fact that I have called," Howard continued, "or that you declined to comment." Howard explained that this arrangement would be of mutual value. "In other words . . . what your friends and well-wishers do not say can often be of as great importance, or greater, than what they do say" (Oct. 23, EM).

To PELAGIUS WILLIAMS   *November 3, 1950*
Personal and confidential

Dear Mr. Williams:[1] Your letter came as an echo from long ago; I cannot tell you how pleased I was to have your message.[2]

With respect to your conclusions about my possible future duties, I have this one obvious remark to make: Any man who says he is not complimented upon learning that any other individual honestly considers him fit or qualified to hold the highest post in the land is either a monumental liar or a complete moron. But, on the other hand, I think that it is easy to see that there may be people who honestly do *not* want to become engaged in the political divisions and struggle of our country. I am one of these, primarily because my life has been given over to a service which would be ruined if it were itself divided by this type of question or problem.[3]

I am working very hard, primarily on the ideas and concepts represented in the American Assembly. I believe so earnestly in the free American system that my only purpose is to assure its health and permanency.[4]

There is little that I can add to the normal and classical phases of education; but possibly I can help bring into closer association the scholars and teachers of our country with the individuals who are engaged in the actual operation of our economy and government. By so doing, in the study and dissection of the vital problems of our time, I think there would be great promise of achieving logical and liberal answers to questions that plague us all. *Sincerely*

[1] For background on Williams, Eisenhower's high school principal and history teacher at Abilene, see Galambos, *Chief of Staff*, no. 1835.

[2] In his handwritten letter Williams had expressed his "great satisfaction" in knowing that his life had touched that of "General and President 'Ike'" (Oct. 23, 1950, EM).

[3] Williams hoped that Eisenhower would consider his former teacher's desire and that of millions of other true American's to "see you again render a great civic service . . . by accepting the presidential nomination in 1952." Williams said that he thoroughly believed the General's leadership could bring America back to the "rule of constitutional government and to safe and sane thinking and acting that was once the American way of life. . . ." On this question see also no. 1050.

[4] Williams had said that Eisenhower's plan to form the American Assembly would bring about a "sane solution" to America's national and international problems (Oct. 23, EM; concerning the Assembly see no. 1039).

1054   *Eisenhower Mss.*

TO GODFREY LOWELL CABOT   *November 3, 1950*

Dear Mr. Cabot: I am grateful for your letter of the 23rd.[1] I am particularly appreciative of your comments on Communism and, more specifically, I share your feeling about the law recently passed by Congress over the President's veto.[2]

In your letter I find that you feel incompetent to offer any advice concerning an Institute for War and Peace studies. It seems to me that, in connection with this particular project, there is one basic purpose that must be accomplished or we will be pursuing a remarkably stupid course. This is to provide an answer to the one simple question:

"How does a democracy of free people organize itself for the emergency of war so as to conduct that war efficiently, effectively and *economically* and in such fashion as to assure that whatever rights and freedoms pertaining to the individual that were voluntarily surrendered in the name of efficiency and for the duration, are returned in undiminished stature at the end of the war?"

So far as I can find out, no civilian group has ever thoroughly and completely studied this question in all of its ramifications.[3]

Thank you again for your courtesy in writing me.[4] *Sincerely*

[1] Cabot had met with Eisenhower in his office on October 10 (for background see no. 975). At that time the two men had discussed various Columbia programs aimed at increasing the university's usefulness to America. Later the General had sent Cabot documents on several of these programs, including an outline of the American Assembly (printed as no. 979); a memorandum from Philip Young, dean of the Graduate School of Business, dated October 13, 1950; the American Assembly announcement to Columbia's deans, directors, and department executives (no. 1039); and a prospectus for the establishment of a conference center at the Harriman estate (copies of the above are attached to memorandum, Sharp to Eisenhower, Oct. 18, 1950, CUF). Cabot's three-page letter (EM) was a reply to the General's request for comments.

[2] Cabot had said that he agreed with President Truman's veto of the enactment of Congress outlawing communism and was sorry to see the veto overridden. He believed that at no time since his graduation from Harvard (1882; he was now ninety years old) had there been less danger from the Communists, and he feared that this latest "unwise" law would draw to their ranks "many men whose sense of justice is outraged by making a label a crime" (for background on the controversial Internal Security Act of 1950, which required registration of Communist organizations, see U.S., *Statutes at Large*, vol. 64, pt. 1, pp. 987–1031; U.S., Congress, House, *Internal Security Act of 1950: Message from the President of the United States* 81st Cong., 2d sess., 1950, H. Doc. 708; and *New York Times*, Sept. 21, 23, 24, 1950).

[3] Eisenhower elaborates on these goals for the Institute of War and Peace Studies in no. 1056. The institute, which would open in 1952, would conduct extensive research on international affairs and U.S. national security policies.

[4] Eisenhower would next see Cabot at a dinner in Boston on November 22, 1950 (see no. 1094).

1055   *Columbia University Files*

To PAUL CLARE REINERT, S.J.   *November 3, 1950*

Dear President Reinert:[1] The psychological difficulty mentioned in your letter of the 30th should not, in my opinion, develop into a critical obstacle in the American Assembly.[2] This is because, first of all, I am a Midwesterner myself and, secondly, the last thing that we propose to permit will be any kind of geographical identification of brains and support that we intend to put into it. Our feeling is that no matter how earnestly we want to have similar institutes established elsewhere, someone should take the lead and be the pilot model in this new kind of development. Mistakes are bound to be made and each successive conference and program should show superiority in technique and in results over preceding ones. Nevertheless, I appreciate the force of your observation that these additional conference centers should be organized quickly.

With respect to your second observation, I have the feeling that at least a very minimum number of these conference centers should be so national in scope and so national in their composition that they could not possibly be accused of narrowness in findings or conclusions.[3] I am keenly aware of what you say about the difficulty of financing private institutions of learning and particularly financing an effort to strike out into such fields as that envisioned in the Assembly program. I most certainly hope that our fund raising efforts in this particular case will not cut severely into the sources of income of local institutions anywhere in the United States. But I strongly feel that, unless this whole broad effort gets started off on the basis that it is a far-reaching investigation into great national problems with almost no self-imposed limits whatsoever, the whole thing will be a miserable failure. I started out with this very strong conviction and I earnestly assure you that it is one point in the development that I consider vital to its success.

I am truly grateful for your letter and for the trouble you took to express your views on this matter that engages so much of my time and attention.

With warm personal regard, *Cordially*

[1] Reinert (Ph.D. University of Chicago 1944) had been president of Saint Louis University, St. Louis, Missouri, since 1949.

[2] Reinert had heard Eisenhower speak about the American Assembly plan at a luncheon given by David R. Calhoun, Jr., in St.Louis on October 24 (for background see nos. 1024 and 1039). In a letter of October 30, 1950 (CUF), Reinert had told Eisenhower that one of the difficulties with Columbia University's sponsorship of the American Assembly was that midwesterners "are frequently irked by the assumption that all the answers to our problems must be found somewhere along the Eastern seaboard." The result, thought Reinert, could be an "increasing lack of enthusiasm" elsewhere, and he suggested that similar projects be inaugurated in other parts of the United States.

[3] A second difficulty, according to Reinert, was that the American Assembly might drain off funds so great that other schools could not finance similar programs. Reinert thought it would be more fair to finance a project chiefly for the area in which it was located.

To George Frost Kennan   *November 3, 1950*

Dear George:[1] Because I was reluctant to hold you on the phone for an extended period this morning, I am writing this note to fill in one or two of the blank spots in what I expected to tell you.

First comes my explanation of why I had to ask you to see Dean Krout instead of making a personal engagement for myself. I leave for Texas on Monday evening and will not return to New York before the middle of November.[2]

I should like also to give a little bit of background about what Dean Krout will want to talk to you about, in the thought that this will make the meeting more purposeful and satisfying for you.[3]

We have been working on establishing an "Institute of Peace and War," although we have not fixed, irrevocably, on this particular name.[4] The purpose is to help in the development of peace and serve the interests of America, through carrying on searching and analytical studies in the causes, conduct and consequences of war. There are numbers of institutions that have made academic and sometimes realistic investigations into the political, social and economic causes of war and have, in numbers of instances, made appeals to mankind to strive toward the elimination of these causes. However, even this part of the proposed program has never been incorporated as an integral part of a broad and continuing study on the phenomenon of war, but has mostly involved sporadic or narrow-based effort.

Moreover, there are those who believe that war and conflict are so deeply imbedded in human nature that there is little to be gained by the kind of study just indicated. However, it is easy to point out that there is a very practical, specific purpose in the study of the *conduct* of war. Obviously, if the military and economic strength of a nation are important in preserving peace—or at least in winning a war—then it becomes vitally necessary that a democracy such as ours devise and design methods for the conduct of war that will achieve victory expeditiously, surely and economically. Here is a vast field for study because, while we have a long history in the organizing of a democracy to conduct war, we have never, in an emergency, had any plan that was more intelligently designed than could be produced almost on the spur of the moment and according to the whim of the individual then serving as President. This is simply not good enough.

On the social and other consequences of war (which presumably we wage only to protect a way of life), it is almost equally important that we have exact knowledge. If we fight to defend freedom, we should certainly plan all our emergency functions so that, at the end of the war, our individual liberties will emerge unimpaired.

With respect to some of the mechanics of the proposition, we are anxious to do much of the work in our Institute, on a Round-Table and Conference basis so that results achieved will not be merely filed away in dusty shelves. We want the whole thing to be a vital, dynamic movement and we have been greatly heartened by the readiness of numbers of individuals to support the proposition financially. The success of any such venture will of course depend, first and foremost, upon the qualifications and standing of its leader. This is the post that John Krout will want to talk to [you] about. Possibly, he may have one or two others of our people at the conference, especially Grayson Kirk, whom I think you know.[5]

As of this moment, we are thinking in terms of a five-year program, to be continued indefinitely if the whole project is as successful as we believe it will be.

There would seem to be little use in my taking up more of your time in an explanation of details. Assuming your interest, Dean Krout will go into all of these so far as we have been able to crystallize plans. We are very enthusiastic about it and I hope you will be. I am truly sorry that I cannot be here next Thursday.[6]

With warm personal regard, *Cordially*

[1] Kennan, while on leave from his duties as counselor to the Department of State, was affiliated with the Institute for Advanced Study at Princeton, New Jersey. For Eisenhower's opinion of Kennan see no. 721.

[2] On the trip see no. 1061.

[3] For background on John A. Krout, dean of the Faculty of Political Science, Philosophy and Pure Science, see no. 361. Krout had sent Eisenhower a four-page summary of plans titled "The Proposed Institute for War and Peace Studies at Columbia University," and he had marked portions of the first two pages, noting that "some of this might be helpful in drafting the Kennan letter." Krout had highlighted the part of the summary mentioning the relative neglect of military studies at colleges and universities in the United States. The opportunity was currently at hand to redress the situation, the summary continued, and with the support of General Eisenhower the idea would be given "scope and force." The plan still included the proposal that the American Military Institute and its journal, *Military Affairs*, come under the auspices of Columbia University (on the origin of that proposition see no. 665). Financial arrangements for the institute would begin on a five-year basis; at the end of that time the university would evaluate the work of the institute and make a decision concerning its future. The final part of the summary that Krout had deemed important listed the following five objectives: "1. Investigation of the causes and conduct of war and more particularly its impact on modern society. . . . 2. Research concerning the formulation of present and future military policies of the United States, especially as they influence foreign policy and international affairs. 3. Periodic conferences and seminars dealing with the relation of military policy to the maintenance of peace. 4. Collection of source material on military history, with special reference to the administrative and military experiences of the civilian and military leaders in World War II. 5. Publication of a quarterly journal and other papers relating to military studies." Copies of the plan are in EM and in CUF.

[4] It would come to be known as the Institute of War and Peace Studies in 1952

(see Gene M. Lyons and Louis Morton, *Schools for Strategy: Education and Research in National Security Affairs* [New York, 1965], pp. 134–36; and Cowan, *A History of the School of International Affairs*, pp. 90–92).

[5] Grayson L. Kirk, vice-president and provost, was a specialist in the field of international relations.

[6] For developments see no. 1116.

1057   *Eisenhower Mss.*

To Fred M. Manning   *November 3, 1950*
Personal

Dear Fred:[01] Thank you very much for the wonderful volume of pictures. They are far above excellent—more than this, they are pleasant reminders of a very enjoyable summer, not to say warm friendships.[2]

You have probably read in the papers about the possibility that I may have to go to Europe.[3] As you know, I would under no circumstances, utter the faintest word of protest against any assignment suggested for me by the Government. After all, I am first and foremost a soldier and I would consider it a disgrace not to respond instantly to any military call made upon me.

On the other side of the picture, the whole thing is so hazy and indefinite that it is far from certain that any such call will ever be sent to me. If it should come, then I will be forced to rely even more heavily on my friends than I have in the past for assistance in making certain that particular programs, to which I have given so much attention, will be successfully carried to completion. In the past, I have talked to you about many of these things and you will understand my feelings. I am quite ready to serve wherever the Government wants me to in the interest of this country to which all of us owe every single opportunity and thing we have. But I am convinced that there is so much for us to do *here* in the interest of our country that I am anxious that the great work go ahead regardless of the location of my particular post of duty.[4]

Thank you again for the wonderful pictures. I am looking forward eagerly to seeing you on the 12th.[5] *Cordially*

[1] For background on Manning see no. 545.

[2] Manning had sent the General an album of photographs of the Eisenhower family taken during their annual summer vacation in Denver, Colorado (see no. 805. See also Manning's letter to Eisenhower of Oct. 30, 1950, EM).

[3] In the same letter (Oct. 30) Manning had said that from what he had read in the papers, it appeared that "one of us will have to travel quite a distance to play golf together next summer."

[4] The "great work" to which Eisenhower refers was the newly announced American

Assembly plan to be sponsored by Columbia University (for background see no. 1039).
[5] Eisenhower's plans to see Manning on November 12 are discussed in no. 1044.

1058   *Eisenhower Mss.*

TO ARTHUR HAYS SULZBERGER   *November 3, 1950*

Dear Arthur:[1] So far as I am concerned, I think that it would be desirable to confer promptly upon both Carman and Finch the additional titles of Dean Emeritus.[2] This opinion is given without any knowledge whatsoever of tradition or former custom.[3] While I would not want to violate such things seriously, particularly if they were well established in such a University as this; from the human angle, I think it would be well to act soon.[4] *Cordially*

[1] Sulzberger was chairman of the Committee on Honors at Columbia University (for background see no. 694).
[2] For background on Harry J. Carman, former dean of Columbia College, and James K. Finch, former dean of the School of Engineering, see nos. 825 and 434, respectively. Both men had relinquished their administrative posts on June 30, 1950, in accordance with the school's new retirement program (see no. 124) and had subsequently resumed teaching duties at Columbia.
[3] As a matter of general practice, the emeritus designation was largely a routine matter. The president of the university referred a proposed list of retiring officers to the chairman of the Committee on Honors, who sought action on each nominee from the committee members. A report was then submitted to the trustees for formal action (Sulzberger to members of the Committee on Honors, Apr. 11, 1950, EM, Columbia Corr.).
[4] Both men would soon receive this honorary designation.

1059   *Eisenhower Mss.*

TO HOYT SANFORD VANDENBERG   *November 4, 1950*

Dear Van:[1] A man named Mr. Edelson is very anxious to see you for an interview. A friend of his—a Mr. Dan Gaines—has just visited my office on Mr. Edelson's behalf.[2] According to Mr. Gaines, Edelson is a supplier of ordnance items, including certain types of equipment for airplanes. Mr. Gaines desired to leave with me a voluminous report—that apparently emanated from Wright Field—concerning a particular item manufactured by Mr. Edelson's company. This I declined to accept and forward to you because of my utter lack of knowledge in such technical areas. However, I did take two short memoranda, more for the purpose of helping you identify Mr. Edelson by position and reputation than for any other reason. These I promised to send on to you, together with the statement made to me that Mr. Edelson has found it impossible to see you personally, even for 20 minutes.

I was given to understand that Mr. Edelson's standing in the business world is excellent and that his reputation as a supplier of ordnance items during World War II was of the highest. I cannot, of course, vouch for any of these statements and, consequently, I make no request whatsoever upon you. I merely send you these things in the belief that, provided Mr. Edelson's position conforms to the reports given to me, you might want to talk to him personally, if for no other reason than because of its possible public relations value.

It seems to me that someone is forever approaching me with the request to bring them favorably to your attention. If I am a bore, I apologize; in this case I am acting, as I have in most others, out of mere politeness and a feeling that you might possibly want to know about such things.

Whatever your decision, please *do not bother to answer this note*. The affair is none of my business. Except that there is always a possibility that there may be some truth to the man's story—that the Government will be the loser if it ignores the particular technical development he claims to have produced—I would not dream of bothering you with such a letter as this. *Sincerely*

[1] For background on Vandenberg see no. 73.
[2] Dan M. Gaines, an executive with Saginaw Furniture Shops of Chicago, Illinois, was a friend of Mrs. Eisenhower's. He had met with the General on November 3.

1060   *Eisenhower Mss.*

To Oscar Henry Brandon   *November 4, 1950*

Dear Mr. Brandon:[1] While I have had but a brief minute to devote to the query posed in your letter of the 26th, I have the feeling that your editor must have lifted a particular statement of mine from its context and so given to it a very restrictive meaning.[2] I am sending to you, therefore, a marked page out of my talk so that you can see that I am not laboring under the delusion that American forces are not needed in such a critical spot as the Western area of Europe.

You will notice that I said "The points where attack could conceivably fall are many." It is in recognition of this obvious truth that one may observe that no nation, however strong, can provide cordon defenses throughout the world. Any such attempt would tie down, irrevocably, all the available forces and would make the entire structure a brittle defense that could be broken easily.

I am sorry that I have not time to discuss in detail all the questions raised or implied in your letter. In such questions as you raise, there is scarcely any answer possible except where accompanied by exhaustive estimates and calculations that show the basis and the purpose of the conclusion. However, no explanation is needed for the statement that the defensive force at the disposal of the Supreme Commander of the Atlantic Forces in Europe should be equal to the task of defending that area until additional military power can be developed in the area or brought to it. On this particular point of the exact strength of this force in divisions, I have not consulted my colleagues who are actively studying it day by day.[3] Consequently, I say only that that strength should be obviously greater than it is now.

I regret that times does not permit a more satisfactory reply to your letter.[4] *Sincerely*

[1] Brandon was chief of the Washington Bureau of the *Sunday Times* (London); his letter to Eisenhower, dated October 26, 1950, is in EM.

[2] Brandon had asked Eisenhower to clarify certain points raised in the speech the General had delivered in Pittsburgh on October 19 (see no. 757). Brandon, noting that Eisenhower had warned against stationing "large-scale permanent" forces outside of the continental United States, asked the General whether he considered the five-to-ten division force currently envisaged as the American contribution to European defense as "large-scale." Brandon also asked Eisenhower, who had called for centrally located mobile strategic reserves, how many such mobile units would be necessary and whether the General thought these forces "could be shifted fast enough in the atomic-war-age when wars may be won within weeks."

[3] On September 9 President Truman had announced that he would increase the strength of American military forces stationed in Europe. His announcement followed presidential approval of a plan, worked out between the Department of State and the Defense Department, that contemplated providing from four to six additional American divisions for Europe (see Acheson, *Present at the Creation*, pp. 437–40; and State, *Foreign Relations, 1950*, vol. III, *Western Europe*, pp. 273–78. For developments see nos. 1112 and 1113).

[4] Brandon would thank Eisenhower in a letter of November 8 and would ask to meet the General in New York. In a staff-drafted reply of November 14 Eisenhower would explain that his crowded schedule made such a meeting impossible. Both letters are in EM.

1061   *Eisenhower Mss., Diaries*

DIARY   *November 6, 1950*

Today I start on a trip to Chicago, Dallas, Texas A&M, Houston, Oklahoma City, Chicago—Home. I travel in interests of American Assembly, a project on which I've been working almost 2 years, but under various names.[1] It's purpose is explained in a memo I'm attaching to this book.[2] It has appealed mightily to business men — and support, both moral & material has been fine. Right now we're working on the money for original capital (though I personally never ask for a dollar) and through my explanations to selected groups we've tagged, already, well over one hundred thousand.

Roy Cullen	25		
Mr. Queeny	25		
Mr. Olin	25		
Bob Woodruff	10	Boots Adams of Philipps Oil	
Pete Jones	10		50
Munitalp (Found.)	10	Tom Watson	35
Bob Kleberg	10		

(in thousands) are just a few of the larger contributors.[3] So I'm encouraged! Philip Young, in direct charge of the project, is a splendid leader![4]

The Allied Conference adjourned in Washington without reaching a conclusion on the German problem. So far as I'm concerned I shall go ahead on my current tasks and let the future (particularly the military future) take care of itself.[5]

A couple of weeks ago Mr. Dewey announced that if elected Governor of NY this year he would try to get the N.Y. Rep. Delegation to urge me as Rep. Candidate for Pres. in 1952. The storm broke out again — within the past few days it has subsided publicly — but in private conversation it never dies.[6]

Have urged universal military service of 2 years duration, without pay, for all 18 year olds. Jim Conant is in general agreement. Marshall does *not* agree, *ditto Lovett.*[7] While sometime I wonder whether I do not exaggerate in my own mind the seriousness of the world situation, I likewise am not certain that some of our office holders are not either complacent or too slow to treat the American people with the _bald_ facts of the world situation. Some of these officials think we can _buy_ security; solvency and security can scarcely be separated — yet I hear talk of 55 billion a year for _several_ years.[8] Tragic.

In Washington I feel that there is some hysteria — certainly one does not gain a lot of confidence when it is hinted that he will probably have to undertake a very serious & prolonged assignment in Europe in order to preserve American security and can obtain no satisfactory answers to such questions as how many divisions, groups and ships are involved in America's planned building programs.[9] Vagueness seems to be no crime or fault — the answer is "In Europe Eisenhower can solve all the problems." Sweet — but valuable only as an opiate! Goddamit — is there no desire to _know_ where we are going. If Forrestal had only had the _stamina_ to equal his honesty and sense!![10] And poor H.S.T.[11] — a fine man who, in the middle of a stormy lake, knows nothing of swimming.

Yet a lot of drowning people are forced to look to him as a life guard. If his wisdom could only equal his good intent!!

Marshall—the best public servant of the lot obviously wants to quit (I don't blame him—he has no children.)

[1] Eisenhower would visit Chicago twice during a week-long trip designed to interest leaders in business and education in Columbia's American Assembly conference plan. On November 7 he would attend a luncheon given for him at the Chicago Club by Rawleigh Warner, chairman of the board of the Pure Oil Company. Later the same day his friend Jerry D. Brandon would host a cocktail party at the same club (correspondence concerning the arrangements for the Warner and Brandon parties, including guest lists, is in EM). On his return to Chicago on November 13 Eisenhower would be honored at a luncheon given by Jonathan Catlett Gibson, vice-president and general counsel, Atchison, Topeka, and Santa Fe Railway Company, Chicago (Gibson's guest list is also in EM. For more information about Eisenhower's visits to Texas and Oklahoma in November 1950 see nos. 895, 989, 1017, 1022, and 1025. See also the Chronology in this volume).

[2] The memo to which Eisenhower refers is not attached to his diary, but it was probably one of two documents we have published as nos. 826 and 1039.

[3] For background on Hugh Roy Cullen see nos. 602 and 989. Four months later Eisenhower would write this comment next to Cullen's name in the diary entry: "(Re-neged) (So far as I know, he has never paid this: March '51)." Edgar Monsanto Queeny was chairman of the board of the Monsanto Chemical Company, St. Louis; his pledge was made through the Monsanto Charitable Trust. For background on John M. Olin see no. 885; on Robert W. Woodruff see no. 258; and on William Alton "Pete" Jones see no. 388. The Munitalp Foundation, of New York City, whose purpose it was to foster pure research in meteorology, had pledged support for the conference plan through a Columbia Associate, Edward H. Green. In October 1950 Green had been named chairman of the Columbia Association Committee for the American Assembly; he was also chairman of the University Development Plan Committee (see Eisenhower to Green, Oct. 19, 1950, EM; for more on Green see no. 488). For background on Robert J. Kleberg, Jr., see nos. 623 and 942; on Kenneth S. "Boots" Adams, of the Phillips Petroleum Company, see no. 1021; and on Tom Watson see no. 31. Correspondence concerning individual contributions from people listed here is in EM, American Assembly.

[4] Young was dean of Columbia's Graduate School of Business and Executive Director of the American Assembly.

[5] The NATO defense minister's meeting had adjourned without reaching a decision about either German rearmament or the person who should command the NATO forces (see no. 1050. For developments see nos. 1112, 1113, and 1134).

[6] On October 15 New York Governor Thomas E. Dewey had endorsed Eisenhower for President (see nos. 1040 and 1041).

[7] Eisenhower had long advocated compulsory military service for American men (see nos. 984 and 985). In September and October he had written Harvard University President James B. Conant and Secretary of Defense George C. Marshall on this subject (see nos. 1006 and 1042). Marshall and Deputy Secretary of Defense (designate) Robert A. Lovett were, however, concerned about the public opposition to such a measure.

[8] In September President Truman had approved the proposed rearmament program outlined in NSC 68 (a reexamination of American policy in light of the Russian acquisition of nuclear weapons). NSC 68 called for a massive build-up of the military strength of the United States and its allies. Estimated costs for the first

year of the program totaled $50 billion; and on November 6 the *New York Times* published a report that the FY51 defense budget would be $55 billion (see Paul Y. Hammond, "NSC-68: Prologue to Rearmament," in *Strategy, Politics, and Defense Budgets*, by Warner R. Schilling, Paul Y. Hammond, and Glenn H. Snyder [1962; reprint ed., New York, 1966], pp. 343–44; Etzold and Gaddis, *Containment*, pp. 383–442; State, *Foreign Relations, 1950*, vol. I, *National Security Affairs; Foreign Economic Policy*, pp. 400, 425–32; and *New York Times*, Nov. 6, 1950).

[9] See no. 1045. Eisenhower had met with the President, Defense Department officials, and military leaders in Washington on October 28–29; they had probably discussed the size of the American commitment to European defense at that time (see also State, *Foreign Relations, 1950*, vol. I, *National Security Affairs; Foreign Economic Policy*, pp. 474–77, 578–80).

[10] James V. Forrestal (see no. 425).

[11] President Harry S. Truman.

1062   *Eisenhower Mss.*

TO CLIFFORD ROBERTS   *November 6, 1950*

Dear Cliff:[1] Supplementing our conversations on the future of the American Assembly in the event that I should again be called upon to return, at least temporarily, to military service, I send you this letter to make of record what I have already told you verbally.[2]

To my mind the success of the plan will become even more important to us all, if America should assume Command responsibilities for the defense of Western Europe. Such action would impose upon us a still greater need for understanding the vital factors at work both for and against us in the world; an understanding that we must obtain or suffer the risk of grave consequences. The concept of the American Assembly will increase in importance according to the duration and intensity of the tensions under which we live.

In this situation I, of course, facing the possibility of returning to uniform must turn to and depend upon my friends even more completely than I have in the past—and I have always because of their loyalty and understanding, depended upon them without stint. If I do have to lay aside, temporarily, official connection with the plan, it will be a wonderful thing to know that all its adherents are more than ever determined upon its success.

Incidentally, I have already suggested to Philip Young, who will continue as the personal and immediate leader of the whole project, the possibility of holding the first conference of the Assembly on some subject connected with American responsibilities in Western Europe. Such a decision would give me specific reason for a hasty visit to the

United States (if I should then be abroad) to participate in the opening of the Assembly. I'd like to see it off to its actual start.[3] *As ever*

[1] For background on Roberts see no. 69.
[2] For background on the American Assembly conference plan see no. 1039, on Eisenhower's concern about a return to military service see no. 1045. Eisenhower and Roberts had played golf the afternoon of November 2. Later that same day Roberts had had dinner and played bridge with Eisenhower and several other friends.
[3] Young was dean of Columbia's Graduate School of Business and the Executive Director of the American Assembly. "The Relationship of the United States to Western Europe" would be the subject of the first session of the American Assembly in the spring of 1951, but Eisenhower, by then Supreme Commander, Allied Powers, Europe, would not be able to attend (see *New York Times*, May 22, 1951).

1063   *Eisenhower Mss.*

TO MERRILL MUELLER   *November 6, 1950*

Dear Red: Thank you very much for the letter that followed your wire of a few days ago.[1] I have your name on my list—if ever I have to go back in uniform, there is bound to be some special niche in the organization that you could fill adequately.

I have no idea when, if ever, I may be called. So don't hold your breath waiting for a message.[2]

Needless to say, I am flattered—I mean proud—that you should send to me such an offer of service. *Cordially*

[1] Mueller, a news broadcaster for NBC, had been a correspondent in Europe during World War II (for background see *Eisenhower Papers*, vols. I–IX). In his wire of October 27 and his letter of the twenty-eighth (EM) Mueller had requested an assignment in Europe as Eisenhower's aide. On the General's impending appointment as NATO Supreme Commander see no. 1045.
[2] Mueller wrote letters of November 1 and 8 (EM) repeating his offer of service. Eisenhower would reply in a note of November 15 (EM) that there was no additional news about the NATO job. For developments see no. 1135.

1064   *Eisenhower Mss.*

TO LAWRENCE B. YOUNG   *November 6, 1950*

Dear Mr. Young:[01] Thank you very much for your thoughtful letter. Perhaps you are right about the German situation; I certainly claim no superior value for my views. However, I cannot agree with the first part of your letter—even though I subscribe wholeheartedly to your final paragraph.[2]

I have great sympathy for the French attitude and I think I can understand it. But I honestly believe that the defense of Western Europe presents such a difficult political-military problem that every nation concerned will have to make *some* concessions (and this most certainly includes the Western Germans) before success is in sight.[3]

Because of the complexities and the conflicting considerations inherent in the whole situation, there seems to be little use trying to present, in a letter, an estimate of current requirements. Perhaps some day you and I may run into each other whereupon we can have a free exchange of views.

I cannot fail to remark that I derived real encouragement from the clear evidence your letter brings that thoughtful Americans are giving their earnest attention to the broad and vital questions that are so important to the world's peace and security. *Sincerely*

[1] Young was an official of Brennan Publications, printers and publishers of several newspapers in the county of Fairfield, Connecticut.

[2] In his undated letter (EM) Young said that he supported the French government's opposition to the creation of large units of West German troops for a European defense force. Young said that he would take the French proposals (the Pleven Plan [see no. 1045]) a step further, however, and allow only individual German enlistments, distributed piecemeal throughout the various armies of the force. His last paragraph concluded: "We have fought German militarism for the total of nine years in the twentieth century at a great sacrifice of lives and property. We shouldn't give nationalism a chance to rise up again in Europe."

[3] For background on the problems of Western European defense see no. 1045. The French cabinet would eventually accept a compromise plan and agree to establish German combat teams organized in mixed divisions, with not more than one team in any division of an integrated Atlantic force (instead of a European army) under a supreme commander. On the following day (Dec. 7) the North Atlantic Council deputies would agree to this plan for the immediate formation of integrated military forces for the Atlantic Alliance (*New York Times*, Dec. 7, 8; see also no. 1112, n. 3). In the meantime, West German Chancellor Konrad Adenauer had insisted on greater equality as the price of Germany's participation in European defense. The West Germans pointed out that their lives and territory would be endangered first in the event of a Soviet attack, and they objected to the terms of the French compromise plan (*New York Times*, Dec. 1, 7, 8. For more on the opposition to German rearmament see Morton A. Kaplan, *The Rationale for NATO: European Collective Security—Past and Future* [Washington, D.C., 1973], pp. 15–23; and James L. Richardson, *Germany and the Atlantic Alliance: The Interaction of Strategy and Politics* [Cambridge, Mass., 1966], pp. 17–23. For subsequent developments see nos. 1112 and 1113).

To Kenneth William Dobson Strong   *November 6, 1950*
Personal

Dear Kenneth: My long delay in answering your letter of the 29th was occasioned by the hope that I would find time to give you the serious answer it deserves.[1] At this moment, however, I have finally decided that I should make some acknowledgment even though the pressure on my time seems never to lessen.

Possibly you know something of the political talks that have been proceeding, with one of their aims—the setting up of a Supreme Commander in Europe. If this comes about, it can easily set in motion a series of circumstances that could easily bring you and me together once more.[2] This particular result would be at least one bright spot in an otherwise drab outlook.

I do not concur most emphatically in the two paragraphs in the middle of your first page where you expressed your opinion about Russia's intentions and in the next paragraph where you urged that we never lose sight of our long term objectives.[3]

Recently I spent two or three days in Washington, during which time I saw Beetle. He is very thin but seems to retain his old fire and spirit. I think that he believes he is fully recovered in health, but it is difficult for me to accept his opinion at face value. He always believed that he was perfectly healthy, even just before he had to undergo two major operations. But I must say that I feel easier with our C.I.A. at least in the hands of such an able individual.[4] *Cordially*

---

[1] For background on Eisenhower's wartime associate Strong see no. 480. In his letter of September 29 (EM) Strong had said that the Korean War would have "a profound influence and on the whole I think for the good." The reverses suffered by the North Koreans would, Strong thought, "tend to prove that war by proxy does not pay and that it is not a great bargain to be placed in the position of acting as Russia's agent."

[2] Eisenhower had learned that he would probably be named the commander of NATO forces in Europe (see no. 1045). Strong had written that he had "no doubt" that eventually he and other World War II comrades of Eisenhower's would have the pleasure of serving with the General again. Strong, Director of the Joint Intelligence Bureau of the Ministry of Defence in London, would, however, not join Eisenhower at SHAPE (see no. 865; see also Slim to Eisenhower, Feb. 14, 1952, and Eisenhower to Slim, Mar. 15, 1952, in EM).

[3] Strong feared "the ignorance of the men in the Kremlin"; he also was afraid of "some miscalculation by Stalin and his friends which may precipitate world war." He did not think that it was in the interest of the Soviet Union to go to war, but he felt that dictatorship made it "impossible to make any firm calculations about their actions." Strong believed that the Western allies should stress the "defensive nature of our re-armament" and avoid provocation. In his opinion, "real danger" from the Soviet Union would come when its power had grown to the extent that Russia could "dominate the world."

[4] On General Walter Bedell Smith, Director of the Central Intelligence Agency, see nos. 950 and 1071. Strong's reply to this letter, dated November 25, is in EM.

1066   *Eisenhower Mss.*

TO MARCELLUS HARTLEY DODGE   *November 6, 1950*

Dear Marcy:[1] I am, of course, grateful for all the kindnesses you showed to my son and his companions, following the unfortunate automobile accident near Morristown.[2] Since then I have learned that you got out of a sick bed to do it and this distresses me mightily. I had gotten on the phone to learn whether there was any use of my going to Morristown in person or whether I should wait until the group returned to West Point. I was doing this telephoning when you called, and the confidence inspired by the knowledge that you were on the job determined me not to make the trip. I cannot tell you how distressed I am, and I hope that any ill effects you suffered will be temporary only.[3]

I leave for Texas this evening but will be back by the fifteenth.[4]

George Warren brought me your note and I will not raise the question of naming a man for Bill Donovan's Committee.[5]

With best wishes for your complete and quick recovery, *Cordially*

[1] Dodge, clerk of the trustees of Columbia University, lived at Giralda Farms in Madison, New Jersey (for background on him see no. 41).

[2] Captain John S. D. Eisenhower, currently stationed at the U.S. Military Academy in West Point, had been slightly injured in an automobile collision near Morristown, New Jersey, while en route with three other Army officers to attend the Army-Pennsylvania football game in Philadelphia. An account of the incident on the morning of November 4 appeared in the *New York Times* on November 5, 1950.

[3] Dodge would thank Eisenhower for his letter and assure him that "the little bit that I was able to do when the boys were hurt means nothing. . . . All in all the whole thing turned out very fortunately" (Nov. 9, EM). On the day of the accident Dodge had sent the General the names of the attending physician and superintendent at the Morristown Memorial Hospital. Eisenhower's letters of appreciation to Frank H. Pinckney, M.D., and Robert G. Boyd, both dated November 6, 1950, are in EM.

[4] Eisenhower would leave New York at 6:45 P.M. to begin an eight-day visit to numerous cities in the Southwest on behalf of Columbia's American Assembly project (see no. 1061).

[5] George E. Warren was associate clerk of the board of trustees. The trustees were to meet later that afternoon, and Dodge had asked Eisenhower to put off the issue of authorizing the selection of an individual for Major General William J. Donovan's development council (Nov. 4, EM). Concerning the formation of and appointments to this council see no. 930.

To Earl Henry Blaik

Dear Red:[1] In our great concern about our son on Saturday evening, I doubt that I was very emphatic in expressing my appreciation for the courtesy of your telephone call. I am sure, however, that you understand how good it makes me feel to know that our friends, and particularly one as busy as you must have been on Saturday evening, should be concerned about us.[2]

This evening I leave for Texas, to return about the 15th.[3] Possibly after that, I may find a free afternoon to run up for a brief practice. If this opportunity should arise, I will telephone you first. I should very much like to see the gang at a day's workout. I enjoy those more than I do games because I find that I am far too partisan for my own good. In fact, that was one reason that I was so delighted when the Army finally let me off my amateurish coaching efforts years ago.[4]

All the best to you and yours, and thank you once more. *Cordially*

[1] Blaik was the head football coach at the U.S. Military Academy (for more on Blaik and his son Robert, the Army team's quarterback, see no. 250; and *Saturday Evening Post*, Oct. 7, 1950).

[2] Concerning John Eisenhower's accident see the preceding document. Blaik had later coached his team to a 28–13 victory over Penn (see *New York Times*, Nov. 5, 1950).

[3] On the trip see no. 1061.

[4] Early in his military career the General had coached the junior varsity at West Point, and later he had held several other coaching jobs (see *At Ease*, pp. 23, 121–22, 180, 196–98 and 203–4; Lyon, *Portrait of the Hero*, pp. 44–49; and no. 250). The General had last attended an Army football game on October 14, when the cadets had rallied to a hard-fought 27–6 victory over Michigan (*New York Times*, Oct. 15, 1950). For further developments see no. 1133.

To Clifford Roberts

Dear Cliff:[1] I am just starting in to write a note to each of the donors named on the list you handed me Sunday evening.[2] Nothing could have given me greater satisfaction than such concrete evidence that my good friends approve of the efforts we here are trying to make in the interests of American progress—I was so in danger of becoming emotional at the party that I was, deliberately, as matter of fact as I could be in responding to your little presentation talk.

But you must know how I felt.

As I told you, I had completed a letter to you on Sunday. Now it appears completely out of date, but I shall send it along anyway just as if I had mailed it before you broke the good news at your wonderful party.[3]

Incidentaliy, you were completely successful in keeping from my knowledge any possible hint of what was to be expected. I never dreamed that the party would turn into such a fine thing for Columbia.

I discovered that, on the list of names you provided me, there are those of a few men with whom I am not acquainted. This includes all of the non-member subscriptions and, in addition, I cannot remember meeting Mr. Osborne, Mr. Marks or Mr. Staley.[4]

For your own generous donation, my everlasting and sincere thanks.

Phil Young[5] is out of town, but this morning I told my other principal associates up here about your efforts and they were completely delighted, of course. *As ever*

[1] For background on Roberts see no. 69.

[2] On Sunday, November 5, Roberts had given a joint birthday party for Dwight and Mamie Eisenhower in the petit salon of the Park Lane Hotel in New York City. The General's birthday was October 14, Mrs. Eisenhower's November 14. Roberts had surprised the General by presenting to him pledges totaling $50,800 from twenty-five donors to the American Assembly conference plan. A committee of solicitors, all friends of Eisenhower's and all members of the Augusta National Golf Club, had included (in addition to Roberts) W. Alton Jones, Ellis D. Slater, William E. Robinson, Clarence J. Schoo, Douglas M. Black, Barry T. Leithead, and Robert W. Woodruff (correspondence concerning the committee and subscription reports from Roberts are in EM, American Assembly Corr., and in EM, Roberts Corr. For background on the Assembly see no. 1039).

[3] See no. 1062.

[4] The non-member subscriptions, that is, pledges from those who were not members of the Augusta National Golf Club, were made by John R. Miller of Oakland, California, and H. W. Gillen, M. J. Meehan, and Winston Paul, all of New York City. Those whom Eisenhower could not remember meeting were W. Irving Osborne, Jr., of Chicago, and Laurence M. Marks and Thomas F. Staley, both of New York City. Eisenhower would send letters of appreciation to all of the donors (all in EM. See also Roberts's report, Augusta National Committee, EM, American Assembly Corr.).

[5] Philip Young was Executive Director of the American Assembly.

1069   *Eisenhower Mss.*

To John Hersey Michaelis   *November 6, 1950*

Dear Mike: I cannot tell you how delighted I am to have your letter. Recently, Mamie had one from your good wife and, additionally, I have been able to keep up with some of your doings through the newspapers. Everything that you have done has made us both very proud. But I felt that you were far too busy fighting to be concerned with correspondence.[1]

The last few days have brought us news of another threat in North Korea, after General MacArthur's messages had shown that he believed the whole mess to be largely over.[2] I do hope that the senseless bloodshed can soon stop. But if we have to be in it, I cannot tell you how gratified I am that soldiers of the caliber of yourself and Johnny Walker, and others like you, are on the job.[3]

Of course, when I advised you to go on Foreign Service while still young, I had no idea that your doing so would put you in the middle of a full-fledged war.[4] As long as it had to be fought, I am sure that you are delighted you could, as a professional soldier, participate. But I do urge you to take care of yourself—no nation is ever rich enough in good leaders to spare any of them.

You were right in your assumption about the nagging effect of the constantly repeated suggestions of a political career for me. Right now, however, the real prospect is that I shall go sooner or later to Europe. There, I shall be expected to organize defensive forces. Quite naturally, after that part of the work is done, there will be plenty of distinguished soldiers volunteering for the job of commander; it is just the drudgery and heartaches of organizing such a force that the boys are so scared of. I think, though, that there are a number of political decisions yet to reach before they want to name a Supreme Commander for the Western Powers.[5]

I do hope that Mary and your youngster are in fine health. Of course, they cannot be enjoying life too much with you still on the battlefront. But they, at least, just like all your friends, have a special reason for being proud of you.

Mamie joins me in very warm regards.

Again, I say, take care of yourself. *Cordially*

[1] In his letter of October 24 (EM) Colonel Michaelis, commander of the 27th Regiment of the 25th Division of the U.S. Eighth Army in Korea, had reported on his recent experiences in the Far East. "The tour in Japan was intensely interesting and Korea, now that it has reached the final stages, has presented a challenge and offered opportunities rarely encountered." Michaelis's regiment had won fame for stopping the enemy's attempts to penetrate the U.N. defensive perimeter during the previous summer (see *New York Times*, Aug. 28, 1950).
[2] Since the U.N. landings at Inchon, South Korea, in mid-September the North Koreans had been in retreat northward toward the border with Manchuria (for background see no. 1046). On October 21 General of the Army Douglas MacArthur had told newsmen that the war was coming to an end (see *New York Times*, Oct. 21, 1950). On October 25, however, as the U.N. forces approached the border, they were engaged in combat by Chinese Communist troops, whose intervention halted the U.N. advance; the number of U.N. troops wounded or killed then rose

from the rate of forty per day in October to 326 per day during the first week of
November (see Schnabel, *Policy and Direction*, pp. 233–39).
[3] Lieutenant General Walton H. "Johnny" Walker commanded the U.S. Eighth
Army in Korea (for background see no. 32).
[4] In his letter Michaelis had recalled Eisenhower's advice in 1948, when he was
Eisenhower's aide (see Galambos, *Chief of Staff*).
[5] For background see no. 1045.

1070   *Eisenhower Mss.*

To ———   *November 6, 1950*

Dear ———: Bedell and I have just had a long talk on the telephone.
As the law now stands, it is not possible for an officer, retired for other
than physical disability, to have a governmental position provided his
retirement pay is more than $2500.[1] There is no provision in the law
for waiving of retired pay by the officer.
Consequently, and if [unless?] Bedell asks for some adjustment in
the law, he cannot employ you in the C.I.A.
Bedell is well aware of your qualifications for the kind of work he
has to do and he suggested that I remind you to be sure to see him
when you come to Washington in the next two or three weeks—and
this, in spite of the fact that, at this moment, he cannot offer you
employment.[2]
Naturally, I am distressed to hear of the death of your fine son.[3] The
older I grow the more I hate the stupidity that permits wars; the only
thing I hate more are the people, like those in the Kremlin, that are
always ready to thrust war upon a long-suffering humanity. You will
have, of course, many fine memories of your boy, but I know from
bitter experience what a burden it is you are carrying.[4] You will have
the sympathy and support of all your old friends but there is little that
anyone can say or do to help.
Do not fail to call on me any time you think I can be useful to you.
While I am traveling a great deal these days and shall be absent from
my office for the next 10, messages directed here will always reach
me.[5]
I am sorry that my reply from Bedell could not be more immediately
encouraging, but I think the case is far from hopeless.[6] *Cordially*

[1] The retired officer in question had asked Eisenhower in September 1950 to
recommend him for a job with the CIA (for background see no. 988). Lieutenant
General Walter Bedell Smith, Director of the CIA, had informed the officer
recently that according to a ruling of the Comptroller General, an officer who
retired for reasons other than physical disability and whose retirement pay exceeded

twenty-five hundred dollars per year could not be employed by the CIA. The officer had insisted nevertheless in a letter of November 4 (EM) that Smith had not been "fully advised as to the means of taking me on if he really wants me."
[2] The officer in question had maintained that he had been highly successful in his previous "operational experience with C.I.A. work" and that he could render greater service to the government in the CIA than in any other agency. He had asked Eisenhower to contact Smith again "if you should consider that the situation warrants."
[3] This officer's son, also an Army officer, had died on September 21, 1950, of wounds received in combat in Korea. The father had written, "You will remember him as the handsome lad to whom you presented one of the three cigarette boxes on behalf of the Class of '15 in June."
[4] On the death of the Eisenhowers' first-born son see no. 37, n. 7.
[5] On the trip see no. 1061.
[6] The officer in question would thank Eisenhower in a letter of November 20 (EM), adding that the Comptroller General "always was a little cantankerous cuss with his decisions." He said, however, that he remained confident that the CIA could utilize his abilities and that he planned to see Smith in the near future.

1071   *Eisenhower Mss.*

To Francis Wilfred De Guingand   *November 15, 1950*

Dear Freddie:[1] No command has yet been offered me and so there is nothing definite to say in response to your nice, and most welcome, letter.[2] I think that there is to be no command set up in Europe, until the needful political agreements have been reached. I am not even aware of the progress of these negotiations and so you can understand how truly impossible it is for me to guess what is to happen to me.[3]

I saw Bedell recently and while I rather think he dislikes his Intelligence job, he does realize that it is vitally important to us to get that particular activity on the rails. Consequently, he is working very hard.[4] He has not recovered his weight following upon the two serious operations he had some months back. And, even if the President were willing to let him go, I doubt that he would be fit for extended field service. (Of course, he does *not* agree with us—Bedell always thinks he is as strong and healthy as a 25-year old.)[5]

If anything positive develops, I shall most certainly write to you about the prospects. In the meantime, good luck and warm regards. *Sincerely*

[1] De Guingand presently held a position with a firm in Johannesburg, South Africa (for background see *Eisenhower Papers*, vols. I–IX).
[2] De Guingand, who had learned the news from a press report, had congratulated Eisenhower on his "unselfish" acceptance of the post as commander in Western Europe. He wished the General every success in "the call which is so necessary

for the West" (Nov. 10, 1950, EM. See *The Times* [London] and *New York Times*, Nov. 9, 1950).

[3] Eisenhower's frustrations concerning his role in the Atlantic Union are discussed in no. 1045; for his official appointment as head of NATO see no. 1134.

[4] Eisenhower had last seen Walter Bedell Smith, Director of the Central Intelligence Agency, on October 30 in Washington, D.C. (for background see no. 950).

[5] On Smith's medical problems see nos. 745 and 776. De Guingand had asked about the possibility of Smith's rejoining Eisenhower in Europe (Nov. 10, EM). This was not to be the case, however, as Smith would remain at his post as CIA Director until 1953 (concerning those who would accompany the General see no. 816, n. 4).

1072   *Eisenhower Mss.*

To George Catlett Marshall   *November 15, 1950*

Dear General: While I, of course, cannot recall the exact terms I used in which to express my convictions to you concerning rejuvenation of French morale, I give you the following as a succinct summing up of my thinking.[1]

"Criticism of the American program for Aid to Europe is shooting wide of the mark when it is based on the allegation that there is no fighting spirit left in Western Europe. The true ultimate purpose of that program is to recreate and sustain Western European morale. When this has been accomplished, the whole problem will have been successfully met. This applies with peculiar force to France.[2]

"The French have seen their army, in which they took tremendous pride, dismally defeated and destroyed. This, followed by an occupation that made further inroads into their national pride, has left them, understandably, with a feeling of helplessness bordering upon complete defeatism. So France becomes an area of weakness, rather than of strength, in any defensive structure until this psychological swamp has been drained.[3]

"What is needed is for the French to review their own history, particularly that of the French Revolutionary days even preceding the emergence, in 1796, of Napoleon as a leader. With all the thrones of Europe seeing their positions in danger by the rights of self-government, there was a spontaneous military movement against France that gave her almost no respite from war and presented a military picture that — by any realistic evaluation — was dark indeed for the French.

"But the French reaction was magnificent. Its universal service law of that time is a model of exactitude and of elan. Its very language was calculated to inspire Frenchmen to the defense of their fatherland, and their performance on the battlefield was magnificent proof of what this kind of morale can do.[4]

"The French need to remind themselves that their former magnificence as a nation flowered in and was a direct outgrowth of peril, danger and disaster. They should recall to their minds their own World War I performances at Verdun and on the Marne. There are brilliant spots, also, even in their record of World War II. Their fighting in Italy was of the highest order, and the French battles around Belfort were characterized as much by the elan and morale of the participating French forces as by the difficulties under which they fought.[5] These are the things on which they must now think and ponder because, in doing so, they will unconsciously relate themselves to the heroic figures of their own military history and they will realize that what they have done before *they can now do.*"

I have a very lively fear, as I finish this dictation, that I have lost the particular emphasis in this subject which apparently intrigued you at your apartment a couple of weeks ago. For this reason I have put it down at possibly greater length than I must have said it then. In this way you can cut őut and piece together whatever you may find of usefulness in this attempt. *Very sincerely*

---

[1] Eisenhower had met with Secretary of Defense Marshall in Washington, D.C., on October 29; at that time they had discussed the problem of French morale. On November 15 Eisenhower had telephoned Marshall concerning another matter, and during their conversation Marshall had asked Eisenhower to put his views on this subject in writing.

On September 28 the *New York Times* had published a report that the Europeans were not acting vigorously to defend themselves. This "feeling of apathy or futility" seemed to be particularly strong in France, where American diplomats, politicians, and soldiers had been concerned about the state of French morale (for background see no. 303; and Forrestal, *Diaries*, pp. 500–502. See also State, *Foreign Relations, 1950*, vol. III *Western Europe*, pp. 358–61, 1369–72, 1379–80, 1383–87; U.S., Congress, Senate, Committee on Appropriations, *Conditions in Europe in the Autumn of 1950: Report of the Special Subcommittee on Foreign Economic Co-operation*, 82d Cong., 1st sess., 1951, pp. 2–4, also in EM, Miscellaneous Routine Corr., "Report—Subcommittee on Foreign Economic Cooperation"; U.S., Congress, Senate, Committee on Foreign Relations, *Executive Sessions of the Senate Foreign Relations Committee (Historical Series)*, vol. II, *Eighty-first Congress: First and Second Sessions, 1949–50* [Washington, D.C., 1976], pp. 411–12, 431; U.S., Congress, Senate, Committee on Foreign Relations and Committee on Armed Services, *Military Assistance Program, 1949: Hearings on S. 2388*, 81st Cong., 1st sess., 1949, pp. 109, 398–99; C. L. Sulzberger, *A Long Row of Candles: Memoirs and Diaries [1934–1954]* [New York, 1969], pp. 598–99; and U.S. Department of State, *Foreign Relations of the United States, 1951*, 7 vols. [Washington, D.C., 1979–82], vol. III, *European Security and the German Question*, pt. 1 [1982], pp. 405, 421).

[2] In November Senator Robert A. Taft (see no. 104, n. 1) had begun to raise doubts about the wisdom of sending American troops and aid to Europe (see *New York Times*, November 11, 14, 1950).

[3] For a description of the French Army after its defeat in 1940 see La Gorce, *The French Army*, pp. 314–74.
[4] For a brief treatment of the wars that followed the French Revolution see Theodore Ropp, *War in the Modern World* (Durham, N.C., 1959), pp. 85–99; see also Crane Brinton, Gordon A. Craig, and Felix Gilbert, "Jomini," in *Makers of Modern Strategy: Military Thought from Machiavelli to Hitler*, ed. Edward Mead Earle (Princeton, 1943), pp. 77–92.
[5] On the battle of the Marne see Robert B. Asprey, *The First Battle of the Marne* (Philadelphia, 1962); and Henri Isselin, *The Battle of the Marne* (Garden City, N.Y., 1966). On Verdun see Alistair Horne, *The Price of Glory: Verdun, 1916* (London, 1962). For the history of the French Army in Europe after 1942 see Chandler, *War Years*; Clark, *Calculated Risk*; Charles de Gaulle, *The War Memoirs of Charles de Gaulle*, 3 vols. (New York, 1955–60), vol. II, *Unity, 1942–44*, (1959) vol. III, *Salvation, 1944–46* (1960), both trans. Richard Howard; and Marcel Vigneras, *Rearming the French*, U.S. Army in World War II, ed. Kent Roberts Greenfield (Washington, D.C., 1957).

1073   *Eisenhower Mss.*

To George Catlett Marshall   *November 15, 1950*

Dear General:[1] I understand that you are having some of the same worries that we had in World War II with respect to the thoroughness of the average young American's understanding of our national history and concepts and of his own duties as a citizen.

For some two years Columbia University has been developing a practical course in Citizenship for inclusion in the high school curricula of the nation. While the whole movement is, to some extent, still in the project stage, we have made great progress and real success has been reported from the cities where pilot courses have been installed. In any event, we have, as a result of all this work, a very fine central group of scholars and leaders — individuals who might be of inestimable value to the Services in designing an effective and highly concentrated course in Citizenship.[2]

Teachers College of Columbia University would be delighted to explore the situation with responsible officers in the Service. I suggest that a small conference be arranged by having someone contact Dr. William S. Vincent, Teachers College, Columbia University. At this first conference only one or two senior Training or Educational officers from each Service should attend. In this way, it can be quickly determined whether or not our personnel will be able to help along practical and useful lines. I assure you again that, if this should prove to be the case, we should all be highly pleased.[3] *Sincerely*

[1] General Marshall was currently Secretary of Defense (for background see nos. 75 and 982).
[2] On the Citizenship Education Project, a program organized to increase civic pride among high school students, see no. 727. The project had been well received in eight cities in New York, New Jersey, Connecticut, and Pennsylvania, and teachers colleges in eight states had initiated similar programs. From August 2 to August 12, 1950, administrators of the project had conducted a workshop for school superintendents, principals, and social studies teachers at Columbia University. Columbia made available to the participants a catalog of films, books, pamphlets, magazine articles, and newspaper clippings that could be used to supplement current courses in citizenship (*New York Times*, Aug. 3 and 13, 1950).
[3] Marshall replied on December 7 (EM) that he had asked two officers to meet with William S. Vincent, executive officer of the Citizenship Project, on December 8, 1950 (for background on Vincent see no. 727). Vincent would report to Eisenhower (letter, Jan. 2, 1951, EM) that he had sent a proposal to the Chief, Armed Forces Information and Education Division, Office of the Secretary of Defense, outlining a plan of collaboration between the Citizenship Education Project and the Armed Forces. The services would join with the project in the formulation of plans for citizenship training early in 1951, and the result would be a program of ten one-hour teaching units called "Hours on Freedom" (see Columbia University, Teachers College, Citizenship Education Project, *Improving Citizenship Education*, pp. 24–27). Eisenhower's appointment calendar indicates that he had a telephone conversation with Marshall on this subject on this same day.

1074

Eisenhower Mss.

To Carl Spaatz

November 16, 1950

Dear Toohey:[1] The telegram, sent out by your office about joining the Iron Curtain Refugee Campaign, has been in my office for two days.[2] Of course, because it is you who asked me to do this, my impulse is to say "Yes" without hesitation. But I have a peculiar, cogent reason for being doubtful as to the wisdom of my doing so.

I have a very small staff here at Columbia, a staff already overworked in its devoted efforts to keep my correspondence up to date and my routine business in some kind of shape. Experience has shown that every time I allow my name to be used as a sponsor for some new and worthy purpose, my volume of mail increases. I simply do not have the ways and means of handling it.

In more than one instance, an organization has asked me to transfer to its headquarters all correspondence relating to my connection with it. This does not work for me, because I answer, personally, the communications that come to me.

I am already identified with the Crusade for Freedom and the Committee for Free Europe, to say nothing of a number of public spirited organizations whose purposes are more nearly domestic in character.[3]

To join more would be far from wise and, in this case, this conclusion is reached with great reluctance because I hold for you an affection and admiration that I reserve for very few people in this world—and I am, in addition, a firm believer in the work you are trying to do.

But—there must be some limits on what I attempt to do.[4] *Cordially*

P.S. Why don't you ever come up to 116th Street and have a few minutes with me?

[1] General Spaatz (USAF, ret.; for background see no. 154) had recently succeeded Admiral Richard E. Byrd as chairman of the Iron Curtain Refugee Campaign of the International Rescue Committee.

[2] Spaatz had asked Eisenhower to join the sponsors of this program to give "immediate emergency assistance to thousands of escapees from Stalin's terror" (Nov. 14, 1950, EM). In his telegram he had mentioned John Dewey, Richard E. Byrd, Robert Sherwood, and Marquis W. Childs among the group of distinguished Americans already supporting this humanitarian cause.

[3] For background on Eisenhower's endorsement of the National Committee for a Free Europe see no. 428; on the Crusade for Freedom project sponsored by this committee see no. 739.

[4] Spaatz would again ask Eisenhower to endorse the Iron Curtain Refugee Campaign in the fall of 1951 (his letter of Sept. 13, 1951, and a statement of appeal to the American people are in EM, Spaatz Corr.). Aide Craig Cannon's declination would cite the General's policy of refusing to endorse any project not directly related to his role as Supreme Commander (Sept. 28, 1951, EM).

1075   *Eisenhower Mss.*

To Ellen Doud Moore   *November 16, 1950*

Dear Ellen:[1] It is true that your Aunt Mamie and I bought a farm. However, we have no horses—in fact, we merely bought some land and a house. All of the cows and other animals on it belong to someone else.[2]

Maybe we will go there to live some day. And if I do, the first thing I shall buy is a horse. Then I shall ask you to come and spend the summer with me and ride as much as you want.[3]

With much love, *Devotedly*

[1] Miss Moore was the daughter of Mrs. Eisenhower's sister Mabel Frances Doud Moore (for background see no. 695). In a handwritten letter to the General, Ellen had asked "Uncle ike" if he had any horses. She said, "I would like to know if I could ride your horses because I have liked horses all my life [and] I know how to ride" (n.d., EM).

[2] The Eisenhower farm in Gettysburg, Pennsylvania, consisted of 179 acres of land, a nine-room red-brick house, a herd of Holstein cows, over five hundred laying hens, and various kinds of farm machinery and dairy equipment (see nos. 1003 and 1080).

[3] Eisenhower recalled that the purchase of the farm in 1950 reflected a "confidence that the balance of my working years would be spent at Columbia, followed by retirement to Gettysburg" (*At Ease*, p. 361). This would not be the case, however, since the General would soon make an exploratory trip to Europe following his appointment as Supreme Commander, Allied Powers, Europe (see no. 1137). Four years would pass before the Eisenhowers would be able to spend an occasional weekend or holiday at the farm, and by that time (1954) their official residence was the White House.

1076   *Eisenhower Mss.*

To Charles Henry Caldwell   *November 17, 1950*

Dear Caldwell:[1] I cannot tell you how deeply shocked and distressed I was to read in my Denver paper, only yesterday, that you had been transferred to Fitzsimons Hospital with some kind of heart ailment. I most devoutly trust, of course, that the attack is a slight one and that you will eventually be returned to full health and strength. From some family experiences with this type of case, I am quite certain of one thing—the more exactly you obey your doctor's orders, the more quickly such a cure can be anticipated.[2]

Obviously, a sudden illness at this particular time brings to you the added disappointment of having to turn over to someone else responsibility for the great expansion program you had undertaken at Lowry Field.[3] Your leadership will be sorely missed, but it is one of those things that you will have to accept as inevitable and, so, try to free your mind of worry so that you may concentrate on the business of getting well.

Both Mamie and I send you our affectionate regards, our sincere wishes for complete recovery and the hope that, if there is anything you believe either or both of us might do for you or any of yours, you will let us know without delay.

With warmest personal regards and my affectionate greetings to Mrs. Caldwell,[4] *Sincerely*

[1] For background on Brigadier General Caldwell, CG of Lowry Air Force Base, near Denver, Colorado, see no. 855.

[2] In a letter to Eisenhower on this day (Nov. 17, EM), Caldwell reported that "everything about the case is typical. An attack which I thought was nothing more than severe and acute indigestion hit me about a month ago. Two weeks later I went to my own hospital to find out why this 'heartburn' persisted and ended up here in Fitzsimons." In a subsequent reply, Eisenhower expressed relief that the case was not "of the kind that practically keeps one on his back forever" (Nov. 21, EM; see also *Denver Post*, Nov. 18, 1950).

[3] Caldwell said that he was disappointed in "having to quit Denver, Lowry, and the Air Force at a time when more than ever before, I really thought I was doing a good

job" (Nov. 17, EM. For discussion of the expansion program at the Lowry base see U.S., Congress, House, Committee on Appropriations, *Military Public Works Appropriations for 1952: Hearings*, 82d Cong., 1st sess., 1951, pp. 179–86).

[4] Caldwell told Eisenhower that following his retirement in January 1951 he and Mrs. Caldwell would move to Tampa, Florida, where they hoped to purchase a small boat and spend much of their time on the water. He commented: "It is most amazing how psychologically we are prepared for this change in our mode of life" (Nov. 17, EM).

1077   *Eisenhower Mss.*

To William Rudolph Gruber   *November 17, 1950*

Dear Bill:[1] Thank you very much for your fine letter. I doubt that there is much to do about the particular point that is disturbing you. Certain self-labeled sophisticates and others are going to ascribe deceitful motives to others—and lack of evidence does not stop them.[2]

More than two years ago, under somewhat dramatic circumstances— possibly even more dramatic than most people realize—I definitely turned my back upon political inducements, including some brought to me by the most prominent political figures of the times. For that there were a number of reasons, some of which I stated in a public letter.[3] One of the lesser but sincere personal reasons—one that I have repeated until I am weary of it—is that I do *not want* any political office. This seems to be one statement that no politician and very few newspaper men will believe. They have been so long and so often kidded by people who use exactly this language to cover up an avid desire for political power that they mentally, if not verbally, say "Oh yeah."

In this situation I long ago decided to go right along, supporting what causes I believed to be worthy and in the interests of the United States, but avoiding to the fullest extent of my ability participation in any argument that could *properly* be labeled as "political," or "partisan." This kind of purpose and reasoning brought me to this great University—I assure you that back in 1947 there were a number of offers that, so far as remuneration and personal ease of living were concerned, were much more elaborate than the one I accepted.[4] But here I believe I can support Americanism and help promote understanding of today's responsibilities and opportunities. I do not want anything else!

It was nice to hear from you again. When you run into the kind of statements that disturb you, I hope you tell people that I am at least a *fairly* honest guy and that there is no use in their getting burned up merely because I do not want something *they* think I should want.

Love to Helen[5] and warm regards to yourself. *Cordially*

[1] For background on Brigadier General Gruber, a veteran of both the first and second world wars, see Chandler, *War Years*, no. 2295. Following his service with the 24th Infantry Division in 1945, Gruber had worked in the Office of the Army-Navy Liquidation Commissioner in Europe (see Chandler and Galambos, *Occupation, 1945*, no. 417). He had retired from the Army on August 13, 1946.

[2] Gruber's letter, written in the spirit of "candor between soldiers and old friends," had alerted the General to a sentiment expressed by the press that "you are 'insincere' with regard to presidential aspirations." Gruber believed that the public was being deliberately dosed with this idea, and he begged Eisenhower not to "allow a feeling to grow that it is dangerous to trust your sincerity" (Nov. 6, 1950, EM).

[3] Eisenhower was referring to the question of his candidacy in the 1948 presidential election (concerning some of his politically prominent advocates see nos. 34, nn. 10 and 11; and 110). To quell the mounting speculation at that time, the General had issued several public statements disclaiming any interest in political office. The full text of his initial declination, in the form of a letter to Leonard V. Finder, appears as no. 1998 in Galambos, *Chief of Staff*. Additional pressure to consider becoming a presidential candidate had evoked a second declination and still a third (nos. 106 and 1041 in these volumes on Columbia University).

[4] Concerning offers from the commercial and financial world see Galambos, *Chief of Staff*, nos. 1274 and 1528; for more on his decision to go to Columbia see nos. 1645 and 1832.

[5] Mrs. Gruber, the former Helen L. Drennan.

1078   *Eisenhower Mss.*

To Philip Young[1]   *November 18, 1950*

I think that you have all the data as to the pledges made in favor of the American Assembly. The question comes as to when and through whom these people should be asked to turn in their money.[2]

I think that, in the case of Cliff Roberts' friends, this has all been taken care of.[3] But I believe there are a few, including Arthur Godfrey, who will be awaiting some further notice. If you should want me to write a note to Mr. Godfrey, let me know when you think I should send it.[4]

[1] Young was the Executive Director of the newly announced American Assembly conference plan (see no. 1039).

[2] For an eleven-page handwritten record of the pledges see EM, American Assembly Corr.

[3] For Roberts's efforts on behalf of the American Assembly see no. 1068; for developments see no. 1086.

[4] For background on Godfrey's pledge see no. 1027; and for Eisenhower's note to him see no. 1103.

TO JOHN HAY WHITNEY   *November 18, 1950*

Dear Mr. Whitney:[1] Cliff Roberts has sent to me a list of individuals who had subscribed, through him, to the American Assembly of Columbia University.[2] It is my personal conviction that the Assembly offers concrete and specific opportunity to do something in America about the great questions that plague and torture us—particularly those questions that will obviously influence our free system.

As a consequence, you can understand how profoundly grateful I am, both personally and as President of this University, for your generous gift. It denotes not only a similar belief in the need for doing something about the great problems of our time but evidences, as well, your determination to support this kind of effort with material means. You have done much, both to encourage us who are working on the program and to assure its eventual success.

Incidentally, I should like to take this opportunity to assure you, in view of the specific comment made in your letter to Cliff Roberts,[3] that no matter where I am or what I may be called upon to do, I shall not abandon my belief in the plan of the American Assembly or my determination to do everything within my power to further it. If I should be called away by official duty, I trust the absence will not be so prolonged that this personal interest and this effort cannot be sustained.[4] Moreover, an added item of information that may be of interest to you is that I am at this moment engaged in the attempt to find some outstanding and dynamic American to take the direct charge of the program that neither the Dean of the Business School nor I could possibly give because of necessary preoccupation in a multitude of other duties.[5] This plan is so important and is so promising for the future that it deserves the full time and devoted efforts of the finest individual we can produce for it.

Again, my thanks and, of course, my personal regard. *Sincerely*

[1] On Whitney and Eisenhower's earlier correspondence concerning the American Assembly conference plan see no. 1026.
[2] Eisenhower's friend Roberts had been an enthusiastic participant in the campaign to enlist subscribers (see no. 1068. For background on the plan see no. 1039).
[3] Whitney's letter to Roberts is not in EM.
[4] See no. 1045.
[5] Philip Young was dean of Columbia's Business School and also Executive Director of the American Assembly. Lewis W. Douglas would head the program (see no. 1081).

To WILLIAM L. MCLEAN, JR.   *November 18, 1950*

Dear Bill:[1] I just have a note from your City Editor, asking me about the farm I have been attempting to purchase near Gettysburg. If you believe the story is of real interest, I see no reason why it cannot be made public because, certainly, when—if ever—the deed is recorded, the news will be out.[2]

The fact is that—while, as I understand it, my representative has made a firm agreement with the representative of the present owner— I have not yet seen a scratch of paper nor have I even been told that finally there is a chance of a halt in the proceedings. What I am trying to say is that I am not attempting to be coy at all—I just do not know anything more than I give you above.[3]

Since representatives of each generation on the paternal side of my family, since 1740, have lived in Pennsylvania, I have a real sentimental reason for wanting to own a piece of ground in that region.[4] It never occurred to me that this would be news. But, if it is, I have no objection whatsoever to publication, once the thing has been completely removed from the realm of possibility and speculation and has become fact.[5]

It is because of the character of the situation that I answer Mr. Taylor's letter through you. Would it not be best if you should merely tell him that I promise to send you prompt word if and when I acquire a deed to the title to any property in Pennsylvania? Whether or not you agree with my solution, please explain to Mr. Taylor the reasons for my decision to answer him in this indirect fashion.[6] *Cordially*

P.S. Since writing the above I've been asked for a "down payment"— so I guess that's final.[7] So you may publish as you please, but *not quoting* me. I merely assume that the story is true—& please thank Mr. Taylor for courtesy in checking!

[1] McLean was vice-president and treasurer of the Bulletin Company, publisher of Philadelphia's *Evening Bulletin* and *Sunday Bulletin* (for further background see no. 839).

[2] *Bulletin* city editor Stuart S. Taylor's letter was returned to McLean (for background on Eisenhower's efforts to buy a farm home in Pennsylvania see nos. 998 and 1003).

[3] See the postscript and n. 7 below.

[4] Eisenhower discusses his ancestral "roots" in the Susquehanna River area and reflects on his wishes to "end his days on a Pennsylvania farm" in *At Ease*, pp. 56–63 (see also no. 824). Additional sentiments prompting the General's choice of a Gettysburg homestead included his early command at Camp Colt and proximity to family and friends (see Eisenhower's correspondence with Edward Martin, U.S. senator from Pennsylvania, Nov. 22 and 24, 1950, EM).

[5] In addition to the Philadelphia news coverage, the story of the Gettysburg farm

purchase would appear in the *New York Times*, November 21, 1950, and in *Newsweek*, December 4, 1950.
⁶ McLean would thank Eisenhower for his cooperative attitude and assure him that "our boys did think the story to be of real interest." The newspaper executive also relayed "Stu" Taylor's one comment on Eisenhower's letter: "What a swell guy" (Nov. 21, 1950).
⁷ Richard A. Brown was the attorney handling the General's purchase of the Gettysburg property; John C. Breen was the real estate agent through whom owner Allen S. Redding would sell his farm. The *New York Times* (Nov. 21, 1950) would report when the down payment was made on the Redding Farm (see also nos. 1075 and 1100).

1081   *Eisenhower Mss.*

To LEWIS WILLIAMS DOUGLAS   *November 20, 1950*

*Dear Lew:*¹ I am writing this to enclose with a much longer letter that Phil Young is writing to you on the subject of the American Assembly.² Except that I feel certain you must take a considerable time—after leaving your present post—for rest and for recuperation, I'd write this in terms of the utmost urgency.³ We want you with us; without you the plan will never be the success it will realize with you in either policy making or executive capacity.

We have no idea as to when you will return to the U.S. Maybe you haven't either.⁴ But in any event—we'd like to know (a) That you plan, after the necessary period of recuperation, to go back into some form of active work, and (b) that you'll give us a chance to talk to you. Here, the admiration we feel toward you is equalled only by our affection for you. We plead this fact as well as the more concrete one that in the American Assembly you'd be doing something vital and challenging.⁵

Good luck—above all, a speedy return to health!

With warm regard. *Always*

¹ For background on Douglas, retiring U.S. Ambassador to Great Britain, see no. 111. A note at the top of the copy of this letter (EM) indicates that Eisenhower wrote the original in longhand.
² Young would report in a letter of November 22 (EM, Young Corr.) on the organization of this conference plan (for background see no. 1039). Selection of the discussion topics would be the responsibility of a national policy board representing business, labor, government, and agriculture. Young would ask Douglas to serve either as chairman of the policy board or as director for the American Assembly. "We have only one first choice for either post," Young would write, "and that is yourself." The directorship would be a salaried job, while the compensation for the chairmanship would vary with "the amount of time that you might be able to give us."

³ On September 26, 1950, Douglas had announced his resignation from the ambassadorship. He had described his plan to return to his ranch in Arizona for several months of rest before undertaking any other government assignment (see *New York Times*, Sept. 27, 1950).
⁴ Douglas would arrive in New York on November 21 (see *New York Times*, Nov. 22, 1950).
⁵ Douglas would acknowledge this letter in a note of November 13 (EM); he would include the addresses at which Eisenhower might reach him in Arizona and add that he planned to visit the General late in January 1951. Douglas would tell newsmen on December 3 that he would not return to government service after his period of rest (see *New York Times*, Dec. 4, 1950). Notes at the bottom of Eisenhower's appointment calendar for November 29 and December 29 indicate that he had telephone conversations with Douglas regarding the American Assembly on those days. Later in March 1951 Douglas would agree to head the National Policy Board of the American Assembly (see no. 1117).

1082   *Eisenhower Mss.*

To JOSEPH H. WILLITS   *November 20, 1950*

Dear Dr. Willits: In a letter dated October 11th and a memorandum dated October 25th, Professor Schuyler C. Wallace, director of the School of International Affairs, has outlined the needs of the Russian Institute of this University.¹ In submitting this memorandum, Professor Wallace fully realized that the amounts involved were so large that it would be unreasonable to ask any one Foundation to underwrite the entire undertaking. The memorandum was designed to indicate to you the scope of the development the staff of the Russian Institute of Columbia University believes to be imperative if the University is to make that contribution to the study of Russian affairs of which it is capable.

The purpose of this letter is to say that, in my opinion, a material expansion of the work now carried on by the Russian Institute is not merely highly desirable from a scholarly point of view but is an urgent national need.

I sincerely hope, consequently, that it will be possible for the Foundation to assist the University in this development. The staff reports this can be done by a grant of $150,000 for the academic year 1951–1952; $75,000 for 1952–1953; $70,000 for 1953–54; $65,000 for 1954–1955; and $60,000 for 1955–1956.² It would be exceedingly helpful also if the grants could be made in such a way as to permit the University to carry over unexpended balances from year to year and to permit shifts between the different categories of activity outlined in the [letter] of October 11th and the memorandum of October 25th.

The University contemplates an expenditure of $94,000 in the Russian field during the academic year 1951–1952. An increase rather than a diminution of this expenditure is anticipated annually. The University plans to make every effort possible to secure additional financing to implement further the program contained in the memorandum of October 25th.

May I take this opportunity to express my very real appreciation of the generous cooperation of the Foundation in the development of the Russian Institute down to date and in the many other developments of national significance undertaken by the University.[3] *Sincerely*

[1] Willits was the Rockefeller Foundation's Director for the Social Sciences. Wallace prepared a draft of this message for Eisenhower, who made numerous changes in the letter (see copies in EM and CUF). For background on the Russian Institute see nos. 48 and 204.
[2] The Rockefeller Foundation would announce on January 16, 1951, that it had agreed to grant $420,00 to the Russian Institute at Columbia University over a five-year period (see *New York Times*, Jan. 17, 1951; and Rockefeller Foundation, *The Rockefeller Foundation Annual Report, 1950* [New York, 1950], pp. 204–7).
[3] In a letter of December 18 (CUF) Willits would inform Wallace that the trustees of the foundation would permit Columbia "as much flexibility as possible" in the use of the grant. Funds for the appointment of additional faculty members might come initially from the grant, but the university would have to pay increases in their salaries and their complete salaries at the end of the grant period.

1083   *Eisenhower Mss.*

To Anna Marie Rosenberg   *November 20, 1950*

Dear Anna:[1] I congratulate the Defense Department on your appointment—but I must say that your leaving New York threw a number of my personal plans into a temporary state of confusion. I had staked out a number of jobs both in counseling and in plain hard work in which I was hopefully counting on you to participate.

For most of these I shall, of course, now have to make other arrangements because there is no doubt in my mind that you are going to be a very busy person. However, there is one in which I must still look to you for real assistance. It involves the securing of proper Labor participation in the American Assembly program. But because, in communicating with representatives of Labor, you may want to give them a quick explanation of the scheme I enclose a few documents which might be helpful to you. If you find no need of them, then, of course, just throw them into the wastebasket.[2]

We have had favorable responses concerning the general idea and readiness to cooperate from Philip Murray, Mr. Jacobsen in Minneapolis, William Green and Matthew Woll. At our New York luncheon, which I was so sorry you could not attend, were Morris Iushewitz,

David Sullivan and Mark Starr. Unfortunately, Messrs. Green and Murray were unable to be there.[3]

What is needed is definite assurance that able representatives of Labor will be ready to participate in discussions of specific problems — in fact, I cannot conceive of any conference being held under the American Assembly program in which Labor is not adequately represented. Beyond this, we need about two representatives on the permanent *Policy Board* of the whole program.

Further, we need the financial support of Labor so that we can truthfully say that Labor is participating not only intellectually, but financially, in the carrying out of this American program under the auspices of Columbia University.[4]

Our most acute *practical* need in the labor field right away is to find the one or two individuals who should serve on the *Policy Board*. I had hoped that you might accept one of these places. But now that you have gone to Washington, I still hope you will give me the names of the individuals I should approach.[5]

With warm personal regard and my best wishes for your complete success in the new and important service you have undertaken. *Cordially*

P.S. You will probably soon be hearing from our Dean Philip Young, who is the son of Owen D. Young, and is the spearhead, within the University, of the Assembly project.[6]

---

[1] On November 11 President Truman had appointed Mrs. Rosenberg Assistant Secretary of Defense in charge of Manpower. Since July 1950 she had been special consultant on manpower problems to the chairman of the National Security Resources Board (see *New York Times*, July 22 and November 10 and 12, 1950. For Eisenhower's request for help from Mrs. Rosenberg regarding the American Assembly see no. 905. For further developments see no. 1123). On November 17 Eisenhower had sent his first draft of this letter to Dean Philip Young with a note: "Will you look this over and let me know your suggestions?" A copy of the draft in EM shows several handwritten changes and additions by both Young and Eisenhower. On Young see n. 6 below.

[2] Eisenhower had probably enclosed his confidential memorandum and his prospectus on the American Assembly, both of which are discussed in nos. 979, 1026, and 1032. See also no. 1039 for background.

[3] On labor leader Murray see no. 330; on R. C. Jacobson, no. 904; on Woll, no. 905. Morris Iushewitz was secretary-treasurer of the New York CIO Council; David Sullivan was president of the Building Service Employees International Union, AF of L; and Mark Starr was educational director of the International Ladies' Garment Workers' Union.

[4] In a reply of November 27, 1950, Mrs. Rosenberg suggested two people from whom Eisenhower could get "both funds and intelligent participation." They were David Dubinsky, president of the International Ladies' Garment Workers' Union, and Jacob S. Potofsky, president of the Amalgamated Clothing Workers of America. These were probably the two richest and most powerful unions in New York City, she said (RG330 [Sec of Defense], Asst Sec of Defense, Manpower, Personnel and Reserve, Executive Office [Chronological File], "Anna Rosenberg," Nov. 1950, [box 10, entry 56]. For more on this subject see no. 1081).

[5] In the same letter, Mrs. Rosenberg told Eisenhower that "if you want labor people, they must come from the ranks of labor." While she was sorry that she could not participate, she assured Eisenhower that "they never would have accepted me as a representative of labor." She asked him to tell her more about the policy board; she would then be better prepared, she said, to suggest people he might approach. In April 1951 Eisenhower would announce that William Green, president of the AF of L, and Jacob S. Potofsky, president of the Amalgamated Clothing Workers of America, were the newly appointed members of the National Policy Board of the American Assembly.

[6] Philip Young was dean of Columbia's Graduate School of Business and Executive Director of the American Assembly. On his father, Owen D. Young, see no. 486. On December 7 Eisenhower and Young would meet for lunch at the Statler Hotel in Washington, D.C., with Anna Rosenberg, William Green, Jacob Potofsky, and Albert J. Hayes of the Machinists' Union (see Eisenhower to Green, Dec. 1, 1950, EM).

1084   *Eisenhower Mss.*

To George Ephraim Sokolsky   *November 20, 1950*

Dear Mr. Sokolsky:[1] I am grateful for the trouble you took in sending me the information contained in your note of November 9th.[2] While I have never seen one of the leaflets, this and similar instances of circulating the page—to which you refer in the West Point 1915 Howitzer—have been called, previously, to my attention. I have never given them any concern because—while it can be easily demonstrated that my clear Pennsylvania Dutch ancestry on my father's side and my Lutheran on the maternal side extend back in this country alone to beyond the 1750's—I would never raise my hand or say a word that could be fairly interpreted as fear of those misguided people who appeal to ancestry in the attempt to create prejudice.[3]

Because of your courtesy, I am impelled to give you, for your personal information, an explanation of how this particular expression happened to appear in my 1915 yearbook. The squib was written by my oldest and best friend in the Army and who was my roommate at West Point for four years. His name is Colonel Paul Hodgson, (Retired).[4] In the graduating class each of us was given the job of writing one or more so-called biographical sketches for the yearbook, and he was assigned the job of writing mine. The expressions that appear on that page are representative of nothing more than his attempt at humor—he was completely and fully aware of my entire family background. In fact, we both came from Kansas—he from Wichita and I from Abilene.[5]

With best wishes. *Sincerely*

[1] For background on Sokolsky, a columnist and lecturer, see nos. 333 and 815.
[2] In his letter (EM) Sokolsky had alerted the General to an anti-Eisenhower

publication that had come to him from the Patriotic Tract Society of St. Louis, Missouri. Sokolsky said a page from the West Point *Howitzer* yearbook of 1915 had been reproduced and entitled "Attention General Eisenhower." "The article," Sokolsky continued, "apparently refers to you as a 'Senor' in front of your name and as 'the terrible Swedish-Jew.' "

[3] Concerning the Eisenhower family see no. 824. The article referred to Eisenhower as "Señor Dwight David Eisenhower . . . the terrible Swedish-Jew, as big as life and twice as natural."

[4] For background on "P. A." Hodgson see no. 940, n. 5; a copy of his "squib" on Eisenhower from the 1915 *Howitzer* is in EM, USMA Corr.

[5] Eisenhower reminisces further about his days at West Point and his former roommate in no. 983; see also Edward M. Coffman's account of their relationship in "My Room Mate is Dwight Eisenhower," *American Heritage* 24 (April 1973), 102–3.

1085   *Eisenhower Mss.*

TO JOSEPH FRANCIS SANTILLI, JR.   *November 21, 1950*

Dear Cadet Santilli:[1] For the past two weeks I have held your letter on my desk because I would really like to answer it in the way you requested. This I cannot do because of the pressure of work.[2]

I definitely believe that education for a well prepared army officer must be broadly based.[3] For many years, it has been realized that West Point can do no more than to give the officer a sound beginning in attaining mastery of his profession. As a consequence of this realization, our service schools have included in their curricula a constantly expanding array of subjects, many of which defy any classification as "military."

I agree with you that we have now further and radical increase in requirements for broadly educated leaders. Indeed, I have some very positive ideas about the need for this education to include instruction in the business of handling conferences with representatives of foreign nations. Perhaps a course in foreign affairs and diplomacy could be profitably given.[4]

Naturally, I am cheered by the evidence, implicit in your letter, that cadets themselves appreciate these ever broadening needs. It is clear that they do not intend to confuse strength with bad manners or to fear that courtesy implies weakness.

The best of luck to your project and, again, my regrets that I cannot even attempt to provide anything that you possibly might find suited to your purposes.[5] *Sincerely*

[1] Santilli (USMA 1952) was editor of *The Pointer*, a biweekly undergraduate magazine published by the cadets at West Point.

[2] In his letter (Nov. 11) Santilli had asked the General for an article to help

explain "this new requirement of an officer—that of being soldier and diplomat." He said that the cadets at the Military Academy recognized the changing role of the American Army officer serving abroad in the postwar era to be that of "both commander of his troops and a representative . . . of the American ways of doing things." Santilli hoped that an article by Eisenhower could enlighten the cadets about this important subject (Santilli's handwritten letter and a typed copy are in EM).

[3] See Galambos, *Chief of Staff*, no. 613, concerning Eisenhower's past recommendations on the Academy's curriculum.

[4] Critics of the Military Academy's curriculum often noted the heavy emphasis on scientific-engineering studies. In 1950 more than half of West Point's course hours were devoted to these subjects; one fourth to social-humanistic studies; and the remaining fourth to professional courses (Weigley, *History of the United States Army*, pp. 552–53). For a more favorable view of the post–World War II changes see Ambrose, *Duty, Honor, Country*, pp. 297–301.

[5] In June 1951 *The Pointer* would feature an article on this topic entitled "The Soldier's New Role." In the story Eisenhower would be named among the prominent West Pointers who at some time in their military career had acted in the capacity of diplomat, governor, or scientist. Others mentioned included Douglas MacArthur, Omar Bradley, Maxwell Taylor, and Matthew Ridgway (letter from Leslie G. Kingseed, Archivist, Oct. 19, 1981, EP).

1086   *Eisenhower Mss.*

TO PHILIP YOUNG[1]   *November 24, 1950*

Clifford Roberts visited me to discuss the financial aspects of the American Assembly program.[2] He believes that, for a number of reasons, our financial push must be quickly assured. He seems to think that, unless this is done within a matter of the next few weeks, radical and prompt action should be taken. Unless our prospects are for early and full success, he wants to have a little conference with you as soon as possible.[3]

[1] On Philip Young see no. 1039.

[2] Investment banker Roberts had been actively involved in raising funds for the American Assembly (see, for instance, Eisenhower's letter to him of November 6, no. 1068).

[3] For Eisenhower's continuing efforts to interest potential sponsors see no. 1119.

To Louis Francis Albert Mountbatten   *November 24, 1950*

Dear Dickie:[1] Just after Alan Morhead visited me in my office a few weeks ago, I made a little resolution to drop you a note—a resolution that, I now realize, I have failed miserably to keep.[2]

Mr. Morhead has probably told you that I agreed to attempt writing a short foreword for your Report if and when you published it in this country. From what he said, I assume that you are publishing the actual official report—not a war memoir or narrative based upon the report.[3] The former kind of document will, of course, be much more valuable than the second as history, and particularly for study by historical and military schools and staffs. It probably will not be so widely read by the public as would a more personal account of your operations.[4]

I assume that you have considered all of these things but the reason I am writing is that, provided you will want me to produce a foreword for your American edition, it would be helpful if you would assure me that my understandings are completely correct or, if I am wrong, in just what respect I have gone off the base.[5]

The hopes we had some six or seven years ago, that the end of hostilities would also bring to us a life of greater leisure and enjoyment, seem to have disappeared in problems of global import and in the smoke and dust of Korea. Maybe it is just the march of years that makes me somewhat more pessimistic, but I am beginning to have the feeling that I could use a good shot in the arm composed of good news and cheerful prospects.[6]

Please convey my greetings to your charming Lady[7] and, of course, with warm regard to yourself. *As ever*

---

[1] Mountbatten had been Supreme Allied Commander, Southeast Asia (SACSEA), from August 1943 to May 1946. He had then served as Viceroy of India (March–August 1947) and subsequently as Governor General (until June 1948). He had thereafter returned to the Navy as flag officer, commanding the 1st Cruiser Squadron, Mediterranean Fleet, and in 1950 was appointed Fourth Sea Lord of the Admiralty (for further background see *Eisenhower Papers*, vols. I–IX).

[2] Alan McCrae Moorehead was a newspaper correspondent and newly appointed Public Relations Officer in the Ministry of Defence in London (for background see Galambos, *Chief of Staff*, no. 1170). He had met with Eisenhower on October 18 to seek advice concerning the publication of Mountbatten's official report to the Combined Chiefs of Staff on the campaign in Southeast Asia (Mountbatten's letter to Eisenhower delivered by Moorehead, Oct. 15, 1950, is in EM).

[3] Mountbatten had objected to the writing of any form of personal memoir outside of his official report. Later, however, after his retirement from active duty in 1965, he would authorize and participate in a biography (see John Terraine, *The Life and Times of Lord Mountbatten* [London, 1968]).

[4] For background on Eisenhower's opinion of the original draft version of the SEAC report see Galambos, *Chief of Staff*, nos. 907, 1161, 1807, and 2041.

[5] Mountbatten would affirm this understanding of the situation (Nov. 29, EM). He said that extensive alterations to the report had resulted in a finished product that was factually correct and encompassed the entire campaign from the inception of the Southeast Asia Command (SEAC) to the surrender of the Japanese at Singapore. Mountbatten would repeat his appeal for a short foreword by Eisenhower (see the following document).

[6] Mountbatten would agree with Eisenhower's pessimism about the deteriorating international relations, remarking, however, that the one compensation would be that this would induce the General to return to high office (Nov. 29, EM).

[7] Edwina Cynthia Annette Ashley Mountbatten.

1088   *Eisenhower Mss.*

To Justus Baldwin Lawrence   *November 24, 1950*

Dear Jock:[1] Thank you very much for sending me the note from Dickie Mountbatten.[2] Apparently, he feels that his official "Report" will have some reader appeal for quite a number of our people. I think there is room to doubt this because I believe that our reading public much prefers a narrative or story as opposed to the report type of document. Certainly, this proved to be the case in the several reports issued by the Chief of Staff and other officers of World War II.[3]

Nevertheless, I did agree to Alan Morhead's suggestion that I might write a short foreword for such a document if Dickie should decide to publish it in this country.[4]

Thank you again for letting me see the note. *Cordially*

[1] Lawrence had gone to England in June 1942 at the request of Admiral Louis Mountbatten to be Chief Public Relations Planner at Combined Operations Headquarters. After Mountbatten's departure for the SEAC, Lawrence had become Public Relations Officer for ETOUSA. He presently was executive vice-president and a member of the board of directors of the J. Arthur Rank Organization (for further background see no. 410; and Chandler, *War Years*, no. 1938).

[2] Eisenhower had complied with Lawrence's request to return the note from Mountbatten. For background on the subject of the correspondence see the preceding document.

[3] Lawrence would agree with Eisenhower on the probable American response to "that type of 'Report.'" He would promise to keep the General informed of further word from Mountbatten (Dec. 1, 1950, EM).

[4] Mountbatten's official *Report to the Combined Chiefs of Staff by the Supreme Allied Commander, South-East Asia, 1943–1945* would be published exclusively by His Majesty's Stationary Office in London in 1951. For reviews of the report by the British and American press see *The Times* (London), February 5, 1951; and *New York Times*, February 4, 1951.

Dear Paul:[1] When you and I first discussed the Pasadena trip, it appeared that the Korean war was, to all intents and purposes, successfully ended.[2] Since then it has broken out anew and only this morning I see in the papers that a general offensive has been undertaken by United Nations troops.[3] This could, of course, develop into a dingdong campaign and, if it should do so, there is still some likelihood that we would be in the midst of sanguinary battle at the New Year.

If this should prove to be the case (and I realize I am talking about a lot of ifs) then I think it would be quite inappropriate for me, a more or less "permanent" soldier, to be participating in a gala ceremony at that particular moment. While I realize that in the minds of the Committee I am being asked, this year, in my capacity as a University President and not as a soldier, yet such distinctions would mean little to others—and they certainly could not add to my own peace of mind. This is particularly true because in recent weeks there has been a very considerable newspaper discussion about the possibility of my going back into uniformed service.[4]

All this is merely another example of the kind of question that is constantly plaguing me, but it does raise again the possible advisability of Mr. Kenworthy[5] deciding upon someone else for Grand Marshal while there is still time to do it without making any explanation to *anyone.* I do urge you—and him—that if this or other possibility of my having to cancel out at the last moment will cause current indecision and doubt in his planning, then he should, in justice to himself and his associates, make this move at once and with the certainty that I will fully understand and will be no less appreciative of his great courtesy in asking me.

Another subject: There apparently has been some leakage (possibly even by me) of information pertaining to my tentative plans for coming to Pasadena and, as a result, I have just received an invitation to participate in a public function in Southern California on January 2 or 3. As of this moment I see no alternative to declining such invitations— even though I had planned to go on a two- or three-day holiday out in the desert, on the morning following the football game. I most certainly do not want to appear disregardful of the wishes of associations and groups in that area, but it it obvious that there are some limits on the number of public appearances an individual can make and still retain any sanity, not to say health.

This letter, which seems to be compounded of doubt, uneasiness and personal problems, is sent to you instead of Mr. Kenworthy because, as we both know, it was only your personal invitation that led Mamie and me to consider acceptance.

Frankly, what we should really have liked to have done would have been to visit you two for a couple of days, "sneaking" in and out of town.

I do want to get your personal reactions to my thoughts as soon as possible, and I want you to know of this additional possible impediment—which did not exist at the time you and I first talked about the matter.[6]

With warm personal regard, *Cordially*

P.S. This morning Mamie saw in the paper that yesterday's temperature in Los Angeles was 110. That may be a misprint, but it certainly threw her into a storm on the matter of "apparel."

[1] Hoffman was managing director of the Ford Foundation (see no. 1007).

[2] Eisenhower is referring to his acceptance of an invitation to be grand marshal of the Tournament of Roses parade in Pasadena, California, on New Year's Day, 1951 (for background on the arrangements see no. 1034).

[3] U.N. forces had been pursuing the North Koreans across the thirty-eighth parallel (for background see no. 1046). When Chinese Communist troops had joined the North Koreans in the fighting, U.S. Army intelligence officers had underestimated the potential significance of the Chinese intervention (see Schnabel, *Policy and Direction*, pp. 233–79). The Eighth Army had begun a new offensive on November 24 (see *New York Times*, Nov. 24, 1950), and on the following day the Chinese had launched a massive counterattack. Four days later the U.N. forces would withdraw to defensive positions. For developments see no. 1096.

[4] See no. 1045.

[5] L. Clifford Kenworthy, president of the Pasadena Tournament of Roses Association (see no. 1034).

[6] Eisenhower's fears were well founded (see no. 1104).

1090   *Eisenhower Mss.*

To Willard Vinton King   *November 28, 1950*

Dear Willard:[1] While it is never "bother" to write to you, with this note I shall cease trying to express my gratitude to you for your continuing and effective support of this great institution. But I cannot refrain from saying, once more, that you have shown a greater appreciation of my personal purposes and problems—as evidenced again in your note of the 25th—and a more complimentary attitude toward the efforts I am making than almost any other of my friends. Your moral support means far more to me than the financial—even though the value of the latter can scarcely be over-estimated.[2] *Cordially*

[1] This was a handwritten note to King, a member of Columbia's board of trustees (for further background see no. 875).

[2] In his letter of November 25 King had asked Eisenhower not to bother to acknowledge his future contributions to Columbia. "I am so full of admiration for you and gratitude for what you are doing for Columbia and for the world in general," King said, "that my one desire is to take off your shoulders any part possible of your burden" (EM). King, who was also a member of the Columbia Associates, had contributed to the American Assembly on October 18, 1950 (for background on the conference plan see no. 1039).

1091   *Eisenhower Mss.*

To WILLIAM D. ROBERTSON   *November 28, 1950*

Dear Lieutenant Robertson: From your letter I am in some doubt as to whether you hope to join the Regular Army or whether your purposes are to go back in the Medical Corps for some limited period of service as an interne, on the order of two or three years.

This lack of knowledge on my part, however, would seem to have little influence on the kind of documentary support you need in your application to the Army authorities.[1]

Of course I remember the incident in my office when there was brought to me the improvised flag, which was used at the time of the link-up with forward elements of the Russian Army. With the concurrence of your immediate commanders I promoted you and the members of your patrol at that time.[2]

I am delighted to learn that you have continued your education since your separation from active service and are now about to graduate from medical school. I have gone over extracts of your official military record[3] and find that it completely supports the assumption I made, at the time of your battlefield promotion, that you were worthy of that mention. I do hope that all goes well with you and that you may realize your ambitions of serving in the Armed Forces once more.[4] *Very sincerely*

[1] Robertson, an officer in the Military Intelligence, Reserve, and a senior at the University of California Medical School, had served under the General's command during World War II. He had gained notoriety in 1945 for leading the American patrol that first made contact with the Russian Army at Torgau, Germany (see n. 2 below). Following separation from the service, Robertson had resumed his medical studies and was presently applying for an internship with the Army Medical Corps. In his letter (Nov. 15, EM) he had asked Eisenhower for a brief recommendation to submit with his application.

[2] See Chandler, *War Years*, no. 2490, and *New York Times*, April 28, 1945.

[3] In addition to the résumé enclosed by Robertson, Eisenhower had asked to see the official record of his military service (see memorandum, McDuff to Schulz, Nov. 22, 1950, EM, Robertson Corr.).

Robertson would be admitted into the military intern program (July 1951–June 1952) and would then be placed on active duty.

1092   *Eisenhower Mss.*

To Neil H. McElroy   *November 29, 1950*

Dear Mr. McElroy:[1] You can well imagine what a lift I gained from your nice note and the news that your campaign in support of the Assembly is progressing favorably. I have visited numbers of cities and from each there has been a response that has been most encouraging. I am delighted to learn that Cincinnati will also be represented among our sponsors.[2]

Quite naturally, I am more than obligated to you, both personally and officially. The American Assembly project lies close to my heart because of my convictions of its usefulness to our country. I have no slightest doubt that the sum you are collecting and will forward to us will produce real benefits for our country.

Won't you please send with the donation a list of the people who helped produce the sum? I should like to write each of them a note of thanks.[3] *Cordially*

[1] McElroy, of Cincinnati, Ohio, had been president of Procter & Gamble Company since 1948; he had been associated with the company since 1925.

[2] In a letter of November 24, 1950 (EM), McElroy had reported that industrial and commercial interests in southwestern Ohio had "rounded up" twenty-five thousand dollars for the American Assembly (for background see no. 1039). Eisenhower had recently toured several states in order to interest Columbia alumni in the newly announced project (see no. 1044); he had visited Cincinnati, Ohio, on October 26. On that day McElroy had honored Eisenhower at a luncheon for twenty people at the Queen City Club (the guest list is in EM, McElroy Corr.).

[3] For an example of this type of correspondence see Eisenhower's November 6 letter to Charles F. Williams, president of the Western and Southern Life Insurance Company in Cincinnati (EM).

1093   *Eisenhower Mss., Diaries*

Diary   *November 29, 1950*

Once in a while, I reach for this particular book to make a notation. Just why, I do not know, for I so rarely write down anything of the day's happenings that my other book will never be filled—if I should live another 30 years!

Last eve I went to dinner with Mr. Clarence Dillon,[1]

Guests (among others)
Mr. Langsley
Lord Brand
Mr. Leffingwell
Mr. Rockefeller (J.D. Jr.)
Mr. Brady
Mr. Dillon (Jr.)
Mr. Millbank
Mr. Schiff[2]

The dinner was arranged to give me an opportunity to describe the American Assembly — thus paving the way for associates to go after these men for financial support for the Assembly program.[3]

Actually, everyone was in such a blue funk over the tragic news from Korea that there was no hope of turning conversational interest into any other channel.[4] So — in response to my host's suggestion that I chat for a while to the others, I took the Korean debacle & tried to show some of the additional problems it imposed upon us as citizens. This led to the conclusion that in most cases we didn't have the facts, the truth, on these problems. And so, finally, I ended up arguing for the American Assembly idea!

[1] Dillon was head of Dillon, Read & Company. A list of the guests is in EM, Dillon Corr.

[2] William C. Langley was head of a New York City investment firm. Robert Henry Brand, First Baron Brand of Eydon, had been head of the British Food Mission in Washington, D.C., from 1941 to 1944 and representative of His Majesty's Treasury in the same city from 1944 to 1946. Russell C. Leffingwell was chairman of the board of J. P. Morgan & Company (for background see no. 208). John D. Rockefeller, Jr., was president of the board of the Rockefeller Institute for Medical Research (see no. 143). James Cox Brady (A.B. Yale 1929) was president and director of Brady Security & Realty Corporation; Clarence Douglas Dillon (A.B. Harvard 1931), son of the host, was chairman of the board of Dillon, Read & Company. Jeremiah Milbank was an investment banker and founder of the Institute for the Crippled and Disabled. John Mortimer Schiff (M.A. Oxford 1927) was a partner in Kuhn, Loeb & Company. The guest list also included Harvey S. Firestone, Jr., chief executive officer and chairman of Firestone Tire and Rubber Company (for another account of the evening see Lyon, *Portrait of the Hero*, p. 414).

[3] On the Assembly see no. 1039.

[4] A counteroffensive by Chinese troops on the western end of the line of battle in Korea had forced U.N. forces to retreat on November 28 (see *New York Times*, Nov. 28, 1950; for background see no. 1089).

To Robert Cutler

Dear Bobby: (After the thoroughly delightful and informal evening that I enjoyed at the Tavern Club, I do not see how I can address you more formally.)[1]

As soon as your letter arrived, I started the wheels to discover what I could about the Army policies that govern the recall of veterans to active service. The first answer I received was merely "Field officers are not needed or desired at this time." This is not enough for me because I quite agree with the final sentence of your next to the last paragraph; so I am digging away to get concrete and specific statements of what might be expected because it seems to me that our young people ought to have a chance to plan their lives with the finest kind of information they can get from the service. You will be hearing from me again in a matter of a couple of days.[2]

As for my day in Boston, it was really quite wonderful. I met so many interesting individuals and was so intrigued by everything I saw and heard that the day was one for me to remember with real satisfaction. Of course, the fact that everyone that I met seemed to take such a specific and objective interest in the American Assembly was most gratifying.[3]

Incidentally, I trust that you did not object to my making, at your dinner, a brief reference to your late brother. Not only did I hold him high in my affection, admiration and respect but I have always felt that his cool courage in the final days of his life provided an example that I should like to be able—under similar circumstances—to emulate.[4]

With warm personal regard, *Sincerely*

---

[1] Cutler, president and a director of Old Colony Trust Company, had given a dinner in honor of Eisenhower in Boston, Massachusetts, on November 22 (a list of the guests is in EM, American Assembly Corr.). Cutler had mentioned in his letter of November 24 (EM) that many of the guests had told him of their pleasure at having met Eisenhower. The main portion of the letter, however, had concerned the qualifications of Cutler's nephew for service either to "the National Security" or to Eisenhower. The nephew, who was a veteran of World War II and an officer in the Massachusetts Reserve Division, faced the possibility of a call to active duty in the Army.

[2] See no. 1102.

[3] For background see no. 1039. On the same day Eisenhower had attended a luncheon at the Somerset Club in Boston as the guest of Henry L. Mason, Jr., a partner in the firm of Herrick, Smith, Donald & Farley, and George D. Aldrich, of Incorporated Investors. Eisenhower had thanked them in letters of November 27 and 29, respectively (EM. The guest list is in EM, Aldrich Corr. See also *New York Times*, Nov. 23, 1950).

[4] On the late Elliott Carr Cutler see Chandler and Galambos, *Occupation, 1945*, no. 76; and Galambos, *Chief of Staff*, nos. 1217 and 1662. Robert Cutler would

thank Eisenhower (Dec. 1, EM) for recalling memories of his brother. He would quote this paragraph of Eisenhower's letter in Robert Cutler, *No Time for Rest* (Boston, 1965), p. 264.

1095   *Eisenhower Mss.*

To Vannevar Bush   *November 29, 1950*

Dear Dr. Bush: Thank you very much for your note and its highly interesting enclosures. While I have already read it, I realize that it deals with matters of such import that I must study it far more carefully. My instant reaction is, of course, that I concur without reservation.[1]

I miss the occasional conversations I used to have with you when I was on duty in Washington. I wish we could have one soon again— particularly about what was discussed in your memorandum to Bob Lovett.[2]

Thank you again for sending it to me. *Cordially*

[1] Bush, president of the Carnegie Institution of Washington, was the former chairman of the Research and Development Board (for background see no. 313). In his note of November 27 (EM) Bush had enclosed a memorandum (Nov. 20, to Deputy Secretary of Defense Robert A. Lovett) on the reorganization of the NATO Military Production and Supply Board (MPSB). The latter agency, according to the memorandum, faced the enormous task of coordinating during the next three or four years the manufacture in Europe of more than ten billion dollars' worth of military equipment. Representatives of the NATO nations were currently transforming the MPSB into the Defense Production Board, which would have a three-part function: "to review the military production plans of member countries, to work out integrated production plans designed to turn out adequate quantities of end items in the most efficient manner, and to follow the progress of production programs." The experience of the MPSB had shown that the second mission was the most difficult to perform. Both the French and U.S. governments had slowed the work of the MPSB by refusing to release certain items of information regarding production of military equipment. The NATO Defense Committee had decided in the autumn of 1950 to place at the head of the Defense Production Board a U.S. industrialist, whose staff would need a two-thirds majority—rather than unanimous approval—for action (see Lawrence S. Kaplan, *A Community of Interests: NATO and the Military Assistance Program, 1948–1951* [Washington, D.C., 1980], pp. 136–37). The memorandum had included descriptions of the qualifications for three key positions that would probably go to the Americans. Prompt action on appointments to those posts would allow the Defense Production Board to proceed with its work and to forestall the tendency of the MPSB "to flounder indecisively." Bush had appended a two-page list of "possible U.S. appointees."

[2] The memorandum had gone to Lovett under a covering letter of November 27 (EM. For background on Lovett see no. 1018).

To Clarence Dillon *November 29, 1950*

Dear Mr. Dillon:[1] There seems to be nothing to add to the newspaper accounts on the Korean mess. When General Marshall made the public statement that our affairs there are in a critical state he was apparently factual, nothing more.[2]

In spite of the pall of gloom hanging over all of us, the evening at your house was a most interesting one—for me it was also helpful. I never fail to gain something out of the effort to test my ideas against the thinking of others who are also concerned in the great questions of the day. You gathered together, for your dinner, such an unusually keen group of individuals that my education and comprehension were both measurably advanced. (At least, I think so!)[3]

My sincere thanks to you for your hospitality, as well as your many kindnesses to me. *Cordially*

P.S. Soon I shall send you a few of our printed brochures on the Assembly.[4]

[1] A note on the copy of this letter in EM indicates that Eisenhower wrote the original letter to the head of Dillon, Read and Company in longhand.

[2] Chinese Communist troops had repulsed a major offensive by the U.S. Eighth Army and the X Corps along a front of more than seventy miles (for background see no. 1089). On November 28, Secretary of Defense George C. Marshall had used the word *critical* to describe both the world situation and the outlook for U.S. forces in Korea (address to the National Women's Press Club in Washington, D.C.). He had predicted that there lay ahead "a long period of tension during which we must maintain a posture of sufficient strength that the situation won't go into full war" (see *New York Times*, Nov. 29, 1950. For developments see no. 1108).

[3] Dillon had been host of a dinner on the previous day (for background see no. 1093).

[4] The brochure would go out to prospective contributors in early December (see no. 1115).

To Amon Giles Carter, Sr. *November 29, 1950*

Dear Amon:[1] I have just written a letter to Sid, thanking him for the fine check in support of the American Assembly.[2] Naturally, I feel toward you the same deep sense of gratitude. Moreover, I take particular pleasure in the fact that you and Sid, my two oldest friends in Texas who were in a position to support the American Assembly financially and to understand and sympathize with its basic purposes, have taken an outstanding place among the supporters of that great program. So your letter, with its two fine checks, was heart-warming encouragement to me as we here struggle to bring the program to completely successful operation.

Shortly after the checks arrived, I received the bundle of pictures. I cannot tell you how much enjoyment I derived from going through them and recalling to my mind the great pleasure I have had out of my association with you and Sid—an association that now extends back some nine years in his case and only a little less than that in yours. There were three pictures that I especially liked. All of these were taken of the three of us, and two of them had Sid sitting at a table while you and I were standing behind him. In each of these two, I think the expression on Sid's face is remarkable. In one he seems to be highly amused, apparently by something being said by his two friends standing behind him. In the other his look is one of complete skepticism or just tolerant boredom.[3]

Certainly, I am most deeply obligated to you for sending on such a nice set of pictures. Those of your dinner party remind me that I *hope* I have written to Minnie to thank her for the nice evening.[4] I always intend to do these things promptly, but once in a while they slip my mind. In this case, if I have been neglectful, won't you please tell her that her dinner was the highlight of the whole day. She was gracious to have us and I enjoyed every minute of the evening.

Again, my thanks and to show you again how I feel about the American Assembly, my congratulations to you for this evidence of your determination to help our universities join more closely with the entire public in doing something about the great problems that plague us all.[5]

With love to Minnie and warm regard to yourself. *Cordially*
P.S. Remember me also to young Amon.[6]

[1] For background on Carter see no. 258.
[2] In a letter of November 22, 1950, Carter had enclosed two checks for the American Assembly, one for ten thousand dollars from Carter himself and one for fifteen thousand from Sid Richardson (for background on Richardson see no. 113 and the next document). "This is a great work you are carrying on," Carter had said, "and if followed through and supported by liberal, patriotic citizens sufficiently to enable you to carry out the program in its entirety, it will be a blessing to our country and humanity in general" (EM).
[3] Carter had sent Eisenhower a set of photographs taken when the General had visited with Carter and Richardson in Forth Worth, Texas, on November 8, 1950 (see no. 1017).
[4] Mrs. Carter (see no. 622). The Carters had entertained Eisenhower at dinner in Fort Worth on November 8. The General had not written to Mrs. Carter, but on November 17 he had thanked Amon Carter for the "family dinner," and in a handwritten post-script he had sent "Love to Minnie!" (EM).
[5] On the conference plan see no. 1039.
[6] Amon Giles Carter, Jr. (see no. 917).

To Sid Williams Richardson   *November 29, 1950*

Dear Sid:[1] Recently there arrived at my desk two pieces of mail, both dispatched by Amon. The first was a "double check" job, the second a group of pictures, mostly of you, Amon and me.[2] Of course, the checks are of greater significance to this University, to the efforts we here are making to assure a healthy, vigorous and free future and, therefore, to the ultimate welfare of the nation.

The pictures, however, intrigue me so much personally that I simply had to take off a half hour to chuckle over them. The two I like best involve the three of us, in each case, you sitting at a table while Amon and I are standing up to examine something that he is apparently holding just behind your head. Your impish look in one of these entitles the picture to be labled "Oh, yeah," while in the other one your look of tolerant boredom seems to say "My God, is he going to tell that one again?" A third picture I like very much simply because it shows that, while you and Amon have plenty to eat, I am living off nothing more substantial than a glass of water. (However, I cannot account for the fact that my face seems to be as much on the full moon side as is yours.)[3]

Of course, I am delighted with the checks. My friends in Texas have paid me the great compliment of listening carefully to the project on which I am working so hard and of supporting it both intellectually and with their check books. I am more than grateful that you, as my oldest friend in Texas who could possibly be in a position to do something of this order, have thus become one of the prominent members of our American Assembly.[4]

Amon's letter to me says that you spent Thanksgiving down on the Island. You cannot imagine what a feeling that news gave me, almost one of homesickness. As you know, I fell in love with your Island and every time my thoughts stray back to it, I am overcome by nostalgic memories.[5]

With warm personal regard and my very sincere thanks. *Cordially*

[1] For background on Richardson see no. 113.
[2] For Eisenhower's reply to Amon Carter see the preceding document.
[3] See the preceding document, n. 3.
[4] See no. 1023.
[5] For Eisenhower's visit to Richardson's island see no 607.

To Alfred Maximilian Gruenther   *November 30, 1950*
Personal

Dear Al: For a very definite reason I have decided not to call you on
the phone any more to discuss the current military situation. This
reason is that everywhere I go I am put on the witness stand to discuss
the details of the tactical situation and I have come to the conclusion
that it is best for me to know nothing except what I read in the papers—
in this way I cannot reveal any secrets that should remain secrets.

Incidentally, I found one encouraging little note in the paper this
morning; it was a statement by General Walker who was giving his
conclusions that our attack had been very fortunately timed. He pointed
out that, had we not attacked, things for us would have been *really*
bad. At least by comparison, therefore, with what might have been,
we seem to be in fairly good shape and, so far as I am concerned, I
am now grasping at any news that shows that we are not at the very
bottom of the hole.[1]

As you know, there is no one I despise quite so much as the fellow
who is always looking for a "goat" on whom he can heap the blame
for everything bad that has happened. This practice is particularly prev-
alent among those who themselves have just a bit of a guilty feeling.
Consequently, I do not go back in my own mind over the past to point
out, with the benefit of hindsight, where such and such individuals
made grave and significant errors. Indeed, I am never so certain that
I, personally, would have done better in similar circumstances than
those I might be tempted to criticize.

In this particular mess, the one thing that does puzzle me is a seeming
lack of urgency in our preparations, starting last June 25. You will
recall the conversations that afternoon about the 28th of June when
Dr. Snyder and I were sitting in your office and when we later talked
to Ridgway, Joe Collins and others. A couple of days later I returned
to Washington at the invitation of the big Chief and I gained some
assurance again that preparations were going to be speedy, effective and
sufficient.[2] So, the subject that I propose for some conversation when
you and I can get together is just what has happened—possibly, what
has not happened—since the Koreans' first attack and the decision was
made to defend the territory south of the 38th parallel. This particular
phase of the matter does intrigue me, although I admit that I have no
information on which to base any critical appraisal.[3]

I do hope that Dick is progressing well and can soon be invalided
home to complete his convalescence.[4]

Love to Grace[5] and the best to yourself, *Cordially*

P.S. Is Pete Carroll there? If we are beginning to talk about a potential staff in terms of personalities—I'd like to talk to him or you upon occasion. Let's prove to someone—(maybe ourselves) that we *can* streamline![6]

[1] Lieutenant General Walton H. Walker, the Eighth Army CG, had stated that if U.N. troops had not attacked the Chinese Communists on November 24, the U.N. commanders would not have known the strength of their forces. According to Walker, he had seized the initiative and had successfully preempted an enemy offensive supported by an even larger build-up of men and supplies (see *New York Times*, Nov. 30, 1950). General of the Army Douglas MacArthur, C in C, U.N. Command, also believed that Walker's attack had forced the Chinese to reveal their intention of intervening for the purpose of destroying the U.N. armies. "Had I not acted when I did," he would later write, "we would have been a 'sitting duck' doomed to eventual annihilation" (see MacArthur, *Reminiscences*, p. 374; and Schnabel, *Policy and Direction*, p. 275).

[2] Eisenhower had visited Gruenther in Washington, D.C., on June 28, 1950, accompanied by Major General Howard M. Snyder, Sr. (USA, ret.), his physician. Eisenhower had also talked with Lieutenant General Matthew B. Ridgway, Deputy Chief of Staff for Administration, and General J. Lawton Collins, Chief of Staff of the Army (for background see no. 870). On July 5 Eisenhower had traveled to Washington to discuss the situation in Korea with President Truman (see no. 886).

[3] For background see no. 1046.

[4] Gruenther's son, Richard, had been wounded in Korea.

[5] Mrs. Gruenther.

[6] Lieutenant Colonel Paul T. "Pete" Carroll was currently assigned to the Army War College at Fort Leavenworth, Kansas (for background see no. 948).

1100   *Eisenhower Mss.*

To Aksel Nielsen   *November 30, 1950*

Dear Aksel: As I wrote you some time back, the only effect the Pennsylvania deal has on the plans you and I were developing last summer is that it tends to limit, a little bit, the amount I could invest out there.[1] The whole thing is in your hands and I shall go into each of these the same level that you do on the projects that you consider the most promising. As you suggest, I shall merely wait for you to tell me about each as it becomes "ripe."[2]

Of course, I shall be glad to see your friend James Rouse. All he has to do when he comes up here is to give Bob Schulz a ring. We will arrange to have him to come up here at the earliest moment.[3]

Give my love to your family. *Cordially*

[1] See previous correspondence with Nielsen, nos. 998 and 1003, concerning Eisenhower's purchase of a Gettysburg farm and its effect on his plans for investments in Denver, Colorado. The General had been attempting to settle on an upper limit

for his cash investment; a longhand note added at the end of this sentence reads: "My guess is that for projects that you consider truly formidable I could still get together 45–50 thousand. Possibly I'll get to see you as X-mas time."

[2] In a letter of November 27 Nielsen had outlined progress on a number of investment propositions in Denver, including the acquisition of farmland outside of the city and construction of several shopping districts. He promised that "as any of the projects get close to final details, I will write you about them . . . and you can decide definitely at that time if you want in and for how much" (EM). Nielsen would continue to send information concerning these projects to the General's headquarters at SHAPE.

[3] In his letter Nielsen had mentioned the name of James Wilson Rouse, "one of the leading mortgage and property management men in the country." Nielsen strongly recommended that Eisenhower meet Rouse, as "he has some very definite ideas about things that might be done so far as world peace is concerned and would like to talk to you about them . . ." (Nov. 27, EM). According to his appointment calendar, the General would see Rouse on the morning of December 12.

1101

Eisenhower Mss.

November 30, 1950

To Mrs. Samuel Huntington Wolcott, Jr.

Dear Mrs. Wolcott:[1] After returning from Boston I found my desk stacked so high with papers that only today has enough of it been cleared away so that I could find a spot on which to write this note. And, in spite of such excuses, if my dear old mother were alive, she'd still scold me for delaying this long to tell you again what a delightful hour I had at your home a few days ago.[2]

You have a charming group of friends[3] — so much so that my planned exploratory tramp about the farm dwindled to a hasty tour from the comfortable seat of an automobile.

Thank you so much—and won't you convey to all the "ex" Miss Wilds,[4] and their husbands (including your own) my best wishes and warm greetings. *Sincerely*

[1] The former Mary Elizabeth Weld was the wife of Samuel Huntington Wolcott, Jr., vice-president and a trustee of the Consolidated Investment Trust. The Wolcotts lived in Milton, Massachusetts.

[2] On November 22 the General had spent the day in Boston (for background on the visit see no. 1094. Eisenhower's original note was written in longhand).

[3] The General had apparently met the Wolcotts and others at a luncheon sponsored by George D. Aldrich, of Incorporated Investors (see no. 1094. The guest list is in EM, Aldrich Corr.).

[4] The General meant Welds.

To Robert Cutler   *December 1, 1950*

Dear Bobby: I have been pushing the Department of the Army to give me more information on their policies involving recall of reserve officers to active duty.[1] I am sending along with this note a couple of documents I have received, but I must say that they still do not give me a completely satisfactory answer to the question that your nephew raises.

It is clear that the Army will not be calling anyone of field grade (that is, except where the individual of field grade belongs to a unit that is recalled to active duty in its entirety). The only probability, therefore, of extended field service for your nephew would seem to be the outbreak of a general war. Aside from this, the only possibility would seem to be an application for reduction to the grade of captain, a move that would seem to me to be entirely out of order unless there was some special and personal reason on your nephew's part, of which I would, of course, know nothing.[2]

I am sorry that my answer cannot be more informative and positive, but it is the Army that says these things.[3]

With warm personal regard, *Cordially*

P.S. Just as I mail this letter, a final piece of information came in through another office where I had lodged inquiries. I attach it also.

[1] Eisenhower had promised to find out whether or not Cutler's nephew could have a tour of duty in Europe if the Army called him to active service (see no. 1094).

[2] The nephew would thank Eisenhower in a letter of December 4 (same file as document), adding that he preferred to retain his reserve status unless an unlimited emergency arose.

[3] Cutler would also express gratitude in a letter of December 5 (EM), reflecting briefly on the dilemma confronting "*any* individual who has seen some service" and who wanted now to be of help to his country.

1103   *Eisenhower Mss.*

To Arthur Michael Godfrey   *December 2, 1950*

Dear Arthur: The time is now here when we can use to wonderful advantage the donation you pledged to the American Assembly. Your ten thousand is deductible by making it out to Columbia University and merely marking it for "The American Assembly."[1]

I am tempted in this letter to try to tell you about the enthusiasm the project has stirred up all over the country.[2] But I am forced to put off such a recitation until you and I can meet again. You will be gratified, I know, to hear the story.

Incidentally, two other people who were at that luncheon at the Denver Country Club, when you pledged your gift, have also proved most helpful. Fred Manning has been busy working among his friends in the Denver region and, the last I heard, had thirty to forty thousand promised from that area.[3] Mr. Rodman, the man who spoke up at the luncheon in such enthusiastic appraisal of the proposition, has been continuing his good work and has been most effective, particularly around Oklahoma City.[4]

I think that my luncheon dates up to the Christmas Holidays are chockablock, but if you are agreeable, why don't we give our respective office forces the job of arranging an informal luncheon for us just after the first of the year? I'd like to have you at my house—and I'll hunt up a friend or two so that you won't have to listen to me exclusively!![5] *Cordially*

[1] On the pledge from Godfrey, a radio and television entertainer, see no. 1027; for background on the American Assembly see no. 1039. Godfrey would reply in a letter of December 8 (EM) that since he had already contributed to charities as much money as he would be able to deduct from his taxable income during 1950, he wanted to wait until January 2, 1951, to send the check. Eisenhower would agree to this in a letter of December 12 (EM).
[2] On the previous day Eisenhower had sent a note (EM) to William L. Pickens, of Dallas, Texas, thanking him for the letters and checks that he had forwarded on behalf of nine Texans interested in the American Assembly.
[3] For background on Manning, of Denver, Colorado, see no. 1044; on the luncheon see no. 1027.
[4] Roland Rodman was president of the Anderson-Pritchard Oil Company in Oklahoma City, Oklahoma.
[5] Eisenhower's appointment calendar indicates that he breakfasted with Godfrey on December 29.

1104   *Eisenhower Mss.*

To FRED G. GURLEY   *December 2, 1950*
Personal

Dear Fred:[1] With the world situation what it is, I have decided against making the Pasadena trip.[2] I have not yet notified the authorities of the Pasadena Tournament of my final decision but I have told them that I am quite likely to send them this kind of a message within a few days.[3] Both Mamie and I regret losing the opportunity to see and be with old friends, with special reference to you and Ruth, Jerry and Peggy and John and Mrs. Whipple.[4] But I simply cannot bring myself to participate in a holiday festival when the Korean war has again broken out into violent action and American soldiers are really suffering on the battle front.

When I first gave my tentative acceptance to the invitation, the reports from General MacArthur's headquarters were that the war was really over and the matter settled, at least temporarily. That condition no longer persists so I feel that I not only have the right—but for me, the duty—to change my decision.[5]

Both Mamie and I send love to you and Ruth. It is still possible that we may go on to Denver for the holidays and, if we do, may come through Chicago. In that event, I shall send you a timely message so that possibly we can have a few minutes' chat.[6] *Cordially*

---

[1] Gurley was president of the Atchison, Topeka and Santa Fe Railway Company.
[2] Eisenhower had accepted an invitation to be grand marshal of the Tournament of Roses parade in Pasadena, California, on New Year's Day, 1951. He gives a full account of his reasons for canceling the engagement in his November 24 letter to Paul G. Hoffman (see no. 1089. For background on the invitation see no. 1034).
[3] On December 6, 1950, Eisenhower would wire Hoffman, who had helped plan the General's Pasadena visit, and ask that he inform L. Clifford Kenworthy, president of the Pasadena Tournament of Roses Association, of his decision to cancel. "It has become crystal clear," he would write, "that there is no hope of the Korean situation clearing up sufficiently to allow me to carry out my original plans. . . ." On December 19 Eisenhower would wire Kenworthy directly to express his regret and to propose that Kenworthy consider asking a combat veteran returned from Korea to be the grand marshal. "In honoring him," Eisenhower said, "we would be honoring all of our men and women in uniform, including the fighting men who are making daily sacrifices for cause of world peace." Kenworthy would reply the same day (Dec. 19) that he would act immediately on Eisenhower's suggestion. The honors would go to Corporal Robert Stewart Gray, a twenty-one-year-old marine who had been wounded in the retreat from the Changjin reservoir in Korea. Correspondence and the telegrams are in EM; see also *Life* magazine, January 15, 1951, which featured Gray on the cover and published an article, "Corporal Does General's Job," pp. 41–42.
[4] In a letter to Eisenhower of November 30, 1950 (EM), Gurley had offered to arrange a private railroad car for the Eisenhowers' trip to Pasadena. Gurley and his wife Ruth were to have been hosts on board; guests were to have included Jerry D. Brandon and his wife Peggy and John Whipple and his wife Elsa. Brandon, of Chicago, Illinois, headed the Brandon Equipment Company, which specialized in railway supplies. Whipple, according to Gurley, was a director of the Santa Fe Railroad.
[5] In September and October 1950, U.N. forces had driven the North Korean Army out of the southern part of the peninsula (for background see no. 1046). The intervention of the Chinese Communists on October 25, however, had slowed MacArthur's advance, and a massive enemy counterattack on November 25 had forced the U.N. armies to retreat southward. The situation of the U.N. troops would worsen (for developments see no. 1108).
[6] In a note of December 4 Gurley would tell Eisenhower that he understood the General's feelings. Gurley had also canceled plans to attend the Tournament of Roses: "I am as worried as worried can be," he wrote, "and I am in no mood for Pasadena" (EM). On December 19 the Eisenhowers would go to Denver, Col-

orado, to visit Mrs. Eisenhower's parents (see no. 1134, n. 2); there is, however, no further correspondence in EM regarding arrangements for a meeting in Chicago with Gurley. On December 11 Eisenhower would write Robert W. Woodruff to tell him of the decision to cancel the Pasadena trip (for background on Woodruff see no. 258; the letter, drafted by aide Robert L. Schulz, is in EM and in EP, Schulz Coll., Drafts).

1105

Eisenhower Mss.

To Russell Wheeler Davenport

December 5, 1950

Dear Russell: Thank you very much for your letter.[1] We had a most interesting conversation the other day, but I never cease to be amazed that thoughtful persons seem honestly to believe that I have something out of the ordinary to contribute to the great problems of our day. I am so conscious of inadequacies, in so many directions, even in discussing intelligently some of the more abstruse questions that plague us that I have great difficulty in avoiding feeling ashamed of myself.[2]

Of course, I am grateful for your sending me a copy of your poem. Your friends really gave it a boost and I am going to read it promptly.[3] *Cordially*

[1] Davenport, moderator of Life Round Tables, had mentioned in his letter of November 28 (EM) his disappointment at missing a recent luncheon meeting at which Eisenhower's future in politics had been discussed. Eisenhower's appointment calendar indicates that the meeting had taken place at Columbia University on November 27 and that there had been five persons present, including the General (for background on Davenport see no. 871). Davenport had heard that the luncheon had been successful, and he attributed this to "almost two years of very humble and painstaking work on the part of Eddie, John and myself." Eddie was probably Edwin N. Clark, a business consultant and executive in New York City, and John was no doubt John Gordon Bennett, a Republican of Rochester, New York (for background on Clark see Galambos, *Chief of Staff*, no. 1456). Davenport argued that it was time to formulate policies "so that the whole thing can become a crusade for principles rather than just another political dog-fight," and he suggested that "John and the Governor" take care of organizational matters. The governor was probably ex-Governor James H. Duff, of Pennsylvania, whose constituents had recently elected him to the U.S. Senate (for background on Duff see no. 937).
[2] For other examples of Eisenhower's ambivalence see nos. 638, 786, and 980. For developments see no. 1159.
[3] Davenport's poem is not in EM.

To Allan Blair Kline   *December 5, 1950*

Dear Mr. Kline: It seems scarcely necessary for me to assure you of my great feeling of distinction in your invitation to address a message to the members of the Farm Bureau, meeting in convention at Dallas. I was even more honored by your suggestion that I appear before your distinguished group to discuss some aspects of today's world situation.[1] My utter inability to avail myself of this privilege moves me, however, to send to them, along with my best wishes and personal greetings, a brief comment on this subject.

In these days, when we are buffeted by rumors and alarms and evil tidings, we shall be heartened if we survey the assets of America. Among these we find the productivity of our industrial economy, unequaled by any combination of enemies; our capacity for global communications and transport; our wealth in skills and science; our broad and fertile acres; above all, the spiritual strength of our people, time and again proved in generations of struggle for freedom and peace among men.

You who are close to the land are the source of a particular and valuable segment of this spiritual strength. You are most direct in descent from the pioneer men and women who courageously and triumphantly advanced the American way across a continent. Their sturdiness of purpose, their self-reliance, their day-by-day courage—all these are still part of the American heritage—and especially of the American farmers' heritage.

So, you can help us all face up to the stark reality that the aggressive forays against the free world can be met only by high purpose, acute comprehension of every danger, and by adequate armed strength. You can help make us realize that confidence in America, unity among Americans, sacrifice for America can today banish from the world the dire menace to our way of life.

Never again, we pray, will the defense of home and country demand that the men and women of America fight a global war. But the spirit of the pioneer, coupled with the realization that peace and freedom are won and maintained only by those who prize them above wealth and life, this spirit, under God, will be our salvation against any threat whatsoever.

With best wishes and warm personal regard,[2] *Cordially*

---

[1] Kline, president of the American Farm Bureau Federation, had invited Eisenhower (letter, Oct. 20, EM) to address the convention on December 12 or 13. Eisenhower had declined in a telegram of December 1 (EM), offering instead to send a message that Kline could read to the convention. (Kevin C. McCann, Eisenhower's assistant, helped prepare Eisenhower's telegram and this document;

a draft of the telegram, with Eisenhower's changes, is in the same file. On Eisenhower's friendship with Kline see no. 581, n. 7.)
[2] In a note of December 16 (EM) Kline would inform Eisenhower that the convention had received his message with enthusiasm.

1107 *Eisenhower Mss.*

To Thomas Richard Garlington *December 5, 1950*

Dear Dick: A few days ago when Mr. Wilcox brought in to me the most wonderful pair of golf shoes I ever saw, he informed me that they were a present from you.[1] I had nursed the faint hope that I was going to be able to come down to Augusta for the governors' meeting and would hunt you up to thank you in person. But I have now concluded that only a miracle will give me a chance to get down there this winter.[2]

In any event, I hope you know just how deeply appreciative I am of your extraordinary kindness. The shoes themselves fit wonderfully and represent complete perfection in the bootmaker's art. Even so, it is the giver rather than the gift alone that makes them so valuable to me.

Lately I have been so very busy that I scarcely know when my friends come to town for a few hours or days. But I do hope that, if you or Bobby[3] should be in the city, you will not fail to give me a ring to see whether we could not have an hour in which to forget some of the cares of the world and to talk about more important things like long drives and short putts.

Again, my grateful thanks for your thoughtfulness.[4] *Cordially*

P.S. Of course, remember me warmly to Bobby.

[1] Garlington, of Atlanta, Georgia, was a member of the executive committee of the United States Golf Association and a member of the Augusta National Golf Club. In a letter of October 25 (EM) he had asked Lieutenant Colonel Robert L. Schulz, Eisenhower's aide, to lend an old pair of the General's shoes to C. L. Wilcox (vice-president of Field and Flint Company, of Brockton, Massachusetts) so that a properly fitting pair could be made for Eisenhower. Schulz mailed the shoes on November 8, and Wilcox returned them on the thirteenth, promising to make a couple of pairs of other styles if they turned out well. Garlington would explain why he had given Eisenhower the shoes in a letter of December 16 (EM): "I found out last Spring in Augusta that you had difficulty with the foot end of yourself, so I thought I would try to help you out a little, because I don't know of anybody in the world that handles the other end any better than you."
[2] Eisenhower had informed the secretary of the Augusta National Golf Club (Nov. 24, EM, Subject File, Clubs and Associations) that he would not attend the meeting of the board of governors on December 9.
[3] Golf champion Robert T. Jones, Jr.
[4] Eisenhower would thank Garlington for another pair of shoes in a letter of January

4, 1951 (EM); Wilcox would also send Eisenhower a pair of combat boots in April (see Eisenhower to Wilcox, May 4, 1951, EM).

My evening schedule for this date is typical of my current life. Invites to 3 dinners, all of which I thought I should accept and (as it turns out after enough talking between my A.D.C. & prospective hosts) I'm *going to all 3*. By arrangement I go to the 1st for cocktails, the second to chat a while and finally make the 3d, supposedly, just as the party is to go to the dinner table. What a mess! The first is an Engineering Smoker; the 2nd a veteran organization honoring my old friend Amon Carter and the 3d (the one I personally accepted a long time back) a dinner honoring my friend Dave Calhoun. Both Amon and Dave have been active in helping the A.A.[1] —

The Korean situation is tragic, although I still believe that MacA can stabilize the situation if he comes back far enough to stretch the hostile lines & expose their communications to incessant air attack.[2] What have we been doing here in the Z of I for 5 mos.??[3] Something is terribly wrong — I feel that my hunch of last July 1 was right — but I was wrong when I supposed that both the Def. Depts & the White House would heed the fine advice I gave on preparation.[4]

[1] The Columbia Engineering School Alumni Association had postponed its annual smoker from November to December to accommodate Eisenhower's crowded schedule. According to correspondence in EM, Columbia University Corr., Kevin C. McCann, Eisenhower's aide, had served as liaison with the alumni association. Eisenhower's appointment calendar indicates that he would leave for the smoker at the Columbia University Club at 6:00 P.M. One hour later he was to be at a dinner sponsored by the American Legion Air Service Post No. 501 at the Savoy Plaza Hotel. Amon G. Carter, president and publisher of the *Fort Worth Star-Telegram*, would receive the Hawks Memorial Award there. At approximately 8:30 P.M., Eisenhower was to be at a dinner honoring David R. Calhoun, Jr., at the Links Club. The hosts would be Harold Holmes Helm, president, and Isaac B. Grainger, senior vice-president of the Chemical Bank & Trust Company of New York (on Carter's interest in the American Assembly see no. 1097; on Calhoun's work see no. 1024).

Philip Young, dean of Columbia's Graduate School of Business, had reminded Eisenhower in a memorandum of this same day (EM) that the General was to speak at the Tax Foundation dinner on December 6. The guests would expect a description of the American Assembly, Young advised, and the occasion might serve as "a very fitting climax" to the fund-raising campaign. Young suggested that Eisenhower comment on "the general world picture, especially Russia," before mentioning the American Assembly. John Wesley Hanes (A.B. Yale 1915), chairman of the Tax Foundation, would thank Eisenhower in a letter of December 7 for his help in making the dinner successful (see also Eisenhower's reply of December 11, both in EM).

[2] For background on the U.N. retreat see no. 1089. On December 8 General of the Army Douglas MacArthur, C in C, U.N. Command, would order the X Corps to evacuate by sea from Hungnam, North Korea, and to reinforce the Eighth Army in its withdrawal below the thirty-eight parallel. U.N. forces would maintain a defensive stance until January 15, 1951, when the Eighth Army would penetrate Chinese lines on the western edge of the Korean peninsula; encouraged by the limited resistance, the Americans would probe the Chinese again on January 25 and February 5. MacArthur's troops would mount Operation KILLER on February 21 with logistical and fire support from the Air Force (see Schnabel, *Policy and Direction*, pp. 326–406; and Futrell, *United States Air Force in Korea*, pp. 314–27). By March the tide of the war would appear to change in favor of the U.N. forces as they accomplished KILLER's objectives.

[3] Z of I ("Zone of the Interior") is a miliary abbreviation denoting the continental United States.

[4] Eisenhower had consistently argued that implementation of President Truman's decision to aid the South Koreans in June 1950 required a rapid and forceful application of U.S. strength. In his discussions with officials in Washington, D.C., on June 28 and July 5 he had emphasized the need for decisive action (see nos. 870 and 886; see also nos. 914 and 1099).

1109   *Eisenhower Mss.*

To WINSTON SPENCER CHURCHILL   *December 6, 1950*

Dear Winston: Thank you very much for sending me a copy of THE HINGE OF FATE.[1] I have, of course, read in my daily paper some of its selected passages, but I am starting now to give it thorough study. A single glance shows it to be as full of meat as are its predecessors in the series.

Your book describes the arrangements that were made at Casablanca for setting up an Allied Headquarters. There is related, a bit later, Brendan Bracken's attitude with respect to the probably public reaction in Britain to any overplaying of the Supreme Commander's role. In these passages more than history is involved—there are valuable hints on human behavior, and there are lessons for the future.[2]

If I were pushed to place a tag on the one lesson on which I feel able to comment with some confidence, I would call it "The Gradual Approach" in developing efficiency in Allied Command machinery. Only tolerance, patience, readiness to conciliate and an ability to look at the other side of the coin can make a success of such ventures. Since these are the qualities that soldiers traditionally abhor (there is no

D'Artagnan flavor to them),[3] there is plenty of room for error and failure, after the headquarters has been theoretically established.

If future war-time Statesmen should become dogmatic in the assumption that through written documents, chock-full of provisos, whereases and conditions, they can assure the success of an Allied Command or of the military operations that are to be directed by that Command, then we shall have nothing but sterile, uninspired and totally unsatisfactory performance. Likewise, if any military individual, designated for a high position in such a headquarters, becomes obsessed with the need for glorifying his particular position (and this they sometimes do in the name of their country's prestige), a similar failure will result. This applies—and I hope that this does not make me appear immodest—with particular force to the Supreme Commander.

I am particularly confident that any man named to Supreme Commander must approach it *studiously* and *gradually* and imbued with an idea to "earn" his way rather than to take the attitude that most of us in the military do when we encounter a routine change of assignment. In the normal case, the size and composition of our commands are specified exactly and the scope and extent of our authority defined accurately by regulation and custom. Consequently, we waste no time in getting on with whatever chore may be given us; we demonstrate without delay "who is boss." That whole attitude must be left behind when an Allied Command is brought into being.

Historically, the peak of mutual confidence and trust—which must exist not only between governments composing an alliance, but between these governments and their commanders in the field and among these commanders as individuals—was reached in the war in Europe when you and the CIGS informed me in no uncertain terms that, if ever I had any dissatisfaction with any British commander, no matter what his rank or his position, he would be relieved instantly upon my request.[4] Incidentally, on that day I saw you with new eyes—in a light that has never since left you, so far as I'm concerned.

When such a situation as this has been brought about through mutual tolerance, understanding and application to duty, the problem has become easy; only disaster clearly traceable to the stupidity of the top man could possibly unhorse him. But the real job is to bring everyone forward to this cooperative attitude.

Forgive me if I have seemed to write to you about this point at excessive length. But I cannot forget that events march fast in the world. Much of what we did in World War II has no application whatsoever to any future conflict into which we might be forced. But these experiences and lessons that deal with human beings—and particularly when these human beings are placed into positions of such responsibility that they involve capacity to damage the coalition as well as to rivet it tightly together—should, if remembered and heeded, do much to smooth out future difficulty and to expedite the true business of soldiers, which is merely to win victories and then to retire to the rear of the stage.

My present personal plans (if not interrupted by a call to duty) will bring me to the United Kingdom in the late spring.[5] I shall then, of course, hope to call upon you to pay my respects. If you should have any interest in the matters I have so haltingly spoken of in this letter, we could talk about them then.

Again, my warm thanks for your magnificent volume. Please extend my greetings to your charming wife and to your nice family.

With warm personal regard,[6] *Cordially*

[1] For background on the fourth volume of Churchill's memoir and publication of excerpts in the *New York Times* see no. 996. There are two drafts of this letter in EM, both heavily reworked by Eisenhower.

[2] Eisenhower refers to agreements made by the CCS at the Casablanca Conference (Jan. 11–25, 1943) concerning reorganization of the Allied command structure. In the new arrangement, Eisenhower, then Commander in Chief, North Africa Theater of Operations, would have three principal subordinates: General Sir Harold Alexander, deputy commander of the Allied forces; Air Chief Marshal Sir Arthur W. Tedder, commander of the air forces; and Admiral of the Fleet Sir Andrew Cunningham, commander of the naval forces (for background see Churchill, *Hinge of Fate*, pp. 674–95; Eisenhower, *Crusade in Europe*, pp. 135–39; and Chandler, *War Years*, nos. 744, 810, and 811). Brendan Bracken, British Minister of Information, had informed Churchill of his concern over British reaction to these command appointments (for background on Bracken see no. 179). In a note to Churchill, Bracken had said that if General Eisenhower's appointment were stressed and Alexander's and Tedder's functions were left "vaguely undefined," then we must expect a "spate of criticism from the British press." Bracken predicted that Americans would resent the "almost inevitably resulting criticism of General Eisenhower's appointment or any comparison between his military qualifications and those possessed by General Alexander." Churchill sent Bracken's note to Roosevelt, saying that he thought the President "should take the rough with the smooth about British public opinion," but the Prime Minister promised to "utter the most solemn warning against controversy in these matters. . . . Please do the like on your side to help your faithful partner" (*Hinge of Fate*, pp. 724–26).

[3] D'Artagnan was the adventurous soldier hero of the Alexandre Dumas triology, *The Three Musketeers* (1844), *Twenty Years After* (1845), and *The Viscount of Bragelonne* (1848–50).

[4] See Eisenhower, *Crusade in Europe*, p. 317.

[5] The call to duty would come on December 19, 1950, when Eisenhower would be designated Supreme Allied Commander, Europe, North Atlantic Treaty Organization (NATO) (see no. 1134; and *New York Times*, Dec. 20, 1950). The General would visit the United Kingdom in January 1951 (*New York Times*, Jan. 14, 1951).

[6] On December 11 Churchill would cable Eisenhower that he was "deeply grateful" for this letter (EM).

To Arthur Hays Sulzberger   *December 8, 1950*

Dear Arthur: To my mind President Miller has answered his own question in the language in which he poses it in the third paragraph of his letter.[1] He says:

"We recognize that America faces in the century ahead vast new problems of world dimension. Accordingly, we must strive for a new comprehension of the role of a private university of the type at Northwestern as it relates to these problems and to the mission of America."

He clearly recognizes that universities can no longer feel that they are discharging their full responsibility to the public that supports them if they confine their activities to the training of "future" leaders and in the "advancing the frontiers of knowledge." Actually, in the paragraph I have just quoted above, Dr. Miller is repeating the song that we here at Columbia have been singing for these many months. (I think Dr. Miller attended one of the meetings in Chicago where the American Assembly was under discussion.)[2]

Consequently, in your place, I would merely write him a little treatise which would take his third paragraph as a text, enlarge upon it a bit and then urge him to initiate some definite concrete plan during their Centennial year.

You note the last three words of the paragraph to which I refer are *"mission of America."* Here, you have in a definite form the same concept that we are dealing with in our Bicentennial, namely, freedom and free access to knowledge, since these are basic to the American system. However, in order to reemphasize our own Bicentennial aim, you might enlarge a bit upon this phase of the program that you would urge him to undertake.[3]

I regret that, at this moment, I do not have time to give you a more logical and detailed outline of my idea but I suspect that, from what I have already written, you can get my basic thought. *Cordially*

---

[1] Sulzberger, a trustee of Columbia University and publisher of the *New York Times*, had asked for Eisenhower's help (Dec. 4, 1950, EM) in answering a letter of November 30 (same file) from James Roscoe Miller (M.S. Northwestern 1931), president of Northwestern University. Miller had observed that his institution would soon celebrate its centennial, and he was seeking new ways for Northwestern to be of service to the nation. Sulzberger was one of ten individuals from whom Miller was soliciting opinions, and he promised not to publicize the publisher's views without first obtaining his permission.

[2] Miller might have heard Eisenhower describe Columbia's conference plan, called the American Assembly, in Chicago, Illinois, on October 23 or November 7, 1950 (for background see nos. 1045 and 1061; on the conference plan see nos.

605, 844, and 1039. On Eisenhower's hopes that Columbia would contribute to the solution of the nation's vital problems see nos. 482, 826, and 979).

[3] Sulzberger was chairman of the committee that was planning Columbia's bicentennial activities (see no. 495).

1111   *Eisenhower Mss.*

To James S. Alexander   *December 11, 1950*

Dear Mr. Alexander: The size of my account has no significance whatsoever except that I just seem to be spending more than I can possibly make.[1] There are so many worthwhile projects in New York that stir my desire to help that I sometimes forget that I am just a poor College President.

In any event, it was more than kind of you to express concern and to write me such a nice letter. I am delighted, also, to have your Season's Greetings which I assure you I return to you in full measure and with an expression of my thanks for your many courtesies and those your organization have continued to show to me. *Cordially*

[1] Alexander, a vice-president of Guaranty Trust Company of New York, had asked in a note of December 6 (EM) whether the low level of funds in Eisenhower's account was an indication that he planned to close the account. Alexander had explained that the bank had taken special interest in Eisenhower's account "because it is one which we are so pleased to have."

1112   *Council on Foreign Relations Archives*

To Harry S. Truman   *[December 11, 1950]*
Confidential

First Paragraph draft by General Eisenhower: H.F.A.[1]

We, members of the Council of Foreign Relations, convinced that our country and the free world are in critical danger of defeat and the extinction of our treasured ideals believe that the nation can restore peace and stability only through unlimited and unified exertion and sacrifice, accompanied by definite risk of global war. In these circumstances and because this institution was established to study problems involved in our relations with other nations, we respectfully submit to you the following as our analysis of the current danger and our profound convictions as to what must now be done.

(A) A disunited free world is certain to fall, piecemeal, under the tyrannical power of Soviet imperialism.

(B) There is today in the nations comprising the North Atlantic Union such pitifully inadequate military force that it is fair to assume that only our possession of atomic weapons and a Russian economic and political unreadiness to risk the consequences of a war of attrition against the U.S. have maintained an uneasy peace.

(C) The only way in which our peaceful intent and moral purposes will be respected by the Soviets is the rapid production by us, and by our friends, of powerful military forces. To this effort the only limit should be national solvency, and we should recognize its price as sacrifice by all in the whole free world to include definite recessions in our standards of living through payment of taxes, longer work hours and military service as an obligation of citizenship.[2]

(D) We warn especially against dependence upon international paper agreements except when these reflect the determined will of cooperating peoples and are speedily implemented by rapid production of forces.

(E) The U.S. must not, under any circumstances, accept national responsibility for military command in Europe except as a consequence of the mutual confidence engendered by successful inauguration of the purposes described in D above.[3]

(F) Our own national efforts must attain maximum effectiveness through:

1. Instituting educational programs concerning all pertinent facts in the problem.[4]

2. Inspire public opinion to respond to the danger of the situation as it has so often in the past.

3. Instituting production programs that will emphasize speed and efficiency and minimize costs, both through careful planning and through recapture of profits in taxes.[5]

4. Produce military forces at maximum speed and economy under a system of universal military service at nominal pay, and building up reserve forces as well as adequate strength in being. We believe we should station in Europe, as soon as possible, about 20 U.S. divisions with adequate air support and cooperating with naval forces equal to controlling sea lanes wherever our interests are involved. Strategic air strength should be equal to the demands of an effective bombing attack against Russia.[6]

5. Doing all things that will produce the strength necessary to carry us through the tensions of the next several decades, without war if possible but capable of waging it effectively if it is thrust upon us. Especially important is the need to do this with full determination that whatever individual liberty is sacrificed to produce and maintain necessary force will be automatically restored when the definite *danger of foreign aggression subsides*. Finally we believe that a Citizens' Committee should be organized under the President, comprised of respected leaders

of American business, professions, education and religion, to sit either constantly or at frequent intervals at the seat of government, to advise with appropriate agencies of government on critical problems of organizations, financing, use of man and woman power, and of public opinion, and in assisting the government in all phases of national activity where their experience, knowledge and effort might prove useful.[7]

[1] Eisenhower drafted this letter on December 11 at a meeting of the Aid to Europe Group of the Council on Foreign Relations. The General was chairman of the group (for background see no. 269). Hamilton Fish Armstrong—that is, H.F.A.— editor of *Foreign Affairs* and a member of the study group, would make major revisions in the first paragraph. There would also be changes in the remainder of the letter after W. Averell Harriman, Special Assistant to President Truman on Foreign Affairs, made suggestions; Allen W. Dulles, another member of the study group, would relay these to Armstrong. A note at the top of the revised draft indicates that Eisenhower would make additional revisions "as a condition of accepting the others" (for background on Armstrong and Dulles see no. 269; on Harriman see no. 852).

According to a digest of the discussion at the meeting on the eleventh, Eisenhower originally proposed the idea of sending a statement to the President (see Council on Foreign Relations, Study Group on Aid to Europe, "Digest of Discussion, Twentieth Meeting, 12/11/50," p. 5, same file as document). Henry M. Wriston, president of Brown University and also a member of the group, would maintain in a memorandum of April 22, 1968, that a comment that he had made at the meeting had "precipitated" the letter (see Henry M. Wriston, "Eisenhower Study Group Letter to President Truman, December 12, 1950," Apr. 22, 1968, p. 1, enclosed in George S. Franklin, Jr., to Eisenhower, Apr. 23, 1968, Council on Foreign Relations Mss., Eisenhower Library, Abilene. For another account of the meeting see Lyon, *Portrait of the Hero*, pp. 415–16).

[2] For Eisenhower's views on military service see nos. 912, 1006, and 1042. The phrase "the productive capacity of a free economy" would replace "national solvency" in the final draft of the letter. That version would include the following additional sentence: "No war premiums should go either to capital or labor."

[3] In no. 1045 Eisenhower had also expressed his concern that the United States not conclude an agreement on forces "that would necessarily remain largely a paper one and would give more opportunity for debate than for action." He probably feared the consequences of a compromise such as that accepted by the North Atlantic Council deputies on December 7, 1950 (see no. 1064). The deputies had agreed that the United States should make a specific commitment of troops to Europe even though the question of French fulfillment of obligations remained unresolved. The plan's appealing feature was its proposal for German participation in the NATO force. The contribution of the Federal Republic would comprise less than one-fifth of the manpower pool, and the German contingents were to be dispersed among the Belgian and Italian forces (see Kaplan, *A Community of Interests*, p. 130; and McGeehan, *The German Rearmament Question*, pp. 84–87. For background see no. 1050).

[4] On Eisenhower's interest in U.S. information programs see nos. 60, 785, 890, and 918.

[5] In its final form, this section would read as follows: "Expedite with all possible urgency the placing of orders for our military requirements and for those of other nations willing to fight with us, emphasizing speed and efficiency and minimum

costs. Cut non-essential spending to the bone." For Eisenhower's views on industrial mobilizaiton see no. 914.

[6] The last two sentences of this paragraph would become parts 5 and 6 in the revised version. Concomitant with the proposal for "a strong U.S. ground force" in Europe there would be a requirement that the Allies contribute "comparable forces." The figure of twenty U.S. divisions would not appear in the final draft. Eisenhower had suggested that number during the meeting, but Harriman would request that Dulles delete it the following day; Armstrong would ask Eisenhower to agree to the change (see Council on Foreign Relations, "Digest of Discussion," p. 6; and Wriston, "Eisenhower Study Group Letter to President Truman," p. 12, both cited in n. 1 above). Eisenhower had argued at the meeting that U.S. acceptance of command responsibility in NATO should be combined with firm pledges of troops. He believed that such questions as which areas would be under the control of the supreme commander and whether the supreme commander would deal directly with heads of governments were less important than commitments of forces. The General had also revealed that Truman and Harriman had described the mission of the supreme commander as that of a "super-ambassador" (see Council on Foreign Relations, "Digest of Discussion," p. 6, cited in n. 1 above).

[7] This would be step 7 in the final draft, and the only significant change would be the omission of the recommendation for a citizens' committee. In his memorandum of April 22, 1968, Wriston would surmise that the deletion had been a consequence of his remark to the study group that the Committee on The Present Danger would issue a statement on December 12. The committee would call for the mobilization of manpower and resources to meet the threat of aggression by the Communists (see *New York Times*, Dec. 13, 1950. See also Schulz, memorandum for record, Nov. 1, 1952, EM, Committee on The Present Danger Corr.).

Armstrong would place a date of December 12 on the final version of this letter and enclose it in a note of the same day to Harriman explaining that the paper was the work of a group of members of the Council on Foreign Relations and that it did not represent the views of the council. The following persons were listed as signers: Hamilton Fish Armstrong, Percy W. Bidwell, William Diebold, Jr., Allen W. Dulles, Edward Mead Earle, George S. Franklin, Jr., Walter H. Mallory, Stacy May, Arthur S. Nevins, Philip D. Reed, Lindsay Rogers, and Henry M. Wriston (copies are in the same file as this document; and in EM, Council on Foreign Relations Corr.).

Truman would send Harriman a memorandum of December 15 thanking him for the letter and calling it "an interesting document" and saying that he had read it "with a lot of pleasure." Harriman would enclose the memorandum in a note of the following day to Armstrong (copies are in the same file as this document; and in EM, Harriman Corr.).

1113   *Eisenhower Mss.*

To GEORGE CATLETT MARSHALL   *December 12, 1950*
Secret

Dear General Marshall: I spent Saturday morning with the Joint Chiefs of Staff and obtained my first slant on their thinking with respect to the prospective European Command.[1] Of course, I have already indicated to the President and to you that I shall undertake the responsibility of Supreme Command in Europe if I am requested unanimously by the Governments concerned, and designated by the President. But, in making this commitment to the President, he clearly indicated that he would not ask me to undertake this task unless the advanced political and military arrangements were such as to give justifiable promise of success.[2]

At the Saturday meeting there was mentioned a "Paper" in which there has apparently been some agreement, at the military level, as to the amount of military force that each participating nation would be expected to contribute as a minimum. But it seemed to me that there was apparent a readiness to rush the United States into a responsibility, namely that of taking over Command in Europe, without a careful evaluation of the situation and without clear comprehension of all that this assumption of responsibility might mean.[3]

The whole venture is one in which the only true basis is, of course, mutual confidence and I quite realize it is hoped that the selection of an individual for Supreme Commander will help to build up and enhance this confidence. But the seeds of it must exist before our country makes any commitment for additional responsibilities, particularly that of assuming command. These seeds must be clearly perceived and there must be logical reason for believing that they can be developed through assumption by America of leadership in the whole venture and by naming to command an individual who will work patiently and tirelessly at the task.

Specifically, I am concerned about the following:

(a) The assumption that any agreement respecting the German question that is reached among Britain, France and America will automatically solve that vexing problem — that the German reaction will be one of pleased acceptance.[4] The Chiefs of Staff, of course, clearly perceive that this is not true but, nevertheless, some of the circumstances of this whole effort give rise to the suspicion that some of them have shut their eyes to the grave consequences of miscalculating badly in this regard.

(b) The failure of any paper, that I have seen, to contain a full, warmhearted pledge on the part of each country that it intends to do its maximum in order to make sure that the project succeeds.

(c) The degree to which some of the papers are filled up with detailed conditions, circumstances and arrangements for command, all of which gives rise to the suspicion that people are more engaged in watching each other and in insisting upon limitations upon unified command than in supporting with their full strength the efforts of the selected commander. For example, there seems to be a "staff" desire to separate the Mediterranean from the main theater.

This shows the kind of attitude in which the problem is being approached.[5]

(d) One trend of thinking seemed to me to indicate uncertainty that the American Army could place in Europe more than three or four divisions, and this out of a planned Army strength of 1,260,000.[6]

If we are going to pursue the old policy of loading up overhead and staff organizations to the hilt and produce out of this number of men so few fighting units that we cannot put in Europe something on the order of 10 to 20 divisions (at least during the critical and risky stages of this venture) then I wonder how we can expect other nations to attain the standards of sacrifice and devotion that we require.

(e) Initially, of course, the American contingent within the Command structure must be largely Air Force and Naval Air Units. These must be as powerful as we can make them.

I have no wish to add to the burdens you are carrying. I hope, also, that I am not too much influenced by my own personal ideas, convictions or by even lesser motives of personal convenience. I am very sure that America is dealing with a project of which the significance may continue to grow, especially in the minds of our own people and, equally important, in the minds of all the people of Europe. Because of this, let us make no commitments involving additional responsibilities, including command responsibilities, except as we can justifiably expect to carry them out. We must expect the same of others.

While I was in Washington, I talked about this problem at some length with Mr. Harriman, but you were on the Hill and I did not get a chance to discuss it with you. In order to give him an inkling of my thinking, I am sending a copy of this letter to Mr. Harriman.[7] He may wish to check my memory and understanding with those of the President, concerning our first meeting. I am certain, however, that there is no possible difference between the two of us.[8]

It was nice to see you at the Red Cross luncheon and I regret that we did not have an opportunity for a real talk.[9] *Very sincerely*

[1] An earlier draft of this letter is in the same file. According to Eisenhower's appointment calendar, he had met with the JCS in Washington, D.C., on Saturday, December 9.

[2] For background see no. 1045.

[3] On October 23 Marshall had approved a JCS paper recommending the major military force levels that each NATO country should achieve in the years to come. The United States, according to this paper, was to raise 14 divisions for NATO by July 1954. The force levels in the JCS proposal were very similar to those approved later that month by the NATO Defense Committee, which comprised the defense ministers of the NATO member nations, when it had agreed upon a Medium Term Defense Plan. This plan had set forth total NATO force requirements for 49⅓ combat-ready divisions, none of which were to be German (Walter S. Poole, *The History of the Joint Chiefs of Staff: The Joint Chiefs of Staff and*

National Policy, vol. IV, *1950–1952* [Wilmington, Del., 1980], pp. 207–8, 213; and JCS 2073/81, Oct. 11, 1950, CCS 092 Western Europe [3-12-48], Sec. 60).

Eisenhower might have been referring to MC 30, Nov. 18, 1950, "Report by the Standing Group to the Military Committee on Military Aspects of German Participation in the Defense of Western Europe," which had received the concurrence of the North Atlantic Council deputies on December 9. This paper stressed the urgency of securing a West German contribution to the NATO force; nevertheless, it also included proposals for limitations on the size of German land formations, on the types of military equipment that could be produced in German factories, and on the responsibilities for services of supply of the German units (see State, *Foreign Relations, 1950*, vol. III, *Western Europe*, pp. 517–18, 531–32).

[4] The North Atlantic Council deputies had arranged a compromise on the question of German participation on December 7 (for background see the preceding document). Within the Federal Republic there was no consensus on the terms under which German units would join the NATO force. In recent speeches Chancellor Konrad Adenauer had insisted on equality for German troops within the proposed army, but he faced the opposition of the Social Democratic Party to any agreement that might lead to a revival of militarism or make permanent the division of Germany (see Konrad Adenauer, *Memoirs, 1945–53* [Chicago, 1965], pp. 304–9; McGeehan, *The German Rearmament Question*, pp. 67–74; and *New York Times*, Dec. 12, 1950. See also JCS 2073/95, Nov. 27, 1950, CCS 092 Western Europe [3-12-48], Sec. 63).

[5] Eisenhower was probably referring to a report that the North Atlantic Military Committee would submit to the North Atlantic Defense Committee on December 12. The former group, consisting of one top military representative from each of the nations belonging to NATO, had proposed that in the Mediterranean there be "a separate overall Naval Command directly responsible to the Standing Group. . . ." The report had included a definition of the latter as "the authority responsible for coordinating the requirements of all Fronts." According to this plan, the Standing Group, consisting of the American, British, and French representatives on the Military Committee, would be the channel through which Eisenhower would deal with matters in the Mediterranean (see State, *Foreign Relations, 1950*, vol. III, *Western Europe*, p. 554).

Deputy Secretary of Defense Robert A. Lovett would inform Secretary of State Dean G. Acheson on December 15 that Eisenhower was "very unhappy at what he assumed was an effort on the part of the British and our Navy to remove the Mediterranean forces and the North Sea forces from the command of the Supreme Commander." The JCS had reassured Eisenhower, according to Lovett, that during an emergency every American serviceman in Europe would come under his command (see memorandum of telephone conversation, by Barbara Evans, personal assistant to the Secretary of State, December 15, 1950, *ibid.*, p. 578).

[6] There were currently two U.S. Army divisions in Europe; four more would go to West Germany after Eisenhower's appointment as Supreme Commander of the NATO forces (see Robert Endicott Osgood, *NATO: The Entangling Alliance* [Chicago, 1962], p. 77).

[7] See the following document.

[8] In a telegram of December 13 Chief of Naval Operations Forrest P. Sherman would inform General of the Army Omar N. Bradley, chairman of the JCS, that he was "disturbed" to hear of Eisenhower's dissatisfaction with the instructions given Sherman by the JCS. Admiral Sherman, who was presiding at meetings of the Military Committee in London, said that the Military Committee had adopted views that were apt to be more in line with Eisenhower's than were the instructions. Moreover, Sherman had persuaded the Military Committee "to pave the way for

review and further changes after recommendations by Supreme Commander Europe." Sherman would return to Washington to discuss NATO matters with the JCS and with Eisenhower on December 14 (see Sherman to Bradley, Dec. 13, 1950, CJCS, Bradley Files, 092.2 North Atlantic Treaty, Nov./Dec. 1950; and *New York Times*, Dec. 11, 1950).

[9] Eisenhower and Marshall had attended a luncheon at the Bankers Club in New York City on December 8. David Sarnoff, national chairman of the Red Cross 1951 Fund, had been the host (see *New York Times*, Dec. 9, 1950. For background on Sarnoff see no. 334).

Eisenhower, Marshall, and Lovett met in Washington to discuss these issues on December 14. Eisenhower criticized the "penny pinching" attitude characteristic of some NATO nations in their efforts to furnish forces for the common defense. He told Marshall and Lovett that he thought the problem of enlisting German support for Western European defense was crucial. Eisenhower also believed that the United States should be prepared to commit ten divisions to NATO if the European countries demonstrated "whole-hearted efforts in self defense." Lovett later told Secretary of State Acheson that Eisenhower, although worried about the sincerity of the British and the French, had been reassured and was willing to become Supreme Allied Commander (State, *Foreign Relations, 1950*, vol. III, *Western Europe*, pp. 578–80). In a letter of December 21 (EM) Marshall would advise Eisenhower that a majority of the problems "have reached a degree of understanding or solution acceptable to you." For subsequent developments see no. 1136.

1114   *Eisenhower Mss.*

To WILLIAM AVERELL HARRIMAN   *December 12, 1950*
Secret

Dear Averell: Herewith the copy of the letter I wrote to General Marshall.[1] I was able to finish it only today, although I started it last Thursday. Naturally, I had to revise it because of my visit to Washington last Saturday.[2]

The basic thing that I want to get across is that America, in accepting Command in Europe, is undertaking a very great responsibility and one that will have a profound effect both upon the people of the United States and the people of Europe.

By no means do I think we should attempt to blackjack European nations or to ignore their pride or their sovereignty. Each should be regarded as an equal partner.[3] But it is certain that their performance will be effective only if each feels an urgent requirement to do the best that is possible. It is only human nature to try to throw responsibility upon others; so, in the same degree that they can feel the United States responsible for them, they will tend to relieve themselves of onerous duty. You will see from the letter that I was quite annoyed to find that staff groups (I do not know *what* staff groups) have been engaged in placing limits upon the area and laboriously spelled out limits upon the authority of the planned headquarters rather than fervently supporting the simple concept of Supreme Command. Such action does not augur well for future success and I should like to know that American representatives understand how important it is that these things get off on the right foot.

I am sure that the ideas I am representing here accord exactly with the tenor of the conversation I had with the President. You know that I am not trying to be difficult. I am merely concerned about a program of vital importance and want to be sure that we do not do anything stupid.[4]

With cordial regard. *Sincerely*

[1] The preceding document.

[2] Eisenhower had met with Harriman after having breakfast with the JCS on Saturday, December 9. The last appointment of the morning had been with Lieutenant General Walter Bedell Smith, Director of the CIA. At 12:30 P.M. Eisenhower had conferred with Lieutenant General Alfred M. Gruenther, Deputy Chief of Staff for Plans and Operations, who was slated to become Chief of Staff to the Supreme Commander of the NATO forces. Eisenhower had lunched with General J. Lawton Collins, Chief of Staff of the Army, at 1:00 P.M., and he later had met again with Gruenther before returning to New York late in the afternoon (for background on Smith see no. 950; on Collins see no. 517).

[3] This was probably a reference to the recent assertions by West German Chancellor Konrad Adenauer that his government would contribute troops to the NATO force only if the Federal Republic were to have rights equal to those of the other powers (for background see no. 1064).

[4] For further developments see no. 1138.

1115   *Eisenhower Mss.*

To Lewis Bergman Maytag   *December 12, 1950*

Dear Bud: Your note gave me the first lift I have had in days. I am delighted both with your continuing interest in the American Assembly and with your suggestions about the hunt.[1]

The date you suggest is one I cannot now quite make. I have cancelled my engagement in Pasadena and, therefore, will not leave New York City until the evening of the 17th.[2] This will put me in Denver sometime late the 19th or early on the 20th since I have to stop for a few hours in Ohio.[3]

If it would be possible for us to go shooting on the morning of, say, the 22nd or 23rd, or on merely one of these mornings, I would be glad to go along. The only anxiety I have is that you shall not change any of your shooting plans merely because of the possibility of my getting there on a particular date. I am very tired and would most certainly enjoy a day in the open with you. Things have gotten to the point where I cannot even count with certainty upon carrying out plans made only for the next day.[4] Therefore, I should like to leave it on the basis that the instant I get to Denver I will call you on the phone and we will then, weather and all other things permitting, make up a plan for one or two mornings of shooting.[5] I will bring along warm clothing against this possibility. But I will count on picking up a gun and such things after I get there. I have plenty of friends in Denver who have all kinds of guns. I am most grateful to you for remembering.[6]

Cordially

[1] Maytag, past president and a director of the Maytag Company, which manufactured washing machines, had thanked Eisenhower in a letter of December 8 (EM) for sending him a copy of a booklet describing the American Assembly (for background see no. 1039). Maytag had also invited Eisenhower to Alamosa, Colorado, to hunt ducks in late December.

Eisenhower had sent the booklet to Maytag under a covering note of December 4 (EM. Similar notes to John L. McCaffrey, James F. Oates, Jr., Colonel Alvin M. Owsley, A. W. Peake, Rawleigh Warner, and Robert E. Wood are in EM). Eisenhower would thank Maytag in a letter of December 13 (EM) for his donation of one thousand dollars to the American Assembly (other correspondents whose recent letters had included checks for the Assembly were Edward H. Green, Charles McNaught, Robert V. New, Clifford Roberts, and Spyros P. Skouras).

[2] Eisenhower had declined an invitation to be grand marshal of the Tournament of Roses parade in Pasadena, California (see no. 1104). The Eisenhowers would leave New York by train (see no. 1140).

[3] On one of the stops in Ohio on the eighteenth see no. 1134, n. 2.

[4] Eisenhower had just turned down (letter Dec. 11, EM) the invitation of Thomas J. Watson, Jr., executive vice-president to IBM, to the "Dawn Patrol" breakfast of the Greater New York Councils of the Boy Scouts of America on January 31, 1951. Eisenhower had attended the event the previous January (see no. 641; on Watson see no. 899). In a letter of December 12 (EM) Eisenhower tentatively accepted the invitation of Albert C. Jacobs, chancellor of the University of Denver, to a dinner honoring Alexander G. Ruthven, president of the University of Michigan, on February 2, 1951. There is, however, no indication in EM that Eisenhower was able to attend the affair (on Jacobs see no. 440; on Ruthven see no. 928).

[5] Maytag would reply (Dec. 14, EM) that he would await Eisenhower's call at his home in Colorado Springs, Colorado, the evening of the twentieth and the morning of the twenty-first. He planned to hunt on the nineteenth and twentieth, but only "to size the situation up and give you a report when you call."

[6] Eisenhower would send the following telegram on December 17 (EM): "Unforeseen circumstances sharply limit vacation time. Impossible to go shooting. Deeply regretful but grateful to you."

To George Frost Kennan *December 12, 1950*

Dear George: Thank you very much for your letter of December 8th. I shall read its attached enclosure at my earliest opportunity.[1]

I have, from time to time, experienced in Washington some of the frustrations that can be discovered between the lines of your letter.[2] In fact, I think it was to some extent the failure of Washington officials, including military chiefs, to understand some of the obvious factors in our global and domestic problems that encouraged me to want to undertake the kind of studies we are now projecting at Columbia—and we hope elsewhere. Possibly the day will come when both you and I may find a leisure hour when we can get together again for a talk. I would value such an opportunity highly. *Cordially*

[1] Kennan was affiliated with the Institute for Advanced Study at Princeton, New Jersey, while on leave from the Department of State. One month earlier, John A. Krout, dean of the Faculty of Political Science, Philosophy and Pure Science at Columbia, had discussed with Kennan the possibility of the latter's taking part in the organization at Columbia of an Institute of War and Peace Studies (for background see no. 1056). Kennan had written to Eisenhower on December 8 (EM) explaining that his plans were still unsettled but that soon he would be able to make a decision regarding his future. He had enclosed with his letter a document that he had received from an anthropologist at Northwestern University. He described it as significant "in these dark days when so much is falling to pieces all around us and when it is evident that we are going to have to start all over again with new humility and new determination and try to correct many of the mistakes of the past." Kennan's enclosure is not in EM.

[2] Kennan had written that he had recently been in the nation's capital "in the thick of it." He had found that U.S. military chiefs were not aware of the extent to which the "intellectual outlooks and reactions" of individuals could have repercussions on the international situation. He suggested that the attitudes and actions of servicemen stationed overseas might be worthy of investigation by the institute of military studies to be organized at Columbia. When the institute came into being in 1952, Kennan would serve as one of its four special consultants (see *New York Times*, Dec. 10, 1951).

To Lewis Williams Douglas *December 12, 1950*

Dear Lew:[1] The other day I saw Roland Harriman at lunch and told him confidentially that I am trying to get you to associate yourself with me in some capacity to discuss the American Assembly. The response I have had, when I have expressed myself similarly to one or two others, has been one of such universal approbation and hopeful anticipation that I am almost coming to feel that you are already one of us. I realize that I have no iota of right to do so, but I am, daily, more convinced that when I see you I shall urge upon you the great opportunity for service that lies in this function of our universities and try to get the support and personal satisfaction that I will feel in your association on any terms that you may feel appropriate.[2]

I do hope that Arizona is working wonders for your health.[3] *Cordially*

[1] Douglas, former U.S. Ambassador to Great Britain, had received an offer to be director of the American Assembly or chairman of its National Policy Board (see no. 1081).

[2] E. Roland Harriman, partner in Brown Brothers, Harriman & Company, investment bankers, chairman of the board of the Union Pacific Railroad, and president of the American Red Cross, had talked with Eisenhower at a luncheon at the Bankers Club in New York City on December 8 (see *New York Times*, Dec. 9, 1950. On Harriman's contributions to the American Assembly see no. 605). Harriman had sent Eisenhower a copy of a letter to Douglas of December 8 (EM, Douglas Corr.) in which he had expressed his hope that Douglas would accept a position of responsibility in connection with the Assembly. Eisenhower had thanked Harriman in a note of December 11 (EM).

[3] Columbia University officials would announce Douglas's acceptance of the chairmanship of the National Policy Board in March 1951 (see *New York Times*, Mar. 14, 1951).

1118   *Eisenhower Mss.*

To EDWARD JOHN BERMINGHAM   *December 12, 1950*

Dear Ed: I enclose copies of three notes I have just written.[1] Also, I am sending back to you the letters from your friends.

After Clarence Dillon's dinner, which was attended by about ten of the prominent financiers of the city, I have done nothing further in his direction except to write a normal "thank you" note. The evening was most enjoyable even though it coincided with the very worst news we had from Korea—I did not get to talk about the American Assembly as much as I would like because I had the job of helping pick us all up from the "mental floor."[2]

I have been uncertain whether I should make any direct request upon Mr. Dillon to act as our agent in following up the men who were his guests that night; temporarily, at least, I have decided against it on the theory that his dinner was so small that he will be bound to do it if he believes in the American Assembly as much as I think he does.[3]

With warmest thanks for your continued interest and with very deep and sincere wishes for a happy Holiday Season for you and yours,[4] *Cordially*

[1] Bermingham was a retired investment counselor (for background see no. 381). The letters were to Sewell L. Avery, chairman of the boards of Montgomery Ward and Company and U.S. Gypsum Company; to General Robert E. Wood, chairman of the board of Sears, Roebuck & Company; and to Merle J. Trees (C.E. University of Illinois 1911), chairman of the board of Chicago Bridge and Iron Company. Each letter expressed Eisenhower's pleasure that they had written to Bermingham expressing interest in the American Assembly (the letter to Avery is in CUF; the note to Wood is in EM. We have been unable to locate a copy of the letter to Trees. For background on the Assembly see no. 1039). Bermingham had notified Eisenhower (Dec. 2, EM) that Wood had promised to make a donation to the American Assembly in 1951. Eisenhower had thanked Bermingham on the fourth (EM), observing that Wood's influence would be decisive with other potential contributors. Bermingham would write again on the seventh (EM) to report on his progress with Avery, who appeared to be on the verge of subscribing.

[2] Dillon, head of Dillon, Read and Company, had been host of a dinner on November 28 (see no. 1093).

[3] See Bermingham's reply (Dec. 14) and his subsequent letter to Dillon on December 20, a copy of which he sent to Eisenhower in an undated note (all in EM).

[4] For further developments on the American Assembly see the next document.

1119   *Columbia University Files*

To Robert Cutler   *December 13, 1950*

Dear Mr. Cutler: Since our delightful Boston visit, we have gone ahead rapidly with the plans for The American Assembly.[1] As you know, we are moving forward on three fronts—conference planning, management, and finance—and I am encouraged to see that we are making excellent progress toward our first conference in 1951.[2]

Our financing is divided into three phases. Mr. W. Averell Harriman has given us a home for the Assembly and he, together with his brother, E. Roland Harriman, are providing the funds to adapt the property and to furnish it for conference purposes.[3]

In order to proceed with our conference planning, we determined that we would need a working capital fund of $500,000. I am happy to say that $320,000 of this amount is already in hand or in firm pledges. I hope that we shall receive at least the major portion of the balance before the end of the year, so that phase two may be considered as completed.

The third step in our financing is to secure conference sponsorships. Although we have made no special effort to date to obtain them, having concentrated on our working capital fund, we already have one in hand and commitments for three others at $25,000 each. In our planning we have decided that we would need fifty such sponsorships to carry the program on the five-year trial basis. I would like to secure these fifty sponsorships as promptly as possible to enable the conference planning staff to go forward with their program.

I am writing to several of my friends in various sections of the country asking them to serve as my personal representative and deputy in obtaining conference sponsorships.[4] I would like to ask you if you would be willing to serve as my representative. I would be most appreciative if you would do so.

I intend to continue my leadership of The American Assembly. No matter where I am or what I may be called upon to do, I shall do everything within my power to further the program. I expect to participate personally in the Assembly discussion.[5]

Dean Young of the Graduate School of Business and I, together with a few friends in various sections of the country, have done most of the work to date in bringing the story of The American Assembly before the people of the country.[6] The program has now reached the point where we are unable to give it the coverage that it requires, and I am asking a few of our friends to assist us. I hope that I may count on you.[7]

If this meets your approval, I will ask Dean Young to talk with you and outline in detail our plan for the conference sponsorships.[8] *Sincerely*

[1] Cutler, president of Old Colony Trust Company in Boston, Massachusetts, had been the host of a dinner for Eisenhower on November 22 (see no. 1094). A note at the top of the copy of this letter in CUF says that Eisenhower wrote the following in longhand on the ribbon copy: "Dear Bobby—This formal dissertation was, as is obvious, prepared by a staff assistant. If you knew, how pressed I am, almost to the point of panic, you'd forgive me for not rewriting it. So far as meaning goes, it expresses my sentiments very well indeed!"

[2] University officials would announce that the topic of the first series of conferences would be United States-Western Europe relations. The *New York Times* (Dec. 20, 1950) would quote Eisenhower's remark that the topic "would actually assist me personally in carrying out my job in Western Europe"—that is, as NATO Supreme Commander.

[3] For background see nos. 605, 844, and 1039.

[4] The other persons to whom Eisenhower was writing were Ralph Austin Bard, Harry A. Bullis, Theodore F. Drury, Samuel Goldwyn, Edward H. Green, Donald S. Kennedy, Fred Lazarus, Jr., Leonard F. McCollum, Elton F. MacDonald, Harvey S. Mudd, John M. Olin, Edgar Monsanto Queeny, and John P. Weyerhaeuser (the letters to Drury, Green, Mudd, Olin, and Weyerhaeuser are in EM; the others are in CUF).

[5] Eisenhower was anticipating serving as Supreme Commander of the NATO forces (see no. 1114).

[6] For background on Young see no. 54.

[7] In a letter of December 24 (CUF) Cutler would present four reasons for declining to serve as Eisenhower's deputy. His enthusiasm for the American Assembly had waned, he said, primarily as a result of his belief that all energies should be directed toward the mobilization of the economy for war. He would also confess his fear that during Eisenhower's tour of duty in Europe the project would falter "without your constant, daily force to breathe life into it." A third factor contributing to his unwillingness to raise funds in Boston was his belief that the city was "not as

rich a field as many other parts of the country" and that its citizens already had charitable commitments that they had difficulty meeting. He protested finally that he was currently involved in two fund-raising campaigns and that Harvard University, his alma mater, might also want him to join a similar effort.

Eisenhower would agree in a note of December 31 (CUF) that Cutler was too busy to raise money for the American Assembly, and he would ask only that Cutler recommend someone from the Boston area upon whom they might rely. In rejoinder to Cutler's first reservation concerning the American Assembly, Eisenhower would write: "Incidentally, I personally believe that it is more important than ever before to push the plan—this is no time to resign ourselves to acting by guess and by God; we must develop the facts and act upon them."

[8] For further developments see no. 1159.

1120   *Eisenhower Mss.*

To Henry Krumb   *December 13, 1950*

Dear Mr. Krumb: The contents of your letter vividly illustrate one type of difficulty that I seem to find almost chronic these days.[1] Universities—at least this one—do not have staffs in the sense that a military organization has. Because of this, most staff work is performed by the heads of departments and divisions, and each of these is so busy with daily administration that he frequently finds it impossible to follow up upon the execution of good intentions, even where these have been translated into specific policy.[2]

A couple of years ago when you first told me about your difficulty in keeping in touch with the beneficiaries of the scholarships you had established, I took this matter up with Mr. Jacobs and Mr. Davis and we thought we had established a scheme that would be almost automatic in providing to a benefactor of Columbia the kind of information that he naturally and justifiably desired. Our plans extended the idea into a policy so that all similar cases would be automatically covered.[3]

Obviously, we have failed and for this I offer you my most abject apologies. I think you can understand the impossibility, in these harried times, of my giving very much personal attention to following up such matters—I grow embarrassed by the inadequacies of time left to me to devote to these administrative features. But I have turned the whole matter over to Grayson Kirk with instructions to produce a system that will insure that money provided by a benefactor is spent for the purposes he specifies and, secondly, that the reports to him will be of the kind he desires.[4]

Incidentally, you will be interested to know that, in almost the same mail, we received another letter from a man who bitterly complained that he had received far too many letters from the University pertaining to a gift he had made to us. By the time his gift had reached its ultimate destination he had received five letters of acknowledgment and thanks, including one from me. You can see that our system seems sometimes to work as far toward one extreme as in other cases it works toward the opposite. We shall try to do better and, certainly, there is no doubt in our mind as to the very great sense of obligation that we feel toward you for your continued help and support.

With warm personal regards, *Sincerely*

[1] Krumb, a consulting mining engineer and a former trustee of Columbia University, had complained in a letter of December 8 (EM) that university administrators did not inform benefactors as to how their gifts were used. He recounted the experience of a friend who had contributed money to establish a scholarship and who had received only a letter of acknowledgment. Krumb had tried to intercede with Columbia officials, but the inquiries that he had directed to Frank D. Fackenthal, acting president, and to Frederick A. Goetze, treasurer, had received a perfunctory reply (on Fackenthal see no. 3; on Goetze see no. 126). Krumb also said that he had signed an agreement on December 19, 1945, donating money for a scholarship; he had, however, not learned what had happened to the fund until, after several inquiries, he had been sent a pamphlet describing the fellowships that the university had awarded during 1949/50. He had been chagrined because he had stipulated that the money be used for scholarships. Krumb also mentioned another unfortunate incident and said that contributors would be more receptive to Eisenhower's entreaties if they knew what had happened to the money that they had already committed. This was a reference to Eisenhower's letter of December 6 (CUF) describing plans for a new fund-raising campaign for the proposed engineering center (for background see no. 242; for developments see no. 1122).

[2] For Eisenhower's views on the current problems of development activities at Columbia see no. 825.

[3] Albert C. Jacobs had been provost and vice-president of the university until November 1949 (for background see no. 440). Paul H. Davis had been vice-president in charge of development until May 1950 (see no. 789). In March 1949 Davis had proposed that Eisenhower acknowledge gifts, grants, and bequests of one hundred dollars or more, as well as all gifts sent directly to him (see Davis to Eisenhower, Mar. 28, 1949, EM).

[4] Grayson L. Kirk, provost and vice-president, would serve as acting president during Eisenhower's tour of duty in Europe (see no. 1141). Eisenhower had already delegated some new tasks to him. For instance, the Educational Policies Commission of the National Education Association of the United States and the American Association of School Administrators had asked the General to vote on a draft of a report on moral and spiritual values, and Eisenhower had written at the top of the request: "Kirk—I simply *cannot* study this. Do you suppose we have anyone who'd be interested in going over it & giving me a *short* memo on it? If not I merely will fail to vote" (see Carr to Eisenhower, Dec. 6, 1950, CUF).

To Carl Raymond Gray, Jr.   *December 14, 1950*

Dear Carl:[1] You may have occasion to notice in yesterday's *New York Times* about a large-scale manpower study which we have under way at Columbia, entitled the "Conservation of Human Resources."[2] I tried to reach you by phone during one of my recent trips to Washington, to talk with you about this matter, but failed to find you in.

One of the most important aspects of this Project deals with the problem of military manpower; specifically, why two million men were rejected for military service and another three-quarters of a million had to be released for inaptitude or psychoneurosis. We are trying to learn as much as we can about this experience so that we can be wiser next time.

The Director of the Project is Dr. Eli Ginzberg, who has worked closely with your people in the medical field; and his senior adviser is Major General Howard Snyder, whom you doubtless know.[3] The Department of Defense is making all of its records available to the Project, and this note is to request you to make the Veterans Administration records available to the extent that they are needed. I am sure that you will find that our Columbia group will only ask for what it absolutely needs to push its studies ahead.

I feel very strongly that this Project can come up with very important answers which will be of great value in the present crisis. I will deeply appreciate whatever help you and your associates will be able to give.[4]

With warm regard,[5] *Cordially*

[1] For background on Gray, who had been the Veterans Administrator since the end of 1947, see *Eisenhower Papers*, vols. I–IX.

[2] This project, which had been initiated by Eisenhower in 1948, was announced publicly for the first time at a press conference on December 12, 1950 (for background see no. 155; see also Columbia University, *Conservation of Human Resources: Progress Report, June 1951*, p. 1).

[3] For background on Ginzberg and Snyder see nos. 155 and 1, respectively.

[4] The Veterans Administration would offer its assistance to the project (see Columbia University, *Conservation of Human Resources: Progress Report, June 1951*, p. 36). Eisenhower had also asked others for help with this undertaking. In November he had written The Adjutant General (TAG), General Witsell, concerning a November 1949 memo that restricted access to the medical records of members and former members of the Armed Forces. Stressing the project's need for these records, Eisenhower argued that "unlike medical research experts, who are usually interested in the details of the individual case, our Columbia Group is in search of broad patterns which will help to explain the behavior of large numbers of people" (Nov. 20). Witsell replied, "Because of your personal interest and my conviction that this study would be of tremendous value to the Army and to all the services, I am happy to advise that an exception to the policy in this instance has been granted" (Dec. 18). He enclosed a memorandum from the Office of the Chief of Staff directing that "individuals designated by Columbia University

be given every assistance practicable by all concerned" (Haas to Comptroller of the Army *et al.*, Dec. 13, 1950; all correspondence is in EM). By 1951 the project was receiving assistance from the Selective Service System, the Department of Labor, the Department of Commerce, the Defense Department, the VA, and other public and private research groups (Columbia University, *Conservation of Human Resources: Progress Report, June 1951*, pp. 32–38).

[5] The first Human Resources Project publication would be Ginzberg and Bray's, *The Uneducated* (1953), which would be followed by Ginzberg, *Human Resources: The Wealth of a Nation* (New York, 1958). Among the subsequent publications would be the highly regarded three-volume study by Eli Ginzberg *et al.*, *The Ineffective Soldier: Lessons for Management and the Nation* (New York, 1959). The questions Eisenhower had raised in December 1948 (no. 300) were answered in these several volumes. Ginzberg and his associates found that the waste of human resources was largely due to four basic conditions: unemployment; underemployment; inadequate training; and arbitrary employment barriers. Moreover, they discovered certain common denominators that helped explain the failure of men to perform. Ginzberg's sweeping recommendations advocated a reevaluation of America's education policies, greater support for health services, and long-range plans for the improvement of personnel management. Eisenhower would later write that his part in the Conservation of Human Resources Project was "one of my proudest memories of life at Columbia" (*At Ease*, pp. 350–51).

1122   *Eisenhower Mss.*

To David Sarnoff   *December 14, 1950*

Dear Dave:[0] Your prompt acceptance of one of the Honorary Chairmanships for our Engineering Center Campaign is a real encouragement and I express my deep appreciation.[1]

A great opportunity lies ahead of Columbia in this Engineering Center project. One of the great strengths of this country in the past, and surely one of its great strengths for the future in the troubled state of world affairs, rests with the development of our scientific and technological prowess. No matter how much the Communist hordes of Europe and Asia may outnumber our own people, I have not the slightest doubt that 150,000,000 Americans, backed by American know-how in the fields of engineering and science, can look to the future with confidence.

Columbia, so far as I have been able to determine in the short while that I have been here, has a great engineering tradition to build on, and potentialities in its men which should make our Engineering Center Program a great force for advancing American engineering in both the teaching and research fields.

I know that the Trustees share my own pleasure in having you identified with this Engineering Center Program as an Honorary Chairman.[2] *Sincerely*

[1] Sarnoff, chairman of the board of RCA, had agreed in his letter of December 8 (EM) to serve as one of the honorary chairmen of the National Committee of Sponsors for the Engineering Center Development Program (for background on Sarnoff see no. 334; on the engineering center see no. 242). In a staff-drafted letter of December 6 (EM) inviting Sarnoff to join the campaign Eisenhower had mentioned the $22,150,000 needed for construction and for additional endowment. Of this amount, the university was seeking $13,650,000 for "the physical needs" in a nationwide appeal that would continue until 1954. Similar letters of December 6 had gone out to Walter H. Aldridge, Richard E. Dougherty, Gano Dunn, Herbert C. Hoover, Robert E. McConnell, Harvey S. Mudd, Edmund A. Prentis, and Andrew W. Robertson (the correspondence with Hoover, Mudd, Prentis, and Robertson is in EM; the other letters are in CUF). Eisenhower had also signed a staff-drafted note to Sarnoff of the sixth (EM) acknowledging RCA's gift of $5,000 to the Conservation of Human Resources project (see no. 1121).

[2] University officials would announce other details of these plans while Eisenhower was on leave of absence in Europe (see *New York Times*, Nov. 5, 1951).

1123   *Eisenhower Mss.*

TO RICHARD BREVARD RUSSELL   *December 14, 1950*
Telegram

I have been informed that you and your Committee have expressed some interest in my opinion of Anna Rosenberg's ability and activities during the period I have known her.[1] This acquaintanceship extends back into the war period when she came to Europe to conduct certain studies for the Government. Since that time I have had many contacts with her in the discussion of problems of universal military training as well as others pertaining to labor and the business of Columbia University. In all of these contacts I have been impressed by her keen thinking, her direct and forthright attitude and her outspoken interest in Americanism and its perpetuation. It has never crossed my mind to question her sincerity, integrity or her devotion to our country.[2] *With personal regard*

[1] Senator Russell, a Democrat from Georgia, was acting chairman of the Committee on Armed Services, which was currently conducting hearings regarding the appointment of Mrs. Rosenberg, a personnel relations consultant, to be Assistant Secretary of Defense (for background see no. 1083). On this same day Eisenhower sent a similar telegram (EM) to Senator Styles Bridges, a Republican from New Hampshire and a member of the Committee on Armed Services. According to Eisenhower's appointment calendar, he had discussed his plans for the American Assembly at a lunch with Mrs. Rosenberg and several labor leaders in New York City on December 7. A note at the bottom of the calendar page for December 8 indicates that Eisenhower received a telephone call concerning Anna Rosenberg from Lieutenant General Walter Bedell Smith, Director of the CIA. Eisenhower apparently telephoned Mrs. Rosenberg to talk about her appointment and the American Assembly and also called Smith to discuss Mrs. Rosenberg's nomination.

Mrs. Rosenberg had recently denied charges that she had been a member of a Communist-front organization in the 1920s. The Armed Services Committee had reported her nomination favorably to the Senate November 29, 1950, but it had reopened its hearings on December 5 after the accusations had come to its attention. On December 7 Russell had ordered that Mrs. Rosenberg's accusers come before the committee to confront her (see U.S., Congress, Senate, Committee on Armed Services, *Nomination of Anna M. Rosenberg to be Assistant Secretary of Defense: Hearings*, 81st Cong., 2d sess., 1950, pt. 2, pp. 29, 37–332; and *New York Times*, Nov. 30 and Dec. 8, 1950. This telegram from Eisenhower was printed in the *Hearings*, p. 344).

[2] Senator Bridges would send a telegram (this same day, EM) thanking Eisenhower for his views and explaining that the Armed Services Committee had voted to report Mrs. Rosenberg's nomination favorably to the Senate. The Senate would vote to confirm Mrs. Rosenberg as Assistant Secretary of Defense on December 21 (see *New York Times*, Dec. 22, 1950).

1124   *Eisenhower Mss.*

To THOMAS BAKER SLICK   *December 14, 1950*

Dear Tom: Thank you very much for your contribution to the American Assembly. You know how close to my heart that project is; so, every time one of my friends gives such concrete evidence of his support, I get an especially satisfying thrill out of it.[1]

Quite obviously, I have no knowledge at all of the intricacies of the tax problems in Mexico. However, as I told you, I was more than devoted to Hal Mangum; for him I held an affection and respect.[2] I saw the way that he dealt and worked with his ranch hands and other employees in Mexico and thought him most enlightened, and concerned with their best interests. Obviously, the only thing I could do would be to express this kind of feeling with respect to my old friend to any Mexican official and on the basis of this feeling to ask for expeditious action in the settling of all tax and estate problems incident to Hal's death. I know that no one connected with the project wants any unusual consideration but, because of the intricacies of the whole affair, they hope that the work of adjudication will be correspondingly pushed.

Thank you again for your nice contribution to the University. *Sincerely*

[1] Slick (A.B. Yale 1938), a rancher in San Antonio, Texas, had enclosed a check for the American Assembly (see no. 1039) in his letter of November 21 (EM). He had met Eisenhower during the latter's trip to Houston, Texas, on November 10.

[2] Slick had reminded Eisenhower of his offer to intercede with the Mexican government regarding the tax situation of the estate of the late Hal L. Mangum, who had owned property in San Antonio, Texas, and in San Geronimo, Mexico (for background see no. 849).

To Milton A. Reckord   *December 15, 1950*

Dear General Reckord:[1] It is completely out of the question for me to undertake, with others, the job of arranging a conference to discuss the subject of Universal Training and Service. Indeed, I did well to get to the Conference of College Presidents in which we worked out a statement of our general conclusions.[2]

Quite naturally, I am very concerned with the views of all organizations that are devoted to the defense of America. However, there is great danger that we will continue to look upon some of our defense and security problems as a mere continuation of those that we have faced in our peace-time years of the past. We are up against something entirely new, more full of risk and danger than anything we have yet encountered. It is to this kind of a situation that we must address ourselves. I believe that we must produce *thorough training*; that in producing this training we must use the system also to provide needed strength in being, and that we must build up our reserve components to an adequate strength with thoroughly trained and fit men. All this we must do with maximum efficiency and economy.[3]

I have been reluctant to express my detailed views in public because I am not certain as to details of plans that are being developed in the Defense Department.[4] Since I am still an officer on the active list, I do not want to appear in open or public conflict with my superiors; so the view I give you are those of one individual officer speaking to another. But I repeat my conviction that we have to attack all of these problems with vigor and without any regard for what we may have believed in the past.[5]

I wish I could participate with you in further deliberation but I simply cannot find the time, in view of the very many duties and responsibilities devolving upon me these days. *Cordially*

[1] Major General Reckord, Adjutant General of Maryland since November 1945, had mentioned in his letter of December 11 (EM) that he was pleased with the action that educators had taken on the subject of universal military training and service. He had liked especially an article that James B. Conant, president of Harvard University, had written on the subject (for background see no. 1006). Reckord had heard that there was a new emphasis on universal military service among officials in the Department of Defense; he expressed hope that Eisenhower would arrange a conference among members of the American Legion, the National Guard Association, and the Reserve Officers' Association to draft a bill on this subject to submit to Congress.

[2] See no. 1016.

[3] Eisenhower had expressed similar sentiments in his draft of a letter to the President (no. 1112).

[4] Eisenhower had written to Secretary of Defense Marshall to this effect. (see no. 1042).

⁵ On December 13 members of the Committee on The Present Danger and of the AAU had met with officials of the Department of Defense to discuss military training and service (see *New York Times*, Dec. 14, 1950. For background on the committee see no. 1112).

1126   *Eisenhower Mss.*

TO CHARLES VINCENT MCADAM   *December 15, 1950*

Dear Charlie: Thank you very much for your letter of December 12th and for the two checks that accompanied it.¹ I am writing a short note to each Mr. Mathes and to Mr. Ludwig and am enclosing them with the request that you send them on to the addressees.

Please do not push any further your campaign to raise some money. As you know, I am tremendously grateful for what you have done and, more especially, for the great interest you have taken in the project. But I insist that the plan is one that presents *opportunity* to people that are in a position to help financially and, consequently, they should *not* under any circumstances be importuned to send in donations. All that should be done is to tell them of the project, show its importance and its requirements in finances and then give them a chance to help. All this you have done—I *would be embarrassed if you should do more.*²

With warm personal regard and a very Merry Christmas. *Cordially*

¹ McAdam, president of McNaught Syndicate, Inc., had forwarded gifts to the American Assembly from Fred Ludwig of New Canaan, Connecticut, and James Monroe Mathes, president and a director of an advertising agency in New York City (for background on the Assembly see no. 1039). According to a note of this day (EM, McAdam Corr.), Eisenhower forwarded the checks and copies of his replies to Ludwig and Mathes to Philip Young, Executive Director of the American Assembly.

² McAdam had reported on his efforts to convince five other individuals to contribute to the American Assembly. "While I have tried to get the big money," he had written, "I guess I will have to be content with whatever I can rake in—if you feel you would like to have me continue to get in the small checks." Concerning recent donations to the American Assembly see no. 1115.

1127   *Eisenhower Mss.*

TO MARTIN MAHER   *December 15, 1950*

Dear Marty: In your case I am going to break a long-standing and inflexible policy and try to write an introduction for you.¹ This I have always refused to do for any American because it was impossible to respond favorably to all of those who wanted me to do it. However, you represent for me, as you do for thousands of other West Pointers, something special.

You will have to give me just a bit of time to complete the job because I am so pushed for opportunity to do such things these days. Because of this, I wonder whether you would have Mrs. Campion send me a suggested draft outline or description of what she believes would be fitting. Since I do not know the type of book it will be, I do not want to trust my own imagination in this matter. I would suggest that whatever she (or Colonel Reeder) might have to say would be best addressed to Miss Sharp of my office. She will bring it in to me as soon as we can find time to work on it.[2]

I assure you that I am complimented that you should want me to write the introduction to your book.[3]

With warm personal regard, *Cordially*

[1] For background on Sergeant Martin Maher, USA (ret.), see no. 559. In a letter of December 12 (EM) he had asked that Eisenhower write an introduction to his—that is, Maher's—autobiography.

[2] Mrs. Nardi Reeder Campion, the sister of Colonel Russell Potter Reeder, Jr., was helping Maher write the book. For background on Colonel Reeder see Galambos, *Chief of Staff*, nos. 721 and 733.

[3] Maher would thank Eisenhower in a letter of December 22 (EM), adding that Mrs. Campion would forward a draft outline of the book. Kevin C. McCann, Eisenhower's administrative assistant, would remind the General in a memorandum of February 15, 1951 (same file), that he had promised to write the foreword. McCann would also attach a draft. Eisenhower would make changes on this, and there would be additional revisions in the final version, which would appear over the date of February 27, 1951, in Sergeant Marty Maher with Nardi Reeder Campion, *Bringing Up the Brass: My 55 Years at West Point* (New York, 1951), pp. vii–viii.

1128   *Eisenhower Mss.*

To Mary Wadsworth Michaelis   *December 15, 1950*

Dear Mary: I am most grateful for your letter. First, because it brought me news of your and my favorite Colonel and, secondly, because it expressed such a sympathetic understanding of the problem Mamie and I now face.[1] These people who seem to think that I should look forward to a possible job in Europe with delighted anticipation and seem to think that it is one designed merely to shed honor and glory on some individual, give me a feeling akin to nausea. You can well imagine how we both face the prospect to [of?] my return to military duty, even if it were to be performed in this country.[2] However, I do not believe that personal feelings have anything to do with such matters these days; indeed, I feel just a little bit guilty even in mentioning their existence to you. It was only your complete understanding that has led me to do so.

I do hope that, before too long, Mike can come home. You must be growing exceedingly tired of having your husband exposed to the risks and dangers of the battle field, and you have been a brick to take these years as stoically and philosophically as you have. My very best wishes to you both.

Please tell Mike in your next letter that I would really prize the opportunity to write to him a long letter, but I simply cannot do it. I am, however, going to put his name down as one of those I should like to get back with me if such should be possible.[3]

I told Mamie I was writing you and she said to give you her love. We trust that you and Mike will have as fine a Holiday Season as is possible under the circumstances. *Cordially*

---

[1] Mrs. Michaelis was the wife of Colonel John H. "Mike" Michaelis, who had been Eisenhower's aide during 1947 and 1948 (for background see no. 1069). In her letter of December 10 (EM) she had mentioned that her husband had sent her a telegram from Seoul, South Korea, that morning saying that he was "fine." On the situation in Korea see no. 1108, n. 2.

[2] On Eisenhower's impending assignment as Supreme Commander of the NATO forces see no. 1134.

[3] Colonel Michaelis, commander of the 27th Regiment of the 25th Division, would become assistant commander of the division in February 1951. After promotion to brigadier general, he would join Eisenhower's SHAPE staff during the summer of 1951.

On this same day Eisenhower replied (EM) to Brigadier General Carl C. Bank (USA, ret.), thanking him for his offer of service (letter of Dec. 9, EM) but adding that he was not yet in a position to act on the matter (for background on Bank see no. 983, n. 12).

Also on this day Eisenhower forwarded to Lieutenant General Alfred M. Gruenther—soon to become Eisenhower's Chief of Staff at SHAPE—a letter of December 12 (EM) from Brigadier General Edwin B. Howard, Chief of Intelligence, Office, Chief, Army Field Forces, since 1949 (for background see no. 241). According to Eisenhower's message to Gruenther, "This is the man [Howard] I really had in mind for the American G–2." Howard would become head of the Intelligence Section of the headquarters of the Allied land forces in Central Europe in 1951.

In a note of December 30, 1950 (EM), Eisenhower would thank General Mark W. Clark, Chief of Army Field Forces, for recommending Elizabeth A. Riley for a position with SHAPE. Miss Riley had been Clark's secretary in Vienna, Austria, and was currently working in Berlin in the Office of the U.S. High Commissioner for Germany.

To Harry S. Truman
Secret

Dear Mr. President: I have, of course, already told you that any military duty assigned me by you as Commander-in-Chief will be promptly and uncomplainingly performed to the best of my ability.[1] But, beyond this, I feel that I have a personal and official duty to you to outline briefly some of my ideas with respect to the world situation, so that I may at least be sure that these points have been considered by you and your advisors in reaching the decisions that are now about to be implemented. I trust that my views are not in any way influenced by personal convenience or desire to avoid onerous service; but, in any event, I give them to you for what they are worth.

The points listed below contain only a minimum of exposition or argument. Though the reasons on which they are based may not always be obvious, I am certain that you will have no difficulty in understanding their import.

Our struggle for survival against Soviet imperialism will continue until either we or the Soviets are destroyed or the other side has recognized the hopelessness of attempting to conquer the free world through force and will seek, with us, a reasonable and practical basis for living together in the world. (This they will never do except to gain time.)

Because the opponent is militant in the political world as well as in the field of force, he develops a many-sided and complex system of attack, using force, deceit, propaganda and subversion. It is against this kind of relentless world-wide attack that the free world must defend itself.

The United States is not only the principal leader of the free world, it is the only one that has disposable means for helping the others reach a position of respectable defense and, in doing so, build up the necessary mutual confidence among them.

The resources of the United States are *not* unlimited and it becomes necessary to determine *a priority of action* in order that our efforts may be most effective and will not finally be defeated through our own bankruptcy, either financial or political.

The traditional counterweights to Russia's long held imperialistic ambitions, now supplemented and used by Communistic doctrine, have been Germany and Japan. These two have been destroyed as military forces, but there now exists a situation under which a reasonable military strength could be restored in Japan; while something might be initiated in the case of Western Germany.

It would seem possible that the American Government could,

by proper Legislative and Executive pronouncement, state that— so far as the United States is concerned—Japan and Germany will be restored to an independent status in the family of nations. It would be recognized that in the case of Germany only Western Germany would be affected.[2]

To support this pronouncement, the United States could also express its intention to help these nations provide decent security for themselves, under some system that *manifestly* could not threaten the peace of the world. In the case of Japan, we have already deployed in that region seven of our divisions, and these units, whether kept in South Korea or moved into Japan, would be most helpful in beginning the reestablishment there of a respectable military organization. The influence of this development would be toward stability in the region, together with some value as a counterweight to Russian ambitions, even to the extent of partially immobilizing a portion of the Russian strength. Its political effect on the remainder of the Far East should be profound.[3] (Admittedly, a terrific amount of preparatory political work would have to be done in Japan and there would have to be a very great deal of economic help given the country for some years. But restoration of the national pride and the opportunity to work decently with the other free nations of the world would be powerful influence.)

In Germany, the approach would have to be cautious, and unquestionably, for a long time that country could do no more than produce for itself adequate police forces, border guards and a central constabulary. Forces of the Western Nations would certainly have to remain inside the country, at Germany's request, for considerable time. Nevertheless, there would be a partial reawakening of *national spirit* while all national rehabilitation would be so well controlled that no one could take offense in this vitally important matter of spirit, and we would be realizing a great advance.

Incidentally, both subversion and propaganda weapons should be developed, for us throughout the world, to a high degree of efficiency. I think that 200,000,000 yearly could profitably be spent on propaganda of OSS—(no govt connection for most of this!) and free govts, collectively, should use info better.[4]

We must never lose sight of the fact that Western Europe is the keystone of the defensive arch we are trying to build up. In this arch the United States is the foundation.

The most necessary thing needed in Western Europe is the *will* to fight—confidence. It is in this realization that we have instituted agreements and pacts and engaged ourselves to participate in the defense for that region.[5] Now we have engaged, also, to assume national responsibility for command in that area, *but we have done this at a time when we are badly extended in the East and there is only a modicum of readily available strength in the United States which can support the promises* involved in assumption of command. There is no opportunity of sending promptly into Europe sizeable military units to support the psychological effect that our diplomats (and staffs) anticipate as a result of naming me to command!

We need to help encourage Europe in every possible way, but we should not *over*-emphasize the favorable consequences of assuming the responsibility for command. It is always possible that this act *might* create even a greater European tendency to sit back and wait, in a renewed confidence that the United States has assumed an inescapable and publicly stated responsibility.

But we can step up materially the rate of military help in terms of munitions, and more important, help Western Europe establish a partial munitions industry of its own. This should include the manufacture of field guns and all small arms; to this, I think that certain types of light planes should be added, as well as light tanks.

In view of the tremendous budgets that America is now contemplating for security purposes, the amounts necessary to implement this portion of the program would not be great, percentagewise, and would not be vital to our solvency.

In the meantime, it is clear that all this would be of no import except as the United States initiates, instantly, a real program of military preparedness.[6] The only limitation upon its size must be the maximum that we can, with utmost economy in every other kind of governmental expenditure, carry through an indefinite period of some ten to thirty years. In my judgment, both a current extension and expansion of the Selective Service law together with an immediate and active universal *service* law can meet our requirements. Roughly, I subscribe to the so-called Conant Plan, supplemented during the initial build-up period by an expanded selective service law.[7] In the matter of compensation, the dependents and disabled should be paid generously. Aside from this, only the professional cadres in each service should be paid a professional wage. Others, aside from their shelter, health requirements, etc., should receive only nominal pay. Comparable munitions programs and reserve organizations must be integral parts of the effort. (In war all on *same* footing.)[8]

All this will impose a tremendous strain upon our economy and I believe that America must be taught to live on an austerity basis in order that we may successfully meet this great challenge to our survival. Every kind of so-called "indirect" control will have to be employed and, most certainly, if we go after this thing on this clear basis, the most direct types of controls will also have to be imposed. Of these matters, of course, I know little; I mention them only to show that I realize that you have tremendous problems in this field as well as in that of international politics and American security.

On the assumption that in a matter of two years the United States would have largely attained the level of preparations that it thereafter intends to maintain, that the European nations have responded effectively to the help the United States has given and have developed confidence among themselves and in us—and we in turn in them— I firmly believe that we will have reached the point where promises and performance will work together so as, constantly, to enhance this confidence and that a serenity will begin to return to our lives and hysteria abolished from our thinking.

Moreover, when we have reached this level of security, we can begin to think of the free world more as partners than as dependents and, *within a few years thereafter, there should be a gradual diminution in the portion of our national production that we must devote to the sterile, negative business of protecting ourselves.*

To sum up:

I believe that our justifiable anxiety for the safety of Western Europe is causing us to take over, at this moment, a responsibility for which we are *not* prepared and that the effect of this taking over will not be as beneficial as we had hoped because its psychological value will be dissipated in a bitter realization that there is no great amount of material help instantly forthcoming. I believe, therefore, that we should establish for ourselves (1) *a definite priority of action* which we keep secret, so far as possible, from those hostile to us. (Russia & satellite)[9] We should go instantly into the business of *building up our military strength: we should not trim our plans to suit what we believe to be public opinion.* On the contrary (2) *we must inform public opinion of the critical nature of our problem* and, therefore, of the radical measures required to meet it.

We should (3) *help Western Europe* with drastic increase in our material help and with special emphasis of recreating in that region a respectable munitions industry.

(4) We should do what we can, at once, to *begin the restoration of the traditional counterbalances to Russian ambition.*

I repeat that I stand ready to carry whatever military duty you may wish to assign me. (This includes the European Command that you have already requested me to assume.)[10]

This paper has been seen only by the two assistants who have helped me in its preparation and may, therefore, be kept as confidential as you desire. On the other hand, I have no objection whatsoever to your showing it to any of your official family. I realize that it contains many points not only with which you are thoroughly familiar.[11] By the same token, it may contain some ideas that are completely impracticable so far as their realization is concerned.

Finally, I am sure that you will perceive that I am not attempting to build up any advance alibis. I merely suggest to you that an entirely *different approach to the great crisis of our time might develop a wisdom in making certain changes in current programs.*

It has been difficult to reach a decision to write this letter to you because it obviously touches on many things in which I am not expert and I do not want to be trespassing on the responsibilities of others. But, because you have told me of your intention of using me in a field that will be practically as broad as our entire policy in Europe, I have come to the conclusion that I should tell you of my deep conviction that, while arming speedily and effectively here at home and supporting and aiding our foreign ramparts to the utmost, *we should not too quickly commit ourselves to arrangements which might possibly have an effect opposite to those we expect.*

With assurance of my continued regard,[12] *Respectfully submitted*

---

[1] For background see no. 1045. Eisenhower wrote a note at the top of this draft of the letter (EM) saying that he had decided not to send it to the President. "Never sent contents largely conveyed to Pres verbally by me & by Averell [Harriman] in conversations," Eisenhower explained (see n. 12 below).

[2] On December 12 the government of the Federal Republic had rejected a U.S. proposal that it contribute troops to an international defensive force. Chancellor Adenauer had insisted on full equality with the members of NATO before Germany participated (for background see no. 1064), but there was some doubt whether even equality would satisfy a majority of his constituents. The East Germans had made the situation more difficult by proposing negotiations regarding reunification and by warning that the Soviets would not permit the rearmament of West Germany (see *New York Times*, Dec. 13, 1950). The North Atlantic Council of Deputies and the Military Committee had reached agreement on the thirteenth on a plan to give the Federal Republic more control over its internal and external affairs (see *ibid.*, Dec. 14, 1950). Yet negotiations regarding West Germany's status would not yield significant results until Britain, France, and the United States agreed to changes in the Occupation Statute and the Charter of the Allied High Commission in March 1951 (see McGeehan, *The German Rearmament Question*, pp. 117–18).

[3] The State Department had announced on September 15, 1950, that no restrictions on rearmament would be included in the peace treaty with Japan which the United States planned to present to a commission representing those nations that had been at war with Japan. The governments of the United States and the Soviet Union had exchanged notes on this subject during the autumn, and on December 27, 1950, American diplomats would inform their Russian counterparts that the treaty should permit the Japanese to "participate with the United States and other nations in arrangements for individual and collective self-defense" (see *New York Times*, Sept. 16 and Dec. 29 and 31, 1950; and Acheson, *Present at the Creation*, pp. 426–35). Negotiations would continue until the signing of a treaty on September 8, 1951 (see Acheson, *Present at the Creation*, pp. 539–50).

[4] Eisenhower inserted in longhand the figure of two hundred million, as well as all the words in this sentence after *propaganda*. OSS had been the Office of Strategic Services during World War II (for background see Galambos, *Chief of Staff*, no. 608. On Eisenhower's interest in propaganda see nos. 60, 785, 890, and 918).

[5] On the North Atlantic Treaty see nos. 375 and 539.

[6] A typewritten note beside this paragraph indicates that this portion of the letter was drafted on December 12. President Truman's radio and television address of December 15 "covers the point *fairly* well," according to the note. In that address

Truman had outlined a plan for increasing the number of men and women in the armed services to three and one-half million and for providing more weapons for the United States and its allies. The President hoped that a speed-up in production in the course of a year would lead industry to turn out planes at five times the current rate and combat vehicles at four times the current rate. Truman proclaimed the existence of a national emergency on December 16, citing the recent setbacks of U.N. troops in Korea as a primary reason for his action. The President ordered "that the military, naval, air, and civilian defenses of this country be strengthened as speedily as possible to the end that we may be able to repel any and all threats against our national security . . ." (see *Public Papers of the Presidents: Truman, 1950*, pp. 741–47, and Truman, *Memoirs*, vol. II, *Years of Trial and Hope*, pp. 420–28; see also no. 1061. On the situation in Korea see no. 1108).

[7] On the plan of universal military service put forward by James B. Conant, president of Harvard University, see no. 1006; on plans to amend the Selective Service Act see no. 1042.

[8] Eisenhower added this parenthetical expression in longhand.

[9] Again, the General added the material in parentheses by hand.

[10] This too was added by hand.

[11] This sentence had concluded with the words "but are thoroughly disgusted" before Eisenhower crossed out the ending.

[12] The following typewritten note appeared at the bottom of the letter: "(Never sent, because this material was largely repeated via telephone to Mr. Harriman on morning of Dec 16, 1950)." Eisenhower wrote in longhand beneath this: "Also given to H.S.T. verbally. He assured me that all these factors had been thoroughly considered!"

1130   *Eisenhower Mss.*

To Arthur Hays Sulzberger   *December 16, 1950*

Dear Arthur: This is a hasty reply to your notes, one dated the 13th and the other the 14th.[1] (Repeating these two dates brings to me the flash of memory that, six years ago today, the Battle of the Bulge broke out in the ETO.)[2]

Concerning the effort to make our Trustees Meetings more interesting, I could fill up half an hour telling you of some of my amusing experiences, which I would be almost compelled to call "reverses." The most I have been able to accomplish is to omit laborious and detailed reading of all the records of appointments, resignations, expressions of sorrow, etc., etc., I have tried to put before the Board—on either a formal or informal basis—matters of University policy and important features of operation. Certainly, I should like to talk to you about this one of these days.

With respect to the I & E program, the single requirement, so far as the military services are concerned, is to get every commander to understand and to accept responsibility for this function within the entire groupment that he controls. Soldiers, traditionally, understand that they are responsible for matters of discipline, for physical development, for technical and professional training and for esprit de corps. They instinctively resist other types and kinds of responsibility and so the real answer is to make them understand that information and education *directly affect* the levels of military efficiency in their commands.

Every commander should, therefore, have a suitable staff officer who keeps needling him about this phase of his training program. But, beyond this, he needs material that is definitely slanted to the requirements of a soldier. (Here is the reason that mere excellence in prior civil education never fully meets the need.) This function of providing the needed material, either directly or by seeing the cooperation of other agencies, and the job of developing applicable techniques and practices furnish the reasons for the existence of the I & E headquarters.

It never occurred to me to examine any Table of Organization to see where this particular office was located, diagrammatically, during World War II.[3] But I do know that it should be on the commander's staff and not on somebody's who has, primarily, a staff function to perform.

Here again is a subject that you and I could talk about for quite a while, but I should warn you that I have a hunch that if things keep getting worse, you might easily find yourself the new "General Osborn" with a mission of writing out your own directive and your own Organizational Table!!!!![4]

With best wishes, *Cordially*

---

[1] Sulzberger, publisher of the *New York Times* and a life trustee of Columbia University, had asked Eisenhower in a letter of December 13 (EM) what the *Times* could do to help to explain to U.S. troops stationed in Europe "why they are away from their own country and those they love." Sulzberger hoped that there would not be a recurrence of the situation in World War II during which the Army Information and Education (I&E) Division had exerted little influence in high echelons. Sulzberger's letter of the fourteenth (EM) pertained to the manner in which meetings of the Columbia University trustees had been conducted. There was no point in changing the procedures, he argued, since Eisenhower would soon be taking up his duties in Europe, but he believed that in a less formal atmosphere the meetings might have been "more interesting and valuable." In particular, he thought that evening sessions were preferable to midday ones and that "with a couple of drinks, the men might have broken down and relaxed. . . ."
[2] On the Battle of the Bulge see Chandler, *War Years*, no. 2177; Cole, *The Ardennes*, pp. 54−55; and John Eisenhower, *The Bitter Woods*, pp. 28−29.
[3] The Information and Education Division had been part of the Army Service Forces during World War II. The scope and organization of I&E had changed twice in the postwar period before James V. Forrestal had brought the agency under the aegis of the Office of the Secretary of Defense (beginning May 1, 1949). It became the Armed Forces Information and Education Division, and its work fell within the purview of the chairman of the Armed Forces Personnel Policy Board (see *New York Times*, Mar. 26, 1949. Regarding Armed Forces I&E's precursors see U.S. Army, *The Army Almanac: A Book of Facts Concerning the Army of the United States* [Washington, D.C., 1950], pp. 715−28).

[4] President Roosevelt had commissioned retired banker Frederick Henry Osborn (A.B. Princeton 1910) a brigadier general in the Army and Chief of the Morale Branch of The Adjutant General's Office in 1941. Osborn had directed the reorganization of Special Services and the Post Exchange Service of the Army Service Forces in 1942; by the end of World War II he was a major general and Director of the Information and Education Division. After leaving the Army he had served as Deputy U.S. Representative on the United Nations Atomic Energy Commission from March 1947 to January 1950.

1131   *Eisenhower Mss.*

To Leonard Townsend Gerow and   *December 16, 1950*
Mary Louise Gerow

Dear Mary Louise and Gee: How nice it was to have a note from you.[1]

We live these days in a shadowland of uncertainty; we have become convinced that I am to be ordered back into some kind of duty, but timing and other things are still undecided. Actually, there is still a chance that we will not receive any orders at all. Add to all this the whole national state of mind and you can understand how we are living.

All this just in order to tell you that we got an unusual lift from having word from old and dear friends.

Good luck and Merry Christmas to you both, and may the New Year bring to you increased health and continued happiness. *As ever*

[1] The Gerows had congratulated Eisenhower on his impending appointment as head of the NATO forces in an undated letter (EM. For background on Lieutenant General Gerow [USA, ret.] see no 888). The Gerows planned to spend the winter in Cocoa, Florida, and then go to Virginia "unless the Army should decide it can use my services in some capacity."

1132   *Eisenhower Mss., Diaries*

Diary   *December 16, 1950*

I'm half way to Europe.

On yesterday morn had a talk with Ferd. Eberstadt at Herbert Hoover's.[1] The latter's theory is "arm to the teeth & *stay home*."

Talked a long time with Averell Harriman.[2] Whole idea was a long range policy in foreign affairs. See 2 memos in back of book.[3]

[1] For background on Eberstadt and Hoover see no. 57.

[2] A note on Eisenhower's appointment calendar for December 15 indicates that he

telephoned W. Averell Harriman, President Truman's Special Assistant on Foreign Affairs, to discuss "SHAPE and authorities" (for background on Harriman see no. 852). There is also a note about a conversation of the same day with General of the Army Omar N. Bradley, chairman of the Joint Chiefs of Staff, regarding "letters of authority from president." On the scope of Eisenhower's authority as SACEUR (Supreme Allied Commander, Europe) see no. 1136.

[3] We have been unable to locate the memoranda to which Eisenhower refers. He was, it seems, familiar with Eberstadt's views prior to their meeting on the fifteenth. He had informed Eberstadt in a note of December 5 (EM) that he had read carefully Eberstadt's speech of October 16 concerning the balance of world power. Eisenhower had called it "a splendid effort . . . really a fine paper." An abridgment had appeared in *Time*, October 30, 1950, p. 30. That version had included an elaboration of Eberstadt's earlier statements on the importance of West Germany and Japan as counterplayers to Russia in the competition for power (for background see no. 951). He proposed "a long-term political program for peace" which would include rearmament of these nations. For Eisenhower's views see nos. 1129 and 1155.

1133   *Eisenhower Mss.*

To Earl Henry Blaik   *December 17, 1950*

Dear Red:[1] While I am quite certain that my telegram would have had little influence in the outcome, still, I am sorry that it was not delivered the evening before, as I had intended it. I sent it Friday evening about six o'clock and asked that it be rushed through.[2]

Of course, I was interested in your estimate and I most emphatically agree with your conclusion that the series is not helped by any West Point defeat.[3] The very best that can possibly be said for the setback is that it may be of some use to you next year when you are hammering home lessons that you want your men to remember.[4]

Your paragraph on the bewilderment of our youth is, in my opinion, both correct and timely. Even so, I really believe that most of our young people are ahead of the oldsters in their thinking. The older man simply refuses to desert a traditional, secure niche that automatically exists for him in his own thinking—in his illusions— and, consequently, he cannot recognize the requirements that a changing world is placing upon each of us. There is a tremendous need for understanding, vocal leaders in our country today.[5]

It appears that, from the papers, I am in more or less immediate range of a call to uniformed duty. Sometimes my reaction is that the world must be in an even sorrier state than I think it is when they have to call back veterans of my vintage to get into active harness.[6]

With the very best of luck and best wishes from the entire Eisenhower tribe for a fine Holiday Season for you and yours. *Cordially*

[1] Colonel Blaik (USA, ret.) was head football coach at the U.S. Military Academy (for background see no. 250).

[2] In his telegram of December 1 (EM) Eisenhower had expressed the hope that the West Point team would win the Army-Navy game the following day. If the cadets exemplified "perfection in teamwork, courage, skill and loyalty," the consequences would include a victory over Navy and a surge of "renewed confidence to everyone who is concerned about the welfare of America." Blaik reported in his letter of December 14 (EM) that the telegram had arrived after the game, and he wished that he could have had it to read to the team between halves. Army had lost by a score of 14−2 (see *New York Times*, Dec. 3, 1950).

[3] The cadets had won twenty-seven games with Navy, lost twenty, and tied four since 1890; their recent loss in the annual encounter was their first since 1943 (see *ibid*.). Blaik had mentioned a friend's remark to him that "perhaps defeat would do much to help the series," and he had answered that the man "was getting far too mellow in his middle age."

[4] Blaik had observed that his team had not played as well as it might have and that the Naval Academy squad had made optimal use of its "physical capabilities." The cadets, on the other hand, had taken a win over Navy as a foregone conclusion, and Blaik argued, "In such an atmosphere no football team could be completely ready."

[5] Blaik had noticed that young men had "no belly" for the war in Korea, and he postulated "that if we are to again become a formidable fighting nation every effort must be made to win over the bewildered young soldier."

[6] See the next document.

1134 *Eisenhower Mss.*

To Bernard Law Montgomery[1] *December 19, 1950*
Cable. Secret

You may have seen the news of my designation to command the new European organization.[2] I hope to proceed to Europe on a trip around the first of the year but as you know it takes a little time to set up a new headquarters and organization for command.[3] I assume that you will carry on in your present regional organization, as you must know how dependent I will be upon you during the initial stages.[4] With all good wishes and a merry Christmas.

[1] Field Marshal Viscount Montgomery was chairman of the Commanders-in-Chief Committee of the Western Union (for further background see no. 14). Lieutenant Colonel Paul T. Carroll prepared this message for the General.

[2] At the unanimous request of the foreign ministers of the North Atlantic Treaty nations (meeting as the North Atlantic Council [NAC] in Brussels, Belgium), President Truman had designated Eisenhower to be Supreme Allied Commander, Europe (SACEUR), on this day (see Truman to Eisenhower, Dec. 19, 1950, EM, and State, *Foreign Relations, 1950*, vol. III, *Western Europe*, pp. 594−95, 604−5. See also nos. 1136 and 1139). The NAC had given Eisenhower authority "to train the national units assigned to his command and to organize them into an effective integrated defence force" (see NAC communiqué, Dec. 19, 1950,

Department of State Bulletin, Jan. 1, 1951, p. 7; and *New York Times*, Dec. 20, 1950).

ˈ A note on Eisenhower's appointment calendar for December 18 summarizes part of a telephone conversation with the President, a talk which took place while the General was in a freight station in Bucyrus, Ohio: "Mr. Pres, as an individual I don't matter; I just want to be certain our Government knows what course it should pursue. . . . Proposed a month's survey trip and return to D.C. for preliminary report. Wm. T. Phillips with DDE during phone call per DDE request." Phillips was assistant to the General Passenger Agent, Traffic Department, Pennsylvania Railroad. General and Mrs. Eisenhower were traveling to Denver, Colorado, by train to spend the holidays with the Douds (see no. 1140).

³ Eisenhower would visit the governments of eleven of the NATO nations between January 7 and 26, 1951 (see *New York Times*, Jan. 21, 24, 26, and 27, 1951).

⁴ On December 20 the Consultative Council of the Brussels Treaty powers would decide to merge the Western Union Defense Organization with the headquarters that Eisenhower would establish (see *New York Times*, Dec. 21, 1950; and Kaplan, *A Community of Interests*, pp. 132–33. For background on the Western Union see no. 375). Montgomery would reply in a telegram of December 23 (EM) that he would "carry on" in the Western Union "until further orders."

Eisenhower had not yet received Montgomery's telegram of this day (EM) congratulating him on the appointment. That message included the assurance that Montgomery would "be delighted to serve under you in any capacity you like."

1135

Eisenhower Mss.,
Merrill Mueller Corr.

To David Sarnoff
Restricted

December 21, 1950

Am planning an exploratory trip of two or three weeks to Europe leaving around two January. Have talked to Red Mueller while in Denver and believe he would be of considerable assistance to me on this survey.¹ Can you spare him?² In the meantime, we are exploring possibilities using Red as my personal adviser public affairs thru State Dept. For initial absence he would probably be on dollar per year basis. Appreciate this means sacrifice to you and sponsors, but you will understand that I need disinterested and expert help. Will you wire answer to me at Lowry Air Force base, Denver.³ *Regards*

¹ Sarnoff was chairman of the board of RCA and a director of NBC (for background see no. 334). Merrill "Red" Mueller was a news commentator for NBC and Director of RCA, Ltd., London. On his request for an assignment with Eisenhower in Europe see no. 1063.

² Frank M. Folsom, president of RCA, would reply in a telegram of December 22 (EM) that the answer was yes (for background on Folsom see no. 334). Eisenhower would respond (telegram, Eisenhower to Mueller, Dec. 23, EM) that arrangements had been made for Mueller to accompany him during January (on

the trip see no. 1137). Mueller would send a telegram on December 24 (EM) reporting that he was awaiting instructions.

[3] Although he is listed as a member of Eisenhower's party on an initial, tentative itinerary (EM), we have been unable to find any evidence that Mueller actually made the January exploratory trip with Eisenhower. The following month Mueller would suggest that Eisenhower "support . . . privately" the idea that Sarnoff should reassign him—that is, Mueller—to Europe (Mueller to Eisenhower, Feb. 6, 1951, EM). Eisenhower would answer on February 12 (EM), however, that Mueller should remain on his assignment in San Francisco, California, because the public relations aspect of Eisenhower's work "will be in a somewhat different category than we first anticipated."

1136   *Eisenhower Mss.,*
                                                        Harry S. Truman Corr.

To Alfred Maximilian Gruenther   *December 22, 1950*
Cable. Secret

Following is draft we worked up here as a reply to the President:

"I write to acknowledge receipt of your letter of December 19, 1950 in which is outlined the scope of the authority you assign me with respect to United States forces in Europe.[1]

The terms seem entirely appropriate and I desire only to state that, while operational command does not involve routine administration, training and supply functions, it will obviously be necessary in the performance of my assigned mission to issue certain guidance in the training field.[2] On the administrative side, I am sure you will agree that, since all senior United States commanders in Europe will be my direct assistants in carrying out assigned missions, I should have definite influence in their selection, relief or replacement. In this view, I am certain the Joint Chiefs of Staff would concur.[3]

Thank you sincerely for your expression of confidence. I can only say that I will give the best that is in me.

With best wishes for a happy Christmas to you and your family. *Respectfully*"

Request your comments.[4]

[1] In his letter (EM) Truman had assigned Eisenhower operational command of U.S. army and air forces in Europe and U.S. naval forces in the Eastern Atlantic and Mediterranean "to the extent necessary for the accomplishment of your mission" (for background see no. 1134). The President had told newsmen on the nineteenth that Eisenhower's position in Europe would be analogous to that of General of the Army Douglas MacArthur in Asia (see *Public Papers of the Presidents: Truman, 1950*, pp. 753–54; and *New York Times*, Dec. 20, 1950). Truman had explained that he meant MacArthur's assignment as SCAP, rather than as C-in-C, U.N. Command (on the former command see Galambos, *Chief of Staff*, no.

729; for background on MacArthur see no. 33. An earlier draft of this letter, with Eisenhower's extensive changes, is in the same file as this document).

[2] The words "in the performance of my assigned mission to issue certain guidance" were omitted from the cable as it was sent out to General Gruenther.

[3] In his letter Truman had directed that the established channels of command of U.S. forces in Europe continue to function "subject to overriding requirements of the Supreme Allied Commander, Europe." The President had indicated that "the missions, routine employment, training and administration" were matters that would not ordinarily fall within Eisenhower's purview.

On December 18 the defense and foreign ministers had approved several proposals for the reorganization of the NATO military structure. These recommendations, which had been presented by the North Atlantic Military Committee (for background see no. 1113), had defined Eisenhower's peacetime authority differently than had Truman's in his directive. The Supreme Commander would have "direct control over the higher training of all national forces allocated to SHAPE in peacetime"—a provision of authority that would become plausible with the consolidation of the regional defense organizations (for background see no. 1134). Moreover, the Supreme Commander was to have direct access to the chiefs of staff of each nation, as well as authority to communicate with their respective defense ministers and heads of government. Finally, the Supreme Commander would have authority "to make recommendations direct to National Chiefs of Staff on the peacetime deployment of National forces placed, or to be placed, under his control, and on logistic and administrative matters affecting the efficiency or readiness of these forces." In time of war, on the other hand, Eisenhower would have "the full powers of a Supreme Commander" in matters of operations and training. The ministers planned to define the latter powers in detail at a future meeting (see State, *Foreign Relations, 1950*, vol. III, *Western Europe*, pp. 559–60, 562–63. For background on Eisenhower's dissatisfaction with the scope of the Supreme Commander's authority see no. 1113, n. 5).

[4] In a telegram of December 26 (EM, Truman Corr.) Lieutenant General Gruenther would advise Eisenhower not to raise the question of U.S. senior commanders in his reply to the President. Gruenther would argue, "You should assume that you have necessary power and you should act accordingly. Your letter to the President should only thank him for his confidence in you and restate your determination to discharge the assignment to best of your ability." Eisenhower would heed Gruenther's suggestion and would send Truman an abridged version of this letter (see no. 1139).

1137

Eisenhower Mss.

To JAMES FREDERICK GAULT[0][1]   *December 23, 1950*
Cable. Restricted

Am planning a preliminary trip to Europe, leaving here about New Year's. Will keep you in touch with Julius Holmes, who has been making some preliminary plans.[2] Hope to have a long talk with you when in London.[3] I want to have you with me in some capacity on my new job.[4]

¹ For background on Gault see no. 14. An earlier draft of this message is in the same file as this document.

² Holmes, Minister in the U.S. Embassy in London, had sent a cable on December 20 (EM) congratulating Eisenhower on his appointment as SACEUR (for background on Holmes see no. 30). He had also offered to make arrangements for the General's visit to London. In a letter of the twenty-second (EM) he had mentioned that Sir Alan F. Lascelles, secretary to King George VI, had told him that the King wanted to see Eisenhower and possibly have lunch with him (for further background on Lascelles see *Eisenhower Papers*, vols. VI–IX). Eisenhower would reply (telegram, Dec. 30, EM) that he would not arrive in Europe as early in January as he had planned and that he would soon inform Holmes of his new itinerary. He also promised to hold a luncheon date open for the King, but as it turned out, the King would not be in London during Eisenhower's visit (see Holmes to Eisenhower, Jan. 5, 1951, EM, Subject File, Trips; and *New York Times*, Jan. 14, 1951).

³ Eisenhower would probably see Gault at a dinner at Holmes's residence in London on January 15, 1951 (see "Itinerary of General Dwight D. Eisenhower, 12–27 January 1951," EM, Subject File, Trips).

⁴ Gault would serve as Eisenhower's United Kingdom Military Assistant in 1951.

1138   *Eisenhower Mss.*

To Frank Stephen Hoag   *December 23, 1950*
Personal and confidential

Dear Mr. Hoag:⁰ Thanks for the editorial you sent me. I read it with a great deal of interest.

I agree completely with your idea of international cooperation. The effort must be cooperative or we will certainly exhaust ourselves in the hopeless task of doing the job alone.¹

Your final paragraph, however, suggests action which I feel I cannot take without overstepping my role as a soldier. It is very important to our democratic system, I think, that the clearly defined role of the soldier be acknowledged and adhered to.²

Thanks again for your letter and please accept my best wishes for a happy holiday season.³ *Sincerely*

¹ Hoag, president of the Star-Journal Publishing Corporation of Pueblo, Colorado, had sent an editorial from his newspaper of December 21 (EM). The editorial began with a summary of former President Herbert C. Hoover's radio and television speech of the previous evening on the subject of U.S. foreign policy and went on to recommend that the administration strictly limit aid to the European nations until they accepted some of the burden of opposing Communist aggression. The editorial said that Hoover's speech embodied the realization that "our own economic welfare should come first before we are bled white in men and money and with a mounting national debt greater than the debts of all other civilized nations combined" (a transcript of Hoover's address is in *New York Times*, Dec. 21, 1950).

² The editorial had concluded with advice for Eisenhower in his new role as

SACEUR: he should "respectfully demand" that the nations of Western Europe contribute to their own defense "on the basis of their respective populations." If these efforts were satisfactory, then Eisenhower should tell the Europeans that "the United States will do as it always has done, namely, it will come to your rescue and cooperate with you to the fullest extent" (on Eisenhower's appointment see no. 1134).

[3] In a letter of December 21 (EM) William E. Robinson (see no. 28 for background) had recounted several remarks that Clarence Dillon had made about Eisenhower at a luncheon on the same day (on Eisenhower's recent interest in Dillon see no. 1118). Dillon had stressed the importance of European contributions to the army that Eisenhower would soon raise.

Robinson had enclosed an editorial by Walter Lippmann which had appeared in the *New York Herald Tribune* of the twenty-first (for background on Lippmann see no. 389). The piece had opened with the hopeful observation that Truman's recent call for mobilization of industry and the North Atlantic Council's compromise on German rearmament would assist Eisenhower in accomplishing his mission in Europe (on the compromise see no. 1064; on the mobilization see no. 1129, n. 6).

1139   *Eisenhower Mss.*

TO HARRY S. TRUMAN   *December 28, 1950*

Dear Mr. President: I write to acknowledge receipt of your letter of December 19, 1950 in which is outlined the scope of the authority you assign me with respect to United States Forces in Europe.[1]

Thank you sincerely for your expression of confidence. I can only say that I will give the best that is in me.

With best wishes for the New Year to you and your family. *Respectfully*

[1] This letter is an abridged version of no. 1136.

1140   *Eisenhower Mss., Family File*

TO JOHN SHELDON DOUD AND   *December 29, 1950*
ELIVERA CARLSON DOUD

Dear Min and Pupah: I will make certain that the barometer and thermometer will be properly mounted and adjusted at the new farm.[1]

I am sure you know what great fun Mamie and I had in spending Christmas with you in Denver. I only hope that we did not disrupt your routine too much.[2]

Mamie, Bob and Cy will keep you posted as we progress in our new venture.[3] The strongest tie that will urge me to complete my tasks early are in Denver, and while I give no promise for the summertime, I hope that we may again be together next Christmas. *Affectionately*

[1] These were no doubt gifts from Eisenhower's parents-in-law. On the purchase of the farm near Gettysburg, Pennsylvania, see no. 1080. In letters of December 16 and 17 (EM, Family File, and EM, Moore Corr.) Eisenhower had thanked his nephews and nieces for their gifts.

[2] The Eisenhowers had returned to New York City on the preceding day. They had been in Denver, Colorado, from December 20 to December 26 (see *Denver Post*, Dec. 19, 1950; and *New York Times*, Dec. 29, 1950).

[3] Bob and Cy were Lieutenant Colonel Robert L. Schulz, Eisenhower's aide, and Cyril C. Croke, a friend of the Douds' (for background on Croke see no. 286).

1141   *Eisenhower Mss.*

TO GRAYSON LOUIS KIRK   *December 29, 1950*

Dear Mr. Kirk:[0] I soon go on indefinite leave of absence on military duty.[1] Under our statutes, Chapter one, paragraph three, the Vice-President of the University is to assume presidential functions and responsibilities "in the event of the death, disability, resignation or retirement of the President . . ." Since my absence will create a "disability" within the meaning of this statutory provision, I am writing officially to inform you that effective with my departure to Europe and pending my return to the University, you, in your capacity as Vice-President, are to exercise the chief executive power of the University.[2] This authorization is, of course, subject to the authority of the Trustees to make other arrangements at any time.[3] *Sincerely*

[1] Kirk was vice-president and provost of Columbia University (for background see nos. 515 and 843).

[2] Eisenhower had previously interpreted this as the provost's responsibility (see no. 361).

[3] The trustees had granted Eisenhower's leave of absence and had confirmed Kirk as acting president on December 19 (see *New York Times*, Dec. 20, 1950). Kirk would forward to Eisenhower in a note of December 30 (EM) a resolution of the University Council expressing its pride, support, and hope for Eisenhower in his role as SACEUR (for background on the appointment see no. 1134).

To Grayson Louis Kirk and   *December 29, 1950*
Joseph Campbell

I have just received word from Mr. Clarence Dillon that the Dillon Fund is contributing $25,000 to the American Assembly. From my many conversations with Mr. Dillon on the subject, I know that he really wants to use this money for the support of the Peace Institute, under the American Assembly.[1] Consequently, please inform all concerned that this money will be reserved for that purpose.[2]

[1] Dillon, head of Dillon, Read & Company, had promised to find ways to finance the work of an institute of war and peace studies at Columbia (see nos. 682 and 810. On the American Assembly see no. 1039).
[2] A thank-you note of December 25 (CUF) had gone out to Dillon from Denver, Colorado.

To George Catlett Marshall   *December 29, 1950*

Dear General Marshall: I am most grateful for the sentiments you express in your letter to me of the 21st.[1] I am certainly determined to do the very best I can in the extraordinary task assigned me.

While I had planned to take off for Europe on an exploratory trip on January 2, I have now been persuaded by members of the Staff and some of our representatives in Europe to postpone my start until the 7th. This will give me two or three extra days for additional briefing in Washington. During that time I shall call at your office. I am counting on the initial trip to last two or three weeks and then to return to Washington for final conferences before going to Europe to undertake actual problems of organization.[2] *Cordially*

[1] In his letter (EM) Secretary of Defense Marshall had offered to be "at your disposal in anyway I can find" during the course of the mission that Eisenhower would undertake in Europe (for background see no. 1134). Marshall had also praised Eisenhower's selflessness and "rare ability to work harmoniously with other people. . . ." He said that the integrity of Eisenhower's efforts in the latter regard made him "rather unique in the world."
[2] Eisenhower would confer with officials in Washington, D.C., from January 1 until his departure for Paris on January 6. He would visit the governments of eleven of the NATO nations between January 7 and January 26 (see State, *Foreign Relations, 1951*, vol. III, *European Security and the German Question*, pt. 1, pp. 392–458; and *New York Times*, Jan. 21, 24, 26, and 27, 1951).

To Arthur Hays Sulzberger   *December 29, 1950*

Dear Arthur: My thanks for your nice note of the 19th.[1] You probably have some comprehension of the distress I feel at the thought of leaving work that has become intriguing, not to say challenging. Moreover, it is a shock for Mamie and me to break up housekeeping once more as we have done so many, many times in the past 35 years. Besides, when I read every day of the divided counsels in our country respecting our responsibilities and opportunities in Europe, I am forced to wonder whether there should not be some preliminary work done *here* before we start something new abroad. But I am convinced that Western civilization is doomed unless the United States, the British Commonwealth and the Western European nations can find a solid, sound basis of cooperation for the common security.

So, I am determined to give my best. *Cordially*

[1] Sulzberger, a trustee of Columbia University and publisher of the *New York Times*, had written (EM) that he hated to see Eisenhower leave but that he was eager to see the General take up the NATO assignment (for background see no. 1136).

To William Averell Harriman   *December 29, 1950*

Dear Averell:[1] Today I was visited by Mr. Horace Flanigan, a good friend of mine, and Chairman of the Board of the Manufacturers Trust Company, 55 Broad Street, here in New York.[2] He is related by marriage to a man who is now a resident of Switzerland and who was formerly a German munitions maker. His name is Bernhard Berghaus. Because of the background of Berghaus, the Swiss Government is apparently using him as a sort of agent in an attempt to procure some needed munitions of war.

It is my understanding—obtained from Mr. Flanigan—that Mr. Berghaus, acting for the Swiss Government, would like to buy, for cash, 500 Patton tanks from the American Locomotive Co. or from any other company experienced in the manufacture of this item and able to undertake manufacture with reasonable promptness. In addition to their readiness to pay cash (I believe $200,000,000 was the figure mentioned.) the Swiss are ready to ship, also, to this country 20,000 tons of steel which they understand to be the approximate equivalent of the steel to be used in the manufacture of 500 tanks.

The only reason that Mr. Flanigan is connected with the case is because his friend, Mr. Berghaus, had no other connection through which to start inquiries as to the readiness of our Government to approve such a purchase. Mr. Flanigan came to ask me about the matter and I venture to write to you only because of the influence that a well-armed and defense-minded Switzerland could have on the military situation in Western Europe. I, of course, know nothing about the international politics of these matters and, consequently, I submit the whole affair to you without additional comment.

I assume that both the State and Defense Departments would have some opinion, but whatever the answer, I merely ask that you communicate it to Mr. Flanigan—or you could even simply tell him with whom he should communicate in any of the established Departments. I volunteered to place this case before you because of a feeling that both Mr. Flanigan and I have that it might be of some importance to our Government.[3]

With warm personal regard, *Cordially*

[1] For background on Harriman see no. 852.
[2] Eisenhower had gone hunting with Flanigan in October 1950 (for background see no. 1008).
[3] We have been unable to locate any additional correspondence on this subject in EM.

1146   *Eisenhower Mss.*

TO FREDERICK COYKENDALL   *December 29, 1950*

Dear Mr. Chairman: I am profoundly grateful for your nice note.[1] I am planning to see something of the central core of Columbia's family before I depart semi-permanently for Europe. I think I shall do this by asking the University Council and a few of their friends plus the Trustees, and representatives of the student body to a reception at the Faculty Club. I am planning to do this late in January after my first trip to Europe. Certainly, before I leave, I shall hope to have a long talk with you on Columbia's affairs. In the meantime Mamie and I send to you and Mrs. Coykendall our very best wishes for a fine New Year. *Sincerely*

[1] Coykendall, chairman of the board of trustees of Columbia University and president of the Cornell Steamboat Company, had written on December 23 (EM) to express his esteem for Eisenhower: "We are proud of and grateful for your leadership and we look forward to your return, free from all care, and full of plans for the future of the University."

To Daniel I. J. Thornton   *December 29, 1950*

Dear Dan:[1] The lady's name of whom I spoke to you is Myrtle Sheahan. Mrs. Sheahan is a machine operator in the Public Utilities Commission. According to her story there are two individuals who figure the road tax for all carriers using Colorado roads. She states that salaries depend upon the length of service and the merit system—but that these are radically influenced by political considerations.

Rather than go into further details, all of which you would want to verify anyway through a proper investigator, I should like merely to say that I have known her for many years and have found her to be a woman of high character, real loyalty and pleasing personality.[2]

I cannot tell you how pleased both Mamie and I were with the opportunity to meet you and Mrs. Thornton, with her mother and to have the opportunity for a real visit with the three of you.

Beyond this, we were most deeply appreciative of your courtesy in coming to see us, with the Mannings, as the train pulled out.[3] Mamie carried her flowers into her house and I returned to my office, as soon as we got here, to get started on a stack of work that is a mile high.

Referring again, for the moment, to the Sheahan case, I am sure that you understand that I am not venturing in any way to urge any particular action on it or even to request anything except an inquiry into the case. In spite of the fact that Mrs. Sheahan has been a long-time friend of the family, I am not possibly qualified to pass upon her capabilities in her present position.[4]

Please remember me kindly to Mrs. Thornton and her mother and with warmest regards to yourself. *Cordially*

[1] Thornton, governor-elect of Colorado, had been guest of honor at a luncheon that Eisenhower had attended on December 22 (a list of the guests is in EM. For background on Thornton see no. 992).

[2] The Eisenhowers had recently been in Colorado on vacation (see no. 1140).

[3] Thornton and Mr. and Mrs. Fred M. Manning, Sr., had been at the station in Denver to say good-by to the Eisenhowers on December 26 (see *Denver Post*, Dec. 27, 1950. On Manning see no. 1023).

[4] Eisenhower would inform Mrs. Sheahan in a note of this day that he had written to Thornton regarding her case.

To Philip Dunham Reed   *December 30, 1950*

Dear Philip:[1] Mr. D. H. Heinemann has become interested in a project we have here at Columbia University—The Institute of War and Peace.[2] He, in turn, has interested Mr. Harrod of the International General Electric.[3] I understand that Mr. Harrod is going to propose some corporate assistance for the project subject, of course, to approval of higher authority in the Company. I assume that you will probably be the deciding influence. Faced with the rather bleak necessity of going off to Europe on military duty and, consequently, of severing my day-to-day connection with a number of our programs which I feel will be of inestimable value to the country, I am hopeful of having some of them launched as going concerns before I make my final departure from this country.

I realize that I cannot possibly ask you to give your approval blindly but if you should be interested in a complete description of the project, I suggest that you have your office call Brigadier General Edwin Clark (32 East 57th Street, New York City, PL 3-7571) who, I am sure, would—as a devoted supporter of the project—be glad to come to your office to explain the whole thing to you.[4] Another whom you could call would be Dean John Krout here at the University (UN4-3200, Ext. 2535).[5]

I shall be off to Washington before you receive this and thereafter will spend a couple of weeks in Europe before coming back here to wind up my affairs and go back to Europe for the next year or so. Needless to say, I hope that when you next come to Europe you will seize the opportunity to drop in at my headquarters. I would most thoroughly enjoy talking to you.[6]

With best wishes for the New Year. *Cordially*

[1] Reed was chairman of the board of the General Electric Company (see no. 721).
[2] Dannie *N.* Heinema*n* was chairman of the standing committee of the Société Financière de Transports et d'Enterprises Industrielles (SOFINA), a holding company that specialized in engineering and development of electric power. In 1914 he had helped to organize the Commission for Belgian Relief, and after World War I he had supported proposals for a United States of Europe. He had also established the Heineman Foundation for Research, Educational, Charitable and Scientific Purposes, Inc.

Columbia University's Institute of War and Peace Studies would sponsor research in international affairs and national security policy (for background on Eisenhower's plans for the institute see no. 1056).
[3] William Rogers He*r*od (Ph.B. Yale 1918) would take a leave of absence from his duties as president of the International General Electric Company after his appointment as Coordinator of the Defense Production Board of the North Atlantic Treaty Organization in January 1951. Herod was an associate fellow of Pierson

College at Yale University and chairman of the Yale University Council's Committee on the Division of Engineering.

[4] Edwin N. Clark was a business consultant and executive in New York City (for background see Galambos, *Chief of Staff*, no. 1456. On his fund-raising efforts see no. 765).

[5] On John A. Krout, dean of the Faculty of Political Science, Philosophy and Pure Science and associate provost, see nos. 361 and 825. Reed would reply on January 3, 1951 (CUF), that would send Eisenhower's letter to the official in the General Electric Company responsible for investigating requests for contributions.

[6] Reed would visit with Eisenhower in Puerto Rico early in 1951 (see Eisenhower to Reed, Feb. 24, 1951, EM).

1149   *Eisenhower Mss.*

To JOHN ARCHBOLD   *December 30, 1950*

Dear John:[01] It was nice of you to think of sending me some of my favorite literature. When the pressures of the day build up, I always look forward to riding in the saddle with the fearless plainsmen of years ago.[2]

Thank you again for your thoughtfulness and with every good wish for a brighter New Year. *Sincerely*

[1] Archbold was a neighbor of the Douds' in Denver, Colorado.

[2] On Eisenhower's interest in Western magazines and books see Galambos, *Chief of Staff*, no. 1179.

1150   *Eisenhower Mss.*

To FORREST PERCIVAL SHERMAN   *December 30, 1950*

Dear Forrest:[1] Over a number of years I have often found it useful to provide background material for individuals engaged in communication activities in our country. This was true while I was on active service and has been since that time.

In these days of tension and of crisis and of arguments as to the character of America's foreign interests, it seems to me particularly important to provide the public, through every means possible, the truth about basic factors in the situation. I refer especially to the economic dependence of the United States upon other regions for certain types of indispensable materials; the tremendous advantage that would accrue to the Communists if they were successful in an invasion of Western Europe; the strength that is implicit in unity and the need for establishing priorities in our essential tasks, inasmuch as the strength of America is not equal to carrying on her back all the rest of the world.

Another field in which much is necessary, in the way of information, if our people are to act wisely, is the relationship between our national security and the intelligence with which we solve our problems at home of preparation, maintenance, taxes, use of manpower, production and so on and so on. Few people, for example, clearly understand the difference between Universal Military Training and Universal Military Service.[2] This is one simple illustration of the prime need for better information if our people are to act intelligently which means, of course, *economically* and effectively.

One very prominent man in the field of communication who has great interest in this type of problem is *Arthur Godfrey*. I have had two or three talks with him and I feel certain that it would be beneficial if, at some convenient time, he could have an opportunity to talk to you, among others in Washington.[3]

Because I believe that much good might derive from this kind of thing, I have suggested to him that he seek an appointment with you sometime in the near future. If he does so, this note will explain the reason. Since it is estimated that his programs reach a total of some 44 million people weekly, it is clear that he could be of great help to our country whenever a piece of important information could be appropriately fitted by him and his experts into his particular type of program.

I feel so sure that much good can come out of this kind of thing that I would be perfectly glad to take Mr. Godfrey to my headquarters for a short tour of duty if, at some future time, you should think it desirable to recall him to active Naval duty and send him on to me. On such a tour he might gather at first hand much information on our foreign problem that would be of tremendous value to our people.[4]

I trust that you will find something of value in this suggestion.

With warm Regard, *Cordially*

P.S. I am sending this same suggestion only to two or three others in Washington.

---

[1] Admiral Sherman was CNO (for background see nos. 345 and 598). On this same day Eisenhower sent similar letters to General J. Lawton Collins, Chief of Staff of the Army; W. Averell Harriman, Special Assistant to President Truman on Foreign Affairs; and Secretary of the Army, Frank C. Pace (all are in EM).

[2] On this difference see no. 912.

[3] For background on Godfrey see no. 1027.

[4] Eisenhower would send a copy of this letter enclosed in a letter to Godfrey of December 31, (EM), asking Godfrey to write to him "when you think it is time for us to arrange for a temporary tour of duty."

To Hamilton Fish Armstrong   *December 30, 1950*
Personal and confidential

Dear Ham: If the European Studies Group is to continue its sessions, you will, of course, have to arrange for another chairman.[1] I understand that persons such as Wriston, yourself and one or two others are considered unavailable because of official positions with the Council on Foreign Relations, while others may be unable to act because of the infrequency with which they can attend meetings. In this situation, I would suggest Philip Reed or, if he could not serve, possibly Grayson Kirk.[2]

This is entirely gratuitous advice and is submitted only because I thought you might like to have my fleeting thought on the point. Please do not show this to anyone else.[3] *Cordially*

P.S. Thank you very much for your letter of the 27th which I have forwarded to General Collins with the request that it be studied.[4]

[1] Armstrong, editor of *Foreign Affairs*, was a member of the Council on Foreign Relations study group, of which Eisenhower was chairman (for background see no. 269).

[2] Henry M. Wriston was president of Brown University. Reed was chairman of the board of the General Electric Company, and Kirk was vice-president and provost of Columbia University.

[3] Armstrong would reply on January 3, 1951, that the Council on Foreign Relations would ask Kirk to act as chairman of the study group (for developments see no. 1157).

[4] Eisenhower's covering letter of December 30 to Collins is in EM, but there is no copy of Armstrong's letter of the twenty-seventh.

To James Wesley Gallagher   *December 30, 1950*
Personal

Dear Wes:[1] I am distressed that I shall miss you due to our passing each other in mid-ocean. I should have liked very much to chat with you. You are mistaken in believing that I know as much as you do about the important things of Europe—the deepseated, underlying sentiment of the people.[2] This whole problem dissolves itself into one of morale, and there is going to be a lot of skillful and energetic work take place before there will begin to develop a morale that will be effective in these troublesome times.

I agree with your evaluation of Gruenther—hence my choice.[3] In fact, I hope that all Europe will soon see that he is a proper replacement for a veteran of my venerable years.

With personal regard. *Sincerely*

¹ Gallagher was Chief of the AP bureau in Germany (for background see no. 573).

² In his letter of December 28 (EM) Gallagher had said that he had intended to write Eisenhower "giving a correspondent's eye view of the difficulties as seen from this end." He had, however, given up the idea because he assumed that Eisenhower was fully aware of the problems.

³ Lieutenant General Alfred M. Gruenther would serve as Eisenhower's Chief of Staff. Gallagher had observed that Gruenther had not received enough recognition for his contributions to the Allies' victory in World War II.

1153   *Eisenhower Mss.*

To Harold Raynsford Stark   *December 30, 1950*

Dear Betty: My apologies for the long delay in answering your nice note of November 3. My days simply are not long enough to get done all of the things I should like to do.[1]

You probably have noted in the papers that I am again to head for Europe.[2] It seems just a bit odd to me that our Government seemingly has to turn to veterans rather than to the younger men on their way up whenever these new and critical jobs loom up. As you may remember, I personally cannot command from the comfortable security of a mahogany desk many miles removed from troops. I have to go to see, to learn, to feel. This means that there is demanded a physical resistance and endurance that every man begins to lose long before he has reached the three-score level. I admit that there are certain positions in which wisdom and experience are mandatory and in which the physical factor is of little importance but actual command of troops demands this third qualification equally with the others, and we must constantly bring along younger people.[3]

This note brings to you and yours my very best wishes for the New Year, as well as assurances from Mamie and me of our abiding affection. *Cordially*

¹ Admiral Stark, currently living in retirement in Washington, D.C., had been CNO at the time of American entry into World War II (for background see *Eisenhower Papers*, vols. I–IX). In his letter of November 30, 1950, he had included a reference to the longhand postscript that Eisenhower had appended to his birthday greeting to Stark (Nov. 9, EM). Eisenhower had written, "The papers imply from time to time, that once again I may have to unfurl my flag. But I hope that, this time, the shooting can be omitted." Stark had responded, "There is another flag that millions of Americans would like to see you unfurl a couple

of years hence—almost everyone I see mentions it—be he of high or low estate and regardless of any former affiliations—never a dissenting view."

2 For background see no. 1134.

3 Eisenhower reiterated these sentiments in a letter of this day (EM) to Major General Ira Thomas Wyche, who had been U.S. Army Inspector General until his retirement in 1948 (for background see Galambos, *Chief of Staff*, no. 1141).

1154   *Eisenhower Mss.*

To Edward Bishop Dudley, Jr.   *December 30, 1950*

Dear Ed:[1] How typically nice of you to send me a set of these new irons. So far, I have been unable to take them any further than the roof of my house but I really believe that I could shoot a par, even on 13, if I just had the chance to use them down at Augusta. I not only am grateful to you but I am instantly following your suggestion and am writing to Don Tait of the Spalding Company.

Of course, you can understand my very great disappointment that I cannot come down to the Club this year. I am afraid that my life is again thrown back into a state of constant movement, high pressure and unsolvable problems. Sometimes, I get dangerously close to feeling sorry for myself—but, so far, I have been fortunate enough to have my sense of humor come to my rescue before I fall completely victim to this dangerous disease.

Again, my thanks for your beautiful present and with very best wishes for a happy and successful New Year.[2] *Cordially*

P.S. By the next time I get to Augusta, I at least ought to have the advantage of a 36-stroke handicap.

1 Dudley, a golf professional, had written in a letter of December 21 (EM) that he had had several golf clubs made for Eisenhower. He had hoped to give them to him at Augusta National Golf Club (Augusta, Georgia), but he realized that the General would not have time to visit the club before taking up his new responsibilities in Europe (on the latter see no. 1136). Dudley had asked that Eisenhower send a note about the clubs to Don Tait, of the Custom Department of A. G. Spalding and Bros. (the note of this day to Tait is in EM. On the set of woods that Spalding had made for the General see no. 829. See also no. 478).

2 Among other friends to whom Eisenhower had sent notes thanking them for their gifts were Edward J. Bermingham, Dale Hull, Lieutenant General John C. H. Lee (USA, ret.), Mary Ann and Bud Nevins, and Clifford Roberts (all are in EM).

To Ferdinand Eberstadt   *December 31, 1950*

Dear Ferd: Thank you very much for following up on the question that bothered me so much.[1] I wish that you and I could have one more talk before I leave, but I scarcely see how it is possible, unless you might happen to be in Washington on the 2nd, 3rd, 4th, or the morning of the 5th of January. If we fail to have such a talk, I shall certainly try to see you when I make a brief visit to this country about the first of February.[2]

I believe that you and I could put down in very simple, almost diagrammatic form, the core or the central structure of our ideas concerning foreign affairs, including national security, and the relationship of these to the many great internal problems that we are now trying to solve. If my impression as to this identity of basic view is correct, it would be encouraging to me to know it.[3]

I am very anxious to see someone of stature take the lead in preaching a positive doctrine for the United States that starts right down almost at the origin of our concepts of government. I should like to see brought out the clear truth that a free form of government is the political expression of an abiding faith by a race in a Superior Power, in a God. Starting from this obviously moral platform, I should like to see someone skillfully develop our aims and purposes, and finally relate these to our physical position in the world and show that a proper foreign policy rests upon both this moral foundation and the physical requirements of our situation.

Such a study as this, pursued to a logical conclusion, would, I firmly believe, lead to certain simple, easily understood conclusions—conclusions by which the average American citizen could guide himself in the exercise of his political freedoms, rights and obligations.

I realize that development of such a policy is a task for devoted and able individuals who can give to it long and undivided attention. But I personally feel that it is only through such an accomplishment that we are going to bring to our people the confidence that is derived from common, positive understandings. We are attracted too much by partisan argument and, as a result, are prone to think in negative terms, of being *against* someone or something rather than *for* something else because of a very clearly understood moral purpose and a system of physical and scientific fact.

I am afraid that, in my haste, this has become a bit jumbled, possibly even confusing. Maybe for that very reason, however, it will be the more accurate.

With best wishes for 1951, *Cordially*

[1] Eisenhower's appointment calendar indicates that he had received a telephone call from Eberstadt on December 29 (for background on Eberstadt see no. 57).

[2] Eberstadt would reply in a letter of January 6, 1951 (EM), that he was sorry that he had not had an opportunity to talk with Eisenhower prior to the latter's departure for Europe.

[3] For Eisenhower's reactions to Eberstadt's views see nos. 951 and 1132. Eberstadt would remark in his letter of January 6 (EM) that he had heard from an authoritative source that the administration planned to sign a peace treaty with Japan in the near future (for background see no. 1129, n. 3). By rebuilding Japanese strength in the Far East, Eberstadt argued, the United States might divert the Soviets' attention from Western Europe.

1156   *Eisenhower Mss.*

TO BERNARD MANNES BARUCH   *December 31, 1950*

Dear Bernie:[1] Tomorrow I go to Washington for a three or four day stay, and then I take off for Europe. I had hoped against hope that I would get to talk to you once more before my departure, but the calendar has been crowding me so severely that I have had to give up, for the moment, the doing of anything that was not of an official nature.

However, I expect to return to this country for a ten-day conference and "closing out" period about the end of January. If it can be arranged then, I want very much to see you. What I have in mind is that I would like to draw again upon your experience, understanding and courage before I hold anticipated meetings with a number of Washington officials upon whose efficiency and productivity I will, in Europe, be manifestly dependent.[2]

This note brings to you my very best wishes for a fine 1951, as well as my appreciation for a friendship that, over these many years, has meant so very much to me. *Cordially*

[1] Baruch was a philanthropist and an adviser to several Presidents (for background see *Eisenhower Papers*, vols. I–IX).

[2] Baruch would reply in a telegram of January 3 (EM) that he hoped to see Eisenhower within the week. On the following day, however, he would send a message (EM) suggesting that they meet after Eisenhower returned from Europe.

To Hamilton Fish Armstrong   *December 31, 1950*

Dear Ham: The calendar begins to crowd me and I doubt that I shall have another opportunity to meet with the European Studies Group.[1] While, at times, I think that each of us has been a little bit impatient with a seeming lack of concrete progress in the Studies, my own enthusiasm has remained at a high pitch, both because of the character of the individuals making up the group and because I always remember the observation of a very successful soldier who said, "Peace-time plans are of no particular value, but peace-time planning is indispensable."

Moreover, since I have been confronted with my new military assignment, I place higher value than ever before on the opportunities I have had to listen to continuing analyses and conclusions respecting the European situation.

Won't you please convey to the members of the group an expression of my thanks for their tolerance toward my shortcomings as a chairman and my appreciation to each for the contribution he has made to the Studies up to this moment? Incidentally, I trust that the Studies will continue to go ahead as long as the members of the group believe there is any reason for their continuance.[2]

With warm personal regard to you and to each of the others. *Cordially*

[1] For background see no. 1151.
[2] Armstrong would reply in a letter of January 3, 1951 (EM), that the members of the group would miss Eisenhower's leadership and that they would continue to send him papers.

1158   *Eisenhower Mss.*

To James Bryant Conant   *December 31, 1950*

Dear Jim:[1] You instructed me not to answer your note, but I simply had to say how much I have missed seeing you these late months when you have been in.[2] More than this, I wanted to congratulate you upon your stand on the Universal Military Service issue—I am on your team.[3]

For the next year Grayson Kirk will be Acting President of Columbia and I have written to Mr. Strong requesting that appropriate action be taken to have him designated as Columbia's representative on the Higgins Board.[4] I did not have time to look up the will and the by-laws and so on. Consequently, if I have made the wrong approach, please serve as my advocate at the next meeting and insist that I "meant well."

My present plans will bring me back to the United States for a few days in late January or early February. If all goes well, possibly I will get a chance to talk to you briefly then. I would like it very much. *Cordially*

[1] James Conant was president of Harvard University (for background see no. 285).
[2] Conant had congratulated Eisenhower on his appointment as SACEUR in a letter of December 21 (EM) (for background see no. 1134). Conant had apologized for adding to the General's mail and admonished him not to reply.
[3] See no. 1006.
[4] Eisenhower had written to Benjamin Strong, president of the United States Trust Company of New York, on December 30 (EM) requesting that Kirk be allowed to serve in his place on the Board of Control of the Eugene Higgins Trust (for background see nos. 328 and 434).

1159   *Eisenhower Mss.*

To William H. Burnham   *December 31, 1950*

Dear Bill: I have been trying to reserve a day in which I could write a personal note to all those individuals who have jumped in so enthusiastically to help us in the development of the American Assembly plan.[1] I find that the calendar has defeated me. I simply cannot find the time to do more than write to a very few. These include Sid Richardson, McCollum, Mr. Dillon, Amon Carter and Fred Manning.[2] I hope that you will undertake to convey a personal word from me to the many, many others that have contributed of their time and brains and money to make the thing a success. While I know that Phil Young will be doing this on the continuing basis, I am merely hoping that you, as opportunity offers, will assure these individuals of my own personal gratification and appreciation.[3]

For what you have done, I have no words that could express my thanks. Moreover, your unselfish offer of service during the coming year, which was made without any kind of strings or limitations, has touched me very deeply.[4] I believe I am to see you again, this afternoon, but I want to take no chances of failing to tell you how much your friendship has meant to me and how dependent I have become upon your unfailing good judgment and your readiness to help in any possible way.[5]

With warm personal regard, *Cordially*

[1] Burnham, a New York City investment banker, had worked closely with Eisenhower in the development of plans for the American Assembly (for background see nos. 826 and 877).
[2] For background see nos. 113, 826, 593, 258, and 545, respectively.
[3] Young, dean of Columbia's Graduate School of Business, would continue to

serve as Executive Director of the American Assembly. For background on his work as Acting Coordinator of Development at Columbia see no. 930.
[4] Eisenhower and Burnham had discussed the possibility of his serving on the General's SHAPE staff, but Burnham thought it would be unwise because of his strong political ties. In 1948 Burnham had headed the National Draft Eisenhower League, which he believe made him "too hot a number" to have on a military staff, "where all political implications should be avoided." Burnham would instead serve as Eisenhower's unofficial "eyes and ears" for political matters in the United States until May of 1951, when he would join SHAPE as a civilian economic analyst (see Burnham to Eisenhower, Dec. 27, 1950, EM; and Lyon, *Portrait of the Hero*, p. 426).
[5] Eisenhower's appointment calendar indicates that he would see Burnham at 7:00 P.M. on this day.

1160   *Eisenhower Mss.*

TO AMON GILES CARTER, SR.   *December 31, 1950*

Dear Amon: I have kept my last few minutes in my Columbia office to write to you and Sid.[1] There is little new to report since I talked to you on the telephone, except that it now appears that my first return to the United States will be delayed beyond the date I gave you. I think now that I shall be back between January 30 and February 8 or 9.

Again, I want to thank you for your very wonderful moral support of the things I have been trying to do here at Columbia, as well as for the generous donation you made to the American Assembly.[2] I hope that you will keep in touch with Philip Young as he develops that project. (I am more than hopeful that Lew Douglas is going to take active direction of that particular project.)[3] I believe that it offers our country a very clear-cut and definite scheme for improving the workings of our free society and for assuring its perpetuation.

Give our love to Minnie and, of course, remember us warmly to Amon, Jr.[4]

I shall miss my frequent contacts with you but, after all, I am still hopeful that this job will not require me to be away forever.[5]

Happy New Year to you all. *Cordially*

[1] Carter was president and publisher of the *Fort Worth Star-Telegram*. For background on Sid W. Richardson, also a Texan, see no. 113.
[2] For background see no. 1097.
[3] Douglas would become chairman of the National Policy Board of the American Assembly, and Young would continue to serve as the Assembly's Executive Director (see no. 1117).
[4] Minnie was Mrs. Amon G. Carter, Sr. (for background see Galambos, *Chief of Staff*, no. 1950. On Amon Jr., see no. 917).
[5] Eisenhower wrote similar letters of this day to Edward J. Bermingham, Clarence Dillon, H. L. Hunt, Fred M. Manning, Sr., L. F. McCollum, and Sid W.

Richardson (the correspondence with Bermingham, Manning, and McCollum is in EM; the other letters are in CUF). Carter would send a telegram of January 3 (EM) wishing Eisenhower a safe trip and promising to be in New York with Richardson when Eisenhower returned.

Bibliography:
Note on Primary Sources

General Eisenhower continued to retain a copy of virtually every important letter that he wrote even after he left the office of Chief of Staff of the Army in February 1948. Consequently, the great majority of documents selected for publication or used for annotation in volumes X and XI are to be found in the prepresidential (1916–52) Dwight D. Eisenhower Personal Papers, located in the Presidential Library in Abilene, Kansas. This collection (a copy of which we have on microfilm) is described at some length in the bibliographical essays in volumes V and IX of *The Papers of Dwight David Eisenhower*. It has been cited in these volumes as "Eisenhower Mss." ("EM" in the footnotes). A recent accession to the Eisenhower Manuscripts is a small file of correspondence and drafts that contains early versions of Eisenhower's letters with his handwritten changes. This file is cited as "EM, Letters and Drafts."

The most important new sources of Eisenhower material used in these volumes were the central files of Columbia University. These files are maintained under the jurisdiction of the secretary of the university and are located in the Low Memorial Library on the Columbia campus in New York City. We cite this collection as "Columbia University Files" ("CUF" in the footnotes). The collection is arranged chronologically by academic years (July 1 to June 30), and the 1948/49 segment contains approximately twenty-two and one-half feet of letters and documents. The files for 1949/50 and 1950/51 are slightly smaller, comprising seventeen and one-half feet and twenty feet, respectively.

Within each segment, the files are arranged alphabetically by correspondent. There are separate "Eisenhower" file folders, but letters written by and to the General may be found throughout all three files. Many letters in the Columbia University Files bear handwritten notations concerning the dates and locations of related correspondence. There is also a comprehensive index to the entire collection. Inquiries concerning the Columbia University Central Files should be addressed to the secretary of Columbia University.

The Columbia Archives do not contain correspondence concerning Eisenhower's activities as military adviser to the Secretary of Defense and as presiding officer of the Joint Chiefs of Staff (JCS). While many letters, memoranda, and reports documenting Eisenhower's role as defense consultant may be found in the Eisenhower Manuscripts, research in this field must include consultation of the voluminous collections in the Military Archives Division of the National Archives in Washington, D.C. The most rewarding collections in which to do research are the extensive files of the Office of the Secretary of Defense (OS/D) in Record Group 330. The records generated by the Secretary's office are divided into a classified portion (the "CD" file), covering the period from September 1947 until June 1950, and an unclassified portion, which spans the years 1947−49. A much smaller collection, the Service Academy Board Subject File, also in Record Group 330, contains verbatim transcripts of meetings in which Eisenhower participated.

Other material relating to Eisenhower's service as defense consultant may be found in the records of three military agencies. The files of the JCS itself, the "CCS" files, begin in 1942 and run throughout the period covered by our volumes. The 1948−50 segment was of most interest to us, although some material related to Eisenhower's activities may be interfiled in a later portion covering the years 1951−53. The CCS files are to be found in Record Group 218, as is a much smaller collection, the records of JCS chairman Omar N. Bradley. We have cited this latter file as "CJCS, Bradley Files." Both the CCS and the CJCS Bradley files use the War Department's decimal filing system (see *Eisenhower Papers*, vol. IX, p. 2261). Equally valuable are the voluminous files of the Army's Plans and Operations Division, which we cite as the "P&O" files (Record Group 319). These files are divided into three major segments: the unclassified through Secret files, the Top Secret files, and a small collection of especially sensitive material called the "P&O Hot File." The 1949/50 Top Secret portion of these records is occasionally (and misleadingly) referred to as the "AC of S [Assistant Chief of Staff] (G−3) Operations Decimal File." All P&O files use the War Department decimal filing system. Finally, the joint planning records of the Director of Plans, United States Air Force (1942−54, in Record Group 341), contain many revealing documents concerning Eisenhower's involvement in the task of securing interservice agreement to a joint war plan. We have cited the most useful file as "AF/PD Project Decimal, HALFMOON," the original code name for the war plan under discussion. Another Air Force collection, the Office of the Secretary of the Air Force Special Interest File (cited in our notes as "OS/AF SI File"), contains a few items of interest not readily available elsewhere.

A few personal manuscript collections also yielded important Eisenhower material: the Arthur Capper Mss., Kansas State Historical Society, Topeka, Kansas; the Milton S. Eisenhower Mss., Dwight D. Eisenhower Library, Abilene, Kansas; the Council of Foreign Relations Archives, Harold Pratt House, New York, New York; and the Hoyt S. Vandenberg Mss., Library of Congress, Washington, D.C. Access to these files may be limited due to varying restrictions imposed by donors or as a result of the levels of security classification of the documents contained in them. Interested researchers are advised to contact the custodians of the particular record collections for information.

Bibliography:
Secondary Sources Cited

Abels, Jules. *Out of the Jaws of Victory*. New York, 1959.

Abrams, Frank W. "How Can American Business Help American Education?" *Association of American Colleges Bulletin* 35, no. 1 (March 1949), 33–40.

Acheson, Dean. *Present at the Creation: My Years in the State Department*. New York, 1969.

Adenauer, Konrad. *Memoirs 1945–53*. Chicago, 1965.

Alderson, William T., Jr. "The American Association for State and Local History." *Western Historical Quarterly* 1, no. 2 (1970), 177.

Alexander, Field-Marshal Earl, of Tunis. *The Alexander Memoirs, 1940–1945*. Edited by John North. London, 1962.

Allen, Robert Sharon. *Lucky Forward: The History of Patton's Third U.S. Army*. New York, 1947.

Allied Forces, Supreme Headquarters. *Report by the Supreme Commander to the Combined Chiefs of Staff on the Operations in Europe of the Allied Expeditionary Force: 6 June 1944 to 8 May 1945*. Washington, D.C., 1946.

"All-Out War Effort Now—The Baruch Plan." *U.S. News & World Report*, August 4, 1950, 60–63.

Alperin, Lynn M. *Custodians of the Coast: History of the United States Army Engineers at Galveston*. Galveston, 1977.

Alsop, Stewart, and Griffith, Samuel B. "We Can Be Guerrillas, Too." *Saturday Evening Post*, December 2, 1950, 32–33.

Ambrose, Stephen E. *Duty, Honor, Country: A History of West Point*. Baltimore, 1966.

————. "Eisenhower as Commander: Single Thrust Versus Broad Front." In *The Papers of Dwight David Eisenhower*. Baltimore, 1970–. Vol. V, *The War Years*, edited by Alfred D. Chandler, Jr., 1970.

————. *The Supreme Commander: The War Years of General Dwight D. Eisenhower*. Garden City, N.Y., 1970.

American Assembly. *The United States and the Far East.* New York, 1956.

American Council on Education. *A Brief Statement of the History and Activities of the American Council on Education, 1948–49.* Washington, D.C., 1948.

Andrews, F. Emerson. *Philanthropic Foundations.* New York, 1956.

Appleman, Roy E. *South to the Naktong, North to the Yalu (June–November 1950).* U.S. Army in the Korean War, edited by Stetson Conn. Washington, D.C., 1960.

Arango, E. Ramón. *Leopold III and the Belgian Royal Question.* Baltimore, 1961.

Asprey, Robert B. *The First Battle of the Marne.* Philadelphia, 1962.

Association of American Universities. *Journal of Proceedings and Addresses of the Forty-Ninth Annual Conference, Held at the University of Pennsylvania, Philadelphia, Pa., October 28, 29, 30, 1948.* Princeton, 1948.

Association of Graduate Schools in the Association of American Universities. *Journal of Proceedings of the Fiftieth Annual Conference (AAU) and the First Annual Conference (AGS), October 27, 28, 29, 1949.* Princeton, 1949.

Baier, D. E. "Interpreting Officer Efficiency Reports." *Army Information Digest* 4, no. 10 (1949), 58–62.

Baldwin, Hanson W. *Battles Lost and Won: Great Campaigns of World War II.* New York, 1966.

Banks, Arthur C., Jr. "International Law Governing Prisoners of War during the Second World War." Ph.D. dissertation, The Johns Hopkins University, 1955.

Barnard, William D. *Dixiecrats and Democrats: Alabama Politics, 1942–1950.* University, Ala., 1974.

Barré, Georges. *Tunisie, 1942–43.* Paris, 1950.

Baruch, Bernard M. *American Industry in the War.* New York, 1941.

————. *Baruch: The Public Years.* New York, 1960.

————. " 'Pacing Ourselves': Cold War Strategy." *Vital Speeches of the Day* 16, no. 13 (1950), 391–94.

————. *Preventing Inflation: Statements and Writings on Controlling Living Costs and Preventing Inflation, Sept. 1941–Dec. 1941.* New York, 1942.

————, and Hancock, John M. U.S. Office of War Mobilization. *Report on War and Post-War Adjustment Policies, February 15, 1944.* Washington, D.C., 1944.

Barzun, Jacque. *Graduate Study at Columbia: Extracts from the Report of the Dean of the Graduate Faculties for 1957.* New York, 1958.

Beard, Charles A. *Toward Civilization.* New York, 1930.

————. *Whither Mankind: A Panorama of Modern Civilization.* New York, 1928.

Belden, Thomas, and Belden, Marva. *The Lengthening Shadow: The Life of Thomas J. Watson.* Boston, 1962.

Ben: Perley Poore. *The Life and Public Services of Ambrose E. Burnside, Soldier—Citizen—Statesman.* Providence, R.I., 1882.

Benton, William. "Self-Portrait—By Uncle Sam." *New York Times Magazine*, December 2, 1945, 13.

Billington, Ray Allen, comp. *Allan Nevins on History.* New York, 1975.

Blackman, Raymond V. B. *Jane's Fighting Ships: 1951–52.* London, n.d.

Blauch, Lloyd E., ed. *Accreditation in Higher Education.* Washington, D.C., 1959.

Blaustein, Albert P., and Zangrando, Robert L., eds. *Civil Rights and the American Negro.* New York, 1968.

Bond, Brian. *Liddell Hart: A Study of His Military Thought.* New Brunswick, N.J., 1977.

Borklund, C. W. *The Department of Defense.* New York, 1968.

Bradley, Omar N. *A Soldier's Story.* New York, 1951.

Brandon, Dorothy. *Mamie Doud Eisenhower: A Portrait of a First Lady.* New York, 1954.

Bright, Charles D. *The Jet Makers: Aerospace Industry from 1945 to 1972.* Lawrence, Kans., 1978.

Brinton, Crane; Craig, Gordon A.; and Gilbert, Felix. "Jomini." In *Makers of Modern Strategy: Military Thought from Machiavelli to Hitler,* edited by Edward Mead Earle, pp. 77–92. Princeton, 1943.

Bryan, T. Scott. *The Geysers of Yellowstone.* Boulder, 1979.

Buhite, Russel D. *Patrick J. Hurley and American Foreign Policy.* Ithaca and London, 1973.

Burgess, John W. *Reminiscences of an American Scholar: The Beginnings of Columbia University.* New York, 1934.

Burkhead, Jesse. *Public School Finance: Economics and Politics.* Syracuse, 1964.

Burrell, John Angus. *A History of Adult Education at Columbia University: University Extension and the School of General Studies.* New York, 1954.

Buss, Claude A. *The United States and the Philippines: Background for Policy.* Washington, D.C., 1977.

Butcher, Harry C. *My Three Years with Eisenhower: The Personal Diary of Captain Harry C. Butcher, USNR.* New York, 1946.

Callaghan, William M. "Unified Sea Transportation." *Army Information Digest* 5, no. 11 (1950), 33–39.

Campbell, John C. *The United States in World Affairs, 1948–1949.* New York, 1949.

Caraley, Demetrios. *The Politics of Military Unification: A Study of Conflict and the Policy Process.* New York, 1966.

Carnegie Corporation of New York. *Reports of Officers for the Fiscal Year Ended September 30, 1949.* New York, 1949.

————. *Reports of Officers for the Fiscal Year Ended September 30, 1950.* New York, 1950.

Carnegie Endowment for International Peace. *Annual Report, 1950–1951.* New York, 1951.

Caro, Robert A. *The Power Broker: Robert Moses and the Fall of New York.* New York, 1974.

Carr, Robert K. *The House Committee on Un-American Activities.* Ithaca, 1952.

Caute, David. *The Great Fear: The Anti-Communist Purge under Truman and Eisenhower.* New York, 1978.

Cave Brown, Anthony. *Bodyguard of Lies.* New York, 1975.

Chalfont, Alun. *Montgomery of Alamein.* New York, 1976.

Challener, Richard D. "New Light on a Turning Point in U.S. History." *University: A Princeton Quarterly* 56 (Spring 1973), 30.

Chambers, M. M. *Charters of Philanthropies: A Study of Selected Trust Instruments, Charters, By-Laws, and Court Decisions.* New York, 1948.

Chambers, Whittaker. *Witness.* New York, 1952.

Chapin, William Wallace. "General Eisenhower and the Presidency." *The Argonaut,* May 5, 1950, 3.

Childs, Marquis. *Eisenhower, Captive Hero: A Critical Study of the General and the President.* New York, 1958.

————. "Why Eisenhower Said No." *Collier's,* August 28, 1948, 14–15.

Christian Century, October 27, 1948.

Churchill, Winston S. *Churchill: His Paintings.* Compiled by David Coombs. Cleveland and New York, 1967.

————. *The Second World War.* 6 vols. Boston, 1948–53. Vol. I, *The Gathering Storm* (1948); vol. II, *Their Finest Hour* (1949); vol. IV, *The Hinge of Fate* (1950); vol. V, *Closing the Ring* (1951); vol. VI, *Triumph and Tragedy* (1953).

Clark, Mark W. *Calculated Risk.* New York, 1950.

————. *From the Danube to the Yalu.* New York, 1954.

Clay, Lucius D. *Decision in Germany.* New York, 1950.

————. *The Papers of General Lucius D. Clay, Germany, 1945–1949.* Edited by Jean Edward Smith. 2 vols. Bloomington, Ind., 1974.

Clifford, Kenneth J. *Progress and Purpose: A Developmental History of the United States Marine Corps, 1900–1970.* Washington, D.C., 1973.

Cline, Ray S. *Washington Command Post: The Operations Division.* U.S. Army in World War II, edited by Kent Roberts Greenfield. Washington, D.C., 1951.

Coffman, Edward M. "My Room Mate is Dwight Eisenhower." *American Heritage* 24 (April 1973), 102–3.

Cole, Alice C.; Goldberg, Alfred; Tucker, Samuel A.; and Winnacker, Rudolph A., eds. *The Department of Defense: Documents on Establishment and Organization, 1944–1978.* Washington, D.C., 1979.

Cole, Hugh M. *The Ardennes: Battle of the Bulge.* U.S. Army in World War II, edited by Stetson Conn. Washington, D.C., 1965.

Coles, Harry L., and Weinberg, Albert K. *Civil Affairs: Soldiers Become Governors.* U.S. Army in World War II, edited by Stetson Conn. Washington, D.C., 1964.

Coletta, Paolo E. "The Defense Unification Battle, 1947–50: The Navy." *Prologue: The Journal of the National Archives* 7, no. 1 (Spring 1975), 6–17.

————. *The United States Navy and Defense Unification: 1947–53.* Newark, Del., 1981.

Coll, Blanche D.; Keith, Jean E.; and Rosenthal, Herbert H. *The Corps of Engineers: Troops and Equipment.* U.S. Army in World War II, edited by Kent Roberts Greenfield. Washington, D.C., 1958.

College Entrance Examination Board of the Middle States and Maryland. *First Annual Report of the Secretary, 1901.* New York, 1901.

Collins, J. Lawton. "Modern Weapons for Today's Army." *Army Information Digest* 5, no. 6 (1950), 3–9.

————. *War in Peacetime: The History and Lessons of Korea.* Boston, 1969.

Collins, Robert M. *The Business Response to Keynes, 1929–1964.* New York, 1981.

"The Columbia Budget." *Columbia Report* 3, no. 4 (1950), 4–6.

Columbia University. *Bulletin of the New York School of Social Work 45, no. 1 (1951), Dean's Report 1950–51.*

————. *Conservation of Human Resources: Progress Report, June, 1951.* New York, 1951.

————. *The Report of the President's Committee on the Educational Future of the University.* New York, 1957.

————. *Report of the Treasurer, June 30, 1947.* New York, 1947.

————. *Report of the Treasurer, June 30, 1948.* New York, 1948.

————. *Report of the Treasurer, June 30, 1949.* New York, 1949.

————. *Report of the Treasurer, June 30, 1950.* New York, 1950.

————. *Report of the Treasurer, June 30, 1951.* New York, 1951.

————, Teachers College. *Improving Citizenship Education: A Two-Year Progress Report of the Citizenship Education Project.* New York, 1952.

Commager, Henry Steele. "English Traits: One Hundred Years Later." *Atlantic Monthly* 182, no. 2 (August 1948), 61–65.

The Commerical Club of Chicago: Year Book 1947–1948. Chicago, 1948.

Conant, James Bryant. *Education in a Divided World: The Function of the Public Schools in Our Unique Society.* Cambridge, Mass., 1948.

———. *My Several Lives: Memoirs of a Social Inventor.* New York, 1970.

Condit, Kenneth W. *The History of the Joint Chiefs of Staff: The Joint Chiefs of Staff and National Policy.* Vol. II, *1947–1949.* Washington, D.C., 1976.

Congressional Digest 23, no. 3 (1944), 67–73, 90–91, 96.

"Convention Addresses." *The Military Chaplain* 21, no. 1 (July 1950), 8–9.

Cook, Ross K. "Eisenhower Family in America." *New York Genealogical and Biographical Record* 76, no. 2 (April 1945).

Cooke, Alistair. *A Generation on Trial: U.S.A. v. Alger Hiss.* New York, 1952.

Coon, Horace. *Columbia: Colossus on the Hudson.* New York, 1947.

Council on Foreign Relations. *Annual Report 1977–1978.* New York, 1978.

———. *The Council on Foreign Relations: A Record of Twenty-Five Years, 1921–1946.* New York, 1947.

Counts, George S. "Whose Twilight?" *Social Frontier* 5, no. 42 (February 1939), 135–40.

Cowan, L. Gray. *A History of the School of International Affairs and Associated Area Institutes, Columbia University.* New York, 1954.

Craven, Wesley Frank, and Cate, James Lea, eds. *The Army Air Forces in World War II.* 6 vols. 1948–55. Reprint. Chicago, 1948–. Vol. I, *Plans and Early Operations, January 1939 to August 1942* (1948; reprint 1958); vol. III, *Europe: Argument to V-E Day, January 1944 to May 1945* (1951; reprint 1958); vol. VI, *Men and Planes* (1955; reprint 1958).

Cremin, Lawrence A.; Shannon, David A.; and Townsend, Mary Evelyn. *A History of Teachers College, Columbia University.* New York, 1954.

Crowl, Philip A. "What Price Unity: The Defense Unification Battle, 1947–50." *Prologue: The Journal of the National Archives* 7, no. 1 (Spring 1975), 5.

Cruickshank, Charles. *Deception in World War II.* New York, 1980.

Cuff, Robert D. *The War Industries Board: Business-Government Relations during World War I.* Baltimore, 1973.

Cunningham, Andrew Browne. "Operations in Connection with the Landings in the Gulf of Salerno on 9th September, 1943." *Supplement to the London Gazette,* April 28, 1950.

———. *A Sailor's Odyssey.* New York, 1951.

Cutler, Robert. *No Time for Rest.* Boston, 1965.

Cutrona, Joseph F. H. "Midshipmen at West Point." *Army Information Digest* 4, no. 10 (1949), 55–57.

Dalfiume, Richard M. *Desegregation of the U.S. Armed Forces: Fighting on Two Fronts, 1939–1953.* Columbia, Mo., 1969.

Daugherty, William E., with Janowitz, Morris. *A Psychological Warfare Casebook.* Baltimore, 1958.

Davenport, Russell W. "The Greatest Opportunity on Earth." *Fortune,* October 1949, 65–69, 200–208.

———. "Pensions: Not IF But HOW." *Fortune,* November 1949, 81–83.

Davis, Kenneth S. *Soldier of Democracy: A Biography of Dwight Eisenhower.* New York, 1945.

Davis, Vincent. *The Admirals Lobby.* Chapel Hill, 1967.

Davison, W. Phillips. *The Berlin Blockade: A Study in Cold War Politics.* Princeton, 1958.

DeConde, Alexander. "George Catlett Marshall (1947–1949)." In *An Uncertain Tradition: American Secretaries of State in the Twentieth Century*, edited by Norman A. Graebner, pp. 245–66. New York, 1961.

De Gaulle, Charles. *The War Memoirs of Charles de Gaulle*. 3 vols. New York, 1955–60. Vol. II, *Unity, 1942–44* (1959); vol. III, *Salvation, 1944–46* (1960). Translated by Richard Howard.

De Guingand, Francis. *Operation Victory*. 3d ed., rev. London, 1963.

De Toledano, Ralph, and Lasky, Victor. *Seeds of Treason: The True Story of the Hiss-Chambers Tragedy*. New York, 1950.

Detzer, Karl. "Kentucky on the March." *Reader's Digest* 55 (October 1949), 67–70.

Dewey, Bradley. "High Policy and the Atomic Bomb." *Atlantic Monthly* 182, no. 6 (December 1948), 37–39.

Diamond, Robert A., ed. *Congressional Quarterly's Guide to U.S. Elections*. Washington, D.C., 1975.

Disraeli, Benjamin, Earl of Beaconsfield. *The Works of Benjamin Disraeli*. 20 vols. London and New York, 1904–5. Vol. XVII, *Lothair* (1904).

Divine, Robert A. "The Cold War and the Election of 1948." *Journal of American History* 59, no. 1 (June 1972), 90–110.

Donnison, F.S.V. *Civil Affairs and Military Government: Central Organization and Planning*. History of the Second World War, edited by J.R.M. Butler. London, 1966.

————. *Civil Affairs and Military Government: North-West Europe, 1944–1946*. History of the Second World War, edited by J.R.M. Butler. London, 1961.

Donovan, Robert J. *Conflict and Crisis: The Presidency of Harry S. Truman, 1945–1948*. New York, 1977.

Downey, Matthew T. *Ben D. Wood: Educational Reformer*. Princeton, 1965.

DuBois, Philip H. *A History of Psychological Testing*. Boston, 1970.

Educational Policies Commission. *American Education and International Tensions*. Washington, D.C., 1949.

Ehrman, John. *Grand Strategy*. Vol. V, *August 1943–September 1944*. History of the Second World War, edited by J.R.M. Butler. London, 1956.

Eisenhower, Dwight D. "An Open Letter to America's Students." *Reader's Digest* 53 (October 1948), 1–5.

————. "An Open Letter to Parents." *Reader's Digest* 54 (February 1949), 11–14.

————. *At Ease: Stories I Tell to Friends*. New York, 1967.

————. *Crusade in Europe*. New York, 1948.

————. *The Eisenhower College Collection: The Paintings of Dwight D. Eisenhower*. Text by Kenneth S. Davis. Critique by Frieda Kay Fall. Los Angeles, 1972.

————. *The Eisenhower Diaries*. Edited by Robert H. Ferrell. New York, 1981.

————. *Eisenhower Speaks: Dwight D. Eisenhower in His Messages and Speeches*. Edited by Rudolph L. Truenfels. New York, 1948.

————. "Lincoln Had the Proper Attitude toward Power: Service to Others the True Essence of Liberty." *Vital Speeches of the Day* 15, no. 8 (1949), 335–36.

————. *Mandate for Change, 1953–1956*. New York, 1963.

————. "Mental Health: Key to World Peace." *Cosmopolitan* 125, no. 2 (August 1948), 35, 91.

————. *The Papers of Dwight David Eisenhower*. Baltimore, 1970–. Vols. I–V, *The War Years*, edited by Alfred D. Chandler, Jr. (1970); vol. VI, *Occupation, 1945*, edited by Alfred D. Chandler, Jr., and Louis Galambos (1978); vols. VII–IX, *The Chief of Staff*, edited by Louis Galambos (1978).

————. *Waging Peace, 1956–1961.* Garden City, N.Y., 1965.

Eisenhower, John S. D. *The Bitter Woods.* New York, 1969.

————. *Strictly Personal.* New York, 1974.

Eisenhower, Milton S. *The President Is Calling.* New York, 1974.

————. *The Wine Is Bitter.* New York, 1963.

Elliott, Edward C., and Chambers, Merritt M., eds. *Charters and Basic Laws of Selected American Universities and Colleges.* New York, 1934.

Ellis, Howard S. *The Economics of Freedom: The Progress and Future of Aid to Europe.* New York, 1950.

Elson, Robert T. *The World of Time Inc.: The Intimate History of a Publishing Enterprise.* 2 vols. New York, 1968–73. Vol. II, *1941–1960.*

Elstob, Peter. *Hitler's Last Offensive: The Full Story of the Battle of the Ardennes.* New York, 1971.

Encyclopedia of Aviation. New York, 1977.

Englebourg, Saul. *International Business Machines: A Business History.* New York, 1976.

Etzold, Thomas H., and Gaddis, John Lewis, eds. *Containment: Documents on American Policy and Strategy, 1945–1950.* New York, 1978.

Farago, Ladislas. *Patton: Ordeal and Triumph.* New York, 1964.

Federal Records of World War II. 2 vols. Washington, D.C., 1950–51. Vol. II, *Military Agencies.*

Feis, Herbert. *The China Tangle: The American Effort in China from Pearl Harbor to the Marshall Mission.* Princeton, 1953.

————. *From Trust to Terror: The Onset of the Cold War, 1945–1950.* New York, 1970.

Ferrell, Robert H. *George C. Marshall.* The American Secretaries of State and Their Diplomacy, vol. XV, edited by Robert H. Ferrell. New York, 1966.

Field, James A., Jr. *History of United States Naval Operations: Korea.* Washington, D.C., 1962.

Finch, James K. *A History of the School of Engineering, Columbia University.* New York, 1954.

Fine, Lenore, and Remington, Jesse A. *The Corps of Engineers: Construction in the United States.* U.S. Army in World War II, edited by Maurice Matloff. Washington, D.C., 1972.

Fleming, Thomas J. *West Point: The Men and Times of the United States Military Academy.* New York, 1969.

Flemmons, Jerry. *Amon: The Life of Amon Carter, Sr. of Texas.* Austin, 1978.

Forman, Sidney. *West Point: A History of the United States Military Academy.* New York, 1950.

Forrestal, James. *The Forrestal Diaries.* Edited by Walter Millis. New York, 1951.

Forrestel, Vice Admiral E. P. *Admiral Raymond A. Spruance, USN: A Study in Command.* Washington, D.C., 1966.

Forster, Arnold. *A Measure of Freedom.* New York, 1950.

Fosdick, Raymond B. *John D. Rockefeller, Jr.: A Portrait.* New York, 1956.

Freeman, Douglas Southall. *R. E. Lee: A Biography.* 4 vols. New York, 1934–35. Vol. I.

Futrell, Robert Frank. *The United States Air Force in Korea, 1950–1953.* New York, 1961.

Galambos, Louis. *Competition and Cooperation: The Emergence of a National Trade Association.* Baltimore, 1966.

Gallup, George H. *The Gallup Poll: Public Opinion, 1935–1971.* 3 vols. New York, 1972. Vol. II, *1949–1958.*

Garber, Ethel. "The Birthright of Every Child." *Education* 69, no. 10 (June 1949), 627–31.

Garland, Albert N., and Smyth, Howard McGaw. *Sicily and the Surrender of Italy.* U.S. Army in World War II, edited by Stetson Conn. Washington, D.C., 1965.

Ginzberg, Eli. "Conservation of Human Resources." *Science*, November 23, 1951, 3.

———. *Grass on the Slag Heaps: The Story of the Welsh Miners.* New York, 1942.

———. *Human Resources: The Wealth of a Nation.* New York, 1958.

———, assisted by Carwell, Joseph. *The Labor Leader: An Exploratory Study.* New York, 1948.

———, and Bray, Douglas W. *The Uneducated.* New York, 1953.

———; Ginsburg, Ethel L.; and Lynn, Dorothy L. *The Unemployed: Interpretation: Case Studies.* New York, 1943.

———; Anderson, James K.; Bray, Douglas W.; Ginsburg, Sol W.; Herma, John L.; Jordan, William A.; Ryan, Francis J.; and Snyder, Howard M. *The Ineffective Soldier: Lessons for Management and the Nation.* New York, 1959.

"Globe Hop Sets B–50's New Role." *Aviation Week*, March 14, 1949, 14–15.

Goebel, Julius, Jr. *A History of the School of Law, Columbia University.* New York, 1955.

Goodrich, Leland M. *The United Nations.* 1959. Reprint. New York, 1966.

Graves, John Temple. "The Why of States Rights." *Southern Fireside*, October 1949, 14–15, 38–40.

Great Britain, Chancellor of the Exchequer to Parliament. *Economic Survey for 1949.* London, 1949.

Green, Charles Henry [Sandhurst, B. G.]. *How Heathen Is Britain?* London, 1948.

Gruber, Carol S. *Mars and Minerva: World War I and the Uses of the Higher Learning in America.* Baton Rouge, 1975.

Gunther, John. *Behind the Iron Curtain.* New York, 1949.

———. *Inside Russia Today.* New York, 1958.

Hall, Donald F. "Psychological Warfare Comes of Age." *Army Information Digest* 4, no. 9 (1949), 29–32.

———. "Psychological Warfare Training." *Army Information Digest* 6, no. 1 (1951), 40–46.

Hamby, Alonzo L. *Beyond the New Deal: Harry S. Truman and American Liberalism.* New York, 1973.

Hammond, Paul Y. *Organizing for Defense: The American Military Establishment in the Twentieth Century.* Princeton, 1961.

———. "NSC-68: Prologue to Rearmament." In *Strategy, Politics, and Defense Budgets,* by Warner R. Schilling, Paul Y. Hammond, and Glenn H. Snyder, pp. 343–44. 1962. Reprint. New York, 1966.

———. "Super Carriers and B–36 Bombers: Appropriations Strategy and Politics." In *American Civil-Military Decisions: A Book of Case Studies,* edited by Harold Stein, pp. 465–545. Birmingham, Ala., 1963.

Hansen, Harry, ed. *Texas: A Guide to the Lone Star State.* American Guide Series. Rev. ed. New York, 1969.

Harbaugh, William H. *Lawyer's Lawyer: The Life of John W. Davis.* New York, 1973.

Harrison, Gordon A. *Cross-Channel Attack.* U.S. Army in World War II, edited by Kent Roberts Greenfield. Washington, D.C., 1951.

Hartmann, Susan M. *Truman and the 80th Congress.* Columbia, Mo., 1971.

Hatch, Alden. *Red Carpet for Mamie.* New York, 1954.

Haynes, Richard F. *The Awesome Power: Harry S. Truman as Commander in Chief.* Baton Rouge, 1973.

―――. "The Defense Unification Battle, 1947–50: The Army." *Prologue: The Journal of the National Archives* 7, no. 1 (Spring 1975), 27–31.

"Headquarters Gazette (continued)." *Military Affairs* 14, no. 3 (1950), 133–59.

Herz, Martin F. "Some Lessons from Leaflet Propaganda." In *Propaganda in War and Crisis,* edited by Daniel Lerner, pp. 416–33. New York, 1951.

Hewes, James E., Jr. *From Root to McNamara: Army Organization and Administration, 1900–1963.* Washington, D.C., 1975.

Hewlett, Richard G., and Duncan, Francis. *A History of the United States Atomic Energy Commission.* Vol. II, *Atomic Shield, 1947–1952.* University Park, Pa., 1969.

Hidy, Ralph W.; Hill, Frank Ernest; and Nevins, Allan. *Timber and Men: The Weyerhaeuser Story.* New York, 1963.

High, Stanley. "Peace, Inc." *Saturday Evening Post,* March 5, 1938, 8–9.

Higham, John, with Krieger, Leonard, and Gilbert, Felix. *History.* Englewood Cliffs, N.J., 1965.

Hirshauer, Victor Bruce. "The History of the Army Reserve Officers' Training Corps, 1916–1973." Ph.D. dissertation, The Johns Hopkins University, 1976.

Hiss, Alger. *In the Court of Public Opinion.* New York, 1957.

Hobbs, Joseph P. *Dear General: Eisenhower's Wartime Letters to Marshall.* Baltimore, 1971.

Hoen, John L. "The Service Academy Board Recommends―." *Army Information Digest* 5, no. 9 (1950), 48.

Hoff, Ebbe Curtis, ed. *Preventive Medicine in World War II.* Vol. II, *Environmental Hygiene.* The Medical Department of the United States Army, edited by John Boyd Coates, Jr. Washington, D.C., 1955.

Holloway, James L., Jr. "The Holloway Plan―A Summary View and Commentary." *United States Naval Institute Proceedings* 73, no. 11 (1947), 1293–1303.

Hoover, Herbert. *Addresses upon the American Road, 1948–1950.* Stanford, 1951.

Hopper, Bruce Campbell. "The Bolshevik Challenge." *Harvard Alumni Bulletin,* March 27, 1948.

Horne, Alistair. *The Price of Glory: Verdun, 1916.* London, 1962.

Hotz, Robert. "Improved B–36 Is Planned by Strategists." *Aviation Week,* March 14, 1949, 12–13.

Howe, George F. *Northwest Africa: Seizing the Initiative in the West.* U.S. Army in World II, edited by Kent Roberts Greenfield. Washington, D.C., 1957.

Hoxie, R. Gordon. *Command Decision and the Presidency: A Study in National Security Policy and Organization.* New York, 1977.

Humphrey, David C. *From King's College to Columbia: 1746–1800.* New York, 1976.

Infantry School, The. *Operations against Guerrilla Forces.* Fort Benning, Ga., 1951.

Ingersoll, Ralph McAllister. *Top Secret.* New York, 1946.

Isley, Jeter A., and Crowl, Philip A. *The U.S. Marines and Amphibious War: Its Theory, and Its Practice in the Pacific.* Princeton, 1951.

Ismay, Hastings L. *The Memoirs of General Lord Ismay.* New York, 1960.

―――. *NATO: The First Five Years, 1949–1954.* Netherlands, 1954.

Isselin, Henri. *The Battle of the Marne.* Garden City, N.Y., 1966.

Iversen, Robert W. *The Communists and the Schools.* New York, 1959.

Jeffery, Arthur. "The Department of Semitic Languages." *A History of the Faculty of Philosophy: Columbia University,* pp. 183–89. New York, 1957.

Johnson, Louis. "Teamwork for Defense." *American Magazine* 148 (July 1949), 131.

Joncich, Geraldine M. *The Sane Positivist: A Biography of Edward L. Thorndike.* Middletown, Conn., 1968.

————. , ed. *Psychology and the Science of Education: Selected Writings of Edward L. Thorndike.* New York, 1962.

Kahn, E. J., Jr. *The World of Swope.* New York, 1965.

Kampelman, Max M. *The Communist Party vs. the C.I.O.: A Study in Power Politics.* New York, 1957.

Kaplan, Lawrence S. *A Community of Interests: NATO and the Military Assistance Program, 1948–1951.* Washington, D.C., 1980.

Kaplan, Morton A. *The Rationale for NATO: European Collective Security—Past and Future.* Washington, D.C., 1973.

Karnow, Stanley. "East Asia in 1978: The Great Transformation." *Foreign Affairs* 57, no. 3, *America and the World 1978* (1979), 589–612.

Kellermann, Henry J. *Cultural Relations as an Instrument of U.S. Foreign Policy: The Educational Exchange Program between the United States and Germany, 1945–1954.* Washington, D.C., 1978.

Kerkvliet, Benedict J. *The Huk Rebellion: A Study of Peasant Revolt in the Philippines.* Berkeley, 1977.

Kilman, Edward W., and Wright, Theon. *Hugh Roy Cullen: A Story of American Opportunity.* New York, 1954.

King, Ernest J., and Whitehill, Walter Muir. *Fleet Admiral King: A Naval Record.* New York, 1952.

Kirkendall, Richard S. "Election of 1948." In *History of American Presidential Elections,* edited by Arthur M. Schlesinger, Jr. 4 vols. New York, 1971. Vol. IV, *1789–1968,* pp. 3099–211.

Kolko, Joyce, and Kolko, Gabriel. *The Limits of Power: The World and United States Foreign Policy, 1945–1954.* New York, 1972.

Kornitzer, Bela. *The Great American Heritage: The Story of the Five Eisenhower Brothers.* New York, 1955.

Kouwenhoven, John. *Adventures of America, 1857–1900: A Pictorial Record from Harper's Weekly.* New York, 1938.

Kriebel, P. Wesley. "Unfinished Business—Intervention under the U.N. Umbrella: America's Participation in the Korean War, 1950–1953." In *Intervention or Abstention: The Dilemma of American Foreign Policy,* edited by Robin Higham. Lexington, Ky., 1975.

Krock, Arthur. *Memoirs: Sixty Years on the Firing Line.* New York, 1968.

Labor's League for Political Education of the AFL. *League Reporter,* December 26, 1949, 4.

La Gorce, Paul-Marie de. *The French Army: A Military-Political History.* Translated by Kenneth Douglas. New York, 1963.

Larrabee, Eric. "Korea: The Military Lesson." *Harper's,* November 1950, 51–57.

Lauer, Walter E. *Battle Babies: The Story of the 99th Infantry Division in World War II.* Baton Rouge, 1951.

Lea, Homer. *The Day of the Saxon.* New York, 1912.

————. *The Valor of Ignorance.* 1909. Reprint. New York, 1942.

Lea, Tom. *The King Ranch.* Vol. II. Boston, 1957.

Lee, Ulysses. *The Employment of Negro Troops.* U.S. Army in World War II, edited by Stetson Conn. Washington, D.C., 1966.

Lefer, Henry. "Navy's Special Devices Center; Better Training, Less Expense." *Aviation Week*, September 26, 1955.

Leffingwell, R. C. "Devaluation and European Recovery." *Foreign Affairs* 28, no. 2 (January 1950), 203–14.

Legere, Lawrence J., Jr. "Unification of the Armed Forces." Ph.D. dissertation, Harvard University, 1951.

Lewis, George G., and Mewha, John. *History of Prisoner of War Utilization by the United States Army, 1776–1945*. Department of the Army Pamphlet 20–213. Washington, D.C., 1955.

Li, K. C., and Wang, Chung Yu. *Tungsten: Its History, Geology, Ore-Dressing, Metallurgy, Chemistry, Analysis, Applications, and Economics*. New York, 1943.

Lichterman, Martin. "To the Yalu and Back." In *American Civil-Military Decisions: A Book of Case Studies*, edited by Harold Stein, pp. 584–97. Birmingham, Ala., 1963.

Liddell Hart, Basil Henry. *The Memoirs of Captain Liddell Hart*. 2 vols. London, 1965.

Lie, Trygve. *In the Cause of Peace: Seven Years with the United Nations*. New York, 1954.

Lilienthal, David E. *The Journals of David E. Lilienthal*. 4 vols. New York, 1964–69. Vol. II, *The Atomic Energy Years, 1945–1950* (1964).

Linebarger, Paul M. A. *Psychological Warfare*. Washington, D.C., 1954.

Lovell, John P. *Neither Athens nor Sparta? The American Service Academies in Transition*. Bloomington, Ind., 1979.

Lyon, Peter. *Eisenhower: Portrait of the Hero*. Boston, 1974.

Lyons, Gene M., and Morton, Louis. *Schools for Strategy: Education and Research in National Security Affairs*. New York, 1965.

MacArthur, Douglas. *Reminiscences*. New York, 1964.

————. *Reports of General MacArthur*. Prepared by his General Staff. Vol. I, *The Campaigns of MacArthur in the Pacific*. Washington, D.C., 1966.

McBane, Robert B. "The B–36—Air Force Global Bomber." *Army Information Digest* 4, no. 8 (1949), 25–33.

————. "Career Compensation for the Services: A Summary of the Hook Commission Report." *Army Information Digest* 4, no. 2 (1949), 39–53.

McCann, Kevin. *Man from Abilene*. New York, 1952.

McCardell, R. A., ed. *The Country Day School: History, Curriculum, Philosophy of Horace Mann School*. Dobbs Ferry, N.Y., 1962.

McComb, David G. *Houston: The Bayou City*. Austin, 1969.

MacDonald, Charles. *The Siegfried Line Campaign*. U.S. Army in World War II, edited by Stetson Conn. Washington, D.C., 1963.

Macdonald, Dwight. *The Ford Foundation: The Men and the Millions*. New York, 1956.

MacDonald, R. St. J., ed. *The Arctic Frontier*. Toronto, 1966.

MacDougall, Curtis D. *Gideon's Army*. 3 vols. New York, 1965.

McGeehan, Robert. *The German Rearmament Question: American Diplomacy and European Defense after World War II*. Urbana, Ill., 1971.

MacIver, Robert M. *Academic Freedom in Our Time*. New York, 1955.

McKeogh, Michael J., and Lockridge, Richard. *Sgt. Mickey and General Ike*. New York, 1946.

Macksey, Kenneth. *Crucible of Power: The Fight for Tunisia, 1942–1943*. London, 1969.

McLane, Charles B. *Soviet Strategies in Southeast Asia: An Exploration of Eastern Policy under Lenin and Stalin*. Princeton, 1966.

McNarney, Joseph T. "Economy Makes Sense." *Army Information Digest* 5, no. 5 (1950), 3–6.

McSurely, Alexander. "AF Pushes Buildup of B–47 Jet Bomber." *Aviation Week*, April 16, 1951, 13–14.

Magat, Richard. *The Ford Foundation At Work: Philanthropic Choices, Methods, and Styles.* New York, 1979.

Maher, Sergeant Marty, with Campion, Nardi Reeder. *Bringing Up the Brass: My 55 Years at West Point.* New York, 1951.

Malnutrition and Starvation in Western Netherlands, September 1944–July 1945. The Hague, 1948.

Manchester, William. *American Caesar: Douglas MacArthur, 1880–1964.* Boston, 1978.

"A Man Who Likes to Give Away Millions." *U.S. News & World Report*, February 11, 1955.

Marshall, S.L.A. "Bastogne: The First Eight Days." In *Rendezvous with Destiny: A History of the 101st Airborne Division,* by Leonard Rapport and Arthur Northwood, Jr., pp. 423–585. Washington, D.C., 1948.

Masland, John W., and Radway, Laurence I. *Soldiers and Scholars: Military Education and National Policy.* Princeton, 1957.

Matloff, Maurice, and Snell, Edwin M. *Strategic Planning for Coalition Warfare, 1943–1944.* U.S. Army in World War II, edited by Kent Roberts Greenfield. Washington, D.C., 1959.

Menninger, William C. *A Psychiatrist for a Troubled World: Selected Papers of William C. Menninger, M.D.* Edited by Bernard H. Hall. New York, 1967.

Meyer, Cord, Jr. *Peace or Anarchy.* Boston, 1948.

Millett, Allan R. *Semper Fidelis: The History of the United States Marine Corps.* New York, 1980.

Millett, John D. *Financing Higher Education in the United States.* New York, 1952.

Montgomery, Bernard L. *The Memoirs of Field-Marshal the Viscount Montgomery of Alamein, K.G.* Cleveland and New York, 1958.

Morgan, Frederick E. *Overture to Overlord.* New York, 1950.

Morgan, Kay Summersby. *Past Forgetting: My Love Affair with Dwight D. Eisenhower.* New York, 1976.

Morison, Samuel Eliot. *Leyte: June 1944–January 1945.* History of United States Naval Operations in World War II, vol. XII. 1958. Reprint. Boston, 1966.

————. *Sicily–Salerno–Anzio: January 1943–June 1944.* History of United States Naval Operations in World War II, vol. IX. 1954. Reprint. Boston, 1964.

Morton, Louis. *The Fall of the Philippines.* U.S. Army in World War II, edited by Kent Roberts Greenfield. Washington, D.C., 1953.

Moses, Robert. *Public Works: A Dangerous Trade.* New York, 1970.

Mountbatten, Louis Francis Albert. *Report to the CCS by the SACSEA, 1943–1946.* London, 1951.

Murphy, Charles J. V. "Treasure in Oil and Cattle." *Fortune*, August 1, 1969, 110–14.

Murphy, Robert D. *Diplomat Among Warriors.* Garden City, N.Y., 1964.

"Naval Center Develops Training Devices for Use by Services." *Aviation Week*, September 17, 1956.

Neal, Steve. *The Eisenhowers: Reluctant Dynasty.* New York, 1978.

Nielsen, Waldemar A. *The Big Foundations.* New York, 1972.

Nixon, Richard M. *Six Crises.* Garden City, N.Y., 1962.

Osgood, Robert Endicott. *NATO: The Entangling Alliance.* Chicago, 1962.

Paddock, Alfred H., Jr. "Psychological and Unconventional Warfare, 1941–1952: Origins of a 'Special Warfare' Capability for the United States Army." Ph.D. dissertation, Duke University, 1980.

Page, James. *Leopold III*. London, 1960.

Paget, Reginald Thomas. *Manstein: His Campaigns and His Trial*. London, 1951.

Paige, Glenn D. *The Korean Decision, June 24–30, 1950*. New York, 1968.

Parmet, Herbert S. *The Democrats: The Years after FDR*. New York, 1976.

———. *Eisenhower and the American Crusades*. New York, 1972.

Patton, George S., Jr. *War As I Knew It*. Boston, 1947.

Paxton, Robert O. *Parades and Politics at Vichy: The French Officer Corps under Marshal Pétain*. Princeton, 1966.

Pemberton, William E. *Bureaucratic Politics: Executive Reorganization during the Truman Administration*. Columbia, Mo., 1979.

Pevsner, Nikolaus, and Lloyd, David. *Hampshire and the Isle of Wight*. Harmondsworth, 1967.

Playfair, I.S.O., and Molony, C.J.C., with Flynn, F. C., and Gleave, T. P. *The Mediterranean and Middle East*. Vol. IV, *The Destruction of the Axis Forces in Africa*. History of the Second World War, edited by J.R.M. Butler. London, 1966.

Pogue, Forrest C. *George C. Marshall*. 3 vols. New York, 1963–73. Vol. II, *Ordeal and Hope, 1939–1942* (1966); and Vol. III, *Organizer of Victory, 1943–1945* (1973).

———. *The Supreme Command*. U.S. Army in World War II, edited by Kent Roberts Greenfield. Washington, D.C., 1954.

Poole, Walter S. *The History of the Joint Chiefs of Staff: The Joint Chiefs of Staff and National Policy*. Vol. IV, *1950–1952*. Wilmington, Del., 1980.

Prawdin, Michael. *The Mongol Empire: Its Rise and Legacy*. Translated by Eden Paul and Cedar Paul. 2d ed., rev. London, 1967.

"Prodding the House of Representatives." *School and Society* 67 (June 19, 1948), 456.

Psychological Warfare Division (SHAEF). *An Account of Its Operations in the Western European Operation, 1944–45*. Bad Homburg, 1945.

Public Papers of the Presidents of the United States: Harry S. Truman, January 1 to December 31, 1948. Washington, D.C., 1964.

Public Papers of the Presidents of the United States: Harry S. Truman, January 1 to December 31, 1949. Washington, D.C., 1964.

Public Papers of the Presidents of the United States: Harry S. Truman, January 1 to December 31, 1950. Washington, D.C., 1965.

Public Papers of the Presidents of the United States: Harry S. Truman, January 1 to December 31, 1951. Washington, D.C., 1965.

Quattlebaum, Charles A. *Federal Aid to Elementary and Secondary Education: An Analytic Study of the Issue, Its Background, and Relevant Legislative Proposals, with a Compilation of Arguments Pro and Con, Statistical Data, and Digests of Pertinent Reports and Surveys*. Chicago, 1948.

Rapport, Leonard, and Northwood, Arthur, Jr. *Rendezvous with Destiny: A History of the 101st Airborne Division*. Washington, D.C., 1948.

"Report of Status of Funds, American Military Institute." *Military Affairs* 14, no. 3 (1950), 164.

Reuther, Walter P. *Selected Papers*. New York, 1961.

Reynolds, Quentin. "Mr. President Eisenhower." *Life*, April 17, 1950, 144–60.

Richardson, F.L.W., Jr., and Walker, Charles R. *Human Relations in an Expanding Company*. 1948. Reprint. New York, 1977.

Richardson, James L. *Germany and the Atlantic Alliance: The Interaction of Strategy and Politics.* Cambridge, Mass., 1966.

Ries, John C. *The Management of Defense: Organization and Control of the U.S. Armed Services.* Baltimore, 1964.

Ritter, Lawrence S. *The Glory of Their Times: The Story of the Early Days of Baseball Told by the Men Who Played It.* New York, 1966.

Roberts, Henry L., and Wilson, Paul A. *Britain and the United States: Problems in Cooperation.* New York, 1953.

Rockefeller Foundation. *The Rockefeller Foundation Annual Report, 1947.* New York, 1947.

—————. *The Rockefeller Foundation Annual Report, 1948.* New York, 1948.

—————. *The Rockefeller Foundation Annual Report, 1949.* New York, 1949.

—————. *The Rockefeller Foundation Annual Report, 1950.* New York, 1950.

Rodgers, Cleveland. *Robert Moses: Builder for Democracy.* New York, 1952.

Rodgers, William. *Think: A Biography of the Watsons and IBM.* New York, 1969.

Rogow, Arnold A. *James Forrestal: A Study of Personality, Politics and Policy.* New York, 1963.

Ropp, Theodore. *War in the Modern World.* Durham, N.C., 1959.

Roseboom, Eugene H. *A History of Presidential Elections.* New York, 1964.

Rosenberg, David Alan. "American Atomic Strategy and the Hydrogen Bomb Decision." *Journal of American History* 66, no. 1 (June 1979), 62–87.

—————. "The U.S. Navy and the Problem of Oil in a Future War: The Outline of a Strategic Dilemma, 1945–50." *Naval War College Review* 29, no. 1 (Summer 1976), 53–64.

Ross, Irwin. *The Loneliest Campaign: The Truman Victory of 1948.* New York, 1968.

Rovere, Richard H. "The Second Eisenhower Boom." *Harper's,* May 1950, 31–39.

Ruppenthal, Roland G. *Logistical Support of the Armies.* Vol. II, *September 1944–May 1945.* U.S. Army in World War II, edited by Kent Roberts Greenfield. Washington, D.C., 1959.

Ryan, Cornelius. *A Bridge Too Far.* New York, 1974.

Saposs, David J. *Communism in American Unions.* New York, 1959.

Saunders, Charles B., Jr. *The Brookings Institution: A Fifty-Year History.* Washington, D.C., 1966.

Schacter, Harry W. *Kentucky on the March.* New York, 1949.

Shechtman, Joseph B. *The United States and the Jewish State Movement: The Crucial Decade, 1939–1949.* New York, 1966.

Schilling, Warner R. "The H-Bomb Decision: How to Decide without Actually Choosing." *Political Science Quarterly* 76, no. 1 (March 1961), 24–46.

—————. "The Politics of National Defense: Fiscal 1950." In *Strategy, Politics, and Defense Budgets,* by Warner R. Schilling, Paul Y. Hammond, and Glenn H. Snyder, pp. 5–266. 1962. Reprint. New York, 1966.

Schnabel, James F. *Policy and Direction: The First Year.* U.S. Army in the Korean War, edited by Maurice Matloff. Washington, D.C., 1972.

Schriftgiesser, Karl. *Business and Public Policy: The Role of the Committee for Economic Development, 1942–1967.* Englewood Cliffs, N.J., 1967.

Schuyler, William M., ed. *The American Yearbook: A Record of Events and Progress, Year 1948.* New York, 1949.

Searle, R. Newell. *Saving Quetico-Superior: A Land Set Apart.* N.p., 1977.

"Seismological Notes." *Bulletin of the Seismological Society of America* 39, no. 3 (1949), 223–24.

Selden, William K. *Accreditation: A Struggle over Standards in Higher Education.* New York, 1960.

———. "The National Commission on Accrediting." In *Accreditation in Higher Education,* edited by Lloyd E. Blauch, pp. 22–28. Washington, D.C., 1959.

Sherwood, Robert E. *Roosevelt and Hopkins: An Intimate History.* New York, 1948.

Simmons, Ernest J. "The Department of Slavic Languages." In *A History of the Faculty of Philosophy, Columbia University,* edited by Dwight C. Miner. New York, 1957.

Sitkoff, Harvard. "Harry Truman and the Election of 1948: The Coming of Age of Civil Rights in American Politics." *Journal of Southern History* 37, no. 4 (November 1971), 597–616.

Slater, Ellis D. *The Ike I Knew.* Baltimore, 1980.

Smith, Gaddis. *Dean Acheson.* The American Secretaries of State and Their Diplomacy, vol. XVI, edited by Robert H. Ferrell. New York, 1972.

Smith, Robert Aura. *Philippine Freedom, 1946–1958.* New York, 1958.

Smith, Robert Ross. *The Hukbalahap Insurgency: Economic, Political, and Military Factors.* Washington, D.C., 1963.

Smith, Walter Bedell. *My Three Years in Moscow.* New York, 1950.

Socolofsky, Homer E. *Arthur Capper: Publisher, Politician, and Philanthropist.* Lawrence, Kans., 1962.

Speake, Dan W. "Effects of Controlled Burning on Bobwhite Quail Populations and Habitat of an Experimental Area in the Alabama Piedmont." *Proceedings of the Twentieth Annual Conference, Southeastern Association of Game and Fish Commissioners, October 24– 26, 1966, Asheville, North Carolina* (Columbia, S.C., 1967), 19–32.

Starobin, Joseph R. *American Communism in Crises, 1943–1957.* Cambridge, Mass., 1972.

Stebbins, Richard P. *The United States in World Affairs, 1949.* New York, 1950.

Stewart, George R. *The Year of the Oath: The Fight for Academic Freedom at the University of California.* Garden City, N.Y., 1950.

"Stratojet Delays Worry Air Force." *Aviation Week,* January 14, 1952, 34.

Sulzberger, Cyrus L. *A Long Row of Candles: Memoirs and Diaries [1934–1954].* New York, 1969.

Summersby, Kay. *Eisenhower Was My Boss.* New York, 1948.

Sutherland, R. J. "The Strategic Significance of the Canadian Arctic." In *The Arctic Frontier,* edited by R. St. J. MacDonald, pp. 256–71. Toronto, 1966.

Syracuse University, Maxwell Graduate School of Citizenship and Public Affairs. *The Maxwell Graduate School of Citizenship and Public Affairs: Twenty-Fifth Anniversary, 1924–1949.* Syracuse, 1949.

Tanner, William R., and Griffith, Robert. "Legislative Politics and 'McCarthyism': The Internal Security Act of 1950." In *The Specter: Original Essays on the Cold War and the Origins of McCarthyism,* edited by Robert Griffith and Athan Theoharis, pp. 174– 89. New York, 1974.

Taylor, Telford. *Final Report to the Secretary of the Army on the Nuernberg War Crimes Trials under Control Council Law No. 10.* Washington, D.C., 1949.

Tedder, Arthur W. *With Prejudice: The War Memoirs of Marshal of the Royal Air Force Lord Tedder.* London, 1966.

Terraine, John. *The Life and Times of Lord Mountbatten.* London, 1968.

Thompson, Edwin A. "Bibliography: Essay on Primary Sources." In *The Papers of Dwight David Eisenhower.* Baltimore, 1970–. Vol. V, *The War Years,* edited by Alfred D. Chandler, Jr., 1970. pp. 17–32.

Tiger, Edith, ed. *In Re Alger Hiss: Petition for a Writ of Error Coram Nobis.* New York, 1979.

Truman, Harry S. *Memoirs by Harry S. Truman.* 2 vols. New York, 1955–56. Vol I, *Year of Decisions*; and vol. II, *Years of Trial and Hope.*

Underhill, Frank H., ed. *The Canadian Northwest: Its Potentialities.* Toronto, 1959.

Union League of Philadelphia. *Handbook of the Union League of Phildelphia from 1862, the Year of Its Organization, to 1931.* Philadelphia, 1932.

United Nations. *Official Records of the Third Session of the General Assembly. Part I. Political and Security Questions Including Regulation of Armaments: First Committee Summary Records of Meetings, 21 September–8 December, 1948.* Paris, 1948.

―――――. *Security Council, Official Records: Third Year, 361st Meeting, 4 October 1948, no. 113.* Paris, 1948.

―――――. *United Nations Bulletin.* Vol. VII, *July 1–December 15, 1949.* Lake Success, N.Y., 1950.

―――――. *The Work of the United Nations International Children's Emergency Fund: Its Origins and Policies.* Lake Success, N.Y., 1949.

U.S. Army. *The Army Almanac: A Book of Facts Concerning the Army of the United States.* Washington, D.C., 1950.

U.S. Bureau of the Census. *Historical Statistics of the United States: Colonial Times to 1957.* Washington, D.C., 1960.

U.S. Commission on Organization of the Executive Branch of Government, Committee on the National Security Organization. *National Security Organization: A Report with Recommendations.* Appendix G. Washington, D.C., 1949.

U.S. Department of Commerce, Coast and Geodetic Survey. *Earthquake History of the United States.* Part I, *Continental United States and Alaska (Exclusive of California and Western Nevada).* Washington, D.C., 1958.

U.S. Department of Defense. *Annual Report of the Secretary of Defense and the Annual Reports of the Secretary of the Army, Secretary of the Navy, Secretary of the Air Force, July 1, 1958 to June 30,1959.* Washington, D.C., 1960.

―――――. *A Report and Recommendation to the Secretary of Defense by the Service Academy Board.* Washington, D.C., 1950.

―――――. *Second Report of the Secretary of Defense and the Annual Reports of the Secretary of the Army, Secretary of the Navy, Secretary of the Air Force for the Fiscal Year 1949.* Washington, D.C., 1950.

―――――. *Semiannual Report of the Secretary of Defense and the Semiannual Reports of the Secretary of the Army, Secretary of the Navy, Secretary of the Air Force, July 1 to December 31, 1949.* Washington, D.C., 1950.

U.S. Department of Labor. *Analysis of Work Stoppages during 1949.* Bulletin no. 1003. Washington, D.C., 1950.

―――――. *Public Social Security Programs in the United States, 1949–1950.* Bulletin no. 982. Washington, D.C., 1950.

U.S. Department of the Navy, Naval History Division. *Dictionary of American Naval Fighting Ships.* 8 vols. Washington, D.C., 1959–81. Vol. IV (1969).

U.S. Department of State. *The China White Paper, August 1949.* Stanford, 1967.

―――――. *Foreign Relations of the United States: Diplomatic Papers, 1944.* 7 vols. Washington, D.C.,1963–67. Vol. IV, *Europe* (1966).

―――――. *Foreign Relations of the United States: Diplomatic Papers, 1945.* 9 vols. Washington, D.C., 1965–69. Vol. IV, *Europe* (1968); vol. V, *Europe* (1967).

―――――. *Foreign Relations of the United States, 1947.* 8 vols. Washington, D.C.,1971–73. Vol. III, *The British Commonwealth; Europe* (1972).

———. *Foreign Relations of the United States, 1948*. 9 vols. Washington, D.C., 1972–76. Vol. I, *General; The United Nations*, pt. 2 (1976); vol. II, *Germany and Austria* (1973); vol. VI, *The Far East and Australasia* (1974); vol. VIII, *The Far East: China* (1973).

———. *Foreign Relations of the United States, 1949*. 9 vols. Washington, D.C., 1974–78. Vol. I, *National Security Affairs, Foreign Economic Policy* (1976); vol. III, *Council of Foreign Ministers; Germany and Austria* (1974); vol. IV, *Western Europe* (1975); vol. VI, *The Near East, South Asia, and Africa* (1977); vol. VII, *The Far East and Australasia*, pt. 1 (1975).

———. *Foreign Relations of the United States, 1950*. 7 vols. Washington, D.C.,1976–80. Vol. I, *National Security Affairs; Foreign Economic Policy* (1977); vol. III, *Western Europe* (1977); vol. V, *The Near East, South Asia, and Africa* (1978).

———. *Foreign Relations of the United States, 1951*. 7 vols. Washington, D.C., 1979–82. Vol. III, *European Security and the German Question*, pt. 1 (1982).

———. *United States Treaties and Other International Agreements, 1952*. Vol. 2, pt. 2. Washington, D.C., 1952.

U.S. Department of State, Office of Public Affairs. *The Berlin Crisis: A Report on the Moscow Discussions, 1948*. Washington, D.C., 1948.

———. *Germany, 1947–1949: The Story in Documents*. Washington, D.C., 1950.

———. *The North Atlantic Pact: Collective Defense and the Preservation of Peace, Security, and Freedom in the North Atlantic Community*. Washington, D.C., 1949.

U.S. National Military Establishment. *First Report of the Secretary of Defense*. Washington, D.C., 1948.

U.S. National Military Establishment, Department of the Army. *Annual Report of the Secretary of the Army: 1948*. Washington, D.C., 1949.

University of Denver. *Biennial Report of the Chancellor from February 15, 1946 to September 1, 1947*. Denver, 1947.

Vandenberg, Arthur H. *The Private Papers of Senator Vandenberg*. Edited by Arthur H. Vandenberg, Jr. Boston, 1952.

Vigneras, Marcel. *Rearming the French*. United States Army in World War II, edited by Kent Roberts Greenfield. Washington, D.C., 1957.

Vinacke, Harold M. *Far Eastern Politics in the Postwar Period*. New York, 1956.

Viorst, Milton. *Hostile Allies: FDR and Charles de Gaulle*. New York, 1965.

Vosburgh, Frederick G. "Shrines of Each Patriot's Devotion." *National Geographic Magazine*, January 1949, 51–82.

Warmbrunn, Werner. *The Dutch under German Occupation, 1940–45*. Stanford, 1963.

Watson, Thomas J., Jr., *A Business and Its Beliefs: The Ideas That Helped Build IBM*. New York, 1963.

Webb, Walter Prescott, ed. *The Handbook of Texas*. 2 vols. Austin, 1952. Vol. II.

Wechsler, James. "Twilight at Teachers College." *The Nation*, December 17, 1938, 661–63.

Weigley, Russell Frank. *History of the United States Army*. New York, 1967.

Weiner, Edward H. *Let's Go to Press: A Biography of Walter Winchell*. New York, 1955.

Weinstein, Allen. *Perjury: The Hiss-Chambers Case*. New York, 1978.

Weld, William Ernest, and Sewny, Kathryn. *Herbert E. Hawkes: Dean of Columbia College, 1918–1943*. New York, 1958.

Wells, John A., ed. *Thomas E. Dewey on the Two-Party System*. New York, 1966.

Weyand, Alexander Mathias. *The Olympic Pageant*. New York, 1952.

Wilbur, Ray Lyman; Sanger, William T.; Krusen, Frank H.; Behrens, Charles F.; Comstock, Carl R.; Coulter, John S.; Hansson, Kristian G.; and Strickland, Benjamin A., Jr., *Report of the Baruch Committee on Physical Medicine, April, 1944*, pp. 1–4. New York, 1944.

Williams, Stillman P., ed. *Panorama of Recent Books, Films and Journals on World Federation, the United Nations, and World Peace.* Washington, D.C., 1960.

Willoughby, Charles A., and Chamberlain, John. *MacArthur, 1941–1951.* New York, 1954.

Wilson, Sir Henry Maitland. *Eight Years Overseas, 1939–47.* London, 1950.

Winterbotham, Frederick W. *The Ultra Secret* New York, 1974.

Wolk, Herman S. "The Defense Unification Battle, 1947–50: The Air Force." *Prologue: Journal of the National Archives* 7, no. 1 (Spring 1975), 18–26.

Woltman, Frederick, "Zoll, Hate-Monger, Promotes New Racket." *New York World-Telegram*, August 25, 1948.

"World Peace Through World Trade." *Arbitration Journal* 5, no. 2 (1950), 96–97.

Yarnell, Allen. *Democrats and Progressives: The 1948 Election as a Test of Postwar Liberalism.* Berkeley, 1974.

Yergin, Daniel. *Shattered Peace: The Origins of the Cold War and the National Security State.* Boston, 1977.

Young, Edward H., ed. *Trials of War Criminals before the Nuernberg Military Tribunals under Control Council Law No. 10.* 15 vols. Washington, D.C., 1949–53.

Ziemke, Earl F. *The U.S. Army in the Occupation of Germany: 1944–1946.* Army Historical Series. Washington, D.C., 1975.

Zoll, Allen A. "Redu-cators at Columbia University." *National Council for American Education*, May 15, 1950.

Glossary

AA BNS	Antiaircraft battalions
AAU	Association of American Universities
AAUP	American Association of University Professors
A/B DIV	Airborne division
ABN	Anti-Bolshevik Bloc of Nations
ACE	American Council on Education
ADA	Americans for Democratic Action
A.D.C.	*Aide-de-camp*
AEC	Atomic Energy Commission
AFHQ	Allied Force Headquarters
AF of L	American Federation of Labor
AFS	American Field Service
AFSWP	Armed Forces Special Weapons Project
AMA	American Management Association
AMGOT	Allied Military Government
ANVIL	Code name for invasion of the south of France in August 1944
AOA	American Overseas Aid
AP	Associated Press
ARC	American Red Cross
ARCADIA	Conference between military representatives of the United States and the United Kingdom that established the Combined Chiefs of Staff, December 24, 1941–January 14, 1942, Washington, D.C.
ARMD DIV	Armored division
AUS	Army of the United States

AVALANCHE	Code name for amphibious assault on Salerno, Italy, in September 1943
B−29	Superfortress; a four-engine medium bomber developed by Boeing
B−36	Peacemaker; a long-range heavy bomber developed by Consolidated
B−47	Stratojet; an all-jet medium bomber that used General Electric's J−47 turbojet engines
B−50	Superfortress; an improved version of the B−29
BB	Battleship
BCOS	British Chiefs of Staff
BJSM	British Joint Staff Mission
BLT	Battalion landing team
BSA	Boy Scouts of America
CA	Heavy cruiser
CAMID	Exercise involving Military Academy cadets and Naval Academy midshipmen
CAV REGT	Armored cavalry regiment
C.B.E.	Commander Order of the British Empire
CBS	Columbia Broadcasting System
CED	Committee for Economic Development
CG	Commanding general
CIA	Central Intelligence Agency
CIGS	Chief of the Imperial General Staff
C in C	Commander in Chief
CINCFE	Commander in Chief, Far East
CINCPAC	Commander in Chief, Pacific Fleet
CINCPOA	Commander in Chief, Pacific Ocean Area
CIO	Congress of Industrial Organizations
CL	Light cruisers
CLAA	Antiaircraft cruiser
CLK	Antisubmarine cruiser
CNO	Chief of Naval Operations
CO	Commanding officer
Cominform	Communist Information Bureau; established in 1947 to exchange information and to coordinate activities
COSSAC	Chief of Staff to the Supreme Allied Commander
C/S	Chief (or Chiefs) of Staff
CUF	Columbia University Files
CV	Aircraft carrier
CVB	Large aircraft carrier
CVE	Escort aircraft carrier
CVG	Fleet carrier air group
CVL	Small aircraft carrier

CVLG	Light carrier air group
DD	Destroyer
D-day	The first day of any military operation
DDR	Radar picket destroyer
DE	Destroyer escort
DIVS	Divisions
DRAGOON	Revised code name for ANVIL, the 1944 invasion of the south of France
ECA	Economic Cooperation Administration
EM	Eisenhower Manuscripts
EP	Eisenhower Project, Milton S. Eisenhower Library, The Johns Hopkins University
EPC	Educational Policies Commissions
ERB	Educational Records Bureau
ERP	European Recovery Program
ETO	European Theater of Operations
ETOUSA	European Theater of Operations, United States Army
FEC	Free Europe Committee
FLEETWOOD	Code name for U.S. war plan in the event of Russian military aggression during fiscal year 1949
FTR BOMB GPS	Fighter bomber groups
FTR INTCPR GPS	Fighter interceptor groups
FTR PENT GPS	Fighter penetration groups
FY	Fiscal year
G-1	Personnel section of divisional or higher staff
G-2	Intelligence section of divisional or higher staff
G-3	Operations and Training section of divisional or higher staff
G-5	Civil Affairs section of divisional or higher staff
Generalfeld- marschall	Field Marshal
GHQ	General Headquarters, United States Army
G.O.C.-in-C.	General Officer Commanding-in-Chief
GOP	Republican party
GP	Group
GSC	General Staff Corps
GYMNAST	Code name for planned invasion of French North Africa in 1942
HALFMOON	Code name for U.S. war plan. See FLEETWOOD
HB GPS	Heavy bomber groups
H-bomb	Hydrogen bomb

HUAC	House Un-American Activities Committee
HUSKY	Code name for Allied invasion of Sicily in July 1943
IBM	International Business Machines
IKE I	Names given to lists of military forces to be maintained during
IKE II	fiscal year 1951
INF DIV	Infantry division
INF RCT	Infantry regimental combat team
INF REGT	Infantry regiment
JCS	Joint Chiefs of Staff
JDCS	Joint Deputy Chiefs of Staff
JIC	Joint Intelligence Committee
KILLER	Code name for U.N. offensive against Chinese Communist and North Korean forces, February 21–March 2, 1951
LIFT	Naval Amphibious Shipping Capacity
LM	Legion of Merit
LOC, L of C	Line of Communication
LT BOMB GPS	Light bomber groups
MAR BLT	Marine battalion landing team
MB GPS	Medium bomber groups
M-day	Mobilization day
MICOWEX	Minor cold-weather exercise; code name for Air Force-Navy exercise in Alaska
MOS	Military occupational specialty
MP	Member of Parliament
MPSB	Military Production and Supply Board
MSTS	Military Sea Transportation Service
MTO	Mediterranean Theater of Operations
NAC	North Atlantic Council
N.A.M.	National Association of Manufacturers
NATO	North Atlantic Treaty Organization
NATOUSA	North African Theater of Operations, United States Army
NBC	National Broadcasting Company
NCAA	National Collegiate Athletic Association
NCCJ	National Conference of Christians and Jews
N.E.I.	Netherlands East Indies
NG	National Guard
NKVD	*Narodnii Kommissariat Vnutrennikh Del* (People's Commissariat of Internal Affairs), secret service of the Soviet Union
NME	National Military Establishment
NROTC	Naval Reserve Officers' Training Corps
NSC	National Security Council

NSO	National Security Organization
NSRB	National Security Resources Board
OCS	Office of the Chief of Staff
OFFTACKLE	Code name for U.S. war plan that did not contemplate holding the U.K.-Rhine-Egypt line
OPA	Office of Price Administration
OPC	Office of Policy Coordination
Op-23	Navy office for unification problems
ORC	Officers' Reserve Corps
	Organized Reserve Corps
OSRD	Office of Scientific Research and Development
OSS	Office of Strategic Services
OVERLORD	Code name for the invasion of northwest Europe in the spring of 1944
P&A	Personnel and Administration Division
PC	Patrol craft
PI	Philippine Islands
PKP	Communist party of the Philippines
P.L.	Public Law
P&O	Plans and Operations Division
POW	Prisoner of war
RA	Regular Army
RAF	Royal Air Force
RASC	Royal Army Service Corps
RCA	Radio Corporation of America
RDB	Research and Development Board
Reclama	Request to authority to reconsider its decision or its proposed action
RN	Royal Navy
ROTC	Reserve Officers' Training Corps
SACEUR	Supreme Allied Commander, Europe
SCAP	Supreme Commander, Allied Powers
SHAEF	Supreme Headquarters, Allied Expeditionary Force
SHAPE	Supreme Headquarters Allied Powers, Europe
SLEDGEHAMMER	Code name for a limited-objective attack across the Channel in 1942 designed either to take advantage of a crack in German morale or as a "sacrifice" operation to aid the Russians
SOFINA	*Société Financière de Transports et d'Enterprises Industrielles*
SS	Submarine
STRAC	Strategic Army Corps
STRAT RCN GPS	Strategic reconnaissance groups
TAC RCN GPS	Tactical reconnaissance groups

TAG	The Adjutant General
TORCH	Code name for Allied invasion of North and Northwest Africa, begun on November 8, 1942
TP CAR GPS	Troop carrier groups
TROJAN	Code name for U.S. war plan that was in most respects identical to its predecessor FLEETWOOD
TWU	Transport Workers Union
UAW-CIO	United Automobile, Aircraft and Agricultural Implement Workers of America
UMT	Universal military training
U.N.	United Nations
UNAC	United Nations Appeal for Children
UNESCO	United Nations Education, Scientific and Cultural Organization
UNICEF	United Nations International Children's Emergency Fund
UNRRA	United Nations Relief and Rehabilitation Administration
USA	United States Army
USAF	United States Air Force
U.S.C.C.	United States Corps of Cadets
USFET	United States Forces, European Theater of Operations
USMA	United States Military Academy
USNA	United States Naval Academy
USO	United Service Organizations
USSR	Union of Soviet Socialist Republics
VA	Veterans Administration
VFW	Veterans of Foreign Wars
V-J Day	Victory in Japan Day
VMF	Marine fighter squadron
VMF (ALL WX)	All-weather Marine fighter squadron
VMP	Marine patrol squadron
VP RONS	Navy patrol squadrons
WAC	Women's Army Corps
WDGS	War Department General Staff
WPD	War Plans Division
WSEG	Weapons System Evaluation Group
YMCA	Young Men's Christian Association
ZI	Zone of the Interior

Chronology

The chronology for volumes X and XI details Eisenhower's years as president of Columbia University. Beginning February 8, 1948, the day following his termination of active service as Chief of Staff, the chronology traces the majority of Eisenhower's daily appointments and activities, ending on New Year's Eve, 1950, when he was preparing to leave the university to assume the post of Supreme Allied Commander of the NATO forces.

We have relied upon Eisenhower's desk calendars to compile this chronology. Only one desk calendar seems to have been kept for the year 1948. This calendar lists anticipated appointments, engagements, and trips. In 1949 Eisenhower's staff kept three separate calendars, two written in anticipation of appointments and events and one written after the fact, noting cancellations and changes in schedule. Incoming and outgoing telephone calls also are noted in this latter calendar. Four calendars were maintained during Eisenhower's final year at Columbia, three after the fashion of the 1949 calendars and an additional typed, after-the-fact calendar where only appointments of an official university nature are noted.

Telephone conversation logs exist for 1949 and 1950 only, and the records of these calls are included here to supplement the information on Eisenhower's daily activities. It is doubtful that these were the only calls made or received by Eisenhower during these two years; it is more likely that they were noted at Eisenhower's direction because he considered them of personal or official importance.

We have attempted to identify every person mentioned in the chronology who has not been identified in the text or notes of these volumes; the full name is given at the first mention, followed by a brief identification in parentheses. In most instances the identification consists of the individual's business or official title. For persons who have been mentioned in the text or notes and those previously identified in the chronology only the initials and last name are given; in the case of military ranks and government and academic titles of individuals who visited frequently with Eisenhower only the rank or title and the last name are given. In cases where there is a similarity of title and last name, initials have been included to avoid confusion.

1948

February 8   Washington.

9   Washington. Morning appointments with L. Little, General Donovan, and E. Anderson; K. D. McCormick at Quarters One. Afternoon dental appointment at Walter Reed General Hospital. To Pentagon office. Late afternoon meeting with members of Pentagon Officers Athletic Club.

10   Washington. Morning appointment with L. V. Finder. To studio of artist Augustus Vincent Tack to sit for mural portrait. Afternoon appointment with J. Wallop at Quarters One. To Hotel 2400 for dinner given by Kansas State Society of Washington.

11   Washington. No appointments.

12   Washington. To General Bradley's office. Morning appointment with General and Mrs. Joyce. To Library of Congress for appointment with Dr. Luther Harris Evans (Librarian of Congress).

13   Washington. Morning appointments at the Pentagon with Senator James Edward Murray (Montana); General and Mrs. Joyce.

14   Washington. To cocktail party given by W. T. Faricy (Association of American Railroads) for General Gray at Wardman Park Hotel.

15   Washington.

16   Washington. Daylong appointment with K. D. McCormick at Quarters One.

17   Washington. Quarters One.

February 18 Washington. Accompanied by General Clark Louis Ruffner (Chief, Legislative and Liaison Division, Department of the Army) to the Capitol to testify on WAC legislation before House Armed Services subcommittee. To Quarters One to pose for Easter Seals photo. Lunch with Messrs. Kimball and Williamson.

19 Washington. Works on *Crusade in Europe.*

20 Washington. Works on *Crusade in Europe.*

21 Washington.

22 Washington.

23 Washington. Morning appointment with K. D. McCormick at Quarters One.

24 Washington. Works on *Crusade in Europe.*

25 Washington. Afternoon appointment with John Denson (managing editor, *Kiplinger* magazine).

26 Washington. Afternoon appointment with D. F. Carpenter. Dinner with J. B. Mintener.

27 Washington. Morning appointment with Elizabeth Draper (interior decorator). Afternoon appointment with K. C. McCann. Evening of bridge at Quarters One with E. Culbertson and Generals Gruenther and Ruffner.

28 Washington.

29 Washington. Afternoon bridge and mah-jong with the B. F. Caffeys.

March 1 Washington. To barber. Afternoon appointments with Frank Owen (editor, *Daily Mail*); J. E. McClure; L. R. Holbrook; Dr. Hsiang Hsi Kung (former Vice-premier of Nationalist China). Dinner with General and Mrs. Haislip.

2 Washington. Morning appointments with K. D. McCormick; J. Barnes.

3 Washington. Dinner at the B. F. Caffeys'.

4 Washington. Afternoon appointment with Secretary Symington.

5 Washington. To the Chevy Chase Club for golf with General Parks.

March	6	Washington. To Burning Tree Country Club for golf with General Parks. Evening cocktails and supper with Colonel and Mrs. Howard.
	7	Washington. Lunch with Mrs. Eisenhower and P. S. Mesta.
	8	Washington. Works on *Crusade in Europe*.
	9	Washington. Afternoon appointment with J. C. Black at Quarters One. Dinner at the H. R. Starks'.
	10	Washington. Works on *Crusade in Europe*. Dinner at J. J. McCloy's.
	11	Washington. Works on *Crusade in Europe*. Dinner at the W. S. Symingtons'.
	12	Washington. Morning appointment with Robert McCurdy (a friend of General Bradley's) and Colonel Hansen. Noon appointment with R. L. Davies. Afternoon appointment with General C. R. "Dinty" Moore.
	13	Washington. Morning appointment with K. C. McCann at Quarters One.
	14	Washington.
	15	Washington. Noon appointment with Dr. Liebman. Afternoon appointments with R. Simon; Richard Clare and J. Dorrance; Colonel Weyand.
	16	Washington. Morning appointments with A. M. Rosenberg; General Parks. Golf with General Parks in the afternoon.
	17	Washington. Daylong appointment with K. D. McCormick.
	18	Washington. Noon appointment (through Dr. Liebman) with E. Epstein. Lunch in office with Professor Ginzberg and General Snyder. Afternoon appointment with Max Goldberg (of Denver).
	19	Washington. To Secretary Forrestal's office for lunch. Afternoon appointment with Richard C. Leib (agent, Northwestern Mutual Life Insurance Company) at Quarters One.
	20	Washington. Dinner with the J. C. Blacks.

March 21 Washington. Afternoon bridge and mah-jong with group of sixteen, including the J. S. Douds, at Quarters One.

22 Washington. Afternoon appointment with Congresswoman Helen Gahagan Douglas (California) and Congressman Chet Holifield (California).

23 Washington.

24 Washington. Finishes manuscript of *Crusade in Europe*. Dinner with Madame Henri Bonnet (wife of French Ambassador).

25 Washington. Morning appointments with Senator Robertson (Virginia); L. V. Finder; General Parks. Golf with J. C. Black and General McClure.

26 Washington. Morning appointments with General Willis Dale Crittenberger; Dr. Duncan Emerick (Library of Congress). To Department of Commerce for lunch with W. A. Harriman. To Commerce Building in the afternoon. Appointment with F. G. Gurley (Santa Fe Railroad).

27 Washington.

28 Washington.

29 Washington. To barber. Appointments with General Persons; D. M. Black and W. E. Robinson; Judith de Mille Fineman (daughter of Mrs. Margaret de Mille Kaplan), to be overnight guest at Quarters One.

30 Washington. Works on *Crusade in Europe*.

31 Washington. Works on *Crusade in Europe*.

April 1 Washington. Morning appointment with Mr. Ferrendow. Noon appointment with Joseph Wright Alsop, Jr. (syndicated columnist). Appointment with W. J. MacFadden for wardrobe fitting. Lunch in office with Professor Earle (Institute for Advanced Study, Princeton). To Quartermaster Depot. Appointment with General Persons, R. Cutler, and Karl Robin Bendetsen (Counsel and Special Assistant to the Secretary of Defense).

2 Washington. Morning appointments with W. Winchell; General M. W. Clark. To Senate Office Building with General Persons. Meeting with Senator Lucas (Il-

April   linois). To caucus room to testify on draft and UMT before Senate Armed Services Committee. Evening cocktails with General Stephen J. Chamberlin (Director, Army Intelligence). Dinner with former Congressman Joseph Edward Casey (Massachusetts).

3   Washington.

4   Washington. To Fort McNair, Virginia, for cocktails with General Spencer Ball Akin (Chief Signal Officer).

5   West Point. Visits the John S. D. Eisenhowers to see new grandson.

6   West Point.

7   Washington. Morning appointments with Vincent E. Sutliff (president, Americana Corporation) and General Sayler; Senator Lucas; K. C. McCann and K. D. McCormick; General Hughes. To Burning Tree Country Club with General Parks.

8   Washington. Lunch in office with J. C. Black. To the Chevy Chase Club for golf in the afternoon. To Belgian Embassy for state dinner given by Baron Silvercruys (Belgian Ambassador) and Prince Regent Charles of Belgium for President and Mrs. Truman.

9   Washington. To the Pentagon for morning appointments with Mr. Lekes; General Snyder. To the Corcoran Gallery of Art with T. E. Stephens at noon. Evening cocktails at Hotel 2400 to meet General G. J. Sas (military attaché, Netherlands Embassy) and bid farewell to General Aleid G. van Tricht (Netherlands Military Mission).

10   Washington. Morning appointment with President Truman at the White House. Appointment with Secretary Symington. To the Chevy Chase Club for golf with General Parks, L. Gassen, and G. E. Allen. To the Statler Hotel for Gridiron Club spring dinner.

11   Washington. Golf at Burning Tree Country Club with General Bradley and brothers J. C. Black and C. R. Black, Jr. To afternoon christening of Sergeant and Mrs. Dry's daughter. To Fort Meyer for christening of Major and Mrs. Cannon's daughter.

12   Washington.

April 13 Washington. Accompanied by Mrs. Eisenhower, departs in the morning for vacation at Augusta National Golf Club with the G. E. Allens. At Augusta until April 24.

24 Augusta. Departure by plane for Manhattan, Kansas. Overnight at the home of Milton S. Eisenhower.

25 Manhattan. Departure by plane for Wichita, Kansas. Visit to Mrs. W. W. McCammon and daughter (friends of Mrs. Eisenhower's). Address to Kansas Junior Chamber of Commerce convention at the Lassen Hotel. Inspection of XL−15 "Scout" liaison plane at Boeing plant prior to return to Manhattan.

26 Manhattan. Morning plane to Washington.

27 Washington. Morning appointments at Walter Reed General Hospital with Frances Kovar; Major Alfred Emerson Toye (D.D.S., Army Dental Corps). Lunch with W. A. Harriman. Afternoon appointments with General Persons; K. C. McCann; General Walker. Accompanies Edgar N. Eisenhower to Union Station. Evening cocktails and bridge with Mrs. Eisenhower at the H. B. Saylers'.

28 Washington. Morning appointments with General Joseph James O'Hare (Army Personnel and Administration Division); Dr. Harold Dean Cater (Army Historical Division, Special Staff); and Lyle Campbell Wilson (United Press) accompanied by General Parks. To Fort Meyer after lunch to serve as honorary pallbearer at funeral service for Colonel Merillat. Appointment with T. E. Stephens. Evening cocktail party at the B. F. Caffeys'.

29 Washington.

30 Washington. Daylong appointment with K. C. McCann.

May 1 Washington. Morning meeting with J. C. Black. Kaffee klatsch. Appointments with Colonel Carroll; General Norstad. To the Chevy Chase Club for golf with General Parks, L. Glasser, and G. E. Allen.

2 Washington. Morning departure from Quarters One, Fort Meyer. Late afternoon arrival at 60 Morningside

May   Drive (president's house on the Columbia University campus, hereafter referred to as #60).

3   New York City. Morning appointments with R. Harron; Dean Carman; M. H. Dodge and F. Coykendall; Provost Jacobs. To Men's Faculty Club for lunch with Dr. Fackenthal and the trustees of Columbia University. Press conference. To Low Memorial Library for trustees meeting. To president's office to meet informally with the trustees.

4   New York City. Morning appointments with Professor Ayres; Dean Pegram. Luncheon at the Union Club given by T. J. Watson for Dean Young. Afternoon appointment with George Peck.

5   New York City. Morning appointments with Captain Timothy Francis Wellings, USN (professor of naval science, NROTC, Columbia University); Dean Gifford; Prince Lippe-Biesterfeld. Accompanied by General Snyder to the University Club for International Congress of Mental Health luncheon.

6   New York City. Morning installation as trustee of Carnegie Endowment for International Peace. Addresses luncheon meeting of the New York State Chamber of Commerce. Afternoon appointments with Dean Finch; Dean Y. B. Smith.

7   New York City. Morning meeting with office staff of P. Hayden. Appointments with General E. N. Clark; Provost Jacobs and P. H. Davis (general secretary of Columbia University); Leon Philipson (editor in chief, 1948 *Columbia Engineer*); Mr. Birnum.

8   New York City. All day at the Blind Brook Club with W. E. Robinson.

9   New York City. All day at #60.

10   New York City. Morning departure for Wyandank Club, Smithtown, Long Island.

11   New York City. Morning appointments with H. M. Schley; representatives of American Overseas Aid—United Nations Appeal for Children headed by S. P. Skouras; Messrs. Sarasohn and Saxon (of Columbia's Public Law and Government Club); Dr. Robinson; Dr. Fackenthal.

May Afternoon appointment with Provost Jacobs, P. H. Davis, and D. M. Black. To Links Club for Columbia trustees stag dinner.

12 New York City. Morning appointments with Professors Rogers and John S. Millet (of Columbia's Department of Public Law and Government); L. Little; K. D. McCormick; William Adams Hance (assistant dean of Columbia College); F. L. Dunne; General Berry. Lunch with W. E. Robinson, C. Roberts, and G. E. Allen at Men's Faculty Club. To Blind Brook Club in the afternoon.

13 New York City. Morning appointments with Mr. Coleman (Health Spot Shoe Company); Florence Nielsen Goodrich (wife of Professor C. Goodrich); J. Gunther; General W.E.R. Covell (a classmate of Eisenhower's). Lunch with A. H. Sulzberger. Afternoon appointment with G. L. Harrison. Accompanied by Mrs. Eisenhower to cocktails with Dean Young.

14 New York City. Morning appointments with Annie Nathan Meyer (senior trustee and founder, Barnard College); T. J. Watson and James Gillespie Blaine (president, Marine Midland Trust Company of New York); Laurence Howard Eldridge (Philadelphia law firm of Norris, Lex, Hart & Eldridge); Mrs. I. O. Sulzberger re the fraternity situation. Lunch with W. E. Robinson. Afternoon appointments with Mr. Kugler (of Boone, Iowa); A. M. Rosenberg; K. C. McCann. Address to Columbia's Public Law and Government Club on organization of the Allied Army in World War II. Accompanied by Mrs. Eisenhower to dinner at home of T. J. Watson.

15 New York City. Morning golf with C. Roberts.

16 New York City.

17 New York City. Morning appointments with D. C. Josephs; Mr. Gussen; K. D. McCormick. Afternoon appointments with R. Harron; A. J. Goldsmith; Robert Fair DeGraf (president and cofounder, Pocket Books, Inc.); former Ambassador Davies. Accompanied by Mrs. Eisenhower to dinner at Men's Faculty Club to meet Columbia deans and their spouses.

May 18   New York City. Morning appointments with Dean Ackerman; students; M. W. Childs; Sevellon Ledyard Brown (editor and publisher, *Providence Journal and Evening Bulletin*). Lunch with Provost Jacobs, D. M. Black, and P. H. Davis. Afternoon appointment with Dr. Hyman.

19   New York City. Daylong tour of Columbia's Teachers College with Dean Russell and staff. Afternoon appointment with P. H. Davis and D. M. Black. Evening departure with Mrs. Eisenhower by train for Chicago.

20   Early afternoon arrival in Chicago. Overnight at home of General and Mrs. Walker, Fort Sheridan.

21   Chicago. To Glen View Club for golf and lunch with Franklin Bliss Snyder (president, Northwestern University), W. T. Faricy, and J. D. Brandon. To Blackstone Hotel for press conference and evening address to the Commercial Club of Chicago.

22   Chicago.

23   Morning train to New York City.

24   New York City. Morning appointment with Dean Russell. Afternoon appointments with F. Coykendall; General Covell; Dr. Russell Potter (Director, Columbia's Institute of Arts and Sciences); P. H. Davis and F. W. Chambers (Alumni Federation). Accompanied by Mrs. Eisenhower to dinner given by T. J. Watson for Ambassador and Mrs. Espinosa de Los Monteros of Mexico.

25   New York City. Poses for pictures for VFW poppy sale. Appointments with Colonel Robert Patrick Hamilton (professor of law); L. Wright; Dr. Finkelstein. Lunch at #60 with J. L. Hennessy. Portrait sitting at studio of Joseph Cummings Chase for collection of World War II commanders displayed at the Smithsonian Institution. Appointments with D. M. Black and P. H. Davis re Columbia Associates; T. J. Watson.

26   New York City. To barber. Appointments with General Pierre Guillain de Benouville (member, executive committee, Rally of the French People); Charles Cheney Hyde (professor emeritus of international law and diplomacy); Professor Mullins; Dean Pegram. Afternoon and evening with W. E. Robinson.

May 27 New York City. Morning appointments with Dumas Malone (professor of history); Professor Wood and Thomas Hambly Beck (magazine publisher); J. H. Moninger; F. L. Dunne. Presents Father of the Year medal to D. Pearson at luncheon given by Father's Day committee at the Pennsylvania Hotel. To studio of Joseph Cummings Chase for portrait sitting. Cocktails and buffet at home of W. H. Burnham.

28 New York City. Morning appointments with Messrs. Cambridge, Parsons, and Anton; P. Carlos Smith (of Columbia's Engineering School Alumni Association). Accompanied by General E. N. Clark to studio of Jo Davidson (sculptor). Lunch with W. S. Paley at Men's Faculty Club. Afternoon appointments with Provost Jacobs and group of touring German broadcasters sponsored by Columbia's Bureau of Applied Social Research; Alex Freeder; Dr. Fackenthal. Evening at #60 with the F. C. Pages.

29 New York City. Morning golf with J. C. Black at the Deepdale Club. Dinner at #60 with the Blacks.

30 New York City.

31 New York City. To Men's Faculty Club for black-tie dinner for recipients of honorary degrees.

June 1 New York City. Morning appointments with Robert Richard Gros (current affairs lecturer/interviewer); Colonel Carroll. To Men's Faculty Club for Commencement Day luncheon, then to 194th commencement of Columbia University. To Men's Faculty Club for dinner.

2 New York City. Morning appointments with Mr. Josefsohn (newsman); Dean Ackerman; P. H. Davis and Lester Darling Egbert (insurance executive); Colonel Thurman. Named honorary member of the Golden Jubilee Committee of West New York in office ceremony. Appointment with Colonel John Nicholas Smith, Jr. (Director, Institute for Crippled and Disabled). Afternoon with W. E. Robinson.

3 New York City. Daylong conference with K. D. McCormick and K. C. McCann. Afternoon meeting with D. M. Black and W. E. Robinson re *Crusade in*

June *Europe*. Cocktails and dinner for General Hodges at the Officers Club, Governors Island, New York.

4 New York City. Morning appointments with Professor Huger Wilkinson Jervey (Director, Parker School of International Studies); Joseph E. Casey; Major Rigor, a military courtesy call; Howard Sidney Meighan (CBS executive); K. C. McCann and General Nevins. Afternoon appointment with General Chanowich.

5 New York City. Morning with R. L. Simon.

6 New York City.

7 New York City. Morning appointments with Albert Gordon Redpath (trustee of Columbia University and partner, law firm of Auchincloss, Parker and Redpath); R. Harron; Dr. Fackenthal; Mrs. Springer. To Trustees Room for ceremony to receive keys to the University and to officially assume duties of president of Columbia. Lunch with W. Benton. Afternoon appointments with P. H. Davis, Provost Jacobs, D. M. Black, and Dean Pegram; F. Coykendall. To Toots Shor Restaurant for Overseas Press Club dinner.

8 New York City. Morning conference with K. C. McCann and General Nevins. To City Hall at noon for photo session with Mayor O'Dwyer in support of A.O.A.-U.N. Appeal for Children. Afternoon fitting with Emanuel Goldman (tailor). Dinner at the T. J. Watsons'.

9 New York City. To barber. Morning appointments with Frank S. Hacket (headmaster, Riverdale Country School); C. M. Chester and E. R. Harriman; J. R. Swann; Professor Catlin (Department of Political Science, Ohio State University); Clark Mell Eichelberger (National Director, American Association for the United Nations). Afternoon meeting with W. E. Robinson. Stag dinner at #60 with G. E. Allen, C. Roberts, and W. E. Robinson.

10 New York City. Morning appointment with J. Davidson. To Montauk Club for luncheon meeting of the Brooklyn Sunday School Union, followed by review of children's Sunday School parade. Accompanied by Mrs. Eisenhower to reception at the Men's Faculty Club. To

June   evening graduation ceremonies of the Institute for the Crippled and Disabled.

11   New York City. Morning appointments with C. Bowles; Walter Edwin Bixby (president, Kansas City Life Insurance Company); Dr. White and his assistants; Professor Krout; P. H. Davis. Afternoon appointments with J. W. Duyff (professor of physiology, University of Leiden, and former resistance leader in Holland); Morris W. Watkins (executive secretary, Alumni Federation of Columbia University); Dr. Walter Walker Palmer (president, American College of Physicians); L. Henderson; Mr. and Mrs. Tadeusz Jarecka (lecturer in music at Columbia and former Director, Musics and Concerts, Polish Government-in-Exile). Fitting with E. Goldman. Accompanied by Mrs. Eisenhower to reception for Columbia College reunion. Dinner and informal talk to joint alumni classes at John Jay Hall.

12   New York City. Morning appointments with K. C. McCann and Dean Russell.

13   New York City. Midmorning departure for Rutgers University, New Brunswick, New Jersey, to receive honorary Doctor of Laws degree at 182d commencement.

14   New York City. With C. Roberts by private plane to Southampton, Long Island.

15   Southampton. Golf. Midafternoon plane to New York City. To dinner given by the National Association of Soil Conservation.

16   New York City. Morning appointments with Deans Pickel and Arnaud; Frank Gavatt; Chancellor Harry Woodburn Chase (New York University); Captain T. F. Wellings; President Allan Willard Brown (College of the Seneca); H. Young. Afternoon appointments with Colonel James Edler; Harry Carlson (Democratic National Committeeman, New Hampshire); Mr. Drummond (Bureau of Internal Revenue); Colonel Robert Rutherford McCormick (editor, *Chicago Tribune*) and Dean Smith; Professor Edwin Howard Armstrong (Department of Electrical Engineering); T. J. Watson, A. W. Page, and Roland Livingston Redmond (president, Metropolitan Museum of Art).

June 17 New York City. Morning appointments with C. M. Eichelberger and Oscar A. deLima (member, executive committee, A.O.A.-U.N. Appeal for Children); Dean Arnaud, Professor Campbell, and Mr. Rogers; Sir Francis Edward Evans (British Consul General); Governor Jester (Texas) and Wright Morrow (Democratic National Committeeman, Texas); Dean Russell; Mr. Ungerleider; J. Alsop. Afternoon viewing of film *Beyond Glory*. Dinner at the D. M. Blacks'.

18 Washington. Daylong visit to National War College. Morning lecture to students, "Problems of Combined Command," followed by informal luncheon at home of Vice-Admiral Harry W. Hill (commandant).

19 New York City. Morning appointment with L. V. Finder. Trip to Poughkeepsie Boat House canceled due to Eisenhower's illness.

20 New York City. Morning train to Williamstown, Massachusetts, to receive honorary Doctor of Laws degree at Williams College commencement. Evening auto to New York City.

21 New York City. Morning appointments with F. L. Dunne; Bishop Gilbert; Dr. William E. Brooks (rector, St. Thomas Church) and Dr. Jacoby; A. G. Carter and Mrs. Electra Waggoner Biggs (sculptress). Afternoon appointments with Elizabeth Faulkner Baker (chairman, economics department, Barnard College); Erik Barnouw and Professor Zanetti; P. H. Davis.

22 New York City. To New Haven, Connecticut, to receive honorary Doctor of Laws degree at Yale University commencement. To Yale alumni luncheon.

23 New York City. Morning appointments with Dean Russell; H. C. Butcher; Professor Lyon. To the Deepdale Club with C. Roberts.

24 New York City. Morning appointments with W. Melville; Mr. Rickey. Presented with Grand Cross of Italy by Italian Ambassador Alberto Tarchiani in brief office ceremony. Afternoon appointments with W. L. McLean, Jr.; D. M. Black; K. C. McCann; E. Goldman. To dinner given by W. L. Kleitz.

June 25 New York City. Morning appointment with Major Cannon. To Trustees Room to greet foreign students sponsored by the American Field Service. Appointment with Raymond Walters (president, University of Cincinnati). To Journalism Building to record VA transcription for July Fourth message. To Rotunda to meet Columbia administrators. To Deepdale Club with J. L. Hennessy.

26 New York City. To Poughkeepsie to attend dedication ceremonies for new IBM plant. Dinner at #60 with J.F.M. Whiteley.

27 New York City. Accompanied by Mrs. Eisenhower to Scarsdale to attend afternoon birthday party for L. Marx's son.

28 New York City. Morning appointments with Tilford Eli Dudley (Assistant Director, CIO Political Action Committee); George Wilfred Hartmann (professor of education, Teachers College); Joseph Cochran (G & C Merriam Company); and R. J. Furey. Greets maintenance personnel. Appointments with H. M. Schley; Dr. and Mrs. Gregg Manners Sinclair (president, University of Hawaii). Accompanied by Robert F. Moore (Director of Personnel) to Rotunda to greet office, clerical, laboratory, and library personnel. To luncheon at #60 for Columbia's Committee on Education. Late afternoon appointment with P. H. Davis, DeWitt Wallace, and Mr. Howard (*Reader's Digest*).

29 New York City. Morning appointments with H. G. Jussen; Senator Olin Dewitt Johnston (South Carolina); Harold Frohn (industrial relations adviser, Vacuum Oil Company, Denmark); Professor Ginzberg; Dean Carman and F. S. Hogan; Dean Russell; Mr. and Mrs. Preston Hotchkis (president, Founders' Fire & Marine Insurance Company); Edward F. Hutton (investment banker). To lunch at #60 with Mr. Hutton. To office of the treasurer for meeting of the Committee on Finance. Evening at #60 with L. Marx. Night train to Washington.

30 Washington. Addresses F. Eberstadt's committee on the NSO (Hoover Commission).

July 1 New York City. At #60 for weekend celebration of

July	the Eisenhowers' 32d wedding anniversary with the "Washington gang."
2	New York City.
3	New York City.
4	New York City.
5	New York City. Afternoon golf with C. R. Black, Jr. Late evening release of statement to R. Harron declining nomination for any public office.
6	New York City. Morning appointments with Provost Jacobs; Dr. R.H.S. Tanriover; Senator Brien McMahon (Connecticut); Professor Lyon; Philip Ferguson; P. H. Davis; Mr. Martinez. To the Rotunda to meet with Professor Ayres and staff of Summer Session, followed by greeting to students. Afternoon appointments with Professor Ginzberg, Deans Young and Pegram; Dr. Sorour; Paul Fairly (son of Viola Hutchinson Fairly, a former Abilene classmate); F. W. Chambers and P. H. Davis; T. J. Watson. Dinner at #60 for University Fund Committee.
7	New York City. To barber. Morning appointments with H. M. Schley and consulting architect; Jean Arachtingi (student); E. Roper; General Genovevo Perez Damera (Chief of Staff, Cuban Army). Afternoon appointment with W. E. Robinson. Dinner with the B. F. Caffeys.
8	New York City. Morning appointments with E. Roper; G. T. Bye; M. H. Dodge and G. E. Warren. To Dean Pegram's office for meeting of Advisory Committee on Educational Policy. Appointment with Wylie Campbell (veteran student). To Waldorf-Astoria for A.O.A.-U.N. Appeal for Children luncheon. Late afternoon appointments with Provost Jacobs; W. H. Burnham. Introduces Mrs. Roosevelt at evening opening of Summer Session Institute.
9	New York City. Morning appointments with Jack Wiener (veteran); C. Meyer, Jr. (United World Federalists); C. Canfield and Alexander Standish (partner, J. H. Whitney & Company). To convocation, followed by luncheon at Men's Faculty Club, for President of Venezuela Romulo Gallegos. Afternoon appointment with Governor and Mrs. Thurman (South Carolina).

July 10 New York City.

11 New York City. Midmorning engagement with Mrs. Eisenhower and Mr. and Mrs. A. H. Sulzberger.

12 New York City. Morning appointments with Dr. Aake Ording (Director, U.N. Appeal for Children) and Sidney Hertzberg (U.S. liaison officer); Mrs. E. W. Biggs. To Teachers College with Dean Russell for conference of school superintendents. Afternoon appointments with Morris Lincoln Strauss (Columbia alumnus, Class of 1897); General Joseph Franklin Battley (USA, ret.). Midafternoon departure with General E. N. Clark for his summer home near Westport, Connecticut.

13 Westport. All-day fishing with General Clark.

14 To Endicott, New York, to address IBM personnel at factory. Guest of honor at company banquet in evening.

15 New York City. To Garden City, Long Island, with K. C. McCann for daylong meeting at Doubleday & Company. Informal stag dinner for the trustees at #60.

16 New York City. Morning appointments with Mr. Reiter; R. Harron; Professor Brownell and Miss R. Evans; General Milciades Contreras (Chilean military attaché) and Colonel Prince; H. F. Gremmel and F. M. Manning re U.N. Appeal for Children. Afternoon appointment with Theodore August Distler (president, Franklin and Marshall College), followed by lunch at #60 with Dr. Distler. Late afternoon appointments with W. L. McLean; H. M. Schley and the Committee on Buildings and Grounds. To the Rotunda to greet one hundred American and foreign educators sponsored by UNESCO.

17 New York City. Departure with Mrs. Eisenhower for West Townshend, Vermont, to visit General and Mrs. Nevins.

18 West Townshend.

19 West Townshend. To Washington by plane for General Pershing's funeral; returns to Vermont by plane in the evening.

20 West Townshend.

July 21 West Townshend.

22 West Townshend.

23 West Townshend. Departure by auto with Mrs. Eisenhower to Pawling, New York, for luncheon with Governor and Mrs. Dewey. By auto to Highland Falls, New York, to visit John S. D. Eisenhower and family.

24 Highland Falls.

25 Returns to New York City.

26 New York City. Morning appointments with D. M. Black, J. Barnes, and K. D. McCormick; Rabbi Isidor B. Hoffman (counselor to Jewish students); Ned Harland Dearborn (president, National Safety Council); W. Melville; Morris Snyder (former chief chef, officers mess, SHAEF); Niles Trammel (president, NBC). To Knickerbocker Club to meet with Herbert Claiborne Pell (former New York congressman).

27 New York City. Morning appointments with Reverend Fuller (Army chaplain); Elmer Quillen Oliphant (Metropolitan Life Insurance Company); Frederick Miller (Director of Buildings and Grounds); General E. N. Clark and L. de Rochemont; General Colwyn Henry Hughes Vulliamy (former staff officer at SHAEF) and Colonel J. J. Duvivier. Lunch at #60 with General Vulliamy. Returns to office to receive souvenir from Brazil from Father Ulysses Galvao (psychology department). Afternoon appointments with P. H. Davis, D. Wallace, William Hard (*Reader's Digest*), and K. C. McCann; Rabbi Hoffman; Colonel Harry Louis Berman.

28 New York City. Morning appointment at #60 with R. J. Furey. Inspection of Baker Field and gymnasium. Appointments with D. M. Black; Provost Jacobs; David Morgan Roderick (student); P. H. Davis and F. W. Chambers. Lunch with T. Perkinson and the directors of the Chase National Bank. Afternoon appointments with K. C. McCann and Major Schulz; Professor Ralph S. Alexander (Columbia's School of Business); Frank H. Bowles (former Director of Admissions).

29 New York City. Late-night departure by train with Mrs. Eisenhower for vacation in Wisconsin and Colorado.

July 30   Travel Day.

31   Arrival in Minocqua, Wisconsin. At home of H. Young through August 7.

August 8   Minocqua. Evening train to Chicago.

9   Early morning arrival in Chicago, followed by noon departure for Denver.

10   Morning arrival in Denver. Press conference at Brown Palace Hotel. Overnight at the J. S. Douds'.

11   To Pueblo, Colorado. Fishing in San Luis Valley with Dr. H. A. Black. At home of Dr. Black through August 13.

14   Late afternoon return to Denver. Stay with the J. S. Douds.

15   Denver.

16   Denver.

17   Denver. Addresses nation in radio broadcast on behalf of U.N. Crusade for Children. On vacation through August 30.

31   Denver. Luncheon at the University Club to address Columbia's Alumni Club of Colorado. Midafternoon dedication of General Rose Memorial Hospital. To Fitzsimons General Hospital to review parade in honor of retiring General Quade. The Eisenhowers continue their vacation in Denver through September 8.

September 9   Return to New York City. To office in afternoon. Evening conference on science, philosophy, and religion with Dr. Louis Finkelstein (president, Jewish Theological Seminary of America).

10   New York City. Morning appointments with Provost Jacobs and Mr. O'Shea (attorney for Columbia); Don Belding, Kenneth D. Wells (chairman and director, respectively, of the Joint Association of National Advertisers—American Advertising Agencies Association Committee on Improvement of Public Understanding of our Economic System), and W. H. Chase; Professor Ginzberg; Father Robert Ignatius Gannon (president, Fordham University) and B. F. Gimbel. Afternoon appointment with Dean Carman. Ceremony to receive

September   decoration for leadership in World War II from Ethiopian Ambassador Ras Imru and First Secretary Haddis Abemayehou.

11   New York City. Late-morning appointment with E. K. Kane.

12   New York City. Afternoon plane to Corning, New York. Dedication of veterans' memorial stadium as part of Corning Centennial Week celebration. Luncheon guest of Amory Houghton (chairman of the board, Corning Glass Works). Late afternoon return to New York City.

13   New York City. Welcomes freshman class at opening of the College of Physicians and Surgeons. Lunch with Dean Rappleye. Afternoon appointments with W. McLean; Dean Pegram; D. M. Black.

14   New York City. Morning appointments with Professor Ginzberg; General Simonds; F. L. Dunne for wardrobe fitting; R. Harron and K. C. McCann. To Metropolitan Life Insurance Company luncheon. Afternoon appointments with P. H. Davis and F. W. Chambers; Provost Jacobs and Professor Campbell.

15   New York City. Morning appointment with Mrs. H. R. Reid. Sitting for photograph by Manny Warman and sketch by Erlich of the *Columbia Jester*. To dedication of Twentieth Century Limited train at Grand Central Station, followed by lunch on board with G. Metzman. Afternoon appointments with Dean Young; Dr. Uccelani and C. R. Miller.

16   New York City. Morning appointments with G. E. Warren; Opal Faulkner and Glen McDaniel (vice-president, RCA); Mrs. A. H. Sulzberger and Joseph Willen (executive vice-president, Federation of Jewish Philanthropies of New York).

17   New York City. Morning appointments with H. M. Schley, R. F. Moore, and Provost Jacobs; Dr. Zook (American Council on Education); Dr. George Paull Sargent (rector, St. Bartholomew's Church); Mrs. John Biggs. Photograph with Air Corps students. Meetings with Peter, Prince of Greece; Dr. Henry Walker (a friend of Milton S. Eisenhower's). Afternoon appoint-

| September | ments with John Lawrence Bogert (alumnus, Class of 1887); Dr. Salmon. Meeting with R. Harron and directors of Ivy League Public Relations. To Baker Field to watch football practice. |

18   New York City. Morning appointments with Roscoe Drummond (chief, Washington News Bureau, *Christian Science Monitor*) and Blair Moody (Washington correspondent and columnist); Miss J. Hearn.

19   New York City. Late afternoon appointment at #60 with Secretary Symington.

20   To Washington for conference on Army organization. Evening return to New York City to attend welcoming dinner for freshman at John Jay Hall.

21   New York City. Morning appointments with Provost Jacobs and P. H. Davis; R. McConnell and Professor Kerr. To meeting of the Advisory Committee on Educational Policy. Appointment with R. J. Furey and Harold A. Rousselot (president, Columbia Varsity "C" Club). To the Roosevelt Hotel to address luncheon meeting of the Sales Executive Club of New York. Late afternoon meeting of the trustees' Development Committee with G. L. Harrison, J. G. Jackson, G. E. Warren, and W. H. Sammis. Evening cocktails with the K. C. McCanns at #60.

22   New York City. Morning appointments with Professor Lyon; R. Herpers and Professor Allen; Melvyn Gordon Lowenstein (secretary, Babe Ruth Foundation); Mrs. Beardsley Ruml and Mrs. Arnstein; Provost Jacobs, Mr. Orton, and Professor Campbell; R. Considine. Afternoon appointment with Dr. D. C. Duke. To the McMillin Theater to address students at opening of Columbia's academic year.

23   New York City. Morning appointments with Messrs. Butler, Milch, and Emerson (students); William I. Nichols (editor, *This Week Magazine*) and Louise Thomas (publicity director, Doubleday & Company); Dr. Rodolfo Mendez Penate (former rector, University of Havana) and Provost Jacobs; Judge John Warren Hill. Noon meeting with Pierre de Gaulle (Mayor of Paris). Address to students at opening of Barnard College. Evening with General and Mrs. Snyder.

September 24	New York City. Morning appointments with Gaston Benac (managing editor, *Paris Press*); Norman Lerner; Mrs. Patricia Blackader (cousin of Colonel Gault's); A. Nielsen; Mr. Thompson and Congressman William Kingsland Macy (New York); Mrs. Lamarr. Afternoon golf with W. E. Robinson at the Blind Brook Club.
25	New York City. To barber. To the RCA Building for luncheon given by E. Anderson, then to Baker Field for Columbia-Rutgers football game. Accompanied by Mrs. Eisenhower to the Plaza Hotel for dinner with Mrs. Jacqueline Cochran Odlum and the John S. D. Eisenhowers. To Madison Square Garden for Air Force anniversary celebration and convention of the Air Force Association.
26	New York City.
27	New York City. Morning appointments with Major J. M. Norwood and group attending Columbia's Russian Institute; Dr. Carl White; General E. N. Clark; Dean Pegram; Boyden R. Sparks (author). Lunch at #60. Afternoon appointments with D. M. Black and W. E. Robinson; F. Coykendall. To early evening ceremony to receive Doctor of Humane Letters degree from the Jewish Theological Seminary of America (presentation by Dr. Louis Finkelstein, president).
28	New York City. Morning appointments with Eugene P. Thomas, William S. Swingle, Robert A. Breen, and James S. Carson (officers of the National Foreign Trade Council); D. M. Black, A. H. Sulzberger, and J. G. Jackson; Mr. McParsons, Louis E. Bloetjes (counselor to veterans at Columbia), and Provost Jacobs. Meeting with editorial group from Latin America. Informal address to Columbia College students in McMillin Theater in the afternoon. Lunch at #60 with J. B. Mintener and Provost Jacobs. Afternoon appointment with Dean Finch, followed by visit from Prince of Siam Prem Burachatr and Princess Ngamchitya.
29	New York City. Morning fitting with F. L. Dunne. Appointments with Adrian P. Levy (business executive, San Antonio, Texas); Professor Ginzberg. To the Deepdale Club at noon for golf with C. Roberts, C. V. McAdam, and R. T. Reed. Dinner for C. V.

September   McAdam, Mrs. J. O. McMahon, C. Roberts, and the
             J. D. Brandons.

        30   New York City. Morning appointments with Professor
             Lyon; Father John H. Murphy (vice-president, Uni-
             versity of Notre Dame); P. H. Davis; Dean Russell and
             Hollis L. Caswell (associate dean, Teachers College).
             Noon appointment with Professor Nevins.

October 1   New York City. Morning with J. C. Black and W. E.
             Robinson. Late afternoon train to Philadelphia to ad-
             dress Newspaperboys Thrift Club at Convention Hall.
             Evening return to New York City.

         2   New York City. Morning departure for West Point
             accompanied by Mrs. Eisenhower and Milton S.
             Eisenhower to visit John S. D. Eisenhower and General
             M. D. Taylor.

         3   New York City. Milton S. Eisenhower visits at #60.

         4   New York City. Morning appointment with Provost
             Jacobs, Associate Provost Zanetti, P. H. Davis, and
             Ossian R. MacKenzie (Director, University Develop-
             ment Program) re Higgins Trust. To the Men's Faculty
             Club for trustees luncheon. Appointment with H. M.
             Schley and the Committee on Buildings and Grounds.
             Late afternoon meeting of the board of trustees.

         5   New York City. Morning appointments with Professor
             Rabi; Kenneth D. Wells, W. H. Chase, and Louis A.
             Novins (executive vice-president, American Heritage
             Foundation). Honored by visiting Tibetan trade mis-
             sion. Informal address to members of New York YWCA
             at Waldorf-Astoria luncheon to open fund drive.

         6   New York City. All appointments canceled due to
             illness.

         7   New York City. Lunch at #60 with W. Benton. To
             dinner at the Waldorf-Astoria to open annual appeal of
             the Federation of Jewish Philanthropies of New York.

         8   New York City. Ill at home.

         9   New York City. Ill at home.

        10   New York City. Arrival of the Milton S. Eisenhowers
             and Edgar N. Eisenhower for inaugural ceremonies.

October	11	New York City. Midafternoon rehearsal for inauguration. Evening reception at Low Memorial Library.

12 New York City. To office in the morning. To #60 for family luncheon. Escorted to Nicholas Murray Butler Library for official installation as thirteenth president of Columbia University. To Men's Faculty Club for reception given by Dean Young for academic representatives, university officers, and trustees.

13 To Uptown, Long Island, to visit Brookhaven National Laboratory for the day.

14 New York City. General Eisenhower's birthday. To the Waldorf-Astoria for the seventy-fifth anniversary dinner of the New York Board of Trade.

15 New York City. Morning appointments with Dr. Russell Potter; Provost Jacobs and W. E. Robinson; Provost Jacobs and H. M. Schley; P. H. Davis and A. T. Koch; Mr. Freeman (*New York Times*). Midafternoon departure for Albany to receive honorary degree in evening ceremonies at the University of the State of New York.

16 New York City. Midmorning talk at dedication of the Hudson River site of the Riverdale Country School. To Baker Field at noon to preside over alumni homecoming reunion at Columbia. Attends Columbia-Penn football game. Evening appearance at homecoming ball.

17 New York City.

18 New York City. Morning appointments with Arthur C. Cronin (Director, Veterans Facilities, Rutgers University); C. L. Bernstein (Hotel Paramount). Lunch at #60 with R. C. Leffingwell, R. G. Wasson, and P. H. Davis. Afternoon appointments with F. Coykendall; Dean Russell and the president of the council of the University of Brussels; F. W. Chambers. To the McMillin Theater to open the Institute of Arts and Sciences.

19 New York City. Morning appointments with Provost Jacobs and Dean Rappleye; Dr. Shotwell (Carnegie Endowment); M. W. Childs; Dr. Peter Zenkl (exiled Czechoslovak Deputy Prime Minister) and Jan Munzer. Award ceremony to receive honorary degree from the

October   University of Santo Domingo. Lunch at #60 with General Wickersham. To the Trustees Room for meeting of the University Council. Appointment with Dr. Henry P. Van Dusen (president, Union Theological Seminary).

20   New York City. Morning appointments with C. B. Jackson (*Time* magazine); Renshaw Smith (president, Devoe Reynolds). Meeting of the Student Council's executive committee. Appointments with R. J. Furey; Brazilian Ambassador Mauricio Nabuco. Afternoon inspection tour of Shanks Village with Provost Jacobs and K. C. McCann. To Men's Faculty Club for welcome dinner.

21   New York City. Morning appointments with Ralph P. Cousins (executive vice-president, Founders' Fire & Marine Insurance) and son; J. D. Wise; Dean Young and P. H. Davis; James E. Day (president, Chicago Stock Exchange); Ecuadorian Ambassador Augusto Dillon and Dr. Wilburn H. Ferguson; E. J. Bermingham. Lunch with David Rockefeller. Afternoon appointment with Dean Smith, D. M. Black, Provost Jacobs, and P. H. Davis. To the Biltmore Hotel for meeting of the National Executive Board of the Boy Scouts of America.

22   New York City. Morning appointments with Dean Russell; D. Wallace and W. Hard (*Reader's Digest*). Afternoon fitting with E. Goldman and Herman Tritz. To evening ceremony to receive African Star Medal at Fellowship of U.S.-British Comrades convention. To reception given by the Association for University Teas.

23   New York City. Morning appointment with Ellen C. Ruthman (former WAC officer). To luncheon of the Barnard alumnae. Afternoon departure for estate of H. Young in Ridgefield, Connecticut.

24   Ridgefield.

25   Ridgefield. Morning return to New York City. Appointments with F. H. Sparks; Sidney Hedley Bingham (Commissioner, New York City Board of Transportation).

26   New York City. Morning appointments with Dean McIntosh; Dr. Counts; E. K. Carter. Fitting with E.

October	Goldman and H. Tritz. Guest speaker at luncheon given by the Association of National Advertisers at the Waldorf-Astoria. To memorial dinner for Professor Kemp at Men's Faculty Club.
27	New York City. Morning plane to Washington. Briefing at the Pentagon, followed by lunch with Secretary Forrestal and Generals J. L. Collins and Vandenberg. Afternoon briefing with General Wedemeyer in his office. Evening bridge with Mrs. Eisenhower, R. B. Butcher, General and Mrs. Gruenther, Mr. and Mrs. Parsons, Mary Allen and General and Mrs. Sayler.
28	Washington. Morning appointment with Mark Skinner Watson (journalist). Visit with General Vandenberg in his office. Lunch with Secretary Royall. Briefing with General Gruenther. Dinner with Mrs. Eisenhower and the Saylers at the Roosevelt Hotel.
29	Washington. Morning dental appointment with Colonel Toye. Visit with General and Mrs. Beach. To the Burning Tree Country Club, accompanied by G. E. Allen, for lunch and golf with C. Roberts and W. E. Robinson. To cocktail buffet given by the G. E. Allens at the Wardman Park Hotel.
30	Washington. Morning visit with General Bradley in his office. Appointments with General Norstad; General Richards; Admiral Denfeld. To the Burning Tree Country Club with G. E. Allen for lunch and golf with J. C. Black and L. D. Gasser. Bridge and mah-jong with the E. S. Hugheses in the evening.
31	Washington. Bridge and mah-jong with the Gruenthers in the afternoon.
November 1	Washington. Morning plane to New York City. Tour of Columbia's Medical Center with Dean Rappleye. To luncheon at Bard Hall, followed by meetings of the board of trustees and of the trustees' Development Committee.
2	New York City. Morning appointments with Dr. L. E. Kling (Department of Public Health); Magnus Ingstrup Gregersen (professor of physiology); General E. N. Clark; B. Andrews. Lunch at #60 with Dean Rappleye, T. J. Watson, and the A. D. Laskers. Dinner

and bridge with G. E. Allen, C. Roberts, and W. E. Robinson.

3   New York City. Morning appointments with Dr. Jean Marx (Plenipotentiary Minister of France) and Norman Lewis Torrey (professor of Romance languages). Luncheon given by the West Point Society of New York. Afternoon appointments with D. M. Black; A. W. Dulles, J. W. Davis, and H. M. Wriston. To dinner given by the Chamber of Commerce of the State of New York at the Waldorf-Astoria. To the home of R. T. Reed for meeting with James T. Lee (banker) and W. E. Robinson.

4   New York City. Morning appointments with Messrs. O'Shaunnessy, Lipman, Silard, and Waldman on behalf of the Sachem Society; Judge Newcomb Condee (Superior Court, Los Angeles); T. J. Watson, Jr., and Charles McCabe. Luncheon at #60 with Sir James Milne (former director, Great Western Railway). Afternoon appointment with Judge Hubert T. Delany (alumnus, College of the City of New York). Accompanied by F. W. Chambers and P. H. Davis, visits Mrs. Georg Unger Vetlesen. Cocktails at #60 with Mrs. Forrestal. Stag dinner given by the American Heritage Foundation.

5   New York City. Morning appointments with P. H. Davis; James Hazen Hyde; Leonard Andrew Scheele (Surgeon General, U.S. Public Health Service); Paul Lachenal (president, Swiss Bar Association); George Daniels.

6   New York City. Accompanied by Mrs. Eisenhower to Army-Stanford football game with the John S. D. Eisenhowers at West Point.

7   New York City. To hearthfire lighting ceremony with Mrs. Eisenhower at Johnson Hall.

8   New York City. To office. No appointments.

9   New York City. Morning appointments with Christian E. Burckell (formerly of Teachers College); Max Gissen and Ruth Mehrtens (*Time Books*); Edward M. Crone (president, Van Nostraud Company). Lunch in office with Pendleton Dudley (public relations executive), P.

November   H. Davis, K. C. McCann, and Provost Jacobs. To the Plaza Hotel to address members of the New England Society at their stag dinner.

10   New York City. Morning appointments with Provost Jacobs and P. H. Davis; Dr. Howard Canning Taylor, Jr. (professor and chairman, Department of Obstetrics and Gynecology, College of Physicians and Surgeons); Frank Bane (secretary-treasurer, Governors Conference). Lunch at #60 with J. L. Hennessy. To Academy of Political Science dinner at the Hotel Astor.

11   New York City. Morning appointments with P. H. Davis; R. Harron and John Neville Wheeler (North American Newspaper Alliance); Professor Austin Patterson Evans (Department of History) and Professor and Mrs. Montgomery (University of Stockholm). Dinner at #60 with General and Mrs. Robert M. Littlejohn.

12   New York City. Morning appointments with R. J. Furey and Dean McKnight; Paul Rich Stewart (president, Waynesburg College); Dr. and Mrs. Benietz (University of Manila); Jessie Jones; Generals Barker and Randolph (Kemper Military Academy); Dr. Hector Zalles Ormachea (Bolivia).

13   New York City. To Columbia-Navy football game with Captain and Mrs. T. F. Wellings in the afternoon.

14   New York City.

15   New York City. Morning appointments with Professor William T. Montague (Barnard); C. V. Dollard and Provost Jacobs; W. E. Robinson and D. M. Black; Professor Kerr, P. H. Davis, Evan B. Lloyd, and Professor Zanetti re Lamont estate. Lunch with Provost Jacobs and the deans of the university at the Men's Faculty Club.

16   New York City. Morning appointments with H. S. Mudd at the Ritz Carlton Hotel; Mr. and Mrs. Rudolph Roesler de Villiers. To dutch treat luncheon at the Century Club. Afternoon appointment with J. B. Mintener. To orientation dinner for the development program at the Men's Faculty Club.

17   New York City. Morning appointments with Norman Collins (a friend of Sir Louis Greig's); Mrs. James L.

November   Clark. To McMillin Theater to greet members of the Institute of Human Relations. Named honorary member of the Lawyers' Club at their luncheon. Presented a complimentary issue of the *Columbia Jester* from student group. Visited by Essex County Alumni Club officers (accompanied by P. H. Davis). To Men's Faculty Club for junior faculty reception. Evening cocktails with Betty Tyson (niece of P. S. Mesta).

18   New York City. Morning golf with W. E. Robinson, C. Roberts, and C. V. McAdam. To Teachers College for meeting of the trustees. Dinner with J. B. Conant.

19   New York City. Morning appointments with Professor Lyon; Professor Norton; Robert Palmer (student, School of General Studies); General Sandy Beaver (president, Riverside Military Academy). Noon meeting with Dean Ackerman, Professor Raymond B. Allen, and R. Herpers. To the Men's Faculty Club for luncheon, followed by presentation of the Maria Moors Cabot awards. Dinner at #60 with H. Young and W. R. Cox. Late night train to Washington with Mrs. Eisenhower.

20   Washington. To Walter Reed Chapel for midmorning funeral services for General Beach. Early evening return to New York City.

21   New York City.

22   New York City. Morning appointments with Mr. and Mrs. Nathan Straus (president, radio station WMCA), Dean Carman, and R. Harron; W. E. Robinson and C. Roberts. To J. P. Morgan and Company luncheon. Afternoon with W. E. Robinson and C. Roberts. Dinner with the D. M. Blacks.

23   New York City. Morning appointment with Frederick Stephens. Addresses Book and Author luncheon sponsored by the *New York Herald Tribune* and the American Booksellers Association. To St. Paul's Chapel in the afternoon to attend funeral of Professor Ayres. To board of directors meeting of Morningside Heights, Inc. (Eisenhower an ex-officio member).

24   New York City. Morning appointments with General E. N. Clark; Dean Arnaud and R. Rodgers; William Loren Batt (president, S.K.F. Industries). Golf with

November   W. E. Robinson in the afternoon. Dinner with Harry Scherman (president, Book-of-the-Month Club).

25   New York City.

26   New York City. Late afternoon meeting with W. H. Burnham's nephew and friends at #60.

27   New York City.

28   New York City.

29   New York City. Morning appointments with R. L. Biggers; F. W. Chambers; Dean Pickel; Maurice Ewing (professor of geology). Afternoon appointments with W. H. Mallory; Dean Russell. To Men's Faculty Club for junior faculty reception. Night train to Washington.

30   Washington. Midmorning appointment with John Wesley Snyder (Secretary of the Treasury), George Jeremiah Schoeneman (Commissioner of Internal Revenue), and Major Schulz. Lunch with Secretary Forrestal. Accompanied by General Bradley to afternoon meeting of Army commanders. Appointment with W. A. Harriman. To the Gruenthers' for bridge in the evening.

December 1   Washington. Lunch with General Bradley. To the White House for afternoon meeting with President Truman and Secretary Forrestal. Appointments with General Bradley; Secretary Royall. Evening train to New York City.

2   New York City. Morning meeting at #60 with P. H. Davis, D. M. Black, and William G. Brady, Jr. (chairman of the board, National City Bank of New York). Afternoon appointments with Professor Ginzberg and Provost Jacobs; General E. N. Clark. Meeting of the trustees' Committee on Reorganization. To the annual award dinner of the Varsity "C" Club with K. C. McCann and Harold A. Rousselot.

3   New York City. Morning appointments with William Ludlow Chenery and Walter Davenport (publisher and associate editor, respectively, of *Collier's* magazine); Harold Korn (Columbia alumnus, Class of 1901). Meeting with group of nineteen Latin American visitors; late afternoon appointment with Dean Pickel re

December fund drive. To black-tie dinner at the A. H. Sulzbergers'.

4 New York City. Morning appointments with Helen Farr (sister of Sergeant John F. Farr); R. Sproul. To meeting of the Association of American Universities at the University Club. Lunch at #60 with General J.C.H. Lee and Dean Ackerman. To Men's Faculty Club for stag black-tie dinner given by the history department.

5 New York City.

6 New York City. Morning appointments with Father Basil (chaplain, First Ranger Battalion); R. McConnell. Noon visit to School of Law with Dean Smith. Trustees luncheon at Men's Faculty Club, followed by meetings of the trustees and of the trustees' Development Committee.

7 New York City. Morning appointments with R. L. Biggers; Mrs. F. W. Metcalf; Professor Lyon; P. H. Davis. Visits to Mrs. Burt at St. Luke's Home; Reverend Frederic Sydney Fleming, D.D. (rector, Trinity Parish), at his home.

8 New York City. Morning appointments with Dr. Shotwell re Carnegie Endowment; B. M. Baruch. To Cardinal Spellman's residence for presentation of checks by the New York City Cancer Committee to Columbia's College of Physicians and Surgeons, followed by luncheon. Accompanied by Mrs. Eisenhower to dinner at home of Mrs. Harold Irving Pratt, then to home of Mrs. Stephen Carlton Clark.

9 Washington. Morning appointments with Secretary Forrestal; H. B. Hinton; Secretary Royall in his office. Lunch with Secretary Forrestal. Afternoon appointment with Secretary Symington. To the White House with Secretary Forrestal and General Vandenberg for meeting with President Truman.

10 New York City. Morning appointments with A. G. Redpath; G. Mead; C. M. Malone. Noon meeting with P. H. Davis.

11 New York City. Morning appointment with André Maurois (author and former French Army officer) to inscribe copies of *Crusade in Europe*. Afternoon appoint-

December ment with General Genovevo Perez Damera (Chief of Staff, Cuban Army) and Colonel Prince.

12 New York City.

13 Washington. Early morning breakfast on train with General Gruenther. Visit to offices of Secretary Forrestal; Admiral Denfeld. Meeting with Secretary Symington, Generals Vandenberg and Norstad, Admiral Blandy. Lunch with W. J. McNeil in his office. Afternoon appointments with W. Webster; Admiral Blandy; Secretary Forrestal with Admiral Blandy; H. B. Hinton. Cocktails with W. E. Robinson at home of General Haislip, Fort Meyer. Dinner with General Gruenther, General Sayler, and W. E. Robinson in the General Officers' Mess.

14 Washington. Morning briefing with General Kenneth David Nichols (Chief, Armed Forces Special Weapons Project). Appointments with Admiral Momsen, Captain Morgan, and Commander Sanchez; Admiral Towers; Secretary Symington in his office. Lunch with Secretary Forrestal, followed by JCS presentation. Afternoon appointments with Admiral Ben Moreell (USN, ret., president, James & Laughlin Steel Corporation); W. Webster; G. Mead; General Eichelberger; Mrs. Dale Hull.

15 Washington. To morning briefing by JCS ad hoc committee on long-range plans for war. Appointment with General Persons. Lunch in office with Major Schulz. Afternoon plane to New York City. To yule log lighting ceremony with Mrs. Eisenhower at John Jay Hall. Annual Links Club stag dinner.

16 New York City. To meetings of the Development Committee and of the Buildings and Grounds Committee. To luncheon meeting of the U.S. Trust Company of New York. Evening cocktails and buffet for the School of Business alumni at the Men's Faculty Club.

17 New York City. Morning appointments with Benjamin Joseph Buttenwieser (trustee, Federation of Jewish Philanthropic Societies) and P. H. Davis; General Efisio Luigi Marras (Chief of the Italian Army General Staff), accompanied by five officers; William Rosenwald, Reuben B. Resnik (honorary president and di-

December	rector of community relations, respectively, United Service for New Americans), and Professor Chamberlain; P. H. Davis. Late afternoon meeting of the Association for University Teas with Mrs. Eisenhower.
18	New York City. Morning appointment with Professor Ginzberg. Recording of message for North Western Chapter of the Fellowship of U.S.-British Comrades. Accompanied by Mrs. Eisenhower to visit Sir James Milne. To luncheon at home of T. J. Watson.
19	New York City.
20	New York City. Morning meeting of the Buildings and Grounds Committee. Appointments with R. L. Wensley and P. H. Davis re Columbia Fund; T. J. Watson. To Rockefeller Foundation luncheon. Appointments with W. D. Shadbourne; P. H. Davis. Late afternoon visit to Mrs. Lamont's home.
21	New York City. Morning appointments with C. M. Spofford; P. H. Davis and Professor Chamberlain. To meeting of the University Council. Afternoon train for Denver with Mrs. Eisenhower.
22	Travel day.
23	Morning arrival in Denver, where General and Mrs. Eisenhower visit with the J. S. Douds for the next eight days.

1949

January	1	Denver. Afternoon departure by train.
	2	Travel day. Brief stop in Chicago.
	3	Early morning arrival in New York City. To trustees luncheon at Men's Faculty Club. Meeting of the trustees' Committee on Reorganization with D. M. Black and J. G. Jackson, then to meeting of the board of trustees. White-tie dinner given by T. J. Watson for the Dodds.
	4	New York City. Midmorning appointment with P. H. Davis. Afternoon appointment with Dr. Fackenthal.

January 5 New York City. Boy Scouts of America Dawn Patrol Breakfast at the Waldorf-Astoria. Appointments with Dean McKnight; Al Overton (international field director, Associated Executives Clubs); Miss Barbara Brady; Dean Russell. Afternoon train to Washington. Evening meeting with Professor Leach. Bridge and mah-jong in the evening with Mrs. Eisenhower at the Gruenthers'.

6 Washington. Morning appointments with Secretary Forrestal; H. Hinton; General Wedemeyer; Secretary Symington. Lunch in Army Mess. To Secretary Forrestal's office for coffee. Afternoon appointments with General J. Hull (Director, Weapons Systems Evaluation Group, Office of the Secretary of Defense); W. Webster; G. Gray. Accompanied by Mrs. Eisenhower to informal dinner with Secretary Forrestal and President Truman.

7 Washington. Morning appointments with Secretary Symington; Ben Gray; Secretary Symington in his office; Colonel John Held Riepe (Army Personnel and Administration, General Staff) re cadet-strength briefing. Afternoon appointments with General J. Hull; Secretary Royall. To Roundtable dinner at the Knickerbocker Club.

8 Washington. Morning appointments with Secretary Symington; General Gruenther. Afternoon plane to New York City.

9 New York City.

10 New York City. Morning appointments with Professor Zanetti and Provost Jacobs; General McClure; David Andrew Weaver (president, Shurtleff College); Dean Russell. To luncheon for General M. D. Taylor given by T. J. Watson at the Union Club. Appointments with J. G. Detwiler (president, Central Cable Corporation); Dean Pegram. To evening meeting of the Council on Foreign Relations with Arthur Nevins.

11 New York City. Morning appointments with W. H. Lane; Prime Minister Peter Fraser (New Zealand). Accompanied by K. C. McCann to film of General Eisenhower's talk before the Association of National Advertisers joint committee on economic understanding. Luncheon at the Columbia University Club. Ac-

companied by Mrs. Eisenhower to the Alexander Hamilton dinner of the Columbia College Alumni Association at the Roosevelt Hotel.

12 New York City. Morning appointments with J. D. Wise, D. M. Black, William Brady, and P. H. Davis; Colonels D. S. Campbell and A. Burch (students, Air War College, Air University); Dean McKnight and Levering Tyson (president, Muhlenberg College); Professor Hays. Accompanied by Mrs. Eisenhower and K. C. McCann to the Chrysler Building for Texaco Roundtable and luncheon. Afternoon appointments with Provost Jacobs and P. H. Davis; Professor Zanetti.

13 New York City. Morning appointments with Professor Zanetti, Provost Jacobs, and P. H. Davis; J. H. Chamberlin, K. C. McCann, and P. H. Davis; Admiral Henry Ken Hewitt (U.S. representative, U.N. Military Staff Committee); Captain Wellings. Receives recordings of D-day wall map ceremony from Admiral Brian Betham Schofield (British Joint Services Mission, Office of the Combined Chiefs of Staff), followed by luncheon at #60.

14 New York City. Afternoon fitting with E. Goldman and H. Tritz. Cocktails at #60 with the Metcalfs. To the Century Association to participate in discussion on higher education sponsored by the Carnegie Corporation of New York.

15 To Rockaway Hunting Club, Cedarhurst, Long Island, for shooting with General Wickersham and Alden Hatch (author).

16 New York City. To afternoon memorial service at St. Paul's Chapel.

17 New York City. Morning appointments with F. W. Chambers, P. H. Davis, V. Cooper (chairman, Alumni Club Reorganization Committee), and Langford Sully (assistant to Mr. Cooper); J. J. McEwan. To General Motors Corporation luncheon at the Waldorf-Astoria. Afternoon appointment with L. D. Egbert (alumni trustee). Meeting of the Buildings and Grounds Committee.

18 New York City. Morning appointments with Dean McKnight; Julio F. Mendez (Venezuela). Meeting of

January   the Alumni Federation Nominating Committee. Appointment with Matthew Fox (executive vice-president, Universal Pictures). Presentation of antique book collection for Butler Library by Athengoras I, patriarchelect of the Greek Orthodox Church. Afternoon appointments with Kenneth Wells; G. V. Cooper. To Men's Faculty Club for meeting of the Alumni Federation board of directors. Dinner with Henry Junior Taylor (journalist) and Mrs. Taylor.

19   New York City. Morning meeting with Dean Pegram.

20   Morning plane to Washington. Lunch with Colonel Harry O. Paxson (military assistant to Secretary Royall). To join Secretary Royall in parade car following inauguration of Harry Truman. To apartment of G. E. Allen in the afternoon. To Inaugural Ball in the evening. Late night "chat" with President Truman. Returns to home of G. E. Allen.

21   Washington. Morning appointments with General Gruenther; Secretary Forrestal; General Bradley; K. T. Compton. Lunch with Generals Bradley and Gruenther.

22   Washington. Morning appointment with Dr. Francis Frank Borzell (assistant professor of radiology, Graduate School of Medicine, University of Pennsylvania). To Secretary Symington's office, then to lunch. Bridge and mah-jong at the Saylers' in the evening.

23   Washington. To the Pentagon with Secretary Forrestal in the morning.

24   Washington. Morning staff meeting with Secretary Forrestal. To the White House for off-the-record talk with President Truman. To Secretary Symington's office. Lunch with General Gruenther and the JCS. To Secretary Forrestal's office. Afternoon appointments with F. G. Wisner and Maynard Bertram Barnes (career Foreign Service officer); J. H. Ohly.

25   Washington. Morning appointment with General F. H. Smith (assistant for programming, USAF Headquarters). War Council meeting with Secretary Forrestal. Lunch. Afternoon appointment with General Lutes.

January 26 Washington. To national security briefing for House Armed Services Committee in the morning, followed by buffet luncheon given by Secretary Forrestal. Afternoon appointments with Secretary Forrestal; Secretary Symington.

27 Washington. Morning appointments with Secretary Symington; General B. E. Moore; Secretaries Forrestal and Symington and Colonel R. J. Wood. To briefing for House Subcommittee on Military Appropriations. Late afternoon train to New York City. Accompanied by Mrs. Eisenhower to dinner given by G. H. Montague for General Hodges and Admiral Kincaid.

28 New York City. Morning appointments with A. G. Redpath; Dean Y. Smith re New York State Bar Association talk; Dean McIntosh re Women's Colleges Conference talk; D. M. Black; H. Masters. To American Press Institute seminar and luncheon at John Jay Hall. Afternoon appointments with P. Davis; Colonel Carroll; Colonel Robert R. McCormick. To Dental School alumni meeting at the Medical Center. To Council on Foreign Relations meeting with General Nevins.

29 New York City. Afternoon appointments with Provost Jacobs; Dean Carman; Charles Edmundson (Washington bureau correspondent, *St. Louis Post-Dispatch*). Lunch at home with Colonel Carroll. To the Waldorf-Astoria for the Women's Colleges Conference in the afternoon and the New York State Bar Association dinner in the evening.

30 New York City. Accompanied by Mrs. Eisenhower to dinner with the Harold Brookses.

31 Morning train to Washington. Lunch with Secretary Sullivan in his office. Afternoon appointments with Admiral Charles Wellborn, Jr. (Deputy Chief of Naval Operations, Administration); Admiral Arthur William Radford (Commander in Chief, Pacific Fleet). To Admiral Denfeld's office for briefing. Returns to office with Admiral Wellborn. Meeting with Secretary Forrestal. Dinner with Major Schulz.

February 1 Washington. Arrives at Pentagon in the morning with General Nevins. Appointment with General Gruenther. To Admiral Denfeld's office for briefing and presenta-

February	tion. Lunch in Secretary Symington's office. Continuation of naval briefing in the afternoon. Meeting with General Bradley. Dinner with General M. W. Clark and J. B. Mintener.
2	Washington. Morning appointments with General McNarney; R. L. Biggers. To the Senate Armed Services Committee meeting. To Admiral Denfeld's office for naval briefing. Lunch, followed by continuation of naval briefing in the afternoon. Appointment with Secretary Forrestal. Dinner with Major Schulz.
3	Washington. To Secretary Forrestal's office in the morning. To Admiral Denfeld's office for naval briefing. To West Point Class of 1915 luncheon at the Army and Navy Club. To Carlton Hotel for dinner and bridge with G. E. Allen, General Gruenther, S. T. Early, and Victor Emanuel (president, Albert Emanuel Company).
4	Washington. Morning appointment with Secretary Symington. To office of Under Secretary of the Navy W. John Kenney. Meeting with Secretary Forrestal. Afternoon train to New York City.
5	New York City. Morning appointments with D. M. Black; P. C. Jessup; General Marshall. To Union Club luncheon.
6	New York City.
7	New York City. Morning appointment with Dean Russell. Wardrobe fitting. Tours the School of Engineering with Dean Finch. Trustees luncheon at Men's Faculty Club. Trustees meeting, followed by meeting of the trustees' Development Committee. Receives Phi Beta Kappa honorary membership. To Carnegie Corporation dinner at the Century Association.
8	Morning plane to Washington. To Secretary Forrestal's office. War Council meeting. Noon appointment with H. Hinton re press inquiries. Lunch with General Bradley. Eye examination with Captain Jacobins. Dinner with Secretary Forrestal.
9	Washington. To Walter Reed General Hospital in the morning to see Generals Marshall and W. B. Smith. Lunch with Secretary Forrestal. Off-the-record meeting

with President Truman at the White House. Appointment with Secretary Forrestal.

10 Washington. Morning appointments with General Gruenther; Secretary Forrestal. Lunch in Army Mess. To Secretary Forrestal's office for budget meeting with C. M. Clifford and F. Pace. Dinner with R. D. Murphy and Major Schulz.

11 Washington. Morning appointments with Admiral Conolly; General McNarney. Lunch in office with W. A. Harriman and General McNarney. Afternoon appointments with M. Leva; H. B. Hinton; Secretary Forrestal. Off-the-record meeting with President Truman at the White House. Bridge with Generals Ruffner, Sayler, and Gruenther at the Statler Hotel.

12 Morning plane to New York City. Appointments with Provost Jacobs; D.M. Black and M.H. Dodge; David Waddington (portrait photographer, London). To Earl Hall for School Boys Conference with Dean Carman.

13 New York City. Late night train to Washington.

14 Washington. To General Bradley's office in the morning. Staff meeting in Secretary Forrestal's office. To Air Force ROTC Advisory Committee meeting. Appointments with General Gruenther; J. H. Ohly. Afternoon meeting of the JCS. Appointments with Secretary Forrestal; General McNarney. Accompanied by Mrs. Eisenhower to dinner at the Forrestals'.

15 Washington. Morning appointment with A. G. Carter. Meeting with the Committee of the Four Secretaries. Coffee in honor of Secretary Forrestal's birthday. Meeting of the National Security Resources Board. To Air Force ROTC Advisory Committee meeting. Lunch in Air Secretary's Mess. To Andrews Air Force Base for air-progress demonstration in the afternoon.

16 Washington. Morning appointments with Dr. Howard M. Smith; Secretary Forrestal; General McNarney. To Secretary Forrestal's office to meet with General Sir W. D. Morgan. Afternoon appointment with General Vandenberg. Returns to Secretary Forrestal's office to meet with M. W. Childs. Appointment with General

February   Gruenther. Cocktails and supper given by the Haislips for General and Mrs. Eisenhower.

17   Washington. Morning appointments with Admiral Denfeld; Generals Gruenther and Lemnitzer. JCS meeting. National Security Council meeting at the White House in the afternoon. To P. S. Mesta's for dinner.

18   Washington. Appointment with D. F. Carpenter, J. H. Ohly, Generals Gruenther and Lutes re foreign military aid. JCS meeting and lunch. To Secretary Forrestal's office. Appointments with Admiral Conolly; J. H. Moninger. To dinner with Milton S. Eisenhower and the L. Eakins.

19   Washington. Morning appointment with K. C. McCann. Meeting of the Joint Intelligence Committee. To Burning Tree Country Club with General Bradley, Secretary Forrestal, and Mr. Barlow for annual crab party given by Congressman Lowell Stockman (Oregon). Dinner at the Belgian Embassy.

20   Washington.

21   Washington. Morning appointments with General William Evens Hall (Director of Intelligence, European Command); K. C. McCann; J. H. Ohly. T. K. Finletter to see General Eisenhower in the afternoon. Showing of Reserve Officers Association film by C. R. Smith (president, Air Force Association). Appointments with former Supreme Court Justice Owen J. Roberts; W. Webster. Dinner with M. W. Childs and Blair Moody at the Statler Hotel.

22   Washington. Appointments with General Lemnitzer; General Gruenther. Lunch with George Williams at the Sulgrave Club. Evening with C. Roberts and W. E. Robinson.

23   Washington. Morning briefing by General LeMay. To War Council meeting, then to Secretary Forrestal's office. Afternoon appointment with Admiral Walter Frederick Boone (Assistant Chief of Naval Operations for Strategic Plans). JCS meeting. Evening preview of television version of *Crusade in Europe*.

24   Washington. Morning appointments with Congressman Samuel Francis Hobbs (Alabama) re Fort McClellan;

February Secretary Forrestal; General Devers. Lunch. Afternoon meeting with representatives of the United World Federalists, including C. Meyers, Jr., C. Canfield, T. K. Finletter, and General McNarney. Plans and Operations Division briefing on oil by Colonels Osmanski and Collins. To Secretary Forrestal's office. Informal dinner with J. J. McCloy.

25 Washington. Morning meeting of the JCS, including lunch. Afternoon appointment with C. Cooper (chairman, Armed Forces Medical Advisory Committee) at Secretary Forrestal's request. Dinner for Senator Brien McMahon (Connecticut) and Mrs. McMahon at the Statler Hotel.

26 Washington. Evening with George Maurice Morris (member, law firm of Morris, KixMiller, and Baar).

27 Washington. To luncheon at P. S. Mesta's with Major Schulz.

28 Morning plane to Chicago. Afternoon arrival at the Blackstone Hotel. Lunch in suite with James E. Day (chairman, 1949 Red Cross Fund), John W. Evers, Jr., Julien H. Collins, R. Douglas Stuart, E. J. Bermingham, and K. C. McCann. Press conference. Reception and dinner, followed by nationally broadcast address to open the 1949 American Red Cross campaign.

March 1 Chicago. Morning appointments with Raymond D. Smith; Thomas Blazina (Adjutant, Allied War Veterans Council); Vice-president Davis. Lunch at the Blackstone Hotel with F. W. Chambers, William Keady, Frederick Hedley Jobbins, Frederic C. Strodel, Vice-president Davis, E. J. Bermingham, and K. C. McCann. To Chicago alumni reception and cocktail party in honor of General Eisenhower at the University Club. To Teachers College dinner with Dean Russell for meeting of the National Association of Secondary School Principals. Leaves with M. J. Trees and R. Douglas Stuart for dinner arranged by E. J. Bermingham at the Chicago Club.

2 Morning plane to Washington. Meeting with Secretary of State Acheson and Secretary Forrestal. Lunch with Secretary Forrestal. JCS meeting. Reception for Sec-

March   retary Forrestal at the Carlton Hotel. To dinner at Secretary Forrestal's.

3   Washington. Morning appointments with Generals McNarney and Gruenther; Robert Henry Hinkley (vice-president and director, American Broadcasting Company); Milt D. Hill. JCS meeting. Afternoon plane to New York City. Deans' meeting in the Trustees Room. Evening address to the New York City Bar Association.

4   Morning plane to Washington. Appointments with General Morgan; Admiral Kincaid; General Gruenther; J. E. Webb and W. W. Butterworth. Lunch with General Gruenther. Appointments with Secretary Forrestal; General J. Garesché Ord; General William Henry Harrison Morris, Jr. (senior member, Joint Brazil—United States Military Commission), and Colonel A. P. Jones; C. P. Cooper; S. T. Early; W. T. Faricy; Admiral Carney. Evening bridge with General Gruenther, E. Culbertson, and Chief Justice of the United States Frederick Moore Vinson.

5   Washington. Morning appointments with General William Dole Eckert (executive to the Under Secretary of the Air Force) and Secretary Symington; Paul Vories McNutt (chairman of the board, Philippine American Life Insurance). To the Armed Forces Medical Center. Appointments with Generals Gruenther and Wedemeyer. Lunch at Army Mess with Secretary Forrestal and W. F. Frye. Afternoon plane to New York City.

6   New York City.

7   New York City. Morning appointments with M. H. Dodge; Provost Jacobs; General Adler, Stanley Marshall Rinehart, and Stanley Marshall Rinehart, Jr. (publisher); F. Coykendall. Tour of Columbia College. To Men's Faculty Club for trustees luncheon, followed by trustees meeting. Meeting of the Council on Foreign Relations.

8   New York City. Morning appointment with J. Campbell. Lunch, then bridge, with C. Roberts, E. D. Slater, and W. E. Robinson.

9   New York City. Evening meeting of the Society of

March   Older Graduates at the University Club. Late night train
to Washington.

10   Washington. To the Pentagon for morning appoint-
ments with General Gruenther; Secretary Sherman. To
Secretary Forrestal's office. Afternoon appointments with
T. D. Campbell; Dr. Robert F. Rinehart (executive
secretary, Research and Development Board); Mc-
George Bundy (political analyst, Council on Foreign
Relations).

11   Washington. Morning meeting of the Educational Policies Commission. Dinner at the French Embassy given
by Ambassador Henri Bonnet for Chief Justice and Mrs.
Vinson.

12   Washington. Morning appointments with Frank Lea-
royd Boyden (principal, Deerfield Academy); W. F.
Frye; Generals Norstad and Gruenther. Golf in the
afternoon with J. C. Black, General Hughes, and G.
E. Allen. Dinner given by the Haislips for John
Nicholas Brown (former Assistant Secretary of the Navy
for Air).

13   Washington. Afternoon appointment with Leland Harrison (diplomat).

14   Washington. Morning appointments with General Gay,
General Hall, and Dr. Philip McCord Morse (Deputy
Director, Weapons Systems Evaluation Group); Sec-
retary Forrestal. JCS meeting. Lunch with Secretary
Forrestal. JCS meeting in the afternoon. Appointment
with Secretary Royall. Returns to office via Secretary
Forrestal's office.

15   Washington. Morning appointments with Charles W.
Jackson; Secretary Symington. War Council meeting.
Lunch in Army Mess. JCS meeting. To Secretary For-
restal's office with Generals Gruenther and McNarney.

16   Washington. Morning JCS meeting. To Secretary For-
restal's office, followed by lunch with him and General
Gruenther. Afternoon appointments with Benjamin
Mosby (editor, *Washington Star*); G. V. Cooper; W.
L. Lippmann. To U.S. Naval Academy for dinner and
informal talk to the midshipmen's Smoke Hall Panel.

March 17   Washington. Dental appointment at Walter Reed General Hospital. JCS meeting. Lunch in Army Mess. Afternoon JCS meeting. Personal visit from Colonel Charles Hardin Anderson. With Mrs. Eisenhower to the Sulgrave Club as guests of the Saylers in the evening.

18   Washington. Daylong meeting of the Service Academy Board. Lunch with Secretary Forrestal in staff dining room.

19   Washington. Morning appointment with R. L. Stearns and J. L. Hoen, followed by daylong meeting of the Service Academy Board. White House News Photographers Association dinner at the Statler Hotel.

20   Washington. Supper and games with General and Mrs. Hughes.

21   Washington. Morning staff meeting. Testifies before House Appropriations Subcommittee on the FY50 military budget. Appointment with General McNarney. To Conference of Mayors at the Statler Hotel. Luncheon given by Eric Johnson in his office for Louis Burt Mayer (motion picture producer). Afternoon appointments canceled because of illness. Remains in Washington until March 28.

28   By President Truman's plane to Boca Chica, Florida, then by auto to U.S. Naval Base in Key West for convalescence.

29   Key West.

30   Key West.

31   Key West.

April 1   Key West.

2   Key West.

3   Key West.

4   Key West.

5   Key West.

6   Key West.

7   Key West. Afternoon meeting with Generals Gruenther and Norstad. Dinner at the Little White House with

April   the Chiefs of Staff. Viewing of film *Secret Life of Walter Mitty*.

8   Key West. JCS meeting at Quarters A-B in the morning. Lunch. Evening viewing of film *Cisco, King of Bad Men*.

9   Key West. JCS meeting.

10   Key West. JCS meeting including Secretary of Defense Johnson. Dinner at the Little White House. Viewing of film *Egg and I*.

11   Key West. JCS meeting including Secretary Johnson.

12   Key West. Morning JCS meeting. Appointments with Sergeants Davies and Moaney; General Snyder and Major Schulz. Afternoon plane (the *Sacred Cow*) to Augusta, Georgia, where Eisenhower recuperates at Augusta National Golf Club until May 11.

May 11   Morning plane to Washington. Afternoon JCS meeting. Evening at the Gruenthers including the Hugheses, Saylers, Snyders, Prichards, and Mrs. R. Butcher.

12   Washington. Morning War Council meeting. Committee for Economic Development luncheon at the Statler Hotel with President Truman, Secretary Johnson, and the Cabinet. Afternoon JCS meeting.

13   Washington. Morning appointments with J. L. Hoen; General Morgan. JCS meeting. Lunch with Secretary Johnson. Afternoon appointments with Luther Lyons Hill (vice-president, *Des Moines Register and Tribune*); F. G. Wisner. To Secretary Johnson's office, then to the White House for off-the-record meeting with President Truman. Plane to New York City.

14   New York City.

15   New York City.

16   New York City. Breakfast at #60 with D. M. Black.

17   New York City. Morning appointments with General Salih Omurtak (Chief of Staff, Turkish Armed Forces); Dr. Dunning; General Joyce. Afternoon appointment with General Gruenther. Accompanied by Mrs. Eisenhower to dinner given by Dr. Fackenthal for General W. B. Smith at the Men's Faculty Club.

May 18 New York City. Morning appointment with Dean Carman and Professor John Andrew Northcott, Jr. (chairman, engineering department, Notre Dame University, Indiana). To Blind Brook Club with General Snyder at noon. To meeting of the Council on Foreign Relations with A. Nevins.

19 New York City. Morning appointments with H. C. Butcher; Boyd DeWolf Lewis (executive editor, Newspaper Enterprise Association); General Ralph Hamilton Tate (USA, ret.; now with Camillus Cutlery Company); Vice-president Davis; General Hawley. Golf at Deepdale Club with C. Roberts, J. L. Hennessy, and W. A. Jones in the afternoon.

20 New York City. Morning appointments with Vice-president Pegram; Vice-president Davis; and Vice-president Dean Krout. Afternoon visit with F. Coykendall. Appointment with J. Campbell.

21 New York City. Golf at Blind Brook Club with Messrs. Cleveland, Royall, and Harris.

22 New York City. Honorary sponsor of dinner for B. M. Baruch by the Brooklyn Philanthropic League, United Order True Sisters.

23 New York City. Morning appointments with D. M. Black, Vice-president Davis, and J. D. Wise; T. D. Brophy. Lunch at #60 with J. D. Brandon and Colonel Frank Albert Allen, Jr. (Office of the Commanding General, New York–New Jersey Military District Headquarters). Golf with C. V. McAdam at Blind Brook Club in the afternoon.

24 New York City. Morning appointments with Dean McIntosh; Dean Finch; Roscoe Drummond; Dean Young; and Captain T. F. Wellings. Afternoon appointment with Dean Krout. Presented with College of Physicians and Surgeons yearbook by two medical students. Late afternoon reception honoring Brazilian President Eurico Gaspar Dutra.

25 Morning plane to Washington. To funeral of James V. Forrestal at Arlington National Cemetery. Lunch with Secretary Johnson and the JCS. Afternoon JCS meeting. Plane to New York City.

May 26 New York City. Afternoon appointments with K. C. McCann; Major Cannon. To Harvard Business School dinner honoring Dean Young.

27 New York City. Morning appointment with Paul R. Mort (professor of education, Teachers College). To Deepdale Club for golf with Edward John Barber (chairman of the board, Barber Steamship Lines), C. Roberts, and E. D. Slater.

28 New York City. Golf at Blind Brook Club with C. Roberts, C. J. Schoo, and G. E. Allen.

29 New York City. To Walker Gentry Buckner's for golf at St. Andrews.

30 New York City. Accompanied by Mrs. Eisenhower to small luncheon given by Mrs. Cornelius Vanderbilt, Jr.

31 New York City. To Dean Carman's office in the morning. Dinner at #60 for recipients of honorary degrees.

June 1 New York City. Morning briefing for Columbia commencement. Alumni trustees meeting, followed by luncheon at John Jay Hall. Commencement in the afternoon.

2 New York City. Morning meeting with Dean Russell. To La Guardia Airport for departure of fifth anniversary D-day flight to Normandy beaches. Afternoon appointment with E. Goldman. Brief appearance at School of Nursing graduation. Cocktails with General John Wilson O'Daniel (military attaché, Moscow) and Mrs. O'Daniel.

3 New York City. Morning appointments with E.J. Bermingham; Dr. Dunning; Dean Young; M. H. Davis (Portland, Oregon). Luncheon at #60 for Doctors Hu Shih, J. Heng Liu, and Magnus I. Gregersen (respectively, honorary president, medical director, and president of the American Bureau for Medical Aid to China). Evening with General and Mrs. H. Harmon.

4 New York City. Morning appointments with Professor B. D. Wood; C. M. Malone. Golf with J. Campbell. To Blind Brook Club with C. Roberts, G. E. Allen,

June and Herbert Weld Grindal (banker). Dinner with the Nevinses.

5 New York City.

6 To Stephensburg, New Jersey, for fishing at Hidden Valley Farm of Frank R. Kelly. Golf in the afternoon. Returns to New York City.

7 New York City. Morning staff meeting with Provost Jacobs, Vice-presidents Pegram, Davis, and Rappleye, Dean Krout, and J. Campbell. Autographs books for Oleg Cherney. Appointments with General F. Trubee Davison (president, American Museum of Natural History); Vice-president Pegram. To U.S. Trust Company luncheon re Higgins Trust. Afternoon appointments with G. E. Allen and F. L. Andrews; Dwight Morse and Mr. Hume. Special meeting of the trustees.

8 New York City. Accompanied by Mrs. Eisenhower to Nevis estate in the morning. Meeting with Professors Rabi, Macmahon, O. J. Campbell, E. J. Simmons, C. Goodrich, and A. W. Thomas. Appointment with Madame Alma Clayburgh. Lunch at #60 with John Bond Trevor (president, American Coalition of Patriotic Societies), Cecil Palmer, and Provost Jacobs. American Heritage Foundation dinner at the Links Club.

9 New York City. Morning appointments with K. D. Johnson; A. Flexner; Mrs. May Eden (deputy chairman and honorary director, Children's Free World Community Chest and Joint European Refugee Committee). President's Council luncheon with Provost Jacobs, Vice-presidents Pegram and Davis, Dean Krout, J. Campbell, and J. T. Cahill. Press conference for Surgeon General Leonard A. Scheele. Afternoon appointment with Dean Young. Meeting of the School of Business Committee on Instruction. Cocktail party for Columbia Ambassadors at the Men's Faculty Club.

10 New York City. Meeting of the Department of Political Science Committee on Instruction. Appointments with F. S. Hogan and F. W. Chambers; General Donovan and J. R. Reuben (general counsel, Metro-Goldwyn-Mayer). Columbia Associates luncheon. Afternoon appointment with H. J. Taylor.

June 11 New York City. Visits with B. M. Baruch in the morning. To Blind Brook Club for golf.

12 New York City. Golf with C. Roberts.

13 New York City. To West Point with Lord and Lady Alanbrooke. Lunch with John S. D. and Barbara Eisenhower. Afternoon return to New York City. Dinner at #60 for the Alanbrookes.

14 New York City. Visit with Malcolm Pratt Aldrich (financial manager). Dinner party given by the Brandons.

15 New York City. Morning appointments with Captain Wellings and Henry G. Moran (professor of naval science, USNROTC, Columbia University); G. V. Cooper. Dinner with Admiral and Mrs. Kincaid.

16 New York City. Morning appointments with Frederick Miller, T. McGoey, and R. F. Moore; Lester Markel (Sunday editor, *New York Times*); M. J. Quill; Dean Arnaud. Golf in the afternoon with C. V. McAdam.

17 Early morning plane to Washington. Addresses National War College graduating class in the morning. Appointment with Sir Dalrymple-Hamilton. Lunch with General Clark in Army Mess. Afternoon JCS meeting.

18 Washington. Meeting of the Service Academy Board. Afternoon plane to New York City.

19 New York City. Night train to Washington.

20 Washington. To Pentagon in the morning. Attends swearing-in ceremony for Secretary of the Army G. Gray. JCS meeting. Afternoon appointments with General Gruenther; Admiral Struble. Afternoon plane to New York City.

21 New York City. Morning appointment with Provost Jacobs. Staff meeting. Appointment with Provost Jacobs, Vice-presidents Pegram and Davis, Deans Krout and Young, Dr. Dunning, and J. D. Wise. President's Council luncheon. Afternoon meeting of the Department of Philosophy Committee on Instruction. Buildings and Grounds Committee meeting. Evening cocktail party for Mr. and Mrs. J. W. Gerard.

June 22 New York City. Meeting of the Library Association Committee on Instruction. Appointments with H. C. Butcher; Dr. Fackenthal. To Deepdale Club for golf with C. Roberts, P. Grimm, E. D. Slater, R. Reed, and W. G. Buckner in the afternoon.

23 New York City. Morning appointments with Charles G. Proffitt (director, Columbia University Press); Vice-president Davis; Earl Kincaid, Mr. Guleck (vice-president, Equitable Insurance Company), and Mr. Pumpelly; E. Goldman. Lunch at #60 with the Douds.

24 New York City. Morning meeting with Provost Jacobs, Vice-president Davis, and J. Campbell re purchase of Sheffield building. Appointments with General E. N. Clark; G. V. Cooper; Captain Henry John Schroeder, Jr. (USA); General Snyder and Professor Ginzberg; Dr. Guy Everett Snavely (executive director, Association of American Colleges); Miss Alice K. Snyder (sister-in-law of Earl D. Eisenhower); General Kerr. To Blind Brook Club with C. V. McAdam, C. Roberts, and General Snyder.

25 New York City. Morning appointments with T. J. Watson; A. Levy; Benjamin Salvosa (president, Baguio College). To Blind Brook Club with C. Roberts.

26 New York City. Inauguration of the Pennsylvania Railroad's new passenger train *The General*. Buffet supper.

27 New York City. Morning appointment with Julian Darst Conover (secretary, American Mining Congress). Lunch at #60 with E. E. Newsom. Meeting of the Department of Pure Sciences Committee on Instruction. To Council on Foreign Relations meeting.

28 Morning plane to Washington. To Armed Forces Industrial College graduation exercises. Lunch at Army and Navy Club. Afternoon appointment with General Morgan. JCS meeting. Evening plane to New York City.

29 New York City. Morning appointments with J. Gunther; R. V. New; J. Campbell, T. A. McGoey, and R. F. Moore. To Deepdale Club for golf with J. C. Black and C. R. Black, Jr., in the afternoon. Dinner given by the Crittenbergers at the Waldorf-Astoria.

June 30   New York City. Morning appointments with Dean Young; C. A. Norgren; A. H. Sulzberger; Roy Holbrook; D. Wallace and Vice-president Davis; Alvin Stokes (investigator, Committee on Un-American Activities). To Deepdale Club for golf with William Starling Sullivant Rodgers (chairman of the board, The Texas Company), J. C. Black, and C. R. Black, Jr. Dinner at home of H. R. Reid.

July   1   New York City. Morning appointments with Frank E. Holman (president, American Bar Association); Roy Holbrook; Dr. Dunning and W. V. King; Vice-president Davis. Golf. Guests arrive for weekend celebration of the Eisenhowers' thirty-third wedding anniversary.

2   New York City.

3   New York City.

4   New York City. Staff meeting with Provost Jacobs, Vice-presidents Pegram, Davis, and Rappleye, Dean Krout, and J. Campbell.

5   New York City. Morning appointment with D. Wallace and Vice-president Pegram. Brief appearance at opening of Columbia's Summer Session.

6   New York City. Morning appointments with E. Goldman; General Chauncey Lee Fenton (president, West Point Alumni Foundation); Vice-president Davis; Vincent Sutliff. Luncheon at #60 for group of eleven re Columbia development.

7   New York City. D. M. Black for morning coffee. Appointments with J. Campbell; Provost Jacobs and R. Herpers. To Blind Brook Club for golf with W. E. Robinson, B. Barton, and W. A. Jones.

8   New York City. Morning appointment with R. F. Moore and L. A. Appley. Daylong seminar at Teachers College.

9   New York City. Morning appointment with General Claire Lee Chennault (USA, ret., chairman of the board, Army Decorations). To Blind Brook Club for golf with W. E. Robinson, B. Barton, and W. A. Jones or C. V. McAdam.

10   New York City.

July 11 New York City. Morning appointment with General C. L. Fenton. Staff meeting with Provost Jacobs, Vice-presidents Pegram, Davis, and Rappleye, Dean Krout, and J. Campbell. Appointment with Professor Dohr. Off-the-record discussion with Standard Oil Company executives, followed by luncheon.

12 New York City. Morning appointment with H. W. Baldwin. By plane to Washington to attend funeral service for General Prichard in the afternoon. Meeting with Secretary Johnson. Returns to office. Overnight at Statler Hotel. Visited by H. A. Blunck.

13 By plane to New York City with Secretary Symington and Major Allen B. Gaston (military aide to Secretary Symington). Lunch at #60 with Secretary Symington. To office in the afternoon. To Chrysler Building to see W. C. Hanway, Jr. (regional manager, Fargo Motor Corporation) re new Chrysler Crown Imperial.

14 New York City. Morning meeting with W. L. McLean. Afternoon train to Washington with G. E. Allen and others. Appointment on board with W. T. Phillips. To Blair House in the evening for off-the-record meeting with President Truman, Vice-president Barkley, Secretary of State Acheson, Speaker of the House Rayburn, D. E. Lilienthal, and members of the Joint Committee on Atomic Energy re British-Canadian cooperation on atomic energy. Night train to New York City.

15 New York City. Morning appointments with Paul Menges (Abilene); Felix E. Larkin (Associate General Counsel, Office of the Secretary of Defense); Magnus I. Gregersen re letter from General Chennault. Golf with J. C. Black and Charles M. White.

16 New York City. To Blind Brook Club with W. E. Robinson and Ed Lane. Accompanied by Vice-president Davis and K. C. McCann to *Reader's Digest* meeting with D. Wallace in Pleasantville, New York.

18 New York City. To barber. Morning appointments with Professor Hacker; M. H. Dodge; Kansas high school group; Kenneth Wells; Benjamin Neal; General E. N. Clark re Army reserve. Afternoon appointment with M. W. Childs. Council on Foreign Relations meeting.

July 19 New York City. Morning appointments with D. M. Black and Roland P. Soule (vice-president, Irving Trust Company) re Engineering School development; R. K. Merton; Dr. Finkelstein; Vice-president Davis; Colonel Edwin Fahey Black (Office of the Secretary of Defense).

20 Early morning plane to Washington. Appointments with General Norstad; Chiefs of Staff and General Gruenther. Lunch in Army Mess with General Bradley. To the Capitol for meeting with Secretary of State Acheson and Secretary Johnson. Brief press conference. To Secretary Johnson's office. Appointment with General Gruenther. Evening plane to New York City.

21 New York City. To barber. Appointments with Provost Jacobs; Vice-president Pegram; Dean Young; and Dr. Dunning.

22 Early morning plane to Rhinelander, Wisconsin, accompanied by G. E. Allen. Eisenhower to be guest of H. Young in Minocqua for the next two weeks.

August 6 By plane for vacation in Denver. Evening arrival at the John S. Doud's.

7 Denver.

8 Denver. Daylong meeting of the Service Academy Board at Lowry Air Force Base. Stag dinner hosted by R. S. Stearns at the Denver Country Club.

9 Denver. Service Academy Board meeting. Accompanied by Mrs. Eisenhower to reception at the home of R. S. Stearns in Boulder. Late night return to Denver.

10 Denver. Visits Colonel J. Miley at Fitzsimons General Hospital in the afternoon. Anniversary dinner in honor of the Douds.

11 Denver. Morning golf with J. A. Culbreath.

12 Denver. To Brown Palace Hotel for appointment with E. S. Graham, C. Chase, W. Glenn Muncy (president, Kansas Jaycees), and E. P. Murphey (of Topeka, Kansas). Lunch at the Denver Club. Golf at Cherry Hills Club with Fred Wallace, Temple Buell, and F. M. Manning.

13 Denver. Golf with J. C. Black, J. A. Culbreath, and

August		Newell Hamilton Orr (vice-president, Colorado Fuel & Iron Corporation).
	14	Denver.
	15	Denver. Golf with J. C. Black, J. A. Culbreath, and N. H. Orr. To the Brown Palace Hotel for Mile High Club dinner.
	16	Denver. Golf with J. C. Black, E. M. Burnham, and J. A. Culbreath.
	17	Denver. Daylong visit with A. Nielsen.
	18	Denver. Golf with E. M. Burnham, J. A. Culbreath, and J. C. Black. To Central City accompanied by Mrs. Eisenhower, the Schulzes, the J. C. Blacks, and the E. M. Burnhams. Dinner and show hosted by Mr. and Mrs. N. H. Orr and James Maintland. Evening return to Denver.
	19	Day trip to Colorado Springs by auto with N. H. Orr, J. C. Black, and E. M. Burnham. Golf at the Broadmoor Club with E. B. Dudley, Jr., L. B. Maytag, General Ross O'Donald, Howard Kneal, and Donald Bathwell (of Oklahoma).
	20	Denver. Morning appointment with William VanDerveer (attorney). Golf at Cherry Hills Club with J. C. Black, E. M. Burnham, and J. A. Culbreath. Luncheon with guests Mrs. Eisenhower, Mrs. J. C. Black, and Mrs. Schulz. Visits with Roy Eisenhower, daughter Peggy, and Milton S. Eisenhower, Jr.
	21	Denver. Golf with Wiley Blair, Jr. (chairman of the board, Holly Sugar Corporation), J. C. Black, and L. B. Maytag.
	22	Denver. To office at Lowry Air Force Base in the morning. By plane to Colorado Springs for lunch and golf with J. C. Black at the Broadmoor Club.
	23	Denver.
	24	Denver.
	25	Denver.
	26	Denver. Morning golf with E. F. Gregory (chairman of the board, Accident and Health Underwriters) and J. A. Culbreath. Afternoon appointment with Professor

August		Dunning re Columbia University. Meeting with Mrs. Lewis F. Wells.
	27	Denver.
	28	Denver.
	29	Denver.
	30	Denver.
	31	Denver.
September	1	Denver.
	2	Denver. By plane to Topeka, Kansas, accompanied by Governor Carlson. Dinner, followed by address before the Kansas Junior Chamber of Commerce.
	3	Topeka. Morning visits with John Hersh (former Abilene classmate); Mamie Witter (cousin); and Minnie Stewart (teacher, Topeka High School). By plane to St. Louis accompanied by Milton S. Eisenhower. Afternoon press conference and photo session.
	4	St. Louis. Open-house meetings with Edwin R. Culver III (Culver Educational Foundation); Frank Rand; Chester Charles Davis (president, Federal Reserve Bank of St. Louis). To cocktail party with Arthur B. Eisenhower.
	5	St. Louis. Addresses American Bar Association in the afternoon. Brief appearance at buffet supper hosted by Frank E. Holman. By plane to Denver accompanied by Secretary Symington, D. R. Calhoun, and Majors Gaston and Schulz.
	6	Denver. Golf in the morning with Secretary Symington, D. R. Calhoun, R. Arnold, and F. M. Manning.
	7	Denver. Golf in the morning with Secretary Symington, J. A. Culbreath, R. Arnold, and William Flenniken. To Fraser, Colorado, for fishing at ranch of A. Nielsen.
	8	Fraser.
	9	Fraser.
	10	Fraser. Late afternoon return to Denver. Accompanied by Mrs. Eisenhower to dinner at the Fred Wallaces'.

September 11   Denver.

12   Denver. Attends Columbia alumni luncheon at the University Club. Visits with E. J. Bermingham. Returns to the Douds' in the evening.

13   Denver. Golf with J. A. Culbreath, Fred Newton, and R. Arnold.

14   Denver. Golf with J. A. Culbreath, Jack Lighthall, and J. G. Dyer.

15   Denver. Morning appointment with Jay E. Shideler (president, City Real Estate, and Columbia alumnus) re Columbia trust. Afternoon departure by train for New York City.

16   Travel day. Morning arrival in Chicago. Afternoon departure.

17   Morning arrival in New York City. Appointment at #60 with K. C. McCann. Lunch with Provost Jacobs.

18   New York City. Late afternoon meeting with W. A. Harriman.

19   New York City. Morning appointments with Professor Kirk; Dean Carman; J. Campbell. Afternoon appointments with George Eisenhower; Mr. Felice. To Council on Foreign Relations dinner, followed by meeting with Ambassador Douglas.

20   New York City. Morning appointments with Mrs. E. W. Biggs; M. H. Dodge; Alexander H. W. Zerban (Columbia alumnus); Judge Levanthal. Luncheon at #60 for deans re Columbia development. Afternoon plane to Washington. To wedding reception for B. A. Horkan, Jr., at Chevy Chase Club. Bridge with Generals Gruenther and Sayler in the evening. Overnight at Wardman Park Hotel.

21   Washington. Morning appointments with General Bradley and Secretary Johnson in their offices. Appointment with General Alfred Bixby Quinton, Jr. Appointment with General J. L. Collins in his office. To Secretary Symington's office for meeting of the Advanced Study Group, including Colonels D. Z. Zimmerman, G. W. Beeler, George Jones, and Frederick William Gibb. Early afternoon appointment with J. L. Hoen.

Lunch with Secretary Johnson. Early afternoon plane to New York City. Passengers include Secretary Johnson; Generals Cates, Hughes, Richard Cox Coupland, James Dennett McIntyre, James Henry Burns, Abraham Robert Ginsburgh, Vandenberg, Bradley, J. L. Collins, Haislip, and Parks; Admiral Albert Gallatin Noble; LeRoy Whitman (editor, *Army and Navy Journal*); W. A. Harriman; Colonels Chester Victor Clifton and Joel B. Olmstead; Captains Steve Watson Mulkey, Jr. (aide-de-camp), and Edgar M. Ramsey (aide-de-camp). Dinner and bridge at W. A. Jones's with W. E. Robinson and C. Roberts.

22 New York City. Morning appointment with R. L. Biggers. Meetings at the Men's Faculty Club with all deans and the trustees; Committee on Development.

23 New York City. Morning appointments with Vice-president Pegram; J. L. Hoen; J. W. Gallagher; Sir Ian Jacob (Director of Overseas Broadcasting for the British Broadcasting Company). To the Waldorf-Astoria for luncheon given by Arthur B. Eisenhower, Palmer Bradley (attorney for the Hughes Food Company), Warren Lee Pierson, Ralph Damon, George Clay, Powell Crosley, Jr. (president, Crosley Corporation), Sidney Maestre (president, Mississippi Valley Trust Company), John A. Collings (executive vice-president, TWA), A. D. Simpson (president, National Bank of Commerce), Harold Brophy (New York attorney), Clarence Dow (New York insurance executive), and N. S. Talbott (Ohio realtor). Leaves for football practice at Baker Field in late afternoon with R. J. Furey and Bob Chernoff.

24 New York City. Morning appointments with General Campbell; H. M. Schley. To the Columbia-Amherst football game in the afternoon with General Snyder and K. C. McCann. Dinner and bridge at #60 with C. Roberts, J. Gould, General Snyder, and K. C. Royall.

25 New York City. Lunch at #60 with T. E. Stephens and General Snyder. To the dedication of the Harlem YMCA in the afternoon. To General and Mrs. Nevins's for bridge in the early evening.

26 New York City. Morning meetings with Provost

September		Jacobs; Harrison Brown (dean of faculties, University of Chicago). Lunch with the Committee on Education. Late afternoon appointment with Vice-president Pegram and Provost Jacobs. Council on Foreign Relations meeting and dinner.
	27	New York City. Morning appointments with Dr. M. Immanuel; G. V. Cooper (Columbia alumnus); President Russell; Mrs. C. B. Luce. Lunch at #60.
	28	New York City. Morning appointments with Professor Kirk; J. B. Mintener; Clifford Hildebrandt Tate (West Point classmate). To McMillin Theater for formal opening of Columbia University's 196th academic year. Accompanied by K. C. McCann to Harkness Hall in the evening for informal opening of the School of General Studies.
	29	New York City. Morning appointments with Dean Maurice John Hickey (Columbia Dental School); Lieutenant and Mrs. L. Moore; Richard Guertis de Rochemont (producer, *March of Time* newsreels) in the Trustees Room. Late morning appointment with Mrs. E. W. Biggs. Luncheon and opening assembly at Barnard.
	30	New York City. Morning appointments with Dean Young; Dean Caswell; Mrs. H. R. Reid; Professor Chamberlin and the New York Association for New Americans with Mrs. David Levy, William Rosenwald, Henry Bernstein; J. Campbell. Lunch at #60 with W. Benton.
October	1	New York City. To Baker Field for lunch at the Boat House. Afternoon golf at the Deepdale Club with J. L. Hennessy, C. N. Hilton, and C. Roberts.
	2	New York City. Afternoon at T. J. Watson, Sr.'s.
	3	New York City. Morning appointment with C. M. Malone. Lunch at #60 with Professor Kirk, Vice-president Pegram, J. Campbell, Dr. Dunning, Dean Krout, and Vice-president Davis. Informal advance meeting of the trustees, followed by formal meeting. To the Men's Faculty Club for evening cocktails with the trustees and members of the School of Business. To the Links Club for dinner honoring Secretary Lovett.

October   4   New York City. Morning appointments with J. W. Alsop, Jr.; General E. N. Clark; M. W. Childs. Lunch. To McMillin Theater for freshman class welcome. Afternoon appointments with R. A. Roberts; Dr. Stewart (college president). Visits Columbia College. Returns to #60. To the Jacobs' for an evening cocktail party for the Kirks.

5   New York City. Morning appointments with Vice-president Pegram; Professor Chamberlin re Nehru; Professor Carl Sumner Shoup (Department of Economics). Lunch with D. C. Josephs, Secretary Lovett, and G. L. Harrison. Afternoon appointment with Dr. Norton (Teachers College). Bridge in the evening at #60 with C. Roberts, C. J. Schoo, and J. Gould.

6   New York City. Thirty-fifth annual meeting of the Educational Policies Committee of the National Education Association.

7   New York City. Early afternoon appointment with George Strecker of Chicago. Lunch at #60 with J. Campbell, J. C. Blaine, and L. Lee. Afternoon appointments with President Russell re field house fund; J. T. Cahill; Dr. Shotwell; Professor J. Chamberlin.

8   New York City. In the morning to Educational Policies Committee meeting and alumni fall reunion. Lays cornerstone at Baker Field. To the Columbia-Yale football game in the afternoon with the Vandenbergs and the Tedders. Cocktails and dinner at #60 with the Vandenbergs, Tedders, and General and Mrs. W. B. Smith.

9   New York City.

10   New York City. Morning appointments with Dr. Dunning; Dean Finch and Engineering School Committee on Instruction. Lunch at #60. Afternoon departure for H. Young's in Ridgefield, Connecticut.

11   Ridgefield. Morning duck and pheasant shoot with H. Young, H. C. Flanigan, Dave Cooper (farm manager), and Arnold Smith.

12   Ridgefield. Recreation. Lunch with K. C. McCann.

13   New York City. To barber. Morning appointments with Professor Wallace; Richard Wilson (Gridiron Club);

October   Dr. Dunning; General E. N. Clark. Luncheon at #60 for Dr. Dunning and group of twelve. In the afternoon Holmes Bannard and H. H. Pevler present a book on Eisenhower's inauguration as president of Columbia. Evening cocktail party at the University Club given by Earl D. Babst in honor of Provost Jacobs. Late evening visit with A. Hatch at #60.

14   New York City. Eisenhower's birthday. Lunch with L. Little and the football team at John Jay Hall.

15   New York City. To the Deepdale Club for lunch and golf with J. L. Hennessy, C. N. Hilton, and J. P. Binns.

16   New York City. Visit by J. D. Rockefeller, Jr., at #60, followed by attendance at layman's service at Riverside Church.

17   New York City. Morning rehearsal for university convocation. Appointment with Congressman Coudert (New York). To dinner honoring Pandit Nehru, followed by university convocation to award degree to Nehru.

18   New York City. Morning appointment with K. C. McCann re "*Herald Tribune* Forum" speech. Meeting in A. H. Sulzberger's office with the Committee on the Organization of the Columbia Bicentennial. To the Deepdale Club with J. C. Black, E. M. Burhman, W. T. Faricy, and F. L. Parks.

19   New York City. Morning appointment with General Duque (Deputy Chief of Staff, Philippine Army). Leaves for meetings with the Boy Scouts Executive Board and the Committee on Foreign Relations. Luncheon at #60 with Dean Hickey, George L. Radcliffe (Baltimore lawyer), A. H. Diebold, William Ralph La Porte (physical education specialist), H. P. Field, and Dr. R. P. Herwick. Afternoon appointments with J. Campbell; Dean Young and student for Nottingham Scholar presentation. To interfaith meeting at Earl Hall. Dinner at #60 for Mr. and Mrs. H. R. Cullen.

20   Morning plane to Washington. To the Pentagon for morning appointments with Secretary Johnson and Generals Bradley and J. L. Collins. Testifies before House Armed Services Committee. Meeting with Sec-

retary Johnson at the Pentagon. Lunch with General Bradley. Afternoon plane to New York City.

21 New York City. Morning appointments with Chaplain Clayton and Humphrey Whitbread; J. Campbell. Lunch at #60 with S. F. Pryor, Jr.

22 New York City. To the Deepdale Club with C. Roberts and W. E. Robinson. Dinner and bridge with C. Roberts, W. E. Robinson, and J. D. Brandon. To the Horace Mann Auditorium at Teachers College for the John Dewey birthday celebration in the evening.

23 New York City.

24 New York City. Morning appointment with J. D. Wise, O. R. McKenzie, and Vice-president Davis. Tour of Pupin Hall with Dr. Dunning. Lunch with L. Marx. To Carpenter Suite at Waldorf-Astoria for W. E. Robinson dinner. In the evening to the "*Herald Tribune* Forum" at the Waldorf-Astoria.

25 New York City. Morning appointments with Vice-president Davis; R. E. Larsen and C. V. Dollard; President Russell and Dr. Vincent; W. A. Johnston (president of the Illinois Central). Afternoon appointment with Robert L. Johnson (president of Temple University) and Dean Peabody. Meeting with the Columbia College Committee on Instruction, including Deans Carman and McKnight, Charles Cole, Jr., Professors Chamberlain, Chiappe, Prohock, Bernard Osgood Koopman (mathematics), Polycarp Kusch (physics), and Jan Schilt (astronomy).

26 New York City. To barber. Morning appointments with William L. White; Arthur Milam (*Yale News*); Gene Tunney and Edward Anthony (publisher, *Collier's* magazine); William Merriam Chadbourne (New York lawyer). To the Blind Brook Club for golf with C. Roberts, E. D. Slater, and Thomas Ivan Taylor (chemistry). Accompanied by Mrs. Eisenhower and Professor and Mrs. Thomas to the Men's Faculty Club for welcome dinner.

27 New York City. Morning appointments with DeWitte Poole (Committee for a Free Europe); Dr. Dunning. Early afternoon plane to Madison, Wisconsin. To Hotel

October		Lorraine in Madison (L. G. Fitzgerald, manager). Evening meeting with Dr. Conant.
	28	Madison. Leaves hotel with Dr. Conant for Association of American Universities business meeting and luncheon. Meeting adjourned in late afternoon; returns to hotel. Conversation with Mrs. Northcott, formerly Florence Eugle, of Abilene. Evening arrival (by plane) in New York City.
	29	New York City. Visit to #60 by General Sayler. Evening bridge with C. Roberts and W. E. Robinson.
	30	New York City. To West Point by auto with General Sayler.
	31	New York City. Morning appointments with J. Campbell; Robert Underwood Johnson; Professor John A. Moore re Dean Pegram's retirement; Mrs. A. H. Sulzberger. Luncheon with the trustees' Committee on Education at the Men's Faculty Club. Afternoon meeting of the College of Physicians and Surgeons Committee on Instruction. Telephone conversations with Congressman Thompson (Texas) re stopping in Galveston during Texas trip; General Hurley. To Council on Foreign Relations meeting in the evening.
November	1	New York City. Morning appointments with R. J. Furey and Dean McKnight; D. R. Calhoun, J. W. McAfee, and J. R. Forgan. Late morning inspection of the New York School of Social Work with Vice-president Pegram. Lunch at #60 with General Donovan and the Greek scholarship group. Afternoon appointments with W. E. Robinson; Edward R. Murrow for television photograph and Veterans Administration film (Trustees Room). To #60 for meeting with J. G. Jackson.
	2	New York City. Morning appointments with A. B. Kline; Congressman H. D. Scott, Jr. (Pennsylvania); M. K. Moir; Professor Powell. Lunch at #60 with Harry F. Guggenheim (president, Guggenheim Nitrate Corporation) and General Doolittle. Afternoon appointment with Y. El Bandak. Telephone conversations with Dean Rappleye; E. J. Bermingham. Evening visit by Mrs. Lamar at #60.

November 3   New York City. Morning appointments with Provost Kirk; W. M. Chadbourne; Admiral Samuel Murray Robinson. Lunch at #60 with Beardsley Ruml (chairman of the board, R. H. Macy Company) and W. Benton. Afternoon appointments with F. E. Wormser and John Meston Lovejoy (president, Seaboard Oil Company); Dr. Yukawa and Vice-president Pegram; Dean Rappleye. Telephone conversations with M. H. Dodge; Secretary Johnson re Admiral S. M. Robinson's plan for special corps of officers. To dinner honoring I. Geist.

4   New York City. Morning appointments with Harris Kennedy Masters (construction engineer); Dean Carman and Mr. Knabe; E. C. Anderson; J. Campbell; Russell S. Rymer (procurement specialist). Lunch with F. Eberstadt. In the afternoon to installation of K. D. Johnson as dean of the New York School of Social Work. Telephone conversations with A. G. Carter re Texas schedule; Colonel Denson (executive officer to General Larkin) re R. Rymer's piano. Evening cocktails with K. C. Royall and Howard McGrath.

5   Morning plane to Indianapolis. Midmorning arrival at Stout Field; met by Legionnaire Albert Starshak, Gene Pulliam (publisher, *Indianapolis Star*), and photographers. To American Legion National Headquarters for address to Legion's National Executive Committee. Lunch at the Antlers Hotel with Commander George Craig, Senator Capehart (Indiana), and ranking Army and Navy commanders. Afternoon visit with Ernest R. Lee (former Eisenhower aide) and his children. Late afternoon plane to New York City.

6   New York City.

7   New York City. Morning appointments with Provost Kirk; R. J. Furey; Professor Hacker; Judge Medina. Lunch with E. J. Bermingham and C. D. Dillon. Telephone conversation with J. Campbell. Afternoon appointment with J. Campbell. To J. Gould's for dinner and bridge with C. Roberts and R. W. Woodruff.

8   New York City. Election Day. To the polls with Mrs. Eisenhower in the morning. To the Blind Brook Club in the late morning for golf with W. E. Robinson, John

| November | | Stephen Burke (president, Altman Foundation), and C. Roberts. |

November Stephen Burke (president, Altman Foundation), and C. Roberts.

9 New York City. To barber. Morning appointments with H. C. Butcher; Ernest Floege (veteran with DSC) for autograph; Provost Kirk, Dean Ackerman, Maria Moors Cabot prizewinners, and photographers. To West Point in the afternoon. To Captain John S. D. Eisenhower's quarters, followed by football rally (with Cadet William Knapp) and dinner with the cadets. Returns to New York City in the evening; arrives at #60. To Pennsylvania Railroad Station for train to Annapolis, Maryland.

10 Early morning arrival in Baltimore, Maryland. Leaves for Annapolis by Navy auto in midmorning. Arrival at commandant's quarters, U.S. Naval Academy. To Commissioned Officers Mess for Service Academy Board meeting. Lunch in mess hall with brigade. Reconvenes Service Academy Board meeting in early afternoon. Viewing of dress parade, followed by reception at the superintendent's home for board members and their ladies.

11 Annapolis. Morning briefing on Academy curriculum, followed by tour. Service Academy Board session on inspection. Lunch on destroyer. Reconvenes Service Academy Board meeting in afternoon. Leaves in late afternoon for Harwood, Maryland, to visit General and Mrs. R. M. Littlejohn.

12 Annapolis. To Thompson Stadium in afternoon for Columbia-Navy football game, followed by reception at superintendent's home. Early evening departure for Baltimore. Train to New York City.

13 New York City.

14 New York City. Mrs. Eisenhower's birthday. Morning appointments with Provost Kirk; C. M. Tsaldaris and Mr. Kyrow re gift of Greek chair; J. D. Wise and Vice-president Davis; J. Campbell. Telephone conversations with S. W. Richardson; Alex Frieder re visiting while in Cincinnati; General Clay; and A. G. Carter re additional Texas invitations. Black-tie dinner at #60; guests include Mr. and Mrs. G. E. Allen, Mr. and Mrs. J. D. Brandon, General and Mrs. E. S. Hughes,

C. Roberts, General and Mrs. A. Nevins, W. E. Robinson, Mrs. L. B. Caffey, General Snyder, Major and Mrs. Schulz.

15 New York City. Breakfast with D. M. Black at #60. Morning appointments with Roy Holbrook (a friend of Eisenhower's from days in the Philippines); Oliver Martin Sayler (drama critic); Victor S. Bryant (member of committee to select president of the University of North Carolina); Provost Kirk; Vice-president Pegram. To U.S. Trust Company for luncheon meeting re Higgins estate. Afternoon appointments with G. V. Cooper; Dean Rappleye. Telephone conversations with General Bradley re Service Academy Board; J. H. Jones re Houston speaking engagement; Secretary Johnson re Service Academy Board; J. L. Hoen re Service Academy Board. Dinner with Mrs. Eisenhower and President and Mrs. Russell.

16 New York City. Milton S. Eisenhower visiting at #60. Morning appointments with J. B. Mintener; Vice-president Pegram; Professor Van Wagenen; J. E. Smith (of Harrisburg). To luncheon given by Advertising Club of New York for presentation of plaque of achievement.

17 New York City. Morning appointments with Dean Young; Professors Simmons and Lotz; Mr. Garrity (Internal Revenue Service); M. Fox. Luncheon meeting at the Waldorf-Astoria re Nutrition Foundation. Dinner at the Harvard Club with Professor and Mrs. E. J. Simmons. Accompanied by Mrs. Eisenhower to concert at the Manhattanville Center.

18 New York City. Morning appointments with L. Little; Vice-president Davis; W. H. Burnham; Mr. Miller (IBM). To the New York State Hospital Association luncheon at the Men's Faculty Club. Early afternoon meeting with Governor Dewey at #60.

19 New York City. Morning recording with Mr. Gannon for the American Cancer Society in the Trustees Room. Appointment with Major Fridtjof Endresen (Norway). Late morning golf at the Blind Brook Club with W. E. Robinson and W. A. Jones. Kickoff for the Columbia-Brown football game in the early afternoon. Eberstadt dinner at River House.

November 20   New York City. Afternoon address to reserves on Central Park Mall. To Johnson Hall in the evening for hearthfire lighting ceremony.

21   Morning departure by train to Valley Forge for presentation of the Freedom Awards of the Freedom Foundation. Met in Philadelphia by K. S. Wells and briefed while en route to Valley Forge. Presentation by park commissioner of relic of Valley Forge. Visit to Washington's headquarters, followed by luncheon at K. S. Wells's home. After lunch, brief talk by Eisenhower and presentation of awards. Early evening departure for Ohio.

22   Cincinnati. Tour by Cincinnati alumni. To Netherlands Plaza Hotel (met by Max Schulman, general manager). Visited by the A. Frieder family; G. V. Cooper; Vice-president Davis. Lunch at the University Club with Charles Finn Williams (president, Western and Southern Life Insurance Company), John Josiah Emery (chemical, railroad, and container company executive), Vice-president Davis, Charles M. Robertson (president, Proctor and Collier Company), William Hayden Chatfield (president, Chatfield Paper Corporation), Daniel J. O'Connor, F. Lazarus, Jr., Walter Clarence Beckjord (director, Cincinnati Gas and Electric Company), G. V. Cooper, Walter Max Shohl (Cincinnati lawyer), Richard Redwood Deupree (corporation official), Albert Peter Strietmann (chairman of the board, United Biscuit Company of America), and John C. Walter. Inspects new Terrace Plaza Hotel (at request of J. J. Emery, owner). Reception and alumni banquet at Netherlands Plaza Hotel. Presented with watch by Benjamin Samuel Katz (president, Gruen Watch Company). Evening train to New York City.

23   Late afternoon arrival in New York City. Dinner honoring H. Young at the St. Regis Hotel.

24   New York City. Thanksgiving.

25   New York City. Morning appointments with Professor Boris Stanfield; Mr. Garrity (Internal Revenue Service); Stanley Arnold; Provost Kirk; Mrs. Elizabeth Fisher and son Robert re appointment to West Point; Charles B. Coates (vice-chairman of Citizens Committee for

November the Hoover Report); School of Law Committee on Instruction. Telephone conversations with A. G. Redpath re personal estate; J. G. Jackson re personal estate and trustee matters; C. E. Wilson (General Motors) re informal dinner in January 1950; W. T. Faricy re Service Academy Board and ROTC matters.

26 New York City. Morning appointments with W. D. Fletcher; Otis Treat Bradley (New York lawyer).

27 New York City. Meets Field Marshal Slim at La Guardia Airport. To West Point in the afternoon with Mrs. Eisenhower for the christening of Barbara Anne Eisenhower.

28 New York City. Morning appointments with C. M. Malone; F. E. Holman; President Wallace Sterling of Stanford University; Field Marshal Montgomery; Dean Krout. Telephone conversations with J. D. Brandon re guns, hunting; J. B. Mintener re invitation from Associated Industries. To the University Club for lunch with the Columbia College Campaign Committee. To the French Embassy for presentation of the Grand Medal of the Society of Engineer Doctors. To Men's Faculty Club for student reception for fellows and graduate scholars. Late afternoon visit with General Sulzman at #60.

29 New York City. To barber. Morning appointments with Professor Rabi; J. Campbell; Provost Kirk; Mrs. William Russell to paint Eisenhower at work; Mr. Rovelstadt; Dr. Haven Emerson (professor emeritus); F. E. Wormser re engineering deanship. To lunch with the trustees at the Century Club. Afternoon appointments with F. W. Chambers; W. D. Fletcher; Mrs. Wagner (widow of a friend of John S. D. Eisenhower's); Christopher Daniels. Telephone conversations with W. D. Fletcher re personal estate; Commander Craig (American Legion) re invitation. Meeting with Council on Foreign Relations, followed by Varsity Club stag banquet at the Men's Faculty Club.

30 New York City. Morning appointments with M. H. Dodge; Dr. Ruth Alexander (journalist); Provost Kirk; Dean Pegram. Afternoon appointments with M. W. Watkins (Alumni Federation); General Donald Arm-

November		strong and K. C. McCann; Dr. Dunning. St. Andrew's Society dinner.
December	1	Morning plane to St. Louis. Late morning arrival at Scott Air Force Base. To Union Station; met by Frank C. Rand, Jr. (president, New Mexico Publishing Company). Mrs. Eisenhower arrives in St. Louis by train in the early afternoon. Lunch in Frisco car no. 2 with Mrs. Eisenhower and W. R. Cox. Leave St. Louis via Frisco/Katy Texas special train.
	2	San Antonio, Texas. Afternoon arrival in San Antonio. Visit with H. L. Mangum at Hotel George. Dinner with H. L. Mangum and Mr. and Mrs. A. A. Seeligson at the St. Anthony Hotel.
	3	San Antonio. St. Anthony Hotel. Mrs. Eisenhower leaves with Mrs. Lewis for Mrs. Seeligson's luncheon. Luncheon in suite with H. L. Mangum, Ragen Houston (president, Alamo National Bank), J. H. Frost, Robert Barclay (National Bank of Commerce), Leroy Denman (lawyer), Raymond Dickson (Houston oil), A. A. Seeligson, R. J. Kleberg, Jr., T. Armstrong, and Major Schulz. Dinner given by H. L. Mangum in Tapestry Room, St. Anthony Hotel.
	4	San Antonio. Early morning hunting with H. L. Mangum, A. A. Seeligson, T. Armstrong, John J. Shenin (host), and Gaines Whittington (guide).
	5	San Antonio. To black-tie dinner given by A. A. Seeligson.
	6	San Antonio.
	7	San Antonio. Early morning train to Houston. At Lamar Hotel in Houston. Late morning visit with the C. Campbells. Press conference. Luncheon at H. R. Cullen's. Addresses Houston Chamber of Commerce.
	8	Houston. To the Houston Club for Columbia alumni breakfast. Visits the University of Houston. To Galveston to address the Galveston Chamber of Commerce.
	9	To St. Joseph Island.
	10	St. Joseph Island.
	11	St. Joseph Island.

December 12 St. Joseph Island. Lunch at S. W. Richardson's with E. O. Thompson and others.

13 To Houston.

14 Houston. Train to Fort Worth.

15 Early morning arrival in Fort Worth. Lunch with Mr. and Mrs. A. G. Carter, Sr., at their home; other guests include A. G. Carter, Jr., S. W. Richardson, J. C. Gibson, and Major Schulz. Addresses Fort Worth Chamber of Commerce. Departure by train for New York City.

16 En route to New York.

17 En route to New York.

18 En route to New York.

19 New York City. To barber. Morning appointments with Provost Kirk and Shigeru Nambara (president, University of Tokyo); Dean Young; Dr. Dunning. To the School of General Studies with K. C. McCann for afternoon Christmas tea, followed by yule log lighting ceremony at John Jay Hall. Dinner honoring the Shah of Iran at the Men's Faculty Club.

20 New York City. Morning appointments with J. F. Dulles; E. J. Bermingham; Dr. Nevins and Mr. Canby; Dean Krout. Afternoon meeting with Professor Redslob (rector, Free University of Berlin). Meeting of the University Council in the Trustees Room, followed by meetings of the trustees and the Committee on Buildings and Grounds. Dinner with J. W. Byrnes.

21 New York City. Morning appointments with Dean K. D. Johnson, Provost Kirk, and Dr. Dunning; Dr. Rudolph De Villiers; Q. Reynolds; Joseph Buhler; G. V. Cooper. To Radio City Music Hall with W. E. Robinson in the evening.

22 New York City. Morning appointment with Provost Kirk and J. Campbell. Telephone conversation with R. A. Roberts. Stag dinner at #60.

23 New York City. Morning appointments with Dean Carman; Martin Philipsborn. Telephone conversation with L. Marx.

December 24 New York City. Lunch at 21 Club. Telephone conversation with General W. B. Smith.

25 Christmas.

26 New York City. Evening with Madge Robinson.

27 New York City. Morning appointment with Ralph Jonas re Jonas Foundation. To the Men's Faculty Club in the afternoon for Mathematical Society tea. Jones Foundation dinner at the Men's Faculty Club.

28 New York City. Morning appointments with Robert E. Merriam of Chicago; Robin Day and Geoffrey Johnson-Smith (Oxford University); President Horace A. Hildreth (Bucknell); Joseph Lindsey Henderson (teacher and author); Q. Reynolds; President Russell; Arthur Hill and Dean Johnson. Lunch at #60 with A. Hill. Telephone conversation with President Robert Sproul (University of California) re Bohemian Grove, 1950.

29 New York City. Morning appointments with Otto Smith (a friend from Kansas) and Mr. Poe; Q. Reynolds; Vice-president Davis. Holiday luncheon at the Columbia University Club, followed by meeting of the Committee on Education. Late afternoon appointment with Major Cannon. Telephone conversations with T. J. Watson re Dawn Patrol Breakfast; C. Roberts re bridge on New Year's Eve; Paul Evans Lockwood (secretary to Governor Dewey). Black-tie dinner at A. H. Sulzberger's.

30 New York City. To Arden House with Dean Johnson, K. C. McCann.

31 New York City.

1950

January 1 New York City.

2 New York City.

3 New York City. To barber. Afternoon meeting with Committee on Finance. Bridge in the evening with G. E. Allen and C. Roberts.

4 New York City. Dawn Patrol Breakfast for the Boy Scouts at the Waldorf-Astoria. Morning appointment

with C. V. Dollard, R. E. Larsen, Dr. W. S. Vincent, and President Russell. Afternoon appointments with Vice-president Davis; Chester Bert Bahn (editor of media journals); Edwin R. Gilliand (professor of chemical engineering, Massachusetts Institute of Technology).

5 New York City. Morning appointments with C. H. Babcock; C. Roberts.

6 New York City. Morning appointments with J. D. Wise and Provost Kirk; C. Mellen and Lester Grant (National Fund for Medical Education); Admiral Ben Morrell (chairman of the board, Jones & Laughlin Steel Corporation); General E. N. Clark. Luncheon given by T. J. Watson to honor Provost Kirk at the Union Club. Afternoon appointment with Vice-president Davis. Meeting on college development program with Dean Carman at the Men's Faculty Club. Cocktails with P. Grimm at #60.

7 New York City. Morning appointment with Dean Krout. Accompanied by Mrs. Eisenhower to luncheon at L. Marx's in Scarsdale, New York, followed by christening of L. B. Marx.

8 New York City. Stag dinner at the Plaza Hotel with C. E. Wilson (of General Motors).

9 New York City. Morning appointments with Mr. and Mrs. E. E. Connor; Ralph Madia to receive sculpture from Italy; Dr. J. E. Zanetti; Colby Chester and Dr. Dunning. Trustees luncheon at the Men's Faculty Club. Afternoon trustees meeting. Appointment with Rabbi Hoffman concerning 50th anniversary of Earl Hall (university interfaith center). To Metropolitan Club stag dinner with W. H. Burnham.

10 New York City. Morning appointments with Dr. and Miss Pavry; Dean White; Sir Robert Grensden; Dr. Dunning; Congressman Hugh D. Scott (Pennsylvania). Luncheon re engineering development at the Men's Faculty Club. To Council on Foreign Relations meeting.

11 New York City. Morning meetings with R. J. Furey and Dean McKnight; Wendell Phillips; B. Barton; Vice-president Davis. Lunch at #60 with J. C. Walter and C. E. Wilson. Afternoon appointments with R. V.

January   New; *Quarto* editors. To black-tie dinner for Society of Older Graduates at the University Club with F. S. Hackett.

12   New York City. To black-tie dinner at G. H. Montague's with Mrs. Eisenhower.

13   New York City. Appointments canceled because of illness.

14   New York City.

15   New York City.

16   New York City. Morning appointments with David Lawrence (editor of *U.S. News & World Report*); Congressman Frances P. Bolton (Ohio); General Wendell Westover (president, Reserve Officers Association, Department of New York); John Clarendon Schraam (managing director, Calvin Kazajian Economics Foundation) and William A. Forbes. Lunch at #60 with M. H. Dodge and A. C. Jacobs. Afternoon meeting with the board of trustees of the Metropolitan Museum of Art.

17   New York City. To barber. Morning appointments with Provost Kirk, Dean Krout, Chaplain Pike, and Vice-president Davis; Professor E. M. Fisher (School of Business) re land and housing studies; General Joyce. Afternoon meeting with Columbia atomic energy group; Dr. Dunning. Accompanied by Mrs. Eisenhower to black-tie dinner given by H. J. Taylor (journalist and economist) and Mrs. Taylor.

18   New York City. Morning appointments with Harry E. Ewing of Buenos Aires re possibility of South American tour for Eisenhower; K. D. McCormick; J. Campbell; Ernestine Evans (documentary film maker) and Professor Robert Morrison MacIver; Jeanne Dixon (former SHAEF employee). Tour of the university campus with Dean Krout. Afternoon appointment with F. Coykendall. Meeting with the New York School of Social Work board of trustees. Informal dinner at #60 for the J. D. Brandons and General and Mrs. Joyce.

19   New York City. By plane to Washington for General H. H. Arnold's funeral service. Return to New York City. Evening train to South Carolina.

January 20 Warrenville, South Carolina. Departure by auto for Augusta National Golf Club, Augusta, Georgia. Remains in Augusta until January 26.

26 Augusta. Morning departure by military aircraft. Early afternoon arrival at Lawson Air Force Base, Georgia. By private auto to E. J. Bermingham's Enon Farm in Midway, Alabama, arriving in the midafternoon.

27 Midway.

28 Midway.

29 Midway.

30 Midway. By auto to Newton, Georgia. Noon arrival at R. W. Woodruff's Ichauway Plantation. Evening bridge with William C. Patter (retired president, Guarantee Trust Company), Richard Tuft (in the real estate business in Albany, Georgia), and Ken Hodges (in the hardware business in Albany).

31 Newton. A note here records that during the twenty-one working days in January 1950, Eisenhower received twenty-one hundred pieces of mail, or an average of one hundred letters a day.

February 1 Newton.

2 By plane to Turner Air Force Base, Albany, Georgia. Lunch in officers' dining room. By plane to Washington, arriving in the late afternoon. By plane to New York City, arriving in the early evening.

3 New York City.

4 New York City. Morning appointment with M. H. Dodge, Vice-president Davis, and Provost Kirk. Telephone conversation with Governor Dewey.

5 New York City.

6 New York City. Morning appointments with President Russell; General E. N. Clark; J. F. Brownlee; Dean Smith; A. Gardner; Dean Krout; M. H. Dodge. Afternoon board of trustees meeting. Telephone conversations with Milton S. Eisenhower; G. L. Harrison.

7 New York City. To barber. Morning appointments with Vice-president J. Campbell; Dean Pickel; Professor Henry Crampton re invitation to H. L. Stimson; General Carl-

February   ton S. Dargusch (public service affairs); J. Gunther. Lunch with William A. Brady and the National City Bank board of directors.

8   New York City. Morning appointments with Dean Krout; K. D. Johnson; W. D. Fletcher; S. Braden re dinner for T. J. Watson. Lunch with A. H. Sulzberger in his office at the *New York Times* Building re Columbia Bicentennial Committee. Departure for New Haven, Connecticut, and *Yale Daily News* banquet.

9   New York City. Morning appointment with Vice-president J. Campbell. Lunch with Mrs. Eisenhower and R. L. Biggers at #60. The Moles dinner at the Waldorf-Astoria.

10   New York City. Morning appointments with Dr. Dunning; Mark Woods (vice-chairman of the American Broadcasting Company). Tours the School of Business with Dean Young. Lunch at the Men's Faculty Club with Dean Young. Afternoon appointments with Provost Kirk; Dr. Dunning; J. T. Cahill and F. S. Hogan; Dean Rappleye. Telephone conversation with Secretary Johnson re naval research and H-Bomb project. Evening bridge with W. E. Robinson, H. C. Flanigan, and John Michael Budinger (president, Commercial Bank and Trust Company).

11   New York City. Lunch with Mrs. Eisenhower and S. P. Skouras, followed by special showing of the film *Twelve O'Clock High*. Dinner with Mrs. Eisenhower at the K. C. Royalls'.

12   New York City.

13   New York City. Morning appointments with G. K. Howard (vice-president, Ford Motor Company, and member of the Council on Foreign Relations); J. L. Hennessy. American Institute of Mining and Metallurgical Engineers luncheon at the Statler Hotel. Afternoon appointments with Vice-president Pegram; Vice-president Campbell.

14   New York City. Morning appointments with Vice-president Campbell; J. M. Kaplan (Welch Grape Juice Company), arranged by Dean Young; Provost Kirk, H. F. Armstrong, and W. H. Mallory re Council on

Foreign Relations; Dean Young. Lunch with H. Ford II at #60. Afternoon appointments with E. O. Thompson (railroad commissioner of Texas); Vice-president Campbell. Telephone conversation with G. K. Howard re H. Ford II visit. Accompanied by Mrs. Eisenhower to dinner given by the D. M. Blacks in honor of General and Mrs. Clay.

15 New York City. Morning appointments with Lord J. Boyd Orr re U.N. food plan; R. J. Furey. Varsity Club luncheon at the Men's Faculty Club. Afternoon appointments with A. W. Berg; Emmet Anderson (a friend of Edgar N. Eisenhower's), Bruce A. Campbell (Illinois lawyer), and James R. Nicholson. Evening Council on Foreign Relations meeting.

16 New York City. Morning appointment with Mrs. E. W. Biggs. To American Red Cross springboard luncheon with Mrs. Eisenhower. Alexander Hamilton dinner at the Ritz Carlton.

17 New York City. Morning appointments with Dean Krout; Professor Christo-Loveanu to sit for portrait; Arthur Bliss Lane. Nutrition Foundation luncheon. Afternoon appointments with Vice-president Pegram; Professor Rabi. Evening cocktails at the Spragues'.

18 New York City. Morning appointment with D. M. Black. Lunch with H. D. Collier, E. M. Burnham, J. C. Black, and Torkild Rieber (chairman of the board, American Gilsonite Company) at #60.

19 New York City. Supper at Women's Faculty Club with Mrs. Eisenhower.

20 New York City. Morning appointments with R. J. Furey; R. Harron; and F. S. Murphy (at request of W. H. Burnham). To Rockefeller Foundation luncheon at the Men's Faculty Club with Professor D. Wallace and C. I. Barnard. Meeting at Russian Institute. Photographer at #60 in early evening for photographs with Mrs. Eisenhower.

21 New York City. To barber. Morning appointments with Chaplain Pike; Dean Krout and General E. N. Clark; R. J. Furey. Afternoon appointments with the University Council and the Committee on Buildings and

February | Grounds; D. Wallace; H. E. Stassen at #60. Telephone conversations with Ambassador Henri Bonnet re invitation to accept membership in French organization; H. B. Swope re talk at American Mining and Metallurgical Association.

22 New York City. Morning appointment with Dean McIntosh and Jean Palmer re the Barnard Development Plan. Campus tour with Dean Carman. Late afternoon meeting with H. B. Swope at #60. Black-tie dinner at the George Vetlesens'.

23 New York City. Morning appointments with M. H. Dodge; E. O. Thompson. Teachers College alumni greeting. Afternoon appointment with Dean Young. Lunch at #60 with Dean Young and R. A. Lovett. By train to Washington with Mrs. Eisenhower. To the Statler Hotel for evening with the Gruenthers, Saylers, Snyders, and Caffeys.

24 Washington. To Walter Reed General Hospital for appointment with Colonel A. E. Toye, and Mrs. Eisenhower's appointment with Major Lewis Humbert Riva. Midmorning appearance before House Armed Services Committee on budget. Meeting with General Arnold. Return to the Pentagon for appointments with W. S. Symington; Secretary Johnson. Lunch with General J. L. Collins in his office. Late afternoon train to New York City.

25 New York City. Morning appointments with Warren Wolf; Dan O'Keefe; Professors Earle and Kerr; Frank McCarthy. Lunch, skeet shoot, and tea with General Wickersham at Rockaway Hunt Club, Cedarhurst, Long Island.

26 New York City. Lunch with W. A. Harriman at #60.

27 New York City. Morning appointments with Mrs. H. R. Reid; John T. Van Sant and Carl H. Pforzheimer, Sr. (of the Horace Mann School); General E. N. Clark and Dean Krout; F. Coykendall. Afternoon appointments with Vice-president Pegram; Dean Krout. Meeting with the Education Committee. Accompanied by Mrs. Eisenhower to black-tie dinner in honor of Mr. and Mrs. C.J.H. Hays at the Men's Faculty Club.

February 28	New York City. Morning appointments with W. Webster; Dean Johnson; G. K. Howard; Mr. Burbank and President Rogers (Brooklyn Polytechnical Institute); Dr. Flexner; Dean Smith, Vice-president Campbell, and A. G. Redpath; C. W. Boyer (of River Brethren Church, Dayton, Ohio). Dinner with Mr. and Mrs. G. A. Sloan, followed by *Tosca* at the Metropolitan Opera House.
March 1	Morning train to Philadelphia. Temple University Moving Up Day.
2	Lancaster, Pennsylvania. Franklin and Marshall College convocation in the morning. By afternoon train to New York City.
3	New York City. Morning appointments with Dean Young; George Shuster (president of Hunter College) and Dean Carman; Vice-president Pegram and M. H. Burkholder (Columbia alumnus from Abilene); Arthur Kroeger; General E. N. Clark and R. W. Davenport; K. G. Crawford. Afternoon appointments with Major Ted Brown; Professor Christo-Loveanu (to sit for portrait) and D. M. Black; A. W. Berg's committee re Columbia's development program. John Jay Forum on Freedom and Democracy dinner.
4	New York City.
5	New York City. To Lambs' Gambol for cocktails, dinner, and theater. The J. S. Douds depart for Denver.
6	New York City. Morning appointments with Provost Kirk, Vice-president Campbell, Dean Krout, Dean Smith, and Dean Wallace; Dr. Dunning; L. Little and Chester LaRoche (advertising executive); F. E. Wormser and J. M. Lovejoy (Seaboard Oil). Lunch at #60 with A. H. Sulzberger and J. P. Binns. Afternoon appointment with F. Coykendall. Board of trustees meeting. Dinner with J. D. Rockefeller III. Telephone conversation with M. H. Dodge.
7	New York City. Morning appointments with Henry Alexander (J. P. Morgan & Company) and E. B. Schwulst (president, Greater New York Fund); General Wickersham, John W. Davis, George Serenbetz, F. R. Coudert, and Hunter L. Delatour re Nassau County

March   Bar Association. Lunch at #60 with A. M. Godfrey. Afternoon appointment with William Augustus Hanway (secretary, International Paper Company). Telephone conversations with W. S. Symington re Eisenhower's report of 3 November 1947; W. W. Aldrich re lunch on March 10. To the University Club for stag dinner forum given by A. Kroeger.

8   New York City. To barber. Morning appointments with President Russell and Professor Shaffer; Vice-president Campbell. Tours Columbia College. Lunch at #60 with E. E. Newsom. To dinner with Mrs. Eisenhower at the J. F. Dulleses'.

9   New York City. Morning appointment with D. M. Black at #60. Lunch at #60 with C. D. Dillon and E. J. Bermingham. W. H. Burnham to #60 for afternoon meeting. Dinner and bridge at #60 with C. Roberts, W. E. Robinson, and E. D. Slater.

10   New York City. Morning appointments with Dr. Tarokawa and Mr. Ushioda (presidents of two Japanese universities); A. M. Massie (trustee); Dean Arnaud; G. W. Buckner, Jr.; R. Rodgers. Lunch at #60 with R. Rodgers and W. W. Aldrich. Afternoon appointment with C. D. Dillon. To *Herald Tribune* dinner meeting with Mrs. H. R. Reid.

11   New York City. Accompanied by Mrs. Eisenhower to luncheon for the Columbia Scholastic Press Institute at the Waldorf-Astoria. Dinner at the R. L. Clarksons'.

12   To Absecon, New Jersey.

13   Absecon. To Seaview Country Club with G. E. and Mary Allen.

14   Absecon.

15   Absecon.

16   Absecon. W. E. Robinson arrives in late afternoon.

17   Absecon. E. D. Slater and Mrs. Slater arrive.

18   Leaves Absecon in the afternoon and returns to #60.

19   Views film *Francis the Mule*.

20   New York City. Lunch at #60 with Dr. Dunning, H. Krumb, W. H. Aldridge, J. M. Lovejoy, and H. S.

March   Mudd. Afternoon meeting of the Metropolitan Museum of Art's board of trustees. Evening meeting of the Council on Foreign Relations.

21   New York City. Morning appointments with President Russell; Harry W. Shacter (of Kentucky) re citizenship. Afternoon meetings with K. C. McCann; Vice-president Pegram and Provost Kirk; E. Goldman; Committee on Buildings and Grounds in the Trustees Room. Evening meeting with Mrs. Eisenhower and the New Jersey Columbia alumni at the Hotel Essex in Newark.

22   New York City. To barber. Morning campus tour with Dean Carman. Lunch at the Men's Faculty Club. Evening meeting of the National Fund for Medical Education at the Cloud Club of the Chrysler Building. Telephone conversation with W. S. Symington re trip to New York. To black-tie dinner at G. H. Sibley's with Mrs. Eisenhower.

23   New York City. Morning appointments with K. C. McCann; Dean Rappleye; David Heyman; Alice Gram Robinson (writer and editor). Evening meeting with Colonel and Mrs. Stack at #60. Gabriel Silver Lecture (given by Eisenhower) at the McMillin Theater.

24   New York City. Morning appointments with Arthur K. Watson; J. M. Bovard (of the Carnegie Institute of Pittsburgh); Robert Christenberry (VFW Security Council); Dean Finch; Major Gault; Vice-president Campbell; R. W. Woodruff. Lunch at #60 with R. W. Woodruff and Dean Young. Afternoon appointment with Vice-president G. B. Pegram. Telephone conversations with General W. B. Smith re personal matters; F. E. Wormser re the engineering program; and W. S. Symington re his visit to New York on March 25. Afternoon trip to Governors Island for visit with General W. B. Smith.

25   New York City. Morning appointments with Ambassador Jessup; Sir Leslie Rowan (Deputy to the British Ambassador and Economic Minister in the Embassy); Dr. Rabi. Visit to artist T. E. Stephens's studio with General Snyder. Afternoon visit by W. S. Symington. Evening visit with the Arthur B. Eisenhowers, W. E. Robinson, and W. S. Symington.

March 26   New York City. Telephone conversation with General
            Gruenther.

27   New York City. Morning appointments with G. K.
            Howard; Dr. Rabi; Committee on Education in the
            Trustees Room; and Commander P. H. Grouleff
            (NROTC). Afternoon appointments with Dean Finch;
            General Wyman; General and Mrs. W. H. Simpson
            (British) at #60. Telephone conversations with Am-
            bassador Jessup re statement of the President on Jessup's
            remaining in the State Department; General Draper re
            a proposed visit by the Minister of Pakistan to the United
            States in mid-April; Colonel James Curtis (aide to Sec-
            retary Gray) re the Signal Corps contracts between the
            Army and Columbia. In the evening bridge at #60
            with G. E. Allen, C. Roberts, and W. E. Robinson.

28   New York City. Morning appointments with Provost
            Kirk and Professor Wallace; Dr. Shotwell (Carnegie
            Foundation); Blinded Veterans. Lunch at Men's Faculty
            Club with military history group. Afternoon meeting
            with B. M. Baruch at his home. Telephone conver-
            sations with General Wyman re General W. B. Smith's
            going into Walter Reed General Hospital; General Wy-
            man to advise Eisenhower that General Smith has agreed
            to go to Walter Reed General Hospital; General C. R.
            Gray (Director of the Veterans Administration) re the
            establishment of a branch of blinded veterans; W. W.
            Aldrich re a meeting with Harold Seymour, R. Rodgers,
            and W. W. Aldrich on university development; General
            Arnold to verify his understanding of Eisenhower's pres-
            entation to the Mahon committee on February 24; K.
            C. Royall re a meeting with General Covell and playing
            bridge. Accompanied by Mrs. Eisenhower to dinner
            with the Westchester County alumni at the Apawamis
            Club.

29   Morning plane to Washington. Dental appointment with
            Colonel Toye at Walter Reed. Morning appointments
            at the Pentagon with Secretary S. T. Early; W. S.
            Symington; and General Gruenther. Lunch with Vice-
            president A. W. Barkley. Open-session hearing before
            Senate Appropriations Committee. Afternoon appoint-
            ments with Secretary Early and W. S. Symington; Gen-

March eral Gruenther, Captain William George Lalor, and General Haislip.

30 Washington. Educational Policies Commission meeting. To Columbia alumni dinner with Mrs. Eisenhower.

31 Washington. Educational Policies Commission meeting. Lunch with S. W. Richardson. Evening held for General Gruenther or G. E. Allen.

April 1 Washington. Educational Policies Commission meeting. To Burning Tree Country Club with J. C. Black and A. A. Seeligson in the afternoon. Early evening visit with the Gruenthers.

2 New York City. To dinner with Mrs. Eisenhower at Mr. and Mrs. Ledyard's (Mrs. Stokes's mother).

3 New York City. Morning meeting with Professor Vincent. Afternoon meetings with the trustees' Honors Committee and the board of trustees in Trustees Room. Telephone conversations with Secretary Johnson re Eisenhower's recommendations in congressional testimony; Dean Smith; Professor Rabi; Dean Rappleye; Professor Irwin Edman; Professors Carter and C. L. Goodrich re proposal to name Provost Kirk successor to Vice-president Pegram and the consolidation of the two positions. To stag dinner at the Links Club with D. R. Calhoun.

4 New York City. Morning appointment with Major Gault. Meeting with W. W. Aldrich, Harold Seymour, and R. Rodgers at the Brook Club. To the Hotel Commodore with General Marshall for International House luncheon. Afternoon visit to John Erskine with Professor I. Edman. Accompanied by Mrs. Eisenhower to cocktails with K. C. and Mrs. Royall. To stag dinner at the Brook Club with K. C. Royall.

5 New York City. To barber. Morning appointments with Vice-president Davis; General E. N. Clark; Provost Kirk; Professors Thomas Bradford Drew (Columbia, chemical engineering), Henry Blood Linford (Columbia, chemical engineering), and Robert Stanley Livingston (University of Minnesota, chemistry). Campus

April	tour. Lunch at the Men's Faculty Club. Afternoon appointments with Professor Erwin H. Amick; E. Goldman and H. Tritz. Telephone conversations with F. Coykendall and Dean Finch re appointment of Dr. Dunning.
6	New York City. Morning appointments with Tex Moore (Law Center); Robert Browning and James C. Olson (Booz, Allen, and Hamilton); and W. H. Burnham. New York State Chamber of Commerce luncheon honoring J. D. Rockefeller, Jr. To Century Club dinner for H. L. Stimson.
7	New York City. Morning appointments with G. W. Buckner, Jr.; W. H. Mallory and H. M. Wriston; C. M. Malone; E. N. Khouri, who presents two Worcester Royal Porcelain birds. Dinner at #60 with the A. A. Seeligsons.
8	New York City. To Cedarhurst, Long Island, for lunch and skeet shoot with General Wickersham. Accompanied by Mrs. Eisenhower to dinner at Mr. and Mrs. Harold Brooks's.
9	Departure by train for Augusta, Georgia.
10	Arrival in Warrenville, South Carolina; by auto to Augusta, Georgia. To stay in Augusta until August 22, when the Eisenhowers depart by train for New York City.
23	New York City. W. A. and E. R. Harriman to lunch at #60 with K. C. McCann, Dean Young, Ken Jackson, Dr. Dunning, Dean Krout, Provost Kirk, and W. D. Fletcher.
24	New York City. To the Waldorf-Astoria for Associated Press luncheon. Afternoon meeting of the Association of American Universities. Evening meeting of the Council on Foreign Relations.
25	New York City. To barber. Morning appointments with C. Arthur Larsen; L. V. Finder; Captain F. Patillo and Cadet Jay Parker (New York Military Academy); C. P. Davis and A. D. Hinckley; Vera Roberts (former interpreter for Eisenhower). Luncheon meeting at the University Club with General E. N. Clark and Dean Krout to discuss the chair for peace at Columbia. After-

April   noon appointments with D. M. Black; Dean Rappleye. To dinner with Mrs. Eisenhower at the Edward L. Tinkers'.

26   New York City. Morning appointments with M. H. Dodge; Committee on Education. To Higgins Trust luncheon. Late afternoon meeting with General Clay at #60. Telephone conversation with W. D. Fletcher re meeting with W. A. Harriman. Accompanied by Mrs. Eisenhower to Academy of Political Science black-tie dinner at the Hotel Astor. After dinner with W. E. Robinson, E. D. Slater, Ed Barber, Gene Tunney, R. Christenberry, C. Roberts, and Frank Willard.

27   New York City. Morning campus tour with Dean Carman. Appointments with General E. P. Curtis; R. A. Roberts. Late morning golf at Blind Brook Country Club with G. E. Allen, Gene Tunney, and E. D. Slater. Telephone conversations with Secretary Johnson; Admiral R. E. Byrd (of Boston); Senator H. F. Byrd (Virginia). Accompanied by Mrs. Eisenhower to reception given by the Association for University Teas at the Men's Faculty Club.

28   New York City. Morning appointments with General Covell, Dr. Eduardo Aranjo, Maurice Dineman, and B. J. McKenna; Captain H. G. Moran to present Commander E. J. Kroeger; John Coalter, F. Eberstadt, and Paul V. Shields (Curtis-Wright); General Kenneth F. Kramer (Chief of the National Guard); Vice-president Campbell, L. Little, and Ferris Booth.

29   New York City. Morning appointments with Roy Rutherford; Richard M. Pittinger (Director of Public Relations, Portland Chamber of Commerce). Telephone conversation with General J. L. Collins. Golf at the Blind Brook Country Club with C. Roberts, W. E. Robinson, and C. Frazer. Accompanied by Mrs. Eisenhower to John Lyon dinner at the Men's Faculty Club.

30   New York City. To the Cathedral of St. John the Divine to attend 100th anniversary celebration of St. Luke's Hospital. Evening supper and bridge at #60 for the J. D. Brandons, G. E. Allens, and C. Roberts.

May   1   New York City. Morning staff conference. Appointment with H. M. Schley. Trustees luncheon meeting

May in A. H. Sulzberger's office. Bridge in the evening at #60 with G. E. Allen, J. D. Brandon, and W. E. Robinson.

2 New York City. Morning appointments with Dean Carman; Vice-president Campbell re Columbia College. Afternoon dedication of the Nevis Cyclotron.

3 New York City. Morning appointments with Dr. Shotwell; Dean Rappleye; representative of Voice of America; Ernest Dale; A. G. Carter. Lunch with General Drum, J. J. Raskob, Mr. and Mrs. L. Marx, and Prince Bernhardi at the Empire State Building. Telephone conversations with C. B. Luce; H. L. Stimson.

4 New York City. Morning appointments with Dr. John H. H. Lyon; Dean Krout. Lunch and annual meeting of the Carnegie Endowment for International Peace. Afternoon appointments with J. B. Mintener; E. J. Bermingham; H. J. Taylor. Early evening appointment with Professor and Mrs. Paul Francis Kerr. Accompanied by Mrs. Eisenhower to Kemp dinner at the Men's Faculty Club.

5 New York City. Morning meeting re development with D. M. Black, J. G. Jackson, A. G. Redpath, and L. D. Egbert. To citizenship conference at Teachers College with H. J. Taylor and R. E. Larsen. To Cold Spring Harbor, New York, in the afternoon to visit H. L. Stimson.

6 New York City. Morning appointments with Dean Krout; Provost Kirk; W. C. Davis; M. W. Childs. Golf at Blind Brook Country Club with W. E. Robinson. To black-tie General Studies dinner with Professor L. M. Hacker.

7 New York City.

8 New York City. Morning appointments with R. Harron; George M. Shuster (president, Hunter College); Professor E. J. Simmons and Russian group; D. M. Black and Professor Christo-Loveanu. Lunch with W. H. Burnham and L. F. McCollum (president, Continental Oil Company). Afternoon appointment with Dean Young. To the Trustees Room to present honorary degree to His Excellency Liaquat Ali Khan. Telephone

May   conversation with General Gruenther re invitation to English Speaking Union meeting in October. Bridge at #60 with G. E. Allen, C. Roberts, and W. E. Robinson in the evening.

9   New York City. The G. G. Moores arrive in early morning at Pier 12, Staten Island. Morning appointments with Dean Carman; Colonel José Ramos; B. F. Gimbel and Football Committee; Henry Morton Robinson (editor). To Fourth Floor Cabinet luncheon with leaders of extracurricular activities at the Men's Faculty Club. Becomes ill in the afternoon.

10   New York City. Appointments canceled due to illness.

11   New York City. Appointments canceled due to illness.

12   New York City. Morning appointment with J. D. Rockefeller III at #60. To bed after meeting.

13   New York City. Appointments canceled due to illness. Telephone conversation with G. Gray.

14   New York City. Eisenhower at home. Christening of C. C. Cannon, Jr., at #60 in the afternoon.

15   New York City. No appointments. Telephone conversation with T. J. Watson. Dinner at E. R. Harriman's with Mrs. Eisenhower.

16   New York City. To barber. Morning appointment with Francis A. Englehart and four other Vermonters. Accompanied by Mrs. Eisenhower to reception and dinner for T. J. Watson (American Arbitration Association).

17   New York City. Morning appointments with Generals E. N. Clark and J. A. Adler; Dean Young; G. E. Sokolsky. Telephone conversations with D. R. Calhoun re fishing trip; S. W. Richardson re hunting in Mexico. Afternoon golf. Accompanied by Mrs. Eisenhower to black-tie dinner with C. R. Black.

18   New York City. All appointments canceled. Golf at Blind Brook Country Club with C. Roberts, W. E. Robinson, and A. Nielsen. To Evening School of Business Seminar with B. M. Baruch in the evening.

19   New York City. Morning appointments with W. T. Faricy; Colonel Richard Stevens; J. H. Crider (editor,

May		*Boston Herald*); A. Wingfield; Provost Kirk, Vice-president Campbell, Frederick Sheffield (New York lawyer), and E. J. Price. Accompanied by Mrs. Eisenhower to review NROTC midshipmen at South Field.

20 Morning plane to Washington. Meeting with Secretary Johnson and General Ridgway. Meeting with the President at the White House. To reviewing stand in late morning for Armed Forces Day parade. Lunch in General Ridgway's office. Early afternoon plane to New York City.

21 New York City.

22 New York City. Morning appointments with Vice-president Pegram; Noel Busch and R. Harron; R. Christenberry; office staff; R. Rodgers; R. Harron re *New York Times* article about Milton S. Eisenhower. Lunch at #60 with J. B. Mintener. Cocktails at #60 with W. H. Burnham, S. B. Flynn, D. S. Kennedy, Frank Potter, and the J. R. Spragues. C. Roberts, W. E. Robinson, G. E. Allen, and W. A. Jones at #60 in the evening for bridge.

23 Morning plane to Hartford, Connecticut. To meet Columbia alumni at Hartford's Bradley Field for the dedication of the airport building at noon. Early afternoon return to New York City.

24 New York City. Morning appointments with Messrs. Frank, Bonyhadi, Elkins, Pinkers, and Preble from Shanks Village Committee; Lindsey Rodgers, W. H. Mallory, and Provost Kirk. Lunch with C. Roberts, R. W. Woodruff, and F. F. Gosden at the Links Club, followed by golf at the Deepdale Club. Evening meeting of the Council on Foreign Relations.

25 New York City. Morning appointments with L. Little; A. M. Hill; Dean Johnson; A. W. Berg and Provost Kirk; Vice-president Campbell; Eugene Sheffer (French House). To luncheon given for P. S. Mesta by T. J. Watson and M. Woll. Telephone conversation with F. G. Gurley re Bohemian Grove. Accompanied by Mrs. Eisenhower to black-tie dinner at the Walter Hovings'.

26 New York City. Morning appointments with District Attorney F. S. Hogan; I. Geist; Dr. Dunning; George

May	Cooper and K. C. McCann. Lunch at #60 with A. Nielsen. Telephone conversation with W. S. Symington re golf at Southampton in June. Afternoon visit with General W. B. Smith at Governors Island.
27	New York City. Morning golf at the Blind Brook Country Club. To Pawling, New York, in afternoon for dinner with the H. J. Taylors and L. Thomas.
28	New York City.
29	New York City. Morning staff meeting. Appointment with R. C. Leffingwell and Under Secretary Tracy S. Voorhees. Lunch with F. R. Coudert and Secretary Finletter at the Century Association. Evening bridge at #60 with E. D. Slater, C. Roberts, W. E. Robinson, and G. E. Allen.
30	New York City. No appointments. To West Point for Barbara Anne Eisenhower's birthday.
31	New York City. To barber. Morning appointment with Dean Krout. Late morning golf. Afternoon appointments with F. Coykendall; Dean Smith. Telephone conversations with General M. W. Clark re his visit on June 9; K. C. Royall re invitation to North Carolina. To stag dinner with W. L. Kleitz and Willis Booth at the Racquet Club.
June 1	New York City. Morning appointments with Dr. Hollington K. Tong (Cairo Conference); General E. N. Clark; Dr. Armand Hammer. Meeting of the President's Examination Committee in the Trustees Room. Appointment with Wesley Hardenbergh (American Meat Institute). Lunch at #60 with M. Woll, Dean Young, and Dean Carman. Afternoon meeting with A. Hatch.
2	New York City.
3	New York City. Early afternoon departure for West Point reunion of the USMA Class of 1915. Late afternoon arrival at West Point. Steak fry.
4	West Point. E. Leone barbecue.
5	West Point. Morning meeting of the trustees of the Association of Graduates, USMA. Luncheon given by the Association and presentation of class gift to the sons

June	of graduates. Telephone conversation with Vice-president Campbell re Arden House.
6	New York City. Morning appointments with Jack Connelly and Ralph Cate; Dean Young. Meeting with Committee on Education in the Trustees Room. Lunch at #60 with W. H. Burnham, L. F. McCollum, and Dean Young. Telephone conversations with W. D. Fletcher re Arden House Project; M. H. Dodge; and Dean Johnson re Arden House Project.
7	New York City. Morning appointments with K. C. McCann and Professor Hacker; General H. J. Collins. Morning Columbia College class day exercises in Hamilton Hall. Lunch with A. C. Jacobs at the Men's Faculty Club. Afternoon appointments with Vice-president Campbell, Dr. Dunning, and Arthur E. Pew, Jr. (oil industry executive); Dr. Aristad V. Grosse (chemist), Dr. Eugene T. Booth, Sr. (physicist), and S. A. Bower. Telephone conversations with Tom Armstrong re invitation to races; S. W. Richardson re Committee for Free Europe.
8	New York City. Morning appointments with Dick McKay; alumni trustee nominating committee in the Trustees Room. Alumni luncheon, followed by University commencement at Butler Library.
9	New York City. Breakfast at #60 with H. A. Bullis, W. H. Burnham, and General Robert Hilliard Mills. Morning appointments with General M. W. Clark; Calvin Clyde Murray (dean, University of Georgia); Miss Katherine Z. W. Whipple and Miss Beatrice Troupier; Dean Krout and K. C. McCann. Afternoon appointments with Senator Lodge (Massachusetts); Isabel Ross re article on Dean McIntosh; Dean Hollis Leland Caswell. Telephone conversations with D. Sarnoff; D. R. Calhoun re Minneapolis trip; W. H. Burnham, also re Minneapolis trip; J. R. Sprague. To musical *South Pacific* with Mrs. Eisenhower and the Jack Carlsons in the evening.
10	New York City. Morning golf. Nassau County Bar Association dinner.
11	New York City. Accompanied by Mrs. Eisenhower to

June   Hofstra College commencement to receive honorary degree.

12   New York City. Morning appointments with Vice-president Davis; Robert Russell (son of W. F. Russell); D. M. Black; R. Harron and Bruno Shaw; Dean Krout. Meets with Central Savings Bank executive committee and trustees in the afternoon. Telephone conversation with C. Roberts re golf. Evening bridge at #60 with C. Roberts, W. E. Robinson, and C. V. McAdam.

13   New York City. To barber. Morning appointments with Brad Davis (son of B. H. Davis); General E. N. Clark; W. S. Symington. Afternoon appointments with W. D. Fletcher re Arden House; A. E. Smith to sit for portrait; Judge William Clark (former staff member of Eisenhower's). Telephone conversation with A. H. Sulzberger re Bicentennial plans. Bridge in the evening at #60 with G. E. Allen, C. Roberts, E. D. Slater, and C. V. McAdam.

14   New York City. Morning appointments with W. H. Burnham; P. Barnum; C. B. Luce. Late morning departure for the Deepdale Country Club for lunch and golf with General J. L. Collins, C. Roberts, and Byron Nelson. Late afternoon return. Dinner with General Collins at #60 before his return to Washington.

15   New York City. To A. E. Smith's studio in morning, followed by appointments with J. C. Black; Dr. Harry Smith and Samuel St. John re kinship of Emma Stover; General E. N. Clark and Major Migel. To luncheon at University Club given by L. F. McCollum and W. H. Burnham. Afternoon appointments with Frederick Adams Virkus (publisher and economist) and Thomas Joseph Downs (lawyer); G. W. Buckner, Jr. Late afternoon meeting at #60 with H. Young.

16   New York City. Morning appointment with F. Coykendall. Noon departure by plane for fishing vacation at Moisie Salmon Club, Seven Island, Canada (guest of W. L. McLean, Jr.).

25   Seven Island. Morning plane to New York City. Afternoon arrival.

26   New York City. Morning appointments with Vice-

June   president Campbell; Buildings and Grounds Labor Committee; Scoutmaster Hill and fourteen scouts from Logan, Utah; A. E. Howse (from Wichita, Kansas) re Eisenhower Foundation. Afternoon appointment with E. Goldman. Dinner and movie at Rockefeller Center with Mrs. Eisenhower, Mary Cullen, Gustav S. Eyssell (executive vice-president of Rockefeller Center), Carolyn Hood, Mr. and Mrs. R. W. Woodruff, Edward James Churchill (business executive, president of Donahue & Coe), and W. H. and Wilma Robinson.

27   New York City. Morning appointments with R. Rodgers; D. Middleton at Hotel Gotham. Meets W. S. Symington at airport, followed by lunch with W. S. Symington, J. P. Binns, G. W. Buckner, Jr., at the Deepdale Club. Telephone conversation with the President. Bridge in the evening with W. S. Symington, W. A. Jones, G. E. Allen.

28   New York City. Morning appointments with Dr. Russell Potter (Director of Columbia's Institute of Arts and Sciences); M. H. Dodge; Colonel Robert Brooks Ennis; R. Harron and David Marke (AP editor for education); M. J. McKeogh. Afternoon plane to Washington. To Walter Reed General Hospital in the afternoon with Dr. Snyder. Appointments at the Pentagon with Generals Haislip, Ridgway, J. L. Collins, and Gruenther. Telephone conversation with G. G. Moore from the Pentagon. Late afternoon flight to New York. Evening telephone call to the President from New York.

29   New York City. Morning appointment with Dean Young. Afternoon meetings with Dean Krout; Kenneth Alfred Greene (Consul General of Canada). Telephone conversations with General Haislip; W. G. Buckner, Jr.; General W. E. Smith re fishing trip.

30   New York City. Morning appointments with Dean Carman and Hal Emerson; Sister Ruth; Vice-president Campbell. Late afternoon golf with W. E. Robinson, C. Roberts, and E. D. Slater.

July 1   New York City. The Eisenhowers' thirty-fourth wedding anniversary.

    2   New York City.

July 3 New York City. To barber. Telephone conversation with the President re July 5 luncheon with General Marshall.

4 New York City. Evening departure by plane for the Boy Scout Jamboree at Valley Forge, Pennsylvania.

5 New York City. Morning plane to Washington. Morning appearance before the Senate subcommittee of the Committee on Foreign Relations, Senator Elbert Duncan Thomas (Utah) chairman. Late morning appointment with W. A. Harriman. Afternoon visit to Blair House. Late afternoon appointments at the Pentagon with General Vandenberg, General Norstad, Secretary Finletter, Mr. McComb; Secretary Johnson. Telephone conversation with W. S. Symington. Evening plane to New York City.

6 New York City. Breakfast with R. W. Woodruff at #60. Afternoon appointment with Vice-president Campbell. Stag supper at W. H. Burnham's. Telephone conversations with S. W. Richardson; D. R. Calhoun; General Gruenther; W. E. Robinson; H. L. Stimson.

7 Morning plane to Minneapolis, accompanied by P. Young, W. H. Burnham, K. C. McCann, and R. B. Whitney. To the Minneapolis Club for cocktails and dinner given by H. A. Bullis.

8 Minneapolis. Afternoon plane to New York City. Supper and bridge at #60 with C. Roberts, W. E. Robinson, and C. J. Schoo.

9 New York City. Morning meeting with R. W. Woodruff at #60.

10 New York City. Morning appointments with M. H. Dodge; E. Rennhback; Colonels James Russell Wheaton and Patton; C. M. Spofford. To Summer Session opening exercises with President Russell at Alma Mater, followed by lunch at #60 with W. W. Aldrich, R. Rodgers, H. Seymour, and Dean Young. Afternoon appointment with President Russell. Sits for portrait with A. E. Smith. Telephone conversation with Jesse H. Jones re invitation to Texas. Bridge at #60 in the evening with C. Roberts, G. E. Allen, and E. D. Slater.

11 New York City. Morning appointments with K. D.

July | Johnson, Dean Dunning, and Dean Young; Dean Dunning, G. A. Sloan, and Dr. C. G. King. Meeting with the Committee on Education in the Trustees Room, followed by meeting with W. H. Lowe, Jr., of Cowles magazines. Lunch at #60 with George Marck, Dewitt Klough, W. H. Burnham, E. E. Newsom, and Dean Young. Telephone conversations with President Russell; Robert A. Lovett; General Clay.

12 | New York City. Morning appointments with J '. B. Lawrence; G. V. Cooper; Dr. V. M. Kraus; Robert Bird and O. R. Reid. Late morning golf at the Deepdale Club with C. Roberts, R. W. Woodruff, W. E. Robinson, C. V. McAdam, and B. T. Leithead. Telephone conversations with W. H. Burnham re California trip; and the President.

13 | New York City. Morning appointments with Colonel Howse re Eisenhower Foundation; W. H. Lowe, Jr., and G. Cowles; General E. N. Clark; T. F. Tsaing; Colonel Richard H. Stevens; M. H. Dodge; L. F. McCollum. Luncheon at W. H. Burnham's with Dean Young, L. F. McCollum, R. J. Kleberg, Jr., H. J. Porter, J. H. Frost, L. Fleming, H. L. Hunt, and W. Golston. Telephone conversations with W. E. Robinson re Eisenhower Foundation; A. M. Rosenberg re Arden House project. Afternoon departure for Cold Spring Harbor, New York, and meeting with H. L. Stimson.

14 | New York City. To barber. Morning meeting with General M. W. Clark. Noon appointment with Dean Young and L. Lee. Lunch at #60 with W. E. Robinson and Governor J. H. Duff of Pennsylvania. Afternoon appointments with Dean Krout and E. M. Earle re military history chair; C. B. Luce. Telephone conversation with W. G. Buckner, Jr. Evening train for the West Coast with Mr. and Mrs. Bannard and Mr. and Mrs. J. C. Black.

15 | En route to the West Coast. Morning arrival in Chicago. Depart Chicago by train in afternoon, accompanied by the F. G. Gurleys, the D. M. Blacks, the J. D. Brandons, and E. M. Burnham. Evening arrival in Kansas City; visit by the Arthur B. Eisenhowers.

16 | En route to the West Coast.

July 17   Day spent touring the Grand Canyon.

18   Afternoon arrival at Yosemite National Park.

19   Late morning departure from Yosemite. Arrive in Oakland, California, in the late afternoon. To Press Club dinner with General Walter Campbell Sweeney, Thor M. Smith, and Mr. Huggins.

20   Afternoon departure for Bohemian Grove, Camp Stowaway. Lunch with H. D. Collier.

21   Bohemian Grove.

22   Bohemian Grove.

23   Bohemian Grove.

24   Departure from Bohemian Grove for Fairmount Hotel, San Francisco.

25   San Francisco. T. S. Petersen luncheon in early afternoon. Evening cocktails with A. Andrews, Jr., and twenty young businessmen.

26   San Francisco.

27   San Francisco.

28   Evening arrival by train in Denver with Mrs. J. C. Black.

29   Denver. Morning meeting with General Caldwell at Lowry Air Force Base.

30   Denver.

31   Denver.

August 1   Denver. To Fitzsimons General Hospital with Mrs. Eisenhower. Golf at the Cherry Hills Club with J. A. Culbreath, F. M. Manning, and R. Arnold.

2   Denver. Morning meeting with T. D. Campbell. Lunch at the officers' club with T. D. Campbell and General Caldwell. Afternoon golf with A. C. Jacobs at Cherry Hills Club.

3   Denver. Fishing with A. Nielsen.

4   Denver. Meeting with the air ROTC graduating class at Lowry Air Force Base. Telephone conversations with Secretary Johnson re Europe defense; E. P. Hoyt re

August	golf and September radio address. Afternoon golf with E. P. Hoyt, D.I.J. Thornton, and R. Arnold.
5	Denver. Morning telephone conversation with C. Roberts. Golf with A. C. Jacobs at Cherry Hills Club.
6	Denver.
7	Denver.
8	Denver.
9	Denver.
10	Denver. Telephone conversations with W. S. Symington; L. F. McCollum; Commander George North Craig (Governor of Indiana and National American Legion commander). Morning meeting with W. H. Burnham in office at Lowry Air Force Base. Lunch with W. H. Burnham at Cherry Hills Club. To Cherry Hills Club for cocktails and dinner to celebrate the J. S. Douds' wedding anniversary.
11	Denver. To luncheon given by L. F. McCollum at Cherry Hills Club.
12	Denver. Friends visiting with the Eisenhowers include C. Roberts, W. E. Robinson, G. E. Allen, C. J. Schoo, E. D. Slater, and F. F. Gosden.
13	Denver. G. E. Allen departs.
14	Denver. Telephone conversation with H. A. Bullis re Crusade for Freedom.
15	Denver.
16	Denver.
17	Denver.
18	Denver. Evening visit with the C. W. Allens in Central City.
19	Denver.
20	Denver.
21	Denver. To luncheon with ladies of Mrs. Eisenhower's class at the Wolcott School.
22	Denver. Morning visit with Vice-president Pegram and

August		Dean Carman at Denver University, then to Cherry Hills Club for golf.
	23	Denver. Morning convocation at Denver University to award honorary degree to Eisenhower. Golf in the afternoon. Telephone conversation with W. A. Jones.
	24	Denver. Telephone conversations with Under Secretary, USAF, John A. McCone (Defense Department); W. A. Jones; Governor H. E. Stassen.
	25	Denver. Telephone conversation with E. P. Hoyt.
	26	Denver.
	27	Denver.
	28	Denver. Morning visit to Fitzsimons General Hospital. To the Denver Club for luncheon with A. Nielsen, A. M. Godfrey, Edward D. Nicholson (manager, United Airlines Denver regional office), R. Rodman, and F. M. Manning.
	29	Denver.
	30	Denver. To luncheon for Mrs. Eisenhower given by Columbia Women's Club at the Denver Country Club. Afternoon visit with war casualties at Fitzsimons General Hospital.
	31	Denver. Afternoon appointment with H. E. Stassen. Telephone conversation with Deputy Secretary of Defense S. T. Early re Crusade for Freedom address.
September	1	Denver. Late morning flight to Colorado Springs to meet W. S. Symington and D. R. Calhoun.
	2	Colorado Springs. Morning meetings with W. S. Symington; D. R. Calhoun; E. B. Dudley; R. Arnold; E. P. Hoyt; L. B. Maytag; Mr. Fleniken.
	3	Colorado Springs. Meeting with W. S. Symington and D. R. Calhoun. Return to Denver.
	4	Denver. Crusade for Freedom speech.
	5	Denver. Morning appointment with Leo M. Clark re application to Regular Army.
	6	Denver.
	7	Denver.

September | 8 | Denver. Evening stag dinner with C. K. Boettcher.

9 Denver. Morning golf with E. M. Burnham, W. L. Johnson, and J. C. Black. Dinner and cards with the E. E. Hartwells (friends of Mrs. Eisenhower's).

10 Denver.

11 Denver. To the University Club for Columbia alumni club luncheon. Golf in the afternoon with E. D. Nicholson, E. P. Hoyt, and Harry M. Anholt (general manager of Denver's Brown Palace Hotel).

12 Denver. Morning golf. Afternoon viewing of preview of film *Farewell to Yesterday*. Late afternoon meeting with young Denver businessmen at the Brown Palace Hotel.

13 Denver. Morning golf.

14 Denver. Breakfast at the Brown Palace Hotel with L. F. McCollum, followed by late morning golf with McCollum.

15 Denver.

16 Denver.

17 Denver. Visit to Dr. H. A. Black in Pueblo, Colorado, via F. M. Manning's plane. Evening train to New York City.

18 New York City. Late afternoon reception for Dan Mumford at the Statler Hotel with Mr. and Mrs. D. R. Calhoun, Mr. and Mrs. W. A. Hanaway, Mr. and Mrs. Atkinson, Mrs. C. G. B. Prichard, J. W. McAfee, W. T. Philips, and Major Schulz.

19 New York City. Morning appointment with Provost Kirk.

20 New York City. Morning appointment with Provost Kirk and the alumni trustee nominating committee in the Trustees Room. Late morning golf. Telephone conversation with B. M. Baruch.

21 New York City. Morning appointments with Dean Young; General Campbell. Lunch with Dean Young, K. C. McCann, and W. H. Burnham. Afternoon appointments with E. J. Bermingham; Norman Loyal McLaren (California accountant and member of the

September   Bohemian Club); Dean Pegram. Telephone conversations with C. D. Dillon re Forrestal diary; F. Eberstadt re Napoleonic postwar history and General Marshall's appointment; M. H. Dodge; H. Ford II.

22   New York City. Morning appointments with M. H. Dodge; Vice-president Campbell, Dean Dunning, and Provost Kirk. Late morning departure for Gettysburg, Pennsylvania, with Mrs. Eisenhower and G. E. Allen. Telephone conversation with F. D. Fletcher.

23   Gettysburg.

24   Gettysburg.

25   New York City. Morning staff meeting with Dean Young, Provost Kirk, Dean L. H. Chamberlain, Vice-president Campbell, Dean Dunning, Dean Krout, and K. C. McCann. Meeting of the Committee on Education in the Trustees Room. Lunch with General W. B. Smith at #60. Afternoon appointment with General Harry H. Semmes (Washington attorney). Telephone conversations with W. S. Symington; General W. B. Smith. Evening bridge at #60 with C. Roberts, W. E. Robinson, and J. D. Brandon.

26   New York City. Morning appointments with five Columbia Eisenhower scholars; Dr. Rabi and Dr. Yukawa; General Donovan. To McMillin Theater in the afternoon for university opening exercises (the 197th year). Evening viewing of film *Broken Arrow*.

27   New York City. Morning appointments with Elliott Hugh Lee (banker); A. P. Levy; Howard Whitman and R. Harron; General Curtis; and D. M. Black. Afternoon appointment with Vice-president Davis, followed by attendance at Barnard's opening exercises. Late afternoon visit to C. D. Dillon. Telephone conversations with Dean Young re American Assembly; S. P. Skouras re St. Lo Church rehabilitation; C. D. Dillon; Senator Tydings (Maryland).

28   New York City. To college presidents' meeting at the Waldorf-Astoria. Late afternoon visit to W. A. Harriman. Dinner at Sherry's given by B. M. Baruch in honor of General W. B. Smith.

29   New York City. Morning appointments with Provost

September		Kirk; General E. N. Clark; Dean Ackerman; Dean Young; Jess N. Dalton; Willard Paulin (of New York Life Insurance Company, a friend of Sergeant M. Popp's). Afternoon golf at the Links Golf Club, Westbury, Long Island, with R. B. Whitney, R. Warner, and several young businessmen. Dinner with R. B. Whitney.
	30	New York City. Morning appointment with R. F. Moore. Golf at the Blind Brook Club.
October	1	New York City.
	2	New York City. Morning appointments with Abbott Joseph Liebling (*New Yorker* magazine); Vice-president Campbell; Professor Zuckerman (a friend of Lord Tedder's); Sir A. E. Grassett; Dean Dunning, Dr. King, and C. Francis. Trustees luncheon, followed by trustees meeting. Telephone conversations with General Clay; R. W. Howard. Evening with C. Roberts, W. E. Robinson, and E. D. Slater.
	3	To University Park, Pennsylvania, for Milton S. Eisenhower's inauguration as president of Pennsylvania State University.
	4	University Park.
	5	University Park.
	6	University Park.
	7	New York City. Morning appointment with Erwin Charles Uihlein (president, Joseph Schlitz Brewing Company). Golf with W. E. Robinson and C. Roberts in the afternoon. To the Roy Howard dinner in the evening.
	8	New York City. To ball game with Lester Bowles Pearson (Canadian Secretary of State for External Affairs).
	9	New York City. Breakfast with W. H. Burnham and William Castleman. Morning appointments with Dean Krout; E. H. Green and Dean Young; R. A. Roberts; Kenneth Robertson; R. B. Whitney. Lunch at #60 with H. R. Luce and General E. N. Clark. Afternoon appointments with General Richard Jaquelin Marshall (superintendent of the Virginia Military Institute); Provost Kirk. Late afternoon visit with Mr. and Mrs. H. D.

October   Collier at #60. To dinner given by the Federation of Jewish Philanthropies.

10   New York City. Morning appointments with General E. N. Clark and Benjamin Gross; G. L. Cabot; Dean C. W. Ackerman; President Russell; William Russell White (USN, ret.). Lunch at #60 with W. H. Burnham, R. Cutler, John Endicott Lawrence (cotton merchant, director of Old Colony Trust Company), Byron Kauffman Elliott (lawyer, director of Old Colony Trust Company), and Dean Young. Afternoon appointments with Merrill Jacob Holmes (president, Illinois Wesleyan University); General Donovan and Dean Young; J. M. Budinger. Telephone conversations with W. A. Harriman; General Gruenther. Accompanied by Mrs. Eisenhower to Mrs. H. R. Reid's dinner for Barnard trustees.

11   New York City. Accompanied by Mrs. Eisenhower to black-tie faculty welcome dinner at the Men's Faculty Club.

12   New York City. Morning appointments with Lord Camrose (a friend of W. S. Churchill's); David Wise (*Columbia Spectator*); Dean Pegram. Late morning golf at the Blind Brook Club with J. C. Black, W. E. Robinson, and C. Roberts. To opening of musical show *Call Me Madam* with the Joseph Caseys of Washington in the evening.

13   New York City. Morning appointments with Charles Ian Orr-Ewing (business executive and member of the British Parliament); Louis Cassius Upton (chairman of the board of the Whirlpool Corporation) and Alred Barnes Connable, Jr. (investment counselor); Donald Redfield Griffin (zoology professor, Cornell University), Richard Kingsbury Stevens (lawyer and Princeton University trustee), and Morris Watkins; Harvey S. Mudd; G. W. Buckner, Jr.; Professor Roy Durham (Kansas State Teachers College). To the Links Club for trustees luncheon. Afternoon meetings with General and Mrs. Kenneth W. Haas (AUS, ret.; Benedictine High School, Richmond, Virginia); German broadcasters; General Gruenther. Dinner and bridge with General Gruenther, E. D. Slater, G. E. Allen, and C. Roberts at #60.

October 14 New York City. Eisenhower's birthday.

15 New York City. No appointments.

16 New York City. Morning appointment with General E. N. Clark and Louis Wasey re War and Peace Institute. Development planning meeting with M. H. Dodge, D. M. Black, E. H. Green, S. E. Warren, Deans Young, Krout, Dunning, and Chamberlain, Vice-presidents Kirk and Campbell, General Donovan, and K. C. McCann. Telephone conversation with W. E. Robinson. Late morning departure for Connecticut.

17 Ridgefield, Connecticut. Evening meeting with H. J. Porter, W. H. Burnham, and L. F. McCollum. Dinner at the home of Mrs. Kermit Roosevelt (the former Belle Wyatt Willard, widow of Theodore Roosevelt's son), followed by visit to English Speaking Union's preview of modern English art.

18 New York City. To barber. Morning appointments with Dr. Oliver Cromwell Carmichael (educator); Daniel Stack (student); R. Harron; G. E. Allen and C. M. White. Columbia Associates luncheon at the Men's Faculty Club. Afternoon meetings with E. Goldman; Alan M. Moorehead; Council on Foreign Relations. Telephone conversations with General Marshall re Pittsburgh speech; Arthur B. Eisenhower; W. S. Symington. Late train to Pittsburgh.

19 Morning arrival in Pittsburgh. Morning meeting with Earl D. Eisenhower. To Schenley Hotel. Press conference and reception, followed by Columbia alumni luncheon. Evening reception and buffet supper at the Carnegie Institute (Founders' Day).

20 Pittsburgh. Luncheon with Henry John Heinz II (president, H. J. Heinz Company). Afternoon plane to New York City. Dinner and bridge at #60 with C. Roberts, Secretary Pace, and General Gruenther.

21 New York City. Morning appointment with R. Harron. Ceremonies at Baker Field for Columbia homecoming. Homecoming ball in the evening.

22 New York City. Accompanied by Mrs. Eisenhower to One Hundred Year Association dinner honoring R.

October   Rodgers and O. Hammerstein. Late evening train to Chicago.

23   Stop in Blue Island, Illinois, then on to Chicago. Alumni tour. Columbia alumni dinner. Telephone conversation with the President. Late evening train to St. Louis.

24   St. Louis. Alumni tour. Morning press conference. Luncheon given by D. R. Calhoun at the Statler Hotel to promote the American Assembly. W. R. Cox dinner at the Log Cabin Club. Late evening train to Indianapolis.

25   Indianapolis. Alumni tour. Late evening train to Cincinnati.

26   Morning arrival in Cincinnati. Alumni tour. Luncheon at the Queen City Club with N. H. McElroy. To Columbia alumni dinner in the evening. Late evening train to Charleston, West Virginia.

27   Charleston. Alumni tour. Lunch at the home of R. S. Spilman. Late afternoon flight to Washington.

28   Washington. Morning appointments with General Gruenther; General J. L. Collins; Secretary Pace; the President. Lunch. Afternoon meetings with W. A. Harriman, Deputy Secretary Lovett.

29   Washington. Meeting with Ambassador Davies.

30   Washington. Morning visit to the National War College. Morning appointments with General Norstad; General W. B. Smith. Lunch with Ambassador Davies. Afternoon appointments with General J. L. Collins; General Ridgway. Afternoon plane to New York City. Telephone conversations with Colonel Guggenheim re hunting; the President. Evening at #60 with C. Roberts, Jay Gould, Ralph Thomas Reed (American Express), R. W. Woodruff, W. E. Robinson, and J. M. Budinger.

31   New York City. Morning appointments with General E. N. Clark; Franz Gruber (Austrian Foreign Minister) and Joseph Murphy; C. A. Anger and Provost Kirk; General Donovan; Dean Young; General M. W. Clark. Lunch with John Luther Cleveland (chairman of the board, Guaranty Trust Company of New York) and the directors of the Santa Fe Railroad.

November 1 New York City. To barber. Morning appointments with Dr. Hacker; W. Hoving. Lunch at #60 with P. G. Hoffman. Afternoon appointment with T. J. Watson, Sr. Telephone conversation with S. W. Richardson. To dinner given by Military Order of Foreign Wars in honor of H. C. Hoover.

2 New York City. Morning appointments with M. H. Dodge; General Fenton; J. B. Lawrence; Dr. Alberto Fuentes Llaguno. Late morning golf at the Deepdale Club with C. Roberts and W. E. Robinson. Dinner and bridge at #60 with C. Roberts, J. Gould, C. V. McAdam, and Frank Henry Willard (cartoonist).

3 New York City. Sits for *Newsweek* cover photograph. Morning appintments with Dean Krout and General E. N. Clark; G. E. Allen. Afternoon appointments with D. M. Gaines; E. Goldman. Telephone conversation with G. F. Kennan. To dinner given by D. M. Black.

4 New York City.

5 New York City. C. Roberts's party for the Eisenhowers at the Petit Salon, Park Lane Hotel.

6 New York City. Morning appointments with Robert L. Shoaf; office staff. Afternoon appointments with Honors Committee; trustees. Telephone conversation with General W. B. Smith. Evening train to Chicago.

7 Chicago. Late morning arrival in Chicago. Visits General Charles Gates Dawes (chairman of the board, City National Bank and Trust Company of Chicago). To the Chicago Club for luncheon given by R. Warner. Cocktails at the Chicago Club with J. D. Brandon. Evening train to Fort Worth, Texas.

8 Fort Worth. Train to College Station, Texas.

9 College Station. Morning review of the corps of cadets at Texas A & M University. Visit with General Lutes. Afternoon radio broadcast address. Afternoon plane to Houston. With W. H. Burnham, R. B. Whitney, J. C. Gibson, and Major Schulz to cocktails and dinner given by L. F. McCollum.

10 Houston. Morning visit to the University of Houston. Lunch at the Shamrock Hotel with Dr. William Ver-

million Houston (president of Rice Institute) and Dr. W. W. Kammerer. Afternoon visit to Rice Institute. Buffet supper at Tejas Club with C. D. Dillon, E. C. Anderson, and J. H. Blaffer. Evening train to Fort Worth.

11 Morning auto to Dallas. Columbia alumni breakfast. Coffee with Henry C. Beck (First National Bank, Dallas), Wirt Davis (Republic National Bank, Dallas), and young Dallas businessmen. Lunch at the City Club. Afternoon visit with F. M. Manning. Cocktails and buffet supper given by H. H. Coffield and W. L. Pickens.

12 Oklahoma City. Luncheon given by D. S. Kennedy at the Oklahoma City Golf and County Club. Evening cocktail party given by R. B. Whitney. Departure by train for Chicago.

13 Chicago. Luncheon given by J. C. Gibson.

14 Early morning arrival in New York City. Mrs. Eisenhower's birthday. No appointments.

15 New York City. To barber. Citizenship conference at Teachers College. Morning appointment with Dean Carman. Lunch at #60 with R. W. Woodruff and General E. N. Clark. Telephone conversation with General Marshall re Citizenship Program, SHAPE.

16 New York City. Morning appointment with Vice-president Campbell. To the Biltmore Hotel for the Auchincloss luncheon. Afternoon appointment with E. Goldman. Late afternoon visit to Morningside Heights offices.

17 New York City. Morning appointments with Walter Pepke; Charles Ruffin Hook, Sr. (chairman of the board, Armco Steel); D. Stack (Columbia College GOP Club); Chaplain Emeritus R. C. Knox and Walter Lemon; Dean Young. Afternoon appointment with E. J. Bermingham. Telephone conversation with General Gruenther re SHAPE. Hearthfire lighting at Johnson Hall in the evening.

18 New York City. Evening with the J. D. Brandons, W. A. Hanaways, G. Metzman, Arthur N. Atkinson (pres-

November   ident of the Wabash Railroad Company), and A. S. Nevins.

19   New York City. To dinner in Rosemont, Pennsylvania, with Martin Withington Clement (chairman of the board, Pennsylvania Railroad).

20   New York City. Morning appointments with G. W. Buckner, Jr.; F. E. Wormser and Dean Dunning re School of Engineering campaign; Provost Kirk and S. C. Wallace; General E. N. Clark. Afternoon meetings with Dean Smith; Staff of Development Advisory Committee. Telephone conversation with General Gruenther re luncheon to discuss SHAPE. Evening meeting of the Council on Foreign Relations.

21   New York City. Morning appointments with Dean Krout and Bishop John Jague of Bermuda; W. H. Burnham and J. P. Weyerhauser, Jr.; General Crittenberger. Luncheon meeting with G. F. Kennan (adviser to the Secretary of State). Afternoon appointments with H. E. Stassen; Committee on Buildings and Grounds. Accompanied by Mrs. Eisenhower to dinner at W. H. Burnham's.

22   Boston. Luncheon for the American Assembly given by G. D. Aldrich and H. L. Mason, Jr., at the Somerset Club. To dinner given by R. Cutler at the Tavern Club.

23   New York City. Thanksgiving.

24   New York City. Morning appointments with General John B. Ackerman and Sir Clive Latham Baillieu (deputy chairman of the English Speaking Union) re Roll of Honour in St. Paul's Chapel, London; Mr. Fultz of Manhattan, Kansas.

25   New York City. Luncheon given by Frank Hoke at the Columbia Club. Bridge at #60 with C. Roberts, W. E. Robinson, C. V. McAdam, and B. Barton in the evening.

26   New York City.

27   New York City. Morning appointments with Professor Christo-Loveanu; D. M. Black; F. Coykendall; L. V. Finder; C. D. Dillon; Committee on Education; A. H.

November   Sulzberger. Lunch at #60 with General E. N. Clark. Afternoon appointments with Dean Young; dentist.

28   New York City. Morning appointments with W. E. Robinson and Marguerite Higgins (journalist, *New York Herald Tribune*); Professor Christo-Loveanu. Afternoon appointments with C. L. Wilcox; Dr. Dee Brul (dentist). Accompanied by Mrs. Eisenhower to late afternoon graduate faculty reception at Men's Faculty Club. To dinner given by C. D. Dillon.

29   New York City. To barber. Lunch with K. C. Royall at Recess Club. Telephone conversations with General Gruenther re Korean situation; A. B. Kline; L. W. Douglas re American Assembly. Bridge at #60 with W. E. Robinson, C. Roberts, and Jack Isidor Strauss (department store executive) in the evening.

30   New York City. Morning appointments with Dr. Hacker; Professor Mark Van Doren and three professors from the University of the Andes, Colombia, South America; Senator Lodge, Jr. (Massachusetts). Telephone conversation with G. E. Allen. Accompanied by Mrs. Eisenhower to black-tie dinner at the W. W. Aldriches'.

December 1 New York City. Morning appointment with Dean Smith. Lunch at #60 with G. E. Allen.

2   New York City.

3   New York City.

4   New York City. Morning meeting of the Association of American Universities at the University Club. Afternoon meeting with Provost Kirk. To Dean Pegram's office for photo session with the trustees, followed by trustees meeting.

5   New York City. Morning appointments with K. C. McCann; Alfred W. Bass (IBM); Dean Chamberlain. Columbia College luncheon and orientation. Afternoon and early evening meetings with W. H. Burnham; the War and Peace Institute organizing committee; Columbia Engineering alumni. Telephone conversation with General Gruenther. To the Savoy Plaza to attend Air Service Post 501 honoring A. G. Carter. To the Links Club for dinner given by Isaac Grainger to honor D. R. Calhoun.

| December | 6 | New York City. Morning appointments with C. R. Blyth; Professors Arthur Warren Hixson (chemical engineering) and Arthur W. Thomas; H. J. Taylor. Afternoon appointments with R. L. Biggers; A. G. Carter and S. W. Richardson; Dean Krout; W. H. Burnham; Dean Dunning. Telephone conversations with Vice-president Campbell; B. M. Baruch re NATO assignment; General Gruenther re SHAPE. To the Plaza Hotel for Tax Foundation dinner. |

7 New York City. Morning plane to Washington. Picks up General M. W. Clark in Philadelphia. Late morning arrival at Camp Pickett, Blackstone, Virginia. Address to the 43d Division. Early afternoon arrival in Washington. Lunch at the Statler Hotel with the American Assembly staff, including Dean Young, W. Green, A. M. Rosenberg, A. J. Hayes, and Mr. Potofsky. To military history lecture in the evening. Late evening return to New York with Professor S. C. Wallace.

8 New York City. Morning appointments with General E. N. Clark; Dean Rappleye; F. Coykendall; Professor B. D. Wood; Russell Moberly (University of Wisconsin). D. Sarnoff luncheon honoring General Marshall and E. R. Harriman at the Bankers Club. Telephone conversations with W. A. Harriman; General Gruenther; General W. B. Smith; and Governor Dewey. Afternoon appointments with H. S. Firestone, Jr.; K. G. Crawford. Milton S. Eisenhower arrives in afternoon. To Pennsylvania State Club to dinner honoring Milton S. Eisenhower.

9 Washington. Breakfast with the Joint Chiefs of Staff. Morning appointments with General Gruenther; Colonel Wood; Colonel Carroll; Colonel Alfred Dodd Starbird; W. A. Harriman. Afternoon appointments with General W. B. Smith; G. E. Allen; General Gruenther, General Schuyler, and Colonel Wood. Telephone conversation with Lord A. W. Tedder. Late lunch with General J. L. Collins. Late afternoon appointment with General Gruenther.

10 Morning train to New York City. Lunch at P. D. Reed's.

11 New York City. Morning appointment with G. W.

December | Buckner, Jr. To meeting of board of trustees of the Endowment for International Peace. Luncheon with the Columbia Bicentennial Committee. Telephone conversation with G. E. Allen re farm. Afternoon appointments with Dean Krout; C. M. Malone. Council on Foreign Relations meeting.

12 New York City. Morning appointments with Dean Krout; L. Little; General Larkin; General E. N. Clark; Colonel Robert E. Wood; Chaplain Pike and the Riverside Church Committee; J. W. Rouse (a friend of Aksel Nielsen's); Professor Christo-Loveanu. Lunch at #60 with Dean Young, A. H. Sulzberger, H. R. Luce, R. E. McConnell, D. M. Black, W. S. Paley, and Mrs. H. R. Reid. Telephone conversations with Secretary Pace and General J. L. Collins, both concerning SHAPE. Afternoon appointment with W. T. Grant, Dean Young, and B. D. Wood.

13 New York City. To barber. Morning appointments with Dean Young, Tom Millian, Roger Flynn, and James McConnell; General Norstad and Colonel Wood. To annual Salvation Army luncheon at the Waldorf-Astoria. Telephone conversation with General Bradley. Afternoon yule log ceremony at Columbia College, then to General Studies tea. Cocktails and dinner with the Barnard trustees.

14 New York City. Morning appointments with M. W. Childs; Roger Owen; B. Mintener; F. Coykendall. To lunch with William Knox (Westinghouse Company). Telephone conversations with General E. N. Clark re SHAPE and politics; A. M. Rosenberg re her appointment and American Assembly labor representation; General W. B. Smith re Rosenberg nomination. Afternoon plane to Washington. Late afternoon meeting with JCS. Early evening return to New York by plane.

15 New York City. Morning appointments with J. B. Lawrence; F. Eberstadt; R. Woodruff. Telephone conversations with R. P. Patterson re Universal Military Service; W. A. Harriman re SHAPE; General Bradley re letter of authority from the President.

16 New York City. Afternoon with C. Roberts, W. A. Jones, E. D. Slater, B. T. Leithead, J. King, C. V.

December		McAdam, and J. M. Budinger. Telephone conversations with A. M. Rosenberg; Dean Young; General Gruenther; General J. L. Collins; R. W. Howard.

17 New York City. Evening train with Mrs. Eisenhower to Tiffin, Ohio. Telephone conversations with F. McCormick, F. Eberstadt.

18 Afternoon arrival in Bucyrus, Ohio, and departure by auto for Tiffin. Telephone conversation with President Truman concerning NATO. Afternoon arrival at Heidelberg College, Tiffin. Luncheon with students, followed by convocation and reception at the president's house. Evening train to St. Louis.

19 Morning arrival at St. Louis. Press conference at the Statler Hotel. Lunch with D. Mumford, D. R. Calhoun, George Hanaway, and A. K. Atkinson. Presents painting of her husband to Mrs. C. G. B. Pritchard. Evening train to Denver.

20 Morning arrival in Denver. To stay at the home of J. S. Douds until evening of December 26.

26 Denver. Evening with Mr. and Mrs. F. M. Manning and Governor D.I.J. Thornton. Departure for New York City.

27 En route to New York.

28 Noon arrival in New York City. Evening meeting with E. Goldman and M. Tritz.

29 New York City. To barber. Breakfast appointment with A. M. Godfrey. Morning appointments with Provost Kirk; General E. N. Clark; Vice-president Campbell; H. C. Flanigan; H. C. Butcher; Major A. Folice; T. J. Watson; Dean Young. Telephone conversations with Governor Dewey re world situation; M. H. Dodge re mobilization and the American Assembly.

30 New York City. Morning appointments with D. M. Black; K. C. Royall; Major Folice; Vice-president Campbell; General Adler; General E. N. Clark. Afternoon appointments with Vice-president Pegram; Governor Duff and General E. N. Clark; R. W. Davenport; J. R. Forgan; J. G. Bennett.

31 New York City. Evening with W. H. Burnham and R. B. Whitney.

Index

E., 1517–18; presidential candidacy, volunteers for E., 841; Republican leadership, concern for, 161–62
Burning Tree Country Club, 303, 1046, 1055, 1057
Burnside, Ambrose Everett, 309
Burt, Mrs. William Bradley, 301–2
Bush, Vannevar, 514; background, 399; Conant committee, 799; JCS, plan for organization of, 399; NATO, Military Production and Supply Board, reorganization of, 1446
Butcher, Harry Cecil, 608, 768–69, 1249–50; Allied Control Council, recollection of first meeting, 109–10; background, 38–40; book by, syndication of, 79–80; Columbia, applicant to, 974–75; Crommelin, E.'s opinion of, 1065–66; *Crusade in Europe*, 395–96; invitation to speak, declined by E., 1065–66; notes from E., addressed to, 366; politics, 39, 974; Summersby book, 395–96
Butcher, Mary Margaret, 38, 40, 1066
Butcher, Ruth (Barton), 608
Butler, Nicholas Murray, 204, 453–54, 689, 988; background, 25, 77; Columbia, 273, 388, 1197
Butterworth, William Walton, Jr., 132–34
Bye, George Thurman, 80, 94–95, 145; *Eisenhower Was My Boss*, 159, 170, 395–96; *Eisenhower's "Girl Friday,"* 145, 159–60, 396
Byrd, Richard C., 907
Byrd, Richard E., 1425
Byrnes, James Francis, 840–41; background, 841; supports E.'s candidacy, 885–86, 888
Byrnes, John W., 608, 610
Byron, Joseph Wilson, 50–51

Cabot, Godfrey Lowell, 1302–3; communism, comments on, 1400–1401
Caeiro da Mata, José, 9–10
Caffey, Benjamin Franklin, Jr.: background, 230; guerrilla warfare, instruction for, 1223–24, 1225; Switzerland's strengths, 229–30; wedding anniversary party for the E.s, 108–9
Caffey, Louise (Battle), 230
Cahill, John Thomas, 817, 937; background, 684–85; Columbia, football program, 942, 962
Cahn, Sidney L., 1076
Caldwell, Charles Henry, 1175–76, 1242; illness of, 1426–27
Caldwell, Jeannette Pendleton, 508
Calhoun, David Randolph, Jr.: background, 809; dinner honoring, 1459; golf with E., 1242; luncheon for E., 1360, 1402; politics, supports E. in, 808–9, 840–41, 885, 888
—Augusta National Golf Club: invitation to join, 954–55, 1004–5; visit with E. at, 881–82, 924, 941
Callan, Edwin C., 1262
Cameron, Velma H., 740–41
Campbell, Craig: advice from E., 1371–72; background, 755; presidential nomination, disavowal by E., 754–55
Campbell, Joseph, 1024–25, 1068, 1102, 1158, 1163–64; American Assembly, gifts to, 1273, 1504; budgetary and accounting procedures, 689; building renovation, 803, 988; Eno bequest, plaque for, 1180; named acting vice-president in charge of business affairs, 535–38; maintenance workers' strike, 1170–72; President's Council, member of, 711; resignation of, 181, 183, 198
—Bicentennial Committee: beautification of Morningside Heights, 972; member of, 686
Campbell, Oscar James, Jr., criticism of E.'s administrative policies by, 727
Campbell, Thomas Donald: Alaskan defenses, concern of, 1115–16; background, 1115; heavy overland transport, problems of, 1258–59; Navy, oil exploration in Alaska, criticism of, 1115–16
Campion, Nardi (Reeder), 1486
Camrose, Lord, 1330
Canfield, Cass, 1238
Cannon, Ann Davis, 201–2
Cannon, Charles Craig, 45, 58, 123, 631, 763, 1425; background, 26; move to Massachusetts, 201–2; NATO, invitation to accompany E., 1124
Cannon, Louise, 201–2
Canol oil distribution system, 584–85
Capper, Arthur, 328–29
Career Compensation Act (1949), 629–31
Carey, James Barron: ADA, coalition to draft E., 42–43; Aid to Europe Group, membership in, 340; background, 43; National Committee for a Free Europe, sponsor of, 583
Cargill, Sergeant, 1117
Carlson, Carolyn, 7–8
Carlson, Frank, 745; background, 135–36; E.'s candidacy, worked for, 1067
Carlson, Joel E., 7–8
Carman, Harry James: background, 478–79; dean emeritus, honorary designation of, 1406; federal aid to education, in support of, 262; state of the university, study of, 1135–36, 1148; student enrollment, concern about, 1182–83; successor to, search for, 713; temporary leave for E., 477–79

difference of opinion with, 20; gift copy to, 312, 314
—portrait of: by Chandor, 948; unveiling declined by E., 1375−76
—U.S. visit, 504−5; E.'s illness, 555; invitations received by, 393, 495, 519−20, 543
Citadel, The, 929−30, 939−40
Citizens Committee on Displaced Persons, 114−15
Citizens Community Council Program, 1119−20
Citizenship Education Project, 914−15, 1007−8, 1008−9, 1071−72, 1074−75, 1079−80, 1119−20, 1170, 1191, 1423−24. *See also* Citizenship training
Citizenship training, 84−87, 476, 614−17, 646−47, 665, 680, 745, 775−76, 779−80, 1144−48, 1174−75. *See also* Citizenship Education Project
City Club of Dallas, 1360−61
Clark, Edwin Norman, 1167; documentary film, represents E. for, 279−80; fishing with E., 139; Institute of War and Peace Studies, supporter of, 1508−9
—American Military Institute: affiliated with Chair for Peace, 1065, 1118; fund raising for, 932−33
—politics: luncheon for E., 1456; supports E. in, 885, 888
Clark, Grenville, 649
Clark, Mark Wayne, 1198, 1397; Army training methods, opinion of, 1377−78; background, 1303−4; *Calculated Risk*, 1168−69, 1238−39; as Chief of Army Field Forces, 1303−4; The Citadel, as president of, 940; *From the Danube to the Yalu*, 1238−39; House Armed Services Committee, testimony before, 896, 905; lunch with E., 638; reduction of Army commanders, 23; Riley, recommendation to E., 1487
Clark, Robert Lincoln, 1222−23
Clarkson, Cora G. (Shields), 1024
Clarkson, Robert Livingston, 1024
Clausewitz, Karl von, 1315, 1317
Clay, Lucius Du Bignon, 121, 441, 1081; American Heritage Foundation, offer to head, 596−97, 619−20; background, 69, 677; book by, *Decision in Germany*, 976−77; Columbia, post for, 1021−22, 1084; Crusade for Freedom, chairman of, 1267−68, 1305, 1328−29, 1336, 1349; friendship with E., 276; Ganeval, post-graduate studies at Columbia, application for, 187−88; Germany, military government in, 919−20; health information foundation, offer to head, 605−6; honorary degree for, 606; IBM, job offer at, 676−77; invitation to

fish with E., 1112; politics, 840−41, 885, 888; retirement of, 605−6; visit with E., 276−77
Clay, Marjorie (McKeown), 188, 276, 619−20, 676, 1022
Clayton, Philip B., 1183
Clayton, William Lockhart, 340
Clerke, John A., 181−82
Clifford, Clark McAdams, 353, 554−55
Clinchy, Everett Ross, 17
Clothier, Robert Clarkson, 235
Coffield, H. H., 1361
Cohen, Lester, 974
Colasanti, Regis J., 1019−20
Cold War, 544−45, 571−72, 627, 779−80, 828, 894−95, 905, 1033−34, 1100−1101, 1126−27, 1248−49, 1254−55, 1256, 1274−75, 1282−83, 1311−14, 1365−66, 1366−67, 1488−93, 1501−2, 1514−15
Cole, Albert M., 1067
Cole, Jean T., 1229
Cole, John Tupper, 1229
Coleman, Arthur Prudden: background, 140; resignation as assistant professor at Columbia, 139−41, 162−66, 167
Coleman, Marion Moore, 140, 164, 166
Colley, J. Meyrick, 864−66
Collier, Harry DeWard: Bohemian Grove, 1068−69, 1111, 1198, 1213, 1326; luncheon for E., 1188−89
Collins, Gladys (Easterbrook), 1264−65
Collins, Harry John, 303
Collins, Joseph Lawton, 382, 384, 775, 1450−51, 1511; Army ROTC courses, 400−401, 718; background, 14; commendation for, by E., 13−14; *Cross-Channel Attack*, E.'s comment on proofs, 811−14; Dry and Moaney, sergeants, assignment of, 1245−47, 1264−65; Godfrey, recommended to, by E., 1510; HUAC, unification and strategy, testimony by, 895−96, 904; interservice debate, 779; lunch with E., 239, 1472; Navy, Bradley's attack on, 798; retired officers, promotion of, suggested by E., 1127−28; Symington, request for declassification of memo approved by, 1005−6; titanium, in production of airborne equipment, discussion of, 1276; Truscott, offer of service in Korean crisis, 1253; trusted by Forrestal, 462; visited by E., 1389, 1391
Collins, Maudie Alice (McAlpin), 302−3
Colorado State College of Education, 1125−26
Colt, Samuel Sloan, 1113−14
Columbia Daily Spectator, criticism of E., 851−52, 874−75
Columbia Engineering School Alumni Association, 1459
Columbia Presbyterian Medical Center:

D-day commemoration ceremony, 1201−2, 1290−91, 1375−76
D. D. Domino (bull): background, 92−93; development of, 288, 594−95; gift of Nielsen, 92−93; illness of, 964−65; selling of, 964−65
Dahlquist, John Ernest, 174, 295
Dale, Ernest, 984−86
Dallas Athletic Club, 1360−61
Dallas City Club, 1360−61
Dalrymple-Hamilton, Frederick Hew George, 637−38
Danaher, John Anthony, 529
Dandison, Basil Gray, 126
Daniell, Raymond, 1124
Darby, Harry, 1067
Darlan, Jean François, 632
Darling, Robert Croly, 481
Das Kapital (Marx), 638−39, 646−47
Davenport, Russell Wheeler: background, 1100, 1191, 1192; community councils, limitation of government intervention, 1191; presidential candidacy, interest in E., 1456
David, Donald K., 404−5
Davies, Joseph Edward, 669; background, 159; counsel for, sought by E., 611−12; invitation to E. by, 562−63; Nutrition Center, appeal for funds by E., 586−88; political prediction by, 159
Davies, Marjorie Merriweather (Post), 562−63, 586−88, 612; background, 563
Davies, Richard L., 30−31
Davis, Don, 1112
Davis, Joseph, 939
Davis, Joseph P., 124
Davis, Nina Eristova-Shervashitze, 355, 707−8, 782−83; health of, 708
Davis, Paul Herbert, 588; Arden estate, 845; Babcock financial plan, investigation of, 858, 920−21; biannual prize for tungsten research, 297; board on university reorganization, member of, 535−36; Columbia Associates, discussion of, with E., 943−44; Columbia Bicentennial Committee, member of, 686; Committee on Corporate Participation, 981−83; "continuous gift procurement," strategy for, outlined by, 264−65; development budget, decrease in, questioned by, 267; Dohr, recommended to E. by, 689; educational scholarships proposal, 290−91; football group, E.'s affiliation with, opposed by, 650; fund-raising letter, E.'s concern about, 936−37; gifts to Columbia, acknowledgment of, 1478−79; Harvard alumni dinner, arrangements for, 405; Higgins Trust, Harvard plan for, 591; Holley gift to Columbia, 1020, 1024−25; Lamont estate, gift of, involvement in, 379; letter to alumni from E., comment on,

444; March of Dimes, E.'s affiliation with, opposed by, 688; meetings with E., 263, 776; National Fund for Medical Education, fund raising for, 530; President's Council, member of, 711; *Reader's Digest*, discussion of articles for, 616; resignation of, 1094; Riverside Church, affiliation with Columbia, member of committee, 932; Shimkin financial plan, comment by, 826−27; trustees, mailings prior to meetings, 770; vice-president in charge of development, appointment as, 196, 487−88, 489−90
—development program: criticism by Bermingham, 707; memorandum, by, 597−98; support from E., 674
Davis, Thomas Jefferson, 707, 1372; background, 355; health of, 355, 708, 782−83; pheasants, raising of, 708, 782−83
Davison, Donald Angus, 1316−17
"Dear Ike" Club, 1092
Decentralization of government, E.'s views on, 571, 608−11, 612−14, 617−18, 665−69, 745, 755−57, 773−74, 933−35, 1325
de Chambrun, René, 348
Declassification of information, 662−63, 770−71, 976−77, 1005−6
Decorations Board, 278−79, 337
de Coubertin, Baron Pierre, 28−29
Deepdale Club, 1217
Defense, Department of, 239−40, 322−23, 365−68, 379−86, 466−73, 477−79, 836−37, 889−906, 1041−48, 1048−50, 1050−51, 1115−16, 1237−38, 1318−19, 1355, 1409−11, 1482−83; budget, 512−14, 515−19, 545−47, 551−52, 582−83, 591−94, 606−7, 645−46, 651−57, 699−704, 735−36, 738−40, 740−41, 746−47, 970−71, 992−94, 1058−59, 1082−84, 1268, 1287−89, 1311, 1313, 1337−38; Special Devices Center, 1148−49; Staff Council, 574−75. *See also* Armed services unification; Forrestal, James Vincent; Johnson, Louis Arthur; Joint Chiefs of Staff; Marshall, George Catlett
de Gaulle, Charles André Joseph Marie, 923
De Guingand, Francis Wilfred, 818−19, 1030−31; background, 420−21, 1031−32; *Crusade in Europe*, review of, 419−22, 438; memoir, *Operation Victory*, 236; NATO command, congratulates E. on, 1420−21
de Jaeger, Albert, 1131−32
De Linie, 73−74
DeMille, Cecil Blount, 1298
Democratic party, 39, 41−43, 78−79, 106−7, 119−20, 125, 129−30, 158−59, 310−11, 645, 755−57, 758, 778−79, 854−55, 883−84
Denazification, 394

Denfeld, Louis Emil: aircraft carrier, U.S.S. *United States*, debate over construction, 560, 561–62; Air Force, officers allocated to, from Navy, 636; anti-submarine equipment, refuses allocation for, 1083; background, 151; budget formulation procedure and basic war plans, 515–19; cooperation of, requested by E., 392; Crommelin, disclosures by, and congressional hearings, 1016; Harmon report, debate over, 569; health professionals and Armed Forces, liaison between, 151; interservice debate, 451, 778–79; meetings with E., 240, 366, 368, 369, 370; Navy, Bradley's attack on, 797–98; opinion of, by E., 545–46; Philippines, naval requirements in, 577; Sherman, successor to, 809; strategic concept and military budget, FY51, 545–46
—defense budget, FY51: E.'s recommendation discussed with, 1044; objections to, by, 739; recommendations of, 593
—House Armed Services Committee, hearings: Navy presentation, E.'s report to Vinson, 906; testimony of, 835–36
—JCS: memos, signer of, 525; military budget responsibilities, 472
Denison Domino (bull): gift to E., 1206–7; progress of, 1394
Denver Country Club, 1454
Denver Post, 1320–21
de Rochemont, Louis, 280
de Toledano, Ralph, *Seeds of Treason*, book by, 1292–93
Devaluation of British currency, 790–91
Devers, Jacob Loucks, 490–92
Dewart, Thomas Wheeler, 888–89
Dewey, Frances E. (Hutt), 146, 185
Dewey, John, 1425
Dewey, Thomas Edmund, 217, 756–57, 1105; background, 39; confidence of E. in, 184; election of 1948, results of, 310–11; endorses E., 1383–85; governorship of New York, attempt to persuade E. to run for, 679, 758; luncheon for, by E., 841; New York State, higher taxes for, statement by, 490; opinion of, by Burnham, 286; political polls (1950), showing in, 1089; presidential aspirations of, 142; visit from E., 146; Wisconsin primary (1948), 39
—presidential candidacy (1952): Gabrielson's opinion of, 1267–68; pressures E. to accept, 677–79, 840–41, 885–87, 1409–10
De Witt, John Lesesne, 749–50
Dickinson, Sidney Edward, 913
Diebold, William, Jr., Aid to Europe Group, report for Truman, 1467
Dillon, Clarence, 1444; background, 825–26; Forrestal, diaries of, 1337–38; Korea,

comment by E., 1447
—American Assembly: E.'s appreciation to, 1517; interest in, 1447, 1475–76
—Institute of War and Peace Studies: contribution to, 1504; financing for, 1117–18; planning for, 950, 959, 961–62, 1011
—NATO: command, E. departs for Europe, 1518; forces, importance of European contribution to, 1502
Dillon, Clarence Douglas, 1444
Dinsmoor, William Bell, 144
Displaced Persons Act (1948), 114–15
Disraeli, Benjamin, 1197
Distinguished Service Medal, 278–79
Dixiecrats. *See* States' Rights Democrats
Dodds, Harold Willis, 777; Higgins Trust, 805–6
Dodge, Marcellus Hartley: background, 52; Baruch gift to Columbia, 473–74; Campbell appointment, 712; Columbia, gift to, 107–8; Dunning appointment, 955–56; J. S. D. Eisenhower, accident and assistance to, by, 1415; installation of E., Rockefeller invitation, 182–83; Jacobs, honorary degree for, 1017–18; Pegram portrait, 955–56; university reorganization, 736–38; Yale, honorary degree for E., 52
—American Assembly: gift to, by, 1341; Grace gift to, 1297–98
—development program, 674–75, 937–38; "little cabinet," proposed by, 1260–61
—trustees: committee on reorganization, member of, 488; J. Grace, retirement from, 996; P. Grace, prospect for, 1297–98; president's council plan, 673–74; D. Strauss, nomination for, 1181
Dohr, James Lewis, 688–89
Dollard, Charles Vernor: background, 256; Citizenship Training Program, interest in, 1007–8; Columbia, Russian Institute, appeal from E., 256–57
Donaldson, Jesse Monroe, Columbia bicentennial, commemorative stamp for, 837
Donaldson, John Wilcox, 1110
Donaldson, Renée du Pont, 1109–10
Donker, L. A., German attack on the Netherlands, investigation of, 980–81
Donner, Robert, 1106
Donovan, William Joseph: background, 74; Columbia, fund raising for, 829; guerrilla warfare, involvement with, 1223–24
—Council on Development and Resources: appointments to, 1415; chairman of, 1260–61
Doolittle, James Harold, 346; background, 270–71
Doriot, Georges Frederick, 1167–68
Dorr, John Van Nostrand, 480

Doubleday and Company, 33–34, 74–75, 87–88, 96–97, 104, 482, 676–77, 1337–38
Doud, Elivera (Carlson): anniversary dinner for, 716, 1270; birthday celebration, 580–81; Christmas with E.s, 377–91, 1502–3; health of, 7–8, 605, 939, 948–49; health of E., 1039–40; paintings, requested from, by E., 765–66, 767–68; visits from E.s, 150, 160–61, 712, 1111–12, 1176, 1227, 1237, 1286–87; visits to E.s, 580, 585, 596, 873–74, 881–82, 966
Doud, John Sheldon: anniversary dinner for, 716, 1270; birthday greetings from E., 298–99; Christmas with E.s, 377, 391, 1502–3; *Crusade in Europe*, gift copy from E., 298–99; death of, 1376; E.'s painting, 765; health of, 6–7, 7–8, 18, 92–93, 605, 924, 939, 948–49, 1016; summer vacation, thanks from E., 765–66; visits from E.s, 150, 160–61, 391, 712, 1111–12, 1176, 1227, 1237, 1286–87; visits to E.s, 580, 585, 596, 873–74, 881–82, 966
Dougherty, Richard E., Columbia Engineering Center Campaign, appeal from E., 1482
Douglas, Lewis Williams, 342, 980; American Assembly, National Policy Board Chairman, 1429, 1431–32, 1474–75, 1518; background, 131; British-American relations, 326–27; *Crusade in Europe*, British review of, 326–27, 345–46; portrait of, 173
Douglas, William O., presidential nomination by ADA, declined by, 130
Dow Chemical Company, 1159
Dowling, Noel Thomas, strained relations at Columbia, concern by, 728
Draper, William Henry, Jr., 429
Drum, Hugh A., 1091; Stillwell mission to China, 1034–36
Drury, Newton B., 969
Drury, Theodore F., American Assembly, appeal from E., 1477
Dry, Geraldine, 1267
Dry, Leonard D.: transfer for, suggested by E., 1245–47; transfer of, 1264–67, 1281–82
Dry, Mary Alice, 1267
Dubinsky, David, 1434; Council on Foreign Relations, Aid to Europe Group, membership in, 338–40
Dudley, Edward Bishop, Jr.: background, 566; golf clubs for E., gift of, 1513; golf lessons for E., 576; new golf clubs for E., 660, 1151
Duff, James Henderson, 1198; background, 1268, 1456; E.'s presidential campaign, interest in, 1456; presidential candidacy

(1952), possibility of, 1268, 1272
Duke, Borghild D., 229
Duke, D. C., 229
Duke, Paul Demetrius, 229
Dulles, Allen Welsh: background, 339; National Committee for Free Europe, sponsor of, 583
—Council on Foreign Relations: Aid to Europe Group, membership in, 338–39, 459–60; report for Truman, 1466–67
Dulles, John Foster, 77, 1100; background, 18; Conant Committee, member of, 799–800; Hiss litigation, 186, 214
Dumas, Alexandre, 1462
Dunn, Charles Wesley, 287
Dunn, Gano, Columbia Engineering Center Campaign, appeal from E., 1482
Dunning, John Ray, 1158; Arden estate, Columbia committee for, member of, 844, 1071; atomic research by, 1257; background, 955, 982; dean, School of Engineering, appointment as, 1022, 1023–24, 1067, 1184; director of scientific research, appointment as, 955–56, 1002–3; Higgins Trust, coordinating scientific projects, Columbia representative for, 437; industrial-university committee, proposed by, 982; Institute of Human Relations, participates in program, 243, 309; Nutritional Center, interest in, 586–87; principal associate of E.'s, 612; university reorganization, proposal by, 711
du Pont, Alice, 1109
du Pont, Francis V., 1110
du Pont, Thomas Coleman, 1109
Durr, Louis, 144
Dutch Investigating Committee, 980–81

Eakin, LeRoy, 149–50
Eakin, Mabel, 149–50, 596
Earle, Edward Mead, 1198; background, 317, 1096; *Crusade in Europe*, review by, 316–17; Institute of War and Peace Studies, consultant to, 1096; Military History, possible chair of, 1095–96
—Council on Foreign Relations, Aid to Europe Group: membership in, 338–39; report for Truman, 1467
Early, Stephen Tyree: background, 13; Crusade for Freedom, reviews E.'s speech, 1281; presidential candidacy (1948), interest in E., 12–13; Under Secretary of Defense, appointment as, 562–63
—Deputy Secretary of Defense: appointment as, 769; resignation of, 1314, 1355
—Senate Appropriations Committee: consults with E., 1046; recommendations by Johnson and E., 1082
Earthquake, 566–67

death of, 47
Eisenhower, Louise Sondra (Grieb) (wife of
Arthur B.), 1210; Columbia, inauguration
of E., attended by, 236–38; wedding anniversary party, 624
Eisenhower, Mamie (Doud) (wife), 51–52,
56, 87, 111, 112, 377, 391, 393, 626,
759, 760, 767–68, 945, 954, 1161, 1229,
1264, 1267, 1392, 1417–18; Augusta vacations, 45, 48, 50–51, 57, 558–59, 562,
984, 1055, 1073; "Best Dressed," E.
named, comment on, 988, 993; birth of
grandson, 36, 45; birthday of, 1357–58;
birthday party for, 1417; Mrs. Black, traveling companion of, 1277; Caldwell's illness, 1426; Chicago trip, 37, 79; dental
work, 765; dinner with Blacks, 76; dinner
for, in Denver, 1176; E.'s assignment in
Europe, 1486–87, 1505; E.'s schedule,
burden of, 1023–24, 1039–40; Fairbanks
speech, sent to, 1101; farewell ceremony,
Fort Myer, 55; father, death of, 1376; father,
illness of, 924; fear of flying, 1031, 1055;
Gault's recovery, 538–39; Gettysburg farm,
1425; health of, 6, 7, 230, 302–3, 1272,
1390; Herrington invitation, 1181–82;
Manhattanville Neighborhood Center, interest in, 223–24; Mesta, plan for visit
with, 1375; news from nephew, 1227;
pheasants, gift of, 783; Puerto Rico, vacation plans, 881–82; Sloans, dinner and
opera with, 1003–4; Stack, condolences
to, from, 929; Texas trip, 824, 832, 843,
853–54, 860, 877; Tournament of Roses,
plans for, 1369–70, 1454–55; USMA,
1915 class reunion, attended by, 1073,
1151; wedding anniversary parties, 108–
9, 112, 238, 607–8; weight of, 783; West,
vacation in, 175, 1188, 1198–99, 1209–
10, 1237
—Douds: anniversary dinner for, 716;
Christmases with, 377, 391, 393, 1286–
87, 1455–56, 1498, 1502–3; summer
vacations with, 596, 712, 765–66, 1112,
1227, 1237
Eisenhower, Milton Stover (brother), 47, 135,
1257–58; Air Force academy, site for, 550;
American Heritage Foundation, offer to
head, 596–97, 620; Americans for E., receives Simmons letter on, 1070; background, 377, 1110; birthday greetings from
E., 1299; Christmas greetings from E.,
377–78; citizenship training proposals,
Naiden correspondence with, 58; Columbia, inauguration of E., 236–38, 243;
conservationists' dinner, 72; Cowles brothers, urges E. to meet, 1056–57; Denver
University, candidate for chancellorship,
455–56; discussions with, helpful to E.,

1244; Eisenhower brothers' reunion, 623–
24; federal aid to education, comment by,
642–43; fishing, invitation from Roberts,
1112; football game, Kansas State vs. Columbia, proposed by, 915–16; junior colleges, argues for, 915–16; political ambitions of, speculation by Butcher, 974;
public speaking, E. vows to stop, 1090;
Stephens, recommendation by E. for portrait of, 946–48; Topeka and St. Louis,
accompanies E., 745; UNESCO, association with, 377–78, 596–97, 768; visit
from E., 45, 1244; visit with E., 225–
26; Wisconsin vacation, plans for, 149–
50, 566–67, 580–81, 596–97, 643
—Eisenhower Foundation: E.'s comment on,
1154–55; report to E. from, 1155
—Kansas State College: citizenship course,
669–70; ROTC programs, curricula for
Army and Air Force, 400–401
—Pennsylvania State College: acceptance of
post by, 946–48, 1110–11; brother's attendance at inauguration, plans for, 1095,
1302; college head, comment by E., 989;
college head, comment by Hazlett, 993–
94; inauguration of, 1056, 1121, 1244,
1328, 1331–32
Eisenhower, Milton Stover, Jr. (son of Milton
Stover), 580–81, 946–47
Eisenhower, Patricia (daughter of Roy). See
Fegan, Patricia
Eisenhower, Roy (brother), 46–47, 946–47,
989; background, 47, 947
Eisenhower, Ruth Eakin (daughter of Milton
Stover), 580–81, 946–47
Eisenhower Foundation, 349–50, 914, 1154–
55, 1174–75
El Bandak, Yusif, 807
Eliot, George Fielding, 1100
Elliot, William: Alexander's dispatch, revi-
sion of, 718–19; background, 705;
Mediterranean operations, revised reports,
704–6
Ellis, Howard Sylvester: background, 683;
Nurkse paper on European currency deval-
uation, opinion of, 682–84
Ely, Richard Royal, 577–78
Encyclopaedia Britannica, Inc., 1186–87
Engel, Albert J., 971
English-Speaking Union, 1290–91, 1375–
76
Eno, Amos F., 1179–80
Epstein, Eliahu, 24
Equitable Life Assurance Society, 445–47
Estéva, Jean-Pierre, 632–33
Etherington, Florence (Musser), 476–77
European Recovery Program, 31, 117, 118,
459–60, 750–51
Evans, Arthur Llewellyn, 649–50

acknowledgment of gifts, 1479; retirement of, 181, 198

Goldberg, Reuben Lucius, 889

Goldman, Albert, 688

Goldsmith, Arthur Jacob, plan to resolve Palestinian conflict, 77

Goldwyn, Samuel, 1147; American Assembly, appeal from E., 1477

Golembe, Harry, 507

Golf, 12, 50–51, 56–57, 72, 75–76, 79, 83–84, 94, 109–10, 110–11, 160–61, 236–37, 325, 342–43, 540, 596, 660, 740, 765–66, 1046, 1090, 1160, 1199–1200, 1217, 1242, 1327, 1358, 1359, 1387–88, 1412. *See also* Augusta National Golf Club

Golston, Walter, 1148

Goodrich, Carter, criticism of E.'s administrative policies by, 727–28

Goodrich, Luther Carrington, 728

Gorham Manufacturing Company, 1152

Gosden, Freeman F., 1130–31, 1286–87

Gottwald, Klement, 166

Grace, Joseph Peter: background, 388; retirement of, as trustee, 995–97

Grace, Joseph Peter, Jr.: American Assembly, gift to, 1297–98; background, 388

—Columbia trustee: father becomes honorary, 996–97; father's retirement as, 387–88; suggested as, 387

Grafton, Susanna, Duchess of, 842–43

Graham, Emmett Schwedner, 349–50, 745

Grainger, Isaac B., 1459

Grant, Edward J., 713

Grant, Ulysses S., 1129

Grant, William Thomas, 1327–28

Grasett, Arthur Edward, 1376; King Leopold III of Belgium, treatment of, by E., 978–79, 1081

Graves, John Temple, article by, 825–26

Graves, Louis, 1396–97

Graves, Rhoda (Fox), federal aid to education, 405–6

Gray, Carl Raymond, Jr.: background, 1239; Conservation of Human Resources, appeal to from E., 1480–81

Gray, Gordon, 1050, 1128; Army Corps of Engineers, take-over by Department of Interior, 879–81; background, 647, 733; E.'s opinion of, 988–89; R. E. Lee, portrait for West Point, 913; Nuremberg trial, declassification of papers, 771; Wake Forest University, move of, 732–33

—Secretary of the Army: retirement of, 943, 1071; swearing-in ceremony, 645, 647

—University of North Carolina: inauguration as president, 1313–14; president of, 943, 993

Gray, James T., 838–39

Gray, Robert Stewart, 1455

Greater New York Fund, 590–91

Green, Edward Henry: American Assembly, 1410, 1473, 1477; background, 675; Columbia, Development Plan Committee, chairman of, 675; Council on Development and Resources, member of, 1261

Green, William: National Committee for a Free Europe, sponsor of, 583

—American Assembly: labor participation in, 1231, 1433–34; National Policy Board, member of, 1435

Greene, Elmer Westley, Jr., 948

Greig, Louis, 977, 1290–91; background, 20; Culzean Castle, management of E.'s apartment, 19–20; Gault, illness of, 332, 363–64, 372

Grew, Joseph Clark: background, 583; National Committee for a Free Europe, chairman of, 582–83, 634, 1336; Polish invasion anniversary message, requested from E., 728–30

Griffith, Major Dison, 191–92

Grimm, Peter: background, 685–86; Columbia bicentennial, committee for, 684–85

Griswold, Erwin N., 948

Groseclose, Elgin, 300–301

Grosvenor, Gilbert Hovey, 174–75

Grosvenor, Melville Bell, 175

Gruber, Helen L. (Drennan), 1427–28

Gruber, William Rudolph, 1427–28

Gruenther, Alfred Maximilian, 1347; address of, for Campbell, 1372; aircraft carrier, U.S.S. *United States*, debate over construction, 560–63; Air Force, unauthorized release of information, 494; B-36 procurement program, 514–15; background, 386, 1225, 1487, 1511–12; birthday greetings to E. from, 792; bridge, 112, 168–69, 237–38, 1289–90, 1319–21; common cap insignia for all services, 574; consults with E., 239–40, 366, 367, 551–52, 647, 1044, 1046, 1190, 1389, 1391, 1472; Director of Joint Staff, JCS, 368, 469; E.'s inauguration at Columbia, attended by, 238; Forrestal trust in, 462; game of "nullo," 238; guerrilla warfare instruction in service schools, 1223–24, 1225–26; invitation from E., 111–12; military medal case, gift of E., 1395; new job for "Mr. Brown," 145–46; Ordnance Department problems, discussed with E., 644–45; Philippine Islands, U.S. relations with, 577–79; "red brick" strength levels, FY51, E.'s unhappiness with, 592–93; Secretary of Defense, principal military adviser to, favored by, 399; Senate Appropriations Committee, Johnson's statement before, 1082–84; Staff Council, designated representative for, 574–75; Strong's letter concerning Shedden visit,

—Coleman case: investigation of, by, 167; resignation of, 139–40
—trustees: composition of board, 152, 155–56; late mailings to, 769–70; policy decisions, 152, 155
—University of Denver: accepts chancellorship, 456, 602–3, 874; honorary degree for E., 1283, 1340; Hoyt address at inaugural luncheon for, 855
—university reorganization, 152, 155; Dunning paper on, 711; duties of provost, 487–89; Organization Committee, E. requests action from, 597–98
Jacobson, R. C.: American Assembly, interest in, 1231, 1233, 1433–34; background, 1231
Jakobson, Roman, 166, 167
James, Frank Cyril, 222
Japan, 428–29; rearmament, 1489, 1492, 1514–15
Jardine, William M., 373
Jasper, George M., 1059–60
Javits, Jacob Koppel, 8
Jeffers, William Martin, Crusade for Freedom, 1335–37
Jefferson, Floyd Wellman, 191–92
Jeffries, William Francis, 1375–76
Jessup, Philip Caryl: background, 713; *China White Paper*, criticism of, 1292; Columbia, declines position of provost, 713, 737; Senate subcommittee, testimony before, 1014, 1033–34, 1333
Jester, Beauford Halbert: background, 107; E.'s candidacy, 106–7, 125; environment, member of advisory committee for, 135
Jewish Theological Seminary of America, 234
Johnson, Arnold, 86
Johnson, Charles Spurgeon, 691–92
Johnson, Edwin Carl, 1276
Johnson, Joseph E., 1114
Johnson, Kenneth Dewey: Arden House, proposed uses of, 844–45, 1070–71; Columbia, New York School of Social Work, dean of, 944–45
Johnson, Leroy, 69
Johnson, Louis Arthur, 738, 800, 941, 1128; accused of incompetence, 1272; Air Force, allocation of officers to, requests recommendations from E., 635–38; appointment of, 361, 546–47, 579–80; background, 546–47; consultations with E., 991–93; Forrestal, admiration of, 546–547; heavy transports, difficulties with, 1258–59; Hook Commission, stresses importance of military pay legislation, 629–31; meetings with E., 579–80, 752–53, 1114–15, 1128, 1211–12; Munitions Board, alters duties of, 500–501; National Committee for a Free Europe, advises E.

to join, 582–83; NATO, receives letter on, from E., 752–53; Nehru, host for visit of, 709–11; new forms of warfare, thanks E. for report on, 800; Nuremberg trial records, orders continuation of publication, 1114–15; Ordnance Department, criticism of Hughes, 644–46; Philippine bases, against abandonment of, 577–79; resignation, 1314, 1326; sworn in, 553–54, 546–47; UMT, tells E. of plan for, 1240–41
—Defense Budget FY51 (*see also* interservice rivalry; reductions in defense expenditures; supercarrier controversy): 591–94, 738–39; aircraft procurement, 746; anti-submarine equipment increase, 1050; Army and Navy figures approved, 657; Bradley urges approval of Air Force figures, 746; development of, explained, 994; dubbed IKE III by, 994; funds assigned by, 699–704; IKE II, submitted to JCS, 699–704; JCS, invited to discussion on, 654; major force limits set by, 699–704; reappraisal ordered by, 1082–84; receives E.'s memo on, 699–704; recommendations on, requests, 1082–84; reduction in, ordered, 1043; submits to Truman, 699–704, 735–36; testimony of E. on, disagrees with, 1047–48, 1288–89
—interservice rivalry (*see also* Defense Budget FY 51; supercarrier controversy), 738–39; admirals' revolt, 744–45, 778; B-36 hearings, 514, 778; Navy, E.'s opinion of attitude toward, 721–22; testimony on, 896–97
—JSC (*see also* Defense Budget FY51; interservice rivalry; supercarrier controversy; unification): chairmanship, desires E. to hold, 706; guided missiles, approves agreement on, 941; House Armed Services Committee, requests advice of, on testimony for, 644–46; Marines, request to assign adviser to, 547–49; submarines, meets with on, 552; strategic bombing, studies by, ordered, 568–70
—Korea: blamed for setbacks, 1313; information, orders services to limit release of, 1285; meets with E. on, 1237–38
—reductions in defense expenditures: civilian jobs eliminated, 735–36; installations closed, 735–36; orders on, 1148–49
—Service Academy Board: bill for third academy to, 550–51, 714–16; continues work of, 1026; final proposal of, approved by, 856, 951; preliminary report of, received, 714–16; suggestions to E. on report of, 692–94; supports recommendations of, 714–16; thanks E. for work on, 856
—supercarrier controversy (*see also* Defense

American Assembly, Dillon gift for war and peace studies, 1504; Amos F. Eno Fund, acknowledgment of gift, 1179–80; appointed provost, 737; Arden estate, meeting on uses of, 1071; background, 713–14; Columbia, acknowledgment of gifts to, 1478–79; Council on Foreign Relations, Aid to Europe Group, suggested by E. for chairman, 1511; development program, decentralization of, 1094; Earl Hall, financial needs of, 802–3; Encyclopaedia Britannica, *Syntopicon*, study of proposal by, 1197; Flexner, fund-raising proposals, 998–1000; football, Columbia vs. Kansas State, memo on proposed game, 916; Gunther gift for cancer research, 748–49; Hacker report on School of General Studies, 1157–58; honorary degree for Videla, arrangements for, 1018; Horace Mann School, reciprocal financial arrangements with Teachers College, 997–98; international relations, expert in, 1405; Jessup letter, assisted E. in drafting, 1014; Liaquat Ali Khan, honorary degree for, opposed by, 1079; luncheon in honor of, 925; maintenance workers, negotiations with, 1170–72; Nevis estate, study of uses for, 1109–10; opinion of, by E., 962; Philosophy Hall, proposal for refurnishing multi-purpose room, 987–88; Presidents of American Association of Universities, meeting of, E.'s report to, 800–802; Riverside Church and Columbia, member of committee on, 932; School of Architecture, Barnum's criticisms of, 1167–68; Stockholm Peace Petition, refuses circulation of, 1279; trustees, late mailings for, 770; University Peace Committee, declines recognition of, 1279–80; Vincents, apartment for, 1008–9; C. E. Wilson (GE), honorary degree for, 1134
— Bicentennial Committee: announcement of observance, 1108; member of, 686; Waldorf-Astoria Hotel, schedule of events, 973–74
— Higgins Trust: administration of, 918–19, 983; request for, to serve in E.'s place, 1516–17
— vice-president: in charge of education and provost, duties of, 1163–64; and provost, overlapping of function, 1001–2
Kleberg, Robert Justus, Jr., 1148, 1255, 1325; American Assembly, 1284–85, 1409–10; background, 868; Columbia, gift to, 1273–74; E.'s political candidacy, 966–67, 1169; meeting with E., 867–68
Klein, Harry T., 453
Kleitz, William Lambert, 1160
Kline, Allan Blair: American Farm Bureau

Federation, E.'s message to, 1457–58; background, 808–9; presidential candidacy, interest in E., 840–41
Koch, Arnold Theodor, 686, 1025
Koehler, Mr., 337
Koenig, Pierre Joseph, 1131–33
Koo, Vi Kyuin Wellington, 350, 444
Korea, 1184–86, 1190, 1199–1200, 1211–13, 1222–23, 1223–24, 1241–42, 1243–44, 1245–47, 1249–50, 1250–51, 1251, 1252–53, 1253, 1262–63, 1264–65, 1267–68, 1278–79, 1294–95, 1311–14, 1320–21, 1356, 1356–57, 1371–72, 1393, 1414, 1417–19, 1438–39, 1440–41, 1444, 1447, 1450–51, 1454–55, 1459–60, 1475–76, 1486–87, 1496–97
Kraus, Victor M., release of atomic energy information to public, 1234–35
Kridl, Manfred, incumbent of Mickiewicz Chair, 141, 166, 167
Krock, Arthur, 129, 1018
Krout, John A., 1065, 1198; administrative personnel, reassignment of, 1002; administrative reorganization, 488; alumni, short courses for, 1286; American Assembly, 1269–70; Arden House project, 1071, 1198; article by, proposed by E., 615–16; associate provost, appointment as, 1209; background, 488; Council on Development and Resources, member of, 1261; *Newsweek* article critical of E.'s administration, 727–28; President's Committee on the State of the University, chairman of, 1136; President's Council, member of, 711; Riverside Church and Columbia University, relationship between, 931–32; School of General Studies, 1158; War and Peace Studies, Institute for, 1403–4, 1474, 1508–9
Krumb, Henry, 1023–24; Columbia, acknowledgment of gifts, 1478–79
Krusen, Frank Hammond, 275
Kulukundus, Manuel, 829
Kunkel, Walter R., 793–95

Labor-management relations, 222–23, 626–27, 751–52, 782–83, 790–91. *See also* Strikes
Labor's League for Political Education, *League Reporter*, 933–35
Lafayette College, 1121–22
Lagens airfield, 9
La Gorce, John Oliver, 175
Lambert, Betty, 26
Lambert, Lloyd Washington, 25–26
Lambs, The, 1001
Lamont, Florence Haskell (Corliss), 378–79
Lamont, Thomas William, 378–79
Lamont Geological Observatory, 378–79, 911–12

of Defense, E. congratulates on appointment, 1355; NATO, memo from Bush, 1446; NATO command, E.'s concerns with, 1470–71; New York Life Insurance, invites E. to join board, 767; universal military training, opinion of, 1385, 1409–10
Low, Andrew Stevenson, Jr., 940–41
Lowe, William Hyslop, Jr., 1238
Lowry Air Force Base, 1175–76, 1259, 1426–27
Loyalty oaths, 601–2, 670–71, 779–80
Lucas, Scott Wike, 659
Luce, Clare Boothe: politics, 755–57, 840–41; *Summa Dialectica*, proposal for, 1186–87; supports E.'s candidacy, 885, 888, 1272; visits to E., 764, 1198
Luce, Henry Robinson, 555, 583, 756; background, 520; Churchill's U.S. visit, 519–20
Ludwig, Fred, gift to American Assembly, 1485
Lutes, LeRoy, 462, 1222; background, 446; recommendation from E., 445–47
Luttwitz, Heinrich von, 815
Luxembourg, 759–60, 1375–76
Lynd, Robert Staughton, 460–61
Lyon, Edwin Bowman, 192–94, 368–69
Lyon, Peter, 37, 125
Lyons, Leonard, 112–13

Mabry, Thomas Jewett, on E.'s candidacy, 106
McAdam, Charles Vincent: American Assembly, fund raising for, 1485; article on E., 874–75; background, 325
McAfee, James Wesley, 841; dinner given for E., 955; politics, offers to help E. in, 808–9, 885–88
MacArthur, Douglas, 718; background, 39; E.'s length of service with, 993–94; Formosa, U.S. policy toward, unauthorized statement by, 304–5; Hurley's assignment, 331; intelligence operations in Far East under, criticism of, 1225; Japan, ban on scholarly activities in, 429; JCS, rank of chairman, discussion with E., 433; MacArthur boom, 39; Miller attack on E., Michaelis view, 60; Philippines, civil administration in liberated areas, policy of, 1092–93; *Pointer* article, named soldier and diplomat, 1437; presidential candidacy of, E.'s objection to interpretation in Forrestal diaries, 1338; Truman comparison of E.'s NATO command and SCAP assignment of, 1499–1500; Wisconsin primary (1948), 39
—Korea: authority to use U.S. Army forces, 1190, 1212; Chinese Communist troops halt U.N. advance, 1418–19; E.'s confidence in, 1459–60; Liu proposals for fighting tactics in Far East, 1256; Operation KILLER, 1460; praise for, from E., 1393; retreat of U.N. forces, 1455; Walker's attack, comment on, 1451
McAuliffe, Anthony C., 348–49, 814–15
McCaffrey, John Lawrence, 1364–65, 1473
McCammon, Bess, 45
McCann, Kevin Coyle, 74, 317, 531, 1020, 1030, 1033, 1044, 1061, 1219, 1221–22, 1228, 1229, 1348, 1349, 1388; alumni association, liaison with, 1459; background, 34; Barnard College, letter to McIntosh, 485; Bicentennial Committee, E.'s memo to, 503; *Columbia Daily Spectator*, criticism of E., defense by, 851–52; federal aid to education, letter to Garber, 642; fishing on the Moisie, accompanies E., 1160; Franco, nephew's admission to Columbia, 768–69; Hacker report on School of General Studies, received by, 1158; Hartford, E.'s visit to alumni, 982; Horace Mann School, E. declines invitation, 997–98; invitations, memo to, 503; Isely correspondence about history of amphibious warfare, 623; job applicant, report to E. by, 1068; Jones interview with E., difficulties in arranging, 601–2; Liaquat Ali Khan, honorary degree for, reply to Kirk by, 1079; Labor Day address by E., assistance in drafting, 1280–81; "little cabinet," proposal by Dodge, 1260; Maher book, foreword by E., 1486; *Man from Abilene*, book by, 366; meeting with Newsom on Columbia projects, 1006–7; National Fund for Medical Education, letter to Conant, 457; NATO, to serve with E. in Europe, 1124; paintings by E., requests for, 218; *Reader's Digest*, series of articles for, 614, 616; Zoll investigation of Columbia, 1106
—*Crusade in Europe:* assistance with manuscript, 96–97, 102–3; conferences concerning publication, 139; file of reviews kept by, 317
McCarthy, Joseph Raymond, 1014
McCarthy-Morrogh, Vera, 94–95
McClatchy, Eleanor, 68
McClellan, John Little, Army Corps of Engineers takeover by Department of Interior, 880
McCloy, John Jay, 291, 1218; background, 293; Baughey, recommendation of, by E., 734–35; Boy Scout movement in Germany, 793–94; secretary of defense, chief of staff to, 292–93
McClure, John Elmer, 109–10
McClure, Robert Alexis, 396; background, 104–5, 397; guerrilla warfare, interest in, 1223–24
McCollum, Leonard Franklin: background,

estate of, request for E.'s assistance, 1483; illness of, 965–66; invitation from E., 772; invitation to ranch, declined by E., 1055; requests recommendation from E. for Biddle, 772

Manhattanville Neighborhood Center, 223–24

Manning, Fred M., Sr., 1507; background, 759–60; Columbia, fund raising for, 1333–34; daughter's meeting with Mesta, 759–60; E.'s Texas trip, 1359; European assignment for E., speculation about, 1405–6; golf with E., 1327, 1359; luncheon with E., 1270; photos of summer vacation, thanks from E., 1405

—American Assembly: appreciation to, from E., 1387–88, 1517, 1518; E.'s hopes for, 1405–6; fund raising for, 1359, 1454

Manning, Hazel, 760, 1359, 1507

Manstein, Fritz Erich Georg von, 393–94

Mao Tse-tung, 350

March of Dimes, 687–88

Marine Corps League, 1314

MARKET-GARDEN. See Arnhem, Battle of

Marks, Laurence M., 1417

Marquat, William Frederic, 430

Marshall, George Catlett, 301, 331, 509, 583, 762–63, 1064, 1212, 1228, 1355; background, 90–91; Christmas greetings to E., 853–54; Citizenship Education Project, E. suggests use of in military, 1423–24; *Crusade in Europe*, gift copy to, 311–12; defense expenditures, calls for increase in, 385; department of peace suggestion received, 1064; French morale, E.'s suggestions to, on improvement, 1421–23; guided missiles program, 1326; International House, chairmanship of, 983–84; Jessup, letter supporting, 1014; kidney operation, 311–12; Red Cross, 853–54, 860–61; Secretary of Defense, appointment as, 1314–15, 1318–19, 1334, 1355; Selective Service law, decision to amend, 1384–86; unification, testimony on, 897

—China: mission to, 350–51; statement on sent to E., 132–34; U.S. intervention in, views on, 132–34; World War II, mission in, 1034–36

—Korea: defeats in, blamed on inadequate reserves, 1385–86; intervention in, supported, 1212; luncheon with E. on, 1212; speech on, 1447

—NATO: approval of forces for, 1467–69; offers aid to E. in assignment, 1504; receives letter on from E., 1467–69; Western Europe, calls for build-up in, 385

—Secretary of State: criticism of performance as, 1105; resignation as, 311–12

—UMT and UMS (*see also* Waldorf-Astoria Conference): appeals for UMT, 1241; opposes E.'s sentiments toward UMS, 1409, 1410; Selective Service laws, seeks amendments for UMT in, 1384–86; speech supporting UMT, 1385–86; World War II, reports on UMT/UMS progress at close, 1312

—U.N.: American Overseas Organization, requests E.'s involvement in, 90–91; Appeal for Children, requests E. to head, 90–91; Berlin blockade, votes to refer issue to, 232; Citizens Day, requests E.'s service on committee, 146–47; E. reports difficulties with, 148

—Waldorf-Astoria Conference (*see also* UMT and UMS): advice on attendance sought by E., 1319; consultation with E. on, 1318–19; invitation to, urged by E., 1318–19; letter on, received from E., 1484; reluctance of E. to attend, 1385–86; report from E. on, 1384–86

—World War II: Drum considered for China post, 1034–36; "eyes only" letters with E., 762–63; Hurley assignment, 301, 331; North African campaign, selection of E. for, 811–14; Telek anecdote, 860–61, 1228; UMT and UMS, tells E. of progress toward, 1312

Marshall, John, American Press Institute program for German publishers and editors, 104–5

Marshall, Katherine Boyce (Tupper) Brown, 91, 312

Marshall, Maple Lee, 148–49

Marshall Plan, 43, 477. *See also* European Recovery Program

Martin, Joseph William, Jr., 122–23, 1268

Marx, Barbara, 1177

Marx, Idella Ruth (Blackadder): background, 869; birth of son, 869; christening of Spencer Bedell attended by E., 869–70, 916; European tour, 1177; luncheon for Prince Bernhard attended by, 1090–91

Marx, Jacqueline, 1177

Marx, Karl, *Das Kapital*, 638–39, 646–47

Marx, Louis: background, 681; christening of Spencer Bedell attended by E., 869–70, 916; European tour, 1177; painting by E., gift to, 869; plastic animals, 1090–91, 1176–77; portrait of E. for West Point, donated by, 681; praise for Stack from, 928–29; Prince Bernhard, invitation to E. from, 1090–91

Marx, Louis, Jr., 1177

Marx, Patricia, 1177

Marx, Spencer Bedell: birth of, 869–70; christening, 916, 928–29

Masaryk, Jan, 166

Masaryk, Thomas G., 166

Randolph, Dorothy E. (Wilson), 175
Randolph, Norman, 174–75
Rankin, John Elliott, 285
Rappleye, Willard Cole: admissions request from Skouras, 1346–47, 1363; background, 126; Baruch Committee on Physical Medicine, study of, 274–75; board on university reorganization, member of, 536; Columbia President's Council, member of, 711; Egyptian universities, request for professors and textbooks, 126–27; financial problems of medical schools, 356, 456–57; Gunther gift for cancer research, 748–49; meeting with E., 287; National Foundation for Infantile Paralysis, grants to Columbia, 687–88; residence hall job, comment on applicant, 1068; vice-president in charge of medical affairs, 489
Raskob, John J., 1091
Rawlings, Edwin William: aircraft procurement, 654; background, 519; Budget Advisory Committee, member of, 519; FY51 budget, controversy over, 656; pilot procurement, 654–55
Rayburn, Samuel Taliaferro, atomic energy, cooperation with Britain and Canada, 702
Reader's Digest, 476, 540, 614–17, 642, 863, 1089
Reagan, Ronald Wilson, 1298
Recipe, 708–9
Reckord, Milton A., universal military training, opinion of, 1484–85
Red-brick budgeting, 497–98, 515–19, 551–52, 591–94, 699–704
Redding, Allen S., 1431
Reed, Philip Dunham: Institute of War and Peace Studies, 1508–9; letter to Truman on current danger, signer of, 1467
—Aid to Europe Group: invitation to join, 1000; proposed by E. to head, 1511
Reed, Ralph Thomas, 1242
Reeder, Russell Potter, Jr., 1486
Rees, Edward H.: E.'s commencement address (1950), 1158; E.'s absentee vote (1948), 1070–71
Refugees, European, 114–15
Reid, Helen Rogers, 672, 797–98; background, 225; *New York Herald Tribune* Forum, invitations to speak, 224–25, 625–26
Reid, Whitelaw, 820
Reid, William, 1102
Reinert, Paul Clare, S.J., 1401–2
Rennell, Lord Francis James, 345–46; background, 327; *Crusade in Europe*, on bad review of, 326–27
Rennhack, Elliott, 1152, 1215–16
Rennhack, Henry F., 1152
Republican party, 38–39, 41–43, 103, 119–20, 141–43, 203–4, 310–11, 502–3, 677–79, 755–57, 758, 778, 804–5, 854–55, 1067, 1091–92, 1267–68
Research and Development Board, 207, 211, 406–8, 432–34, 512–14, 568–69, 574–75, 940–41
Reuther, Victor George, 1281
Reuther, Walter Philip, 440
Revenue Act (1950), 1229–30
Reynolds, Quentin, 1096–97
Reynolds, Russel Burton, 151
Rice Institute (Rice University), 1324–25, 1334–35
Rich, Robert F., 1158
Richards, George Jacob: background, 240, 400; JCS, proposal to abolish, 400
Richardson, James Otto, 891, 904
Richardson, Sid Williams, 1247–48; background, 136; Columbia, E.'s goals for, 665, 669; conservation of natural resources, 135–36; lunch with E., 1046; politics of, Mangum's concern, 1169; visits from E., 853, 866–67, 966–67, 1354
—American Assembly: appreciation of E., 1517, 1518–19; gift to, 867, 1447–48, 1449
Rickenbacker, Edward Vernon, 872
Ridgway, Matthew Bunker, 1127–28, 1190, 1437; background, 836; Columbia, School of Business, Army participation in, 836; Korea, 1450–51; NATO forces, commander of, 1392; Netherlands, German attack on, investigation of, 980–81
Rieve, Emil, ADA coalition to draft E., 43
Riley, Elizabeth A., 1487
Ripka, Hubert, 634
Ripka, Noemi, 633–34
Riverdale Country School, 251
Riverside Church, 931–32
Roberts, Clifford, 924; bridge, 858–59, 1225; financial problems of private schools, 857–58; investments, discussions with E., 1159; Republican presidential candidate, argues for E.'s declaration, 888; sends article to E., 874–75; Stephens portrait of Bobby Jones, 725–26; tax-free donations to universities, 921; trip with E., 758; visit with E., 1286–87
—American Assembly: appreciation to, from E., 1513; birthday party, surprise pledges to, 1411–12, 1416–17; gift to, from, 1473; procedure to process pledges, 1428; subscribers to, 1429; suggests financial push to E., 1437
—Augusta National Golf Club: membership for Bermingham, 1004–5; membership for Calhoun and Symington, 940–41, 1004
Roberts, Ernst Edward, 314–15, 321
Roberts, Roy Allison: background, 200; cur-

rent national and international problems, editorial by, 1366–67; Eisenhower draft, comment by, 887; E.'s candidacy, works for, 1067; Future Farmers of America, invitation to E., 199–200; invitations from, declined by E., 1111–13

Robertson, Absalom Willis, E.'s presidential candidacy, support for, 106

Robertson, Andrew Wells, 1373–75; Columbia, Engineering Center Campaign, appeal from E., 1482

Robertson, Brian Hubert, 794

Robertson, Walter Melville, 348

Robertson, William D., 1442–43

Robeson, Paul, 695

Robinson, Beverly, 1129

Robinson, Geroid Tanquary: background, 62–63, 256; Russian Institute, as director, E.'s opinion of, 62

Robinson, William Edward, 45, 84, 225, 566, 758, 924, 1198, 1281, 1357, 1502; American Assembly, gift to, 1417; background, 34; bridge with E., 1225; Butcher book, Clay's memoir, 676–77; Forrestal diaries, serialization of, 1337–38; golf, 236–37, 325; invites articles by E., 540–41, 911; Newsom, recommendation for, 969–70; politics, 841, 885–88; speech by E., comment on, 757; visit to E. in Denver, 1286–87

Rockefeller, David, 1297–98; background, 272; Morningside Heights, Inc., president of, 972

Rockefeller, John Davison, Jr.: Campbell's resignation, 181, 198; Columbia, installation of E., invitation to, 182–83; dinner with E., guest of Dillon, 1444; Flexner, adviser to, 999; International House, established by, 984; New York State Chamber of Commerce, luncheon honoring, 1073–74; President's Committee on the State of the University, 1208–9; Riverside Church and Columbia, relationship between, 931–32

—Columbia Associates: contribution to, by, 312–13; honorary presidency of, 247–48, 271–72, 295–96

Rockefeller, John Davison, Sr., 999, 1209

Rockefeller, John Davison, III, 135; background, 136; Citizenship Training Program, financial support of, 1007–8; Columbia, gift to, 876; Greater New York Fund, Columbia participation, 590–91

Rockefeller Foundation, 104–5, 396–98, 1432–33

Rodgers, Richard, 1178–79

Rodman, Roland, 1454

Rogers, Lindsay, Aid to Europe Group, report to Truman, 1467

Rogers, Will, 323

Romberger, Ira, 1134–35

Romulo, Carlos Pena, E. as "Man of the Half Century," nomination by, 887, 908

Roosevelt, Anna Eleanor: Crusade for Freedom, interest in, 1348–49; dinner honoring, 24; public service broadcast, E. declines participation in, 925–26

Roosevelt, Elliott, ADA, coalition to draft E., 42

Roosevelt, Franklin Delano, 13, 17, 547, 922, 926, 948, 1169–70, 1349, 1462, 1495; Army Corps of Engineers, debate over, 880; Hurley's assignment, 300, 330–31; politics, 42, 679, 874; TORCH, London conference on plans for, 813

Roosevelt, Franklin Delano, Jr., 659; ADA, coalition to draft E., 42

Roosevelt, James: ADA, coalition to draft E., 42; "Dump Truman" movement, 125; presidential nomination, E.'s refusal of, 129–31

Roper, Elmo Burns, Jr., 129

Rose, Maurice B., 161

Rosenberg, Anna Marie: American Assembly, labor's participation in, 1232–33, 1433–35; Assistant Secretary of Defense, appointed as, 1433–34; recommendation from E., 1482–83

Rosenwald, Lessing Julius, 114–15

Ross, William Robert, 1125–26

ROTC (Reserve Officers' Training Corps), 400–401, 490–92, 635–38, 717–18

Roth, Irving, 1288–89

Rouse, James Wilson, 1451–52

Rovere, Richard H., 1097

Royal Air Force. *See* RAF

Royal Army Service Corps (RASC), 131–32

Royall, Kenneth Claiborne: background, 60, 775; birthday flowers for E., 240; Bradley, opinion of, by, 797; candidacy, disavowal by E., 125; Chevy Chase Club, recommended by E. for membership, 910; China, U.S. policy toward, 132–34; conferences with E., 239–40, 367, 382; consolidation of Navy and Air Force, proposal by, 282; House Armed Services Committee, B-36 investigation, 774–75; Japan, ban on scholarly activity, 428–30; Korea, statement by E. urged by, 1267–68; military assistants for five-star generals, 59–60; Republican presidential candidates, speculation on, by, 1267–68; resignation as Secretary of Army, 429, 647; Service Academy Board, composition of, 424; Truman's inaugural parade, rides with E., 446

Rundstedt, Karl Rudolf Gerd von, 393, 474–75. *See* Ardennes counteroffensive

Runyon, Mefford Ross, 248–49

Scotland. *See* Culzean Castle

Scots Guards, 1153–54, 1161–62, 1162–63

Scott, Hugh Doggett, Jr., 809

Scott, Richard Underhill, 723, 725; background, 49

Scottish Trust. *See* Culzean Castle

Scripps-Howard newspaper chain, 886, 888

Scrivner, Errett P., 952–53

Scudder, Townsend, 295

Scully, Leonard Tyson, Higgins Trust, rules of procedure, 983

SEAC report, 1438–39

Secretary of the Air Force. *See* Finletter, Thomas K.; Symington, William Stuart

Secretary of the Army. *See* Gray, Gordon; Pace, Frank C., Jr.; Royall, Kenneth Claiborne

Secretary of Defense. *See* Forrestal, James Vincent; Johnson, Louis Arthur; Marshall, George Catlett

Secretary of the Navy. *See* Matthews, Francis Patrick; Sullivan, John Lawrence

Secretary of State. *See* Acheson, Dean Gooderham; Marshall, George Catlett

Security Review Branch, 494

Sedalia, Missouri, proposed site for Air Force academy, 549–51

Seeligson, Arthur A.: background, 810; invitation to E., 810-11, 824–25; visit to E., 1055, 1057

Seeligson, Ramona, 811, 1055

Selective Service Act (1948), 31, 333, 499–501, 1245–47, 1283–84, 1294–95, 1384–86, 1490–93. *See also* Universal military service; Universal military training

Senate: Appropriations Committee, 118, 1041–48, 1048–50, 1050–51, 1082–84, 1287–89; Armed Services Committee, 38, 116, 123, 553–54, 1482–83; Banking and Currency Committee, 1243; Finance Committee, 1229–30; Foreign Relations Committee, 1014, 1033–34, 1211–12, 1216–17

Service Academy Board, 373–74, 383, 385, 422–26, 426–28, 490–92, 501–2, 549–51, 635–38, 692–94, 714–16, 717–18, 720, 724, 855–56, 951, 1026–28

Servicemen's Readjustment Act (1944), 293–94

Service pay, 629–31

Severinghaus, Aura Edward, 748–49

Seymour, Charles: background, 51–52; Higgins Trust, comment on definition of, 805–6; honorary degree for E., informed by, 51–52; Human Relations Area Files, urges E.'s participation, 829–30; National Fund for Medical Education, mentioned in E. letter on, 530; retirement, 957

Sfax Project, 704–6

SHAEF, 474–75, 761–62, 976–77, 978–79, 980–81, 1349–50

Shanks, Carrol Meteer, 135–36

SHAPE, 1396–97, 1499–1500. *See also* NATO

Sharp, Willow, 1486

Shaw, Irwin, *The Young Lions*, E.'s comment on, 559–60

Sheahan, Myrtle, 1507

Shedden, Frederick Geoffrey, 976–77; Australia, requests defense information for, 662–63

Sheerin, John J., 811

Shellenberger, George, 1203–4

Sheperd, Howard C., 1148

Sheppard, Harry R., 971

Sheridan, Philip, 1129

Sherman, Eleanor Boyle (Ewing), 113

Sherman, Forrest Percival: anti-submarine defense, 1044, 1083; appointed CNO, 808–9; background, 462, 808–9; Columbia projects sponsored by U.S. Navy, 1329–30; conference with E., 1212; Crommelin affair, 1015–17; E.'s opinion of, 993–94; Godfrey, communications expert, recommended to by E., 1509–10; Hazlett's opinion of, 834–36, 863–64; on Marshall's appointment, 1329–30; NATO matters, 1470–71; security at naval shipyards, 1208; trusted by Forrestal, 462

Sherman, I. S., 258–59

Sherman, John, 113, 663

Sherman, Sherrill, 1061

Sherman, William Tecumseh, 678, 1129, 1027–28; background, 1028; "General Sherman statements," attributed to E., 113

Sherwood, Robert Emmet, 1425; *Crusade in Europe*, comments on reviews, 340–41

Shields, William S., 724

Shimkin, Leon, Columbia, fund-raising proposal by, 826–27

Shotwell, James Thomson: background, 214–15, 1114–15; Hiss case, role in, 214–15, 1254; Nuremberg trial records, fears over access to, 771, 1114–15

Shown, Robert J., 161, 175–76

Shryock, Thomas J., Jr., 126

Shuffler, R. Henderson, 1222

Sibert, Edwin Luther, 192–93

Sibley, George H., 1023–24

Sibley, Harper, 147

Sicily campaign, 26–27, 1330–31

Sikes, Robert L. F., 971

Silis-Ozolins, Mirdza, 1345–46

Silver, Leo, 1024

Simmons, David Andrew, Americans for E., activities with, 1069–70, 1091–92

Simmons, Ernest J.: background, 140; Cole-

1424–25; loyalty of Negro troops in World War II, 695; Miller case, review of, by, 193; on Universal Military Training, 1063–64; U.S. foreign policy conference, invitation to, 1296–97

Spaatz, Ruth (Harrison), 1063

Sparks, Frank Hugh, 176

Sparks, Joseph Stanley, 710

Spaulding, Francis Trow, 573

Speers, Wallace C., 1152–53

Spellman, Francis (cardinal), 1122

Sperrle, Hugo, 394

Spilman, Robert S., 1391

Spofford, Charles Merville, 384, 386

Sporn, Philip, 663–65, 1184

Sprague, John Russel: background, 887; supports E.'s candidacy, 885

Sproul, Robert Gordon, 424; background, 135–36; Bohemian Grove, sends invitation to E., 1068–69; comments on E. fund-raising letter, 1269

Spruance, Raymond Ames: Army ROTC, evaluation of, 717–18; background, 716, 724; E.'s opinion of, 720; Military Education Panel, chairman of, 715–16

Stack, Carol Lee, 582

Stack, Elsa, 581–82, 929

Stack, James, 581–82, 928–29

Stack, Linda, 582

Staff Council, 574–75

Staley, Thomas F., 1417

Stalin, Joseph Vissarionovich, 22, 1425

Standard Oil Company of New Jersey, 534–35, 690, 698

Standley, William Harrison, 259–60; urges E. to seek presidency, 1103

Stark, Harold Raynsford, 1512–13

Starr, Mark, 1434

Stassen, Harold Edward, 135, 858; background, 39, 142; Burnham's hope, 286; candidacy of (1952), 1089, 1268, 1272; election of 1948, 142–43; encouragement from E., 142–43; National Fund for Medical Education, supporter of, 530; scholarships for careers in public service, 669–70; United Nations Week, proposed by E. to head, 147; U.S. foreign policy conference, 1296–97, 1318–19, 1353, 1366; Wisconsin primary (1948), 39

States' Rights Democrats (Dixiecrats), 130, 310–11, 826

Stearns, Robert Lawrence, 716, 1026; ROTC, E.'s letter on, 718; Service Academy Board, work as chairman, 714, 951

Steffanson, Hokan Bjornstrom, 1179–80

Steffanson, Mary Pinchot (Eno), 1179–80

Steichen, Edward, *Crusade in Europe*, photographs for, 104

Steinhardt, Laurence Adolph, 963

Stennis, John C., ADA, coalition to draft E., 42

Stephanidis, Stephen, 829

Stephens, John Allen, 1075–76

Stephens, Thomas Edgar, 131, 173, 288, 1128–29; background, 65; E.'s painting, 765–66; Jones portrait, 725–26; opinion of, by E., 681; recommendation of, by E., 946–48

Stevens, Francis Bowden, 165

Stevens, George A., 749–50

Stewart, William Robert, 1182–83

Stieff, Gideon Numsen, 29

Stilwell, Joseph Warren, 216, 1034–36

Stilwell Mission to China, 1034–36

Stimson, Henry Lewis, 1036; background, 1034; E.'s visit with, 1217–18; State Department employees, Senate investigation of, 1033–34

Stipp, George Michael, 474–75

Stirling, Frances Marguerite (Wilson), 25

Stirling, William Gurdon, 24–25

Stockholm Peace Petition, 1279

Stoddard, Arthur Ellsworth, 870–71

Stoddard, George Dinsmore, 425; background, 304–6; West Point, study of curriculum, 1026

Stone, William A., 1219

Stover, Nettie, 253–54

Strategic Air Command, 533–34, 568–69, 699–704

Strategic bombing, 568–70, 778–79, 792–93, 894–99. *See also* B-36

Straus, Helen (Sachs), 321–22

Straus, Nathan, 321–22

Strauss, Lewis Lichtenstein, 1180–81

Streptomycin, 331–33, 363–64, 371–72, 538

Strikes, 324–25, 783, 785–88, 790–91, 1170–72, 1184–85, 1188

Stromberg, Marie, 45

Strong, Benjamin: background, 437; E.'s request that Kirk be named to Higgins Board, 1516–17; Higgins Trust, administration of, 434–37, 590–91, 806

Strong, Kenneth William Dobson: associates of the war days, E.'s comments on, 976–77; background, 662, 790–91; Culzean Castle, E.'s wish to invite, 818; Korea, E.'s views on, 1184–86; NATO, E.'s probable appointment, 1414; Shedden visit, 662–63, 976; Soviet Union, fear of, by, 1414

Strong, Walter W., 1011–12

Struble, Arthur Dewey, 545–47, 647

Stuart, J. R., 391

Stuart, John Leighton, 350

UNESCO. *See* Eisenhower, Milton Stover
Ungerleider, Samuel, Sr., 118
UNICEF, 90–91, 146–48
Unification. *See* Armed services unification
Union Club, 68
Union League of Philadelphia, 804–5
Union Pacific Railroad Company, 1234
United Automobile Workers, 460–61
United Europe Movement, 1344–45
United Mine Workers, 135
United Nations, 43, 1235–37, 1344–45;
  Appeal for Children, 90–91, 148–49;
  Crusade for Children, 160–61; Day Com-
  mittee, 146–47; E.'s view of, 1396–97;
  Relief and Rehabilitation Administration,
  91, 133–34. *See also* Eisenhower, Milton
  Stover
United Service for New Americans, 328, 386
United Service Organizations, 907–8
United States Air Force, 38, 123, 233, 280–
  83, 291–92, 379–85, 448–51, 472–73,
  482–84, 512–14, 526, 544–45, 547–
  49, 550–51, 551–52, 561–62, 568–69,
  574, 591–94, 635–38. *See also* Armed
  services unification; B-36; United States Air
  Force Academy
United States Air Force Academy, 373–74,
  383, 422–26, 549–51, 692–94, 714–
  16, 855–56. *See also* Service Academy Board
United States Army (Regular Army), 280–
  83, 448–51, 510, 512–14, 547–49, 551–
  52, 574, 577–79. *See also* Armed services
  unification; Historical Division; Troop
  Carrier Command; United States Military
  Academy
United States Marine Corps, 498–99, 792,
  895–96, 904–5; in Korea, 1393. *See also*
  Armed services unification
United States Military Academy, 604–5,
  1026–28, 1152, 1153–54, 1161–62,
  1162–63, 1215–16, 1315–18; *Howitzer*, 1317, 1435–36; letters to sons of
  class members, 82–83, 113–14; *Pointer*,
  1436–37; portraits, 680–81, 912–13; reunions, 1072–73, 1126–27, 1150–51.
  See also Army-Navy game; Service Academy Board
United States National Academy of Sciences,
  430
United States Naval Academy, 539, 635–39,
  1215–16. *See also* Army-Navy game;
  Service Academy Board
United States Navy, 230–34, 280–83, 365–
  68, 373–74, 401–3, 448–51, 461–62,
  465–66, 482–84, 515–19. *See also* Armed
  services unification; Supercarrier; United
  States Marine Corps; United States Naval
  Academy

United States Seniors' Golf Association, 1060–
  61, 1112
United States Steel Corporation, 1003–4
United States Steel Corporation of Delaware,
  1075–76
United Steelworkers of America, 1075–76
United World Federalists, 595, 1009–10,
  1235–37
Universal military service, 1222–23, 1240–
  41, 1312–13, 1341–42, 1365–66, 1384–
  86, 1409–11, 1484–85, 1490–93, 1510,
  1516. *See also* Selective Service Act (1948)
Universal military training, 31, 38, 1222–
  23, 1240–41, 1312–13, 1341–42, 1365–
  66, 1384–86, 1482, 1484–85, 1510. *See
  also* Conant Plan; Selective Service Act
  (1948)
University of Chicago, 353–54, 1186–87
University of Denver, 377, 455–56, 602–
  3, 1283, 1340
University of Glasgow, 1290–91, 1375–76
University of Houston, 1324–25, 1334–35
University of Illinois, 303–6
University of Michigan, "Atoms for Peace
  Day," 1256–57
University of North Carolina at Chapel Hill,
  943, 988–89, 993, 1313–14
University of Northern Colorado, 1125–26
University of Pennsylvania, 669–70
University of the State of New York at Albany,
  251
Urban League Service Fund, 217–18
Urwick, Lyndall Fownes, 985–86
U.S. News and World Report, 754–55, 781–
  82, 1285
U.S.S.R., 21–22, 28, 66–67, 230–34, 239–
  40, 255–56, 367, 448–51, 485–86, 508–
  9, 515–18, 545, 552, 561–62, 568–70,
  591–94, 627, 654, 724, 738–40, 773–
  74, 1048–50, 1115–16, 1248–49, 1274–
  75, 1312–14, 1396–97, 1414, 1464–
  67. *See also* Cold War
U.S.S. *United States.* See Supercarrier

Vail, Robert William Glenrole, 143–44
Valley Forge Park, 174–75
Van Amringe, John Howard, 345
Van Amringe medal, 344–45
Vandenberg, Arthur Hendrick, 120; background, 751; talk by, E.'s comment on,
  750–51; talk by E., comment on, 756–
  57; Vandenberg Resolution, 509
Vandenberg, Gladys Rose, 559
Vandenberg, Hoyt Sanford, 239, 366, 370,
  528–29, 559, 739, 1006, 1044, 1212;
  air defenses, invitation from E. to "chat"
  about, 1057, 1058, 1059; Alaskan defenses, 1116; B-36 bomber, 775, 792; back-

ground, 88; Bissell, recommendation by E., 88–89, 90; budget formulation procedure and basic war plans, 515–19; consultation with E., 383; Edelson, ordnance supplier, 1406–7; Flying Wing, cancellation of contract, 1059–60; Harmon Report, objection to, 569; health professionals and Armed Forces, liaison between, 151; interservice debate, 450–51, 483–84, 991, 994; JCS, military budget responsibilities, 472; Miller, promotion of, 368–69; Navy, Bradley's attack on, 798; ROTC, Air Force units of, 401; U.S.S. *United States*, supercarrier, 283, 560, 561–62
—Air Force: officers, allocated from service academies, 636; performance, under FY 51 budget, 593; reduction of operational groups, 380

Vandenberg Resolution, 509
Van Fleet, James Alward, 83
Van Fleet, James Alward, Jr., graduation gift to, 82–83
Van Sant, John T., 997–98
Van Zandt, James E., 645
Velde, Harold Himmel, 647
Verdun, Battle of (World War I), 1421–22
Versailles, 474–75
Veterans Administration, 294, 525–26, 1338, 1480–81
Veterans of Foreign Wars, 1304–5
Videla, Gabriel Gonzales, 964, 1018–19
Viking Press, 1338
Vincent, Janet (Newton), 1008–9
Vincent, William Shafer: Citizenship Education Project, executive officer of, 1007–8, 1120; development of project with Army, 1423–24; housing for, requested by E., 1008–9
Viner, Jacob: Aid to Europe Group, membership in, 338–40, 459–60; background, 339
Vinson, Carl, 509; B-36 investigation and, 775; House Armed Services Committee, chairman of, 904, 1127–28; revised service pay bill, action on, 630–31; UMT, presses for legislation on, 1241
—JCS chairmanship: opposes establishment of, 367; questions E.'s appointment to, 509
Virginia Polytechnic Institute, 31–32
Vivian, John Charles, 1177–78
Voice of America, 68–69, 1087–88
Volk, Albert A., letter from E. on collectivism, 612–14, 624–25, 650–51
Vyshinsky, Andrey Yanuaryevich, 239–40

WAC, 12, 116
Wade, Mason D., Sr., United World Federalists, 1235–37

Wadsworth, James Wolcott: letter of commendation from E., 1166; universal military training, legislation for, 1241
Wagley, Charles Walter, human relations files group, Columbia membership in, 829–30
Wagner, John Peter, 777
Wagner, Robert Ferdinand, 658
Wake Forest College, 732–33
Waldo, Gretchen H., 1063–64
Waldorf-Astoria Hotel, 973–74; conference, 1296–97, 1318–19, 1319, 1341–42, 1353, 1355–56, 1362, 1366–67, 1367–68, 1368–69, 1373–75, 1384–86, 1467, 1484–85
Walker, Walton Harris: background, 37–38; Korea command, 1418–19, 1450–51; visit to, by E., 37–38, 79
Wallace, DeWitt: background, 616; E.'s presidential candidacy, 1089; *Reader's Digest* articles, E.'s suggestions, 614–17
Wallace, Henry Agard, candidate of Progressive Party, 130, 310–11
Wallace, Schuyler Crawford: Arden House, proposed uses of, 844
—Columbia: Center for Iranian Studies, 759; Russian Institute, Rockefeller grant to, 1432–33
Wallop, John Douglass, III: background, 34; *Crusade in Europe*, 34, 75
Walter, John Charles, 916, 1133–34
War Council, 484–85, 510, 574–75, 576, 662–63
War criminals, 392–94
War Manpower Commission, 499–501
Ward, Orlando: Army Historical Division, becomes chief of, 505; background, 1034–36; China, E. comments on manuscript sent by, 1034–36; *Cross-Channel Attack*, requests E.'s comments on manuscript, 814, 927–28; errors in World War II section of almanac pointed out to, by E., 927–28; Liddell Hart book, comments on author's letter to E., 691–92; SHAEF, requests E.'s permission to transmit documents from, to British, 761–62
Warner, Rawleigh, 1410, 1473
Warren, Albert Henry, 1316–17
Warren, Earl: background, 142, 310; candidacy of, 1268; comment on statement by E., 122; polls, 1089, 1272
Warren, George Earle, 273, 674, 937–38, 1415; Council on Development, service on, 1260–61; investigates amending Columbia charter, 317–18; nominates Mudd to trustees, 273, 307–9; vice-president for business affairs, role in creation of post, 361–62, 363, 712
Washburn, Abbott McConnell, 1280

Wilson, Charles Edward: background, 916, 952; monopolies, testimony on, 951–52; Harvard professorship in honor of, 1123
—Columbia: committee on corporate participation, 981–82; honorary degree from, 1133–34
Wilson, Charles Erwin: background, 916; honorary degree, 1133–34
Wilson, Earl, 1389, 1391
Wilson, Henry Maitland, 977; *Eight Years Overseas*, memoir, E.'s foreword to, 172
Wilson, Leroy A., 1148
Wilson, Lyle Campbell, E.'s presidential candidacy, 106–7
Wilson, Thomas Woodrow, 1373–74
Winant Volunteers, 1183
Winchell, Walter, 1105; background, 28; Soviet Union, diplomatic relations with, 28
Wind, Herbert Warren, 1159
Wingfield, Alvin, Jr., 1016–17
Winiewicz, Josef M., Mickiewicz Chair, role in founding of, 141
Wisconsin presidential primary (1948), 38–39
Wise, James DeCamp, 686; background, 272; Columbia Associates, contributions to, 944
Wisner, Frank Gardiner, 582–83
Witsell, Edward Fuller, 337, 831, 940; background, 278; Columbia, Conservation of Human Resources Project, research for, 1480–81
Witter, Guy, 1204
WMCA Radio, 321–22
Wogan, John Beugnot, 1316–17
Wolcott, Mary Elizabeth (Weld), 1452
Wolcott, Samuel Huntington, Jr., 1452
Wolcott School, 1178
Wolf, Walter Reid, 369–70
Woll, Matthew, 1233, 1433–35
Women's Armed Services Integration Act (1948), 116–17
Women's Army Corps. *See* WAC
Wood, Benjamin DeKalbe, 1149; background, 454–55; collegiate testing, 453, 454–55; Ford Foundation grant for Columbia, 570–73
Wood, John Stephens, 220
—HUAC: American Negro soldiers in World War II, loyalty of, 694–95; proposed legislation to combat subversive activities, E.'s opinion on, 1028–30; textbook investigation, 638–39, 646–49
Wood, Robert Elkington, 1119, 1473, 1476; American Assembly, interest in, 1473, 1476; background, 447
Wood, Robert Jefferson, 548; background, 485; B-36, capability of, 485–86
Wood, Rose, 810, 1198
Woodall, Edward Corbet, 270–71

Woodruff, Robert Winship, 962, 1456; background, 322–23; *Crusade in Europe*, gift copy to, 343; dinner with E., 369; Forrestal, name suggested to by E. for panel of businessmen, 322–23; luncheon with E., 1148; medical education, E. writes to, regarding support for, 1098–1100; Owen Young Chair at Harvard, E. writes concerning, 1108–9, 1123; shotgun, presents to E., 1211
—American Assembly: donation to, 1409; pledge as birthday gift for E., 1417
—Augusta National Golf Club: E. informs of planned trip to, 924; Jones, agrees to pay for portrait of, for club, 725–26
—Ichauway, estate of: E.'s description of hunt, 957–59; hunting with E. at, 364–65, 954, 1362–63; invitation to E., 342–43
Wordsworth, William, 44
World Almanac, The, 913–14, 927–28
World War II. *See* Ardennes counteroffensive; Arnhem, Battle of; Normandy campaign; Northern Africa campaign; Salerno, Italy, campaign; Sicily campaign; Southern France campaign
Wormser, Felix Edgar, 1084
Wright, Fielding L., 130
Wright, Loyd, 72–73
Wright, Zayle (Donaldson), 362
Wriston, Henry Merritt, 647, 649, 857–58, 1373, 1374; Carnegie Endowment, recalls E.'s agreement with trustees' action in Hiss case, 214; HUAC textbook investigation, 647, 649; Internal Revenue, E. suggests name as contact concerning, 857–58, 920–21; Waldorf conference, presides over, 1353, 1373, 1374
—AAU: appoints E. to committee on university financing, 457–58; draft deferment resolution of, 352–53; India Conference, invitation to E., 628–29; urges E. to attend meetings, 319
—Council on Foreign Relations, Aid to Europe Study Group: chairmanship, unable to accept, 1511; invitation to join, 340; Truman, report to, 466–67
Wyche, Ira Thomas, 1513
Wyman, Ethel Mae (Megginson), 708–9
Wyman, Willard Gordon, 17, 709

Yale University, 51–52, 121, 434–37, 590–91, 918–19
Yellowstone National Park, 1227
Young, Howard, 149–50; vacations with E., 712, 777, 1343–44
Young, John Orr, 1344–45
Young, Lawrence B., 1412–13
Young, Owen, 612, 672, 836, 1164, 1434;

background, 673; professorship in honor of, 1108–9, 1123

Young, Philip, 377, 612, 664, 844, 1071, 1080, 1123, 1198, 1260–61, 1401, 1417; acting coordinator, Office of Development, appointment as, 1094, 1156; alumni dinner given for, 404–5; assistant sought for, 1156; background, 67–68; economic mobilization course offered by, 672–73, 773–74; Owen Young, professorship in honor of, 1108–9, 1123

—American Assembly, 1382, 1437, 1477; Arden House Project, meeting on, 1071; deans and directors, report written for, 1382, 1401; donations, fund raising, and pledges, role in, 1333–34, 1386–87, 1409–11, 1428, 1485, 1517–18; Douglas, selection for board, 1429, 1431, 1518; E.'s opinion of work on, 1409–11; executive director of, 1517–18, 1518; first assembly topic, 1411–12; Harriman, informs E. of funds from, 1299–1300; Harriman estate, on committee for use of, 844, 1164–65; labor, efforts to secure participation in, 1233, 1433–35; lunch on, 1148; planning for, 1164–65; reports to E. on progress, 1277–78, 1433

—Conservation of Human Resources Project: advisory committee chairman, appointment as, 664, 1277–78; American Management Association, investigates cooperation with, 689–90; report to E. on, 1277–78; suggestion for study, 377

—Graduate School of Business: Army participation in suggested, 836–37; dean, service as, 67–68; expansion of school, proposal for, 67–68; fellowship established, 1025; tour of, with E., 985

Young, Spencer C., 1101–2

Youngberg, Gilbert Albin, service academies, military education plan for, 501–2

Young Lions, The, 559–60

Yukawa, Hideki, atomic research of, 1257–58

Zanetti, Joaquin Enrique, 74, 397, 996–97, 1002–3, 1078

Zeinert, Oliver B., 161

Zhdanov, Andrei Alexandrovitch, 22

Zhukov, Georgi Konstantinovich, 511–12; Allied Control Council, details of first meeting, 109–10

Zimmerman, Don Zabriskie, 697

Zoll, Allen Alderson, II, communism in the schools, 1105–6

Zook, George Frederick, 648